PRINCIPLES OF GENERAL PSYCHOLOGY

PRINCIPLES OF GENERAL PSYCHOLOGY

5TH EDITION

GREGORY A. KIMBLE
Duke University

NORMAN GARMEZY
University of Minnesota

EDWARD ZIGLER
Yale University

JOHN WILEY & SONS, INC.
New York Chichester Brisbane Toronto

Library of Congress Cataloging in Publication Data

Kimble, Gregory A
Principles of general psychology.

Bibliography: p.
Includes indexes.
1. Psychology. I. Garmezy, Norman, joint author.
II. Zigler, Edward Frank, 1930- joint author.
III. Title.

BF121.K5 1980 150 79-23269
ISBN 0-471-04469-5

Printed in the United States of America

10 9 8 7 6 5 4 3 2

To Lucille, Edith, and Bernice

ABOUT THE AUTHORS

Gregory A. Kimble is at present professor and chairman of the Department of Psychology at Duke University. He was formerly the director of undergraduate and graduate studies at this university. Earlier he taught at Brown and Yale universities and was professor and chairman of the Department of Psychology at the University of Colorado. Dr. Kimble frequently contributes to professional journals on topics pertaining to learning and memory. He edited the book *Foundations of Conditioning and Learning* and is the author of *Hilgard and Marquis' Conditioning and Learning, How To Use (and Misuse) Statistics,* and the forthcoming *The Departmental Chairmanship: A Survival Manual.* Dr. Kimble has served as chairman of the Experimental Psychological Research Review Committee, of the National Institute of Mental Health, and was a NATO fellow at Cambridge University. He is a member of the Society of Experimental Psychologists.

Norman Garmezy is now professor of psychology at the University of Minnesota; he previously directed its Center for Personality Research. Earlier appointments were clinical professor of psychiatry at the School of Medicine, University of Rochester, and professor of psychology at Duke University. He has been honored with the 1974 Distinguished Scientist Award, Section III (Experimental), Division of Clinical Psychology, American Psychological Association; and with the Stanley Dean Award for basic behavioral research in schizophrenia. Dr. Garmezy is a past chairman of the Board of Trustees, Association for the Advancement of Psychology; and a past president of the APA's Division of Clinical Psychology. He has published widely on topics concerning personality and psychopathology. His book-length monograph, *Children at Risk,* is distributed worldwide by the National Institute of Mental Health.

The current appointments of Edward Zigler at Yale University are Sterling Professor of Psychology and head of the Psychology Section of its Child Study Center. He was the first director of the Office of Child Development and headed the United States Children's Bureau, Department of Health, Education and Welfare, from 1970 through 1972. Dr. Zigler was one of the planners of this country's Head Start Program. His many contributions to professional journals concern cognitive development, mental retardation, and compensatory education. He is coauthor of the textbook *Socialization and Personality Development*. He has won the Dale Richmond Memorial Award from the American Academy of Pediatrics, the first Gunnar Dybwad Distinguished Scholar in the Behavioral and Social Sciences Award, bestowed by the National Association for Retarded Children, and the G. Stanley Hall Award, given by the Division of Developmental Psychology of the American Psychological Association. Dr. Zigler was named one of the honorary commissioners of the United States Commission for the International Year of the Child.

PREFACE

When the three of us began our work on this fifth edition of *Principles of General Psychology,* our principal aim was to bring the book up to date. We had been reasonably well satisfied with what had been covered in the fourth edition, but we recognized that new research had led to significant advances in many areas of psychology. As a result of our updating efforts, about 25 percent of the references cited in this edition were published in 1974—the date of the fourth edition—or later. These new materials and our rethinking of issues are reflected on every page of the revision.

Although there is a considerable amount of new information in this edition, our major emphasis continues to be the interaction between the biological and environmental origins of behavior. In support of this emphasis, we have developed a new chapter sequence which we believe serves it better. The relatively more biological topics appear early in the book. Environmental factors become increasingly more important in the later chapters. For some instructors this change will be the most important one of this revision.

For others the most important change in the textbook will be its greatly enhanced appeal for students. As the number of people listed in our Ackowledgments reveals, we have had a great deal of help on this revision. The result is a text that is more readable and more in touch with the interests of undergraduate students.

Gregory A. Kimble
Norman Garmezy
Edward Zigler

Durham, North Carolina
Minneapolis, Minnesota
New Haven, Connecticut

ACKNOWL-EDGEMENTS

A number of people have contributed vitally to this revision. First and foremost were the invaluable contributions of R. Bruce Masterton, Florida State University, who wrote Chapter 2, "The Nervous System and Behavior," and of Edward E. Jones, Princeton University, who prepared Chapter 13, "Social Psychology." We also wish to thank the other professionals who reviewed the manuscript and provided helpful suggestions for improvements: James Butcher, University of Minnesota; David W. Carroll, University of Wisconsin, Superior; Rosa Cascione, Yale University; Ruth Day, Duke University; David Elmes, Washington and Lee University; Michael L. Epstein, Rider College; Karen K. Glendenning, Florida State University; Steve Hollon, University of Minnesota; Donald Jensen, University of Nebraska; Philip Kendall, University of Minnesota; Mark McGee, Texas A & M University; Victoria Seitz, Yale University; James E. Spivey, University of Kentucky; Sally Styfco, Yale University; and Auke Tellegen, University of Minnesota.

The following persons contributed generously of their time in the preparation of the manuscript: Shari Alexander, Edna Bissetts, René Burton, Hazel Carpenter, Chris Greene, Darlene Harvey, Pat Johnson, Amby Peach, and Marge Williams, all of Duke University; Nancy Roche of Durham, North Carolina; and Linda Wallace of the University of Minnesota. Special thanks are given to Lucille L. Kimble for preparing the indexes. And finally, we are much indebted to the staff of John Wiley and Sons for its strong support throughout the project—to Priscilla Todd for her sensitive editing of the final manuscript; to Stella Kupferberg for her role in photographic research; to Rosie Hirsch for her efforts in moving the manuscript through production under the usual pressures of time; and to Jack Burton for his sponsoring support and coordination of the project throughout.

G. A. K.
N. G.
E. Z.

TO THE INSTRUCTOR

This textbook is one of a number of items available to you for use in planning an effective course in introductory or general psychology. The others are an *Instructor's Resource Book,* prepared by the authors; a *Test File,* a set of about 1500 test items, prepared by Mark G. McGee and Gregory A. Kimble; a *Study Guide,* developed by William F. Hodges and Richard Olson; and a series of 160 color slides with an accompanying *Instructor's Manual,* created by Richard A. Kasschau.

Although the chapters of the textbook are organized according to our preferred sequence, other arrangements are practicable, as are adjustments of the text material to fit courses with special emphases. The *Instructor's Resource Book* describes some of these possibilities. The primary substance of the *Instructor's Resource Book* consists of a set of "Lecture Modules" and materials for demonstration. There is probably enough of this material to cover over half of what you will need for classroom presentations.

The separately bound *Test File* consists largely of multiple-choice items. For each chapter, however, there are thirty items to be matched with descriptions. These same test items could be converted to the fill-in form. The *Test File* will also be available on computer tape to adopters of the text.

Hodges and Olson maintain in the *Study Guide* the same style that helped their guide for the fourth edition win such universal approval. Many regarded it as the best in the field. This supplementary aid provides students with detailed guidance in how to study as well as giving them practice in taking objective examinations.

Richard Kasschau's series of slides illuminate topics from every chapter in the book.

CONTENTS

CH. 1

Psychology and Human Concerns

Psychology began its existence as a separate discipline a little over a hundred years ago. Many people set the beginning date as 1879, the year in which Wilhelm Wundt founded the first psychological laboratory at Leipzig University, in what is now the German Democratic Republic. In the earliest days of its history, psychology concentrated on the study of the sensory processes, perception, simple learning, and memory. Gradually, however, the field has expanded to the point that it now covers a range of topics so broad it touches the lives of all of us. In the days of Wundt, psychology was almost exclusively confined to the laboratory and its principal activity was research. As the field has grown, however, large segments of psychology are now involved in practice.

We shall pick up threads of the history of psychology in succeeding chapters. This first chapter covers materials designed to illustrate methods, procedures, and points of view. The examples chosen illustrate the diversity of the field.

In 1875 Wilhelm Wundt (1832-1920) came to Leipzig. Four years later he began research that would be his first published in psychology. The date 1879 is usually given for the founding of his laboratory and of the discipline.

PSYCHOLOGY: FROM RESEARCH TO PRACTICE

This heading is the title of a new volume (Pick et al., 1978) that grew out of discussions held by the Board of Scientific Affairs of the American Psychological Association (APA). The members of the Board, recognizing that the public often misunderstands the role of basic research in science, decided that the time was ripe to prepare a book of case studies that would show how research methods and findings are applied to important human problems. We would like to borrow three examples from this book to illustrate the transition from traditional laboratory research to practical studies.

Breast Feeding and Taste Preferences in Infants

The study of the sensory processes, including taste sensitivity, is a field of research with a long history. Psychologists and physiologists have learned a great deal about the operation of the gustatory system, through traditional laboratory work. We know, for example, that the sense of taste is fully developed at birth and that infants discriminate among the primary tastes, salt, sweet, sour, and bitter (see page 63). Research by Lewis Lipsitt at Brown University now points to the practical significance of this knowledge.

Lipsitt studied the sucking behavior of infants by presenting them with a sequence of different taste experiences: sugar water, plain water, sugar water, plain water. This research not only established the infant's preference for the sugar water but also demonstrated a disinclination to suck for water alone after having had sugar water. For Lipsitt (1978) the implications of these results are clear.

> This result tells us what some nurses working with newborns knew already. Perhaps many more will know it now. If the baby is [given] sugar-water just before being offered for nursing to the mother, as is sometimes done, this works against the success of breast feeding. To the extent that . . . unsuccessful [breast feedings] tend to discourage the mother from further breast-feeding attempts, as we think sometimes occurs, there could be enduring effects. Infants may turn away from their mothers if they have just previously experienced a sweeter taste than that obtainable from mother's milk.

The feeding of the infant by its mother fosters the bond of attachment between the two so important for the baby's social and physical development. Everything possible must therefore be done to enhance the mother's attractiveness to her infant and to make breast feeding satisfactory. Breast feeding also of course enhances the infant's chances of survival (see page 18).

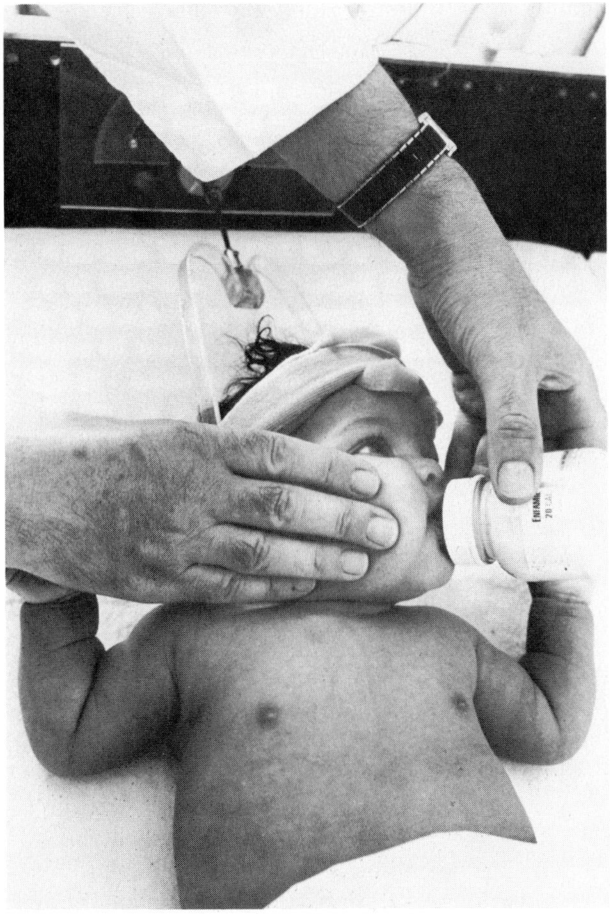

One of the babies whose taste preference for sugar water was studied by Lewis Lipsitt in his laboratory at Brown University.

Television and Aggression

In 1975 almost 80 percent of all television network programs contained some violence. Every hour of network viewing confronted its audience with an average of 7.4 violent incidents. On Saturday morning, the children's hour, 93 percent of all programs had violent episodes, at an average rate of eighteen per hour (Huston-Stein, 1978). By the time children finish high school in America, they will have watched the screen for more than 15,000 hours, have been exposed to 350,000 commercials, and observed 18,000 murders (*Newsweek,* February 21, 1977). Never has there been a more aggressive intruder into the American home. If this intrusion has been worrisome to some parents, so too has it concerned many child and social psychologists, who have contributed most of the more than 2300 studies and reports about the medium and its influence.

Does video violence encourage aggressive behavior? The applied research of those who have studied the consequences of televised aggression owes a great deal to earlier basic work done at Stanford by Albert Bandura and his co-workers. They demonstrated that normal children readily imitate aggressive models. In a now classic study (Bandura, Ross, and Ross, 1963) some nursery school children watched an adult model kick, punch, and verbally abuse a large inflated "Bobo" doll. Other children did not have this experience. Later on, under mild frustration induced by taking toys away from the children, those who had witnessed the adult's aggression were themselves more aggressive toward Bobo than were the other children.

Further studies of aggression conducted by Leonard Berkowitz (1964, 1970) at the University of Wisconsin have added to our basic knowledge. These studies show that a person who becomes anxious when angered is also likely to become violent and that observing the violent behavior of others may make the viewer more violent. These findings have helped investigators plan their studies on the effects of televised violence.

One ten-year longitudinal study (Lefkowitz et al., 1972) of children ages eight to eighteen found first that aggressive behavior in third-grade boys was related to the amount of violence they preferred to watch on television at home. Ten years later these children were still more aggressive than their peers, who had not watched as much television violence when young. In fact, and this is especially worrisome, the pattern of television viewing was a better predictor of later aggression in the children than any of the parental child-rearing practices or family characteristics that were studied. This research suggests that aggression may be self-stimulating, with its consequence even more aggression.

Other studies suggest that television can be a force for good as well as evil. Some television programs, after all, are gentle. Such programs, although in shorter supply, do influence children. "Mr. Rogers' Neighborhood," seen on public television, is presided over by a gentle figure who talks about understanding the child's feelings as well as those of others, about empathy, altruism, sharing, and the like. Preschoolers who watch this program persist more at assigned tasks, are more cooperative and sharing, and obey the rules of the nursery school more dependably than children who do not watch the program.

Visual Illusions and Air Safety

In the fall of 1965 the Boeing Company introduced the 727 jet. Within months of its introduction this plane, which had received the highest grades in test flights, had had a series of accidents over four major cities, Chicago, Cincinnati, Salt Lake City, and Tokyo.

Initially the structural design was blamed, but a careful review of each accident suggested that the true cause was human error. In each case it seemed probable that the pilot had made a mistake in judging the approach path and the plane's altitude as he neared the airfield. Apparently the pilots were the victims of a spatial misperception, of a visual illusion possibly created by cues outside the aircraft. In all instances these cues had been city lights visible in the distance; below the planes had been dark areas of land or water. In each city the lights seen had been on a slope, which could have affected the pilots' judgments of altitude.

Conrad Kraft (1978), an experimental psychologist in the field of vision research with the Boeing Company, was called in to try to isolate the factors that might have caused the accidents. One interesting fact quickly uncovered related to the very stable performance of this new model aircraft. Its descent was so quiet that it failed to provide pilots with the usual auditory, kinesthetic, and vibratory cues that would ordinarily alert them to a too rapid descent.

In his search for other possible factors, Kraft used an aircraft simulator, a life-size model of the cockpit of the 727 complete with controls, instruments, and a way to simulate the outside environment in operational flights. The simulator was placed in a dark room to allow the experimenter to control illumination. The description by Kraft indicates how realistically the conditions of the world can be created in the laboratory.

> The pilot looking through the windows of the simulator viewed a pattern of lights representing a hypothetical city. The platform on which these lights were mounted could be moved so that the visual scene, from the pilot's position, appeared very similar to an actual night visual approach. Movement of the platform was controlled by a small home-made computer that produced a visual effect similar to that which would be experienced in a 727 aircraft weighing about 136,000 pounds. Fortunately, from the point of view of simulation technology, the changes in appearance of the visual scene are essentially the same irrespective of whether the motion is produced by movement of the visual pattern or, as in the case of actual flight, by movement of the aircraft itself (p. 369).

A series of carefully designed experiments showed that pilots judged their altitude by using the distant light cues, but that these cues were accurate only when the terrain was flat. If the terrain sloped upward the pilots responded as though it were flat and thus overestimated their altitude; if the slope was downward the pilots underestimated the altitude. Once the spatial misperception had been identified, the research findings were published in technical journals

This simulator makes it possible to create for a pilot the illusions of approach, climb, and descent as well as a variety of realistic night scenes.

and safety magazines to alert pilots around the world to the visual illusion that posed dangers to their passengers and crews.

SUMMARY ☐

In the century of its existence as a separate discipline, psychology has expanded its interests and turned from an exclusive devotion to laboratory research to research that has application. We have presented three examples of how work originally done in the laboratory has been demonstrated to have important application. Studies of the taste preferences of infants have a bearing on social development and even the probability of survival. Studies of aggression, originally carried out in artificial situations, have serious implications for the effects of viewing television violence. Studies of visual perception have helped to explain a series of airplane accidents and have provided the means of preventing them.

THE METHODS OF PSYCHOLOGY

As psychology broadened its perspective, it also began to use a wider variety of investigative methods. It has moved into the clinic, the classroom, and industrial organizations and has developed methods appropriate to each.

The Case History Method

One of the oldest methods, borrowed from medicine, is the **case history.** You will all recognize the following abbreviated description of the man responsible for an event in November 1978 that spread across the front pages of every major newspaper in the world.

> Jim Jones was born in 1931 in a small hamlet in Indiana, in what has been described as "little more than a shack." His mother, who married a man seventeen years older than she, believed that it was her son's destiny to become a messiah who would undo the wrongs in the world. The family was poor, and the mother worked in factories and waited tables to provide much needed support in the home. As Jim grew up, his mother nagged him to make something of himself. His father belonged to the Ku Klux Klan, hated blacks, and once beat him for bringing a black friend home to play.
>
> From early childhood the young boy initiated games in which he played the role of preacher, delivering sermons to other children and demanding obedience from them. Through the relatively uneventful years of high school, Jim showed a growing interest in religion and turned away from medicine, which had been his mother's goal for him. For ten years, while working for his bachelor's degree, he served as the pastor of a small church in Indianapolis. His strong integrationist views earned him the enmity of others in the community, however, and he was forced to leave this post and form his own church. The church he created was a liberal-minded one which offered a haven for the poor and friendless: a soup kitchen to feed them, an employment service to help them find jobs, a nursing home for the aged and the sick. Those who knew the young pastor remember him as a charismatic figure capable of making others devout and trusting believers.
>
> But then changes began to take place. Jones insisted that his parishioners be totally committed to him. He urged that he be called "Father," his wife "Mother." Dissidents in the church were questioned by special interrogation committees. Some left because they believed Jones was attempting to don a mantle of godliness. Stories and rumors of fake healings and of Jones's exorcising the cancers of church members started to circulate. He attacked members of the church for putting more credence in the Bible than in him as their spiritual leader. He began to collect substantial tithes from the congregation but never accounted for these funds.
>
> Fearing a nuclear holocaust, Jones went to Brazil where he founded a new church. While in South America he visited Guyana and saw in the jungle a site for a future utopian settlement. Shortly after his return to the United States, he started to speak of his ability to perform "miracles." He moved his church and seventy followers to California, where in 1971 he established a "People's Temple" in San Francisco and later another in Los Angeles.
>
> Jones's vision of himself as a living "God" took on even larger proportions and he fabricated more dramatic healings. He preached to his congregation in lengthy marathon-like services during which he declared that, were it not for his power, they would become victims of the KKK or the CIA. Church members were urged to inform on family members and neighbors. Rumors grew that members of the group were turning over their bank accounts and earnings to Jones.
>
> Sexual grandiosity also came to dominate Jones's harangues to the congregation. He dwelt on the "curse of his huge penis," which he declared made him the object of women's desires. Women close to him were called on to engage in sexual relations with him, some of whom complained that he was a sadistic lover. Parents were asked to sign away their possessions and their children. On occasion parents signed false confessions that they had molested their children. In supposedly cathartic sessions, dissidents were ridiculed and beaten with paddles for their intransigence. When reports of these abuses leaked out, a West coast magazine began to prepare an exposé for publication. But Jones arranged to move his followers to a tract of land

The People's Temple, its pastor, the Reverend Jim Jones, and the scene at Jonestown, Guyana, on November 20, 1978.

he had leased in Guyana. The group left the United States before publication of the article.

In Guyana Jones, who had previously used amphetamines, now began to abuse drugs heavily. Word filtered back to families in California of human rights violations in the settlement, and there were demands for an investigation. Relatives of some of the settlers prevailed on their congressman, Leo J. Ryan, to look into the rumor that Jones was rehearsing his followers in "mass suicide procedures." Ryan and his party flew to Guyana where some members of the settlement asked to be taken back to the states. As the congressman and his party prepared to fly home from a small nearby airstrip, they were fired upon by some of Jones's followers. Ryan and several in his party were killed. Informed about what had happened, Jones called his followers before him and urged them to commit suicide. More than 900 preceded their leader into death.

This, like other case studies, demonstrates one unequivocal fact. Of all the materials that the student encounters in psychology, few are more fascinating than the case history. But our concern is with the case history as a *method,* with its values and deficiencies as a source of psychological information. We begin with the deficiencies.

Weakness of the Method The case history is *retrospective.* It is based on the contemplation of an event after it has occurred. Events of great traumatic intensity are often distorted in memory, selectively forgotten, and actively repressed. This limits the confidence we can place on the history. In the preparation of a case history, even the assembly of materials can be modified by knowledge of a person's later life. Did Jones as a child truly command his playmates to obey him? That small bit of information fits so smoothly into Jones's adult life that it gives us pause. Too many histories are made to "fit" the outcome of a person's life, as though the clinician or the biographer wants to ensure that the pattern of the individual's life has a sense of continuity.

The case history is *unique.* No single case history ever exactly duplicates another. There are suggestions in Jones's case history of the factors that might have caused his breakdown, but these factors are elusive. Although the mother's conviction that her son would become a new messiah may have played an important role in Jones's development, it is equally plausible to blame the later abuse of drugs, which we know can precipitate a paranoid psychosis (see page 433). But there is no way to be certain that these factors were the most important ones or that they were important at all.

The case history emphasizes the *unusual.* Jones's paranoid reaction, his grandiosity, his delusions are worthy of recounting; less striking facts tend to be bypassed. One of the giants in the history of animal psychology, Edward Lee Thorndike (1911), made this point in connection with case histories in the area of animal behavior.

> . . . Nor is that all. Besides commonly misstating what facts they report, they report only such facts as show the animal at his best. Dogs get lost hundreds of times and no one ever notices it or sends an account of it to a scientific magazine. But let one find his way from Brooklyn to Yonkers and the fact immediately becomes a circulating anecdote. Thousands of cats on thousands of occasions sit helplessly yowling, and no one takes thought of it or writes to his friend, the professor; but let one cat claw at the knob of a door, supposedly as a signal to be let out, and straightway this cat becomes the representative of the cat-mind in all the books (p. 24).

The case history admits a *variety of interpretations.* Given the richness and complexity of a person's life, the case history writer can almost always find the evidence to advance a particular theory. If the psychologist has a theory emphasizing sexual factors in maladjustment, some will be found in the case history. If the psychologist believes that significant events center in family life, such circumstances are recorded in the case history. To determine the importance of particular factors would require the collection of many case histories. Only if people with particular symptoms always had the same kind of history could elements of that history be considered causative.

Strengths of the Method Despite these limitations, case histories have important virtues. One of their chief values is that they provide a rich source of hypotheses which can be investigated in situations that allow some control. Moreover, from even the skimpy evidence available in Jones's case history, several general suggestions emerge. We note, for example, that the onset and characteristics of Jones's disorder follow a pattern that has been repeatedly observed in paranoia.

1. Early belief in the importance of being the center of attention precedes the belief at a later stage in life that others are plotting one's destruction.
2. Early feelings of inadequacy and of being different are followed later by an unrealistic, exalted sense of importance.
3. Early failure that tends to be blamed on poor circumstances is later transformed into the belief that there is a plot by others to cause one to fail.
4. A righteous, crusading zeal for the betterment of others changes in the final stages of paranoia into an urge to kill the enemies of society.

These four generalizations sum up what has been called *paranoid crystallization.* They were drawn not from a single case history but from many of a similar kind. Thus the case method is frequently the first step in a process of classification that is essential for creating a scientific account of disordered behavior.

The Experimental Method

Since the case history method provides us only with a starting point, we must look for more definitive methods if our knowledge of psychology is to progress. The strongest candidate is the traditional method of **experimentation.** Before treating such methods more abstractly, let us consider an example, an experiment conducted by Clive Seligman and John Darley (1977), which we introduce with a passage from their report of the study.

> The world is in an energy crisis! Energy costs are increasing rapidly and will continue to do so. Energy shortages have been experienced; conservation techniques are needed. The present study tests the effectiveness of an energy conservation technique in residential housing. For several reasons this is important: First, in the United States, the residential sector consumes approximately 20 percent of the total energy demand, and almost 60 percent of residential energy use is accounted for by space heating and air conditioning. . . . It is estimated that half of the energy consumed by the residential sector can be conserved. . . . Second, voluntary techniques will be preferred ones for producing energy conservation in the private sector. It will be well for social science to have some demonstrably effective voluntary techniques to recommend (p. 363).

The experiment performed was very straightforward. For about a month Seligman and Darley monitored the consumption of electricity in two groups of comparable homes. In both groups the residents were urged to save energy. One group of residents, however, received periodic information on how they were doing; the other residents did not. At the end of the experiment, it was determined that the informed group used about 10 percent less electricity on an average day than the uninformed group. Apparently one practical approach to energy consumption will be to provide homeowners feedback on energy consumption.

Traditional Experimental Design This study on energy conservation was the simplest type of experiment. It involved two groups, an **experimental group** which was treated in a special way, receiving feedback on energy consumption, and a **control group** which was not. The experiment had three stages.

Stage 1: Equating groups When an experiment is begun, it is almost always with the belief that the special treatment settled on will have an effect. Usually this comes down to the hope that groups initially the same will be different after the special treatment of one of them. The assumption of initial equality is crucial. In our sample experiment the outcome, 10 percent less electricity consumption, could not have been attributed to the experimental treatment if the residents of the first group of homes had generally used less electricity than residents of the second group. To guard against this, the experimenters took two important precautions. (1) They chose comparable homes for the two groups. "Each home was a three-bedroom townhouse located in the interior of a row of townhouses. In these homes electricity is used for central air conditioning, lighting, refrigeration, and whatever other electrical appliances the owner has purchased." (2) They measured electricity consumption before the experiment began and found that daily consumption was nearly identical in the two groups of homes. The averages were 68.33 kilowatt-hours in the homes that were to become the experimental group and 69.14 kilowatt-hours in those that would constitute the control group. Although from home to home electricity consumption differed, the extent of the variability was similar in the two groups.

Stage 2: Experimental treatment In the second stage of the study the experimental group received feedback about its consumption of energy. Each day plastic numbers indicating the amount of electricity consumed were inserted into a Lucite holder that was visible to the occupants of the home through a window. We commonly refer to the special treatment in an experiment as an **independent variable.** A variable is any aspect or condition that can vary or any quantity that can change in value. It is called an independent variable if the experimenter has chosen to manipulate it. The experimenter wants to know what effect this manipulation has on behavior, more specifically on another variable called the dependent variable. In any simple experiment it is important to manipulate only one variable at a time. If more than one treatment were employed, it would be impossible to tell which was responsible for any differences that were evident at the end of the experiment. Because of this, experimenters go to great lengths to keep all conditions other than the manipulated one the same. The most important **controlled variables** in this experiment were the following. (1) Energy consumption in the two groups was observed over the same period of time so that different weather conditions could not affect the results. (2) Homeowners in both groups were told that they were in the experiment and urged to conserve energy. They were also told that the most important way to conserve energy would be by cutting down on electricity used for air conditioning. This stipulation was meant to control for the "guinea pig effect," which sometimes confuses the results of an experiment (see page 15).

Stage 3: Evaluating outcomes Attention is finally focused on the effects of the independent variable on the phenomenon of interest, energy conservation in this case. The "phenomenon of interest" just referred to is the **dependent variable** in an experiment. It is called dependent because it is affected by the manipulation of the independent variable and is, therefore, dependent on it. In psychology the dependent variable is usually a measure, direct or indirect, of the behavior of people in the experimental situation. In this case the measure was fairly direct, consumption of electricity in kilowatt-hours. At the end of the experiment it was found that homeowners in the experimental group had used a daily average of 48.56 kilowatt-hours; those in the control group used 54.25 kilowatt-hours. The difference of 5.69 kilowatt-hours represents a saving of about 10.5 percent. This outcome raises a question. Of what significance is an energy saving of 10.5 percent? There are two answers to this important question.

Statistical significance. The first answer addresses the dependability of the result. No matter how carefully an experiment is done, accidents can happen. It is possible that were the experiment to be performed again, the difference between experimental and control groups would disappear. There are statistical methods of evaluating this possibility. Without going into detail here (see page 507), these methods provide an estimate of the probability that the result obtained was an accidental one rather than being attributable to the special treatment given one group. In this experiment the probability was only 1 in 25 that the experimental group consumed less electricity by chance rather than because they had been kept informed of their consumption. Thus the investigators concluded that the result was **statistically significant,** that the result obtained is real in the sense of being reliable.

Practical significance. A 10.5 percent saving is not a large one; in many situations it would not be of much importance. In this case, however, with energy costs running to billions of dollars, a saving of this magnitude would be of great practical significance. It has been estimated that with a 10 percent reduction in energy consumption, the Dow Jones stock average would increase, the value of the American dollar would improve on the foreign money markets, and inflation at home would ease—quite a large return for a small investment based on a psychological principle of providing feedback.

Additional Examples The design of the experiment just reviewed, consisting of an experimental group and a control group and three procedural stages, is extremely simple but basic. Several additional examples will serve to review the principle points and to introduce some new ones.

Credibility of testimony The first example is from the growing field of forensic psychology, which examines the psychological factors connected with the legal, judicial, and correctional systems. In this experiment (Erickson et al., 1978) the investigators used linguistic criteria to distinguish subtle differences between what they call the "powerful" and "powerless" speech used by witnesses at a trial. The questions and first answers given in Table 1.1 came from the actual questioning of a witness who had responded with powerless answers. Actors recorded these powerless responses and also the second powerful versions, which were created by omitting the powerless phrases. The participants in this experiment were 152 students at the University of North Carolina, divided into two groups. One group of students listened to the powerless versions of the testimony, the other to the powerful, after hearing a discription of the case.

TABLE 1.1
Sample "Powerless" and "Powerful" Speech

Q.	Then you went next door?
A.	(Powerless): And then I went immediately next door, yes. (Powerful): Yes.
Q.	Approximately how long did you stay there before the ambulance arrived?
A.	(Powerless): Oh, it seems like it was about uh, twenty minutes. Just long enough to help my friend Mrs. Davis you know, get straightened out. (Powerful): Twenty minutes. Long enough to help get Mrs. Davis straightened out.
Q.	Now how long have you lived in Durham?
A.	(Powerless): All my life, really. (Powerful): All my life.
Q.	You're familiar with the streets?
A.	(Powerless): Oh yes. (Powerful): Yes.
Q.	You know your way around?
A.	(Powerless): Yes, I guess I do. (Powerful): Yes.

> The . . . case involved a collision between an automobile and an ambulance. The patient in the ambulance, already critically ill and en route to the hospital, died shortly after the accident. Subjects were instructed that the patient's family was suing the defendants (the ambulance company, its employees, and the driver of the automobile) to recover damages for the patient's death. The witness was a friend and a neighbor of the patient who had been in the ambulance at the time of the collision. The lawyer [asking the questions] was said to be representing some of the defendants in the case. The substance of the witness' testimony described the events taking place before, during and after the collision (p 272).

The participants in the experiment were asked to rate the witness in several ways, one of them for credibility. The average ratings revealed that the witness was much more credible when her responses were powerful than when they were powerless. Appropriate analyses showed that this result was statistically significant. The chances were less than 1 in 20 that the results could have occurred by chance.

Small variations in the way in which a witness delivers testimony can affect its credibility.

Now to make our principal points. (1) The independent variable in this experiment is the difference between powerful and powerless speech. The dependent variable is the rating of credibility. (2) As happens more often than not, the distinction made earlier between experimental and control groups does not apply well in this experiment. One group was not singled out for special treatment. Rather each was treated differently. One group heard the powerless expression of information, the other group the powerful. (3) The experiment consisted of three stages only by argument. The groups were equated by selecting as subjects students from the same university who were fairly similar to one another, but no explicit equating stage was included. In the second stage the two groups of students listened to the different testimonies. In the third the students rated the credibility of the witness, and the ratings of the two groups were compared.

Poverty and reading If our greatest resource is our children, there is reason to fear that we are squandering this resource, just as we have squandered the lesser ones represented by our forests, wildlife populations, and mineral reserves. In particular, our children are being short-changed by the educational system, emerging from it with less than minimal basic skills. The poor and otherwise disadvantaged suffer the most in this situation. The experimental work to be described suggests a possible way of helping children learn to read (Wallach and Wallach, 1976), hopefully correcting an important educational problem of disadvantaged children.

The children in this study came from the first grades of two inner-city public schools on the south side of Chicago. They were predominantly from low-income families and black. The scores that these children had obtained on a test of reading readiness were so low that it was doubtful that they would learn very much in the first grade. Two groups of thirty-six children each were matched child by child for sex, reading readiness, and the classroom from which they came. This accomplished the equating of groups required in the first stage of an experiment.

In stage 2 of the study, thirty-six of these children were assigned to a control group and thirty-six were placed in an experimental group. Those in the experimental group were tutored in reading, according to a special program developed by the Wallachs. This program emphasizes the skill of recognizing the sounds that letters stand for and using them in words. The Wallachs believe that deficiences in this skill are at the root of reading difficulties and that these difficulties must be removed if a child is to learn to read. The children in the control group did not receive this tutoring.

In stage 3 of the study, the children's ability to read was assessed in several ways. One measure was their score on a test requiring them to read twenty-five sentences correctly. Children in the experimental group had an average score of 16.08; those in the control group had an average score of 9.97. Statistical analysis showed the difference to be statistically significant. The probability that it was accidental was only 5 in 10,000! The practical significance of helping children learn to read requires no comment.

Small-*N* Designs By now you may have begun to wonder where the individual participant is in these experiments that use anywhere from dozens to hundreds of subjects! In reporting averages, have we not lost the contributions of single people? If you have thought of these questions, you are in good company. In recent years many psychologists have posed the same question and have advocated the use of what are called **small-*N* designs.** In statistical notation the letter *N* stands for the number of individuals in a study. In the traditional designs of the three studies discussed in the previous section, *N* was pretty large: 29, 152, and 72. In small-*N* designs the number of participants is much reduced, even to an *N* of one, a single individual. The following examples of small-*N* research are summarized in a recent book by Paul W. Robinson and David R. Foster (1979).

ABAB designs Experiments with single or few subjects often have very practical applications. In one instance (Allen et al., 1964) two nursery school children had been a worry to their teacher because they played alone, refusing to interact, even with each other. Observation suggested that this isolated play was a device for getting attention from the teacher. An experiment which supported this general hypothesis and also corrected the problem was devised. It consisted of four stages.

Stage 1: Observe baseline activity. Before they were given any special treatment, the children were observed for an hour on each of five days. During these periods the investigators made note of the percentage of their activities that was shared with other children. This was the dependent variable in the experiment. Stage 1 provided a measure of **baseline** activity to compare with activity produced by the introduction of an independent variable. In the ABAB design the letter A refers to the baseline condition.

Stage 2: Introduce independent variable. In stage 2 the teacher for six days paid attention to the children only when they interacted with other children. This procedure was the independent variable in the experiment, represented by the letter B. The children began to interact with other children when the teacher withheld attention unless they did so.

Stage 3: Return to baseline. In traditional experiments, whether the outcome is attributable to the experimental treatment or chance is dealt with by statistics. Although statistical analyses are usually possible in small-*N* studies, it is more common to answer this question by a **return to baseline,** that is, to withdraw the special treatment given in stage 2. If the behavior also returns to what it was originally, the change in behavior observed during stage 2 is attributed to the independent variable. So in this experiment the teacher stopped paying attention to the two children when they played with others. The two again isolated themselves in their play.

Stage 4: Reintroduce the independent variable. Finally, for another nine days, the teacher again paid attention to the children only when they interacted with other children, thus completing the ABAB design.

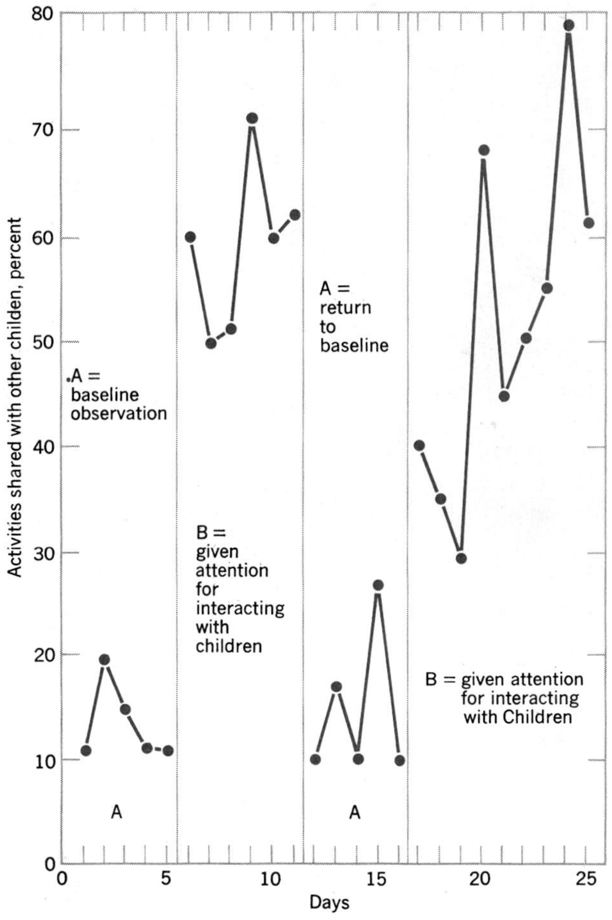

FIGURE 1.1

ABAB study of isolated behavior. The ordinate of the graph is the percentage of time that two children spent with other children. The abscissa is the series of 25 days over which the experiment was conducted. Section A, baseline observation, was a period when the children received no special treatment. In section B the independent variable was introduced. The teacher paid attention to the children when they played with other children. The third and fourth sections show what happened in a return to baseline (A) and in a reintroduction of the independent variable (B). (After Allen et al., 1964.)

Results. Much of what is stated verbally in this book, and probably much of what your instructors present, will also be given in graphic form. Do not ignore or pass lightly over such presentations. They are important because they convey information very concisely.

Figure 1.1 shows what happened in the four stages of this experiment. The dependent variable, the percentage of activity shared with other children, is given on the vertical axis, the ***y*-axis** or **ordinate** of the graph. The horizontal axis, the ***x*-axis** or **abscissa,** rep-

A child may be alone in the classroom because of shyness or unhappiness, because she has been rejected by other children, or because she chooses aloneness as a means of attracting attention.

resents the twenty-five days of the experiment. The four panels in the graph lay out the ABAB design: baseline, independent variable, return to baseline, independent variable. You can see at a glance that more activities were shared with other children when the teacher paid attention to such behavior and fewer when she did not.

The line plotted in the last panel of Figure 1.1 suggests that the two youngsters may have been developing a tendency to give up their isolated play and to interact more with other children. Follow-up observations over a period of weeks indicated that this was indeed the case. The fairly straightforward psychological treatment of rewarding social interactions had improved the behavior of the children.

Chaos in the classroom An experiment that demonstrated a way of reducing the noise level in a fourth-grade classroom (Schmidt and Ulrich, 1969) will review the ABAB design. The experiment was carried out on a particularly unruly class whose typical activities created an amount of noise that made instruction impossible. Baseline observations (A) consisted of monitoring the level of noise for ten sessions before the introduction of a procedure designed to reduce this level. This procedure (B) was to give the pupils extra gym time and a break from classroom activities for keeping noise at a level considerably lower than normal. During this period, which lasted for seven sessions, a whistle was blown whenever the pupils were making more noise than they were supposed to. Following these seven sessions there was a return to baseline (A) for six sessions, during which the pupils

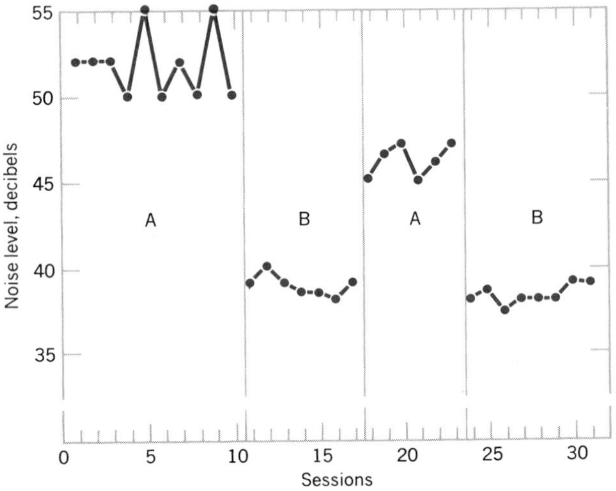

FIGURE 1.2
ABAB study controlling noise in a classroom. (After Schmidt and Urlich, 1969.)

were not rewarded for quietness, and then a series of sessions (B) in which rewards for being more quiet were offered again. This completed the ABAB experiment.

The horizontal axis of the graph in Figure 1.2 is marked off in sessions, each consisting of several days. The vertical axis is noise level in decibels, a measurement of loudness. The A and B phases of the experiment are indicated as panels. As you can see, the classroom became much quieter when the children were rewarded for being quiet. The abrupt shift in noise levels indicates that the independent variable does, in fact, control the noisiness of the pupils.

Variations The ABAB experiment is one of a family of designs that are used in small-*N* research. Some of the designs in this family cut down on the number of phases. Others increase the number of phases. Still others allow the investigator to study the effect of more than one independent variable and to phase in these variables in ways that permit the investigator to observe their cumulative effects. Our final example follows an ABCB design. In this design, the letter A, as usual, stands for a period of baseline observation, and B represents the introduction of an independent variable. In stage C there was a different type of independent variable. The final stage B was a return to the earlier stage B conditions.

Using this design, a research-minded group of psychiatrists and psychologists (Agras et al., 1974) sought to treat a life-threatening medical condition with a behavior modification procedure. The disorder, *anorexia nervosa,* is a comparatively rare condition but one whose incidence appears to be increasing. It is best described as self-inflicted starvation. In 1868 the first clinical reports of a condition of extreme emaciation afflicting young women between the ages of sixteen and twenty-three appeared. The symptoms have not changed much in the interim: severe reduction in food intake, emaciation, cessation of menses, constipation, slowed pulse and respiration, the absence of other somatic or bodily pathology, at least in the beginning stage of the disorder, and restless activity. Weight loss can be so great that accompanying physiological changes are difficult to reverse; the disorder can bring death. The cause of the disorder has still not been determined. Various forms of treatment, such as forced tube feeding, drugs, psychoanalytic therapy, and harsh discipline, have been attempted with varying degrees of failure.

The patient in this study, a five-foot-tall, thirteen-year-old girl, was admitted to the hospital after her weight had dropped from 117 pounds to 77 pounds. The severe weight loss had followed upon a diet which her mother had insisted that she adhere to. The girl's menses had ceased, she now ate very little, and she had grown depressed.

Stage A: Baseline observation. At the beginning of treatment, the patient was told that the staff was concerned about her, that she was expected to eat as much as possible, and that four meals of 1500 calories each would be served at set times during the day. She was asked to count and plot on a graph the mouthfuls of food swallowed. After she had entered the number on the graph, she was given a card that informed her of the number of calories she had consumed. In addition, each morning she was told her weight. During this baseline phase the patient was given a minimum amount of nursing attention and was confined a large part of the day to her room, except for three scheduled periods when she could go to the dayroom. Her room was without reading or writing materials, television or radio, for reasons that will become apparent as the next phase is described.

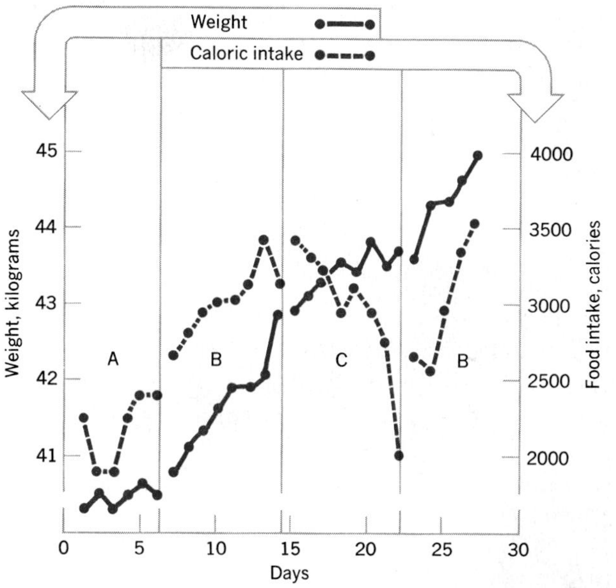

FIGURE 1.3
Control of anorexia nervosa through reward for eating. The four panels are A, baseline observation; B, privileges depend on eating; C, privileges continue but are not contingent on eating; B, privileges are again contingent on eating.

Stage B: Introduction of the independent variable, privileges for weight gain. During this second phase, for each 3½-ounce gain in weight over the previous high weight, the patient received privileges for the day. She could leave her room or have a radio or television brought to it, play games with the nurse, or converse with other patients in the dayroom. But as stage B progressed, in order for the patient to have a day of privileges, the necessary additional weight that she had to gain slowly rose to 8.8 ounces.

Stage C: Privileges given whether or not weight was gained. Stage C was an interesting modification of stage B. The treatment team wanted to know whether weight was gained in stage B because being allowed privileges *depended on it.* One way of answering this question is to give the patient the same privileges in stage C as in stage B, whatever the patient's daily caloric intake and weight gain.

Stage B: Reintroduction of the independent variable, privileges again made contingent on weight gain. Making privileges again contingent on weight gain will confirm their power to encourage eating. The final stage B is simply a repeat of the earlier stage B.

Weight, expressed in kilograms, is measured along the ordinate on the left side of Figure 1.3, caloric intake on the right ordinate. In stage B the increase in food intake and weight gain was steady. In stage C, however, when receiving privileges was no longer dependent on eating, caloric intake dropped markedly, and weight gain slowed considerably. When receiving privileges depended again on weight gain in the second stage B, both food intake and weight increased once more.

SUMMARY □

The wide-ranging interests of psychologists have led to the development of methods appropriate to them. We have considered two traditional methods, case histories and experiments. Case histories suffer from several deficiencies as a scientific method. They are retrospective and subject to errors of memory. Because they are unique, no general conclusions can be drawn. They emphasize the peculiar aspects of behavior. They are complex and seldom allow a single interpretation. But case histories do provide a rich source of information for psychologists. They often yield the ideas with which other investigations begin.

In the most traditional experiments one group of individuals, an experimental group, receives some special treatment and a control group does not. The treatment is considered an independent variable because the investigator manipulates it to determine its effect on behavior, or more narrowly on another variable which is dependent on it. Experiments proceed in three stages: equating groups, treating experimental and control groups differently, and assessing the effect on the behavior in which the psychologist is interested.

In recent years a variety of experimental designs have been developed and applied to small groups of individuals or even single persons. In these small-*N* experiments the same subjects undergo the two different conditions of the experiment. In the ABAB form of such experiments, the baseline observations of activity are made (A), experimental treatment is introduced (B), it is withdrawn and conditions are as they were at first (A), then the experimental treatment is reintroduced (B).

In both types of experiments, the effects of experimental treatment on behavior are determined. In traditional experiments the assessment whether the effect is attributable to the treatment or could have occurred by chance is usually statistical. In small-*N* experiments the analysis is often graphic.

THE ISSUE OF ARTIFICIALITY

It is important to recognize that the value of experiments comes from certain of their features. Two of these are especially significant. First, the fact that the conditions of the experiment are manipulated by experimenters means that they can pick any condition, arrange for it to happen, and determine the result. Second, by creating an artificial and limited situation, experimenters control the circumstances of behavior more exactly than by any other method. This second feature increases the precision of experiments but it also raises a question. In setting up such limited situations, do we sacrifice all relevance to everyday life?

Increasing the Realism of Experiments

A classic experiment by Roger Barker, Tamara Dembo, and Kurt Lewin (1941) demonstrates the problem. They studied the constructiveness in play of young children under nonfrustrating and frustrating conditions. During the first part of the experiment, the children played with a standard set of toys, such as dolls, telephones, and crayons. Psychologists observed them and rated their play for constructiveness, depending on its quality. Subsequently, the children were allowed to play in a more attractive situation—in a large, furnished dollhouse which they could enter and at a nearby table set for a party. As the children's absorption in the new play situations grew, frustration was introduced by having them return to the standard set of toys while the more attractive dollhouse and party table remained visible through a screen.

The important laboratory finding was that after the children had become frustrated, the constructiveness of their play declined. Clifford Fawl (1963), however, using records of children's behavior in natural settings, later found that frustration was infrequent and did not have the negative consequences observed in the controlled laboratory situations of the earlier experiment.

What do such discrepancies imply? Simply that the experimental situation may not be entirely representative of the real world. In this example we suspect that the original experimental situation was too artificial to capture important processes that must be taken into account, which suggests a second question. Can we make the experimental situation more realistic and lifelike so that we will feel greater confidence in generalizing laboratory findings to real-life situations? The answer is that we can, but carrying out such experiments raises moral problems. Putting subjects under stress that is strong enough to have powerful effects on behavior raises ethical questions. One highly realistic experiment has been heavily criticized on ethical grounds.

Investigators doing research for the army (Berkun et al., 1962) wanted to study the responses of recruits under conditions that would simulate the stressful pressures of war. To accomplish this they selected at random groups of army recruits being trained in the techniques of radio communication. One group of recruits was placed aboard a transport plane. While in flight, they were told that a crash landing was imminent. Another unit was informed that accidental nuclear radiation was being emitted in the area. Other recruits were told that a forest fire was engulfing their forward outpost, a threat made more realistic by the use of artificial smoke machines. Still others heard a fictitious report that their outpost was being subjected to misdirected artillery fire, which they could clearly hear. Each recruit had been given a radio transmitter. In each of the crises, however, the transmitter, the recruit's most likely tool for securing help, failed, although he continued to receive stressful messages of the impending disaster.

In each crisis the recruit was told that he could avoid the disaster by repairing his transmitter; this would enable him to send a rescue message to a helicopter which was hovering over the area. The effectiveness with which the potential victim responded to stress was measured in several ways. How quickly did he begin to work on his radio? How well was he able to read a wiring diagram and absorb the instructions necessary to repair the instrument? And how effectively could he make satisfactory, simple repairs to put the equipment back in working order?

Of the various crises, the misdirected artillery fire condition proved the most stressful. The recruits in this situation first expressed shock and disbelief. Then they made urgent efforts to protect themselves. Most stood by their sets on command and attempted to reestablish communication with headquarters. Once they began the constructive task of trying to repair the set, many of the subjects concentrated less on the dangerous situation. Ten soldiers, however, overwhelmed by the apparent danger confronting them, were unable to cope and fled, an unfortunate but powerful testimonial to the reality of this experimental simulation of wartime stress.

Was it ethical experimental procedure to inflict an individual with this level of stress? Should not a person give informed consent before being expected to endure suffering? Was the information gained of sufficient import to warrant the procedures used to obtain it? We return to these questions more directly at the end of the chapter. For now it will be enough to note that experiments have the potential of raising very worrisome ethical problems. Such concerns have led many investigators to seek answers to their questions in the accidental experiments that happen in everyday life, in **naturalistic observation.**

Naturalistic "Experiments"

In the experiments described so far in this chapter, the investigator has taken an active hand in the procedures, creating the conditions whose effects were to be determined. In some situations it is possible to let nature produce the experimental manipulations. Here is an example.

If you have gone as a member of a large group to a good restaurant, you may have been infuriated to discover that an automatic 15 percent gratuity is added to the bill in some of these places. Restaurants have established this policy because the size of a customer's tip tends to vary inversely with the number of people in the party. The automatic gratuity forestalls dissatisfaction on the part of poorly tipped waiters. In one naturalistic experiment, which made the basic point, the investigators kept track of the tips left by parties of different sizes and plotted the percentage of the tip against number of people in the party (Figure 1.4).

Obviously this study has most of the features of a true experiment. There is an independent variable, number of people in the party, and a dependent variable, size of the tip. The study was carried out in the same restaurants to control a number of other important variables. The chief difference between this and a true experiment was that the investigators could not manipulate the independent variable and had to accept, instead, the naturally occurring values of this variable, the number of people in the dinner party, as they happened.

The most important message of this study is not so much the results obtained as what everyone will recognize to be a more general implication. People alone or in small groups are identifiable, and if they leave a small tip the waiter will know it. Thus, under the waiter's eagle eye, they behave differently than they would in the relative anonymity of a dinner party

FIGURE 1.4

Cheaper by the bunch. As the number of people in a restaurant dinner party increases, the size of the tip goes down. (After Freeman, Walker, Borden, and Latané, 1975.)

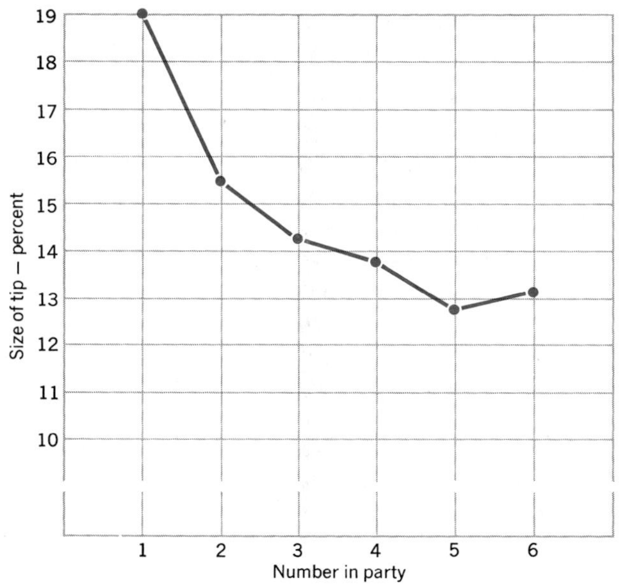

of six or eight. More generally, this means that, when people know that their behavior is being observed, this fact alone influences their behavior. Recognition of this fact has altered methods of psychological experimentation and the look of experimental design.

Demand Characteristics of Experiments

Human participants in research treat the experience as though it places them under certain obligations, which may have nothing to do with the investigator's purposes. Their behavior may reflect these **demand characteristics** of the experiment rather than the hoped-for effect of the experimental treatment.

One experimenter's efforts to develop a set of tasks so meaningless or boring that college students would give up in disgust provide an amusing example. The experimenter gave each of a group of students a stack of 2000 sheets of paper. Each sheet contained rows of random digits, which they were to add. The experimenter departed, and the students proceeded to tackle this Herculean project. Five and a half hours later, the students were still at the task! The experimenter surrendered.

Next he proceeded to make the task even more frustrating. The research participants were told that when they had finished adding the numbers on each sheet, they were to draw a card from a large pile, which would give them further instructions. Every card in the pile carried the same instruction.

> You are to tear up the sheet of paper which you have just completed into a minimum of thirty-two pieces and go on to the next sheet of paper and continue working as you did before; when you have completed this piece of paper, pick up the next card, which will instruct you further. Work as rapidly and accurately as possible.

Certainly a meaningless task, but once again the students persisted.

A postexperimental inquiry explained this remarkable stamina; invariably, the participants perceived the task as a test of endurance. It is plain that research participants develop their own hypotheses about the experiments in which they serve, and these hypotheses may have little or no correspondence to the experimental intensions of the investigator.

Demand Characteristics and Sensory Deprivation

In experiments on sensory deprivation, individuals are isolated for extended periods of time. Insofar as possible all stimulation is eliminated. The person may be immersed in tepid water with a mask covering the eyes and ears; or the individual may lie on a bed with eyes covered, ears plugged, and extremities encased in tubes to eliminate tactile stimulation. In these circumstances some people suffer hallucinations and extreme panic. Because of the possibility of such traumatic effects, experimenters always provide the individual with a means of escaping from the isolation chamber.

In an ingenious experiment Martin Orne (1962) demonstrated that many people will behave in a manner comparable to that of individuals subjected to sensory deprivation, even though their situation does not actually shut them away from any of their sensations. Male college students in the experimental group came to the laboratory believing that they were to participate in "a psychological experiment in meaning deprivation." The students were greeted by the experimenter, who was dressed in a white medical coat; in the course of taking a medical history, the experimenter asked questions about past history of dizziness, fainting spells, and so on. In plain view as the information was gathered was a tray of drugs and medical instruments labeled "Emergency Tray."

The instructions given the subjects emphasized what a person might possibly experience during sensory deprivation—fantasies, difficulties in concentration, hallucinations, disorientation, and the like. A critical component of the instructions was this provision. "If at any time you feel very discomforted you may obtain release immediately by pressing the button which I will show you once we enter the chamber. Do not hesitate to use this button if the situation becomes difficult. However, try to stick it out if you can."

The control group heard the same set of instructions, but the white coat, emergency tray, and medical history were omitted. Moreover, these individuals were told that they constituted a control group for a sensory deprivation experiment. Members of both groups were placed one at a time in the same room. The room itself was not at all like a sensory deprivation chamber. The participating individuals could hear voices, footsteps, the sound of cars and planes, and the chirping of birds; they could move about freely in the large and well-lighted area.

Ten tests successfully used by previous investigators to detect the effects of sensory deprivation were administered before and after the stay in the experimental room. Comparing the answers given by two groups, Orne found that on thirteen of fourteen measures, answers of members of the experimental group differed from those of the control group, always in the direction of accounts previously obtained after sensory deprivation. Some reported perceptual aberrations—"The walls of the room are starting to waver"; periods of "blankness" during which they failed to remember things; and claustrophobic anxiety, spatial disorientation, and restlessness. Some gave "an impression of almost being tortured." Orne believed that the panic cues provided by the experimenter—white coat, medical history, and emergency tray—

had made members of the experimental group expect discomfort and stress, and so they found them.

The Placebo Effect The demand characteristics of a situation, as indicated in Orne's experiments, derive from cues that inform individuals what is expected of them. Nowhere are such cues more important than in the doctor-patient relationship. The doctor's confident assertion that a proposed treatment will make the patient well can have more to do with recovery than the drugs prescribed or any other physical remedy the doctor may suggest. This is the **placebo effect.** Typically, it operates in the direction of cure, for the doctor is by stereotype a healer.

The word *placebo* in Latin means, "I shall please," and a placebo has been defined as a medicine given "merely to humor the patient." It contains no active pharmacological substance but is administered for its psychological effect. A "sugar pill" is the well-known example. But the placebo effect applies to psychotherapies as well as to physical agents. Here, too, a cure may have nothing to do with the particular type of psychotherapy employed.

It is important to recognize that expectations other than the patient's may be involved. The clinical researcher usually has a heavy emotional investment in the worth of a particular therapy and may see more improvement in a treated patient than the objective facts warrant. The general term for this second effect is **experimenter bias.** Thus, in order to evaluate the success of any program of therapy, it is important to control for the overly optimisitc evaluations of the therapist as well as for those of the patient.

In drug research, which will serve as an example, the usual method is a **double-blind procedure,** which exercises two types of control. (1) To control for effects on the patient of knowing that he or she is receiving a drug, experimenters give some patients placebos that are indistinguishable from the drug by sight, smell, and taste but have no pharmacological properties. Other patients receive the drug. (2) To control for effects on the investigators, judges who do not know which patients have received the drug and which the placebo rate their improvement.

Unobtrusive Measures

The message in all these studies, once again, is that scientific psychologists must always be alert to the possibility that obtained results may reflect their own biases or those of their research participants rather than the psychological process allegedly being studied. For a long time psychologists have been aware of the danger that their results are at least contaminated by a sort of "guinea pig effect." If people know that they are being studied or tested, they may try to make a good impression, or sometimes a bad one. If the procedures suggest certain types of responses, people tend to comply or resist, depending on their perception of themselves and the situation. Some psychologists have been so impressed with these effects that they have proposed the complete abandonment of laboratory experimentation. Most psychologists do not go this far, but they do propose that we rely to a greater extent on **unobtrusive measures.**

Unobtrusive measures make use of records which participants need not know are being made. They consist of evidence that accumulates in the course of everyday living and has a bearing on questions of

Patterns of seating in the lunchroom may indicate that segregation exists in a supposedly integrated school.

psychological interest. E. J. Webb and his colleagues (1966) have given some examples.

- Racial attitudes in college students were assessed by noting the degree of clustering of black and white students in lecture halls.
- The increasing fear of children being told a ghost story was measured in terms of the shrinking diameter of the circle of seated children.
- Rate of alcohol consumption in a "dry" town was determined by counting discarded liquor bottles in ashcans.
- One investigator studied the effects of television on library withdrawals by comparing them before and after television came to a community. Fiction dropped off. Nonfiction was unaffected.
- Interest in a chick-hatching exhibit at the Chicago Museum of Science and Industry was evident from the fact that floor tiles in front of the exhibit lasted only six weeks, as compared to years before most other displays.
- Records of parking meter collections indicated the effect of a strike on business. There was a marked drop in revenue during the period of the strike.
- Measures of water pressure provided an index to patterns of television viewing. A marked periodicity of water pressure was linked to the beginning and end of programs, when people drew water for a drink or flushed the toilet.
- Even more dramatically, power blackouts in the United Kingdom coincided with the commercials on television. Apparently people simultaneously took that moment to plug in water heaters for making tea and overloaded the circuits of the national power system.

Correlational Methods

It has been claimed that a survey carried out in the state of Montana revealed a positive correlation between the number of saloons and the number of churches in a town, the more saloons, the more churches. This discovery raises a question of cause and effect. Do saloons create a need for churches, or is it the other way round, that churches create a need for saloons? Actually, the answer is "neither" but, before we explain the answer, this example will serve to illustrate the concept of correlation. Things like the number of churches and saloons are correlated when they are co-related, when they go together, when one thing varies systematically with variation in the other. **Correlational studies** search for such covariation. No variable is manipulated. The measures are often unobtrusive, but they need not be.

Positive and Negative Correlation The correlation between churches and saloons in Montana, and probably everywhere, is a **positive correlation.** Large numbers of churches go with large numbers of saloons. Small numbers of churches go with small numbers of saloons. Events sometimes show a **negative correlation.** Large values of one thing go with small values of the other and vice versa. One significant example is a negative correlation, community by community in Bavaria, between the percentage of babies who are breast-fed and infant mortality rate: the greater the percentage of babies who are breast-fed, the lower the mortality rate (Knodel, 1977).

Degree of Correlation The only remaining point to be made about correlations is that they vary in degree. Whether positive or negative, the correspondence between the correlated measures can be anywhere between perfect and nonexistent. The degree of such correspondence is represented by a correlation coefficient, for which the symbol is r, standing for "relationship." Correlation coefficients fall somewhere on a scale that goes from $r = -1.0$, perfect negative relationship; through $r = 0$, no relationship; to $r = +1.0$, perfect positive relationship. The scale, of course, includes numbers in between these three values, for example, $r = .95$, $r = .36$, $r = .47$, and $r = -.80$. The Statistical Appendix explains where these numbers come from (see page 503). For the purposes of this chapter, it will be sufficient to illustrate the meaning of varying degrees of relationship by citing some examples, which will either be familiar or easy to understand.

- The IQs of pairs of identical twins are very similar. The chances are 50–50 that these two IQs will differ by no more than about 5 points . . . $r = +.90$.
- Ratings of the qualities of jug wines by expert tasters and the costs of these same wines are closely correlated. At least in the case of jug wines, we get about what we pay for . . . $r = +.85$.
- There is no relationship between the IQs of individuals and their physical strength . . . $r = .00$.
- In a selection of districts in England, there was a close negative relationship between the amount of open park space and accident rates for children. The more open space, the lower the accident rate . . . $r = -.85$.
- As mentioned earlier, the higher the percentage of breast-fed children in German communities, the lower the infant mortality rate. The negative relationship is surprisingly high . . . $r = -.90$.

Applications of the Method The correlational methods are an important source of information in psychology and are basic in the field of psychological testing. Suppose that a new test claims to measure aptitude for engineering. How would its formulator go about determining whether it really tests for this aptitude? The concept of correlation is central to the answer to this question.

The test formulator would begin by gathering a group of people who want to be engineers, administering the test to each of them, and keeping a record of their scores. Then it would be necessary to wait until some measure of their performance in an engineering situation became available. Grades in an engineering school might serve the purpose. If those who do well on the test also do well in the practical situation, and if those who do poorly on the test also do poorly in an engineering school, it would seem that the test actually does measure the capacity of interest. The accuracy with which it measures this aptitude would be indicated by the size of the correlation between test scores and engineering school grades.

As another example, A. Davids and S. DeVault (1962) studied the relationship between certain personality traits of pregnant women and the difficulty of childbirth. They first gave a series of personality tests to a group of women in their seventh month of pregnancy. After the babies had been born, they consulted the obstetricians' records to determine whether the personality traits of the mothers predicted anything at all about ease of delivery. They found a rather strong relationship between level of anxiety and two indicators of difficulty in delivery. Highly anxious women tended to remain longer in the delivery room, and the attending physicians noted a greater number of unusual circumstances associated with the birth.

Correlation Is Not Causation The existence of a correlation between two measures does not mean that one measure causes the other, or even that one measure does not cause the other. There is a strong positive correlation between the number of fire engines in the several boroughs of New York City and the number of fires in these same boroughs. If there is a causal relationship in this case, of course, it is that the fires are responsible for the number of fire engines, not that the engines cause fires. This example makes the point that, even though a causal relationship exists between correlated data, *the direction of causation is ambiguous.*

For the correlation between saloons and churches, with which this section began, *a third factor is the causal one.* Numbers of saloons and churches both increase as the size of the city increases. Per thousand of population, the number of saloons and the number of churches are about the same, whether the city is large or small.

There are ways to obtain causal information from correlational data, but they are pretty much beyond the scope of this book (see page 506). The essential point to remember is that, usually, correlations provide little useful information about causation.

SUMMARY □

The artificiality of laboratory experiments is a source of strength and a source of weakness. On the side of strength, artificiality allows a high degree of control in the experimental situation. On the negative side, this control may make experiments so different from real life that the results do not apply to real situations. One way to assure that experiments will be relevant is to conduct realistic ones. Studies of this type have been done, but they sometimes raise difficult ethical questions.

Even in naturalistic experiments the demand characteristics of experiments raise other questions about the credibility of experimental results. Subjects in experiments too often behave as they think the situation demands. This point was made dramatically in a study in which the experimenters led subjects to anticipate sensory deprivation and to expect it to be stressful. The participants found the situation so, even though there was no sensory deprivation. The placebo effect, commonly encountered in medical research, is a related example. Patients expect the treatments to cure them and this expectation may produce a cure. Along with the placebo effect on patients, the medical researcher treating them has a strong tendency to detect improvement, rather than worsening or no change. Such problems have led to the development of double-blind procedures in which neither patients nor investigators know the particular role played by a particular subject in the experiment. The problems associated with experiments have also encouraged research that requires no manipulations but relies instead on unobtrusive measures.

The correlational methods are not experimental methods, because they examine naturally occurring relationships between variables. The degree and direction of such relationships are expressed by a correlation coefficient, ranging from -1.0 to $+1.0$. The absolute size of the correlation ranging from 0 to ± 1.0 indicates the closeness of the correlation. Correlations of $+.60$ and $-.60$ represent equally close relationships. The sign of the correlation, plus or minus, indicates the direction of the correlation. An important point to remember is that correlations do not mean causality.

THE ETHICS OF PSYCHOLOGICAL RESEARCH

As we have already noted, there are times when psychological research begins to raise moral issues. In one study the privacy of the home was invaded to determine energy consumption. In another some disadvantaged children received tutoring in reading, while others were deprived of the same opportunity. In a third study children who were inclined toward isolation were influenced to become more sociable, something that may have been against their nature. In another experiment individuals were allowed to discover their cowardice in a situation of contrived emergency. Is it ethically acceptable to carry on such research?

On the other hand, is it ethically acceptable *not* to do such research? Many of the current ills of society have a psychological component. If these ills are to be understood and corrected, there must be studies of the psychology of energy consumption, of techniques for increasing the educability of deprived children, and of reactions of people to stress. This means that the participants in psychological research will sometimes be placed in a position of jeopardy. Protecting the welfare of these participants is a matter of considerable importance.

A Code of Research Ethics

For several years a committee of the American Psychological Association, under the chairmanship of Professor Stuart W. Cook, devoted itself to the development of a code of ethics to cover the treatment of human subjects. Both the method of developing this code and the code itself are important.

The code was developed empirically. Almost 20,000 members of the association were asked to contribute actual incidents that they believed raised ethical problems. The committee received thousands of examples, which they sorted into such groupings as stress, invasion of privacy, and deception. With these categories established, the next step was to develop guidelines for psychologists to use in handling the ethical issues involved. In this process the committee called in experts from medicine, other fields of social science, and philosophy as consultants.

It quickly became clear that the psychological investigators are in a situation of conflict. The most effective contribution that they can make to the betterment of society is through research, but any research requires at least some impositions upon the participants. Moreover, the more important the research question, the more serious these impositions are likely to be. Studies of learning and memory seldom raise ethical questions of serious proportions. Research on obedience, social conformity, stress, and pain do. Thus psychological investigators must weigh the possible benefits to society that a particular study may yield against the demands that are placed on the participants. They should proceed only if their evaluation, aided by outside advice if necessary, is clearly supportive. To guide this judgment of pros and cons, the committee made available an ethical code, as well as a longer discussion of the problem (American Psychological Association, 1973).

Stuart W. Cook directed a study that led to the formulation of a code of ethical principles to guide research with human subjects.

Guidelines for Research

The code itself provides a set of ten principles designed to serve as guidelines for the conduct of research with human beings.

- The researcher is personally responsible for the ethical acceptability of each study that is undertaken.

- This ethical responsibility extends to the behavior of assistants and colleagues.
- The researcher should inform participants of all features of the research that might influence a decision whether or not to participate.
- If deception is required in a study, the deception and the reason for it should be explicitly explained once the experiment is completed.
- Participants should not be coerced to participate, and they should have the freedom to discontinue participation at any point if they wish to do so.
- At the beginning of the experiment the investigator should present a clear description of the procedures to be employed and of what the participant is expected to do.
- Participants should be protected from physical discomfort, harm, and danger, and from all forms of mental stress. If the potential for such consequences exists, the investigator should inform participants of this fact, secure their consent to proceed, and take all possible measures to minimize the distress that may be experienced.
- At the end of an experiment, the investigator has the responsibility to explain the experiment and to remove any misconceptions that may have arisen.
- The experimenter has responsibility for detecting and correcting any undesirable outcomes of a person's participation in a study.
- Complete confidentiality about individual participants in research must be maintained.

SUMMARY □

The knowledge to be acquired through psychological research is potentially relevant to the ills besetting society. To the extent that the problems we are trying to solve have to do with pain and stress, these conditions may have to be imposed on people in order to collect needed information. The experimental procedures may very well be harmful to research participants. The ethical dilemma is obvious. A code of ethics for research with human beings has been developed. The aim of this code is to foster research and at the same time to protect the welfare of the people who participate in it.

AN INVITATION TO PSYCHOLOGY

In bringing this chapter to a close, we offer a bit of guidance which may increase the value of your study of psychology. The rest of this book consists of five major parts and a Statistical Appendix. When you have finished reading this chapter, it would be a good idea to page through the rest of the book, in order to get a general impression of its content. Along the way you may want to read pages 165 to 170 in Chapter 7 carefully. They present some practical hints on memory which should be useful.

A major problem for us as authors and for many students is the topic of statistics. Our solution has been to present statistical materials as they are needed and to present them nonmathematically. You have already encountered most of these materials in this chapter. Although this type of coverage is adequate for an understanding of the psychological materials we present, that understanding will be enriched by reading the Statistical Appendix. It will pay off if you do so early.

Each chapter in this book ends with two end notes. The first item is always a list of the major concepts covered in the chapter. These concepts are listed in roughly the order in which they came up in the chapter. If you really know the contents of a chapter, you will be able to use these concepts as cues and reproduce its content. If you find that you cannot do so, although you feel that you understand the materials, the problem is likely to be with the standards you are setting for yourself when you conclude that you know the materials (see page 165).

The second item suggests additional materials to study in this book and elsewhere. It will deepen your understanding of psychology if you do some of this extra study. We know, however, that your time is limited. Depending on your personal schedule, we suggest that you do as much as possible of the following, in this order. (1) Review recommended materials that you have already studied. This will be a very useful way to help pull things together. (2) Read ahead in this book when that is recommended. Sometimes you will be referred to materials that your instructors have not assigned. (3) At least browse through some of the other recommended readings. Particularly if you are going on in psychology, they will help you get an impression of what more advanced courses will be like. Our recommendations will frequently be the textbooks in these courses.

TO BE SURE YOU UNDERSTAND THIS CHAPTER △

As we mentioned in the last section of this chapter, the major concepts will be listed in roughly the order in which they came up. In the text itself, these items almost always appear in boldface type. You should be able to define each concept. If your instructor uses objective tests, such definitions will go a long way toward preparing you for such tests. But your understanding of these concepts should go beyond the level of definition. You should be able to state the points the text makes about each concept, in effect to reproduce the contents of the chapter. Here are the concepts for Chapter 1.

Case history
Experimentation
Experimental group
Control group
Independent variable
Controlled variable
Dependent variable
Statistical significance
Small-*N* design
Baseline
Return to baseline
Y-axis (ordinate)
X-axis (abscissa)
Naturalistic observation
Demand characteristics
Placebo effect
Experimenter bias
Unobtrusive measures
Correlational studies
Positive correlation
Negative correlation

In addition to these major concepts, there will always be some minor ones that your instructor may or may not expect you to know. They will almost always be *italicized* in the text. Examples from Chapter 1 are the following.

Paranoid crystallization
ABAB and ABCB designs
Anorexia nervosa
Placebo

Some materials do not lend themselves to recall with only the aid of major, and even minor, concepts as cues. Examples from Chapter 1 are

Strengths and weaknesses of case history method
Stages in a typical experiment
Positive and negative values of artificiality in experiments
Correlation versus causation

TO GO BEYOND THIS CHAPTER △

In this book What might be included here has been covered in part in the final section of the text. If we have a single, strongest recommendation to make, it would be to read the Statistical Appendix. Other related materials are to be found throughout the book. Chapter 17 presents a good many case histories which illustrate the method further. Examples of experimentation are most numerous in Parts 2 and 4 of the text. Examples of correlational methods are most numerous in Parts 3 and 5.

Elsewhere This paragraph directs you to other books that you might find useful. Usually we give just the title and author, listing complete references in the bibliography at the end of the book. This time we cite the complete reference here and make just one recommendation: Patricia Lunneborg,

Why Study Psychology? Monterey, Calif.: Brooks/Cole Publishing Company, 1978. This reference, a brief paperback booklet, addresses most of the issues confronting college students, the audience for *this* book, as they begin their study of psychology.

PART 1

THE WORLD OF AWARENESS

CH. 2

The Nervous System and Behavior

The Neuron
Communicative Action of the Neuron
Integrative Action
Excitation and Inhibition
Summary

The Fundamental Plan of the Nervous System
Spinal Cord
Function
Reflex Action
Summary
Hindbrain
Midbrain

Cerebrum
Old Forebrain
New Forebrain
Connections Between the Hemispheres
Summary

This chapter was written by R. Bruce Masterton, Florida State University.

The most direct information about the functioning of the human nervous system has been collected in the aftermath of damage and disease. The most common type of injury to the adult brain, and the one most familiar to the general public, is disruption of the blood supply. This disruption may be the plugging of an artery with fatty material, called *cerebral atherosclerosis;* by a clot that has formed at a site so narrowed, a *thrombosis;* or by a clot that has traveled from elsewhere and become lodged, an *embolism.* Or an artery may burst and *hemorrhage.* Any of these events quickly kills the nerve cells that depended on the interrupted blood supply for oxygen and glucose. The individual falls unconscious, as if struck by a blow, and is said to have suffered a "stroke." If the patient recovers, behavior is often altered dramatically. The patient may appear dazed and inattentive; one side of the face may droop and one arm and one leg may be immobile, a condition known as *hemiplegia.* Speech is sometimes markedly disturbed, which indicates that the patient has one of the several forms of *aphasia.* From the study of the relationship between symptoms such as these and the location of the damage in the brain, it is possible to gain considerable knowledge about how the nervous system works. Since the fundamental structure and function of the human nervous system are the same as that of our vertebrate ancestors, the general principles of neural action discovered in studies of animals apply to the human nervous system as well.

Overview of Structure Our particular version of the basic vertebrate nervous system (Figures 2.1 and 2.2) consists of two principal parts, the **peripheral nervous system** and the **central nervous system.** There are, in turn, two parts of the central nervous system, the **brain** and **spinal cord,** which are contained within the skull and bony spinal column. Together they control all bodily activity via the peripheral nerves. The peripheral nervous system is divisible into four *functional* parts: the **somatic sensory** nerve fibers, which carry information from the external receptors—the eyes, ears, nose, skin, and so on—to the central nervous system; the **somatic motor** fibers, which carry commands from the central system to the skeletal muscles, those attached to bones, instructing them to move the body; the **visceral sensory** fibers, which carry information regarding the internal state of the body and viscera to the central system; and the **visceral motor** fibers, which carry commands from the central system to the smooth muscles of the blood vessels and internal organs, to heart muscles, and to glands. The visceral motor fibers are usually referred to as the **autonomic nervous system;** it plays a surprisingly large role in a person s reactions to situations that are of psychological importance. The sympathetic and parasympathetic divisions of the autonomic nervous system have functions to be discussed later.

Overview of Function Examination of the most obvious physical features of the nervous system, such as the size of the brain, reveals little or nothing about psychological function. The brains of most adult males weigh about 3 pounds (1400 grams), but some weigh as little as 2 pounds (900 grams), others as much as 4 pounds (1800 grams). We wonder immediately, of course, whether these differences might not be related to intelligence. A number of brains of brilliant men have been weighed after death, and these weights have been compared with the weights of the brains of average, or even subaverage, persons. They are neither heavier nor larger (Donaldson, 1900). Moreover, for at least a hundred years investigators have studied the pattern of furrows and fissures in the brain, hoping to discover intimations of intelligence, personality, and moral fiber, but nothing of the sort was ever demonstrated (Mettler, 1956). This means that the search for a relationship between brain and behavior must turn to a more detailed examination of the nervous system, of its cellular elements, the interconnections among these elements, and the functionings of particular parts of the system.

The almost infinite number of specific functions of the nervous system can be divided into two general categories, *communication* and *integration.* As a communicative network, the nervous system allows organs at one place in the body to respond to events occurring elsewhere. As an integrative system, it deals with the enormous amount of simultaneous stimulation that impinges upon the individual from inside as well as outside the body. It continuously evaluates the importance of all incoming stimulation and directs the activities of the organs into a unified and appropriate course of action.

THE NEURON

The entire nervous system is composed of only two kinds of cells, **glia cells** and **nerve cells** or **neurons.** Glia cells provide a mechanical framework supporting the networks of neurons; they insulate one neuron from another; they police the nervous system for foreign materials and debris resulting from injury or infection; and they provide a chemical barrier, **the blood-brain barrier,** which prevents some substances in the blood from contacting the sensitive nerve cells. Recent discoveries suggest that glia may play a role in functions such as memory, but the extent and nature of these other functions are still a matter of conjecture.

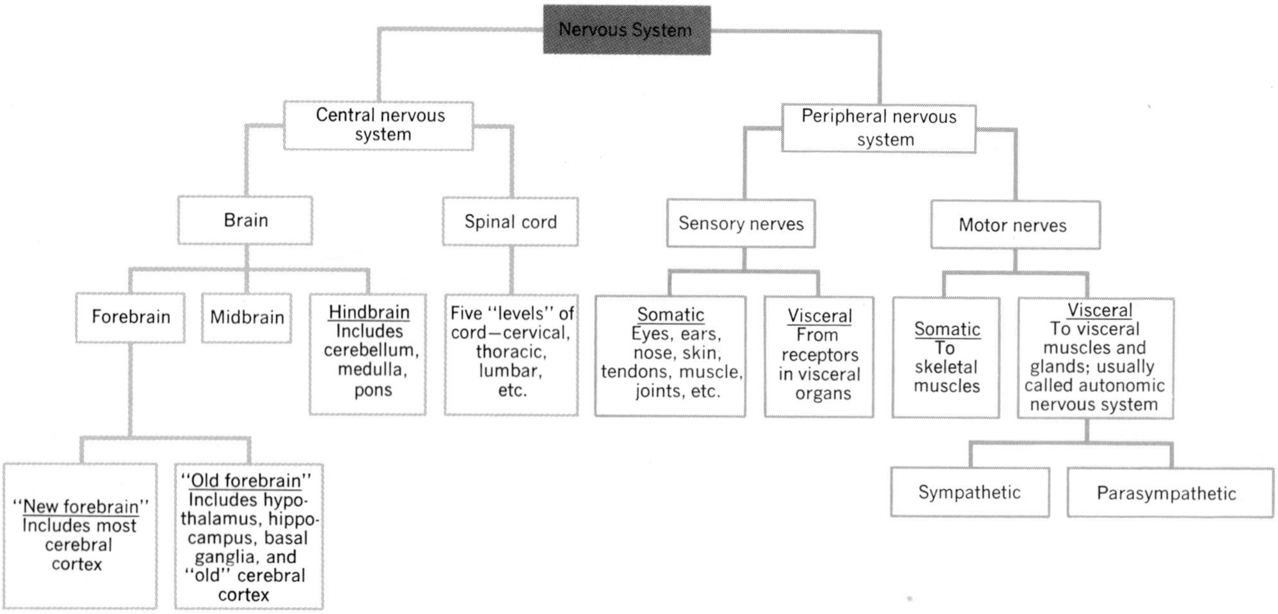

FIGURE 2.1
Major subdivisions of the nervous system. This chart provides an overview of the various sections of the nervous system to be covered in this chapter. Figure 2.2 presents some of the same materials in an anatomical form.

The active elements of the nervous system are the neurons. The nervous system contains many billions of them and they take numerous specialized forms, one of which is shown in Figure 2.3. There are four main parts of a neuron: (1) the **cell body,** which contains the nucleus of the nerve cell and its nutritional mechanisms; (2) several **dèndrites,** which are usually short and thick extensions of the cell body; (3) a single **axon,** which is a thin cylinder of cytoplasm extending for some distance from the cell body and eventually branching; and (4) numerous terminal buttons, each a small swelling at the end of one of the axon's many fine terminal branches. A neuron receives stimulation at its cell body and dendrites, conducts a signal along its axon and emits its responses at the terminal buttons. The axon of a neuron is usually sheathed in a white, fatty, insulating substance called **myelin,** which is produced by the glia. In general, the conductive part of the neuron is myelinated and insulated; receptive parts and the fine terminal branches are not.

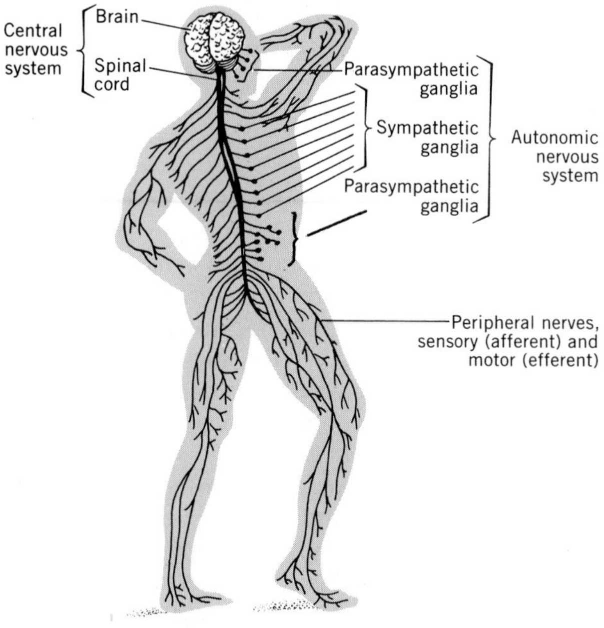

FIGURE 2.2
Plan of the human nervous system. The brain and spinal cord are the two parts of the central nervous system. Sympathetic and parasympathetic ganglia are two parts of the autonomic nervous system. Every organ of the body is connected with every other through the central nervous system.

Communicative Action of the Neuron

The axons of most neurons are less than a millimeter long, but some neurons have axons or nerve fibers several feet in length. For example, the sensory neurons whose dendrites are in the skin of the feet have cell bodies near the spinal cord and terminal buttons near the base of the brain. Thus the site of a neuron's stimulation is usually at some distance, and may be a considerable distance, from the site at which it responds. Obviously, there must be a communicative mechanism by which stimulation of the

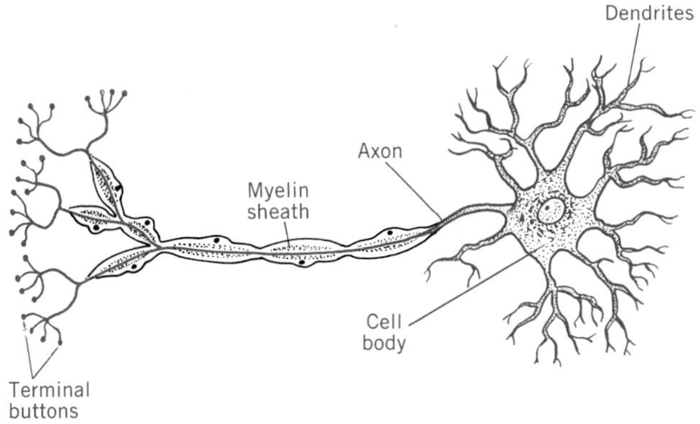

FIGURE 2.3
Schematic drawing of a neuron. The cell body and dendrites are receptive and integrative parts; axons are communicative parts; terminal buttons are transmitting parts. Insulating myelin sheaths the axon. Terminal buttons secrete a transmitter substance, the neurotransmitter, upon arrival of an impulse.

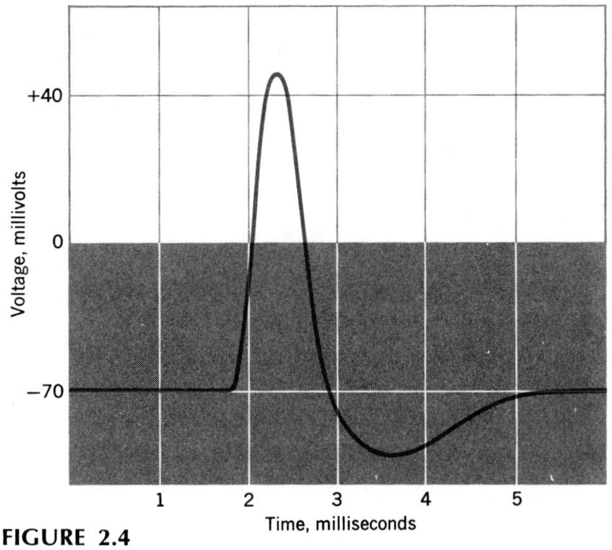

FIGURE 2.4
Tracing of an action potential. The action potential is a reliable pattern of electrical changes that accompany the nerve impulse.

dendrites and cell body of a neuron can trigger a reaction fairly far away. This communicative mechanism is the **nerve impulse.**

The Nerve Impulse When a neuron is adequately stimulated, an electrochemical reaction occurs in the walls of the axon near the place where the axon leaves the cell body. This reaction is the nerve impulse; once established, it traverses the entire axon. The speed of the nerve impulse is fairly slow, 10 to 250 miles per hour, depending on whether the diameter of the axon is small or large, and the thickness of the myelin sheath.

The nerve impulse is accompanied by small electrical changes called an **action potential.** The existence of action potentials makes the nerve impulse relatively easy to observe and measure. A small wire electrode is placed near the axon. Electrical activity in the vicinity of the electrode tip is detected, amplified, and recorded in visual form (Figure 2.4).

One fact revealed by these recordings is that the actual potential of any given neuron is always the same size and shape and has the same speed as it travels the length of the axon. This means that the axon conducts whole impulses or none at all, sometimes called the **all-or-none law** of nerve conduction. The nerve impulse does not die out as it travels because it is a chemical reaction that takes its energy from within the axon itself. In this respect, the axon of a neuron is something like the fuse of a firecracker. The chemicals in the fuse provide the energy that maintains the fire throughout its length.

This total absence of any variation in the action potential as it traverses the length of the axon raises a question. How can the nervous system react differently to stimuli of different strengths, as the fact that we perceive intensity differences suggests it must? One part of the answer to this question is that, as the intensity of stimulation increases, a sensory neuron increases the *rate* at which it generates impulses, up to the limit of its capacity—as many as 200 to 1000 impulses per second. A second part of the answer is that, as the intensity of stimulation increases, more and more nearby neurons generate impulses. Therefore weak stimuli evoke low rates of response, few impulses in only a few neurons. Strong stimuli evoke high rates of response, many impulses in many neurons.

A final point about the action of the neuron is important. Even when there is no obvious stimulation whatsoever, for example, during sleep or even coma, almost every neuron in the nervous system conducts impulses. This spontaneous activity provides a refinement in the neuron's mechanism of communication. The neuron, like a gauge whose pointer rests at the center of its scale instead of at one end, can signal changes in stimulation either by increasing or decreasing its rate of response. That is, the impulse rate of a neuron may be either *excited,* sped up, or *inhibited,* slowed down, by stimulation.

Synaptic Transmission So far we have described only the mechanism by which a neuron communicates within itself, from its cell body to its many axon terminals. How do neurons communicate with each other or with the muscles or glands that they ultimately control?

The mechanism by which neurons stimulate other neurons is called **synaptic transmission.** Figure 2.5 illustrates a junction between two neurons in sufficient detail to reveal its typical structure and function. The entire junction is the **synapse,** the transmit-

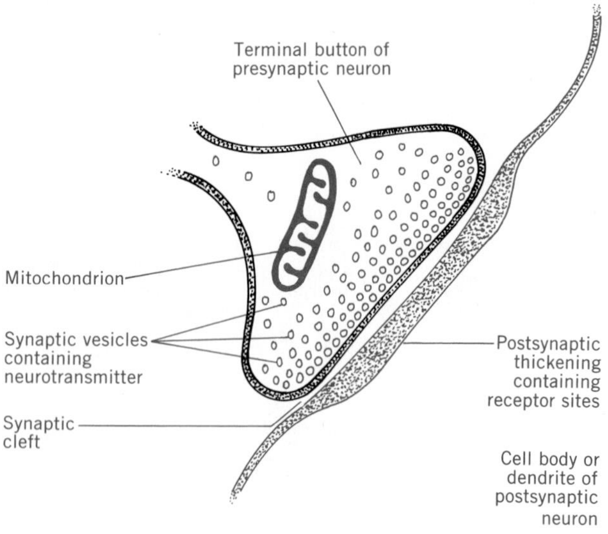

FIGURE 2.5

A synapse. The synaptic junction of the terminal button of one neuron with the dendrite of another neuron is the site of transmission.

ting cell is the **presynaptic neuron,** the receiving neuron is called a **postsynaptic neuron,** and the space in between is the **synaptic cleft.** The terminal button of the presynaptic neuron contains many **synaptic vesicles** full of the neuron's chemical transmitter substance, called a **neurotransmitter.** The membrane of the postsynaptic neuron contains the synaptic **receptor sites.**

When an impulse in the axon of the presynaptic neuron reaches the terminal button, one or more of the synaptic vesicles release their contents, the neurotransmitter, into the synaptic cleft. Upon reaching the other side of the synaptic cleft, the neurotransmitter molecules react with the receptor sites to stimulate the postsynaptic neuron.

After the neurotransmitter has stimulated the postsynaptic neuron by reacting with its receptor sites, the molecules are ejected or fragmented by another chemical, the **deactivating enzyme.** These fragments along with any free or unused molecules of neurotransmitter are then taken up once more by the presynaptic neuron and reformed into whole molecules of transmitter to be used again. This final process increases the efficiency of the synapse by preserving the store of neurotransmitter in the terminal. The duration of the process from arrival of the impulse to stimulation of the postsynaptic neuron is only about 0.5 millisecond (thousandths of a second, msec).

The chemical reactions that take place at synapses are of a very precise kind: one and only one neurotransmitter can fit into and react with a given kind of postsynaptic receptor site; and one and only one kind of receptor site can accept and react with a given neurotransmitter molecule. This ultraspecific kind of chemical reaction is common in biological systems and is called **lock-and-key specificity.** This lock-and-key specificity at synapses provides insurance against the synapse being either accidentally activated or "jammed" by foreign molecules such as neurotransmitters from nearby synapses.

Figure 2.6 illustrates the sequence of chemical reactions at a synapse. The important features are (1) the matching shapes of the neurotransmitter molecules and the receptor sites they activate; (2) the specificity of the deactivating enzyme for the neurotransmitter; and (3) the uptake of the neurotransmitter molecules and the fragments of molecules for restoration and reuse by the presynaptic terminal button.

Although there are a number of different neurotransmitters in the central and peripheral nervous system, each neuron manufactures and secretes only one of them. Depending solely on the effect of this substance on other neurons, the neurotransmitter and the neuron that secretes it can be characterized in general terms as either *excitatory* or *inhibitory*. Since many terminal buttons from many different neurons converge on any one neuron, both excitatory and inhibitory neurons are themselves bombarded by both excitatory and inhibitory neurotransmitters from other neurons.

Integrative Action

The communicative functions of a neuron are only one part of its total contribution to the nervous system. As we have already stated, each part of the nervous system has a second function, integration. The neuron integrates or weighs simultaneous and successive stimuli. Since the cell bodies and dendrites of most neurons are in synaptic contact with axon terminal buttons of a large number of other neurons, this means that most neurons receive stimulation from many other neurons and, in turn, stimulate many others. This complexity of interconnections in the nervous system provides for the great flexibility that characterizes behavior. But for any single neuron it means that neurotransmitters at hundreds of synapses may be bombarding it at any one moment (Figure 2.7).

The cellular mechanism of integration, like the communicative mechanism, can be observed by means of electrical recording. When an electrode small enough to avoid killing the neuron is inserted into its cell body and a second electrode is attached to some other tissue, it is possible to detect an electrical charge called the cell's **resting potential.**

The resting potential of a neuron is measured in volts, as is the charge in a battery, but the voltage is very small. A neuron has a resting potential of about

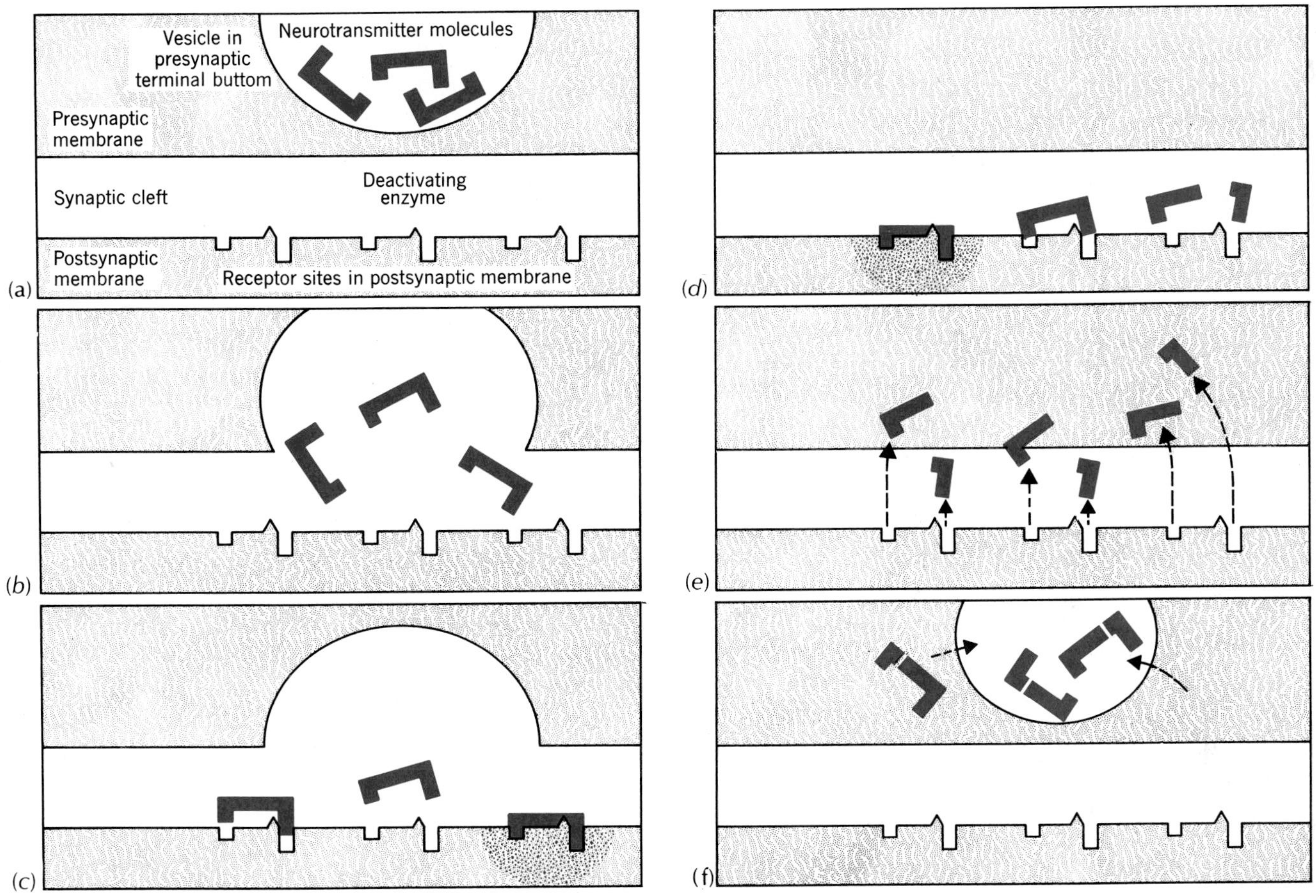

FIGURE 2.6
Sequence of events during activation of a synapse. (*a*) Neurotransmitter molecules are stored in the presynaptic vesicle before the impulse arrives. (*b*) When the impulse arrives, molecules are released into the synaptic cleft. (*c* and *d*) Transmitter molecules, the keys, fit into receptor sites, the locks, and stimulate postsynaptic neuron; then molecules are fragmented by a deactivating enzyme, shown here as a spike on the receptor site. (*e* and *f*) Molecule fragments are taken up by the terminal button, resynthesized, and stored in vesicles for reuse. Not all synapses make use of a deactivating enzyme that fragments the transmitter molecules. Whole molecules may be ejected from receptor sites, taken up by the presynaptic terminal, and stored again in the vesicle for further use.

−70 millivolts (thousandths of a volt, mv). The inside is electrically negative with respect to its outside. As long as a neuron remains unstimulated and healthy, the resting potential stays at −70 mv, but any event that irritates the dendrites or cell body upsets the neuron's chemical balance and there is a change in the potential. Figure 2.8 shows the effect upon the neuron's resting potential of irritations produced by electrical shocks of various intensities. Up to a point increasing intensities produce a higher and faster rise in the cell's potential, but it always returns to its resting level within a few milliseconds after the shock. Beyond this point, however, an entirely different set of events begins. A shock strong enough to raise the cell's potential to a level of about −40 mv produces the reaction in the walls of the axon that is the nerve impulse.

Temporal Summation If two or more stimuli are applied to a neuron in sufficiently quick succession, the rise in potential will be greater to the series of stimuli than it is to one of them alone. A series of successive stimuli, individually too weak to trigger a nerve impluse, is capable of raising the cell's potential to −40 mv and generating a nerve impulse (Figure 2.9). This ability of the neuron to allow the effects of many single stimuli to add together over short periods of time is called **temporal summation.** Since the effects of any one stimulus are over after only about 5 msec or so, the stimuli in a train must be separated by

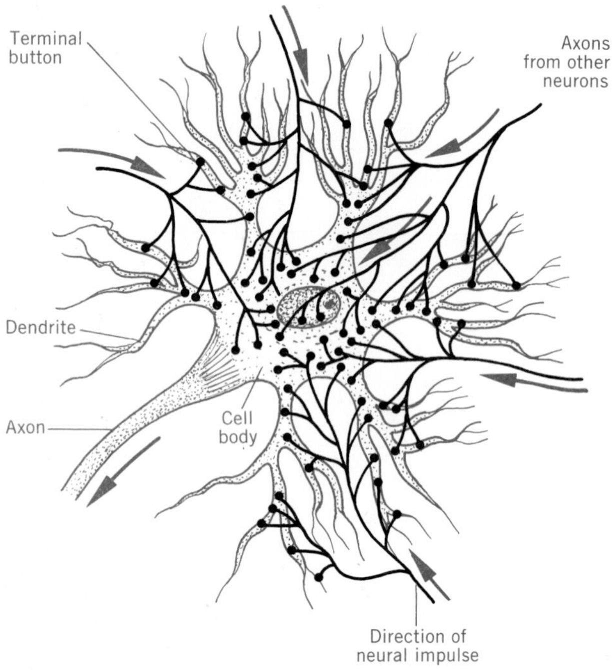

FIGURE 2.7
Synaptic terminals at the cell body of a neuron. In reality, the cell body and dendrites are almost completely covered by terminal buttons. The many synaptic connections allow for the integrative function of the neuron.

less than this amount of time if temporal summation is to occur.

Spatial Summation Figure 2.10 is a schematic drawing of a neuron with a *recording* electrode inside it near its axon and three stimulating electrodes that mimic terminal buttons located at three different places on its surface. With this arrangement it is possible to study the effect of stimulating the neuron at each point individually or at two or three points in combination. Even though the intensity of the stimulus is the same at each point, the effects are different, depending on the distance between the stimulating and recording electrodes. The greater the distance, the less the effect. Thus the terminal buttons contacting a neuron near the origin of the axon will have a greater effect on the axon's activities than those that make contact farther away. Terminal buttons with synapses far out on a dendrite have only a slight effect on the axon's activities.

So far we have considered the effects of stimuli occurring at only one place at a time. For a neuron in its natural state, however, this would be a very unusual event. At any one moment a neuron may be bombarded with stimulation at many different places on its surface. We have already seen in Figure 2.10 that stimulation at point 1, 2, or 3 alone does not produce a nerve impulse. If points 1 and 2, 1 and 3, or 2 and 3 are stimulated together, the effects add and the change in potential is larger; but again, the effect is not enough to fire the neuron and the potential soon subsides to the resting level. If points 1, 2, and 3 are stimulated together, however, the potential rises to −40 mv and an impulse is generated. The effects of simultaneous stimuli at different places on the neuron's surface add together, which is called **spatial summation.** For the integrative action of the nervous system, this is the neuron's most crucial ability.

Excitation and Inhibition

So far we have seen that three factors work together to determine whether or not a neuron generates an impulse. These are (1) the rate of excitatory stimulation (temporal summation), (2) the distance of this stimulation from the origin of the axon, and (3) the number of simultaneous stimuli (spatial summation). To this list we must add a fourth factor. (4) The stimulation received by a neuron may not be **excitatory stimulation,** which tends to raise the neuron's potential and to trigger a nerve impulse. It may be **inhibitory stimulation,** which works against the production of a nerve

FIGURE 2.8
Effects of stimulation on neuron's potential. Stimuli of increasing strengths have been applied at the arrows. The length of the arrow suggests the increasing strength. When the potential reaches −40 mv, an impulse is generated and an action potential is recorded.

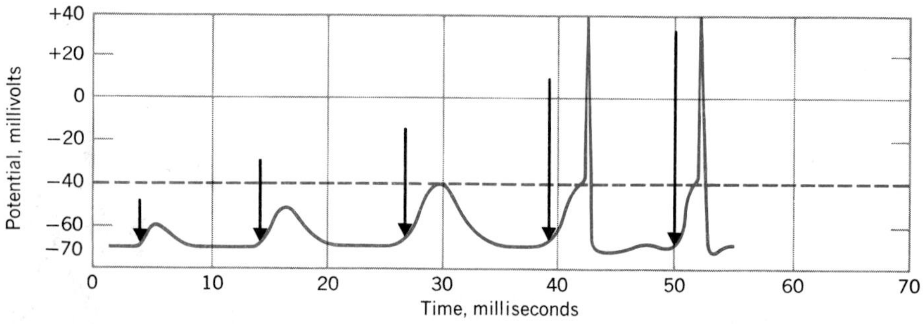

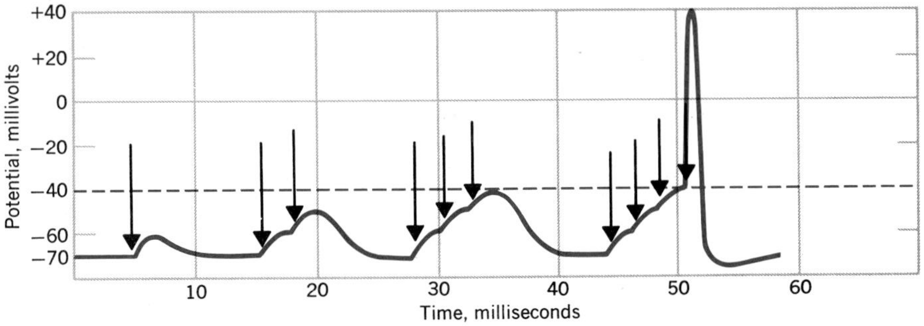

FIGURE 2.9
Temporal summation. A single stimulus does not raise the potential enough to trigger an impulse, but trains of successive stimuli do. Repeated stimulation has a staircase effect on the neuron's potential.

impulse. Excitatory and inhibitory neurotransmitters which are chemically different from each other have these opposing effects.

As a usual thing, the increases and decreases in potential brought about by excitatory and inhibitory transmitters cancel one another, and the neuron's potential remains at or near its resting level. It is only when the total amount of excitation far outweighs the total amount of inhibition that the neuron's potential rises far enough for a nerve impulse to be triggered.

SUMMARY □

Neurons or nerve cells are the active elements of the nervous system. A neuron receives stimulation at its dendrites and cell body in the form of small amounts of chemical neurotransmitter substances secreted onto its surface by the terminal buttons of many other neurons. If the excitatory component of this stimulation exceeds the inhibitory component, and the excitatory stimulation is persistent and widespread enough, the neuron will generate an impulse which travels down its axon and triggers the release of its own transmitter substance at each of its many terminal buttons. In this manner each neuron *integrates* the simultaneous and successive stimuli from a wide variety of sources and *communicates* its information to other neurons. The net effect of this process is an integrative and communicative network which is capable of weighing considerable, often contradictory, information, making decisions, and executing motor activities appropriate to each situation that arises.

THE FUNDAMENTAL PLAN OF THE NERVOUS SYSTEM

Much of what the nervous system does is to process information provided by sensory inputs and initiate appropriate action in the form of motor outputs. Thus a basic distinction of function in the nervous system is

FIGURE 2.10
Spatial summation. The inset shows the location of three stimulating electrodes and one recording electrode. The effects of individual stimuli add together to produce a larger potential change, but only the simultaneous stimulation of points 1, 2, and 3 raises the potential to −40 mv and triggers a nerve impulse.

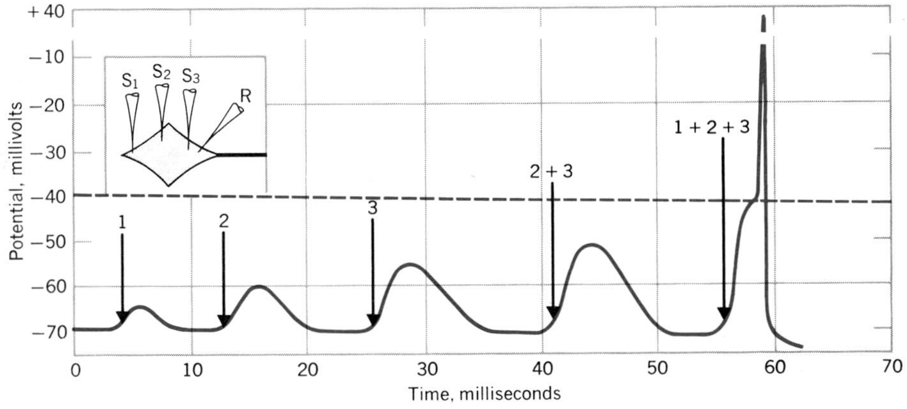

between *sensory* activity and *motor* activity. This functional distinction is imposed on the nervous system by other organs of the body—by **receptors,** such as the eyes, ears, and nose, and by **effectors,** the muscles and glands. In the peripheral system it is possible to make a distinction between sensory and motor neurons. The sensory neurons are **afferent.** They carry impulses from receptors into the central nervous system. The motor neurons are **efferent.** They carry impulses originating in the central system outward to effectors. Once inside the central nervous system, however, the clarity of the distinction begins to blur.

In the sections to follow, we shall examine five progressively higher levels of the central nervous system (Figure 2.11). Proceeding from the lowest of these levels to higher and higher levels, we find the peripheral or first-order sensory neurons making synaptic connections with more central second-order neurons, these with still more central third-order neurons, and so on. These higher-order neurons are not directly attached to a receptor. They receive inputs from lower-order sensory neurons and other sources. Thus first-, second-, and third-order neurons are progressively less completely sensory in their function. Proceeding *backward* through the motor system, function becomes similarly diffused. Strictly motor neurons synapse directly upon effectors, but these neurons are usually stimulated by neurons whose entire lengths are in the central nervous system; these neurons correspond to the higher-order neurons in the sensory system.

The pattern described then is one in which the distinction between sensory and motor functions becomes more and more vague as neurons are synapse by synapse more central. Nevertheless, it is still useful to retain terms with which to distinguish neurons that are most closely connected to receptors from neurons that are more closely connected to effectors. Therefore "relatively sensory" and "relatively motor" will serve to describe the functions of many higher-order neurons. Indeed, this disctinction can be applied to neurons after an indefinitely large number of synapses if damage to the neurons in question results in behavioral changes that are relatively restricted either to perceptual or to motor functions. Later on we shall describe some effects of these kinds. We must be prepared, however, for the fact that the alterations of perception and action that result from damage to higher-order neurons may have little in common with the changes brought by damage to peripheral sensory or motor neurons.

FIGURE 2.11
Schematic diagram of functional plan of the nervous system. Circles represent collections of nerve cell bodies or gray matter and are communicative in function. The left column represents structures that are relatively sensory, the right column structures that are relatively motor. The lower four levels are common to all vertebrates. The top level is unique to mammals.

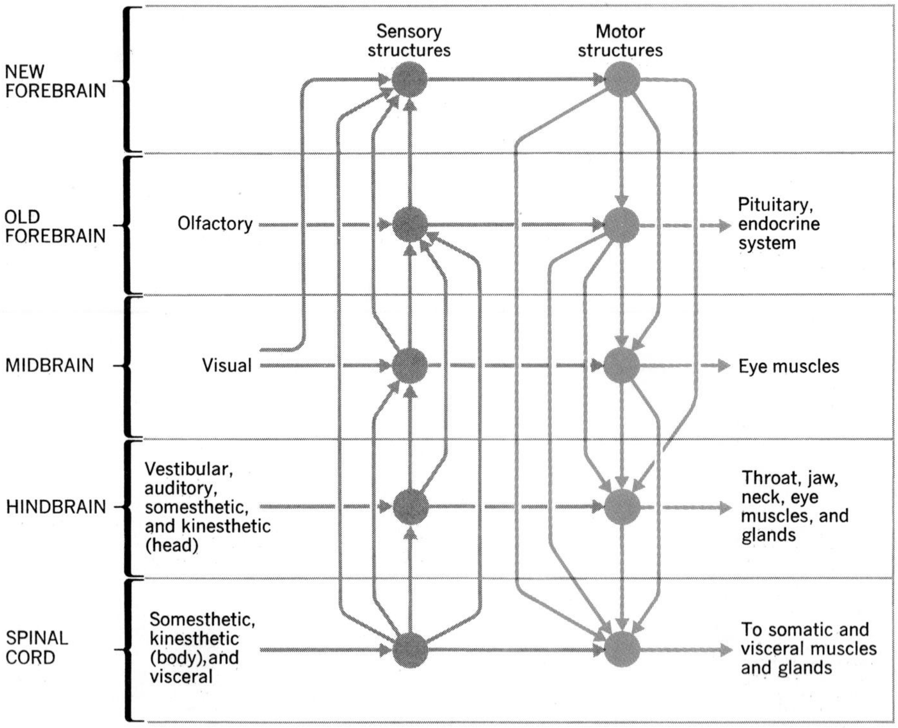

SPINAL CORD

In a six-foot man the spinal cord is about the diameter of the little finger and two feet long. A cross section of the spinal cord at any level reveals the same basic internal arrangement (Figure 2.12). There is an area of **white matter** near the outside and an H-shaped core of **gray matter.** White matter gains its color from the myelin sheath around axons. Thus the more exterior part of the cord consists of axons of nerve fibers and is communicative in function. The gray core consists of unmyelinated nerve cell bodies and dendrites and is integrative in function.

There are thirty-one pairs of peripheral **spinal nerves** connected to the spinal cord. Bundled together in each nerve are thousands of individual axons, some sensory and some motor in function. The sensory branches of the spinal nerves enter the cord at the back, or dorsal, portion (top of cross section in Figure 2.12). They bring into the spinal cord information originating in the sensory receptors in the skin, joints, muscles, and viscera. Following synaptic connections in the cord, the sensory activity flows toward the brain. The motor branches of the spinal nerves leave the front, or ventral, portion of the cord (bottom of cross section in Figure 2.12) and control the action of nearby muscles and glands.

Function

The communicative and integrative functions of the spinal cord can be deduced from observing the actions of a patient who has survived a complete transection of the spinal cord. The resulting condition is called *quadriplegia* if the cut is above the level of exit of the spinal nerves to the arms and legs and *paraplegia* if the cut is below the arm level but above the leg level. Because neurons within the central nervous system do not regenerate their axons after they are cut, both conditions are permanent—there is no recovery. The most dramatic effects of quadriplegia or paraplegia are complete anesthesia and paralysis of the body below the level of the cut. There is anesthesia, an absence of feeling, because axons of first- and second-order sensory neurons that run up the spinal cord to the brain have been severed. The paralysis, an inability to make voluntary movements, is evidence that the axons of second-order motor neurons running down the cord from the brain have been cut.

Although transection of the cord destroys voluntary movement in the part of the patient's body below the cut, reflexive movements are not lost. In paraplegia the patient's limbs will respond reflexively to a variety of stimuli; for example, if a toe is pinched or pricked with a pin, the leg withdraws. If the sole of the foot is tickled, the response is opposite; the toes splay and the leg extends. If the tendon below the knee is tapped, the knee-jerk reflex occurs. The presence of these reflexes in a patient whose spinal cord has been cut illustrates the integrative capacity of the spinal cord itself. Obviously, it is capable of responding appropriately to simple stimuli. It is also capable of responding differently to different stimuli and performing a crude kind of decision making. For if two stimuli, such as a pinprick and tickle, are applied simultaneously to one foot, the severed spinal cord will respond by withdrawing the leg, the response to the prick, while inhibiting the competing response to the foot tickle.

A part of what is lost in paraplegia is the capacity to perform these actions upon command. Also lost is the moderating influences of the higher centers. Normally reflexes are under some sort of descending inhibition from the brain. In paraplegic or quadriplegic patients the reflexes are larger and more sudden than they are in intact individuals.

The ability of the brain to inhibit actions originating in the spinal cord is just one example of a more general principle that holds true at all levels of the nervous system. The successive levels form a chain of command. Each higher level is capable of achieving a more complete integration of sensory input than is available to lower levels. If, on the basis of this more complete integration, a better or longer-range plan of action arises, the higher levels can supersede the actions initiated by the lower levels. This mode of organization allows the body to react differentially after the higher levels of the nervous sytem have evaluated the wide and subtle array of stimulation.

FIGURE 2.12
Cross section of spinal cord. This schematic cross section of the spinal cord shows gray matter and white matter, roots, and a typical reflex arc consisting of sensory neuron, interneuron, and motor neuron.

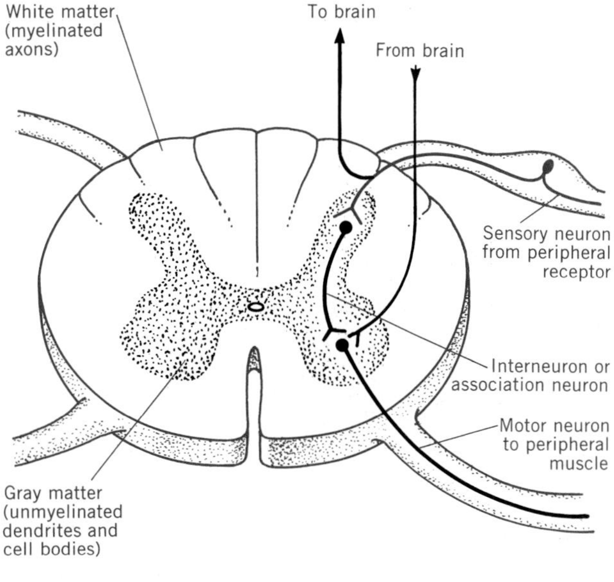

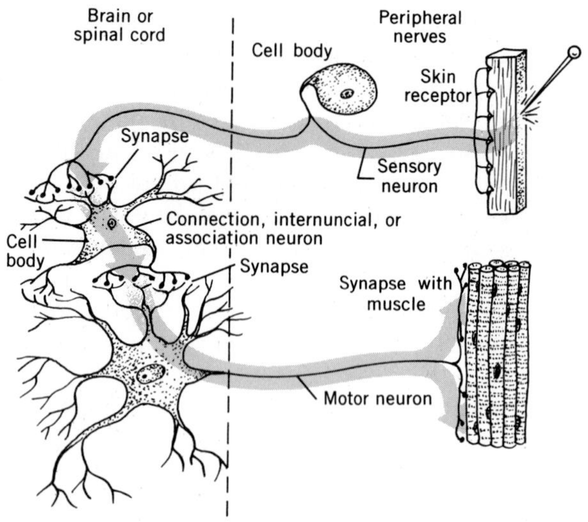

FIGURE 2.13

The reflex arc. Effects of stimulation are transmitted to the spinal cord by sensory neurons. These synapse with connecting neurons, which in turn synapse with motor neurons, which in turn activate the muscle. A reflex act requires the stimulation of hundreds of neurons.

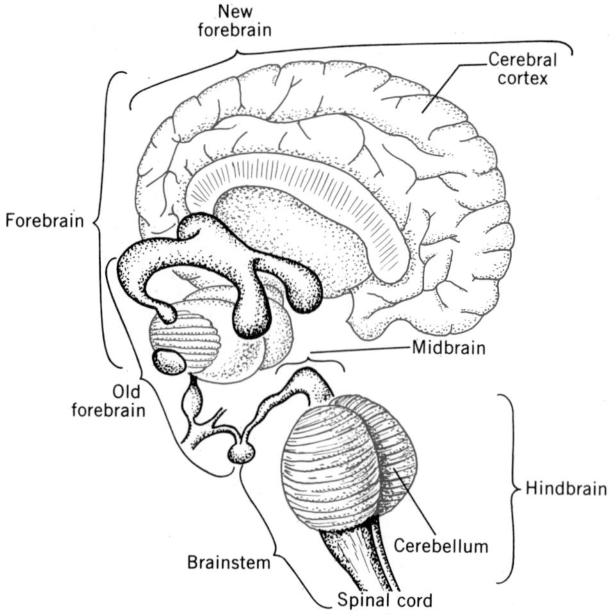

FIGURE 2.14

Levels of the human nervous system.

Reflex Action

In Figure 2.13 are diagramed some of the spinal cord interconnections for the reflex withdrawal of the leg to avoid pain. When the foot is pricked with a pin, for example, sensory neurons carry impulses to **internuncial** or **association** neurons in the cord. These neurons connect the sensory neurons to motor neurons. Receiving stimulation from sensory neurons by way of the association neurons, the motor neurons cause the leg muscle to contract.

The three-neuron model of the **reflex arc** shown in Figure 2.13 is correct as far as it goes, but the sketch is simplified and incomplete. There are several additional points to make. (1) The action of just one neuron would have no effect at all. Simultaneous activity in many neurons is necessary to produce overt action. (2) Opposed or antagonistic muscles must also act. For the leg to withdraw reflexively, muscles that ordinarily extend the leg must relax as the muscles that make it bend contract. A reflex arc relaxing the extensor muscle must operate in parallel with the arc producing flexion. If both relaxation and contraction did not proceed in a coordinated fashion, the leg would not withdraw but become rigidly locked. (3) Stimulation of the foot would create impulses in sensory axons not shown in Figure 2.13. This neural activity goes to the brain and translates into the conscious experience of pain. (4) Impulses from the brain, traveling down the cord on motor neurons not shown in the figure, also influence the internuncial and motor neurons in the reflex arc. They can often inhibit the reflex.

HINDBRAIN

The hindbrain consists of the *cerebellum, medulla,* and *pons* (Figure 2.14). The medulla and pons constitute the lower part of the *brainstem.* The upper part of the brainstem includes the *midbrain* and a portion of the *forebrain.* The cerebellum is behind the brainstem and is connected to it through three large pairs of nerve tracts.

The brainstem portion of the hindbrain occupies a key position in the nervous system. The narrow medulla serves as the main line of traffic for nerve tracts originating in the brain and descending to the spinal cord, and nerve tracts originating in the spinal cord and ascending to still higher brain structures. Nerve tracts are bundles of axons within the central system. In addition to these tracts that are passing through, the hindbrain directly receives sensory nerve fibers from the ears, the skin, the mouth, and muscles of the head and sends motor nerve fibers directly to the face, jaw, throat, neck, and some visceral muscles and glands. Beyond the hindbrain these fibers course together as peripheral nerves. They are called **cranial nerves** because they are confined for the most part to the skull, but in structure and function they are essentially similar to the thirty-one pairs of spinal nerves.

The cerebellar part of the hindbrain receives stimulation from many different receptors relayed to it from other parts of the nervous system. Some of the stimulation comes from the visual, auditory, and skin receptors, but the largest portion originates in muscles and in the receptors near the inner ear that are responsible for the sense of balance (see page 66).

Since the brainstem portion of the hindbrain provides the only route for communication between the receptor organs of the head and the effector organs of the trunk and limbs, its communicative function is a large part of its total contribution. The hindbrain does have integrative functions, however, which can be grouped into three orders. The first of these consists of a wide variety of sensory-motor reflexes—withdrawal reactions to noxious stimuli to the head, eyeblinks to stimuli near the face, the tensing of muscles in the ears to loud sounds, gagging or coughing to a clog in the throat, increasing the depth of breathing when the level of carbon dioxide in the blood rises, and dilating the arteries when blood pressure increases. Each of these reflexive actions, like those controlled by the spinal cord, serves a protective or maintenance function; like the spinal reflexes, each is subject to some measure of inhibition from higher levels of the nervous system.

Second-order integrations of the hindbrain mix stimulation from various sensory receptors and direct the product to higher or lower levels of the system. The stimulation from the two ears is mixed to localize a sound source, and the stimulation from the two sets of vestibular organs is mixed for the analysis of head movements.

The highest order of integrative activity of the hindbrain is much more complex than any integration accomplished by the spinal cord. The cerebellum, receiving information from skin receptors and those sensitive to muscle tone, monitors the pressures on the skin in each limb and the current state of contraction of each muscle. In addition, the eyes and vestibular organs inform it of the body's position in space and its balance. Integrating all this information, the cerebellum helps to keep the body upright and balanced and the muscles in the slightly contracted condition necessary for their prompt and smooth coordinated action. When the body is in motion, the cerebellum maintains its posture and refines its movements even as they are being made.

MIDBRAIN

The midbrain (see Figure 2.14) is the part of the brainstem just above the hindbrain. The optic tract from the eye sends axons here, providing the only direct sensory input to the midbrain. There are only two pairs of motor nerves leaving the midbrain. They control some of the muscles for moving the eyes and also the muscles of the eye's iris and lens. The interior of the midbrain, as well as of the hindbrain below it, is gray matter interlaced with crisscrossing groups of axons. This structure is called the **reticular formation,** which is a strictly descriptive term. When viewed through a microscope, the core of the brainstem resembles white netting or lacing on a gray background. Many thin myelinated nerve tracts crisscross the gray matter; it is, therefore, "reticulated."

The communicative function of the midbrain is much like that of the hindbrain. Tracts of the motor system originating in the forebrain stream down through the midbrain on their way to lower motor structures, and tracts of the sensory systems entering the spinal cord and hindbrain stream upward into the forebrain. The midbrain also has important integrative functions. Some of these are reminiscent of spinal reflexes and hindbrain function. A number of important visual responses are reflexive. Other functions are of an order of integration not met in any lower level. One of these higher-order integrations can be illustrated by imagining the picture of the world that would be obtained with a movie camera hand-held in a moving car. The camera would jog with every bump in the road. If the film shot by this camera were then projected onto a screen, these bumps would make the world appear to jump and jerk. When you are riding in a car, your head and eyes are subjected to the same bumps as the camera, yet the world still appears steady. The difference is that every slight movement of the head is sensed by the vestibular system and the eyes themselves and integrated by the neurons of the midbrain. Vision is momentarily suppressed, and the eyes are instantly adjusted to the new point of view. In spite of bumps, the world appears stable. In professional moviemaking elaborate machinery is required to smooth the movements of a camera. In human beings the entire mechanism is contained in much less than a cubic inch of nerve tissue.

Axons ascending from the reticular formation activate the forebrain and thus play an arousing role in the life of an individual. When the midbrain reticular formation of an intact but sleeping animal is stimulated, the animal awakes with a bound and gives every indication that something has awakened it. But if the midbrain reticular formation is damaged, the animal falls into a prolonged coma. For this reason the ascending fibers have come to be called the **reticular activating system** (Magoun, 1952).

SUMMARY □

The anesthesia and paralysis of paraplegic patients indicate how the communicative and integrative functions of the spinal cord must be organized. Because sensory neurons that communicate between sense organs and the brain have been severed, such individuals lose all sensitivity to stimulation below the point at which the cord is cut. They also lose the ability to initiate voluntary movements of their legs, for neurons that run from the brain to the spinal cord neurons serving the muscles in these limbs have been cut. On the other hand, not only do paraplegic and quadriplegic patients have reflexes but they are exaggerated. Reflexes are still possible because their mechanisms are located entirely within the cord and the connecting spinal nerves. Similar responses cannot be initiated voluntarily, however, because there are no connections with the higher centers of the nervous system. Nor can higher centers exert their usual inhibitory control over reflexes.

The hindbrain consists of the medulla, pons, and cerebellum. The first two of these structures serve both communicative and integrative functions; the cerebellum is solely integrative. The conspicuous communicative functions of the hindbrain make it possible to react to stimuli presented to the eyes, ears, and other head receptors. Integrative functions are of three kinds. The simplest integrations are reflexive in nature. In addition, the brainstem portion of the hindbrain participates in the mixing of stimuli, as is required, for example, in sound localization. The cerebellum contributes more complex integrations, maintaining posture and muscle tone. Thus the hindbrain is crucial to almost every action of the body. It permits communication between the spinal cord and all higher levels, integrates a wide variety of stimulation in order to provide reflexive protection and maintenance, and makes coordinated and skilled movements possible.

The midbrain adds still another level of integration to those already achieved by the spinal cord and hindbrain. The simplest integrations are reflexes for the visual system. The midbrain also makes reflexive adjustments of posture in response to visual and auditory stimulation. The reticular formation of the hindbrain and midbrain arouses the entire nervous system, awakening the individual through ascending connections to the forebrain.

CEREBRUM

Old Forebrain

The *forebrain* or *cerebrum,* the largest part of the human brain, can be divided into an old and a new portion. The old forebrain consists of structures similar to those that constituted the entire forebrain of our ancient vertebrate ancestors. From its evolutionary history, the old forebrain can be expected to tend to bodily functions and regulation common to all vertebrates, such as appetite and thirst, water balance, sleeping and waking, temperature control, reproductive cycles, and activity cycles. And, of course, it oversees the lower levels in their more reflexive actions. It also has much to do with the patterns of the basic emotions, rage, terror, pleasure, and sexual arousal. The new forebrain, the cerebral hemispheres with their differentiated lobes covered with surface gray matter or cortex, evolved later. For this reason it may be expected to provide higher-order integrations which allow the behavior that is unique to mammals and particularly to human beings.

The largest part of the old forebrain is the **limbic system.** Although this system receives fibers indirectly from every sensory system, its most direct sensory input is from the olfactory system and from the sensory system originating in the viscera. It also sends out a pathway of fibers to the autonomic nervous system controlling the viscera. The limbic system consists of many parts, but only the hypothalamus will be discussed here. The hypothalamus, no larger than a peanut and positioned in the base of the forebrain, receives some fibers from the viscera and sends back others in return. It is also directly connected to the pituitary gland, which, in turn, controls the activities of the other endocrine glands throughout the body. Thus the hypothalamus is the structure by which the old forebrain maintains control over the body's interior.

Function In turning from the contributions to behavior of the spinal cord, hindbrain, and midbrain to those of the old and new forebrain, we need a new set of descriptive categories. Whereas the lower structures support behavior we might call "automatic" or reflexive, the higher structures control behavior that is "emotional," or "affective," and "thoughtful," or "cognitive." In general, the old forebrain serves more emotional or affective functions; the new forebrain serves more thoughtful or cognitive functions. The sympathetic and parasympathetic divisions of the autonomic nervous system carry out many of the emotional and motivated activities initiated by the old forebrain and in particular by the hypothalamus.

Autonomic nervous system The **autonomic nervous system** consists of peripheral motor fibers running to a variety of organs (Figure 2.15). Fibers leaving the brainstem and sacral regions of the cord comprise the **craniosacral system** anatomically and the **parasympathetic system** functionally. Fibers leaving the central portion of the cord comprise the **thoracicolumbar system** anatomically and the **sympathetic system** functionally.

The sympathetic and parasympathetic systems tend to act in opposing ways. The sympathetic system prepares the body for action; the parasympathetic system usually functions when the body is at rest. When the sympathetic system is active, heartbeat increases to pump more blood. Blood is shunted away from the viscera to the muscles, providing extra oxygen and nutrients where they are most needed during activity. Breathing becomes deeper and more rapid, which ensures a plentiful supply of oxygen. The pupils of the eyes dilate to allow for better vision. The liver releases sugar for energy. All these actions mobilize the body's resources.

The parasympathetic system helps the body's organs to protect and conserve their resources. The heart slows down, blood is shunted from the muscles to the viscera, the pupils of the eyes contract, breathing is more relaxed and shallower. Because of the nature of the physiological processes that they initiate, the two systems tend to be associated with emotional states. Sympathetic arousal is interpreted as "nervous tension," anxiety, fear, and excitement, parasympathetic arousal as calmness.

Pituitary and endocrine system The autonomic or visceral motor system is the means by which the old forebrain controls the body's internal state *quickly*.

FIGURE 2.15

The autonomic nervous system. The sketch indicates sympathetic innervation by red lines, parasympathetic innervation by black lines. When the fibers of the sympathetic system leave the spinal cord they synapse almost immediately with other motor neurons located in the ganglia on either side of the vertebral column. These side banks of ganglia have connecting fibers to make them a coordinating chain. Fibers of the parasympathetic system synapse in ganglia close to the organs to be innervated. Notice that most organs receive both sympathetic and parasympathetic nerves.

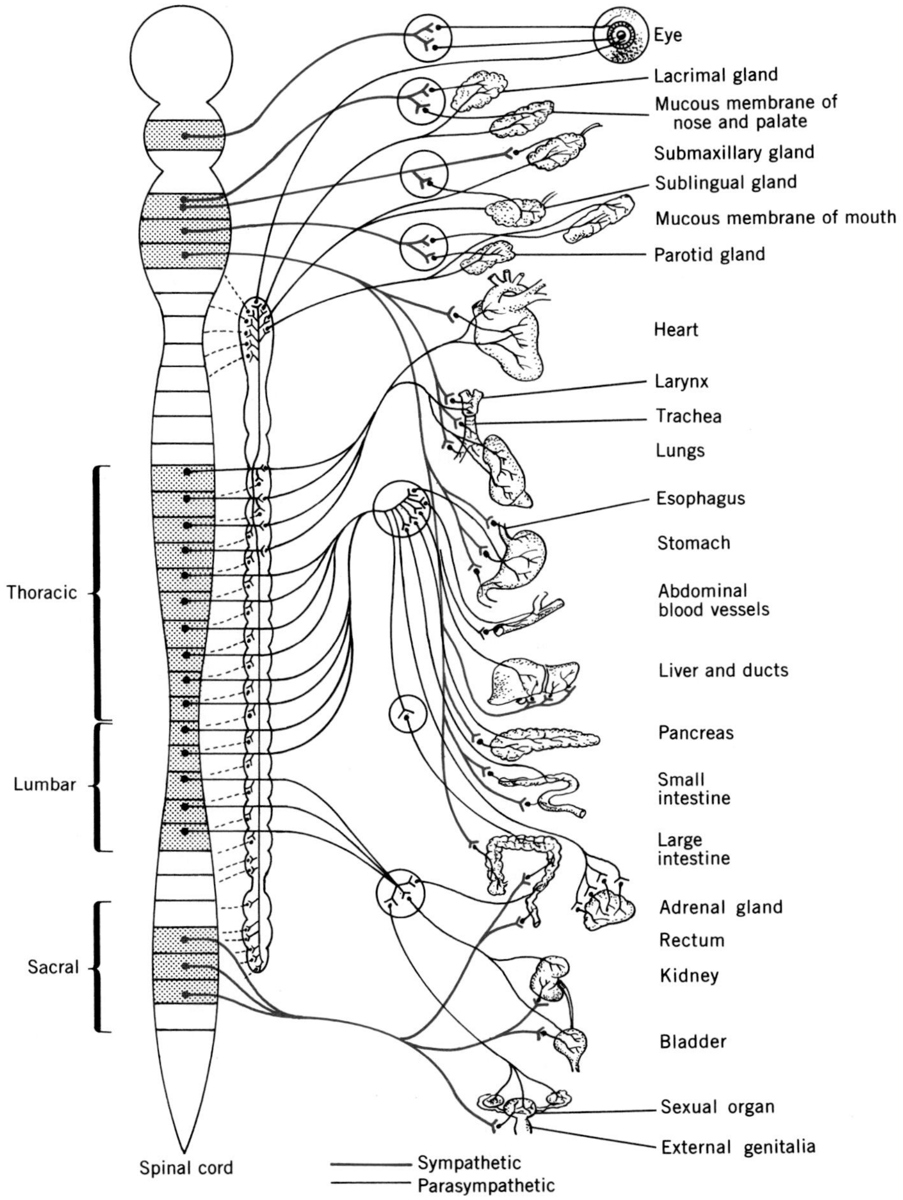

For internal states that are to be sustained, the hypothalamus activates a second system, the endocrine or internal gland system. Eight glands, four of which are paired—gonads, adrenals, thyroid, and parathyroid—and four unpaired—kidney, pancreas, pineal, and pituitary—make up the endocrine system. The secretions of these glands, called *hormones*, pass directly into the bloodstream and are carried to all the body's tissues.

Of all the endocrine glands, the pituitary is foremost because it secretes many different hormones; furthermore, many of them trigger the secretions of the other endocrine glands. This role of the pituitary makes it the kingpin of the entire endocrine system. But the pituitary itself functions mostly under the control of the hypothalamus, to which it is attached. The hypothalamus stimulates the pituitary to action in either of two ways. It stimulates some parts of the pituitary via neurons. This neural system sets in motion reactions of the endocrine system that must be executed relatively fast. To initiate reactions that can proceed more slowly, the hypothalamus stimulates the pituitary via its own hormones. The hypothalamus secretes a very small amount of hormone into a blood vessel which passes through it on the way to the pituitary. The pituitary senses the presence of the hypothalamic hormone and secretes its own hormones into the bloodstream. When these hormones reach their targets throughout the body, the necessary changes are effected, including stimulating still other endocrine glands to secretion. Thus the pituitary and endocrine system provide a second, largely nonneural route by which the hypothalamus maintains control of the body's interior.

Electrical Stimulation of the Brain Peripheral nerve fibers of the sympathetic and parasympathetic systems terminate on many of the same organs. Elsewhere, however, the two systems are quite separate. In the old forebrain the front and sides of the hypothalamus are parasympathetic, the back part sympathetic. The evidence for this division comes in part from observations of the behavior of animals when one of these regions is stimulated electrically. Small electrodes are inserted into the hypothalamus through a hole in the skull (Figure 2.16). Wires can then be attached to the electrodes, and groups of cells in the hypothalamus can be stimulated directly.

Stimulation applied through an electrode in the back half of the hypothalamus brings sympathetic reactions. The animal becomes watchful, crouches, its hair erects, and by every other standard it acts frightened. Stimulation applied to the front part of the hypothalamus, on the other hand, induces parasympathetic activity. Stimulation of slightly different locations to the left or right makes the animal eat or drink, even if it has just eaten or drunk its fill. With stimulation in still other locations, there is sexual posturing.

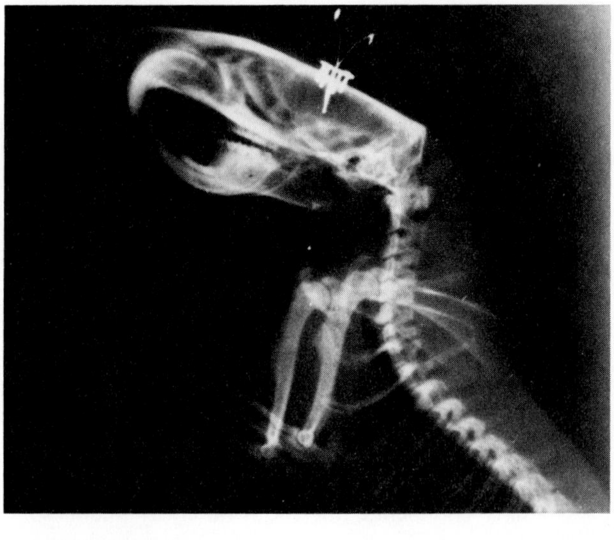

FIGURE 2.16
The technique of brain stimulation. This X-ray photograph shows the permanent placement of an electrode in the skull of a rat.

A slightly different technique, called **self-stimulation** (Olds and Milner, 1954), also demonstrates that the old forebrain is intimately associated with emotion and motivation. An electrode is inserted in the same manner as before, this time into the septal area in front of the hypothalamus. Instead of being controlled by the experimenter, the stimulation is now under the control of the animal itself. Typically, the animal is provided with a pedal that it can press. Every time it presses the pedal, a small shock is delivered through the electrode.

Animals provided with this means of stimulating their own brains fall naturally into one of two groups. Either they stimulate themselves only once, or they stimulate themselves constantly. There seems to be little middle ground. The animals that stimulate themselves more than a few times stimulate themselves excessively and often at the expense of their true needs. Hungry animals stimulate themselves rather than eat. Thirsty animals stimulate themselves rather than drink. It is difficult to imagine any stimulus other than an extraordinarily pleasurable one that would have this effect. Similarly, the careful avoidance of stimulation to other areas suggests that the feelings evoked are probably aversive.

Although the experiments just described provide clear evidence that the old forebrain participates in emotion and motivation, other experiments have shown that it exerts excitatory and inhibitory control, in somewhat the same way that lower-level functions are controlled. Stimulating one area may make an animal eat. Stimulating a slightly different location may make even a very hungry animal stop eating. Still other locations excite or inhibit drinking, excite or inhibit sexual activity, arouse or inhibit fearful reactions.

New Forebrain

The new forebrain consists of all the cerebrum that can be seen in either a side view or a top view of the brain and the thalamus below. The thalamus, a larger structure above the hypothalamus, has traffic with the new forebrain. The back part of the thalamus is the major relay center for all the somatic sensory tracts coming from below and for the entering optic tracts. The thalamus projects all their sensory signals on, by means of its own fibers, to specific areas of the cortex. Through the front part of the thalamus pass motor nerve tracts, in direct pathways from the cortex to the spinal cord.

The two cerebral hemispheres are the largest part of the human brain. Their gray-matter covering, the cerebral cortex, is deeply fissured, folded upon itself and into itself, allowing for a very large surface. To our complex human behavior—our acute sensitivities and our dexterity, our language, our extensive memories and learning, our sense of time and interest in our own history, our reasoning, our imagination—the contribution of the cerebral cortex is correspondingly large.

The cerebral cortex has many parts and many functions. Some areas are most closely connected to the receptors and serve a relatively sensory function. These areas are called **primary sensory cortex.** Another area, called **primary motor cortex,** is most closely connected, via only two synapses, with the body's muscles. Immediately surrounding primary sensory and motor cortex are areas that are less directly sensory and motor in function but whose damage also results in perceptual or motor deficit. These areas are called **secondary sensory** and **secondary motor cortex** (Figure 2.17). Most of the cerebral cortex, however, is neither clearly sensory nor clearly motor in function. This vast area is usually referred to as **association cortex.**

Organization of Sensory Cortex The sensory areas in each hemisphere are connected to the receptors in such a way that the right side of a person's perceptual world is predominantly represented in the left hemisphere, and the left side of the world is represented in the right hemisphere. For example, the visual system is arranged so that the right half of what each eye sees is represented in the left visual cortex. Stare at a point on the wall. Everything to the left of a vertical line through that point is represented in the visual cortex of your right hemisphere, and everything to the right is represented in the left hemisphere. A patient in whom the right visual cortex has been destroyed can-

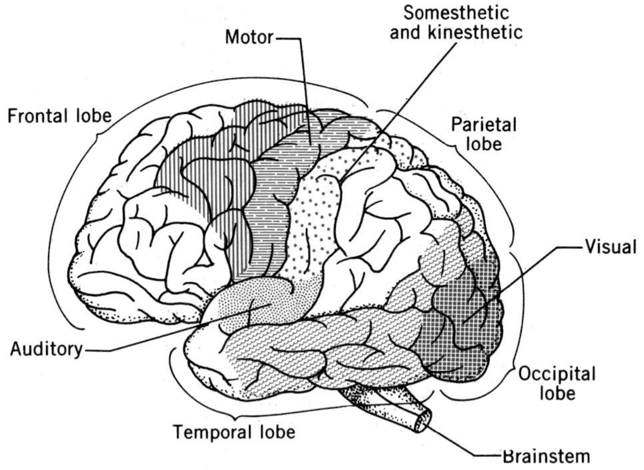

FIGURE 2.17
Lateral view of human cerebral cortex. Primary and secondary sensory and motor areas are shaded. Unshaded areas of cortex are "associative."

not see anything to the left of the vertical line (Berkley, 1978). Similarly, sounds coming from places to the left of the same line are represented for the most part in the auditory cortex of the right hemisphere, and skin sensitivity on the left side of the body is represented in the right somatosensory cortex. Consequently, damage to the right auditory or somatosensory cortex disrupts these perceptions on the left side (for example, Thompson and Masterton, 1978; Vierck, 1978).

The secondary sensory areas surrounding primary sensory cortex receive a large part of their input from the primary areas and provide a higher level of perceptual organization. The symptoms of damage to secondary sensory cortex reveal something of the nature of this higher organization. The general name for these symptoms is **agnosia** (Greek *agnosia,* ignorance). We speak of visual agnosia when secondary visual areas are destroyed, auditory agnosia when secondary auditory cortex is destroyed, and somesthetic agnosia for the destruction of secondary somesthetic cortex (Carpenter, 1976).

In each of these syndromes the ability to understand or speak about what is being perceived is lost. People with visual agnosia are unable to understand or recognize what they see, although their sight is mechanically intact. Such individuals, for example, can see a book as well as they ever could, but they cannot call it a book or describe what it is used for. If, on the other hand, these patients hear the word *book* or are allowed to feel a book, they can then say "book" and describe its use. In short, patients with visual agnosia can see but cannot recognize what they see.

Organization of the Motor Cortex The motor cortex, like sensory cortex, is crisscrossed in its connec-

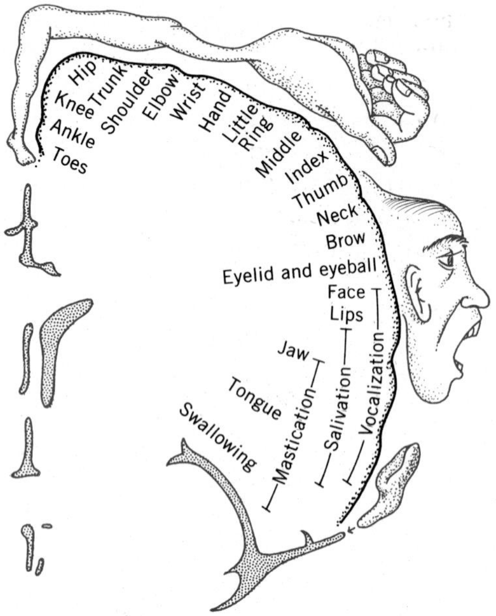

FIGURE 2.18

The motor homunculus. The size of the body part suggests the amount of cortex devoted to control of that part. The cortex controlling the toes is deep within the longitudinal fissure dividing the hemispheres. (Adapted from Penfield and Rasmussen, 1950.)

tions with muscles. The right motor cortex controls muscles in the left half of the body and vice versa. Damage to the left motor cortex, for example, produces **hemiplegia,** half-paralysis of the right side of the body. Motor cortex has an orderly upside-down arrangement by body part, which is suggested somewhat metaphorically in Figure 2.18. Because this organization is not really as precise as depicted in the figure, a small area of damage in the motor cortex may appear to cause only a slight weakening of the muscles controlled by that area rather than a complete loss of their voluntary movements. This means that the adjacent area, which has some, but less efficient, control over the muscles, can compensate for the focal damage, at least to a degree. Such compensation, however, is probably never perfect, although the remaining deficit may be noticeable only in certain kinds of cases. For example, a pianist with damage in the area that controlled the little finger of the right hand would probably lose the very precise control that is needed to perform, although somewhat more gross activities, such as writing, would appear to be unaffected. More extensive damage in primary motor cortex, of course, produces correspondingly larger deficits, and recovery is correspondingly less complete.

Damage to secondary motor cortex, the area just in front of the primary motor area, brings a subtler kind of motor deficit, involving whole categories of action rather than limited specific movements. With damage to secondary motor cortex, the pianist in our example is still able to move each of his fingers correctly and perform all the basic movements needed in playing; these are controlled by primary motor cortex. But now he is unable to execute a musical passage, or play a scale, or even drum his fingers rhythmically. In short, a higher order of motor organization, the timing and ordering of movements, is disrupted.

Cortical Areas Associated with Speech and Language Speech, the utterance of sounds with symbolic meaning, appears to have two components. First, there is the mere utterance of a sound, say to attract attention or denote displeasure. Second, there is the utterance of a sentence, complete with subject and predicate, symbolically conveying an idea with a possibly unique combination of sounds. The mere physical act of making sounds is a function of brainstem structures; coherent speech is a function of the cerebral cortex—in fact, of a special area quite dissimilar to any found in other animals.

In almost everyone the speech area is confined to the left hemisphere (Figure 2.19). Damage to this region brings about a disturbance of speech called **aphasia.** Aphasia is an inability to speak in coherent symbolic sentences, even though the ability to make speech sounds is unimpaired. This inability to speak correctly may have a variety of underlying causes, only two of which will be considered here. The entire speech area can be roughly divided into a front half and a back half. Although damage in either of these parts disturbs speech, the symptoms of the aphasias are quite different. The difference provides a basis for understanding the cause of the speech difficulty.

Sensory aphasia The rear part of the speech area includes the primary and part of the secondary auditory sensory cortex. Damage in this general region results in a syndrome called **sensory aphasia** or **receptive aphasia.** The most glaring deficit produced by damage in this area is the patient's inability to understand spoken words, a special kind of auditory agnosia called auditory verbal agnosia. The patient cannot repeat sentences or take dictation and may perceive spoken words in a jumbled way, much as we do when we hear someone speaking rapidly in a foreign language.

The inability to understand speech also extends to the patient's own speech. Normally, we listen to the sounds we are uttering and correct our lip, tongue, and throat movements to make the sounds we want and to say the words we want with proper enunciation and in proper grammatical sentences. After damage in auditory cortex on the left side or the back part of the speech area, however, patients do not under-

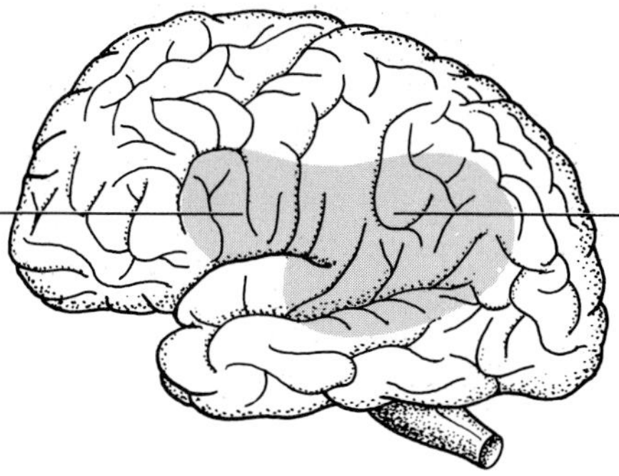

FIGURE 2.19
Speech areas of brain. The sensory and motor aspects of speech are represented in different locations.

stand the words they are saying and cannot be sure that what they wanted to say was in fact said. With their speech perception so muddled, patients begin to speak and then slow down. They stutter and stumble until the coherence of the intended message is lost. Since this is a speech deficit, patients have an aphasia as an indirect result of auditory agnosia.

Motor aphasia Damage in the forward part of the speech region also causes aphasia, but without an accompanying sensory deficit. Because such a patient's difficulty seems to be confined to the motor act of speaking, the resulting syndrome is called **motor aphasia** or **expressive aphasia.** Pure motor aphasia is easily distinguished from pure sensory aphasia. The critical question is whether the patient can understand spoken words. Although neither a motor aphasic nor a sensory aphasic can speak in answer to a spoken question, a motor aphasic can give intelligent answers in writing or with gestures but a sensory aphasic cannot. The difficulty underlying pure motor aphasia seems to be an inability to put thoughts into speech. Since motor aphasia still allows verbal contact between the patient and the world, motor aphasia is not as disastrous a deficit as sensory aphasia (Peele, 1977).

Frontal Lobe The very large area of the frontal lobe that lies forward of the motor area (see Figure 2.17), the **prefrontal association area,** has proved to be a most perplexing part of the cortex. We know little about its function. The prefrontal cortex is *not* sensory in function because no sensory system projects directly to it, nor does the stimulation of any sensory receptor evoke immediate neural activity within it. It is also *not* motor in function. Few fibers project from it directly to the spinal cord, and direct stimulation produces no noticeable body movements. Damage to prefrontal cortex brings no marked deficits. Patients with injuries to this area have no detectable motor or sensory disturbances.

It now appears, however, that damage to prefrontal cortex has subtle but important consequences. One such consequence is a **perseveration deficit,** a loss of the ability to stop an activity when it is inappropriate. The symptom can be illustrated in this manner. Suppose you had a standard deck of playing cards with the usual four suits, clubs, diamonds, hearts, and spades, and the usual thirteen cards in each suit, ace through king. There are two obvious ways of subdividing the cards in the deck, by suits or by the denominations of the cards. If you were asked to start dividing the cards into piles but were not told in which of the two ways to do it, you would probably choose one of the two ways and start building the appropriate piles. Then if, after you were halfway through the deck, the request came to stop sorting the cards by the method chosen and to sort the remainder of the deck by the other method, you would have no trouble complying.

Patients with damaged prefrontal areas have great difficulty making such a shift, although they can sort the cards on either basis as well as a normal person. Once started on a method of sorting, the patient perseverates. The prefrontal patient cannot shift from one rule of sorting to the other, in spite of seeming to know that the rule has changed. The patient may say, "I know this is wrong," but continue sorting card after card by the old rule (Milner, 1962).

The perseveration deficit suggests that one of the functions of prefrontal cortex is to inhibit plans of action initiated at other places in the nervous system. The inhibitory influence, if brought to bear on relatively automatic reactions or even acquired habits, would assure the deliberate thoughtfulness that is characteristic of much human behavior. Indeed, the behavior of prefrontal patients is more automatized. They are unable to resume an activity at the point of interruption. If they are interrupted while counting, they start again at the beginning. Ordinarily, individuals begin again only when a highly practiced series of movements or an extremely well-known pattern of words is interrupted.

A final deficit has to do with abstract thinking. It can be illustrated by asking the patient to copy a simple arrangement of sticks. Normal individuals have no difficulty reconstructing any of the arrangements, but prefrontal patients have great difficulty with some arrangements and no difficulty with others. Their comments about the problems are a clue to the nature of the deficit. Each construction that they can copy reminds them of a concrete object such as a "ladder" or a "house." The arrangements that they cannot reconstruct remind them of "nothing." Apparently the attachment of a concrete title to the stick arrangements is necessary if they are to be reconstructed (Figure 2.20). Patients find it impossible to

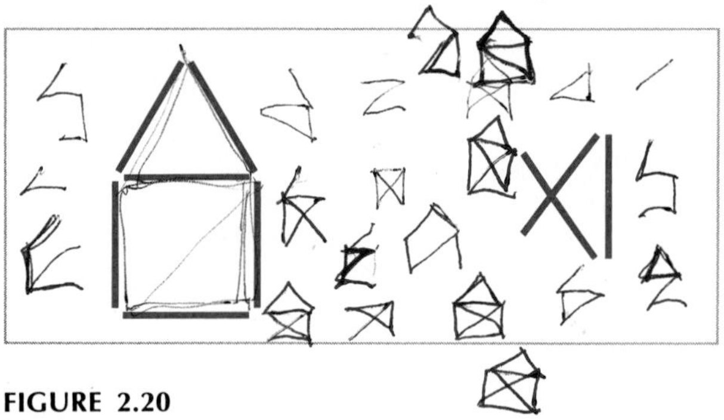

FIGURE 2.20
Stick arrangements for testing prefrontal patients. Meaningful arrangements such as one suggesting a house are easy for the patients to copy, but meaningless arrangements are not.

duplicate arrangements that are not reminiscent of a concrete object.

Connection Between the Hemispheres

The two hemispheres of the forebrain are interconnected by bundles of fibers called **commissures** (Figure 2.21). These commissures can be seen in cross section after the two hemispheres have been divided to expose the inside or medial surface. The largest commissure is the **corpus callosum,** which interconnects the cortical parts of the two hemispheres. The smaller commissures, the anterior and hippocampal, connect the left and right halves of the old forebrain, and the smallest one, the posterior commissure, connects the two sides of the midbrain.

In a normal person the commissures allow the integration of sensations from both halves of the body and also assure coordinated movements of the two halves. These commissures are sometimes severed to alleviate the symptoms of severe **epilepsy.** The "electrical storm" of discharging neurons in one hemisphere is then unable to pass over and excite those of the second. For a time after these operations were first performed, no differences in the behavior of these individuals were noticed. The symptoms of the so-called "split-brain" syndrome are revealed only by a very special set of tests. As we shall see, these symptoms raise profound questions about such basic matters as the concept of self. In fact, experiments with split-

EPILEPSY

The single term epilepsy covers a wide variety of disorders whose symptoms are loss of consciousness and convulsions. The immediate cause of epilepsy is an excessive activity of neurons in the brain. The epileptic seizure often begins with abnormal activity in one area of the cortex, but the excessive activity may spread to more and more tissue until it takes over the entire brain. The more basic causes of epilepsy vary. A part of the etiology is genetic. If one of a pair of identical twins has epilepsy, the chances are nearly 40 percent that the other twin will have it too. By contrast, if one of a pair of fraternal twins has epilepsy, only 2 percent of the co-twins do. Brain damage, congenital defects of the brain, endocrine disorders, and diseases such as meningitis and encephalitis can cause epilepsy. The electroencephalograph (EEG), which electronically records the brain's electrical activity as marks on paper, will register the excessive discharging of the epileptic's brain that takes place during seizures, and sometimes between them, providing an essential means of diagnosis.

Three broad categories cover most of the clinical forms of epilepsy. **Grand mal** is what we usually think of as epilepsy. It is the "sacred sickness," the "falling disease" that afflicted such past greats as Julius Caesar. Grand mal seizures sometimes begin with an aura, a "warning" which lasts for perhaps a few seconds. It may consist of visual or auditory hallucinations or sometimes a vague feeling that the world is becoming unreal. The seizure itself is accompanied by a major generalized convulsion. Patients become rigid and lose consciousness, falling to the ground. Almost at once they begin to writhe violently. The jaws open and close rhythmically and forcefully. After the attack, which usually lasts about five minutes, patients have no recollection of the seizure at all. They emerge from it confused and sleepy and possibly with a headache.

Petit mal epilepsy is marked by a brief loss of consciousness. People stop whatever they are doing and stare. The eyes may appear glazed. There may be a generalized jerking and sometimes a loss of muscle tone, which will make people stagger but rarely collapses them. Petit mal occurs most frequently in children and rarely has its onset after the age of about twenty. The attacks themselves last about fifteen seconds and may occur many times a day. In extreme cases the attacks run together and cause a lapse of consciousness several minutes in length.

Psychomotor epilepsy begins with an aura, which may be an unpleasant smell or taste or an auditory or visual hallucination. Patients lose touch with their surroundings, but they appear conscious and engage in a confused type of activity, such as picking at their clothes or staring at objects around them. The attack is usually brief but occasionally becomes a prolonged state of confusion lasting for hours or even days. Patients actively resist any attempt to restrict their rather mechanical movements.

About 85 percent of all epileptics are able to control their seizures with drugs. In all other cases surgical removal of damaged brain tissues has been successful. The most extreme therapy, of course, is the severing of the commissures between the hemispheres.

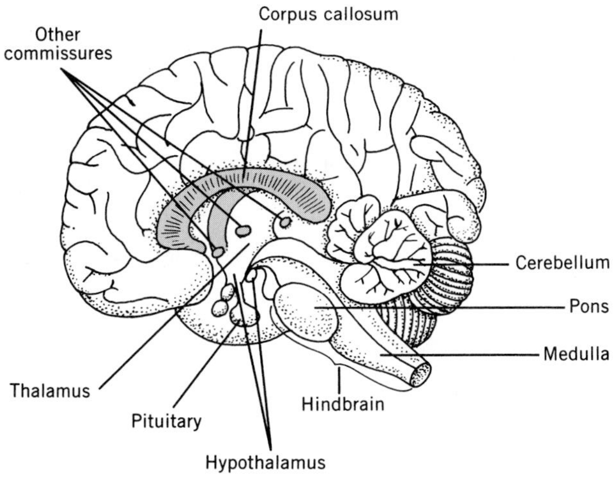

FIGURE 2.21
Medial view of human forebrain. The corpus callosum and other commissures connect the two hemispheres.

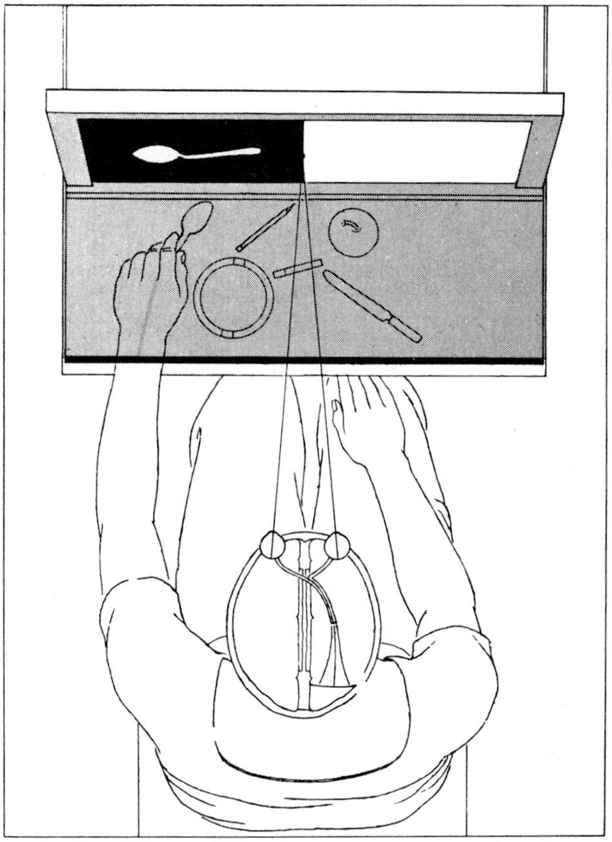

With a fixation as indicated, the retinal image of the spoon on the left goes to the right hemisphere. The patient cannot name the object as a spoon but can identify it by touch.

brain patients are about as astonishing as any you will meet in the study of psychology.

In order to comprehend the behavior of the split-brain patient, it is important to remember a number of things. (1) Sensory effects of stimulation and motor control remain normal in these patients. The transection of the commissures does not disconnect the cortex from receptors or effectors. (2) For seeing, hearing, or feeling, the right sensory field has its principal effect on the left hemisphere, the left sensory field on the right hemisphere. (3) Acts performed with the right hand are controlled through the motor cortex of the left hemisphere; control of the left hand is from the right hemisphere. (4) The left hemisphere contains the language areas. What is lost in split-brain patients is the normal ability to integrate the activities in the two halves of the brain. Consequently, left and right parts of sensory fields and the movements of left and right parts of the body are not integrated.

If split-brain patients are presented with a list of six digits, three coming to the right ear and three coming to the left, they will be able to report only those delivered to the right ear. Patients are not deaf to those in the left ear, but the left ear projects predominantly to the right hemisphere, which is without the speech center required to report them. The fact that their difficulty is in responding verbally becomes clearer when they are confronted with visual stimuli.

If the stimulus HE/ART is presented in such a way that HE is in the left visual field and ART in the right visual field, split-brain patients will be able to *read* ART and say it on request, but they cannot read or say HE. By contrast, when shown a collection of test words, these patients will be able to *point* with the left hand to HE, as something they have seen, but they cannot point to it with the right hand. They will not be able to point to ART with the left hand, but they can with the right hand. Of course they cannot read or report HEART in any manner (Gazzaniga, 1967).

Stimuli in the *right* visual field, ART in our example, are projected to the left visual cortex. Since the speech areas are also in the left hemisphere, patients can read ART and say the word. The HE coming from the left visual field, however, is registered only as a design by the right hemisphere, which has been disconnected from the language areas of the left hemisphere. Although patients cannot deal verbally with stimuli coming to the right hemisphere, they can deal with them in other ways, for example, by pointing to them with the left hand, but not the right.

If the left hemisphere is required for language-related tasks, is the right hemisphere best at any particular activity? The answer is yes. The right hemisphere is superior for many tasks requiring spatial perception. Suppose split-brain patients are given the task of solving a block design puzzle (Figure 2.22). The right hemisphere, and therefore the left hand, is good at this kind of perceptual task, as long as words are not involved. The left hemisphere, and the right hand, is poor at such tasks, however. Because of this difference patients are usually unable to do these puzzles when allowed the use of both hands, although they can solve them easily with the left hand alone. When they are free to use both hands, the right hand tries to help but often undoes the superior accomplishments of the left hand (Gazzaniga, Bogen, and Sperry, 1965).

When the two hemispheres are separated by damage to the commissures, the person becomes "two" individuals, a right-sided one, connected to the left hemisphere, who can talk, read, understand speech, and operate the right arm and leg; and a left-sided individual, connected to the right hemisphere, who is entirely without language but can operate the left arm and leg and can perform certain nonverbal perceptual and motor tasks in a manner superior to that of the right-sided individual.

Outside the laboratory, and to some extent within it, these two individuals tend to get along very well because each is attentive to the activities of the other and each makes use of the other's skills. But as we might anticipate, peace and harmony do not always reign.

Although both hemispheres in these people can have emotions, there are differences. The left hemisphere can describe and explain the basis for the emotion; the right hemisphere cannot. Moreover, the emotions can be different in the two hemispheres. One of these patients, the right-hemisphere individual, once got angry with his wife, grabbed her with the left hand, and shook her violently while the left-hemisphere individual and right hand tried to intercede and bring this other half of himself under control. Suppose that the right hand had been unsuccessful and that the left hand had murdered the wife. Who would be guilty of homicide in such a case? Who should be punished, perhaps even put to death (Gazzaniga, 1970)?

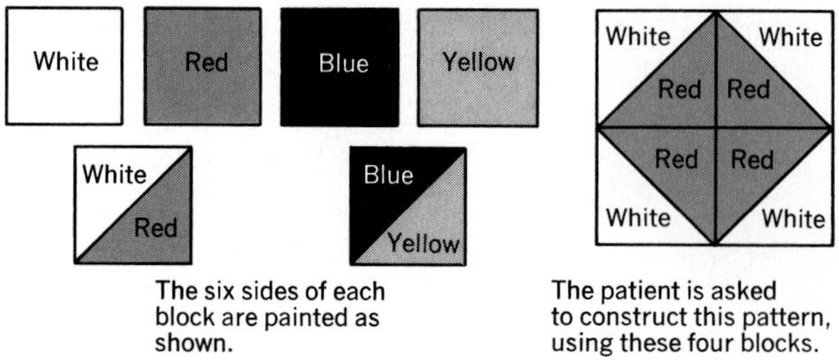

FIGURE 2.22

A block-design test showing superiority of right hemisphere for spatial perception. A patient is given blocks with each of their six sides painted differently. The patient's task is to arrange these blocks so that they copy a pattern presented on a card.

SUMMARY □

The old forebrain integrates a greater range of stimulation than the spinal cord, hindbrain, and midbrain, for it initiates sequences of activity, such as eating; its actions are more complex and of longer duration than any controlled by lower levels of the nervous system. Via the hypothalamus the old forebrain controls food intake, regulates the water balance and temperature of the body, and adjusts the circulatory system to the needs of the body musculature. The hypothalamus exercises quick control over the viscera through the sympathetic and parasympathetic divisions of the autonomic nervous system. The divisions act separately either to mobilize or to protect and maintain bodily resources. Through the endocrine glands the hypothalamus regulates sustained internal states. Chemical and electrical stimulation of relevant sites in the old forebrain provide additional evidence of its contributions to motivation and emotions. Some activities of the old forebrain so resemble those associated with emotion that it may be the seat of the emotions themselves.

The new forebrain is the largest part of the human brain. One area of the gray matter covering it, the primary sensory cortex, is most closely connected with sensory receptors. Destruction of this cortex causes perceptual deficits. Primary motor cortex is most closely connected to effectors. With its destruction voluntary movement is lost. Still other areas surrounding the primary sensory and motor areas, called secondary sensory and secondary motor cortex, are necessary for recognition of what is sensed and the execution of acts requiring sequences of movements. A large part of one hemisphere, usually the left, contains mechanisms necessary for speech and language. Damage to this area causes sensory or motor aphasia, depending on the exact site of the damage. Finally, the frontal lobe contains a large amount of cortex that is neither sensory nor motor. Subtle deficits in thoughtfulness and abstract thinking are noticeable after its destruction, but its function is still largely unknown.

In the normal individual the activities of the two hemispheres are integrated by the corpus callosum and other connecting fiber tracts. Studies of patients with surgically bisected brains have revealed the special capabilities of the two hemispheres. These patients can deal verbally only with stimulation coming to the hemisphere containing centers for speech, usually the left hemisphere. The right hemisphere is found to be superior to the left in spatial perception. In the split-brain patient integration is lost. The person becomes two individuals, living with the same body but with a skull that has two brains within it.

TO BE SURE YOU UNDERSTAND THIS CHAPTER △

This chapter contains a very large number of concepts. The list that follows includes the most important. They are given in the approximate order in which they appeared in the chapter. If you can define them all in order, you will reproduce most of the content of the chapter.

Peripheral nervous system
Central nervous system
Brain
Spinal cord
Somatic sensory fibers
Visceral sensory fibers
Somatic motor fibers
Visceral motor fibers
Glia cells
Neuron
Blood-brain barrier
Cell body
Dendrite
Axon
Terminal button
Myelin
Nerve impulse
Action potential
All-or-none law
Synaptic transmission
Synapse
Presynaptic neuron
Postsynaptic neuron
Synaptic cleft
Synaptic vesicles
Neurotransmitter
Receptor site
Deactivating enzyme
Lock-and-key specificity
Resting potential
Temporal summation
Spatial summation
Excitatory stimulation
Inhibitory stimulation
Receptor
Afferent neuron
Effector
Efferent neuron
White matter
Gray matter
Spinal nerve
Internuncial neuron
Reflex arc
Cranial nerve
Hindbrain
Midbrain
Reticular formation
Reticular activating system
Old forebrain
Limbic system
Autonomic nervous system
Parasympathetic system
Craniosacral system
Sympathetic system
Thoracico lumbar system
Endocrine system
Self-stimulation
Primary motor cortex
Secondary motor cortex
Primary sensory cortex
Secondary sensory cortex
Association cortex
Agnosia
Hemiplegia
Aphasia
Sensory aphasia
Motor aphasia
Prefrontal association area
Perseveration deficit
Commissure
Corpus callosum
Epilepsy
Grand mal epilepsy
Petit mal epilepsy
Psychomotor epilepsy

TO GO BEYOND THIS CHAPTER △

In this book Chapter 3 on the sensory processes is the chapter most closely related to this one. Additional related materials are to be found in Chapters 4 on perception, 5 on states of consciousness, 6 on conditioning and learning, and 8 on language and thought.

Elsewhere The subject matter in this chapter is drawn from material of several disciplines, each of which is an entire science in itself and has its own name, such as physiological or biological psychology, psychobiology, neuropsychology, neurophysiology, neuroanatomy, neurochemistry, neuropharmacology, and so on. Texts with any of these words, or any other words with the prefix neuro-, in their titles will contain wider-ranging and more detailed discussions of the phenomena described here. Perhaps a hundred new books on these subjects are published each year. Examples of the more general ones are *Functional Neuroscience,* by Michael Gazzaniga, Diana Steen, and Bruce Volpe; *The Brain,* by C. U. M. Smith; *Handbook of Behavioral Neurobiology,* edited by F. A. King; and *Biological Psychology,* by Philip Groves and Kurt Schlesinger.

CH. 3

Sensory Psychology

More than 2000 years ago Heraclitus held that everything we know comes to us through the doors of the senses. Since then this empirical view that knowledge comes from experience has been the dominant one. The best-known expression of the doctrine is that of the British philosopher John Locke. In *An Essay Concerning Human Understanding,* published in 1690, Locke maintained that the mind is a blank tablet, a *tabula rasa,* and that it becomes whatever experience writes on it.

> Let us suppose the mind to be, as we say, white paper, void of all characters, without any ideas: —How comes it to be furnished; Whence comes it by that vast store which the busy and boundless fancy of man has painted on it with an almost endless variety? Whence has it all the *materials* of reason and knowledge? To this I answer, in one word, from EXPERIENCE.

Locke went on to say that the content of the mind consists of *ideas* provided by *sensations* on the one hand and by the mind's *reflections* on its own operations on the other. Later, such theorizing would make the study of the senses a topic of fundamental importance in early psychology, and it still is.

Developments in European physiology a little over a century later gave the sensory processes tangible reality. In 1811 and 1822, Sir Charles Bell, in England, and François Magendie, in France, discovered independently that peripheral nerves are of two kinds. There are sensory nerve fibers that enter by the dorsal roots of the spinal cord and motor nerve fibers. They exit by way of the ventral roots. This discovery provided the sensory processes with a general physiological existence apart from behavior.

Then, in 1826, Johannes Peter Müller gave the specific senses separate reality in his doctrine of the **specific energy of nerves.** This doctrine states that each sense responds only in terms of its own specific quality, no matter how the sense is stimulated. Should a blow to the head, for example, stimulate the visual and auditory systems, they will respond in their own terms, as a flash of light and a sound. The stage was set for the study of the individual senses.

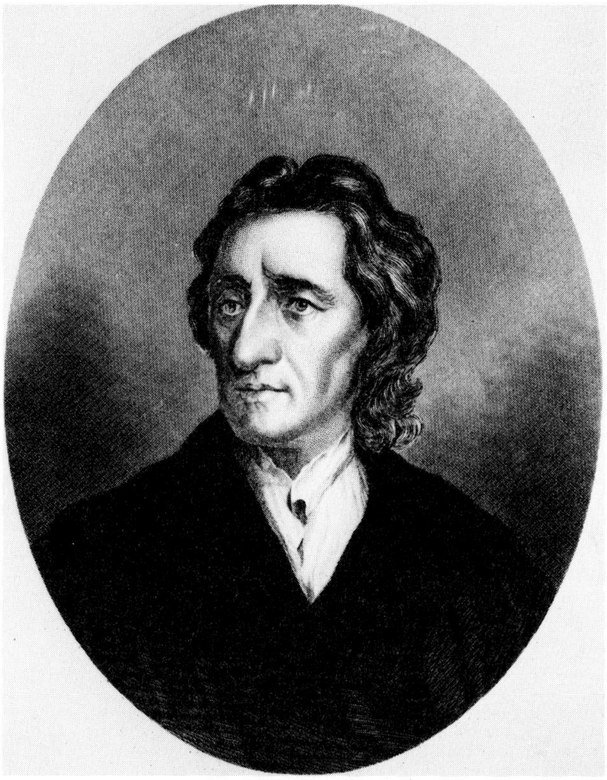

John Locke (1632-1704) believed that understanding the way in which the human mind works is a prerequisite to understanding anything else.

VISION

The visual system will be examined in some detail, the other senses more generally. There are two principal justifications for this. Far more is known about vision than the other senses. Furthermore, vision provides us with an especially rich source of psychologically meaningful information. The organ of vision, the eye, collects the energy called light and brings it to focus on a small region of the retina called the fovea. If the analogy is not pushed too far, the eye can be thought of as a simple camera (Figure 3.1).

The Iris The amount of light entering the eye is controlled by the **iris,** which corresponds to the diaphragm in a camera. The iris is the structure responsible for the color of the eye. It surrounds the **pupil,** the opening through which light enters. In very bright light the iris closes to reduce the amount entering the eye. In dim light it enlarges to allow more light to enter.

The level of illumination is not the only factor controlling pupil size. There are at least two others. When we do close work, even under good light, the iris closes down still further because this increases the sharpness of the visual image. The other factor is emotion. Emotional arousal or interest of any kind will markedly increase pupil size.

The Lens System of the Eye The lenses of the eye are a system, consisting of several elements. The first element is the **cornea,** a curved transparent membrane which is continuous with the tough, white opaque coat of the eyeball; the second is the **aqueous humor,** a clear fluid just behind the cornea. Next in order is the **crystalline lens,** which with the help of the ciliary muscles flattens and bulges to obtain a

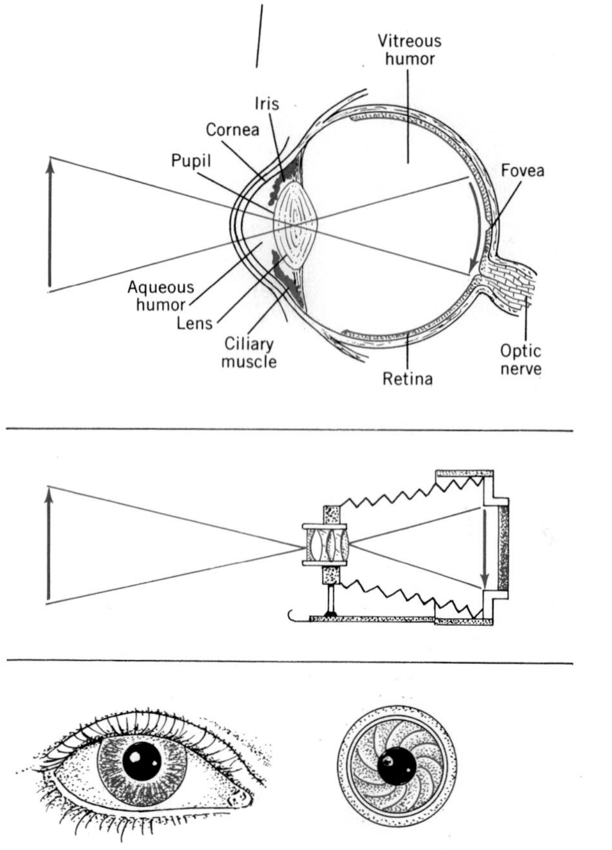

FIGURE 3.1
The structure of the eye and its similarity to the camera. The operation of the iris has been imitated in the diaphragm of the camera. The images formed on the retina and the film are both upside down.

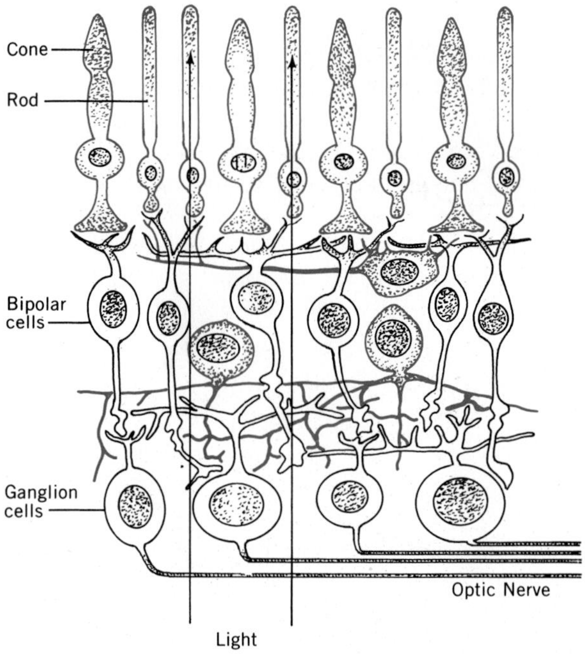

FIGURE 3.2
The retina. Light travels through a complex network of cells before arriving at the rods and cones. Impulses generated in these receptors are transmitted to the bipolar cells and then to the ganglion cells. Lateral connections are made at the level of the bipolar and ganglion cells.

sharp focus for objects distant and near. Finally, in the ball of the eye, between the lens and the retina, lies the **vitreous humor.** This is a jellylike substance which maintains the degree of focus produced by the earlier elements in the system and also maintains pressure that helps keep the retina in place. The cornea provides about two thirds of the focusing power in this system, sharply decreasing the size of the visual image. The lens takes over at that point and operates like a fine tuner, making precise adjustments as required.

The Retina The photosensitive part of the eye corresponding to the film in a camera is the retina. The retina (Figure 3.2) is a thin sheet made up of several layers of interconnected nerve cells. The receptive cells of the retina, the **rods** and **cones** – named for their distinctive shapes – are at the back of the retina. Light must pass through the various layers of blood vessels, of fibers and cell bodies of intermediate neurons, before reaching the rods and cones, which are also neural structures. As we shall learn in more detail later, the cones respond in bright light, in terms of color, the rods in dim light, in terms of white, black, and shades of gray. The cones are most heavily concentrated in the **fovea,** a small indentation only about 0.5 millimeter across, where the image of an object viewed falls directly. The fovea contains only cones. The density of cones drops off drastically just beyond the fovea, however; few inhabit the periphery. The rods become greatest in density a short distance out from the fovea, and then they too become fewer in number in the periphery.

The photoreceptors, the rods and the cones, translate the light energy that falls on them into a neural impulse, which they pass on, to **bipolar cells** and then to **ganglion cells** (Figure 3.2). This is the direct path of transmission. There are also **lateral connections** at the levels of the bipolar cells and ganglion cells. These connections make it possible for cells in different retinal areas to influence one another. The most important psychological contribution of these horizontal connections is to sharpen our perception of borders and edges. If you cover all but one of the stripes in Figure 3.3 and look at it alone, you will see that the stripe is a uniform shade of gray. In the whole figure, however, the stripes appear darker to the right and lighter to the left. At the step where one gray stripe is replaced by a lighter one, the edge of the darker gray is enhanced, and so too is the edge of the new lighter gray. These dark and light edges are called **Mach bands,** after the Austrian physicist Ernst Mach.

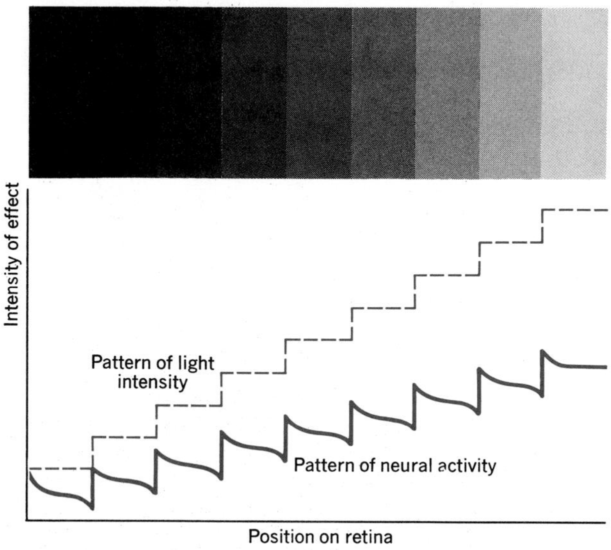

FIGURE 3.3
Mach bands. The individual vertical stripes in the top figure are each a uniform gray from left to right. The stimulation directed toward the retina is also uniform for each stripe. Because of the action of the lateral connections in the retina, however, the pattern of neural activity is less for the edge near the lighter gray neighboring stripe and greater for the edge near the darker neighbor. These bands of enhanced dark and light gray are called Mach bands.

FIGURE 3.4
Locating the blind spot. Close the left eye and fixate the red spot on the space ship. Move the book toward and then away from you. When the planet disappears, its image is falling on the blind spot. Now close the right eye and fixate the red arrowhead. Move the book as before. When the bar of the arrow appears to be continuous, the white space is falling on the blind spot. The brain at this point takes over and fills in the visual field.

Neural activity in one retinal cell is inhibitory to the neural activity of its neighbor. In other words, neighboring retinal cells mutually suppress each other's activity. They pass this inhibition to each other through their lateral connections; the phenomenon itself is called **lateral inhibition.** Of course, for the gray stripes we are examining, retinal cells registering a dark gray are receiving less stimulation than retinal cells registering light gray. The inhibition to cells registering the shade of gray near the border of the darker gray area comes both from neighbor cells registering dark gray and from neighbor cells registering light gray. Their inhibition is therefore greater than inhibition of the cells farther away from the border. Receiving less stimulation, these cells register an enhanced dark gray.

The first lines of cells registering the lighter gray just beyond the step receive less inhibition than their neighbors farther forward, for part of it comes from cells registering the lesser stimulation of the dark gray. The total stimulation to these first lines of cells is therefore greater and is seen as a line of brighter light gray. This special lessening and enhancement of stimulation to cells registering borders makes it much more certain that we will see the borders.

The retina contains about 6 to 8 million cones and at least 120 million rods, but only some 800,000 ganglion cells. Clearly impulses from rods and cones must converge on ganglion cells. Such convergence is greater in the periphery of the retina than in the fovea, and greater for rods than cones. In the fovea the bipolar and ganglion cells are nearly one to one with the cones. In the peripheral portions of the retina, several hundred rods may connect to one bipolar cell. The pooling of impulses to a ganglion cell increases the likelihood of its firing, which means that the eye is given greater sensitivity in low illumination. But the impulse passed on by the ganglion cell is less precise. It is an accumulation of information rather than the discrete details originally supplied by each individual rod. The pattern of light from the object observed is not meticulously conveyed.

By contrast, the cones in the fovea, whose individual impulses will only originate and be passed on when illumination is high, can relay considerable detail. The independently stimulated cones pass on, through their one-to-one connections, single impulses which convey exact information about their sources. Impulses established by patterns of light are maintained throughout the relay to give a well-differentiated image. When we want to examine anything in detail, we turn our head so that that object is in our direct line of vision, which means that its image falls on the fovea.

The axons of the ganglion cells run along the surface of the retina and collect together at the **blind spot,** where they leave the eye as the optic nerve. Because the blind spot contains no rods or cones, it is, in fact, blind. With the aid of Figure 3.4 you can locate your own blind spot. The existence of the blind spot means that there is actually a gap in the visual field of each eye. We are usually unaware of it, however, because when we are using both eyes, an object never falls within both blind spots at once.

The closeness with which cones are packed together in the fovea—they are narrower in this area than elsewhere—and their one-to-one connections account for visual acuity. Everyone who has had his or her eyes examined is familiar with one of the commonest measures of visual acuity, the Snellen eye chart, rows of letters which diminish in size and which the individual being tested attempts to read. Another way of measuring visual acuity is pictured in Figure 3.5.

FIGURE 3.5
One measure of visual acuity. The task is to locate the position of the break in the circle when the figure is viewed from a distance.

Elementary Visual Experience

What we call light is an extremely small, intermediate portion of electromagnetic energy in the complete range of such energies. All electromagnetic energy is radiant, traveling through space at approximately 186,000 miles per second. For our purposes it will be convenient to think of the radiant energy of our universe as moving in waves which can be measured by their length, the distance from the crest of one wave to that of the next. Radio waves, at one extreme, are thousands of meters in length, gamma rays at the other a mere ten-trillionths of a meter. The range is called the electromagnetic spectrum (Figure 3.6, color plate). Besides **wavelength,** electromagnetic waves have **amplitude,** their height from trough to crest (Figure 3.7). Amplitude indicates the strength or intensity of the wave.

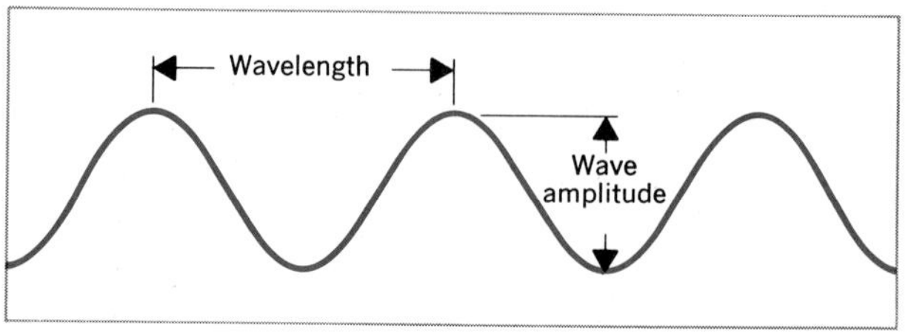

FIGURE 3.7
Wavelength and wave amplitude. In vision wavelength is the principal determiner of the psychological dimension of hue. Wave amplitude is the principal determiner of the psychological dimension of brightness.

The radiant energies from the sun that are able to penetrate the earth's atmosphere and reach sea level have a range that peaks within the wavelengths comprising the visible spectrum. **Light waves,** so-called because they are the only ones of the electromagnetic spectrum that translate into vision, hit and are absorbed by or reflected back from objects in the world. Most of what we see is the vision of objects, which comes to us by means of the incident light that they reflect back. But some objects in the world are also sources and emit light. Whatever their ultimate source—sunlight, moonlight, which is itself reflected from the sun, fire light, or lamp light—emitted and reflected light waves enter the eye by way of the pupil and are focused by its lens in the receptor cells, the rods and the cones.

The rods and cones contain light-sensitive pigments. That of the rods is **rhodopsin,** sometimes called visual purple. The name given to the cone pigments is **idopsin.** When the light waves reach the visual pigments, they are absorbed and initiate a chemical reaction which breaks down pigments, in effect bleaching them. These reactions in turn activate membranes of the receptor cells, initiating the nerve impulses of vision which will eventually arrive in the occipital lobes of the brain.

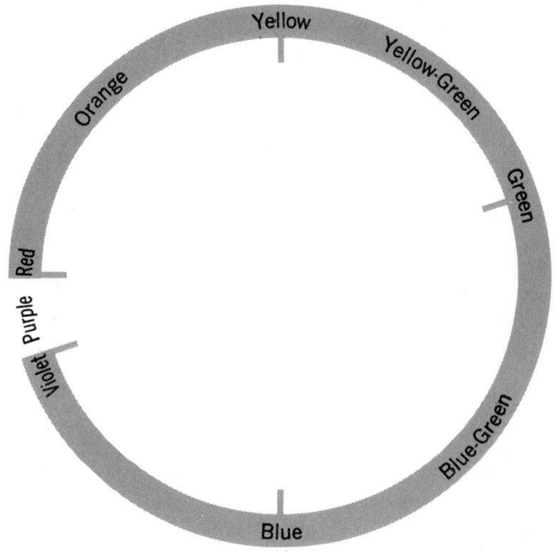

FIGURE 3.8
The color circle. The circle is broken in the region that corresponds to purple, which is a nonspectral color produced by mixtures of red and violet.

Wavelength and Hue The wavelengths of energies in the visual spectrum extend from about 380 to 760 nanometers (billionth of a meter, nm). The length of the light wave determines the perception of **hue,** what we refer to by the common color names, blue, green, yellow, red, orange, blue-green, and so on. The shorter wavelengths are seen as violets and blues, the longer of them as red. The visual spectrum can also be depicted as bent into a circular form (Figure 3.8). The **color circle** is not a complete circle, however. Between red and violet it is left open. In this portion would fall the bluish reds and purplish hues that do not appear in the physical spectrum and can be produced only by mixing long wavelengths with short ones, those that separately translate into reds and into violet.

The objects of the world absorb much of the in-

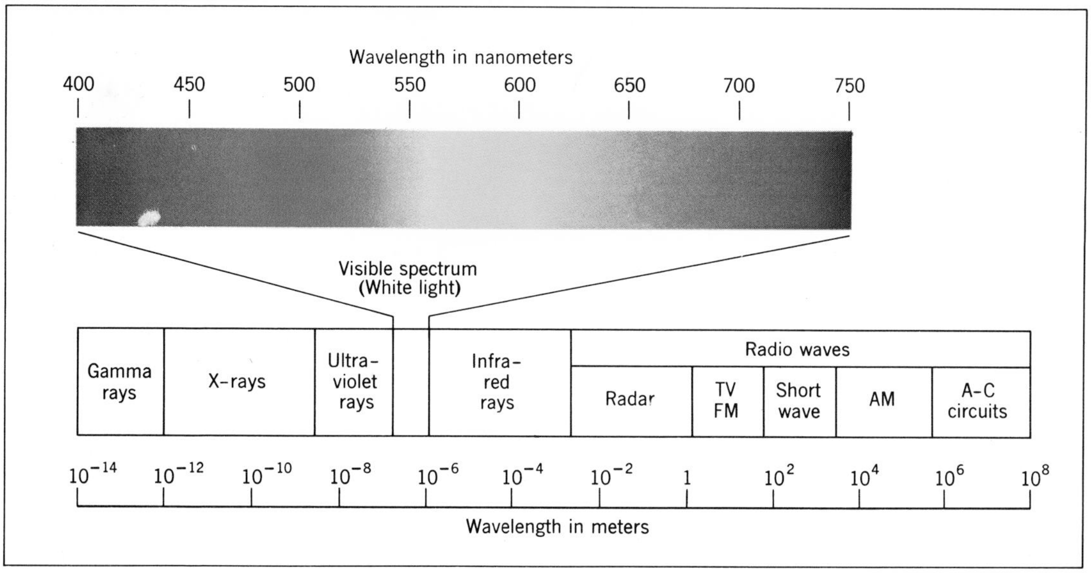

FIGURE 3.6
The electromagnetic spectrum. The visible portion of the spectrum is shown enlarged in the upper part of the figure.

FIGURE 3.11
The principal complementary colors. Colors exactly opposite each other on this circle produce white or gray when mixed. They are called complementary colors. The mixture of any other two colors produces a hue halfway in between them on the circle, with a loss of saturation that is greater for colors far apart than for colors close together.

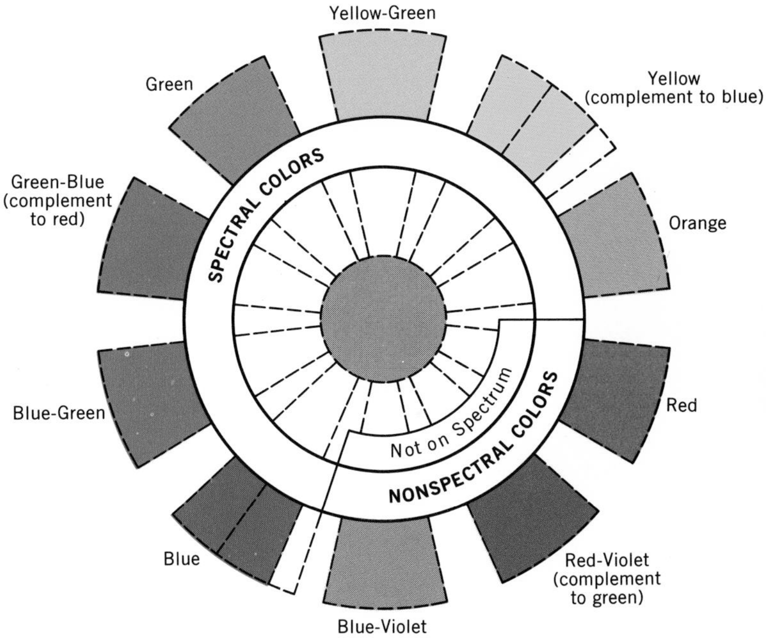

FIGURE 3.12
When lights of physical primary colors combine, the wavelengths of the three add together in the middle as white. When pigments are mixed and when color filters transmit light, the pigments and filters cross-absorb one another's reflected and transmitted wavelengths. Three primaries acting together absorb all wavelengths and are seen as black.

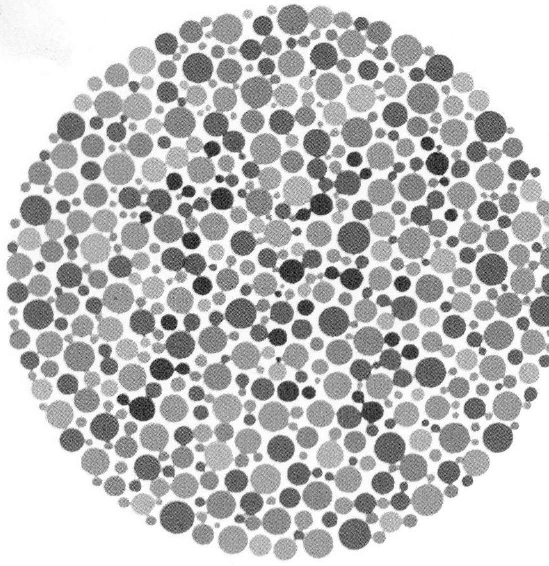

Courtesy of Graham Field Surgical Company, Inc.

FIGURE 3.14
A plate from the Ishihara test for color blindness. A person with normal vision sees the number sixteen.

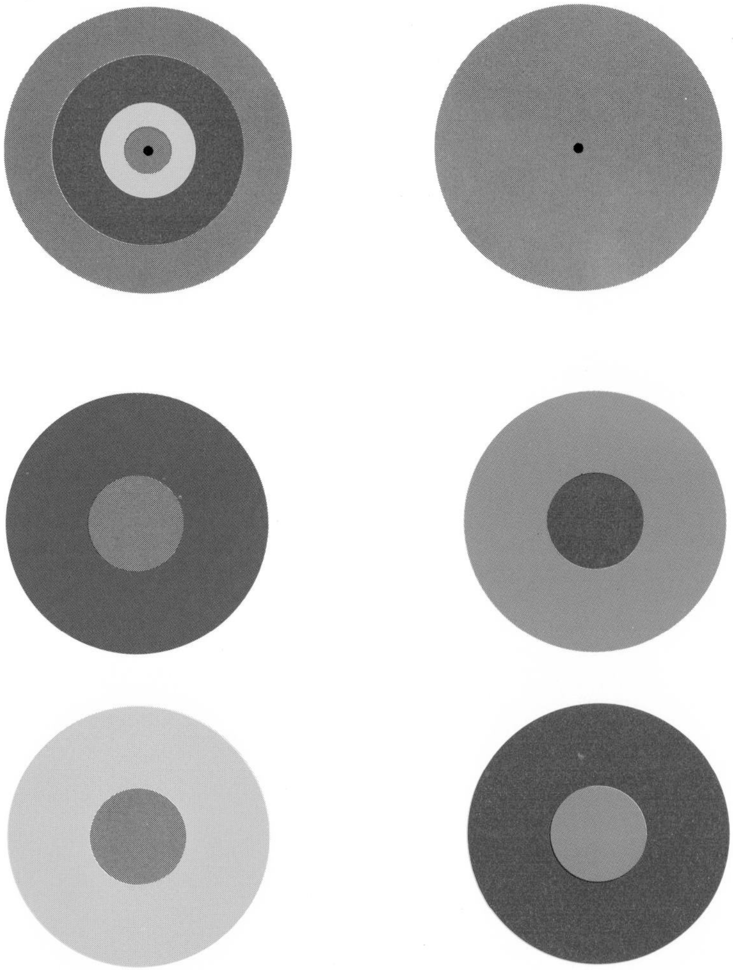

FIGURE 3.13
Stare at the black dot within the red and yellow rings (*top*) for thirty or forty seconds and then at the black dot on the gray circle. (e) A gray circle within a colored one (*left*) takes on a faint hue complementary to that of the surrounding ring. When a colored circle is surrounded by a ring in its complementary color (*right*), both colors are enhanced through contrast.

YELLOW	RED
GREEN	GREEN
BLUE	YELLOW
RED	GREEN
YELLOW	BLUE
RED	YELLOW
GREEN	YELLOW
BLUE	RED
YELLOW	BLUE
BLUE	GREEN
GREEN	BLUE
GREEN	GREEN
BLUE	RED
YELLOW	YELLOW

FIGURE 4.27
Sample Stroop test. It is difficult to ignore the words and report only the colors. The words seem to take over and are responded to automatically.

cident sunlight. We see only the wavelengths that objects selectively reflect back. Thus objects achieve their color, their pigment, from the wavelengths that they reflect. An object that is seen as pure green, for example, is a good absorber and poor reflector of other wavelengths, but a poor absorber and excellent reflector of green wavelengths.

Wave Amplitude and Brightness Colors that are identical in hue may differ in **brightness.** The differences between maroon and pink will give meaning to this dimension. It would be possible to find a maroon and pink that contain the same proportion of red. The maroon will appear blacker, however, the pink whiter, which suggests one way of describing brightness: it is the dimension from black to white.

The principal physical determiner of brightness is the intensity or amplitude of the light wave. Light waves that are identical in length can differ in amplitude. Those of high amplitude are perceived as brighter than those of low amplitude. A secondary determiner of brightness is wavelength; certain colors are intrinsically brighter than others. In ordinary daylight the brightest color is a somewhat greenish yellow; reds and blues are noticeably duller (Figure 3.9). That is, when this particular yellow and any other hue whose waves have the same amplitude are compared, the yellow appears brighter.

Wave Complexity and Saturation No color that you experience in everyday life is a pure color. The yellowest yellow you have ever seen contains some red and some green. Reflected light waves predominantly 575 nm long, with low concentrations of other lengths, will translate as a very highly saturated yellow. Light waves still principally 575 nm long, but made more complex by added portions of other wavelengths, are seen as grayed yellow. Reflected light made up of many wavelengths has no hue whatsoever and translates visually as gray. All the achromatic colors, the colorless colors from white through the grays to black are unsaturated colors. Reflected light waves of complete complexity and great amplitude are seen as white, those of great complexity and medium amplitude as gray, those of complexity but minimum amplitude as black. For this reason change in the brightness of a hue can be expected to affect its saturation. As the reflected 575-nm wave is deeper, translating as a lighter yellow, or shallower, translating as a darker yellow, saturation is also lost. The most saturated colors are of medium brightness.

The double cone in Figure 3.10 summarizes these elementary aspects of visual experience. The circumference of the cone is hue; its radius is saturation; the vertical dimension is brightness. This figure shows, as just mentioned, that a maximally bright, or dull, fully saturated color is an impossibility. The least and greatest degrees of brightness are black and white, which are colorless, that is, without saturation.

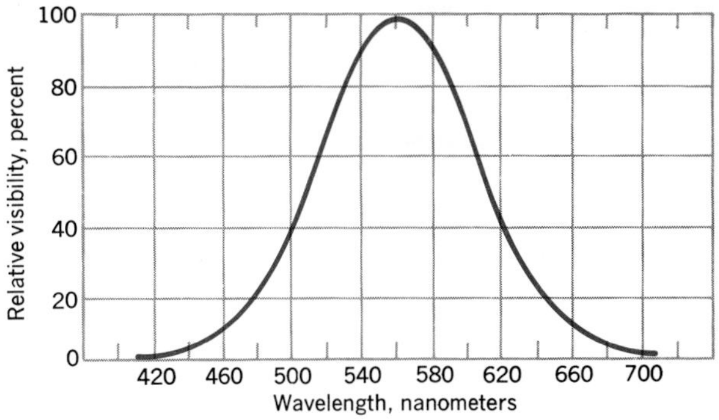

FIGURE 3.9
Visibility of colors in daylight. Waves of different lengths but of the same amplitude differ in apparent brightness. The brightest color is a greenish yellow with a wavelength of about 550 nm.

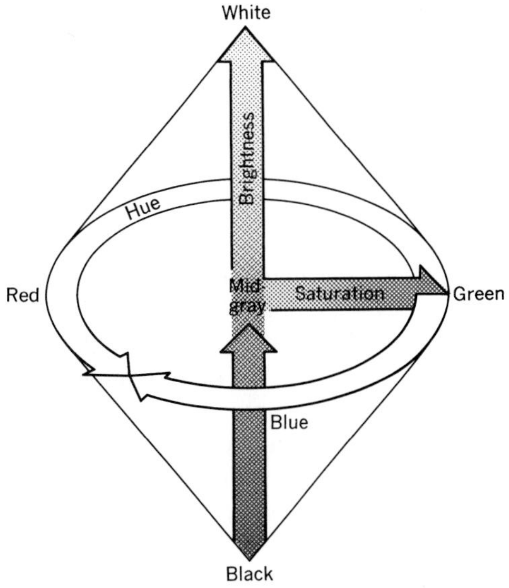

FIGURE 3.10
Dimensions of vision. This color solid is a schematic representation of all possible visual experiences.

Color Mixture

The bluish reds and purples already mentioned are examples of the result of mixing wavelengths. There are two general kinds of color mixing to consider, mixtures of lights and mixtures of pigments. The results of mixing any two colored lights are easiest to explain with the aid of the color circle (Figure 3.11, color plate). In general, when any two lights are mixed, or more commonly when in reflected light two wavelengths are mixed, the resulting color is halfway between them on the circle, and there is a loss of saturation that depends on the distance between them. Consider the mixture of red and yellow wavelengths. Draw a line from red to yellow on the circle and notice where the center of this short line falls. As you could have predicted, it is in the range of hues called orange. The eye receives both wavelengths, which add together as orange. The result of mixing wavelengths for red and green, a yellow of very low saturation, is more surprising. The center of the line connecting red and green is in the range of hues called yellow, but the line passes very near the center of the color circle, which means that the color resulting from the mixture will be very low in saturation, almost a neutral gray. Colors that are exactly opposite to each other on the color circle are called **complementary colors.** When wavelengths of such hues are mixed, they have no detectable color and are seen as an achromatic gray or white. Yellow and blue wavelengths are complementary and mix together as gray.

Mixtures of lights and mixtures of paints do not always produce the same result. The most dramatic case is that of blue and yellow. A mixture of blue and yellow lights produces gray; a mixture of these pigments is seen as green. The color seen can be understood in terms of the wavelengths absorbed and reflected by the two pigments. The blue pigment reflects blue wavelengths predominantly, but some for violet and *green;* it absorbs the other wavelengths in the spectrum. The yellow pigment reflects predominantly yellow wavelengths, but some for *green* and red, and absorbs the other wavelengths. When these two pigments are mixed, the blue pigment absorbs the red and yellow wavelengths reflected by the yellow pigment, and the yellow pigment absorbs the violet and blue wavelengths reflected by the blue pigment. The only wavelengths reflected back in any quantity are those for green. The mixture of lights or of reflected wavelengths is sometimes called **additive mixture.** The eye receives both wavelengths. The mixture of pigments is sometimes called **subtractive mixture** because the pigments cross-absorb and the eye receives only leftover wavelengths (Figure 3.12, color plate).

Other Phenomena

If you stare at the small black dot in the upper part of Figure 3.13 (color plate) for thirty or forty seconds, and then at the gray background, you will soon see an ephemeral blue ring surrounded by a green one. These faint sensations are **negative afterimages.** The hue of the negative afterimage is always the complement of the fixated hue. A closely related effect is seeing **induced colors.** If a patch of gray paper appears against a colored background, the gray takes on a faint tinge of the color that is the complement of the background hue. If we replace the gray paper with a patch that is itself the complement of the background color, the hue of this patch intensifies. This is the phenomenon of **simultaneous contrast.**

Finally, there are the phenomena of color blindness, which comes in many gradations, ranging from the complete absence of color vision through seeing all colors, but red and green only weakly. The completely color-blind individual sees the world entirely in shades of gray. This condition is rare and most often occurs in albinos, whose bodies lack all pigments. Since their cones do not contain the usual photosensitive pigments, the cones in effect do not function. Another extremely rare form of color blindness, usually caused by disease, is the inability to distinguish yellows and blues. The most frequent types are several hereditary varieties of red-green color blindness affecting 7 to 8 percent of males but less than one percent of the female population. Those with this defect cannot distinguish green from red, seeing them both as yellowish brown (Figure 3.14, color plate).

Theories of Color Vision

These various phenomena of color vision have been known for centuries, and scientists from many disciplines have attempted to explain them. The nineteenth century saw the development of two different classical theories of color vision, which still influence our thinking about the topic. As is fairly standard in scientific theorizing, these theories attempt to explain diverse phenomena in terms of a limited number of elements. In theories of color vision the elements are primary colors.

Physical and Psychological Primary Colors The selective mixture of beams of colored light from different thirds of the spectrum will produce all the other colors. Three commonly cited wavelengths are a red of 650 nm, a green of 530 nm, and a blue of 460 nm. Mixtures of these lights with careful attention to proportions can reproduce the entire spectrum. For this reason red, green, and blue have been called **physical primary colors.** It is important to understand that the selection of physical primaries is somewhat arbitrary. Other widely separated wavelenghts can also be mixed to reproduce the entire spectrum. The mixtures would have to be in different proportions for different physical primaries, however.

For the **psychological primaries** there is less flexibility. The psychological primaries, red, green, blue, *and yellow,* are primary in the sense that they are unique and seem a single hue. Particular shades of

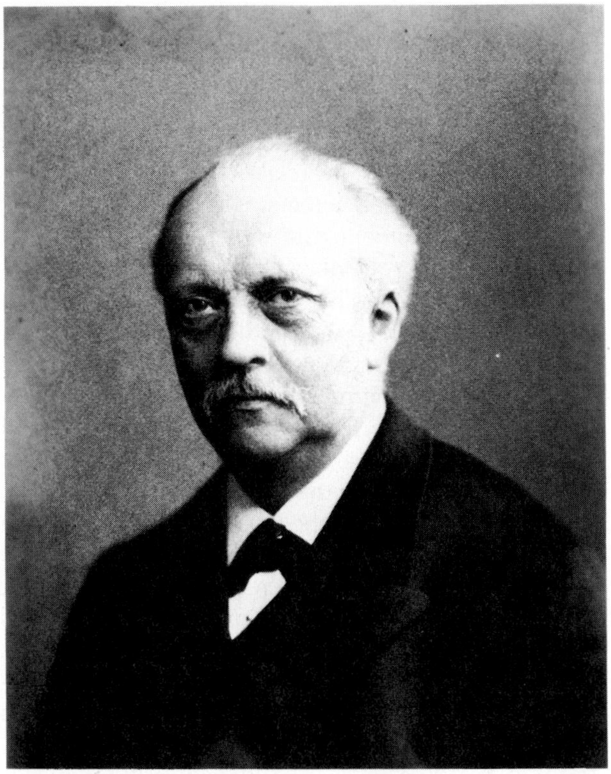

Hermann Ludwig Ferdinand von Helmholtz (1821-1894) was one of the great men of science. Theoretical physics, neurophysiology, optics and vision, physiological acoustics, and the psychology of the senses were all encompassed by his genius.

red, green, blue, and yellow are seen as purely these colors, untinged by any trace of their neighbors in the spectrum.

Trichromatic and Opponent Process Theories The two classical theories of color vision were developed on the assumption that the primaries, physical in one theory and psychological in the other, are fundamental to color vision. Early in the nineteenth century an English physicist, Thomas Young, proposed that the retina contains three kinds of "particles" which "vibrate" to the wavelengths of the three physical primaries, red, green, and blue, and that the eye mixes these stimulations to see the other hues. Initially, the theory received only limited acceptance. Fifty years later, however, the great German physiologist Hermann von Helmholtz revived Young's theory and revised it. Helmholtz proposed that the three receptors, Young's particles, respond maximally to the wavelengths for the primary colors, but that each also responds less strongly to a range of wavelengths (Figure 3.15*a*). Since it assumes three receptors, the Young-Helmholtz theory can be called a **trichromatic theory.**

The second classical theory of color vision was put forward by Helmholtz's compatriot and fellow physiologist, Ewald Hering. Hering also proposed a three-component system, but with each component capable of a dual response. He theorized that three sets of receptor cells deal individually with the three linked visual experiences, blue-yellow, red-green, and black-white. Hering proposed that these receptors respond in one but not both of two mutually antagonistic ways. The blue-yellow cells, for example, can provide the experience of blue or yellow, but not both at the same time. When these receptors respond in one way, the other reaction tends to be canceled. For this reason Hering's theory can be called an **opponent process theory** (Hurvich and Jameson, 1957).

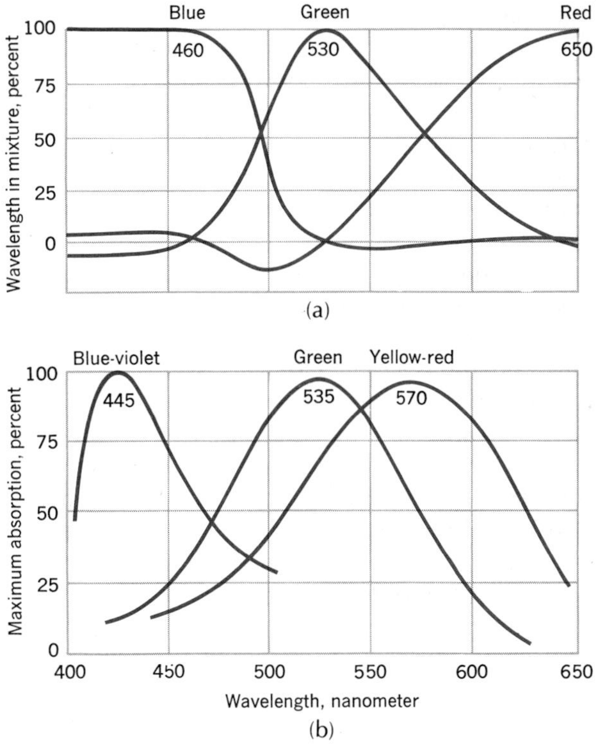

FIGURE 3.15
Three-color retinal processes. (*a*) The proportion of three colors required to produce any color on the spectrum. If the curve goes above 100 or below 0, the mixture must contain some of the complementary color to obtain the hue. (*b*) The absorption spectra for three types of cones. The fact that the two sets of curves are not identical means two things. (1) Nonretinal processes contribute to the experience of color reported in color-mixing experiments. (2) Physical primaries selected for mixing happen not to have exactly the same wavelengths to which the cones are maximally sensitive. (From various sources.)

Evaluation of Theories The Young-Helmholtz and Hering theories had both taken definite form by about 1870. From then, until the middle of this century, the two theories were in competition, each with its own adherents. For the greater part of this period, the Young-Helmholtz trichromatic theory was the dominant one. Both theories explained a range of visual phenomena very well, but trichromatic theory was more widely accepted, partly because of the enormous respect that science held for Helmholtz, but more importantly because the assumption of three receptors, each with just one function, seemed simpler than the assumption of three sets of receptors, each with opposing functions.

The Young-Helmholtz theory assumed that the three types of receptors are maximally responsive to wavelengths for red, green, and blue, but that they also respond less strongly to the other wavelengths in the spectrum. These ideas handle the facts of color perception and color mixture very nicely. When any one of these Young-Helmholtz receptors is stimulated more strongly than others, red, green, or blue would be seen. Yellow would be seen when red- and green-sensitive receptors are stimulated simultaneously. For nonprimary colors other combinations of receptors are excited, for white and gray all three.

The theory explained the fact that negative afterimages have a color that is the complement of the fixation stimulus, assuming that receptors are subject to fatigue. Fixating the red stimulus in Figure 3.13 would tire the red-sensitive receptors and render them incapable of a maximal response. The gray background looked at after the fixation period would normally excite all three receptors equally. Since the red receptors are fatigued, however, they would respond with less vigor than the blue and green; hence the bluish-green hue of the negative afterimage for red.

Color blindness might be explained as a malfunction of one or more of the three kinds of Young-Helmholtz receptors. Furthermore, since the experiences of red and green are produced by different receptors, two kinds of red-green color blindness could be expected, one in which the red receptors do not function properly, and another in which the green ones are insensitive. This prediction is borne out. In color-mixing experiments some people who are red-green color blind are relatively insensitive to red. In matching yellow with mixtures of red and green, they require an unusually large amount of red. A second kind of red-green color blindness is revealed as insensitivity to green.

Up to this point trichromatic theory handles color blindness reasonably well. Other evidence, however, creates difficulties. One of the most important problems is that the red-green color-blind can see yellow. Since the experience of yellow would presumably depend on the simultaneous stimulation of the red and green receptors, weakness in either of these sets of receptors should distort perception of yellow. This does not seem to be the case. Red-green color-blind people, and the few individuals who are red-green blind in one eye only, report that red and green resemble the yellowish shades. There must be additional mechanisms to accomplish color vision. Recent research has thrown considerable light on this issue.

Physiological Evidence The cones of the retina were discovered well after the classical theories of color vision had postulated three sets of receptors. Today we have an instrument with which to study stimulation of the cones. A device called a microspectrophotometer makes it possible to study the absorption of light in a single cone. Such studies have revealed that each cone in the human retina contains one of three iodopsins which differentially absorbs wavelengths of the visual spectrum (Figure 3.15*b*). The absorption accomplished by one pigment peaks at approximately 445 nm, a blue; that of the second at 535 nm, a green. The third absorbs maximally at 570 nm, a yellow, but it also absorbs all the long wavelengths up to 650 nm, covering the reds (MacNicol, 1964). This finding lends strong support to a three-process interpretation at the level of the retina.

At the level of the thalamus, however, microelectrode studies have detected neurons that operate on what appears to be an opponent process principle. The thalamus is a major relay station in the transmission of nerve impulses from receptors such as the eye to sensory cortex (page 41). As is true of neurons elsewhere in the nervous system, those in the thalamus respond continuously, at a relatively slow rate, even though they have not been stimulated (page 29). Russell DeValois and his associates have discovered that firing in some thalamic neurons can be stepped up or halted, depending on the wavelength of the stimulus (DeValois, Abramov, and Jacobs, 1966). These investigators inserted microelectrodes into single cells in the thalamus of a monkey and then presented flashes of light of different colors (Figure 3.16). Presenting a blue or green light to a particular neuron might halt its firing; a yellow or red light would increase it. The firing of other cells follows the opposite pattern.

The physiological data strongly suggest that trichromatic theory describes visual mechanisms very well at the level of the retina but that, at higher levels of the visual system, three-color retinal information is recoded into opponent neural processes.

Two Visual Systems

The rods and cones make up, in effect, two visual systems. The cones are daylight receptors, requiring bright illumination if their lesser amounts of pigment are to absorb wavelengths. The rods, which contain deeper stacks of pigment, operate in dim illumination. Although the rod pigment absorbs wavelengths differentially, it records them as black and white film

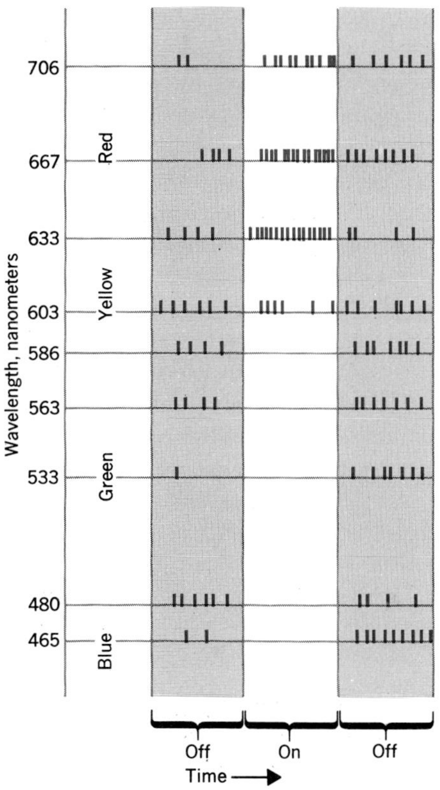

FIGURE 3.16

Opponent processes in the thalamus. The short vertical lines indicate the responses of a single microelectrode-implanted cell in the thalamus to stimulations of nine different wavelengths. The cells are of two kinds. Firing spontaneously at a fairly slow rate, the cell increases the rate of firing, decreases the rate, or ceases firing altogether when the stimulus is given. This particular cell increases its rate of firing at the presentation of yellow and red lights and ceases at the presentation of blue and green lights. (After DeValois, Abramov, and Jacobs, 1966.)

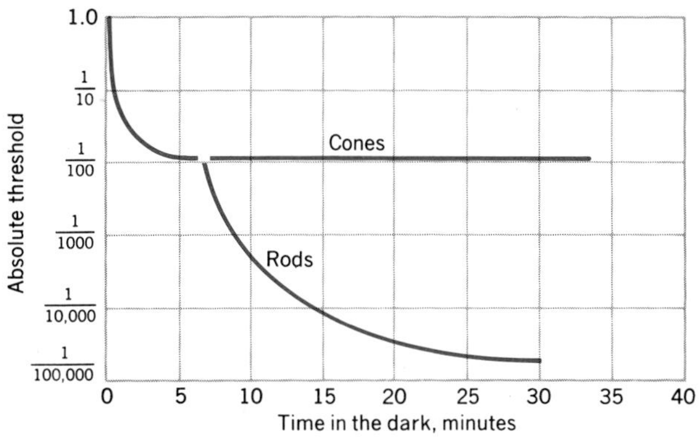

FIGURE 3.17

Dark adaptation. The vertical axis is in fractions of the intensity of light that is visible to the light-adapted eye, set at 1.0. Until the rods and cones have been about 7 to 8 minutes in the dark, the curves for them are identical. Then they diverge. The cones adapt no further. The rods become very much more sensitive.

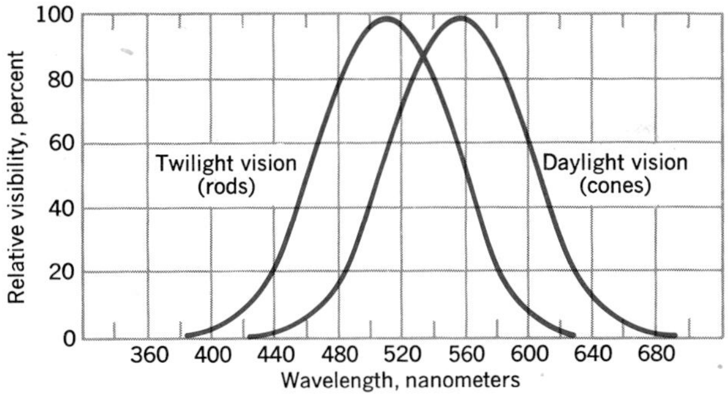

FIGURE 3.18

Visibility function for rods and cones. The right-hand curve is the same as that in Figure 3.9. The left-hand curve shows the shift in the visibility of different wavelengths in twilight vision, when the rods take over.

does, in black and shades of gray. It is important to note in passing, however, that cones also produce achromatic experiences when groups of them respond together.

Dark Adaptation Bright illumination subjects the rods and cones to continual stimulation, which reduces their sensitivity to anything less. Much of the pigment within the receptors has been broken down, and little can be reconstituted before it again absorbs light. In darkness this process reverses itself. As the visual pigments reconstitute themselves, color vision becomes somewhat more sensitive to dimmer light and achromatic vision becomes very much more sensitive. In short, the eye becomes dark-adapted. **Dark adaptation** is measured by determining the dimmest light a person can see (absolute threshold, page 67) after successive amounts of time in the dark (Figure 3.17). The dark-adapted eye is about 100,000 times as sensitive as the light-adapted eye.

Dark adaptation has different time courses in the two visual systems. When we first enter a dark room after being in bright light, we can see absolutely nothing. The light is insufficient to be absorbed by what pigment the cones contain, and the rhodopsin of the rods has been completely bleached. Cone pigments, however, reconstitute themselves rather rapidly in the dark, and soon there is enough of them to absorb the much fainter light. In five to seven minutes cones have become fully adapted. Beyond this point adaptation takes place only in the rods. The transition from rod to cone adaptation appears as a **rod-cone break** in the dark adaptation function (Figure 3.17). The rods do not reach their maximum sensitivity until they have been thirty to forty minutes in the dark. After that amount of time, rhodopsin has been completely reconstituted and we make out our surroundings fairly well, despite the darkness.

The fact that the rods are responsible for dark-adapted vision following the rod-cone break can be

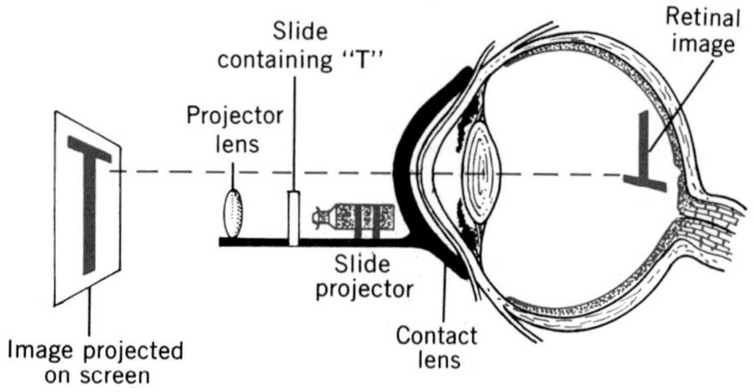

FIGURE 3.19
Stilling physiological nystagmus. With a tiny slide projector attached to a contact lens, the image projected to the retina falls on the same area however the eye moves. (After Cornsweet, 1970.)

demonstrated by tracing the course of adaptation in low-intensity red light. Rods are relatively insensitive to long wavelengths, those for red, but the cones are sensitive (Figure 3.18). After the five to seven minutes required to adapt the cones, there is no further increase in sensitivity to red lights.

The Purkinje Shift The differential sensitivities of the rods and cones account for the changing brightness of different colors with dark adaptation. A red and green matched for brightness in daylight appear to differ under dim illumination, the green appearing much brighter than the red. This phenomenon may be observed easily as twilight falls in a rose garden. The green leaves remain bright for some time after the red blossoms appear black. The fact that the red roses are seen as black in dim illumination confirms again that the rods are totally unresponsive to red. This shifting of the relative brightness of the different colors in low illumination is called the Purkinje phenomenon or **Purkinje shift,** after the physiologist who discovered it.

Certain practical implications follow directly from the fact that the rods are insensitive to red. Rods can become dark-adapted in the light, if that light is red. While the unstimulated rods are adapting, the cones are used for seeing, since they respond to red. One way of making all light reaching the eyes red is to have the person wear red goggles. This procedure is widely used in preparing sentinels who must go on watch duty during the night. Forty minutes or so before they are to go on duty, the sentinels put on red goggles. The last ten minutes of the forty they spend in complete darkness, to adapt the cones. They are able to see in the dark as well as they could had the entire forty minutes been spent in complete darkness.

Physiological Nystagmus

The eye is continually in motion, a fact referred to as **physiological nystagmus.** This tremor actually blurs vision to a slight degree, but it is also essential to the proper functioning of the rods and cones. Both of these facts can be demonstrated by removing the tremor of the eye optically. In one demonstration of this, experimenters attached a tiny slide projector to a contact lens worn by the observer. A slide was projected onto a screen (Figure 3.19). Since the contact lens and the projector moved with the individual's eye, the image from the screen always fell on the same area of the retina, which meant that the pattern of rods and cones stimulated was always exactly the same. In short, the movements of physiological nystagmus could no longer have their usual effect of switching stimulation to neighboring rods and cones. At first, acuity improved somewhat, confirming that this eye tremor does in fact blur the image. Soon, however, the image faded and disappeared. The fading of perception as the pigments of particular rods and cones are depleted gives physiological nystagmus an important function. If it did not exist and we looked at an object for more than a few seconds, the object would not be visible.

SUMMARY □

The eye is sensitive to wavelengths of light that range from about 380 to about 760 nm. Different wavelengths produce the experience of different hues. Other characteristics of the physical stimulus translate as other aspects of simple visual experience. Wave amplitude, but also to a degree wavelength, is responsible for brightness. Saturation depends on the purity of the wave, but also to a degree upon brightness.

At the level of the retina, color perception depends on three cone pigments which absorb selectively blue, green, and red wavelengths. At the level of the thalamus, there are nerve cells that respond in terms of opponent processes—red versus green and blue versus yellow.

The rods and cones are receptors for two different visual systems. The cones function in bright illumination, the rods in dim illumination. The rod pigments are about 100,000 times more sensitive than those in the cones. With dark adaptation the eye shifts from cone vision to rod vision, allowing us, after a time, to see more clearly. The rods and cones also differ in their sensitivity to different wavelengths, the rods being more sensitive to shorter wavelengths and totally insensitive to the longest. This difference is responsible for the Purkinje phenomenon, a shift in the relative brightnesses of colors at twilight. Physiological nystagmus, a continual tremor of the eye, shifts the visual image as it falls on the receptors, preventing the depletion of the pigments in the rods and cones.

Lorrin A. Riggs. A professor at Brown University, Riggs was a pioneer in the study of the effects of physiological nystagmus on visual acuity. He and a student, Floyd Ratliff (Ratliff and Riggs, 1950), reported the initial sharpening and subsequent fading of stopped images.

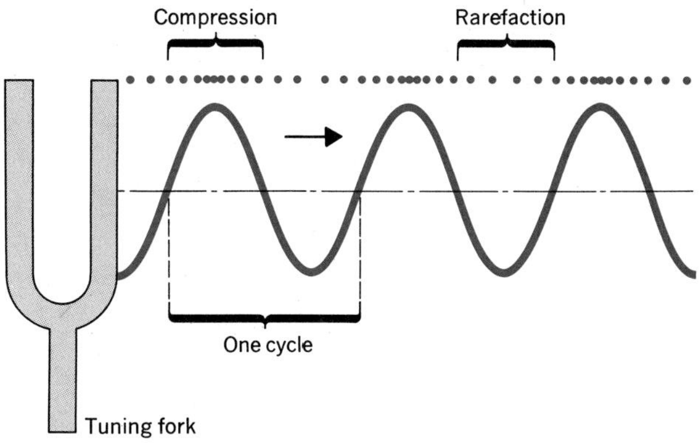

FIGURE 3.20
The nature of sound waves. As the tuning fork vibrates, it produces waves of successive compression and rarefaction of air molecules, represented schematically by dots at the top of the figure. The horizontal line extending from the middle of the fork indicates the normal concentration of molecules. Denser concentrations are represented by the wave peaks above this line, less dense concentrations by the troughs below.

AUDITION

The stimuli for hearing are sequences of compression and rarefaction of the air. Consider, for example, the vibrating tuning fork shown in Figure 3.20. As the fork vibrates to the right, it pushes the molecules of air, which are represented by the dots, to the right. When it moves to the left, a partial vacuum is created. Successive vibrations produce the pattern of compression and rarefaction indicated by the density of the dots. As in vision, sound stimuli can be represented as waves of energy. These pressure waves radiate outward in all directions from the source, however, and they are mechanical rather than electromagnetic. Another important difference between the description of auditory and visual stimuli is that the waves for sound are specified in terms of frequency, cycles per second (**hertz, Hz**), rather than wavelength, although both could be described either way. One cycle is a single complete compression and rarefaction.

Physical Characteristics

Particular sound waves may differ in frequency, amplitude, and complexity, and these differences are responsible for certain aspects of auditory experience. The correspondences between vision and audition in terms of their dependence on the physical characteristics of stimuli are given in Table 3.1.

Pitch The human ear is sensitive to frequencies ranging from about 20 to 20,000 Hz, the greater the frequency, the higher the **pitch.** One interesting phenomenon that is easy to understand in terms of this relationship is the **Doppler effect,** the change in pitch that a person who is stationary hears as a moving sound source approaches and then speeds past. The pitch of a train whistle or automobile horn, for example, rises as the vehicle nears and falls as it passes by. As an automobile approaches, the sound waves are, in effect, more frequent because the forward movement of the car crowds the compressions of the air together; as the car passes, the time between compressions increases (Figure 3.21). Since frequency is the physical basis for pitch, it is to be expected that the pitch of the sound will increase and decrease, exactly as it does.

Loudness **Loudness** in the field of audition corresponds to brightness in vision, both of them reflecting wave amplitude. The amplitude of a sound wave depends on the degree of displacement of the vibrating body from its resting position. It is the strength or intensity of the wave, the extent of compression and rarefaction. The loudness of a sound is usually expressed in terms of decibels (db), a unit of measure related to that for physical pressure (see page 71). The ear is most sensitive in the frequency range

TABLE 3.1
A Comparison of Psychophysical Correlations for Vision and Audition

Vision		Audition	
Physical Feature	**Psychological Dimension**	**Physical Feature**	**Psychological Dimension**
Wavelength	Hue	Wave frequency	Pitch
Wave amplitude	Brightness	Wave amplitude	Loudness
Wave complexity	Saturation	Wave complexity	Timbre

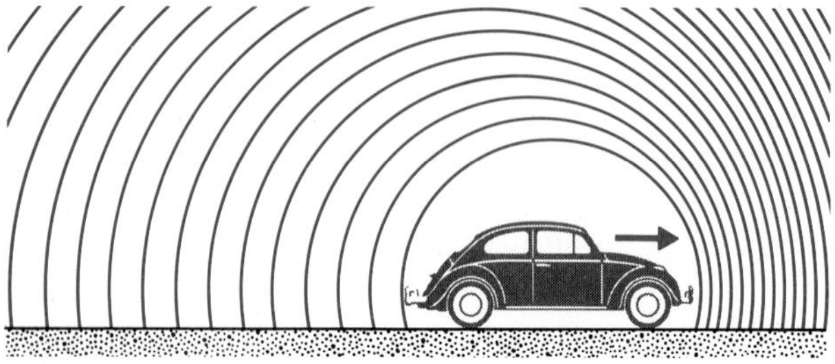

FIGURE 3.21
The Doppler effect. As the car moves forward, the sounds of its horn and engine are heard as high in pitch because the movement of the car, in effect, pushes the sound waves together. As the car speeds past, the waves stretch and the pitch lowers.

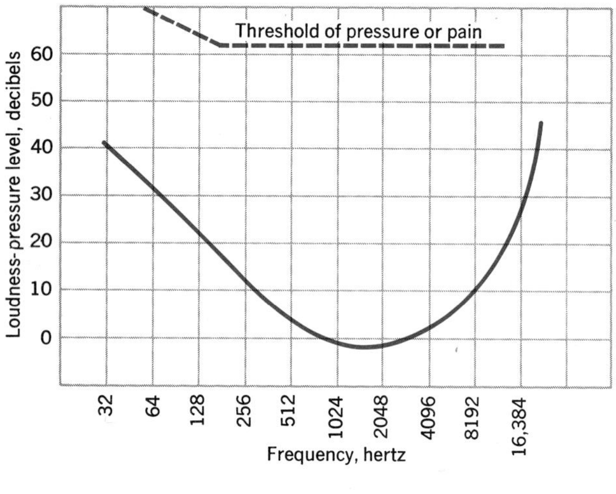

FIGURE 3.22
The audibility function for normal hearing. The vertical axis shows sound pressure, as measured in decibels, the horizontal axis the pitch of pure tones. The ear is the most sensitive in the range from approximately 500 to about 4000 Hz.

around 500 to 4000 Hz (Figure 3.22). Higher or lower tones require a great deal more intensity to make them audible.

Timbre **Timbre** is the tonal quality of sounds that makes it possible to distinguish between different musical instruments that are all sounding the same note. When a violinist draws the bow across the open A-string, the string vibrates at a basic frequency of 440 Hz. This produces the dominant pitch or **fundamental tone** in what the listener hears. At the same time, however, the string also vibrates in segments that are exactly 1/2, 1/3, 1/4, 1/5, and so on of its entire length. These vibrations produce **overtones** of a higher pitch. With the fundamental tone taken as 1, these overtones stand in the ratio 1:2:3:4:5. Thus the overtones produced with a fundamental tone of 440 Hz would have frequencies of 880, 1320, 1760 Hz, and so on. For different musical instruments the number and intensity of the overtones vary. Figure 3.23 shows the difference in form of the sound wave for several instruments on which the same note is being played. As you can probably tell intuitively from looking at the figure, there is a mathematical way, called Fourier analysis, of breaking down any wave form, and thus *any* tone, into its components.

The most complex waves are heard as what we call noise. A completely pitchless noise can be produced by generating a sound that contains all the frequencies in the audible spectrum. By analogy to white light, which contains all wavelengths of the visible spectrum, such a noise is called **white noise.** The nearest approximations to white noise encountered in everyday life are the hissing sounds of air or steam escaping from pressure, as in the sound of a tire slowly going flat.

The Auditory Receptor

Tracing the path of sound through the ear will serve to describe its principal functions (Figure 3.24). The pressure waves are first collected by the external ear and are carried to the **eardrum,** which they force to vibrate at the same frequency. Between the eardrum and another membrane, the **oval window,** are three small bones (ossicles): the **malleus,** or hammer; the **incus,** or anvil; and the **stapes,** or stirrup. These bones, fastened together by ligaments, amplify the pressure vibrations and transmit them to the oval window, which is at the entrance to the inner ear or cochlea.

The bony and coiled cochlea is divided into three canals, each filled with fluid. The perilymph in the

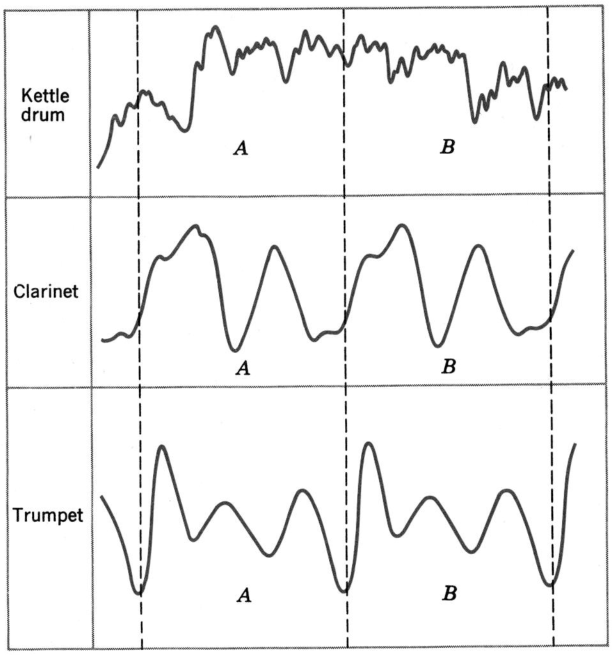

FIGURE 3.23
Timbre. Different musical instruments make characteristically different sounds. Sections *A* and *B* mark off identical periods of time. The trumpet and clarinet produce repetitive, orderly, rhythmic waves consisting of a fundamental tone and several overtones; they are the same in both periods. The kettle drum produces a pattern close to that of noise.

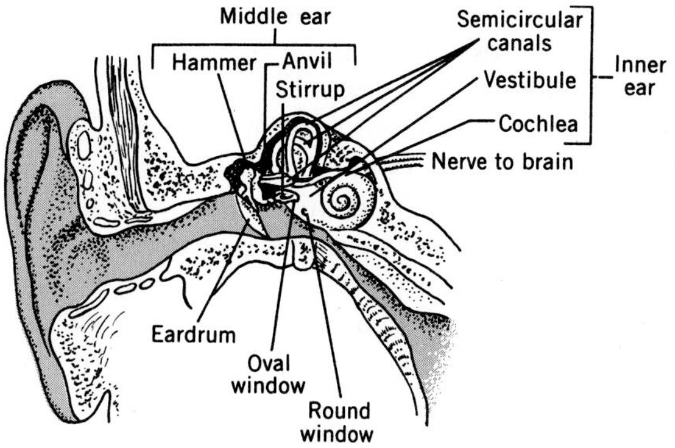

FIGURE 3.24
Anatomy of the ear. The inner ear is sometimes called the bony labyrinth. In addition to structures for hearing, it contains the vestibule and semicircular canals, which are concerned with equilibrium (see page 66).

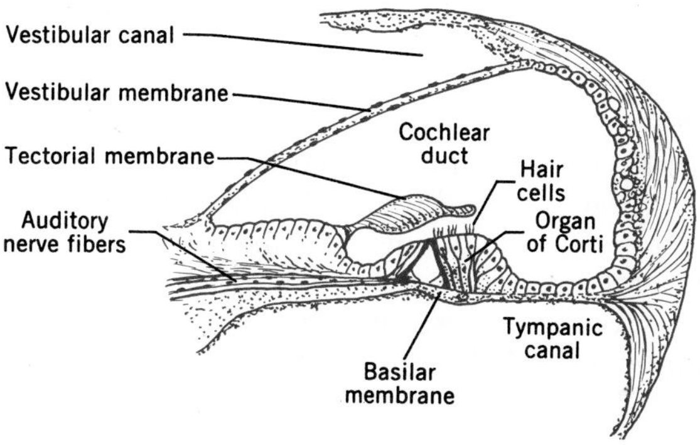

FIGURE 3.25
Structure of the cochlea. The vestibular and tympanic canals contain perilymph; the cochlear duct contains endolymph.

vestibular canal is set into motion by the vibrations of the oval window (Figure 3.25). These vibrations cause waves to travel up the vestibular canal and back down the lower tympanic canal, with which it is connected at the apex of the cochlea. The true auditory receptors are in the cochlear duct, which lies in between. They are tiny **hair cells** located on the organ of Corti, which rests on the basilar membrane dividing the duct from the lower canal. As the fluid waves travel through the upper and lower canals, they displace this tough but flexible membrane. These movements in turn shear the stiff protruding hairs of the hair cells against an overhanging tectorial membrane. These shearing movements of the hair cells translate into impulses. Nerve fibers connecting with the bottoms of the some 25,000 hair cells join together to form the auditory nerve and send their messages to the brain.

The loudness of perceived sound depends on the amplitude of the wave of energy transmitted to the fluids of the cochlea. The perceived pitch depends on the region of the basilar membrane receiving the strongest stimulation. Near the entrance to the cochlea, the basilar membrane is narrow, and it becomes progressively wider toward the tip. The short fibers on the narrow portion of the basilar membrane respond to high-pitched sounds, the longer fibers at the apex to lower sounds. Support for this interpretation comes from studies of stimulation deafness. Guinea pigs subjected for long periods to loud, relatively pure tones have localized deterioration in the structures of the organ of Corti, the site depending on the pitch of the tone.

Impaired Hearing

Difficulty with hearing is a common physical affliction, affecting perhaps 5 percent of the population. Accumulations of wax in the outer ear, imperfect functioning of bones in the middle ear, damage to the receptive mechanism of the inner ear, and defects in the auditory nerve pathways are all possible causes. Some cases of impaired hearing are genetic in origin; some appear as a common symptom of aging. Before the days of penicillin, deafness often followed middle-ear infection in children. Continued exposure to loud sounds, whether in the boiler room or at a rock concert, can cause stimulation deafness.

The first step in dealing with impaired hearing is to assess the extent and kind of hearing loss. The degree of loss is usually greater at certain frequencies than others. In order to obtain the necessary information, the examiner determines the absolute threshold of hearing for the range of pitches most essential in day-to-day living—from 125 or 250 to about 8000 Hz. With these data available, the individual's pattern of sensitivity can be plotted in an **audiogram,** which shows hearing loss throughout a range of pitches. The degree of loss is the increase above the intensity normally required to make a sound of a given pitch audible.

The audiogram for a typical patient, a fifty-four-year-old man, indicates normal hearing within speech frequencies but substantial loss of sensitivity at the higher frequencies. Does this pattern (Figure 3.26) represent a serious problem and is there a remedy?

The patient had come to the Hearing Evaluation Clinic because he had some difficulty understanding speech in noisy surroundings for the past twenty-five years, and it seemed to be getting worse. His complaint strongly suggests that the hearing loss was **sensory-neural deafness,** resulting from some defect in the organ of Corti or in the higher neural pathways. Masking of speech is typical of sensory-neural impairment. At the present time little can be done to correct these disorders. Hearing aids are of limited usefulness, and no other corrective measures have been developed.

The other principal class of hearing disorder is **conduction deafness.** As the name implies, such deafness stems from problems in the mechanical transmission of sounds to the oval window. There are several causes of conduction deafness and several corresponding cures. If wax has accumulated in the auditory canal, a simple cleaning and flushing of the canal may restore normal hearing. In cases of middle-ear infection, the area may fill with liquid, hampering the function of the malleus, incus, and stapes. The physician will frequently pierce the eardrum of such patients, allowing the liquid to drain out.

Many cases of conduction deafness are caused by a hereditary disease called **otosclerosis.** A spongy growth in the middle ear turns to bone and fixates the stapes in the oval window or fuses the ossicles. Hearing aids that utilize the bones of the skull to transmit vibrations to the cochlea will help these people hear.

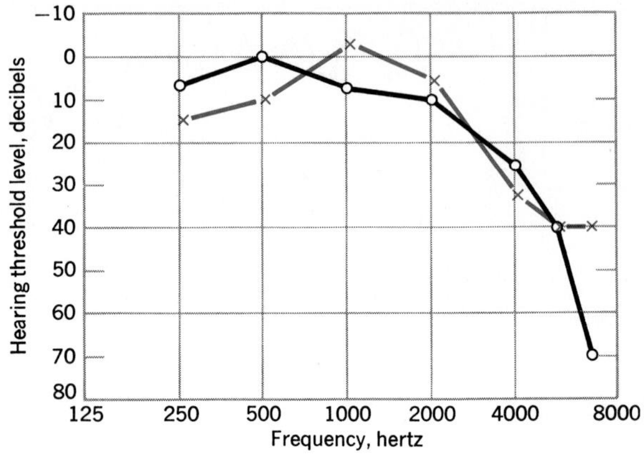

FIGURE 3.26
An audiogram. The vertical axis is a measure of hearing loss, showing in decibels the increase in intensity necessary to produce normal hearing at each frequency. O's are for the right ear, X's for the left.

Now it is also possible to remove the immobilized middle ear bones surgically and to install a plastic and wire replacement, all under local anesthesia. Recovery in these cases is sudden and spectacular. Even during surgery the patient may report the return of useful hearing.

SUMMARY ☐

The ear responds to successive compressions and rarefactions of the air over a range of about 20 to 20,000 Hz (cycles per second). The frequency of the changes in air pressure determines pitch. The amplitude of the sound wave determines loudness, although perceived loudness also depends on pitch. With the intensity of sound waves equated at a generally comfortable level, tones in the range from 500 to 4000 Hz are most easily heard. The complexity of the sound wave determines timbre.

The receptor for hearing works as follows. Sounds are collected by the outer ear and carried to the eardrum. Vibrations of the eardrum are amplified and transmitted to the oval window of the inner ear by three small bones. Waves established in the fluids within travel up and down the canals of the inner ear. The true auditory receptors, the hair cells, are located on the basilar membrane. Pitch is registered according to the portion of the membrane maximally affected by these fluid waves. Loudness is registered through the intensity of the disturbance. Defects in the transmission of sound energy from the eardrum to the oval window produce conduction deafness. In sensory-neural deafness functioning of the inner ear or neural mechanisms is impaired.

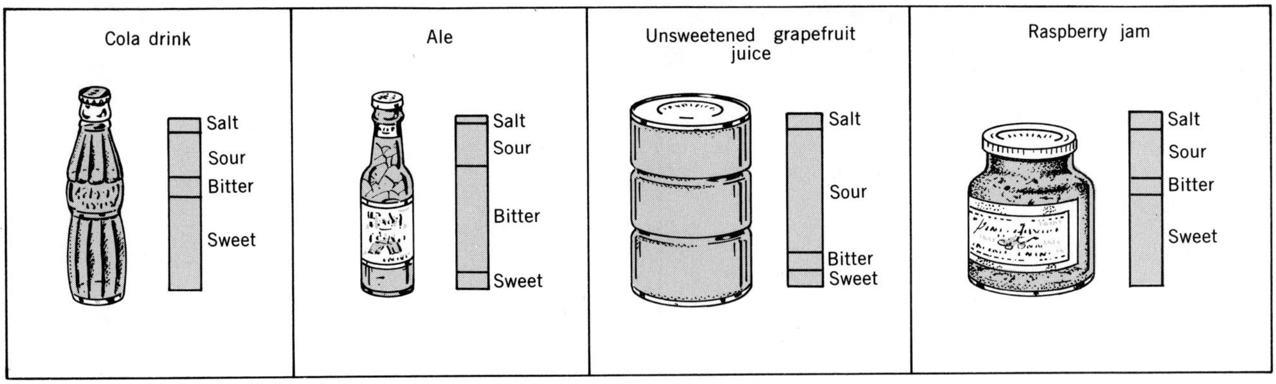

FIGURE 3.27
Compositions of familiar tastes. The rules on the right indicate the relative amounts of salt, sour, sweet, and bitter in the flavors of these substances. The size of the contribution is indicated by the vertical distance.

THE OTHER SENSES

Our description of the other sensory systems will be quite brief for several reasons. These senses do not usually dominate experience in the way that sight and hearing do. Possibly this explains why they have been less thoroughly studied and remain more of a mystery. In most cases the psychological dimensions of sensory experience have been only incompletely mapped out, which in turn has meant that the physiological mechanisms responsible for such experience remain unknown.

Taste

When the effects of smell are eliminated, the sense of taste seems to yield four psychologically primary qualities: salt, sweet, sour, and bitter. The exact taste of a substance in solution depends on how these four basic qualities are combined (Figure 3.27). The receptors for taste are spindle-shaped cells collected in a group to form a **taste bud.** Taste buds are especially dense in the small but visible bumps on the upper surface of the tongue (Figure 3.28). Each bump or papilla is a flat, disk-shaped elevation surrounded by a moatlike furrow, within which the taste buds lie. But taste buds are also found in pits and grooves of the soft palate, the floor of the mouth, the insides of the cheeks, and the underside of the tongue. The tip, sides, and rear of the tongue are the areas most sensitive to tastes, the tip of the tongue being particularly sensitive to sweet, the sides to sour, and the rear to bitter. There is sensitivity to salt along the edges of the tongue.

Although the psychologically primary tastes tend to be sensed most heavily in certain areas of the tongue,

FIGURE 3.28
(a) *Papilla* with taste buds in its walls and in those of neighboring papillae. (*b*) *Structure* of an individual taste bud. Sensory nerve fibers enter the taste bud, then entwine and contact one or more taste cells. The taste cells project hairlike microvilli into the taste pore. (*c*) *Tongue areas* most sensitive to the four primary tastes.

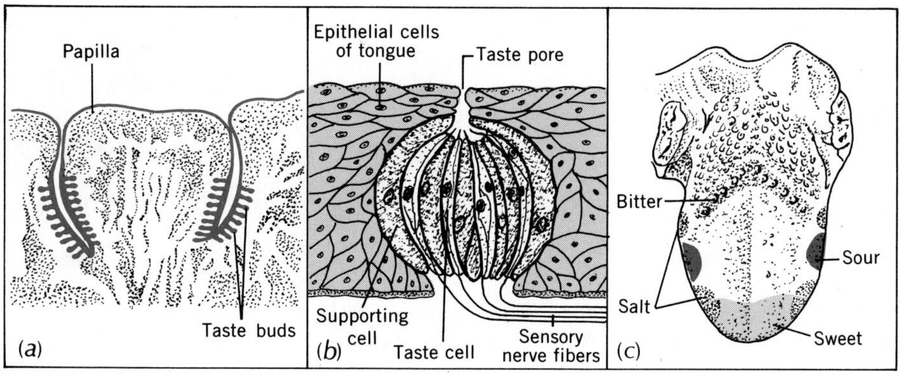

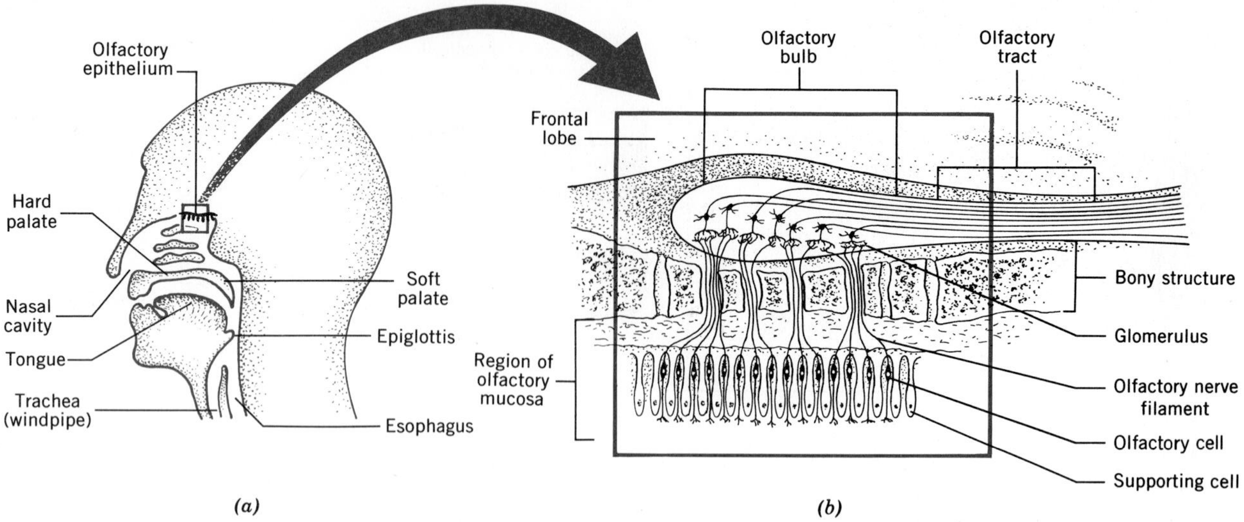

FIGURE 3.29

The olfactory system. (*a*) The human olfactory epithelium measures about half a square inch in each nasal cavity. (*b*) The olfactory cell is neurosensory, which means that it is a more primitive type of receptor having its own nerve filament. Neurosensory cells are able both to receive and to conduct stimulation.

there is no evidence that individual receptors or neural mechanisms respond to particular taste qualities. In short, no set of receptors corresponding to the cone pigments that register the blue, green, and red of vision exists. The taste cells with their nerve fibers respond to a broad range of stimuli. Single taste cells show mixed sensitivity, responding, for example, to sour and salty or to sour, salty, and sweet stimulation. In addition, evidence suggests that some substances may excite taste cells and other substances inhibit their firing. The neural code for taste apparently depends on a pattern of firing in a number of fibers.

Smell

About all that can be said with certainty concerning the stimulus for smell is that odorous substances must be in a gaseous state to reach the receptors and water- and fat-soluble to penetrate the film covering them. Psychophysical studies have failed to produce any dependable system of primary odors. The odor-sensitive **olfactory rods** are at the top of the nasal passage (Figure 3.29). There are perhaps ten million of these long, narrow, column-shaped neurosensory cells, each with six to twelve delicate hairs projecting down into the fluid covering of the mucous membrane. There they contact the dissolved odoriferous molecules. Extending from their other ends are nerve fibers; these course to the olfactory bulbs of the brain directly above them. The olfactory epithelium is accessible both from the nostrils and from the mouth, which is what makes it possible for the sense of smell to contribute to taste.

The Skin Senses

Pressure The classical instrument for studying the sensitivity of the skin to "touch" or pressure is a set of small sticks to which are attached at right angles a graded series of hairs which differ in stiffness. If the skin is explored with a hair of moderate stiffness, it will be found that, within a small area, some spots respond with a clear sensation of pressure; others do not (Figure 3.30). Other sensitivities of the skin, for warmth, coldness, pain, itch, tickle, and vibration, can be similarly mapped, with instruments testing for them. When the maps for sensitivity to pressure, warmth, cold, and pain of a particular area are compared, the points that are maximally sensitive to these

FIGURE 3.30

Pressure-sensitive areas on a small section of skin. Circles on the map are points that yield a sensation of pressure when stimulated. They are often near hairs.

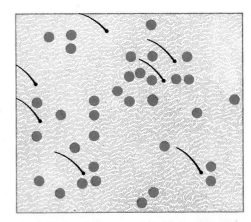

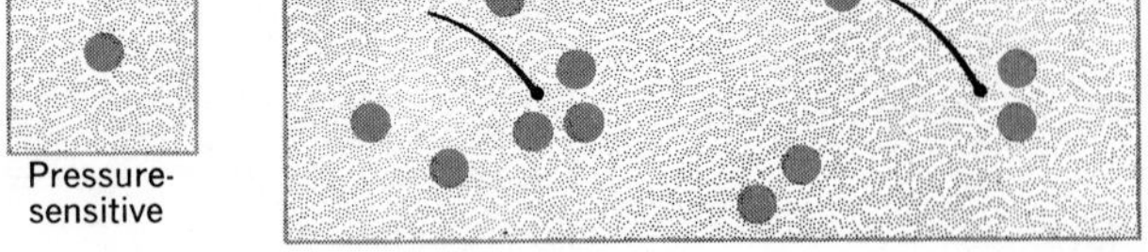

four types of stimulation do not match. For this reason these senses are considered separate. Maps for itch, tickle, and vibration, on the other hand, so overlap the others that they are usually considered derived senses. An itch is experienced when pain spots are gently and repeatedly pricked, or when they react to a chemical. Light, rapid strokes of pressure spots are felt as tickle, even faster and rhythmical stimulation of them as vibration. Thus itch, tickle, and vibration appear to be the experience of light and rapid excitations of the receptors for pain and pressure.

The tip of the tongue, the lips, the fingertips and the hands, the inner forearm are all extremely sensitive to pressure; the upper arm, outer thigh, and back are considerably less so. The more mobile the area, the greater precision in its detection of touch.

Pain Pain can be elicited by many different stimuli —mechanical, thermal, electrical, and chemical. It is also experienced in many different ways. A distinction is commonly made between "bright" pain, which is felt in the superficial layers of the skin, more pervasive "burning" pain, and "dull" pain, coming from the deeper layers of the body. Bright pains are usually well localized and are of the sort produced by brief electric shock, a pinprick, or a superficial burn. Burning pain is slow to develop, lasts longer, and is less easily localized. Dull pains are poorly localized and have an aching, intensely unpleasant persistence.

The experience of pain plays such an important role in life that it has been the object of much theoretical speculation. Until recently, however, theories were all quite unsatisfactory because of their inability to handle many of the facts. One making assessment especially difficult is that pain involves the brain in important ways. For example, hypnosis appears capable of eliminating the experience of pain. Moreover, the relief delivered by the inserted and twirled needles of acupuncture probably depends on related phenomena. And almost everyone has had the experience of not feeling pain from a wound acquired in circumstances that provoked great emotion. The ability of the **gate-control theory** of Ronald Melzack and Patrick Wall (1965) to explain such happenings makes it very convincing.

According to this theory, the experience of pain depends on the frequency of impulses sent to the brain by a set of "transmission cells" in the spinal cord. Two types of neurons running from the skin to these transmission cells carry the messages of pain. One type of neuron transmits the impulses for sharp pain, as well as those corresponding to other skin sensations, over large-diameter, rapidly conducting axons. The second type of neuron transmits the impulses for dull, burning pain over small-diameter, slowly conducting axons.

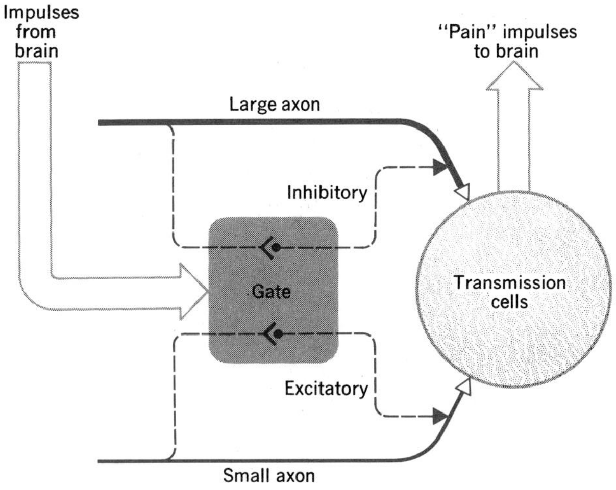

FIGURE 3.31
Gate-control theory of pain. Large axons rapidly send messages of bright pain and other skin sensation to transmission cells. Collateral connections through a theoretical gate inhibit the action of the large axons. Small axons carry more slowly conveyed messages of deep and dull pain to transmission cells. Their collateral connections facilitate the transmission of pain impulses to the brain.

In addition to making synaptic connections to the pain-transmitting cells, both types of neurons make other connections to a gating mechanism which modulates their effects on the transmission cells. Through these collateral connections the large fibers reduce their own capacity to fire the transmission cells and, in effect, close the gate to the experience of pain. The small fibers tend to open this gate, increasing their capacity to fire the transmission cells.

The experience of pain then depends on the balance of activity in the large and small fibers. Usually activity in the large fibers predominates, the gate is closed, and no pain is felt. High levels of activity in the small fibers open the gate and we feel pain. Pain is sharp but short lasting when painful messages carried by the large fibers reach the transmission cells and manage to fire them before the gate can be closed.

In the gate-control theory fibers coming down from the brain also help to close or open the gate. Through these fibers' attitudes, stimulation of the other senses, hypnosis, and the like affect the degree of pain perceived (Figure 3.31).

Temperature Senses The normal temperature of the skin varies from one part of the body to another, ranging from perhaps 82°F in the ear, which is exposed and poorly supplied with blood, to 98°F in protected areas such as the armpit. On the hands and face, which have been most used for experimental investigation, the normal temperature of the skin is about

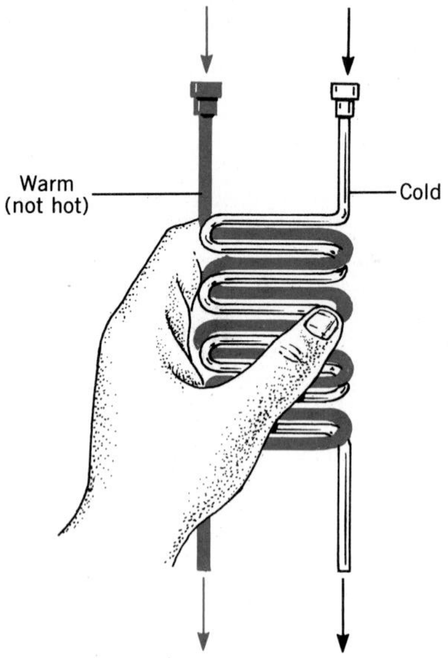

FIGURE 3.32
A heat grill. Cold water circulates through one tube; warm, not hot, water circulates through the other. Together the warm and cold stimulations produce the sensation of intense heat.

90°F. The temperature of the skin area under investigation is taken as **physiological zero.** Temperatures that depart from physiological zero feel warm or cold, depending on the direction of the departure.

The experience of heat, as opposed to warmth, is ordinarily produced by stimuli much above physiological zero. Heat is also experienced in another way, which has implications concerning the mechanism of thermal reception. The alternate tubes of a heat grill (Figure 3.32) can simultaneously present the skin with warmth, not heat, and coldness. If such a grill is applied to a large area of the skin, the heat felt is intense enough that the limb or other body part is quickly withdrawn. In this experience of heat, nerve fibers for transmitting both warmth and coldness are apparently stimulated.

Receptors for the Skin Senses The obvious method of determining the receptors for the various skin senses is first to map the skin for particular sensitivities and then to look for specialized receptors beneath these spots. Because different and identifiable nerve endings in the skin have been found, earlier investigators believed that the sensitivities of the skin depended on certain specific receptors. This position proved overly optimistic. We are now less confident that experiences of touch, temperature, and pain depend on the activation of specific receptors. The physiology of the skin senses appears similar to that for taste. Their neural codes are probably patterns of stimulation carried by several neurons, rather than the simpler arrangement whereby a stimulus excites a very specialized receptor, which in turn fires a very specialized neuron.

Two Senses of Movement

We experience two kinds of movement, that of parts of the body and that of the whole body through space. These experiences come from two quite different sensory mechanisms, kinesthesis and vestibular sensitivity.

Kinesthesis The joints, muscles, and tendons contain receptors that give us immense but unobtrusive awareness of where the parts of the body are and how they are moving. We know the position of our fingers, wrist, limbs, trunk, and other mobile parts of the jointed skeleton, as well as their precise and larger motions. Kinesthesis also tells us of muscle tensions and strains, of a poorly aimed hand movement, and of a trunk pitched too far forward, allowing us to relieve and right them. Through this sense we coordinate our movements automatically, putting one foot before the other as we walk, alternately lowering legs the correct distance as we negotiate stairs, stretching out a hand to an exact spot when picking up an object.

Receptors in the linings of the mobile joints are stimulated as the angles at which bones are held change. Free nerve endings among the muscle fibers signal when a muscle stretches. And in the tendons connecting muscles to bones there are nerve endings which signal when muscle contracts and puts pressure on them.

Vestibular Sensitivity Detection of the position of the whole body and its motion in relation to gravity depends on five connecting structures of the inner ear. Together they give us equilibrium, our sense of balance, and tell us about changes in direction and rate of motion. The nonauditory **vestibule** and **semicircular canals** of the inner ear are continuous with the auditory cochlea (Figure 3.33). The vestibule is in the central position of the inner ear at the "entrance" to the cochlea and consists of two sacs; beyond lie the three semicircular canals, at approximately right angles to one another so that they register the three planes of the head and body.

The cutaway portion of Figure 3.33 reveals something of the inner structure of the vestibule and semicircular canals. Within the outer bony structures, called the **bony labyrinth,** is a **membranous labyrinth;** the two are separated by a fluid, **perilymph.** The membranous labyrinth itself contains another fluid, **endolymph.** In both of the endolymph-filled membranous sacs of the vestibule are tiny crystals of bonelike calcium carbonate. Because of their inertia,

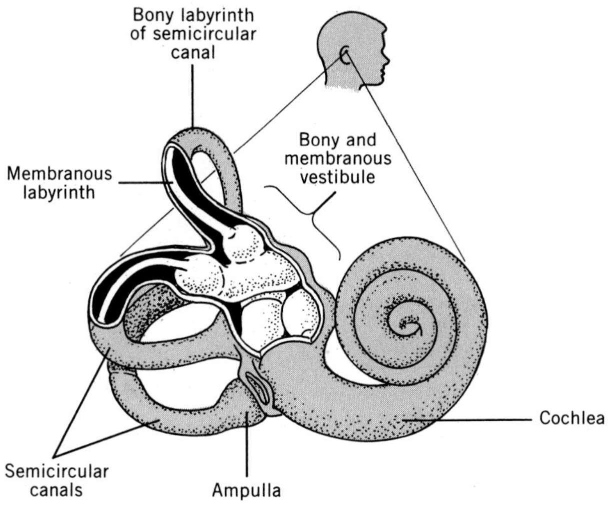

FIGURE 3.33
The bony and membranous labyrinths of the semicircular canals and vestibule.

the crystals bend the hairs against which they rest in the opposite direction whenever the head is tilted, or when the body is speeding up or slowing down in straight-line motion, whether that motion is up-down, forward-backward, or side-to-side. The base end of each semicircular canal swells to form an **ampulla,** within which is a crest of hair cells and their tufts embedded in a gelatinous mass. When the head is turned or rotated and when it comes to rest, the hair tufts are deflected in the opposite direction by the pressure of the lagging endolymph.

The nonauditory portion of the inner ear produces no sensations of its own. Instead, stimulation of the receptors in the semicircular canals and sacs provokes sensations elsewhere. In everyday life dizziness is the most frequent experience associated with vigorous labyrinthine stimulation. Dizziness, upon analysis, turns out to be compounded of pressure in the chest, head, and viscera; a pulsating sensation from the blood vessels; and rapidly shifting visual experiences—the eyes move slowly in a direction opposite that of rotation and rapidly back to the normal position.

SUMMARY □

The stimuli for taste are substances in solution. They register as four primary tastes: salt, sweet, sour, and bitter. These primaries are sensed most strongly by taste buds at different parts of the tongue, but no differentiating receptors that might account for this fact have been discovered. Similarly, neurophysiological studies show that single taste cells can be fired by a variety of taste stimuli, although they may respond more vigorously to certain stimuli than to others. All this suggests that the neural code for taste consists of a pattern of neural activity rather than the firing of single fibers for single tastes.

We know even less about the sense of smell. There is no generally accepted system of primary odors and little understanding of how the odoriferous molecules stimulate the hair cells of the olfactory epithelium.

Maps of the skin, obtained with appropriate stimuli, suggest that pressure, pain, warmth, and coldness may be primary sensations. Others, such as heat, tickle, itch, and vibration are derived sensations. Unique receptors for even the primary sensations have not been found when the skin underlying spots with particular sensitivities has been examined. As with taste, it seems likely that a pattern of stimulation provides the neural code.

The kinesthetic sense, registered in the joints, muscles, and tendons, serves two important functions, providing information about the movements of the body and cues that aid in their coordination. Vestibular sensitivity, registered by minute hair cells in the nonauditory portions of the inner ear, gives us our equilibrium. It informs us when linear movements of the head, and body, are accelerating or slowing down, and when the head and body are beginning to rotate or coming to rest. This stimulation affects other senses in a complex way, as we learn by analyzing the symptoms of dizziness.

PSYCHOPHYSICS

With our discussion of the individual senses complete, it will be useful to explore briefly the field of **psychophysics,** the study of how psychological events depend on physical ones. One of the oldest areas of study in psychology, psychophysics asks two basic questions. How weak a stimulus can a person detect? How small a difference in stimulation can a person detect? These are questions about the absolute threshold and the difference threshold, respectively, in any sensory system. The study of psychophysics has also contributed to the measurement of psychological experience, measurement being a primary goal of all science. The sensations by which the senses register the stimulation of physical energies are quantified in psychophysics; the intensity of a sensation is related to the magnitude of the physical energy.

The Absolute Threshold

The **absolute threshold** in any sensory system is the weakest stimulus that it can detect. For any sense it is the smallest amount of physical energy that will produce a sensation. Studies of the absolute threshold

TABLE 3.2

Approximate Absolute Thresholds

Sensory Modality	Threshold
Vision	A candle flame at 30 miles on a dark, clear night
Hearing	The tick of a watch at 20 feet in a quiet room
Taste	One ounce of quinine sulfate in 250 gallons of water
Smell	One drop of perfume diffused throughout a six-room house
Touch	Wing of a bee falling on the cheek from a distance of 1 centimeter

for various senses have shown that they respond to levels of stimulation that are remarkably low, so low in fact that greater sensitivity would be maladaptive, given the nature of the physical world. If the dark-adapted eye were any more sensitive than it is, visual experience would be very peculiar. Steady light would appear to flash, and we would perceive, in visual terms, the chemical changes that take place within the eyeball. The absolute threshold for hearing is so low that, were the ears only slightly more sensitive, we would be able to hear the collisions of air molecules against the eardrums. The receptors in the inner ear detect movements less than one percent of the diameter of a hydrogen molecule. Threshold values for the different senses in terms that may be more meaningful are listed in Table 3.2.

Although the study of absolute thresholds has a long and honorable history in psychology, and although the exceeding lowness of actual thresholds is impressive, there is a problem with the concept. In order to make the essential points, we need to consider one of the techniques for determining an absolute threshold, the *method of limits,* as it is applied in a practical way for the clinical diagnosis of deafness.

The important equipment for measuring the acuity of hearing, as explained in less detail earlier, is a tone generator that can present sounds of different pitches and intensities. The individual being tested listens to the sound being presented through earphones and indicates whether he hears it, usually by pressing a key. First a given tone is presented at an intensity so low that it cannot be heard. Then, trial by trial, the intensity is gradually raised, by small but constant increments, until the individual always reports hearing the tone. On other trials testing starts with an intensity well above threshold, and the stimulus is decreased in stepwise fashion until the observer fails to hear it. The absolute threshold determined by the method of limits would be the intensity at which experience changes from not hearing the tone to hearing it, and vice versa.

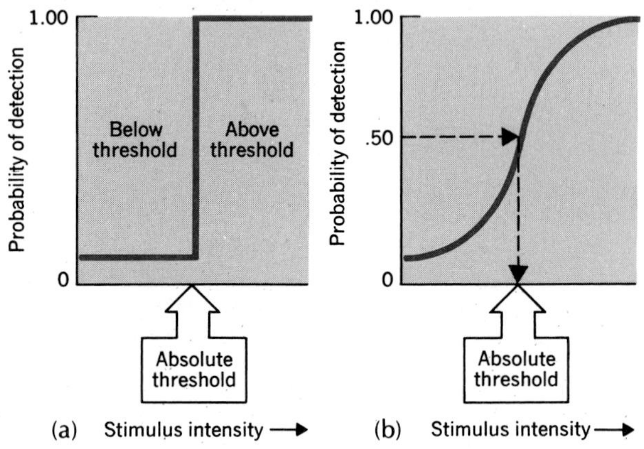

FIGURE 3.34

Two concepts of absolute threshold. (*a*) If the absolute threshold were absolute, there would be an abrupt shift from not sensing a stimulus to sensing it as the intensity of stimulation increases. (*b*) Actually the increase in the probability of detecting a stimulus is gradual. The absolute threshold is determined by reading from the point on the vertical axis where the probability of detection is .50, over to the curve, and then down to the intensity.

The individual's responses can be plotted as a curve which indicates the probability that the subject will report hearing the sound against the intensity of the sound wave. If there were an absolute threshold, in the most obvious sense of that expression, the results would take the form illustrated in Figure 3.34*a*. There would be a range of intensities that the individual never detects and, above some single threshold intensity, an abrupt transition to a range of intensities that he always hears.

Such results are never obtained, however. Instead, as the intensity of the tone increases, there is a gradual increase in the probability that the listener will detect it (Figure 3.34*b*). It has become conventional to define the absolute threshold as the level of stimulation that is detected 50 percent of the time. Such results mean that *the absolute threshold is not absolute.* Because of this basic ambiguity, procedures for studying the detectability of stimuli that avoid the concept of absolute threshold have been developed.

Theory of Signal Detectability

If you have ever had your hearing tested, you will remember that the experience is a strange one. You sit there, in an utterly silent room with the earphones on, and soon discover that your head is a noisier place than you would have thought. There is a constant background of noise, created partly by the testing equipment, partly by spontaneous neural activity in the auditory system, and partly by the sound of blood coursing through the arteries and veins. Sometimes this sound is indistinguishable from what you hear when the very weak signal that you are listening for is sounded.

Now suppose that you are a subject in an experiment consisting of a series of trials, in which this very weak signal is sometimes present, sometimes absent. On each trial you must indicate with a "yes" or "no" whether you hear the signal. Although the intensity of the impression that a signal is present will be greater, trial to trial, you are never absolutely certain whether it is there or not. So what do you do?

In general, you set a **criterion** by deciding how intense the impression of hearing the signal must be before you will say "yes." The criterion you set will depend in several things: your sense, based on experience, of the likelihood that a particular trial will or will not be one with a signal; how much it matters to you whether you miss a signal when it is present or say falsely that a signal was present when it was not; your general tendency to be cautious or reckless in situations such as this one. Individual differences in such matters are large.

However you set your criterion, you are in a no-win situation. As Figure 3.35 shows, the intensity of the impression that a signal is present will be greater, on the average, on trials with a signal present than with it absent. But this is not always so, and no criterion you select will produce a perfect performance. You will sometime miss a signal and at other times report one when none is there.

Figure 3.36 summarizes your situation in another way. There are two kinds of trials in such experiments: trials without the signal, called **noise** trials because the only stimulation present is the background noise; and **signal-plus-noise** trials, in which the effects of the signal are added to those of the noisy background. On each trial you make one of two responses: "Yes, I hear the signal," or "No, I don't." Two kinds of trials on which you can make two different responses add up to four identifiable outcomes:

Hit—a "yes" response on a signal-plus-noise trial (a correct response).
False alarm—a "yes" response on a noise trial (an error).
Miss—a "no" response on a signal-plus-noise trial (an error).
Correct rejection—a "no" response on a noise trial (a correct response).

The methods of signal detectability use two of these outcomes, hits and false alarms, to obtain a relatively pure measure of the sensory process, one which is bias-free or, in other words, independent of the individual's criterion. The methods are easy to understand if you will keep two points in mind. (1) Any conditions that influence the criterion a person sets

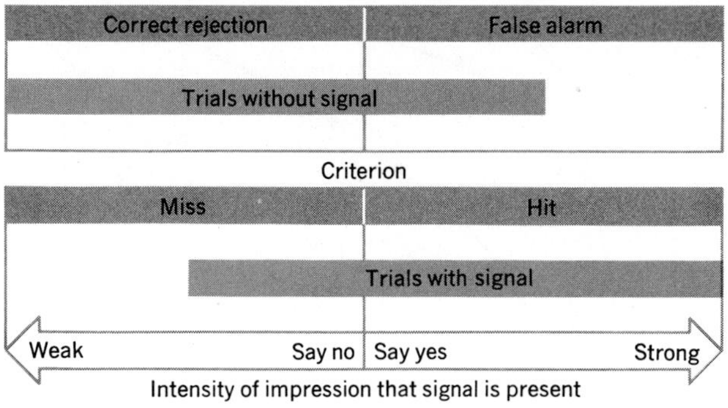

FIGURE 3.35
Basics of signal detectability. As intensity of stimulus increases, so does the impression that a signal is present. This impression is usually weaker when the signal is absent (upper horizontal bar) than when it is present (lower horizontal bar), but the ranges of the strengths of these impressions overlap. The observer's solution to this dilemma is to set a criterion and respond negatively when the strength of the impression is below this criterion and positively when the impression is stronger.

		Response	
		Yes	No
Type of trial	Signal plus noise	Hit	Miss
	Noise	False alarm	Correct rejection

FIGURE 3.36
Possible outcomes on signal detection trials. Two kinds of trials with two possible responses add up to four kinds of outcome.

for saying yes will influence in a similar way the number of hits and the number of false alarms. A lenient criterion, one toward the left of Figure 3.35, will mean a high proportion of hits on trials when the signal is present but also a high proportion of false alarms on trials when the signal is absent. A strict criterion, one toward the right in Figure 3.35, will reduce the number of false alarms but also the number of hits. (2) To the extent that the individual detects the signal, the proportion of hits will exceed the proportion of false alarms. This excess of hits may reflect the strength of the signal, the sensitivity of the observer, or both.

ROC Curves A graphic way to make this point is called a **receiver-operating characteristic curve** or, abbreviated, **ROC curve** (Figure 3.37). The expression comes from electronic engineering, where it refers to the signal-detecting capabilities of equipment. The most direct way to explain the construction of an

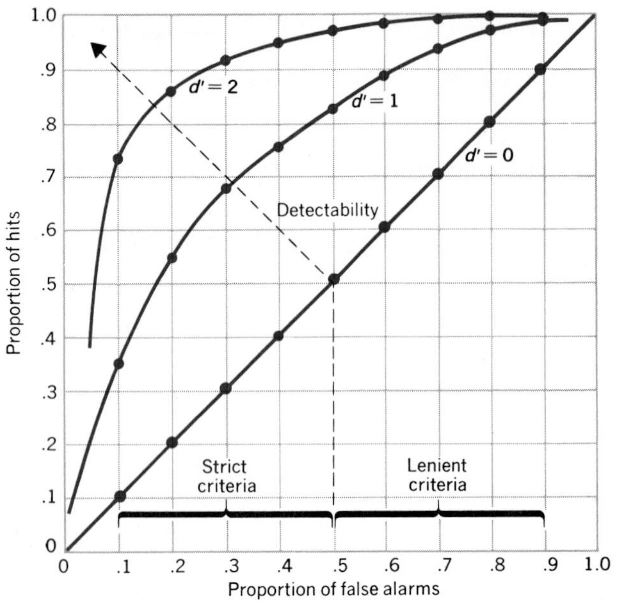

FIGURE 3.37
An ROC curve. Imagine a study with nine observers having very different criteria. On a trial with an undetectable stimulus ($d' = 0$), they have proportions of hits and false alarms of .1, .2, .3, and so on. With stronger signals these biases persist, but the proportion of hits now exceeds the proportion of false alarms. With a weak stimulus the curve bows ($d' = 1.0$), and with a strong stimulus it bows even more ($d' = 2.0$). The partial diagonal in the upper left part of the graph indicates detectability.

ROC curve is to ask you to imagine an experiment with many observers, whose criteria range from strict to lenient. Each observer provides two measurements to be represented in the ROC curve, his or her proportion of hits and proportion of false alarms. The horizontal and vertical axes represent these proportions. A single point expresses the proportion of hits plotted against the proportion of false alarms. People with strict criteria have points to the left of the horizontal axis and toward the bottom of the vertical axis. Those with lenient criteria have points toward the upper right. The method is similar to that used to construct a scatter plot (see page 501).

Response Bias and Criteria Imagine, in the experiment that we have been discussing, that the signal is so weak that the observers cannot detect it at all. Under these conditions all they can do is guess, and performance will depend entirely on the observer's criterion. Individuals with lenient criteria will say "yes" on most trials; individuals with conservative criteria will usually say "no." As we have just seen, the first group will have many hits but also many false alarms, the second group few false alarms but also few hits. The diagonal moving from lower left to upper right in Figure 3.37 represents this relationship, showing that hits and false alarms increase together when the signal cannot be detected.

Detectability, Sensitivity, and *d′* Now consider what can be expected as stronger and stronger signals are presented. The individual's bias will still influence the proportion of hits and false alarms, but with a signal the observer can sometimes detect, the proportion of hits will exceed the proportion of false alarms. The stronger the signal, the greater will be the excess of hits over false alarms.

The two ROC curves in Figure 3.37 represent the detection of signals of two strengths, the upper curve being for the stronger signal. When the signal is stronger, the curve arches higher above the diagonal. The measure of the degree of arching above the diagonal is d'. Both curves summarize the performances of individuals whose criteria varied from extremely strict to very lenient but whose sensitivities are the same. Every point on each curve represents exactly the same degree of sensitivity to the signal. This is the great power of the methods of signal detectability. They provide a measure of the pure sensory process that is independent of criteria.

Differential Sensitivity

The second major question to which psychophysics addresses itself is that of differential sensitivity, the accuracy of our perception of differences among stimuli. Interest in this problem dates back more than a hundred years. In the course of his study of what we now call kinesthesis, Ernst Heinrich Weber performed experiments to determine the smallest difference between two weights that could be discriminated. On the basis of his investigation, he concluded that the discrimination of stimuli is relative rather than absolute. To illustrate the meaning of this proposal, let us suppose that a person can just barely detect the difference between a 50-gram weight and a 51-gram weight. In absolute terms the difference is 1 gram; in relative terms it is one-fiftieth of the smaller weight. Now suppose that we want to predict the weight that a person can just barely discriminate as heavier than 500 grams. If such discriminations were on an absolute basis, requiring as before a 1-gram difference in weights, the detectably heavier weight would be 501 grams. In actual fact, however, the discrimination is relative; the detectably heavier weights will be more like one-fiftieth greater than 500 grams or 510 grams.

A more formal statement of the concept that discriminations between stimulus intensities are relative is sometimes called **Weber's law,**

$$\frac{\Delta I}{I} = K$$

where I is an intensity of stimulation taken as a reference, ΔI is the difference in stimulation required to make the two intensities just noticeably different, and K is a constant. The equation says that ΔI will be a constant fraction (K) of I, no matter what the absolute value of I. In the examples give, in which the differences between 50- and 51-gram weights ($\Delta I = 1$ gram) and 500- and 510-gram weights ($\Delta I = 10$ grams) turn out to be just barely discernible, the formula applies as follows:

$$\frac{\Delta I}{I} = \frac{1 \text{ gm}}{50 \text{ gm}} = \frac{1}{50}$$

and

$$\frac{\Delta I}{I} = \frac{10 \text{ gm}}{500 \text{ gm}} = \frac{1}{50}$$

It is conventional to refer to the absolute value (ΔI) necessary to produce a detectable difference as the **difference threshold** or as a **just noticeable difference,** often abbreviated j.n.d. The fraction $\Delta I/I$ is sometimes called the *Weber fraction.*

The value $1/50$ used in our example is approximately correct for sensing differences in lifted weights. Rough values of the Weber fraction for other senses are brightness vision, $1/60$; pain, $1/30$; skin pressure, $1/7$; odor, $1/4$; and taste, $1/3$. Research has established these constant fractions, but it has also revealed that they do not hold when stimulus intensity is very high or very low. In the middle ranges, however, the proposed relationships hold quite well.

Measurement of Sensation

Weber's work was enlarged upon by Gustav Theodor Fechner, who thought he saw in Weber's law a universal statement of the relation between the mental and physical worlds. Fechner believed that it should be possible, by applying Weber's proposition, to measure the *intensity of sensory experience* in terms of the magnitude of the physical stimulus. He assumed, as had Weber, that all j.n.d.s are equal, whether the two sensations being compared are registrations of small amounts or great amounts of physical energy. The j.n.d. becomes in effect a unit of measurement for sensation. It would follow that the intensity of any particular sensory experience is the sum of all the successive just noticeable differences between the absolute threshold and the stimulus responsible for the sensation whose value is to be stated. Fechner proposed that **sensation level** (S), as the intensity of a sensory experience is sometimes called, is a logarithmic function of stimulus intensity,

$$S = K \log I + A$$

where S is sensation level, I is the intensity of the physical stimulus, A is the absolute threshold, and K is a constant that depends on the sensory system. In other words, as each arithmetic increase in sensation is registered, the amount of physical energy necessary to initiate the sensation has increased geometrically.

An example of measurement based on Fechner's law is the decibel scale for measuring the relative intensity or loudness of sounds. The decibel scale is logarithmically related to that for measuring physical pressure. The range of decibels is from zero to about 140 db, extending from the threshold of hearing to an intensity strong enough to produce pain. Each increase of 20 on the decibel scale represents a tenfold increase in the amount of physical pressure. The decibel scale, together with some psychological landmarks, appears in Figure 3.38.

Difference thresholds have the same problem as absolute thresholds. If you glance back at Figure 3.33 and think of the horizontal axes as relabeled "stimulus difference," instead of "stimulus intensity," the point will be clear. The difference threshold is just as ambiguous as the absolute threshold. For this reason the definition threshold is usually arbitrary too, being the difference in stimulation that can be detected 50 percent of the time. And the methods of signal detectability provide the same solution for this problem as they do for that of the absolute threshold.

SUMMARY □

Psychology operates on the empirical assumption that our knowledge of the world is based on experience. Since the senses provide our only contact with the world, an understanding of how the senses operate is basic to psychology. Two questions about the operation of the senses were among the earliest ones raised in the field. What for any sensory system is the weakest stimulus a person can detect? What is the smallest difference in stimulation that a person can detect? These questions concern the absolute and difference thresholds, respectively.

Experimental work has shown that absolute thresholds are all very low, which means that our receptor systems are extremely sensitive. The same work has also indicated, however, that there is no absolutely identifiable absolute threshold. Instead, the probability of detecting a stimulus increases steadily with increases in stimulus intensity. For this reason the absolute threshold of a sensory system is usually defined arbitrarily as the stimulus a person detects 50 percent of the time.

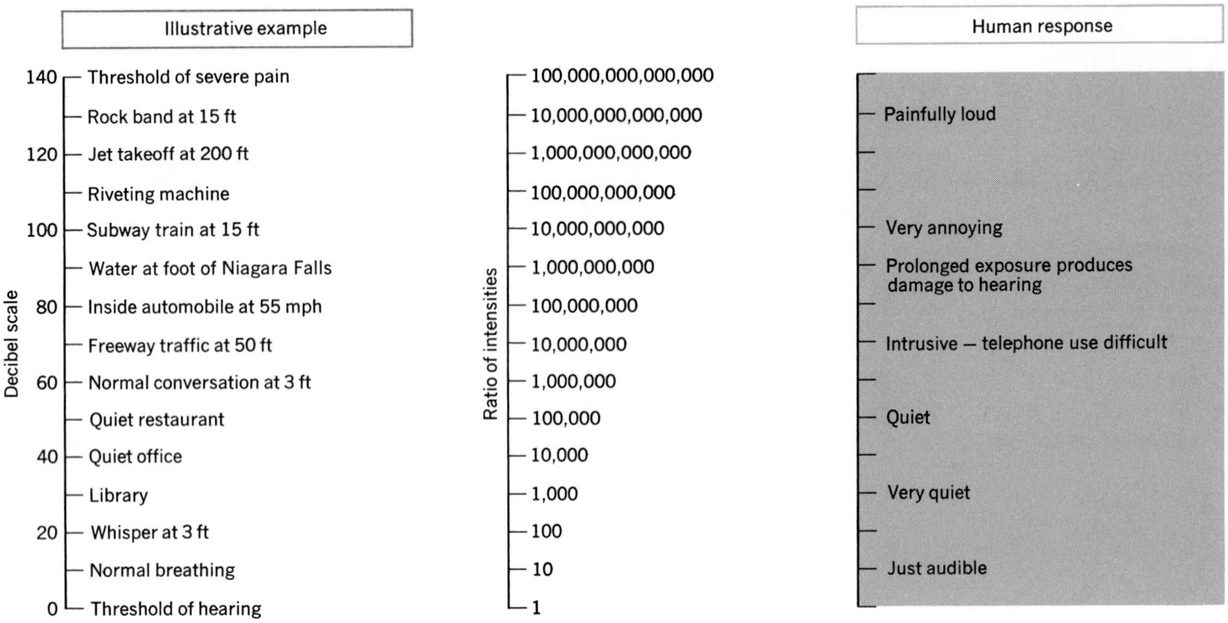

FIGURE 3.38
The loudness of some familiar sounds and ratios of intensity required to produce them.

The absolute threshold poses another problem. In most methods of determining it, the results fail to separate sensitivity to the signal from the observer's criterion for giving a positive response. The methods of signal detectability have helped to solve this problem. Working with "hits," reporting the presence of a signal correctly, and "false alarms," reporting a signal when none is there, makes it possible to obtain a measure, *d′*, of sensitivity that is bias free. The receiver operating characteristic curve (ROC) plots hits against false alarms to provide a graphic picture of sensitivity.

The concept central to the study of the detection of differences in stimulation is the difference threshold, or the just noticeable difference, a unit for measuring sensation first conceived by Weber. Within a wide middle range of stimulation of any sensory system, an increment that registers as a just noticeably different sensation is roughly a constant fraction of the intensity of the stimulus given first. Fechner enlarged upon Weber's work to indicate that the intensity of sensation has a logarithmic relation to the magnitude of the physical stimulus. The difference threshold, like the absolute, requires a statistical definition, the difference that can be detected 50 percent of the time.

TO BE SURE YOU UNDERSTAND THIS CHAPTER △

The following concepts are listed in the approximate order in which they appear in this chapter. You should be able to define these new concepts and state the points made about each in text discussion.

Specific energies of nerves
Iris
Pupil
Cornea
Aqueous humor
Vitreous humor
Crystalline lens
Retina
Rod
Cone
Fovea
Bipolar cells
Ganglion cells
Lateral connections
Mach bands
Blind spot
Wavelength
Hue
Light wave
Wave amplitude
Brightness
Wave complexity
Saturation
Rhodopsin
Iodopsin
Color circle
Complementary colors
Additive mixture
Subtractive mixture
Negative afterimage

Induced color
Simultaneous contrast
Physical primary colors
Psychological primary colors
Trichromatic theory
Opponent process theory
Dark adaptation
Rod-cone break
Purkinje shift
Physiological nystagmus
Pitch
Hertz (Hz)
Doppler effect
Loudness
Decibel (db)
Timbre
Fundamental tone
Overtone
White noise
Eardrum
Oval window
Malleus
Incus
Stapes
Hair cells
Audiogram
Sensory-neural deafness
Conduction deafness
Otosclerosis
Primary tastes
Taste bud
Olfactory rod
Gate-control theory
Physiological zero
Kinesthesis
Vestibular sensitivity
Vestibule
Semicircular canals
Bony labyrinth
Membranous labyrinth
Perilymph
Endolymph
Ampulla
Psychophysics
Absolute threshold
Criterion
Hit
Miss
False alarm
Correct rejection
ROC curve
d′
Weber's law
Difference threshold
Just noticeable difference
Sensation level

TO GO BEYOND THIS CHAPTER △

In this book A review of Chapter 2 at this point will reveal that the materials in this chapter contribute to your understanding of that one. Chapter 4 carries the discussion into the area of perception.

Elsewhere There are several new and excellent volumes on sensation and perception that treat sensory psychology materials in greater depth. Three are Coren, Porac, and Ward (1978), McBarney and Collings (1977), and Schiffman (1976). In the field of vision the two books by R. L. Gregory, *The Intelligent Eye* (1970) and *Eye and Brain* (1973), are particularly useful.

CH. 4

Perception

One of the most amazing facts about human experience is that we move in a world of stable objects that maintain their sizes, shapes, and colors at almost any angle or any distance from which we view them. What makes this dependability of perception remarkable is that such changes in angle and distance have profound effects on the pattern of stimulation reaching the receptors. We refer to energies in the physical world that excite the sense organs as **distal stimuli.** The light waves reflected by objects in space and the sound waves produced by vibrating bodies are examples. When these energies strike an appropriate receptor, they bring about **proximal stimulation.** Thus the pattern of light energies reflected by the print that you are now reading is a distal stimulus; the image of the print cast on your retina is a proximal stimulus. Restated, the amazing fact of human perception is that, although the proximal stimuli representing the same distal stimulus vary greatly from time to time, we interpret them in ways that usually yield dependable information about the world. It is clear that knowledge of the senses discussed in the previous chapter takes us only a short distance in the understanding of perception. Sensory stimulation provides the raw materials out of which we construct perception. But perception adds a great deal to these raw materials. It is useful to view **perception** as the interpretation of sensory information.

PERCEPTION OF OBJECTS

The most basic perception of all allows us to recognize that there is something out there. The first question to ask, then, concerns the circumstances under which the perception of objects occurs. One way of working toward an answer to this question is to start with a world without objects and see what happens when we introduce some of the features of objects into this objectless world.

Vision in the Ganzfeld

The German word **ganzfeld** (*ganz,* entirely; *feld,* field) is often applied to such a world without objects. For experimental purposes a ganzfeld has been produced in different ways. In some studies individuals have worn halves of Ping-Pong balls over their eyes or looked into a translucent globe. They see light but no sharp impressions of form. In other studies subjects have looked into a hemisphere so constructed that light is evenly distributed over the entire surface. The experience is something like looking into a large mixing bowl standing on end, with even illumination across it.

Suppose now that the ganzfeld is illuminated with a gradient of light so that, from side to side, it changes from brighter to darker. If the gradient is very gradual, an observer does not notice it and the whole field seems to have a uniform brightness midway between the greater and lesser brightnesses on either side. Although differences in brightnesses of adjacent areas is one feature associated with the existence of objects, this condition alone is not enough for the perception of an object. Suppose, however, that a thread is stretched through the field just described, so that it bisects the imperceptible gradient. Now perception changes, and the two halves of the field appear to have distinctly different brightnesses separated by an apparent step at the line of the thread. What this demonstration begins to tell us is that contours and edges provide essential information contributing to the perception of objects. As we saw in Chapter 3 (page 50), retinal functions contribute to the clear definition of borders and edges. Other research has shown that neurons in the visual cortex detect the existence of lines, edges, contours, angles, and motion in these elements (Hubel and Wiesel, 1965). The mechanism of such detection is considerably beyond what we can cover in this book. Briefly, these cells respond to spatial frequencies, into which visual patterns can be analyzed, somewhat as complex tones can be broken down into component frequencies (DeValois, Albrecht, and Thorell, 1979). Using this knowledge of what is necessary for object perception makes it possible to depict impossible objects, such as the two shown in Figure 4.1. These drawings contain contours and edges that usually mean the existence of objects, but here they are cues to mislead the observer.

Perceptual Organization

To describe the perception of an object in terms of joining together edges and angles is in the tradition of structural psychology, which dominated the field at the turn of the century. **Structuralism** took a part-to-whole approach to the interpretation of perceptual events, in the belief that this was the only acceptable

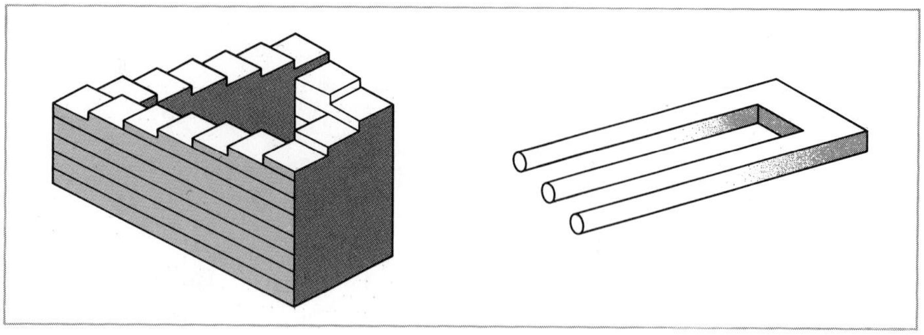

FIGURE 4.1
Going up the down staircase and the impossible tuning fork.

scientific one. From this point of view of the structuralists, psychology's aim would be to develop a sort of "mental chemistry," in which the mental elements would be sensory—hues, loudnesses, and the like. Psychology's program of study would be to discover these elements and the laws by which they combine to create the contents of a mental experience.

A few years later, about 1910, a group known as the **Gestalt psychologists** began to argue for the opposite whole-to-part position. *Gestalt* is a German word with no exact translation in English, although form, organized whole, and configuration are close. The Gestaltists argued that objects are perceived as complete, unitary shapes, not as elementary constituents adding together. When we perceive an apple, it does not appear as a rounded contour with so much redness, so much greenness, and a stem on top. Rather it appears to be an apple, which has these characteristics.

Figure-Ground Relationships Our experience of figure-ground relationships serves to emphasize the wholeness of perceived objects. In the visual field certain parts usually stand out in a distinctive manner from the rest. The distinguishable part is called a figure; what it extends against is called a ground or background (Figure 4.2). Figures tend to have a distinct shape, to be more solid and substantial, and to be in front of the ground. Boundaries seem to belong to the figure rather than to the ground, which is seen as formless. A reversible figure-ground makes this point. Figure 4.3 can be perceived either as a white vase against a colored ground or as two human profiles against a white background. As perception of it shifts from one version to the other, the boundary switches and the newly bounded figure acquires shape and a forward position.

Figure 4.4 is a more complicated demonstration of a reversible figure. The drawing shifts back and forth, being seen as a picture of a young woman, then as that of an old woman. The phenomenon illustrated in these examples has been applied to artistic creations. The works of M. C. Escher offer the most impressive examples (Figure 4.5), but the same methods have been used in more primitive art (Figure 4.6).

Perceptual Grouping The Gestaltists called attention to other organizing principles at work in perception. Items that have *proximity* are likely to be seen as

FIGURE 4.2
Figure on ground.

FIGURE 4.3
An ambiguous figure. Notice that as the view shifts from vase to profiles and back again, the boundary always belongs to what you see as figure.

FIGURE 4.4
The wife and the mother-in-law. (From Boring, Langfeld, and Weld, 1948)

belonging together and forming a group. So too are any constituents that have a point of *similarity*. Items of the same size, shape, and color group together as parts of a pattern. *Continuity* of line in an established direction will make the line seem unitary. And when enough of a pattern is present that a whole can be guessed at, *closure* takes over and fills in. We see incomplete figures as though they were complete (Figure 4.7).

Influence of Context Although these simple demonstrations make a persuasive case that we perceive forms whole, the part-to-whole theorists have a very difficult question for the opposition. How physiologically is it possible to perceive objects except in terms of elementary features? As we saw in the last chapter and early in this one, there are reasonably well-understood physiological mechanisms for detecting hue, brightness, and contours. There are none at all for detecting apples, vases, and mothers-in-law. The only answer the whole-to-part theorists have to this is a stubborn, "Somehow we do!"

As so often happens in psychology, battles over an issue have down through the years led finally to the recognition that both sides of an argument have merit. The sense in which this could be true in the structuralist-Gestalt debate is demonstrated with the materials in Figure 4.8. In each of the three paired examples, the same pattern of lines takes on a different meaning and even a different appearance, depending on the context. At first blush such phenomena suggest that wholes are affecting the perception of parts. But once more we must face the hard-nosed structuralist observation that, as far as anyone knows, human beings have no detectors for words, series of symbols, or even individual symbols. Rather, they have detectors that respond to parts of symbols, to lines, angles, and the like.

Faced with this problem, current theorizing to explain such effects goes like this. The raw perceptual materials picked up by our visual system are information of the kind that the nervous system is sensitive to. These data initiate a part-to-whole mecha-

FIGURE 4.5
Reversible perspective in a print by M. C. Escher.

FIGURE 4.6
Reversible perspective in a primitive Ecuadoran weaving.

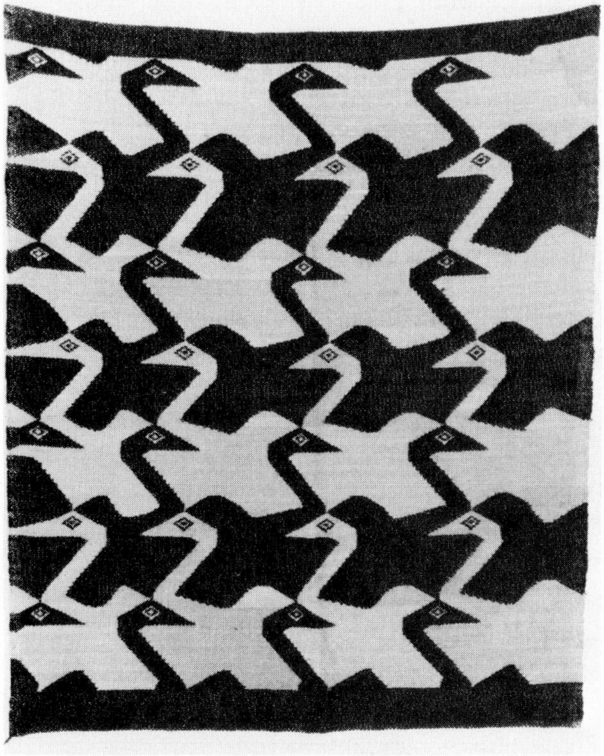

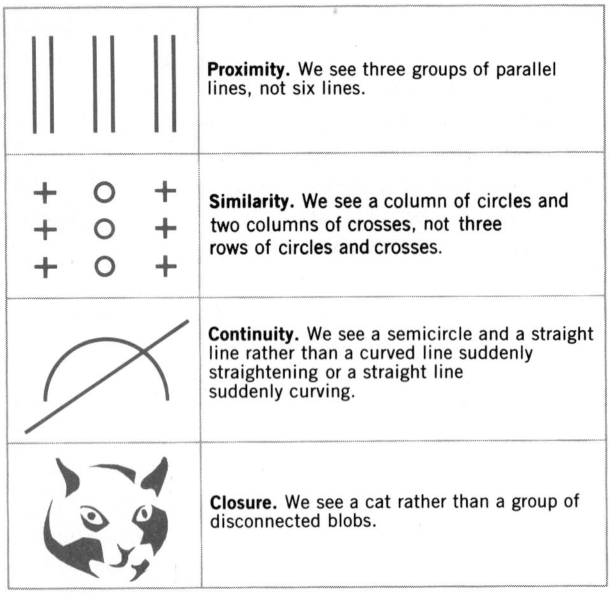
Proximity. We see three groups of parallel lines, not six lines.
Similarity. We see a column of circles and two columns of crosses, not three rows of circles and crosses.
Continuity. We see a semicircle and a straight line rather than a curved line suddenly straightening or a straight line suddenly curving.
Closure. We see a cat rather than a group of disconnected blobs.

FIGURE 4.7
Gestalt principles of perceptual grouping.

nism—sometimes called a "data-driven" or "bottom-up" process—which makes numbers, letters, and words out of the information provided. Almost immediately, however, as the symbols take form, a whole-to-part—"conceptually driven" or "top-down"—mechanism enters the picture. This whole-to-part process brings the results of past experience to bear on perception. Seeing one string of symbols made up of 12 – 14, 15, 16, and another made up of A – C, D, E the individual perceives the same item, which fills the second position of each string, as a different symbol. It becomes the number 13 in the first string, the letter B in the second. These different completions fulfill the expectations created by the concept of letter in the first string, that of number in the second. This is why the interpretation is "conceptually driven."

Adaptation Level The phenomena just described make it very clear that contexts can influence perception and that contexts are provided by earlier experience with similar objects. Put another way, past experience gives us a certain **adaptation level** with respect to the *dimensions* of objects; we consider them great or small in terms of this level. Thus we judge a course as easy or difficult, a salary as high or low, a person as above or below average in attractiveness, the traffic in the city as light or heavy on the basis of such frames of reference.

Experimental procedures make it possible to examine the influence of adaptation levels under conditions of better control. Harry Helson had observers lift and judge the weights of a series of objects whose actual weights were 200, 250, 300, 350, and 400 grams. Subjects were requested to make their judgments by categories ranging from very, very light to very, very heavy. In one series subjects made their judgments after lifting a 900-gram weight, in another series after lifting a 90-gram weight. Judgments fell predominantly toward the light and heavy ends of the scale, depending on whether the weight originally lifted was heavy or light (Figure 4.9).

SUMMARY □

Although the difference between sensory processes and perception is somewhat arbitrary, a roughly useful distinction holds that sensory processes provide the raw materials and that perception provides an interpretation of these materials. Both processes begin with distal stimuli in the physical world; they activate receptors, thus creating proximal stimuli.

The most basic perceptual interpretation tells us that there are objects in the world. Psychologically, the basic condition for perceiving objects is the existence of contours. Physiologically, the detection of contours is accomplished by brain cells that respond fairly specifically to lines, edges, and angles, as well as to their movements through their specific fields.

Structuralism, a classical position in psychology, assumed that the perception of objects is accomplished by combining simple elements, the aspects of sensations. An opposing position, Gestalt psychology, held that perception is not atomistic but provides an immediate interpretation in terms of whole units. The very obvious figure-ground relationships, perceptual groupings, and the effects of contexts on perception provide evidence for the Gestalt position. The differences in the two schools can be summarized by saying that for the structuralists perception is a part-

FIGURE 4.8
Part-to-whole versus whole-to-part processing.

12 13 14 15 16
A B C D E
THE CAT

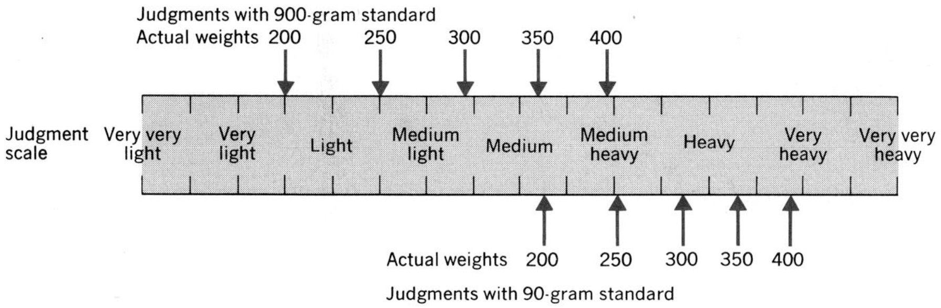

FIGURE 4.9
Adaptation level. Different subjective scales of weight were developed by observers, depending on whether the standard weight was very heavy or very light. The standard weights are sometimes said to anchor the scale of a subjective judgment. (After Helson, 1948.)

to-whole process, for the Gestaltists a whole-to-part process. Current theorizing holds that perceptual experiences begin with the detection of elementary constituents. As these are combined to produce the impressions of objects, previous experience supplies an interpretation that controls to some extent what we actually perceive. Perception consists of both the structuralist's elements of sensations and the Gestalt psychologist's wholes interacting together.

PERCEPTION OF DEPTH, DISTANCE, AND MOTION

Having seen something of the processes by which we form perceptions of objects, we come to an important question. How do we know where these objects are—at what angle and at what distance? Any proximal stimulus is ambiguous because it can actually represent an infinite number of external states of affairs. Representation of the size of the objects is a good illustration, for a retinal image of a given size could be produced by any number of objects differing in physical size and distance (Figure 4.10). But obviously we have little tendency to become confused about such matters. Our perception of the sizes of objects is usually very accurate because our estimates of size always take distance into account. A number of cues aid us in our estimation of distance.

Primary Distance Cues

Some of these cues, frequently called **primary cues** to distance, depend on the functioning of the visual system. Three are accommodation, convergence, and retinal disparity. A fourth important primary cue, motion parallax, will be described at the end of the next section.

Accommodation The shape of the lens of the eye changes in order to produce a sharp image on the retina. For near objects the lens bulges, for far objects it flattens. Called **accommodation,** these changes are initiated by the ciliary muscles surrounding the lens. Kinesthetic receptors in these muscles detect tension when the eye is viewing near objects but none when it is viewing from afar. Accommodation is a useful cue to distance only when the object at which we are looking is fairly near. Beyond 3 or 4 feet accommodation is relatively unimportant. Accommodation is a monocular cue; the lens of one eye will focus whether or not the other eye is being used.

Convergence The two eyes must turn toward each other, or **converge,** to fixate on a near object. Beyond a distance of 30 or 40 feet, the lines of sight of the two eyes looking at an object are essentially parallel, but to look at a near object, they must converge. Muscles attached to the eyeballs turn them and are in different states of tension for viewing near and distant objects. Kinesthetic receptors again send impulses, but this time they must come from both eyes. Convergence cues to distance are binocular.

Retinal disparity The retinas of the two eyes are separated by about 2.5 inches. This means that in normal binocular vision they receive disparate images of the same scene. In spite of this difference, we see the world as though we had a single Cyclopean eye in the middle of the forehead. We are al-

FIGURE 4.10
What retinal images fail to tell us. The same retinal image can be produced by an infinite number of objects of different sizes.

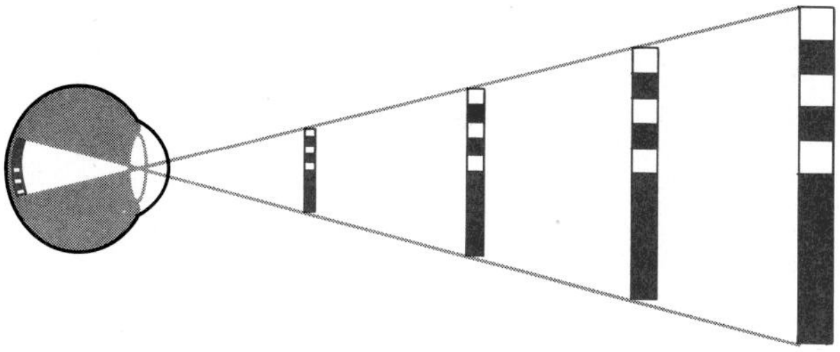

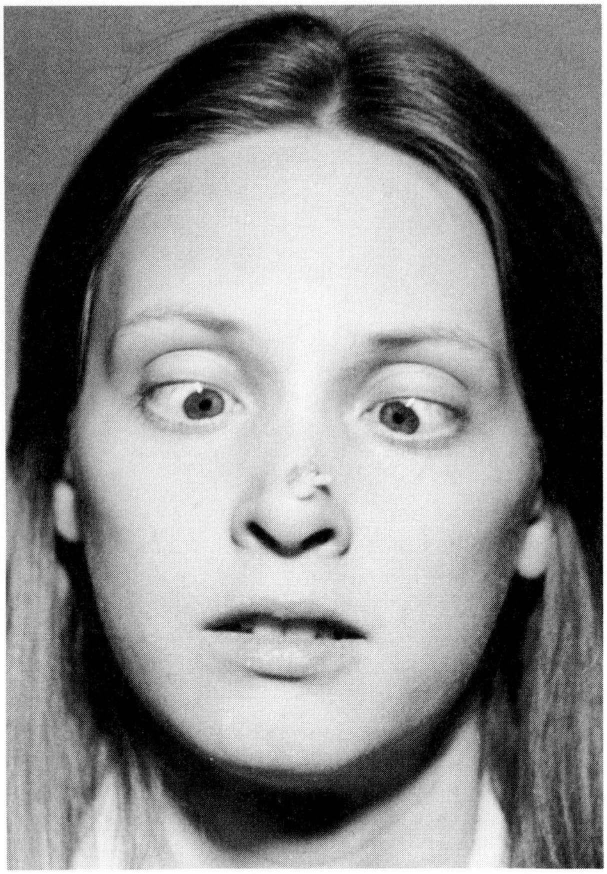

Convergence is a binocular cue to distance and depth.

most never aware of **retinal disparity,** the fact that the two eyes are actually receiving two different views. The right eye sees more of the right side of the scene, the left eye more of the left side. When the brain combines these two scenes as a single view, it is in three dimensions and objects have solidity. Thus retinal disparity provides a binocular cue to depth and distance.

A simple demonstration will make the point that images are actually double. Hold up two pencils, or two fingers will do (Figure 4.11). Fixate either the near pencil or finger, or the far one, but pay some attention to the other. You will discover that there are two images of the nonfixated object, for the reason explained in the right half of Figure 4.11.

Secondary Distance Cues

Other distance cues can be described independently of the functioning of the visual system. These cues, called **secondary cues,** are provided by the physical arrangement of objects and all are monocular cues, available separately to each eye.

Linear perspective Parallel lines, such as the two sides of a road, appear to converge as they stretch into the distance. As objects become more distant, they decrease in size and appear closer together. Objects farther away also appear higher in the horizontal plane.

Aerial perspective Objects in the distance appear blurred and bluish. The dust and water vapor of the atmosphere are diffracting the reflected light waves coming from them. For this reason whatever we see in more detail we perceive as being closer.

FIGURE 4.11

Double images of nonfixated objects. The figure on the left shows the procedure described in the text. The figure on the right explains the effect. Assume that fixation is on the near object. The image falls on the fovea (*F*) of both eyes. The images of the nonfixated objects falls on the nasal retina, toward the nose, and not on the fovea. Since the lens of the eye reverses the world, the two objects are interpreted as being to the two sides of the real object. The solid lines represent light reflected by the two objects, the dashed lines the paths of the projected images. Although such double images exist, they are usually suppressed and we pay attention only to objects whose images are foveal.

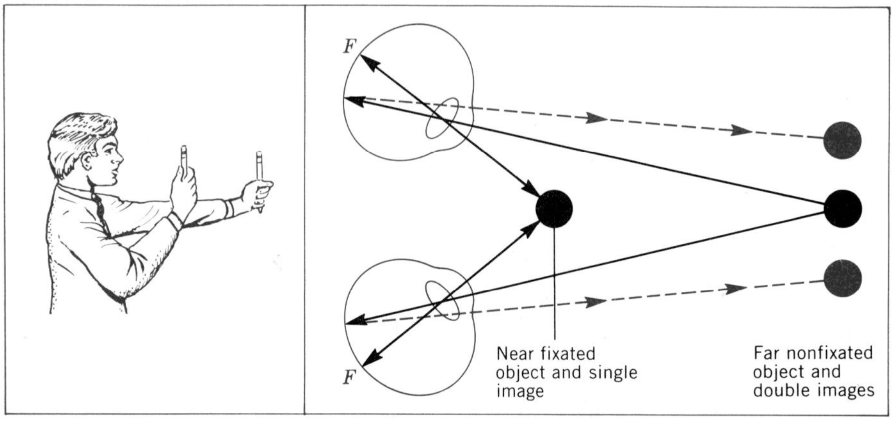

Illustration for Just So Stories, *by Rudyard Kipling, London, 1902.* Linear perspective and the relative sizes and interposition of the trees all contribute distance information.

Relative size of the retinal image When images of objects of the same or similar shapes reach the retina at the same time or in quick succession but differ in size, the object projecting the larger image is judged to be closer.

Interposition If one object obstructs our view of another object in the same line of vision, the fully exposed one appears closer than the obscured one (Figure 4.12).

Gradients of texture Most surfaces have a texture or grain. The texture gradually loses roughness or detail as the surface extends into the distance. The elements making up the texture become denser and finer the farther away they are. Figure 4.13 gives two representations, one an artificial texture, the other from nature. The illusion of depth in the first is impressive.

Patterns of light and shade Since the sunlight and most sources of artificial light are above us, there is a certain dependability to the pattern of highlights and shadows on an object. They provide a cue to small differences in depth. The parts of an object that are lower and recede from the light are usually in shadows. Figure 4.14 illustrates the operation of this cue photographically. Turning the photograph upside down reverses the pattern of light and shade; the indentations become bumps, and vice versa, because we continue to assume an overhead light source.

Auditory Localization

Whenever we turn toward the source of a sudden, unexpected noise, we demonstrate the fact that the

The progressive haziness called aerial perspective can be a beautiful cue to distance.

FIGURE 4.12
Distance and interposition. This figure makes several points. In the left-hand drawing relative size and linear perspective make one card seem farther away. The same is true in the middle drawing; presented here to show how this demonstration works. In the right-hand drawing the small card fills the cutout in the large card. Now it seems *closer,* illustrating the effect of interposition. It also seems smaller, although the size is unchanged. You will understand why after you read the discussion of the moon illusion later in the chapter.

auditory system also provides information that is useful in locating objects in space. Our two separate ears are remarkably sensitive to differences in the sounds that reach them. As small a difference as 0.0001 second in the time of arrival of the sounds at one ear and then the other can be detected. This difference indicates that the sound source is on one side of the head. Moreover, because the second ear is in a "sound shadow" created by the head, which absorbs part of the intensity of the sound waves, sound reaching this farther ear is also less intense (Figure 4.15). Finally, with lower-pitched sounds the length of the sound waves may be greater than the width of the head. One ear receives one *phase* of the waves, say the crest, the farther ear the trough. Although most of us make little use of our ears in locating objects in space, blind people learn to use these cues effectively.

Motion Perception

A condition necessary for the perception of motion is the stimulation of a series of rods and cones in quick succession. Any object that moves across the visual field has this effect (Figure 4.16). This is the situation

FIGURE 4.13
Gradients of texture as cues to distance. (Drawing after Gibson, 1950).

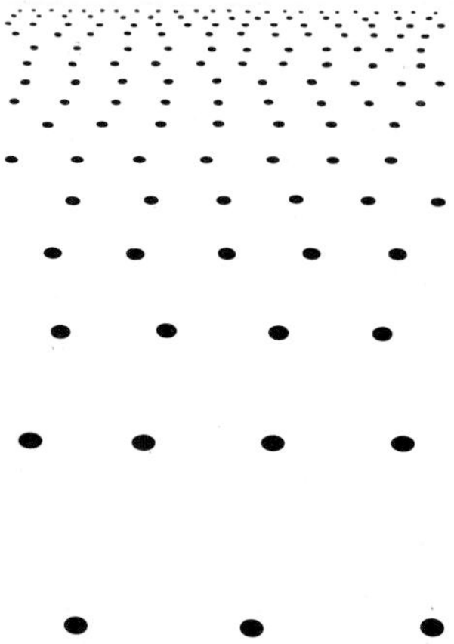

FIGURE 4.14
Light and shade as cues to depth. Turn the picture upside down and see the reversal of depth.

in which the perception of motion usually occurs. Rods and cones are also successively stimulated when the eye rotates in its socket to track a moving object, but in this instance the sources of this stimulation are in the background and are regarded as stationary. The voluntary messages to the eye muscles instructing rotation apparently moderate the retinal messages. The relatively fixed images registered by the focusing fovea are perceived as those of a moving object, and the shifting images registered by the rest of the retina—still necessary for the perception of mo-

FIGURE 4.15
Cues for sound localization. Sounds from a source straight ahead affect the two ears equally. A sound from one side reaches the near ear sooner, in greater intensity, and in a different phase than it reaches the far ear. (After Schiffman, 1976.)

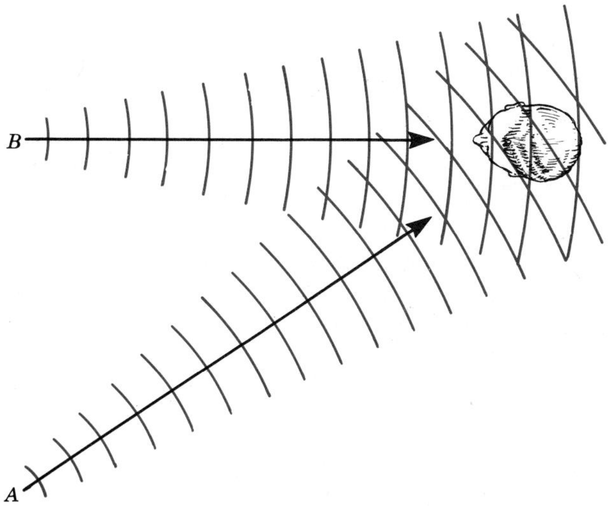

FIGURE 4.16
Motion perception. (*a*) Motion is perceived when rods and cones are stimulated in quick succession, which happens when an object moves across the field of vision. (*b*) The retina of the tracking eye receives quite uniform stimulation to the fovea as well as the quick successive stimulations.

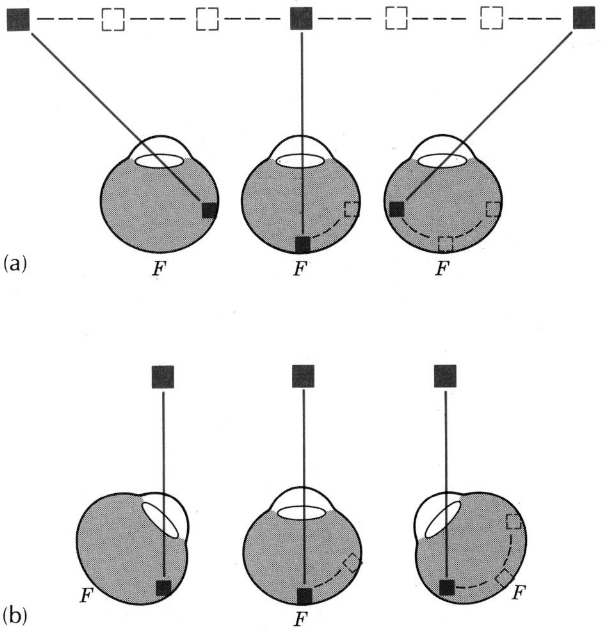

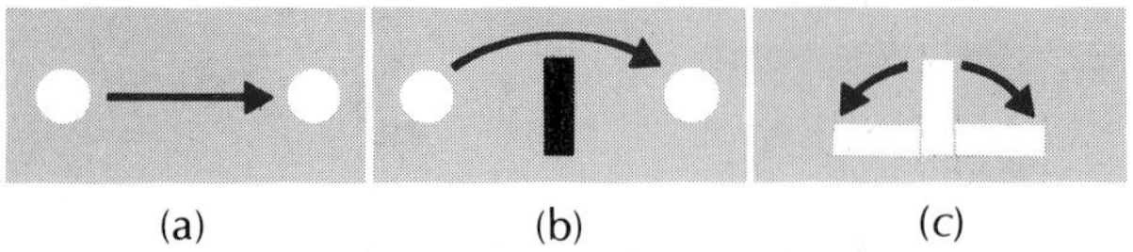

FIGURE 4.17
Apparent motion. (*a*) Flashing on first the left-hand light and then the right-hand light produces apparent motion from left to right. (*b*) If a barrier is interposed between the two lights, the light may seem to jump over the barrier. This is called bow movement. (*c*) If the center vertical bar of light comes on and then the two horizontal bars are flashed on simultaneously, the center light may appear to split and become two horizontal bars. This is sometimes called split movement.

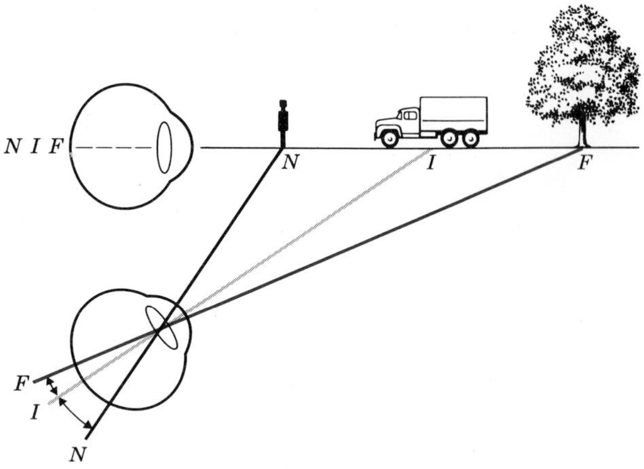

FIGURE 4.18
Motion parallax as a cue to distance. The diagram shows the shifts in retinal stimulation that make near objects appear to flash by in an opposite direction and far objects to "go along with us" as we ride in an automobile or on a train.

tion—are seen as those of stationary background objects. The voluntary messages to the head and eye to move to survey a room in effect also still the succession of images registered by the retina. The objects in the room projecting these images are perceived as motionless.

When the head and unfocused eye are moved in space other than through their own volition, however, the shifting images on the retina are interpreted as motion. The surroundings are erroneously seen as moving. You can observe the perceptions of the passively moved eye in a simple experiment. Close one eye and gently place a finger across the bottom lid of the open eye, just below the eyeball. Move the eyeball slightly upward. The visual field will be observed to move downward, since retinal events are the opposite of those in the outside world. The images of objects in the field now fall on a higher region of the retina, which is interpreted as a downward motion.

Apparent Motion In certain other circumstances objects that are standing still are seen to move. Suppose that two lights, A and B, represented by the circles at the top of Figure 4.17, are flashed on one after the other and that the time interval separating the two flashes is about 0.06 second, which is nearly optimal. Under these conditions—the distance between the two lights and their intensity must also be controlled—we see not first one light and then the other but one light moving across the field of vision from A to B. This is the **phi phenomenon.** Such apparent motion makes it possible to construct animated electric signs, in which "moving" arrows point to the entrance to a cafe or lights seem to travel around the periphery of the theater marquee. The phi phenomenon demonstrates well that the perception of motion depends on the successive stimulation of spatially separated retinal points.

The phi phenomenon, or stroboscopic motion as it is sometimes called, is basic to the motion seen in moving pictures. As almost everyone knows, the figures on the motion picture screen do not really move. The film consists of a series of still frames of people and objects in slightly different positions. When the frames are projected in rapid succession, usually at least twenty-four frames per second, continuous and smooth movement is perceived. Flicker would be evident, however, if the intense projecting light were not flashed three times for each frame. Projection is really at seventy-two flashes per second (Schiffman, 1976).

Motion Parallax The phenomenon of the **motion parallax** is the fourth primary cue to distance, mentioned earlier. When we are riding in a rapidly moving automobile, we look out to the middle distance. Distant objects appear to move with us, those at the intermediate distance appear to remain fixed, and those nearest appear to move in a direction opposite that in which we are traveling. The top part of Figure 4.18 shows a near (*N*) figure of a person, a truck at an intermediate (*I*) distance, and a far (*F*) tree all lined up along a single line of sight. At this moment the figure, truck, and tree all stimulate the same spot on the retina. A moment later the eye is in a new position. Assuming that fixation on the intermediate object is maintained, the point on the retina occupied by the intermediate object remains unchanged. With respect to the image of this intermediate object, however, that of the near object has moved in the same direction that the eye has traveled; the image of the far object has moved in the opposite direction. But the movements of objects are interpreted as being in the direction opposite to that in which their retinal images move. Far objects appear to move with us, even the moon, and near objects flee past us in the opposite direction. The blurred images of near objects and the stately immobility and clarity of the middle and distant countryside are important cues to their distances.

SUMMARY □

Proximal stimulation is basically ambiguous, because any such stimulus can be produced by a variety of distal stimuli. A retinal image of a given size, for example, may represent any of an infinite number of objects of different sizes at different distances. In spite of this ambiguity, we judge sizes and distances remarkably accurately. The cues to distance fall into two categories. Primary cues—accommodation, convergence, retinal disparity, and the motion parallax—depend on the functioning of the visual system. Secondary cues depend on the physical arrangement of objects. Linear and aerial perspective, the relative size of the retinal image, interposition of objects, gradients of textures, and patterns of lights and shade all help us judge distances. Auditory cues supply distance information which blind people use effectively.

An essential condition for the perception of motion is the successive stimulation of rods and cones, as happens when an object moves across the visual field. When the eye rotates in its socket to track a moving object, the voluntary messages to the muscles of the rotating eye moderate retinal messages, however. They in effect still the shifting images from background objects. The fixed images of the focusing fovea are perceived as those of a moving object. In the phi phenomenon the stationary eye sees apparent motion when lights of a certain intensity and closeness are flashed at correct fractions of a second. In the motion parallax the rapidly traveling eye focused on the middle distance perceives faraway objects as moving with it, intermediate objects as stationary, nearby objects as speeding by in the opposite direction.

PERCEPTUAL CONSTANCY

What Constancy Achieves: Stability

The size of the retinal image varies inversely with the distance from which an object is viewed. Figure 4.19 indicates what happens to the retinal image of an object viewed at two different distances and also what happens to perception. When the square is near, the image on the retina is large. When it is far away, the image is smaller. Our perceptions, however, have a

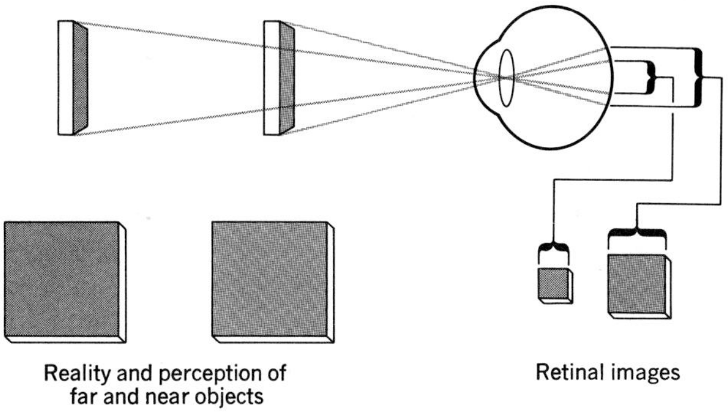

FIGURE 4.19
Retinal images of near and far objects. Although the two objects are the same size, they produce retinal images of different sizes. We tend to see objects in an appropriate constant size, however, as the lower part of the figure indicates.

way of compensating for this difference in the size of the retinal image. Perceptual processes reinterpret the proximal stimulus to provide an object with **size constancy.** For familiar objects such as automobiles, people, animals, and the like, learning is important. As soon as we recognize an object for what it is, we judge it to have an appropriate size, whatever its distance. We automatically correct the size of the retinal image, or we do so at least partially. Certainly the size perceived is closer to that of the object than to that of the retinal image. Our judgment of the size of unfamiliar objects apparently always takes into account the distance at which the object is viewed. The sizes of surrounding objects and background depth are estimated on the basis of the distance cues described earlier. Experiments in which cues to distance have been eliminated demonstrate that size constancy then breaks down, and perception of the size of an object corresponds to the size of the retinal image.

When we view objects and people from the top of a very tall building, we do not have a mechanism for size constancy. We are not accustomed to judging distance in the vertical. The impression that cars are toys and people ants, a miniaturization not evident in a horizontal view, is pure retinal image, with no adjustment for distance.

Retinal images also vary when we look at an object from different points of view. Yet from many angles objects are perceived as maintaining about the same shape. **Shape constancy** is another of our valuable perceptual reinterpretations of the proximal stimulus. An opening door looks to have the same rectangular structure even when viewed edge on, although the retinal image changes considerably (Figure 4.20). The integrity of a coin's round outline is maintained, though the retinal image of its surface becomes an ellipse. The order and stability of the visual world depends on this object constancy, this perception of objects as existing in the same size and shape, whatever the size and pattern of the retinal image.

Objects also tend to maintain their appropriate colors and brightness, in changing illumination. In the special case of **brightness constancy,** a white shirt looks white in bright light or in the shade, although much less light is reflected from the shirt when it is in shadows. A black suit looks black even in bright sunlight, when it reflects a great deal of light. The perception of blackness and whiteness depends not on the absolute intensity of stimulation reaching the eye but on relative intensities. If the amplitudes of the light waves reflected by two adjacent objects differ by a ratio of about 16 to 1, the object reflecting the smaller amount appears black. An interesting application of this principle is the special signs used along some of our superhighways. They have white lettering, in ordinary paint, against a background of green paint which contains small particles of a light-reflecting material. At night, when the headlights of an automobile strike these signs, the lettering appears to be black on a white background, for the special green paint reflects much more light than the white lettering.

When Constancy Fails: The Illusions

Although our perceptions are usually quite accurate, they are also subject to distortions called illusions. Illusions take a great many fascinating forms. Some visual illusions are called illusions of extent and direction (Figures 4.21, 4.22). Illusory experiences also beset the other senses. The Müller-Lyer illusion shown in Figure 4.21 has been demonstrated on the skin (Bekesy, 1967). Aristotle noticed long ago that the blunt end of a stylus inserted between the tips of crossed adjacent fingers can be felt as two styli.

Attempted Explanations Some illusions are explained by well-known physical principles. If you put a straight rod into a glass of water, it appears bent at the surface of the water. This is a purely physical optical phenomenon; oblique incident and reflected light waves are deflected from a straight path when

Size constancy. Bringing the background figure close to the foreground figure shows how small the man really is when viewed from a distance. In both pictures the figure of the man is the same size.

they enter and leave water. In the Doppler effect (page 59) the movement of the sound source compresses and expands sound waves, producing the physical bases for higher and lower tones. For most illusory experiences, however, physical explanations are inadequate, suggesting that psychological processes are at work. Attempts to explain the illusions in such terms have been only partly successful.

The moon illusion One illusion has been noticed and has generated speculation for milleniums. Near the horizon the moon looks larger than it does high in the sky, although the size of the retinal image is the same in both cases. A favorite explanation can be traced to Ptolemy, the second-century astronomer and mathematician. He maintained that an object seen through space that is filled with objects, as the terrain leading to the horizon is, is seen as farther away than an object at the same distance seen through empty space. The horizon moon therefore

Viewed from a great height, people and cars are seen in miniature proportions.

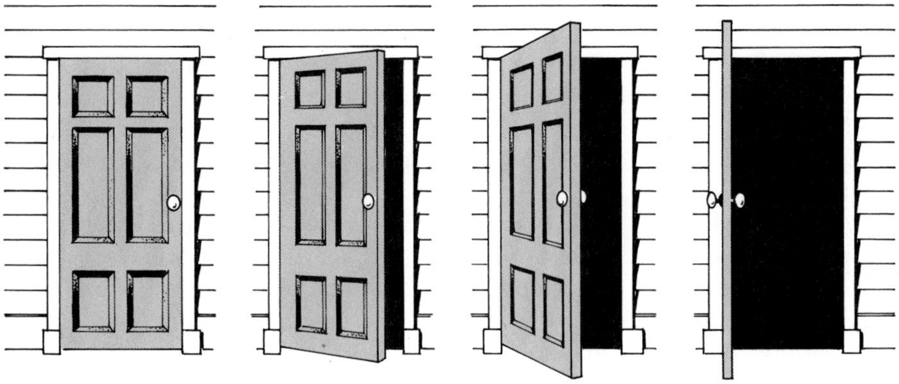

FIGURE 4.20
Shape constancy. The opening door is perceived as retaining its rectangular shape, despite the markedly different images projected on the retina.

Shape constancy. The ovals below the coins indicate the actual shapes of their outlines.

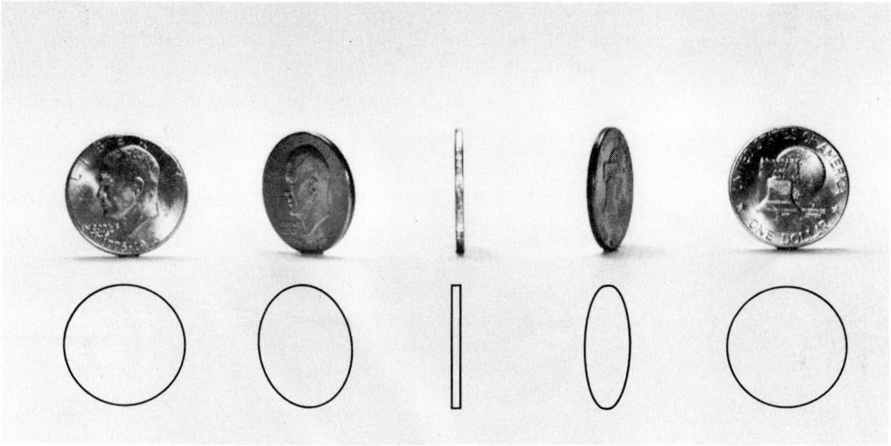

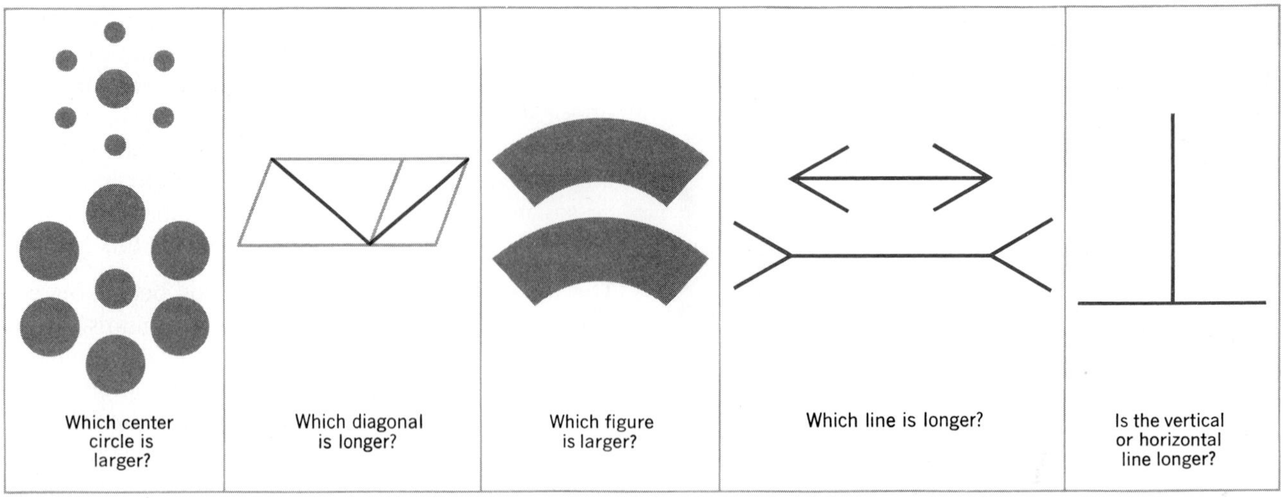
Which center circle is larger?
Which diagonal is longer?
Which figure is larger?
Which line is longer?
Is the vertical or horizontal line longer?

FIGURE 4.21
Illusions of extent. In every instance one of the two identical sizes appears to be larger. The figures with the angles at the ends make up the Müller-Lyer illusion.

looks farther away and for this reason seems larger.

As we have indicated earlier, a large object far away or a small object that is closer can produce retinal images of the same size (Figure 4.23). If for some reason the horizon moon seems farther away than the zenith moon, the moon illusion could be understood in these terms. People would interpret the retinal image as having a *larger* size because they see the horizon moon as at a greater distance. There is good reason to suppose that the horizon moon might seem farther away. Many more of the secondary cues to distance are present in a view of the horizon moon, interposition of objects, gradients of texture, linear and aerial perspective, to name the most important. If people do perceive the horizon moon as farther away, their conception of the arching heavens might be that illustrated in Figure 4.24. Now they would interpret the same retinal image as that produced by the horizon moon as being *smaller* because the vault of the heavens has been misjudged.

But now we must raise a question of fact. Does the moon at the horizon actually look farther away than when it is at its zenith? Unfortunately for any simple theory of the moon illusion, the answer to this question is "No." People usually report the horizon moon as seeming nearer than the zenith moon. The horizon moon should then seem smaller instead of larger. So where does this fact leave the theory? Obviously, with a problem but the problem is an old one. Scientists interested in perception have long emphasized that how a particular situation is registered and what the individual reports need not be perfectly related. It could be that the nervous system makes the **unconscious inference,** to use Helmholtz's expression, that the moon is farther away when it is on the horizon. Since the cues to distance are present, the nervous

FIGURE 4.22
Illusions of direction. In these illusions straight lines appear distorted. Lay a ruler along the diagonal in the left figure to see where it actually goes. Do the same on the edge of the bent square to see that the line is actually straight.

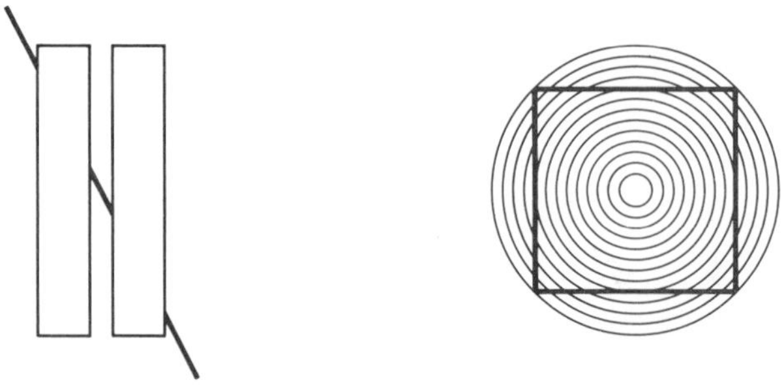

FIGURE 4.23
Basis for the moon illusion? Images of the same size can be projected to the retina by a small near object or a large distant object of the same kind. When retinal images are of the same size and we think that we know the distances of the objects, one theory holds that we automatically see the far objects as larger. Thus seeing the horizon moon as farther away than the zenith moon can only make the horizon moon seem larger.

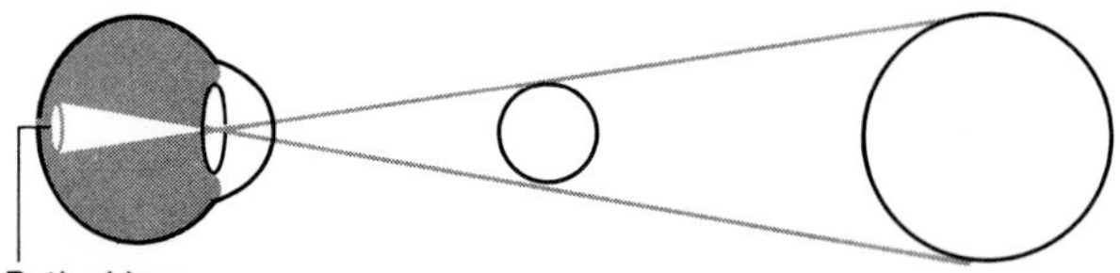
Retinal image

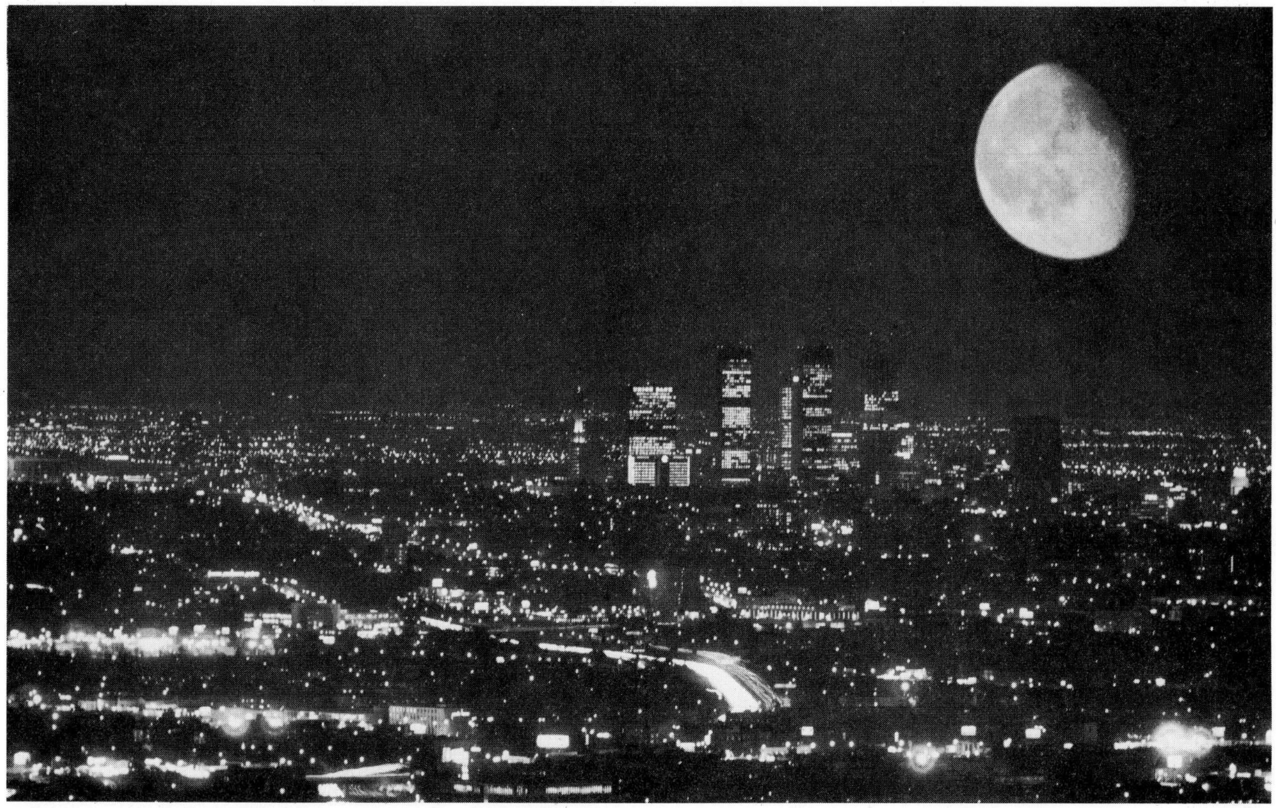

The horizon moon can appear truly enormous.

system might take them into account and arrive unconsciously at that interpretation. The individual then perceives a larger moon, which in turn seems nearer.

Other illusions of extent The Müller-Lyer illusion, the two figures with standard and reversed arrowheads in Figure 4.21, has also been interpreted in terms of false adjustments for size constancy. In normal perspective the apparently longer line often means "far corner" of a room, and the apparently shorter one often means "near corner" of a building (Figure 4.25). The explanation resembles that developed for the moon illusion. Although the retinal images of the two principal lines are the same, the size-constancy mechanism goes to work and adjusts the one farther away to a larger size. The retinal image supposedly coming from close by is similarly shrunk in size. These correction processes are so ingrained that they are applied even when they are inappropriate. Some people contend that the Müller-Lyer illusion can be explained without bringing in depth. They say that the converging and diverging end contours by themselves induce the perceived distortions in length. Moreover, the Müller-Lyer illusion

FIGURE 4.24
Imagined distant horizon and low-vaulted heavens. As the moon moves in its orbit, it may be considered farther away at the horizon, nearer at its zenith. Cues to distance are far fewer looking straight up than looking toward the horizon.

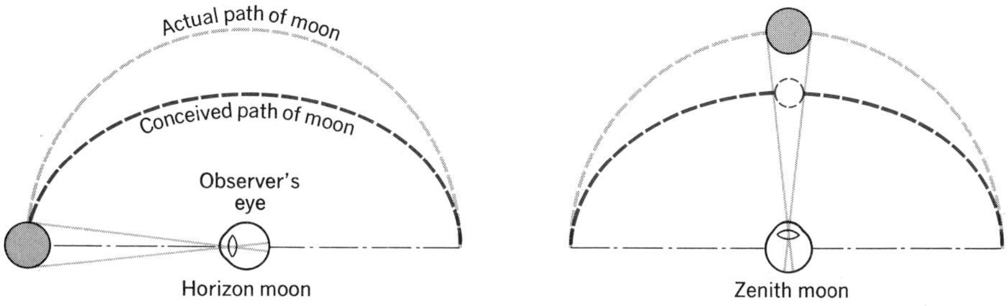

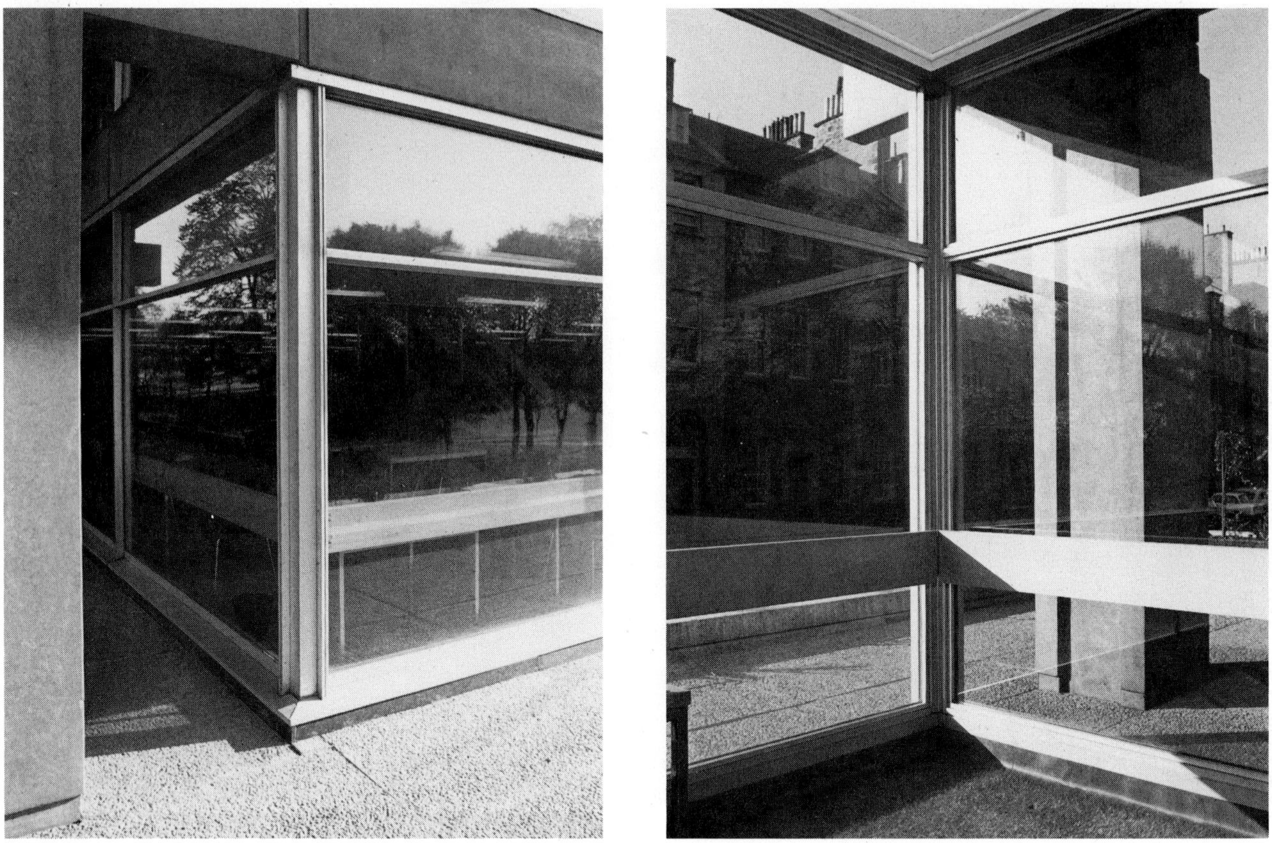

FIGURE 4.25
Interpreting the Müller-Lyer illusion. The photography indicates how the arrowheads in the Müller-Lyer illusion usually mean "near corner" of a building and "far corner" of a room.

when presented on a flat surface has no noticeable depth effect. But Richard Gregory (1970) has shown that when these illusion-producing figures are constructed of wire coated with luminous paint and presented in a dark room, they do appear to have depth.

The Ponzo illusion, sometimes called the "railroad track" illusion, has converging lines which introduce a powerful cue to distance, linear perspective. On this basis the top horizontal line, or boat, in Figure 4.26 is considered to be farther away. Therefore, since the upper and lower objects make the same-sized projections to the retina, the upper one is perceived by ingrained processes as not only more distant but also larger.

Automatization In our opinion, at least by now, but perhaps earlier, you have found yourself saying, "I don't believe it! Much of what I am reading seems too unlikely to be true. You try to tell me that I make objects out of meaningless lines and edges, that concepts and expectations determine what I see. And now *unconscious inference*? I don't believe it!" Our answer to you is, "Of course you find these processes difficult to accept because they are unconscious, out of awareness, and automatic. This is one of the most difficult aspects of behavior confronting psychology. We know very little about such matters, except that behavior does tend to become automatic with very

FIGURE 4.26
Ponzo illusion. A powerful cue to distance, linear perspective, indicates that one of two identical lines and boats is farther away. Since the second line and boat project the same retinal images as the first, they are considered to be larger as well as more distant.

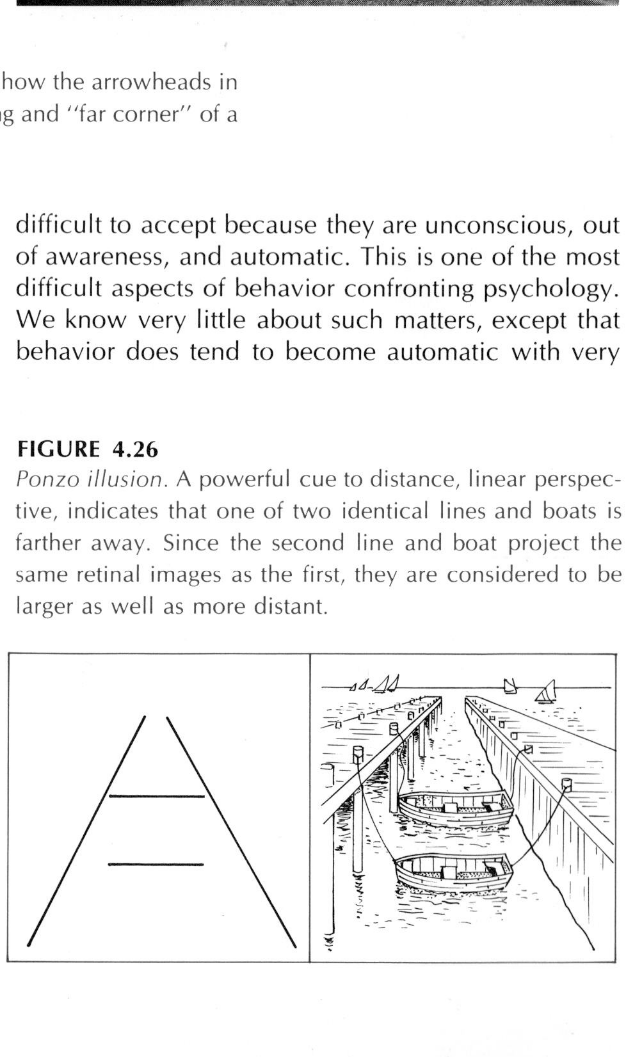

Les Promenades d'Euclide. The two cones in this painting have the same physical height, but cues to distance make us see the second as a lengthy but spectral avenue.

extended practice." Perhaps an example of another automatic process will help establish this point.

J. R. Stroop (1935) devised the test shown in Figure 4.27 (color plate). These materials consist of a list of color names printed in colors that do not match the names. The task of the individual taking the Stroop test is to name the colors in the order shown, rather than read the mismatched words. Try it, and get someone else to try it. You will discover that the task is difficult because the printed words tend automatically to elicit themselves, which interferes with the recitation of the names of actual colors.

SUMMARY ☐

Perceptual constancy has been demonstrated for a host of attributes of objects. Size constancy is possible in part because of numerous cues to distance. Our perceptions of the sizes of objects take this distance information into account. If the object is recognized, familiarity provides an additional cue. The shape, color, and brightness of an object are also perceived with some constancy, matching our vision to reality.

Although perception is usually accurate, sometimes it is subject to distortions, the so-called illusions. Some of these illusions are well understood, but most of them are not. A particular class of illusions, of which the moon illusion is one, have a currently accepted explanation. Two objects that are actually the same size seem to be different sizes because the situation leads the perceiver to infer unconsciously that one object is farther away. Because the retinal images for these objects are the same size, it is necessary to see the more distant object as larger. All this mistaken perceiving goes on automatically and unconsciously, an aspect of behavior which raises difficult problems for psychology.

THE NATIVISM-EMPIRICISM ISSUE

Any list of the most important questions that psychology has to face will always include this one. To what extent is behavior governed by hereditary, inborn, unlearned factors, to what extent by environmental, acquired, learned factors? The **nature-nurture** issue, as it is sometimes called, will come up at several points in the book. (The end notes for this chapter give specific references.) In the field of perception this question is usually called the **nativism-empiricism** and asks more specifically whether perception is inborn or learned.

Visual Experience in "First Sight"

John Locke, the British empirical philosopher, once received a letter from his friend William Molyneaux posing the now celebrated question.

> Suppose a man born blind, and now adult, taught by his touch to distinguish between a cube and a sphere of the same metal, and nighly of the same bigness, so as to tell, when he felt one and the other, which is the cube, which the sphere. Suppose that the cube and sphere placed on a table, and the blind man be made to see: query, whether by his sight, before he touched them could he distinguish and tell which is the globe, which the cube? (Locke, 1690.)

Both Molyneaux and Locke believed the man could not.

In recent years interest in the effects of learning on perception has prompted experiments with lower animals and studies of newly sighted human beings that bear on this issue. Pigeons have been raised for a period of time with their eyelids sewn shut or with translucent hoods over their heads. When sight is restored, these birds assume unusual postures as though they are disoriented in space; they find it impossible to avoid bumping into obstacles. Similar perceptual abnormalities have been observed in rabbits and chimpanzees reared in darkness and in fish brought from dark pools into lighted aquariums.

One important line of evidence comes from the study of persons who have had severe cataracts since childhood and have been given sight by surgical removal of the cataracts. Such evidence is less satisfactory than we might wish, however. For one thing, these patients have never been truly blind. Rather, their vision has been obscured by cataracts, which usually allow them to see clouded patches of light but no patterns. Second, the sight restored is often in a physiological sense defective. Finally, there is an enormous problem in communicating with these patients. They do not have the vocabulary to describe their world, and we do not have the experience to understand what they are trying to say.

In spite of these difficulties, we now know that the perceptual abilities of these patients are seriously impaired. Perception of such geometric forms as circles, squares, and triangles is very poor. In order to distinguish a triangle from a square, the patient has to count the corners or trace the outline. A second difficulty encountered by those who are given new sight is an inability to generalize as normal persons do. If, after months of training, such patients learn to recognize a triangle that is on a desk, they may fail to recognize the same triangle when it is outdoors in the grass. A triangle of a different color or the original triangle turned upside down may not be identified. Distance perception is usually a problem. Moreover, years after the operation the patient may know the faces of only a few very close friends.

Gregory and J. G. Wallace (1963) have given a detailed case history of a Mr. S. B. The patient, an Englishman, had lost effective vision in both eyes at the age of ten months and had his vision restored surgically at the age of fifty-two. Gregory and Wallace saw him about one month after his operation. They discussed with him his visual experience following removal of the cataracts and conducted a number of visual tests. Describing his first visual experience, the patient said that he had heard a voice coming from in front of him and to one side. He turned to the source of the sound and saw a "blur." He realized that this must be a face. Upon careful questioning, S. B. seemed to think that he would not have known that this was a face had he not previously heard the voice and known that voices come from faces.

The strengths and weakenesses in the patient's vision were instructive. S. B. seemed not to have most of the illusions. The lines in the Hering illusion (Figure 4.28*a*) did not bend; the two "arrows" in the Müller-Lyer illusion seemed much more nearly the same length than for most people; the reversible staircase (Figure 4.28*b*) portrayed no depth for him and did not reverse. S. B. could make little or nothing of most photographs, and card 1 on the Rorschach test (see page 411) was merely a design. He misjudged depths badly, thinking that it would be easy to step from a second-story window to the ground, a distance of some 30 to 40 feet.

The patient's performance on the Ishihara test for color blindness (Figure 3.14, color plate) was excellent. He read all the numbers accurately, including the most difficult ones. He could read a clock correctly and drew a recognizable picture of a bus, although he omitted the radiator and hood.

The less-than-obvious fact tying all the patient's perceptual strengths together was that every accurate perception was of objects with which he had become familiar by touch. He had learned to read a watch by feeling the position of the hands, and this transferred to sighted clock reading. The blind are taught to read numerals and capital letters by touch because these skills are useful in reading embossed signs; this skill transferred perfectly to the Ishihara test, although there the numbers are made up of dots. The patient was able to draw a picture of a bus and his drawings improved in quality, but they never included the

FIGURE 4.28
(*a*) *The Hering illusion.* Check it with a straight edge. (*b*) *Reversible perspective.* Fixate the near edge of the middle stair for a while and notice the change.

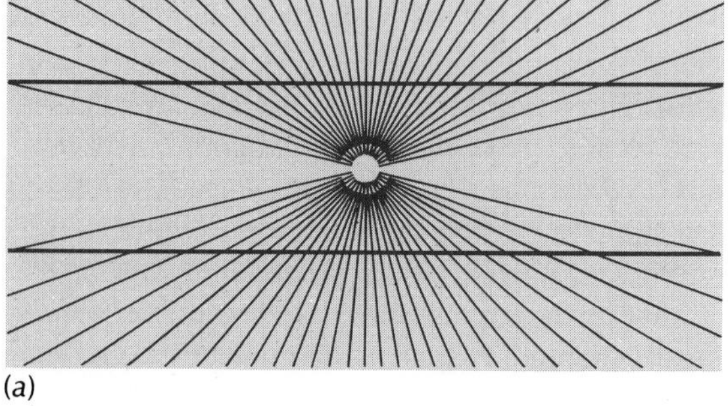
(*a*)

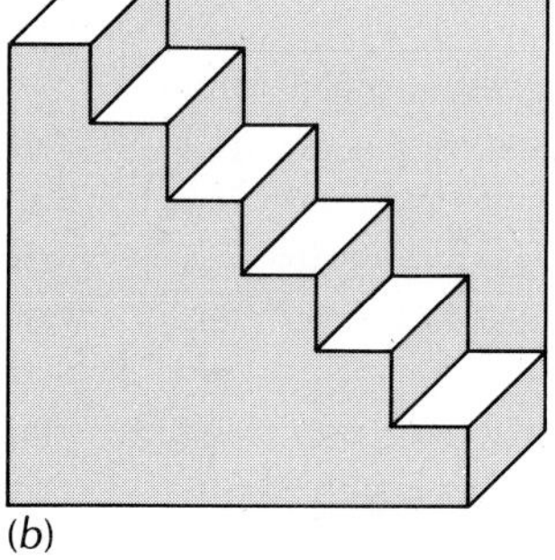
(*b*)

hood, the one part of a bus with which he had never come in contact. These observations seem to prove that Locke and Molyneaux were wrong; knowledge acquired by touch alone does transfer to the visual sphere.

A final point to be made about this case has nothing directly to do with perception. Although, in medical terms, the operation was a success and, in terms of perception, S. B. showed marked improvement after the operation, as was common in other cases mentioned by Gregory and Wallace, the restoration of sight to the patient ended in tragedy.

> Before the operation he was regarded by everybody as a cheerful rather dominant person, and we independently formed this opinion when we first saw him at the hospital. He seemed changed when he came to London; dispirited and bored. It seemed to all of us that he was deeply disturbed; yet too proud to admit or discuss it. . . . His story is in some ways tragic. He suffered one of the greatest handicaps, and yet he lived with energy and enthusiasm. When his handicap was apparently swept away, as by a miracle, he lost his peace and self-respect (pp. 36-37).

Less than two years after the operation, the patient died.

Turning the World Upside Down and Backward

Other evidence supporting the role of learning in perception comes from a very famous experiment by George Stratton (1897). For a period of eight days Stratton wore over one eye a lens that reversed the visual world from right to left and from top to bottom. The other eye he kept blindfolded. At the beginning of the experimental period, the upside-down and backward nature of his world made it extremely difficult for Stratton to carry on his daily activities. He could perform tasks guided by sight only slowly and laboriously. To pour a glass of milk at the table was a major undertaking. Particularly interesting is his report that, initially, the world lost its stability. Head and eye movements seemed to make the world move and swing about.

With respect to uprightness and the inversion of things, Stratton perceived the world as being upside down but he experienced the orientation of his body as it had been before he donned his lens. Whereas we usually judge the orientation of our bodies by reference to the outside world, Stratton now took his body as the standard and perceived the world as inverted and movement as reversed.

As the experiment wore on, Stratton became better able to function in his new environment. Movements were made with less deliberation. He ran into things less often and was able to wash his hands, sit down, and eat, which had been extremely difficult at the beginning of the experiment. Although Stratton never said that the world came to look right side up, he did learn to get around in it adequately and eventually came to regard the orientation of his body as consistent with that of his surroundings.

The Importance of Movement

The studies just described point to an aspect of perception that seems very important today. Our perceptual capacities are the complex consequence of a history of moving about in the perceptual world. The new vision of the Englishman described by Gregory and Wallace was most effective with materials with which he had had previous tactual experience. Stratton became perceptually competent in his inverted world after he had moved about in it and tried a number of activities. Many investigators have added information of this type to our knowledge of perception.

There is, for example, a brilliantly simple demonstration of the importance of locomotion within a lighted area to the development of perception. Richard Held and Alan Hein (1963) reared twenty kittens in darkness until they were mature enough to pull a bit of weight, a matter of eight to twelve weeks. At this age the kittens, two at a time, spent three hours a day in an illuminated carousel apparatus (Figure 4.29). One kitten wore a body harness which allowed it to move of its own accord in a circular path within the cylindrical enclosure. The other was transported in a suspended carriage as the first kitten moved. The idea behind this procedure was to provide the two kittens with nearly the same view as they circled within the cylinder but allow only one of them an opportunity for visual-motor coordination.

Tests conducted after each pair had spent an average of about thirty hours in the apparatus indicated that the perceptual capabilities of the kittens that had been moved passively through their surroundings were much impaired. The other kittens blinked at approaching objects, extended their forepaws in anticipation of contact as they were lowered onto a table, and evidenced depth perception by avoiding the "deep" side of the "visual cliff" (see page 95). The passive kittens did not blink or extend their forepaws in these circumstances, and they walked unconcernedly across the visual cliff. But all their deficiences were righted after a few days of free movement in a lighted room. At a minimum, such results indicate that self-produced movement in lighted surroundings is necessary for the development of fundamental perceptual abilities; visual experience alone is not enough.

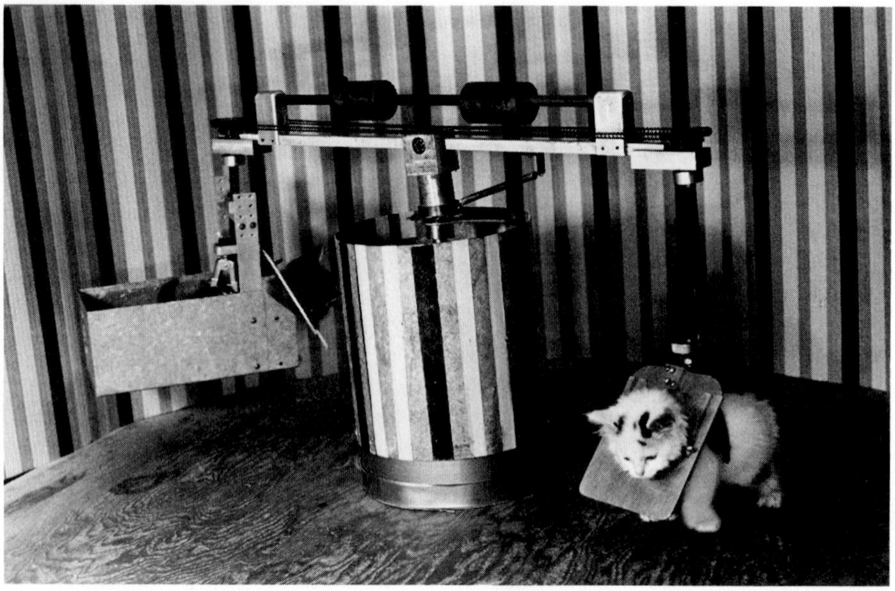

FIGURE 4.29
The kitten carousel. The active and passive kittens had essentially equivalent visual experiences as they moved within the vertically striped cylinder, but for one kitten these experiences were initiated by its own locomotion.

But a more difficult question remains. Just what does such self-produced movement contribute to the development of perception? In a general way the answer to this question is becoming clear. Held and Bauer (1967) performed another rearing experiment, this time with infant monkeys. Within twelve hours of birth, the infant was transferred to a confining apparatus (Figure 4.30) which made vision of the hands impossible, although it did of course provide for feeding the infant and contained a bar covered with soft fur which the infant could fondle. We know that this kind of stimulation is necessary to prevent severe emotional disturbances in the monkey (see page 366).

After a monkey had been in this apparatus for thirty-five days, which is somewhat longer than the normally reared monkey needs to develop good eye-hand coordination, one hand and arm was exposed to view and the infant was handed a bottle. The baby monkey reached for the bottle, but the moment its hand came into view, it stopped reaching and for minutes at a time watched its own hand with apparent fascination. For the next twenty days the visually guided reaching of that limb for the nursing bottle was tested. The infant was also allowed to view the exposed arm for one hour each day.

With time the hand watching abated, and it was possible to determine the accuracy of the visually guided reach. It turned out to be much poorer than that of normally reared monkeys, but with practice it improved. A series of ten similar sessions with the other, previously unexposed hand followed training of the first limb. The sequence of events was similar. Reaching was inaccurate at first. With training, however, the ability to use the second limb improved rapidly. This study effectively demonstrates that for the visually guided movements of the very young to be accurate, both perceptual and motor practice are required.

Perception in the Neonate

The studies presented so far argue for nurture in the development of perception. Other evidence, however, leaves little doubt that human infants, and

FIGURE 4.30
Perceptual restriction in the monkey. The apparatus kept the infant monkey from seeing its limbs and their movement for thirty-five days. (After Held and Bauer, 1967. Copyright © 1967 by the American Association for the Advancement of Science.)

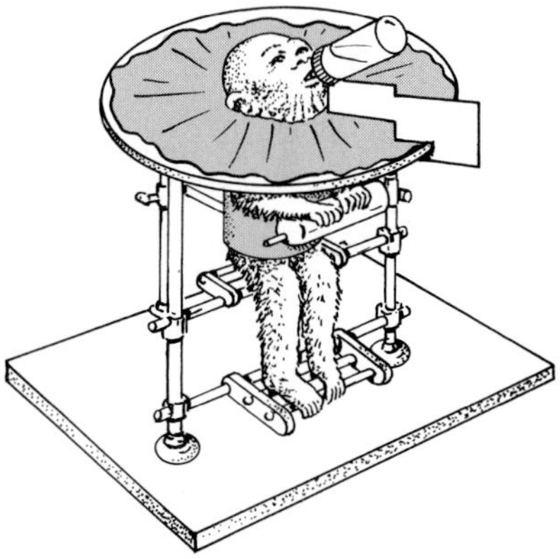

neonates of other species, are born with a fair amount of perceptual power. For one thing, every sensory system apparently is functional at or soon after birth. Studies in which careful attention has been paid to what babies look at demonstrate that they have visual perferences and must, therefore, be able to detect differences among visual stimuli. Infants as young as one week show a strong preference for complexity. They look longer at a bull's-eye, a checkerboard, and horizontal stripes than at simpler figures such as a square, circle, or triangle (Fantz, 1961). At least at a very young age infants have form perception.

Other evidence indicates that infants also have depth perception. The most interesting and important studies to make this point are those of Eleanor J. Gibson and her associates at Cornell University, using an apparatus called the visual cliff (Gibson and Walk, 1960). In these experiments the infant is placed on a ledge spanning the middle of a heavy plate glass table top. On one side of the slightly raised ledge, checkerboard-patterned material extends flush with the undersurface of the glass. This side of the table appears to be solid. Below the glass on the other side there is a dropoff of a few feet; the side of the cliff and the floor below are covered with the checkerboard material. In an experiment with human babies ages six to fourteen months, only three of thirty-six infants could be coaxed to the "deep" side of the cliff by their mothers' calls and offerings of toys. Apparently, the perception of depth is present at least by the time the baby begins to crawl. We suspect that depth perception is present at birth or soon thereafter. Day-old chickens, goats, and lambs can stand, and they perceive and avoid the visual cliff. Other animals have been tested as early as they can stand or walk, and they too shy away from the cliff. The cue responsible for depth perception in infants is now assumed to be motion parallax, available to them when they move their heads. An obvious alternative explanation, retinal disparity, was rejected after a ten-and-a-half-month-old infant who had a cancerous eye removed behaved on the visual cliff like a normally sighted child (Walk and Dodge, 1962).

There is a final important point to make, which can be introduced as a question. If form perception and depth perception are present at birth or very soon after, why do the patients whose sight has been restored not have these abilities? The answer almost certainly is that there is a **critical period** during which such perceptions must be used. Otherwise they are lost.

The visual cliff. The child avoids the "deep" side, revealing depth perception.

SUMMARY □

Studies conducted in laboratories allowing close control provide very direct evidence that perception can be affected by learning. Newly sighted people have the most accurate perceptions of objects that they have previously learned to know through touch. Stratton's tribulations with a vision-distorting lens also suggest that experience is essential in adjusting perceptual processes. Moreover, kittens do *not* develop important visual reactions—they will not blink at approaching objects, extend a paw when lowered to a table, or avoid the visual cliff—if they have not had a chance to develop visual-motor coordination. Finally, monkeys need to be able to watch and practice reaching and grasping if these movements are to become accurate. Movement and observation of it is essential to the development and application of perceptual processes.

Other evidence supports the notion that some competencies are inborn. The sensory systems of the infant function at birth or soon after. Moreover, complex perceptual capacities such as form and depth perception are present very early.

TO BE SURE YOU HAVE MASTERED THIS CHAPTER △

The following concepts are the important ones introduced in this chapter. You should be able to define them and state the points made about each in text discussion.

Distal stimulus
Proximal stimulus
Perception
Ganzfeld
Structuralsim
Gestalt psychology
Figure-ground relationship
Adaptation level
Primary cues to distance
Accommodation
Convergence
Retinal disparity
Secondary cues to distance
Linear perspective
Aerial perspective
Relative size
Interposition
Gradient of texture
Auditory localization
Patterns of light and shade
Phi phenomenon
Motion parallax
Size constancy
Shape constancy
Brightness constancy
Illusion
Moon illusion
Unconscious inference
Müller-Lyer illusion
Nature-nurture issue
Nativism-empiricism issue
Critical period

TO GO BEYOND THIS CHAPTER △

In this book A review of Chapter 3 at this time would be appropriate. The nature-nurture issue comes up again in various contexts. Chapter 9 covers behavior genetics and develops the topic very fully. The discussion continues in Chapter 10, on the nature of intelligence. The question of the innateness of motives is examined in Chapter 15. Chapter 18 deals with the heritability of mental disorder.

Elsewhere The references given for Chapter 3 are all appropriate for this chapter as well.

CH. 5

States of Consciousness

When, about a century ago, psychology first took the form of a separate discipline, independent of philosophy, its stated purpose was to discover the structure of the mind. The goal of this **structural psychology** (page 75) was to analyze consciousness into its elements and then to discover the laws by which they combine to create the contents of a mental experience. The structuralists believed that the elements making up the structure of the mind and its contents were the attributes of sensation, what E. G. Boring (1933) would later call the physical dimensions of consciousness. The method chosen to discover these elements was **introspection;** trained observers examined the personal subjective experiences brought about by specific stimuli and reported on the properties of each. The aspects of sensory experience reported by the introspectionists were first the quality of the sensation—red, sour, pressure, and so on—then the intensity, extent, duration, and clarity of the experience. In addition to these properties, other, less physical dimensions were reported, such as feelings of pleasure and displeasure, tension and relaxation, and excitement and depression.

If there was a problem with this approach, it seemed to be that the number of elements might be unmanageably large. As research progressed, it was estimated that the number of experiential elements was some 33,000 for vision alone and 12,000 for audition. Presumably similar numbers of elements for the other senses would be discovered. In spite of this problem, structuralism was the reigning theoretical position in the new discipline at the turn of this century and for a short time thereafter, lasting longer in Europe than it did in America.

The Fall of Consciousness What finally led to the fall of consciousness were related objections to the introspective method and the concept of consciousness. The introspectionist reports on experiences that are entirely private. How can a method so subjective and so personal be expected to come forth with general knowledge of experience? It is impossible to verify and compare different people's subjective observations, and public knowledge is the essence of science. Moreover, it is difficult to see how the structuralists could ever have accounted for the mental experiences of animals, children, the mentally retarded, and the mentally disturbed; for them introspective reporting would be either impossible or, if accomplished, untrustworthy. The objection to the concept of consciousness was that it is subjective, just as the introspective method is. All the data concerning consciousness are evident only to the persons experiencing it. How can there be a *science* of personal experience?

The final blow to consciousness was delivered by John B. Watson. In 1913 Watson published the behaviorist manifesto, "Psychology as a Behaviorist Views It," proposing a psychology of stimuli and responses to replace the one of consciousness.

John Broadus Watson (1878-1958). Often called the father of behaviorism, Watson rejected all mentalistic concepts, including that of consciousness.

> I believe that we can write a psychology and never use the terms consciousness, mental states, mind . . . imagery and the like. It can be done in terms of stimulus and response, in terms of habit formation, habit integration and the like. Furthermore, I believe that it is really worthwhile to make this attempt now.

Psychologists did make the attempt. Under the new banner of **behaviorism,** they turned to a militant **stimulus-response (S-R)** psychology. Learning and habit formation became the most important subject matter for the field. Pavlov's work on conditioned reflexes was taken as a model for research and theorizing. Concepts as foreign to S-R theory as consciousness were discarded. Only a few said that behaviorism had thrown out the baby with the bath water.

The Recovery of Consciousness Today the concept of consciousness is again respectable, for several reasons. In their experiments psychologists found that subjects pay attention, use images when attaining concepts, entertain hypotheses, make decisions, and the like. All these processes go on in the course of experiments on habit formation and habit integration. Thus to carry out the program that Watson had recommended, they found it necessary to bring back the very concepts the program had intended to eliminate.

A number of other circumstances have helped psychology regain consciousness. Psychoanalysis had never abandoned the concept. Indeed, the analysts enlarged upon it, proposing that there are three levels of consciousness: the **unconscious,** the repository for repressed thoughts; the **preconscious,** which contains memories and information that we are not aware of at the moment but can summon when needed; and the **conscious,** which contains thoughts of which we are fully aware. Through the years much of the attention of psychoanalysts had been directed at what they consider to lie buried below the level of awareness. To study the unconscious is, of course to touch upon consciousness through its opposite state.

The importance of the concept of consciousness was also urged upon psychology by interesting observations of what are now called altered states of consciousness. During the 1950s and 1960s, people who had taken psychedelic drugs reported having what they called "mind-expanding" experiences. Advances in neurophysiology suggested new ways of studying sleep and the sort of consciousness we have when dreaming. When the corpus callosum of epileptic patients was cut, split consciousness could be investigated (page 44). Such physiological processes as heart rate, once believed beyond conscious control, yielded somewhat to voluntary actions reinforced by biofeedback. Finally, through the persuasiveness of Abraham Maslow, Carl Rogers, Gordon Allport, and others, humanistic psychology has become a major contemporary movement. These men urged psychologists to reassert the importance of human experience. Each individual, according to them, is quite unique and worthy and can control the life course through the conscious exertion of free will. What individuals are conscious of may be more important than their physiology and their environment in realizing human potential. These conceptions stand in sharp contrast to the mechanistic views of traditional behaviorists.

THE NATURE OF CONSCIOUSNESS

Definitions of Consciousness

As the title of this chapter suggests, it is not possible to define consciousness as any single aspect or process of the mind. Moreover, to different psychologists it means or has meant different things. As a condition of the mind, consciousness is being awake, aware, alert, attentive. When it means contents of the mind, consciousness pertains to what can be described in words. In this sense we are conscious of a state of happiness, of our perceptions of our surroundings, and of fleeting memories and images, but not of the physiology underlying them. At the level of behavior, consciousness refers to voluntary acts as opposed to automatic. An individual is conscious of selecting the clothes to wear on a given day but often not of the act of dressing, conscious of ordering a steak medium rare but not of the movements made in eating it. At a more philosophical level, consciousness is mental substance. It is the "mind stuff" that thoughts and dreams are made of.

Altered States of Consciousness

As dreams and periods of heightened mindfulness tell us, consciousness varies in an individual from time to time. It also varies from person to person. These variations have come to be called **altered states of consciousness.** These altered states give us insights into normal consciousness and have been studied for this reason and because any departure from ordinary awareness is intrinsically interesting. Drugs, the major agents for altering consciousness, will be discussed at the end of this chapter. Two others are mental disorders and meditation.

The Altered Consciousness of the Schizophrenic

The consciousness of a mental patient can differ from ordinary consciousness in a number of ways. A psychiatric nurse's description of her descent into a schizophrenic breakdown provides a vivid account of the content of her consciousness in the course of this psychosis (MacDonald, 1960).

> What I do want to explain, if I can, is the exaggerated state of awareness in which I lived before, during, and after my acute illness. At first it was as if parts of my brain "awoke" which had been dormant, and I became interested in a wide assortment of people, events, places, and ideas which normally would make no impression on me. Not knowing that I was ill, I made no attempt to understand what was happening, but felt that there was some overwhelming significance in all of this, produced either by God or Satan, and I felt that I was duty-bound to ponder on each of these new interests, and the more I pondered the worse it became. The walk of a stranger on the street could be a "sign" to me which I must interpret. Every face in the windows of a passing street car would be engraved on my mind, all of them concentrating on me and trying to pass some sort of message. Now many years later, I can appreciate what had happened. Each of us is capable of coping with a large number of stimuli, invading our being through any one of the senses. We could hear every sound within earshot and see every object, line, and colour within the field of vision, and

so on. It's obvious that we would be incapable of carrying on any of our daily activities if even one-hundredth of all these available stimuli invaded us at once. So the mind must have a filter which functions without our conscious thought, sorting stimuli and allowing only those which are relevant to the situation in hand to disturb consciousness. And this filter must be working at maximum efficiency at all times, particularly when we require a high degree of concentration. What had happened to me in Toronto was a breakdown in the filter, and a hodge-podge of unrelated stimuli were distracting me from things which should have had my undivided attention (p. 218).

Multiple Personality: Divided Consciousness A rare type of mental disturbance called multiple personality, in which a person takes on two or more distinct and separate personalities, reflects a dramatic division of consciousness. Each personality is independent of the other, and yet each is a relatively stable one with its own thoughts and feelings. One of the personalities is usually dominant over the others. The co-selves are generally quite aware of the behavior of the dominant self, but the dominant personality may remain unaware of the activities of its lesser partners.

One case of multiple personality became evident when a twenty-seven-year-old black man, Jonah—was admitted to a university psychiatric hospital after prolonged complaints of severe headaches. These headaches lasted for varying periods of time, and during them Jonah was unable to "remember things." Three weeks before his hospital admission, the patient had attacked his wife with a butcher knife, chasing her and his three-year-old daughter out of the home. Although the patient could not recall these events, his wife reported that during such episodes of violence, the patient referred to himself as Usoffa Abdulla, son of Omega. The patient's history contained many such acts of violence. While a soldier in Vietnam, he had suffered a lapse and fired his gun wildly in all directions until he was subdued. These and other episodes had led to his honorable discharge for medical reasons.

The ward physician in the university hospital noticed that each of the patient's lapses of memory was accompanied by a marked personality change. To the psychiatrist's surprise, one of four separate and distinct personalities would appear, each bearing a different name.

Jonah, the "square," was the primary personality, a shy, sensitive, conventional, fearful individual who appeared confused and whose emotional responses were shallow.

Sammy, the "lawyer," claimed to be aware of the other personalities but knew Jonah best. He was the rationalist, intellectual, legalistic, and capable always of talking his way out of trouble. This personality had emerged when Jonah was six years old, after Jonah's mother and stepfather had fought violently and she had stabbed her husband. When the family was finally reunited, Sammy emerged, announcing to both parents that their irresponsible behavior was bad for their children and urging that they never fight in front of them again. Jonah reported that from that day onward he had never again witnessed a fight between his parents.

King Young, the "lover," claimed that he appeared whenever Jonah was unable to "make out" with women. Pleasure-oriented, King proved to be a ladies' man who was incapable of taking "no" for an answer to his demands. King had also appeared when Jonah was six or seven years old. Jonah's mother had in those years taken pleasure in dressing him in girl's clothes, which had confused him about his sexual identity. When in first grade Jonah had expressed confusion over the identities of Jerry and Alice in the stories in his school reader, King had emerged to "set Jonah straight." Ever since then, King indicated, he had looked after Jonah's sexual interests.

Usoffa Abdulla, the "warrior," was a "god" who appeared briefly whenever Jonah was unable to defend himself physically. Usoffa, cold, belligerent, and protective, first came on the scene when Jonah, then nine years old, was attacked by a gang of white children who beat him for the "sport" of it. Terrified, Jonah thought it was his end and lost consciousness. Usoffa emerged and fought so viciously that he almost killed two of his attackers. From that moment on, Usoffa exercised a protective watch over Jonah.

Through therapy the personalities of Jonah were encouraged to fuse together as a single individual, Jusky, a name made up of the first letters of all four of Jonah's names. Unfortunately, Jusky turned out to be, if anything, more disturbed than any of the earlier personalities.

Self-portraits were drawn by each of the four personalities (Figure 5.1). The psychiatric investigator (Ludwig et al., 1972) concludes that their separate functionings may have been a more effective way of handling the patient's problems. Four heads, he suggests, may be better than one.

Meditation: Pure Awareness Zen is the Japanese pronunciation of a Chinese word for *meditation.* This branch of Buddhism was introduced into Japan in the thirteenth century. The Zen masters attempt to guide students to a point of sudden enlightenment, *satori,* a state of consciousness which is the spiritual goal of Zen Buddhism. Beginners are required to spend two periods of the day sitting with their eyes closed, motionless and in intense concentration. Claudio Naranjo and Robert Ornstein, in their book *On the Psychology of Meditation* (1977), describe the first exercise, counting breaths from one to ten and

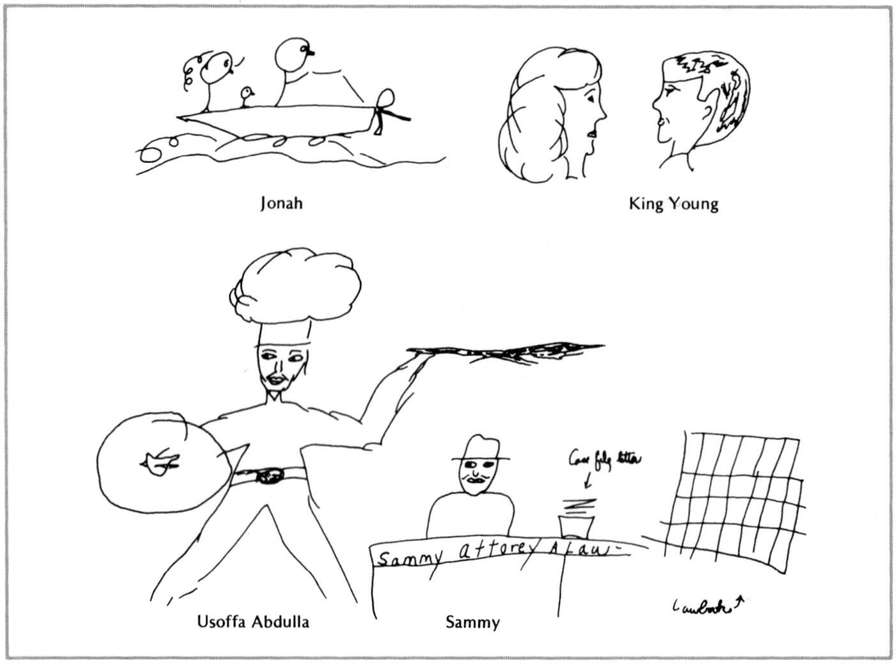

FIGURE 5.1
Self-portraits by each of Jonah's multiple personalities. (Courtesy of Professor Arnold Ludwig.)

then repeating the exercise. Beginners tend to lose count and must begin over again. Once novitiates have successfully concentrated on counting breaths, they shift their complete attention to the *process* of breathing, the progress of air into the lungs and its exhalation. The goal is to shut out from awareness everything but this process. In the words of a Zen master,

> At the beginning you will find it extremely difficult to bring your mind to concentrate on your breathing. You will be astonished how your mind runs away. It does not stay. You begin to think of various things. You hear sounds outside. Your mind is disturbed and distracted. You may be dismayed and disappointed. But if you continue to practice this exercise twice a day, morning and evening, for about five or ten minutes at a time, you will gradually . . . begin to concentrate your mind on your breathing. After a certain period you will experience just that split second when your mind is fully concentrated on your breathing, when you will not hear even sounds nearby, when no external world exists for you. This slight moment is such a tremendous experience for you, full of joy, happiness and tranquility, that you would like to continue it. But still you cannot. Yet, if you go on practicing . . . , you may repeat the experience again and again for longer periods. That is the moment, when you lose yourself completely in your mindfulness of breathing. As long as you are conscious of yourself you cannot concentrate on anything (p. 146).

This is the beginning point for the student of Zen, on the way to mastering concentrative meditation.

Meditation of course comes from the East. Its practitioners believe that we live in a world of illusion. In our desire to seek pleasure and avoid pain, our perceptions and thoughts have become distorted. All our interpretations and meanings are out of kilter, though our sensory systems are still intact and are able to put us in contact with the real world.

The aim of concentrative meditation is to shut down the usual processes of perception and thought by focusing all attention, as in beginning Zen, on the natural movements of the belly in breathing. In the popular Westernized form, transcendental meditation, the person quietly concentrates on a *mantra,* a particular, perhaps soothing, pattern of sound. Some meditators choose visual patterns, called *yantras.* Advanced Zen meditators may concentrate on a *koan,* or paradox, such as "What is the sound of one hand clapping?" The koan is meant to make meditators despair of reliance on reasoning and force them to a break in the conceptual mind and an intuitive enlightenment. When the meditator is truly concentrating, all sensations and perceptions cease, leaving clarity and emptiness. No thoughts fill this void. What remains is pure awareness without any particular content.

In the aftermath of concentrative meditation, the practitioner feels in fresh contact with the world and the self. Perception seems direct rather than through the usual selective filters.

In opening-up meditation, an advanced Zen tech-

Meditation. A class of trainees and a Zen master.

nique, the practitioner sits with eyes closed and gives full attention to whatever happens and to his or her reactions. Unpleasant thoughts and experiences are faced rather than allowing the mind to drift off into the daydreams and illusions of ordinary consciousness. The mind attains great alertness, a heightened state of awareness which is exhausting and cannot be sustained for more than half an hour. But perception is clarified immediately rather than in the aftermath of meditation.

Studies have revealed that during concentrative meditation a number of physiological processes slow down. Less oxygen is consumed, less carbon dioxide exhaled; respiration, blood pressure, and heart rates are lower. There is also a drop in the blood level of lactate, a by-product of muscle activity. Electroencephalograms of some meditators reveal a greater proportion of brain waves of the alpha rhythm, a desired pattern associated with resting wakefulness. The reduction in body metabolism is about 20 percent, greater than the reduction that is found during sleep.

SUMMARY □

In the early days of psychology, the concept of consciousness was central and was studied by the method of introspection. Although the pronouncements of the behaviorist J. B. Watson led psychology to give the concept up for decades, both personal experience and laboratory research indicate its importance. Consciousness is now once again of considerable concern to many psychologists.

Consciousness is difficult to define. The term can refer to the condition of the mind, its alertness; to its unsummoned contents, to feelings, perceptions, fleeting memories and images; to volition, and to what we call to mind, the summoned substance of thoughts and daydreams. Alterations in consciousness, brought about through mental disorders and meditation, are fascinating in themselves.

SLEEP AND DREAMS

Throughout the ages of recorded history, poets and playwrights and ordinary men and women have likened sleep to a temporary death. In the minds of our earliest ancestors, what have been called the two great biological mysteries—the appearance of the human form in dreams and visions and the enigma of life and death—probably became linked. Primitive human beings may have had their first views of a "ghost soul," an apparition separate from the body yet so like it, because they had already encountered their fellows in their dreams. From these beginnings, anthropologists have suggested, may have come the supposition that human beings have souls which survive the body and exist after death (Diamond, 1962).

As sleep has become better understood through psychological research, we have learned that any comparisions between sleep and death are inappropriate. Sleep is far too active a condition, being

> . . . punctuated with movements, talking, snoring, smiling, waking. The sleeping person makes subtle discriminations, and may slumber through a thunderstorm yet awaken to a baby's whimper . . . Sleep has generously poured out revelations

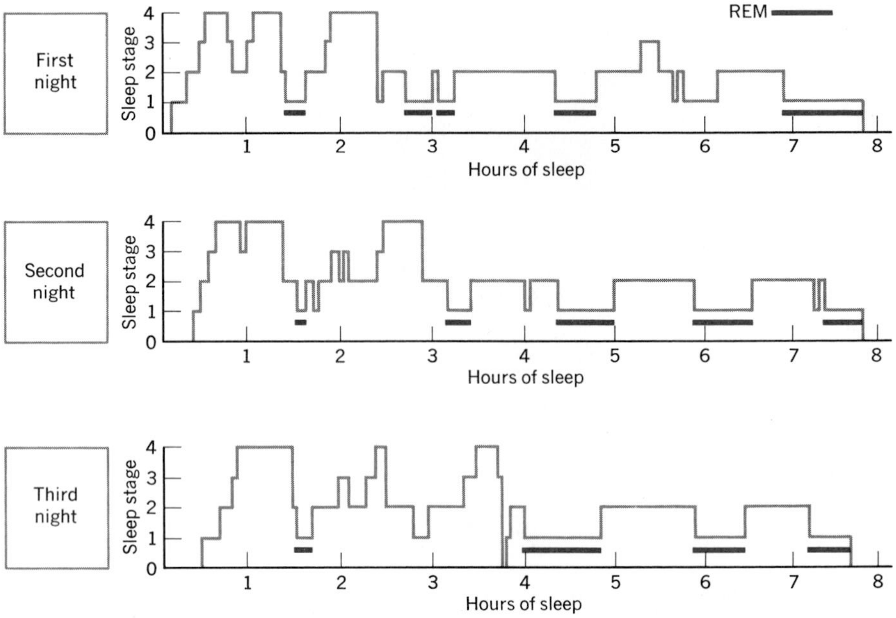

FIGURE 5.2
The course of a night's sleep. An hour-by-hour account of three nights of sleep by a single research participant indicates clearly that stage 4 sleep happens early in the night and drops out as it proceeds. Stage REM, by comparison, is relatively infrequent early in the sleep cycle but more frequent as the hours of sleep lengthen. (Adapted from Webb and Agnew, 1968.)

> about man's waking nature, his mysterious capacities, his nightly edge of madness and remarkable daytime talents (Luce and Segal, 1966, pp. 16-17).

Biological Clocks and Patterns of Sleep

Although the amount of time individuals sleep and when they do so varies extensively, the sleep-waking cycle is roughly regular and tied to the twenty-four-hour light-darkness cycle of the world in which we live. The world over people generally sleep five to eight hours of every twenty-four, and they usually choose to do so at night. The sleep-waking cycle is therefore said to have a **circadian rhythm** (*circa,* about; *diem,* day). Activities tied to wakefulness—attentiveness, eating, and energy of movements—and basic physiological measurements—pulse rate, body temperature, and blood pressure—have similar rhythms, increasing and diminishing with twenty-four-hour periodicities. The regulation of these rhythms is believed to be by the pineal gland (page 40). For a long time this function of the gland was unknown, but research on fish and amphibians provided a clue to its role. Apparently in these classes the pineal gland serves as a light-sensitive "third eye." As night falls, the reduction of illumination triggers the gland to release a hormone which darkens the animal's skin, thus matching its color to diminished light intensity and providing an effective camouflage. In human beings the gland may store up and then release chemicals which in turn control the activity rhythms of bodily systems. Information about the lightness and darkness of the outside world is probably provided by the visual system.

Dreaming

Rapid Eye Movements Within the sleep period are shorter regular cycles, which were discovered by Nathaniel Kleitman working in collaboration with a graduate student, Eugene Aserinsky (Aserinsky and Kleitman, 1953; Kleitman, 1963). In the course of their research on patterns of sleep in infants, they noticed an interesting phenomenon. Sometimes eye movements from side to side could be seen beneath the infants' thin lids. These periods were followed by some thrashing of the body and limbs. Subsequently on the two men observed the same recurrent pattern of intermittent **rapid eye movements (REMs)** in adults. Aserinsky, suspecting that these REMs were connected with dreaming, awakened sleepers during REM and non-REM periods and asked whether they had been dreaming. Dreams were reported by about 80 percent of the sleepers awakened during REM periods, rarely by the other sleepers, tying dreaming quite firmly to periods of rapid eye movements.

In young adults REM states occur several times a night at approximately ninety-minute intervals and last an average of twenty to thirty-five minutes (Figure 5.2). By awakening participants in sleep experiments at different points within these REM periods, inves-

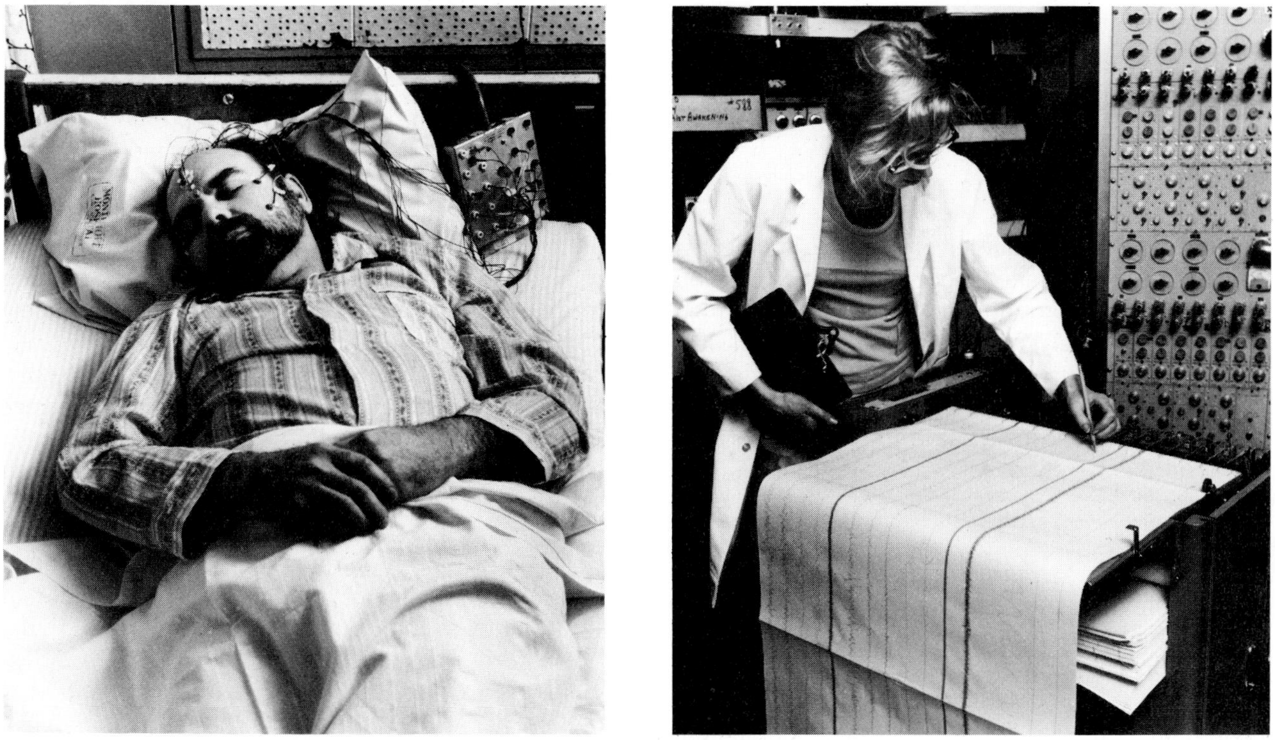

A sleep laboratory. A sleeper with electrodes for recording EEG and eye movements in place. The experimenter monitors the record produced on moving chart paper.

tigators have demonstrated that people dream throughout them. This fact argues against the common idea that dreams last only a few seconds. It also suggests that all people dream, since all people have rapid eye movements, including those who cannot recall their dreams upon awakening.

Psychoanalysis and the Content of Dreams As the opening sentence of his greatest work, *The Interpretation of Dreams* (1900), Sigmund Freud wrote "In the pages that follow I shall bring forward proof that there is a psychological technique which makes it possible to interpret dreams. . . ." Freud's psychological technique consisted of instructing the patient to make free associations to the **manifest content** of an actual dream. Then together the patient and psychoanalyst would examine these associations. Freud believed that the associations would lead back to the **latent content** of the dream, the thoughts for which the dream itself was a substitute. Focusing on the less guarded dreams of children, Freud concluded that the dream represents a conflict between a wish denied in reality and the desire not to be disturbed by its intrusion into consciousness. The purpose of a dream was to allow the individual to remain asleep. Freud believed that in adults free associations to the manifest content of the dream would usually reveal that the latent content was sexual.

We now have a certain amount of information on the manifest content of dreams. Sleep researchers have approached the problem as researchers typically do. They have collected dream logs of large numbers of people and tabulated the contents of the dreams. The reports of 1650 dreams by college students (Hall and Van de Castle, 1966; Snyder, 1970) have contributed the following interesting facts.

- Most dreams are brief and commonplace; only infrequently are they "exotic" and only rarely are they "fantastic."
- The dreamer has company in 95 percent of his or her dreams, usually one person, less frequently several. On more than half of these dream occasions, the other people are known to the dreamer.
- Animals may appear but "monsters" of frightening dimensions almost never.
- Only rarely do movie stars, sports figures, and political figures populate a dream.
- In one-third of all dreams the level of activity is not strenuous and is even passive.
- Dreams have bad news, misfortune, and failure as their themes more often (46 percent) than they have success (17 percent).
- Aggressive encounters (47 percent) marginally outweigh friendly ones (38 percent).
- As for sex and erotic content, Snyder's subjects reported it in only 6 of 620 dreams, the Hall–Van de Castle study in only 76 of 1000. If the latent content of dreams is sexual, this content is *very* latent.

- Emotionally, most dreams are bland even when outrage is expressed. The emotions felt in dreams are more likely to be fear and anxiety rather than anger.

Summing up, Wilse Webb (1975) states: "Dreams do have strange qualities. However, when their components are placed under the microscope of objective analysis, the particular elements of the dream turn out to be remarkably prosaic" (p. 143). To this comment we might add that adults rarely sleepwalk or sleep talk or have nightmares and night terrors, whatever the general impression of their frequency is. These phenomena are most common to the sleep of children and are usually outgrown by adolescence.

Stages of Sleep

The dreaming stage is part of a larger cycle consisting of four other **stages of sleep** (Figure 5.3). The cycle begins with *stage 0,* a pleasant state of relaxed wakefulness. The electroencephalogram shows the alpha rhythm, large regular changes in voltage dominating the pattern of brain waves. The alpha rhythm is present when a person's eyes are closed and the mind is not thinking or attending to things. If an individual falling off to sleep begins to think of a problem, the alpha rhythm will disappear and the EEG pattern will look like that of stage 1.

As *stage 1* begins, the muscles relax, the pulse slows, and the individual feels drowsy. As the sleeper begins to fall off, the alpha rhythm becomes intermittent, gradually disappears, and is replaced by a pattern of small, rapid changes in voltage. Electrodes placed near the eyes record slow rolling movements of the eyes.

Within a few minutes *stage 2* of sleep is underway. Voltage shifts grow slower and larger, but they are interrupted by sleep spindles, bursts of rapid synchronized fluctuations evident as short runs of sharply pointed waves. Most investigators take the appearance of the first spindle of the night as an indication of the onset of true sleep. If awakened during stage 1, the sleeper may deny sleeping and may suggest that he or she was merely drifting off. But if aroused after the appearance of the first spindle, the sleeper usually confirms having been asleep.

Now the descent into deep sleep, *stage 3,* begins, and attempts to awaken the sleeper grow more difficult. Within thirty minutes delta waves have appeared. These are slow waves of great amplitude. There are still sleep spindles, however. If less than half the waves are delta, the sleep is classified as stage 3. If more than half are delta, sleep is considered stage 4. During each of these stages the muscles of the sleeper are relaxed, breathing is even, and the temperature, blood pressure, and heart rate drop. In stage 4 the delta waves are very large and steady and synchronous, with slow rises and deep falls, sometimes only one wave per second. In the rich prose of an earlier volume, "They have the profile of mountain ranges, and they signify the silent darkness of the ultimate depths" (Luce and Segal, 1966).

During the first stage 4 sleep of the night, before there have been any rapid eye movements, children may have their nightmares and night terrors. Children rouse screaming from a night terror and are intensely afraid, agitated, and inconsolable for twenty minutes, but they are not really awake, and they have forgotten the incident by morning. This first episode of *stage 4* sleep may last thirty to thirty-four minutes. It usually terminates with an abrupt body movement, which sleep researchers recognize as a sign of momentary arousal and a precursor to the renewal of stage 2 sleep. The sleeper does not reenter stage 3. About an hour to ninety minutes after falling asleep, the brain waves start to take on the pattern of stage 1, the spindles of stage 2 disappear, and rapid eye movements begin. The sleeper dreams and stage REM is underway. At this point a number of physiological changes belie the apparent flaccid state of the musculature of the body; heart rate and blood pressure become irregular; pulse and respiration increase as they would in wakeful tension or fright.

The first REM period of the night lasts five to ten minutes. After the next ninety minutes, there is a second, somewhat longer REM period. As the night wears on, deep stage 3 and 4 sleep almost disappears, but the sleeper spends more time dreaming. The last dream of the night may be from half an hour to an hour long.

Disturbances of Sleep

Dream Deprivation What happens when a person is partially deprived of the opportunity to experience a given sleep stage? In 1960 William Dement reported fascinating findings about the effects of REM deprivation. By awakening research participants whenever eye movements and EEG patterns signaled the beginning of sleep, Dement was able to reduce by about 80 percent the amount of time individuals spent dreaming. If a person appeared already to be dreaming, he or she was allowed to sleep through the dream and awakened after its completion. After five successive nights of such awakenings, each person was allowed a "recovery" night of uninterrupted sleep. In order to be certain that any noticed effects could be attributed to REM deprivation and not simply to disturbed sleep, the same persons had been awakened during non-REM periods in an earlier succession of five nights.

During the night of interrupted sleep following the control sessions—when the sleeper had been awakened during non-REM periods—the average amount of time devoted to dreaming did not exceed the predeprivation average. During the five nights of REM deprivation, however, the results were very different. As the experiment proceeded, it became necessary to awaken the eight participants more and more frequently in order to suppress their REM sleep. On the first night the average number of awakenings for the group was 10.9; on the final night it was necessary to arouse the participants an average of 21.7 times. Furthermore, during the succeeding recovery night of uninterrupted sleep, the participants averaged 27.3 percent of the night in dreams, compared to a predeprivation average of only 19.4 percent. That night only one of the eight participants failed to show a sharp increase in the amount of time spent in REM sleep. This **rebound effect,** as it has been called, has also been demonstrated in animal sleep studies.

Dement's initial observations suggested that after REM deprivation not only did participants spend more time dreaming but their waking consciousness was profoundly altered. Some individuals suffered a variety of agitations—hallucinations, disturbances in motor coordination, heightened tension and anxiety, memory disturbances, increased irritability and hostility, and distortions of the time sense (Fisher, 1965). Dement reported that when the deprivation period was extended to fifteen or sixteen nights, behavior became psychotic. But this dramatic report, while true, was confounded by two important factors. First, amphetamines were used as part of the deprivation procedure. Second, one of the research participants was reported to have indicated a schizoid personality pattern prior to the sleep study (Webb, 1969). Subsequent studies under more rigorous test conditions have failed to confirm pervasive personality changes.

FIGURE 5.3
Brain wave patterns in different sleep stages. The EEG patterns for waking and sleep stages and the plottings for ordinary eye movements (EM) and rapid eye movements differ markedly. (Adapted from Webb and Agnew, 1968.)

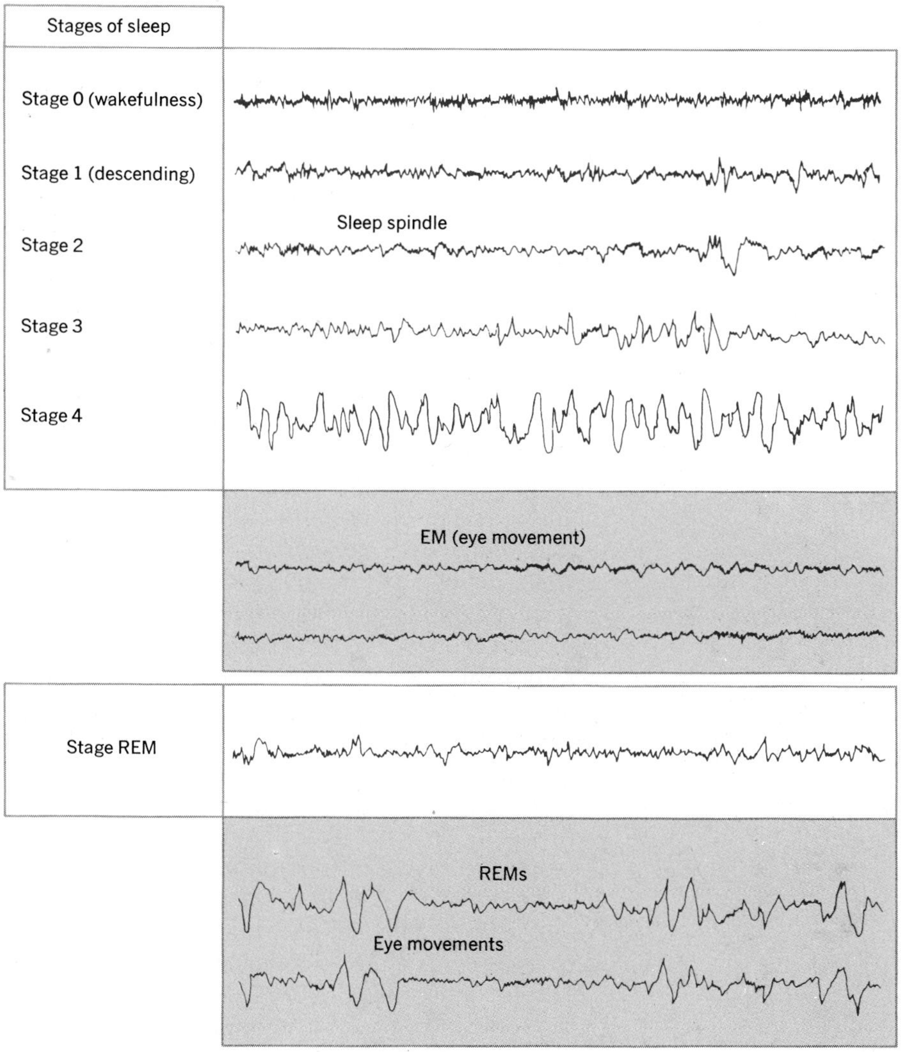

Sleep Disorders Two primary sleep disturbances that sometimes afflict people are narcolepsy, an uncontrollable and disabling tendency to fall asleep, often many times a day; and sleep apnea, an inability to breath while asleep.

Narcolepsy attacks are both dramatic and inopportune. A person who is completely awake, although usually a bit bored or agitated or even at the point of laughter, suddenly falls asleep and may stay asleep for as long as fifteen or twenty minutes. Often accompanying the attack is muscular weakness. In its extreme form the individual collapses in a heap before falling asleep and is unable to move on awakening. The onsets of half these sleep episodes are marked by unusual visual and auditory sensations, called hypnogogic hallucinations. Usually narcolepsy attacks younger people between the ages of fifteen and twenty-five and only rarely after age forty. Research suggests that the narcoleptic goes immediately into REM sleep, and that the hallucinatory experiences are made up of the same stuff as the vivid dreams of REM sleep (Dement, 1974). Narcolepsy is believed to be caused by an inherited abnormality of the brain's REM sleep system. Stimulants can help narcoleptics stay awake.

Sleep apnea is a very curious condition in which the patient can only breathe while awake! Dement (1974) reports the case of a man who had for thirty years had been tortured by insomnia and was eventually brought to the sleep laboratory.

> We could not contain our astonishment when we found that the patient breathed *only when he was awake*. Watching the chart paper unfold, we stared open-mouthed as the patient fell asleep and stopped breathing for nearly 100 seconds. Then, huge scribbles were inked on the respiration chart as he awoke to take gasping breaths into his air starved lungs. This patient was unable to breathe and sleep at the same time. He had to wake up hundreds of times in order to get enough oxygen to survive the night (p. 74).

Disturbances of breathing during sleep may have a higher incidence than was earlier believed to be the case. A recent study of thirty men and nineteen women, all of normal health, found that during sleep men often breathe irregularly and sometimes stop breathing for several seconds at a time (Block et al., 1979). Such a reduction in oxygen intake can make the heart beat irregularly and bring on nighttime heart attacks. This finding backs up earlier reports that a number of deaths from heart attacks occur at 6 A.M., the peak of REM sleep and of oxygen desaturation. Twenty of the men had 264 episodes of abnormal breathing or low oxygen levels, and three of the women had a total of nine similar episodes. Apnea—defined here as not breathing for ten seconds or longer—was evident in twelve of these men and all three of the women. Older and fatter men appear to be at greater risk.

SUMMARY □

Sleep researchers have dispelled some of sleep's mysteries. The sleep cycle has a definite circadian rhythm, whatever the more particular preferences of individual sleepers. Moreover, the contents of dreams emerge as prosaic and bland when dreams are studied in large numbers. Major studies of sleep have delineated a five-stage cycle, each stage with its own brain wave pattern. Research has focused extensively on stage REM, in which rapid eye movements indicate the onset of dreaming. REM sleep apparently serves a significant adaptive function. When denied the opportunity for REM sleep, individuals will on the succeeding night spend more of their sleeping time in this stage. Medical sleep researchers have turned their attention to two primary disorders of sleep, narcolepsy, an uncontrollable tendency to fall asleep many times a day, and sleep apnea, the inability to breathe when asleep. These disorders are slowly yielding up their secrets of prevalence and etiology and of how to treat them.

HYPNOSIS

Hypnosis was once likened to a "sleeping trance," for the stuporous hypnotic state resembles the sleeper's unresponsiveness during deep slumber. The likeness is only apparent, however. At the neurophysiological level sleep is marked by changes in the brain wave pattern and by a lessening of heart rate, muscle tone, pulse rate, and motility. By contrast, when an individual is in a deep hypnotic state, the EEG pattern is dominated by the alpha rhythm, a rhythm of the waking state, and heart rate, blood pressure, and motility remain relatively the same.

These differences extend to the psychological level as well. In a hypnotic state learning can occur. Little evidence supports the supposition that learning can take place at deeper levels of sleep. Russian investigators, for example, have worked assiduously to demonstrate such a phenomenon by playing a tape of paired Russian-English words to sleepers throughout the night. If any learning occurred, it was apparently accomplished by highly motivated individuals who were merely drowsy rather than truly asleep.

People who have been hypnotized recognize that their experience differs from sleep. One student told Professor Ernest Hilgard, "My body felt a little as if it were asleep, but my mind remained unusually alert." Moreover, under hypnosis the individual assumes assigned roles and engages in complex activities related to these roles. This cannot be done by the sleeper. The hypnotized person becomes highly suggestible, reacting in ways suggested by the hypnotist. About all the sleeper ever does is to awaken at the command of the researcher, which has nothing at all to do with increased suggestibility.

The Images of Hypnosis

The layman's image of hypnosis contains a large dramatic component. The authoritarian hypnotist, powerful and dominating, with penetrating gaze and extended hand, manipulates the will of another person and commands his or her passive obedience. But the hypnotist has another, more positive image, as a therapist in a close helping relationship with a patient. For more than a century hypnosis has been a therapeutic technique. It may be helpful to pause for a moment to examine the early history of hypnosis.

The Authoritarian Image: Mesmer and Magnetism When Franz Anton Mesmer (1734–1815) graduated from the Medical Faculty of Vienna in 1765, his dissertation carried the imposing title, "The Influence of Planets on the Human Body." The dissertation, a large part of which we are sad to say was pirated, committed Mesmer to his life work and eventually brought a new word to the vocabulary of a number of languages. The English verb *mesmerize* means to spellbind, fascinate, to compel by fascination. Then in 1843 the word hypnotism was coined by Dr. James Braid. Mesmer believed there to be a tie between the gravitational forces of the planets and the health and general condition of the human body. Just as there are tides in the sea, Mesmer asserted, so too are there tides in the atmosphere. Air moves upward twice during the twenty-four-hour cycle and thereby exercises an influence on small particles of fluids and solids in the body. Mesmer later called this influence animal magnetism.

In 1774 Mesmer, using magnets provided by a Jesuit astronomer with the unlikely name of Maximilian Hell, successfully treated a young woman who had numerous hysterical complaints (see page 427). Her symptoms waxed and waned; Mesmer blamed the "flux and reflux" of the animal magnetism in her body. Passing the magnets borrowed from Hell over her body and feet appeared to free the young woman of this flux. The patient reported feeling surging sensations, which Mesmer believed confirmed the movement and redistribution of the "subtle fluids" within her body.

As one historian has noted, had Mesmer been at all scientifically minded and used a wooden magnet as an appropriate control treatment, he would have witnessed the same effect and might not have become so blind to the psychological components of his treatment (Pattie, 1967). At a later point, when objects to which magnets had been applied, such as teacups and people, appeared to help his patients, Mesmer suggested that "magnetic material" could be transferred from one subject to another. Father Hell, more of a scientist, suggested that a better test of the theory would be to magnetize some objects and not others in the absence of the patient and then to test the patient's response to each object. But Mesmer, convinced of his theory, would have none of it.

Franz Anton Mesmer believed that the stars emanate a magnetism affecting human lives.

A year later Mesmer gave up Hell's magnets because he found he could induce the same effects by stroking or passing his hands over his patient's body. He sought to convince the medical faculty of Vienna of the usefulness of his technique, but they proved to be nonbelievers. In 1778, when Mesmer was forced to leave Austria, he chose Paris and the more liberal atmosphere of Louis XVI's court. There Mesmer decorated his salon in the height of fashion, chose his male assistants for their physical attractiveness, and cloaked himself in magnificent trappings. Soon he had his patients sitting around a *baquet,* a large covered wooden tub filled with bottles floating in magnetized water, in an eighteenth-century version of an encounter group. Mesmer circled about the group, touching each individual in turn with a magnetized wand and inducing trances and convulsions with his touch.

All this was scarcely designed to gain the approval of the medical fraternity. Members of the French Academy who tested the method on themselves felt little at the touch of Mesmer's magic wand and concluded that "magnetism minus imagination" is nothing. A commission of distinguished men, including the American ambassador Benjamin Franklin; Antoine Lavoisier, the discoverer of oxygen; Joseph Guillotin, inventor of the cutting tool that bore his name; and Jean Bailly, the astronomer, investigated and wrote a report for the French Academy of Science. They concluded that "man can affect man. . . almost at will by stimulating his imagination" but disparaged the concept of animal magnetism. The seductive aspects of the treatment when applied to women were attacked, and Mesmer was again forced to abandon a flourishing practice.

The Healing Image Through Mesmer hypnotism acquired an aura of quackery, which has remained with it to some extent. The British physician James Braid helped establish a more positive reputation for hypnosis. After witnessing a seance, Braid concluded that the hypnotic trance was induced not by the imagination but by physiological effects. He became a practitioner and first called the process neuro-hypnotism. Braid denied that he and other hypnotists had any special powers but admitted that he had no adequate explanation for the phenomenon. Braid wrote careful observational accounts emphasizing the docility and attentiveness of his patients. Although Braid's work brought a needed dignity to the study of hypnosis, its legitimacy as a medical technique was not established until the early 1880s, after Jean Charcot, the most famous neurologist in France, had found a likeness between the hypnotic trance and hysteria and used hypnotism to study the state of the nervous system in hysterical patients. When Sigmund Freud went to Paris on a fellowship to study with Charcot, Freud learned hypnotism from him. Later the use of hypnosis to treat hysteria became one of the bases for Freud's classical collaborative work with Josef Breuer, *Studies in Hysteria* (see page 388).

The Scientific Study of Hypnosis

A growing interest in altered states of consciousness has encouraged scientists to study hypnotic states and to raise a number of critical questions. Are some people more susceptible to hypnotic induction than others? What are the personality traits of susceptible individuals? What theories best explain the susceptibility?

Hypnotic Susceptibility If you have ever watched a hypnotist-entertainer at work, you know that he calls for volunteers from the audience and quickly engages in some brief tests of "susceptibility." He retains on stage those he believes he can put into a trance and sends the rest back to their seats. For the scientific study of hypnosis, a more valid and reliable test of these individual differences is needed. The Laboratory of Hypnosis Research at Stanford University, headed by Dr. Ernest R. Hilgard, has conducted careful investigations of hypnotizable people. Dr. Hilgard and his collaborator, Dr. Andre M. Weitzenhoffer, spent eight years developing and refining several forms of the Stanford Hypnotic Susceptibility Scales, which identify people susceptible to hypnosis. Some representative items from Form C of the scale, together with a brief description of the procedure for administering and scoring them, appear in Table 5.1.

Correlates of Susceptibility With a scale for measuring hypnotic susceptibility on hand, people of high, moderate, and low susceptibility could be brought to the laboratory and administered other tests in order to discover their personal characteristics. The results (Hilgard, 1965) have served to destroy a number of stereotypes. For example, the history of hypnosis and its imagined ties to hysteria have long suggested that women were more hypnotizable than men, but they are not. It was also believed that mentally deficient people, because they lack verbal skills and are unable to concentrate, could not be hypnotized. They can be. Finally, neurotics were believed highly susceptible to hypnosis, but the susceptiblity scores for a neurotic group are similar to those for normal people.

Dr. Josephine Hilgard, a co-partner in marriage as well as research with Professor Hilgard, is a psychiatrist with psychoanalytic training. She carried out extensive clinical interviews with the persons who participated in the research studies on hypnotism. Her clinical sensitivity and experimental sophistication provided her with the insight to recognize a very interesting pattern in the highly susceptible individuals. Since childhood they had had "imaginative involvements." The depth of their sensory experiences and their appreciation for reading and drama allowed them to identify strongly with characters in novels and plays. Moreover, their fantasy lives, active in childhood, had continued to be so. Here are two of their statements (Hilgard, 1970).

> A male student's reaction on reading Orwell's *1984:* "I identify myself with the character in 1984, with Winston Smith, who was tortured at the end, fearing rats. His head was in a cage and he felt he would have to submit. I felt the fear that he felt as it came closer, closer. Walking

back from the Union after finishing the book, I had a problem relating myself to my present environment, to the stuff around me, for I was so entangled in the story that I had become exhausted" (p. 26).

A women student's reaction on reading Golding's *Lord of the Flies:* "Toward the end when Ralph was being chased by the rest of the boys and they met a naval officer, [I] was suddenly aware that [I] had been the height of the young boy, that [I] had been running with the boys, and that all of a sudden, when the young naval officer appeared, I felt I grew a couple of feet" (p. 28).

These readers are highly receptive to the author's effort to depict mood and circumstances. They "experience" in a way that may be similar to Abraham Maslow's account of the "peak experience." Events move them; their imagery is vivid and has, in Hilgard's words, an almost "hallucinatory quality." These people are not lost in unreality, however. When the real world impinges, they are aware of its demands. People easily hypnotized are very different from the weak and compliant individuals of the stereotype. Their childhoods were made enjoyable by imaginary companions, their adult fantasy world embraces a spirit of adventure, and they possess a wealthy imagination and potential for creative expression. Auke Tellegen and G. Atkinson (1974) call this characteristic of hypnotizable people **absorption.** Such people acting in a play "become" the characters they portray, forgetting both themselves and the audience. For them a story can seem as real as an actual incident. They look for experiences beyond the realms of logic and reason. They give total attention to whatever situation they are in.

TABLE 5.1
Some Items from the Stanford Hypnotic Susceptibility Scale, Form C

Item	Procedure	Criterion for Passing
Moving hands apart	Have the person extend hands close together. Then suggest that the person imagine a force acting to push them apart.	Score (+) if hands are six or more inches apart in ten seconds.
Mosquito hallucination	Suggest that a mosquito buzzing nearby will alight on the person's hand and that he will wish to brush it off.	Score (+) for any grimacing, movement, or acknowledegment of effect.
Taste hallucination (sweet,sour)	The person is told to imagine that something sweet and then something sour is in the mouth, the taste growing stronger.	Score (+) if both tastes are experienced and if either one is evidenced by overt signs or reported as a strong taste.
Age regression (to fifth and second grades of school)	Suggest that the person is first in fifth grade and then in second grade. Inquire as to age, place, and activity, teacher's name. Have person write name.	Score (+) if handwriting of one of the regressed ages is clearly different from present handwriting.
Anosmia to ammonia	Give the person a small bottle containing ammonia and suggest that the person will be unable to smell the odor.	Score (+) if odor of ammonia is denied and there are no overt signs of person's smelling it.
Hallucinated voice	Suggest that a person in the room will ask about age, place of birth, etc. No questions, however, are asked.	Score (+) is subject answers voice realistically at least once.

Adapted from Weitzenhoffer and Hilgard, 1962.

SUMMARY □

Hypnosis has often been compared to deep sleep, but the comparison is an illusory one. The brain wave pattern of hypnotized people, their heart rate, blood pressure, motility, and ability to learn and retain new information are those of the waking state.

Hypnosis holds a fascination for most people, for one person appears to have dramatic and compelling power over the will of another. This is the mesmeric, occult image of hypnotism. Hypnosis also has therapeutic and scientific status, and the old notion of a contest of wills between the hypnotist and the hypnotized appears to be invalid. People who are susceptible to being hypnotized have had pervasive "imaginative involvements" since childhood. A personality trait tentatively identified as absorption allows them to give their complete attention to situations and to empathize and identify readily with others.

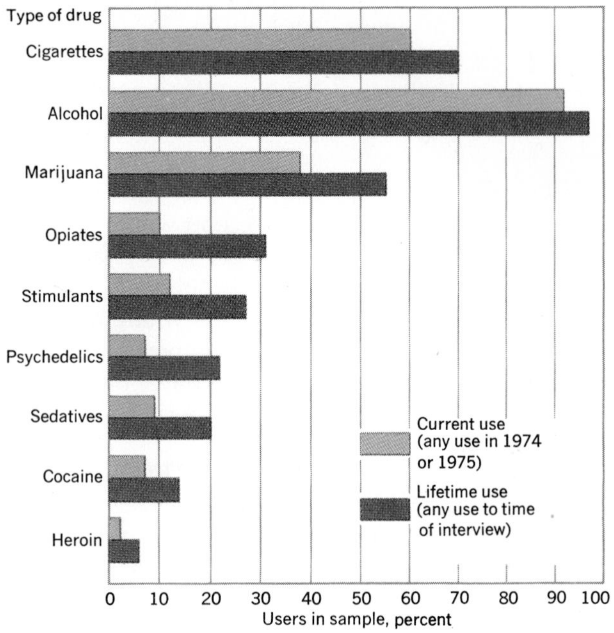

FIGURE 5.4
Use of drugs by a representative sample of American men. Lifetime use is any use to the time of the interview; current use is any use during 1974 and 1975. (Adapted from O'Donnell et al., 1976.)

DRUGS, SOCIETY, AND INDIVIDUAL BEHAVIOR

We live in a drug culture. Television advertisements blare forth their pronouncements of how to gain relief from pain and discomfort. All aches and pains, we are assured, can be miraculously eliminated. One or another nonprescription drug will bring quick relief from sleeplessness, tension, and the emotional and physical discomforts of everyday living. One result of these promotional campaigns is that at least one-third of all Americans between the ages of eighteen and seventy-four have at some time used some form of psychoactive drug. Every year they spend tens of billions of dollars for tens of billions of doses, many of which serve no useful medical purpose. These data are for the legal, sometimes called **licit,** drugs. Data on the use of **illicit drugs** are more difficult to obtain, but Figure 5.4 presents some information on the prevalence of their use by a sample of 3000 men between ages twenty and thirty. The percentages range from a low 2 percent for heroin to a high of 92 percent for alcohol. The percentages are not surprising. All these illicit drugs—the use of cigarettes and alcohol is of course not illegal—breach the blood-brain barrier and affect the mind. In every culture throughout history, people have ingested drugs to disrupt their perceptions of reality, whether to enhance them or to cloud them. Once they have discovered that a particular substance will alter consciousness, mood, and thinking processes, they do not readily give it up.

Members of the drug culture of the late 1960s.

Alcohol

Alcohol *per se* is not a problem, but the alcoholic or problem drinker is. Estimates of the number of severe problem drinkers in the United States vary. In 1974 the prevalence figure was set at 9 million. More recent estimates extend the range to 12 to 15 million.

TABLE 5.2
Representative Reports of Teenage Drunkenness

Definition	Age or School Grade			
Ever	Teenagers Both sexes 50%			
In last year	Grades 7 to 9		Grades 10 to 12	
	Male	Female	Male	Female
	33%	27%	70%	69%
Last month	Teenagers Both sexes 20%			
Last week	Teenagers Both sexes 7%			

Adapted from Demone and Wechsler, 1976; Marden and Kolodner, 1977; and Blane and Hewitt, 1976.

The incidence appears to be rising, with some 200,000 new alcoholics being reported annually. This rise appears to be greatest among young people (Table 5.2).

The reasons why young people drink are readily evident. Drinking is part of the process of socialization; young people are mimicking the drinking that they see done by adults and their peers. Drinking provides a temporary means of coping with the discomforts of adolescence, with the threats to self-esteem, the fear of failure, and the sense of alienation from family and adults faced by young people in the transition between childhood and maturity.

Is there a "natural history" in the progression to alcoholism? It was once believed that the prognosis for the problem drinker was inevitably a grim one, but recent evidence contradicts this view. Surveys of drinking practices indicate that within three years of initial reports of problem drinking, 20 percent of individuals state that they have solved the problem and have an improved level of social and physical functioning (Mendelson and Mello, 1979). The widespread belief that alcoholics cannot return to social drinking after treatment may be a myth. The Rand Report (Armor et al., 1976), based on a nationwide survey of 14,000 persons who were being treated in alcohol treatment centers, concluded that of those who had cut down on their drinking, only a small number were total abstainners. The majority of the people were ingesting moderate amounts of alcohol, but at levels far below what could be described as problem drinking, or they were alternating between periods of drinking and abstinence. This conclusion runs so counter to the "disease" view of alcoholism and the demand for total abstinence advocated by Alcoholics Anonymous that the subject is now a matter of considerable controversy and intense debate.

Can the sudden cessation of drinking be dangerous? Persons with a chronic history of severe alcoholism, or any person who has been drinking heavily for two weeks, may suffer delirium tremens (DTs) three to four days after they have stopped drinking. With the sudden drop of alcohol in the blood, the brain does not receive the supply to which it has grown physiologically accustomed. Individuals become disoriented and extremely agitated, sweat profusely, are severely tremulous. They have a high fever, a racing heart, and they see and feel small animals and insects crawling over walls and up their bodies, advancing to destroy them. The condition requires immediate hospitalization and may cause death.

Is there a typical alcohol abuser? Problem drinkers are a heterogeneous lot. No special personality type, family background, social class, or stressful experience predicts the development of alcoholism. When people who have an alcohol problem are sober, their thinking, judgment, memory, insight, and appearance are no different from those of people without one.

Is there a genetic factor in alcoholism? It was Aristotle who declared that drunken women "bring forth children like themselves." More recent information supports the view that alcoholism runs in families. One expert in the genetics of alcoholism indicates that with only a single exception, "Every family study of alcoholism, irrespective of country origin, has shown much higher rates of alcoholism among the relatives of alcoholics than in the general population"

(Goodwin, 1979). Such evidence does not *prove* that a genetic factor is at work, for drinking by parents, the attitudes they express, and the level of stress they put their children under are not always controlled in family studies of alcoholism. Studies that have incorporated such controls suggest a modest genetic predisposition to alcoholism, although the precise nature of the inheritance is not clear. A lack of tolerance for alcohol has been suggested (Goodwin, 1979).

The Sedatives

Sedatives such as alcohol and the synthetic barbiturates act as depressants on the central nervous system. The barbiturates—representative trade names are Luminal, Amytal, Nembutal, Seconal—account for 25 percent of mood-changing prescriptions and are powerful sleep inducers. Unfortunately, the barbiturate hangover affects activity into the next waking day Oakley Ray (1978) indicates that the barbiturates have the unfortunate effect of reducing the time spent in REM sleep and thus in dreaming. When barbiturates are discontinued, dreaming and nightmares may increase. Barbiturates are physiologically addictive. With prolonged use tolerance develops, and larger doses must be taken for the drug to have the same effect. And if prolonged use of a barbiturate is abruptly terminated, the withdrawal reactions are severe. The person may go into convulsions and die or suffer a prolonged toxic psychosis.

In testimony before a United States Senate investigating committee, a noted expert in the field of drug abuse, Dr. Sidney Cohen, spoke of the overuse of barbiturates by the young.

> For the youngsters barbiturates are a more reliable high and less detectable than "pot." They are less strenuous than LSD, less "freaky" than amphetamines, and less expensive than heroin. A school boy can "drop a red" and spend the day in a dreamy, floating state of awayness untroubled by reality. It is drunkenness without the odor of alcohol. It is escape for the price of one's lunch money (quoted by Ray, 1978, p. 292).

Small doses of the barbiturates induce a euphoric "high" and sometimes aggressive behavior; higher dosages can bring confusion, cognitive impairment, exaggerated emotionality, and a loss of motor coordination. Barbiturates are used by people who wish to commit suicide. They are responsible for 5000 deaths annually and five times that many trips to hospital emergency rooms. As drugs of abuse, the barbiturates are bad medicine indeed.

The Stimulants: Amphetamines and Cocaine

The amphetamines are synthetic drugs that act as stimulants to the central nervous system, bringing a sense of euphoria and heightening activity. Used to prevent sleepiness, to suppress appetite, and to counteract depression generally, the amphetamines are the "ups" in a world of ups and downs, but they are dangerous "ups." In large doses the amphetamines can cause convulsions and also heart attacks by affecting the heart muscles.

Most threatening of all the amphetamines is "speed" or Methedrine, which is injected intravenously by "speed freaks." Hyperactivity, eventual exhaustion, paranoid thinking, and destructive, violent behavior may all be aftermaths of this "mainlining." In the 1960s the danger of methamphetamine was tellingly conveyed by the watchword "Speed kills." The attraction of speed lies in its ecstatic "high," but to maintain it requires heavier and heavier doses of the drug. The "speed freak" injects the drug every few hours for several days and goes without sleep and food. Irritability, confusion, and fears mount, culminating in collapse or sometimes a paranoid psychosis. Of all the drug-induced mental aberrations, amphetamine psychosis, although uncommon, is the one that most clearly resembles paranoid schizophrenia. Unfortunately, the prognosis for recovery from the psychologically addictive power of speed is a poor one.

Whether the drug in smaller doses enhances motor activity is open to debate. For the individual in a state of fatigue it appears to do so, but when a person is well rested such favorable effects have not been observed. Its use among athletes to counteract fatigue and to make them able to perform at higher levels has caused considerable concern and necessitated legal action to prevent its use.

Cocaine was one of the earliest stimulants to be used medicinally, and one of its prime advocates was Sigmund Freud. He had read an account of the isolation of cocaine, an active ingredient of coca leaves, at a time when he was suffering a bout of depression and fatigue. He decided to try the drug and found that it not only relieved his depression but gave him newfound energy with which to continue his work. Freud became a proselytizer for the drug. In his *Cocaine Papers* (1885) Freud wrote of its numerous therapeutic benefits. Not only was it exhilarating and an aphrodisiac, but it was effective, he stated, as a local anesthetic and for treating asthma, digestive disorders of the stomach, and alcohol and morphine addiction. Freud's enthusiasm vanished after he had spent a night nursing through an acute cocaine psychosis a physician friend who had taken the drug on his recommendation. Thereafter he was bitterly opposed to the drug.

Cocaine is now the extremely expensive "in" drug for inducing a sense of euphoria and intense stimulation. Inhaled or "snorted" into each nostril, the drug is absorbed from the mucous lining into the bloodstream and reaches the brain almost immediately. The short high peaks within minutes and may be over within thirty. A more dangerous method for ingesting cocaine is by intravenous injection, either alone or in combination with heroin. Cocaine increases heart rate and blood pressure; it may make the abuser feel strong and become talkative. Prolonged use can induce a psychosis and terrifying tactile hallucinations not unlike those of delirium tremens.

The Narcotics or Opiates

Addiction In the latter part of the nineteenth century, the dispensing of opiates was so open in this country that, in the words, of one distinguished journalist, America was a "dope fiend's paradise." Opium was sold legally, costs were low, usage high; in fact, morphine, a derivative of opium, had been administered so extensively in treating the wounded of the Civil War that by the end of the conflict 45,000 soldiers were addicts. Not only drugstores but grocery and general stores sold opiates across the counter; if no store was nearby, mail-order houses were ready to fill the need. Patent medicines containing opium and morphine were abundantly available, ranging from Mrs. Winslow's Soothing Syrup to McMann's Elixir of Opium. Teething syrups for children and medicines for "women's troubles" contained opiates (Brecher, 1972).

Heroin, much stronger than the morphine from which it is derived, may induce a sense of euphoria and contentment which lasts for some four to six hours. Sometimes the reaction includes a "rush," "kick," or "bang," which is often sensed as a sexual equivalent, an "abdominal orgasm." Individuals vary widely in their reactions to this drug; it may be quite unpleasant to some. The proportion who derive immediate pleasure may actually be quite low, for only 2 to 3 percent of first users go on to abuse the drug.

Treatment Many narcotic addicts go untreated. Those who do receive therapy are often handled in ways that provide little basis for encouragement. Addicts are allowed to spend months or years in a "therapeutic community," as long as they remain free of drugs and their behavior meets the standards set. These residences lean heavily on daily group encounter sessions (see page 488) in which the staff and peers confront the addicts and critize their personality patterns. Few survive the regimen; most drop out and return to the streets and to their addiction.

An alternative treatment that looked promising for a time was the potent synthetic drug **methadone,** used medically as a substitute for morphine. The effects of methadone are similar to those of heroin but

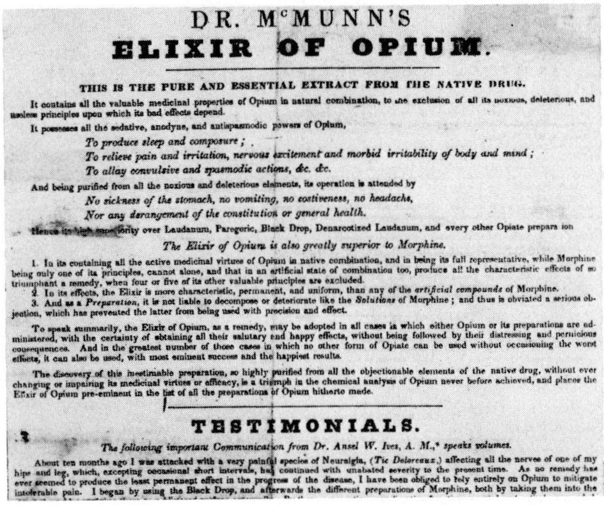

DR. M^cMUNN'S

ELIXIR OF OPIUM.

THIS IS THE PURE AND ESSENTIAL EXTRACT FROM THE NATIVE DRUG.

It contains all the valuable medicinal properties of Opium in natural combination, to the exclusion of all its noxious, deleterious, and useless principles upon which its bad effects depend.

It possesses all the sedative, anodyne, and antispasmodic powers of Opium,

To produce sleep and composure;
To relieve pain and irritation, nervous excitement and morbid irritability of body and mind;
To allay convulsive and spasmodic actions, &c. &c.

And being purified from all the noxious and deleterious elements, its operation is attended by

No sickness of the stomach, no vomiting, no costiveness, no headache,
Nor any derangement of the constitution or general health.

Hence its high superiority over Laudanum, Paregoric, Black Drop, Denarcotized Laudanum, and every other Opiate prepara ion

The Elixir of Opium is also greatly superior to Morphine.

1. In its containing all the active medicinal virtues of Opium in native combination, and in being its full representative, while Morphine being only one of its principles, cannot alone, and that in an artificial state of combination too, produce all the characteristic effects of so triumphant a remedy, when four or five of its other valuable principles are excluded.
2. In its effects, the Elixir is more characteristic, permanent, and uniform, than any of the *artificial compounds* of Morphine.
3. And as a *Preparation*, it is not liable to decompose or deteriorate like the *Solutions* of Morphine; and thus is obviated a serious objection, which has prevented the latter from being used with precision and effect.

To speak summarily, the Elixir of Opium, as a remedy, may be adopted in all cases in which either Opium or its preparations are administered, with the certainty of obtaining all their salutary and happy effects, without being followed by their distressing and pernicious consequences. And in the greatest number of those cases in which no other form of Opiate can be used without occasioning the worst effects, it can also be used, with most eminent success and the happiest results.

The discovery of this inestimable preparation, so highly purified from all the objectionable elements of the native drug, without ever changing or impairing its medicinal virtues or efficacy, is a triumph in the chemical analysis of Opium never before achieved, and places the Elixir of Opium pre-eminent in the list of all the preparations of Opium hitherto made.

TESTIMONIALS.

The following important Communication from Dr. Ansel W. Ives, A. M., speaks volumes.*

About ten months ago I was attacked with a very painful species of Neuralgia, (*Tic Doloreaux*,) affecting all the nerves of one of my hips and leg, which, excepting occasional short intervals, has continued with unabated severity to the present time. As no remedy has ever seemed to produce the least permanent effect in the progress of the disease, I have been obliged to rely entirely on Opium to mitigate intolerable pain. I began by using the Black Drop, and afterwards the different preparations of Morphine, both by taking them into the

Over-the-counter drugs in America in the middle of the nineteenth century.

side effects are less severe and withdrawal symptoms are milder.

The first major test of the effectiveness of methadone in counteracting the addict's craving for heroin was conducted by Doctors Vincent Cole and Marie Nyswander at the Rockefeller Hospital in New York. In this study a large group of hard-core addicts were kept on a high level of methadone for a period of four years. During this time the addicts became more constructive in their activities, attending school or achieving some employment stability. Very few were arrested. Since methadone is both legal and inexpensive, it permitted the addicts to pursue a life free from the crime, despair, and terror so often a part of maintaining a heroin habit.

Unfortunately, two things happened after the first methadone programs were initiated. First, as the number of programs with their supportive social services expanded, their costs to government rose. Cutbacks were then made in the ancillary programs devoted to counseling and employment and recreational services. Second, methadone began to be sold on the streets and itself became a drug of abuse. A majority of heroin addicts in the great urban centers returned to the streets, for a $10-a-day methadone habit was of course easier to sustain than the far more expensive heroin habit.

Methadone also has its own serious disadvantages as a treatment. Methadone is itself addictive; when discontinued, a craving for heroin, not methadone, becomes intense. Pregnant women who are methadone users frequently give birth to infants whose withdrawal symptoms are not unlike those of infants born to mothers on heroin. Moreover, although they tend to be mild, methadone does have physical side effects; overdosages can be fatal. Most important, 50 percent of street addicts on methadone maintenance reject the programs and prefer heroin.

The British program, called heroin maintenance, has long been advocated as the ultimate solution. In Great Britain heroin addicts are treated as sick individuals; clinics dispense the drug to them free. The number of addicts in England is extremely small, 3000, the rate of addiction has been slowed, and drug-connected crime is minimal by American standards.

The Psychedelics and Hallucinogens

The Psychedelic Drugs In 1943 a chemist in Basel, Switzerland, Dr. Albert Hofmann, was experimenting with *d*-lysergic acid diethylamide and somehow, without his knowing it, some of this substance got into his system. Hofmann's report of the experience is as follows.

> Last Friday, April 16, in the midst of my afternoon work . . . I had to go home because I experienced a very peculiar restlessness which was associated with a slight attack of dizziness. At home I went to bed and got into a not unpleasant state of drunkenness which was characterized by extremely stimulating fantasy. When I closed my eyes (the daylight was most unpleasant to me) I experienced fantastic images of an extraordinary plasticity. They were associated with an intense kaleidoscopic play of colors. After about two hours this condition disappeared (Ropp, 1957).

The **hallucinogens** are a class of drugs known for their power to produce disorders in perception, thinking, emotion, and behavior, as well as for expanding consciousness. These effects are sometimes called *psychotomimetic* because they appear to mimic some of the symptoms of psychosis (see page 431). Within this class of drugs LSD was one of the most abused in the 1960s. Other psychedelics popular in these years were mescaline from the peyote cactus and psilocybin from a Mexican mushroom. Today they have been replaced by a drug of infinitely greater power for human destruction. Its chemical name is *phencyclidine* (PCP), but on the street it has many bynames: angel dust, dust, crystal, cyclone, embalming fluid, elephant or horse tranquilizer, killer weed, super weed, mint weed, mist, monkey dust, Peace Pill, rocket fuel, goon, surfer, KW, and scuffle. Highly variable in appearance, it may be sold in other guises, as cannabinol, mescaline, LSD, and even cocaine or amphetamine (Petersen and Stillman, 1978). It is today the number one street drug of abuse in the United States (Domino, 1978).

A very powerful case against PCP recently appeared in a monograph published by the National Institute of Drug Abuse. Here is an excerpt.

> A young man smokes some PCP and proceeds to rob a gas station at gunpoint. A juvenile smokes PCP and rapes his baby sister. . . . A police officer encounters a young man who may have ingested an analog of PCP. The man, naked and unarmed, reportedly becomes combative and assaultive and is shot to death by the officer. Two lovers are smoking PCP alone in their bedroom; within a few minutes one is bleeding to death from a knife wound which may or may not have been self-inflicted. A middle-aged woman takes some cocaine which has been adulterated with PCP and tries to rob a bank armed only with a broom which she manipulates as if it were a gun (Siegel, 1978, p. 272).

These are actual recorded tragedies, all blamed directly on the ingestion of the drug. Small doses of PCP can generate either striking psychotic symptoms or the moderate impairment associated with brain damage. The drug users, disassociated from their surroundings, may be both analgesic, insensible to pain, and amnesiac, without memory; they may believe that their bodies have been altered in some way and feel completely estranged and isolated (Lerner and Burns, 1978). Attention span is minimal, coherence of thought lost, and learning grossly impaired. Severe language disturbances may be evident. Ray (1978) quotes a reflection on PCP taken from *Time* magazine.

> It's hard to understand why people are taking PCP. They don't take it to get high. They don't take it to make sex better. They take it to zonk themselves out. In a way it's a disguised death wish (p. 387).

Marijuana and Hashish Marijuana is derived from the leafy portion of *Cannabis sativa*, the hemp plant, which is widely distributed across the world's temperate and tropical areas. The major psychoactive element of the plant, tetrahydrocannabinol, is concentrated in its resin, which is found in the plant's flowering tops. The leaf contains less of the resin and the fibrous portion of the plant the least of all. Marijuana is prepared from the leaf, hashish or hash from the flowering portion. The greater concentration of resin in hashish explains why it is likely to be anywhere from three to ten times more potent than marijuana, although each of these drugs as sold on the street may vary considerably in potency.

Charles Tart (1969) had 150 college students who were fairly habitual users of marijuana anonymously complete questionnaires on the marijuana experience. He then tabulated the sensations and feelings that had been reported by more than half the group. Most striking were perceptual alterations which made objects focused upon seem to have greater clarity. Auditory perception underwent a similar change, with sounds seeming to possess new vividness; musical notes became purer in tone. The senses of touch, taste, and smell were all similarly enhanced. Memory appeared to be impaired, but it returned as the effects of the drug began to wear off. Sexual pleasure was reported to be greater, apparently through a heightened sense of communion with the partner combined with the heady sensory awareness induced by the drug. Sleep came readily, bringing vivid dreams to the user.

More objective studies of marijuana's effects are relatively few in number but are on the increase. Smoking the amounts of marijuana commonly used is detrimental to driving, whether performance is measured in laboratory studies or on city streets (Peterson, 1977; Klonoff, 1974). This impairment of driving skill by marijuana has now been firmly established as contributing to fatal accidents (Sterling-Smith, 1976). Despite such findings, today more marijuana users, 60 to 80 percent, drive while intoxicated than did in previous years. Airplane pilots high on marijuana have also been tested in flight simulators. The results are similar; piloting deteriorated markedly (Janowsky et al., 1976).

SUMMARY □

Alcohol is the most common drug of abuse in most segments of society. Research has revealed that most of the common beliefs about alcoholism are probably incorrect The majority of cured alcoholics may be social drinkers rather than abstainers. There is no standard pattern in the development of alcoholism and no standard alcoholic personality. Some evidence suggests a genetic predisposition to alcoholism.

The barbiturates, which are sedatives and physiologically addictive, and the amphetamines, which are stimulants and psychologically addictive, are both dangerous to the body and mind. The narcotics too are powerfully addictive, making it difficult to treat abuses. Heroin addicts do not remain long in therapeutic communities, and methadone itself is addictive. The British system that allows clinics to dispense free heroin to addicts may be the best means of caring for them.

Of the psychedelic drugs, the newest one on the street, phencyclidine or angel dust, is a menace. It has been directly implicated in violence and murder. Research on marijuana, the most widely used, is beginning to show that its effects on behavior are as dangerous as those of alcohol.

DRUGS AND THE NERVOUS SYSTEM

Neurons in the central nervous system are the most fragile cells of the entire body. They are easily killed by mechanical shock, by oxygen deprivation, and by foreign chemicals. Because of this fragility of neurons, the body goes to great lengths to protect them. The brain is protected from mechanical damage by the skull and by a membrane full of fluid which insulates it from this bony enclosure. It is protected from oxygen deprivation by oxygen detectors in the arteries carrying blood to the brain. Should the oxygen content happen to fall, breathing rate and blood pressure are increased until the proper level of oxygen is reestablished. If this system fails even for a few moments, the neurons begin not to transmit; the person feels light-headed and then faints, losing consciousness completely. If the oxygen supply falls to a low level for more than three or four minutes, some neurons die; with longer periods of unconsciousness, more and more neurons perish.

Vulnerability to Drugs

Vulnerable as neurons are to mechanical shock or to disruptions in the blood or oxygen supply, they are even more vulnerable to foreign chemicals. Just as we will not tolerate chemical fumes in the air around us, neurons will not tolerate unusual molecules in the fluid surrounding them. Their lives and their ability to function depend on having exactly the right amount of each of several substances in the surrounding fluid. If alien substances are present in a high concentration, or if they are there persistently and repetitively, the neurons begin to die.

Because of the great damage that foreign molecules do to neurons, the body has erected, among others, the **blood-brain barrier.** This barrier is in the central nervous system itself and is one of the functions of the glia cells (page 27). The glia cells serve as an intermediary or "middleman" between the blood supply on one side and the neurons on the other. They absorb molecules from the blood and pass on only those that are appropriate for the neuron to use.

Although the blood-brain barrier works effectively for almost all natural substances that might find their way into the bloodstream, a few, perhaps twenty or thirty, can breach this barrier. The most notable come from the tobacco plant, the coffee plant, the opium poppy, the coca plant, the hemp plant, the peyote cactus, and *Psilocybe mexicana,* a mushroom. Lysergic acid comes from ergot, a rust that attacks rye grasses. It is these substances, along with the many artificial ones made by pharmaceutical laboratories specifically to breach the blood-brain barrier, that are neuroactive drugs.

Dosage

When drugs are taken *systemically,* by placement in the bloodstream, they flood the entire body. Their action is not confined to any one place, and their concentration is diluted by the body's own fluids. Thus a given amount of drug administered systemically is much more concentrated in a small person than in a large person. What is a moderate dose for a 200-pound man can be a lethal dose for his 120-pound girlfriend. The effect of a given dosage of a drug also varies widely in different people, even those of the same body size. For this reason the effect of a given dosage cannot be predicted exactly. As dosage levels are gradually increased, more and more people are affected. The dosage at which 50 percent of the population are affected is the drug's **effective dose** or ED. Thus a drug's ED is completely ineffective in one half of the population and effective in the other half.

As dosages of a drug are increased still further, another even more important level is reached; this one is the drug's **lethal dose** or LD. The LD is also defined statistically, as the dose at which 50 percent of the population is killed by the drug. Like the ED, the LD varies. Some people are killed with dosages that are below the effective dosage of others (Figure 5.5). The ED and LD curves are exactly like the psychophysical functions discussed in Chapter 3 (page 68), and the ED and LD are similar to absolute thresholds.

Dangerous drugs are those whose ED and LD curves are close together, even overlapping. A dose that is too low to affect some people will kill others. With the individual response to dosage added to variation in response because of body size, avoiding a lethal dose becomes an obviously tricky business.

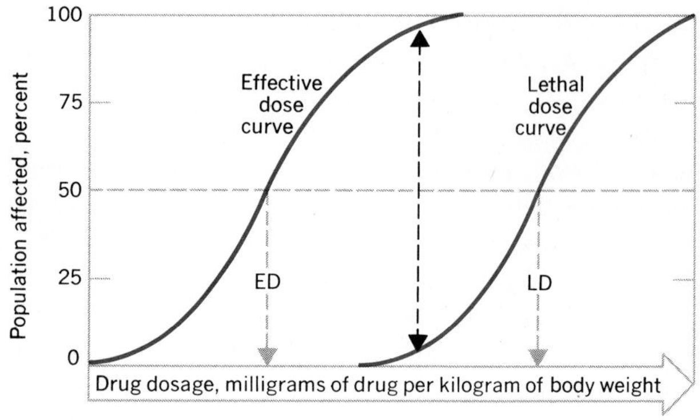

FIGURE 5.5
Effective and lethal dose curves. These curves show the percentages of the population affected (*left curve*) and killed (*right curve*) by increasing dosages. The effective and lethal doses are those that affect and kill half the population respectively. If the difference between effective and lethal dose curves is small, the drug is "dangerous." If the difference is larger, as here, the drug is "safe." Even for this drug, however, a dose that does not affect a small percentage of the population kills a small percentage. These percentages are those above and below the double-headed arrow.

Drug Action

Drugs can be classified in several overlapping ways: by their psychological effect—hallucinogenic, sedative, and so on: by the site of action on the neuron—synapse, axon, membrane, or cell body; by their mechanism of action—synaptic blockers, impulse blockers, neurotransmitter mimics, neurotransmitter depleters, and so on; by the swiftness and duration of their effect—fast-acting or slow, short-acting or long; by whether they are specific or general in their effects. Especially important is their addictive power—the degree to which the body becomes tolerant of a drug, requiring more for the same effect, and accustomed enough to the drug that bodily functions are disrupted when it is not administered.

Disruption of Synaptic Transmission Since synaptic transmission is entirely chemical, it is the most vulnerable spot to foreign molecules in the entire neural process. Of course, the lock-and-key specificity of the chemical reactions at the synapses serves to protect these processes from disruption by foreign molecules, and, in a sense, this specificity amounts to a fourth barrier against neuroactive drugs. But as with other protective barriers, this one too can be breached. If drug molecules have the proper shape, they can imitate either the lock or the key or some part of one or the other. The lock-and-key specificity of synaptic reactions means, however, that a drug affecting a synapse using one neurotransmitter will probably not have the proper molecular shape to affect a synapse using another neurotransmitter. This means that synaptic drugs usually affect one or another system of neurons in its entirety, leaving other systems unaffected at first. Since the many neural systems cooperate in controlling the body, however, when a drug affects one, it almost always throws the whole nervous system, and the body, out of balance in one way or another.

Amphetamines mimic the effects of the neurotransmitter norepinephrine, firing all its postsynaptic neurons and spreading excitation in the brain and throughout the sympathetic nervous system. Amphetamine has another effect too. It causes the neurons that use norepinephrine to leak this substance from their terminal buttons. This leakage, besides stimulating the postsynaptic neurons still further, depletes the store of norepinephrine in the terminals. This depletion can be made up only by transport of the substance down the axon from its manufacturing site in the cell body, a very slow process. Thus, even after the drug molecules have eventually been cleansed from the system, the drug's effect can linger for hours or days as the store of norepinephrine slowly reaches its proper level in the presynaptic terminals. Because the presynaptic neuron cannot stimulate the postsynaptic neuron at the normal level, a net depression of activity is the consequence. This is the cause of the "hangover," "let-down." "crash," or depression that follows amphetamine usage. It is also the basis of amphetamine psychological addiction, for another dosage of amphetamine can partly relieve the hangover by causing what little norepinephrine has accumulated to leak out once more.

Besides stimulating the postsynaptic neuron and making the terminal button leak, molecules of synaptic drugs can clog the receptor sites of the postsynaptic neuron or interfere with the uptake of the neurotransmitter after firing. The molecules of other drugs stick to those of the neurotransmitter so that they no longer fit into the receptor sites. Still others mimic the action of the deactivating enzyme, fragmenting the transmitter before it reaches the receptor site. Still other drug molecules interfere with the deactivating enzyme, flooding the synaptic cleft with neurotransmitter. Almost all neuroactive drugs, whether hindering the body or benefiting it, work in at least one of these ways. For example, caffeine and nicotine molecules mimic those of different neurotransmitters. Nicotine mimics acetylcholine, the neurotransmitter of the neuromuscular junction, causing tenseness, muscle twitching, and spasticity of the muscles. Chloropromazine, a major tranquilizer which has calmed many schizophrenics, blocks the receptor sites for the neurotransmitter dopamine. LSD may block that for serotonin. Drugs disrupt all the synapses of a particular transmitter, unbalancing or rebalancing the nervous system in different ways.

Disruption of Impulse Transmission Cocaine and its commercial derivatives—Novocaine, Procaine, Xylocaine—block the conduction of impulses along axons. If one of these substances comes in contact with a neuron anywhere along its axon, the neuron's impulses will be blocked at that point. Regardless of the number of impulses generated by the neuron, none will pass the block and none will reach its terminal buttons. Apparently these substances change the axon's membrane in some way that makes it lose its ability to conduct an impulse.

Cocaine itself passes the blood-brain barrier, so it affects the central nervous system as well as the peripheral. The commercial derivatives do not; so their effects are confined to peripheral nerves only. It is this property that gives them medicinal value and allows them to be used as local anesthetics. An injection of one of them in the vicinity of a peripheral nerve renders that nerve inactive for a period of time. A dentist can block the nerves from the teeth and save a patient the pain of drilling, or an obstetrician can block the nerves from a woman's pelvis and save her the pain of childbirth.

If, however, the cocaine derivative is given systemically, so that it is distributed throughout the body, all axons will be affected, although to a lesser degree because of the dilution of the drug. When cocaine is administered systemically, it affects not only peripheral axons but, because it passes the blood-brain barrier, axons in the central nervous system as well. Like its derivatives, cocaine blocks impulses rather quickly, but in addition it blocks the uptake of the neurotransmitter norepinephrine. This action gives a user the "rush" and also causes a depressive hangover, for eventually the terminal buttons are depleted of norepinephrine.

Disruption of the Neuron's Cell Body Processes Although their mode of action is not yet known for certain, opium and its derivatives, morphine and heroin, may affect the body cell of the neuron, interfering with its normal respiration, metabolism, and maintenance. Molecules of these drugs adhere to particular points on the membrane of neurons, much as neurotransmitters do at synapses. Once attached, they somehow affect the internal processes of the neuron. Why these so-called narcotics are so very addictive is not known, but addicts' reports of generalized pain and malaise when deprived of these drugs suggest that they may mimic certain natural hormones called **endorphins.** These hormones are normally secreted into the bloodstream in response to injury or persistent pain. It is possible that opiates somehow damage this natural pain-relieving system so that it can no longer protect a person from the many small external and internal injuries accumulated from moment to moment throughout normal life.

SUMMARY □

Although the blood-brain barrier protects the nervous system from most foreign chemicals, the neuroactive drugs breach this barrier and affect neural functioning. There are great individual differences in the effects of drugs. The most important of these are differences in effective doses and lethal doses, which can be shown graphically as effective dose (ED) curves and lethal dose (LD) curves. As dosage increases, the percentage of individuals affected at all and the percentage of individuals killed increase. On the basis of such curves, effective and lethal doses are defined statistically as the dosages that respectively affect or kill 50 percent of the population. Dangerous drugs are those whose ED and LD curves lie close together.

Drugs may influence the nervous system in a number of ways. Some drugs—amphetamine, for example—mimic the effects of neurotransmitters. Cocaine and its derivatives block the conduction of nerve impulses. Morphine and heroin probably affect the cell bodies of neurons and interfere with the physiology of the neuron. Recent research suggests that narcotics have addictive power because they simulate the action of endorphins which normally protect the individual from injury and pain.

TO BE SURE YOU UNDERSTAND THIS CHAPTER △

The following concepts are the major ones introduced in this chapter. You should be able to define them and state the points made about each in text discussion.

Structural psychology
Introspection
Behaviorism
S-R psychology
Unconscious
Preconscious
Conscious
Altered states of consciousness
Schizophrenia
Multiple personality
Meditation
Biological clock
Circadian rhythm
Rapid eye movements (REM)
Manifest content of dream
Latent content of dream
Stages of sleep
Dream deprivation
Rebound effect
Narcolepsy
Sleep apnea
Hypnosis
Hypnotic susceptibility
Absorption
Licit drugs
Illicit drugs
Alcoholism
Sedatives
Stimulants
Narcotics (opiates)
Methadone
Heroin maintenance
Psychedelics
Hallucinogens
Blood-brain barrier
Effective dose (ED)
Lethal dose (LD)
Endorphin

TO GO BEYOND THIS CHAPTER △

In this book Chapter 17, "A Casebook of Psychopathology," and Chapter 18, "Understanding Psychopathology," treat mental disorders more completely. Chapter 16, "Personality," describes the work of Freud and the humanistic psychologists mentioned in this chapter. Chapter 2 has a section on split-brain studies and the implications for consciousness. Chapter 19, "Treatment and Therapy of Disordered States," provides a wide-ranging description of various forms of therapy, including behavioral therapy methods of managing the addictive disorders.

Elsewhere Several basic books covering states of consciousness are recommended. First there is Robert Ornstein's *The Psychology of Consciousness,* which discusses split-brain research, the esoteric psychologies, mediation, self-regulation, and the like. Ornstein has also edited a book of readings on the subject, *The Nature of Human Consciousness,* now available in paperback. Ernest Hilgard's *Divided Consciousness* provides a masterly account of such intriguing topics as states of possession, multiple personality, and other types of disassociative phenomena. The editors of *Scientific American* have brought together under the title *Altered States of Awareness* a series of authoritative articles which originally appeared in the magazine.

Two paperbacks are recommended reading for sleep states and dreaming, William Dement's *Some Must Watch While Some Must Sleep* and Wilse Webb's *Sleep, the Gentle Tyrant.* Both authors are major contributors to sleep research, and both write with clarity and a robust enthusiasm which captures any reader's interest.

If your interest runs to hypnosis, you may wish to read Ernest Hilgard's *The Experience of Hypnosis* and Josephine Hilgard's *Personality and Hypnosis.*

A broad fascinating overview of drugs is provided by Oakley Ray's *Drugs, Society and Human Behavior.* Donald Goodwin's *Is Alcoholism Hereditary?* gives the background of research into an intriguing and complicated problem and can be easily understood by the undergraduate reader.

PART 2

LEARNING AND THINKING

CH. 6

Conditioning and Learning

As you begin the study of learning, it will be useful to look at events in the world in a special way, asking in effect about the extent to which your behavior controls them. There are a few events over which you have almost no control. Thunder follows lightning, however strongly you may wish away its awesome cracks and rumbles. Pain is a likely prospect once the dentist applies the drill. For many people an uncontrollable queasiness follows the sight of blood. There are no means of keeping each of these second events from following the first.

More commonly what you do has consequences. You study hard for an examination and get a good grade. You leave your bicycle unlocked on campus and somebody steals it. You go to the auditorium early and find an eighth-row seat on the aisle. In such circumstances you are rewarded or punished, depending on how you have behaved.

Other situations seem to represent a combination of these two states of affairs. A certain look on a mother's face means punishment is imminent, unless the child switches to behavior that forestalls it. The light and crackling of a fireplace mean warmth and comfort in a chilly house on a cold evening, but only if a person moves near enough to feel it.

These examples suggest that, in any given situation, two rather different things may be learned: the sequences of events to be expected and what to do about them. Probably most, and possibly all, learning in practical situations involves both of these components. This makes the study of learning complicated. In order to simplify things, psychologists who study learning have developed two separate experimental procedures that seem to capture the essentials of these two processes. These procedures are called classical and operant conditioning. In **classical conditioning** sequences of events in the experiment occur no matter what the subject does. In **operant conditioning** specific behavior brings reward or punishment.

Ivan Petrovich Pavlov (1849-1936), skeptical about psychology, avoided mentalistic and subjective terms and insisted his work on conditioning was physiological.

PROCEDURES FOR STUDYING LEARNING

Classical Conditioning

The systematic study of classical conditioning began in Russia with the work of Ivan Petrovich Pavlov. A doctor of medicine and physiologist by training, Pavlov won a 1904 Nobel prize for his work on the physiology of digestion. During the course of his study of the functioning of the salivary and gastric glands, his laboratory happened upon a troublesome but intriguing phenomenon. In order to stimulate these glands, the laboratory assistants would place food powder in a dog's mouth. They soon became aware that, after a few repetitions of this treatment, the dog began salivating at sight of the powder, before it had been tasted. Then the dog began salivating as soon as it saw its feeder and eventually even earlier, when it heard his footsteps. Pavlov had the wit to be curious about this course of events and determined to study it. And indeed that is how he spent the last thirty-six years of his professional life.

The details of Pavlov's procedures for the study of conditioning are familiar to almost everyone. In order to record the salivary response, the dogs first received a minor surgical operation which brought a salivary duct to the outside of the cheek. After recovery from the operation, the dogs were introduced to the laboratory: to the harness that would restrain them, and to the other apparatus that would make measurement during the experiment possible. When they had adjusted to these conditions, the dogs were experimented upon in a room shielded from extraneous vibrations and noise.

In a typical procedure (Figure 6.1) the animal was first presented with a neutral stimulus such as light, which produced no salivation. After the light had been on for several seconds, food was placed within

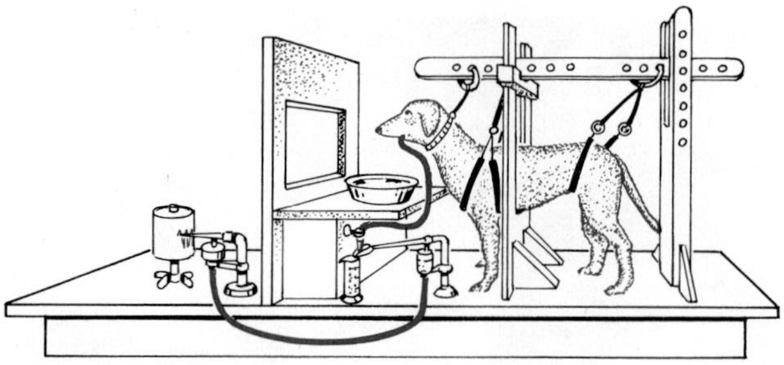

FIGURE 6.1
Dog in conditioning apparatus. The dog is restrained by a harness attached to a stand. The tube connected to the dog's cheek covers a salivary gland brought surgically to the body surface. Saliva can be collected in the test tube. Each drop of saliva, as it contacts the channel leading to the test tube, activates a lever and stylus, which records the secretions on the revolving drum at the left.

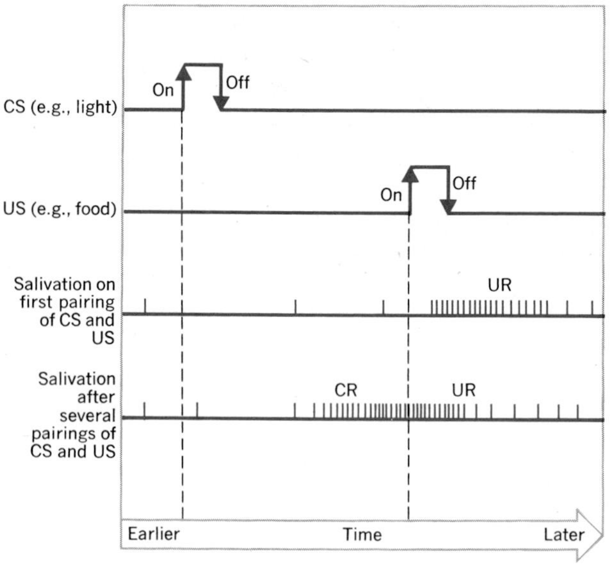

FIGURE 6.2
Hypothetical records obtained in salivary conditioning experiment. This diagram shows what goes on in time in a conditioning experiment. First the CS comes on. In this example it goes off after a brief period. In some experiments it remains on and overlaps the US. Then the US is offered. Early in the experiment, before many pairings of CS and US, salivation occurs only as a UR to the US. In records of this type each short vertical line indicates one drop of saliva. After several pairings salivation occurs in anticipation of the US, as a CR, and blends with the UR made to the US.

the dog's reach. The chewing and swallowing of food typically produced copious salivation. After the light and food had been paired in this manner a number of times, the light alone gradually came to elicit salivation. Such a response, called forth by a previously neutral stimulus, is a **conditioned response** or **conditioned reflex**.

Pavlov's experiment provides us with a means of introducing the basic vocabulary of conditioning. The most important terms in this vocabulary are the following.

Unconditioned stimulus (US) Any stimulus that produces a dependable response at the outset of an experiment. In the Pavlovian experiment just described, the US was food. Pavlov spoke of the US as a **reinforcer** to convey the idea that it strengthened and supported the conditioned response that was acquired in these experiments. With time the term came to refer to any reward or punishment employed to obtain learning in any situation.

Unconditioned response (UR) The consistent reaction to the US just mentioned. Salivation was the UR in the Pavlovian experiment.

Conditioned stimulus (CS) A stimulus that, for experimental purposes, is paired with the US and, at the outset of the experiment, does not produce the UR. In the experiment just described, the CS was the light. Such stimuli often do elicit a response which the Pavlovians call an **orienting reflex** (OR) and equate with giving attention to the CS. With conditioning the OR tends to disappear.

Conditioned response (CR) A response similar to the UR, now elicited by the CS. Of principal interest in the study of conditioning are the circumstances under which such reactions develop. Figure 6.2, which is the kind of record Pavlov obtained, presents a comparison of the salivary response before and after a series of conditioning trials. Figure 6.3 shows Pavlov's neurological conception of conditioning. For Pavlov conditioning involved the development of a "temporary connection" or association between the neural centers registering the CS and the US. Learning depended on this condition of linking, hence the term conditioning. Pavlov's neural connection would be the basis for the expectancies mentioned earlier.

Two Examples Although classical conditioning is a laboratory procedure, it is easy to find real-world examples. These two come from a book by Edwin R. Guthrie (1952) and were chosen because they make important additional points about the process of classical conditioning.

> In a Pacific Coast city . . . a number of dogs succumbed to strychnine poisoning. Poisoned chunks of beef were found in the neighborhood. Several owners of good dogs undertook to train their animals not to indulge in stray tidbits by scattering about many pieces of beef to which there were fastened small mousetraps of the familiar spring variety. For the time, at least, they had a quick success. The dogs developed a very supercilious attitude toward stray meat.

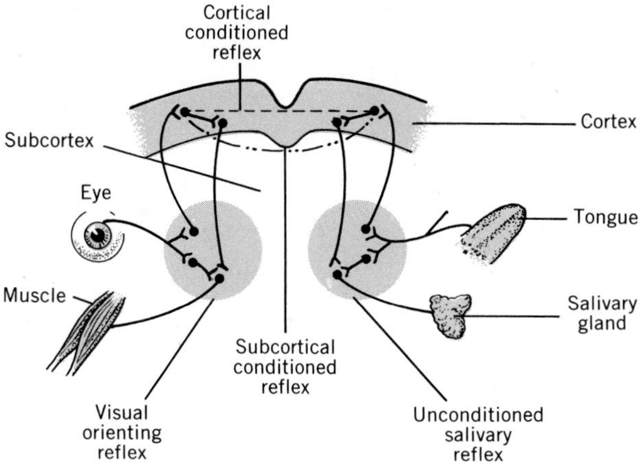

FIGURE 6.3
Pavlov's conception of the conditioned reflex. The materials on the left represent a visual orienting reflex, from eye, to the central nervous system, to muscle. This reflex might be a blink. The materials on the right represent the unconditioned reflex, from tongue, to central nervous system, to salivary gland. The conditioned reflex, represented by dashed lines, is at both higher cortical levels and subcortical levels. This representation of conditioning takes account of a good bit of what is known (page 36) about reflex behavior. (Adapted from Asratyan, 1953.)

In this example the conditioned stimulus is the meat. The unconditioned stimulus is the pain produced by the springing of the mousetrap. The unconditioned response is withdrawal produced by this pain. And the conditioned response is the avoidance of meat based on its association with pain. In this example, by contrast with the original Pavlovian experiments, food (meat) is a CS rather than a US. Initially, the meat did not produce the avoidance reaction elicited by the mousetrap, but eventually, through pairing, it did.

> Two small country boys who lived before the day of the rural use of motor cars had their Friday afternoons made dreary by the regular visit of their pastor, whose horse they were supposed to unharness, groom, feed and water and then harness again on the departure. Their gloom was lightened finally by a course of action which one of them conceived. They took to spending the afternoon of the visit retraining the horse. One of them stood behind the horse with a hayfork and periodically shouted "Whoa" and followed this with a sharp jab with the fork. Unfortunately, no exact records of this experiment were preserved save that the boys were quite satisfied with the results.

In this example, as in the previous one, the CS was not a neutral stimulus. In fact, the initial response to "Whoa" was the exact opposite of the response that replaced it.

Significance of Classical Conditioning These two examples should indicate the most significant aspect of classical conditioning. It is very important in emotional learning. Many psychologists believe that it is the only way in which emotions can be acquired. One of the most famous studies in the entire history of psychology helps to make this point.

This was the experiment in which the eleven-month-old Albert learned a conditioned fear of a white rat after its presence was paired with an unconditioned fear-producing stimulus. When Albert was first introduced to the tame white rat (CS) as he sat playing on a mattress, he showed no fear and indeed appeared happily curious. But just as he reached out to touch the rat, the experimenter struck a large steel bar immediately behind the child's head. At the sound of the very loud noise (US), Albert started, fell forward, and buried his head in the mattress (UR). When Albert had recovered enough to reach for the rat a second time, the bar was again hammered forthwith. This time Albert jumped, fell forward, and began to whimper. One week later Albert reached for the rat when it was first put down near him but withdrew his hand before touching it, even though he had not seen the rat in the meantime. That day a few more of their encounters were paired with the loud noise. Albert was soon crying and crawling away from the rat as fast as his knees would carry him (CR) even when the bar was not struck. He also appeared to be afraid of objects resembling the rat, such as a fur coat, a ball of absorbent cotton, and a dog (Watson and Rayner, 1920).

The early date of this experiment is significant. The ethical codes developed since then would almost certainly prevent carrying out such a study today. As a matter of fact, the experimenters had originally intended to remove Albert's fear, again through conditioning, but unfortunately Albert was taken from the hospital where he had been living before they could do so.

Since fear or anxiety is a common symptom of mental disturbance, we are led correctly to anticipate that classical conditioning figures in the development of such disorders. A famous clinical case of *phobia* illustrates the point.

> A female patient had an unreasonable fear of running water, particularly if it made a splashing sound. She could give no reason for the phobia, nor could she control it. When it was finally uncovered, the explanation went back to a childhood experience. The patient had gone on a picnic with an aunt who was visiting the family. Against the specific warning of her parents, she had gone wading in a stream where the current was swift. Later she was discovered by her aunt trapped beneath a waterfall with the water splashing over her. More concerned with her disobedience than

Edward Lee Thorndike (1874-1948) put Harlem alley cats in his puzzle box, for he was still earning his degree. His study, a classic of the literature, was his dissertation.

anything else, the child pleaded with the aunt not to tell. The aunt agreed, but when the little girl returned home she repressed the incident and the phobia soon appeared.

Although a great deal more is involved in this case, the element of classical conditioning is obvious. A neutral or even pleasant stimulus, water, was established as a CS evoking a strong emotional CR (Bagby, 1928).

Operant Conditioning

Thorndike's Cats At about the time Pavlov was beginning his experiments on classical conditioning in Russia, work on operant conditioning began in America. Edward Lee Thorndike, at Columbia University, was putting chicks, cats, dogs, and monkeys into a variety of experimental situations. The best-known of Thorndike's work was that on cats in a puzzle box (Figure 6.4).

The puzzle box was a cage with a door so latched that a cat could open it from the inside by pulling a string or turning a button. When a cat was first put into the box, it became extremely agitated, clawing and scratching at the sides of the box and anything within, and trying to push its head and paws through

FIGURE 6.4
Puzzle box used by Thorndike. In this version the cat can escape from the box and get food outside by pressing the treadle inside the box. A cord and pulley system unlocks the door.

the spaces between the slats. Sooner or later, in the course of its struggles, the cat, more or less by accident, released the door and escaped. In the typical Thorndikean experiment, the cat was rewarded with a bit of fish, but then immediately put back into the box and required to escape again. On this second trial the cat engaged in the same set of agitated movements but confined them for the most part to the region of the box that contained the release mechanism. Escape usually occurred sooner. On later trials the unrewarded activities gradually dropped out, and the act of opening the door of the cage became more and more precise. The usual measure employed by Thorndike was the amount of time required by the cat to escape from the puzzle box. With practice, this measure steadily decreased (Figure 6.5).

This experiment was an early one on operant or instrumental conditioning, for getting out of the puzzle box and being rewarded with food depended on the cat's making a specified response. The learning of Thorndike's cats has been called **instrumental conditioning** because the response that is learned is instrumental in solving a problem and in earning a reward.

Skinner's Boxes Burrhus Frederick Skinner of Harvard chose the term operant conditioning for such learning because it occurs while the learner is operating on the environment. Skinner is probably the most influential psychologist of the twentieth century, in terms of his impact on the field. In the 1930s Skinner began an extensive series of studies, first of rats learning to press a bar (Figure 6.6) and then of pigeons learning to peck at an illuminated window (Figure 6.7). The apparatuses, both of which have been called **Skinner boxes** by people other than Skinner, are similar. In the bar-pressing experiment a hungry rat is put into a small compartment containing a short,

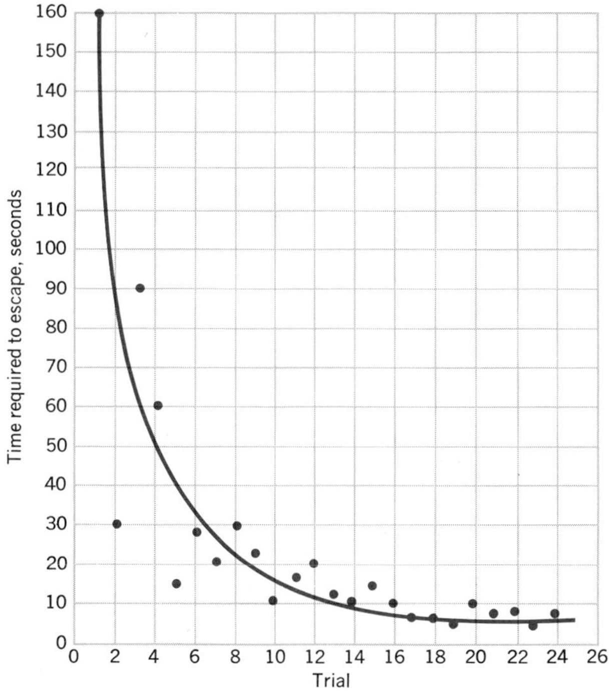

FIGURE 6.5
Learning curve for a single cat's escapes from the puzzle box. Although the cat's escape time decreased in a somewhat irregular fashion, Thorndike believed that learning is a regular continuous process. The smooth curve represents this idea.

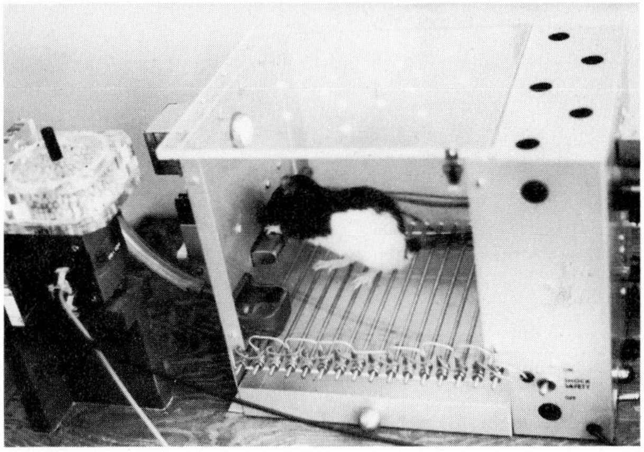

FIGURE 6.6
A Skinner box for rats. The apparatus was developed by Skinner (1938) and called an operant chamber by Skinner himself, a Skinner box by others. Pressing the bar delivers a pellet of food from the hopper on the left.

Burrhus Frederick Skinner.

FIGURE 6.7
Pigeon in a window-pecking apparatus.

movable lever on an inside wall. When the rat depresses the lever, an electrical device releases a pellet of food into a food tray. In this experiment food is the reinforcer. Sooner or later the rat learns to press the lever to obtain reinforcement. In the window-pecking experiment a hungry pigeon is placed in a cage which has a small round window in one wall, located at about eye level for the pigeon. The window can be illuminated as a signal that food is available. If the bird pecks the window a door below opens, permitting the pigeon to peck from a dish of bird seed for two or three seconds. Again the most important outcome is that pigeons quickly learn to peck the illuminated window for reinforcement in the form of food.

Biofeedback and Self-Control The responses made in operant conditioning are almost always of the type that we would call "voluntary." Pressing a bar and pecking at an illuminated window in the Skinner boxes are examples. In recent years there has been considerable interest in the question of whether "involuntary" responses can also be conditioned through operant techniques.

For centuries reports have been reaching us from the East of the impressive accomplishments of the Yogis in gaining control of normally involuntary responses. It is claimed, for example, that the practice of Yoga permits voluntary control of heart rate, blood pressure, oxygen consumption, skin temperature, and a variety of other bodily functions that are normally involuntary. The same sources report impressive alterations in mental states. Within the last decade the accomplishments claimed by the Yogis have been investigated in the laboratory. The general result came as a surprise to many psychologists; the reports of the Yogis are true. The achievement of altered states of consciousness and of voluntary control over involuntary processes are actually quite easy for almost anyone. The method is a version of the operant conditioning procedure.

The secret of gaining such control is to provide people with some way of knowing what is happening to the bodily process they are trying to influence. Normally, involuntary responses are also beyond awareness; we do not notice changes in blood pressure, heart rate, body temperature, and the like. But modern electronic technology makes it possible to monitor such functions and to let the individual know their state. The collection of techniques for giving a person knowledge of these physiological functions has come to be called **biofeedback.** With the development of these methods, a new specialty has appeared in psychology, the study of biofeedback and self-control.

A representative experiment is that of Jasper Brener and Roger Kleinman, who quickly trained a group of college students to lower their blood pressure. The procedure was quite simple. Blood pressure was monitored by equipment of the type a physician uses to take blood pressure. An electronic counter made the readings accessible to individuals in an experimental group. They were told what the tickings meant and were asked to keep their blood pressure as low as they could. Individuals in a control group received the same feedback, but they did not know the significance of the tickings and were asked simply to lie still during the experiment. In less than half an hour the members of the experimental group succeeded in reducing their blood pressure by about 15 millimeters of mercury (Figure 6.8).

EEG control and meditation The normal rhythmic electrical activity on the brain can be detected by the electrodes of the electroencephalograph placed suitably on the scalp of the person (page 131). As we have already seen, the frequency of the amplified and recorded brain waves varies considerably during the stages of sleep and with changing levels of alertness. The range is from about 4 hertz (cycles per second) to about 26 hertz. In the study of self-control of the EEG, the alpha rhythm, 8 to 13 hertz, is of particular interest, for the tranquil mental states achieved through transcendental meditation are reportedly associated with a high proportion of alpha waves (page 103).

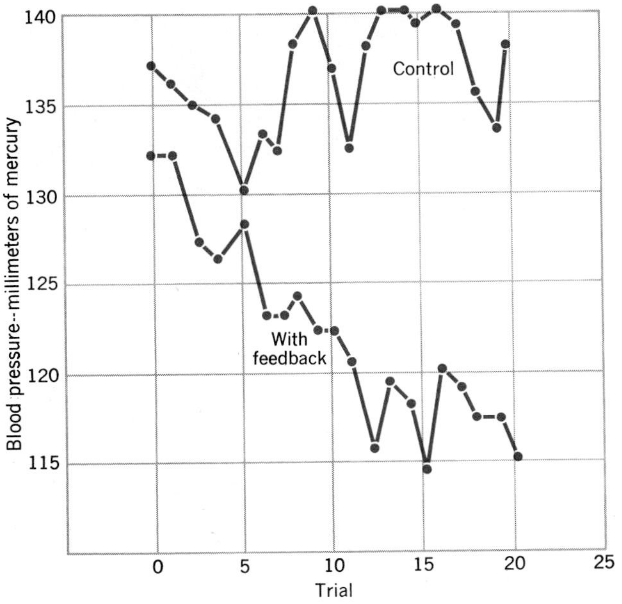

FIGURE 6.8
Biofeedback and self-control. Members of the control group received the same feedback as individuals in the experimental groups, but they were not told the significance of the information or instructed to control blood pressure. (Adapted from Brener and Kleinman, 1970.)

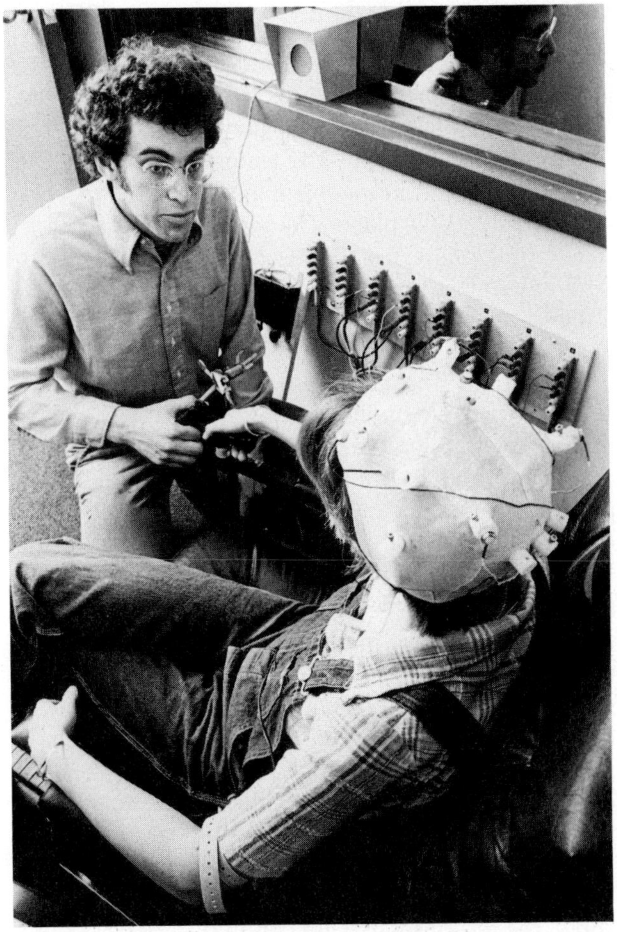

Equipment for monitoring brain waves. The subject is being prepared for an electroencephalogram. The cap on her head ensures that the recording electrodes contact the proper locations on her scalp. Most brain waves are recorded from the cortex, which is immediately below the skull.

The brains of most people produce spontaneous alpha waves only part of the time. This fact led Joe Kamiya (for example, 1969) to wonder whether we can learn voluntarily to increase or decrease the proportion of the alpha in the EEG. The first problem was to find a way of letting people know when their brains are producing alpha. Electronic equipment was devised to monitor the frequency of brain waves and to activate a buzzer whenever alpha waves occur. Kamiya found that, given feedback, people can learn to recognize alpha and nonalpha states and to produce alpha waves or suppress them. Many people reported the alpha state to be rewarding. They found enhancement of alpha to be associated with feelings of detachment and tranquility, not unlike the experience reported by people who practice some form of meditation.

Direct control versus mediation The most interesting question raised by these studies concerns the mechanism of control. Is it direct or through some mechanism of mediation? What we mean by mediation can be illustrated with this example. Suppose that you are a participant in a biofeedback experiment in which you are supposed to elevate your heart rate on command. Striving to do your best for science, you jump up and down vigorously whenever the command is given. Your heart rate goes up and you receive feedback to that effect. In this way you learn to control your heart rate by jumping up and down, and you contribute to the positive outcome of a study on biofeedback and the self-control of heart rate. But this, you say, is cheating! The increase in heart rate was **mediated** by the response of jumping up and down. This is the important point, but it should be made a bit more subtly. Suppose you found that you could elevate your heart rate by *imagining* that you were jumping up and down. Would it be cheating to produce the desired response this way? It would also be a case of mediation. Jumping up and down in the imagination is merely less obvious than physically jumping up and down. Whatever position you wish to take on this issue, there are now these points to make. (1) Imagined exercise can as a matter of fact influence cardiac responses. (2) It is very difficult to eliminate such effects in studies of biofeedback. (3) The organs of the body function together; one affects others, adding to the possibilities for mediation. For all these reasons the question whether the control of involuntary responses in biofeedback experiments is direct control is still unanswered.

SUMMARY □

Both in real life and in the laboratory, it is possible to identify some situations in which a person's behavior has control over rewards and punishments. In other situations the individual has almost no control. The first of these is the arrangement in which operant conditioning may take place. The second is that for classical conditioning, usually associated with Pavlov. In laboratory classical conditioning experiments a neutral conditioned stimulus (CS) is paired with a nonneutral stimulus (US) which produces a dependable response (UR). The result of such pairing is that the CS becomes capable of eliciting a response (CR) resembling the UR. Such conditioning is a simple but important form of learning. Classical conditioning appears to provide the mechanism by which emotional responses are acquired. It accounts, in part, for the fear or anxiety that are symptoms in many cases of psychological disorder.

The distinguishing feature of operant conditioning is that such learning takes place under conditions in which the learner's behavior brings reinforcement in the form of reward or punishment. E. L. Thorndike's studies of cats escaping from a puzzle box were conducted at the end of the nineteenth century. B. F. Skinner's more recent experiments on bar pressing by rats and the pecking of an illuminated window by pigeons are contemporary examples. As these studies show, the responses that are conditionable by operant methods are usually "voluntary" responses. This fact raises the interesting question whether "involuntary" responses can be conditioned in this way. For example, can we learn to control blood pressure, heart rate, and brain waves by the methods of operant conditioning? People have learned such control quite readily when provided with feedback that indicates the state of the system over which they are attempting to establish control. An important question, which remains unanswered, is whether biofeedback provides direct control over involuntary responses or whether this control is mediated by voluntary processes. Because of the many subtle opportunities for mediation, this question is difficult to answer.

BASIC PHENOMENA

Now that the procedures of classical and operant conditioning have been described, we are in a position to discuss the basic psychology of learning, to explain the phenomena and principles that have been discovered in experimental work on classical and operant conditioning.

Acquisition

Although learning is sometimes sudden and insightful, it is more commonly gradual. This fact makes it natural to present the course of learning in the form of a **learning curve.** The horizontal axis of such a graph is always some measure of practice, either the number of practice trials or the amount of time devoted to practice. The vertical axis is always some measure of performance. Some of the most common measures of learning are the percentage of conditioned or correct responses; the strength or magnitude of the response; the time required to complete a response, such as a run through a maze; and response latency, the time between some signal, such as a CS, and the response. Depending on the measure, the learning curve may increase or decrease. Magnitude and percentage measures increase; time and latency decrease.

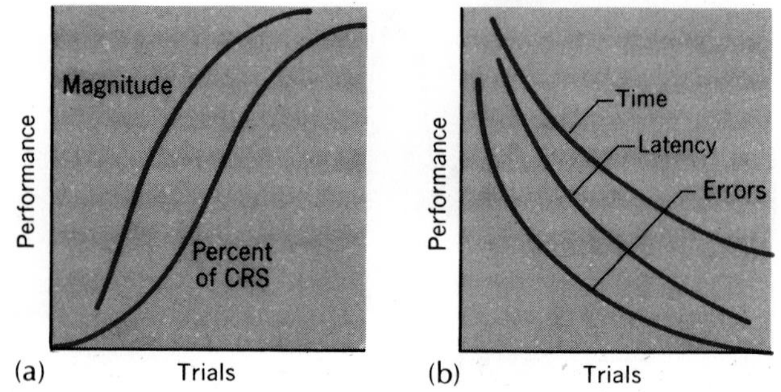

FIGURE 6.9

Characteristic forms of learning curves. (a) Percentage of CRs and response magnitude increase with practice. (*b*) Latency measures and other time measures decrease, as do errors. Errors can decrease to zero.

Cumulative Response Curves The curves in Figure 6.9 show the progress of learning in experiments in which there are separate trials. In the Skinner boxes, in which animals are free to respond as they choose, there are no trials. The animal remains in the experimental situation for a period of time and responds as it will. Performance in such experiments is often recorded automatically, as a **cumulative response curve.** A long sheet of recording paper moves continuously at a constant rate beneath a pen (Figure 6.10). Every time the animal responds, the pen moves upward by a small fixed step. A learning curve revealing the rate of responding is produced automatically. The faster the rate of responding, the steeper the slope of the record.

Reinforcement and the Details of Performance Training a pigeon to peck at the window in order to obtain food in the operant situation is often handled in a succession of steps. Such training begins by teaching the bird to eat from the food dish. This is accomplished in a series of trials in which the experimenter occasionally opens the food magazine so that the bird can learn where the food is. Training of the desired response begins when this first stage is com-

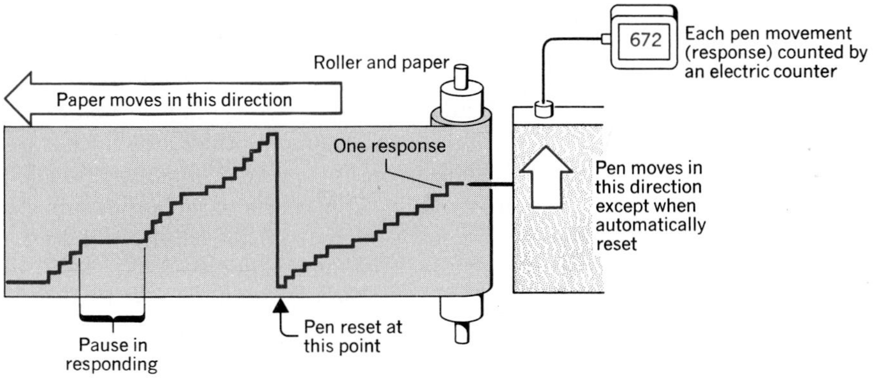

FIGURE 6.10
The operation of a cumulative recorder. The paper moves at a constant speed in the direction indicated. A response, the bar press or window peck, operates an electromagnet, which moves the pen one step upward. When the pen reaches the top of the paper, it activates a switch, which causes the pen to move back to the bottom of the paper. In this way the animal draws its own learning curve. Responses are also counted by an electric counter.

plete and the bird shows only positive reactions to the sounds and sights produced by the food-delivery mechanism as it offers the reward of bird seed. At first the experimenter opens the food hopper whenever the pigeon is near the illuminated window. This keeps the pigeon near the window. In the next step the pigeon must be very near the window to receive reinforcement. And, finally, it is required to peck at the window, which opens the food hopper automatically. These three stages, near the window, very near the window, and pecking at the window, represent a series of gradual approximations to the response that the pigeon is to learn. For this reason the method is called the **method of successive approximations** or, more often, **shaping.** The second term suggests a gradual molding of the response to the form desired by the experimenter.

The shaping procedures indicate that the conditions of reinforcement determine the detailed form that a learned response takes. This means that it is possible to teach animals to respond rapidly or slowly or vigorously or delicately. In one method referred to as a **DRL Schedule** (**D**ifferential **R**einforcement for **L**ow rates of responding), the animal receives food for its responses only if it makes them slowly, separating them by a specific amount of time.

Schedules of Reinforcement The DRL schedule is only one of a family of **schedules of reinforcement** studied in great detail by Skinner and his associates. Most of them are schedules of **partial** or **intermittent reinforcement.** In the operant procedures described so far, the organism received reward every time it made the required response. Such **continuous reinforcement,** however, is not typical of learning as it goes on in the everyday world. Even the well-trained mouser only rarely catches mice. The gambler at the card table wins only part of the time. In either of these situations, the reinforcement schedule is what would technically be called a partial one. Partial reinforcement refers to any arrangement by which the learner is rewarded only a fraction of the time for making a certain response. The variety of schedules of partial reinforcement developed for rats and pigeons performing in Skinner boxes is enormous. Four schedules, however, are basic. These are the fixed-ratio, variable-ratio, fixed-interval, and variable-interval schedules. Rewards are given after fixed and variable numbers of responses and after fixed and variable amounts of time.

In the **fixed-ratio (FR) schedule** the learner must make a fixed number of responses to receive reward. For example, in a bar-pressing experiment a reward might be given for every second, tenth, or thirtieth response, in which case the fixed ratios are 2 (responses): 1 (reward), 10:1, or 30:1. In the terms employed by those working in this field, these schedules would be referred to as FR (fixed ratio) 2, FR 10, FR 30.

In the **fixed-interval (FI) schedule** reward follows the first response to occur after a certain amount of time, such as thirty seconds (FI 30).

In the **variable ratio (VR) schedule** rewards are irregular, but they come after a number of responses that average out to some particular number. On a VR 10 schedule reward might be given for the first response or the thirtieth after the previously rewarded response, but on the average after ten responses. For example, five rewards might occur after one, four, ten, fourteen, and twenty-one responses. Averaging,

1 + 4 + 10 + 14 + 21 = 50; 50 ÷ 5 = 10. Hence the designation VR 10.

In the **variable-interval (VI) schedule** rewards follow the first responses after varying amounts of time that average out to a certain value. If the average of these varying amounts of time were thirty seconds, the schedule would be called a VI 30 schedule.

Typical performances under these schedules are illustrated in Figure 6.11. In the fixed-interval and fixed-ratio schedules there is a characteristic pause immediately after a reinforcement. Such a pause does not usually occur in the variable-ratio and variable-interval schedules. The probable reason is that *immediately* following a reinforcement on one of the fixed schedules, there is never another one. The animal learns this and acts accordingly. Under the variable schedules rewards are more randomly distributed in time; a reward may be offered at almost any moment. Intermittent reinforcement has an important effect on extinction, which we turn to next.

Extinction

As we have seen, classical conditioning takes place when CS and US are paired, operant conditioning when reward or punishment follows a given response. The omission of the US in the classical procedure, or the discontinuing of reward or punishment in the operant, extinguishes the conditioned response. In the Pavlovian experiment the drops of saliva secreted by the dog gradually decrease in number when the light comes on but no meat powder follows. The course of **extinction** of a salivary CR is shown in Figure 6.12*a*.

The extinction of an operant response is similar. If bar pressing and pecking at the lighted window no longer bring an offering of food, the rat and pigeon may continue these responses for a while, but eventually the rate falls off. The rat will press the bar, the pigeon peck the window only in the ordinary and haphazard explorations of their boxes.

FIGURE 6.11

Hypothetical but fairly typical, cumulative response curves under different schedules of reinforcement. Facts to note (1) The vertical lines marked R mean "reinforcement." (2) Performance under the variable-interval schedule is very steady. (3) Performance under the fixed-interval schedule shows a pronounced scallop. The animal has probably learned that it is never rewarded again immediately after receiving one reward. It responds slowly at this point, but it speeds its rate of responding as the moment of reward approaches. (4) On a variable-ratio schedule the animal responds very rapidly because it learns that rewards can be received soon after a previous reward, and that increasing the number of responses increases the number of rewards. (5) The difference between rates of responding early and late in training indicates that the animal learns that rapid responding brings reward quickly.

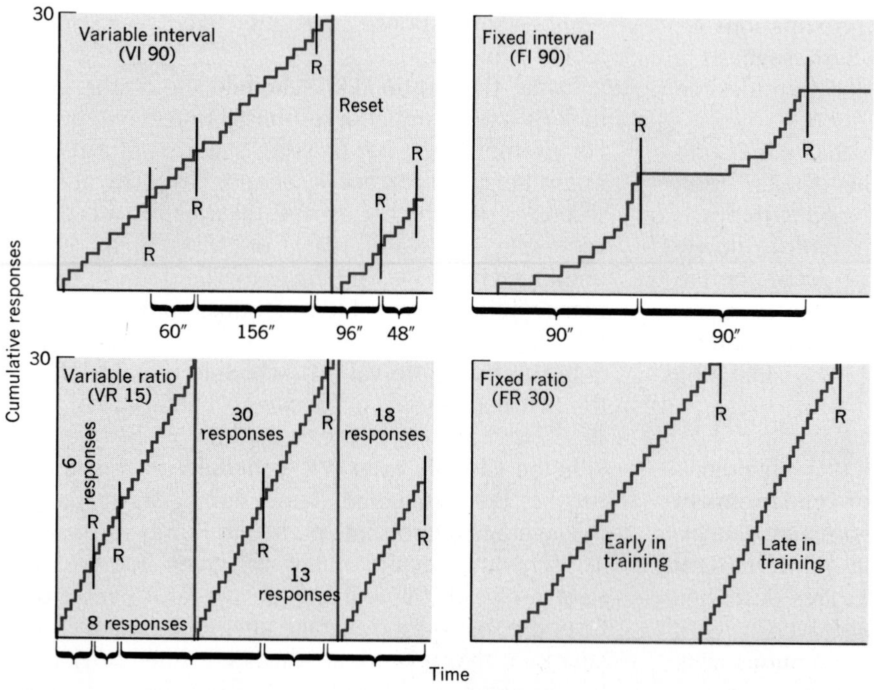

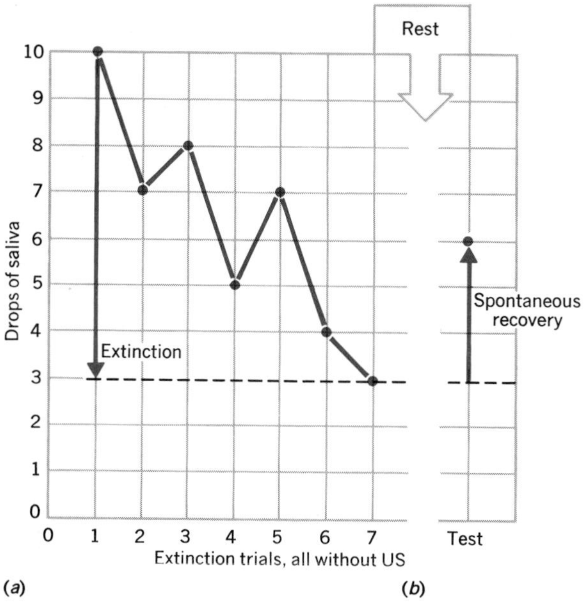

FIGURE 6.12
Extinction and spontaneous recovery. The data are for a single dog described by Pavlov (1927). The arrow pointing downward indicates that unreinforced trials reduced the number of drops of saliva from 10 to 3. The arrow pointing upward indicates that, after rest, the number of drops increased from 3 back up to 6 through spontaneous recovery. Such incomplete recovery, 6 drops rather than 10, is usual.

The number of unreinforced trials or responses that are necessary to obtain extinction depends on many variables. In general, it is more difficult to extinguish well-learned responses than weak ones. A special condition that increases resistance to extinction is a prior schedule of partial reinforcement. That is, the individual who learned under a schedule of partial reinforcement persists longer in responding without any reinforcement at all than an individual who learned originally with continuous reinforcement. This heightened resistance to extinction is called the **partial reinforcement effect.** Human gambling is probably the most important manifestation of the partial reinforcement effect. Gambling persists even when the gambler experiences a long streak of bad luck, probably because the gambling habit was learned with partial reinforcement. If it had been established with continuous reinforcement in the first place, the gambler would probably give up after a few substantial losses.

The partial reinforcement effect is explained by several factors that are not entirely different from one another. (1) During acquisition the individual learns to persist in the face of considerable nonreinforcement, and this persistence continues when there are no rewards at all. (2) The shift from continuous reinforcement to none is much more noticeable than the shift from partial reinforcement to none. (3) During acquisition under partial reinforcement, memories of earlier nonreinforced trials are among the conditions present on reinforced trials. Thus nonreinforcement becomes one of the stimuli for responding. Therefore for a long time during the extinction process nonreinforcement continues to be a cue that encourages a response.

Habits acquired through partial reinforcement are very persistent.

Spontaneous Recovery

Extinction often only temporarily suppresses the conditioned response. With the introduction of a rest interval following extinction, the CR may reappear spontaneously. During the rest period the previously extinguished CR regains strength and, on a new trial with a CS, the CR may again be made. After this **spontaneous recovery** it will persist for a few more trials without reinforcement. The following example from Pavlov illustrates the point. A dog was conditioned to salivate to the sound of a metronome (CS). Then, on seven extinction trials, the metronome ticked on without the presentation of food (US). During this period the drops of saliva produced in response to the metronome decreased from ten to three; the salivary CR was extinguishing. At this point the dog was given a rest, and twenty-three minutes later the metronome was started again. On the first trial after the rest interval, six drops of saliva were secreted, indicating a stronger response than on the last extinction trial (Figure 6.12*b*).

In operant conditioning the rat's bar pressing and the pigeon's window pecking also show spontaneous recovery after these responses have been extinguished. Given a period of time away from their Skinner boxes and then put back, they will often go immediately to the bar and window and begin responding.

In practical terms the phenomenon of spontaneous recovery is important because it shows that a person cannot count on the permanent disappearance of an extinguished habit. With lapses of time it may reappear. As the data in Figure 6.12*b* indicate, however, the spontaneously recovered response tends to be weaker than responses before extinction began. This means that a second extinction will occur more rapidly. If the spontaneously recovered CR is not now reinforced by the US, it quickly reextinguishes. With a series of such extinctions, the response may disappear completely and be beyond spontaneous recovery. If the US is reintroduced, however, the reaction reconditions rapidly and reattains its original strength.

Figure 6.13 is a summary of the materials on the phenomena of conditioning covered so far. The left-hand portion of Figure 6.13 shows the acquisition of the learned response. The intermediate portion demonstrates the process of extinction. The extreme right-hand portion shows what happens to a response that has spontaneously recovered and then is reinforced (upper curve) or not reinforced (lower curve).

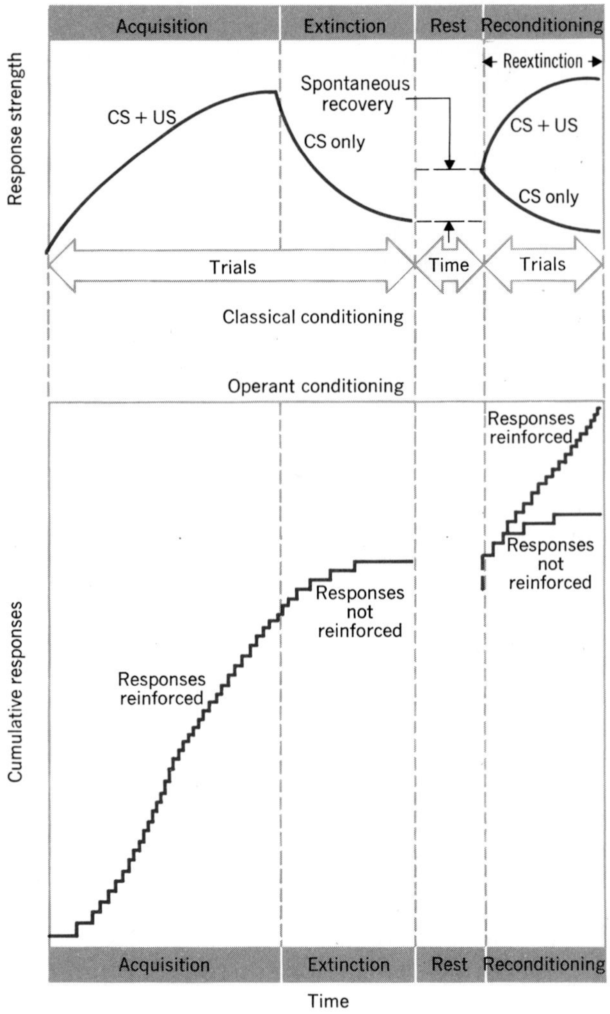

FIGURE 6.13

Review of some basic phenomena. The upper graphs are for classical conditioning. The lower graphs are the cumulative response curves for operant conditioning. You should notice the lengths of the horizontal lines for the various operant responses. Shorter lines mean more rapid responding, that is, responding in a shorter time, than longer lines. Both graphs will repay careful study.

Stimulus Generalization

The CS in a classical conditioning experiment is usually a very specific one, a light of a certain hue and brightness, or a sound of a certain pitch and loudness. In the operant conditioning experiment the pigeon pecks at a window illuminated with a light of a certain color, giving the situation aspects of a CS. A very natural question concerns the ability of other, more or less similar stimuli to evoke the CR. A variety of experiments has shown that a CR can be elicited by such stimuli. This phenomenon is called **stimulus generalization.**

We have already met one example of stimulus generalization in a classical conditioning situation. This was the transfer of Albert's fear of the rat to other furry objects. Pavlov also reported several instances of stimulus generalization. In an operant experiment pigeons were trained to peck at a window illuminated with a green light. Then the pigeons were tested with lights of different colors. The birds did tend to peck at

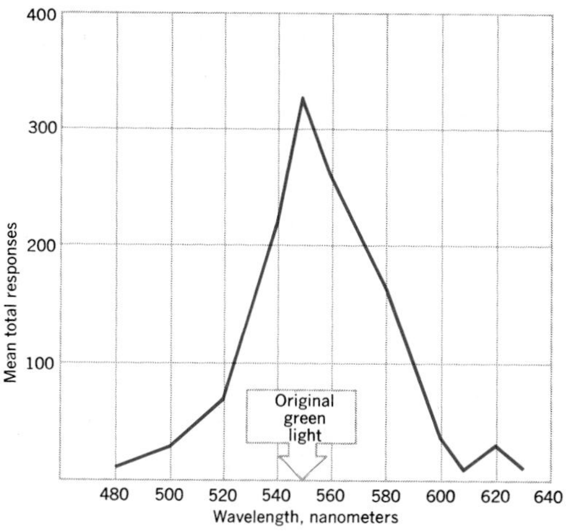

FIGURE 6.14
Stimulus generalization. A generalization gradient for window pecking of the pigeon. Originally the window was illuminated with a greenish light. Pigeons were tested with lights ranging from blue to red. (Data courtesy of Dr. Norman Guttman.)

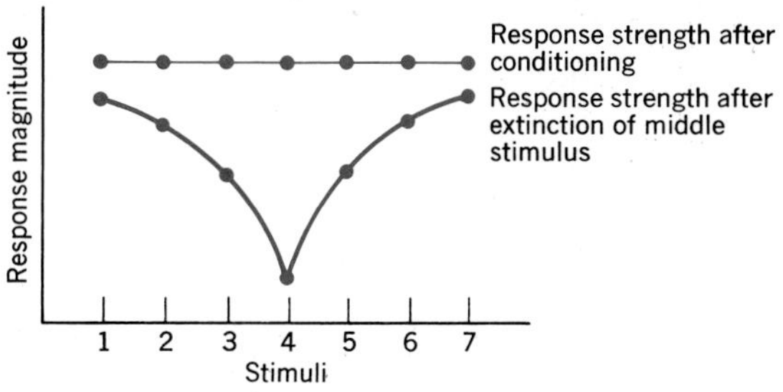

FIGURE 6.15
Generalization of extinction. First a response was conditioned to seven stimuli, all in the same dimension. Then the middle stimulus was subjected to extinction. The graph is a plot of response strength to each stimulus after the original conditioning and after extinction.

any illumination (Figure 6.14), but the number of window pecks fell off as the difference between the color of the training stimulus and that of the test stimulus increased. This symmetrical falling off of the number of responses as the test stimulus becomes more and more different from the training stimulus is called a **generalization gradient.**

The process of stimulus generalization also applies to extinction. If a response is conditioned to a whole range of stimuli and then one stimulus is extinguished, the response will be weakest to that stimulus and stronger to the others (Figure 6.15). This second form of generalization becomes important in a form of behavior therapy, systematic desensitization, to be discussed later in the book (see page 477).

Discrimination

The concepts of acquisition, extinction, and generalization can be used in combination to account for the development of **discrimination.** An animal can learn to respond to a particular stimulus and not to a slightly different one. Pavlov described a discrimination experiment using the methods of classical conditioning. A dog was conditioned to salivate at the tone of a specific tuning fork. After such training conditioned salivation was generalized to other neighboring tones, although the responses were not so strong as to the tone used as a conditioned stimulus. Then in a new procedure the original tone and a second one were presented on randomly alternated trials. Food continued to follow the original tone, but the second tone was never reinforced. As a result, the generalized response to the second tone extinguished, but the response to the original stimulus was maintained. This process of reinforcing one tone and withholding reinforcement for the other thus gradually led to a state of affairs in which the reinforced tone evoked salivation but the second one did not.

As this example shows, the technique for developing a discrimination combines several of the processes described in previous sections. The pairing of a certain tone with the US leads to (1) the acquisition of a CR that (2) generalizes to a similar stimulus. The omission of the US following the presentation of this similar stimulus leads to (3) extinction. A discrimination is established by reinforcing a response to a particular stimulus and extinguishing generalized responses to similar stimuli.

Discriminations can also be taught by operant methods. A pigeon will learn, for example, that only when a green light illuminates the window does pecking at it allow access to bird seed. The green light is called a **discriminative stimulus.** In these circumstances the pigeon can be trained to peck only very rarely at the window illuminated with a yellow or even a yellowish-green light.

One of the most dramatic observations to come from Pavlov's famous conditioning studies were those of animals required to make very difficult discriminations. In one of these studies, Pavlov first conditioned a dog to salivate upon the presentation of a circular figure. Then he established a discrimination between the circle and an ellipse. Whenever the circle was presented, food followed; whenever the ellipse appeared, food failed to follow. Soon the dog came to salivate to the circle but not to the ellipse. When the discrimination was strongly established, the situation was changed and the experimenter began, day by day, to widen the ellipse so that it became more and more similar in shape to the circle. Finally, the two stimuli were so similar that the dog could not distinguish between them. At this point the dog's performance began to deteriorate. Salivation, the conditioned reflex, disappeared and, at the same time, the entire behavior of the animal underwent a marked change. Previously quiet and docile, the dog began to squeal in the restraining apparatus and tore at the equipment and at the tubes for measuring saliva. The dog also showed signs of anxiety—whimpering, trembling, and refusal to eat—as well as drowsiness and yawning. And it barked violently whenever it was taken to the experimental room. Pavlov called this stage **experimental neurosis.**

Pavlov described experimental neurosis as a clash between excitation and inhibition. Translated into slightly more modern phrases, **excitation** is the animal's positive tendency to respond, acquired through reinforcement. **Inhibition** is its tendency to withhold a response because it has not been reinforced. This interpretation was very much in line with the view that human neuroses relfect conflict, a position held in Pavlov's time by Sigmund Freud.

Higher-Order Conditioning

The final phenomenon to be described is **higher-order conditioning.** One of Pavlov's experimental demonstrations consisted of the following steps. A dog was conditioned to salivate at the ticking of a metronome. After this CR had been very well established, the ticking was paired with a black square brought into the dog's field of vision. Food, the original US, was no longer given. In other words, the sound of the metronome, which was the original CS, now served as the US. The black square became a second-order CS. Through this pairing of the black square and the metronome, the dog eventually came to salivate at the sight of the black square, even when there was no ticking. In this demonstration the amount of saliva secreted when the metronome was paired with food in the first-order conditioning procedure was about twelve drops. After ten pairings of the black square with the metronome in the second-order conditioning procedure, the black square evoked six drops of saliva, although the square had never been paired with food directly. Pavlov was successful in obtaining third-order conditioning as well. When the black square was next paired with a tone, salivation eventually followed its sounding. Pavlov had great trouble obtaining third-order conditioning and was never able to achieve higher than third-order conditioning in dogs. The trouble with higher-order conditioning is that the procedure extinguishes the original CR because food is never provided. The dogs will not salivate to a higher than third-order CS because this response has already been extinguished.

Work on secondary reinforcement, to be described more fully in the next section, reveals that something like higher-order operant conditioning is also possible. In operant conditioning we say that the animal may learn to work for a *secondary reinforcer* because it has been associated with a *primary reinforcer*. For example, if the rat presses the bar and hears a click at the same time that the food pellet, the primary reinforcer, slides into the tray, the animal will eventually contine to press the bar just to hear the click, even though food is no longer offered.

SUMMARY □

The phenomena described in this section begin to show the rich variety of influences that learning brings to behavior. (1) Acquisition occurs as a result of reinforcement, when CS and US are paired in classical conditioning or when reward or punishment follows a response in operant conditioning. Reinforcement can be manipulated to control the rapidity and strength of a response as well as its occurrence or nonoccurrence. The progress of learning is often represented in graphic form, a learning curve which shows how some measure of performance changes with the amount of practice. (2) Nonreinforcement leads to a disappearance of the conditioned response, or extinction, but resistance to extinction varies with a number of conditions, the most important of which is the previous schedule of reinforcement. Partial or intermittent reinforcement, of which the four principal types are fixed-interval, fixed-ratio, variable-interval, and variable-ratio, increases persistence and slows up the extinction process. (3) An extinguished response is often spontaneously recovered if the subject is allowed a brief rest following extinction. This indicates that the extinguished response was suppressed rather than completely erased. (4) The responses conditioned to a particular CS in classical conditioning, or controlled by a particular discriminative stimulus in operant conditioning, display stimulus generalization. They appear in response to similar stimuli. The greater the difference between training and test stimuli, however, the weaker the response to the test stimulus. A graph of this relationship is called a generalization gradient. (5) Discrimination, whether in classical or operant conditioning, takes place when reinforcement maintains the responses to one stimulus and nonreinforcement extinguishes generalized responses to similar stimuli. (6) Higher-order conditioning can be obtained when the CSs from earlier stages of a classical conditioning experiment become the USs in a later stage. In operant conditioning stimuli associated with primary reinforcers become secondary reinforcers and are sought for themselves.

CLASSICAL-OPERANT INTERACTIONS

As we mentioned in the first pages of this chapter, classical and operant conditioning procedures represent a simplification of the learning process as an aid to investigation, but in most actual learning situations both forms of learning occur. Moreover, the two forms of learning affect each other. We turn to such interactions now.

Secondary Motives and Rewards

Some motives and their corresponding rewards are **primary motives and rewards.** They depend very little on experience. Hunger and food, thirst and water, pain and escape from pain are obvious examples. Other motives and satisfactions, including most of those that are important to human behavior, are acquired through experience. The needs for power, approval, and achievement and the means of their satisfaction are examples.

No doubt the mechanism for the establishment of these **secondary motives** and **secondary reinforcers** is as complicated as learning itself. It appears, however, that classical conditioning will be a part of the story. Stimuli that are associated with primary rewards become secondary rewards and stimuli associated with primary motives become secondary motives. A description of some of the best-known studies on these topics will help to clarify these abstract statements.

Conditioned Positive Reinforcement One of the investigations of secondary reinforcers—called conditioned positive reinforcement—is now a classic. In these studies (Figure 6.16) chimpanzees first learned to insert small discs, about the size of poker chips, into a vending machine to obtain a grape or other pieces of desirable food. Through this experience, which associated the tokens with food, tokens came to be secondary reinforcers. The chimpanzees learned a variety of responses, for which the only reward was a token. One such response was the lifting of a weighted lever. Another required the animals to pull in a sliding tray, baited with a token, by means of a cord. The animals would continue to work for and save these tokens, even though they could not be exchanged for food until later.

An important incidental point made by this study is that the motive-reward distinction is not a completely sharp one. Although the association of tokens with food made the tokens secondary rewards in this study, they were obviously also functioning as motivators. The animals were willing to work for them. In terms that are generally used, the tokens became **incentives** at the same time that they acquired secondary reinforcing power.

Token economies created for the management of hospitalized psychiatric patients represent a direct application of these ideas at the human level. In the token economy of the mental hospital, the patients re-

FIGURE 6.16
The "Chimp-O-Mat." If the chimpanzee puts a token into the slot, it receives a reward in exchange.

ceive plastic or metal chips, or sometimes paper money, for desired behavior. These tokens are then exchangeable for specific goods from the commissary, for privileges such as a better room or choice of dining partners, for activities such as participating in recreation programs and excursions, and for time away from the institution. The most dramatic successes of these methods have been with psychotic patients who have been kept out of sight in the back wards of state mental hospitals for a decade or more. Such people are out of social contact, slovenly, uncooperative; they spend their hours sleeping, in stuporous thought, or in aimless motor activity. If you have read *One Flew Over the Cuckoo's Nest* or seen the movie, you have the picture. With the installation of token economies, the attitudes, behavior, and appearance of patients have been considerably improved (Krasner, 1976).

Possibly because of their origins in studies of animal learning, these programs have sometimes been criticized on the ground that they "dehumanize" the participants. Such criticism is difficult to understand on logical grounds in a free-enterprise society that tolerates the institution of green stamps. It is even more difficult to understand on moral bases, for participation in token economies appears to *humanize* the patient rather than the opposite.

Conditioned Fear and Avoidance Learning **Avoidance learning** is a form of operant conditioning in which the particular response to be learned will allow the animal to avoid punishment. It is sometimes studied with an apparatus which has an electrified grid in the floor and, in one wall, a wheel that will turn off the electricity if it is rotated (Figure 6.17). In a typical experiment the procedure is as follows. A rat is placed in the apparatus and a warning signal such as a light is presented five or ten seconds before an electric current passes through the grid in the floor. If the animal rotates the wheel during this interval, the current does not come on and the animal receives no shock. On the very first trials, of course, the rat has not learned this. There is no response to the light, and when the current is turned on, the animal shows considerable agitation. It jumps, defecates, urinates, crouches, squeals, and finally, clawing or bumping against the wheel, rotates it. When the rat succeeds in turning the wheel, perhaps thirty or forty seconds after the beginning of the trial, the warning light and the shock both go off immediately. On subsequent trials the escape response is made more and more promptly until the rat turns the wheel within a fraction of a second after the onset of shock. With further training the rat learns to turn the wheel as soon as the light comes on and thus avoids the shock completely.

When the animal learns to turn the wheel to avoid shock, it learns two things. One is the connection between light and shock. This is a form of classical conditioning in which the light is the CS and the shock is the US. From the similarity of this procedure to the experiment with little Albert, you will recognize that it leads to the conditioning fear, a secondary motive. In the avoidant situation the CS thus becomes capable of arousing fear. This is important because now the animal has been given a motive for responding before the shock comes on. The motive is fear evoked by the light.

The other thing to be learned is the timing of the operant wheel-turning response. At first this response is a means of escaping shock after the shock comes on. With practice, however, this response becomes dominant in the situation and, motivated by fear of the CS, the animal turns the wheel *before* the shock comes on. When it does, the light goes off and fear subsides; the wheel-turning response is no longer rewarded by eliminating shock but by reducing fear. This account is a **two-factor theory** of avoidant behavior. The avoidant reaction is *motivated* by conditioned fear and is *reinforced* by fear reduction.

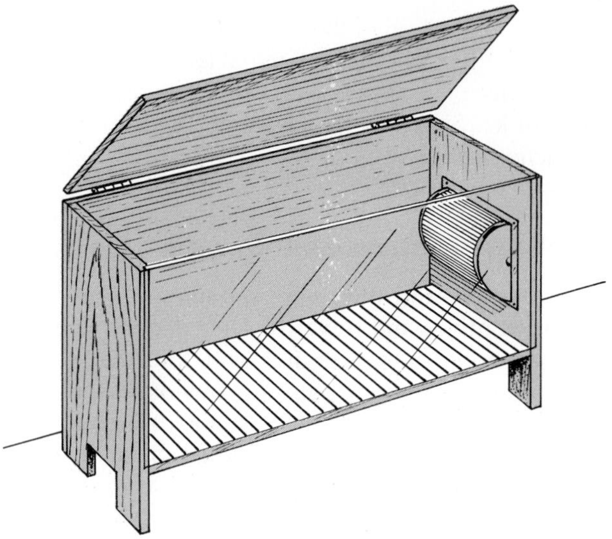

FIGURE 6.17
A wheel-turning apparatus for studying avoidance learning. In the usual procedure a conditioned stimulus (light or sound) comes on, and then 5 or 10 seconds later an electric current passes through the floor grid. Rotating the wheel after the shock comes on turns it off. A response to the CS allows the animal to avoid the shock.

A Conditioned Compulsion

Again, simple learning processes have important applications to human behavior, this time to the development of neurotic symptoms. The case of Mrs. A, described by John Dollard and Neal Miller (1950), will show the connection.

> Mrs. A, a strikingly beautiful twenty-three-year-old married woman who came for psychotherapy, complained of a number of fears, the strongest of which was a fear that her heart would stop beating. Because of this fear she had developed the annoying neurotic symptom of compulsively counting her heartbeats. Born an orphan, Mrs. A had been brought up by a harsh foster mother whose exceedingly repressive sex training had made her feel that sex was evil and dirty. In spite of this Mrs. A developed unusually strong sexual urges. Before her marriage she had slept with a dozen different men, on every occasion feeling painfully guilty.

Enough of Mrs. A's background has now been presented to allow us to trace the development of her neurotic symptoms. Mrs. A was highly motivated sexually, but the stimuli of sexual arousal had been conditioned in the past to bring on an intense anxiety reaction. The conditioning sequence was CS (sexual stimuli) → US (punishment at hands of repressive foster mother). Mrs. A's predominant symptom, counting her heartbeats, was an avoidant response, motivated by anxiety and rewarded by anxiety reduction. Whenever a sexual thought came to mind, Mrs. A started counting. Since this took all her attention, the sexual fantasy and the resulting anxiety disappeared from consciousness.

SUMMARY □

The materials in this section have now spelled out the meaning of the assertion with which this chapter began, that in any learning situation there are two somewhat different things to learn: the sequence of events to be expected and what to do about them. As developed here, the first of these learning processes establishes first events, previously neutral stimuli, as secondary reinforcers. Having been associated with primary reinforcement, such stimuli take on secondary reinforcing properties themselves. They also acquire motivational or incentive value. In a similar way, stimuli associated with pain take on negative properties.

Such conditioning plays an important role in the establishment of operant responses. The mechanisms have been worked out best for avoidance learning. In such learning the animal acquires a fear of stimuli associated with an aversive stimulus, usually shock in experimental work. Motivated by such fear, the animal then learns any response that removes the stimulus provoking fear or allows it to leave the situation provoking fear.

The roles played by conditioned positive reinforcement and conditioned fear have surprisingly direct parallels in human behavior—in the workings of token economies in the first case and in the selection of neurotic symptoms in the second.

LEARNING THEORY

The questions to which we finally turn concern the nature of learning. When a person learns something, exactly what is learned? What role do reward, punishment, and motivation play in learning? What contributions do the biologically given traits of the individual make to the process? Does learning happen gradually or all at once? Are all cases of learning the same, or must we discriminate among different forms of learning? These questions have been the object of intense research, and sometimes bitter dispute, for most of a century. Instead of reviewing this history of controversy, we shall describe what we believe to be the currently accepted positions on several of these issues. This will provide you with a brief synopsis of current learning theory.

Contiguity or Contingency?

For the dogs in Pavlov's classical conditioning experiment, the CS and US are linked together through time. For the rats and pigeons in Skinner's operant conditioning boxes, the response to be learned and reinforcement follow one after the other. The traditional view of learning maintains that such **temporal contiguity** of CS and US or response and reinforcement is an essential condition of learning. There is considerable evidence to support this view. For example, the classical conditioning of many responses is possible only if CS is followed by US, separated by no more than a second or two. A host of operant studies have shown that little or no learning occurs if reward or punishment is delayed, even by a few seconds.

Although temporal contiguity between CS and US or response and reinforcement is the most obvious condition for learning, a different type of relation is also present. This second one is a **contingent relationship.** In most classical conditioning experiments the US (food for Pavlov's dog) is given if and only if the CS (tone or light) has preceded it; that is, the occurrence of the US is contingent on the CS. In most operant conditioning experiments, reinforcement (food for Skinner's rats) follows if and only if a certain response (bar pressing) is made; that is, the occurrence of reinforcement is contingent on the designated response. Contiguity and contingency are present together in situations in which effective learning takes place. Without doing a very special type of experiment, however, we cannot tell whether the necessary condition for learning is contiguity, contingency, or both.

If we limit ourselves to taking classical salivary conditioning as an example, an experiment to decide whether *contiguity* is a necessary condition would require two groups of dogs. An experimental group would be conditioned in the normal way, with *contiguous pairings* of CS, a light, and US, food powder. For the control group of dogs, the CS and US would not be paired. They would see the light and be offered food powder the same number of times as the experimental group, but light and food would never be given closely together in time. Many experiments of this type have shown that the experimental group is conditioned but not the control group, which would seem to indicate the contiguity must be the important condition for learning.

In 1967, however, Robert Rescorla of Yale University called attention to the fact that, although the control procedure just described eliminates contiguity, a contingency remains. The presentation of the CS absolutely guarantees that the US will not be given. In other words, food is offered to the control group if and only if the light *has not* been turned on. Or, vice versa, seeing the light signifies that food *is not* forthcoming. If contingencies are the basis of learning, the subjects in the control group could be learning the negative contingency, that the light signifies no food. In this sense they would be conditioned just as the subjects in the experimental group were. Since they have learned that CS means no US, however, they are not likely to make a response that suggests an association between light and food.

On the basis of this argument, Rescorla proposed an experiment that would indicate whether the contingency between CS and US was the essential condition for learning. Dogs were first trained to shuttle back and forth in a two-compartment apparatus (Figure 6.18) with electrified floor grids and a half partition between the compartments. The dogs were trained on a **Sidman avoidance schedule** (Sidman, 1953), which works in this way. An electric shock is mechanically programmed to come on, say, every twenty seconds, first in the floor grid on one side of the shuttle box and then in that of the other. If the dog stays in the compartment on one side of the apparatus for as long as twenty seconds, it receives a shock. If the dog jumps over the partition and goes to the other side of the apparatus before the twenty seconds are up, however, the next scheduled shock is postponed, say for ten seconds. Under this regime dogs develop a very steady rate of jumping from one side of the box to the other and back again, one that allows them to avoid shock almost completely.

After the dogs had been trained on this schedule in the shuttle box, they were divided into three groups and given further training outside the box. One group of dogs went through a series of regular conditioning trials, with a light as the CS and shock as the US. A second group, considered the control group, saw a light go on and received shock, but the two stimuli were never paired. As we have already seen, this procedure eliminates CS-US contiguity, but it allows a negative contingency for CS predicts perfectly that US is not imminent. Rescorla called the third group a "truly random" control group. These dogs saw the light and received shock, but on a random schedule. Seeing the light predicted *neither* the imminence of shock *nor* its absence. The two stimuli were programmed randomly and separately. Usually they did not occur together, but once in a while they did. The important point is that the light indicated in no way whether shock would be given.

Now the dogs were returned to the original apparatus, where they resumed the steady shuttling back and forth. As they did so, the light was turned on from time to time. How the dogs responded to the light depended on the second period of training. The dogs in the traditional conditioning group jumped back and forth at a faster rate, as though the light were a warning of shock to come, which it had been in the procedure carried on outside the shuttle box. The dogs in the control group, for whom light and shock had been explicitly not paired, slowed down in their rate of jumping. For them the light seemed to be a safety signal, indicating that shock would be omitted. Those in the "truly random" control group showed no change in their rate of shuttling, as though the light had no significance. These results argue convincingly that what is learned in a conditioning situation is the contingency between CS and US, that the major function of the CS is to provide predictions of things to come. CSs that make no such predictions are ineffective.

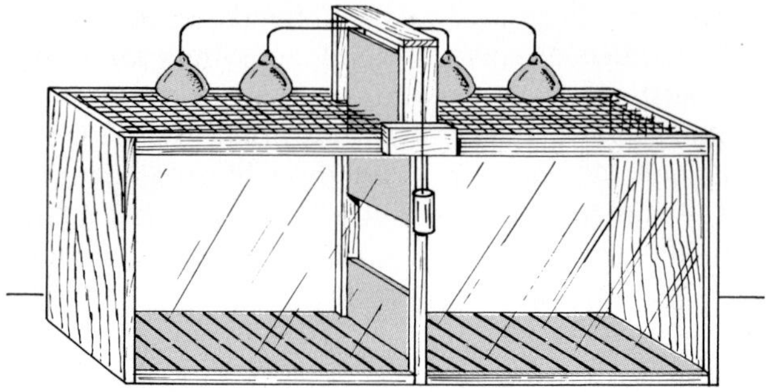

FIGURE 6.18
Avoidance apparatus for dogs. The animal is placed on one side or the other of the apparatus and must jump the partition to escape or avoid shock. In some versions of the experiment the dog merely shuttles back and forth. In others the lights come on as a warning signal. (Adapted with permission of Richard L. Solomon.)

There are data to suggest that rats and pigeons, as well as dogs, are capable of learning that in some circumstances contingencies are lacking and that events happen unpredictably. We should not conclude that a stimulus having no predictive value has no consequences, however. Especially when the stimuli are severe and painful, uncertainty about when they will happen is very stressful. For example, animals from several species have developed stomach ulcers when given unpredictable electric shock.

Learned Helplessness

An interesting phenomenon has been observed in an operant situation which removes the contingency between a response and escape from punishment. Steven F. Maier and Martin Seligman (1976) conducted their experiment with three groups of dogs. All dogs were eventually put in the shuttle box shown in Figure 6.18, but earlier they had had varied experiences with electric shock. One group received no shock at all. Another group received shocks that were escapable. They were strapped into a harness and given shocks which they could turn off by moving their heads and pressing a panel. The final group was a **yoked control group;** these dogs were also harnessed and were subjected to electric shock at the same time as the dogs in the second group. They could not control shock by pressing a panel, however. By means of electrical wiring, the animals receiving the escapable shock turned off the shock for their partners in the yoked control group. Maier and Seligman found that when the dogs in the three groups were put into the shuttle box, they behaved in the following ways.

> When placed in the shuttle box an experimentally naive dog (and also one that has experienced escapable shock), at the onset of the first electric shock, runs frantically about, until it accidentally scrambles over the barrier and escapes the shock. On the next trial, the dog, running frantically, crosses the barrier more quickly. . . . Within a few trials the animal becomes very efficient at escaping and soon learns to avoid shock altogether. . . . But the dogs first given inescapable shock. . . show a strikingly different pattern. Such a dog's first reactions to shock in the shuttle box are much the same as those of a naive dog. He runs around frantically for about 30 seconds, but then stops moving, lies down, and quietly whines. After 1 minute of this, shock terminates automatically. The dog fails to cross the barrier and escape from shock. On the next trial, the dog again fails to escape. At first he struggles a bit and then, after a few seconds, seems to give up and passively accept the shock. On all succeeding trials, the dog continues to fail to escape. . . .
>
> We believe that these phenomena are instances of "learned helplessness," instances in which an organism has learned that outcomes are uncontrollable by his responses and is seriously debilitated by this knowledge (p. 4).

The phenomenon of **learned helplessness** suggests again that the animal understands the contingencies, or lack of them, in a situation, and that this understanding is an important aspect of learning.

Biological Constraints on Learning

Novel-Taste Aversion In the introduction to his book *Biological Boundaries of Learning* (1972), written with Joanne Hager, Seligman tells this personal story.

> Sauce Béarnaise is an egg-thickened, tarragon-flavored concoction, and it used to be my favorite sauce. It now tastes awful to me. This happened several years ago, when I felt the effects of the stomach flu . . . after eating filet mignon with Sauce Béarnaise. I became violently ill and spent most of the night vomiting. The next time I had Sauce Béarnaise, I couldn't bear the taste of it. At the time, I had no ready way to account for the change, although it seemed to fit a classical conditioning paradigm: CS (sauce) paired with US (illness) and UR (vomiting) yields CR (nauseating taste). . . (p. 8).

Experiments with lower animals support Seligman's interpretation. In a typical experiment an animal—usually a rat, but cats, mice, and monkeys have shown the same reactions—is allowed to taste and consume some substance with a novel taste. Water flavored with saccharine is a common example. Then, several hours later, the animal is made sick by subjecting it to X-radiation or by administering a sublethal dose of poison. When the animal recovers from the effects of this treatment, it is given access once more to the substance with the novel taste. Now the animal avoids it, as though it thought the substance had made it sick (Seligman and Hager, 1972).

These results are very much different from those obtained in other experiments. For one thing, associations between CS (taste) and US (sickness) are made after an interval of an hour or more. Usually conditioning does not occur if the time between stimuli is more than a few seconds. For a second thing, learning in this situation happens all at once, in a single trial. These results bring to mind the "belongingness" that Thorndike referred to years ago. Thorndike believed that certain pairs of events naturally belonged together and were easy to associate. The work on taste aversion seems to prove that taste and sickness are such a pair. Control studies have demonstrated that rats *do not* learn to avoid a *place* as a result of being made sick there, although they do avoid the place where they have experienced electric shock. Just as Thorndike proposed, there apparently are certain sympathies between stimuli: sights and pain are easy for the rat to associate, as are tastes and sickness.

This research on conditioned taste aversions suggests that there are, as Seligman and Hager (1972) put it in the title of their book, "biological boundaries of learning." These boundaries have a profound influence on the ease with which certain responses can be learned. In extreme cases learning becomes so easy that almost no practice is necessary or so difficult that learning is virtually impossible. For example, pigeons are rarely able to learn to peck to avoid shock. Pecking for food, however, is so natural for the pigeon that it will do so without any special training. This interesting phenomenon, called **autoshaping,** has been demonstrated in the Skinner box. The window is illuminated for a few seconds and then food is delivered no matter what the pigeon does. The pigeon nevertheless begins spontaneously to peck the window after it has been illuminated only a few times. Window pecking persists even when, later on, conditions are arranged so that it prevents the delivery of food.

Taste aversion and autoshaping experiments challenge what was once a generally accepted view of learning, the **premise of equipotentiality.** According to this premise, just about any stimulus an organism is able to detect can be linked to just about any response the organism can make. On the basis of the evidence just described and similar phenomena, Seligman and Hager propose replacing the principle of equipotentiality with a **principle of preparedness,** which they introduce this way.

> . . . An organism brings to any experiment certain equipment and predispositions either more or less appropriate to the situation. It brings specialized sensory and response apparatus with a long evolutionary history. . . . Often forgotten is the fact that in addition to sensory-motor apparatus, the organism brings associative apparatus which also has a long and specialized evolutionary history. This specialization may make certain contingencies easier to learn about than others, more difficult to forget, more readily generalizable, and so on (p. 3).

This theory that associative processes are an evolutionary specialization has some support. The stimuli that are easiest to condition to reactions of nausea are not the same in all species. The pigeon, a highly visual animal, easily develops aversions to visual stimuli if they are associated with nausea, but it does not develop aversions to flavors that are followed by sickness. For the rat, as we have seen, exactly the reverse is true.

Skinnerian Superstitions Additional evidence of the way in which biological factors contribute to learning comes from studies that, at first, seemed to require quite a different interpretation. Some years ago B. F. Skinner (1948) described an important experiment on superstitious behavior in the pigeon. The pigeons were placed in the Skinner box and the food hopper was opened at fixed intervals, allowing the animal to eat, no matter what else it did; that is, there was no actual contingency between any response the birds could make and reinforcement. Under these circumstances what the pigeons did was very interesting. They developed individual patterns of "ritualistic" behavior, which they performed as though they believed that food was contingent on these particular responses. These superstitious responses consisted of such things as circling the chamber, bowing, flapping the wings and stretching the neck, all in ceremonial sequence.

Skinner's interpretation of these actions was that the pigeon repeated whatever it happened to be doing when the hopper opened. Its chance activities of the moment, reinforced in this way, were automatically strengthened and organized into a chain of reactions that the pigeon performed to bridge the temporal gap from one reinforcement to the next.

At first blush these data seem to lend powerful support to the principle of equipotentiality. Reinforcement apparently dictated the selection of whatever movement the pigeon was making as it was offered. Later work was to show that, although there is more truth to this interpretation than the work on biological constraints may suggest, important qualifications still need to be made.

Instinctive Drift John Staddon and Virginia Simmelhag (1971) repeated Skinner's experiment on superstition, but they made much more detailed observations of the pigeons' responses. They obtained the same results as Skinner had, but with one important addition: the ritualistic sequences of behavior always ended with pecking, a feeding response, in every pigeon except one, whose reaction was to move its head toward the food hopper. Such behavior seemed to occur more and more dependably as training progressed.

The appearance of these food-related responses is an example of what might be called **instinctive drift.** In animal training it is common to find that an animal learning to make a specific response will gradually drift into quite different actions that are normal components of the food-getting behavior of the species. The "dancing chicken" is an example.

> The chicken walks over about 3 feet, pulls a rubber loop on a small box which starts a repeated auditory stimulus pattern (a four-note tune). The chicken then steps up onto an 18-inch, slightly raised disc, thereby closing a timer switch, and scratches vigorously, round and round, over the disc for 15 seconds, at the rate of about two scratches per second until the automatic feeder fires in the retaining compartment. The chicken goes into the compartment to eat, thereby automatically shutting the door. The popular interpretation of this behavior pattern is that the chicken has turned on the "juke box" and "dances."
>
> The development of this behavioral exhibit was wholly unplanned. In the attempt to create quite another type of demonstration which required a chicken simply to stand on a platform for 12-15 seconds, we found that over 50 percent developed a very strong and pronounced scratch pattern . . . we were able to change our plans to make use of the scratch pattern, and the result was the "dancing chicken" [just] described. . . .
>
> In this exhibit the only real contingency for reinforcement is that the chicken must depress the

platform for 15 seconds. . . (Breland and Breland, 1961).

SUMMARY □

The basic process in simple learning appears to be the development of a knowledge of contingencies: CS-US contingencies in classical conditioning and response-reinforcement contingencies in the operant case. Important insights into the nature of learning have come from studies that have kept animals from establishing such contingencies. Animals receiving truly random presentations of the stimuli used as CS and US in a classical conditioning experiment learn that the CS has no bearing on when the US will occur. Presenting the stimulus while these animals are moving routinely to avoid shock has no effect on their behavior. Animals trained under conditions in which the CS predicts that the US either will or will not follow speed up or slow down their movements accordingly.

Animals that cannot avoid operant punishment, whatever movements they make—because the contingency between their responses and avoidance has been removed—become helpless. They later fail to learn to avoid punishment when avoidance becomes possible. These animals behave as though they believe that nothing they do is effective.

These studies have to do with the cognitive or intellectual side of conditioning. They show that understanding contingencies is important. Other research calls attention to the powerful effects of biological factors. Studies of taste aversion in rats demonstrate that a novel taste and a sickness that develops hours later can be associated after a single experience. Visual stimuli and sickness are not associated. These results are among those that argue against the traditional principle of equipotentiality, which supposes that associations between any stimulus an organism can detect and any response it can make are formed with equal ease. They argue, instead, for a principle of preparedness according to which some stimuli and responses "belong" together and are easily and naturally associated.

Detailed observations of the "superstitious" behavior of pigeons add to the evidence that unlearned biological factors restrict what animals are likely to learn in a given situation. Pigeons will continue to repeat ritualistically whatever movements they happened to be making when the food hopper opened, but their chain of movements will end with pecking, a feeding response. Even when other responses are reinforced by food, the pigeon will gradually start to peck. Pecking may even replace the response that is specifically reinforced. Such "instinctive drift" has been put to use in training animals for public exhibitions of their skills. A chicken that scratches a performing platform instinctively appears to have been deliberately trained to dance.

TO BE SURE YOU UNDERSTAND THIS CHAPTER △

The following concepts are the important ones presented in this chapter. They are listed in the approximate order in which they appeared. You should be able to use them to reconstruct the discussion of the chapter.

Classical conditioning
Operant conditioning (instrumental conditioning)
US (unconditioned stimulus)
Reinforcer
UR (unconditioned response)
CS (conditioned stimulus)
CR (conditioned response)
Skinner box
Biofeedback
EEG
Alpha rhythm
Mediation
Acquisition
Learning curve
Cumulative response curve
Schedules of reinforcement (FR, FI, VR, VI)
Partial reinforcement effect (PRE)
Extinction
Spontaneous recovery
Stimulus generalization
Generalization gradient
Generalization of extinction
Discrimination
Discriminative stimulus
Experimental neurosis
Higher-order conditioning
Secondary reinforcement
Primary reinforcement
Secondary motivation
Incentive
Token economy
Avoidance learning
Two-factor theory
Contiguity
Contingency
Sidman avoidance schedule
Yoked control group
Learned helplessness
Biological constraints
Autoshaping
Premise of equipotentiality
Principle of preparedness
Superstition
Instinctive drift

TO GO BEYOND THIS CHAPTER △

In this book Applications of the principles of conditioning and learning appear in Chapter 15, on motivation and conflict; Chapter 17, on psychopathology; and Chapter 19, on therapy. A review of pages 35 to 36, on reflexes, will add meaning to Pavlov's conception of the conditioned reflex.

Elsewhere Pavlov's 1927 book is well within the comprehension of the beginning student. For a contemporary treatment of conditioning and learning with more of an emphasis on operant conditioning, we recommend *Psychology of Learning and Behavior,* by Barry Schwartz. There are many other excellent books on this topic. You can locate them easily by a bit of browsing in the library.

CH. 7

Human Information Processing

Immediate Memory
Iconic Memory
The Magical Number Seven
The Time It Takes To Think
Attention
Summary

Short- and Long-Term Memory
Limits of Short-Term Memory
Storage
Retrieval
Summary

Representation of Information in Memory
Dual-Coding Theory
Organization of Memory
Summary

Forgetting
Measures of Retention
Interference
Summary

Toward a Better Memory
The Feeling of Knowing
Overlearning
Subjective Organization
General Overviews
Mnemonic Devices
Individual Differences
Summary

From time to time psychologists discover people whose memories are truly astonishing. One such individual was studied by two psychologists at The University of Washington. This man, whom they call "VP," plays up to seven chess matches *blindfolded.* He can simultaneously play bridge and chess and read a book. Without referring to notes, he can carry on sixty correspondence games of chess. In the laboratory VP's performance is equally outstanding. In one test he studied for several minutes normal and staggered matrices of numbers such as the following.

Standard matrix	*Staggered matrix*
0 3 4 7 4 3	3 6 96 4 7
9 7 7 4 2 4	2 7 073 1
3 1 6 7 6 6	42 1 0 5 0
1 2 5 6 8 5	2 6 2 78 6
5 5 5 9 5 6	1 24 1 9 4
1 6 2 2 7 7	9 3 0 21 8
8 4 4 2 1 7	5 9 3 38 2
0 3 0 1 7 8	7 6 709 0

He was then able to repeat either matrix without error and to give any row, column, or diagonal series of numbers upon request. Two weeks later he could still repeat the normal matrix without a mistake, except for the reversal of two numbers (Hunt and Love, 1972).

Such impressive performances raise questions, some of them about the specific individual being studied. Are people like VP a great deal more intelligent than ordinary mortals, or are their accomplishments ones that many of us could aspire to? Are there special circumstances in the histories of such individuals that appear to account for their mental feats? Are particular aspects of personal makeup important?

More general questions also come to mind. In what form do memories—for example, of the matrix—exist? As mental pictures, verbal sentences, or what? How does a person go about retrieving materials from memory? Why do we forget certain things and remember others? What skills might we develop to improve our memories? The study of information processing concerns itself with such questions. In this chapter we shall describe some of the basic knowledge about the phenomena of memory. As we do so, we shall answer some of these specific questions and now and again cite other feats of VP's impressive memory.

Stages The term information processing expresses the idea that an individual works on or processes materials as they are presented, putting them into a form that allows them to be stored in memory. One important hypothesis about information processing is that it happens in a series of stages. As materials are presented to a person, they exist first for a few seconds in *immediate memory.* For these few seconds immediate memory contains more information than the system can handle. Only the materials to which we pay attention survive for further processing. These attended-to materials enter *short-term memory,* where they remain for half a minute or so before those that receive still further processing enter *long-term memory.* There they may remain forever, more or less available for use as needed.

Processes What goes on in information processing can also be described in terms of the processes involved, which are often called *encoding, storage,* and *retrieval.* Encoding is putting materials into a form that the memory system can handle. Storage is the process of committing encoded materials to memory. Retrieval is taking the materials that are stored in memory out again.

Level In one way or another, all these processes raise the question of the form or code in which materials exist in memory. The representation is apparently complex, since it can be at a number of different levels. The printed word CHICKEN, for example could be described as a physical object consisting of a collection of marks on a page that have a certain set of geometric features and patterns of light intensity. Or it might be described as a string of letters with individual identities. But CHICKEN is also a certain animal. It is an item on the menu. It is a synonym for cowardice. And it sometimes denotes a reckless, now and then fatal, game that people play with automobiles.

These ways of describing the word CHICKEN range from mere physical features to meaning. This dimension from physical representation to meaning, sometimes referred to as depth or level, sometimes as elaborateness, is central to much of the discussion that follows. The discussion itself, however, is organized according to the proposed stages of memory.

IMMEDIATE MEMORY

Anyone who has ever been to a movie with dialogue in a language with which he is only vaguely familiar has probably found himself wishing from time to time that he could stop the sound for a moment in order to translate what is being said. This suggests that auditory impressions remain available in awareness for at least a brief period of time, constituting a sort of **echoic memory** of sounds just heard. There is also evidence of a similar **iconic memory** (icon-, from the Greek *eikon,* image), of fleeting images of our visual impressions. Both of these are examples of immediate sensory memory.

Iconic Memory

For brief periods of time this immediate sensory memory provides us with a great deal of information that will soon be lost. In an experiment that illustrates this point, George Sperling presented three short lines of letters and numbers for very brief periods of time (Figure 7.1*a*), asking observers to report as much as they could of the material in the complete display. Participants were able to report between four and five items correctly. If, however, immediately *after* the presentation of the materials, when they were no longer visible, participants were given a signal that told them to report the letters and numbers in the first, second, or third lines, they were able to do so almost perfectly. This result suggests that all or almost all the twelve items in the display were available in memory for a brief moment of time. But sensory memory is indeed fleeting. The entire effect disappears in a little over a second. When subjects were asked to remember the whole array, the sensory memory vanished while they were observing and reporting four of the items, and they could report no more.

A person participating in experiments of this type is very briefly able to inspect an image of the display after it has vanished from the visual field. To demonstrate just how fleeting this image is, the experimenter gave the instruction indicating which line was to be reported at various intervals before and after the presentation of the materials (Figure 7.1*b*). Given the instruction to report, for example, lines three, *before* the array was flashed, the observers were able to identify the items very precisely. When the signal *followed* the flashing of the array, performance deteriorated rapidly and after a second's lapse reached the same level as trying to remember the whole array.

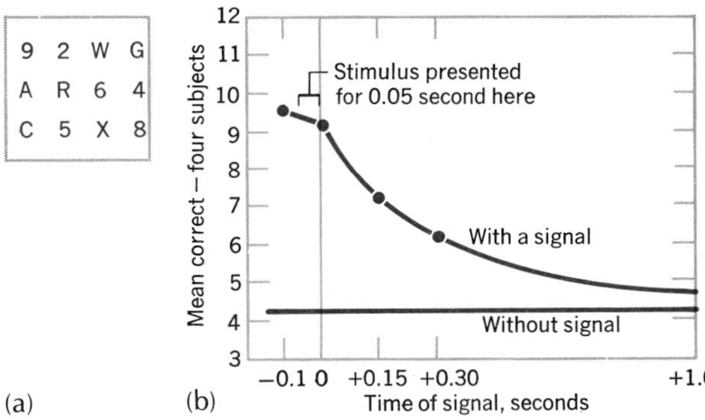

FIGURE 7.1

A study of immediate memory. (*a*) The displays were flashed by means of a tachistoscope, a machine which can expose a visual stimulus for very brief and precise periods of time. (*b*) Without instructions to limit their reporting to a specific line, people gave about four of the items correctly after an exposure of one-twentieth of a second. Instructed after the exposure to report the items in the first, second, or third line, however, they do much better. The number of items plotted for this condition is the *total* obtained on three trials, in which recall of the three lines was tested, one line at a time. (Adapted from Sperling, 1960.)

The Magical Number Seven

One important thing revealed by the study of immediate memory is that the processing capacity of the individual is limited. In Sperling's experiment the observers were able to handle about four items effectively. Usual estimates, however, are larger than this. As early as 1859, Sir William Hamilton, the Irish mathematician and physicist, noticed that if a handful of six or seven marbles is thrown onto the floor, it is possible to perceive the correct number in a single glance, without counting. When more are thrown, the number cannot be instantly perceived. More recent work has shown that Hamilton's claim also applies to the number of things we can remember. With just one presentation we can remember an average of about seven numbers, letters, or simple words. The **span of immediate memory** is so stable that George Miller, writing in 1956, referred to this span as the "magical number seven." But people do vary in capacity, and materials do vary in memorability. In recognition of this fact, Miller modified the expression and referred to the "magical number seven plus or minus two."

The fact that the span of immediate memory is the same for letters and words suggests an important point of interpretation: words must be remembered *as words,* not as collections of letters. If they were remembered as letters, we would remember fewer of them. Obviously, dealing with words enlarges our processing capacity enormously. One way to put it is to say that as letters become words they undergo a process of **recoding** in which small bits of information, the letters, are collected together and dealt with as larger chunks. Deliberate use of something like recoding can increase immediate memory span greatly. As an example, most of us would find a string of ten numbers, say 2034178935, impossible to remember unless we thought of grouping the numbers and recalling them as 203-417-8935. As you have probably noticed, we do this frequently in our recall of telephone numbers broken down into area code (203), exchange (417), and individual number (8935).

The Time It Takes To Think

In 1796 at Greenwich, England, the astronomer royal, Nevil Maskelyne, dismissed his assistant Kinnebrook for 0.8-second "errors" in his observations of the moment at which stars crossed a certain point in the heavens. Before the development of modern astronomy, an observer watched the progress of a star through a telescope and used the beat of a metronome to estimate the exact fraction of a second when the star crossed a point in the sky. Although it was not known in the eighteenth century, there are huge individual differences in such perceptual judgments, sometimes as much as a second or more.

It was nearly a hundred years later when James McKeen Cattell (1860-1944), after taking an undergraduate degree at Lafayette College and studying for a year at the Johns Hopkins University, marched into the laboratory of Wilhelm Wundt at Leipzig, Germany, and informed the professor in *ganz amerikanisch* fashion that he, Wundt, needed an assistant and that he, Cattell, would be it (Boring, 1950). In the meantime, the implications of the Maskelyne-Kinnebrook incident had been duly considered and had launched two important areas of study in psychology. The first was the investigation of what was first known as the "personal equation," the differences so dramatically illustrated by the disagreement between the astronomer and his assistant. Today we call this the study of individual differences. The second was the study of information processing. Cattell was an important contributor to both fields.

Reaction Time In early work on what we would now call information processing, an experimenter would present a highly practiced observer with a stimulus, say a white light, and have the observer press a key as quickly as possible in response to the light. An average time to make this simple response, technically the **reaction time,** might be 0.20 second. The simple reaction time experiment with just the white light provided a sort of baseline, the time required to detect any stimulus and react to it. Then the experimenter would make the task more complicated and require more of the individual. On different trials he would present a variety of lights, perhaps red, green, yellow, blue, and white, asking the individual to react only when the stimulus was the white light. Now, because additional processing was required, the observer's reaction time might be 0.35 second, even though the stimulus was the same one that could be responded to 0.15 second faster in the simpler procedure. Presumably it took the observer 0.15 second to perform the simple mental operation of deciding whether the stimulus presented was the one to respond to. Together these two procedures appeared to provide a promising beginning for the study of thought. In a classic paper published in 1887, Cattell referred to these methods as offering a measure of "the time it takes to think."

Letter Recognition Time passed, nearly three-quarters of a century during which research of this type went out of fashion, along with "mentalistic" concepts like thinking. More recently, however, psychology has again developed interests much like those that motivated the earlier work. The following experiment provides an example. We ask an observer to tell us by pressing one of two keys, as quickly as possible after two letters appear on a screen, whether the letters are the same or different. If we ask the individual to respond on the basis of physical features—AA = same, Aa = different — a typical reaction would be about 0.450 second. If we ask for a response on the basis of the name of the letter — Aa = same, AE = different — reaction time will increase to 0.550 second. The difference between the reaction time of 0.550 second for distinguishing names of letters and 0.450 second for distinguishing physical shapes of letters suggests that it may take 0.100 second to identify a letter in terms of its name as opposed to its physical characteristics. To report that A and E are the same because they are both vowels may take as long as 0.900 second (Posner, 1969).

Although this experiment is not very complicated, the results have considerable significance. *First,* they reestablish the usefulness of reaction times and the subtraction of one from another as a means of studying what goes on in information processing. *Second,* they provide an example of the levels of processing mentioned earlier and offer the first indication of their importance. The three levels identified here are a physical level, a level of names, and a level of concepts, of vowels and consonants. *Third,* they show that the stages of information processing cannot be independent of one another. The name of a letter is in long-term memory. If an individual is to respond "same" or "different" on the basis of names, immediate memory must in some sense make contact with long-term memory in order to perform this task.

Attention

Many situations provide us with an amount of stimulation that far exceeds our capacity to process. **Attention** is the mechanism that selects some materials for processing and filters out the rest.

The "Cocktail Party Phenomenon" Think of a cocktail party or any other noisy gathering at which you were confronted with several conversations going on around you all at the same time—one about America's foreign policy, another about somebody's favorite sports event, a third about sex, and a fourth about the cinematography in a recent film. Because of limited processing capacity, you found it impossible to listen to all these conversations at once. But you found it easy to exclude the other conversations and to attend to the one of greatest interest. This suggests the great functional value of attention. It selects certain stimuli for processing, excludes others,

Of all the conversations we might overhear at a cocktail party, attention allows us to select and listen to just one.

and allows us to monitor materials that are interesting or important.

At a cocktail party the listener has many cues available to help keep the messages separate: they are spoken in different voices; they come from different directions; they are accompanied by visual information, such as lip movements which may be read and gestures which may be interpreted. What would happen if these cues were eliminated? In a classic study E. Colin Cherry (1953) obtained information on this point by having people try to sort out two messages that had been spoken by the same individual and then recorded on the same tape, one message over the other. The procedure eliminates all cues except those in the message. Although the task was very difficult, the subjects were in most cases able to separate out the messages when the tape was replayed several times. This means that linguistic structures alone carry enough information to allow the listener to make the separation.

More specifically, Cherry proposed that his subjects used their knowledge of what is likely to follow what in speech as the basis for sorting the two messages. To support this interpretation, Cherry would need to show that two messages that fail to provide such information cannot be separated. He did this with messages created by stringing together clichés selected from speeches reported in the newspaper. With the help of a few connectives, Cherry patched together meandering passages such as, "I am happy to be here today to talk to the man on the street. Gentlemen, the time has come to stop beating about the bush—we are on the brink of ruin, and the welfare of the workers and the great majority of the people is imperiled." He recorded two such speeches, one over the other, and again asked people to separate them. The subjects were able to identify the clichés with good accuracy. Hearing just one or two words, they could predict the rest. The assignment of clichés to the two messages was impossible, however. Hearing a given cliché provided no information about the specific cliché that might come next. The term *specific* here is important. The political-sounding rhetoric of the passages made up of clichés reminds us that, in certain contexts, the probability that *some* cliché will follow the one being uttered is great. But in Cherry's experiment, in order to separate the two messages, the listener needed to predict that a specific bit of speech was likely to follow what was being said at the moment. No such predictions could be made.

Shadowing and Dichotic Listening The situation of the people in these experiments of Cherry's was unusual in that they were given the opportunity to process both messages. More commonly, when two messages are being delivered, we attend to one and tune out the other. This raises some interesting questions about what is comprehended in the speech that is not attended to. Cherry obtained information on this question from **dichotic,** or two-ear, listening experiments which employ the method of **shadowing.** In this method different messages are delivered to the two ears through earphones (Figure 7.2). The observer is asked to repeat each word delivered to one ear immediately, that is, to "shadow" the message being delivered to one ear or to the other, whichever the investigator chooses. "Shadowing" is a way of

FIGURE 7.2
Dichotic listening. Separate messages are recorded on two channels of the tape and played one to each ear.

being sure that the observer is actually paying attention to the message that the experimenter wants him or her to listen to. Then the experimenter can manipulate the unshadowed message delivered to the other ear to determine what sorts of information may be picked up when attention is directed elsewhere.

The earliest shadowing experiments suggested that very little of the information in the unshadowed message got through. The observers knew that there was a message delivered to the unattended ear and that the message was speech. They remembered nonverbal signals, such as a whistle, but they usually did not notice when a voice was changed from a man's to a woman's. They were unable to recognize, as belonging to the message, a short list of words that had been repeated thirty-five times. Even if bilingual, they could not report the language of the rejected message or tell whether the language had changed during the course of the tape.

All this might suggest that only physical features are processed by the unattended ear. There is, however, a commonsense problem with such a conclusion. If it were true, and the meaning of an unattended message were not processed at all, we would never notice important bits of information in another cocktail party conversation, and we would never be able to redirect attention to messages more important than the ones we are listening to.

We now know that the message to the unattended ear is, in fact, processed somewhat more deeply than the early data indicate. Apparently the unattended message remains in echoic memory for a few seconds and is briefly interpreted in terms of meaning. Then it fades away, just as iconic visual memories do. The evidence that the unshadowed message is briefly available is quite direct. If the experimenter stops the messages and immediately asks for a report of material in the unattended ear, observers can remember the last few words. The evidence for deeper processing comes from several observations. If a message to the unattended ear is preceded by the listener's name, he or she is likely to recall at least part of it later on. If a coherent message changes ears, the observer may follow it briefly. Suppose that the messages to the right (R) and left (L) ears are familiar ones, and that the observer is supposed to shadow the message delivered to one ear or the other:

R When in the course of MAINLY ON . . .
L THE RAIN IN SPAIN STAYS human events . . .

When the message being shadowed switches to the unattended ear, there is a tendency for observers also to switch ears and follow the familar sentence briefly.

Finally, Donald McKay (1973) had subjects shadow sentences like, "They threw stones toward the bank yesterday," and, at the same time, presented either "river" or "money" to the unattended ear. Later on the subjects could not recall the word presented in the unshadowed message. But when they were asked to choose one of two sentences as having been the one that they shadowed,

> "They threw stones toward the side of the river yesterday,"
> versus
> "They threw stones toward the Savings and Loan Association yesterday,"

the observers chose the sentence that was consonant with the word presented to the unattended ear.

SUMMARY □

Information processing is a term that describes the operations by which an individual puts information into a form that allows it to be stored in memory. These operations can be treated from different points of view: as stages of memory, immediate, short-term, long-term; as a set of processes, encoding, storage, retrieval; and as levels of processing, ranging from the superficial physical aspects of pieces of information to their deeper meanings. Our discussion so far has concentrated on immediate memory and encoding, although levels of processing have had to be considered at several points.

The individual is constantly bombarded with stimulation, but only a small fraction of this stimulation "gets through." There is evidence that much more information than is ever processed remains briefly in immediate sensory memory—perhaps all that the eyes can see or the ears can hear—but even then is rapidly fading away.

The processing capacity of immediate memory is severely limited, however, five to nine items for most people and for many kinds of material. This limited processing capacity makes it important that the human observer have a filtering device, that is, attention, to select some information for further processing and reject other information. Studies have shown that when two messages are delivered by the same voice, people are able to separate one verbal message from another on the basis of the linguistic structure of the information alone. These studies and dichotic listening experiments employing the method of shadowing —immediately repeating the words received by one ear—indicate that for the most part we are able to attend to only one of two messages received simultaneously and that we reject the other. We remember very little of the information in the unattended message, although during its brief existence in echoic memory it is processed fairly deeply.

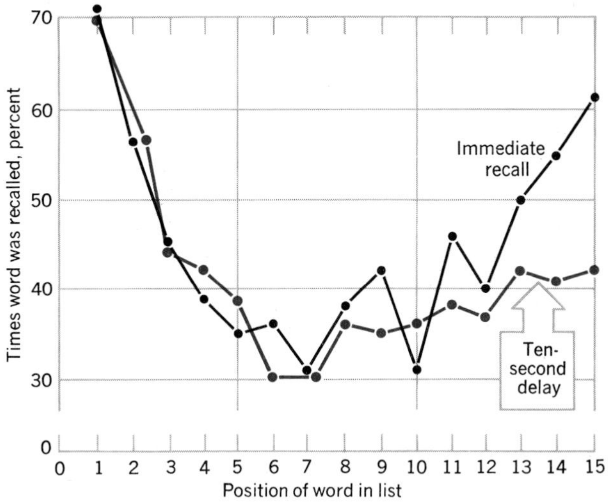

FIGURE 7.3
Serial position curve. Memory is best for the first few items in a list and the last few—primacy and recency effects—when retention is tested immediately after presentation. With a delay of only 10 seconds, the recency effect has almost disappeared. With a 30-second delay, it disappears completely. (After Glanzer and Cunitz, 1966.)

SHORT- AND LONG-TERM MEMORY

Attention provides the link between immediate sensory memory and additional stages of information processing. For only the items that attention selects from immediate memory survive for such processing. The next stage in the sequence is short-term memory, which is familiar to all of us. We look up a telephone number, go to dial it, and for some reason it is gone and we have to look it up again. We are introduced to a man at a meeting but cannot recall his name when another person asks it moments later. Some materials are attended to, identified, and briefly memorized, but nevertheless disappear within a few seconds. Such experiences illustrate the operation of **short-term memory,** or primary memory, as it is sometimes called. **Long-term memory** is sometimes referred to as secondary memory.

Limits of Short-Term Memory

One type of evidence for the existence of two forms of memory comes from studies of free recall. The investigator has subjects first listen to a long list of words, then attempt to recall as many of the words as they can, usually by writing them down. The probability that a word will be recalled depends on its position in the list. If the attempt at recall is made immediately, the first few words and the last few tend to be remembered best (Figure 7.3). The better recall of the first items on the list is called a **primacy effect,** that of the final items a **recency effect.** If the test of retention is delayed for even a matter of seconds, the recency effect disappears. This indicates that the final items were in short-term memory and were lost, just as a telephone number sometimes is in the few seconds between looking it up and beginning to dial it.

In an experiment that is now a classic, Lloyd and Margaret Peterson (1959) of Indiana University studied short-term memory in a different way, one best presented by quoting from their instructions.

> . . . In front of you is a little black box. The top or green light is now on. The green light means that we are ready to begin a trial. I will speak some letters and then a number. You are to repeat the number immediately after I say it, and begin counting backwards by 3s from that number in time with the ticking you hear. I might say ABC 309. Then you say 309, 306, 303, etc., until the bottom or red light comes on. When you see this red light come on, stop counting immediately and say the letters that were given at the beginning of the trial. . . .

Under these circumstances retention of the letters lessened with each passing second, and forgetting was nearly complete after eighteen seconds (Figure 7.4).

Materials, at least verbal materials, exist in short-term memory predominantly in acoustic form, a fact that has been demonstrated by errors in recalling letters. Even if letters are presented *visually,* the errors in recall are most often acoustic in nature. Consider the two sets of letters BCPTV and FMNSX. Those in the first set sound like one another but not like those in the second set and vice versa. Reuben Conrad presented these ten letters visually at a rate of 0.75 second per letter and then immediately asked subjects to write them down in the order that they had seen them, guessing wherever necessary. When he examined errors later on, Conrad found that most of them represented acoustic confusions (Table 7.1). Errors

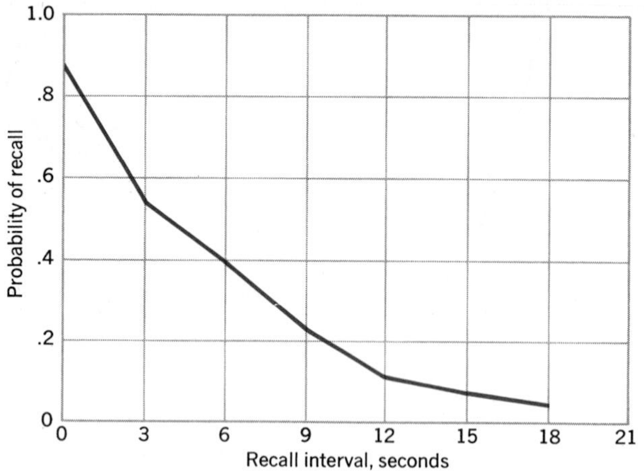

FIGURE 7.4

The course of short-term memory. Short-term retention declines very rapidly when counting keeps subjects from repeating an item to themselves. (After Peterson and Peterson, 1959.)

TABLE 7.1

Frequency of Acoustic and Nonacoustic Confusions in Recalling Letters in Order

Erroneous Responses	Stimulus Letters: B C P T V	Stimulus Letters: P M N S X
B C P T V	198	42
F M N S X	51	190

The data in the four cells are numbers of errors averaged across letters. After Conrad, 1964.

made in reporting "sound alike" letters were four times more frequent than confusion of letters that did not sound alike.

Although a persuasive case can be made that verbal materials are represented acoustically in short-term memory, obviously some short-term memories must exist in other forms. If, after fifteen seconds, we recall a powerful painting, the smell of a rose, the taste of honey or a kiss, there is probably not much that is verbal, much less acoustic, about what we remember. At least a part of short-term representation must concern what sensations and experiences mean to the individual.

Storage

The fleeting forms of memory discussed so far are only the beginning of the series of processes that put materials into long-term memory. One way of looking at it is to say that immediate and short-term memory supply the code that we use to store materials in more lasting memory and later on to retrieve them. Psychologists are just beginning to know a bit about the means by which materials can be effectively stored in long-term memory.

Rehearsal One of these means is the rehearsal of materials to be remembered. Rehearsal may take either of two forms, which serve two rather different purposes. The mere repetition of new information, over and over again, without thinking about it, is sometimes called **maintenance rehearsal.** This form of rehearsal keeps information in short-term memory at least until it has served its purpose. This is the type of rehearsal by which we say a phone number again and again between the time of looking it up and making the call. After that the number is likely to be lost, as is any item in short-term memory.

A more effective form of rehearsal is **elaborative rehearsal,** in which the individual deals with the new information in terms of its meaning. The individual may associate it with something else or imagine it in some context. Elaboration is quite different from maintenance rehearsal because it is processing at a deeper level.

Processing by Level In the early pages of this chapter, we called attention to the fact that materials that might be remembered can be described in a number of ways, which we referred to as levels. A word, for example, can be described as marks on paper, as a string of letters, or as having a certain meaning. As it turns out, people will follow instructions to deal with words, that is, to process them, at these different levels when the words are being committed to memory. The **level of processing** determines how well the words are remembered. Fergus Craik and Endel Tulving of the University of Toronto presented college students with lists of forty words to be remembered. Sometimes they told the students that there would be a memory test, sometimes not. The results were similar in both cases. As each word was first presented to them, the students were asked a question about it. The questions for the words were designed to make the students process them at different levels. The case and rhyme questions, as indicated in Table 7.2, required processing the word in terms of fairly superficial physical characteristics. The sentence question required deeper processing of the word according to meaning.

The results obtained on a test of free recall (Figure 7.5), given shortly after presenting the list, indicated that words processed at a deeper level were better retained than the others. The words processed at the two superficial levels were recalled with about the

Fergus Craik and Endel Tulving.

same frequency. In each kind of processing, more words for which the answer to its question was "yes" were recalled than were words for which the answer was "no."

In attempting to explain why questions answered by yes led to better memory for words than those answered by no, Craik and Tulving proposed that *elaborateness* was probably a better term than depth for effective processing, and that questions with positive answers brought about elaboration. Obviously, the ideas called up by meeting a friend in the street (Table 7.2) are richer, more personal, and more full of meaning than any connected with meeting a cloud in the street. To test this interpretation, Craik and Tulving conducted additional experiments. In one they asked questions—"Is it bigger than a breadbox?"—about words for which the amount of elaboration would probably be the same, whether the answer was yes (*house*) or no (*mouse*). With these questions the yes-no effect disappeared. Recall was about 40 percent for both groups of words.

In another experiment they manipulated elaborateness more directly by using the sentence form of processing and comparing recall of words processed by means of simple and elaborate sentences. For example, "He dropped the ______" and "The old man hobbled across the room and picked up the ______ from the mahogany table" produced about 40 percent and 80 percent recall respectively for the target word *watch*.

TABLE 7.2
Questions and Answers for Different Levels of Processing

		Answer	
Type	**Question**	**Yes**	**No**
Case	Is the word in capital letters?	TABLE	table
Rhyme	Does the word rhyme with SOUR?	flower	CARPET
Sentence	Would the word fit in the sentence: "He met a ____ in the street?"	FRIEND	cloud

After Craik and Tulving, 1975.

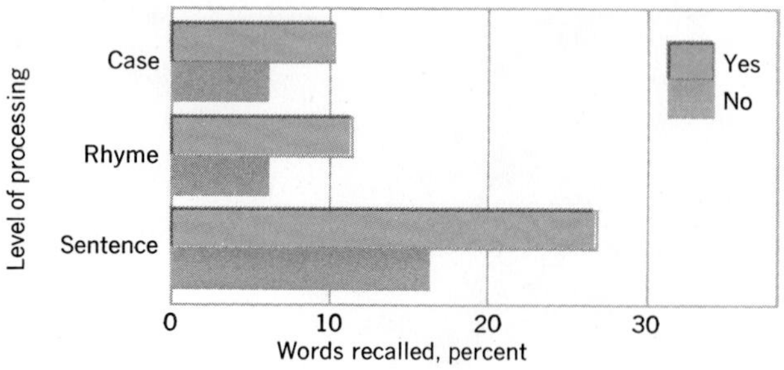

FIGURE 7.5
Recall after different methods of processing. Words processed by putting them into sentences, or even finding that they did not fit, were recalled best. With all methods recall was better for words whose processing question was answered by "yes" rather than "no." (After Craik and Tulving, 1975.)

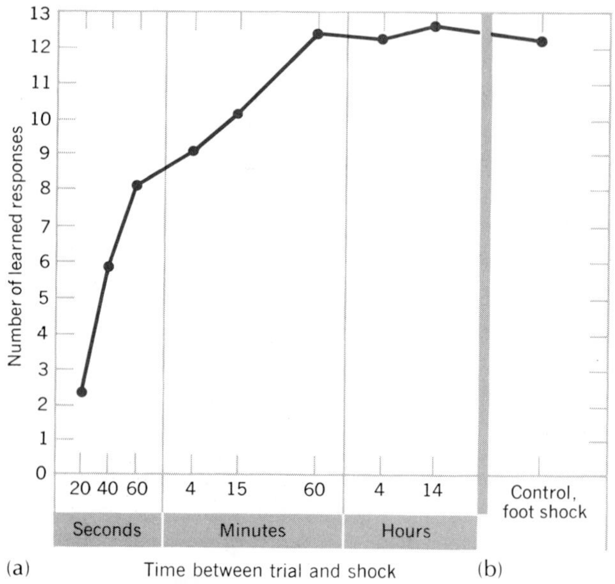

FIGURE 7.6
Effect of electroconvulsive shock on learning. The longer a shock is delayed after a learning trial, the better the learning. One interpretation of these results is that shock interferes with consolidation. Whatever the explanation, shock given 15 minutes or more later has very little effect on earlier learning. The intervals on the abscissa are in logarithmic units to shorten the graph. (Data from Duncan, 1949.)

Consolidation Other evidence points to a process very different from elaboration as contributing effectively to the storage of information in memory. Robert S. Woodworth, for years a professor of psychology at Columbia University, told the story of taking a fall and being knocked unconscious when he was mountain climbing with friends. When he recovered consciousness and overcame the daze that followed recovery, he found he had no memory at all for events that had happened during the fifteen minutes or so that preceded the fall (Woodworth and Scholsberg, 1954). Such **retrograde amnesia,** as it is called, is a common aftermath both of accidents that render a person unconscious and of epileptic seizures. To become permanent, learning apparently requires a period of **consolidation,** a time during which it is somehow prepared for storage. Traumatic events can interfere with the process and make the individual forget.

The phenomenon of retrograde amnesia also occurs in connection with electroconvulsive shock therapy (ECS), sometimes used in treating deep depression in psychiatric patients. In this form of therapy a brief electric shock is passed through the head of the patient, producing a convulsive seizure and unconsciousness. Memory of happenings just before and after the shock is lost permanently. Memories of events extending for a period before the shock are often lost temporarily.

The amnesic effects of ECS have been studied in lower animals. One of the first experiments was that of Carl P. Duncan (1949) at Brown University. In this experiment white rats learned to go from one compartment of a shuttle box to another to avoid electric shock to the paws, which was delivered through a grid in the floor of the first compartment. A light came on ten seconds earlier, to warn them that shock was imminent. Trials were administered at the rate of one per day. The rats in a control group learned the avoidance reaction easily. Animals in eight experimental groups were taken from the shuttle box and given electric shock through the head, at times ranging from twenty seconds to fourteen hours after each day's trial. Learning was slower for all five groups that received head shock within fifteen minutes. Those that received shock to the head twenty seconds after the trial failed to learn that the light warned them of foot shock to come (Figure 7.6*a*).

In another procedure, which served as an additional control, rats that had just been given a learning trial were then taken from the box and received shock to the feet again, instead of through the head. These animals learned very well (Figure 7.6*b*). This means that fear of a second shock could not have been responsible for the deficit in learning in the first five groups. Apparently a process of consolidation goes on for at least several minutes following learning, and nothing is retained if this process is interrupted within twenty seconds, which is roughly the span of short-term memory.

Retrieval

Having completed our sketch of the sequence of processings that get information into memory, we turn to the opposite question, how we get it out again. This is the process of **retrieval,** the incredible talent that each of us has of being able, upon command, to call up from a multitude of memories exactly the one that meets the particular requirements of a particular situation. Of course, there are times when we "remember" the wrong things and others when we cannot quite remember something that we are certain we know. A study of these instances in which retrieval fails may well be as instructive to the study of memory as failures of function have been to the study of the nervous system.

A familiar situation in which memory fails is the **tip-of-the-tongue phenomenon.** We try to recall a name we know we know, but it refuses to be remembered. Technically we say that the name is **available** in memory but that it is not **accessible.**

Roger Brown and David McNeill (1966) studied this phenomenon by reading to a group of students the definitions of a series of difficult words, such as *ambergris, apse, cloaca, nepotism,* and *sampan,* and asking them to supply the word. For example, one definition was, "A navigational instrument used in measuring angular distances, especially the altitude of the sun, moon, and stars at sea." The students were asked, upon hearing the definition, to indicate whether they knew the word, were sure that they did not know it, or had it "on the tip of the tongue" but could not produce it. In the event that they reported being in the last-mentioned state, the experimenters questioned them further. How many syllables do you think there are in the target word? What is the initial letter? What words that possibly sound like the target word are occurring to you? What words are you thinking of that may have a similar meaning?

Given the definition of the navigational instrument just stated, students with the word on the tip of the tongue were likely to guess correctly that it had two syllables rather than any other number; to guess, also correctly, that the first letter was "s"; to think of words like *sextet* and *secant,* which sound like the word; and to think of others, such as *compass,* which are related in meaning. Twice as many "sound like" words occurred to them as "mean the same" words.

These responses suggest something about the nature of storage and the process of retrieval. It would seem that an item in memory is stored in a form, or code, that includes certain of its physical features or attributes, such as number of syllables, initial letter, and general sound, as well as its meaning. Moreover, a word's location in memory apparently places it in networks of related items. The word *sextant* is stored in a way that puts it in contact with words with similar physical features, such as *sextet* and *secant,* and with words related in meaning, such as *compass* and *protractor.* This description of storage suggests that retrieval must consist of a search through a region of memory with a particular range of meaning for an item with particular physical features.

SUMMARY □

The fraction of incoming information that we pay attention to enters short-term memory, where it remains for less than a minute. As one demonstration of the limits of short-term memory, the last items of a list are partially lost after a matter of only ten seconds, although these items, and the very first, are best remembered when the attempt at recall is made immediately. In another demonstration subjects were asked to recall three-letter sequences after extremely short periods of time, during which they were distracted by the task of counting backward from some numbers by threes. Under these circumstances retention of the letters declined essentially to zero in eighteen seconds. Finally, there is evidence that short-term memory holds verbal materials primarily in acoustic form.

The transfer of new information from short-term memory to long is promoted by processing it for meaning. Depth is one term chosen for the process of committing the meaning of a word to memory. The details of this processing suggest, however, that elaborateness may better describe it. Studies of retrograde amnesia after accidental blows to the head and of memory failure after electroconvulsive shock indicate that new information must undergo a period of consolidation as a part of entering long-term storage. Blows and shock to the head prevent this consolidation.

Once in long-term memory, information is usually both available and accessible; it is there and we can get to it. In the interesting tip-of-the-tongue state, however, information is available but temporarily inaccessible. Studies of the tip-of-the-tongue phenomenon suggest that retrieval is a search through a region in memory for items that sound a particular way.

REPRESENTATION OF INFORMATION IN MEMORY

The question we turn to now is how materials are represented in memory. The rudiments of an answer have already been suggested. Time and again the discussion has concerned the processing of the physical features of new information, on the one hand, and its meaning on the other. It should come as no surprise to discover the same emphases on the physical and the conceptual in theories concerning the nature of memory.

Dual-Coding Theory

Dual-coding theory (Paivio, 1971) proposes that information is represented in memory in two separate but interconnected systems or codes, a system of visual images and a verbal system. The theory goes on

Allan Paivio believes that when we think we constantly form images in conjunction with words.

to say that the system of images handles concrete, spatial, imaginable objects and events. The verbal system handles abstract linguistic units and structures. To the extent that information has both of these characteristics, it will be represented in both systems.

An important application of dual-coding theory concerns verbal materials and the image they call up. Consider the words *apple, daffodil, arrow,* and *mountain* on the one hand and *bravery, instance, happiness,* and *obedience* on the other. All are fairly familiar. The first group, however, consists of words that are concrete and capable of evoking a vivid image of the object to which they refer. The second group of words has less of this quality. The considerable research done on this point indicates that words evoking images are easier to learn than words that do not. Dual-coding theory explains this ease by assuming that a concrete word, represented both in terms of images and verbal meaning, enters into both memory systems, whereas an abstract word is put only into the verbal system. Double representation also doubles the number of ways in which the concrete words can be retrieved. Hence the better memory for such words.

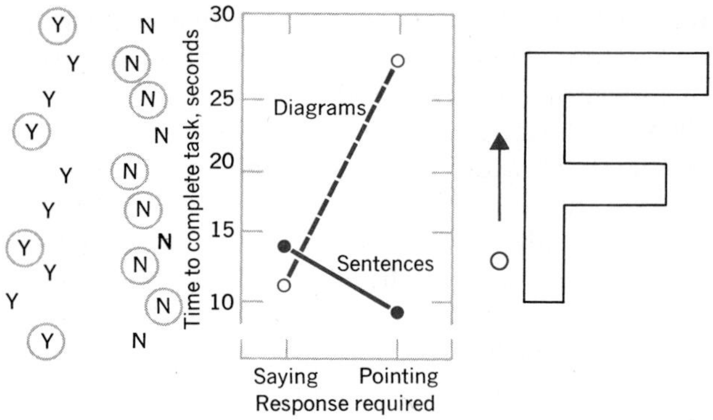

FIGURE 7.7
Interference with memory for words and forms. The letters on the left were used in the pointing task. Those circled form the correct pattern for the sentence in the text example. The letter F at the right is one of the spatial patterns whose image was traced in memory. The graph indicates the time taken to complete the four "thinking through" tasks. The verbal task, saying yes or no, interfered most with memory of a sentence. The spatial task, pointing to Y or N, interfered even more with memory of a diagram. (After Brooks, 1968.)

"Thinking Things Through" Evidence for separate components of memory has come from studies of interference in the remembering process. Verbal activities interfere with "thinking through" linguistic memories; spatial activities interfere with thinking through imaginal memories. Lee Brooks (1968) demonstrated such interference in a study in which subjects made simple judgments about verbal and pictorial materials that they had memorized. In a test of what interfered with remembering words, the subjects first committed sentences to memory, for example, "Rivers from the hills bring fresh water to the cities." Then, with the sentence in memory, they went through it mentally, indicating whether each word in the sentence was a noun. They were instructed first to close their eyes and say "yes" or "no" as they recalled each word. For the sample sentence a correct performance would have been the sequence "Yes," "No," "No," "Yes," "No," "No," "Yes," "No," "No," "Yes." Then, with their eyes open, they simply pointed to "Y" for "yes" or "N" for "no" on a diagram like that on the left of Figure 7.7

The test of interference with remembering an image had the subjects make "yes" and "no" judgments about a figure in memory, such as the F at the right of Figure 7.7. With eyes closed, they began at the open circle and went mentally around the figure, saying "yes" whenever they came to an outside corner and "no" when they came to an inside corner. Then, with eyes open, they pointed to "Y" and "N" on the diagram. For the figure given, the sequence would be "Yes," "Yes," "Yes," "No," "No," "Yes," "Yes,"

"No," "Yes," "Yes." The measure of the interference with remembering was the amount of time required to complete the two "yes" and "no" tasks for sentences and diagrams.

The results appear graphically in the center panel of Figure 7.7. Verbal responses interfered with remembering the sentences; pointing interfered with remembering visual images. Once more these data indicate the limited capacity of processing mechanisms. Apparently the two components of memory had about all the processing that each could handle with the verbal task of thinking through a sentence and the imaginal task of thinking through the figure. Adding another processing task of the same kind made a greater demand on the same mechanism and slowed it down. But the fact that the alternate form of processing interfered less serves to confirm the existence of the two types of memories proposed by dual-coding theory.

Effects in Time Some interesting experiments carried out at the University of Colorado, by Walter Kintsch and his colleagues, increase our understanding of the representation of information in memory. In these experiments one group of college students was presented with materials that expressed a proposition explicitly; a second group saw materials that expressed it only by implication. In one study (Keenan and Kintsch, 1974) sentences contained a proposition, for example, "The discarded cigarette started the fire," presented in two ways.

Explicit: "A carelessly discarded burning cigarette started a fire. The fire destroyed many acres of virgin forest."

Implicit: "A burning cigarette was carelessly discarded. The fire destroyed many acres of virgin forest."

As you can see, the second version actually fails to state the proposition.

In a parallel experiment conducted by Pat Baggett (1975), the materials were series of pictures. The two experiments allow a comparison of verbal and pictorial memories. Obtaining comparable results with the two procedures would mean that verbal memory and pictorial memory function in similar ways. Baggett's pictorial series told stories. One of them was about a long-haired youth entering a barber shop, getting his hair cut, and emerging with a crew cut. The explicit version of this story contained a picture of the youth getting his hair cut; the implicit version did not.

In both of these experiments, the subjects were presented later with the target proposition—"The discarded cigarette started the fire"; the picture of the haircutting episode—as well as with sentences and pictures concerning other subjects. They were asked to say as quickly as they could whether the item was

Walter Kintsch.

"true" or "false" on the basis of what they had seen earlier. These tests came immediately, within 30 seconds, for half the students in each group and later on for the others. For the verbal materials the delayed test was given after approximately twenty minutes. Because pictorial materials are remembered much better than verbal materials, the delay for them was three days.

The results are very similar for the two experiments (Figure 7.8). On the immediate test verification was much more rapid by the subjects who had seen the explicit versions of the propositions. This seems to mean that the proposition as presented was still in memory and available to compare with the test sentence or picture, allowing a rapid check on its truth. When the proposition had been presented only by implication, it took an additional second to interpret and verify the picture, an additional two seconds to interpret the meaning of the test sentence and recognize its truth. But after a delay the literal memory of the item as presented had disappeared. However the materials had first been presented, explicitly or implicitly, the observer was forced to make an interpretation, which took time.

Organization of Memory

Generalized somewhat, to any situation in which a piece of information is acquired, say from a newspa-

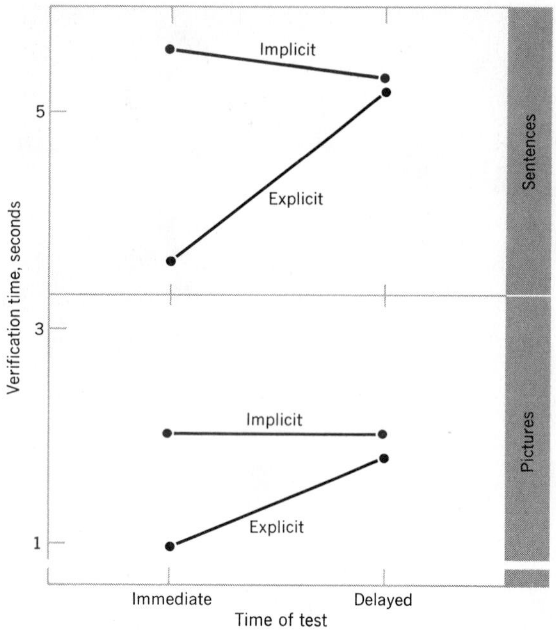

FIGURE 7.8
Verification times for propositions. The propositions to be verified had been presented earlier, either explicitly or only implicity, in sentences or pictures. The very fast verification times in immediate tests with items that had been presented explicitly indicate the contribution of literal, explicit representation in short-term memory. (Adapted from Keenan and Kintsch, 1974; Baggett, 1975.)

per, the differences between immediate literal memory and later interpretations are evident. Immediately after reading a newspaper story, say of a specific forest fire started by a discarded cigarette, a person has a *memory* of reading the story, the information it contained, and a good bit of the precise phraseology: "The discarded cigarette started the fire." Later on the individual has the *knowledge* that the cigarette started the forest fire, but the precise phraseology is gone and even the fact that the information came from a newspaper story may have been forgotten. Perhaps it was heard on radio or television.

Episodic and Semantic Memory Tulving (1972) calls immediate memories of personal experiences episodic memory and later knowledge semantic memory. Put briefly, **episodic memory** is memory for temporally dated, autobiographical experience; **semantic memory** is organized knowledge about the world, including the verbal world of words and how they are used. Semantic memory contains information that is not associated with a particular time or place. The information has been coded in words that allow it to be retrieved in a form different from the one in which it was originally stored. After any bad happenstance with a cigarette left burning, whether the experience was personal or recounted to us, we know that above and beyond the immediate circumstances, a burning cigarette can cause a fire. As we see from this example of the discarded, burning cigarette, the distinction between episodic and semantic memory cannot be a sharp one. Unless we have innate knowledge of the world, all memories must start out as episodic. Nevertheless, the distinction does provide a useful way of dealing with certain important phenomena in the study of memory.

Encoding specificity Episodic memory includes the context in which an item was stored in memory, as well as the item itself. There is evidence that the item can be retrieved only in the context in which it was coded. Tulving and Donald Thompson (1973) interpret this fact in terms of an **encoding specificity principle:** "What is stored is determined by what is perceived and how it is encoded, and what is stored determines what retrieval cues are effective in providing access to what is stored." This idea needs to be put more concretely. Suppose that you are a participant in an experiment that takes place in a series of steps.

Step 1. You are instructed to learn a long list of words presented in capital letters. Each word is presented with another word, a cue word, that "may help you remember it." One example is train—BLACK, in which the cue word is *train* and the word to be remembered is *black*.
Step 2. You are presented with a list of new words and asked to write down as many associations as you can to each. One of the words is white, and you come up with *snow, wedding, black, paper,* and *china*.
Step 3. You are asked to encircle any of the words that you have just written down should you recognize it as a word you are supposed to be remembering. *You fail to encircle black.*
Step 4. On a final test the cues are presented again, but without the words to be remembered. When *train* appears, you immediately remember *black*.

This phenomenon of failing to recognize words that can in another context be remembered is surprising, for recognition is usually much superior to recall. Here memory for the word *black* depends on the specific context of its encoding, appearing with its partner word *train*. In a different context, in association with the word *white*, it is not even recognized.

Clustering in free recall Here is a little experiment that you might try on a group of friends. Read the following list of words to them fairly rapidly—one per second or less—and ask your friends to remember as many of the words as they can: *bed, rest, awake, tired, dream, night, pillow, comfort, slumber, snore, drowsy, quiet, nightmare.* Then ask your subjects to write down the words that they remember. You will probably find that about half of them include *sleep* among the words they "remember," in spite of the fact that *sleep* was not one of the words in the list. This demonstration indicates that words go together in associative clusters and categories. The members of these groupings tend to be recalled together.

In an early demonstration of this point, students at the University of Connecticut were presented with a list of sixty nouns. The list was made up of fifteen items in each of four categories: animals, vegetables, names, and professions. In recalling the words, the students tended to report them in categories, finishing one before moving on to the next (Bousefield, 1953). The recall of words in categorized lists takes place in two stages. First the individual recalls the category, then the items in the category. Remembering one item in a category usually means that the majority of the other items in the category will come to mind. Lists that are made up of words falling into categories have a natural organization for recall. If the materials lack such an organization, subjects in recall studies will invent one. They create a *subjective organization,* a consistent order in which they come to recall the items in the list (see page 166).

Elizabeth F. Loftus.

TABLE 7.3
Responses to Question, "Did you see any broken glass?"

Response	**Verb in Question Asked One Week Earlier** Smashed	Hit
Yes	16	7
No	34	43

Semantic-Episodic Interactions: Eyewitness Testimony The recall of words by categories illustrates the fuzziness of the distinction between episodic and semantic memories. The experimental task is an episodic one, to remember the words that have been learned at a particular time and place. Categories, however, are items of semantic memory, a part of our knowledge about the world. In this case it is a knowledge of what things group together because of their similarities. Semantic memory obviously can have considerable control over how our episodic experiences are perceived, interpreted, and stored.

The manner of such control can be subtle. In an experiment on eyewitness testimony, Elizabeth Loftus and Steven Palmer (1974) had students watch a short film of a traffic accident and then asked them questions about what they remembered. On one point subjects were asked slightly different questions: "About how fast were the cars going when they smashed into each other?" or "About how fast were the cars going when they hit each other?" The subjects who were asked the first question gave much higher estimates than those asked the second. Apparently "smashed" in semantic memory implies higher speed than "hit."

Would the verbs of these two questions affect how the subjects remember the film? Loftus and Palmer called the subjects back a week later for a second interview. The critical question asked them this time was whether they had seen any broken glass in the film of the accident. There had been none. Responses to this question differed, depending on the verb of the critical question asked a week earlier (Table 7.3).

Apparently the episode of the accident has been stored according to the meaning of words applied to it. Subjects asked about the cars that "smashed" into each other have it stored in terms of greater damage than subjects asked about the cars that "hit" each other. After this initial storage, memory will be constructive. Details will be included to fit the event as it is stored. The implications of this point for investigations and for courtroom proceedings are of great importance and are just now beginning to be studied.

SUMMARY □

Dual-coding theory proposes that information in memory is represented by two systems, a system of images and a verbal system. Both the theory and the topic of imagery have generated a great deal of experimental work. The theory maintains that recall will be better for materials that are represented in both systems rather than in just one. The better recall of concrete words, which can be served by both systems, than of abstract words, which are served for the most part by the linguistic system, is supporting evidence. The theory also receives support, in its assumption of two systems, from experiments showing that verbal activities tend to interfere with verbal memories and spatial activities with imaginal memories.

Studies that test memory both immediately and after a delay reveal something else about how information is represented there. They show that, with time, the representation usually becomes less sensory and literal and more semantic and meaningful. This change is related to the distinction between episodic memory and semantic memory. Episodic memory stores the events of personal experience and of experiences recounted by others. Semantic memory stores knowledge. Research reveals that semantic memory has a strong influence on episodic, one instance being eyewitness testimony.

Hermann Ebbinghaus (1850-1909). Fechner's *Elements of Psychophysics* gave him the idea of applying the scientific method to the study of processes "higher" than sensations.

FORGETTING

The first significant scientific experiments on verbal learning and memory were performed toward the end of the last century in Germany. The important pioneer was Hermann Ebbinghaus. Ebbinghaus was a loner. Having completed a doctorate degree in philosophy at Bonn in 1873, he spent the next seven years studying on his own. During this period his scientific work on memory took form. In 1880 he went to the University of Berlin as a docent, or lecturer, and in 1885 he published *Über das Gedächtnis* ("On Memory"), reporting a long series of experiments done entirely on himself.

Ebbinghaus realized that the meaningfulness of materials would have an effect on how easily they could be learned and how well they could be remembered (page 178). He set out to control for this problem by eliminating meaning. To that end he used nonsense syllables, typically three-letter, consonant-vowel-consonant sequences like LUN, ZIV, WEK, which are nearly devoid of meaning. Ebbinghaus made up lists of these syllables, learned them in order, and tested himself for recall after different amounts of time.

Among Ebbinghaus's many contributions was the first careful tracing of the course of forgetting (Figure 7.9). The striking thing about forgetting is the speed with which it obviously occurs. The first point on Ebbinghaus's curve was obtained nineteen minutes after learning, but already 42 percent has been forgotten. Or, as the graph also expresses it, retention is 58 percent. Although the absolute amount forgotten in a given period of time depends on many variables, much of forgetting takes a course similar to Ebbinghaus's curve.

Measures of Retention

The extent of forgetting usually depends on the method by which it is tested. In general, **recall tests,** which require a person to retrieve something from memory, are more difficult than **recognition tests,** in which materials are presented and subjects only have to indicate whether each item is one that they have learned or encountered earlier. An interesting experiment by Harry Bahrick and his colleagues (1975) at Ohio Wesleyan University makes the point very nicely. These investigators studied the memory of high school graduates for the names and faces of their classmates at periods after graduation that ranged from three months to forty-eight years. Their subjects ranged in age from seventeen to seventy-four. In one measure of memory, the graduates were asked to *recall* the names of their classmates when shown a series of ten pictures drawn at random from their yearbooks. In two measures of *recognition,* they had to select first the picture of a classmate from sets of five pictures, and later the name of one from sets of

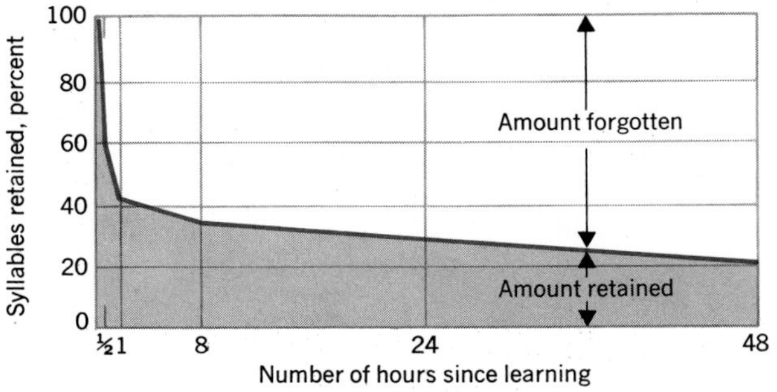

FIGURE 7.9
A typical retention curve for nonsense syllables. The amount forgotten is the difference at any point between the level of the curve and 100 percent. The amount retained is the difference between this same point and zero.

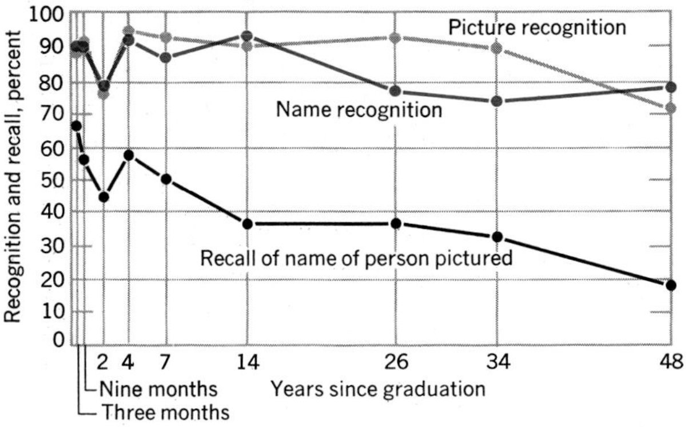

FIGURE 7.10
Memory for classmates after retention intervals ranging from three months to forty-eight years. As usual, recognition is better than recall. (Data from Bahrick et al., 1975.)

five names, four in each set being those of individuals who had not gone to their school.

People who had graduated almost half a century earlier were still able to recognize 75 percent of the names and photographs of their classmates correctly (Figure 7.10). During the same period, however, recall of names declined to under 20 percent.

Interference

What causes forgetting? Although personal experience suggests that memories simply fade in time and eventually disappear, experimental studies tell us that this is not the case. What actually happens is that things we learn before and after a given event interfere with our recall of it.

Retroactive Inhibition One of the earliest hints that retention of something learned might be subject to some sort of interference from whatever followed learning came from the famous experiment of John Jenkins and Karl Dallenbach, who compared re-

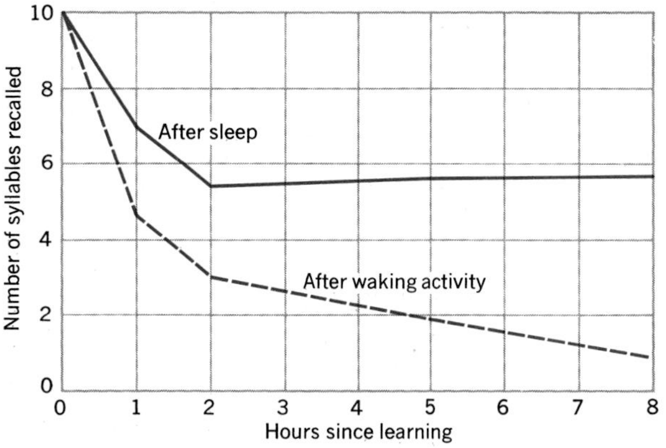

FIGURE 7.11
Retention after sleep and waking. These results were important in developing the concept of retroactive inhibition. (After Jenkins and Dallenbach, 1924.)

tention after various periods of sleep and waking. The participants in this experiment were two male college students who worked with the experimenters over a period of almost two months in order to provide the necessary data. During this time they slept in a room next to the psychological laboratory so that they would be available for the experimental sessions that came at night. The materials were lists of ten nonsense syllables. The syllables were exposed briefly, one at a time, and the learner pronounced each syllable as he saw it. After each run through the list, he attempted to recall the syllables in order. The list was considered learned when the participant remembered all the syllables in the correct order. The students learned some of the lists in the morning, between 8:00 and 10:00 A.M., and the other lists at night, between 11:30 P.M. and 1:00 A.M. For the late-night sessions, the participant got ready for bed and learned the list just before retiring. The daytime sessions were fitted into the normal course of daily activity. Tests for recall were given at one, two, four, and eight hours after learning. Half the periods during which forgetting might take place were filled with sleep, the other half with waking activity.

Recall was shown to be much better after a period of sleep than after a comparable period of being awake (Figure 7.11). Forgetting then is not a passive function of the passage of time after learning. Intervening activity determines to a considerable degree how much the individual remembers.

More recent studies of **retroactive inhibition** have been carried out under conditions that allowed better control. The experimental design employed to demonstrate retroactive inhibition proceeds in three stages and requires at least two groups (Figure 7.12). In this design the two groups first learn the same materials, typically to a stated criterion, such as 80 percent correct. In the second stage of the experiment,

Group		Stages of experiment I	II	III
	Experimental	Learn materials to be remembered	Learn new materials	Test for recall
	Control	Learn materials to be remembered	Unrelated activity	Test for recall

FIGURE 7.12
Design of an experiment on retroactive inhibition. The two groups learn the same materials to the same degree of mastery in stage I and receive the same test in stage III. Thus any difference in recall is the result of the different activities in stage II.

Group		Stage of experiment I	II	III
	Experimental	Learn first materials	Learn materials to be remembered	Test for recall
	Control	Unrelated activity	Learn materials to be remembered	Test for recall

FIGURE 7.13
Design of an experiment on proactive inhibition. The two groups learn the same materials to the same degree of mastery in stage II and receive the same test in stage III. Thus any difference in recall is the result of the different activities in stage I.

the experimental group learns a second set of materials; the control group spends the same amount of time in some unrelated activity, such as solving a mechanical puzzle. In the third stage both groups are tested for recall. Typically, the control group remembers much more than the experimental group, showing that the interpolated learning interfered with the recall of the experimental group.

Proactive Inhibition In retroactive inhibition later learning hinders the recall of materials learned earlier; in **proactive inhibition** materials learned earlier hinder recall of those learned later. The experimental design for studying proactive inhibition appears in Figure 7.13. Somewhat surprisingly, proactive inhibition is responsible for a great deal of forgetting. In 1957 Benton Underwood presented a summary of experiments by a dozen or more investigators. In all these experiments retention had been tested after twenty-four hours, but some of the individuals tested for recall in any particular experiment had previously learned different numbers of other lists. Since the interval between learning the critical list and the test for recall of it had been the same in all these studies, any differences in retention could be attributed to previous experience in learning and recalling such materials. This effect was very great (Figure 7.14). Individuals without previous experience retained about 75 percent of the syllables; those who had learned as many as twenty earlier lists retained only about 15 percent.

In these studies the retention interval was twenty-four hours. Proactive inhibition also hinders short-term memory. In experiments on short-term memory, there are usually many trials with different items to be remembered and tests after various intervals. This means, of course, that the materials learned on early trials could interfere with memory on later ones. We know now that this actually happens. The memory of individuals tested after eighteen seconds on six suc-

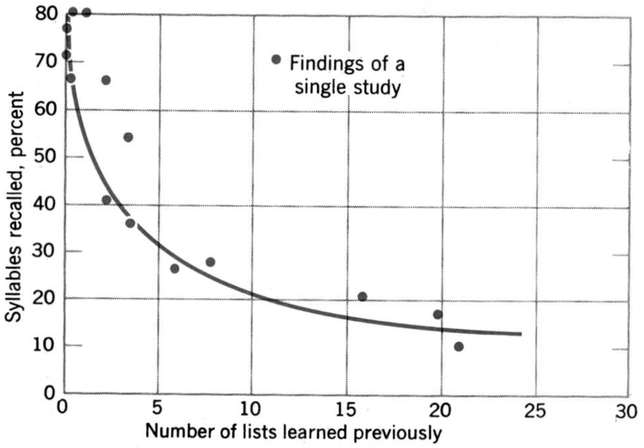

FIGURE 7.14
Cumulative interference by previous learning. The graph shows 24-hour retention of a list as a function of the number of lists learned previously. The greater the number of lists learned earlier, the lower the retention. The data are from many different experiments. This is our most impressive demonstration of proactive inhibition. (After Underwood, 1957.)

cessive lists gradually deteriorated. On the first test their recall was nearly perfect. On the last list it had reduced to 40 percent, and there was every indication that practice on more lists would have interfered even further (Keppel and Underwood, 1962).

The extraordinary memory of VP, reported by Earl Hunt and Tom Love, provides an interesting sidelight on this process of proactive inhibition. Among the tests given to VP was the classic one of short-term memory. First a syllable made up of consonants, such as TGV, was presented. Then VP did the successive subtractions by threes for the interval required and finally tried to recall the syllable. VP's performance in a series of such tests was superior. Whereas college students could report only 50 percent of the syllables during the course of the experiment, at the eighteen-second interval VP was able to report 85 percent of them. Further study showed that VP's performance was like that of the college students on their first test. The difference was that he showed no susceptibility to proactive inhibition. Asked to explain this, VP said that, knowing several languages, almost every syllable suggested a word to him and he could therefore treat the three-consonant item as a single unit.

SUMMARY □

Although subjective experience tells us that we forget because memories simply fade away in time, experiments reveal that other processes are able to interfere. An early hint of this fact came from studies of memory following periods of sleep and of waking. Memory after sleep was better, suggesting that waking activity somehow interfered with retention of earlier learning. Technically, such an effect is called retroactive inhibition: new learning acts back upon earlier learning and inhibits memory of it. Retroactive inhibition has been demonstrated many times in controlled laboratory experiments that employ a standard three-stage design, consisting of (1) original learning by two groups; (2) interpolated learning by the experimental group and unrelated activity by the control group; and (3) a test of the recall of both groups.

By a comparable process, earlier learning interferes with the recall of more recently learned materials. This type of interference, proactive inhibition, is even more powerful than retroactive inhibition. It has been shown to hinder both short-term memory and recall after many hours.

TOWARD A BETTER MEMORY

In nearly the following words, Gordon Bower, a psychologist at Stanford University, relates a story to begin a discussion of the practical uses of memory.

Simonides, a Greek poet, was commissioned to compose a poem praising a Roman nobleman and to recite it at a banquet attended by a multitude of guests. After he had recited the poem, Simonides was briefly called outside by a messenger from the gods Castor and Pollux, whom he had also praised in his poem. While he was absent, the roof of the hall collapsed, killing all the guests. The corpses were so mangled that relatives were unable to identify them. But Simonides stepped forward and named each of the many corpses on the basis of his memory of where they had been sitting in the huge banquet hall (Bower, 1970).

Later on we shall describe the "method of loci," which Simonides used to perform this feat of memory. But there is a good bit of other practical material to present first. If you are willing to work at it, the content of these next few pages may help to make you a slightly better student and a slightly better memorizer in general. But it will require work. The points made here are simple, but putting them to use takes practice.

The Feeling of Knowing

As a student you have the task of mastering a vast amount of material. Along the way to such mastery, you have probably already encountered the problem of judging when you have learned the materials well enough to handle the examinations that your professors inevitably inflict upon you. In the tip-of-the-tongue experiment described earlier (page 157), students were asked to decide whether they were certain that they did or did not know the word being defined, and they were able to do so readily. Other research has shown that our sense of what we know, perhaps even only marginally, is really quite remarkable. But this skill is not perfect. Particularly in the social sciences, the materials are of a kind that can seduce students into thinking that they know them when they do not. This is because so many of the concepts of social science are quite familiar ones. Psychology, for example, is about such things as learning, memory, motives, emotion, intelligence, madness, and the like. Most of the topics are ones that you knew something about even before you took a course in the subject. Under such circumstances it is not surprising that students can mistake familiarity with the topics for an understanding of what psychology has to say about them.

Have you ever gone to a friend, or if you are brave enough, to your instructor, and said, "I really studied for that last test and I really knew the materials, but somehow the test just didn't allow me to show what I knew"? Although there are times when you will be correct in this judgment, you should consider a possible alternative, that you did not know the subject matter as well as you thought. Your criteria for "knowing the materials" may have been too lenient; you may have known them well enough to meet your own standards of knowing but not well enough to meet those of the instructor.

What to do about it, if you decide that you have been lax in setting criteria? Clearly, you should try to find out what the instructor's criteria are like. If exams from previous years can be secured, try to take them. If a study guide is available to accompany your textbook, its most useful function may be to help you decide whether you know the materials as well as you should. Finally, having come to terms with the question of criteria, you should keep the following truism in mind: a good memory is really good initial learning. The only way to sharpen your memory is to develop techniques of effective learning. We turn to some of them now.

Overlearning

The process of mastering materials well enough to handle them on a test may very well mean overlearning them, that is, practicing beyond the point of bare mastery. An important question concerns the value of various degrees of such extra practice. Degrees of overlearning are usually expressed as percentages. If it takes ten trials to learn a list of words, and a person practices for five trials more, this is 50 percent overlearning; ten extra trials is 100 percent overlearning, and so on. In the best-known study of the effect of overlearning, people learned lists of nouns, just to the point of mastering them, with no overlearning, and to overlearning percentages of 50 to 100. There were recall tests after one, two, four, seven, fourteen, and twenty-eight days.

Three things are worth noting about the results (Figure 7.15). The first is that 50 and 100 percent overlearning clearly allows better recall than mere mastery of the materials. The second is that 50 percent overlearning produces a great improvement in recall, but 100 percent overlearning does not add many more additional words to the number remembered. More than 100 percent overlearning would not be an economical procedure when learning lists of nouns, for the amount of extra time required to overlearn them would be out of proportion to the additional number recalled later on. Finally, the value of overlearning increases as the amount of time for forgetting increases; that is, the advantage of overlearning is greater after fourteen or twenty-eight days than after one or two. This last fact is of considerable practical importance. Overlearning is most beneficial with materials that must be remembered for a long time.

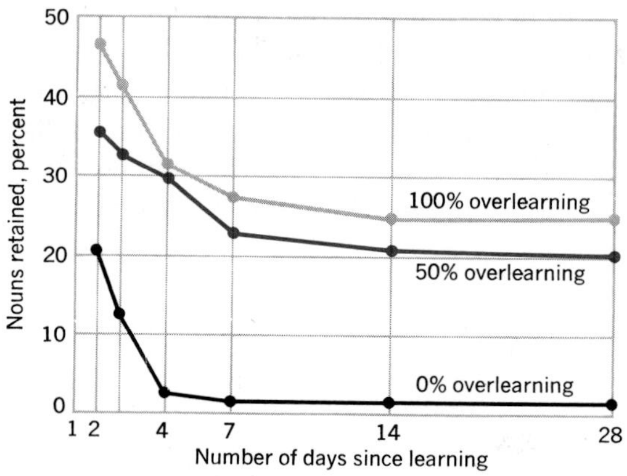

FIGURE 7.15
The effect of overlearning on retention. Overlearning aids retention, especially over long intervals. But these benefits probably follow a law of diminishing returns. Fifty percent overlearning adds a great deal to retention, but 100 percent overlearning does not improve recall that much more.

Subjective Organization

Why should overlearning aid retention? Probably there is more than one reason. Perhaps the most important is that learners impose their personal or **subjective organization** on materials as they memorize them, and this organization is strengthened through practice beyond the point of mastery. Practice on any set of materials to be memorized may soon bring learners to the point that, given a test, they could reproduce them all. But this does not mean that no further learning takes place with additional practice. On a number of successive practice runs learners may put materials into ever-better subjective order so that they feel surer of remembering them.

This point has not been studied as completely as it should be. The data plotted in Figure 7.16, however, are suggestive. The figure shows two measures of performance obtained when people were memorizing a list of words. One measure is simply the number of words produced trial-by-trial in free recall. The second measure is an index of subjective organization, showing the degree to which the learners organized the words and recalled them in the same order on successive trials. It reflects the degree of organization used by each person without revealing the type of organization employed. Recall continues to become better ordered for some time after the list is nearly mastered. The curve for organization suggests, in fact, that a great deal more of it would have occurred with still further practice. Given the importance of organization to memory, it seems to be one of the important contributions of overlearning.

General Overviews

Another kind of organization is a recognized aid to learning. Most how-to-study treatises tell you that you should begin your study of any substantial set of materials by getting a general impression of what these materials are about. If your assignment is a chapter in a book, you should begin by paging though it, noticing headings, glancing at illustrations, and, finally, reading the summary. All this is to be done before you begin detailed study. This is good advice. To get an impression of how important an overview is, please read through the following paragraph quickly, asking yourself how much of it you think you could reproduce, if you had to, after this quick reading. You will find yourself saying, "Not much!"

> The procedure, actually, is quite simple. First you arrange things into different groups. Of course, one pile may be sufficient, depending on how much there is to do. If you have to go somewhere else due to lack of facilities, that's the next step. Otherwise, you're pretty well set. It is im-

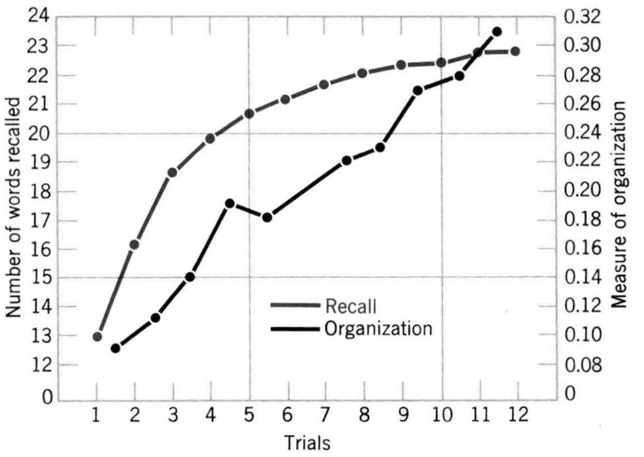

FIGURE 7.16
Organization and memory. The amount of material recalled (left-hand axis) and its organization (right-hand axis) are functions of practice. The measure of organization is a number indicating the extent to which the ordering of words is the same from one trial to the next. The important point to notice is that the organization of terms is still increasing rapidly when the number of them recalled has nearly reached an upper limit. The experiment was not carried out far enough to determine the extent to which ordering would continue. The pattern established suggests, however, that considerably more could be expected. (Data courtesy of Dr. James Pellegrino, University of California, Santa Barbara.)

> portant not to overdo things. That is, it is better to do too few things at once than too many. In the short run, this may not seem important, but complications can easily arise. A mistake can be expensive as well. At first, the whole procedure will seem complicated. Soon, however, it will become just another fact of life. It is difficult to foresee an end to the necessity of this task in the immediate future, but then one never can tell. After the procedure is completed, one arranges the materials into different groups again, and then they can be put into their appropriate places. Eventually, they will be used once more, and the whole cycle will have to be repeated; however, that is a part of life.

The trouble with this passage, of course, is that the wording is so general that it could be about a great many different things. John Bransford and Marcia Johnson (1973) used it in an experiment in which they showed that subjects who had been told that the paragraph was about washing clothes remembered about twice as much of it as those without this information. With this activity as the specific topic of the paragraph now in mind, you may want to reread it, noting how it has changed. You will probably find two important improvements. Now the words call up visual images that aid memory (page 158); and now the paragraph is organized in a way that it was not before. One things follows another in a sensible order.

Mnemonic Devices

Discussions of organization lead naturally to **mnemonic devices,** or aids to memory, because most of them provide some sort of artificial organization. Usually they take advantage of some commonplace organization already in memory and let it provide a way of organizing an unfamiliar set of materials.

"Chunking" For materials greater in numbers than can be handled by immediate memory, an effective mnemonic practice is grouping the materials so that they become few enough to handle. As we have seen, the span of immediate memory is small—seven items plus or minus two, according to popular psychological thought (page 149). Yet each of us remembers longer sequences with little difficulty. Earlier we mentioned familiar ten-item sequences, telephone numbers together with their area codes. Another example is your social security number. In both of these cases, the grouping is provided for us. In others you will have to do the recoding yourself. Such grouping is commonly referred to as **"chunking."**

Our friend with the wonderful memory, VP, offered some additional suggestions for increasing the span of immediate memory. When originally tested, VP's immediate memory span was nine digits—high, but no higher than that of many college students. Given the task of trying to increase his memory span, he did so, reaching a span of seventeen numbers in just five trials. When asked how he accomplished this, he said that he (1) paid strict attention to the number of digits to be expected on each trial; (2) grouped the digits in sets of three and five, depending on their number; (3) decided his strategy of grouping before each trial; (4) made verbal associations to each group of numbers—weights, dates, anything he could think of; and (5) when he could, he made associations between groupings. Provided with these hints and given eleven trials of practice, a selected group of college students increased their span from nine to twelve digits.

The Method of Loci The **method of loci** (*loci,* plural of Latin *locus,* place) was the means by which Simonides achieved perfect recall of all the guests at the banquet, in the tale of catastrophe with which this section began. Simonides was able to retrace in his mind's eye the seating of the guests at the long tables in the banquet hall. The seating arrangement provided a spatial structure wherein he could remember the guests. Any familiar spacial structure or setting can be used to help you remember a number of items.

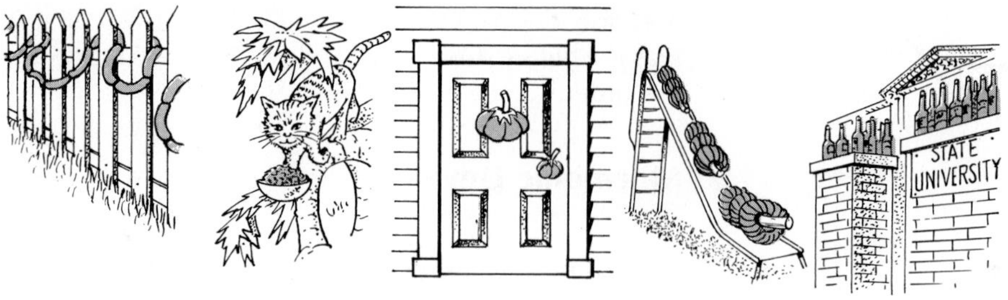

FIGURE 7.17
The method of loci. Putting images of items to be remembered at various places in a recalled scene would be an effective way to remember a grocery list.

Take a mental tour of some place you know well and imagine the things you need to remember located at various places (loci) in this setting. For example, you might imagine that you are taking a tour from home to campus. Now suppose that you have a set of things to remember, perhaps a shopping list consisting of hot dogs, cat food, tomatoes, bananas, and whiskey. The method of loci requires you to place each item to be remembered at some definite location on your mental tour, and to form a vivid image of the item in its spot.

Your route from home to campus might pass a picket fence, a huge tree, the entrance to an elegant house now used as a doctor's office, a children's park with a slide, and the main entrance to the college, marked by pillars on either side. Using the method of loci to memorize the shopping list, you might imagine long chains of hot dog links topping the fence, a cat eating cat food in the tree, tomatoes, replacing the door knocker and doorknob on the elegant house, a parade of bananas sliding in bunches down the slide, and bottles of whiskey topping the pillars at the campus gates (Figure 7.17). A common recommendation is to develop bizarre associations, but this is not necessary. The method of loci, by its very nature, however, will often have you imagining objects in places where it would be very unusual for them to appear.

Experiments have shown the method of loci to be quite effective. In one study students associated lists of forty items with forty locations on campus, taking thirteen seconds to form each association. On an immediate recall test, the average person remembered thirty-eight of the forty items and a day later remembered thirty-four (Ross and Lawrence, 1968). Obviously these averages mean that for many individuals recall was perfect. Such excellent recall depends on three important factors: (1) using a previously mastered organization, (2) taking a fairly long time to deal with each item, and (3) making an effective use of imagery. Choosing a familiar organization freed the students from the necessity of making a new organizing structure. You may wish to note, as a review of a previous point, that remembering the list calls upon episodic memory. The organizing structure is provided by knowledge in semantic memory (page 143).

Numerical Pegs You probably already know the following little series rhyming numbers and objects, or one something like it.

One is a bun,
two is a shoe,
three is a tree,
four is a door,
five is a hive,
six is sticks,
seven is heaven,
eight is a gate,
nine is a line, and
ten is a hen.

Such a series can become a mnemonic device. The procedure is not unlike that employed in the method of loci. Again, as each to-be-remembered item is presented, the individual forms an image that relates it to the corresponding object in the series. If the list of objects consists of an ashtray, firewood, and a football, he or she might imagine an ashtray as the filling for a sandwich, made with a bun (one), a huge shoe (two) filled with firewood, a football lodged in a tree (three), and so on. Again, the method works. Individuals after just one presentation can usually remember every item, sometimes to their surprise.

Narrative Stories Another very effective mnemonic device is to put items that are to be remembered into a story form. In an experiment which makes this point very impressively, students learned twelve different lists of simple words. Students in an experimental group put the lists into the story form. The second group was a *yoked control group* (page 143). Each member studied the words for the amount of time a partner in the experimental group needed to make up stories. Instructions to the members of the experimental group were as follows.

> A good way to learn a list of items is to make up a story relating the items to one another. Specifically, start with the first item and put it in a setting

which will allow other items to be added to it. Then, add the other items to the story in the same order as the items appear. Make each [of the twelve stories] meaningful to yourself. Then, when you are asked to recall the items, you can simply go through your story and pull out the proper items in the correct order.

Three typical stories appear in Figure 7.18.

The results of the experiment can be stated quickly. On recall tests that were given immediately after each list was learned, there was no difference between the two groups; both remembered over 99 percent of the words. After all twelve lists had been memorized, however, the students who made up stories remembered 93 percent of the words in the correct order; the students in the control group remembered only 13 percent.

One explanation for this difference readily suggests itself. Learning twelve lists of words puts the individual into a situation in which retroactive inhibition and proactive inhibition would create powerful interference (page 155). The creation of a story made it possible to keep the lists separate and prevent the accumulation of retroactive and proactive inhibition. Moreover, stories tend to call up images which aid memory, as demonstrated by the clothes-washing example cited earlier.

Finally, making up stories applies elaborate processing to the words in the list. The stories created by the students accomplished the same thing as the elaborate sentences used by Craik and Tulving to improve recall for words (page 155). The relevance of this point to study, that you must engage yourself in it, is worth emphasizing. Whenever you find yourself "just reading words" as you study, your processing is superficial. The time has come to take a break, start over, and read for meaning.

Individual Differences

We come now to a point from which some of you will take comfort. For, as with all psychological processes, there are great individual differences in what makes for effective memorization. These are those, for example, for whom visual images are a mystery. These people claim not to have them and therefore cannot use them as an aid to learning. One such individual was VP, who was not much of a visualizer and did not depend heavily on images. He was very sensitive to linguistic similarities and made heavy use of semantic features, even when tested for recall of pictures. He was tested with a set of materials used by Nancy Frost (1971) to study clustering in the recall of visual scenes. The sketches shown in Figure 7.19 are arranged in rows by physical orientation and in columns by semantic content.

A LUMBERJACK DARTed out of the forest, SKATEd around a HEDGE past a COLONY of DUCKs. He tripped on some FURNITURE, tearing his STOCKING while hastening toward the PILLOW where his MISTRESS lay.

A VEGETABLE can be a useful INSTRUMENT for a COLLEGE student. A carrot can be a NAIL for your FENCE or BASIN. But a MERCHANT of the QUEEN would SCALE that fence and feed the carrot to the GOAT.

One night at DINNER I had the NERVE to bring my TEACHER. There had been a FLOOD that day, and the rain BARREL was sure to RATTLE. There was, however, a VESSEL in the HARBOR carrying this ARTIST to my CASTLE.

FIGURE 7.18
Sample stories. (From Bower and Clark, 1969.)

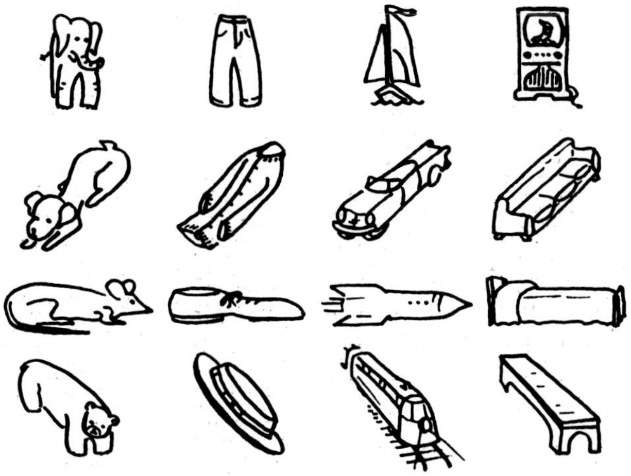

FIGURE 7.19
Clustering in visual memory. Row by row the sketches have the same orientation—vertical, at an angle downward to the left, and so on. Column by column the sketches are of objects belonging to the same category—animal, clothing, and so on. Clustering in memory was by orientation for college students. VP clustered by categories. (Sketches courtesy of Dr. Nancy Frost.)

When most people are shown these materials and later asked to recall them, they remember objects with the same orientation—vertical, horizontal, and so on. VP, in contrast, used semantic clustering, recalling the animals, articles of clothing, means of transportation, and pieces of furniture together.

VP believed that the development of a memory as powerful as his begins early and depends on being placed in situations in which memorizing facts rather than manipulating them is the prized performance. For this reason he said that excellent memorizers are likely to be rather passive people, who are willing to abide by the "rules of the game." When these rules are to memorize, they do so without rebellion. Since current education places more emphasis on interpretation than memorization, VP believed that people like himself may be on the decrease. A willingness to work hard at memorizing is also essential. Whenever possible, VP would devote more time and effort to memorizing than most people. Another of VP's skills was a great ability to note details quickly. In VP's case this aptitude was particularly conspicuous with respect to semantic details.

SUMMARY □

The study of human information processing has progressed to the point that we understand a fair amount and can make modest recommendations about how to develop an effective memory. Our recommendations have much more to do with learning or storage than with memory or retrieval. As a point of departure, we called attention to the fact that the feeling of knowing some set of materials is usually accurate, but that it is not always entirely so. This is the origin of some of the problems students have with study. Setting the criteria for knowing too low, they have a feeling of knowing when materials are less than completely mastered.

Among the procedures that may help correct this error is overlearning, which puts the materials to be learned more firmly into memory and, furthermore, improves the way that they are subjectively organized for recall. Reviewing the organization of a discussion before beginning to study a topic also helps the individual absorb material.

The so-called mnemonic devices employ artificial but familiar forms of organization. The simplest procedure is to group or "chunk" materials. This reduces the number of elements so that they are within the span of immediate memory. More elaborate mnemonic aids include the method of loci, imagining items to be recalled in familiar places; the method of numerical pegs, imagining items in relation to the elements provided by the little rhyme that begins, "One is a bun"; and the method of narrative stories, creating a story to connect the items to be remembered. In all these methods imagery as well as organization contributes to superior recall. A narrative story also puts items through deep or elaborate processing, known from laboratory studies to improve recall.

We end with an escape clause: there are huge individual differences in what makes for effective memory. Students will need to shop around among these recommendations, selecting those that suit their individual talents best.

TO BE SURE YOU UNDERSTAND THIS CHAPTER △

Here are the principal concepts presented in this chapter. You should be able to define them and state the points made about each in the text discussion.

Immediate memory
Encoding
Echoic memory
Span of immediate memory
Recoding
Reaction time
Attention
Cocktail party phenomenon
Dichotic listening experiment
Shadowing
Short-term memory
Long-term memory
Primacy effect
Recency effect
Storage
Maintenance rehearsal
Elaborative rehearsal
Level of processing
Consolidation
Retrograde amnesia
Retrieval
Availability of memory
Accessibility of memory
Tip-of-the-tongue phenomenon
Dual-coding theory
Episodic memory
Semantic memory
Encoding specificity principle
Subjective organization
Recall test
Recognition test
Retroactive inhibition
Proactive inhibition
Overlearning
Mnemonic device
Chunking
Method of loci
Numerical pegs
Narrative story
Yoked control group

TO GO BEYOND THIS CHAPTER △

In this book This chapter is a fairly self-contained unit. The most closely related materials are to be found in Chapter 4, on perception; Chapter 6, on conditioning and learning; and Chapter 12, on cognitive development. The ties are not extremely close, however.

Elsewhere Dozens of books covering information processing have come out in the last five or six years. Some that you may find particularly useful are the following: *Memory and Cognition,* by Walter Kintsch; *Human Memory: Structures and Processes,* by Roberta Klatzky; *Human Memory: The Processing of Information,* by Geoffrey and Elizabeth Loftus; and *Human Information Processing,* by Peter H. Lindsay and Donald A. Norman.

CH. 8

Language and Thinking

We sometimes hear that language is the principal thing distinguishing the human organism from lower forms of life. Although recent studies with the chimpanzee suggest that the gap between us and our nearest evolutionary neighbors may not be so great as we once thought, there is no doubt that our linguistic talents are truly impressive. Consider, for example, the following passage from *Alice in Wonderland,* by Lewis Carroll, who was often preoccupied with issues considered basic in the psychology of language. The speakers in this conversation are Alice and the Knight.

> "The name of the song is called 'Haddocks' Eyes.' "
>
> "Oh, that's the name of the song, is it?" Alice said, trying to feel interested.
>
> "No, you don't understand," the Knight said, looking a little vexed. "That's what the name is *called.* The name really is, 'The Aged Aged Man.' "
>
> "Then I ought to have said 'That's what the *song* is called'?" Alice corrected herself.
>
> "No, you oughtn't: that's quite another thing! The *song* is called 'Ways and Means': but that's only what it's called, you know!"
>
> "Well, what is the song, then?" said Alice, who was by this time completely bewildered.
>
> "I was coming to that," the Knight said. "The song really is 'A-sitting on A Gate': and the tune's my own invention."

To follow the subtleties of this conversation requires remarkable **linguistic competence,** that is, an understanding of how the language operates. Very few of us could put into words the nature of this understanding. We sense how language works without being consciously aware of all its devices.

The name of the song is called "Haddock's Eyes," but the name really is "The Aged Aged Man," the song really is "A-sitting on A Gate."

Language as a Set of Rules Whether we know them or not, sets of rules do prescribe all aspects of our linguistic endeavors. These rules cover language at different levels of complexity.

Some of them are rules of **phonology,** which has to do with the units of sound that make up the stream of speech. For example, only particular sounds can be combined in making words. The rules differ somewhat for different languages. In English *trick* is a word. *Twick* is not but it could be, because *tw* is an acceptable phonological combination. In fact, some children who have not yet learned to pronounce *trick* find *twick* a simpler substitute. *Tbick* is not a word in English because the phonological rules do not allow the *tb* combination at the beginnings of words (But compare *basketball.*) Although the phonological rules are fairly standard in a given language, they are not absolute. For example, *sr* is a prohibited initial combination in English, but in some part of America the natives plant *srubs.*

Other rules concern **syntax.** They cover the ways in which words may be combined into phrases, clauses, and sentences that convey meaning. As an illustration, the improbable "Colorless green ideas sleep furiously" is a sentence in a way that "Furiously sleep ideas green colorless" is not (Chomsky, 1957). The first string of words obeys the rules that dictate the locations of adjectives, nouns, verbs, and adverbs in a sentence, but the order of the second string of words is completely haphazard. Words must be put into a sequence that indicates their mutual relations, and syntax is this ordering.

Another set of rules are those of **semantics.** By these rules meaning is put into our own utterances and extracted from the utterances of someone else. Consider the following pairs of sentences.

John envied Henry.	Henry was envied by John.
Fred married Emily.	Emily married Fred.
Arthur loved Amy.	Amy loved Arthur.
Harold killed Walter.	Walter killed Harold.

Our knowledge of semantic forms tells us that the sentences in the first two pairs mean the same thing, but that those in the last two pairs may not.

The same skill allows us to recognize the ambiguities in some sentences. For example, "They are eating apples" has one meaning as an answer to the question, "What are they doing?" and quite another in answer to "Are those apples better for cooking or for eating?"

Finally, some rules are rules of **pragmatics.** They describe the use of language in a social context, such as the fact that speakers take turns when carrying on a conversation. They also take the situation into account. The same language may mean quite different things in different circumstances. When your professor tells you that your grade in his course is a C and you say "Thanks a lot!" the inflection in your voice will indicate gratitude if you had expected a grade of F but something quite different if you had expected an A. When I say, "Can you open the window?" I probably mean it literally ("Are you able to?") if we are trying to get back into a house after locking ourselves out. But if we are inside and the room is hot, I may really mean, "Will you please open the window to cool the room off." When you tell me that your head is spinning, you may mean, depending on the situation, that you are dizzy from a car trip on a winding mountain road, that you have consumed more of some intoxicant than you should have, or that you have had just about all the psychology of language that you can handle.

LANGUAGE COMPREHENSION

The chief function of language is to serve as a means of communication between and among individuals. A distinction can be made between the comprehension and generation of speech, however, for the process of communication requires a person to be sometimes the perceiver, sometimes the generator of the means of communication. Following an organization suggested by this distinction, we shall look first at the ways in which speech is perceived and comprehended, then at the process of speech generation.

Speech Sounds

When you talk to someone on the telephone, you recognize that the speech you hear is distorted. In spite of this, it is possible to understand the person to whom you are talking. You can distinguish people by their voices and tell how they react to what you say. This is really quite remarkable because the auditory signal you interpret is very much different from the one that would be heard in face-to-face conversation. Studies have shown that as much as half the physical stimulus can be filtered out of a message without seriously degrading its intelligibility. This means that nonacoustic, psychologically meaningful factors

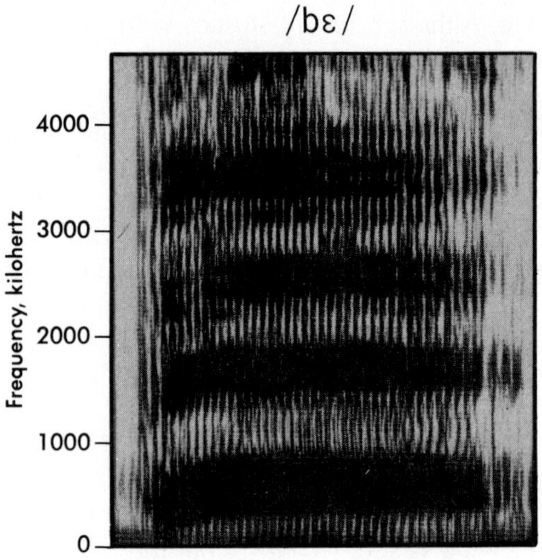

FIGURE 8.1
Sound spectrogram. The energies for most speech sounds, more particularly for their vowels, are concentrated in four clear concentrations, called formants. The darkness of the band reflects the intensity of that pitch in the speech sound. The ℰ in "bet" has four heavy concentrations of energy at 500, 1500, 2500, and 3500 kHz.

must contribute to speech perception. We shall consider what these factors might be after we have discussed the elementary speech sounds.

Physical Attributes of Speech Sounds From our discussion of auditory stimuli (page 61), you already know that every complex sound is constructed of a set of tones and overtones that vary in terms of intensity. The composition of any sound can be represented in a variety of ways, one of which appeared in Figure 3.23 (page 61). Another way is more common in studying the sounds that make up speech. Figure 8.1 is a sound spectrogram of the syllable "bℰ" as in bet. The horizontal line of this figure covers the brief time, about 0.3 second, required to say the syllable. The vertical axis covers the range of frequencies, in kilohertz, making up the syllable. The darker the smudged bar for a particular frequency, the greater the intensity of the tone at that frequency.

The auditory signals for the syllable "bℰ" consists of a pattern of energies changing in time. The sound spectrogram for a longer utterance would present a string of aligned resonant bars (Figure 8.2), similar to the single alignment in Figure 8.1. Detailed study of sound spectrograms reveals that the same person saying the same syllable on different occasions produces slightly different patterns of sound. When different speakers utter the same syllable, the recorded patterns vary even more. In fact, these patterns are of in-

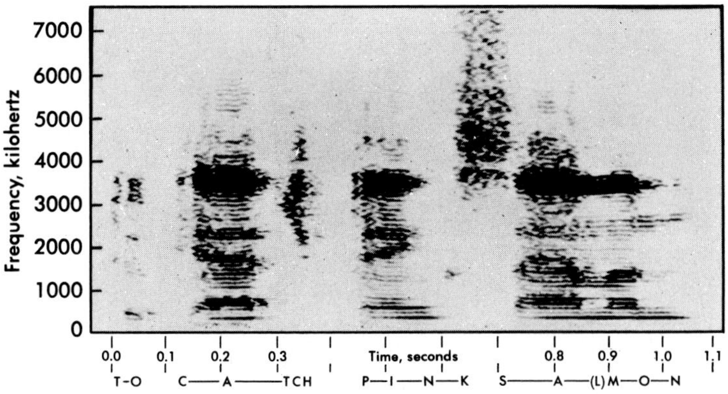

FIGURE 8.2

Sound spectrogram. The portions of the spectrogram associated with the a's in catch and salmon are quite similar. The consonant sounds tch and s have higher pitches than the other vowels and consonants.

finite variety and are unique to individual voices. Just as fingerprints are a means of identification, so too does the sound spectrogram serve as a sort of voice print by which to identify a speaker.

The fact that speech sounds can be graphed so exactly means that the process can be reversed. With a sound spectrogram of an utterance available, a computer can be given this description and then programmed to operate sound equipment to reproduce speech. This is the basic nature of a speech synthesizer. The computer instructs the auditory equipment every few milliseconds (thousandths of a second) to produce sounds made up of such and such frequencies in such and such relative intensities. In Figure 8.3 natural and synthesized speech are compared.

A speech synthesizer can reproduce speech fairly accurately but, perhaps more importantly, it can also modify speech sounds. It can speed speech up or slow it down. It can raise or lower the dominant pitch, thus speaking in a high voice or a low one. Being able to manipulate speech in such controlled ways allows us to determine the effects of these manipulations on how speech is perceived. Although data are sparse, those available indicate that rate and pitch of speech may affect our evaluation of a speaker's personality. One study found, for example, that increasing the rate of a male's speech made him seem less benevolent; decreasing the rate of speech made him seem less competent. When the pitch of the male's voice was raised, he was judged less benevolent and less competent (Brown et al., 1974).

Phonemes The simplest *functional* speech sounds in any language are called **phonemes.** They are the pronunciations of vowels, consonants, and diphthongs and are the smallest units of sound that distinguish one utterance from another by signaling a difference in meaning. Examples of phonemes are the "k" sound in *keep, cool, account, back,* and *liquor,* and the "t" sound in *atlas, gently, tulip,* and *fault.*

If you say the two words *keep* and *cool* and listen carefully as you do so, you will discover that the two "k" sounds are slightly different. Considered just as physical events, they are different phones, a phone being any individual and distinct speech sound, irrespective of how it fits into the structure of the language. The two "k"s are considered forms of the same phoneme, technically **allophones,** because the

FIGURE 8.3

Sound spectrogram for natural speech and synthesized speech. According to Dr. A. M. Liberman, who supplied the figure, "The schematized version at the bottom produces a rather highly intelligible synthetic version of 'Many are taught to breathe through the nose' when converted to sound by the Pattern Playback." Check the pattern for ℰ in "many" against that for ℰ in Figure 8.1 and notice the similarity.

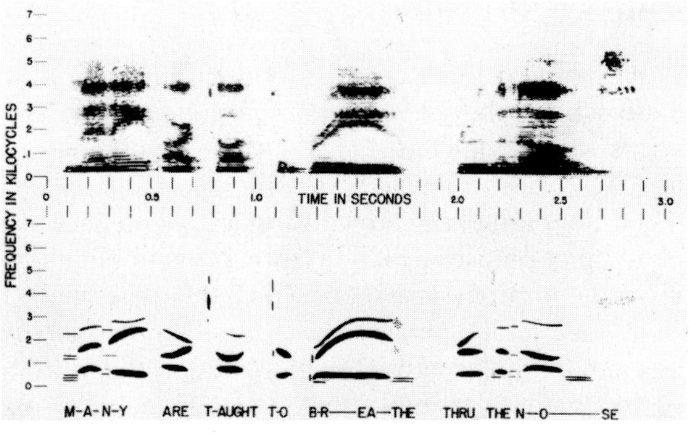

difference between them has no linguistic significance.

In Arabic things are different. The word for "dog," *kalb,* begins with the "k" as in *keep.* The word for "heart," *qalb,* begins with the "k" as in *cool.* Thus in Arabic the two "k"s are separate phonemes because they signal a difference in meaning. It is for exactly this reason that /k/ and /r/ are different phonemes in English. In Arabic *kalb* and *qalb* are different in the same way that *keep* and *reap* and *cool* and *rule* are different in English (Glucksberg and Danks, 1975). The English language has approximately forty-five phonemes. Some languages use as few as twenty phonemes, others as many as sixty.

There is now strong evidence that phonemes have separate psychological reality. The nature of the evidence is as follows. With the aid of an electronic speech synthesizer, it is possible to control the physical composition of simple speechlike sounds very exactly. For example, the syllable "ba" can be altered in very gradual steps so that is becomes the syllable "pa." Through this same set of small transforming steps, the phoneme /b/ becomes the phoneme /p/. The person listening, however, does not hear a gradual transformation. Instead, the syllable continues to sound like "ba" through a considerable range and then, more or less abruptly, shifts to "pa," which it continues to be through any additional small alterations (Eimas and Corbit, 1973). In short, the two phonemes /b/ and /p/ have a kind of integrity that permits them to be heard only in these terms and not as blends. The perception of them contrasts sharply with the continuous nature of the perception of other qualities in the world, even ones that can be categorized. If a person looks at a series of lights in which the dominant wavelength gradually shifts from yellow through orange to red, this is exactly what is seen. There is no abrupt shift from one color to the other, as there is for phonemes. Moreover, some evidence indicates that babies only one month old hear phonemes in the same categorical way (Eimas et al., 1971). Phonemes may very well be unitary sounds and also innately recognizable.

Sentence Structure

As we learned them (and learned to hate them) in grade school, the rules of grammar tell us how sentences *should be* constructed. In the psychology of language, these rules tell us something slightly different, how sentences *are* constructed. Sentences are made up of phrases which, in turn, are combinations of words. A phrase is a set of words that represents a single idea. Since phrases do represent single ideas, they can be replaced by a single word, as the following treatment of a simple sentence will show.

The dog	buried	the bone
He	buried	it
He	acted	

The sentence "The dog buried the bone" consists of three phrases, "the dog," "buried," and "the bone." The phrase "the bone" is a unit and "buried the" is not, for the single word "it" can be substituted for "the bone," but there is no similar substitute for "buried the." Pushing the point further, we can substitute "he" for "the dog" and the one word "acted" for "buried the bone." Units that serve a single function in a sentence and can be replaced by one word are called constituent structures or simply constituents.

The idea of constituent structures can also be represented as a diagram which indicates that a sentence possesses a hierarchical organization.

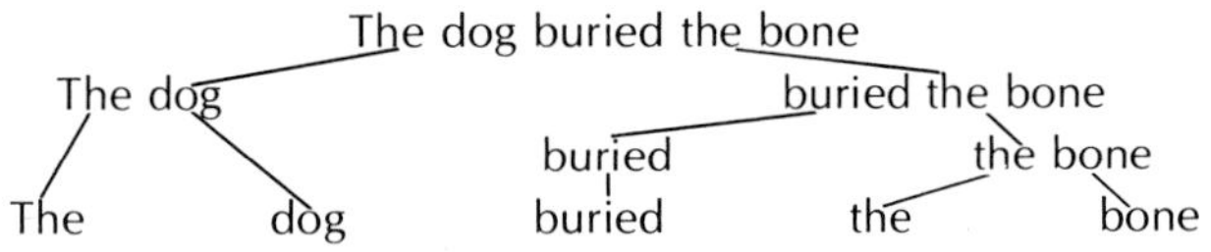

The analysis of sentences into constituents is a linguistic analysis. An important question to ask is whether the constituents of a sentence have psychological meaning. The answer from a number of studies is that they do. In a representative investigation, Richard Graf and Jane Torrey (1966) broke the same materials up into lines in the two ways illustrated by the following sentence.

During World War II,
even fantastic schemes
received consideration
if they gave promise
of shortening the conflict

During World War
II, even fantastic
schemes received
consideration if
they gave
promise of shorten-
ing the conflict

The lines in the left-hand version correspond to constituents of the sentence. In the right-hand version they do not. In the experiment a machine exposed each line for a very short time. One group of participants read the passage broken into constituents, the other group the randomly broken passage, and immediately took a multiple-choice test of comprehension. The subjects who read the passage given in constituent form did better on the test.

Morphemes

The simplest units of language that have recognizable meaning are called **morphemes.** Morphemes are words and meaningful segments of words. Thus *pill* and *bill* are morphemes, as are *pillow* and *billow,* because none of them can be analyzed into simpler meaningful units. *Pills* and *pillows* both contain two morphemes, *pill* and *pillow,* and the final pluralizing "s." Other multimorpheme words are mark/s, mark/ed, mark/ing, mark/er, un/mark/ed, mark/er/s, and re/mark/able. Root words like *pill, mark,* and *dream* are referred to as **free morphemes,** because they can occur alone. Inflections that make a noun plural and indicate that the activity of the verb is ongoing or finished; prefixes such as un- and re- indicating the negative and "again"; and suffixes such as -er and -able signifying agent and ability are called **bound morphemes.** They cannot stand alone and must be bound to free morphemes. Bound morphemes add to or change the meaning of the free morpheme to which they are attached. Studies of morphemes and the meaningfulness of words, the earliest semantic studies conducted in psychology, have indicated that it is useful to consider several types of meaning, denotative, associative, and connotative.

Humpty Dumpty, an early semantic theorist.

Denotative Meaning The **denotative meaning** of a word is the thing, event, or relationship that a word stands for or refers to. Hence it is also called referential meaning. Denotative meaning sometimes seems pretty arbitrary.

> "When I use a word," Humpty Dumpty said, in a rather scornful tone, "it means what I choose it to mean—neither more nor less."
> "The question is," said Alice, "whether you can make words mean so many different things."
> "The question is," said Humpty Dumpty, "which is to be master—that's all." Alice was too puzzled to say anything. . . .

Although Humpty Dumpty was mostly correct in his observation, he was not entirely so. Sometimes there is a connection between the sound of a word and its meaning that makes the meaning less than completely arbitrary. In an important early book on language, Roger Brown (1959) dealt with this point as **phonetic symbolism,** the term he chose to express the idea that the sounds of words sometimes reflect attributes of the objects to which they refer. To illustrate, if speakers of English are told that one of the two objects in Figure 8.4 is a "takete" and that the other is a "maluma," they generally agree that the first is a "maluma" and the second a "takete." Other studies have tested the ability of subjects to choose the correct translation of words in languages with which they are unfamiliar. These studies indicate that subjects tend to agree on appropriate translations, and that the agreed-upon translation is correct much more often than not. For example, if English-speaking people are told that the two Chinese words *ch'ing* and *ch'ung* refer to our two concepts "heavy" and "light" and are asked to guess which is which, they will usually offer the correct translations, *ch'ing*—light and *ch'ung*—heavy. At a more informal level, Brown points out that there could hardly be a better onomatopoeic rendition of the sound of water splashing back and forth in a flask than the German word *geschleudert,* that the very structure of the English word *God,* or even better of *Jehovah* and *Gawd,* implies enormity, and that *tweeter* and *woofer* in hi-fi terminology suggest the functions of such speakers.

Associative Meaning Words may call up associations with considerable speed and in considerable numbers, or they may not. If we are asked to respond to "house" as rapidly as we can with as many associations as possible, we will come up with "home" quickly and easily move on to "family," "school," "live," "window," and so give a substantial number of associations to "house." For "zuren," which is not even a word, we may need a full five seconds to think

FIGURE 8.4
Phonetic symbolism. Which is a "takete" and which a "maluma"? (After Kohler, 1925.)

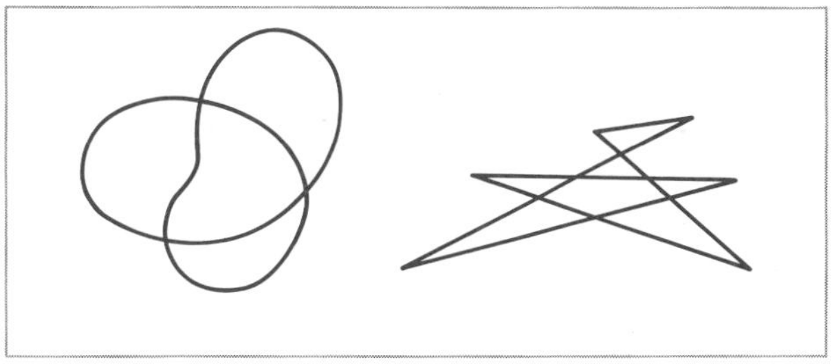

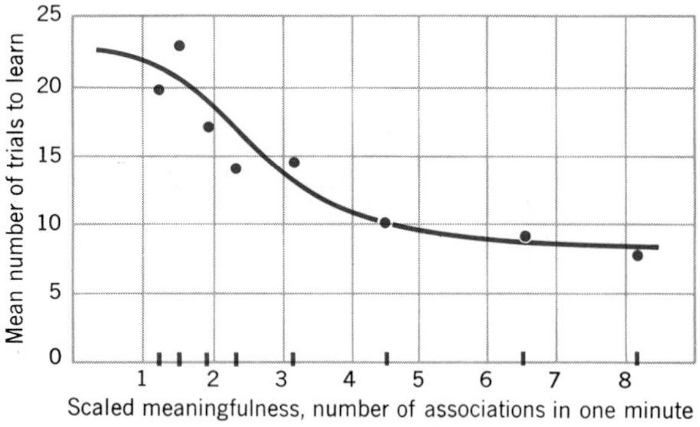

FIGURE 8.5
Learning and associative meaningfulness. Meaningfulness was measured by Noble's procedure. Learning was measured by the number of trials to master the list. The smooth curve is typical of the function obtained in several studies.

of "zebra" or some other word, probably one beginning with z, then draw an utter blank. Both the number of associations and the speed with which they are given have been used as measures of the meaningfulness of words in this sense of having **associative meaning.**

For example, Clyde Noble (1952) chose as a measure of meaningfulness the average number of associations people could make in one minute. He used two-syllable words that varied all the way from the very familiar "kitchen" to sequences like "gojey," which are not words at all. A few of his words, together with the average number of associations made to them, were kitchen, 9.61; uncle, 6.57; sequence, 3.21; flotsam, 2.19; polef, 1.30; gojey, 0.99. The associative meaningfulness of words largely determines the ease with which they are committed to memory. Lists of highly meaningful words are easy to learn. Lists of words with few associations are difficult (Figure 8.5).

Connotative Meaning The simple listing of such terms as *poverty, freedom, nasty, elegant, slipshod,* and *success* will serve to make the point that words differ tremendously in the emotions and judgments they evoke. Charles Osgood and his associates have provided a method for measuring differences in connotations, the **semantic differential.** Subjects are asked to rate a series of verbal concepts that could be almost anything—for example, *polite, eager, burning, lady, Russian.* The scales on which they are rated, usually twenty to fifty of them, consist of two polar adjectives connected by a line divided into seven positions from left to right. The subject decides whether the concept is near one or the other of the pair of contrasting adjectives in its connotations and chooses one of the seven positions to indicate the strength of the connection. The average placements of two concepts, *polite* and *burning,* on ten such

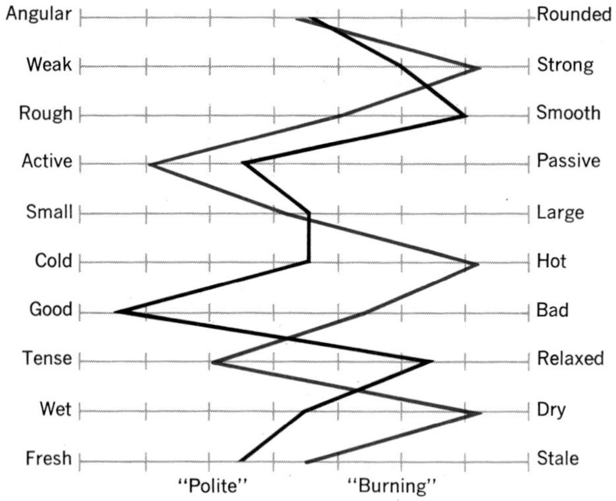

FIGURE 8.6
Semantic-differential profiles. The figure shows the placement of "polite" and "burning" on ten semantic-differential scales. (Adapted from Osgood and Suci, 1955.)

scales are indicated in Figure 8.6. Both concepts were regarded as neutral on the angular-rounded scale and both were rated relatively strong and active. On the other hand, the concept *polite* is midway on the cold-hot scale, *burning* near the hot end. *Polite* is rated as relatively good, whereas *burning* is rated as relatively bad. On the wet-dry scale, *polite* is neutral and *burning* relatively dry. Comparisons of the profiles for different words provide a picture of how concepts vary and are similar in their connotations. From an analysis of a large number of concepts rated by many subjects on many different scales of contrasting adjectives, Osgood and his associates concluded that the scales can be collected into three groups, depending on whether they indicate *evaluation,* good-bad; *potency,* strong-weak; or *activity,* active-passive. For a great number of words and the concept they represent, these appear to be the major dimensions of their **connotative meaning.**

SUMMARY □

The psychology of language is a study that goes on at many different levels. At the level of speech sounds linguists have described the nature of elementary speech sounds and how they combine to form words. Syntax consists of the rules by which words combine to form phrases and sentences. Semantics is the study of meaning. Pragmatics concerns the use of language in real situations by real speakers and listeners.

Evidence suggests that we have an unconscious understanding of the linguistic rules that apply at each of these levels. Thus at the level of speech sounds we understand that *shamble* and *scamble* could both be

English words (both are) but that *sgamble* could not. At the level of syntax we know that "Mary hit John" is an acceptable sentence but "Hit Mary John" is not. At the level of semantics we can find out that the denotative meaning of *scamble* is "to struggle greedily for something," then guess that an associated word might be *scramble,* and that its connotations might place it at the bad end of the evaluative scale, the active end of the activity scale, and the strong end of the potency scale on the semantic differential. Still at the level of semantics we know that "Mary hit John" and "John was hit by Mary" mean the same thing, but that "John hit Mary" means something different. At the level of pragmatics we know, as William James once said, that it is one thing to step on a person's toe and apologize but quite another to apologize and then step on his toe.

Linguistic analyses have provided us with information that has psychological significance. The phonological characteristics of a person's speech affect our judgments of personality. The basic units of sound that distinguish one utterance from another, the phonemes, are perceived categorically, as separate units of speech. The structures identified in syntactic analyses of sentences divide these sentences into units. Text arranged in short lines corresponding to these units is easier to understand than text that is not. The familiarity and meaningfulness of language, as revealed by semantics, affect its comprehension and the ease with which it is learned and recalled.

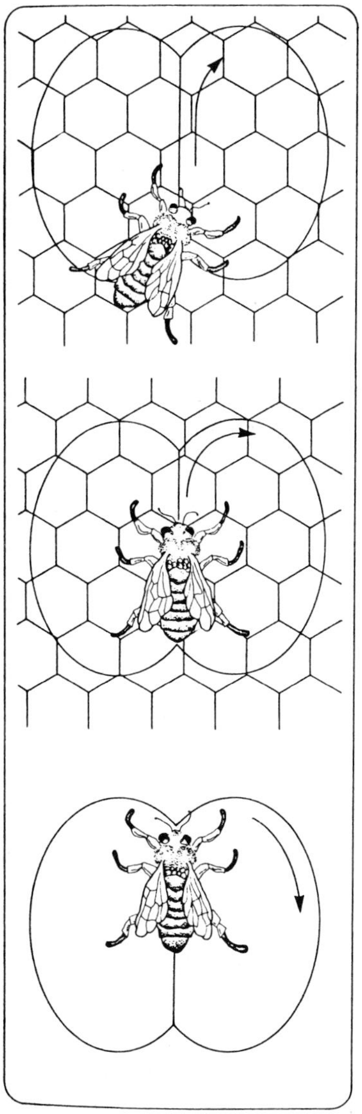

The language of the bees. The direction of the dance indicates the direction, with respect to the sun, in which nectar can be found; the speed communicates distance.

THE GENERATION OF SPEECH

The other side of the communication coin is the generation of speech. In thinking about how language is acquired and used, psychologists are naturally interested in communication in animals other than ourselves. In this context the most interesting question of all is whether other animals can be taught to understand and generate something like human language.

Animal Communication

It is clear that animals of many species communicate. They announce the location of food, state their claims on territory, proclaim a condition of sexual arousal, indicate their recognition of an acquaintance, and perhaps even reassure with sociability. Small shrimplike creatures of the deep, the euphausids, will in a chain reaction light up the luminous spots on their eye stalks, as though to inform one another of each's presence. In southeast Asia the fireflies of the night lift their wings to luminesce in unison. Animals put their means of communication to many of the same gregarious uses that we put language.

The "Language" of the Bees One of the most carefully worked out studies of animal communication is that of the foraging bee. Karl von Frisch (1950), the great Austrian naturalist, had concluded that bees must be able to communicate, for when one bee found a supply of food and then departed, others from the same hive soon arrived in hordes. To find out how they communicated, von Frisch constructed a special hive that made it possible to observe the behavior of the bees directly.

Patient observation eventually revealed that a bee returning to the hive after discovering a new source of food can communicate its closeness at hand by a simple but vigorous circling dance, or the food's distance away and its direction from the hive with a more complicated sequence of straight runs, loops, and abdomen wagging. The platform on which the dance is performed is usually the vertical surface of a honeycomb within the hive. When the food is more than 150 yards away, the scout bee first runs in a straight line for a short distance, wagging its abdomen from side to side. Then it takes a semicircular loop in the clockwise direction, again makes the straight-line, abdomen-wagging run, now loops again, this time counterclockwise. And so on.

The angle of the straight-line run from the vertical communicates the direction of the food with respect to the sun. If the bees must fly with the sun 30 degrees to their left, the straight-line run of the bee scout points to about one o'clock. To indicate greater distance of the food from the hive, the bee dances ever more slowly. It makes a turn every second and a half when the food is a hundred meters away, every three seconds when the food source is a thousand meters distant.

Interestingly, the scout bee performs its remarkable feat in complete darkness and can dance its information about as well on a cloudy day as a clear one. Polarized light from the sky apparently indicates to the bee the correct location of the sun. And the bee's companions in the hive, receiving the information provided by touch—for they feel the dancing movements of the scout with their antennas—are able to find their way to a food source as many as three and a half miles away.

Communication of Primates The number of vocalizations made by our fellow primates for purposes of communication is quite large. As many as thirty-two vocalizations of the chimpanzee can be distinguished. Apparently these sounds are uttered to express temporary emotional states, and other chimpanzees respond appropriately. The vocalizations evoked by social contact or made in an attempt to establish it are distinctive. So are vocalizations that express fright or assert superiority, that complain about isolation, strangeness, and suddenness, that herald aggression against hostile companions. There are also pained cries of frustration and the urgent calls for mating.

Attempts to teach chimpanzees language A number of years ago psychologists began to raise chimpanzees in their home, providing them with as close an approximation of a human environment as they could. Two well-known earlier studies were those of Winthrop and Luella Kellogg (1933) and Cathy and Keith Hayes (1951). Both couples made an effort to determine whether the chimpanzee could develop human speech. The baby chimpanzee Gua, raised along with the Kelloggs' infant son David, learned to understand some commands but never uttered any English words. The chimpanzee Viki, raised by the Hayeses, did learn to produce three recognizable words—"papa," "mama,"and "cup"—but only with great difficulty and after very patient training which included manipulating her lips directly. The failure of these studies led psychologists to conclude that chimpanzees must lack some part of the biological equipment required to develop speech. Either the chimpanzee's vocal apparatus was inadequate or the deficiency was in the animal's brain.

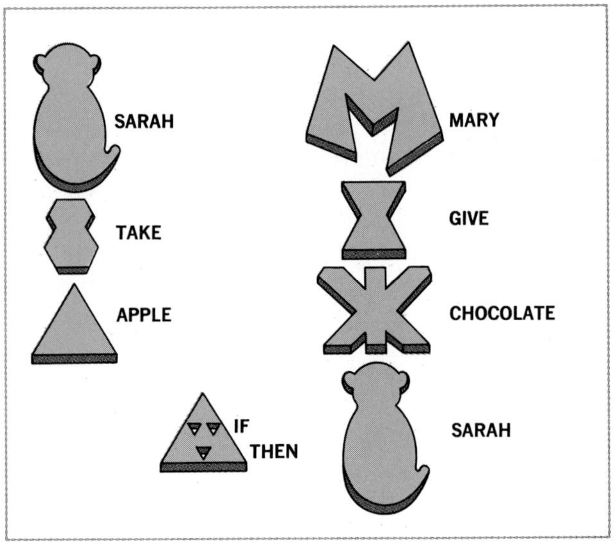

FIGURE 8.7
Sarah's vocabulary. This figure shows a few of Sarah's "words" as she arranged them to form a complex sentence. (From Premach, 1972.)

More recent attempts to teach language to a chimpanzee have begun with the assumptions that the problem at least in part is the inability of the animals to control lips and tongue and that the chimpanzee does have the potential for true language. The psychologists have therefore sought ways to circumvent the need for vocalization.

David Premack, working first with a young chimpanzee named Sarah and later with three others, used as "words" variously shaped symbols cut out of colored plastics (Figure 8.7). The animals could "write" by placing the metal-backed symbols on a magnetized board. With practice they learned the meaning of a hundred symbols or more, among them the question mark, and put them together in particular orders that resembled sentences. In the following examples the parentheses enclose the words denoted by each symbol.

"(Apple) (name of) [picture of apple]"
"(Mary) (insert) (banana) (bowl)"
"(Square) (not) (shape of) (banana)"
"(Red) (color of) (apple)"
"(Sarah) (drop) (glass) (if then) (glass) (break)"

The identification of symbols with words and ideas and the construction of such sentences indicate that chimpanzees are capable of learning fairly sophis-

FIGURE 8.8
Washoe being shown a picture and then making the sign for "cat."

ticated concepts—agency, color, shape, questioning, conditions. Premack's training of Sarah stressed correct word order. It is questionable whether she actually learned syntactical rules, however, for she only constructed sentences that had already been shown her. Never on her own did she put new words in old orders, so to speak. Even so, her accomplishment was far more impressive than any chimpanzee's verbal behavior previously described (Premack, 1976).

In the meantime, Allen and Beatrice Gardner were taking a different approach to the problem. They began to teach the sign language of the deaf to a chimpanzee named Washoe (Figure 8.8). No one ever spoke in Washoe's presence. In a little over four years she had mastered 132 signs (Table 8.1) and had learned to combine some of them in sentences, such as "Please tickle more," "You me go out there hurry," and, in conciliation after a wrongdoing, "Come hug-love sorry sorry." Washoe often seems to chat with herself. When looking at pictures in magazines, she apparently enjoys making the signs for objects she sees, and sometimes she signs "Hurry" as she rushes to her potty chair. She has also put two signs together to describe a new object, calling a swan a "water bird."

Finally, Duane Rumbaugh and his colleagues, working first with Lana, and later with two other chimpanzees, Sherman and Austin, have taught their

TABLE 8.1
A Few of the Signs Used by Washoe

Sign	Usage
Come-gimme (1)	For a person or an animal to approach, and also for objects out of reach. Often combined: come tickle, gimme sweet.
Please (16)	Asking for objects and for activities. Frequently combined: please open, please flower. Also, when ordered to, ask politely.
Cat (34)	For cats and for meowing.
Enough (71)	Spontaneously, when rejecting food at end of meal. At the end of other routine activities such as bath or a drill session on signing, when asking, you finished?
Time (97)	Equivalent to the English word "now," as in time food, time tickle, time out.
Hot (warm) (115)	For hot objects such as furnace or electric heater, and for hot substances such as soup or meat.
Mirror (117)	For mirrors.

Selected from Gardner and Gardner, 1975. The number following each sign indicates its order of appearance in Washoe's repertory.

primates to do their communicating with the aid of a computer, which responds appropriately to their needs (Figure 8.9). Rumbaugh and his associates (1974) describe Lana's situation this way.

> For Lana, the world is a plastic cube, seven feet in each dimension. Her interactions with and adaptations to this unnatural plastic niche concentrate upon use of keyboard console that now holds 75 keys. On each key there is a geometric

FIGURE 8.9
Lana's computerized world.

configuration or *lexigram* that represents a specific word. . . . As the locations of the keys are altered from time to time, Lana cannot rely upon the position of a key to define its functions or word meaning. She must attend to the lexigram on the keys to find her way to successful linguistic expressions. . . . Whenever the keys are randomly reassigned to the console, Lana's visual search for the locations of the word keys . . . becomes pronounced, but the search is basically accurate.

Pressing these keys in a correct order instructs the computer to deliver a requested substance or service. Lana might, for example, send the message: PLEASE MACHINE GIVE LANA BANANA (or M & M) PERIOD or PLEASE MACHINE MAKE MOVIE (or MUSIC or WINDOW OPEN) PERIOD. The PLEASE and PERIOD instructions are necessary to inform the computer that the message is beginning or ending. Lana developed a vocabulary of several dozen items and, like Premack's chimpanzees, she acquired more abstract linguistic concepts such as "name of." Lana lived in a situation in which she had to rely more on her linguistic skills than the chimps in most studies. Rumbaugh and his colleagues have described how well she applied them.

> . . . And probably most important of all, she has learned to use the system on a [24-hours-a-day] basis to get the good life. . . . we know, for example, that not infrequently she gets up during the night for a drink of water and entertains herself with slides and music in the early hours of the morning. Perhaps she's just a swinger at heart. She also seems to ask for the window to be opened when the first light of morning is sensed. And when there is something novel to view outdoors—lawn mowers, trucks, people on the lawn, etc.—the requests for the window to be opened come hot and heavy.

But is it language? Those who question whether chimpanzees are using language are usually asking whether their speech is somehow the same as *human* language. Behind this question often lies a concern that, with the work of the Gardners, Premack, and Rumbaugh, yet another mark of human uniqueness and dignity has been taken from us. First there was Darwin, who turned us into animals, perhaps the most highly evolved animals, but animals nonetheless. Next came Freud, who took away our special status as rational beings and exposed the primitive sexual motives that drive our simplest actions. Then there was Skinner, who robbed us of free will and left us the undignified victims of response-reinforcement contingencies. And now Sarah, Washoe, Lana, and company seem ready to tell us that there is nothing unique about our greatest talent, language. Are we to be diminished to the point that our only uniqueness is being the one creature who worries about such matters?

Certainly the "language" acquired by the chimpanzees has many of the qualities of human speech. (1) It makes sense. When Sarah says that an apple is red but a banana is not, she is correct. (2) The sentences created by the chimps show acceptable grammatical structure. Washoe, whose syntax is sometimes erratic, uses the order "You tickle me," as opposed to "I tickle you," appropriately. (3) Washoe's utterances have a self-determined beginning and an end. At the end of a sentence she drops her hands. (4) Washoe (W) responds appropriately to the so-called "wh-" (who, what, where) questions, as indicated by the following exchanges with an experimenter (E) (Gardner and Gardner, 1975).

Question	*Answer*
E: Who you?	W: Me Washoe.
E: Who pretty?	W: Washoe.
E: Whose that?	W: Shoes yours.
E: Now what?	W: Time drink.
E: What you want?	W: You me out.

(5) Two chimpanzees will communicate with each other in the language taught them. After a considerable amount of simpler training in simpler exchanges, the two chimpanzees Sherman and Austin learned to tell each other about the food available from a container, using the computer keyboard (Figure 8.10).

> But could they simply ask one another for food on the keyboard? To answer this, we gave only one animal a variety of foods and allowed the other animal to watch through the window between the rooms [in which they were separately housed]. The observing animal spontaneously used the keyboard to request food. We encouraged the second animal to observe this request and comply with it. We then reversed the roles, giving food to the other animal. Again the observer spontaneously used the keyboard to request food and the animal with the food was encouraged to comply. From this point on, the animals began to exchange roles and comply with each other's requests. . . . The initial encouragement was necessary to facilitate the social behavior of giving, but was not needed to facilitate the use of symbols or the nature of the communication. . . . Accuracy ranged across sessions from 70 to 100 percent, depending upon the willingness of the animals to comply with each other's requests. In general, the lower-ranking animal, Austin, always complied with Sherman's requests. Sherman also complied with Austin's requests but needed more frequent encouragement to do so (Savage-Rumbaugh et al., 1978).

All this sounds very much like human verbal behavior, so much so that a cautious word or two may be in order. (1) Although the "languages" taught to chimpanzees have allowed them an impressive handling of abstractions, the skill imparted so far still falls short of the linguistic flexibility of human beings. As yet no chimps have developed the ability to use such concepts as *principle, justice,* or *abstraction.* (2) One distinctive feature of human language is what has been called its self-reflexive aspect: it can talk about itself. No chimpanzee, so far, has acquired the ability to use its language to speak about language. (3) Probably most important of all, the chimpanzee acquires language only with great difficulty. What the human child picks up naturally, quickly, and spontaneously takes years of patient tutoring of the chimp.

The Acquisition of Language

The question of how children acquire their language has intrigued scientists and laymen alike for centuries. Salimbene, a thirteenth-century monk and chronicler, wrote of his contemporary, Frederick II, king of Germany,

> . . . He wanted to find out what kind of speech and what manner of speech children would have when they grew up if they spoke to no one beforehand. So he bade foster mothers and nurses to suckle the children, to bathe and wash them, but in no way to prattle them, or to speak to them, for he wanted to learn whether they would speak the Hebrew language, which was the oldest, or Greek, or Latin, or Arabic, or perhaps the language of their parents, of whom they had been born. But he laboured in vain because the children all died. For they could not live without the petting and joyful faces and loving words of their foster mothers (quoted in Ross and McLaughlin, 1949, p. 366).

Only in recent years have there been many answers to the basic questions what children acquire when they master a language and how they acquire it. The progress made has paralleled the new devel-

FIGURE 8.10

Communication between chimps. Sherman reads Austin's request for a specific piece of food. He takes it from a tray of various foods. He feeds it to Austin, not a common thing for chimps to do. Sherman accepts social praise for his performance.

opments in psycholinguistics, developments which have called into question some commonsense "truths" that most of us and an earlier psychology of language accepted.

The Traditional View of Language Acquisition The commonsense view of language acquisition, as well as the older psychological view, makes a number of assumptions, all of which appear either to be wrong or to be overstatements. Language is (1) learned (2) by experience, which includes the child's receiving (3) rewards and punishments as part of the teaching process. Let us consider these points in order.

Learning Since the language we acquire is the language of our parents rather than some other, the conclusion that language is learned is inescapable. At the same time, however, there is considerable reason to suppose that biological factors are important. We mentioned earlier that phonemes may be innately recognizable, which suggests an inborn disposition to make certain of the perceptions that are basic to language acquisition. Moreover, the child acquires language during the critical period when brain development is rapid, a further indication that physiology is important.

By experience Most of the language we create or comprehend is new to us. Direct previous experience with new expressions is a contradiction in terms. Beyond that, it is easy to show that a lifetime would not be long enough to provide such experience. In a landmark paper that revolutionized the psychology of language, George A. Miller (1965) put the arguments against experience this way.

> By a rough, but conservative calculation there are 10^{20} sentences 20 words long, and if a child were to learn only these it would take him something on the order of 1,000 times the estimated age of the earth just to listen to them. . . . Any attempt to account for language acquisition that does not have a generative character will encounter this difficulty. . . .
>
> Since the variety of admissible word combinations is so great, no child could learn all of them. Instead of learning specific combinations of words, he learns rules for generating admissible combinations (pp. 176, 178).

Rewards and punishments The principal point to be made against the theory that children acquire language because their utterances are approved or disapproved is a factual one. Parents use rewards and punishments not so much to establish correct language habits as to influence the content of their children's speech. Studies have shown that parents tend to reward statements that are factually accurate much more often than they do linguistic correctness.

George A. Miller. Nothing we could do...would be more relevant to human welfare...than to discover how best to give psychology away (1969, APA presidential address).

The following fragment from a description of the language development of two children, Adam and Eve, illustrates this point.

> . . . Gross errors of word choice were sometimes corrected, as when Eve said, "What the guy idea." Once in a while an error of pronunciation was noticed and corrected. More commonly, however, the grounds on which an utterance was approved or disapproved . . . were not strictly linguistic at all. When Eve expressed the opinion that her mother was a girl by saying, "He a girl," mother answered, "That's right." The child's utterance was ungrammatical but the mother did not respond to the fact; instead she responded to the truth . . . of the proposition the child intended to express. . . . Adam's "Walt Disney comes on, on Tuesday" was disapproved because Walt Disney comes on, on some other day. It seems then to be truth . . . rather than syntactic well-formedness that chiefly governs explicit verbal reinforcement by parents. Which renders mildly paradoxical the fact that the usual product of such training . . . is an adult whose speech is highly grammatical but not notably truthful (Brown, Cazden, and Bellugi, 1969).

Beyond this, there is evidence that the interventions of parents are not particularly effective if the child is not ready to move from one stage of linguistic development to a more advanced one.

Child: Nobody don't like me.
Mother: No, say "Nobody likes me."
Child: Nobody don't like me.
Eight repetitions of this dialogue.
Mother: No, now listen carefully; say "Nobody *likes* me."
Child: Oh! Nobody don't likes me (McNeill, 1966).

The child has learned the rule that adding "don't" makes a statement negative but cannot yet absorb a new form, one in which "nobody" expresses negation and the rest of the sentence should remain declarative.

Caretaker Speech Since adults helping children to acquire a language do not function chiefly as dispensers of rewards and punishments, the question is what they do do. The answer is straightforward enough. They provide the child with a model of how language is spoken. The model provided in the speech of caretakers is not that of adult speech, however.

Phonologically, caretaker speech is higher in pitch than normal speech. Intonations are exaggerated. Caretakers speak slowly and very distinctly. When children are very young, some words may be simplified to eliminate consonant sounds that are difficult for them—"mommy" for "mother," "wawa" for "water," and "tummy" for "stomach."

Grammatically, caretaker speech is also simplified. Sentences are short, perhaps at a level of complexity no more than six months or so in advance of the child's own level (Moskowitz, 1978). Some words and word endings are omitted, such as the articles "the," "a," and the plural and possessive "s" (Clark and Clark, 1977).

Semantically, caretaker speech is concrete. It tends to be about the here and now and to avoid complex abstractions. The caretaker chooses subjects at the level of the child's comprehension.

Pragmatically, caretaker speech is directed at helping the child use language in socially proper ways. As we have already seen, caretakers reward truthfulness in children's speech. From the beginning they also emphasize the turn-taking character of conversation.

Mother: Hello. Give me a smile (gently pokes infant in the ribs).
Infant: (Yawns).
Mother: Sleepy, are you? You woke up too early today.
Infant: (Opens fist).
Mother: (Touching infant's hand). What are you looking at? Can you see something?
Infant: (Grasps mother's finger).
Mother: Oh, that's what you wanted. In a friendly mood, then. Come on, give us a smile (Clark and Clark, 1977).

Although this "dialogue" is entirely one-sided as far as actual words spoken are concerned, the mother has treated anything that the child does as though it were a verbal "turn."

The Chronology **Crying and babbling** At birth the infant has only a limited repertoire of sounds. Its vocalizations are little more than undifferentiated crying and perhaps a few grunts and gurgles. Within four to six weeks, noises that are not exactly cries are heard. They may well be of two very general types, narrow, nasalized sounds of discomfort and relaxed, back-of-the-mouth sounds of comfort. This ability to express dissatisfaction and satisfaction appears to be an accident of the general muscular and physiological state of the tense and relaxed baby (Menyuk, 1971).

As the sounds uttered by babies become more differentiated, those initially most prominent are vowels. Consonant sounds are in the minority. This ratio gradually changes, however, with consonants becoming more frequent as the baby begins to use consonant-vowel combinations and to repeat these syllables again and again. Some babblings resemble words—ma-ma-ma, choo-choo-choo, bye-bye-bye—and some do not—hey-hey, bup-bup-bup, erdah-erdah. The babblings of babies the world over are the same. The same initial sounds are uttered by infants of all cultures, whether or not they will find their way into later speech. Eventually, at about nine months, babies whose language will be English start to lose their French nasals and German gutterals, largely because their parents do not make and cannot mimic them, and babies hear the sounds only from themselves. As babbling continues, the structure of what the infant utters changes. The baby begins to produce sentencelike strings of sounds with patterns of stress and inflection that resemble the cadences of adult speech. At about the same time sounds that others interpret as words also begin to be heard with increasing frequency. If parental reinforcement is ever important in language development, it is at this stage. The attention and affection bestowed upon babies for producing wordlike vocalizations probably encourage the repetition of such sounds.

First words The age at which the baby speaks its first words is difficult to determine because of this tie to babbling. Sixty weeks has been suggested as the average, but the range is considerable. Whatever the language of the child, the first words spoken are likely to contain the consonants p, t, b, m, and n, those for which the tongue is at the front of the mouth; and the

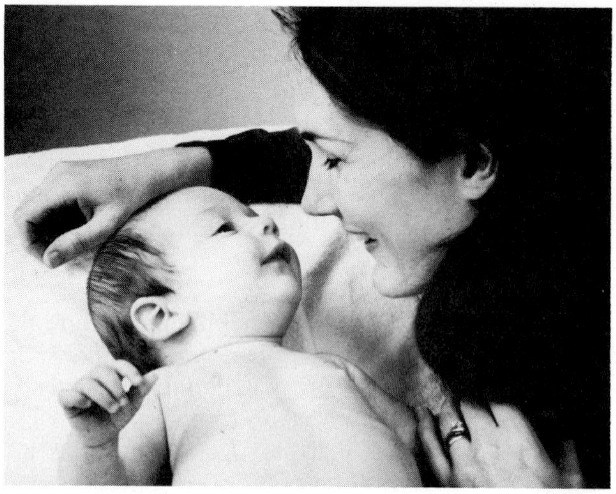

My, don't we look debonair and lively after our afternoon nap. Oh, yes, I know, dear, you've spent enough time in your bed. Now you want to get up and see what the world is doing. What? It looks the same as before your nap? Well, then, of course, you just go ahead and make your own fun. You're showing me what a strong little fellow you are, aren't you?

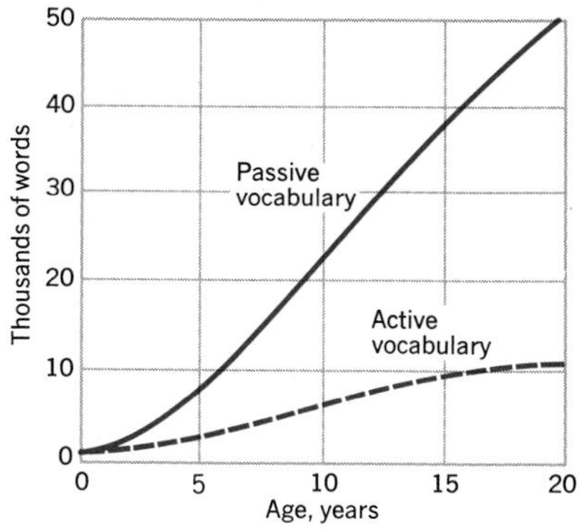

FIGURE 8.11
The development of active and passive vocabulary. As is common in language acquisition, understanding, as indicated by the size of the passive vocabulary, is always far ahead of usage, indicated by active vocabulary.

vowels a and e, which come from the back of a relaxed mouth. The child has already made many of the other vowels and consonants when playing with sounds, but purpose apparently adds difficulty to utterance. The first-mastered words contain the sounds most easily formed. Vocabularies increase rapidly after the baby says its first word. Figure 8.11 makes the useful distinction between the child's active and passive vocabulary. The **passive vocabulary** or receptive vocabulary contains the words understood, the **active vocabulary** or expressive vocabulary contains the words used.

The first words of children function as complete sentences. Depending on how and where it is uttered, "Doggy" may be a simple declarative—"It is a doggy"; or a demand—"I want the doggy"; or a question—"Doggy, where are you?" Spectrographic analyses have shown that babies inflect these simple word sentences in different ways, and, it is assumed, with different linguistic intentions. Although these one-word sentences have meaning in themselves, they are often strung together in sequences to express ideas that we eventually handle with complex sentences.

Acquisition of grammar As soon as children begin to put two words together as sentences, they indicate their earliest concepts of syntax. At this point, however, their brief sequences may be their own and do not always imitate those in adult speech. All the world's children—speaking English, Swedish, Spanish, Hebrew, Russian, German, Japanese, Finnish—apparently go through this stage in which they string two words together to express a wide variety of relationships. At a year and a half, when children first pair words, they do so rarely, but within a few months new combinations are added daily. By age two children may be using two to three hundred word pairs. The same sentence can mean different things, depending on the context. Lois Bloom (1970) reports that one of the children she studied, Kathryn, used the sentence, "Mommy sock," twice in the same day, once when she picked up her mother's stocking and again when her mother put Kathryn's own sock on her. In the first sentence "Mommy" was used as a possessive: "This is Mommy's sock." In the second she was an agent: "Mommy put the sock on Kathryn." Or Kathryn might say "Allgone doggies," "More milk," "Go store," "Pretty dress," "Where ball?" "There Daddy," "Byebye please" to communicate other important happenings and aspects of her life.

Children's early speech is called *telegraphic speech*. Many of the connecting words, the auxiliary verbs, articles, prepositions, and pronouns that serve a grammatical function, are omitted. The reason for omitting them parallels that for leaving words out of telegrams. There they cost money. In children's speech they cost equally precious processing capacity. Children at this age hold two units of information in mind, three at the most. They therefore construct their sentences of the bare essentials, of words carrying the most meaning for them. The frills can come later.

And come they do. The functional words omitted from telegraphic speech appear. Sentences increase in length, complexity, and precision. The child is struggling harder to cope with the linguistic world, and linguists have found that mastery is gained in a rather remarkably consistent sequence. In fact, three children studied by Roger Brown, Eve, Adam, and Sarah, added fourteen grammatical morphemes to their sentences in nearly the same order (Brown, 1973).

In the period from twenty-two months to thirty-two, children begin to use an occasional article, the definite pronouns "I," "me," "you," "we," and some demonstratives and modifiers—"I want candy," "Daddy, new book," "That a flower." They are adding inflections, the grammatical morphemes, to nouns and verbs—"Mommy changes sheets," "Car backing up"; and a few prepositional phrases—"Doggie in box," "We goed to the store." Children can be heard constructing their sentences, so to speak. About a cat they may say, "Stand up. Cat stand up. Cat stand up on table." But they do not yet use auxiliary verbs and indefinite pronouns or embed clauses within sentences. By the age of three, however, many children use sentences in which verbs follow nouns and both have inflections, verbs have auxiliaries, there are indefinite pronouns, and clauses are both joined and embedded. "My daddy is making pennies." "I'm going to empty it." "You lookit that book and I lookit this book." "Make the car go." "Now let me draw you a lady."

Children begin to learn transformational rules. They form questions by inverting subject and verb,

"Is Daddy coming?" They are unable to make two transformations at once, however. In learning the wh-question, they begin it with the question word but do not immediately shift subject and verb: "When Daddy is coming?"

Overregularization Children may move from correct usage to incorrect usage before mastering the problem of word order. One syntactic rule the child appears to learn early is that the order of words in sentences is *agent-action-object.* This is correct for sentences in the active voice—John hit Mary—but incorrect for those in the passive voice—Mary was hit by John. Although children at an early age understand the difference between these two sentences, they may **overregularize** when they become conscious of this rule. They then believe that the passive sentence actually means that Mary hit John. Eventually, of course, they solve this problem.

Children have similar difficulties with the plurals that are formed in irregular ways—foot, feet; child, children; deer, deer—and with irregular verb forms. Although many verbs change from present to past tense by adding "ed"—change, changed; smile, smiled; cry, cried—some of the most basic verbs in the language—go, went; come, came; fall, fell; bring, brought; take, took—are exceptions. Again, children have usually learned the correct irregular form at first. Later on, as vocabulary enlarges, children discover that the majority of words have a regular way of becoming plural or past. With the acquisition of this knowledge, they overgeneralize in applying these rules. The child who once said "Daddy came" and referred to "my feet" now says "Daddy comed" and speaks of "my foots" or "my feetses." The child is not a passive receptacle into which linguistic rules are poured by experience but rather an active creator, attempting to construct a theory of usage that will make him or her a competent speaker of the language.

Pronunciation The ability to pronounce a sound correctly can lag behind knowing what it should be. This sometimes amusing effect has been called the **fis phenomenon,** after an incident reported by Jean Berko and Roger Brown (1960).

> One of us . . . spoke to a child who called his inflated plastic fish a *fis.* In imitation of the child's pronunciation, the observer said: "This is your fis?" "No," said the child, "my *fis.*" He continued to reject the adults imitation until he was told, "That is your fish." "Yes," he said, "my *fis.*"

In another exchange a little boy asked whether he could come along on a trip to "the mewwy-go-wound." An older child, teasing him, said, "David wants to go on the mewwy-go-wound." "No," said David firmly, "you don't say it wight!" (Maccoby and Bee, 1965).

FIGURE 8.12
Method for studying children's inflections. After children are shown a picture of a Wug and then a picture of two of them, the experimenters says, "Now, there are two ____." The fact that children normally respond Wug/z/ suggests that they know the rule for creating this plural. (From Berko, 1958.)

But children eventually acquire correct pronunciation that is quite subtle in its distinctions. Adding -s to form plurals is putting morphemes together in a way that obeys a rule of grammar. Children also learn the correct phoneme for the added morpheme. Given a problem such as the one shown in Figure 8.12, kindergarten and first-grade children rather invariably give the correct ending wug/z/. Words ending with most voiced phonemes form their plurals with the voiced sibilant /z/, as in dogs, rows, bells, birds. Words ending with voiceless consonants add a voiceless /s/—cats, socks, pups. When English is learned by an older person, this distinction may never be mastered, even though the correct combinations are in fact easier to pronounce.

Semantic development Something very much like overregularization happens to the meanings of words. Children the world over extend the meaning of a word to a number of things that have a perceived similarity but may also be much broader in aspect (Table 8.2). Later, when the child learns another word for one of the overextensions and notices other more specific attributes, the process reverses and the meaning of the word narrows.

Three-year-old children have lost many of their overextensions, but they have trouble with antonyms. The meaning of one may be extended to cover both, as though the words really were synonyms. Margaret Donaldson and George Balfour (1968) showed three- to five-year-old children two toy apple trees, one with more apples on it than the other, and asked which tree had more apples and which tree had fewer. To answer *both of these questions,* the majority of the children pointed to the tree with more apples. Testing

TABLE 8.2
Examples of Overextension

Word	Language	First Referent	Extensions in Order of Occurrence
Bébé	French	reflection of self in mirror	photograph of self; all photographs; all pictures; all books with pictures; all books
Buti	Russian	ball	toy; radish; stones; spheres at park entrance
Bow-wow	German	dog	toy dog; fur piece with animal head; fur piece without head
Fly	English	fly	specks of dirt; dust; all small insects; his own toes; crumbs of bread; a toad

From E. V. Clark, 1973.

with other pairs of opposites, wide and narrow and tall and short, have revealed similar confusions.

One possible explanation for this phenomenon is that children first acquire general concepts on amount, more–less; breadth, wide–narrow; and height, tall–short, and know that the two adjectives, which are opposite in meaning for us, apply to the same dimension. But they have not sorted out the quantitative meanings of the specific adjectives. Children apparently prefer whatever is more, and this preference together with their vaguely developed sense of general concept makes them select the greater when asked which is less.

The language of adults contains some evidence that this interpretation is less bizarre than it seems at first. Consider the two adjective pairs, tall–short, old–young, and watch what happens when each of the four fills in the blank in the query "How ___ is he?" The sentences completed with short and young imply that the individual is at the "short" and "young" end of the height and age dimensions. The sentences completed with tall and old carry no such implication. These sentences are neutral and merely ask for information. Adjectives of the first type, short and young, are said to be **marked,** those of the second **unmarked.** Children apparently learn the unmarked form first and overgeneralize it to the marked form.

But markedness is also a continuum. Consider the adjective pairs intelligent–stupid, honest–dishonest, and rich–poor and put them into the sentence, "How ___ is he?" Intelligent, honest, and rich may seem unmarked, but not as definitely so as tall and old.

SUMMARY □

All but the simplest animals communicate, which raises the question whether animals other than ourselves might develop something comparable to human speech. Because of their evolutionary proximity, our fellow primates are the obvious animals of whom to ask this question. Early attempts to teach chimpanzees human vocalization failed, but these same creatures communicate with considerable success by means of American sign language, plastic word forms, and symbols on a computer. The languages acquired so far by chimpanzees have many of the characteristics of human languages, but they are less abstract and have not been used to discuss the nature of language.

The human child acquires language by interacting with other human beings who provide an appropriate linguistic model. Although the process obviously involves learning, we may have an inborn disposition to acquire language. Certainly language is learned quickly and most easily during the early years when the brain is still developing. Rewards and punishments are relatively ineffective in language acquisition, except perhaps in the very earliest stages. It is more important that the children's caretakers provide plentiful examples of correct speech that are only a little beyond the child's current level of development.

The linguistic development of children is a constructive struggle. At every stage and in every process the child appears to test hypotheses about appropriate usage, sometimes overgeneralizing rules of construction and overextending the meaning of words, but eventually mastering the language.

LANGUAGE AND THOUGHT

Language provides the individual with a tremendous advantage in coping with the world. By means of language, events and objects in the world can be expressed in a set of verbal symbols. These symbols can then be manipulated in a way that physical reality cannot be. This manipulation of the world at a symbolic level is an important part of thinking. To observe these processes in your own thinking, try solving the arithmetic puzzle presented by Sir Frederick Bartlett of Cambridge University in England and keep a record of the steps in your solution. Bartlett's problem is this:

> DONALD
> GERALD
> ROBERT
>
> The problem is to be treated as an exercise in simple addition. All that is known is: (1) that D = 5; (2) that every number from 0 to 9 has its corresponding letter; (3) that each letter must be assigned a number different from that given for any other letter. . . ." (Bartlett, 1958, p. 51).

The answer appears at the end of the chapter (page 196). You may want to try to solve it on your own.

Concept Formation

A **concept** is a symbol that stands for the common properties of objects, events, or ideas that are otherwise distinguishable. Day by day we deal effectively with a vast array of concepts. Some of them are simple and objective, concepts like "dog," "automobile," "house," and "shoe." Other concepts are abstract and elaborate, like "avarice," "faith," "justice," and "mercy." Adding to the complexity of concepts is the fact that they exist in hierarchies. The concept "dog" includes the concept "poodle" but is included in the concept "animal." The concept "faith" includes "faith in God," "faith in the free-enterprise system," and "faith in the power of reason," but at least "faith in God" is included in the larger concept "cardinal virtue." Certainly the hierarchial ordering of concepts is anything but tidy.

Concept Attainment The definition of a concept as a symbol that stands for the common properties of things indicates the process by which concepts are acquired. We form concepts by noting common properties and allowing the concept name to cover all objects that have these attributes. The experimental study of concept attainment takes the formation of concepts into the laboratory and makes the process somewhat simpler than what happens in everyday life.

To illustrate the general procedure, let us consider a famous old experiment by Kenneth Smoke (1932). He presented figures to help his research participants develop concepts such as DAX, which consists of a circle with one dot inside and another dot outside (Figure 8.13). The figures employed by Smoke have certain features: shape, size, number of dots, and location of dots. Some of these attributes are relevant —shape, number of dots, location of dots; others are irrelevant—size, aspects of dot location except for being inside or outside the figure. In order to attain this concept, it is necessary to figure out what attributes are relevant and reject those that are irrelevant.

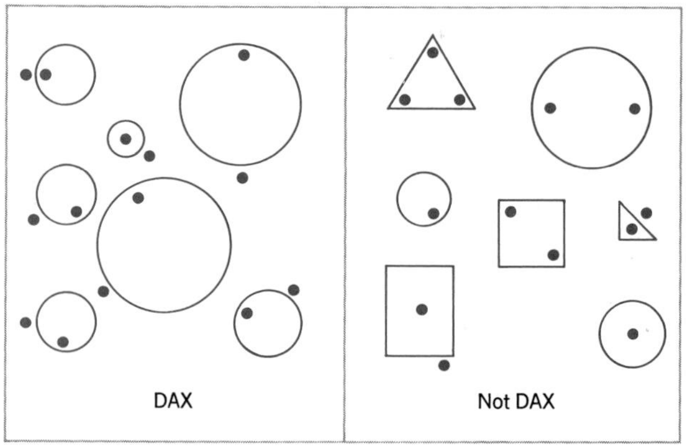

FIGURE 8.13
Samples of DAX *and non-*DAX *figures.* (After Smoke, 1932.)

In concept attainment, not only are there relevant attributes to detect, but the rule or principle governing them must be ascertained. DAX is a figure that is circular *and* has two dots, *and* the two dots are one inside, one outside the circle. Depending on the rules that apply to them, it is possible to identify different types of concepts. Three examples are the following. (1) Some very simple concepts, for example, the concept of "red," have only one attribute. Thus red is the feature shared in common by lipsticks, fire engines, sunsets, and blood. (2) Concepts like DAX are based on the conjunction of attributes. That is, an exemplar of the concept must have this attribute *and* this attribute—for as many attributes as define the concept. "Science fiction," "boring lecture," "cute dumb broad," and "male chauvinist pig" are all examples. (3) Other concepts are disjunctive: exemplars must have this feature *or* that *or* some other or others. A "natural" in a game of craps is a 7 *or* an 11. In baseball a strike is a pitch that is swung on and missed, *or* a pitch that passes over home base at a height between the knees and shoulders of the batter. Investigators in the field of concept attainment have identified other rules that define more complicated types of concepts, but the varieties presented here will help to make certain further points.

Difficulty of Concept Attainment An experiment on concept learning presents a series of examples and nonexamples of the concept, and the learner indicates whether each individual example represents the concept or not. Depending on this response, the experimenter provides appropriate feedback, telling the learner whether the response was right or wrong (Figure 8.14). Correct examples of the concept usually carry more information and aid concept learning more than do those that are incorrect. It would be extremely difficult to acquire the concept DAX without seeing an example of it.

Edna Heidbreder studied concepts of three different kinds, illustrated in Figure 8.15: concrete or

Trial		Response	Feedback
1	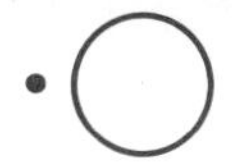	"DAX"	Wrong
2	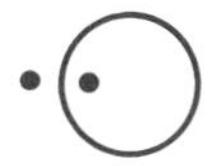	"Not DAX"	Wrong
3		"DAX"	Wrong
4		"DAX"	Right
5	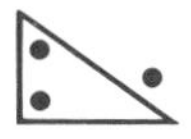	"DAX"	Wrong
6		"DAX"	Right
7		"Not DAX"	Right
8	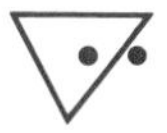	"Not DAX"	Right

FIGURE 8.14
Concept attainment. An experiment for identification of the concept DAX would consist of such a hypothetical series of trials. Successive rows show, trial by trial, the stimulus presented, the response given, and the feedback provided by the experimenter. By trial 6 the research participant has mastered the concept.

object concepts—for example, a *face;* spatial concepts—for example, canes, pennants, flowers all *criss-crossed* over one another; and number concepts—for example, *seven of anything*. She found the ease of achieving the concepts to be in this order: concrete concepts were easiest, spatial concepts were next, and number concepts were the most difficult. Other investigators have not uniformly obtained the same results, however. At the present time it is impossible to rank these particular concepts for ease of attainment.

Conceptual Fuzziness As they are studied in the laboratory, concepts are usually quite definite; a given object is or is not an exemplar of the concept. In real life things are less clear-cut. Consider for example the conjunctive concept of *bird*. Birds fly, they are of a standard size, they have two longish legs, they have feathers, they build nests, they sing, they go to warmer climates when the weather turns cold. Now consider the following representatives of this concept: *robin, sparrow, eagle, crow, pheasant, goose, chicken, penguin*. You will recognize that the order in which they are given is a decreasing order of "birdness." *Robin* and *sparrow* are very good examples of the concept bird; *chicken* and *penguin* are less good. The first examples have more of the attributes of the concept *bird;* the last examples have fewer of them (Rosch, 1977).

Eleanor Rosch (1973) and others have demonstrated the importance of the difference just described in studies in which people are asked to respond "true" or "false" as quickly as possible to sentences like

A robin is a bird.
A penguin is a bird.

Less time is required to say "true" when the objects are good examplars of the concept than when they are poor ones. The time required to decide that sentences like

A bat is a bird.
A stone is a bird.

are false makes the same point. It takes longer to reject the first sentence than the second, theoretically because bats have many of the attributes of birds whereas stones have none. In fact, some subjects in studies asking them to list examples of birds have included bats in their lists.

Linguistic Relativity Another important fact about real-world concepts is that conceptual categories vary from culture to culture. The Eskimos have three words for snow, depending on whether it is falling, covering the ground, or made into igloos. We have only one. The Aztecs go in the other direction and use the same word for cold, ice, and snow. We identify nouns and verbs as very separate parts of speech. Certain of the natives of Vancouver Island make no such distinction. They generally make verbs of nouns, as we might of "flame." Just as it is correct for us to say "it flames," for these people "it houses" is the correct way to refer to the building of a house. The Hopi have a noun that refers to everything that flies except birds. Where we have dozens of words for colors, certain African tribes have four or even only two (Figure 8.16).

Examples such as these led Benjamin Lee Whorf to the hypothesis of *linguistic relativity,* which proposes that language determines the content of thought. In its strongest version the hypothesis holds that these peculiarities of language determine the content of thought, that what the individual can possibly think depends on the categories of language. Most psychologists take a position that is less extreme. They tend to maintain that such linguistic conceptual groupings help or hinder certain types of thinking. In short, although it may be possible to have the same thoughts

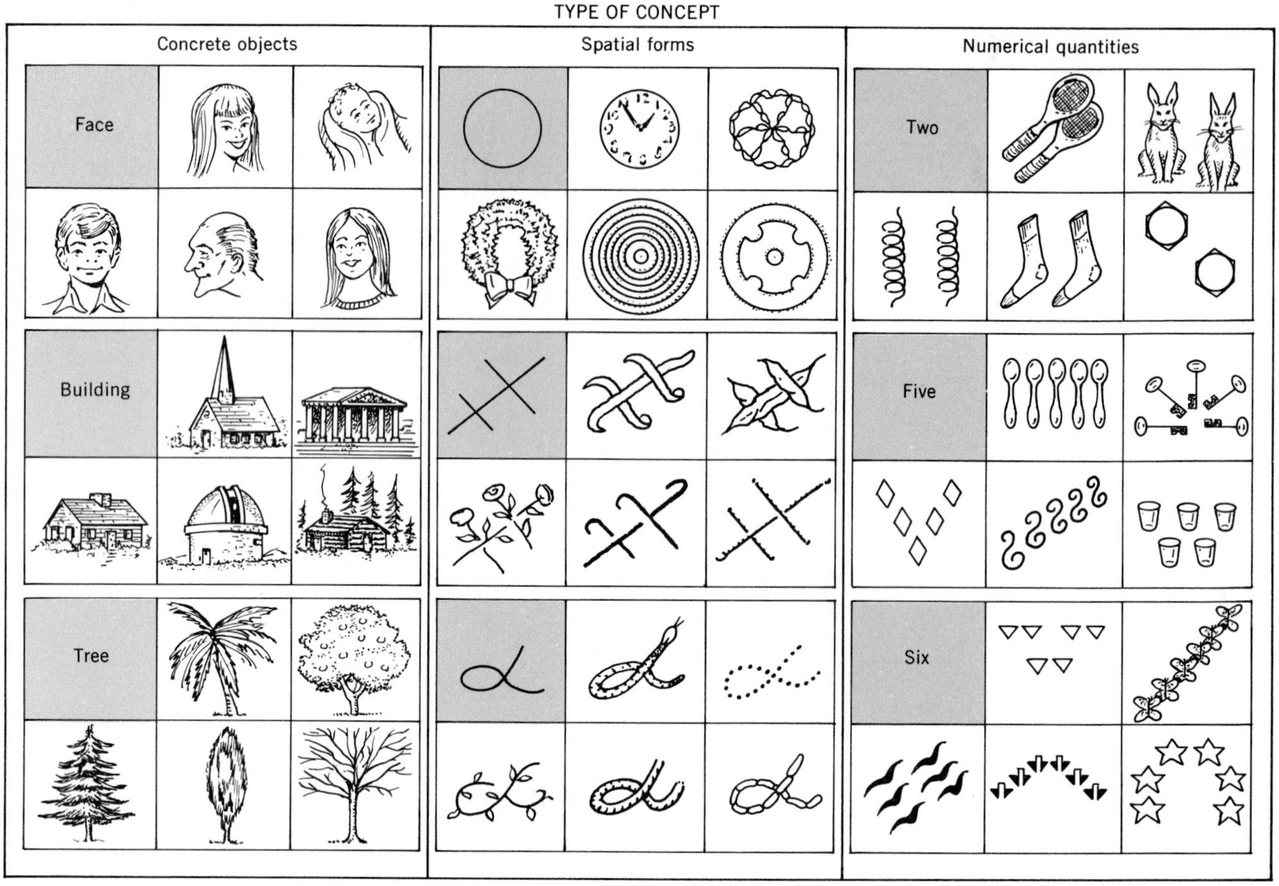

FIGURE 8.15
Five exemplars of each of nine concepts of the sort studied by Heidbreder (1947). The concept is identified by the item in the upper left-hand corner in each panel.

We have the same word for falling snow, snow on the ground, snow packed hard like ice, slushy snow, wind-driven flying snow....To an Eskimo, this all-inclusive word would be almost unthinkable; he would say that falling snow, slushy snow, and so on...are different things to contend with; he uses different words for them...(Whorf, 1956).

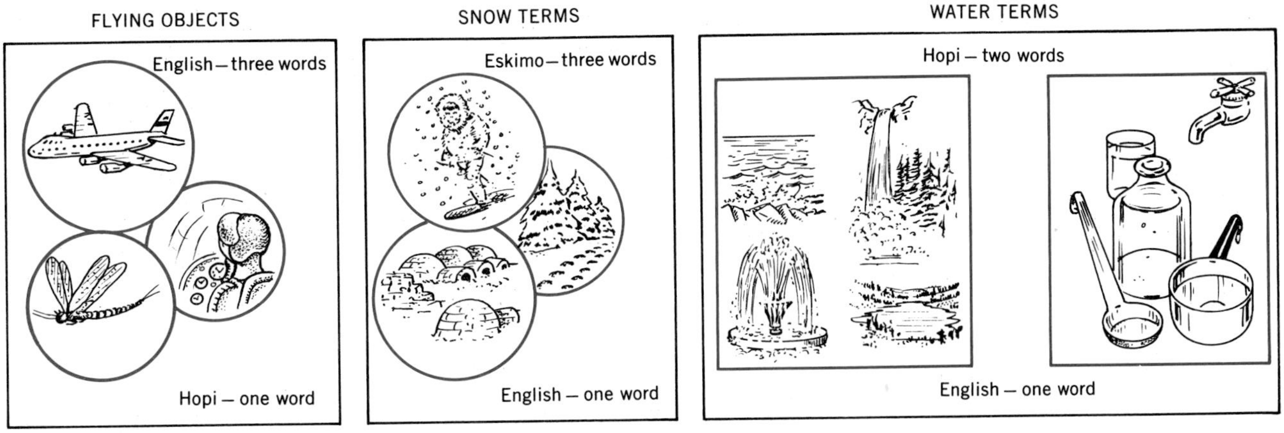

FIGURE 8.16
Linguistic relativity. Certain concepts are handled differently in the English, Hopi, and Eskimo languages. We use three different words for a dragonfly, an airplane, and an aviator; the Hopi use one. We use one word for water; the Hopi have two. (Adapted from Whorf, 1940.)

in all languages, certain thoughts will be easier in some than in others. The most recent experimental work on the topic supports this less extreme point of view.

Consider the following passage from Breyne Arlene Moskowitz's (1978) article on language acquisition: "Throughout the acquisition process a child continually revises and refines the rules of her internal grammar, learning increasingly detailed subrules until she achieves a set of rules that enables her to create the full array of complex adult sentences." The gender-conscious use of *she* and *her* where common practice uses *he* and *his* almost insists that we think of language acquisition as something that happens only to females.

There is a psycholinguistic point to make here. The English language uses the masculine pronouns as though they were unmarked and the feminine pronouns as though they were *marked* (page189).That is, when their associations are general, the masculine forms are seemingly neutral. We have already seen, however, that the quality of markedness is not all or nothing. In the context provided by the hypothesis of linguistic relativity, we might question whether the "neutral" use of masculine pronouns makes people think in masculine terms.

In an experiment that obtained evidence on this point, students made up stories on two themes suggested by these sentences:

> In a large coeducational institution the average student will feel isolated in ____ introductory courses.
>
> Each person knows when ____ appearance is unattractive.

For different groups of male and female participants, the blanks in the alternate versions of these sentences were filled in with "his," "their," or "his or her." The results of interest were the percentages of female characters appearing in the stories prompted by the different pronouns (Figure 8.17). The most potent variable was clearly the gender of the individual making up the story. Women made up stories about women, men stories about men. In support of the hypothesis of linguistic relativity, however, all groups introduced female characters more frequently when the blanks in their sentences were filled with "his or her."

Problem Solving

One of the most important uses to which we put concepts is manipulating them to solve problems. To show that this is what goes on in problem solving, let us begin with a simple example. The problem is to indicate which of a set of four words "does not belong":

ADD SUBTRACT INCREASE MULTIPLY

We see at once that there are two possible solutions. (1) If we group exemplars of the concept "arithmetic operation," INCREASE is the term that is out of place. (2) If, on the other hand, we decide to eliminate the term that does not belong to the concept "implies an increment," SUBTRACT is the one to go (Cofer, 1961). Although this problem is simple, it is not unrelated to those of everyday experience. Some take exactly this form—which card to discard in gin rummy, whom to invite to your next social function, which activity to eliminate from a busy schedule. In gin rummy, making the decision in terms of one concept, such as "three of a kind," indicates one type of discard; a decision on the basis of another concept, say "a run in hearts," indicates another.

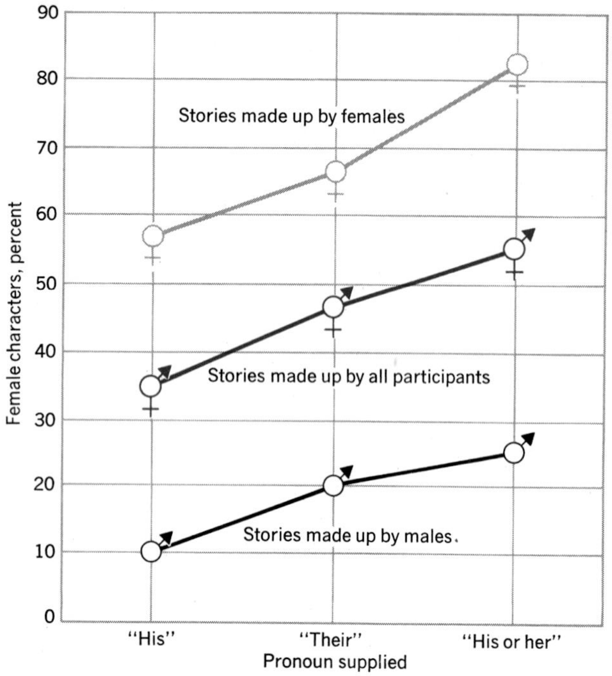

FIGURE 8.17
Effect of pronouns on gender of characters in stories. Although female subjects made up stories that were most often about females and men made up stories about men, the pronoun in the sentence suggesting the story did affect the frequency with which male and female characters were used. (Data from Moulton et al., 1978.)

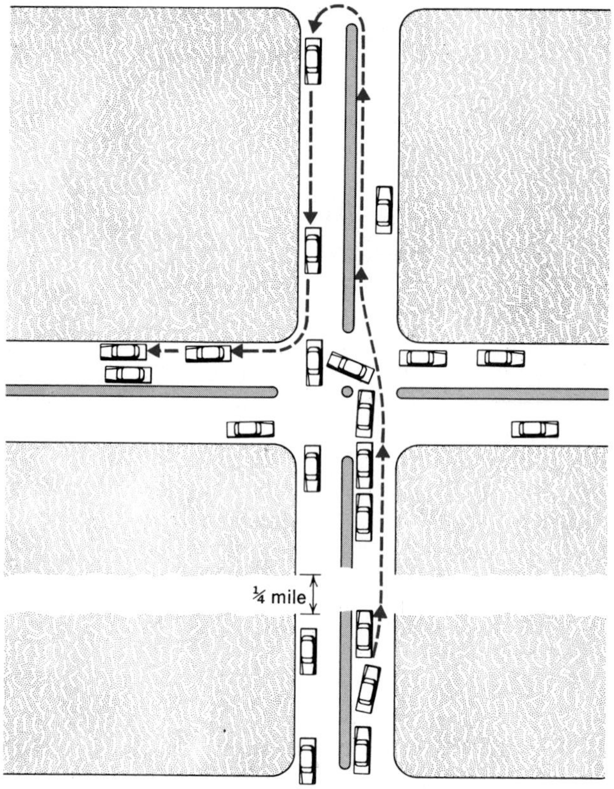

FIGURE 8.18
A problem-solving situation. The driver of the car wants to make a left-hand turn at the intersection, but a combination of heavy traffic and the stop light makes his progress slow. He solves the problem by pulling into the right lane and following the path indicated by the arrows. (Reproduced by permission from *Personality and Psychotherapy,* by J. Dollard and N. E. Miller. Copyright 1950, McGraw-Hill Book Co., New York.)

Symbols and the Real World Examples of problem solving are particularly effective in their support of the point made at the beginning of this section, that the availability of verbal symbols allows us to cope with the world in ways that would be impossible without them. John Dollard and Neal Miller (1950) made the point this way.

> In the heavy traffic leaving a football game, a driver was caught in a long line of cars all waiting to make a left turn on a four-lane highway. [The situation is shown in Figure 8.18.] There was just enough traffic coming from the other direction to make the left turn difficult so the line was advancing quite slowly. . . .
>
> As the long line of cars crept slowly ahead, the man became increasingly impatient. . . . He noticed that the few cars coming in the opposite direction had no difficulty in making their right turns onto this road and driving rapidly on down it. He said to himself, "If I were only going the other way, it would be so easy." This led to the further question, "How could I be going the other way?" From here on he was dealing with a problem that he had had a great deal of practice in solving. He immediately thought of pulling out into the outside line, driving up the highway, finding a place to turn around, coming back the other way and making the right turn onto the other highway. . . .

In his book *Galton's Walk,* Herbert Crovitz (1970) points out that problem solving often requires us to see the conceptual elements of the problem in a new relationship to one another. In the example just presented, the solution required the driver to put his car, one element, into a new relationship to the highway onto which he wanted to turn, the second element. According to Crovitz, language provides only forty-two relationships between two elements. These relationships are defined by the terms *about, across, after, against, among, and, as, at, because, before, between, but, by, down, for, from, if, in, near, not, now, of, off, on, opposite, or, out, over, round, still, so, then, though, through, till, to, under, up, when, where, while, with.* Spelling out these relationships, in the form "Take the (element 1) (relationship) the (element 2)," might suggest the possible solutions to many problems. Thus

"Take the car about the highway"
"Take the car across the highway"
. . . .
. . . .
"Take the car before the highway"

Obviously the compulsive rehearsal of all forty-two of the possible relationships would be a tedious chore. Crovitz makes a good case, however, that the method is useful when a person fails to see the solution to a problem. He also points out that practice with this method of manipulating concepts might help children to become better problem solvers.

Restricting the Manipulation of Concepts Any condition that limits the ways in which a person can manipulate concepts is likely to interfere with problem solving. This fact is well illustrated by Luchins's experiments with problems which were versions of the following: "A mother sends her son to the well to get three quarts of water. She gives him a five-quart and eight-quart can. How can the boy get exactly three quarts of water, using only these containers and not guessing at the amount?" The solution to the problem is to fill the eight-quart can, empty out enough to fill the five-quart can, and take the rest home. Luchins's problems were more complicated in that they involved three containers and numbers a little more difficult to handle. Eight of them are presented in Table 8.3. In order to get the point of the experiment, you should work through all eight of the problems. Begin with problem 1 and work down through the list.

Problems 1 and 7 follow a common pattern. Expressed algebraically, the solution is always of the form $b - a - 2c$; that is, to get 100 units of water as required in the first problem, you fill the 127-unit container, fill the 21-unit container from it once and the 3-unit container from it twice: $127 - 21 - 2(3) = 100$. Problems 1 through 5 can be solved only in this way, but problems 6 and 7 have much simpler solutions, algebraically $a - c$ and $a + c$. The eighth problem can only be solved in a simpler way, $a - c$ (Luchins, 1942).

The basic question asked by Luchins's experiments is whether solving problems 1 through 5 has any effect on the solving of subsequent problems? The answer is "yes." Luchins used two groups of problem solvers. About 80 percent of the people in the experimental group, who were presented with all eight problems, continued to rely on the same method that had solved the first five, in spite of the fact that the last three had an easier solution. Many actually failed to solve the last problem in the time allowed because the method would not work. A control group, presented with only the final three problems, had little trouble with the last one, and they almost always used the simpler method for solving problems 6 and 7. The set developed by solving problems 1 through 5 in a certain way restricted the individual's manipulation of concepts.

TABLE 8.3
Luchins's Problem

Problem	*a*	*b*	*c*	To Obtain
1	21	127	3	100
2	14	163	25	99
3	18	43	10	5
4	9	42	6	21
5	20	59	4	31
6	23	49	3	20
7	15	39	3	18
8	28	76	3	25

From Luchins, 1942.

A set may also hamper logical reasoning. One experiment (Morton, 1942), for example, used abstract terms and emotionally loaded terms to state similarly faulty syllogisms. The following resemble those used in the study.

1. All *x*'s are *y*'s.
   All *z*'s are *y*'s.
   Therefore all *z*'s are *x*'s.
2. All communists are radicals.
   All labor leaders are radicals.
   Therefore all labor leaders are communists.

Which conclusion follows logically? Actually, neither, for the two problems are similarly faulty syllogisms. Should a logically false conclusion match a strong attitudinal bias, however, it is more readily accepted than an identical false conclusion expressed in terms of *x*'s, *y*'s, and *z*'s. If you believe that all labor leaders are communists, you are likely to accept the statement as following from the premises, even though you would not accept the abstract equivalent that all *z*'s are *x*'s. An attitude is said to have an atmospheric effect on reasoning.

The Nature of Thought

The intimate relationship between language and thought led the early behaviorists, for example, John B. Watson, to propose that the two skills are identical—that language is just silent talking to oneself. This view consigned thought to the periphery. It held that the essential mechanism of thought is not neural activity in the brain but muscular activity in the vocal apparatus. There are many objections to this view, one of which is based on an experiment which was quite dramatic. In a classic display of heroism for the scientific good, an anesthesiologist, Scott Smith, allowed himself to be curarized to the point of complete paralysis and then introspected on his own thought processes.

Curare is a chemical that eliminates all muscular and skeletal activity by blocking the neural junction at which nerve impulses pass on directions to the muscles. Curare has been used as a poison by several South American Indian tribes, who put it on the tips of their arrows for battle and hunting. An enemy or quarry shot with a poisoned arrow dies almost immediately because breathing ceases. Smith took enough of the curare that he had to be kept alive with artificial respiration. In these bereft circumstances, Smith reported later, his mind was clear and he could solve problems (Smith et al., 1947). Thinking then can proceed when muscular activity is absent, belying the view that it is subvocal speech. Thoughts originate in the brain, and language expresses them.

SUMMARY □

One of the great powers of language is that it provides a set of symbols by which to manipulate what we call thought. In large part the manipulations employed in thinking are the manipulations of concepts, that is, of the symbols which stand for the common properties of things that are otherwise distinguishable. Concepts develop as an individual notices these common properties and learns to treat objects that possess them in the same way. In laboratory research concepts are defined in terms of arbitrary attributes, and subjects are provided with positive and negative instances of the concept until they master it. The same processes probably account for concept attainment in everyday life. There are complexities, however. Examples vary in the degree to which they represent the concept. Moreover, different cultures develop different concepts. There is modestly convincing evidence that this process affects thinking.

The manipulation of concepts in problem solving very clearly shows the power of language for creative thinking. The solution of a problem usually requires manipulating concepts, putting them into a new relationship to one another. Anything that limits such manipulations interferes with problem solving and reasoning.

The close relationship between language and thought suggested to the early behaviorists that thought might be nothing more than subvocal speech. Introspective observations made by an individual under curare, a paralyzing drug which would have eliminated any traces of the speech that this theory proposed as thought, confirmed that thinking must be a function of the brain. The solution to the puzzle with which this discussion began is

DONALD = 526485
<u>GERALD</u> = <u>197485</u>
ROBERT = 723970

TO BE SURE THAT YOU UNDERSTAND THIS CHAPTER △

The following concepts are the important ones presented in this chapter. They are listed in the approximate order in which they appeared. You should be able to use them to reconstruct the discussion of the chapter.

Linguistic competence
Phonology
Syntax
Semantics
Pragmatics
Phoneme
Allophone
Morpheme
Free morpheme
Bound morpheme
Phonetic symbolism
Denotative meaning
Associative meaning
Connotative meaning
Semantic differential
Passive vocabulary
Active vocabulary
Overregularization
Fis phenomenon
Marked expressions
Unmarked expressions
Concept
Linguistic relativity

A good many other important points made in Chapter 8 should be added.

Phrase structure of sentences
Hierarchical organization of phrase structure
Meaningfulness and learning
Communication and "language" in animals
Role of learning in language acquisition
Characteristics of caretaker speech
Methods of studying concept attainment
Effects of set on problem solving

TO GO BEYOND THIS CHAPTER △

In this book This chapter ties in very nicely with Chapter 12 on cognitive development. The two chapters supplement each other and should suggest a number of interesting connections.

Elsewhere The psychology of language is a rapidly changing field, and many treatments are very technical. A recommended recent book is *Psychology and Language,* by Herbert and Eve Clark. The article on language acquisition by Breyne Arlene Moskowitz, referred to in the text, is first rate.

PART 3

INTELLIGENCE AND ITS DEVELOPMENT

CH. 9

Behavior Genetics

Man is an animal, a unique and particularly complex one, but an animal nonetheless. Human beings are programmed by their genes to become people, just as elephants are programmed by their genes to become elephants. So much of human nature is determined by this genetic template that a full understanding of human behavior is impossible without consideration of its genetic foundations.

The differences in appearance and behavior distinguishing species are governed almost entirely by genetic factors. Variations in members of the same species, however, come from a combination of differences in genetic inheritance and in environmental conditions. The particular influence of genetic and environmental factors differs from trait to trait; some depend more on genes whereas others depend more on environment. Yet every trait and behavior of human beings and other animals partake of both of these great forces, heredity and environment.

For some human traits genes seem especially important. No amount of training or effort would allow most of us to run a four-minute mile or become a great musical virtuoso. A particular genetic predisposition is required for these feats, but this predisposition does not in itself guarantee that they will be accomplished. Individuals genetically blessed with the potential to develop the physical constitution required to run a four-minute mile will never realize this potential unless they receive adequate nourishment. By the same token, without musical training the potential virtuoso will make Carnegie Hall only as a paying customer.

Other important variations in our behavior do not seem to depend so strongly on genetic inheritance. Although a tendency toward general aggressiveness may have a genetic base, an individual's hatred of others because of their skin color or political philosophy appears to have much more to do with learning than with genes.

A major theme of this chapter is that a complete understanding of behavior requires an appreciation of both genetic and environmental factors and of the complex interactions between them.

BASIC GENETIC MECHANISMS

Mendel's Laws

The father of modern genetics was Gregor Mendel (1822–1884), who published in 1866 certain laws of inheritance that he had deduced from his study of peas. This work went relatively unnoticed at the time and was not rediscovered until 1900.

Mendel's laws were stated in terms of hypothetical elements which were later called **genes.** In his experimental work, Mendel crossed pure strains of peas

Gregor Johann Mendel, an Austrian monk educated in Vienna in mathematics and biology, bred his peas in the gardens of his order's monastery.

which differed in single contrasting traits: purple versus white flowers, yellow versus green seeds, and smooth versus wrinkled seeds. In the first generation of offspring — the **F_1** or first filial generation — the trait of one of the parents was usually dominant, whereas the trait of the other parent did not appear. For example, when the purple-flowering plants were crossed with white-flowering plants, all the offspring had purple flowers. When the F_1 hybrids produced offspring (F_2), Mendel discovered that the dominant (purple) and recessive (white) grandparental traits reappeared in the F_2 progeny in a ratio of three dominants to one recessive. This finding gave rise to Mendel's first law, the **law of segregation,** which is represented in Figure 9.1. This law states that genes occur in pairs, and that one member of the pair is contributed by each parent. When a mature organism produces **germ cells** — cells for reproduction such as pollen, sperm, or ova — the paired genes segregate, and each germ cell receives only one member of the pair. When a sperm and ovum unite, a new and unique gene pair is transmitted to the offspring.

This law was to bring about a revolution in scientists' thinking about heredity. Prior to Mendel's work, it was thought that heredity was transmitted from parents to offspring by blood. The blood referred to here is the "blood line" of folklore rather than the red fluid flowing within the body. The parental bloods

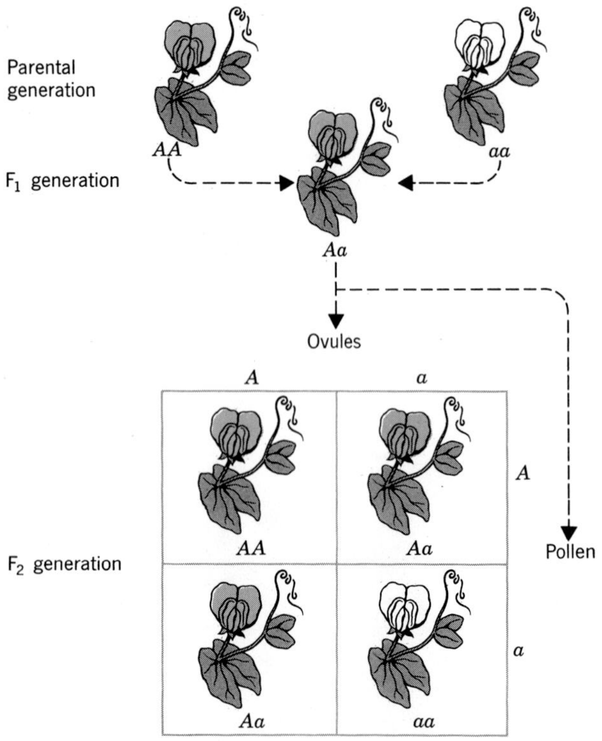

FIGURE 9.1

Mendel's law of segregation. Pure strains of purple-flowering and white-flowering peas are crossed, and the purple color is dominant in the first generation of hybrids (F_1). In the second generation (F_2) there is segregation of the purple and white colors. The allele for purple is represented by *A* and the allele for white by *a*. (After Dobzhansky, 1955.)

were thought actually to mix in the child. Thus it was assumed that each parent contributed a complete hereditary endowment, and that the child received a combination of the parents' heredities, which included the blood of all grandparents and other ancestors.

Segregation of the parents' traits in Mendel's F_2 generation of hybrids indicated that these traits are inherited not through mixable bloods but by discrete bodies, namely the genes, which do not mix with or contaminate each other. We now know that genes can exist in two or more alternative states called **alleles.** In Mendel's peas, for example, the gene for flower color has two alleles, purple (*A*) and white (*a*). When the alleles inherited from each parent are the same (*AA* or *aa*), the offspring is **homozygous** in respect to the trait. When the alleles are different (*Aa*), the offspring is **heterozygous.** Many genes behave in a pattern of dominance and recessiveness. When both a **dominant gene** and a **recessive gene** for a particular trait are present, the dominant gene determines the trait.

That independent physical entities are the vehicle of genetic transmission was further affirmed for Mendel by evidence that led him to postulate his **law of independent assortment.** Mendel crossed some varieties of peas that differed in two traits, for example, yellow, smooth seeds versus green, wrinkled seeds. Since yellow was dominant over green and smooth over wrinkled, the F_1 generation seeds were all yellow and smooth. In the F_2 hybrids seed color was segregated in the ratio of three yellow (dominant) to one green (recessive). Similarly, the F_2 hybrid seeds segregated in a ratio of three smooth to one wrinkled.

The interesting question here was whether the yellow color was linked in segregation with the smooth surface and the green with the wrinkled surface. This proved not to be the case. Mendel demonstrated that color and surface traits segregate independently, since the proportions of yellow and green colors among the smooth seeds were the same as those among the wrinkled ones. This showed that heredity is transmitted through germ cells by a collection of independent genes, and that different genes undergo segregation independently of one another.

Applications to Human Traits

Mendelian laws of inheritance have now been established for many human traits, including eye color, baldness, certain hereditary diseases, and a condition called **albinism.** The albino individual is born with a virtually pigmentless skin, almost white hair, and eyes that are usually pink. To illustrate the inheritance of this condition, we will let *N* represent the allele for normal pigmentation and *n* the allele for albinism. Albinism is known to be caused by a recessive gene, since albino children are usually born to parents who have the dominant, normal pigmentation but who are both heterozygous (*Nn*) for the albinism gene. In a union of two albinos, both of whom must be homozygous (*nn*) for this recessive gene, all the children will be albinos. As with many traits caused by recessive genes, albinism represents a weakness for the individual. The pigmentless skin makes albinos very sensitive to sunlight, and their vision is always poor.

Another human trait inherited according to Mendelian laws is the ability to taste the substance phenylthiocarbamide (PTC). To 70 percent of the population this substance has a very bitter taste, but 30 percent cannot taste it at all. The phenomenon of tasting or not tasting PTC is under the control of a gene pair in which one allele (*T*) is dominant and imparts the ability to taste, and one allele (*t*) is recessive. Only individuals with two recessives (*tt*) are nontasters. From Mendel's principle of dominance, we know that nontasters can only be *tt*, but that tasters can be either *TT* or *Tt*. If the parents' genes for tasting PTC are known, we can apply the Mendelian principles just discussed to calculate the percentage of their offspring who will be either tasters or nontasters (Figure 9.2). As we shall see, this type of calculation is useful

African mother and albino child. Because a gene is not properly constructed, neither is an enzyme, and the melanin pigments do not form from the amino acid tyrosine.

in determining the likelihood that parents will pass certain hereditary diseases or undesirable traits to their children.

Since there is a genetic basis for tasting or not tasting PTC, it seems possible that the taste of other substances might also vary as a result of genetic differences among people. For example, could it be that to a friend who hates spinach this food may actually taste different than it does to someone who likes it? Similarly, does alcohol taste better to an alcoholic than to a nonalcoholic? There is some evidence that alcoholism has a hereditary basis (page 113). We wonder whether this disease could be transmitted in part through genes that make the taste of alcohol especially appealing.

Genotype versus Phenotype

The material presented in Figure 9.2 helps to draw a distinction between a person's **genotype** and **phenotype.** The genotype refers to the genetic makeup the individual inherited from his or her parents. The phenotype refers to the observed characteristics of the individual. Thus we see in Figure 9.2 that different genotypes, either *TT* or *Tt,* bring about the same phenotype, that is, the ability to taste PTC.

Up until now our examples, such as pea traits and tasting PTC, have concerned phenotypes which are seemingly inexorable readouts of the underlying genotypes. For many physical characteristics and especially behavioral traits, however, the phenotype is influenced both by genotype and by the environment. Environment refers to all the external events to which the individual is subjected, including prenatal and neonatal conditions, nutrition, medical care, parents' child-rearing practices, cultural milieu, educational experiences, type and place of occupation, and even the climate of residence and epoch in which the person lives.

The importance of environment in determining even physical traits can be seen in a study of Himalayan rabbits (Sinnott, Dunn, and Dobzhansky, 1958). When raised under natural conditions, these rabbits have a white body with black extremities. When raised in a warm cage, however, they do not have the black pigmentation. Thus rabbits with the same genetic makeup can have different phenotypic appearances as a result of environmental factors. This example should put us on guard against the error of viewing any phenotypic trait as mirroring the genotype.

For many human traits the phenotype is constantly changing, depending on the nature of the interaction between the genotype and the environment. For example, a man's physique is strongly determined by genetic factors, but environmental influences such as nutrition have an important effect on his size and weight at any given time. Similarly, a very intelligent person may through stress or lack of rest experience a temporary inability to remember or reason abstractly.

The importance of the interaction between genotype and environment in determining the phenotype introduces another important concept, the **norm of reaction.** As can be seen in Figure 9.3, each genotype may exhibit a variety of phenotypes, depending on the particular environment experienced. This variety, however, is not infinite. The norm of reaction sets a limit to the range of phenotypes which are possible for a single genotype. For example, an individual whose genotype does not include great musical ability may benefit somewhat from musical training but will never have the phenotype of a musical genius. Later in this chapter the genotype-phenotype distinction, and the differential effects of environment, will help to make clear the general principle that genes are inherited but not necessarily behavior.

Complex Traits and Multiple Genes

In a previous section we have seen how Mendel's theories apply to traits that can be classified into two

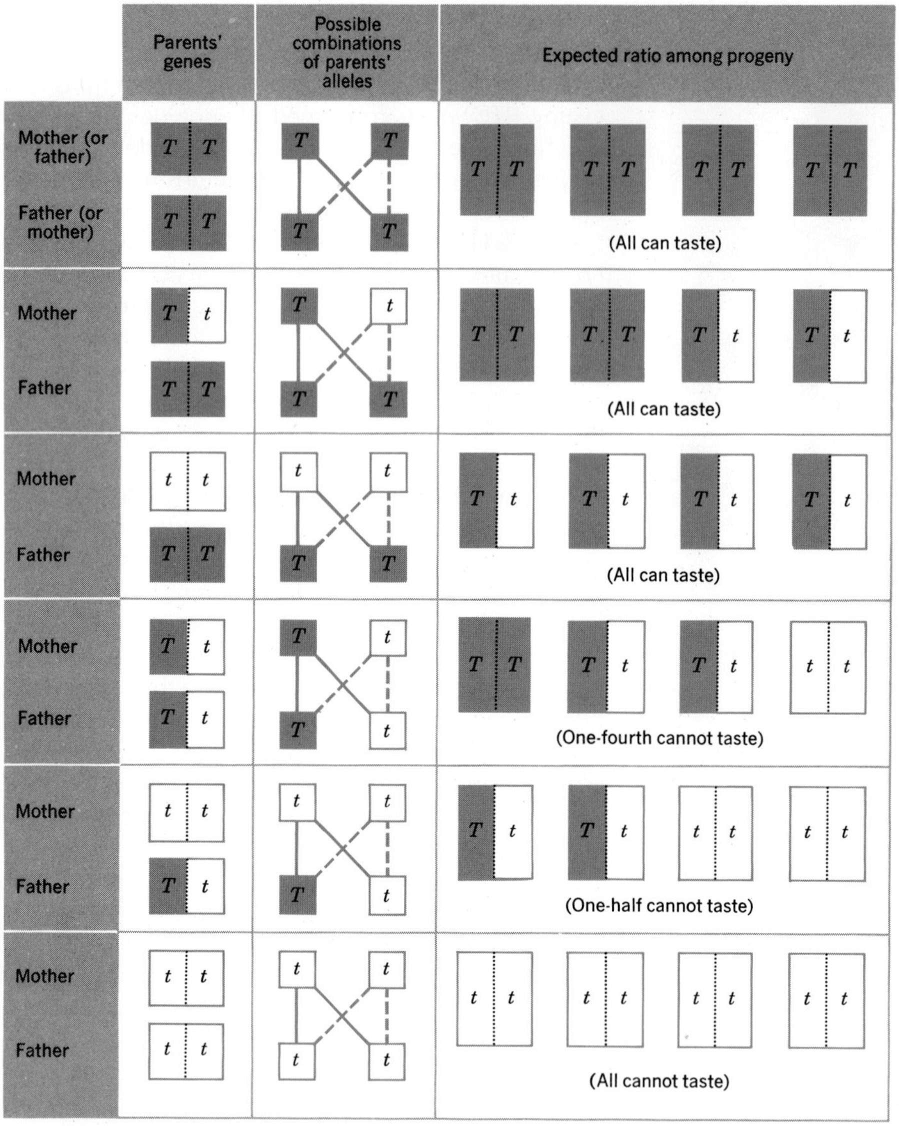

FIGURE 9.2

Inheritance of the ability to taste PTC. There are six possible parental combinations of the dominant gene for tasting (*T*) and the recessive gene for not tasting (*t*) PTC. Notice that the combinations of the parents' alleles would be the same if the genes indicated in the first column belonged to the opposite parent. Each type of mating yields an expected frequency of tasters and nontasters among the progeny.

distinct categories—for example, tasting and not tasting PTC. Many traits, such as human height or intelligence, do not fall into distinct categories but rather show a continuous variation. There are not two clear and separate classes of short people and tall people. Instead, the distribution is continuous, with relatively few very short and very tall people, and with most people having heights near the middle value of the distribution (Figure 9.4).

This normal distribution of a trait can be explained if the trait is determined by the additive action of many genes, a phenomenon known as **polygenic inheritance** (poly-, many). When a trait is polygenically determined, each of the genes involved makes a small positive or negative contribution to the phenotype. Individually, the genes underlying traits that are continuously distributed are assumed to obey basic Mendelian laws.

A model for polygenic inheritance was provided by Irving Gottesman (1963) for the trait of intelligence. For the sake of simplicity, we will assume that the intelligence quotient (IQ) is determined by only three pairs of genes and that a person with the genotype *AaBbCc* has an average IQ, that is, 100. We will also assume that each gene represented by a capital letter can increase IQ by 10 points, that the genes represented by a small letter have no influence, and that the effects of the genes are additive. The highest pos-

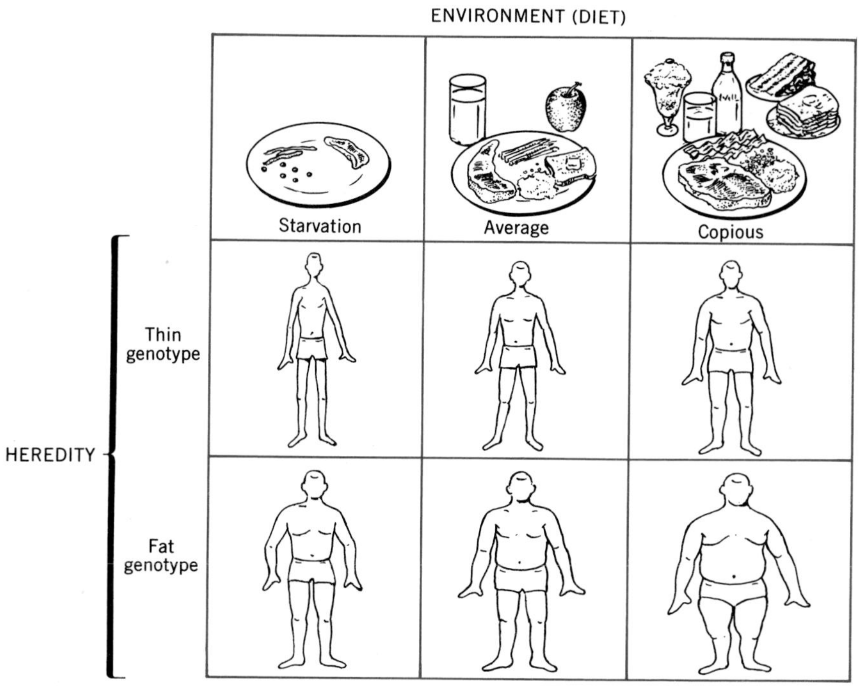

FIGURE 9.3
The norm of reaction. Although the environment is influential in determining the phenotype, heredity sets a limit to the range of possible phenotypes. In this illustration the two different genotypes for physique limit the effect of diet on actual appearance. (After Dobzhansky, 1964.)

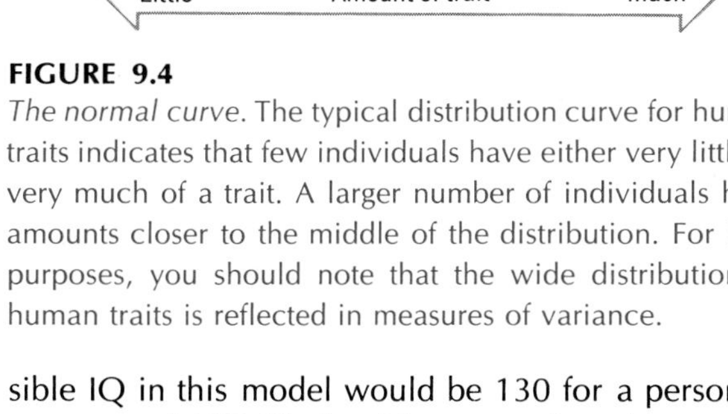

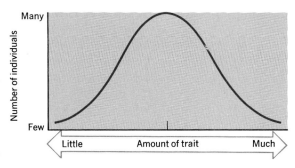

FIGURE 9.4
The normal curve. The typical distribution curve for human traits indicates that few individuals have either very little or very much of a trait. A larger number of individuals have amounts closer to the middle of the distribution. For later purposes, you should note that the wide distribution of human traits is reflected in measures of variance.

sible IQ in this model would be 130 for a person of genotype *AABBCC,* for this person has three more capital-letter genes than the average person. The lowest possible IQ would be 70 for a person of genotype *aabbcc,* since this person has three fewer capital-letter genes than the average. If you are puzzled by the 100 IQ of the *AaBbCc* individual, it may be helpful to note that this person's IQ has been increased 30 points by the three capital letters.

The completely heterozygous person (*AaBbCc*) could produce eight different types of gene combinations to be passed along to his or her children (Figure 9.5). If such heterozygotes mate, there would be sixty-four (8 × 8) possible genotypes for their offspring, some of which are represented in Figure 9.5. The relative frequency of all possible genotypic values from such matings—the genotypic value is the number of capital letters—is given in Figure 9.6. In this distribution each phenotype appears distinct and separable from the phenotype next to it, for we have assumed that only three pairs of genes determine IQ. If we had assumed instead that fifteen or more pairs determine IQ, the resulting distribution would be an excellent approximation of the normal curve. Such an assumption is not farfetched, since it has been estimated that there may be close to five million genes in a human cell (Cavalli-Sforza and Bodmer, 1971).

The normal distribution of many important traits is also ensured by the role of environmental factors. Remember once again that the phenotype is not merely an expression of the underlying genotype. Thus in Figure 9.6 there would be some intermediate cases between the bars as a result of environmental influences—variations in educational opportunities, for example.

Chromosomes

In the decades between Mendel's work and its rediscovery, scientists had sighted small, threadlike bodies

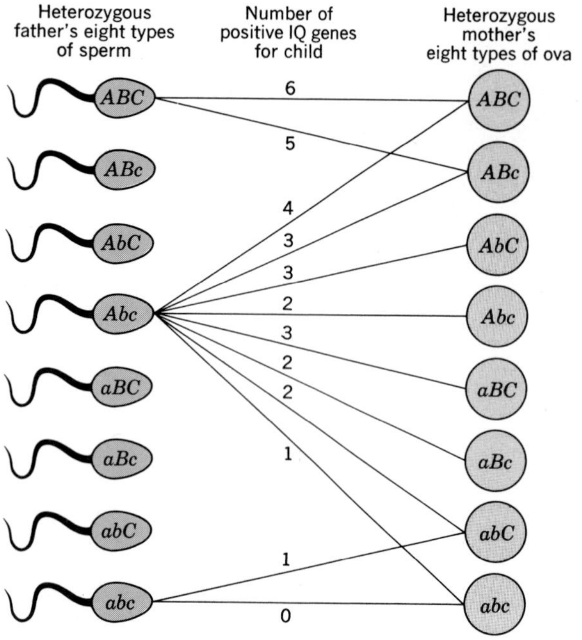

FIGURE 9.5
Possible results of matings between heterozygous persons. IQ is assumed to be controlled by three pairs of genes. For pictorial clarity, only a few of the possible unions of sperm and ova are shown. Lines may be drawn from any type of sperm to any type of ovum (a total of $8 \times 8 = 64$ possible lines). The total number of capital letters accrued by adding those of sperm and ovum denotes the genotypic value for the child. There are many ways (twenty) to produce a child with a genotypic value of 3, but only one of sixty-four combinations produces a child with a value of 0 or of 6.

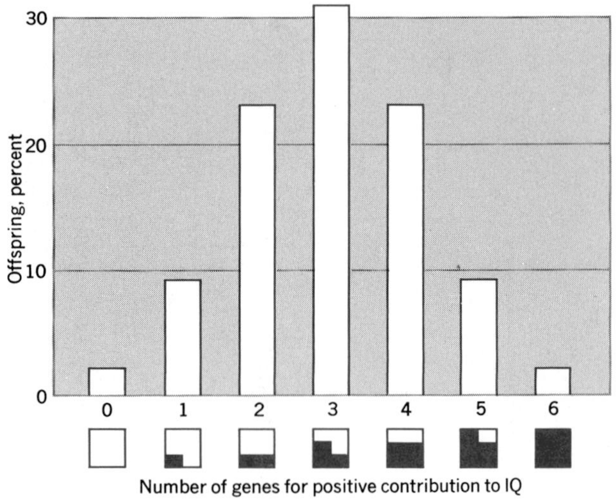

FIGURE 9.6
The inheritance of IQ from matings of heterozygous parents. The bars indicate the frequencies of possible genotype values when IQ is assumed to be controlled by three pairs of genes.

located within the nucleus of cells and clearly visible under the microscope. These bodies, called **chromosomes,** were thought to be involved in genetic transmission. As the importance of Mendel's work was recognized, the connection was made between the laws of his "elements" of heredity and the function of chromosomes. Research has now shown that the thousands of physically much smaller genes, linearly arranged along each chromosome, are the basic units of inheritance.

Genes are made up of chemical molecules technically known as deoxyribonucleic acid, or *DNA,* which contains the "genetic code." The cracking of the genetic code by James Watson and Francis Crick, for which they received a Nobel prize, represents one of the greatest breakthroughs in the history of biology. As with so many great discoveries, the story of DNA is elegantly simple in its final explanation. This genetic material proved to have a surprisingly small number of components; minute variations in the way only four of the DNA elements are arranged were found to provide the code and thus account for all the differences among genes.

Normal Complement The entire genetic message of a human being resides in the single cell called the **zygote,** with which life begins. The zygote is formed when the male's sperm penetrates the egg or ovum produced by the female. The ovum and sperm each contain twenty-three chromosomes. When the zygote is formed, the chromosomes of the ovum and sperm combine. Thus the zygote contains twenty-three pairs of chromosomes—forty-six chromosomes in all—which become the normal complement of every cell in that person's body with the exception of the germ cells, the sperm or ova.

Twenty-two chromosomes from the sperm and twenty-two from the ovum are always pairs in that they determine the same traits. The twenty-third is the sex chromosome. The ovum always contributes the X chromosome, so called because of its distinct shape; the twenty-third chromosome in the sperm can be either an X or a Y chromosome. If the sex chromosome of the sperm is an X, the resulting XX combination guarantees that the zygote will develop into a female. If the sex chromosome of the sperm is a Y, the resulting XY combination guarantees that the zygote will be a male.

Chromosomes may be photographed through a microscope and then cut out of photographic enlargements and arranged into pairs according to their lengths. This arrangement is known as a **karyotype** (Figure 9.7). From a karyotype a trained examiner can observe gross abnormalities such as missing, broken, or additional chromosomes.

Sex Chromosome Abnormalites **Gametes** are mature germ cells—an ovum that is ready to be fertilized

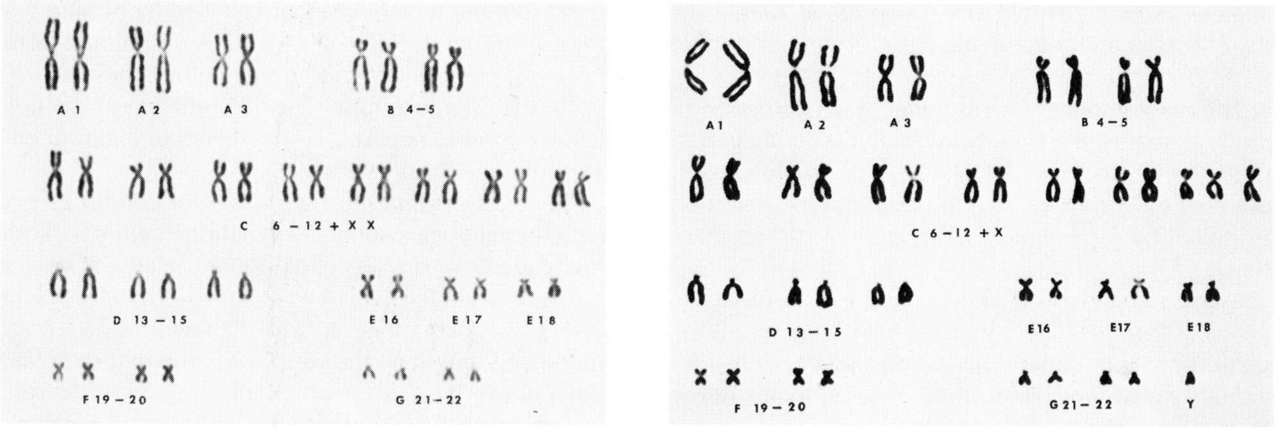

FIGURE 9.7
Karyotypes of the normal female (left) *and male* (right). The sex chromosomes of the female karyotype are in the second line; the Y chromosome of the male karyotype is the last one.

or a sperm that is capable of doing so. Ordinarily, the complex process of gamete formation takes place smoothly and perfectly, with the genes on the chromosomes properly segregated and distributed. On rare occasions, however, gametes form that do not have the normal number of sex chromosomes. Sometimes there is no sex chromosome, or an ovum may contain an extra X chromosome, a sperm an extra Y chromosome. When such an abnormal gamete joins with a normal gamete (or with another abnormal one), the resulting zygote will have either too few or too many sex chromosomes. Although the offspring resulting from such unions may survive, they often have a variety of physical and mental characteristics that mark them as abnormal.

The abnormality that results from the absence of an X chromosome (XO instead of XX) is known as the **Turner syndrome.** These women are short, have incompletely developed breasts, and are sterile. Since the development of secondary sex characteristics such as pubic hair and breasts can be induced through doses of the hormone estrogen, women with the Turner syndrome can be helped to a more normal appearance and are able to live relatively normal lives.

In another abnormality males have an extra X chromosome, a condition called the **Klinefelter syndrome.** These XXY men have an abnormal hormonal balance and are usually sterile. They are tall, thin, and have long arms and legs; their testicles are small. Psychologically, many have low IQs and show poor social adjustment. It is not known whether this poor adjustment is a product of genetic makeup or of the social consequences of the genetic abnormality.

A much-publicized abnormality is the extra Y chromosome found in some men. Early studies of **XYY males** suggested that there was a higher frequency of this chromosomal disorder among men in prison populations and in populations of mentally retarded patients. These findings were widely reported by the press, and throughout the world an image emerged of the XYY male as a tall individual of low IQ, with strong tendencies toward criminality, aggression, and violence. In nations as far afield as Australia and France, criminals with XYY karyotypes were defended on the premise that they were the helpless victims of their genetic inheritance and therefore could not be held accountable for their offenses. This view retains a considerable degree of popularity.

A number of more recent studies have seriously called into question the stereotypic view of the XYY male. Many of these studies have reported that the prevalence of XYY males among criminals is no higher than in the general population, and that many XYY men have no criminal tendencies. In the scientific community, then, the current view of the XYY male is much more cautious and guarded. Some researchers still feel that there might be a slight criminal propensity in such men, but others do not (Hook, 1973; Jarvik, Klodin, and Matsuyama, 1973; Owen, 1972; Witkin et al., 1976).

SUMMARY □

The origins of the scientific study of heredity may be traced to Mendel, who introduced the concept that discrete and independent entities, now called genes, are the true basis for hereditary transmission. In his law of segregation he postulated that genes exist in pairs of alleles within the organism, and that one allele of each pair is contributed by each parent. His law of independent assortment indicated that gene pairs for different traits segregate independently of one another. An individual may have two identical alleles for a trait – homozygosity; or have two different alleles—heterozygosity. In heterozygous organisms the effects of a dominant allele are expressed but not those of a recessive.

The environment may also affect the expression of the trait, that is, its phenotype. The underlying genes, or genotype, may exhibit a variety of phenotypes in different environments, but the extent of this variation is limited by a principle known as the norm of reaction.

Many human traits depend on a multiple system of genes, a form of inheritance called polygenic. Polygenic traits are continuously distributed, with individuals showing a wide range of phenotypes rather than falling into discrete classes or types.

Every ordinary human body cell contains twenty-three pairs of chromosomes, one of which is the pair of sex chromosomes. The specialized reproductive cells, the sperm and ova, contain only half the normal number of chromosomes. The successful fertilization of an ovum by a sperm unites two sets of unpaired chromosomes into a paired set to form a zygote.

NATURE VERSUS NURTURE

Is human behavior an outgrowth of nature, that is, of genetic factors, or is it a result of nurture, that is, the totality of environmental events that a person experiences? Posed in this either-or manner, the question is meaningless. There could be no behavior without an individual who inherits a genetic structure, nor could any behavior occur in the absence of an environment. At the most obvious level, then, all behavior is the outcome of the effects of both heredity and environment.

Less obvious may be the fact that the relative contribution of these two factors differs from one behavioral trait to another. Knowing that one trait is strongly influenced by heredity tells nothing about other types of behavior. Thus the real issue in understanding behavior is a question of how heredity and environment interact and how this interaction differs for various traits, not the pseudoquestion of whether people are a reflection of their heredities or their environments.

Inheritance of Behavioral Traits

Genetic studies of behavior have been conducted much more often on animals than on human beings. This is understandable for several reasons. (1) The behavior of animals is not nearly as complex as that of humans, and therefore the relation between genes and behavior can be more easily understood; (2) the environments of animals can be more readily controlled than those of human beings; and (3) the breeding rate of animals is faster. A generation of lower mammals may grow to maturity within a few months instead of the twenty years or so taken by human beings. Although the results of studies on animals cannot be applied directly to human beings, they are important for demonstrating the different ways in which genetic inheritance may be expressed in different environmental circumstances.

Genes are primarily responsible for certain physical characteristics such as eye color in animals both high and low on the evolutionary scale. In lower forms of animals, such as one-celled organisms and insects, a good percentage of behavior is also very much dependent on the genotype. Even in these creatures, however, the environment plays a critical role by providing the stimulus that elicits particular behavior. For example, bees communicate by means of complex dances (page 179), a system which appears to be completely genetically determined (von Frisch, 1965). Yet the environment provokes the dancing by providing the situation that calls for communication.

All members of a species low on the evolutionary scale may behave in highly stereotypic patterns. But animals of a species higher on the scale may show marked individual differences in their behavior. Whenever individuals of the same species differ in a particular trait, the heritability of that trait may be studied by means of **selective breeding.** This technique requires that animals similar in the degree to which the trait is manifested or not manifested be mated with each other.

For example, in a study to determine whether activity level is inherited, very active males would be mated with very active females, and very inactive males would be mated with very inactive females. In the next generation some of the progeny of the active animals would be very active, and some of the progeny of the inactive animals would be very inactive. Only the most active offspring of active parents, and the most inactive offspring of inactive parents, would be further inbred. The procedure could continue for as many generations as necessary to establish the fact that either there is or is not an inherited component for activity level. Selective breeding methods have also been used in many investigations of the inheritance of emotionality and of learning ability (intelligence) and of the relation between these two important traits.

Emotionality When rats are put into a novel situation—for example, a large, brightly lit area—many of them show evidence of marked emotional upset. They cower and "freeze," remain immobile in a fixed position, and have an increased tendency to defecate and urinate. To study the inheritance of these tendencies, Calvin Hall began with an initial selection of 145 rats and inbred the most and least emotional of them. His mating criterion was simply the presence or absence of urination and defecation during each of a

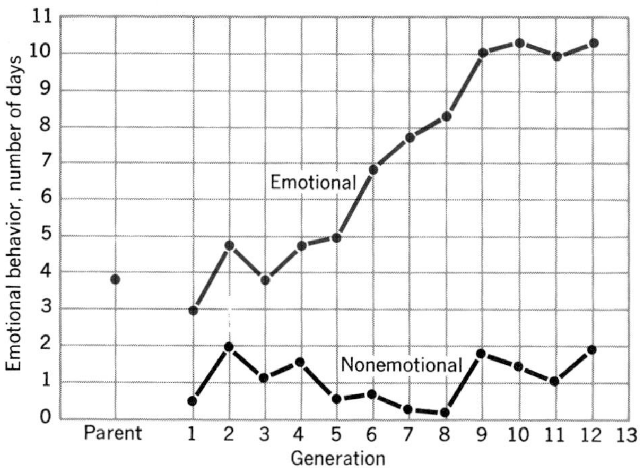

FIGURE 9.8

The inheritance of emotionality for twelve generations of rats. (Constructed from data in Hall, 1951.)

series of twelve daily tests in an open field. The unselected parent generation showed such evidence of emotional upset on an average of 3.86 days. In a series of successive generations the strains gradually drew apart, until the emotional rats continued to be upset for ten and eleven days and the unemotional rats for only two days (Figure 9.8). Emotionality in rats thus appears to have a genetic base.

Maze Learning One of the classic experiments in behavior genetics is Robert Tryon's study of the maze learning of rats. Tryon initially selected 142 rats and gave them 19 trials in a complex maze. Some animals learned the maze very quickly, making few errors; others learned very slowly, making many errors. The frequency distribution of errors—entrances into blind alleys—obtained from the original parent population showed a considerable range in ability to learn the maze (Figure 9.9*a*).

The "bright" rats were then mated with each other, as were the "dull" rats, and both sets of offspring (F_1 generation) were tested in the maze. This process was repeated for eight generations. Figure 9.9*b* presents the error distributions for the F_1, F_3, and F_8 generations. By the eighth generation there was practically no overlap in maze learning ability between "brights" and "dulls."

Clearly, heredity and maze learning are related, and selective breeding can demonstrate that a genetic substrate is involved. But a caution is in order. What is inherited in these experiments is quite specific, as subsequent research by Lloyd Searle (1949) showed. "Brights" were not bright on everything, nor were "dulls" altogether dull. Drawing from the twenty-second generation of the Tryon strains, Searle tested ten "brights" and ten "dulls" for some thirty different traits, including emotionality, activity level, discrimination learning, and performance in Tryon's maze as

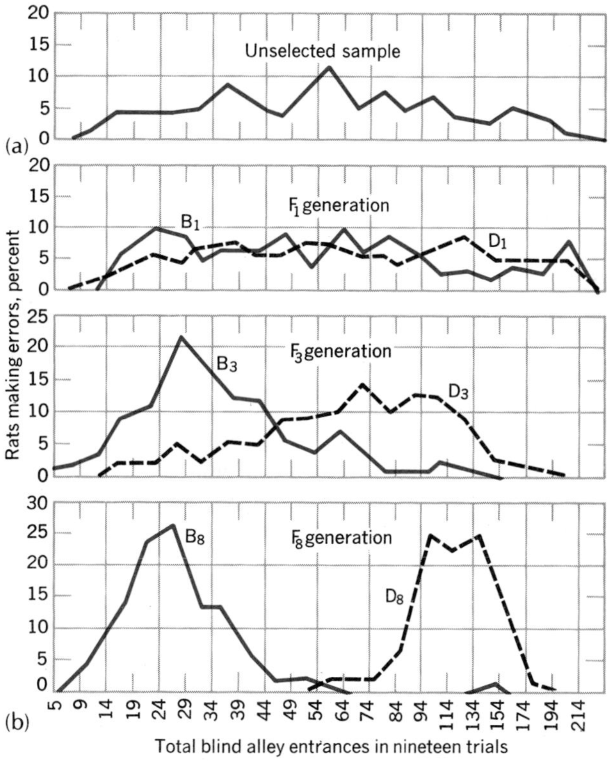

FIGURE 9.9

The maze performance of bright (B) and dull (D) rats. (*a*) The upper graph shows the distribution of errors for the parent population. (*b*) The lower graphs show the performances of first-, third-, and eighth-generation progeny. (From Tryon, 1942.)

well as in a number of other types of mazes.

Searle confirmed Tryon's findings for error and time scores on the original maze, but on other mazes the differences in learning ability disappeared and differences in emotionality became apparent. In some tests the data suggested that the "brights" might be more emotional than the "dulls." Even this trait appeared to be quite specific, since "dulls" were subsequently found to be more fearful of the maze. Table 9.1 summarizes some of the differences obtained by Searle. Obviously, the two groups varied in many ways, almost any of which might have affected maze performance one way or the other.

Another experiment on descendants of Tryon's two strains (Krech et al., 1954) revealed that the "brights" and "dulls" also differed in the level of cholinesterase activity in the brain. Cholinesterase is an enzyme that is important for efficient transmission of neural impulses. The "bright" rats had higher levels of cholinesterase than the "dulls" in every part of the cerebral cortex. These findings suggest that the different patterns of ability of the two strains of rats may have been inherited in part through the genes which determine the level of cholinesterase activity in the nervous system.

TABLE 9.1
Some Differences Between "Brights" and "Dulls" on a Variety of Behavior Measures

Behavior	Brights	Dulls
Food drive	Above average	Below average
Escape from water drive	Inferior	Superior
Spontaneous activity	Relatively low	Relatively high
Emotional responsiveness	Fearful in "open-space" situations	Fearful of mechanical apparatus; emotionally reactive in maze
General intelligence	No evidence of a general superiority in capacity	No evidence of a general inferiority in capacity
Response to elevated structures	Greater timidity	Less timidity
Running speed	Above average	Below average

Adapted from Searle, 1949.

Effects of Environment

Many animal studies have examined how differences in environment interact with genotypic differences in determining behavior. In one study (Freedman, 1958) pups of four breeds of dog—representing four different genotypes—were reared under either indulgent or disciplined regimens. At eight weeks each pup was tested for inhibition of eating by having the person who was rearing the animal punish it for eating and then leave the room. Basenjis ate as soon as the trainer left, regardless of whether their rearing had been indulgent or disciplined. Shetland sheep dogs did not eat the food, however they had been reared. Thus early environment had no effect on these two genotypes. Beagles and fox terriers, on the other hand, were influenced by their early environmental regimen. The indulged beagles and terriers were more inhibited by the punishment than were the beagles and terriers raised under strict discipline.

John Fuller (1967) studied the effects of early environment on the maze learning of two breeds of dog. Some pups of each breed were raised normally, others in isolation. Interestingly, the effects of isolated rearing and emergence from it varied with breed of dog, again illustrating that environmental events have different effects on animals of different genotypes. Fuller found that dogs reared in isolation demonstrated a poorer learning ability, but that they were hindered by emotionality rather than any deficit in intelligence. When their emotionality was overcome, their maze performance improved.

Fuller's work is extremely important. Earlier studies of dogs raised in isolation had also shown them to be poor at learning a maze. On this basis the hypothesis that deprivation keeps animals from developing an effective sensory and cognitive apparatus was formulated. These early studies did much to shape thinking in our country about the relation between deprivation and the low intelligence scores of children raised in impoverished circumstances. Fuller's work demonstrates the dangers of loose analogizing between dogs and children.

In another study of environmental effects on maze learning, strains of bright and dull rats were reared in three markedly different early environments (Cooper and Zubek, 1958). An enriched environment was provided by slides, tunnels, balls, and considerable sensory stimulation. The restricted environment consisted of cages which contained only a food box and water pan and faced a gray wall. The third group of each strain was raised in the natural habitat of a laboratory rat. At sixty-five days of age, each group was tested for maze learning. The enriched early environment helped the "dulls" but not the "brights;" the restricted environment had no effect on the "dulls" but hurt the "brights." Thus, under the restricted condition, even the rats with high genetic potential were prevented from developing it. Again we see that the phenotype is a result of the interaction between genotype and environment.

Nature-Nurture Interaction

These studies help to demonstrate a principle referred to earlier—that what an organism basically inherits is a range of modifiability, a norm of reaction (page 203). Each genotype specifies a range of phenotypes which are possible under different environmental circumstances. If this norm of reaction is narrow for a partic-

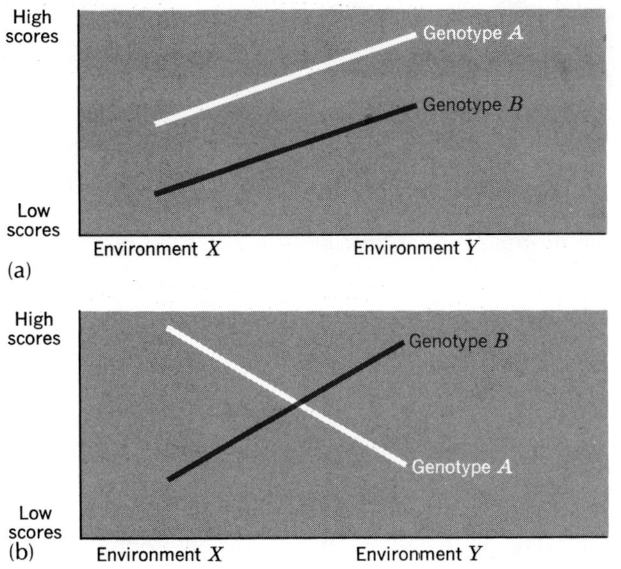

FIGURE 9.10

Norms of reaction between heredity and environment. (*a*) Genotype *A* scores higher than genotype *B* in environments *X* and *Y*, although environment *Y* improves the scores of both genotypes. (*b*) Genotype *A* scores higher in environment *X*, and genotype *B* scores higher in environment *Y*. Here the two environments have different effects on different genotypes.

ular physical or behavioral trait, environmental differences will have little influence on its development. If the norm of reaction is broad, changes in environment will bring about markedly different outcomes. Thus for some traits the range of expression and the power of the environment to influence the phenotype are much greater than for other traits.

Another important principle to emerge from geneticists' studies of the **nature-nurture interaction** is that the same environment may have either the same or different effects upon different genotypes. J. B. S. Haldane (1946) illustrated this principle with some theoretical norms of reaction. In Figure 9.10*a* individuals with genotype A always score higher than those with genotype B, but the scores of individuals with both genotypes improve markedly if they are exposed to environment Y rather than environment X. For example, better nutrition increases the height of both men and women, although on the average men remain the taller sex.

In another possible heredity-environment interaction (Figure 9.10*b*), genotype A is not superior to genotype B, nor is environment X superior to environment Y. Rather, the two genotypes react differently in different environments. An example is how the life expectancies of Europeans and blacks differ from one environment to another. In European cities Europeans outlive blacks, partly because of their greater immunity to tuberculosis. But in many parts of Africa the blacks have the advantage, largely because of their resistance to yellow fever (Haldane, 1946).

In other situations environmental differences may have no effect on one genotype but dramatically affect another. This type of interaction is illustrated by a study of the effectiveness of two methods of teaching reading to eighteen pairs of twins (Naeslund, reported in Vandenberg, 1965). Some of the twin pairs were of average intelligence and some were of superior intelligence. The individual twins in each pair were separated and assigned to different classrooms. Reading was taught by the phonics method in one room and by the sight method in the second room. Within each room, then, the same environmental treatment was given to children of the two genotypes for intelligence, average and gifted. The average children learned to read better with the phonics method than with the sight method. The gifted children did equally well with both methods. Thus two different environments had the same effect on children of one genotype (gifted), but had different effects on children of another genotype (average).

An underlying assumption of all these studies is that the environment can act on the genotype, but that the genotype does not act on the environment. The genotype is considered to be full of potentialities but an essentially passive agent. The environment, on the other hand, is the active agent which operates on the genotype and selects which phenotype will finally emerge. This assumption is not completely true, particularly in respect to behavioral development. Growth does not proceed in a simple reflex fashion to fixed environmental inputs. Rather, there is increasing evidence that the individual actively participates. Each person can manipulate and change the external world and thereby exert some control over the environment that he or she will experience. The view that behavioral and other personal traits develop as a result of reciprocal actions between the individual and the environment is known as the **transactional model of development** (Sameroff and Chandler, 1975).

An important way in which individuals act on the environment and contribute to their own development is by influencing the behavior of others toward themselves. Many cases of child abuse are unfortunate examples. Parents who are likely to abuse their children tend to be impulsive, immature, self-centered, self-critical, and low in intelligence. Not all children having parents with this constellation of attributes will be abused, however. It appears that only children having certain personal characteristics that irritate these parents, such as low birthweight, serious medical illnesses, being difficult or unmanageable, are abused.

Even among theorists who accept the transactional model or at least recognize that neither heredity nor environment is the sole determinant of behavior, some continue to advocate that we focus our attention on one factor or the other. For example, Boyd McCandless (1964) has argued that although heredity and environment interact, we need only concern ourselves with environment since we can more easily do something about it. Behavior geneticists would take issue with this argument, since it generates the expectation that a change in the environment would have the same consequences for all individuals. We have seen that this is certainly not the case. In the words of the prominent behavior geneticist Theodosius Dobzhansky, we should understand that "there are about as many different human natures as there are persons living," and then "take steps to provide conditions in which everybody, or as nearly everybody as possible, is able to do his best" (1968, p. 130).

SUMMARY □

One of the oldest questions in psychology is whether human behavior is determined by a person's ancestry or by upbringing. This question is unanswerable when stated in such extreme terms, for neither heredity nor environment can act independently of the other. The questions of greater interest are how and how much do genetic and environmental influences interact in determining behavior.

An important goal of the behavior geneticist is to separate the contributions of heredity and environment to particular traits. One method is the selective breeding of animals on the basis of marked presence or absence of a specific trait. Typically such matings are carried through successive generations, always mating the animals that are most similar behaviorally. Activity level, emotionality, and maze learning have all been investigated in the white rat, and the gradual separation of the offspring into distinct strains after generations of interbreeding indicates a genetic substrate to such behaviors. Other studies, however, have shown that these behaviors are not necessarily independent. Thus it is difficult to infer exactly what traits are transmitted from parent to offspring. The role of environment in determining particular behaviors is also indefinite. Environmental factors such as discipline and stimulation have been found to affect the behavior of different animal strains in different ways.

The norm of reaction is a key concept in discussing the nature-nurture interaction. It specifies that each genotype has a range of expression. No amount of environmental impact can cause a trait to exceed the upper or lower limits of this range, but the environment can determine its degree of expression within the range. For some traits the range of expression and the power of the environment to influence the phenotype are much greater than for the other traits. In addition, the same environment may have different effects upon different genotypes. The transactional model of development holds that individual traits are a product of the continual interplay between the genotype and environment over time.

INHERITANCE OF INTELLIGENCE

One of the most controversial topics in the field of psychology concerns the inheritance of intelligence. Much of the controversy has been fueled not so much by discrepancies in facts as by differences in ideologies. The extreme views that intelligence is fixed by heredity or that it is shaped by environment have been supported more by the proponents' philosophical, social, or political ideals than by any existing data. The evidence that has been collected in many types of studies indicates that intelligence *is* influenced strongly by heredity. But this does not mean that intelligence is unmalleable. As we shall see, environment also has a very real impact on intellectual functioning.

The evidence that intelligence has a genetic component comes from numerous correlation studies which have examined the following proposition. If heredity influences intelligence, there should be a greater similarity in intelligence among individuals who have more genes in common. Figure 9.11 summarizes the results of fifty-two separate studies that have correlated the intelligence test scores of individuals who have varying proportions of genes in common. Very similar IQ scores have been found for identical twins, who develop from a single fertilized egg and thus have identical genes. Scores of parents and their children, siblings, and fraternal twins, all of whom have about 50 percent of their genes in common, show a moderate degree of similarity. There is no correlation among the intelligence test scores of unrelated persons.

Heritability

Let us now move beyond the position that heredity is important and begin answering the question of how important. Central to this assessment is a statistical measure called a **heritability ratio.** This index provides a numerical estimate of the relative contributions of heredity and environment to the **variance (*V*)** of a given trait in a specific population. In a qualitative sense variance refers to the different expressions of the trait by the individuals of the population. In a quantitative sense a crude index of variance is the range of values for the trait. For IQs this range is

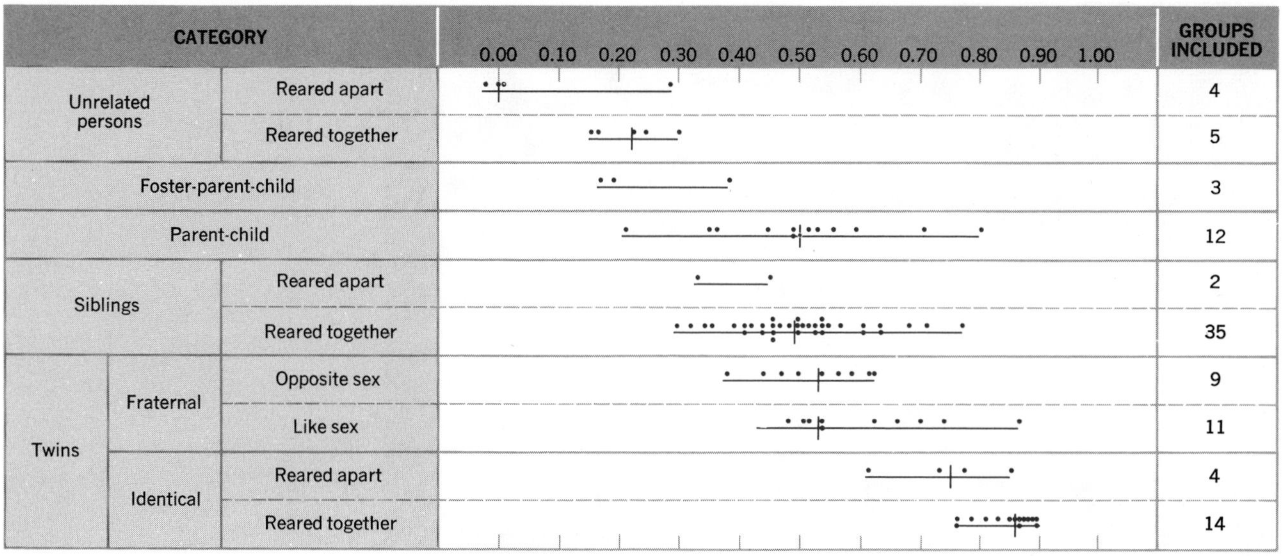

FIGURE 9.11

Correlation coefficients for "intelligence" test scores from fifty-two studies. Some studies reported data for more than one relationship category; some included more than one sample per category, giving a total of ninety-nine groups. Over two thirds of the correlation coefficients were derived from IQs, the remainder from other types of mental-ability tests. Correlations were made between each child's score and the mean of the parents' scores, when available. Otherwise, mother-child scores were employed. Correlation coefficients obtained in each study are indicated by dots; medians are shown by vertical lines intersecting the horizontal lines that represent the ranges. (From Erlenmeyer-Kimling and Jarvik, 1963.)

some 200 points, from nearly zero to over 200. As variance is applied in studies of heritability, it is a statistical measure with a very useful property; it can be separated into additive components that reflect different causes. (The actual statistic is described in the Statistical Appendix, page 498)

In the case of intelligence, for example, it is possible to separate total or phenotypic variance into a component reflecting heredity and a component reflecting environment. *The two separate components are themselves both variances.* Imagine a large number of individuals, all with identical inheritances but raised in different environments. Their IQs would vary as a result. The variance thus created would be **environmental variance,** symbolized by $V_{\text{environmental}}$. Individuals in a population usually have many different genotypes, however. Even if they could be reared in identical environments, they would not have the same IQ because of this genetic variation. This source of variance is **genetic variance,** symbolized by V_{genetic}.

The total **phenotypic variance,** $V_{\text{phenotypic}}$, is the sum of these components:

$$V_{\text{phenotypic}} = V_{\text{genetic}} + V_{\text{environmental}}$$

The heritability (H) of a trait is defined as the proportion of the total phenotypic variance that can be traced to genetic variance:

$$H = \frac{V_{\text{genetic}}}{V_{\text{phenotypic}}}$$

When genetic variation is more important than variations in environment in determining the trait variation, the **heritability ratio** will be large. When the variability of a trait comes more from the different environments experienced by the population members, the value of the heritability index will be small.

Twin Studies Most estimates of the heritability of human traits lean heavily upon comparisons of identical and same-sex fraternal twins. Identical twins are also known as **monozygotic twins** because they develop from a single fertilized egg; fraternal twins are known as **dizygotic twins** because they develop from two fertilized eggs. The logic behind the comparisons is as follows. Since identical twins have the same genes, they can show no genetic variation; any differences between the two members of each twin pair must come from environment alone. Fraternal twins, on the average, are identical in only 50 percent of their genes. Like identical twins, fraternal twins are assumed to have experiences that differ to some degree. Thus hereditary and environmental influ-

Tom and Dick Van Arsdale, identical twins, are strikingly alike physically and are both professional players.

ences together bring about differences in fraternal twins.

We have now isolated components very close to those required to compute an index of heritability: (1) a total variance reflecting both heredity and environment, based on the differences between pairs of fraternal twins, and (2) a variance caused by environment alone, based on differences between identical twins. The first value gives us the denominator we need for the heritability index, $V_{\text{phenotypic}}$. We can obtain the numerator V_{genetic} by subtracting the environmental variance based on identical twins from the total variance (heredity + environment) based on fraternal twins. From this information we can compute a heritability ratio. Usually the ratio is computed directly from correlation coefficients that express similarities between pairs of identical twins on the one hand and fraternal twins on the other.

Heritability ratios can range from a minimum of 0 to a maximum of 1.00. In general, when identical twins resemble each other in a trait much more than do same-sex fraternal twins, the heritability ratio is high. When differences between identical twins are the same as those between fraternal twins, heritability is zero. When similarities are modestly greater for identical twins than for fraternal, the heritability ratio is somewhere in between.

In Table 9.2 are listed heritability ratios for the trait of intelligence obtained from studies comparing twins. As can be seen, the ratios vary from study to study. This is true for two reasons. (1) The index is very sensitive to the genetic and environmental variations that actually exist in the population on which it is computed, and (2) the index varies when studies use different measures of a trait. It is clear, however, that for the populations studied and the tests used, variability in intelligence does have a substantial genetic component.

TABLE 9.2
Correlations and Heritability Ratios from Studies of Intelligence in Twins

Country	Year	Monozygotic (MZ) *r*	Dizygotic (DZ) *r*	*H*
England	1958	.97	.55	.93
U.S.A.	1932	.92	.61	.80
France	1960	.90	.60	.75
U.S.A.	1937	.90	.62	.74
Sweden	1953	.90	.70	.67
U.S.A.	1965	.87	.63	.65
U.S.A.	1968	.80	.48	.62
Sweden	1952	.89	.72	.61
England	1954	.76	.44	.57
England	1933	.84	.65	.54
Finland	1966	.69	.42	.51
England	1966	.83	.66	.50

Adapted from Vandenberg, 1971a.

Identical Twins Reared Apart A particularly powerful means of estimating heritability is through the comparison of identical twins who by some quirk of

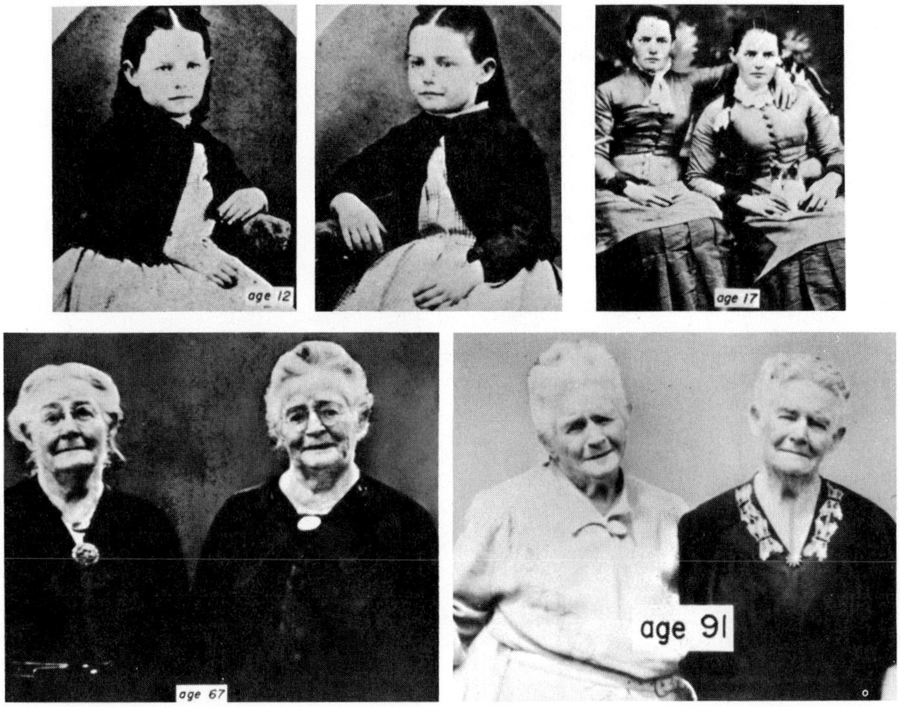

Identical twins before and after they had been separated for a long period of time, from the age of eighteen until they were sixty-five.

fate have been separated early in life and who have had different upbringings. If identical twins who are raised together are very similar in a trait, but those raised apart differ a great deal, this is strong evidence for the importance of environmental influences; the heritability ratio will therefore be low. If identical twins who are raised apart nevertheless resemble each other almost as much as those raised together, the evidence is strong that the trait is primarily influenced by genetic factors; the heritability ratio will thus be high. As can be seen in Figure 9.11 and Table 9.3, correlations of the IQ scores of identical twins reared apart remain quite high, thus providing further evidence of a hereditary influence on intelligence.

Heritability versus Actual Intelligence Scores

To gain a more realistic perspective of the relative contributions of heredity and environment to intelligence, we must consider the absolute scores underlying the correlations and heritability ratios just presented. It has been estimated that the average difference in IQ scores of identical twins reared together is 3 IQ points; for identical twins reared apart it is 6 points; for the same individual tested twice, 5 points; and for unrelated children paired randomly and drawn from the same community, 15 points (Tyler, 1965).

TABLE 9.3
Correlations of IQ Scores for Identical Twins Raised Together and for Identical Twins Raised Apart

Country	Year	Raised Apart	Raised Together
U.S.A.	1937	.77	.98
England	1958	.86	.92
England	1962	.77	.76
Denmark	1965	.62	—

Adapted from Vandenberg, 1971b.

In studies of monozygotic twins reared in markedly different environments, differences of 15 IQ points or even more have been obtained. In one study (Newman, Freeman, and Holzinger, 1937) a difference of 24 IQ points was found for thirty-five-year-old twins who had been separated in infancy. One of the twins had been reared in a backwoods rural community where she received only two years of formal schooling; the other twin had lived in a well-to-do farming community and received a college education. In this same study, however, only one IQ point separated two male twins, one of whom was raised by a truck farmer and the other by a well-to-do physician. Unfortunately, such diverse findings provide the raw material for any argument that the overcommitted hereditarian or environmentalist chooses to make. The environmentalist notes the case of the twins differing

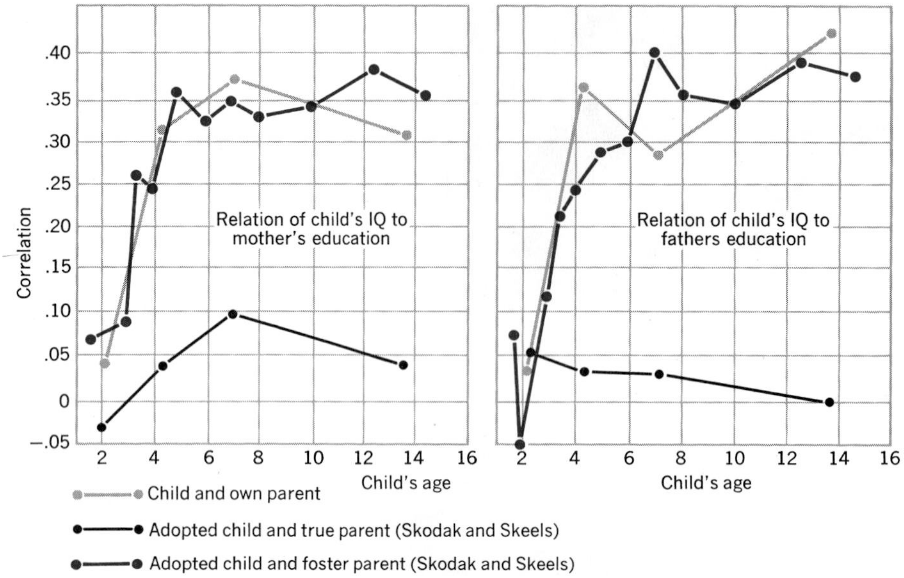

FIGURE 9.12
Intellectual resemblance of adopted children to true and foster parents, and of children to their own biological rearing parents. (Adapted from Honzik, 1957.)

by 24 IQ points, the hereditarian the pair differing by only one point.

In a general way, correlational studies tend to illustrate the genetic contribution to intelligence, whereas a focus on absolute scores illustrates the effects of environment. A series of studies of intelligence in adopted children made this point. Marie Skodak and Harold M. Skeels (1949) examined the intelligence scores of 100 adopted children who were tested at repeated intervals for a period of sixteen years. Educational level, which correlates highly with IQ, was available for both the biological and adoptive parents. With increasing age the adopted children's IQ scores became more highly correlated with the educational level of their *biological* parents than with that of their adoptive parents (Figure 9.12). In fact, a later study (Honzik, 1957) showed that the correlation found for adopted children and their biological parents in the Skodak and Skeels study was not very much different from that for children and their biological parents who had reared them (see Figure 9.12).

These findings have been interpreted as providing one of the strongest arguments that heredity is much more significant than environment in determining intelligence. An examination of the absolute scores, however, provides evidence for the importance of environment. The mean IQ of the sixty-three biological mothers of the adopted children was 86. The mean IQ of their children tested at adolescence was 106, a difference of 20 points! Although no hereditarian would expect parents and children to have equal IQs, even a high heritability ratio for intelligence could account for no more than half of this difference.

Special Intellectual Abilities

In the studies discussed to this point, intelligence has been treated as a unitary trait which can be represented by a single score. Intelligence, however, is not a unitary trait (page 239) but a collection of intellectual abilities. On the typical IQ test these abilities are measured separately, and the scores are then added to provide an omnibus intelligence score. Even if workers could agree on the value of the heritability ratio for such omnibus scores, this value would not indicate how much each intellectual ability is influenced by hereditary factors. Louis L. Thurstone (1941) found that seven intellectual abilities seemed to comprise intelligence, and he made them the focus of his *Primary Mental Abilities Tests*. These abilities are verbal comprehension (vocabulary), word fluency, spatial perception, numerical ability, reasoning, memory, and perceptual speed.

Four twin studies have examined the heritability of these abilities (Table 9.4). As do the heritability ratios for total IQ scores, those for specific abilities often differ markedly from study to study. The data suggest, however, that verbal ability, word fluency, and spatial ability have large genetic components. Evidence of strong genetic effects for number ability, reasoning, and memory is less consistent. (Perceptual speed was excluded from these studies.)

SUMMARY □

Populations show variability in a trait for both genetic and environmental reasons. One method of deter-

TABLE 9.4
Heritability Indices from Four Twin Studies for Six Primary Mental Ability Scores

Ability	Blewett (1954)	Thurstone (1955)	Vandenberg (1962)	Vandenberg (1966)
Verbal	.68	.64	.62	.43
Word fluency	.64	.59	.61	.55
Spatial	.51	.76	.59	.72
Number	.07	.34	.61	.56
Reasoning	.64	.26	.28	.09
Memory	—	.39	.20	—

Vandenberg, 1971a.

mining the relative importance of these two factors is the heritability ratio, which is actually an estimate of the proportion of trait variance having genetic causes. A high heritability ratio indicates that the trait has a large genetic component; a low ratio indicates that environment is of greater importance.

Most ways of computing the heritability of a trait rely on comparisons of identical twins, who differ because of environment alone, with fraternal twins, who differ for both genetic and environmental reasons. Studies of identical twins reared apart also provide evidence that traits remaining similar are more dependent on genes, whereas traits on which the twins differ are more influenced by environment. The comparison of adopted children with their biological and with their adoptive parents is another useful means of studying the relative importance of nature and nurture.

For the trait of intelligence, no final consensus has been reached on the relative contributions of heredity and of environment. In general, correlations of IQ scores among relatives increase in size as the degree of genetic relatedness increases. Heritability ratios and correlational data from studies of twins and adopted children also indicate that there is a sizable genetic component to intelligence. Changes in absolute scores demonstrate that environment is important.

RACE AND THE INHERITANCE OF BEHAVIOR

Current social and political issues, such as desegregation in our public schools and our attitudes and national posture toward newly emerging nations, make the question of racial differences in behavior an important one. Unfortunately, the problem is one of great complexity. At least three difficult questions are involved. (1) Are there measurable racial differences in behavior? (2) Are any differences that may be discovered inherent in the race, or can they be traced to cultural variations? Put in this way, the question is a part of the continuing dialogue that surrounds the nature-nurture problem. (3) Do any discovered differences in the races justify keeping various groups in a socially subservient position? This is not a scientific question, but it is one that cannot be ignored, for its presence in the background of what should be a straightforward scientific evaluation has often tainted the interpretation of data.

Evolution of Races

Before we can begin to address the problem of racial differences in behavior, it would be helpful to understand how the races came to be in the first place. Different races are formed when groups of people are isolated from one another in differing environments. Over time the group comes to differ from other groups in the frequency of one or more genes. A biological definition of a **race,** then, is a group distinguished by the frequency of certain genes or traits, a frequency different from that found in other populations.

Natural Selection The most important process that brings about the difference in gene frequencies among races is **natural selection.** Within every population there are persons with different genetic makeups. Certain genetic traits help the individual adapt to and survive in the particular environment. People with genes that provide such an advantage are more likely to survive and to reproduce than are individuals whose genetic makeup does not give them this advantage. Thus, over time, genes disadvantageous for adaption become fewer, whereas genes that provide a survival advantage become more numerous, until they come to characterize the **gene pool,** the collection of genes available to the population. Furthermore, since environments differ, it would be expected that genes advantageous in one environment might not be advantageous in another. Therefore, over the course of evolution, populations in different geographic regions have come to vary from one another in their genetic makeups.

For example, early man's skin was the filter that controlled the absorption of sunlight. Sunlight causes a layer of tissue just under the skin to produce vitamin D. If too little vitamin D is produced, the individual suffers from the softening of the bones associated with rickets. With too much vitamin D, bones become brittle and are easily broken. Thus in northern climates there was a selective pressure favoring fair skins that could pass the faint rays of the northern sun. Nearer the equator, however, natural selection favored a heavy pigmentation that reduced the amount of sun penetrating the skin. Since individuals suffering from either rickets or frequent bone fractures are less likely to produce offspring than are healthy individuals, the genes underlying the right degree of pigmentation for the particular climate came to multiply through progeny until they were representative for the population.

To cite another example, the long-limbed, slim bodies of African black populations yield a high surface-to-volume ratio that allows heat to dissipate into the environment. The short-limbed, fleshy body of the Eskimo is equally valuable in a cold climate, since it conserves heat. The survival value of many traits, such as the distinctive shapes of eyes, ears, and lips found in different populations, is not clear, however. Nor is it evident why males in some South American Indian tribes have blue penises (Goldsby, 1971).

Behavior and Evolution Given the many physical differences among races, might not various racial groups possess different genes for social and psychological traits as well? Certainly the social behavior of the Bantu tribesman differs from that of the Alaskan Eskimo, and the manner of neither resembles that of the Rotarian on Main Street, U.S.A. It would be an error, however, to assume that these marked differences in behavior are necessarily related to differences in genetic structure. It would seem more realistic to explain them in terms of widely varying environments and cultural histories.

Nevertheless, there is a certain appeal to the notion that in the process of natural selection differing racial groups found certain psychological traits to be valuable in adapting to their particular environments. For example, aggression could be construed as a more essential trait in hunting populations than in those whose diet is mainly vegetarian. That natural selection does act on behavioral traits is being demonstrated in animals by the new science of sociobiology. But whether natural selection has determined human behavior remains unknown. A number of sociobiologists have generated a heated controversy by suggesting that many human behavioral traits are genetically determined and subject to the same evolutionary principles that govern the inheritance of biological structure. Before this view can be accepted, however, it must be shown that the behavioral traits are not transmitted through cultural experiences and learning.

Race and Intelligence

By far the largest number of investigations on behavioral differences in races have had to do with the intelligence of American whites and blacks. Since these two groups differ in respect to the frequencies of particular genes, they satisfy the definition for being different races. On the other hand, they are far from pure races in that there has been considerable intermating. As B. E. Ginsburg has noted, ". . . American Negroes have received 20 to 30 percent of their genes from the white population . . . [and] we are, therefore, closer to being brothers under the skin than phenotypic appearance would suggest" (1971, p. 232).

The empirical finding of countless studies that American blacks and whites do have IQ differences has never been in dispute. Yet the interpretation of these findings has for many decades constituted one of the bitterest controversies in psychology. Across all studies the difference between the two groups is about 15 IQ points, with whites having a mean IQ of approximately 100 and blacks a mean of approximately 85. This 15-point difference is quickly reduced to 11 points if one takes the minimal trouble of seeing that the blacks and whites being compared are of the same socioeconomic status.

What is responsible for this 11-point difference? There is no clear answer to this question, because such an answer could only be obtained in an experiment that is impossible to conduct. That experiment would involve testing the intelligence of equally healthy black and white children reared in virtually identical environments; the children would even have to be matched for the quality of their prenatal care and surroundings. The children's homes would have to be the same in all respects related to intellectual growth, and their experiences would have to be totally devoid of prejudice directed against any race.

Although this situation is a fantasy, one procedure used to study racial differences in intelligence at least attempts to control for environmental differences. One way of meeting the criterion that homes be "the same in all respects related to intellectual growth" is to study the IQ scores of black children raised in white homes. In one such study (Scarr and Weinberg, 1978) black and interracial adolescents who had been adopted in their first year of life by white middle- or upper-class families were found to have a mean IQ of 110. There was no reason to believe that the biological parents of these adolescents were above average in intelligence. Thus being raised by white, well-to-do families raised the IQ scores of these blacks 10 points above the mean IQ of the white population and approximately 25 points above the mean IQ of black children raised by their own families.

These results are very difficult to interpret. Do parents who adopt children of a different race try harder? Do the children? What about the effects of prejudice against interracial adoption, which in many ways can be worse than that directed against minorities? Studies of interracial adoption hold promise for illuminating the causes of the IQ difference between blacks and whites, but this approach needs considerable refinement lest it raise more questions than it answers.

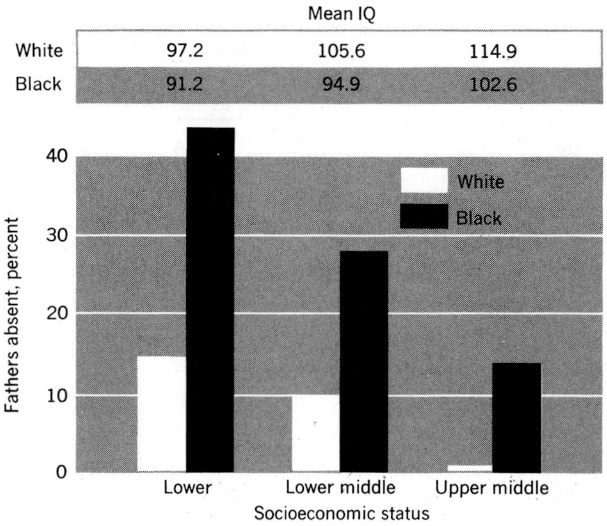

FIGURE 9.13
Nonverbal IQ scores of white and black children of different socioeconomic status, and the percentage of their fathers absent from home. (Adapted from Deutsch and Brown, 1964.)

The Jensen Controversy In 1969 Arthur Jensen, an educational psychologist, published a monograph that captured the nation's attention and created a furor. The bulk of the monograph was a scholarly discussion of the evidence concerning the genetic component in intelligence and had nothing to do with racial differences in IQ. Jensen concluded that the genetic component was substantial and thought that the best estimate of the heritability ratio for intelligence was .80. This figure, you will recall, is on the high side, but within the range of values reported in Table 9.2 (page 214).

Had Jensen written no more than this, his paper would have created no furor and would have been counted as one more analysis indicating that heredity is indeed important in determining intelligence. In a relatively brief section of his paper, however, Jensen went beyond this and hypothesized that since the intelligence of individuals is so influenced by inheritance, the mean IQ differences of the races might be caused by differences in their genetic endowment for intelligence. Jensen argued that the greater the variation in a trait known to be ascribable to genetic factors, the greater the likelihood that the difference in that trait in two populations is caused at least in part by the genetic differences of the two groups.

The great controversy aroused by Jensen's paper led John Loehlin, Gardner Lindzey, and James Spuhler (1975) to undertake an extensive review of the research on racial and ethnic group differences in intelligence. They examined studies of heritability of intelligence in black and white persons, studies of intelligence in mixed-race children, and studies of patterns of abilities among different racial and ethnic groups. Their conclusion was that the observed average differences in the intelligence test scores of American racial and ethnic groups could not be explained on the basis of genetic differences alone. Other factors, such as differences in the environmental conditions of the groups and inadequacies and biases in the tests, also affect performance. These factors will be discussed in turn.

Social status We have seen that grossly equating whites and blacks on socioeconomic status reduces their average IQ difference from 15 to 11 points. Even this matching, however, does not truly equate the groups on their environmental experiences. Important differences remain.

- Even within the same social class, the two racial groups often have markedly different environments. In terms of health factors, for example, black children often have a poorer prenatal and early postnatal environment than white children of the same class, as evidenced by the higher infant mortality rate among blacks.
- Of special importance for the type of achievement reflected in test scores is whether the child comes from a stable family headed by both parents. In all social classes there are more broken homes among blacks, defined by the absence of the father (Figure 9.13).
- The stultifying effects of prejudice itself are especially difficult to eradicate. Until our society divests itself of the view that blacks are second-class citizens—and the destructive behavior that emanates from such a view—we will never know exactly how much white racism has itself attentuated the IQ scores of black children.

Tests Differences in the intelligence of blacks and whites are only differences in scores on particular tests of intelligence. These tests have been constructed on the basis of the performance of whites and

TABLE 9.5
Mean IQs of Black Children with Varying Periods of Residence in Philadelphia

	Mean IQ at Grade Listed					
Group	**N**	**1A**	**2B**	**4B**	**6B**	**9A**
Born in Philadelphia —no kindergarten	424	92.1	93.4	94.7	94.0	93.7
Southern-born—entered Philadelphia schools in grade: 1A	182	86.5	89.3	91.8	93.3	92.8
1B-2B	109		86.7	88.6	90.9	90.5
3A-4B	199			86.3	87.2	89.4
5A-6B	221				88.2	90.2
7A-9A	219					87.4

Adapted from Lee, 1951.

therefore have a cultural bias which favors whites (page 237). For instance, many of the words in the vocabulary portions of the tests are much more likely to be encountered in the white culture than in the black.

A more basic problem with intelligence tests is whether they really measure intelligence. Intelligence is all the processes that assist the individual in adapting to the environment. Our standard IQ tests sample just a few of the abilities known to comprise intelligence (see page237).Perhaps when more comprehensive intelligence tests are developed, differences in the test scores of blacks and whites will disappear.

Motivation and test-taking behavior Test scores are not perfect indicators of a child's ability to answer test items correctly. In interpreting any test score, we must distinguish performance from ability. A variety of factors has been found to depress the test scores of black children. They have less motivation to score highly on tests because their aspirations are lower (Katz, 1968); they have greater anxiety in the test situation (Zigler, Abelson, and Seitz, 1973); and they are perhaps inhibited when tested by an adult member of a different race (Sattler, 1970). Given these drawbacks, the test scores of black children may very well be less adequate indicators of their intellectual abilities than are the test scores of white children.

Educational opportunity There is geographical variation in the IQ scores of blacks and whites. This variation is probably related to the different amounts that states spend for education and to the amounts spent within each state to educate blacks and whites. Spuhler and Lindzey (1967) found higher intelligence scores for both blacks and whites who were residents of states that had a higher per capita expenditure for education. Although within states whites consistently scored higher than blacks, some groups of Northern blacks scored higher than some groups of Southern whites.

The effects of better schooling in the North were seen in a study of black children who had migrated to Philadelphia. As indicated in Table 9.5, the longer children lived in Philadelphia, the higher their IQs became. The group who entered school in the first grade (1A) had a mean IQ of 86.5; this had increased by 92.8 by the ninth grade (9A). Furthermore, in virtually all grades the earlier children had begun their studies in the schools, the better they did in comparison with those who were latecomers to the school system.

These four factors are at least partially responsible for the 11-point difference in the IQs of blacks and whites. How much of this difference such factors can account for is currently unknown. But it is clear that a thorough evaluation of the impact of environmental experiences on racial differences in IQ needs to be made.

Race Differences and Racism

If racial differences in psychological functioning are eventually established, they will be differences between average values for groups and will reveal little about the traits of any one member of a particular race. Average differences between races are one thing; differences between individual members of the same race are another matter entirely. The student will do well to learn and remember the following general principle because it is so basic. *The variation in psychological traits among individual members of a race is always greater than the average difference between races.*

This principle is clearly demonstrated with IQ scores. For white children variations in IQ range approximately from a rare low near zero to an equally rare high above 200. For black children the range is exactly the same. The 15-point difference in mean IQ scores of blacks and whites is therefore much less than the variability among members of the same race (200 points). In addition, the fact that the range of IQ scores for blacks and whites is the same means that there is tremendous overlap in the scores of the two races.

Of late, the pejorative term racist has been used so gratuitously as to rob it of all meaning. In an attempt to restore a measure of sense to the discussion, we make the following distinction. An individual who investigates racial differences, while at the same time appreciating the variation within a race, is not a racist. A **racist** is an individual who ignores individual variation and concludes that because members of group A get a higher average score on some measure than members of group B, every member of group A is "superior" to every member of group B.

Whatever the outcome of investigations of racial differences, there is clearly no ethical basis for allowing either proven or unproven group differences to affect how people are treated.

SUMMARY ☐

Biologically, races are groups that differ in a variety of traits because of different frequencies of particular genes. These varying genetic makeups emerged over the course of evolution as natural selection acted on groups living in different environments.

Studies of racial differences in behavior have been numerous, but their results have been difficult to interpret since so many factors are uncontrolled or uncontrollable when comparing races. For example, although racial differences in IQ are frequently found, there are also racial differences in factors known to affect test performance. Among these are socioeconomic standing, medical care, nutrition, and prejudice. In addition, cultural bias in tests, motivational factors influencing test-taking behavior, and quality of schooling favor the white group. An important principle to consider when comparing behavioral differences of races is that the variability found within any given race is large compared with the variation between any two races.

APPLICATIONS OF GENETIC PRINCIPLES

With rapid gains in knowledge in the fields of genetics and reproduction, we may soon attain incredible power over our genetic future. Before long we may be able to overcome genetic diseases, improve particular genes, and alter gene frequencies in the population. These possibilities evoke both enthusiasm and fear—enthusiasm that genetic manipulations may greatly improve the lot of humankind, and fear that this new power, if not used wisely, may become yet another tool that can ultimately destroy the human race.

Eugenics

Concern for the genetic potential of the human species has a long history. The ancient Greek philosopher Plato wrote in his *Republic* that if we do not wish to see the human race degenerate, we should apply some lessons learned from breeders of hunting dogs and birds of prey. That is, we should encourage unions between the better members of the population and limit matings of the worse. This concern for our genetic potential and methods for improving it have come to be known as **eugenics,** a term coined by Sir Francis Galton in 1883. Galton also made some rather pragmatic proposals to improve the human gene pool, such as urging men and women of superior family stock to have large families and giving fellowships to good students so they could marry and produce children.

The eugenics movement was very influential in many parts of the world in the early part of the twentieth century. In America many states enacted compulsory sterilization laws to prevent the reproduction of "sexual perverts," "drug fiends," "diseased and degenerate persons," and "drunkards." In addition, restrictive immigration laws were written to limit the number of southern and eastern Europeans who could settle and thereby "mix" in the population. In England Karl Pearson, a disciple of Galton, continually employed genetic arguments in an effective effort to stem the immigration of Polish and Russian Jews. He wrote, "Taken *on the average,* and regarding both sexes, this alien Jewish population is somewhat inferior physically and mentally to the native population" (quoted in Hirsch, 1970, pp. 92–93). It is interesting to note that less than fifty years after Pearson's assertion of the genetic inferiority of Jews, another distinguished Englishman, C. P. Snow, argued that in light of the large number of Jewish Nobel laureates, Jews must be a superior people. We thus see how tenuous indeed are those assertions that a particular group is inferior or superior.

Eugenic principles were carried to their ultimate extreme in Nazi Germany, where some six million people, most of them Jews, were murdered so they would not contaminate the "superior" German race. Worldwide shock over this tragedy, coupled with the realization that genetic worth is largely in the eye of the beholder, has led most societies to abandon the eugenics movement.

Medical Genetics

Today scientists have moved beyond the simplistic notions of genetic superiority and inferiority to the more humane problems of preventing and ameliorating genetic disease. About one in ten gametes in the general population carries bad genetic news, caused by a **mutation** or change in a gene or chromosome (Gardner, 1975). The majority of mutations are deleterious, and most embryos bearing abnormal genes are miscarried. About 2 percent of newborns, however, suffer recognizable genetic defects. Agents that can cause mutations include environmental radiation, certain drugs, some of the compounds in smog, and viral infections. The most effective single way of preventing genetic disease is to prevent mutations by eliminating hazardous materials from the environment and protecting people from those that cannot be totally eliminated.

Genetic Screening and Counseling There are numerous genetic diseases that are caused by defective genes already present in the population gene pool. Some of these genes are more frequently found in certain ethnic groups and family lineages than in others. Jews of eastern European descent, for example, are more likely than the rest of the population to carry the gene for *Tay-Sachs disease.* This disorder causes blindness, brain deterioration, paralysis, and finally death within the first two or three years of life. The disease is inherited as a recessive trait and only appears in children who receive the Tay-Sachs gene from both parents. A blood test now available can determine whether a man and woman planning a family are carriers of the gene. If only one of them is a carrier, none of their children will have the disease, although one in two will be carriers. If both husband and wife are carriers, each child will have a 25 percent chance of inheriting the disease.

Blood tests are also available to detect carriers of other genetic disorders, including *sickle-cell anemia,* a blood cell disorder typically found in the black population, and *thalassemia,* a related anemia, generally of persons of Mediterranean origin. Individuals who are discovered to be carriers of particular genetic diseases, and those who have genetic disorders in their family backgrounds, can receive advice from genetic counselors on the risk of passing these on to their children. On the basis of the odds, the individual can decide whether or not to have any children.

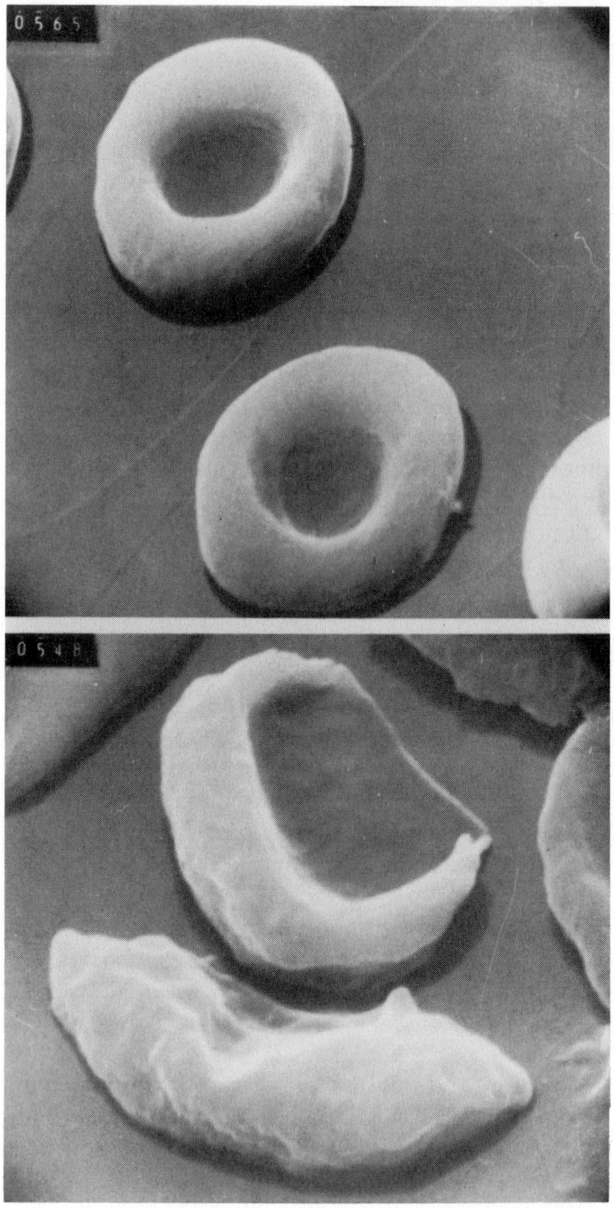

Normal red blood cells *(top)* and sickle cells *(bottom)*, enlarged 17,000 times by the electron microscope. Defective hemoglobin of the sickle-cell patient precipitates when deoxygenated; aggregating crystals distort the cell.

Prenatal Diagnosis and Treatment Those at risk for passing on certain genetic diseases can take the gamble with greater confidence now that specific tests to determine whether an unborn child has a particular disorder are available. Some prenatal diagnostic tests can be carried out on the blood of the pregnant woman. For example, spina bifida, a crippling and fatal neurological disorder, and anencephaly, the lack of a major portion of the brain, can be detected in this manner.

A procedure that has enabled the prenatal detection of many more genetic abnormalities is **amniocentesis.** In the uterus the baby is surrounded by the amnion, a fluid-filled sac which contains, among other things, skin cells shed by the fetus. In amniocentesis some amniotic fluid is withdrawn from the uterus of the expectant mother through a special needle. Both the fluid and cells are then tested for a variety of biochemical abnormalities that signal the presence of a genetic defect. Close to eighty biochemical disorders can now be detected prenatally, including Tay-Sachs disease and thalassemia.

The cells of the fetus can also be tested for chromosomal abnormalities. The cells are grown in the laboratory to a certain stage of cell division when chromosomal analysis can be performed. For example,

Down syndrome, a condition characterized by a broad face, slanted eyes, shortened limbs, and mental retardation, can be detected in a karyotype by the presence of an extra number 21 chromosome. A woman's chances of having a baby with Down syndrome increase dramatically each year after the age of thirty-five. For this reason it is recommended that older pregnant women undergo amniocentesis so that the fetal chromosomes can be analyzed.

Sickle-cell anemia and some other genetic disorders cannot be detected either in the amniotic fluid or through analysis of the fetal cells; the blood of the fetus itself is needed. A new technique, which is currently being perfected, enables a doctor to collect a few drops of fetal blood and test it for these disorders.

An important goal of diagnosing a genetic defect prenatally is to treat the child while still in the womb or soon after birth. Treatment can now be administered through the mother or directly to the fetus for a few disorders such as *Rh blood disease* and *methylmalonic aciduria,* a biochemical defect which causes poor muscle tone and mental retardation and prevents the infant from thriving. No prenatal treatment is yet possible, however, for the majority of serious and fatal genetic diseases, although progress is being made. As more knowledge is gathered and as genetic counseling becomes more widely available, it is hoped that many of these tragic disorders can some day be eliminated.

Genetic Engineering

Over ninety human disorders are associated with specific enzyme deficiencies that are known to be genetically determined. These disorders are sometimes called inborn errors of metabolism. One of them is *phenylketonuria* (PKU), in which a single gene defect causes an insufficiency in the enzyme phenylalanine hydroxylase. Because of the lack of this one enzyme, which metabolizes the amino acid phenylalanine, the brain becomes badly damaged and mental retardation results. Currently, newborns may be screened for PKU by a simple blood or urine test. Children who have the disorder are maintained on a very specialized diet. Although this treatment is effective in preventing the retardation, it is very expensive and must be strictly observed for a number of years.

A far simpler way of treating PKU and similar genetic disorders would be to repair defective genes, if only we had the ability. Gene manipulation may not be as far off as we would imagine. Already bacteria have been given the ability to form the gene that carries instructions for producing the hormone insulin. Bacteria in nature do not have this gene. This feat has been accomplished by splicing into the genetic material of the bacteria the section of DNA from rat cells that specifies the hormone.

Given the progress already made in **genetic engineering** techniques, we might one day be able to restore the genes for producing phenylalanine hydroxylase or other necessary chemicals, either by synthesizing the genetic code for the chemical and adding it to the cell or by transplanting a normal gene for the chemical from a healthy cell. Of course, much more research needs to be done before any gene repair can successfully be carried out.

Despite the possible benefits, many scientists and laymen are urging that research in the area of transplanting and recombining genes of different animal species be discontinued. They fear that unnatural organisms harmful to humans may be produced in the laboratory and escape into the environment. Since adequate safeguards are so essential, most recombinant DNA research is being conducted in conformity with government safety guidelines.

Another extreme form of genetic engineering is **cloning.** This is an asexual form of reproduction in which all progeny are genetically identical. Several years ago an African clawed frog was produced by cloning. The experimenter, J. B. Gurdon (1968), obtained an unfertilized egg cell from a frog, destroyed the nucleus, and replaced it with the nucleus from an intestinal cell of a tadpole. The egg, now containing the full complement of chromosomes characteristic of its species, began to divide and grow as though it had been fertilized. The resulting frog was an identical replica of the tadpole that served as the nuclear donor.

Recently, a science writer caused a stir by claiming that the cloning of a man has already been achieved. The consensus of scientific opinion is that, for now, cloning techniques have this degree of sophistication only in science fiction. This kind of publicity and the fear that particular individuals and their many "carbon" copies will try to take over the world have made people want to restrict further research on cloning. With adequate safeguards, however, cloning may prove useful in research on chromosomes, cancer, aging, and organ transplants.

Cloning and manipulating genes are the most spectacular but not the only means of altering heredity material. Even the relatively simpler procedures of genetic counseling, amniocentesis, abortion, artificial insemination, test tube conception, and contraception are powerful tools for tampering with the genetic inheritance of our species. These techniques can be used to increase our understanding and control of genetic disease, and they can greatly alleviate human suffering. Indiscriminate use of these tools to gratify selfish and temporary needs can be extremely dangerous, however.

The choice of a baby's sex is an example. An older pregnant woman reportedly underwent amniocentesis to discover whether her child had Down syndrome. Upon receiving the chromosomal analysis, the doctor gave her the good news that she was carrying a perfectly normal baby girl. The woman promptly elected to have an abortion, hoping that the next child she conceived would be a boy.

Most couples would probably be reluctant to undertake the expense and inherent physical danger of repeated amniocenteses and abortions for the mere pleasure of selecting their child's sex. If, however, a simple technique could increase the chances of their having either a boy or a girl, many couples might give it a try. Such a technique is now under study, but let us consider what might happen if a foolproof method was indeed available.

It is well known that in most societies sons are preferred to daughters. If many couples practiced some technique to increase the probability of their having sons, drastic changes in society could conceivably occur. First there would be a decrease in the population, since fewer women would be available to have babies. This of course could alter the entire economic system. The institutions of marriage and the family might have to be revamped, or even replaced by a system of polyandry, with women having more than one husband. Thus even a simple procedure for genetic control could have a tremendous impact on the whole structure of a society.

Of perhaps greater significance is the impact that procedures to control our reproduction and genes might have on the genetic pool and ultimately on the survival of our species. If we were to decide that a particular combination of traits was valuable, we could use all the genetic engineering techniques at our disposal to promote these traits in the population. These efforts would in time decrease our genetic diversity. Since there is no way of knowing what the nature of the environment will be in the far future, we could breed out genes that might someday have survival value for our species.

As the techniques for choosing who shall or shall not be born and what traits they shall have become better developed and more widespread, we will have to examine the implications that these choices may have for our society and for humankind's genetic inheritance. It is clear that in applying even the simplest of these techniques, we are adding our hand to the force of natural selection. The question is whether we can ever be wise enough to direct the future evolution of the human race.

SUMMARY □

People have long wanted to improve human genetic potential. The eugenics movement of the early part of the twentieth century focused on how to safeguard the quality of our gene pool. With gains in knowledge in the fields of genetics and reproduction, concern has shifted to the prevention of genetic disease. Today individuals can be screened to determine whether they are carriers of particular genetic disorders and counseled on the risk of passing on genetic defects to their offspring. Certain genetic diseases can be detected prenatally by examining a sample of the amniotic fluid surrounding the fetus, some of the fetal cells found in this fluid, or the maternal or fetal blood. A few diseases may even be treated while the child is still in the uterus.

Research on gene repair and cloning may someday help to alleviate the human suffering caused by genetic disease. The indiscriminate and widespread application of genetic engineering techniques, however, may have serious consequences for society. It is essential that human genetic diversity be maintained in order to preserve our ability to adapt in future environments.

TO BE SURE YOU UNDERSTAND THIS CHAPTER △

The important concepts of this chapter listed here are also defined in the dictionary at the end of this book. You should know the meaning of all of them.

Gene
F_1, or first filial generation
Law of segregation
Germ cell
Allele
Homozygous
Heterozygous
Dominant gene
Recessive gene
Law of independent assortment
Albinism
Genotype
Phenotype
Norm of reaction
Polygenic inheritance
Chromosome
DNA
Zygote
Karyotype
Gamete
Turner syndrome
Klinefelter syndrome
XYY male
Selective breeding

Nature-nurture interaction
Transactional model of development
Variance
Environmental variance
$V_{\text{environmental}}$
Genetic variance
V_{genetic}
Phenotypic variance
$V_{\text{phenotypic}}$
Heritability ratio (H)
Monozygotic twins
Dizygotic twins
Race
Natural selection
Gene pool
Racist
Eugenics
Mutation
Amniocentesis
Genetic engineering
Cloning

This chapter contains a number of more minor concepts that you should know to help fill in the picture.

PTC
Primary Mental Abilities Tests
Tay-Sachs disease
Sickle-cell anemia
Thalassemia
Down syndrome
Rh blood disease
Methylmalonic aciduria
Phenylketonuria

Finally, several points that are not well covered by a listing of concepts should be reviewed.

Selective breeding studies of emotionality and maze learning
Twin studies and the inheritance of intelligence
The Jensen controversy
Variation in psychological traits among and within races

TO GO BEYOND THIS CHAPTER △

In this book The nature-nurture issue comes up in connection with every psychological topic. There are briefer discussions of the heritability of psychological functions in Chapter 4, on perception, and in Chapter 5 in connection with alcoholism. Chapters 10, 11, and 12 add to the discussion in the context of cognitive development. In Chapter 14 the issue becomes whether motives are inborn or learned. Chapter 15 examines the degree to which heredity and learning influence the development of emotions, temperament, attachment, and sex roles. Chapter 18 has substantial material on the inheritance of mental disorders. The Statistical Appendix presents one easy formula for the calculation of heritability.

Elsewhere An excellent textbook of genetics is Eldon Gardner's *Principles of Genetics,* which contains detailed accounts of genetic mechanisms and genetic engineering. A clear and readable discussion of medical genetics can be found in Aubrey Milunsky's *Know Your Genes. Evolution, Genetics, and Man,* by Theodosius Dobzhansky, provides a thorough treatment of how natural selection and adaptation to the environment are important in the process of evolution. For a clear discussion of polygenic models of inheritance, G. E. McClearn's chapter in *Psychology in the Making,* edited by Leo Postman, is recommended. A book that brings together the best literature on the nature-nurture controversy over intelligence is N. J. Block and Gerald Dworkin's *The IQ Controversy.* A standard reference on behavior genetics, John Fuller and William Thompson's *Foundations of Behavior Genetics,* contains an excellent discussion of genetic principles and of animal and human behavior genetics studies.

CH. 10

The Nature of Intelligence

Intelligence is a human trait or characteristic that we all possess. When the term is used in everyday conversation, no one has difficulty comprehending it. Variations in intelligence were probably recognized by the earliest cavemen who knew that their animal hunt would be more successful if dumb Throg were left at home and smarter Zeeg went in his place. But what abilities did Throg lack and Zeeg have that led to this evaluation by their peers? A better sense of smell? Tracking ability? Courage? Speed of foot? Whatever the specific answer, intelligence to the caveman was intimately related to the individual's effectiveness in carrying out real-life tasks.

In this general sense, not very much has changed in what we consider to be intelligence. To the layman the intelligent person still is one who effectively meets life's challenges and the unintelligent person is one who does not. What has changed are the specific abilities that are useful for coping with life's problems. In this age of high-speed communication and the computer, intelligence has much more to do with verbal and mathematical abilities than it does with the ability to track large animals. Thus modern definitions of intelligence tend to emphasize cognition, the capacity to think, reason, remember, and understand. This discussion illuminates an important aspect of our conceptions of intelligence. They are arbitrary and culture-bound. Intelligence consists of the abilities that a society values because they are useful in meeting the society's current needs. When these needs change, the abilities that define intelligence change. Intelligence tests reflect these practical interpretations of intelligence. They also reflect opinions about the nature of intelligence.

In 1889 Alfred Binet cofounded the first French psychological laboratory at the Sorbonne. His early interests were hypnotism, the abnormal personality, and suggestibility.

HISTORY OF INTELLIGENCE TESTING

The very earliest tests of intelligence were based on the assumption that intelligence has a physiological basis. At the time many scientists were convinced of the heritability of intelligence. Moreover, physiologists had discovered that neural impulses took time to traverse the nervous system, and some thought that speed of neural functioning might determine intelligence. It made sense, then, to attempt to assess intelligence by measuring physiological processes.

Early mental measurement consisted of tests of sensorimotor functioning, sensory acuity, and reaction time. Even muscular strength and breathing capacity were sometimes tested, perhaps because of Sir Francis Galton's belief that the fine tuning of the nervous systems of intelligent people extended to their bodies and made them physically vigorous. By the end of the nineteenth century, however, psychologists were aware that such tests did not adequately assess mental functioning in the practical sense of the concept. Performance on these tests was not related to how well children did in school or how intelligent their teachers thought them to be. It became clear that to be adequate indicators of intelligence, tests would have to assess higher mental abilities rather than physiological processes. This view was the central tenet of the work by Alfred Binet (1857–1911), the French psychologist who developed the first widely used tests of intelligence.

Alfred Binet

Binet devoted his career to the study and measurement of intelligence and was particularly interested in the intellectual differences among individuals. Although he never totally abandoned tests of sensorimotor behavior, Binet rejected such tests as the ultimate measure of individual differences in intelligence. Instead, he suggested that ten "mental functions" be tested in assessing intelligence: memory, imagery, imagination, attention, comprehension, suggestibility, aesthetic appreciation, moral sentiments, muscular force (will power), and motor skill. Binet did not view these functions as independent and unrelated elements of the mind, but rather as spe-

TABLE 10.1
Computation of MA from a Hypothetical Distribution of Test Items Passed on the Stanford-Binet Intelligence Scale

Year Level of Test		Number of Items Passed	Credit	
			Years	Months
Basal level	– Year 8	All items	8	0
	– Year 9	4	0	8
	– Year 10	3	0	6
	– Year 11	2	0	4
Terminal level	– Year 12	0	0	0
		Total MA =	8	18
			or 9 years, 6 months	

cific abilities that reflected some more basic underlying general ability.

By 1900 Binet had developed a number of intelligence tests. He administered many of these to his two adolescent daughters over a three-year period, and in 1903 he published *The Experimental Study of Intelligence*, an exhaustive report of the test results.

Over the course of this investigation, Binet could not help noticing that the girls performed better on the tests as they grew older. Herein lay the seed of a major breakthrough in our understanding of intelligence. As obvious as it now seems, it was extremely important to recognize explicitly that whatever intelligence might be, older children have more of it than younger ones. Intelligence therefore became conceptualized as age-related, and test constructors defined the difficulty of a test item by the ability of children of different ages to respond to it correctly.

The Binet-Simon Tests During Binet's time French schools were confronted with the problem of determining which children could benefit from normal schooling and which could not. Compulsory education had been established, and since classes were age-graded, less intelligent children often fell behind their age-mates in school performance. The Ministry of Education wished to set up classes for "dull" children so that they too could gain the "benefits of instruction."

Binet was given the task of developing an instrument that could objectively identify children in need of special education. In 1905, in collaboration with Théophile Simon, Binet constructed a formal test which consisted of thirty items in an ascending order of difficulty. For example, item 1 required the child to follow a lighted candle with the head and eyes, item 4 to recognize the difference between a square of chocolate and a square of wood; item 20 was a comparison of two lines of slightly unequal length; item 30 called for the definition of abstract words. Binet and Simon again found that older children could pass more of the items than younger children.

Binet and Simon published two subsequent revisions of the 1905 test scale. The 1908 revision included almost twice as many items as the original scale and was organized in a way that was to be embodied in all future versions of the test. The items were classified by age levels extending from three to thirteen years. An item's age placement was determined by the percentage of children—ranging from 50 to 90 percent—of that age level who could pass it. The 1911 version, except for one instance, included five different items at each of the age levels.

The Concepts of Mental Age and IQ The way was thus paved for the development of a measure of intelligence that is still in use, namely the **mental age (MA).** The MA was computed by first finding the age level at which the child passed all the test items—now known as the **basal age** or basal level. More difficult items were then given until the child reached an age level, called the terminal or **ceiling level,** at which all the items were failed. Since there were five items at each age level, the child's MA was the basal age plus one fifth of a year for each of the items passed above the basal. Table 10.1 presents an example of the MA computation on the Stanford-Binet Intelligence Scale, an American revision of the 1911 Binet test. Since the Stanford-Binet has six items at most age levels instead of five, one sixth of a year, or two months, of MA credit is given for each item passed beyond the basal level.

The MA is interpreted quite literally. A nine-year-old child who receives an MA of six is functioning at the intellectual level expected of the average six-year-old and would be considered below average in intelligence. A six-year-old child who attains an MA of nine is functioning at a level expected of the average nine-year-old and would be considered quite bright.

The MA is thus a measure of the *absolute* level of intelligence. For many purposes, however, it is useful to assess *relative* intelligence by considering the relation between the individual's mental age and **chronological age (CA).** A relative measure indicates how a child's absolute level of intelligence compares to that of other children of the same age. Such a brightness ratio was first computed in 1912 when the German psychologist Louis Stern recommended the division of MA by CA. This measure was later developed into the **intelligence quotient,** or **IQ,** which is obtained by multiplying the MA/CA ratio by 100 in order to eliminate decimals. The formula IQ = MA/CA × 100 was used for many years to compute intelligence scores.

American Revisions of Binet's Scales

The major force in bringing the Binet test into the mainstream of academic psychology in America was Lewis Terman of Stanford University. In 1916 Terman issued the first American revision of the Binet, which was called the Stanford-Binet Intelligence Scale. This version was quite similar to Binet's 1911 scale, but some changes in it made the test more appropriate for American children. Terman revised, dropped, added, and modified the age placement of many test items on the basis of the performance of children in the United States. The Stanford-Binet consisted of ninety items that tested for ages three through ten, plus items that tested for ages twelve and fourteen and for "average" and "superior" adult levels. In this revision scores were computed for mental age as well as for the new brightness ratio, the IQ.

We know now that the search for an ever-better intelligence scale had barely begun. The 1916 Stanford-Binet was to be replaced by the more refined 1937 revision, which appeared in two different forms, L and M. Thus this revision was actually two intelligence tests with items that differed in content but were designed to assess the same aspects of intelligence. In 1960 the Stanford-Binet again became a single test, called Form L-M, composed of the most satisfactory subtests from the two 1937 tests. The latest changes came in 1972, when the scoring methods were revised to make the test a better indicator of the intelligence of American children regardless of ethnic or socioeconomic background. Table 10.2 presents a comparison of sample items from the 1908 and 1960 Binet scales.

Wechsler Scales

An important point that was implicit even in Binet's work is that intelligence is a complex trait made up of many contributing talents. For an effective measurement of intelligence, it is essential to sample performance on a wide array of intellectual tasks. David Wechsler has constructed several intelligence tests which assess a broad range of abilities and are appropriate for different age groups. The best known of these are the Wechsler Adult Intelligence Scale (WAIS) and the Wechsler Intelligence Scale for Children (WISC).

Wechsler's original problem was to devise a test to evaluate the intelligence of patients at Bellevue Hospital in New York. Most of them were adults, and many were from the working class and had been poorly educated. Wechsler clearly needed a means of tapping their mental abilities in a nonverbal way, although verbal skills certainly could not be ignored.

Wechsler's current tests contain a variety of subtests which measure verbal as well as performance abilities (see Figure 10.1). The verbal section poses questions on general information, comprehension, recall, finding similarities, mathematical reasoning, and vocabulary. In the performance section, which assesses perceptual and perceptual-motor skills, the individual is asked to substitute unfamiliar symbols for letters according to a supplied code, name the missing parts of incomplete pictures, copy printed designs by arranging multicolored cubes, order a series of pictures so they make a story, and assemble jigsaw pieces to form an object.

Wechsler's tests provide three types of intelligence score: a verbal IQ, a performance IQ, and a composite IQ based on all subtests combined. Verbal and performance IQs show a high positive correlation, but the magnitude of the relation (+.77 to +.81) suggests that the two scales, to some extent, measure different abilities.

Although Wechsler was able to construct different subtests for use with children and adults, he found that the meaning of certain capabilities differed with age. For example, his "memory span for digits" test requires the individual to repeat series of numbers of graduated length. For a child this test is surely relevant in an assessment of intelligence. After the mind matures to a point that it can retain say six or seven digits, however, the test measures memory rather than the internal capacity it tapped earlier. As old age approaches, memory itself becomes a useful indicator of intellectual functioning. Not only do Wechsler's tests pose different problems for children and adults, but the scoring systems are constructed so that appropriate credit is given for performance at different ages.

The Wechsler scales represent a major advance in intelligence testing. Wechsler's use of verbal and performance measures, his recognition that the curve of mental growth and decline differs for various intellectual functions, the excellence of the procedures used in developing his tests, his use of deviation IQs (see page 233), and the fact that his adult scale allows the examiner to observe how the adult approaches tasks and solves problems are assets of a high order.

Intelligence Test Scores

Intelligence tests are constructed so that the average person will receive an IQ score of about 100. That is, the average child will achieve an MA on the test that equals his or her chronological age. Children who are

TABLE 10.2
A Comparison of Test Items for Years 5, 8, and 12 in the 1908 and 1960 Revision of the Binet Scale

1908 Binet Test (Binet and Simon)	Form L-M, 1960 Stanford-Binet (Terman and Merrill, 1960)
Year 5*	Year 5
1. Compares two boxes of different weights.	1. Completes a drawing of a man with leg missing.
2. Copies a square.	2. Folds a paper square twice to make a triangle after demonstration by examiner.
3. Repeats a sentence of ten syllables.	3. Defines two of the following three words: *ball, hat, stove*
4. Count four sous.	4. Copies a square.
5. Puts together two pieces in a "game of patience."	5. Recognizes similarities and differences between pictures.
	6. Assembles two triangles to form a rectangle.
Year 8	Year 8
1. Reads selection and retains two memories.	1. Defines eight words from a standard vocabulary list. Some of the easier examples are: *orange, straw, top.*
2. Counts nine sous (three single and three double).	2. Remembers most of the content of a simple story.
3. Names four colors.	3. Sees the absurdities in such statements as, "A man had flu (influenza) twice. The first time it killed him, but the second time he got well quickly."
4. Counts backward from 20–0.	4. Distinguishes such words as *airplane* and *kite, ocean* and *river.*
5. Compares two objects from memory.	5. Knows what makes a sailboat move, what to do if you find a lost three-year-old, etc.
6. Writes from dictation.	6. Names the days of the week.
Year 12	Year 12
1. Repeats seven figures.	1. Defines fourteen words, such as: *haste, lecture, skill.*
2. Finds three rhymes.	2. Sees absurdity in such items as, "Bill Jones's feet are so big that he has to pull his trousers on over his head."
3. Repeats a sentence of twenty-six syllables.	3. Understands the situation depicted in a fairly complicated picture.
4. Interprets pictures.	4. Repeats five digits reversed.
5. Solves problems of facts.	5. Defines such abstract words as: *pity, curiosity.*
	6. Supplies the missing word in such incomplete sentences as, "One cannot be a hero . . . one can always be a man."

*The average child of the ages for which items are given, five, eight, and twelve, can do the problems correctly.

David Wechsler and the materials for administering the performance section of his intelligence scale for children. This test was first published in 1949, his for adults a decade earlier in 1939.

above average, relative to their age group, will receive IQs above 100. Those below the average for their age receive IQs below 100.

The IQ is more than a measure of relative brightness, however; it is also a measure of the individual's *rate* of intellectual development. An IQ of 100 indicates the rate of intellectual development of the average person in the population. For example, the eight-year-old child who attains eight years of MA credit on the test (IQ = 100) is average in rate of development. The child of twelve who attains eight years of MA credit (IQ = 66) is slow in rate of development since this child took twelve years to acquire the intellectual ability found in the average eight-year-old.

The Normal Curve Intelligence test scores are normally distributed. That is, the majority of people have IQs in the neighborhood of the average, 100. The farther the score is above or below this average, the smaller the number of people obtaining it.

What has come to be called the "normal curve" had its historical origins in the mathematical study of some very practical questions raised by wealthy eighteenth-century English gamblers. The resulting laws of probability, developed to predict the outcomes of games of chance using cards, dice, and roulette balls, have been found useful in studying biological events. Whenever in a number of similar cir-

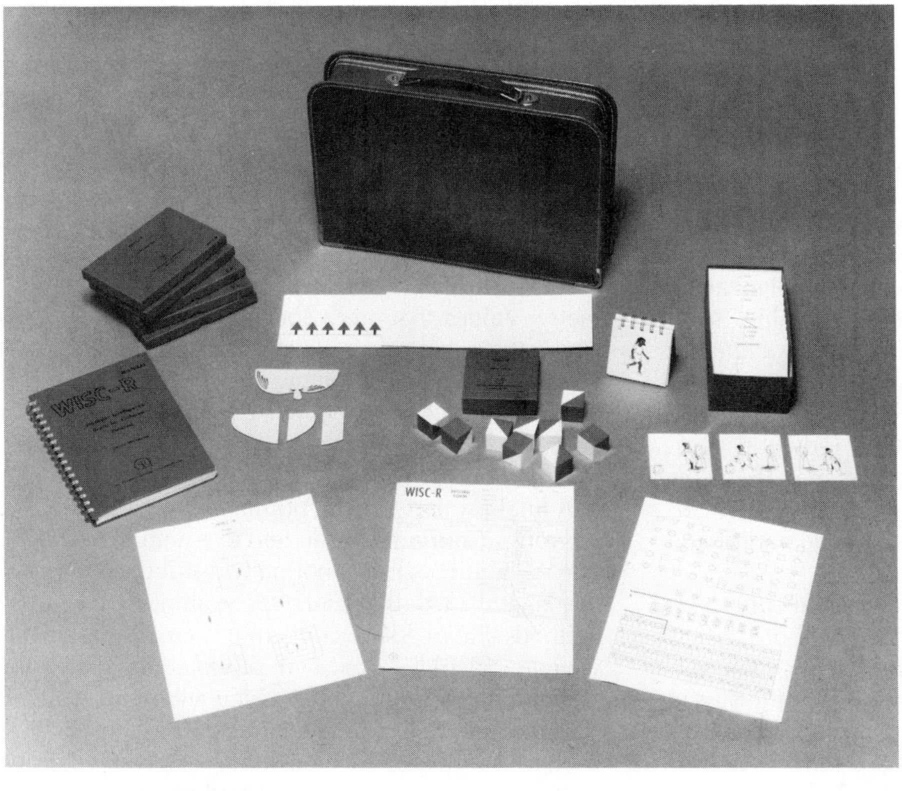

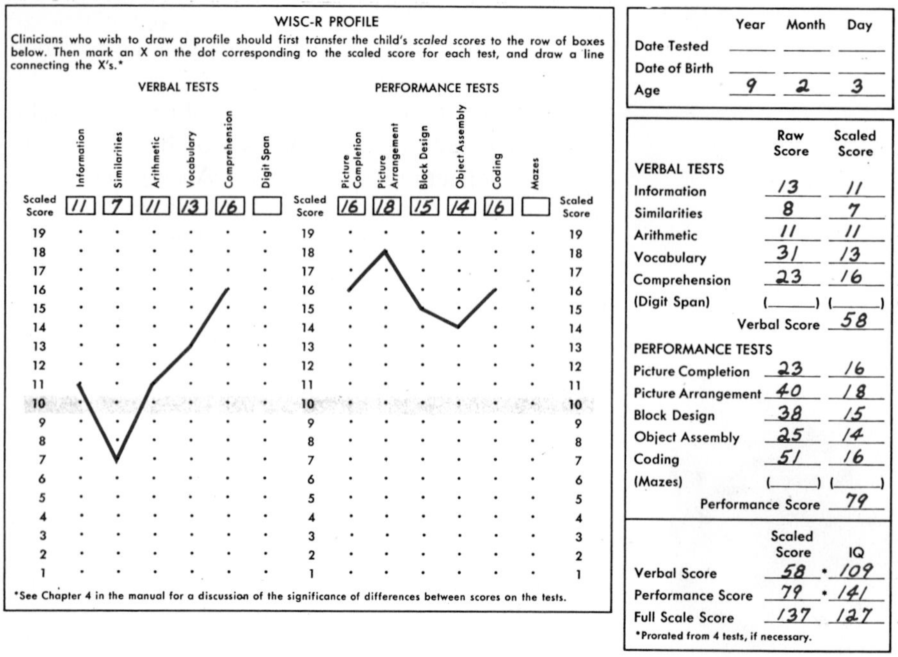
WISC-R PROFILE

Clinicians who wish to draw a profile should first transfer the child's *scaled scores* to the row of boxes below. Then mark an X on the dot corresponding to the scaled score for each test, and draw a line connecting the X's.*

	VERBAL TESTS						PERFORMANCE TESTS					
	Information	Similarities	Arithmetic	Vocabulary	Comprehension	Digit Span	Picture Completion	Picture Arrangement	Block Design	Object Assembly	Coding	Mazes
Scaled Score	11	7	11	13	16		16	18	15	14	16	

*See Chapter 4 in the manual for a discussion of the significance of differences between scores on the tests.

	Year	Month	Day
Date Tested			
Date of Birth			
Age	9	2	3

	Raw Score	Scaled Score
VERBAL TESTS		
Information	13	11
Similarities	8	7
Arithmetic	11	11
Vocabulary	31	13
Comprehension	23	16
(Digit Span)	( )	( )
Verbal Score		58
PERFORMANCE TESTS		
Picture Completion	23	16
Picture Arrangement	40	18
Block Design	38	15
Object Assembly	25	14
Coding	51	16
(Mazes)	( )	( )
Performance Score		79

	Scaled Score	IQ
Verbal Score	58	109
Performance Score	79	141
Full Scale Score	137	127

*Prorated from 4 tests, if necessary.

FIGURE 10.1

The Wechsler Intelligence Scale for Children. Test scores of a nine-year-old as entered on the WISC record form. Mazes may be substituted for the coding test; the digit span test is optional.

A cartoon simulation of the picture-ordering subtest of the WAIS. The correct ordering of the panels is given on page 249. (Drawing by CEM; ©1974 by The New Yorker Magazine, Inc.)

cumstances many variables act independently and at random, the outcome can be summarized by a normal curve. The curve itself is a mathematical ideal, an abstraction never perfectly achieved in reality. Yet it provides a surprisingly good description of a number of real-life events, provided the number of cases studied is large. Among these diverse and otherwise unrelated happenings are heights of redwood trees, lengths of daisy petals, most body measurements such as chest sizes, reaction times in stopping a car, numbers of red cards in a series of bridge hands, and human intelligence test scores.

It is helpful to examine an actual normal curve (Figure 10.2) in order to deduce some of its properties. The first property, readily apparent, is that certain values occur much more commonly than others, and that the common values cluster together around a middle point. This middle point (100 in the IQ distribution) is the mean or average value for the distribution. Values far distant from the mean are rare. The fact that one-half of the curve is a mirror-image reflection of the other is a property known as symmetry. Values that are a specific numerical distance above the mean occur exactly as often as values that are the same distance below the mean. For example, the same number of people have an IQ of 85 (15 below the mean) as have an IQ of 115 (15 above the mean).

A final property of the normal curve is variability. IQs range from a low near zero to a high of over 200. The variability of other normally distributed values—the lengths of daisy petals, for example—is less. By methods that need not concern us here (see page 498) we may calculate a measure of variability called the **standard deviation.** By such calculations the standard deviation of the IQ distribution, for the most widely used tests, is about 15. You should understand, however, that the value of the standard deviation is a fac-

The block design test of the WISC. The child is attempting to arrange the varicolored blocks to match the designs in the spiral-backed copybook.

tual matter. Some tests and some samples of subjects have yielded slightly different values. With this understanding we have used the value of 15 consistently here.

The most essential property of a normal curve is that it permits us to specify exactly what percentage of values will lie between any two points, as long as we know the mean and the standard deviation for the values. (With the help of special tables, such calculations are easily made.) For example, in an ideal normal curve exactly 68.26 percent, or more than two thirds of the values, are found between one standard deviation below the mean and one standard deviation above the mean. This figure confirms our observation that the majority of cases cluster about the mean. In addition, exactly 99.93 percent of the values in an ideal normal curve are found between three standard deviations below and three standard deviations above the mean. In our example, since the standard deviation is 15 and the mean is 100, a full 99.93 percent of the IQ scores would be predicted to lie between 55 and 145. Since the percentage 99.93 includes nearly all cases, a practical range of values in a normal distribution is only six standard deviations wide, three above and three below the mean. This fact helps in predicting which values are actually likely to occur. Although IQs below 55 and above 145 have been recorded, their relative frequency is low.

Deviation IQs An important innovation originated by Wechsler and incorporated into the 1960 Stanford-Binet test was the **deviation IQ** based on normal-curve statistics. The deviation IQ indicates how an individual compares with others of the same age by taking into account the actual test performance of persons in that age group. To calculate a deviation IQ, we first convert the individual's test score to a ***Z*-score** by the formula

$$Z = \frac{\text{Individual's score} - \text{Mean score for persons the same age}}{\text{Standard deviation of distribution of scores for persons the same age}}$$

The Z-score for each individual indicates how far the test score is above or below the mean in terms of standard deviations. Z-scores range from approximately -3.0 to $+3.0$. It is a simple matter, however, to transform these scores into a distribution with a mean of 100 and a standard deviation of 15. The equation is $IQ = 100 + 15Z$, and the IQ obtained is roughly similar to that determined with the traditional formula. The distribution of these scores of intelligence is thus the same as that shown in Figure 10.2. The Statistical Appendix (page 500) gives further information on Z-scores.

Two problems led to the replacement of the MA/CA ratio by the deviation IQ. The first was the discovery that intelligence as measured by IQ tests does not increase steadily with chronological age but increases more slowly in late adolescence and eventually levels off. With the MA/CA formula the only way an intellectually average person could attain an IQ of 100 across the age span was by the rather artificial trick of assigning that person the CA for the upper limit of intellectual growth. When the 1937 Stanford-Binet was constructed, this upper limit was thought to be age sixteen, so for anyone older 16 was used as the denominator in the computation of the IQ. Since intelligence may develop for a longer period of time, and different intellectual abilities may develop at different rates, any arbitrarily selected age poses a problem. The deviation IQ, which assesses the individual's test performance in terms of the particular distribution of test scores of others of the same age, avoids this problem.

The second problem with the MA/CA formula was that, because of certain statistical factors connected with it, children received different IQ scores at different ages, even though they maintained the same position compared to other children their age. With the deviation IQ the individual who maintains his or her relative position within each succeeding age group will always have the same IQ. For example, an

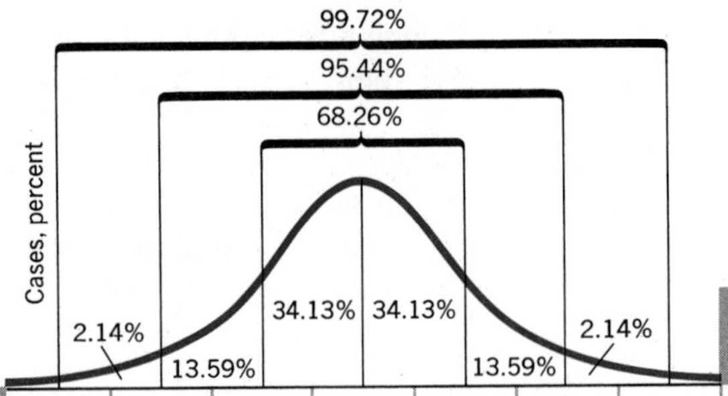

								Mean	Standard deviation
IQ	55	70	85	100	115	130	145	100	15
Z-score	−3.0	−2.0	−1.0	0	+1.0	+2.0	+3.0	0	1.0
Raw score	20	30	40	50	60	70	80	50	10

FIGURE 10.2

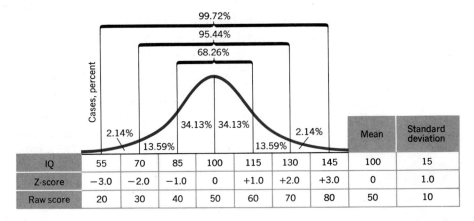

The normal curve of intelligence. This figure is important at several points in the text. Notice first the IQ scale. The figure shows the percentage of cases within three ranges of IQ. This distribution is approximately correct for all the most widely used tests of IQ. The raw score and Z-score scales indicate the procedures involved in calculating deviation IQs. Imagine a test whose raw scores have a mean of 50 and a standard deviation of 10. The transformation first to Z-scores (middle scale) and then to IQs (top scale) gives these scores values that correspond to the normal IQ scale.

intellectually superior person who maintains a Z-score of +3.0 on the Stanford-Binet will always be assigned an IQ of 145, regardless of whether the person is five or fifty years old.

Although the deviation IQ met certain problems inherent in the MA/CA ratio, it created others. The deviation IQ is a good indicator of the individual's level of intelligence compared to that of others of the same age, but it can be misleading in respect to a person's absolute level of intelligence. For example, at the age of seventy an individual may still obtain an IQ of 100, even though this score represents a lower level of absolute intelligence, as measured by the number of test items passed, than was evident at the age of thirty.

Standardizing Intelligence Tests In order to assure that the intellectually average person will receive an IQ of 100, intelligence tests must be standardized in a way that places test items at the age level at which the average person of that age can pass them. **Standardization** is an arduous procedure; the test constructor begins with many more test items than will eventually be used. These items are given to a sample of persons known as the **standardization sample.** If the same percentage of people of differing ages can pass an item, it is considered a poor item and is not included in the final test. On the other hand, if an item is passed by 10 percent of four-year-olds, 60 percent of five-year-olds, and 90 percent of six-year-olds, the item is an ideal one for inclusion at the fifth-year age level. Here a sufficient number of children answer the item correctly and a sufficient number fail it for the test constructor to conclude that a correct answer reflects the intellectual ability of the average five-year-old.

The characteristics of the standardization sample should be as similar as possible to the characteristics of the total population in which the test will be used. There should be the correct proportion of males to females, of urban to rural dwellers, and of people residing in various parts of the country. The standardizing sample must fairly represent persons of various socioeconomic classes and ethnic backgrounds.

The adequacy of the standardizing procedure increases as the number and representativeness of the individuals in the standardizing sample increase. By this criterion Binet and Simon's 1908 scale was poorly standardized, since their sample included only 300 children. Over 3000 children were tested to standardize the 1937 Stanford-Binet. Although some care was taken to make this sample representative of the total population, unfortunately only American-born whites were included. For this reason the test proved to be of doubtful validity (see page 235) in evaluating the intelligence of foreign-born and black children and for comparing their intelligence with that of native-born white children. Some 4500 individuals participated in standardizing the 1960 Stanford-Binet, but once again the sample was limited to whites. This problem was addressed in 1972, when the test was standardized with samples of English-speaking Americans of varying ancestries (Terman and Merrill, 1973).

For IQ scores to remain accurate indicators of intellectual level, intelligence tests must be restandardized at periodic intervals. Changing social conditions may alter the amount or type of knowledge expected at different ages. For example, television has significantly increased the information available to preschoolers, and compulsory education has made today's teens more knowledgeable than their age-mates tested a few decades ago. Restandardization is also necessary since particular items may get easier or more difficult with time. Take, for instance, the question, "What is Mars?" At one time this was a relatively difficult item, but with the advent of the space age, even very young children have heard so much about Mars that they can give the correct answer. On the other hand, the word "coal" was once familiar to the smallest of children, since coal was used in many homes, but today's children may not encounter the word until later in life.

Reliability and Validity Whatever the type of test, it must meet the two statistical criteria of reliability and validity if it is to be of much use.

Reliability A test is reliable if it measures anything consistently, that is, if it produces the same score whenever it is given. Since an individual's traits are assumed to remain fairly constant from day to day, psychologists strive for a reflection of this consistency in their tests. A test of intelligence would not be reliable, and would certainly not be useful, if individuals commonly received an IQ of 150 on one testing and an IQ of 75 on a second testing administered soon afterward.

The most direct way of determining the **reliability** of a test—the **test-retest method**—is to administer it to the same group of individuals twice to see whether their scores are similar on the two testings. If the scores correlate highly, the test is reliable. A reliability coefficient of about +.80 is commonly accepted as the minimum level for a psychological test, although the reliability of many tests is higher than this. That of the Stanford-Binet IQ is about +.90.

Two other methods are also used to assess reliability. In the **split-half method** scores on one half of a test are correlated with scores on the other half. For example, scores on the odd-numbered items may be correlated with scores on the even-numbered items. The third method of measuring reliability, the **alternate-forms method,** can be used only when there are two versions of the same test. If scores on the two tests correlate highly, it is evident that they measure the same thing. The correlation between scores on Forms L and M of the 1937 Stanford-Binet is +.91.

Validity A test's **validity** concerns *what* the test measures and *how well* it does so. A test may be called an intelligence test, but unless performance on the test conforms with other independently observed facts about this trait, it will not be a very good test of intelligence. Psychologists recognize four different types of validity: predictive validity, concurrent validity, content validity, and construct validity.

Predictive validity is a measure of how well a test predicts some future behavioral event. As we have seen, intelligence tests were originally developed to predict school performance. Today the criterion of school success is still used to determine the predictive validity of intelligence tests. A number of studies have shown that the correlation between IQ scores achieved on the Stanford-Binet and school grades is about +.60. In other words, this test of intelligence is a valid predictor of school performance, although not as accurate a predictor as we might desire.

There seem to be three reasons why the correlation between tested intelligence and school grades is no higher than it is. (1) School performance depends on many factors in addition to intelligence, including motivation, interest, and the quality of instruction. (2) Measures of school performance are not completely reliable because teachers make errors and also have their own standards in assigning grades. (3) The reliability of intelligence tests, although high, is not perfect.

We speak of **concurrent validity** when a test is validated by comparing scores obtained on it with scores obtained on another test of established validity. If the scores received on a new intelligence test correlate highly with Stanford-Binet or Wechsler IQs, for example, the new test has concurrent validity.

Content validity is achieved if a test has adequate and appropriate coverage of a given area. A comprehensive achievement test for a specific subject such as a foreign language, vocabulary, or mathematics is a good example of a test that strives for content validity.

Finally, **construct validity** is achieved if a test produces scores that conform to what is generally known or understood about the trait, or construct, being tested. For example, since most theories assume that intelligence increases with age, an intelligence test will not have construct validity if scores obtained by older children are lower than those obtained by younger children.

Whatever the special method employed, establishing the validity of a test comes down in the final analysis to the computation of a correlation coefficient (or some comparable statistic) that provides an estimate of the accuracy with which test scores predict behavior in some criterion situation, either in real life or on another test. Some tests may have validity established by more than one method. College boards, for instance, have predictive validity if their scores correlate with later performance in college, and content validity if scores for sections on particular subjects relate to other academic standards of achievement in those areas.

SUMMARY □

Binet, who produced the first successful instrument for measuring intelligence, was able to do so through a series of brilliant insights. First, he aligned intelligence not with sensorimotor functioning, the traditional notion, but with the complex higher mental processes. Second, he measured the effectiveness of his tests against an important criterion, the ability to achieve in school. Third, he viewed intelligence as age-related, as a configuration of different functions that matured as the child grew older.

Intelligence test constructors generally recognized that intelligence consists of many abilities, but Wechsler was the first to develop effective tests to measure a broader range of talents. His scales included many types of verbal and performance subtests. Wechsler also put into practice the important notion that intellectual functioning has different characteristics at different ages by constructing separate tests for children and adults.

Test scores expressed in terms of mental age provide a measure of absolute intelligence, but they do not indicate an individual's relative intelligence compared to that of others of the same age. This drawback was originally corrected by defining IQ as 100 (MA/CA), but the resulting measure had certain inherent limitations. Because of these difficulties, the deviation IQ was developed. The deviation IQ expresses a person's relative intellectual status within his or her age group and is independent of the variability of scores from age to age.

Standardization is a process by which test items are selected and ordered so that they accurately assess the abilities of persons of different ages. Many possible test items are administered to a large sample of individuals who are representative of the population with which the test will be used. The performance of the standardization sample is used to select the final test items as well as to place them at the appropriate age or difficulty levels. The value of a test, whether of intelligence or anything else, depends on the degree to which it meets the criteria of reliability and validity. Reliability is the dependability of the measures obtained on a test. Validity is the extent to which scores are related to some other criterion of measurement. "Test-retest," "split-half," and "alternate forms" identify different procedures for assessing reliability. "Predictive," "concurrent," "content" and "construct" are different types of validity.

PROBLEMS OF INTELLIGENCE TESTING

Although most existing intelligence tests have been standardized and possess the qualities of reliability and validity, there are a number of unsolved problems in using them as measures of intelligence. Many of the problems revolve at least indirectly around the criterion of intelligence. As we have seen, for historical reasons school performance came to be used as the ultimate criterion of an intelligence test. Although the cognitive processes assessed by the standard intelligence test are useful both in and out of school, it should surprise no one to learn that the test scores are much better predictors of school performance than they are of everyday adult functioning. One reason may be that a variety of cognitive processes important in later life are probably not important in determining school success and are therefore not sampled by intelligence tests.

This raises the question whether an individual's "true" intelligence would be more adequately assessed by some other collection of cognitive tasks. For example, standard tests thought to assess intelligence are not highly related to tests thought to assess creativity. We might conclude that the creative person is not necessarily the "intelligent" one. It makes just as much sense, however, to argue that creativity *is* intelligence more broadly defined, and that our standard measures of intelligence do not include enough items that assess creative intellectual ability.

Intelligence versus Achievement

Another aspect of the intelligence criterion problem concerns the degree to which tests have been successful in separating intelligence as the capacity for learning from achievement, or knowledge already acquired by the individual. Binet was clear that he was trying to assess an ability that was independent of instruction. He was aware that two children of the same intellectual aptitude could differ in their intellectual achievements if one had had more of an opportunity than the other to acquire this or that piece of information or particular skill. He and Simon took great pains to include in their tests only items requiring a minimum of experience to master. But did children from impoverished French homes really see as many squares of chocolate or hear the abstract words included in the test with the same frequency as wealthier children?

To make this distinction between intelligence and achievement clear, suppose that an intelligence test includes the information item, "What is a cable car?" More children in San Francisco than in New York would answer this item correctly, but this certainly would not mean that San Francisco children are more intelligent. Rather, the West coast children would be showing greater achievement because they live in an environment where cable cars are an everyday fact of life. Thus this test item is a measure of achievement but not of intelligence or the ability to achieve.

Theoretically, then, if two people have had the same opportunity to acquire certain information or skills assessed on a test, and if one of them has learned these but the other has not, the test is a measure of their intellectual aptitude. But if they have not have had the exact same opportunities to acquire test is more correctly a measure of their achievement. Of course it would be rare to find two people who have had the exact same opportunities to acquire every bit of information. In practice, therefore, intelligence tests are measures of both intellectual ability and achievement, although the emphasis clearly strives to be on the former.

Culture Fairness

A test does not assess intelligence fairly if passing the items depends on belonging to one particular culture rather than another. Unfortunately, there is considerable reason to believe that our standard intelligence tests contain items that give an advantage to middle-class white children and place minority groups at a disadvantage.

Jerome Kagan (1971) has noted a number of culturally biased items which are included in our current tests. Vocabulary items, for example, are often words most likely to be heard in middle-class white homes. Children are asked how a piano and a violin are alike, not how a tortilla and a frijole are alike. On a reasoning problem they are asked, "What should you do if you were sent to the store to buy a loaf of bread and the grocer said he didn't have any more?" Kagan points out that the correct answer—"Go to another store"—assumes a middle-class, urban environment with more than one grocery store within safe walking distance. Rural or ghetto children who answer "Go home" receive no credit, even though this is a perfectly reasonable solution in their environments.

Culturally unfair tests can underassess a child's intelligence, with very serious consequences for the child's future. As in the days of Binet, intelligence tests are still employed to determine who is mentally retarded and who is not. Jane Mercer (1975) has pointed out how this use of tests may operate to the disadvantage of children from minority groups and lower socioeconomic levels. She notes that a disproportionate number of these children are labeled mentally retarded and placed in special-education classes. Mercer has argued that many minority children assigned to these classes are there because IQ tests have been improperly used. That is, she believes it is unfair to use an IQ test to assess the aptitudes of children whose sociocultural backgrounds are significantly different from that of the majority of children on whom the test was standardized.

To prove her point, Mercer classified Mexican-American and black children into five categories according to how closely their family backgrounds corresponded to the dominant Anglo-American culture. She found that children whose homes were more similar to the Anglo-American mode indeed scored higher on IQ tests than children whose homes were less Anglicized. For example, Mexican-American children from the most Anglicized homes had a mean WISC IQ of 104.4 compared to a mean of 84.5 for children from the least Anglicized homes. Similarly, black children from the most Anglicized homes had a mean IQ of 99.5, whereas those from the least Anglicized homes had a mean score of 82.7.

In an effort to reduce the influence of culture to a minimum, a number of so-called **culture-fair tests** have been constructed. One such instrument is the IPAT Culture-Fair Intelligence Test devised by Raymond Cattell at the Institute for Personality and Ability Testing (hence IPAT). Samples of items from the test's three scales appear in Figure 10.3. Research suggests that the test has been only partially successful in providing a measure of innate ability uncomplicated by cultural influences. Although the scores of persons in Taiwan and France appear to be comparable to those gathered in the United States, scores of other nationality groups show marked differences.

Taking culture-dependent items out of tests has proved to be a difficult if not impossible task, and to date no test has been devised that can be considered totally free of cultural influences. In interpreting intelligence test performance, therefore, we must consider the disparity between the groups on which the test was standardized and the specific group to which the test taker belongs. Even if a perfectly culture-fair test were invented, it probably would be a poorer predictor of school performance than our present tests, inasmuch as successful school performance is also culturally biased. Schools encourage the achievements and ways of performing considered valuable in the white middle-class culture.

Motivational-Emotional Factors

Another criticism of intelligence tests is that they include items sensitive to personality and motivational factors. For example, some test items require persistence or the close attention of the test taker, but these are not necessarily intellectual abilities. Persistence and attention are important for good school performance, however, so it could be argued that they should be measured in intelligence tests.

Emotional factors can also have a dramatic effect on intelligence test performance. One group of researchers (Zigler, Abelson, and Seitz, 1973) found that when economically disadvantaged children were given an intelligence test one week and then retested a week later, their average scores increased a full 10 points. Other children had an opportunity, before the initial testing, to acclimate themselves by playing

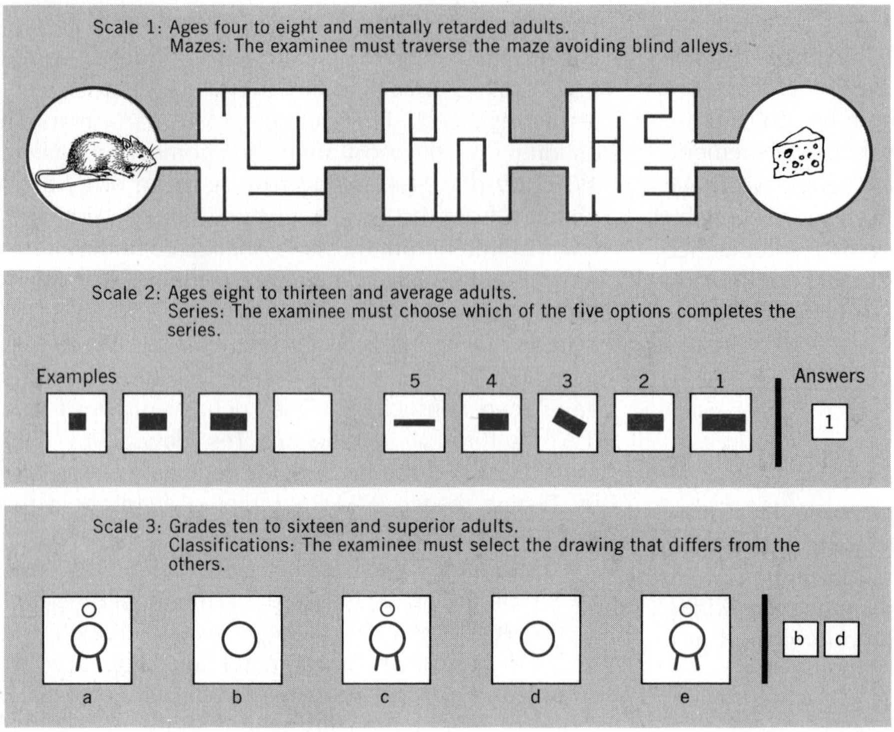
Scale 1: Ages four to eight and mentally retarded adults.
Mazes: The examinee must traverse the maze avoiding blind alleys.
Scale 2: Ages eight to thirteen and average adults.
Series: The examinee must choose which of the five options completes the series.
Examples
5 4 3 2 1
Answers
1
Scale 3: Grades ten to sixteen and superior adults.
Classifications: The examinee must select the drawing that differs from the others.
a b c d e
b d

FIGURE 10.3
Culture-fair measures of intelligence. These sample items are from the IPAT Culture-Fair Intelligence Tests. (Reprinted with permission of Professor Raymond B. Cattell and the Institute for Personality and Ability Testing. Copyright 1949, 1953.)

games with the examiner in a warm and friendly session. The first IQ scores of these children were not much lower than their retest scores. These results suggest that in an unfamiliar testing situation, the children's feelings of fear or anxiety may have impaired their performance. When the children were more familiar with the testing environment, as during the retest or after having a pleasant interaction with the examiner, their scores were substantially higher.

The results of this study indicate that with special care the examiner may be able to alleviate some motivational-emotional factors detrimental to test performance. It is impossible, however, to keep testing totally free of the influence of such factors. The individual's willingness to perform on a test and his or her general emotional state will always be important determinants of the test score achieved.

SUMMARY □

Although standard tests of intelligence are useful predictors of school achievement, they are less successful in predicting everyday adult functioning. Clearly intelligence cannot be defined on the basis of abilities related to school performance alone, since other cognitive abilities are important in other situations. One problem with standard intelligence tests, then, is that they fail to measure all the cognitive abilities that contribute to intelligence, broadly defined.

A second problem with these tests is that they inevitably measure both intellectual ability and achievement. Unless two people have had similar opportunities to learn the information and practice the skills measured by an intelligence test, their differing IQ scores are not valid indicators of their intellectual abilities but merely reflections of their differing experiences.

A related problem is that performance on standard intelligence tests, rather than indicating basic cognitive ability, is partially dependent on the culture in which an individual has been raised. Despite improved standardization, our current tests may give an advantage to middle-class whites and penalize those from minority and lower socioeconomic groups. Although efforts have been made to develop culture-fair tests, the results thus far are not completely satisfactory. Items requiring specific knowledge have been eliminated to some extent, but testing still depends on culturally derived motives, attitudes, and values.

Individual personality traits can also affect performance on intelligence tests. Since motivational and emotional factors can have a pervasive influence not only on test scores but on school performance, any test's sensitivity to such traits probably cannot be eliminated. Adverse emotional effects are thus more likely to be removed by changes in the testing procedure.

THE STRUCTURE OF INTELLECT

Questions such as those we have just been discussing — culture fairness, intelligence versus achievement, effects of emotional factors on test performance — imply that intelligence needs to be considered in two different ways. One way is in terms of "true" intelligence, which represents a person's potential. The other way is in terms of "measured" intelligence, which may reflect true intelligence only approximately. Donald Hebb made such a distinction in his recommendation that we consider **intelligence A** and **intelligence B** in our thinking about the topic. Hebb wrote,

> The term *intelligence A* refers to an innate potential for the development of intellectual capacities and *intelligence B* to the level of that development at a later time, when the subject's intellectual functioning can be observed. Intelligence A cannot be measured, for intellectual functioning is not observed in the newborn; the IQ, therefore, is a measure of intelligence B only. The student should note that A and B are not wholly separate; on the contrary, intelligence A enters into and is a necessary factor in intelligence B. What these two terms distinguish is not two different things but two different ways in which the more general term, intelligence, is used (1972, p. 163).

A similar theory was advanced by Raymond Cattell and his associates (Cattell, 1963; Horn and Cattell, 1967), who drew a distinction between "fluid" and "crystallized" intelligence. **Fluid intelligence** is the type of cognitive analytic ability, relatively uninfluenced by prior learning, which shows up the most clearly on tasks requiring adaptation to new situations. **Crystallized intelligence,** on the other hand, involves skilled habits and is much more influenced by prior learning experiences.

General Trait versus Specific Abilities

Psychologists have long argued whether intelligence is a single ability that permeates all basic cognitive processes or whether it is the sum total of many independent abilities. Early workers attempted to answer this question by determining whether individuals who score high on one type of intellectual task also perform well on others. They found that the scores were significantly related, but not perfectly so.

To explain these findings, Charles Spearman (1904) advanced a two-factor theory of intelligence. He thought that there was a general ability employed by the individual when coping with a variety of intellectual tasks. Spearman called this general ability *g,* for **general factor,** and described it as something analogous to basic mental energy. But, since an individual does not perform equally well on all types of cognitive tasks, he thought that each kind, such as mathematical tasks and verbal tasks, requires a specific intellectual ability as well. Spearman called these specific abilities *s,* for **specific factors.** Thus Spearman thought of intelligence as composed of the *g* factor and a number of *s* factors.

Other psychologists have challenged the view that there is any general ability which is reflected in a number of intellectual functions. Edward Thorndike, for example, argued that intelligence is best conceptualized as a large number of independent abilities. Somewhere between the theories of Spearman and Thorndike was the view of Louis L. Thurstone (1938), who thought that the intellect was comprised of specific abilities, but so few of them that each had broad generality. He termed these **primary mental abilities** and subdivided Spearman's general factor, *g,* into seven of them: spatial perception, perceptual speed, verbal comprehension, numerical ability, memory, word fluency, and reasoning. Thurstone found that an individual's scores on tests of these primary abilities were often interrelated, however, which again pointed to some factor in intelligence reminiscent of Spearman's *g.*

One of the most elaborate schemes for classifying intelligence into special abilities was proposed by J. P. Guilford (1967). Guilford argued that to understand intelligence we ought to consider three dimensions of thought: (1) what the person is thinking about — the *contents* of thought; (2) how the person thinks about them — the *operations* of the thinker; and (3) what kinds of *products* result — the ideas that occur to the thinker. Using a statistical technique known as factor analysis, Guilford isolated four types of contents, five kinds of operations, and six varieties of products.

Guilford's proposed structure of the intellect can be illustrated with a **cubical model** (Figure 10.4). The three dimensions of the intellect are plotted along the three dimensions of a cube. The intersection of lines drawn for each of the four types of contents, five operations, and six products yields 120 ($4 \times 5 \times 6$) cells representing different abilities. Each ability thus consists of a combination of three categories, one from each of the three dimensions. Theoretically, each ability should be measurable by a specific task. Tests constructed in Guilford's laboratory have been able to demonstrate close to 100 of these abilities (Guilford and Hoepfner, 1971).

Some examples of tests used to measure various abilities will help clarify Guilford's model. Suppose

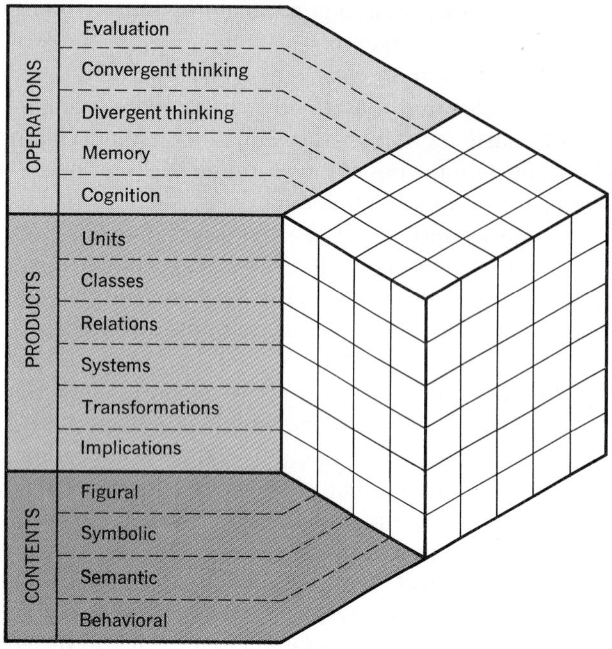

FIGURE 10.4
Cubical model representing Guilford's structure of intellect. The 120 cells of the cube represent individual intellectual abilities. (From Guilford, 1959.)

that a person is shown ten designs for five seconds each and is later asked to sketch them. The content of this task is figural since it involves visible forms. The operation is memory since it involves recall. The product is units since the person must recall a number of individual items. Another ability is probed when a person is asked to choose which of the following three alternatives is most related to both jewelry and bell: (*a*) ornament, (*b*) jingle, or (*c*) ring. The content of this task is semantic, because it utilizes verbal meanings; the operation is cognitive, because the person must discover or recognize; and the product is relations, since a connection between two things must be found. The answer is (*c*) ring.

Guilford made a unique contribution to the understanding of intelligence by including in his model the operation of "divergent thinking." Most standard IQ tests measure only convergent thinking, that is, the ability to search for the most appropriate or most conventional solution to a problem. Divergent thinking, on the other hand, involves the ability to produce a variety of ideas or solutions to a given problem. This type of thinking is generally considered creative (see page 268). An example of a test of divergent thinking is Guilford's Plot Titles Test, which requires a person to create as many titles for a story as possible. A premium is placed on unusual and clever ideas. The cell representing this ability in Guilford's cube would be at the juncture of the divergent thinking, semantic, and transformations (shifts or changes in meanings) categories. An example of one of these stories and some divergent and nondivergent titles are given in Table 10.3.

TABLE 10.3
Plot Titles Test

Plot: A missionary, captured by a tribe of cannibals, is confronted with the choice of marrying the tribal princess or being boiled alive. He chooses the latter. Title the story.

Clever Titles	Commonplace Titles
Pot's Plot	African Death
Potluck Dinner	Defeat of a Princess
Stewed Parson	Eaten by Savages
Goil or Boil	The Princess
A Mate Worse Than Death	The African Missionary
He Left a Dish for a Pot	In Darkest Africa
Chaste in Haste	Boiled by Savages
A Hot Price for Freedom	

After Guilford, 1959.

Little relation has been found between scores obtained on standard IQ tests and scores achieved on tests of divergent thinking. Whereas individuals who perform well on divergent thinking tasks (and are therefore presumably creative) usually have high IQ scores, individuals who obtain high IQs do not necessarily do well on divergent thinking. This brings us back to the basic issues of whether there really is a general factor in intelligence, and whether IQ tests assess a broad enough range of abilities.

Adaptation and Profiles of Abilities

Throughout the history of mental testing, most test constructors have emphasized individual effectiveness in their definitions of intelligence. Binet, for example, saw the essence of intelligence in the ability of the individual to become oriented toward a goal, to make adjustments in the process of achieving the goal, and to be aware when the goal had been reached. He noted that this ability requires judgment, initiative, and reasoning. This problem-solving orientation can also be seen in Henry Goddard's definition of intelligence as "the degree of availability of one's experiences for the solution of immediate problems and the anticipation of future ones" (1946, p. 68). Terman saw as the essential ingredient of intellectual effectiveness the ability to think abstractly. Wechsler maintains that intelligence is "the capacity of an individual to understand the world about him and his resourcefulness to cope with its challenges" (1975, p. 139). The most recent version of this view is that of William Charlesworth (1976), who holds that intelligence consists of specific cognitive abilities that enable an individual to adapt to the environment. One

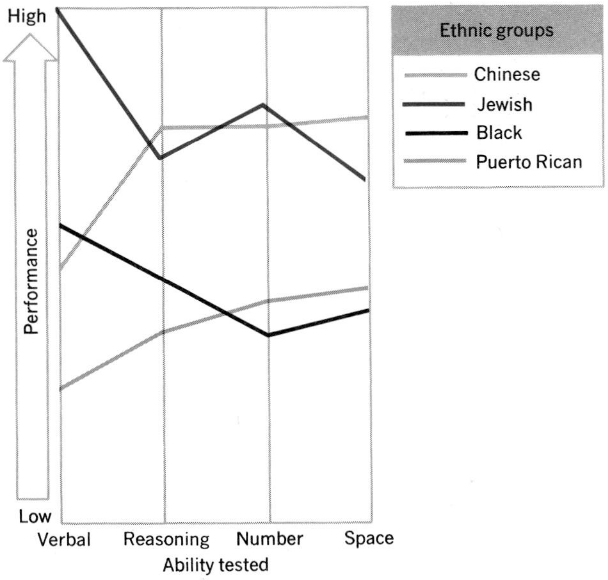

FIGURE 10.5
Patterns of ethnic and racial intelligence. These profiles show that different groups have different patterns of intelligence. Jews and blacks are highest on measures of verbal ability. Chinese and Puerto Ricans are strongest in spatial intelligence. (Adapted from Lesser, Fifer, and Clark, 1965.)

difference between Charlesworth's view and earlier ones turns on the difference between being effective and adapting. To be effective is to have a set of unchanging capacities that allows one to cope with a changeable environment. To adapt is to change one's self in response to unchanging physical reality. A second difference is a somewhat expanded concept of environment.

Although the early proponents of the effectiveness view recognized a broader environment, their research for the most part was limited to the school. Even in preparing tests for adults, they assumed that the cognitive abilities important for children's success in school would also determine adults' success outside of school. The proponents of the adaptation view of intelligence, however, argue that different demands are made by the school and nonschool environments. Further, they point out that the environment outside of school is not homogeneous, and that different groups of people often have very different life experiences. For example, the environments of the American black, poor Appalachian white, and Peruvian peasant differ greatly from one another and certainly from that of the middle-class American white. There would be no reason to expect that the cognitive abilities that enable individuals to be effective in one of these environments would be equally useful in the others. Thus in different groups of people intelligence may actually consist of different patterns of abilities.

Evidence that different profiles of cognitive abilities may in fact exist was provided by a study of four ethnic-racial groups of children living in the United States (Lesser, Fifer, and Clark, 1965). Six- and seven-year-old black, Chinese, Jewish, and Puerto Rican children were tested on verbal ability, reasoning, number facility, and space conceptualization. No group performed uniformly well or poorly on all the tests. Rather, the groups ranked differently on each of the cognitive abilities (Figure 10.5). Furthermore, although lower-class children scored below middle-class children on each of the tests, both classes of children within each ethnic-racial group obtained the same overall pattern of scores.

Intelligence over the Life Span

As we noted earlier, a part of Binet's great contribution to the study of intelligence was the clear demonstration that intelligence changes with age. This general observation lies behind a more specific set of questions. How early in life can intelligence be measured? Do all components of intelligence grow at the same rate? Does intellectual growth continue throughout the life span?

Tests of Infant Intelligence A number of intelligence tests have been constructed for use with infants. Most of the items on infant tests, like those of the very earliest adult tests, are of sensorimotor skills. What the infant tests measure is probably not the same thing as is measured by adult tests of intelligence.

The most important infant test is Arnold Gesell's Developmental Schedules. As with the Binet and Wechsler scales, Gesell's schedules contain items which show a clear age progression; the age levels are from one month to two years. The tests at each age level are divided into four categories: motor, adaptive, language, and personal-social. The motor category assesses such behavior as head balance, standing, walking, jumping, and the child's ability to reach for, grasp, and manipulate objects. Adaptive tests determine reactions to objects such as toy cubes and a dangling ring, and the ability to fit variously shaped blocks into forms on a board. Language items cover prelinguistic vocalizations, comprehension of the speech of others, and the ability to point to objects and pictures named by the examiner. Personal-social items are administered for the most part by interviewing the mother. They cover smiling, self-feeding, toileting, play, and how the infant asks for things.

Gesell viewed his tests as measuring not intelligence but the child's level of development. The score an infant obtains is therefore called a **developmental quotient (DQ),** which is calculated with the

Arnold Lucius Gesell (1880-1961) obtained a medical degree the better to understand the physical basis of development. He established sequential steps of maturation.

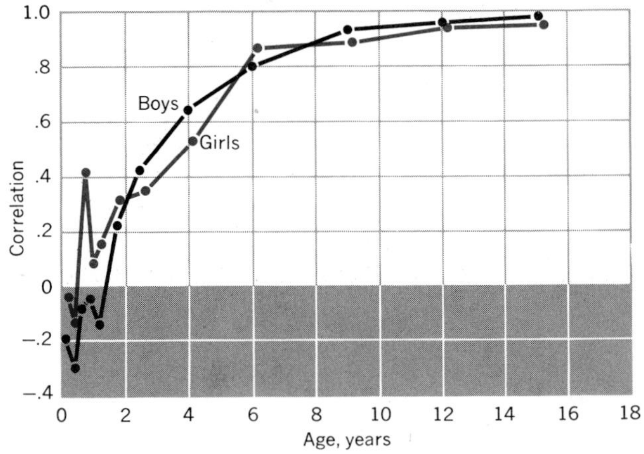

FIGURE 10.6
Correlations of earlier mental test scores with sixteen-to-eighteen-year scores. Before age four the correlations are low and for boys negative. Not until age seven does the correlation of early scores with late scores become sufficiently high to have predictive utility value for both boys and girls. (Data from the Berkeley Growth Study, Bayley and Schaefer, 1964.)

same formula used for IQ. That is, performance is scored in months and is expressed as a developmental age (DA), which is divided by CA and multiplied by 100. For example, if a twelve-month-old girl passes all the items passed by the average sixteenth-month-old, her DQ equals 100(16/12) or 133.

An important question is whether the infant who shows accelerated development in terms of DQ will be brighter later in life than the infant who is not so advanced. Study after study has failed to find evidence for such a relationship. Although children do vary widely in their rates of development, the DQs obtained early in life do not correlate with IQs achieved at maturity. Representative of these studies is the Berkeley Growth Study (Bayley and Schaefer, 1964), in which children were tested every month for the first fifteen months, then every three months up to three years of age, and finally semiannually from three to eighteen years. Figure 10.6 charts the correlations of IQs obtained at ages sixteen, seventeen, and eighteen with the DQs and IQs of the same individuals obtained at several earlier ages. There is no relationship between the earliest scores and those obtained later. From age four on, the relationship becomes increasingly greater, and by age seven the correlation is useful for predicting adult intelligence.

The failure to find a strong relation between infant DQs and later IQs indicates that the two scores reflect different abilities. These studies suggest again that intelligence is not a single capacity that a person gets more of with age but rather a collection of abilities, some being found in the young child and others only in the older child. Guided by this general orientation, several investigators have attempted to isolate the specific abilities assessed by early and later tests. The results of the studies have been unanimous on the point that scores on the two types of tests do indeed reflect different talents. Moreover, the relative contributions of the abilities sampled change with age. In one study (Hofstaetter, 1954), for example, early test scores were found to depend primarily on sensorimotor alertness, whereas measures of persistence were important in determining test scores from ages two to four (Figure 10.7). The influence of verbal reasoning ability rose rapidly through the preschool period and became the more important determinant of test scores as the child became older. These findings indicate that as intelligence grows, mental functioning changes qualitatively as well as quantitatively.

Intelligence in Later Life When the Binet intelligence tests were first given to individuals of different ages, it was considered surprising that average scores reached an upper limit at about age sixteen. On the Wechsler scales they peaked at about age twenty. After that performance remained at a plateau until age forty-five or so and then began to decline. These findings seemed to mean that people are as intelligent as they will ever be in the late teens, and that there is a serious loss of capacity in later life.

These data came from **cross-sectional studies;** people of very different ages were tested at about the same time. Participants were a cross section of the

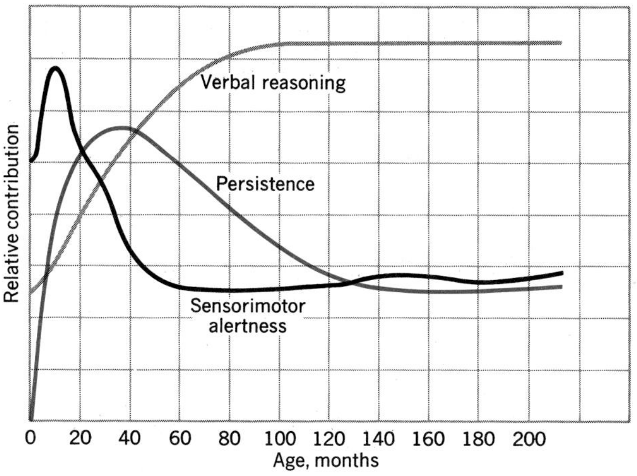

FIGURE 10.7
Three factors differently related to intelligence scores at different ages. The height of each curve at each age indicates the relative importance of the factor in determining the total score at that age. (Adapted from Hofstaetter, 1954.)

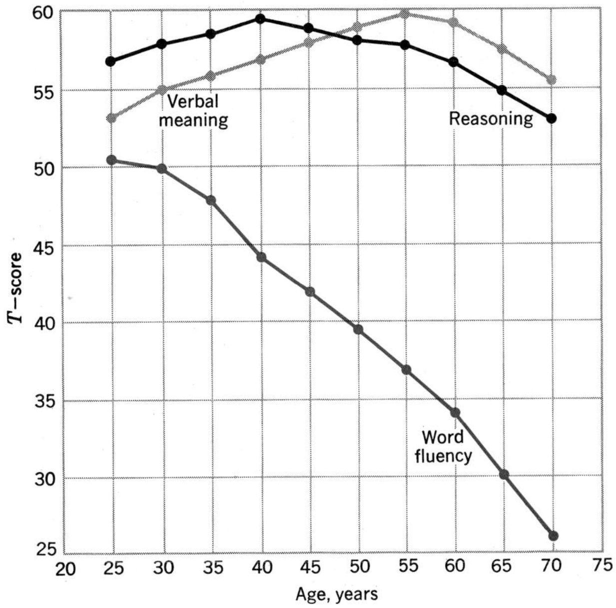

FIGURE 10.8
Estimated change over time for three intellectual abilities. The data are based on longitudinal findings. A *T*-score is a standard score (resembling a deviation IQ) which has a mean of 50 and a standard deviation of 10. (Adapted from Schaie and Strother, 1968.)

population in that period. This means that the older and younger individuals had been educated in very different eras. The younger participants would have grown up in an age of greater educational opportunity than the older people. The schooling of the older people had probably been much less demanding. Differences such as these are a serious criticism of cross-sectional methods.

Longitudinal studies retesting the same individuals at various points in their lives have indicated that general intelligence increases all the way up to age fifty or so, but that various abilities show a different course of development over the life span. Figure 10.8 charts the longitudinal results from tests of three intellectual abilities (Schaie and Strother, 1968). The verbal meaning test examined understanding ideas expressed in words. This ability did not peak until age fifty-five, and at seventy verbal understanding was still better than it had been at age twenty-five. The reasoning test assessed the ability to solve logical problems. Although problem solving peaked at forty, it showed no substantial decrement until age sixty. The word fluency test required individuals to write as many words beginning with a certain letter as they could in a brief period of time. This ability declined markedly and consistently with age.

In general, longitudinal studies have shown that capacities that depend on the accumulation of experiences, such as vocabulary and a store of general information—what Cattell called crystallized intelligence—increase with age and decline only with the approach of senescence (very old age). Capacities that depend on speed, flexibility, and adaptation to the novel and unfamiliar—fluid intelligence—peak much earlier in life. Even these general statements are subject to qualification, however. The curve over the life span depends on the individual's educational level and general richness of life experiences. The older person who maintains an active interest in ideas and continues to engage in intellectual pursuits will probably show much less of a decline than the older person who does not.

SUMMARY □

Most current intelligence tests are based on definitions of intelligence that emphasize an individual's effectiveness, a concept which implies a difference between pure intelligence and measured intelligence. Several psychologists have recognized this difference and have distinguished between two types of intelligence. One is an innate, biological intelligence, relatively uninfluenced by the environment. The other is the actual functioning level of intelligence, which is dependent on prior learning experiences. It is important to recognize that IQ tests measure only the second type of intelligence and that as yet we have no satisfactory measures of innate capacity.

A controversial issue in the field of intelligence testing is whether intelligence is a general trait that permeates all realms of functioning, or whether it consists of a number of specific abilities. Spearman theorized that there is both a g factor and several *s* factors; Thurstone identified seven primary mental abilities; and Guilford proposed a structure of intellect containing 120 separate abilities.

A relatively recent definition of intelligence emphasizes adaptation, as opposed to effectiveness. Since different groups of people must adapt to greatly different environments, the groups will not require the same abilities. Intelligence is thus conceptualized as different patterns of abilities for various groups. Identical levels of overall intelligence might reflect very different profiles of specific abilities.

Since infants cannot perform the tasks required by later intelligence tests, special ones have been devised to assess their rate of development. Infant tests, which emphasize sensorimotor abilities much more than later intelligence tests do, yield a developmental quotient, an index of the relative rate at which the tasks of infancy are mastered. Little relation has been found between DQs and later IQs, indicating that with growth of intelligence mental functioning undergoes qualitative changes.

Although intelligence develops the most rapidly during childhood, longitudinal evidence indicates that general intelligence continues to increase until the later adult years. This pattern of increase is particularly characteristic of certain abilities, those requiring the accumulation of information. Other abilities depending on flexibility of mental functioning peak relatively early in adulthood and decline.

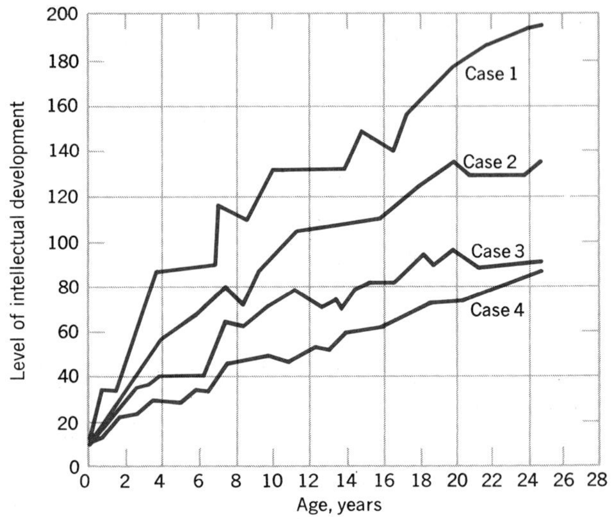

FIGURE 10.9
Individual mental growth curve. (After Bayley, 1955.)

FACTORS RELATED TO IQ CHANGES

The growth of intelligence for any one individual is much more idiosyncratic than descriptions of group intellectual development would seem to indicate. Group curves depict a gradual and smooth growth of intelligence in the early years, with the increase slowing as the person grows older. Individual growth curves, however, often have spurts, plateaus, and even drops (Figure 10.9). Thus an individual may register a high IQ if tested in the middle of an intellectual growth spurt, but a lower one during a plateau or drop.

Some of the fluctuations in an individual's IQ scores can be traced to intelligence tests themselves. Recall that the difficulty level of test items is determined by the performance of large groups. Any one individual may just happen to know an item that the standardization procedure indicated to be difficult and not know an item assessed as easy. Such chance knowledge or lack of it at various testings will make a person's IQ fluctuate somewhat.

Sometimes changing life circumstances can also make IQ vary. In one study of over 200 children, such factors as physical illness, environmental stress, and certain child-rearing practices of their parents were found to correspond to shifts in IQ scores (Honzik, Macfarlane, and Allen, 1948). One child's IQ improved markedly after the child's father had regained employment. That of a child with an overprotective and oversolicitous mother dropped from an above-average level to the borderline retarded. A boy who compensated for his physical problems through intellectual achievements raised his IQ from the below-average range to the superior range. As intriguing as these cases are, other children who experienced marked changes in environmental circumstances did not register corresponding fluctuations in IQ. Moreover, for striking changes in children's IQ scores discovered in another study, investigators were unable to find associated changes in life circumstances (Goodenough and Maurer, 1942).

Since environmental conditions and the circumstances of life do not account completely for changes in IQ, some theorists have offered an alternative explanation modeled on individual patterns of physical development. For example, children who walk at an early age may or may not reach puberty before their peers. Acceleration in intellectual development at one age might similarly fail to predict the pattern of development later on. Although this interpretation has merit—the lack of a substantial correlation between early and later IQ supports it—few scientists would view the growth of intelligence in completely biological terms. Much more frequently psychologists hold that a mix of biological and environmental factors is responsible for fluctuations in the IQ. On this basis they have examined a variety of personality, constitutional, and sociocultural factors as possible contributors.

Personality and Sex Differences

Personality Some evidence indicates that changes in IQ are related to the child's general pattern of adjustment or personality. In a longitudinal study conducted at the Fels Institute, 140 children were tested at intervals between two and twelve years of age (Sontag, Baker, and Nelson, 1958). The 35 children whose IQs rose the most sharply over the years and the 35 children whose IQs showed the greatest decrease were rated on several personality measures. Children whose IQs had increased were found to be aggressive, independent, self-initiating, and competitive. Those with decreasing IQs lacked these traits. Other studies have indicated that the aggressiveness that accompanies an increasing IQ pattern must be of a socially acceptable sort rather than the destructive, uncontrolled, acting-out kind. For example, children who have temper tantrums also have drops in their IQs (Peskin, 1964). To function well intellectually, a person must be able to harness emotions and utilize them in a constructive manner.

Sex Differences Whatever the personality differences of the two sexes, the scores of boys and girls on standard intelligence tests are markedly similar. One reason for this similarity is that the tests were standardized to ensure that both sexes would receive the same IQs; any item on which one sex did better than the other was rejected. Nevertheless, there is some evidence that on certain subtests females are superior to males, whereas on others males are superior to females. On the average girls do better on verbal tasks, but boys as a group excel on numerical and spatial tasks. Although neither sex is superior, the two sexes do display different patterns of abilities.

Some argue that the ways boys and girls are reared and what they are taught to regard as important explain their intellectual differences. A striking finding of the Fels study clarifies this point. Of the 35 children with sharply ascending IQs, a disproportionate number (23) were boys, and of the 35 whose IQs descended, a disproportionate number (22) were girls. Among those with decreasing IQs was a subgroup whose IQs dropped relatively late in the developmental period. This group consisted entirely of girls; the drop in IQ occurred at an age when they might consider exercising their new-found femininity much more self-satisfying than intellectual achievement.

In light of these findings, we should reexamine the personality traits found to be associated with increasing IQs. These included aggression, competition, and self-reliance, traits that are typically nurtured in boys but discouraged in girls. The fact that intelligence is related to such traits might explain why intellectual achievement if often considered a masculine characteristic.

That this is indeed the case was confirmed in a study by Gloria Carey (1958), who found that college women considered problem solving less acceptable behavior than did men. Carey attempted to change these attitudes by conducting group discussions with both men and women, during which she emphasized that it is socially acceptable to excel at problem solving. After these discussions the problem solving of women improved but not that of men. Thus the women's attitudes had been an impediment, one which was overcome once they felt that problem solving was appropriate behavior. The women's movement has been attempting to remove many such impeding attitudes; such efforts may enable women to pursue achievements previously held in psychological abeyance.

Not everyone would agree that male-female differences in such traits as intelligence and aggressiveness are explained solely by social learning. Others argue that basic constitutional differences in males and females also have a role. For example, boys commonly reach puberty a good two years later than girls. One study by Deborah Waber (1977) has provided evidence that the better spatial ability of men may be related to this physiological fact. Waber found that teenagers of *both* sexes who had reached puberty late performed better on spatial tasks than did those who had matured early. Interestingly, the late maturers also differed from the early maturers in a test of ear advantage, something which is thought to reflect the degree of asymmetry in the functioning of the cerebral hemispheres. Although such a test is not a comprehensive indicator of brain functioning, the results of this study do suggest that differences in the maturation rates of the sexes may bring about certain neurological and psychological changes.

Social Deprivation

Some theorists believe that social experiences are of utmost importance to intellectual development, and that social deprivation can cause IQ changes. One of the most frequently cited investigations of social deprivation was conducted by Harold Skeels (1966). He studied twenty-five children who as infants had been placed in an overcrowded orphanage where they received little stimulation or personal attention. They saw only their busy nurses, who barely had time to feed and change their wards. At the age of eighteen months, thirteen of these children, who had an average IQ of 64, were transferred to an institution for retarded women. Here they were considered "house guests," and each was "adopted" by a retarded woman who lavished considerable attention and affection on her child. These children also received additional stimulation in the new setting, for they had toys to play with and were taken on excursions. After two years these children showed an average IQ increase of 28 points. In the meantime, the IQs of the twelve children who had remained in the orphanage during this period dropped 26 points, from a mean of 87.

The two groups also had quite different patterns of adjustment as adults. Those who had been removed from the orphanage were normal in intellectual functioning and social adjustment. Most had completed high school and some had attended college. All were employed or married to wage earners. As adults, the twelve who had remained in the orphanage had a retarded or borderline level of intellectual functioning. Only one finished high school, only one was married, and just half of them had jobs. Four were still wards of the state.

This study raises two controversial and still unresolved issues concerning the relation between social deprivation and intellectual development. The first concerns just what components of social deprivation hamper intellectual growth. Some argue that the culprit is inadequate mothering, holding that the child needs a consistent caretaker with whom to identify. Others say that the lack of sensory input is more damaging to the developing child. Adding to the confusion is the fact that not all children subjected to depriving environments are intellectually retarded. Apparently certain conditions are socially depriving to some children but have no effect on others.

The second unresolved issue is whether the effects of early deprivation are reversible. Some studies have indicated that the effects of severe deprivation in childhood are permanent and even cumulative. For example, the IQs of English children raised on canal boats and of American children raised in extremely isolated and impoverished regions of Appalachia have been found to decline with age.

Such evidence is on the side of the irreversibility of the intellectual damage done by early deprivation, but other data promote the opposite conclusion. Jerome Kagan's (1972) study of the rearing of children in Guatemalan villages is especially convincing. In these villages infants are confined to dark huts, for their parents believe that allowed outside they will catch diseases. Adults seldom play with or even talk to the infants, nor can the children see well to reach and crawl. At the age of two they are listless, apathetic, and retarded in development. But when these children do learn to walk, they leave the huts and begin to participate in community life. By the age of eleven they are active children and intellectually competent.

A study by Wayne Dennis (1973) may help to clarify the inconsistency in these studies. Dennis found that children raised in a foundling home or crèche in Beirut, Lebanon, under extreme social deprivation—the ratio of adults to care for them was one to twenty—became mentally retarded. If the children continued to live in these deprived conditions *through adolescence,* their mean IQs never went much beyond 55. But children who were adopted before the age of two subsequently achieved a completely normal development. In between were those adopted after the age of two. These individuals had varying degrees of intellectual impairment in adulthood, depending on how long they had lived at the crèche: the older the child at the time of adoption, the lower the adult IQ. Thus the effects of social deprivation may depend in part on how long it is endured. If children live in deprived circumstances for only a short period of time, up to approximately two years, the effects can probably be reversed. But deprivation experienced for longer periods of time will have permanent and increasingly detrimental effects.

Socioeconomic Status

Related to the social deprivation issue is the repeated finding that the higher a father's socioeconomic status, typically defined by such measures as occupation, income, and type of dwelling, the higher is his IQ and that of his children. Data collected during World War II indicate that, on the average, professional positions are filled by people with higher IQs (Table 10.5). These data raise an important question.

TABLE 10.5
Average Scores on the Army General Classification Test Obtained by Men in Various Occupations

Occupation	Mean Score
Accountant	128.1
Engineer	126.6
Chemist	124.8
Teacher	122.8
Pharmacist	120.5
Purchasing agent	118.7
Salesman	115.1
Receiving and shipping clerk	111.3
Sales clerk	109.2
Mechanic	106.3
Machine operator	104.8
Bartender	102.3
Auto mechanic	101.3
Chauffeur	100.8
Truck driver	96.2
Lumberjack	94.7
Miner	90.6
Teamster	87.7

Adapted from Harrell and Harrell, 1945.

Do people have high IQs because of greater economic means, or greater status because they have high IQs?

At least four hypotheses, by now familiar to us, have been offered to explain the social-class–IQ relationship. The first is that intelligence tests contain culturally unfair items which underestimate the IQs of those in lower socioeconomic classes. This possibility was assessed in a large-scale study (Eells et al., 1951) in which the performances of low and higher-status children were compared test item by test item. Some culturally unfair items were found that by their very nature guaranteed that children of higher status would do better than those in the lower classes. Many other test items passed by high-status children but not by the others were not ones for which the children had differential familiarity. These items tended to assess the ability to think abstractly.

A second explanation is that the personalities and motivations of persons of different social classes influence their approaches to intelligence testing, as well as their performance. A recent study (Yando, Seitz, and Zigler, 1979) found that economically advantaged children differed from economically disadvantaged children on tasks measuring curiosity, creativity, self-confidence, and dependency. The advantaged children were more curious and self-confident in their approach to academic tasks and more concerned about the quality of their responses. They were less fluent and creative on verbal creativity tasks and less confident of their physical abilities, however. The disadvantaged children, on the other hand, were more spontaneous and flexible in their approach to problems, but they were less self-confident on academic tasks, even when they had the same level of ability as the advantaged children. These findings indicate that children of lower and higher socioeconomic status bring different attitudes and styles to problem solving that could indeed affect their performance on intelligence tests.

Another explanation of social-class differences in IQ is that children of higher status are exposed to a more enriching environment and as a result develop more intelligence. Unfortunately, there are few clues to what particular "enriching" experiences produce more intelligence. A host of circumstances have been advanced as indicators of enrichment, such as greater availability of books and educational materials, and greater aspiration levels conferred upon children by parents, who themselves have high aspirations. Many homes and parents can be so described, whatever their socioeconomic level. The lower intelligence of children who have experienced at least a fairly decent environment cannot be explained by life circumstances.

The fourth explanation is that social-class differences in intelligence reflect genetic differences among the classes. Table 10.6 reports the IQs of children of differing socioeconomic groups as they grew up. The considerable stability of these average IQs at all ages has been pointed to as evidence that heredity explains their different levels. If the quality of the environment were the reason for the different levels, its effects would be cumulative; the IQs of higher-class children would increase with age and those of lower-class children would decline.

This genetic hypothesis was tested in a unique study (Schiff et al., 1978). French school children of unskilled, working-class parents were compared with their half-siblings who had been adopted early in life into upper-middle-class families. The mean IQ of the adopted children was 111, that of their unadopted half-brothers and sisters 95. In spite of the genetic similarity of these two groups, the differences in their IQs and in their failure rates in school were close to those of upper-middle-class and working-class children in the population at large. These findings therefore suggest that the social classes do not differ significantly in the intellectual endowment needed for social skills. An alternative interpretation, however, is that the genetic disadvantage of the children born to working-class parents was allayed by the environmental advantages given them when they were adopted into upper-middle-class homes. There is also

TABLE 10.6
Mean IQs of Children Grouped by Fathers' Occupations

Father's Occupational Level	Chronological Age			
	2–5½	6–9	10–14	15–18
Professional	114.8	114.9	117.5	116.4
Semiprofessional and managerial	112.4	107.3	112.2	116.7
Skilled trades, clerical, and retail business	108.0	104.9	107.4	109.6
Semiskilled, minor clerical, and business	104.3	104.6	103.4	106.7
Slightly skilled	97.2	100.0	100.6	96.2
Day laborers	93.8	96.0	97.2	97.6

Adapted from McNemar, 1942.

the very real possibility, in this and other studies, that adopted children receive extra amounts of care and attention from parents who are truly committed to them.

Whatever combination of causes eventually emerge to explain socioeconomic-class differences in IQ, it must be emphasized that the correlation between IQ and social class is relatively small, only .30. Moreover, the IQ differences are *average* differences and have nothing to do with the IQ of any one individual in any socioeconomic class. As a group the teamsters have the lowest average IQ, but one man in the group represented in Table 10.5 had an IQ of 145, far above the average for individuals in professional occupations. It should also be recognized that although the proportion of high-IQ individuals will be greater in very high-status groups, the absolute number of high-IQ individuals will be greater in lower-status groups for the simple reason that these groups contain so many more people.

SUMMARY □

Group curves depict intellectual development as a smooth and continuous process. Individual curves, however, show sudden increases, times of stability, and even declines in intellectual growth. Some of these fluctuations occur for technical reasons related to the construction of the tests. IQ scores can also shift with changes in life circumstances, although these have not been found to affect children in a predictable manner.

Changes in IQ may also be related to personality factors. Aggressiveness, independence, and competitiveness are more characteristic of children who show a rise in IQ than of those who show a decline. These personality traits may be differentially exhibited by males and females, but there are no sex differences for overall IQ. Such sex differences as have been found are in patterns of ability. Females tend to do better on verbal tasks, whereas males do better on mathematical and spatial tasks. Both cultural and biological factors have been advanced to explain these differences.

Extreme and prolonged social deprivation produces intellectual impairments that are not reversible. Deprivation experienced for shorter periods of time, particularly when the child is very young, has less severe effects. Social deprivation has sometimes been blamed for the existence of socioeconomic-class differences in IQ. This explanation pointing to dissimilar life circumstances is only one of four offered. The others are possible cultural biases of the tests, personality and motivational differences among the members of different economic groups, and possible genetic differences. Whatever the explanation, it should be emphasized that the relation between socioeconomic status and IQ is only moderate and that individuals with high and low IQs can be found in any socioeconomic group.

TO BE SURE YOU HAVE MASTERED THIS CHAPTER △

The important concepts in this chapter are listed below. You should know the meaning of all of them. The last section of the chapter contains no new concepts. You should review that section by noting how it applies the concepts introduced earlier.

Mental age (MA)
Chronological age (CA)
Basal age
Ceiling level
Intelligence quotient (IQ)
Standard deviation
Z-score
Deviation IQ
Standardization
Standardization sample
Reliability
Test-retest method
Split-half method
Alternate-forms method
Validity
Predictive validity
Concurrent validity
Content validity
Construct validity
Culture-fair tests
Intelligence A
Intelligence B
Fluid intelligence
Crystallized intelligence
General factor (*g*)
Specific factors (*s*)
Primary mental abilities
Cubical model of intelligence
Developmental quotient (DQ)
Cross-sectional studies
Longitudinal studies

The final section of this chapter does not lend itself to review in terms of single concepts. You might find it valuable to review the following factors and relationships related to IQ change.

Personality
Social deprivation
Socioeconomic status
Sex differences

TO GO BEYOND THIS CHAPTER △

In this book Chapter 11 applies these materials in a discussion of different levels of intelligence, and Chapter 12 looks at the growth of cognitive abilities in a different way. Chapter 16 covers personality testing, for which problems of reliability and validity come up again. Finally, a review of Chapter 9 on behavior genetics will be useful at this point. This chapter will have added to its significance.

Elsewhere A comprehensive treatment of intelligence is contained in H. J. Butcher's *Human Intelligence*. Much of this clear discussion is also relevant to Chapters 11 and 12. A very readable history of the intelligence testing movement is provided by Allen Edwards's *Individual Mental Testing*. This book traces the development of measures of intelligence and discusses the work and theories of the major psychometricians. *Studies in Individual Differences,* edited by James Jenkins and Donald Paterson, is another history, dealing particularly with the many individual and social factors thought to be related to intelligence and performance on intelligence tests. Statements of current views of intelligence are contained in Lauren Resnick's *The Nature of Intelligence*. An examination of infant intelligence from biological, social, cognitive, and emotional perspectives is presented by M. Lewis, in *Origins of Intelligence*. Another book, *Intellectual Functioning in Adults,* edited by Lissy Jarvik, Carl Eisdorfer, and June Blum, contains the results of various long-term studies of intellectual changes with aging.

(Drawing by CEM; ©1974 by The New Yorker Magazine, Inc.)

CH. 11

The Range of Intellect

Individual variation in intellectual abilities is impressively large. In the present chapter we shall examine the two extremes of this range of intellect—mental retardation and giftedness. Conventionally, persons who obtain low scores on IQ tests are considered to be retarded, whereas those who score very high are called gifted. Within both the retarded and the gifted groups, however, there is again much individual variation, and two persons with the same IQ may be very different in their everyday behavior and accomplishments. To understand the meaning of individual differences in intellect, therefore, we must consider both the problem of definition—how categories of intelligence are established—and the personality factors that can influence how effectively individuals use the intellectual abilities they possess.

MENTAL RETARDATION

Mental retardation is a problem of serious social concern. In view of the large number of persons in our society considered mentally retarded, such interest is certainly justified. Unfortunately, our knowledge and understanding of retardation do not yet equal our concern. The capabilities of retarded individuals are sometimes underestimated, and retarded persons are often the victims of injurious myths and prejudices. Clearer insight into the nature of retardation requires separating fact from fiction, and careful attention to how retardation is defined.

Definitions and Myths

Intellectual Subnormality **Mental retardation** is most often defined by arbitrarily drawing a line through the distribution of intelligence so that individuals with scores above the line are considered intellectually normal and those with scores below it are considered retarded. For many years there was general agreement that individuals whose IQ scores were in the lowest 3 percent of the population were retarded. Then in 1959 the American Association on Mental Deficiency (AAMD) defined mental retardation to include persons whose IQ test scores were more than one standard deviation below the mean, that is, less than 85. According to this definition, about 16 percent of the population was retarded, since IQs are normally distributed (page 231). This simple act of changing the definition increased the number of retarded persons in the United States from approximately 6 million to over 30 million! In 1973 the AAMD shifted the IQ criterion of mental retardation again, this time to *two* standard deviations below the mean, or below about 70 on the most widely used tests of intelligence. On the basis of this most recent criterion, an all-time low of about 2.3 percent of the population is considered mentally retarded.

It is obvious from the drastic shifts in cutoff points in these definitions that there is nothing in the nature of mental retardation to tell us where to draw the defining line. It is important to note, however, that the higher we draw the line, the more mental retardation we "produce." The drawbacks of such arbitrariness are exacerbated when society treats a dividing line as though it had been decreed from on high. For instance, in many states a cutoff point becomes the legal definition of mental retardation and is used to determine whether an individual qualifies for a variety of special services. The nonsense in rigidly adhering to such a definition is obvious. Does a child with an IQ of 69 really differ in kind from a child with an IQ of 70?

Mental retardation is actually characterized by a rather wide intellectual range. Table 11.1 presents the levels into which mental retardation has been subdivided in several classification systems, together with the labels applied to these subdivisions. Retarded individuals do not appear in these four subdivisions in equal numbers. The great majority are in the mildly retarded range (Figure 11.1).

Deficits in Adaptive Behavior Although lowered intellectual functioning is the salient feature of mental retardation, it is not the only criterion currently used by the AAMD. To be considered mentally retarded, an individual must also have deficits in adaptive behavior. That is, in addition to having an IQ below 70,

TABLE 11.1
Classifications of Mental Retardation

Educational Classification	AAMD Intellectual Levels	IQ Range (Wechsler)	Mental Age Expectancy	American Clinical Classification*	AAMD Levels of Adaptive Behavior
Educable	Mild	55–69	8–12	Moron	1
Trainable	Moderate	40–54	3–7	Imbecile	2
	Severe	25–39	0–3		3
Custodial	Profound	Below 25		Idiot	4

*Now obsolete.
From Cleland, 1978, p. 13.

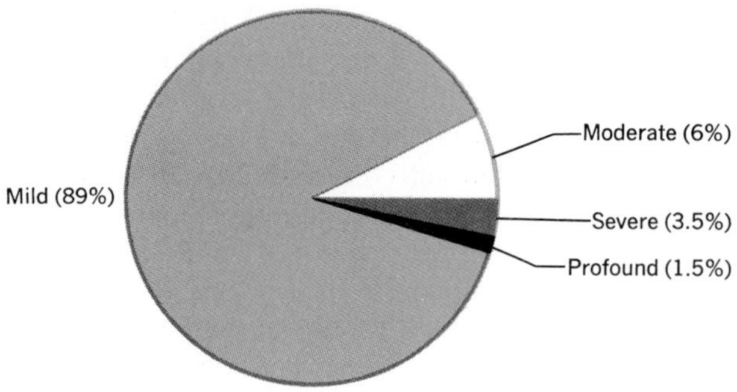

FIGURE 11.1
Makeup of the intellectually retarded population. The great majority of mentally retarded persons are only mildly retarded. (From Report of the President's Committee on Mental Retardation, 1967.)

the person must be unable to meet the standards of personal independence and social responsibility expected of his or her age and cultural group. A third criterion is that these deficiencies become manifest during the period of development, that is, before the age of eighteen. Excluded are individuals who become incompetent later in life, through brain damage or disease.

The AAMD has defined four levels of **adaptive behavior deficits;** they coincide with the intellectual categories of mild to profound retardation. Since the measurement of behavior is not as precise as intelligence testing, clinicians must rely on their own judgments of each individual's adaptive abilities. Observations are made of behavior in several categories such as communication, independence, and self-direction. Judgments in all categories are then compiled, and the adaptive behavior level is classified according to guidelines set by the AAMD. For example, a fifteen-year-old's abilities in the category of economic activity would be classified as follows (Grossman, 1973).

Level 1 (Mild): Can go to some stores and purchase several items; makes change correctly; may earn a living but needs help managing income.
Level 2 (Moderate): Can go on a shopping errand for several items and make minor purchases; handles bills and coins fairly accurately.
Level 3 (Severe): Can go on simple errands with a note to the shopkeeper; may use coin machines; realizes money has value but does not understand how to use it.
Level 4 (Profound): Not capable of economic activities.

These descriptions bring us to one of the myths most destructive to the everyday lives of retarded persons—that they are totally incapacitated and socially incompetent human beings. Nothing could be further from the truth. Just as there is a wide range of intellectual capacity among retarded individuals, there is also great variation in behavioral competence. Only the very small percentage of severely and profoundly retarded individuals are as helpless as the stereotype depicts them. The great majority, who are mildly retarded, are able to meet many of their own needs, hold jobs, and run a household with only minimal aid.

Why then is the view so persistent that all retarded persons are dependent? One culprit may be the familiar mental age concept. As Table 11.1 shows, the mental age achieved by the mildly retarded individual is approximately twelve years. What is often forgotten is that in the calculation of mental age the normal adult is considered to have the ability of an average sixteen-year-old. With this fact in mind, a mental age of twelve seems sufficient to meet most of the social demands of adulthood as well as the requisites of many types of employment.

When both intellectual and adaptive behavior are criteria for deciding whether an individual is mentally retarded, prevalence figures for mental retardation are inconsistent in different age groups (Table 11.2). The percentage of individuals judged to be retarded before they are five is very low. Most come to be considered retarded during their school years, and their numbers begin to decline again as they leave school. This changing prevalence rate reflects the fact that societal expectations vary with age group. Children under five years of age face very few social demands. When they reach school age, however, they encounter many, the most important being that they do well in school. Since this expectation is greatly dependent on intellectual ability, a child who has a low IQ is unlikely to do well in school. This child will thus meet the criteria for being classified as mentally retarded.

Many workers in the field of mental retardation speak of the "six-hour retarded child." They refer to children who are obviously retarded in academic activities but who perform quite normally outside of school. When these individuals are old enough to leave school, most of them are able to find work that is less intellectually demanding than their studies had been. If they succeed in becoming self-supporting and are able to meet the expectations of their social milieux, they will no longer be considered retarded. Brendan Maher (1963) described this situation succinctly when he stated that

> An individual who does not create a problem for others in his social environment and who manages to become self-supporting is usually not defined as mentally retarded no matter what his test IQ may be. Mental retardation is primarily a socially defined phenomenon, and it is in large part meaningless to speak of mental retardation without this criterion in mind.

TABLE 11.2
Percentage of Persons under Age 20 Classified as Mentally Retarded

	Locality		
Age	**England (1929)**	**Baltimore, Maryland (1941)**	**Syracuse, New York (1955)**
Under 5	0.12	0.07	0.45
5–9	1.55	1.18	3.94
10–14	2.65	4.36	7.76
15–19	1.08	3.02	4.49

After Zigler and Harter, 1969. Data from Report of the Mental Deficiency Committee, 1929; Lemkau, Tietze, and Cooper, 1941; New York State Department Mental Hygiene Technical Report, 1955.

A child with Down syndrome.

Organic Disorders

Once a line has been drawn to designate at what point in the distribution of intelligence and adaptive behavior retardation is thought to begin, those falling below it are often incorrectly considered a homogeneous group, all suffering from the same ailment. That mental retardation is a single entity having a single cause is a common misconception. Actually there are at least 200 different *etiologies* or causes of mental retardation, and knowing an individual's IQ and adaptive behavior tells us nothing about the origin or nature of the retardation.

The many etiologies of mental retardation can be classified into two basic types, retardation associated with a recognized organic disorder and retardation for which no organic cause can be distinguished. The **organic** type of mental retardation may be attributed to chromosomal anomalies and genetic disorders, to brain damage, and to a variety of insults from the environment. These diverse etiologies, which will be considered in this section, have one factor in common: in every instance examination reveals an abnormal physiological process.

In addition to people with disordered physiological processes, who make up a minority of all retarded individuals, there are the approximately 75 percent who are called **cultural-familial** retarded persons. The diagnosis of cultural-familial retardation is made when an examination reveals no organic cause, and when parents, siblings, or other relatives are similarly retarded. Very often the diagnosis can be made on both bases. Cultural-familial retardation is described in a later section.

Down Syndrome Approximately one infant of every 700 live births suffers from **Down syndrome** (page 223). Physical appearance alone is usually distinctive enough to permit a rapid diagnosis. The infant typically has a broad but short skull, rather flat at the back; the face is round, the nose low-bridged. Eyes are almost almond-shaped and slant upward and outward, the corners of the mouth droop, and the rather thick and furrowed tongue may protrude a good deal of the time. As the child grows older, stubby hands, fingers, legs, and feet, small stature for age, and a general loose jointedness become evident. The child usually does not walk until two or three years of age and then with a shambling gait. Many children with Down syndrome have congenital heart defects, and a number of them die young from these and other ailments. Individuals with Down syndrome have a rather wide range of intelligence, and there is evidence that those raised at home attain higher IQ scores than children who are institutionalized early in their lives (Stedman and Eichorn, 1964). But many individuals with this syndrome are in the severe and moderately retarded ranges and do require close supervision. About 10 percent of all retarded persons residing in institutions are there because they have Down syndrome. Postmortem examinations reveal that in most cases their brains weigh less than normal, and that the frontal lobes, brainstem, and cerebellum are particularly small (Crome and Stern, 1972).

This type of mental retardation was first described by Langdon Down, an English physician with some quaint and misguided views concerning the intelligence of various racial groups. The slanting eyes of the retarded children he had observed reminded him of the Mongolian eye fold. He concluded that these children had undergone some sort of evolutionary regression from the Caucasian race to what he believed to be the inferior "Mongol" race. These children were therefore thought to suffer from mongolism and to this day are often incorrectly referred to as mongoloids.

The major cause of Down syndrome was not discovered until 1959, when it was found that afflicted individuals have forty-seven chromosomes rather than the normal complement of forty-six (Figure

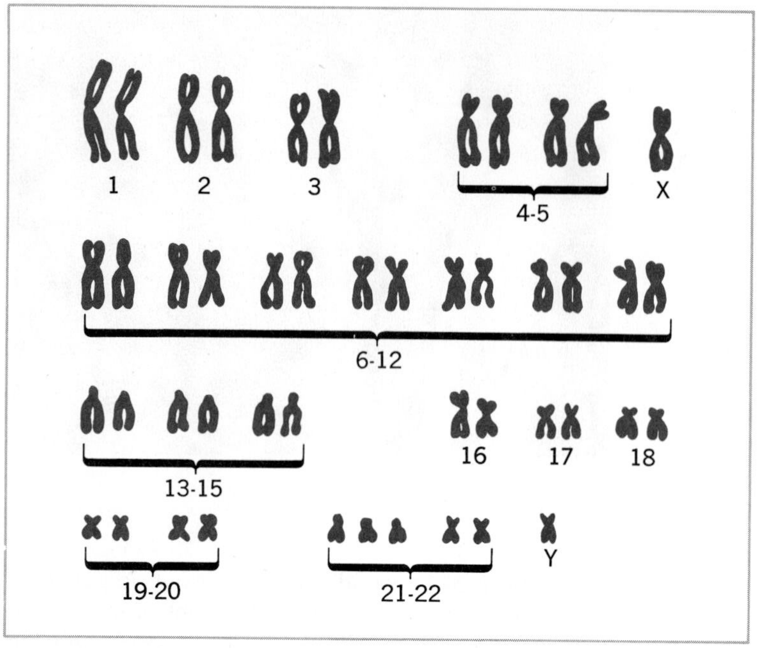

FIGURE 11.2

A karyotype of chromosome pairings from a boy with Down syndrome. Notice that there are forty-seven rather than forty-six chromosomes. The extra chromosome (trisomy) appears in group 21. Karyotypes of fetal cells obtained through amniocentesis (page 222) can now reveal the syndrome in the fourth month of pregnancy. (Adapted from a photograph by Dr. Jorge J. Yunis, Medical Genetics Laboratory, University of Minnesota Medical School. Reproduced with permission of New England Journal of Medicine.)

TABLE 11.3
Incidence of Down Syndrome According to Maternal Age

Mother's Age in Years	Approximate Risk per Pregnancy
Less than 29	1 in 3000
30 to 34	1 in 600
35 to 39	1 in 280
40 to 44	1 in 70
45 to 49	1 in 40

From Motulsky and Hecht, 1964.

11.2). Instead of two there are three chromosomes in group 21, so Down syndrome is often referred to as **trisomy 21.** The genetic material in the extra chromosome is thought to be responsible for the physical and mental abnormalities characteristic of Down syndrome.

An important clue to why these individuals receive an extra chromosome was provided by the discovery that the incidence of Down syndrome is related to the age of the mother. The risk of giving birth to a child with Down syndrome rises as a woman becomes older and increases dramatically after she reaches the age of forty (Table 11.3). A woman's immature egg cells are as old as she is, and their chromosomes have been suspended all that time in the first phase of meiosis, the process by which their number is halved and the gamete is formed. Thus the older she is, the greater exposure her egg cells have had to environmental insults such as irradiation, viruses, and certain chemicals known to cause chromosomal damage. The combination of these environmental factors as well as metabolic changes that occur with age may be responsible for the fact that the smallest pair of chromosomes do not separate when the ovum is formed. Men are not born with all their sperm, but instead they produce new ones, ready daily, by means of a seventy-four-day meiosis. Until quite recently it was thought that the father's sperm was unlikely to contribute the extra chromosome. New evidence, however, suggests that up to 25 percent of all cases of Down syndrome are from faulty sperm produced by the father (Magenis et al., 1977). Studies are currently underway to determine whether the father's age may increase the possibility of his contributing an extra chromosome.

Inborn Errors of Metabolism Inborn errors in the ability of the body to metabolize certain substances were mentioned in Chapter 9. Many of these disorders are inherited through a single pair of defective recessive genes and all are rare, but some may interfere profoundly with the development or maintenance of the brain.

The best-known disorder of this type, *phenylketonuria,* which occurs in about one of every 10,000 to 20,000 live births, has already been discussed (page 223). It is one of the few that can be treated (Figure 11.3). Phenylketonuria, which gives a musty odor to

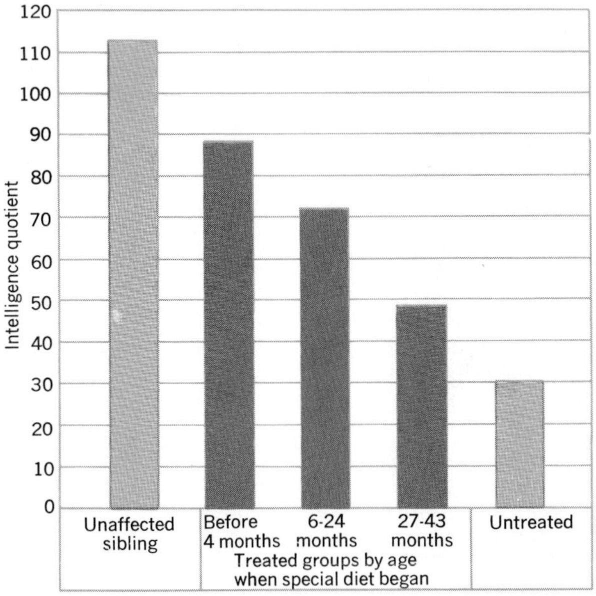

FIGURE 11.3

Effects of treatment of PKU. The graph shows mean IQ scores of children with PKU who were given a special diet starting at different ages, of PKU children who were not treated, and of their unaffected siblings. (Adapted from Berman, Waisman, and Graham, 1966.)

the urine, is the failure to metabolize an amino acid. A number of amino acids are not metabolized normally in *Maple Syrup Urine disease;* infants with this disorder suffer muscle and brain deterioration and die within their first year. In *Tay-Sachs disease,* also mentioned earlier, fats are not metabolized and collect in the nerve cells, causing blindness, brain deterioration, and early death. The infant's troubles begin to be noticeable between the third and sixth months. The metabolic disorder in *Hurler syndrome* causes mucopolysaccharides to accumulate in cells. After several months of normal development, the infant's head becomes abnormally large and the limbs become deformed. Mental retardation is usually severe, although there are milder forms of the disorder. Most children do not survive their teens.

Cretinism. **Cretinism** is a syndrome so distinctive that all who have suffered it from birth physically resemble one another. Their round and yellowish faces have a wide, flat nose, thick lips, and an enlarged, often protruding tongue. Skin is cool and dry, and the body is dwarflike, with a grossly swollen abdomen and short, stubby extremities. Cretinism also brings a sluggish disposition and severe retardation. In the nineteenth century the physical attributes of cretinism were thought to be so characteristic of retarded persons that all of them were called "cretins."

Cretinism is often caused by a pair of recessive genes; the thyroid glands that form are unable to synthesize the hormone thyroxine. But the condition may also develop when the body is deprived of thyroxine, whether through damage to the thyroid gland or its congenital absence, or through iodine deficiencies in the mother's diet during pregnancy and in the child's diet after birth. Iodine is essential in the synthesis of the hormone. Cretinism was at one time much more prevalent in the United States, for in some regions soil, air, and water have low concentrations of iodine. Today iodine is added to table salt. An infant born with a deficient thyroid can be given thyroid hormone, but early diagnosis is imperative, for even a few months of hypothyroidism will diminish intelligence.

Environmental Causes A variety of prenatal and postnatal circumstances can also cause organic forms of mental retardation. Prenatal factors potentially detrimental to the brain include inadequate maternal nutrition and exposure of the mother to drugs, toxins, or diseases such as syphilis and rubella. Radiation also poses a risk, which is why pregnant women are advised to avoid repeated X-rays and are among the first to be evacuated in the event of nuclear accidents. In addition, prematurity, anoxia or lack of oxygen at the time of birth, and birth injuries can significantly reduce intelligence, as can head injuries, lead poisoning, and certain illnesses in infancy and childhood. Two severe brain damage syndromes induced for the most part by environmental insults are microcephaly, in which neither the brain nor skull expands to normal size, and macrocephaly, in which the head becomes large through abnormal growth of supportive tissues. Microcephaly may be inherited through a pair of recessive genes. The mother's exposure to radiation or X-rays during the first three months of pregnancy, her infection with rubella during the same period, and injury or asphyxia of the infant at birth are other causes.

Not all these potential threats from the environment make mental retardation a certainty. Anoxia, for example, is likely to cause the limited motor control known as cerebral palsy, but many of its victims have average and superior intelligence. Rubella and irradiation have their most detrimental effects if the fetus is exposed during the first three months of pregnancy. In rare cases a developing syndrome can be treated and severe retardation avoided. One such syndrome is hydrocephaly. Tumors or disease are usually responsible for the condition. If left unchecked, the skull grossly enlarges as excess cerebrospinal fluid accumulates within the cranium. Draining off the excessive amounts of this fluid through a neurosurgical procedure may prevent mental retardation. Special diets that diminish the accumulation of fluid also help. These treatments are the most beneficial if begun as soon as the problem is discovered.

Children growing up in extremely depriving environments may have low IQs.

Cultural-Familial Retardation

"Retardation due to psychosocial disadvantage"—"psychosocial retardation" for short—is a current term for what has long been known as **cultural-familial retardation.** We shall continue to use the older term because it better reflects the dual nature of this form of retardation. Unlike those with organic disorders, cultural-familial retarded persons are invariably mildly so, having IQs above 50. The cause of this type of retardation remains a great mystery. Although there is some consensus that a combination of environmental and hereditary factors account for it, the relative contributions of the two are difficult to assess, just as are their contributions to intelligence itself and to social-class differences in IQ scores.

Environmental Evidence Some workers insist that cultural-familial retardation can be traced solely to the environment. Studies have found that this type of retardation is more prevalent in the lower socioeconomic classes, most particularly in those who live in extreme poverty and squalor. Moreover, studies such as that of Harold Skeels (page 245) indicate that children raised in extremely depriving circumstances can have low IQs. The current ascendancy of this view is reflected in the new terminology for this type of retardation. "Retardation due to psychosocial disadvantage" implies that only environmental factors are important. But what the extreme environmentalists fail to recognize is that very few of the children classified as cultural-familial retarded have been as socially deprived as were the institutionalized children investigated by Skeels. Furthermore, many children who score in the 50-to-70 IQ range live in homes which, although not affluent, should fulfill their developmental needs adequately enough. The only shortcomings of the hard-working parents who care for such children appear to be that they themselves do not score very high on intelligence tests.

A somewhat different environmental argument has been advanced by workers (for example, Kugel and Parsons, 1967) who are not convinced that cultural-familial retarded individuals are free from organic difficulties. These workers point out that mothers in impoverished circumstances are often in poor physical condition, are probably malnourished, and very certainly receive poor obstetrical care. Thus many children labeled as cultural-familial retarded may actually have organic damage from a variety of prenatal and postnatal circumstances. Some evidence supports this point of view. In one study (Kugel, 1967) it was found that 62 percent of a sample of cultural-familial retarded children had abnormal medical histories and 50 percent had mild neurological dysfunctions, such as abnormal EEG, difficulty with fine motor coordination, and reflex disorders. In another study of all eight-to-ten-year-old mentally retarded children in the city of Aberdeen, Scotland (Birch et al., 1970), central nervous system damage was indicated in one third of those who were mildly retarded. Unfortunately, neither of these studies examined control groups of children and therefore their evidence cannot be considered definitive—some children of average IQ may also have undetected central nervous system abnormalities. Nevertheless, these studies do suggest that what has traditionally

TABLE 11.4
Percentage of Children in Various IQ Ranges Who Were Born to Retarded Parents

	Children's IQs						
Parents	**0–49**	**50–69**	**70–89**	**90–110**	**111–130**	**131+**	**Average IQ**
Both parents retarded	7%	33%	40%	19%	1%	0	74
One parent retarded	2%	10%	28%	45%	13%	1%	92

Data from Reed and Reed, 1965.

been regarded as cultural-familial retardation may not be homogeneous in makeup.

Genetic Evidence Emphasis on the hereditary nature of nonorganic retardation has a long history. In 1877 Richard Dugdale published his book on the genealogical study of a family he called the Jukes. From generation to generation, Dugdale found in this family a very high incidence of criminality, pauperism, and mental retardation. Some forty years after Dugdale's report, Arthur Estabrook followed up the more than 1200 living members of this family and found half of them to be retarded. Both Dugdale and Estabrook noted the poor environmental conditions in which the generations of Jukes children had been raised and felt that both environment and heredity were to blame for the incompetencies of the Jukes family.

Another famous genealogical study, conducted by Henry Goddard (1912), traced two lines of descent from Martin Kallikak, a Revolutionary War soldier. Kallikak is a dubbed name, from the Greek *kalos,* "good," and *kakos,* "bad." One line of descent began when Kallikak took a brief respite away from the war and sired an illegitimate child by a retarded tavern waitress. The second line stemmed from Kallikak's later marriage to a woman of normal intelligence and some social standing. As with the Jukes family, among the descendants in the first line were a number of drunkards, harlots, paupers, convicts, and horse thieves, plus a high incidence of retardation. The descendants of the legitimate marriage were normal, and some were of outstanding reputation. Goddard ignored the differences in rearing and background in the two lines of descent and interpreted his findings as evidence that heredity was the overriding determinant of intelligence and social competence.

Polygenic Explanation In view of current thinking concerning the inheritance of complex traits such as intelligence, Goddard's genetic arguments were much too simplistic. His reasoning implied that intelligence is a single thing inherited in an all-or-nothing fashion. More recent thinking, that intelligence is a polygenic trait determined by a number of genes (page 204), appears to predict the range of intelligence more accurately than attributing it to a single gene or to the environment. The simplistic genetic position generates an expectation that all offspring of two retarded parents will be retarded. So too will all children raised in a poor environment, if the environment is blamed. The polygenic model predicts that the children will range in intelligence, with many but not all testing low in IQ. It also predicts that the average IQ of the offspring should be higher than that of their parents, for with a number of genes acting together there will be a regression, in this case a "progression," toward the mean. Studies of the IQs of retarded parents and their children do indeed bear out these predictions (Table 11.4).

The polygenic model of the inheritance of intelligence, when applied to the general population, predicts an IQ distribution of approximately 50 to 150. Since the lower limit of cultural-familial retardation is an IQ of 50, this group in all likelihood represents the lower portion of the normal distribution of intelligence. This is not to deny the importance of the environment as a factor in determining an individual's IQ score but merely to point out that biological variability does guarantee that the range has a lower end. Individuals with cultural-familial retardation may be quite "normal" in the sense that they are an integral part of the distribution of intelligence produced by variation in our population's gene pool.

The polygenic model is not readily applicable to those with organic retardation, many of whom have IQs below 50. Large-scale surveys have indicated that more individuals have very low intelligence than a simple normal curve would predict. For these reasons considerable clarity could be brought to the field of mental retardation by doing away with the practice of conceptualizing the distribution of intelligence as a single, continuous, normal curve (Figure 11.4*a*). A more appropriate representation might consist of two curves (Figure 11.4*b*). The intelligence of the bulk of the population, including those with cultural-familial retardation, would be depicted as a normal distribution having a mean of 100 and a range of approximately 50 to 150. Superimposed on this curve would be a second, somewhat normal distribution having a mean of approximately 35 and a range from zero to 70. The first curve would represent the poly-

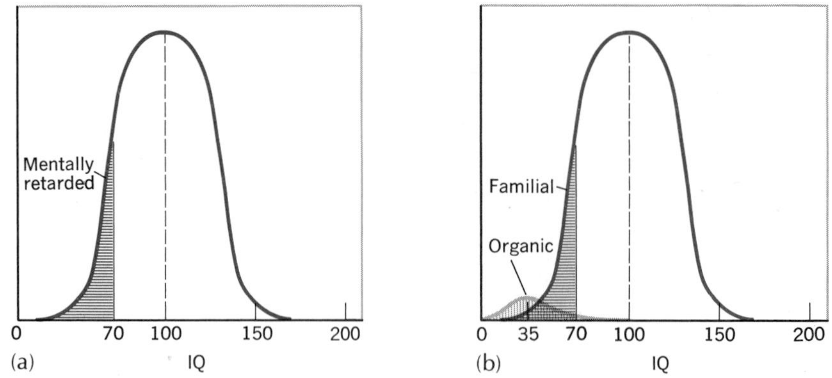

FIGURE 11.4

Two conceptions of the IQ distribution in mental retardation. (*a*) The conventional representation of the distribution of intelligence. (*b*) The distribution of intelligence represented by the two-group approach. The cultural-familial retarded group is seen as part of the normal distribution, whereas the organically retarded group has a separate distribution. (After Penrose, 1963.)

genic distribution of intelligence; the second would reflect the intellectual functioning of individuals in whom an identifiable physiological defect completely overrides normal polygenic expression.

Personality Factors in Retardation

Another common myth about mentally retarded persons is that their behavior is an inexorable product of their low intelligence—that they behave the way they do simply because they are retarded. Actually their behavior is no more totally determined by their IQs than is the behavior of individuals with average or superior intelligence.

Social Adjustment Indeed, many studies have revealed that in mildly retarded individuals social adjustment depends as much on personality as on level of intelligence. One particular study surveyed the adjustment of 8000 retarded recruits in the United States Army (Weaver, 1946). Fifty-six percent of the males and 62 percent of the females made a satisfactory adjustment to military life. The average IQs of the successful and unsuccessful groups were 72 and 68, respectively. The investigator concluded that "personality factors far overshadowed the factor of intelligence in the adjustment of the retarded to military service." More recent studies reveal that the personality characteristics associated with poor social adjustment as compared to good include anxiety, overdependency, poor self-evaluation, hostility, hyperactivity, resistance, and failure to follow orders, even when requests are well within the individual's intellectual ability. Unfortunately, there have been few investigations of how such personality traits might develop in retarded persons, but we have some insight into the process.

Personality and Intellectual Performance Retarded individuals frequently do less well on cognitive tasks than might be predicted from their absolute level of intelligence. For example, twelve-year-old retarded children with a mental age of eight may do more poorly on intellectually demanding tasks than average eight-year-old children with a mental age of eight. A possible explanation is that retarded children develop a variety of maladaptive motives, attitudes, and ways of solving problems which interfere with optimal functioning, a not surprising outcome inasmuch as their everyday experiences have often been quite different from those of children of average intellect. From their earliest years retarded persons are almost certain to experience a greater amount of failure in all their endeavors, which may then compound into discouragement and continual failure. The evidence has begun to spell out the details of the ways in which failure affects retarded children.

Anticipation of failure Several studies (for example, Turnure and Zigler, 1964) have now indicated that the many defeats experienced by retarded individuals give them a high expectancy of failure. They try harder to avoid failure than to achieve success and appear satisfied with performance that is below their intellectual capabilities. For example, in discrimination learning tasks (page 282) retarded children will often continue to choose a stimulus that was once correct rather than experiment to find the right pattern or solution.

Outerdirectedness A high rate of failure also gives retarded children an outerdirectedness when they are presented with a problem. They come to distrust their own solutions and seek guidance from their surroundings. Compared to nonretarded children of the same mental age, they are more sensitive to smiles, frowns, praise, and other cues from an adult and imitate the behavior of adults and peers to a greater extent. This **outerdirectedness** may explain the great suggestibility so frequently observed in retarded children. But when retarded children are guaranteed success and are rewarded for independent thought, they can give up their overreliance on external cues, develop more trust in their own abilities, and solve problems as well as nonretarded children of the same mental age (Achenbach and Zigler, 1968).

Overdependency Many retarded children are more socially deprived than are children of a higher level of intelligence. They receive less attention and support from adults and are more frequently punished by them. A long-lasting and deleterious effect of this early deprivation is an almost insatiable craving for adult attention and affection. All young children need reassurance and love, but as they develop they become more competent and autonomous, and therefore less dependent on adults. Socially deprived retarded children often do not show this typical progression from dependence to independence; relatively late in their development they still hunger for attention and nurturance from others. When someone gives them a problem, they are more interested in socializing with the person than they are in solving the problem. As a result, they do less well in their problem solving than might be expected from their intellectual level.

Wariness Although the social deprivation of retarded children apparently gives them a strong desire to interact with a supportive adult, it can have opposite effects as well. Many retarded children are suspicious, mistrustful, and fearful and avoid strangers. Wariness and mistrust can be detrimental to the everyday effectiveness of the children. In many situations they cannot behave optimally until they feel secure and certain that no harm will befall them.

Although groups of retarded and nonretarded children differ in their general personality patterns, this does not mean that all retarded children have one pattern and all nonretarded children another. Rather, the individual personalities of both normal and retarded children are unique to the extent that they have all led their own particular lives. But the retarded group does have a higher incidence of atypical social histories, which apparently foster a different set of personality traits than are found in others.

SUMMARY □

According to the American Association on Mental Deficiency, mental retardation is a condition in which intellectual functioning is significantly subaverage, the ability to behave adaptively is diminished, and these problems are first manifested during childhood.

The causes of retardation are numerous. Conventionally, a division is made between organic and cultural-familial retardation. About one quarter of retarded persons are in the first group, having recognized organic causes for their lower level of functioning. Included in this group are individuals with Down syndrome, PKU, Hurler syndrome, cretinism, hydrocephaly, and microcephaly, to mention a few. Cultural-familial retardation encompasses the three quarters of retarded persons for whom no organic defect can be identified. The cause of this type of retardation remains unclear, but it seems safe to reject explanations that point just to heredity or just to the environment.

On the average, organically retarded individuals have lower IQs than those with a cultural-familial diagnosis. The latter may represent the lower portion of the normal curve of polygenically determined intelligence, whereas organically retarded persons constitute a separate group. The inherited potentials of these individuals may cover the entire range of intellect, but unfortunately they are overridden by damaging physiological processes.

A number of distinctive personality traits are often found among retarded persons, such as a very strong need for attention and support, expectancy of failure, limited aspiration, and imitativeness. These characteristics probably do not stem from a lowered intellectual ability in itself but rather from a lifetime of social deprivation and efforts marked by failure.

CARE AND TRAINING OF RETARDED PERSONS

Earlier Attitudes

Throughout history the care and training of retarded persons has been determined as much by superstition, religion, fear, and various social aims as by any understanding of retardation. Treatments have ranged from infanticide and flagellation to worship and tender care. The work of Jean Itard in the early nineteenth century was the first systematic attempt to educate and train mentally retarded persons (Itard, 1807; Lane, 1976). Itard was a French physician who undertook the task of teaching "the wild boy of Aveyron." When captured in the woods, Victor, as the boy was later named, was twelve or thirteen years old and could not speak. He grunted and shrieked, crouched and trotted like a beast, and even when still swayed back and forth incessantly. Dirty and naked, indifferent and inattentive, he had subsisted on roots and raw potatoes. The medical authorities of the time diagnosed him as an "idiot" and felt that he had probably been abandoned for this reason. Itard, however, believed that the boy might have become retarded as a result of his social isolation. By providing Victor with the necessary educational and social experiences, Itard hoped to bring about his mental and moral development. Itard worked on the boy's senses, his intellect, and his emotions. Victor did learn to discriminate objects by sight, touch, and taste, to connect objects to abstract symbols, and to be aware of color, size, weight, and other distinctions. He communicated by writing the few words he understood. He eventually responded to fondling and affection and enjoyed his successes.

Although Itard was unable to educate Victor to the point of normalcy, the success he achieved with his training methods created much enthusiasm for educating mentally retarded persons. Itard's work was carried on and extended by his student Edouard Séguin, who was later put in charge of the world's first training school for retarded individuals. In 1848 Séguin brought his methods to the United States, where he helped establish several training institutions for retarded persons.

Later in the century Alfred Binet, the acknowledged "father of intelligence testing," also devoted his energies to special education. He formulated an educational methodology called mental orthopedics; it was designed to strengthen attention, memory, perception, judgment, and will. Exercises included games in immobility, speed tests of making dots with a pen, and other interesting and highly motivating tasks.

Despite notable advances, it soon became apparent that these educational techniques could not cure mentally retarded persons. Enthusiasm for training declined, and interest focused on protecting these unfortunates from society. But before long this new attitude was completely reversed. Instead of protecting retarded individuals from society, the new goal was to protect society from them. Here is how Walter Fernald, one of America's pioneer figures in the field of mental retardation, described retarded people in 1912.

> The social and economic burdens of uncomplicated feeblemindedness are only too well known. The feebleminded are a parasitic, predatory class, never capable of self-support or of managing their own affairs. The great majority ultimately become public charges in some form. They cause unutterable sorrow at home and are a menace and danger to the community. Feebleminded women are almost invariably immoral and . . . usually become carriers of venereal disease or give birth to children who are as defective as themselves. . . . Every feebleminded person, especially the high-grade imbecile, is a potential criminal, needing only the proper environment and opportunity for the development and expression of his criminal tendencies (reported in Davies and Ecob, 1959).

The impact of such indictments was profound; they led to radical movements to segregate and sterilize retarded persons so as to protect the rest of society and control the birth rate of potentially retarded children.

Such an alarmist view largely prevailed for four decades into the twentieth century, until retarded citizens inducted into the army (page 258) and working in defense industries did better than expected. Retarded individuals are now recognized not as inherently evil but rather as persons of low intelligence whose eventual role in society is heavily influenced by the care and training that society provides. Since World War II public school programs and special classes for retarded children have proliferated. These special programs provide curricula appropriate to the children's mental ages and often emphasize self-help skills.

Normalization

Today much of the care and training of retarded individuals is guided by the principle of **normalization.** This concept, which originated in Sweden, is described by Bengt Nirje (1969) as "making available to the mentally retarded patterns and conditions of everyday life which are as close as possible to the norms and patterns of the mainstream of society." A related idea is **mainstreaming,** which means integrating handicapped with nonhandicapped persons in schools and in the community whenever possible.

Education Largely in response to these concepts, the United States Congress passed the Education for All Handicapped Children Act of 1975, which makes it mandatory for public schools to provide appropriate educational services to all children, including those with the most profound handicaps. The law also specifies that handicapped children be educated with nonhandicapped children to the greatest extent possible. Separate classes or schools for handicapped children are permitted only if the regular educational environment plus supplementary services are not sufficient to serve their needs.

This law has become a source of great controversy among educators and psychologists. Those who champion mainstreaming view it as a necessary program for providing equal rights and opportunities to all handicapped children and for reducing the stigma attached to being in a special education classroom. Those who attack the program, on the other hand, argue that these children's needs are best met by the more individualized instruction of specially trained teachers in separate classrooms. They say that the children endure greater stigma in a regular classroom,

Normalization, making the conditions of everyday life available to the mentally retarded, may help them lead more satisfying lives.

where their limitations are more evident in comparison with the abilities of their classmates.

To date, research on the consequences of mainstreaming has done little to abate this controversy, for the results have been mixed. Some data indicate that mainstreamed children do as well academically as children in special classes, but there is little evidence that they are taught more effectively. Indeed, deaf children in special schools have scored higher on standardized achievement tests than deaf children in regular schools (Martin, 1978).

The expectation that mainstreamed retarded children would be less stigmatized by their peers has not been borne out. Most research indicates that mainstreamed retarded children are less well accepted by their peers than are children in self-contained special-education classes (Gottlieb and Budoff, 1973), although one study found that peers of mainstreamed retarded children in urban areas were more accepting than their counterparts in the suburbs (Bruininks, Rynders, and Gross, 1974). Furthermore, another study found that retarded children in mainstreamed classes had higher expectancies of failure than those in special classes (Gruen, Ottinger, and Ollendick, 1974). Clearly, research that will establish which children can best benefit from mainstreaming and which are best served by special-education programs is urgently needed.

Residential Care The normalization ideology has also figured prominently in current social policy concerning institutions and other residential facilities for retarded individuals. The first institutions for retarded people were established in the United States in the

This is a typical scene in a state school for the mentally retarded before massive public protest led to the improvement of such conditions.

mid-nineteenth century. Initially, the goal of these facilities was to train the residents to be self-sufficient so they might return to the community. By the end of the nineteenth century, however, these facilities had become primarily custodial in nature. Large institutions, built far from population centers, were intended to be total-care facilities, serving the educational, health, recreational, and social needs of the residents. This philosophy of care for retarded persons was dominant until the 1960s. Since that time dissatisfaction with large centralized institutions has grown. Certainly the whole pattern of life common in large institutions—the extreme regimentation, the limited choices, and the almost complete lack of privacy—is in conflict with the normalization principle. Just how dehumanizing these living conditions actually are has been well documented by Burton Blatt and Fred Kaplan in their book *Christmas in Purgatory* (1966) and by Blatt in *Exodus from Pandemonium* (1970) and *Souls in Extremis* (1973). In addition, the courts have asserted the right of retarded individuals to treatment in "the least restrictive habilitation setting" (for example, in *Wyatt* v. *Stickney*, 1972). The current trend is to shift many retarded individuals into smaller community-based group homes, halfway houses, and foster homes. Mildly retarded persons who can function more independently may have their own private apartments.

Civil Rights The normalization principle has extended enormously the civil rights of retarded persons. An earlier "reminder," one typical of those given to retarded individuals when they were allowed to work outside the institution, reflects the strictures placed on them as late as the 1950s (Cleland, 1978, p. 292).

> A Reminder
> We congratulate you on being given the chance to take your place in society. During this period you will be on probation and you must obey not only the laws of your community but also the following rules of our school:
> 1. You must not leave your present place without first notifying us.
> 2. You must not drive or own a car.
> 3. You must not drink alcoholic beverages or enter any tavern.
> 4. You must not get married.
> 5. You must not get engaged or go steady or date.
> 6. You must not make any written contract to purchase articles on time payments without first talking to your social worker.
> 7. You must be home by 12:00 p.m., or earlier.
> 8. You must not leave the state of ________.
>
> Carry this reminder with you at all times and read it frequently. Violation of any one of the above rules can result in your return to the school.
>
> ________________
> Superintendent's signature

Today a retarded individual is assumed to have the same rights as any other citizen, although many of them have had to be fought for by retarded persons and their advocates. Some newly won through litigation and legislation in the United States in the 1970s include the rights to education, to treatment, and to remain free from harm; the right to be trained, employed, and paid for work; the rights to have physical access and not to be discriminated against because of mental or physical handicaps. Various states do, however, impose certain restrictions, depending on the person's intellectual competency, on getting a driver's license, voting, signing a contract, and marrying.

Providing care, training, and rights to mentally retarded persons in our society is not only humane but also sound social policy. Follow-up studies of adults who had been classified as retarded in childhood found that more than 75 percent of them were self-supporting and making a good social adjustment. This is not to say that retardation is reversible, but that retarded persons can contribute more than the negative view of their potential, commonly held in the past and still held today by some people, would acknowledge.

SUMMARY □

There have been great shifts in society's attitudes toward retarded persons. We have gone through times of much enthusiasm and high expectations, as well as periods when retarded persons were feared, degraded, and locked away in institutions. Now we have arrived at today's more humanistic views and constructive attempts to improve the lives of retarded citizens. The current concepts of normalization and mainstreaming have guided our efforts to educate, care for, and generally ensure retarded persons the same opportunities and patterns of living that the rest of the population enjoys.

Special-education classes are now giving way to the practice of keeping retarded children in regular classrooms and providing supplementary educational services. Large, total-care institutions are being replaced by small, community-based facilities and residences whenever possible. The most significant change is the granting of basic human rights and freedoms to all retarded persons.

Our more enlightened views and practices can benefit not only retarded persons but society as a whole. Guarantees of care and training can enable retarded persons to fulfill the potential they do possess and to live happier, more productive lives.

GENIUS AND GIFTEDNESS

Just as one end of the distribution of intelligence consists of a small percentage of individuals whose IQs are considerably below average, the other consists of an equally small percentage of individuals who have very high IQs. These individuals are often referred to as gifted. Within this numerically select group is a small subgroup considered geniuses. Although hav-

"I never thought my daughter could live without me."

"Michele is retarded. I've worried about her future because I know I won't always be around to take care of her. The idea of putting her in an institution was out of the question; and yet I didn't know of an alternative until I found out about group homes for the retarded."

Michele's 24 now and has been living in a group home for three years. It's a nice house in a neighborhood close to where she used to live. Here she is as independent as any woman and still gets the care she needs. There's always companionship when she wants it. Her days are spent in a special work center, and this too strengthens her sense of accomplishment. Now when she spends a weekend with her mother there is a lot for the two to talk about, and her mother knows that Michele can live on her own.

The School of Visual Arts Public Advertising System

Poster made possible by One to One.

ing a very high IQ is almost a requisite, being considered a genius implies more than numbering among those in the gifted group having the highest intelligence.

A High IQ Is Not Enough

At one time designations of genius were made on the basis of IQ scores somewhere above the 150 mark, but such a judgment is simply inappropriate. The academic woods are filled with faculty and students with very high IQs, but these same woods are notably devoid of geniuses. For an individual to become a **genius,** an exceptional pattern of basic talent must bring transcendent accomplishment. Furthermore, the individual's accomplishments must stand the test of time, for what is judged original and creative in one period may be considered derivative and unimportant by succeeding generations. Persons who receive widespread recognition for their accomplishments in their own lifetimes are more appropriately called "eminent" rather than geniuses.

The term genius is often applied to individuals whose accomplishments in a specialized area such as music or art have been impressive. For example, *Life* magazine wrote of Louis Armstrong.

> It is a simple fact of jazz music, the only art form America ever wholly originated, that virtually all that is played today comes in some way from Louis Armstrong. . . . More than any other individual, it was Armstrong who took the raw spontaneous folk music of the honky tonks and street parades and, quite unconsciously, built it into a music beyond anything musicians had previously imagined. It was a spectacular outpouring of born, unschooled genius (quoted in Ashby and Walker, 1968).

Even though Armstrong was a key figure in originating a new art form and one who enriched the lives of millions, it remains to be seen whether future generations will continue to consider this rare and inspired human being a true instance of genius.

A Superior Environment Is Not Essential

There does seem to be something extraordinary about geniuses, and their special qualities are often observed early in their lives. Some hold to the myth that children with exceptional talents will never fulfill them unless their abilities are recognized early and they have the further good fortune to spend their childhoods in relatively advantaged homes, nurtured by diligent parents whose principal concern is their giftedness. Yet many geniuses have lived their early years in other surroundings. Armstrong was a neglected child whose father deserted the family and whose mother was "out on the town" (Goertzel and Goertzel, 1962). As a child he was caught firing blank cartridges from his stepfather's revolver and placed in the New Orleans Colored Waifs Home for Boys, where he was taught to play an instrument. Isaac Newton's father was a humble yeoman farmer who died before his son was born; Karl Gauss, perhaps the greatest mathematician of all time, was the son of a bricklayer; James Watt and Abraham Lincoln were sons of carpenters, Martin Luther and John Knox sons of peasants; and Johannes Kepler's father was a drunken innkeeper (Burt, 1955).

The circumstances of these lives lend credence to the "great person" view of the genius as a dedicated individual who overcomes all obstacles to fulfill an inspired, burning destiny. Others have argued that a genius is simply a highly intelligent person whose famed accomplishment is only the final inevitable step in work brought to near fruition by numerous individuals who have lived and labored earlier. Being considered a genius is largely a matter of luck for these individuals, who have happened to be at the right place at the right time. Both views appear to pierce through to a truth; geniuses are probably both born and shaped by circumstance.

Francis Galton: A Case History of Genius

> My dear Adele,
>
> I am 4 years old and can read any English book. I can say all the Latin Substantives and Adjectives and active verbs besides 52 lines of Latin poetry. I can cast up any sum in addition and can multiply by 2, 3, 4, 5, 6, 7, 8, [9], 10, [11].
>
> I can also say the pence table. I read French a little and I know the clock (reported by Terman, 1917, p. 210).

So wrote Francis Galton to his sister on "Febuary" (his only spelling error) 15, 1827, the day preceding his fifth birthday. There are brackets around the numbers 9 and 11 because little Francis scratched out one with a knife and pasted some paper over the other, apparently in an effort to appear less boastful.

Galton's extreme precocity in a number of intellectual spheres has been colorfully described by Lewis Terman (1917). That Galton read at five, not mechanically but with real comprehension, is attested to by his ability to offer quotations appropriate to given situations. One day the five-year-old Francis was found keeping a group of bullying boys at bay, shouting,

> Come one, come all. This rock shall fly
> From its firm base, as soon as I.

Terman also reports a delightful story about Galton at

The mark of true genius is a lasting contribution such as those made by Albert Einstein, Marie Curie, Georgia O'Keefe, and Louis Armstrong.

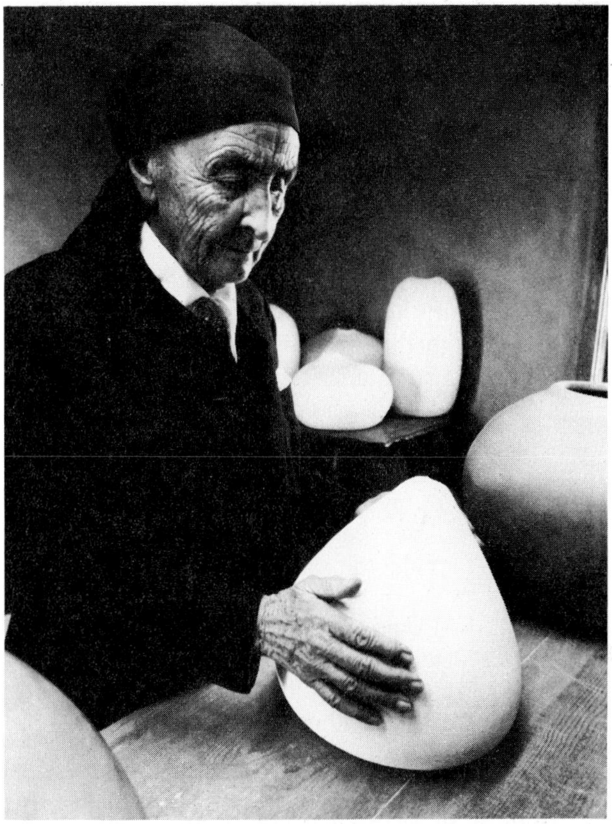

age six, when he had already attained a scholarly understanding of the Iliad and Odyssey.

> At this age, a visitor at the Galton home made Francis weary by cross-questioning him about points in Homer. Finally, the boy replied, "Pray, Mr. Horner, look at the last line in the twelfth book of the Odyssey" and then ran off. The line in question reads, "But why rehearse all this tale, for even yesterday I told it to thee and to thy noble wife in thy house; and it liketh me not twice to tell a plaintold tale" (pp. 211–212).

Young Galton grew up in advantaged circumstances. His early intellectual interests and his family's support of them are evident in the following letter written at the age of ten.

> December 30, 1832.
>
> My Dearest Papa:
>
> It is now my pleasure to disclose the most ardent wishes of my heart, which are to extract out of my boundless wealth in compound, money sufficient to make this addition to my unequaled library.

The Hebrew Commonwealth by John . . .	9
A Pastor Advice	2
Hornne's commentaries on the Psalms . .	4
Paley's Evidence on Christianity	2
Jones Biblical Cyclopedia	10
	27

In spite of all these clear indications of extremely high intelligence, Galton was not considered a child prodigy. Karl Pearson described one amazing intellectual boyhood feat after another, in a four-volume biography, but nevertheless wrote of Galton's childhood,

> The letters we have quoted from these early years . . . are, indeed, just what a healthy normal child would write. . . . Need we attempt to see . . . foreshadowings of future achievement in these outpourings of healthy childhood? I do not think we can say more than that Francis Galton was a normal child with rather more than average ability . . . (quoted in Terman, 1917, p. 214).

Indeed, as Terman points out, since the intellectual feats that earned Galton his reputation were accomplished late in his life—he made breakthroughs in meteorology, anthropology, and genetics; he established the field of eugenics; he devised the correlation coefficient in statistics, a heliograph or mirror for signaling with the sun's rays, a "wave engine" for harnessing the power of waves, as well as a technique for identifying individuals through their fingerprints—he was often referred to as a late-maturing genius. Interestingly, although most geniuses are extremely bright as children, the exceptional intellectual abilities that characterize their genius often do mature relatively late (Figure 11.5). As children they do nothing truly amazing in terms of creative accomplishment. But to be able to read and write at age five, as Galton did, suggests that he had then a mental age of ten and thus an IQ of 200! Just to indicate the rarity of his intelligence, when Terman examined thousands of children, the highest IQ he discovered was 170.

The Price of Genius

Throughout history there has been a popular belief that geniuses pay a price for their creative intellect in madness and emotional instability. The view that "the line between genius and insanity is very thin" is based on striking instances of emotional instability among the ranks of the gifted. Galton, for example, suffered nervous symptoms throughout life and had two breakdowns. Mendel suffered several breakdowns or depressions, and Darwin was plagued by a chronic and mysterious illness which depleted his energies and made him nervous and unable to sleep. Isaac Newton, the father of modern physics, and Michael Faraday, one of the greatest physicists of the nineteenth century, both became psychotic around the age of fifty, although after a period each recovered his sanity. The lives of such greats as Van Gogh, Blake, Da Vinci, Nietzsche, Socrates, Swift, Kant, Coleridge, Raphael, and Rousseau all had their dark aspects. Some gifted individuals have even felt that their accomplishments stemmed from their instability. Thus Edgar Allan Poe wrote,

> I am come of a race noted for vigor of fancy and ardor of passion. Men have called me mad; but the question is not yet settled, whether much that is glorious, whether all that is profound, does not spring from disease of thought, from moods of mind enacted at the expense of general intellect (quoted in Marks, 1925, p. 22).

It has even been suggested that creative giftedness may be genetically linked to schizophrenia. In a review of the empirical findings in support of this claim, Jon Karlsson (1974) established that the degree of association between the incidences of schizophrenia and giftedness in families is high; that individuals having schizophrenic family members are more creative thinkers than the rest of the population; and that schizophrenics are more likely to have been the top graduates in their high schools and to have earned doctorate degrees.

W. Ross Ashby and Crayton Walker have noted that seeming madness "may be not so much the price of genius as the result of mismanaged lives" (1968, p. 219). The single-mindedness with which geniuses focus on their talents may make them ignore or mismanage the details of everyday living, which seem insignificant in comparison to their work. Moreover,

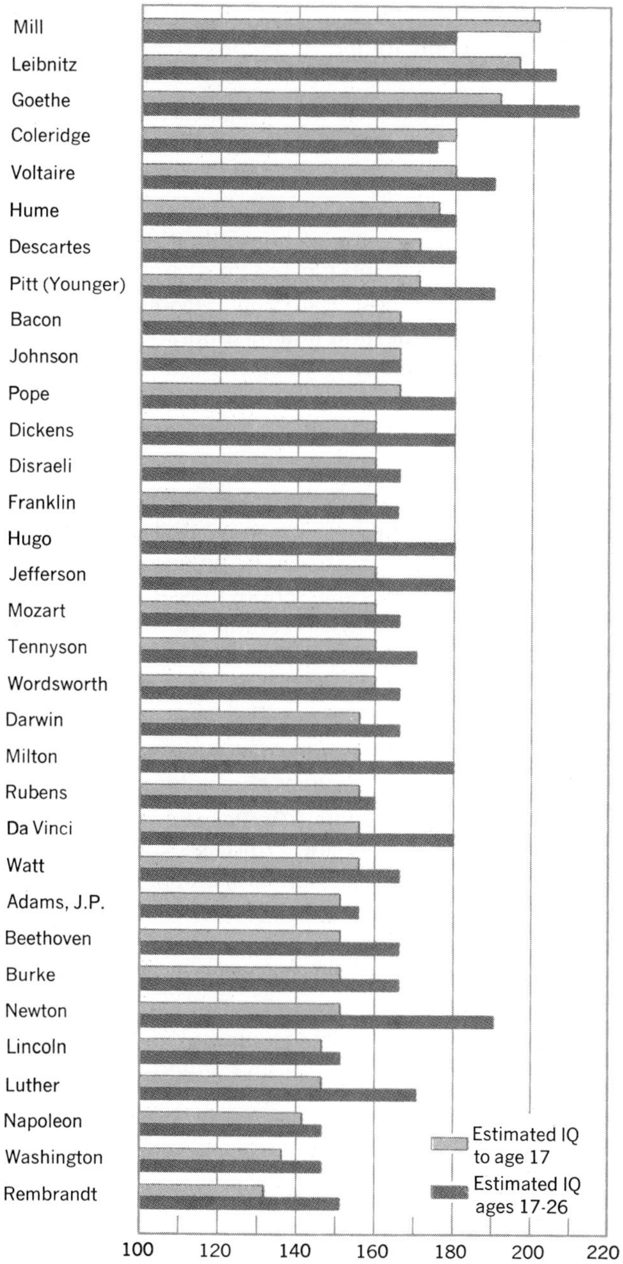

FIGURE 11.5
Estimated IQs of great men of the ages. The judgments were made by Cox, Terman, and Merrill on the basis of achievements of each person at ages 17 and 26. Many were "late bloomers," although all showed great potential at a very early age. (Adapted from Cox, 1926.)

the prodigious labors necessary to bring forth monumental achievement leave little time for society and friendships. Michelangelo illustrates the extreme of the solitary genius in his statement "I have no friends of any kind, nor do I wish any, and I have not so much time that I can afford to waste it" (quoted in Clements, 1963, p. 114). We can only conjecture whether Michelangelo would have been better adjusted had he socialized more and created less.

Studies of Giftedness

Although there may be some connection between *genius* and madness, no such relationship exists for **giftedness** in general. Longitudinal studies of individuals who had exceptionally high IQs as children have found no evidence at all of an inordinately high incidence of maladjustment. The most notable is Terman's (1925; Terman and Oden, 1947, 1959) monumental study, which has set to rest many of the popular stereotypes about the extremely gifted individual. In 1922 Terman reported the results of an initial study of 1470 school children with IQs of 135 or over. They were for the most part in grades three to eight and averaged eleven years old when they were selected. In comparison with a control group of children of average intelligence, members of the gifted group were found to be taller, heavier, more socially poised, more outstanding in educational accomplishments and more avid readers, more active in play, and less prone to headaches, nervousness, tics, and stuttering. All in all, members of the gifted group were remarkably well adjusted. Terman's collection of data shattered the erroneous belief that some mythical law of compensation would hold and preserve a brilliant mind in a fragile, weakened body.

Follow-up studies of these children were made every five to ten years, with the last one done in 1972, when these individuals were entering their sixties. These subsequent studies were equally telling. Educationally, the gifted children grew up to excel on all counts. About two thirds of them went to college. By comparison with the average college graduate, six times as many who graduated continued their studies and received doctorate degrees. Occupationally, over 70 percent found positions in professional and semiprofessional fields. Many had international reputations. Social, marital, and sexual adjustments were as satisfactory as in the general population.

Not all the gifted individuals Terman studied could be counted as successes, however. Some failed in college, some drifted aimlessly from job to job, and some committed crimes. What factors distinguished the successful gifted individuals from the unsuccessful? Certainly IQ was not the critical element, since those considered most successful had an average adult IQ of 139, whereas those considered least successful had an equally potent average of 133. What did seem to separate the unsuccessful gifted group from the successful was poorer motivation and poorer emotional adjustment. Thus, as with a retarded person, the gifted individual's IQ score is outweighed by other personality factors in determining everyday social effectiveness.

Gifted Women Terman's original sample included 671 girls. Although as women many became eminent individuals, they did not over the years report as many easily identifiable accomplishments as did the men. Nonetheless, at the time of the last survey in 1972, more of these gifted women were employed than were homemakers, and compared to other United States women their own age, they had higher incomes, better educations, and more of their numbers in the professions. According to Pauline Sears (1976), who analyzed the women's responses in the 1972 survey, the women achieved less because many of them were less ambitious than the men. They were more likely to settle for work that they enjoyed rather than to strive for success. Moreover, this generation of women had not been offered the same opportunities, or the social encouragement, to develop their full potential that the men had. Undoubtedly, as women are given equal opportunities and more encouragement to develop and apply their abilities, more of them will join the ranks of such famous achievers as Marie Curie, Eleanor Roosevelt, and Margaret Mead.

Personality in the Gifted Several studies have attempted to discover the personality traits of the gifted, and in particular of the gifted who are not socially adjusted. These studies have confirmed that, in general, the gifted do not have an abnormally high incidence of maladjustment. When maladjustment was discovered, the complaints were of "too much time spent in reading, of being self-centered and bossy, and in a few instances of mixing poorly, being teased easily, [and being] solitary, resistant, or bumptious" (Miles, 1954, pp. 1025–1026). In addition, the gifted who were maladjusted often failed to develop good work habits and appeared stifled when forced to live in circumstances that provided too little stimulation (Witty, 1940).

One psychoanalyst found in the gifted a hypersensitivity to stimuli in the external world, a disparity between intellectual and emotional development, and a deep unhappiness with their own exceptionality (Keiser, 1969). Part of the unhappiness of gifted children may be explained by the greater demands that they make upon themselves, and surprisingly, by the fact that they consider themselves less adequate than less intelligent children view themselves (Katz and Zigler, 1967). This disparity between the high aspirations of very intelligent children and their low self-assessment may make them feel considerable guilt and personal dissatisfaction. Whether it also makes them maladjusted depends on whether their reaction to self-dissatisfaction is adaptive, for example, working harder, or maladaptive, perhaps withdrawing from social situations. Brilliant individuals by very dint of their brilliance can make more problems for themselves, but they bring to the solution of such problems tremendous intellectual resources. In light of these resources, we might expect them to attain better personal adjustments rather than worse.

Training the Gifted Of the brilliant Isaac Barrow—who preceded Newton as professor of mathematics at Cambridge—it was said, "Endowed with a restless body and a vivid mind, he so plagued his teachers and was so troublesome at home that his father . . . prayed that if it pleased God to take away any of his children, he could best spare Isaac" (Moore, 1924, p. 3). There is little question that the budding genius can sometimes be difficult and a trial to parents and teachers. Yet it is clearly to society's advantage to ensure that these difficult gifted children develop their full potential.

Unfortunately, there is little agreement about what form of education is best for the gifted child. Some feel that these children should be given special attention but remain in regular school classrooms. Others champion track systems, teaching the exceptionally talented children together in groups. Still others favor "acceleration," promoting children until they reach a grade offering activities commensurate with their intellectual abilities. This, of course, means that gifted children are a much younger chronological age than their classmates, which may or may not be damaging, depending on whether the child has the emotional preparation to meet the social demands of an advanced class.

Whatever methods are chosen, the fact remains that our nation does rather poorly in nurturing the abilities of the gifted. A report from the United States Office of Education (1971) concluded that a very small percentage of the nation's gifted children receive any kind of special services. Gifted children among minority groups and in economically disadvantaged populations appear to be particularly neglected.

Gifted individuals themselves are often unhappy with their school experiences. When questioned in adulthood, three fifths of the 400 most eminent men and women of our century, the majority of whom had had exceptional talent as children, remembered being dissatisfied with school and teachers (Goertzel and Goertzel, 1962). Assigned work that did not challenge them, they probably became bored, frustrated, and disinterested.

Creativity

Creativity has been described in various ways, but most definitions view as its essence placing things in new perspectives and seeing connections that were previously unsuspected. It is often a product of divergent thinking, the process of seeking multiple ideas or solutions to a problem which Guilford has described (page 240). New perspectives may also come about unexpectedly in a flash, during meditation, daydreaming, intoxication, dreams, or through association, logical deduction, and external stimulation. Originality is not always creativity, however. The thinking of mentally ill persons, particularly schizophrenics, is marked by originality and uniqueness, but it is hardly creative. The same holds for most of the new and unusual thoughts that people have. To be creative, an idea or product must be original *and* appropriate—it must fit the context or make sense in light of the demands of the situation. Although the process by which creative insights are achieved is little understood, research has provided some understanding of the attributes of the most creative persons and the factors in the environment that may enhance creativity.

Frank Barron (1958) has conducted intensive studies of persons considered "highly original scientists and artists." Among those tested were painters, writers, biologists, economists, anthropologists, physicists, and physicians. In these studies subjects were assigned many tasks: interpreting inkblots, creating mosaics from colored squares, creating a stage design on a miniature stage, completing unfinished drawings, and expressing an artistic preference for various figures and designs. They were also asked to suggest new uses for commonplace objects and to wrestle with the consequences of untoward events, such as "A nation finds a way to increase the average IQ of its citizens by 50 points—what would the consequences be?" Or they might be expected to create a story using as many words as possible from a list of randomly drawn nouns, adjectives, and adverbs.

Among the findings of these studies were the following. The creative person, whether artist or scientist, prefers drawings that are asymmetrical, complex, and vital rather than those of balanced simplicity (Figure 11.6*a*). Their preferences in paintings are similar, and their own mosaics and drawings (Figure 11.6*b*) have the same asymmetrical and complex qualities. What Barron considered the "most difficult and far-reaching ordering" were the efforts to interpret inkblots in a single comprehensive and synthesizing percept. "It . . . illustrates the creative response to disorder, which is to find an elegant new order more satisfying than any that could be evoked by a simpler

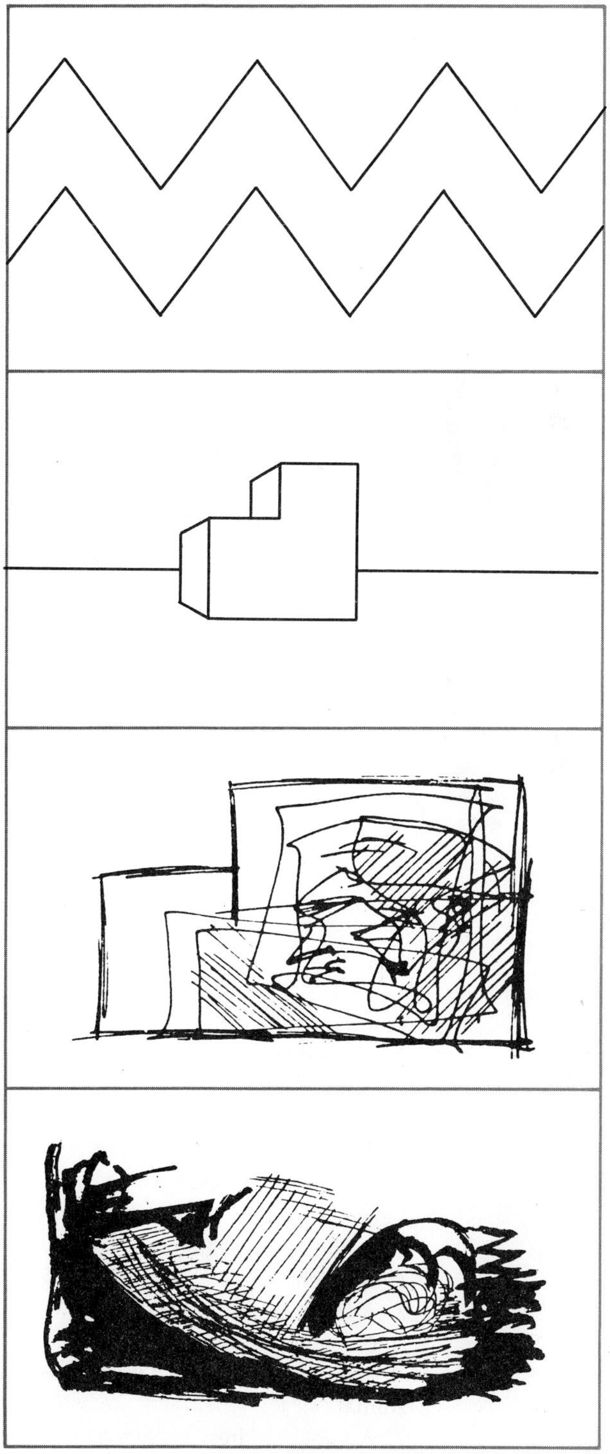

(a)

FIGURE 11.6
Test responses of creative persons and individuals chosen "at random." (a) In the Welsh Figure Preference Test people state whether they do or do not prefer abstract line drawings shown them on cards. Persons chosen at random liked those at the top, creative persons those on the bottom. (*b*, page 270). In the Drawing Completion Test individuals elaborate on sample figures. Creative persons did those on the far right. (Created by Kate Frank.) (*c*) For the Inkblot Test people describe what they perceive in the configuration. (Created by Frank Barron.)(*d*) In the Symbolic Equivalent Test they say what a "stimulus image" brings to mind. (Adapted from the Welsh Figure Preference Test, by George Welsh, copyright 1949, in Barron 1958. Reproduced with permission of the author, *Scientific American*, and Consulting Psychologists Press, Inc.)

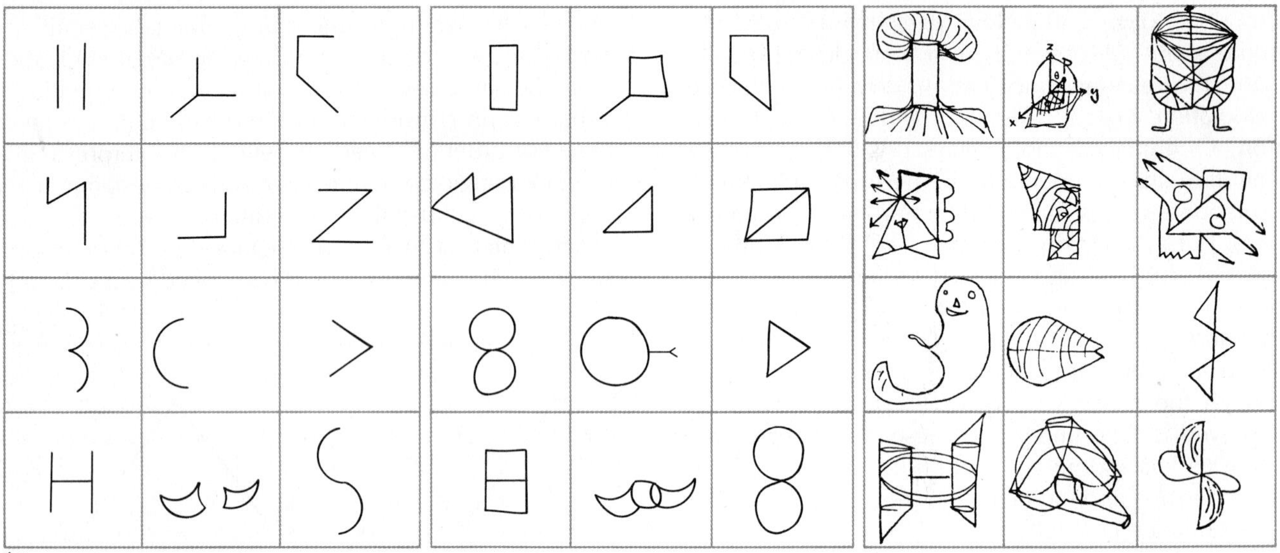

(b)

Common responses
1. Smudges
2. Dark clouds

Uncommon responses
1. Magentized iron filings
2. A small boy and his mother hurrying along on a dark windy day, trying to get home before it rains.

Common responses
1. An African voodoo dancer
2. A cactus plant

Uncommon responses
1. Mexican in sombrero running up a long hill to escape from rain clouds
2. A word written in Chinese

(c)

Stimulus Image

Empty bookcases

Common responses
1. An empty mind
2. A deserted room

Uncommon responses
1. The vacant eyes of an idiot
2. An abandoned beehive

Sound of a foghorn

Common responses
1. A belch
2. A frog's croak

Uncommon responses
1. The cry of despair of a great unseen animal
2. A public address system announcing disaster

(d)

configuration" (Figure 11.6*c*). A symbolic meaning test (Figure 11.6*d*) revealed the same quality of originality.

We can also gain some insight into the creative person from responses to Barron's questionnaire.

- I like to fool around with new ideas, even if they turn out later to be a total waste of time. (True)
- The unfinished and imperfect often have greater appeal for me than the completed and polished. (True)
- A person should not probe too deeply into his own and other people's feelings, but take things as they are. (False)
- Young people sometimes get rebellious ideas, but as they grow up they get over them and settle down. (False)

TABLE 11.5
Personality Correlates of Intelligence and Creativity in Children

Creativity	Intelligence: Low	Intelligence: High
High	". . . in angry conflict with themselves and with their school . . . feelings of unworthiness and inadequacy. In a stress-free context . . . can blossom forth cognitively."	"These children can exercise . . . both control and freedom, both adultlike and childlike kinds of behavior."
Low	"Basically bewildered . . . engaged in various defensive maneuvers ranging from useful adaptations such as intensive social activity to regressions such as passivity or psychosomatic symptoms."	". . . addicted to school achievement. Academic failure . . . perceived . . . as catastrophic. So they must continually strive for academic excellence."

Adapted from Wallach and Kogan, 1965a.

The image of the creative person that emerges from research findings is of an individual who challenges the unknown, willingly attempts tasks that are too difficult and test the limits of his or her abilities, seeks to impose order where it does not exist, and is independent in judgment, nonconforming in views, and often open and honest in expression.

Another important research finding is that the creative person is not necessarily the most intelligent person. Michael Wallach and Nathan Kogan (1965*b*) have succeeded in constructing tests of the creativity of children that correlate positively with one another but not at all with traditional tests of intelligence. Their data suggest that essential to the creative process in children are the ability to make multiple and unique associations and a playful and permissive attitude toward intellectual tasks. Wallach and Kogan found children who are both creative and highly intelligent to be confident, able, and sociable. Children with considerable creativity but not so considerable intelligence are not as well adjusted (Table 11.5).

Is it possible to increase our creativity? Countless popular books contain advice on how to become more creative, and Sunday newspaper supplements regularly feature articles or quote experts on this topic. But whether creativity can actually be learned by practicing prescribed lessons remains unclear. As is true for intelligence, we can probably do little to increase our basic creative potential; we can only hope to exercise that potential to its fullest capacity. Earlier we noted that a superior environment is not essential for geniuses to express their creativity. But obviously certain minimum means must be available to the individual. Louis Armstrong could not have become a musical genius had he not been able to study music adequately. Most of Galton's accomplishments would have been impossible in a preliterate society. The psychoanalyst Silvano Arieti (1976) has observed that a society, by its values and resources, can promote or inhibit the creativity of its citizens. He has specified several factors that foster a "creativogenic" society: the availability of cultural means to all citizens, without discrimination; an openness, tolerance, and interest in diverging views; and a stress on becoming, not just on being. By emphasizing becoming as well as being, society would make individual growth and development as important as immediate gratification, pleasure, and comfort.

SUMMARY □

Gifted individuals are those whose IQs are at the upper end of the distribution of intelligence. A few gifted people are considered geniuses, but their special qualities are difficult to stipulate. The requisites for genius are very high intelligence and accomplishments of such great significance that they continue to be recognized long after the individual's death.

Gifted individuals are often precocious as children. There is no evidence that they must be raised in a superior environment if they are to fulfill their potential, for many geniuses have bloomed in impoverished circumstances. Nor is there strong support for the popular notion that giftedness or genius is akin to madness. Although many creative geniuses have been severely maladjusted, the group of gifted individuals studied by Terman were, in general, better adjusted than the average.

Creativity is an important aspect of giftedness and has been investigated extensively in its own right. Although the extremely bright individual is often creative, creativity and intelligence are not equivalent, and an individual can have much more of one than the other. Highly creative individuals dare to undertake tasks at which they may fail and to examine ideas in new ways. Creative persons have a high tolerance for ambiguity, that is, for situations that are not clearly defined; their aesthetic preferences are for complexity rather than for ordered simplicity.

INTERVENTION PROGRAMS

A great deal of effort has been invested in determining whether special intervention programs can substantially alter a cycle that begins with poverty in childhood and leads to poor school achievement and then unemployment and poverty in adulthood. Probably the most famous of these programs is Head Start, but other programs have also been developed and implemented.

Head Start

In the mid-1960s there was a growing awareness that children from urban and rural slums did poorly in school. There was also a conviction that the impoverished circumstances in which these children were raised had a great deal to do with their school problems. At the same time, some psychologists (for example, Bloom, 1964) were emphasizing the preschool years as a critical period in the intellectual development of the child. These and other factors encouraged the development in 1965 of the most important intervention program in the United States, **Project Head Start.**

Originally, Head Start was an eight-week summer program for children who were about to enter school. It soon became apparent that such a short-term program could have little lasting impact on the children it served. Although continuing to be a summer program for some children, Head Start has become a year-round program which currently serves about 350,000 four- and five-year-old children each year. For approximately two-thirds of these children it is a half-day program for five days a week; for the remaining third it is a day-long program offering both compensatory education and day care, which permits their mothers to work.

Goals of Head Start The goals of Head Start are spelled out in the following description of the five components comprising a Head Start program.

1 *Health* A child who is in poor health will function at a level considerably lower than that of a well child. Since poverty and poor health frequently go hand in hand, Head Start centers provide complete medical and dental examinations, immunizations, and follow-through to ensure correction of health problems.

One of the goals of Operation Head Start was to lay the foundation for future experience in school.

2 *Nutrition* Head Start children are frequently undernourished, and again, hungry children cannot learn. The nutrition program in Head Start centers normally provides at least one hot meal and a snack each day, and also gives parents an opportunity to learn how to prepare well-balanced meals.

3 *Education* Teaching methods are developed to meet the particular needs of each group of children. With one teacher and two aides to every fifteen children, individual problems can get individual attention. Self-reliance, self-esteem, and self-confidence are encouraged and fostered. Unfamiliar objects become familiar, and a solid groundwork is laid for the future school experience.

4 *Parent Involvement* Each program is required to invite the participation of parents in every phase of planning and operation. Parents can observe what their children are doing in the classroom, and they often serve on a paid or volunteer basis as aides to teachers, nurses, and social workers, as

clerks, cooks, storytellers, and supervisors of recreational activities. Fathers sometimes participate in activities with the children and also construct and repair the physical facilities. Frequently, classes are held for parents in home economics, in the purchase and preparation of surplus foods, in child care, and in improving the home environment. Language classes for non-English-speaking parents are often arranged at the centers.

5 *Social and Psychological Services* The social service part of the Head Start program is one of the most important. The Center staff works closely with all appropriate community agencies (for example, church, family counseling) and uses its own expertise to help resolve problems of the child and family (paraphrased from Office of Economic Opportunity, 1968, pp. 2, 4).

The initial reaction to Head Start was euphoric; children were found to make 10-point gains in IQ scores. But enthusiasm for the program began to wane following reports that the IQ gains disappeared soon after the children entered school (Bronfenbrenner, 1974; Westinghouse Learning Corporation, 1969). Although this finding would appear to be more of an indictment of schools than of Head Start, it fostered the belief that Head Start was a failure. The Head Start program, however, was not mounted in hopes of dramatically raising IQ scores or of guaranteeing that all graduates would be reading at their age level at grade five. Rather, the creators of Head Start hoped to give disadvantaged children greater *social competence,* that is, greater everyday effectiveness in all aspects of their lives—in mastering formal concepts, learning well in school, behaving responsibly, and relating well to adults and other children. In many instances children's failures can be traced to a negative self-image, to an "I can't do it" philosophy, and to a wariness or hostility toward others. Thus Head Start's goals concerned the social, motivational, and emotional factors in development as much as they did cognitive factors. Keeping these goals in mind, we can perhaps assess more accurately Head Start's success or failure.

A General Evaluation Most Head Start centers provide curricula to improve children's numerical, spatial, and abstracting abilities as well as their memory and use of language. Many studies have indicated that at the end of the Head Start program, before they enter school, Head Start children do make higher scores on specific measures of these abilities, as well as on IQ tests, than do comparable children who have not taken the program. In the few studies that have attempted to assess impact on socioemotional adjustment, children who attended the centers have usually been found to be better adjusted than those who did not. As for health care, tens of thousands of poor children have been screened, diagnosed, and treated for various physical problems. They are unquestionably better off physically than they would have been without Head Start.

The mere fact that Head Start exists in a community apparently focuses citizens' attention on the services delivered to children. This was demonstrated in a survey of fifty-eight communities having Head Start and seven comparison communities that did not (Kirschner Associates, 1970). Where there was Head Start, considerable community activity centered around family health and education. The study identified nearly 1500 institutional changes introduced in the fifty-eight communities. Two thirds were improvements in education, one third improved delivery of health services. How much community change was precipitated by the presence of a Head Start program appeared to be related to (1) whether parents participated in the program; (2) whether it was highly visible and its personnel were willing to relate to other institutions, such as the public school and the community health center; and (3) whether the community climate was conducive to change.

When we consider the broad and long-range goals of Head Start and examine what has been achieved in the short term, the program must so far be considered a success. Which is not to say that this rather fragile effort during one year of a child's life can be viewed as the ultimate counterforce to poverty, illiteracy, underachievement, racism, deliquency, and failure in later life. We must respect the complexity and continuity of human development. The Head Start year in the child's life is important; the first five years are important. So are the next five, and the five after that.

Other Intervention Programs

The quick and erroneous judgment of Head Start based only on its impact on IQ scores did have one healthy effect. It made us aware that too much had been expected of a single short-term program. Other kinds of programs that can be dovetailed with Head Start and provide more extended intervention have been introduced. One is Follow-Through, in which educational intervention is continued from kindergarten through the third grade. Another is the Parent and Child Center Program in which educators work with both parent and child during the first three years of the child's life. One program has a somewhat different thrust. Educators do not work with youngsters at all but rather train the mother to stimulate her children as much as possible during their early years. In this effort—called Home Start—children are not taken from the home and placed in centers but instead are helped through their families. The common sense of such an approach has considerable appeal. Mothers working with their own children for many hours a day and over a period of many years should be more effective agents for improving their children's intellectual development than educators who see them for a few hours a week over the course of one year.

These programs, as well as Head Start, have been national efforts sponsored by the United States government's Office of Child Development, now known as the Administration for Children, Youth and Families. Other intervention programs have been developed by individual investigators and implemented on a much smaller scale. Like the national programs, they have varied in a number of ways, such as the age at which intervention is begun—anywhere from birth to five years of age; the length of intervention—less than one year to five years; the number of hours per week—anywhere from two to thirty; whether the children attend a center or are taught at home; whether individualized or group training is provided; and the amount of family involvement in the program. A review of the scholastic effects of ten of these programs, including one combination of Head Start and Follow-Through, has recently been made (Palmer and Andersen, 1979). The investigators of each of these programs have followed the children for ten or more years after the treatment was introduced, and the last time data were collected the majority of the children were in elementary and junior high schools. According to the review, participating children (1) were more likely to be in the correct grade for their age, (2) were less likely to be in special-education classes for the learning disabled, (3) had higher reading and mathematics achievement scores, and (4) had higher IQs than comparable children who had not been in the programs. Preschool intervention can produce long-lasting improvements in children's cognitive functioning, even though no single program was found effective in all the ways by which the review measured them.

This review suggests that benefits may be obtained whatever the age at which intervention begins, its duration in years or frequency of sessions, and even the degree of parental involvement. The only variable that seemed to make a difference was the amount of individual attention given to the child. Individualized training brought more improvement than group training. Other reviews (Bronfenbrenner, 1975; Karnes and Teska, 1975), however, have found that better and more lasting intellectual gains are made the earlier in the child's life the instructional program begins and the greater the parents' participation in the project. Obviously, more research is needed to determine which type of intervention program has the greatest benefits. But the studies already carried out have brought the good and clear word that preschool intervention *can* produce long-term intellectual gains in economically disadvantaged children.

Can Cultural-Familial Retardation Be Prevented?

The majority of preschool intervention programs conducted in the United States have been designed primarily to improve the cognitive functioning of economically disadvantaged children. Although these children generally achieve lower IQ scores than middle-class children do, the great majority of them are not now, nor ever will be, mentally retarded. If, however, in addition to poverty, these children live in broken homes, have many illnesses, receive no intellectual stimulation, and come from families in which one or more members are mentally retarded, they will be at high risk for developing cultural-familial retardation. Two intervention programs have been instituted specifically to try to prevent this type of retardation.

The Milwaukee Project The children who participated in the **Milwaukee Project** were identified as **at risk** (see page 454) of becoming retarded because they lived in extreme poverty and their mothers' IQs were below 75 (Garber and Heber, 1977). The project was a six-year comprehensive effort to rehabilitate the family and to improve the children's surroundings, in hopes of allowing normal intellectual development. Project personnel began working with each mother and child shortly after the child reached three months of age. The mothers received vocational training for themselves and were taught to stimulate and encourage their children's cognitive development. During the first year a trained adult also met one to one with each child for several hours daily to provide stimulation. When older, the children attended a center and were trained there in language and cognitive skills.

During the six years of the project, the children in it scored an average of 29 points higher in IQ than a group of comparable children who had not received the regimen. The differences appear to persist even after completion of the program. At eight years of age the mean IQ of the project children was 105, whereas that of the control children was 82. Approximately one third of the control children at this age had IQs below 75, placing them among those for whom special-education classes are provided. In contrast, the lowest IQ score for the project children was 88. Although some methodological criticisms have been leveled against this project (Page, 1972), the results offer hope that an intensive compensatory program, beginning early in life, may counteract depriving conditions.

North Carolina Abecedarian Project Now in progress is the **North Carolina Abecedarian Project** (Ramey and Finkelstein, 1978; Ramey and Smith,

1977). The children at risk for becoming retarded have been divided into experimental and control groups. Both groups have received free supplements of food and medical care, as well as social services when the families have requested them. Only the children in the experimental group, however, have received preschool education, which in fact begins shortly after birth. At twelve months of age, the two groups of children did not differ on measures of infant development. The mean DQ was 106 for the experimental group and 105 for the control group. By thirty-six months of age, however, the mean DQ of the experimental group was significantly higher than that of the control group, 96 compared to 81. The control group is apparently declining into subnormality through time, whereas the development of the experimental group, although not as good as formerly, has kept an almost normal pace. The information collected so far is only preliminary, but it is consistent with findings reported from the Milwaukee Project. If the developmental records of the children in both projects are maintained as they grow older, this will constitute strong evidence that some psychosocial retardation may be prevented by intensive early education in the preschool years.

The Role of Teacher Expectations

The gains in IQ achieved by the children in the majority of intervention programs reviewed have been made possible only through considerable cost and effort. The findings of a study by Robert Rosenthal and Lenore Jacobson, published as *Pygmalion in the Classroom* (1968), captured considerable national interest, for they seemed to indicate that large IQ gains could be accomplished by a cost-free and relatively minimal, although psychologically important, tactic.

The children in this study were in grades one through six. Rosenthal and Jacobson informed teachers that they were administering a test that could identify children who were on the verge of a spurt in their intellectual functioning, but it was actually only a group test of general intelligence. Children were arbitrarily assigned to different groups, one of which was labeled "late bloomers." Teachers were given the names of the children whose "test results" had indicated that they would blossom intellectually over the subsequent school year. Others who were comparable in every other way constituted a control group. At issue was whether this built-in teacher expectation would actually have an effect on the intellectual performance of the children arbitrarily identified as "late bloomers."

Several months into the school year, the IQ increases of the "late-blooming" children were found to be far higher than those in the other group. Although the process by which teachers' expectations might have encouraged the so-called late bloomers actually to bloom was not spelled out, the study did indicate that teacher expectancy was largely responsible. As Rosenthal and Jacobson stated,

> Nothing was done directly for the disadvantaged child. . . . There was no crash program to improve his reading ability, no special lesson plan, no extra time for tutoring, no trips to museums or art galleries. There was only the belief that the children bore watching, that they had intellectual competencies that would in due course be revealed. What was done in our program of educational change was done directly for the teacher, only indirectly for her pupils. Perhaps, then, it is the teacher to whom we should direct more of our research attention. If we could learn how she is able to effect dramatic improvement in her pupils' competence without formal changes in her teaching methods, then we could teach other teachers to do the same. (1968, p. 181)

A number of methodological criticisms, presented in *Pygmalion Reconsidered* (Elashoff and Snow, 1971), have cast doubt on Rosenthal and Jacobson's findings. Moreover, none of nine subsequent studies (reviewed by Baker and Crist, 1971) that attempted to raise children's IQs by modifying teachers' expectations was successful. Although intelligence proved recalcitrant to improvement through being anticipated, these other studies did indicate that when teachers expected more of their pupils, the children often did better schoolwork.

There is considerable evidence that raising the teacher's expectations changes the teacher's everyday behavior. The teacher who works with children considered to be intellectually promising attends to the children more, expends more effort in eliciting and rewarding their responses, interacts more positively with them, and does a greater amount of actual teaching. By the same token, expecting little of the children could prove a self-fulfilling prophecy, for then the teacher might not try as hard to stimulate and challenge them. The children, in turn, are forced to spend day after day in the presence of a teacher who expects only failure from them, which is utterly devastating to self-image and discourages them from any effort to learn. The original enthusiasm for the Rosenthal and Jacobson findings may have been inappropriate, but we are certainly indebted to them for underlining the importance of teachers' expectations and pioneering an area of research worthy of considerable further effort.

SUMMARY □

Project Head Start, a major preschool education effort, seeks to improve the quality of the lives of disadvantaged children. In addition to attending to their health and nutritional needs, the aim of Head Start is to give these children greater social competence and to help them reach their potential. Head Start seeks to achieve these broad goals by working directly with the children as well as with their families and the community.

Although Head Start had no specific intent to raise children's IQs, these scores became the focus of most efforts to evaluate the success of the program. These evaluations suggested that children who attend Head Start programs may make small gains in IQ, but that these are probably transitory, disappearing when children enter a regular school program. Recent evidence, however, indicates that Head Start and other compensatory intervention programs may help children achieve enduring scholastic gains. Further, early and intensive intervention efforts may be able to prevent psychosocial retardation to some degree.

There is also evidence that teachers' expectations of what children can accomplish in school may have something to do with what they do achieve. The evidence gathered so far, suggestive rather than clear-cut, indicates that teachers who expect intellectual gains in children may work with them in ways that facilitate such gains.

TO BE SURE YOU UNDERSTAND THIS CHAPTER △

The following are the major concepts employed in this chapter. You should be able to use them to reconstruct some of the discussion of the chapter.

Mental retardation
Adaptive behavior deficit
Etiology
Organic retardation
Down syndrome
Phenylketonuria
Maple Syrup Urine Disease
Tay-Sachs disease
Hurler syndrome
Trisomy 21
Cretinism
Cultural-familial retardation
Psychosocial retardation
Outerdirectedness
Normalization
Mainstreaming
Genius
Giftedness
Creativity
Project Head Start
Milwaukee Project
At risk
North Carolina Abecedarian Project

Much of the content of Chapter 11 concerns relationships and contrasts, which you should also understand. These are some of the important ones.

Test scores (IQ *and* MA) versus adaptive behavior
Genetic and environmental interpretations of cultural-familial retardation
Personality traits that may either contribute to or be the result of retardation
Attitudes of general population toward retarded persons
Giftedness versus genius
Genius and maladjustment
Giftedness and maladjustment
Personality traits of the gifted
In programs of intervention, gains other than gains in IQ
Teacher expectations and school performance

TO GO BEYOND THIS CHAPTER △

In this book The materials in Chapters 9, 10, and 11 form a unit. You might want to review the first two of these chapters at this point. The organic versus cultural-familial distinction reappears in discussions of psychopathology (Chapters 17 and 18). It might be of interest to look at some of those materials (particularly pages 451–453) now. The technical concept at risk, mentioned briefly here, is treated more fully on pages 454–455.

Elsewhere For a comprehensive treatment of the field of mental retardation, see Peter Mittler's three-volume work, *Research to Practice in Mental Retardation*. Volume 1 is devoted to issues of care and intervention, volume 2 to education and training, and volume 3 to biomedical aspects of mental retardation. Robert Edgerton's *The Cloak of Competence* and Edgerton and S. Bercovici's follow-up report in the *American Journal of Mental Deficiency* (1976) provide an insightful account of how retarded adults attempt to adjust to community living after being discharged from an institution.

A history and assessment of Head Start can be found in Edward Zigler and Jeanette Valentine's *Project Head Start: A Legacy of the War on Poverty.* Philip Vernon's *Creativity,* a book of readings, shows the range and variety of approaches to the study of creativity.

CH. 12

Cognitive Development

Historically, the study of intellectual development has been approached in two ways. The **psychometric approach,** with its emphasis on standardized test scores, was discussed in Chapter 10. The **cognitive-developmental approach** has quite a different orientation. Whereas psychometricians emphasize individual differences in intellect, often focusing on extremes of retardation and giftedness, cognitive-developmental psychologists are more interested in how thinking and related mental processes develop in the average individual. They find that test scores can be informative, but in attending to them alone intellectual processes may go unnoticed. A "wrong" answer may sometimes reflect a level of thinking superior to that leading to a "right" answer. Thus, instead of asking how many items the child answered correctly, cognitive developmentalists are more concerned with how children arrive at their answers.

Although these seem to be opposite approaches, both have contributed a great deal to our understanding of cognitive development. Both psychometricians and cognitive developmentalists have been interested in similar questions. How is early intelligence related to later intelligence? What is the pattern of cognitive abilities at different ages? Is there a single basic factor that permeates a variety of intellectual processes? Furthermore, as we shall see, certain basic principles of mental growth have been affirmed independently by the studies done by each group.

COGNITIVE STAGES

Everyone agrees that with normal cognitive development the child becomes a more adequate individual, capable of an increasingly larger number of intellectual accomplishments. A basic point of controversy, however, is whether cognitive power is gained in a steady, gradual accretion or in a sequence of stages, each qualitatively different from the others. Although psychologists continue to argue whether cognitive stages have any reality, much of value is gained by examining cognitive development from such a point of view. As we shall see in this chapter, Jean Piaget, Jerome Bruner, and Alexander Luria have provided noteworthy stage theories.

One useful means of identifying cognitive stages is to ask children of different ages carefully selected questions that require answers which will reveal their reasoning processes. For example, when we ask a child how a peach and an orange are alike, the child must engage in a series of mental operations, recalling from memory what a peach and an orange are, discriminating between their similarities and differences, and then generating a high-level *abstraction*. If the child says that they are both fruit, we conclude that these mental operations have been conducted successfully. A very young child, however, may tell us that a peach and an orange are alike because they are both round. This child's categorization of the two objects is based on their inherent physical attributes, a mode of thinking called *concrete*. At a somewhat higher level of intellectual functioning, a child may answer our query with "You could eat them both." This child has used a *functional principle* in classifying the objects, based on what can be done with them. Thus we see a sequence in which the child employs ever more intellectually demanding operations in response to our query. The child graduates from one operation to another—from the concrete to the functional to the abstract—as he or she grows older.

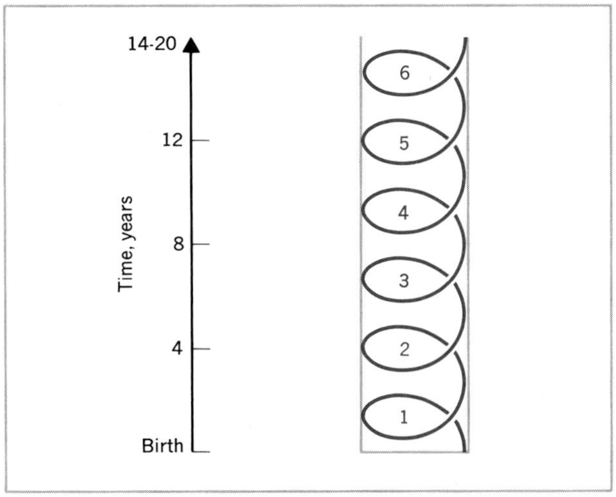

FIGURE 12.1
Simple model of stages of cognitive development. The vertical arrow represents the passage of time. The individual's cognitive development appears as an internal ascending spiral, in which the numbered loops represent successive stages of cognitive growth. This model deals only with the growth of intelligence, not with its decline. The time arrow stops in the 14–20 year range, when a number of cognitive abilities have been found to peak.

Models of Cognitive Stages

A simple model of cognitive development helps to clarify several of its important features (Figure 12.1). First, there is a certain definite sequence of cognitive growth. Stage 2 is always preceded by stage 1 and always followed by stage 3. The child always moves from the concrete to the abstract but never in the reverse order, to use our earlier example. Second, the stages are qualitatively different, as though the individual uses quite different processing systems at different stages of cognitive development. Finally, this model serves to eliminate a potential confusion about the relation between cognitive development and age.

Cognitive development is a continuous process that takes place over time. The individual does not, however, go through the sequence of stages merely as a function of getting older. Time is simply a backdrop against which the rate of cognitive growth is assessed. To understand cognitive development, we must ask what causes the individual to move from one stage of development to the next.

Maturation versus Learning The model presented in Figure 12.1 would be perfectly adequate for an extreme maturationist view of human development. This position considers development, both physical and cognitive, the inevitable expression of an internal plan which propels the human being through a sequence of stages, each stage being reached at a particular point in the life cycle. The term **maturation** refers to growth that depends entirely on physiological development. Few psychologists take such an extreme position with respect to cognitive development.

A second model is more in keeping with current views on the nature of cognitive development (Figure 12.2). The arrows that have been added represent impinging experience as the individual develops. In this **interactionist model** cognitive development is considered an outgrowth of the interaction between internal factors and external experience. By placing different relative emphases on the two sets of factors, individuals holding quite different views about the nature of cognition can be comfortable with this model.

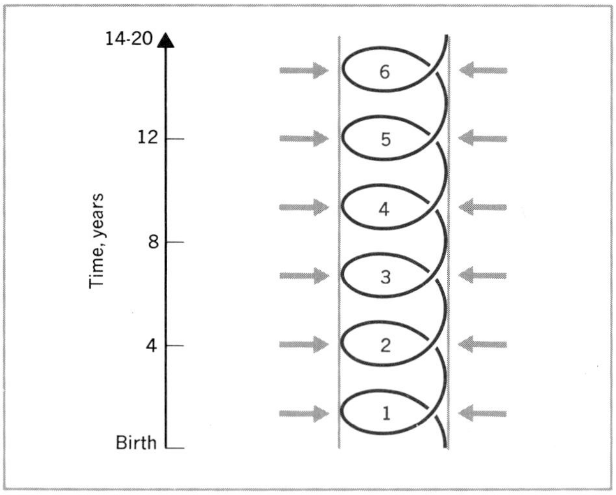

FIGURE 12.2
Interactionist model of cognitive development. The horizontal arrows represent the environmental experiences affecting the developing individual.

Extreme environmentalists, who view the mind of the newborn as a *tabula rasa*, a blank tablet (page 49), attribute all cognitive development to external experience. They would explain the sequence of stages as being totally determined by the arrows in Figure 12.2. What happens at any stage depends on what the child has learned up to a particular point in time. But why then do the cognitive stages seem to form an invariant sequence?

The environmentalists answer that the invariance is not in the nature of human beings but in the sequence of experiences to which they are subjected. Our present methods of educating children tend to force a particular sequence upon them. The environmentalists would explain progression from concrete thought to functional to abstract as a process in which the child is taught to discriminate simple dimensions such as shape first and more abstract dimensions such as function later. Environmentalists would argue that children could move from one stage to any other were we to subject them to the appropriate learning experiences.

Most workers in cognitive development reject this view, just as they do the extreme maturational position. Instead, they take a middle ground and consider the stages to emerge in an invariant order through a process of organism-environment interaction. They view the infant's mind not as a *tabula rasa* but as coming equipped with a primitive structural organization which allows the child to process information in a certain way. With maturation and more contact with the environment, this structure is reorganized. We refer to this reorganization as a new stage.

Although the cognitive-developmental approach has much to recommend it, one of its weaknesses is the minimal attention given to individual variation. Individuals go through the stages at their own pace, and they attain different upper limits. Another model, depicting courses of development for dull, average, and bright individuals, takes this variation into account (Figure 12.3).

Differentiation and Cognitive Stages Early in life there is a gross, all-or-none quality to thinking. Later, it becomes much more fine-grained, discriminating, and complex. One of the most striking examples is the lack of differentiation in very early childhood between the "me" and the "not me." Even body boundaries are fuzzy to very young children, and they have great difficulty differentiating what is inside themselves and therefore private, from what is outside and therefore public. It is not uncommon to find young children who believe that their thoughts can be seen by others. Even after they have successfully differentiated the "me" from the "not me," they are still not differentiated enough to step outside of their own existence, to take the perspective of someone else and view themselves as objects distinct from other objects. John Nash's conversation with six-year-old Pippa illustrates this phenomenon. " 'Pippa, what is your sister's name?' 'Heather.' 'And who is Heather's

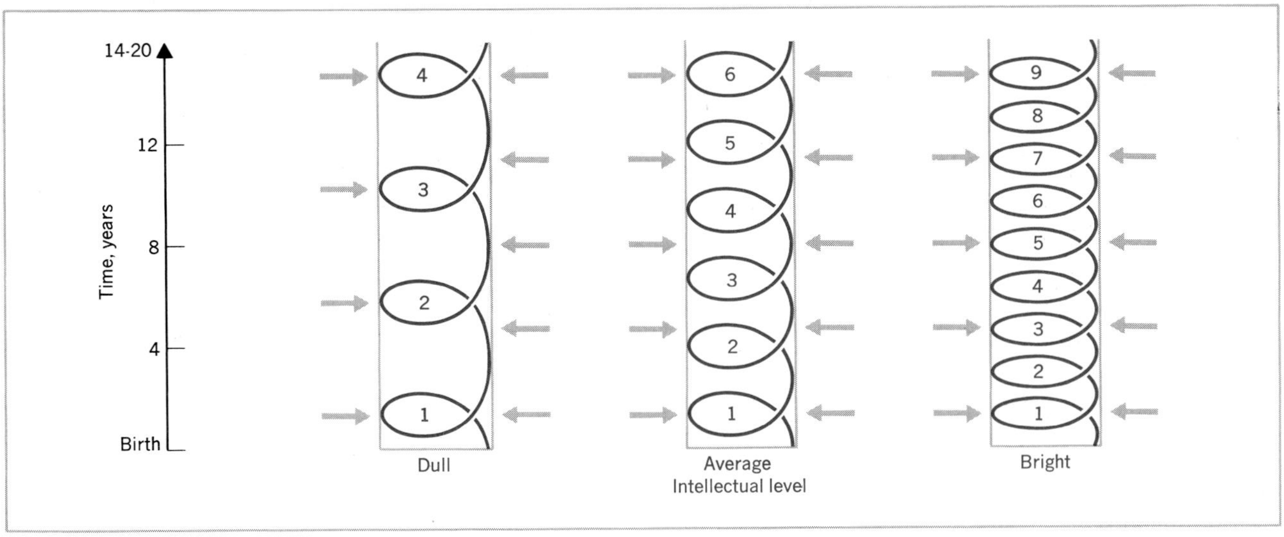

FIGURE 12.3
Developmental model showing individual variation in rate of intellectual growth and in final level attained. The number of stages at each intellectual level has been selected arbitrarily. The actual number of stages that can be identified varies with the particular cognitive process being examined.

sister?' 'Heather hasn't got a sister.' 'But who are you then? Aren't you Heather's sister?' 'No, I'm Pippa' " (1970, p. 359). Pippa is still so central to her perception of things that we can say she has not totally escaped her egocentricity.

Differentiation then is enhanced as thinking develops. When we say that with development cognitive processes change, we refer to just such formal features as degree of differentiation. If we add to our model certain aspects of one suggested by Kurt Lewin (1936), it will express the view that each cognitive stage is more differentiated than the one preceding it (Figure 12.4).

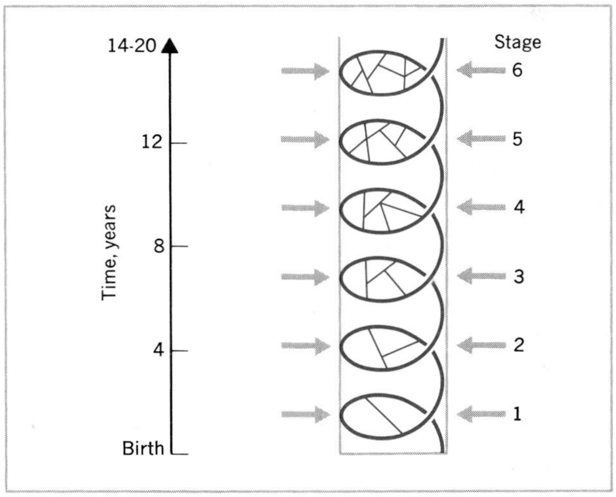

FIGURE 12.4
Developmental model showing greater cognitive differentiation at each successive stage. The increasing number of "regions," as Lewin called them, indicated by the subdivisions at each stage represent the increasing number of cognitive activities of which the person is capable.

Illustrations of Stagelike Thinking

Children's explanations of one phenomenon, their dreams, clearly show a progression through stages and also demonstrate that greater differentiation is present at each higher stage. If adults are asked where their dreams come from, they have no difficulty identifying them as events stemming from themselves. Such comprehension is a demanding cognitive task, however, one young children are incapable of. Even if children are told the adult explanation, they cannot conceptualize dreams in adult terms because they do not yet have the ability to engage in this level of thinking. At every stage, in comprehending and dealing with the phenomena they experience, children can use only the abilities they possess at the time. A bright five-year-old boy explained dreams in this way.

> Dreams come from God. God makes the dreams and puts them in balloons. The balloons float down from heaven and enter a dream bag under your stomach. In the dream bag there are some little men and a sergeant. They have a cannon that shoots the dream-balloons up into your head where they burst into pictures outside your head (reported by Kohlberg, 1971, p. 112).

We can be fairly certain that no adult taught the child this intricate and appealing yet nonetheless inadequate explanation of dreams. It by no means approximates some adult standard explanation that might be learned through training. Rather, the boy has actively attempted to come to grips with the problem of dreams by using the cognitive abilities available to him.

Children only gradually sort out their dreams from other happenings (Laurendeau and Pinard, 1962). At the age of four, children believe that dreams are real events existing apart from themselves and taking place in their room. In the next stage of comprehension, when they are about six, children recognize that the dream is not taking place in the room but rather is in their eyes or in their head. If another person could look inside their head, that person would see the dream, like a little show, being played there. By the age of eight, children realize that dreams take place inside of themselves, cannot be seen by others, and are produced by their own thoughts or imagination.

Studies have shown that children's conceptions of dreams have an invariant order. Children who have passed a particular step in their thinking about dreams have also passed all the earlier steps in the sequence. Lawrence Kohlberg (1969) has pointed out that these steps in the understanding of dreams represent progressive differentiations, which logically cannot have any other order. In the first step the real and the unreal are differentiated; the dream is not an actual, physical event. Then the dream is differentiated as internal rather than external; the dream is like a movie taking place inside the person rather than outside. Finally, the dream is differentiated as psychic and immaterial rather than as physical and material; it is no longer a picture projected in the head but a psychic projection of the imagination.

The ability of children to learn shows stages of differentiation similar to those in which they understand dreams. As children develop, they become more competent in many tasks. One task frequently employed to assess learning capacity is the two-choice size discrimination problem (Figure 12.5). In this problem children are confronted with two wooden squares of different sizes. On each trial they see the same two squares, but the positions vary; the larger square is sometimes on the right, sometimes on the left. A reward such as a marble or small piece of candy is always placed under a square of a particular size, either the larger or the smaller one. Children are told to find the hidden object as often as possible.

Children need several cognitive abilities to solve this problem correctly. They must have advanced from the egocentricity of the very early years and realize that the blocks and rewards are in the external world, that they cannot make rewards appear simply by wishing them to be there. They must have the verbal skills to understand the instructions and to sense that there is a problem to be solved. They must be able to perceive the difference between the two blocks, for the problem is not solvable unless they re-

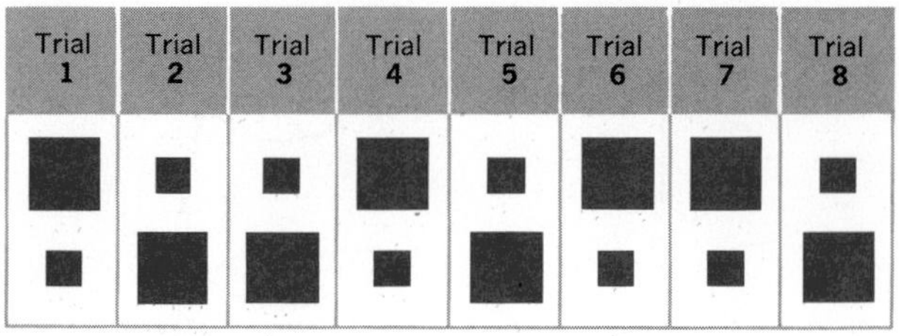

FIGURE 12.5
The first eight trials on a size discrimination problem. The child must learn always to pick up the same-sized block, either the larger one or the smaller, whichever the experiment has determined will be correct.

alize that one block is larger than the other. The children must also be able to develop hypotheses about the solution of the problem.

Suppose that the experimenter decides to reward a young girl for picking up the larger block. Assume further that on trial 1 the child by chance picks up the larger block, which happens to be on the left. At this point she might generate any of three hypotheses that would affect her behavior on trial 2. One is that the experimenter is a nice person who likes to give her candy, and that she will get candy for picking up any block. A second hypothesis is a position hypothesis, that the candy is always on the left. A third hypothesis is that the candy is under the larger block.

To avoid getting bogged down with erroneous hypotheses, the child must be flexible enough to reject hypotheses that bring only occasional reward. The older the child, the greater the likelihood that she can generate the correct hypothesis as well as reject erroneous hypotheses. But, as the cognitive system becomes more differentiated, the child is able to generate a much greater number of hypotheses. For example, the child can hypothesize that the correct pattern of responding is to alternate between choosing the block on the left and the block on the right. Many extremely complex hypotheses are also possible, such as one choice on the left, two on the right, three on the left, and so on. The number of hypotheses that can be generated is limited only by the cognitive ability of the individual confronted by the task.

For this reason greater cognitive capacity is not always helpful in solving problems. If the individual entertains a succession of complex hypotheses, rejecting one after several trials and then selecting another, the large number of hypotheses generated may slow down solution of the problem. Thus for a while children might very well improve their problem solving, yet eventually reach an age at which their ability to generate hypotheses would be a hindrance. This was actually observed in an experiment comparing the performances of individuals of different ages on a simple two-choice task. Children in grades five to eight needed only about one-third as many trials to

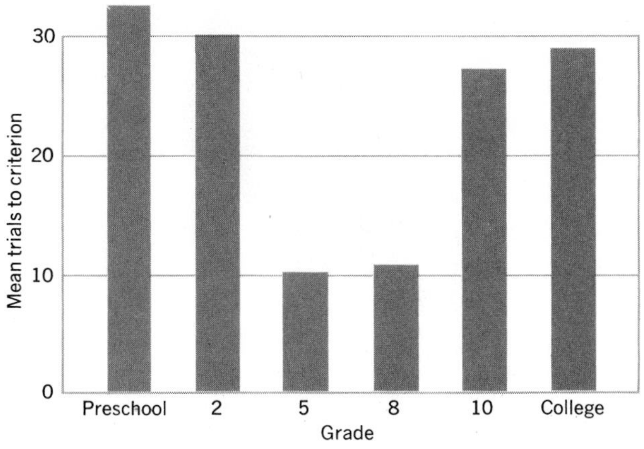

FIGURE 12.6
Mean number of trials required by individuals in different grades to solve a two-choice size discrimination problem. Mean trials to criterion were nearly as great for college students as for preschoolers. (After Stevenson, Iscoe, and McConnell, 1955.)

learn the correct hypothesis as did preschool or second-grade children (Figure 12.6). Tenth-grade and college students, however, required almost as many trials as the youngest children. Questioning of these older students revealed that they were hypothesizing complex sequences of alternating positions or sizes or both. Interestingly, some of the older students hypothesized that there was actually no solution and that success depended on chance alone. This in itself is a very differentiated cognitive hypothesis.

SUMMARY □

It is useful to describe cognitive development as a progression through a series of stages. A simple cognitive stage model emphasizes that development is a continuous process which shows a definite sequence. More complex models may indicate that at every stage the individual is actively interacting with the environment, leading to further growth, and that individuals proceed through the stages at different rates. The principle of differentiation can also be included in a complex model, with higher stages showing more differentiation than lower stages.

Children's reasoning in explaining dreams and their use of increasingly complex hypotheses in problem-solving tasks indicate a progression through cognitive stages.

DIFFERENTIATION IN COGNITION AND PERCEPTION

Differentiation is central to a basic law of development, the **orthogenetic principle,** advanced by Heinz Werner. This principle, which incorporates the ideas presented in Figure 12.4, states that development proceeds from a relative globality, in which all elements are involved, to increasing *differentiation, articulation* or clarification of elements, and *hierarchic integration,* the arrangement of elements according to importance. This principle can clearly be seen in the development of a physical skill—for example, the ability to pick up a piece of string. At first the child's attempt to pick up the string is global, engaging the entire body—hands, arms, torso, and even mouth. Later the child uses only the hand, but all five fingers and the fist are brought into action. Finally, the child adeptly uses only the thumb and forefinger in picking up the string.

Heinz Werner.

Werner's Stages of Development

Werner and his students have demonstrated that perceptual and cognitive development also proceeds in similar stages (Werner, 1957b). Initially, children perceive in an undifferentiated, global manner. They respond to objects as amorphous totalities without parts. In the next stage children have the ability to divide a perception into individual parts and to direct their attention to these parts. In the ultimate stage they are able not only to direct perception toward parts but also to recreate the whole out of the parts in a hierarchically integrated manner. That is, it becomes possible to subordinate some parts of perception to other parts, forming a hierarchy, and to make the whole object meaningful.

An example should help clarify this discussion. Look at the inkblot in Figure 12.7 and decide what it looks like. You have just engaged in a perceptual-cognitive act. Whatever your answer, Figure 12.7 is not exactly the object or objects it reminded you of. To find meaning in the blot, you had to impose your own thought processes onto the figure and construct something from it. For this reason your answer tells us something about the pattern of thinking that you employed when dealing with the task, although no one would expect your response to a single item to give a good indication of the nature of your cognitive functioning. When collections of such inkblots are presented to individuals of different ages, however, the thought processes evident in their descriptions indicate a sequence that supports Werner's orthogenetic principle of differentiation and integration.

Very young children might respond that Figure 12.7 is a "blob" or a "messy thing." This response is global and undifferentiated, for the child considers the whole blot but imposes no structure on it. Responses at the second stage break the inkblot into discrete pieces and examine each segment independently. Thus a young boy might see several unrelated objects in the inkblot. He might, for example, separate the top of the inkblot from the remainder and say that this section looks like the heads of two soda bottles side by side. Then he might interpret the outside bulge in one of the lower quadrants as a hill. Finally, he might say that the two appendages at the bottom look like two fingers. These replies indicate that the child has differentiated the blot and has imposed some realistic restrictions on the individual segments that he has examined.

In the most advanced stage the blot is broken down into pieces which are then recombined into an integrated whole. Suppose that an individual describes the figure by saying, "It's Casper the ghost and his girlfriend who have gone to a ghost party and are whirling around on the dance floor." Although such a description certainly shows imagination, we must examine the individual's reasoning to determine whether it also indicates a high level of intellectual functioning. We could conclude that it does if the person went on to tell us that the top section of the blot represented the heads of Casper and his girlfriend, who are of course dressed in sheets as any self-respecting ghosts would be. The middle sections of the blot are the ghosts' bodies, entwined in an embrace. Our observer might then say that clearly they are dancing, for the two lower appendages are the bottoms of the two dancers' sheets, which are being twirled outward as Casper and his date revolve during a dance step. This observer indeed has demonstrated the high-level ability to disassemble the blot into differentiated features and to reassemble them into a meaningful whole.

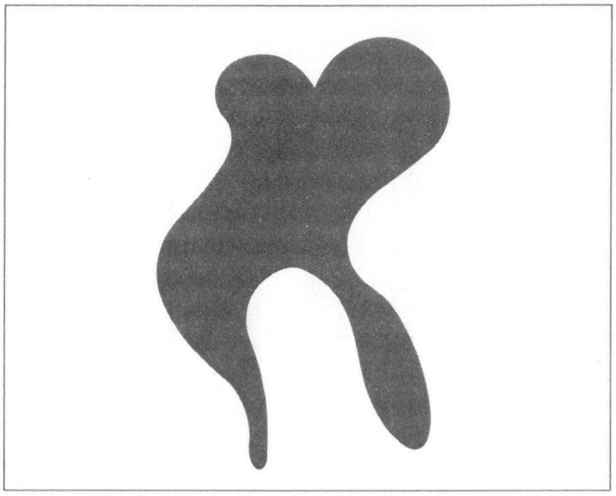

FIGURE 12.7
A perceptual-cognitive task. What is it? Decide what the inkblot reminds you of, and then subject your answer to the analysis in the text.

Although cognitively immature individuals cannot produce high-level responses, the individual at a high level of cognitive functioning is perfectly capable of producing responses at the lower cognitive levels. You may think that the blot looks like an amoeba, which is not an uncommon response for an adult. In terms of formal properties, however, this description is cognitively undemanding and global. Some structure has been imposed on the blot, but since the shape of amoebas is so amorphous and vague, almost any inkblot would qualify for this description. But this is only a single response. When such low-level responses are interspersed with high-level responses to other inkblots, we think of the individual's cognitive functioning as being more flexible and richer than that of adults who do not employ a variety of levels in their responses.

The ability to use cognitive functioning of an earlier level is implicit to the progression through cognitive stages. Remnants or aspects of the earlier stages are found at every succeeding stage. Cognitive functioning is like a collapsed telescope in which each small segment is contained in the next larger segment. Thus, under great stress or when the demands for reality are relaxed, as in fantasizing, the mature individual may engage in the undifferentiated thinking of an earlier age. This has been called **dedifferentiation** or **regression** in thought.

Perceptual Differentiation

Two perceptual phenomena are found much more frequently in children than in adults—synesthesia, when stimulation of one sense is also experienced as sensations of another or other senses; and eidetic imagery, when images have the clarity and accuracy of a perception. These phenomena, which are difficult to investigate, are extremely striking when encountered. They must indicate that something important is happening in the perceptual-cognitive system as it develops.

Synesthesia In **synesthesia** a stimulus registers not only as an appropriate sensation but also in one or more other sensory systems as sensations inseparable from the first. This experience is rare in adults, in whom the sensory systems are usually differentiated so that specific stimuli register only as appropriate and discrete sensations. In early childhood, however, an auditory stimulus may produce both auditory and color sensations, or an olfactory stimulus may also produce a visual sensation.

Probably the most common form of synesthesia is color hearing, which has been estimated to occur in 40 to 50 percent of children (Marks, 1975). Werner (1957a) reported hearing children refer to "light- and dark-red whistling" and the "gold and silver striking of the hour." Color and smell may also be merged. For example, one child whose mother was wearing grape perfume said that her mother smelled purple. For children these are not poetic metaphors but descriptions of very real experiences. The child's sensory system is so undifferentiated that sensations are able to merge. It must be emphasized, however, that synesthesia does not refer merely to an association between two sensations. Rather, in synesthesia two or more sensory systems are registering connected sensations. As Werner has stated,

> If a synesthetic individual who asserts that a certain vowel is blue for him is asked where he sees this blueness, he does not say that he sees it near the vowel, hovering about it in some fashion or other, but that he sees the vowel itself as blue (1957a, p. 93).

Recent analysis by Lawrence Marks (1975) suggests that a definite correspondence may be found between the different sensations experienced in synesthesia. For example, the visual sensation that accompanies a vowel sound seems to be related to its pitch. High-pitched vowels such as /i/ and /e/ produce visual sensations that are brighter and smaller in size than the low-pitched /o/ and /u/. In another study, of the visual impressions connected with words, Anglo-American, Navajo Indian, Mexican-Spanish, and Japanese individuals were asked to evaluate verbal concepts such as good, bad, white, and black on visual scales such as light-dark, large-small, up-down. Anglos, Navajos, and Japanese agreed that "white" is thin and calm; "fast" is thin, bright, and diffuse; and "heavy" is down, thick, dark, and near. Since the sounds of the stimulus words differ from culture to culture, the generality of the findings indicates that the visual impressions were related to the meaning of the words. Thus just as a sound can register as a visual perception, so too can a word register cognitively as a visual impression. Marks's findings are related to the phenomenon of phonetic symbolism discussed earlier (page 177) and also to the interpretation of concepts in terms of their attributes (page 190).

According to Marks, synesthesia may be an early form of cognition which registers important multiple dimensions of a given stimulus. It may be similar to our ability to perceive that an object is light or heavy by the sound of its fall. However economical this mode of information processing may be, it is generally imprecise, and as the child grows older, it is replaced by a more flexible and differentiated mode of cognition.

Nevertheless, some degree of synesthesia may persist when the individual attains higher cognitive stages; many of the metaphorical expressions of poets are synesthetic. Synesthetic experiences are also quite common to persons under the influence of the drugs mescaline and hashish. Even when not intoxicated, it appears that all of us retain some small degree of synesthesia. Most of us could readily answer the question, "What is the color of the sound that a trumpet makes?" Viewed objectively, the blare of a trumpet can produce no color sensation. Most individuals, however, describe the color as red, orange, or yellow. They never call it green, black, or white.

Eidetic Imagery An individual who is able to evoke a vivid and detailed visual image of an object or an event after having experienced it is said to have **eidetic imagery.** Thus, after looking at a picture on a screen, the individual can still see the picture on the screen, or out in space or "on a screen in his head," after it has been removed. The person can scan the image before him or her and describe in great detail the components of the picture.

This phenomenon is often referred to as a photographic memory, but a clear distinction can be made between a memory image and an eidetic image. When we call to mind a memory image of a past experience, we use our memory to construct "something like" what we saw. The eidetic image is more nearly a real perception; the object being recalled is actually there before the person. Furthermore, the eidetic image is susceptible to imaginative embellishment and alteration. For instance, an eidetiker—the individual who can produce eidetic images—can be shown a face, produce the face in an eidetic image, and then be told to put a beard on the face. The eidetiker then reports seeing the chin disappearing and being replaced with a beard. Recent studies suggest that up to 11 percent of children may have eidetic imagery, and that this ability is rarely found after adolescence (Gray and Gummerman, 1975). A variety of explanations of eidetic imagery have been advanced; an especially appealing one is that eidetic imagery, like synesthesia, is the product of an undifferentiated cognitive system. Early in the development of a child's cognitive functioning, sensory and imaginative phenomena have not yet become differentiated, and the two types of experiences are merged. This undifferentiated state gives way later in life to a cognitive system in which the individual has no difficulty distinguishing between perception of the outer world and a memory image formed by the inner world of cognitive processes.

Since the most obvious aspect of cognitive development is that the thinking processes become more effective with age, we might wonder why a phenomenon such as eidetic imagery usually drops out of the individual's repertory relatively early in life. Surely it would be a great advantage to be able to reconstruct vividly and accurately earlier experiences. Further reflection suggests, however, that eidetic imagery is actually a rather inefficient way of storing and processing information. Rather than memorizing both important and unimportant details of a series of experiences, it is more efficient to analyze each experience, abstract its most important qualities, and store these conceptualizations in refined, coded form. Eidetic imagery may indeed be more of a barrier than an aid to optimal cognitive functioning. For instance, in one study it was found that third-grade children with eidetic imagery were more likely to have reading difficulties (Zelhart and Johnson, 1959). These children may rely on their imagery rather than learning the general rules, the letter combinations, and the words that make the complex process of reading possible.

As is true of synesthesia, a few adults retain considerable eidetic imagery, and perhaps all adults retain some small remnants of it. It is not uncommon, for example, to call up an image of the page of a textbook when attempting to answer a test question. The image is seemingly before us, and we have a sense that the answer is on a particular portion of the page—there on the left side, halfway down. Unfortunately, our eidetic ability deserts us at this point, and we cannot quite make out the exact words occupying that position.

This common experience has the support of experimental data (Rothkopf, 1971). In one study students read passages of prose material. Later some were asked to describe the part of the page on which certain material had appeared. Others were asked to describe the information that appeared on specific areas of the page. Individuals found it easier to recall locations rather than words. In this faint remnant of eidetic ability, we see once again the principle that as we move from stage to stage in cognitive development, aspects of earlier stages of functioning are forever with us.

SUMMARY □

Differentiation is an important process in cognitive development. In general, children progress from an undifferentiated, global way of conceptualizing stimuli through a more differentiating period in which they respond to separate parts of a stimulus. Finally, they reach an abstract, integrating stage in which they not only can analyze the parts of stimuli but can also reassemble these parts into a complex and meaningful whole. Heinz Werner has named this progression the orthogenetic principle of development.

Synesthesia and eidetic imagery, two striking phenomena found more commonly in children than adults, seem to reflect the lack of differentiation in early stages of development. Synesthesia is the fusion of sensations from different sensory sytems, such as the auditory and visual, in response to a stimulus that would register as a single sensation in adults. Eidetic imagery, commonly referred to as photographic memory, may represent a lack of differentiation between sensory and memory systems. Adults occasionally show traces of both synesthesia and eidetic imagery, demonstrating the general principle that earlier processes may persist even when individuals have attained higher stages of cognitive functioning.

LANGUAGE AND COGNITIVE DEVELOPMENT

The child's growing ability to use language is intimately related to the increasing differentiation of the cognitive system. Being able to conceptualize experiences in words is an important differentiating process.

Verbal Mediation in Problem Solving

Verbal mediation is the use of language to intervene between our perception of outside events and our acting upon them. Using words to label or name objects is an example. This skill is extremely valuable in helping children discriminate among the phenomena that they encounter. In studies of this skill, children are given tasks in which they must learn to discriminate between two stimuli, say two blocks of differing shapes. Children learn such discriminations more easily if they are trained to give each object a separate name. The stimuli thus acquire an additional distinctiveness. If children are trained to give the same name to each of the two stimuli, they find it more difficult to discriminate between them, apparently because the two stimuli acquire a similarity or equivalence for the children.

Concept Shift Studies A form of verbal mediation that goes beyond the simple labeling of stimuli has also been examined. Howard and Tracy Kendler have conducted a number of concept shift studies (for example, 1962, 1970). In these studies children are asked to figure out the solution to one problem which uses certain materials, then to shift to a second problem using the same materials and figure out the new solution. Suppose, for example, that the materials are large and small red and white squares (Figure 12.8). On the first problem pairs of these four squares are shown to the child, who must learn to choose the larger ones, ignoring their color. In this problem color is irrelevant. Once the child has mastered this problem, the experimenter presents the second problem. This second problem will require a **reversal shift** in concepts if the dimension significant in the first problem, size, is still relevant, but the opposite choice, small rather than large, is correct. The problem will require **nonreversal shift** in concepts if the previously irrelevant attribute is now relevant, and the child must learn to choose the red (or white) squares and to ignore size.

The Kendlers asked which type of second problem is easier to master, one requiring a reversal shift or one requiring a nonreversal shift. They found that the answer depends on the age of the individual. College students find the reversal shift very much easier. With kindergarten children, about half find the reversal shift easier and half find the nonreversal shift easier. Between kindergarten and college age the proportion of children who prefer the reversal shift increases steadily.

These studies and a good bit of other evidence suggest that when the reversal shift is easier, verbal mediation is the reason. Some of the very young children do not put into words the principle that is correct for solving the first problem. They have made no verbal investment, so to speak, when deciding which square to choose. They switch more easily from the size of squares to their color. As children grow older, however, they acquire greater verbal facility. They can more easily verbalize the relevant principle, for example, "Choose the larger and not the smaller." The reversal shift does not require abandoning this mediating principle but only a slight modification of it: "Do the opposite," or "Before it was larger, now it's small." The same dimension and mediating principle are relevant; only the object selected is different. On the other hand, the nonreversal shift is more difficult, for both the mediating principle and the object selected are different.

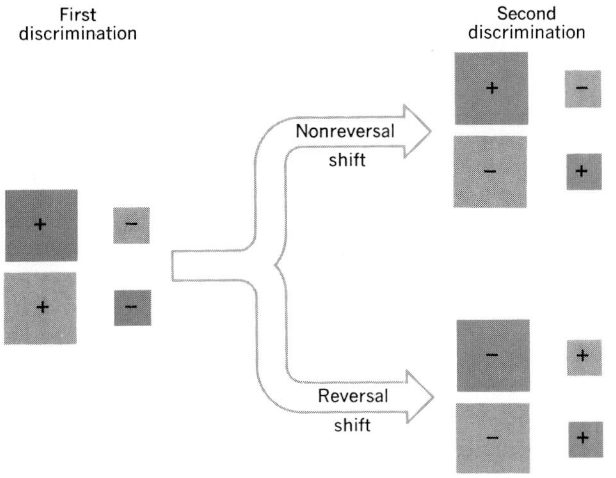

FIGURE 12.8
Reversal and nonreversal shifts. In this diagrammatic representation, plus signs indicate correct choices. The two possibly revelant dimensions are size and color. Size is relevant on the first problem. For the reversal shift in concepts, size is also relevant on the second problem. For the nonreversal shift, color becomes relevant on the second problem.

Failure To Apply Words Many investigations (reviewed by Flavell, 1970) have found that kindergarten-age children who know the names of objects do not necessarily apply them in situations in which such mediators would help them. For example, when asked to memorize the order in which some common objects are presented to them, second graders spontaneously say the names of the objects more often than do the kindergarten children. Fifth graders in turn name more of the objects than do the second graders. There is also a transitional stage, at about age seven, when some children do and some do not produce verbal mediators. At this age children who do not spontaneously give objects names will do so if asked, and their performance improves markedly. When told that they may either use words or not use them during the task, however, children in this transitional stage typically do not verbalize (Keeney, Cannizzo, and Flavell, 1967). For these children more cognitive development must take place before they spontaneously produce the verbal mediators that can make their behavior more effective.

Luria's Stages of Language-Action Relationship

The fact that language is available to children long before they use it effectively to direct their behavior

FIGURE 12.9
Luria's bulb-squeezing task. This apparatus is used to investigate the relationship between language and action. In its simplest use, the child is instructed to squeeze the bulb when the light on the display panel comes on. An event recorder keeps a sequential record of the child's responses, including when he squeezes the bulb, the number and duration of his squeezes, and his verbalizations.

was convincingly demonstrated by Alexander Luria, a distinguished Russian psychologist. Much of Luria's work was concerned with how language comes to control behavior. Luria's investigations (1961) highlighted a developmental sequence which appears quite consistent with Werner's orthogenetic principle. Luria believed that children begin with a relatively undifferentiated system in which motor responses can be made in the absence of language. With the advent of language, children are somewhat more differentiated, for they now have at least two systems at their disposal. What remains to be accomplished is the interlacing of the two systems. Much in keeping with Werner's general description, a hierarchical integration of the motor and verbal systems is attained in the ultimate stage.

Luria demonstrated this developmental progression by studying how well verbal instructions direct behavior in children of different ages. For example, he put various toys before children and said, "Give me the fish." Six-month-old babies were not at all influenced by this command, or at most simply looked at the experimenter. By twelve months of age, the children might also look at the fish. At eighteen months the children almost always oriented to the fish and would sometimes give it to the experimenter. The command was not carried out appropriately until the children reached two years of age. But even when children are two, language is not truly regulating behavior but merely *impelling* it. That is, language is simply stimulating them to act, but the action is not necessarily what is called for. After the children were asked for the fish several times, the instruction was changed to, "Give me the horse." The children often continued to hand Luria the fish.

In a more complicated experimental procedure, a child sat before a panel containing a light bulb. There was a rubber bulb for the child to squeeze and a means of recording the child's squeezes (Figure 12.9). Children were given commands such as, "When the light comes on, squeeze the bulb," or "When the light comes on, don't squeeze the bulb." Most two-year-olds would look at the light whenever they heard "light" and squeeze the bulb whenever they heard "squeeze." They could not appreciate the full meaning of the instructions; their behavior was guided by the meaning of individual words. Moreover, when children were following instructions to squeeze the bulb and were then told, "That's enough," they did not stop squeezing but rather intensified it! Thus, although language can direct simple activities in the two-year-old child, the motor system is clearly dominant during this stage. Adult speech may impel children to initiate an activity, but it cannot inhibit actions they have already started or make them switch from one action to another.

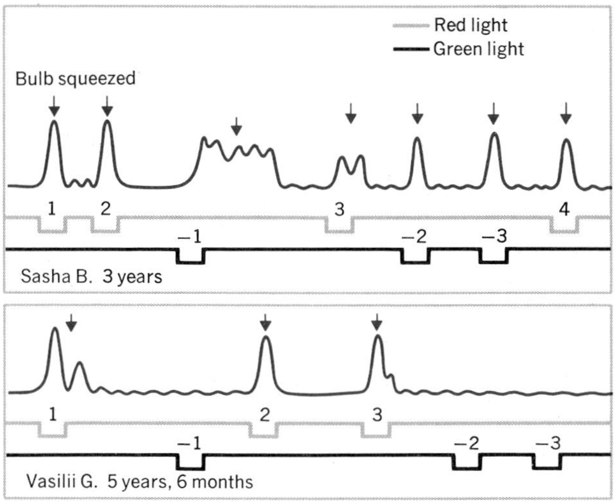

FIGURE 12.10
Two records from Luria's bulb-pressing experiment, illustrating how language gradually comes to control behavior. Children are asked to squeeze the bulb when the red light goes on but not when the green light goes on. Three-year-old Sasha squeezes when either light is on. Language has an impelling function for him, regardless of its meaning. Five-and-a-half-year-old Vasilii, on the other hand, squeezes when the red light is on but is able to refrain from squeezing when the green light goes on. (Adapted from Luria, 1961, p. 69.)

Jerome Bruner.

By the time children are three, however, Luria found that most were able to follow instructions to squeeze the bulb, to stop squeezing, and to wait until the light came on before squeezing. They failed, though, when instructions became more complicated. For instance, given the instruction to "Squeeze when the red light comes on but not when the green light comes on," they usually squeezed to both lights (Figure 12.10). If the command was, "When the light comes on, squeeze twice," they were likely to squeeze more than two times. They perseverated, not because they did not understand the meaning of twice but because, like younger children, they could not stop an activity once they had begun it. Performance on these tasks could often be improved by having the children verbalize when they were supposed to act. For example, if trained to say "Go" when the red light came on, but not when the green appeared, they were more likely to squeeze the bulb at the correct times. Similarly, the children squeezed only twice if they were trained to say "Go, go."

Only when the child reaches five or six years of age does language gain a genuine regulatory function over behavior. When children of this age are given the bulb-squeezing tasks, they respond appropriately to the *meaning* of the verbal instructions. By this age language not only activates children but can direct varied patterns of action—"Squeeze when the red light is on but not when the green is on"—and also terminate action. The meanings of words are now more dominant than the motor system.

Paralleling language's shift from impelling the activity of children to directing its course is a shift from an external to internal mode of verbal control. At first, much of the child's behavior is directed by the spoken instructions of others. Later, Luria observed, children will give themselves overt verbal instruction, and finally, at about the same time that language begins to exert its semantic influence, they begin to internalize speech. This internalized speech, which according to Luria (1957, p. 117) is "indissolubly linked" to thinking, continues to fulfill the function of regulating behavior.

Bruner's Stages of Cognitive Growth

It is clear from the discussion so far that language gives children greater flexibility and power in solving problems and regulating their own behavior. But how does language do this? Jerome Bruner views language as a tool which is provided by the culture and which actually expands the use of the mind. Language provides a means of processing information and the individual's experiences in symbolic form. Children grow cognitively, according to Bruner, as they acquire techniques that enable them to represent the regularities and consistencies of their surroundings with greater efficiency. The use of language, and symbols in general, to code and process past experience is achieved in the third and ultimate stage of cognitive growth.

Before reaching this stage children use two other means of representation. At first infants understand the world only by the actions they perform—what Bruner calls **enactive representation.** To a baby girl in this stage, a rattle exists only when she is playing with it. If she accidently drops the rattle over the edge of the crib, she will look puzzled and seemingly attempt to regain the object by repeating the shaking movements she made just before the rattle disappeared. It is as though the rattle will be in her hand because she is making the movements that the rattle represents to her.

During the first half year of life, babies cry if a rattle is removed only after they have begun reaching for it, but a few months later they will cry if the rattle is shown to them and then hidden from their view. To Bruner, this change in behavior indicates that the children now have an image of the rattle that persists independent of their movements in connection with it. They can now form a picture of the rattle in their minds. The children have advanced to Bruner's second stage of cognitive development, that of **ikonic representation.** During this stage, which usually begins toward the end of the first year of life, imagery is the most effective means of processing information.

The third stage, **symbolic representation,** begins around age three when children first start speaking grammatically. Symbols are much more flexible than images. Words not only allow children to represent their experiences more efficiently but also permit them to organize, to transform or rework those experiences.

Bruner and Helen Kenney (1966) have studied how children in the ikonic and symbolic stages proceed when given simple matrix-ordering tasks. These investigators presented three-to-seven-year-old children with nine plastic glasses, varying in three degrees of diameter and three degrees of height, arranged in a matrix (Figure 12.11). Bruner and Kenney acquainted the children with the matrix by removing one, two, and then three glasses at a time from the matrix and asking the children to replace them. The children were also asked how the glasses in the rows and columns were alike and how they differed. Then the investigators scrambled the glasses and asked the children to make "something like what was there before"—that is, to reproduce the matrix. Finally, they scrambled the glasses once again but placed the glass that had previously been in the southwest corner in the southeast corner. They asked the children once more to make something like what was there before, but to leave this particular glass in its present position.

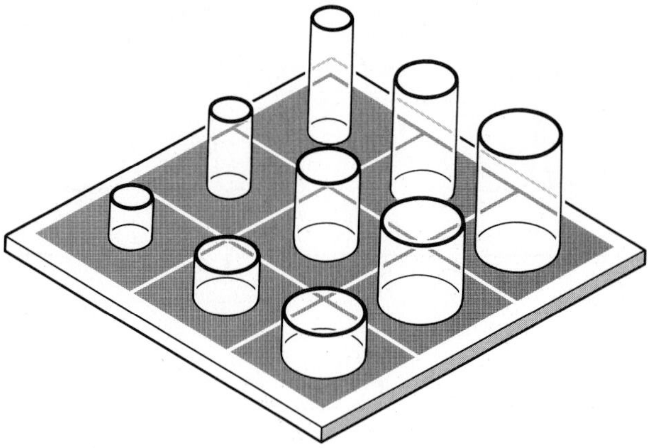

FIGURE 12.11
The matrix of glasses used in an ordering task. (After Bruner and Kenney, 1966.)

The three- and four-year-olds were very poor at such tasks. They did not really grasp the meaning of the instructions, but they eagerly went about moving glasses around, putting them here and there. The five-, six-, and seven-year-olds were all adept at replacing the missing glasses, and they could reproduce the matrix once it had been scrambled. The only difference among them was that the older children were quicker.

The five-, six-, and seven-year-olds differed substantially, however, in their ability to construct the matrix once one of the glasses had been put in a different corner. None of the five-year-olds and only a small percentage of the six-year-olds were able to reconstruct the matrix, but most seven-year-olds succeeded.

The five-year-olds failed on this task because they seemed to rely on an image of the original matrix. Many of them would put the transposed glass "back where it belongs," or they rotated the cardboard base on which the glasses were placed so that it would "be like before." Some five- and six-year-olds simply built the original matrix around the transposed glass. In contrast, the seven-year-olds were more likely to view the transposition as a problem that required thought and did not rely on their mental images of the earlier matrix.

The language that the children used to describe the dimensions of the matrix had no bearing on how they replaced glasses, or reconstructed the matrix, but it did seem to correlate with how well they carried out the transposition task. When the children were asked how the glasses were alike and how they differed, they answered in three ways. The most precise terms were *dimensional.* These children used words that described two ends of a continuum, such as "fat" and "skinny," "tall" and "short." Some descriptions were *global;* children chose undifferentiated terms such as "big" and "little" to describe differences in both diameter and height. Other children used *confounded* terms. One end of a continuum was described globally and the other end dimensionally: "That one is tall, and that one is little." Among the five-to-seven-year-olds, those who used confounded descriptions were the most likely to fail on the transposed-matrix problem.

These findings suggest to Bruner that the five- and six-year-olds can develop an image of the two-dimensional array and can reproduce it quite efficiently. If asked to alter the image, however, they cannot do so because they are not yet capable of translating the matrix into a verbal or symbolic formula. The seven-year-olds who use the correct dimensional language, on the other hand, are provided with a principle for ordering the matrix that helps them deal with the transformation. They find it a simple matter to build new structures according to the rule that governed the arrangement of the original matrix.

Jean Piaget.

SUMMARY □

One of the earliest uses of language is in labeling objects. Labels help the child to make discriminations and to form concepts. Through verbal mediation it is possible to form concepts that help in the solution of a problem. For example, the Kendlers' studies of problems requiring reversal and nonreversal shifts in concepts have indicated that with increasing age, and thus with increasing powers of verbal mediation, the reversal shift of a concept becomes easy to formulate. Thus problems requiring this shift in concepts are easier to solve.

There is considerable evidence that children acquire language long before they use it effectively in regulating their behavior. Luria has traced a developmental sequence in the relationship between language and action and has found a progression that is in keeping with Werner's orthogenetic principle of differentiation and later integration. Initially, the child's response to language is undifferentiated; an adult's words serve merely to stimulate general activity. As children develop, however, they respond in an increasingly appropriate and differentiated manner to the meaning of words. Children also learn to direct their behavior by their own internalized speech.

For the first six months of their lives babies understand the world in terms of their activities. The movements in which objects engage them represent the objects themselves. This representation of the world Bruner calls enactive. Soon, however, infants have ikonic representation. They are able to form images of objects in their heads. At three, when children begin speaking grammatically, they begin to have more flexible symbolic representation. Bruner views language as a tool that actually expands the use of the mind because it permits individuals not only to represent their past experiences but to transform them as well.

THE WORK OF PIAGET

Jean Piaget is the world's most renowned investigator of cognitive development. Born in Switzerland in 1896, Piaget is one of the truly germinal thinkers of our age. He has utilized concepts from biology, psychology, philosophy, and mathematics to examine one of the great eternal mysteries, how individuals come to know the world.

Piaget gave early signs of genius. As a boy, he was interested in biology, and his first article describing an albino sparrow which he had seen in the park was published when he was only eleven. Throughout his adolescence Piaget mixed his interest in biology with his interest in epistemology—the development of a theory of knowledge. Piaget has never abandoned his biological orientation, and his investigation of the method and grounds of knowledge is cast solidly within the framework of biology.

Epistemology and biology merged in his growing interest in psychology. As a young investigator, Piaget accepted a position as assistant to Théophile Simon in Alfred Binet's laboratory in Paris. His initial assignment was to standardize Cyril Burt's reasoning tests by giving them to Parisian grade school children. This work allowed him to observe first hand the psychometric approach to the understanding of cognitive development. That he found this approach limited is made clear by the following account.

> . . . from the very first questionings I noticed that though Burt's tests certainly had their diagnostic merits, based on the number of successes and failures, it was much more interesting to try to find the reasons for the failures. Thus I engaged my subjects in conversations patterned after psychiatric questioning, with the aim of discovering something about the reasoning process underlying their right, but especially their wrong answers. I noticed with amazement that the simplest reasoning task involving the inclusion of a part in the whole or the coordination of relations or the "multiplication" of classes (finding the part common to two wholes), presented for normal children up to the age of eleven or twelve difficulties unsuspected by the adult (1952, p. 244).

Thus Piaget realized that complete information about the nature of the evolving mind could not be gained by test responses alone. His verbal probing technique has come to be known as Piaget's *méthode clinique.*

Piaget had been launched on his life work. Since 1921 he has been doing important studies of child psychology, logic and causal reasoning, the development of language and thought, the growth of moral judgment, the child's conception of the world, and the emergence of intelligence during infancy and early childhood. Through these efforts Piaget has evolved a theory of intelligence and its development.

Piaget's Theory

For Piaget the function of intelligence is adaptation to the world. The cognitive apparatus is like an adaptive structure with which individuals can regulate their interactions with the environment. Piaget observed that since the use of intelligence is so crucial in the adaptive process, intellectual activity may be considered a basic biological urge.

Perhaps Piaget's most significant contribution has been his demonstration of how fundamentally different the intellect of children is from that of adults. At birth infants are conscious neither of themselves nor of objects as independent, permanent structures. Beginning at this primitive level, children's cognitive systems change and grow to become more adaptive and thus provide a more realistic understanding of the world. Central to Piaget's theory is the view that knowledge of the world is not simply a "copy" of what is out there. Rather, our understanding of the world at any time depends on and is limited by the cognitive structure, the mental processes that we have developed up to that time. For example, a two-month-old baby has only a few ways of knowing—by sucking, by touching, and by focusing on round facelike objects. The infant's understanding of the world cannot go beyond what is provided by these scant cognitive resources.

To consider sucking and touching cognitive activities is rather unusual. But for Piaget actions—at first actual physical actions and later in life mental actions as well—are the basis of all knowledge and cognitive growth. Actions are so important in Piaget's theory that he has adopted a special terminology in referring to them. He speaks of **schemes,** of organized patterns of physical action, such as sucking or grasping. The scheme, however, is not a specific motor action but a *generalization* of what different instances of a specific physical action have in common. For example, a child's scheme of grasping is not any individual grasp but the features that are characteristic of all the child's potential grasps. When schemes are carried out in the head—becoming mental actions—they are called **operations.** Both schemes and operations are specific ways of knowing available to the individual.

Cognitive growth takes place as schemes and operations change and become more complex. The process by which this is accomplished consists of two complementary components, assimilation and accommodation. When a child encounters an object or event never before experienced, it is incorporated or assimilated into the child's existing cognitive framework. The cognitive structure may then reorganize or change to accommodate the new experience. **Assimilation** is thus the process of taking in new information and interpreting it—sometimes even distorting it—to make it agree with the available mental organization. **Accommodation** is a changing of the internal cognitive system to provide a better match to outside information. For example, when newborn infants are given the breast, they are equipped with a reflex that causes them to suck. They literally assimilate the breast into their existing prescriptions for behavior. If a corner of a blanket is placed on their lips, they also suck the blanket. They thus continue to assimilate objects into one of the few organized responses that they possess. In the process of sucking the blanket, however, they must reorganize their responses and their cognitive representations, their schemes, of it, for to continue treating a blanket as though it were a breast is ineffective. They must shape their lips differently and, in so doing, change their schemes of

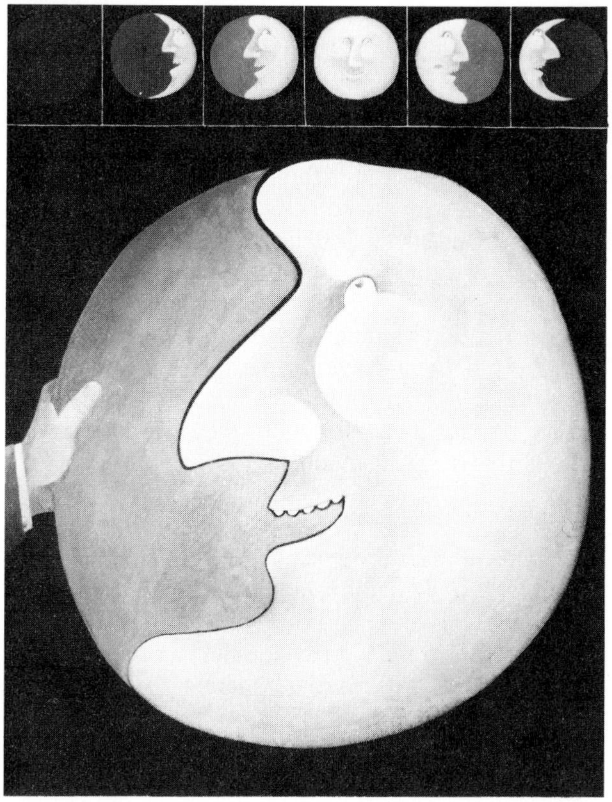

...several children in the four to six age-group told me that the sun and moon were "made" by a gentleman who lighted them up (Piaget, 1971).

sucking. This reorganization in response to the new demands presented by the alien object is an example of accommodation.

The child's explanation of dreams is another example of cognitive growth through assimilation and accommodation. The boy who said that dreams come in balloons sent from God (page 281) has assimilated the experience of dreaming into his existing cognitive framework. Since dreams have certain visual qualities, which make them similar to external events, he has associated them with balloons, external objects with which he is familiar. In saying that the balloons "burst into pictures outside your head," the boy indicates a relatively undifferentiated cognitive structure which makes inadequate distinctions between internal and external events. But even by telling us that dreams take place outside, the child has begun to show some degree of accommodation; he has made a distinction between inside and outside. Later he will be forced to come to grips with certain unstable and eventually unacceptable aspects of his explanation, and he will then have to make further accommodations. For instance, after having had a number of dreams, he will come to recognize their unrealness and the other unsubstantial qualities that separate dreams from events taking place outside the head. The differences that he notices between dreams and nondreams, as well as the greater differentiation of the cognitive system, will lead the boy to the next level of interpreting dreams.

Each instance of assimilation and accommodation stretches the mind a bit, and this stretching enables the individual to make new and somewhat different assimilations and accommodations in the future. These in turn bring additional small increments in mental growth. Thus by repeated assimilations and accommodations, the cognitive system gradually evolves and provides the child with an increasingly accurate view of the nature of things. When the child makes a startling leap in understanding phenomena, he or she moves onto the next stage of cognitive development.

Piaget obviously views the development of intelligence as an active and constructive process. Mental growth is not simply the net result of passively receiving and registering "facts" from the world. Rather, children play an active role in learning about the world and in altering their cognitive processes. Piaget believes that the interaction of environmental experiences and an internally maturing structure help to make the cognitive system more differentiated and complex.

Piagetian Stages

Piaget has charted four major stages of cognitive development. These are the sensorimotor stage, the preoperational stage, the stage of concrete operations, and the stage of formal operations. During each certain critical cognitive abilities are achieved, clearly indicating that the child is processing information in a way that was previously impossible. The age ranges cited are rough guidelines, for there is considerable variation from child to child and task to task.

Sensorimotor Stage—Birth to Two Years During this stage the most fundamental and rapid changes in cognitive structure take place. Piaget calls this the **sensorimotor stage** because the term reflects his belief that knowledge is initially built up directly from sensory perceptions and motor actions.

At birth the infant has no self-awareness—no sense that "I" can act on the world—and no sense of the world as a separate entity. The infant is the center of the universe, which consists of ever-changing perceptions but no permanent objects. Piaget (1973) has described what happens during this stage as a Copernican revolution. Cognitively, the child is dethroned as the center of the universe and becomes an object among other objects. Children also learn that objects and they themselves exist in space and that they may cause something to happen to another object. Children gain all this knowledge before there is any language.

At birth there are only isolated actions and isolated schemes. As the actions are repeated and coordinated, the schemes are elaborated by new assimilations and accommodations. One example of sensorimotor intelligence that develops during this stage is pulling a blanket on which a toy out of reach rests in order to obtain the toy. This task may appear quite simple on the face of it, but Piaget has shown what a cognitive feat it really is. Before children can perform this task, they must have constructed and mastered several relationships, in particular "resting upon" and "moving an object from one place to another," and then coordinated them for their purposes.

Perhaps the most significant achievement during this period is the development of the **object concept** or a sense of object permanence. As noted earlier, infants do not at first realize that objects, including people, have an existence independent of their perceptions of them. They may gaze at a toy which is held within their view, but when the toy is removed they do not search for it. The object simply ceases to exist once it leaves their visual field. This explains the delight infants derive from playing peek-a-boo. If a mother removes her face from her infant son's view and then allows him to see it again, he is surprised and pleased by her re-creation. Later in this stage children will gaze at the point where an object disappeared, and by the end of the sensorimotor period they will actively seek to find an object after it has vanished. By this time children have a sense that objects exist, even when they cannot see or find them.

Their inadequate concept of objects explains why infants less than a year old cannot successfully play the "guess which hand" game. When they watch you hide a coin in your hand, place your hands behind your back, and return an empty hand, they will begin the search where they believe the coin disappeared. Early in the sensorimotor stage children will think it disappeared when you first hid it in your hand, and they will begin the search among your fingers. By the end of the sensorimotor period, they look behind your back, for by now this is the place where they lost knowledge of its whereabouts.

Preoperational Stage—Two to Seven Years of Age

During the **preoperational stage** children become capable of symbolic activities such as mental imagery, language, and drawing, none of which was possible before. Children can now mentally represent to themselves an object when it is not visually present. Consequently, intelligence is no longer restricted to physical actions. During this stage children construct in conceptual terms everything that they have acquired at the level of actions. Instead of schemes as the only generalizing instrument, they now have conceptualization as well. By the end of this period, children are able to talk about objects, draw them, tell stories, and assemble three-dimensional constructions. They also learn to use language to direct their behavior. The stage is called preoperational, however, because children are unable to engage in certain basic mental operations. They cannot put themselves in another's place; focus on two dimensions, such as height and width, at the same time; and reverse or change actions mentally. They can repeat old actions in their minds, but they cannot think of actions that they have not yet engaged in or seen themselves.

Use of language in these young children is very different from that in adults. When children first learn that objects have names, they believe that names are an essential part of the objects. For instance, the word "ball" is considered just as much an inherent property of the ball as its physical characteristics of shape and color. This mode of thinking about the names of things is called **nominal realism.** In the earliest stage of nominal realism, the child finds nonsensical the question why certain objects have the names they do. Since the name is part of the object, the child reasons, the object could have no other name. Furthermore, children feel that the object could not have existed prior to the time it had its name. In later stages children will abandon this view and realize that names are assigned to objects. It is not until much later, however, when they reach the age of eleven or twelve, that children fully comprehend how arbitrary the naming process is. Until then, they will insist that the names of objects were assigned by God or by the men who made the objects and could not have been other than the names they have learned.

In addition to language, the preoperational child acquires **identity constancy.** The child comes to realize that an object remains qualitatively the same, despite alterations in form, size, and general appearance. Rheta DeVries (1969) used an interesting means of studying the development of this concept in three-to-six-year-old children. The children were individually shown a very docile cat. After they had identified it as a cat and petted it, the experimenter told them that soon the animal was going to look different. She asked the children to look only at the tail end of the cat. Then, while screening the front end from their view, she placed a mask of a ferocious-looking dog over the cat's head (Figure 12.12). The cat was turned around, and the children were asked what animal it was now. DeVries found that the older children had a definite appreciation for the identity of the cat. Many of the younger children, however.

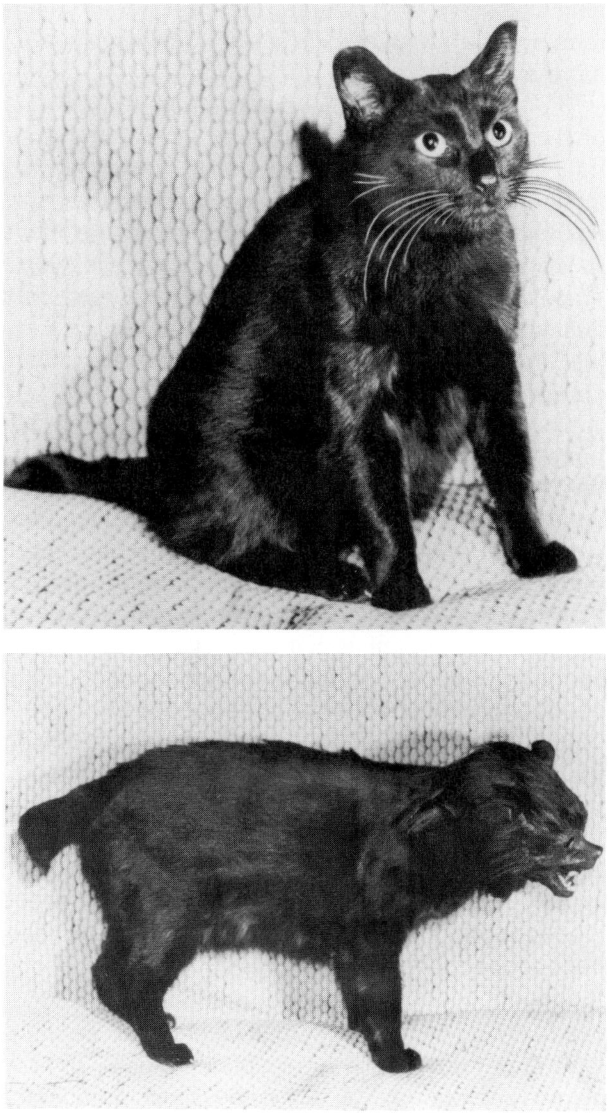

FIGURE 12.12
In a study of identity constancy, a cat was masked as a dog.

really thought that the cat had become a dog, even though its tail end had been visible to them while the mask was put on. They often seemed fearful of the animal and refused to pet it. When questioned, they asserted that it was indeed a real dog, could bark, and had a dog's insides. The older children were more likely to think that a trick had been played, that a cat could not possibly become a dog, not even "by magic."

Piaget has shown that the preoperational child also acquires a grasp of functions. In mathematics, x is said to be a function of y, that is, $x = f(y)$, if the value of x depends on and covaries with the value of y. During this stage children develop the ability to understand simple functional relationships among observed events. They learn that this happens when that happens, and that changes in one thing are associated with changes in another. Children in this stage, however, do not yet have a quantitative idea of functional relationships. In one experiment Piaget and his colleagues (1968) gave children different-sized toy fish—5, 10, and 15 centimeters in length—and fifty beads representing their diet of meatballs. The children were told to feed the medium-sized fish and the largest fish twice and three times as much food, respectively, as they did the smallest fish. By the age of five, most children understood that they ought to give a fish an amount of food that related to its size. They gave the largest fish more food than the medium-sized fish, and the least amount went to the smallest fish. At this age, however, the children did not attempt to quantify the relationship precisely. Only when they had reached the next developmental stage did they know that when they gave two beads to the smallest fish, they ought to give four to the middle fish and six to the largest.

Concrete Operations Stage—Seven to Eleven Years of Age In the next stage children organize into structural wholes many of the scattered schemes and conceptualizations developed during earlier periods. They form mental representations that adequately reflect possible actions and transactions in the physical world. Piaget calls this the stage of concrete operations. As indicated earlier, operations are mental actions, schemes carried out in the head. Now the child is able to act on objects and transform situations mentally. The operations are concrete, however, because the child at this time can only reason about physical things like liquids, blocks, and pieces of clay. Reasoning about abstractions such as words and mathematical symbols is not possible until the next stage of development.

Flexibility During this stage children develop the concept of **hierarchical structures,** the ranking of classes within classes, and they develop the ability to order objects or people on more than one dimension. For instance, when ten red and five green wooden beads are shown to preoperational children, they can tell us that there are more red beads than green. When asked whether there are more red beads or wooden beads, however, preoperational children often reply that there are more red beads than wooden ones. This simplistic approach to classification is overcome in the stage of concrete operations, when the child develops a more abstract notion of class of objects as well as the concept of multiple classification. For example, during this stage children learn that people can be classified into more than one category, that a father can also be somebody's brother, an accountant, and a golfer. An example of the earlier inability to do so has been given by David Elkind, a major interpreter of Piaget to American psychologists. Professor Elkind (1973) asked a preoperational child whether he (Elkind) could be a Protestant and an American at the same time. The child replied "No," but then after a second's thought added, "Only if you move."

Since a child's cognitive structure is an adaptive mechanism for dealing with all aspects of the world, it is not surprising that social interactions take on a different quality as the child develops cognitively. During the concrete operations stage children become less egocentric; they are able to consider the views of others as well as their own. They can share their thoughts with others, adopt others' perspectives, are less contradictory and inconsistent, and engage in meaningful and prolonged communication with others.

We see this change in the child's use of and attitude toward rules. Early in the stage of concrete operations, the child regards rules as absolute and unchangeable, often considering them to have been handed down by God. Rules are thought to exist in the very fabric of the universe, to have existed always, and to permit no deviation. Piaget (1932) investigated children's conceptions of rules by playing marbles with youngsters of various ages and seeing whether he could induce them to change the rules. It was clear from the young children's responses that they viewed Piaget as a troublemaker who simply did not comprehend the inviolability of these rules. Despite their verbal commitment to rules, however, these children often break them in practice. Toward the end of the concrete operations stage, a more abstract and viable approach to rules develops. Children come to realize that rules are established because they are in the best interests of those who construct them, and that since rules are made by people, they can be changed by people, including themselves. Once this transition has been accomplished, Piaget has noted, children much more consistently adhere to the stated rules in practice.

Conservation Perceptually, the world is full of flux and change. We have learned that an object projects radically different images on the retina, depending on its distance from us and the angles at which it is viewed. Yet we know that an object remains the same size and shape, no matter where it exists in our visual field (Chapter 4). Similarly, we know that an object continues to exist despite the fact that its image has disappeared from our retina, and that it remains the same thing despite changes in its appearance. The ability to construct invariants from all the perceptual flux is an indispensable cognitive activity for an adapting individual (Flavell, 1977). The individual able to discern consistencies and regularities in surroundings—to find order in the world—can deal more effectively with it.

The invariants that have been acquired by the end of the preoperations period—size and shape constancy, object permanence, identity constancy, and functions—are fundamentally qualitative rather than quantitative in nature. During the concrete operations stage a notion of quantitative invariants develops. That is, the child learns to maintain a concept both qualitatively and quantitatively in the face of perceptual transformations. Piaget has called this ability **conservation.**

During the concrete operations stage children acquire the ability to conserve such concepts as number, substance, and quantity. Until they have this ability, children do not possess a complete understanding of these concepts. Let us use the concept of number as an example. By the concept of number, Piaget is not referring to the child's ability to count from 1 to 10 or to tell us that 2 + 2 are 4. These can be learned by rote and do not in themselves indicate that the child is really aware that 2 is less than 5 or that the abstraction 7 means the same thing, whether there are seven mice or seven battleships. Shown pictures of seven mice and seven battleships, the young child may well feel that there are more battleships than there are mice because the battleships are so much bigger.

In mastering the concept of number, the child must first be able to utilize one-to-one correspondence. Suppose that we place five wooden balls in a row before the preoperational girl, give her a box containing a large number of square wooden blocks, and ask her to put out on the floor the same number of squares as there are balls. For an individual who has mastered the concept of number, this is an extremely simple task; the adult would immediately grasp that there are five balls and simply count out five squares. This task is beyond the young child, however; she engages in quite a different process in order to solve the problem. Typically, she takes a block and places it directly under the first ball in the row, then places a second block directly beneath the second ball in the row. When she has put a block beneath every ball, she tells us that there are the same number of blocks as there are balls. She has utilized a strategy of one-to-one correspondence in order to produce two collections of objects, each collection having the same number.

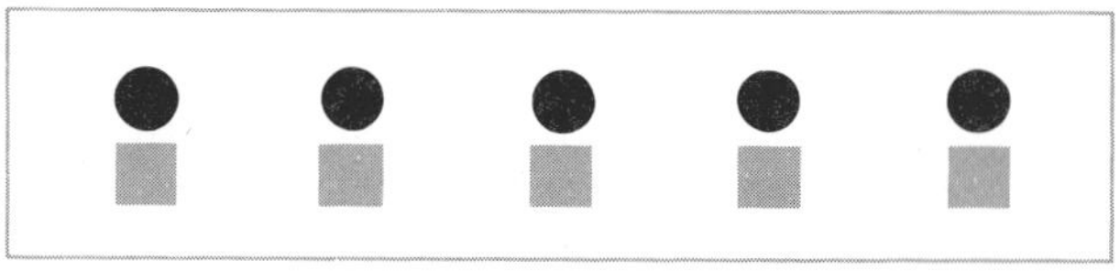

Being able to employ one-to-one correspondence does not mean that the child has mastered the concept of number. Suppose we rearrange the objects this way:

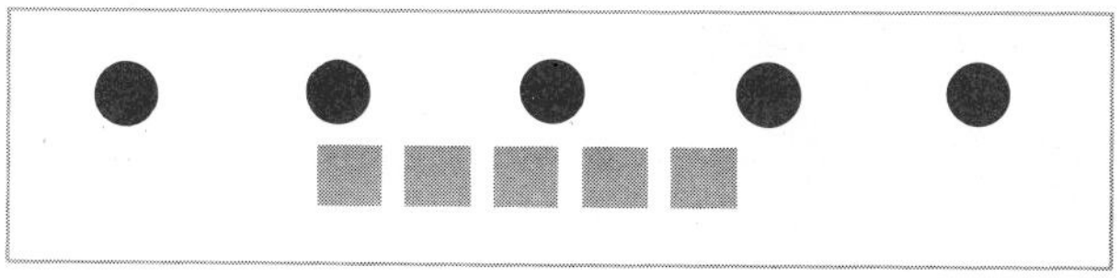

Now when the child is asked whether there are as many squares as balls, she will answer that there are more balls. She may even insist on adding more squares so that they will match the balls in number. Since this simple difference in physical arrangement alters the child's answer, we know that she has not mastered the equivalence between the number of squares placed directly beneath the balls and the number of squares as they are now grouped. The child's perception of length is overriding her conception of number; she reasons that there must be more balls than squares because the row of balls is longer. This single-minded riveting of attention on one particularly salient or interesting perceptual attribute Piaget calls **centering.** Only when children can **decenter** and focus their attention simultaneously on several perceptual aspects of a thing or of an array of things will they be able to conserve concepts.

The principle of conservation of substance is mastered when the child becomes aware that an amount of material stays the same even when the shape is changed. If a child is given two equal balls of clay and asked whether they contain the same amount of clay, the child will usually examine them closely and reply that they do. Then, while the child watches, one clay ball is rolled into a sausage shape. Asked which has more clay, the child who has mastered conservation is often amused at the stupidity of the question and replies that of course the two objects still contain the same amount of clay. A few years earlier, however, while in the preoperational stage, this same child would have replied that the round ball had more clay because it was fatter, or that the sausage had more clay because it was longer. Again, children in the earlier stage center so much on the one dimension of length or breadth that they cannot conserve the concept of substance.

Closely related to the conservation of substance is the child's ability to conserve a quantity of liquid. Two glass beakers of the same size are filled with the same amount of water. The child agrees that they contain the same amount. As the child watches, the water in one of these containers is poured into a shorter and wider beaker. The child who cannot conserve believes that the shallow glass does not contain as much water. When the same liquid is poured into a tall beaker, she believes that this glass contains more water. She even indicates that when the water is poured back into the original container, the liquid will reach a higher level on the glass.

Pouring the liquid into the other beakers transforms the perceptual aspects of the liquid, making it appear shorter in the shallow container, taller in the other. The preoperational child, tied to her perceptions, will say that the liquid has changed in amount, even though she has observed the actual pouring. The child who has reached the stage of concrete operations, however, is able to reason about the act of pouring and conserve the quantity of liquid despite perceptual alterations.

Two other general advancements that are connected with the ability to conserve are made during the concrete operations phase. One is a shift of attention from states to transformations, from how things appear to how they come to appear that way. Piaget has observed that when younger children are solving problems, they are more likely to focus their conceptual energies on states. They are less likely to recall how objects appeared in the past or to anticipate possible future changes in appearance. Children who are able to conserve, on the other hand, are more disposed to keep in mind the process of transition from one state to another. In justifying a conservation judgment, they can point out that the liquid was merely poured from one container to another. The pouring transformed its appearance.

In another advancement children become able to reverse thought. They can interrupt a sequence of thought at any point and return to the beginning of the sequence. Young children cannot conceive that the two pieces of reshaped clay or the amounts of water in different-sized beakers are identical because they are unable to think them back to their original states. In contrast, conservers recognize that the two different-sized beakers contain the same amount of liquid, for in their original states the amounts of water were identical. They also recognize that pouring the liquid back into the original container reverses the earlier action. Therefore the act of pouring cannot permanently change the volume of the liquid. The principle of reversibility is important to a number of mental operations. The child's numerical ability is greatly enhanced once he or she can reverse $4 \times 2 = 8$ by performing the operation $8/2 = 4$. The process of reversibility is also a prerequisite for engaging in transitive reasoning, which takes this form: if A is smaller than B, and B is smaller than C, then A must be smaller than C. If Kirk is heavier than Loren, and Loren is heavier than Mark, who is heavier, Kirk or Mark? Conservers have the ability to reason transitively.

Failure to conserve quantity. (*a*) Two equal volumes of fluid (*b*) poured into different containers may not be recognized as still equal until (*c*) they are returned to identical containers.

(*a*)

(*b*)

(*c*)

The principle of conservation, holding for concepts of number, quantity, volume, weight, space, and time, is pervasive in its scope and significance. It is easy to see why Piaget has indicated that as children grow older, they begin to learn that the world is orderly and that they can profit by differentiating what appears to be so perceptually from what is really so cognitively. For growing children this process has two effects. It strengthens their awareness of the orderly and logical nature of the world, and it fosters their confidence in the power of rational thought, foresight, and planning.

Formal Operations Stage—from Eleven Years On During the final stage of development, children become able to consider a problem in the abstract without needing a concrete representation of it. They will search for alternatives in trying to solve problems, rejecting those that seem inappropriate without physically testing their inadequacy. Children now understand the meaning of logical propositions and arguments and are free to manipulate all sorts of conceptual hypotheses about the world. They can think not only about what is but about what could be. When younger children are confronted with the supposition, "If coal is white, snow is ____," they will respond by insisting that coal is black. The adolescent will answer that snow is black. This problem makes cognitive demands. The reality of the situation is that coal is not white and snow is not black. Through formal operations children free themselves from such physical "givens" and are able to consider a totally hypothetical realm of possibilities, which nevertheless retains some orderliness. This new ability of the person to deal in hypothetical terms is described by John Flavell.

> No longer exclusively preoccupied with the sober business of trying to stabilize and organize just what comes directly to the senses, the adolescent has, through this new orientation, the potentiality of imagining all that might be there—both the very obvious and the very subtle—and thereby of much better insuring the finding of all that is there (1963, p. 205).

Formal operations make possible thoughts about thinking, a grasp of truth, beauty, and immensities, a delving into probabilities and improbabilities, imagining other worlds, conceiving ideals. Exactly these abilities bring about some of humanity's most impressive achievements.

The formal operations stage is the ultimate stage of cognitive development; formal operations are the basis of adult thought. Both the psychometricians and the cognitive developmentalists agree that by late adolescence individuals have developed all the cognitive processes that they are ever to possess. They can of course learn new things, and unquestionably may become wiser with added years, but the processes that underlie cognitive interchange with the world are pretty much established by the age of twenty.

Cross-Cultural Piagetian Studies

Over the past ten years there has been a considerable number of cross-cultural studies on Piagetian theory. The basic question asked by these studies is whether human cognition follows the same course of development in all societies or varies from one culture to another. Piaget's notions of cognitive development have recently been criticized for being a theory of the cognitive development of a Western scientist (Greenfield, 1976). The sequence unraveled by Piaget may in fact be merely an ethnocentric description of the development of mind in the urban technological culture of Europe and North America. People of other societies may have other cognitive processes more adaptive to their own surroundings and of greater cultural value to them. This possibility has not yet been explored, however, for at this still early stage the cross-cultural studies have focused on the cognitive capabilities of children in other cultures and their rates of development, comparing them to those of Western children. Cross-cultural studies have so far been conducted in countries as far afield as Thailand, Rwanda (Africa), Papua (New Guinea), Iraq, Iran, Jordan, Ghana, Australia, and Mexico. Two general statements can be made on the basis of this collection of studies (Dasen, 1977). One is that the developmental stages first observed by Piaget in Switzerland are also observed in very different civilizations. The sequence of cognitive development—sensorimotor to preoperational to concrete operations and finally to formal operations—appears to be a universal phenomenon. This universality suggests to Piaget (1977) that laws of cognitive development have the same generality as other biological laws of development.

The second finding is that the *rate* of cognitive development, or the age at which most children reach a certain level of development, may vary from one society to another. Tasks may be mastered at different ages, even the tasks that Western children usually master during the same cognitive stage, and children may pass from one stage to another at different ages.

Differences in rate of development have been related in some instances to specific cultural variables. For example, infants aged five to thirty-three months living in rural Baoule on the Ivory Coast were found to have greater sensorimotor skills than their contemporaries in France, even though they were unfamiliar with the plastic toy cars and dolls that were used in the evaluation (Dasen, 1977). The motor precocity of many African babies does not extend to all aspects of motor development, however, but only to those that are valued by the culture.

Since intelligence fosters adaptation to the environment, Pierre Dasen (1975) predicted that nomadic, hunting, subsistence economy populations would gain spatial concepts, an achievement requiring concrete operations, earlier than would sedentary, agricultural groups, whereas the latter would learn to conserve quantity, weight, and volume more rapidly than the former. This prediction was generally supported in Dasen's study comparing six-to-fourteen-year-old Canadian Eskimo, Australian Aborigine, and Ebrie African (Ivory Coast) children. Certain specific experiences and activities have also been observed to accelerate specific skills. As an example, growing up in pottery-making families had helped a group of Mexican children learn conservation of substance (Price-Williams, Gordon, and Ramirez, 1969). The particular experiences, ways of life, and values of a cultural group can affect the rate of cognitive development.

Within the same general cultural group, however, cognitive development may also be affected by whether residence is urban or rural and by the extent of education. One study found that Thai rural children showed a "time lag" compared with urban children in mastering several concepts requiring concrete operations (Opper, 1977). The extent of the lag varied from concept to concept. In general, however, urban children acquired the concepts gradually over a period of five years, beginning at the age of six, whereas the rural children did not begin to acquire the concepts until the age of nine and then mastered all of them in a period of only three years. Similarly, among a rather homogeneous group of children in Rwanda, a country in central Africa where mandatory education had only recently been instituted, schooling was found to help children master tasks requiring concrete operations (Laurendeau-Bendavid, 1977).

Accelerated Progression Through the Stages

Whether special training will accelerate children's progression through Piaget's cognitive stages is a subject of continuing debate. There is a clear similarity between a stage, defined by the child's ability to perform certain Piagetian tasks, and an MA level, defined by the ability to give correct answers to items on a test such as the Stanford-Binet (page 229). Thus if children attain a Piagetian cognitive stage or a particular MA level at an earlier chronological age, their intelligence quotients will be raised. The issue of accelerated stage progression reintroduces the nature-nurture argument concerning the development of intelligence. Those who emphasize inherited and maturational factors would argue that specific experiences and training would not be effective in hurrying children from one Piagetian stage to the next. The environmentalist would argue that such experiences would indeed be effective in accelerating cognitive development.

Despite fifty years of work and thousands of published pages, Piaget himself does not take a clear position on the feasibility of acceleration. Whether stage progression can be accelerated hinges for the most part on exactly how and why a child moves from one cognitive stage to the next. Although Piaget has described the process in a generalized manner, his explanations have not been very explicit. In an incisive critique William Kessen (1962) pointed out that Piaget frequently examines the child and finds him or her now at this stage of cognitive functioning and later at another stage, without presenting a satisfactory account of the move from one stage to the other.

In fairness to Piaget, it should be recognized that his aims are not entirely congruent with those of most psychologists. As has frequently been noted, Piaget has been more interested in developing an epistemology than a psychology. Or as Kessen has stated,

> . . . Piaget has little interest in individual variation among children in the rate at which they achieve a stage or in their over-all capacity during it; he is a student of the development of thinking more than he is a student of children (1962, p. 77).

Whatever Piaget's goals might be, American psychologists have remained extremely interested in the related issues of individual variation in rate of cognitive development and the possibility of providing children with experiences that will accelerate cognitive growth.

Many investigators have attempted to help children develop certain concepts by providing specific training; a number of them have apparently succeeded. One of the best demonstrations has been carried out by Rochel Gelman (1969), who trained five-year-old children in conservation of number and length. First, she pretested the children on four standard Piagetian tasks to ascertain that they could not conserve. She then exposed the children to one of three situations. Children in the control group were presented with sets of three toy objects, two identical and one different, and were asked to point either to two objects that were the same or to two that were different. They were given a prize whenever they chose correctly. Children in a second group were also shown sets of three items. Two of the items were always identical in number or length, and the third item differed. For example, there might be two rows of five chips and one row of three chips, or two six-inch sticks and one ten-

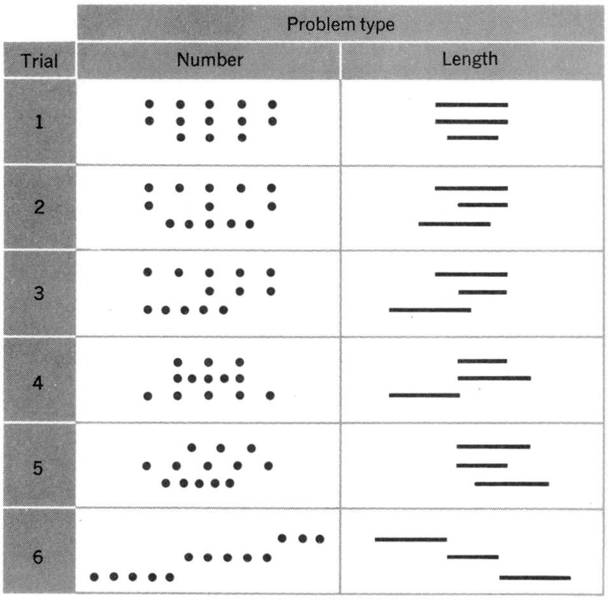

FIGURE 12.13
Examples of the sets of three items given children in number and length discrimination training. (Adapted from Gelman, 1969.)

inch stick. In half the sets number was the feature to be discriminated; in the other half it was length. The children were asked to point either to two sticks that were the same, or different, in length or to two rows that had the same number, or different numbers, of chips. Since preoperational children often define number in terms of length, Gelman deliberately varied the distance between the chips in the number problems, so as to confound quantity with the length cue (Figure 12.13). Color, shape, and geometrical arrangement were also varied. Again, the children were rewarded for all correct responses. Children in the third group were shown exactly the same sets of items and asked the same questions as children in the second group, but they received no reward for correct responses. Thus children in the third group had no reliable way of learning when they had succeeded or failed in making the necessary discriminations.

During the training session the children in the first group performed almost perfectly. Apparently the five-year-old subjects came to the training session with an understanding of "same" and "different." Those in the second group quickly began to learn the required discrimination between length and number. The children in the third group, however, learned very little.

All children were given posttests of conservation the day after training and again two to three weeks later. The results were quite remarkable. Neither the children in the first group, who were not trained to discriminate the appropriate dimensions, nor the children in the third group, who received no feedback to guide their attention, demonstrated much capacity for conservation. In contrast, the children in the second group performed almost flawlessly on both posttests. Moreover, although they had been trained specifically to conserve number and length, they were now able to conserve liquid and mass as well.

Gelman's study is a powerful demonstration that training and experience may facilitate early acquisition of the principle of conservation. The results meet several stringent criteria for deciding that this was accomplished. The children in the second group gave appropriate explanations for their conservation judgments; their ability to conserve persisted for some time after training; and conservation was generalized to problems not encountered in the training session. Howard Gardner (1978) points out, however, that Gelman used only five-year-old subjects. It is possible that these children were already on the verge of learning conservation on their own, and Gelman's procedures may have simply nudged them a bit prematurely into operational thinking. Gardner did not think it likely that the training would have had any significant effect on four-year-olds.

This criticism may be valid. But Piaget's theory would not predict that specific training might be able to bring about the same cognitive capacities in all children. Piaget believes that human reason grows through the interaction of environmental inputs and an internally maturing cognitive structure. Inputs do not act on a *tabula rasa* but on a cognitive organization that varies in children of different ages. Children interpret and use their experiences in light of their own mental frameworks. Thus in the five-year-olds the cognitive structure had evolved to a level of complexity at which added training effectively stimulated the development of conservation. The more immature cognitive systems of young children could not be expected to make such an advance.

We must await additional research to learn the extent to which mental growth can be accelerated and what conditions may allow it. At this time the best conclusion appears to be that children will attain the cognitive abilities charted by Piaget, providing they have had broad enough experiences and have reached the maturational level of the stage in question. Hurrying the child needlessly from one stage to the next could possibly interfere with normal cognitive development, and such acceleration could become a barrier to the child's optimal cognitive achievements. Joachim Wohlwill (1970) has noted a phenomenon frequently alluded to in this chapter, namely that the reasoning of very young children, although generally outgrown, may be useful to them later in life, especially in their imaginative and creative acts. If children are hurried through early stages, these early processes may not be properly incorporated in the overall cognitive apparatus, making certain useful ways of thinking unavailable to them as adults.

SUMMARY □

Piaget has emphasized the biological, adaptive significance of intelligence and has charted its growth through an apparently invariant series of four stages. Each of these stages is distinct in important respects from those preceding and following it.

Piaget has stressed that human beings have an existing cognitive structure which they use in their interactions with the outside world. They are never passive receptors for environmental input. Even infants have behavioral sequences and generalizations, which they attempt to use in coping with the demands of their surroundings. To some extent they will be able to deal successfully with the environment using their existing abilities and schemes, for they will incorporate or assimilate new experiences into existing patterns of thought and action. When an outside stimulus fails to conform to their expectations, they will have to adapt, to modify some of their schemes. Such a changing of the cognitive apparatus is called accommodation. Through these two processes cognitive growth will occur. With certain major reorganizations of the cognitive processes, the child is said to enter a new stage.

In the first cognitive stage of life, the sensorimotor, infants acquire the concept of an object as a permanent structure whose existence is independent of their perception of it. Intelligence at this time is restricted primarily to the level of physical actions. During the preoperational stage children begin to use symbols such as imagery and language, and they come to understand identity constancy and functions. In the concrete operations period the greatest acquisition is the ability to conserve number, weight, volume, space, and time. And finally, in the stage of formal operations, the child becomes capable of considering a problem in the abstract without needing a concrete representation of it.

Cross-cultural studies have indicated that the stages Piaget has observed in Western children are also found in children of very different societies. The rate of development, however, appears to differ, depending on schooling, cultural values and experiences, and whether residence is urban or rural.

TO BE SURE YOU HAVE MASTERED THIS CHAPTER △

The most important concepts introduced in this chapter are in the list below. They follow the order in which they appeared in the chapter slightly less exactly than usual. You should concentrate on the relationships of some of the terms now listed together—for example, Piaget's stages of development.

Cognitive stages
Maturation
Differentiation
Dedifferentiation (regression)
Orthogenetic principle
Synesthesia
Eidetic imagery
Verbal mediation
Reversal shift
Nonreversal shift
Enactive representation
Ikonic representation
Symbolic representation
Scheme
Operation
Assimilation
Accommodation
Sensorimotor stage
Preoperational stage
Concrete operations stage
Formal operations stage
Object concept
Nominal realism
Identity constancy
Hierarchical structures
Conservation
Centering
Decentering

TO GO BEYOND THIS CHAPTER △

In this book The tie between the materials in this chapter and those in Chapter 8 is very close. It will be useful to review the earlier discussions of language acquisition and concept formation (page 190), putting the context of the two chapters together. Stagelike development is hypothesized too for personality (Chapter 16), which is also studied both psychometrically and developmentally. Research of biofeedback and self-control (page 130) raises questions related to mediation in another context.

Elsewhere The following books give detailed accounts of theories and empirical data in the field of cognitive development: *Cognitive Development,* by John Flavell; *The Growth of Competence,* edited by K. J. Connolly and Jerome Bruner; *Piaget's Theory of Intelligence,* by Charles Brainerd; and *Jean Piaget: The Man and His Ideas,* by Richard Evans.

PART 4

SOCIAL BEHAVIOR

CH. 13

Social Psychology

This chapter was written by Edward E. Jones, Princeton University.

Social psychology is a distinctive subdiscipline of psychology, concerned with responses to the conditions created by the presence and the actions of other human beings. Many of the aspects of life studied by psychology are affected by social factors. It has long been clear that perception, thinking, and recall are all influenced in various specific ways by socially derived motives and expectancies. The understanding and acquisition of language is also very much a social process. In the next chapter we shall deal at length with the role of parents and peers in social development; insight into social determinants will help us understand succeeding chapters on personality and psychopathology. Nevertheless, a distinctive area of psychology is concerned with interpersonal events. This chapter will cover a few of their more basic aspects and show how social psychologists have tried to understand them. Since social influences are so ubiquitous, it is not surprising that social psychology has been called the "psychology of everyday life." Our treatment will highlight everyday social phenomena.

You hardly need to be reminded that your daily moment-to-moment behavior is greatly affected by social considerations. The clothing choices you made this morning were probably influenced by your expectations for the day to come. The persons you expected to run across and the settings you saw yourself probably getting into may have tipped the balance toward the shetland sweater rather than the torn sweatshirt. In the supermarket your familiarity with brand names touted by the commercials on television and advertisements in newspapers—two of our media which are inordinately and self-consciously concerned with social effects—is likely to guide your choices. It has probably crossed your mind that it might not be too good an idea to argue with your psychology instructor or your section assistant, at least until the grades are in. You are irritated by the thoughtless behavior of a friend. Shall you express your anger? How? You find yourself on a committee charged with a set of complex decisions. How should the committee be organized? Who should assume leadership? Your classmates elect you to the judicial board. A friend is accused of plagiarism under cloudy circumstances. How do you sort out all the many moral and social pressures acting on you in order to reach decisions with which you can comfortably live?

Such concrete, everyday, social incidents illustrate the broad range of topics about which social psychology has much to say—conformity, social comparison, self-presentation, persuasive communication, aggression, affiliation, group organization, and the attribution of responsibility.

UNDERSTANDING OUR SOCIAL ENVIRONMENT

The Perception of Persons

Characteristically, the behavior of others affects us in different ways, depending on the meaning we assign that behavior. This meaning in turn is conditioned by our perceptions of the behavior itself, but also by our perceptions of the motives, intentions, and broader personal dispositions of the person so behaving. The account of an automobile breakdown can be a tragic recital of unfortunate facts, a hilarious account of the driver's own mechanical ineptitude, or a plaintive plea for help, depending on the circumstances surrounding the telling. Not surprisingly, a great deal of research and theorizing has concerned the perceptions of persons, their motives, and dispositions; and if we accept the reasonable position that the behavior of persons observed is conditioned by social stimuli *as perceived* by them, person perception is as good a place as any to enter the realm of social psychology.

People are, of course, perceived as physical objects just as surely as we perceive rocks, trees, and skyscrapers as objects. People emit sound, they reflect different wavelengths of light, they have three-dimensional solidity and palpable texture. Typically, however, people are important because of the psychological significance of what they communicate verbally and nonverbally. Moreover, some people are capable of making decisions and carrying out actions that strongly affect the perceiver's well-being. The perceiver's task is therefore to process the witting and unwitting communications of others and to make inferences about their intentions and dispositions. For these inferences to be reasonably accurate, complex cognitive processes must relate behavior to its context. One of the fascinating aspects of social behavior is that perceivers themselves typically provide an important part of the context to which these others in their environment are responding.

Examples of momentary perceptual decisions are readily at hand. Is she really mad at me? Am I involved with him in a test of power? Does he really think Nixon was honest or is he pulling my leg? Will he be embarrassed if I tell him he is attractive? Will she laugh at me if I tell her I need her help? Such private questions as these point up the importance of our perceptions of the social environment in making behavioral decisions. Fritz Heider, a distinguished student of interpersonal behavior, has emphasized (1958) the importance of our need to control, and thus to be able to predict, the various states of our environment. We are not passive in registering the effects of the environment. In our role as perceivers we actively attempt to find stable categories for explaining behavioral variations. We impose stability on perceived variability by attempting to discover dispositions and underlying motivational reasons behind behavior. If someone opposes us and helps our opponent, we are likely to perceive him as hostile rather than "sometimes hostile" and "sometimes friendly." We infer a single disposition "to explain" varying behavior.

The perceiver of persons reaches then for hidden or latent constructs to explain what is manifest. We hypothesize psychological states in order to give behavior coherence. Heider, in particular, has argued that this process is indeed perceptual, for we immediately attach causal significance to observed behavior. He finds this impression of causality as basic as the perception of the other properties of objects.

Attribution Theory

When Heider argued for the basic, even primitive perception of what he called "units" of cause and effect, he set the stage for what later became known as **attribution theory,** so-called because we attribute surface behavior to underlying causes. Perhaps the major distinction made by attribution theory, as it applies to person perception, is whether a given action is seen as caused by the person or by the environment. Now of course the philosophical question of what *really* causes behavior is a nest of unsolvable riddles. Attribution theory, however, concerns perceived causes. It attends to the assumptions people make and is moot regarding the validity of these assumptions.

Most people would agree that behavior can tell us either a little or a lot about the unique dispositions of the actor. If the situation is seen as causing a person's action—"anyone would have behaved the same way"—the attribution implies that the behavior reveals little about this particular person. If the person is regarded as determining the course of action, on the other hand, we conclude that the individual is telling us something very revealing.

This reasoning is put forth in the version of attribution theory known as **correspondent-inference theory.** According to Edward E. Jones and Keith Davis (1965), we assume that behavior tells us something distinctive about the person when there are few reasons for engaging in the behavior, and these reasons would not impel everyone to behave in the same way. By choosing between equally attractive and unattractive alternatives, a man reveals more about himself than he would were the choice an obviously popular or normative one, or were there no alternatives and he was "forced" to act in a particular way. In making an unusual choice, the man "wears his heart on his sleeve." A corresponding or similar disposition is inferred directly from his act.

An example might be helpful here. John Thibaut and Henry Riecken (1955) conducted an early experiment in which each male subject was induced by the experimenter to try to persuade two other "subjects," who were actually accomplices of the experimenter, to a course of action. One of these accomplices had presented himself as high status, as a graduate or law student, whereas the other student had presented himself as a lowly freshman. In one experiment subjects attempted to persuade the two to give blood to the blood bank. They both complied, and the subjects were then asked to evaluate each student for a number of pertinent characteristics signifying perceived intent and personal attractiveness. The subjects tended to see the compliant behavior of the high-status accomplice as for the most part internally caused—he complied because he spontaneously wanted to. The low-status accomplice was seen as complying because he was constrained by the situation and had no alternative. The subjects also reported increased liking for the high-status accomplice. The correspondent-inference theorist would say that the low-status accomplice had more reasons for complying and therefore less choice than did the high-status accomplice. The behavior of the high-status complier was consequently more informative about his intrinsic generosity, spontaneous good will, and related personal traits. Harold Kelley later christened this the **discounting effect:** "The role of a given cause in producing a given effect is discounted if other plausible causes are also present" (1971, p. 8).

Another early experiment makes a similar point. Jones, Davis, and Kenneth Gergen (1961) tape-recorded a simulated job interview in which the interviewee behaved either in a very outgoing way or in a very introverted way. Some subjects listened to a tape in which the interviewee's responses were preceded by the description of a job, that of submariner, which put a premium on outgoingness. Other subjects heard the job of astronaut described in a way that made it clear that introverts would be better qualified. When the interviewee behaved in a manner compatible with the stated job requirements, subjects felt that they learned little or nothing about him. But when the interviewee was very outgoing while applying for a job that required an introverted person, subjects felt that he was being himself and was a very outgoing person indeed (Figure 13.1).

Attribution Errors The judgments that we make concerning the personalities of others are subject to **attribution errors.** For one thing, we tend to underestimate situational factors and to overestimate personal dispositions as causes of behavior. If subjects are shown essays clearly described as prepared under conditions that allowed the writers no choice—for

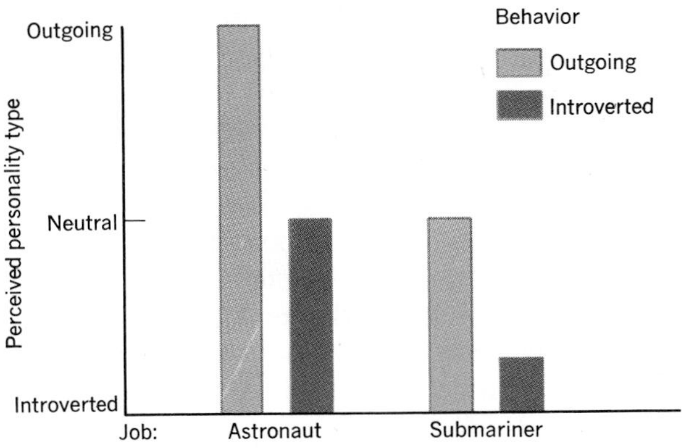

FIGURE 13.1

Perception of an outgoing personality versus an introverted personality. In this study the job of astronaut was described as requiring an introverted personality, the job of submariner as requiring an outgoing personality. Applicants whose behavior countered these requirements were seen as *very* outgoing or *very* introverted. Those whose behavior matched the requirements were perceived as falling at the midpoint of the scale. (Adapted from Jones, Davis, and Gergen, 1961.)

TABLE 13.1
Questions for a Quiz Game

1. Who was originally supposed to play Dorothy in *The Wizard of Oz* movie?
2. Who was the author of *As I Lay Dying?*
3. Who was president of France during World War I?
4. Who makes Crayola crayons?
5. "I buried Paul" can be heard at the end of what Beatles song?
6. Which weighs more, a proton or a neutron?
7. What was Richard Adam's next book after *Watership Down?*
8. Who was the only United States president to be elected, having lost the popular vote?
9. Which trilogy won the Hugo award as the best science fiction series of all time?
10. Who was the last player to bat against Tom Seaver while Seaver was still a Met?

Is the person who thought up these questions, after being asked by the experimenter to devise ten "challenging but not impossible" questions, more knowledgeable than you are? Try to think of ten such questions yourself and see whether a friend finds them any easier to answer.

example, as an assignment of a political science instructor or the debating coach—they will still usually assume that the essayists believe in the position taken. This turns out to be a serious error when the subjects' estimates are compared to the self-rated attitudes of the people who actually wrote the essays (Snyder and Jones, 1974).

A more dramatic example of this "fundamental attribution error," as it is called by Lee Ross (1977), has been demonstrated by Ross, Teresa Amabile, and Julia Steinmetz (1977). These experimenters asked pairs of subjects to participate in a quiz game. One member of the pair was randomly assigned to the role of "questioner" and the other to the role of "contestant." *In the presence of the contestant,* the questioner was instructed to make a list of the hardest questions he or she could think of and knew the answers to. These questions were then given to the contestant as a quiz. During the quiz the contestant, naturally, did not fare very well, After the questioning both subjects were asked to evaluate their own general knowledge and that of their partner. Observers who had watched the proceedings also evaluated the general knowledge of both participants. The questioner considered the contestant's knowledge and his or her own to be that of the average student. The contestant as well as the neutral observers, however, saw the questioner as much more knowledgeable than the contestant, even though the observed discrepancy in knowledge was to an important degree preordained by the arbitrary role assignments. Ross and his fellow experimenters have speculated that for just this reason doctoral students invariably finish their oral exams feeling like dunces, whereas the examiners are impressed with the wisdom of their colleagues (Table 13.1).

Actor-Observer Differences Jones and Richard Nisbett (1971) have proposed that the fundamental attribution error contributes to a socially important divergence of the opinions of people who observe a bit of behavior from those of people doing the behaving. They theorize that actors tend to attribute their behavior to the situation, whereas observers see the same behavior as reflecting personal dispositions. Although this theory that actors are more aware of the situation and observers more aware of personal dispositions remains somewhat controversial, considerable evidence compatible with it has been collected. Clear discrepancies in actors' and observers' causal accounts of behavior appear to be the seeds of misunderstandings in many circumstances. Whereas the angry man feels that he has been clearly provoked, and assumes that anyone would have reacted the same way he did, the bystander sees him as dispositionally hostile and "trigger tempered." Whereas the failing student blames the circumstances of a broken love affair, his adviser is convinced of his fundamental academic inertia. Whereas the cabinet officer attributes his own ineffective behavior to the political pressures brought to bear on him, the observer explains it in terms of a lack of courage, persistence, and resourcefulness. Fortunately for the the mutual understanding of actors and observers, these differences in the perception of causality may be partly overcome by inducing observers to put themselves in the shoes of actors. For example, the better the observer knows the actor and the more they empathize, the more comparable their perceptions of causality will be.

SUMMARY □

When social psychologists refer to person perception, they usually imply inferences made about the dispositions, motives, and intentions of a person. These inferences are derived from complex attributional processes that integrate information about behavior with information about the situation. It has been well established that people are prone to the error of attributing causality too readily to the disposition of a person and underestimating the role of the situation. Observers are more likely to make this error than people who are acting. Such divergent explanations for a given action raise the possibility of serious misunderstanding. It is assumed that a better scientific knowledge of how people perceive each other and make causal attributions for behavior will clarify many of the phenomena of social interaction.

STEREOTYPES AND SELF-FULFILLING PROPHECIES

The preceding account clearly implies that the perception of persons is an active, constructive process. The perceiver goes well beyond immediate information to construct an impression of unseen personal traits and environmental forces that control behavior. Psychologists have long understood that these constructed impressions are a combination of the given and of the expected. Perceivers do not confront the social environment empty-handed—or empty-minded. On the contrary, they have richly developed expectancies about people in general, about classes or types of people, and about people who engage in certain behavior in certain situations. The network of expectancies that guide a particular perceiver is sometimes referred to as an **implicit personality theory.** Some of us have better-elaborated or more articulate theories than others, but from time to time when we meet people we all think in facile stereotypes of "redheads," "tycoons," "women's libbers," Chicanos, and "preppies."

To Justify Prejudice

We may think of **stereotypes** as the components of implicit personality theory that are based on inadequate information, that are overly concrete and specific, and that are relatively unaffected by attempts to disconfirm them. Stereotypes often accompany and "justify" ethnic prejudices and, as such, they bring disadvantage to whole groups or classes of people. The study of prejudice and stereotypy has a long history because of their obvious importance in interpersonal and group relations. Social scientists have often, and rightly, deplored premature judging of others, although they have come to recognize prejudgment as a normal and pervasive cognitive tendency (Allport, 1954).

The avoidance and antagonism associated with prejudice are always buttressed by cognitive stereotypes, which provide a rationale for discrimination. Central to the construction of a prejudicial rationale is the tendency of people to see greater personal variety within their own group than in other groups. A Yale student is likely to feel that Iowa State students are more similar to one another than Yale students are; the Iowa State student no doubt feels the same way about "Yalies." This tendency to perceive "outgroups" as more homogeneous than the "ingroup" is undoubtedly explained in part by our limited contact with outgroup members, but merely increasing contact may be insufficient to break down stereotypes. Extended and favorable contacts and the opportunity and leisure to observe personality differences in members of the outgroup are probably necessary if the stereotype is to be eroded away.

Impact on the Target of Prejudice

It has become increasingly clear that negative stereotypes have great impact on the actions and self-concepts of members of the targeted groups. As Gordon Allport (1954) has noted, prejudice often creates traits of victimization: "One's reputation whether false or true, cannot be hammered, hammered, hammered into one's head without doing something to one's character" (p. 142). More specifically, many social expectancies or stereotypes are self-fulfilling in nature. Not only can prejudice affect and determine certain traits in the targets of prejudice, but this group's subsequent manifestation of these traits can convince prejudiced people that they were right all along.

Our next task is to examine the processes whereby a perceiver's expectancy about a person can actually bring about changes in the person's behavior that confirm this expectancy. This enterprise has relevance beyond illuminating the role of prejudice and stereotypy. The social expectancy that leads to its own confirmation is a classic and striking example of interpersonal influence and the interplay between person perception and behavior. We shall argue that perceivers' impressions affect their actions in ways that shape the nature of what is perceived. This happens without their being aware of the social consequences of their own behavior.

It was Robert Merton who in 1948 first argued that prophecies about social events may affect those events. In some cases social prophecies increase the probability that the events prophesied will actually happen. According to Merton's **self-fulfilling prophecy,** a false definition of a situation may invoke new behavior which makes the originally false conception come true. The prophet may then cite the actual course of events as proof that the prophecy or hypothesis was correct. For example, an authoritative public figure might predict a stock market decline, thus causing a frantic wave of selling. Thereupon he claims to have prophesied the decline. It should be emphasized that the final outcome is *not* misperceived—the prophecy actually does come true—but the prophet and other observers remain insufficiently aware of the causal significance of the prophecy itself.

If we translate this theorizing into a typical interaction situation where person A meets person B, there is a possibility that A will act on a hypothesis about B and elicit a response from B that confirms and therefore strengthens the initially false hypothesis. Does this actually happen? And if so, why does it happen?

Circumstances in which responses generate reciprocation are the most obvious examples. If A thinks B does not like him, he will either avoid B or behave in an antagonistic way. B is likely to respond to A's negative behavior with similar avoidance and antagonism, readily confirming A's initial hypothesis. Or if A thinks B is highly competitive and therefore himself adopts a very competitive stance, this competitiveness is highly likely to elicit the very behavior from B that A expected (Kelley and Stahelski, 1970). Nor does the cycle have to be a vicious one. If A thinks B likes him, he may share intimate revelations, which encourages B to reciprocate the intimacy. Or A may devote time and attention to B, bringing positive, attentive responses in return.

Experimental demonstrations of such reciprocating behavior require that there be independent evidence in B's behavior that A's hypothesis has affected it. It is not enough that A *thinks* B has behaved competitively, aggressively, or warmly, though there is ample evidence that our social hypotheses are even more readily confirmed subjectively than objectively. It must be shown that B has actually been induced to behave as A predicted.

One experiment (Snyder, Tanke, and Berscheid, 1977) fulfills this criterion. Pairs of undergraduate students, one male, one female, carried out spontaneous conversations by microphone and headphones, the two of each pair supposedly getting acquainted with each other over the telephone. Males were shown a snapshot, allegedly of their female partner, and each believed that a Polaroid snapshot of himself would be shown to her. In fact, the females knew nothing about any photographs. The experimenters showed the men one of several specially selected snapshots; the women in one group of photographs were very attractive, in the other rather unattractive, as judged by other undergraduates. The spontaneous conversations were tape-recorded, with each voice on a separate channel. The male subjects shown a photograph of an attractive woman were expected to find their partner warmer, more sociable, poised, and humorous than were the men with an unattractive partner. The results confirmed this expectation.

Twelve introductory psychology students subsequently evaluated the conversation of the females for intimacy, enthusiasm, and other similar qualities. Although these judges knew nothing about the hypothesis, and neither heard the male side of the conversations nor saw the pictures, they considered the "attractive" females warmer, more sociable, poised, and humorous, just as the male subjects had. In ways that can only be guessed at, the males were able to elicit from the females the kinds of verbal responses that confirmed their own stereotypes about attractive and unattractive coeds, stereotypes which had been triggered in the first place by randomly assigning photographs of the women.

Two related experiments (Ward, Zanna, and Cooper, 1974) show that a prophecy can become self-fulfilling through nonverbal as well as verbal means. In the initial experiment white male subjects were given a plausible reason for interviewing either a white or a black male job applicant. The applicants were accomplices carefully trained to behave in a standard way in all interviews. Systematic observations revealed that the interviewer's efforts at contact were less "immediate" when the applicant was black than when he was white. Interviewers placed themselves farther from the black applicants than from the white, the interviews with blacks were shorter, and the interviewers of black applicants made more speech errors than those seeing white applicants. In the companion experiment naive subjects served as job applicants; the accomplice interviewers were trained to strive for immediacy or distance in their interviewing techniques. The interviewer striving for immediacy sat closer to the applicant, made fewer speech errors, and took longer to give his interviews. In other words, he behaved as had those interviewing the white applicants in the first experiment. Judges who could see only the applicants considered those confronting a direct, approachable interviewer to be more competent and composed than those confronting remote interviewers. It is easy to conclude from these experiments that black job applicants may perform less impressively than white solely because of the white interviewer's behavior. It is also likely that the white

TABLE 13.2
Hypothetical Sequence by Which Expectancies Are Self-Fulfilled

Perceiver A	Partner B
1. Expectancy or hypothesis a. Beauty means socially adept. b. Blacks are inadequate. c. He is a competitor.	
2. Behavior in line with expectancy a. Warm, affiliative comments. b. Distance, aloofness. c. Competitive actions. →	
	3. Reciprocation a. Warm sociability. b. Awkward fumbling. c. Arousal to competition.
4. Strengthened expectancy ← ("I was certainly right.")	
5. More behavior in line with now-strengthened expectancy →	
	6. More reciprocation a. Warm sociability. b. Awkward fumbling. c. Competitive behavior. ↓ Eventually??? ↓
	7. New self-definition a. I am sociable, attractive. b. I am inadequate, worthless. c. I am competitive, aggressive.

interviewers in the first experiment were totally unaware that their own behavior might affect the interviewee. The evidence that a prophecy about the lesser ability of a black applicant can be self-fulfilling is in this instance circumstantial but nevertheless quite compelling.

Expectancies and Self-Concepts

The episode that makes a prophecy about a person self-fulfilling may induce a change in the person's self-concept, locking in the new behavior for future occasions. Some evidence for such an outcome has been obtained (Snyder and Swann, 1978). In a complicated experiment male subjects participated in a reaction time contest with male partners whose performances they could try to disrupt with a "noise weapon" at their disposal. Before the contest began, one partner was arbitrarily informed that his partner was either a hostile, competitive person or a mild, gentle person. The other partner was told that the first man's use of the noise machine would depend on the kind of person he, the second partner, was, as well as on what he considered to be the best way of winning in competitive tasks. The men each had a number of turns at pressing a button as soon after hearing a bell as possible. As the contest proceeded, the perceiver who thought that he confronted a hostile partner delivered louder, more disruptive noises than the perceiver with a supposedly nonhostile partner. The partner understandably responded in kind when it was his turn, thus confirming the perceiver's belief that his partner was hostile or gentle. The supposedly hostile or gentle person was then asked to engage in a similar contest with a third person, who had no advance expectations about him. Now the man who had been initially, and quite arbitrarily, labeled as hostile was much more aggressive in his use of the noise weapon than the person initially labeled gentle.

The Snyder and Swann study indicates that in certain well-defined circumstances, in which the actions of another are to be attributed to the self rather than to the situation, the perceiver can induce a response in his partner in line with an arbitrarily assigned disposition. Then the responder will continue to make that response when confronting another partner, thus showing that he has internalized the newly established disposition, in this instance to be competitive and hostile or noncompetitive and gentle (Table 13.2).

Although much more research is needed to assess the conditions under which induced changes in behavior become internalized dispositions, this experiment may typify what happens in important socialization situations. Children are commonly induced to view themselves in line with the hypotheses rightly or wrongly held by their parents, siblings, or teachers. In an earlier chapter (page 275) the so-called "Pygmalion effect," the possibility of raising children's IQs by making teachers expect more of them, was discussed. Questions remain about the possibility of affecting basic intelligence in this way, but there is solid evidence that classroom performances do differ depending on teachers' expectations. Children expected to do especially well do better than children considered less promising, even though the initial expectancies are randomly and arbitrarily assigned (Meichenbaum, Bowers, and Ross, 1969; Beez, 1968; Anderson and Rosenthal, 1968).

We are now in a better position to see that such prophecies are self-fulfilled without the teacher appreciating his or her own contributions to the process. Once again the fundamental attribution error rears its head. Teachers link children's behavior to manufactured causal dispositions, at the same time underestimating the role of situational factors and even *their own behavior*.

SUMMARY □

The self-fulfilling prophecy represents a set of important social phenomena, important enough to justify the careful study of person perception and attribution. Our expectancies about others affect our social behavior in ways that may create the very reality we expect. And yet we remain unaware of our own contribution to the behavior of others that we think we only observe. Not only does an expectancy produce confirming behavior; the person expected to act in a certain way may actually internalize dispositions to account for this behavior, for he or she too fails to realize the controlling impact of perceivers, their expectations, and the actions they tend to instigate.

SOCIAL INFLUENCE AND CONFORMITY

One of the striking features of social life are culturally determined uniformities in behavior and attitudes. When the anthropologists compare cultures and stress their diversity, they also imply the relative homogeneity of values, beliefs, speech, dress, and economic organization *within* cultures. Cultures are typically defined in terms of shared norms or a consensus about appropriate behavior. It has long been understood that these shared norms are established and maintained through social pressures conveyed by the actual or expected responses of others. The very fact that every culture has terms for the person who is deviant, terms overwhelmingly negative in connotation, suggests that norms are enforced by various expressions of approval or disapproval. Social psychologists call it the **application of social sanctions.** What is true of cultures at large is also true of generations, classes, and subgroups within a culture. Even in our free-opportunity, highly mobile society, class distinctions are rather clearly maintained through dress, other patterns of consumption, and dialect or speech inflection. We are amused at movies about adolescents of the fifties, struck by the quaint homogeneity of their dress and manners, less aware that our own generation of adolescents had its own distinctive homogeneities. Thus pressures toward uniformity are ubiquitous, whenever and wherever we look at groups of people functioning together.

Of equal interest to social psychologists, however, are the phenomena of resistance to group pressures. There is diversity even in the most homogeneous groups, and individual personalities are certainly more than the subjective manifestations of culture. Any theory of social influence must come to terms with instances of personal autonomy and uniqueness as well as the more familiar instances of imitation and conformity. Jack Brehm (1966) has proposed that certain circumstances arouse **psychological reactance:** we strive to assert our freedom when someone threatens to exert control over our options. Children told not to play in a rubble-strewn vacant lot fuss about not being allowed to go there, although they might otherwise have preferred the playground. We may become more determined to see a play when an acquaintance tries to persuade us it is not worth our time. We are likely to show resistance when anyone attempts to persuade us in ways that threaten our freedom to hold any opinion we want to.

William McGuire (1964) conducted a brilliant sequence of studies on the vulnerability to attack of truistic beliefs, one such being "It is good to brush your teeth twice a day." In fact, because truisms have seldom if ever been challenged, these beliefs are surprisingly vulnerable. McGuire set out to show how the believer's capacity to resist a persuasive attack on a truism can be increased by "inoculating" him or her before the attack. An effective kind of inoculation is first to give the individual a brief one-sentence argument attacking the truism, such as "Too frequent brushings tend to damage the gums and expose the vulnerable parts of the teeth to decay." McGuire showed that this procedure can stimulate the individual to find ways to rebut the argument,

Conformity in hairstyles and dress in the 1950s and 1970s.

with the result that the truism, no longer a truism, is nevertheless more resistant to a subsequent full-scale attack. On the other hand, an attempt to defend the truism by offering arguments that directly bolster or support the truism is less effective in protecting the truism against subsequent attack (Figure 13.2).

Dependence on Others

Looking carefully at the ways in which people depend on others provides a clue to the means by which social pressure is exerted. Children are early dependent on their parents for the satisfaction of a variety of tangible needs, such as food and physical comfort, and some not so tangible, such as affection and approval. Soon children are also dependent on others for information about their surroundings because the attainment of important goals depends on such information. Children depend first on their parents and later on school teachers, siblings, and peers for this information. Once they have the necessary information, they can sometimes satisfy their own needs. These two forms of dependence are intertwined and

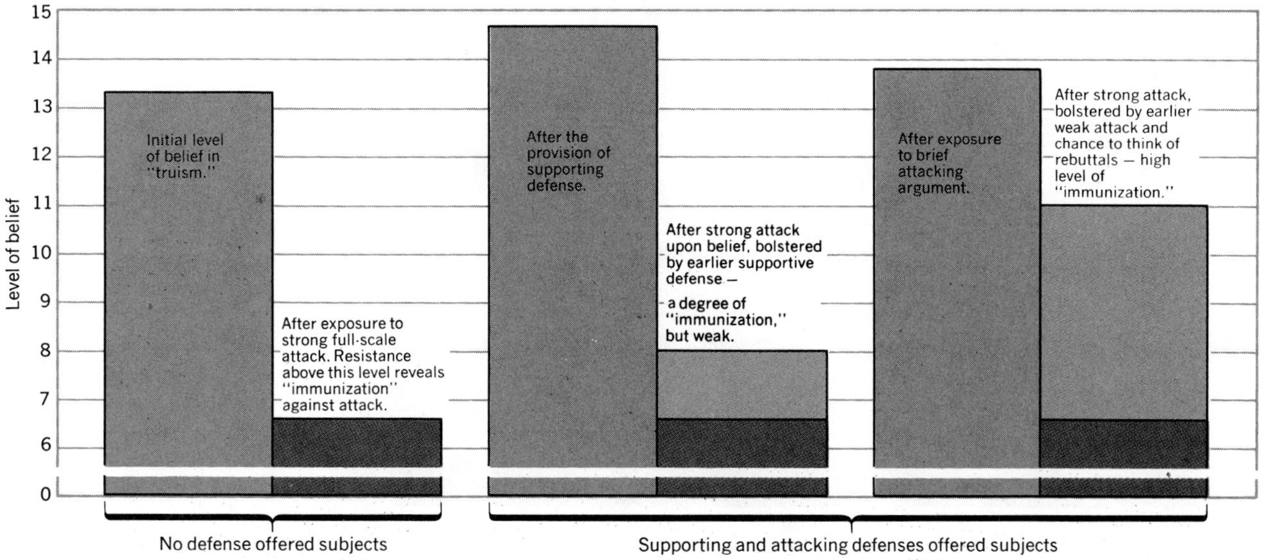

FIGURE 13.2

Immunization against persuasion. This experiment demonstrated that hearing earlier weak arguments against a truism allowed subjects to build up a defense against stronger arguments. (Data from McGuire, 1964.)

difficult to separate when the individual becomes an adult, but it is nevertheless useful to maintain their theoretical distinctness in analyzing how social pressures are exerted.

Social Comparison Defines Reality Leon Festinger was one of the first to emphasize that social pressures have diverse origins. The major contribution of his 1954 analysis was a detailed description of how we are dependent on others for information. Festinger emphasized that people have a powerful need to know the nature of their world, and much of this knowledge necessarily comes from others. If we want to know how heavy an object is or whether it is flammable, we can perform obvious physical tests without the help of other people. If we want to know what happens to the self-concept at the moment of death, or whether job opportunities in psychology are good or bad, we must seek such information through communications with others.

One of Festinger's key assumptions was that our sense of confidence in the accuracy of our socially derived knowledge depends strongly on the degree to which others agree with us. The process of reaching such agreement is a major source of social pressure and has important attitudinal consequences. If there is a discrepancy between what others believe or see and what we believe or see, it is natural for us to reason that one of us must be wrong. Festinger's **social-comparison theory** holds that we will try to reduce this disconcerting discrepancy by trying to win others to our point of view or by changing our own position to conform to the consensus. Sometimes we may decide that those who hold views different from our own are not really relevant judges, and we may cease to compare our opinions with theirs.

Conforming to a Unanimous Majority The pressures that groups exert on members is strikingly clear in the classic conformity studies of Solomon Asch (1956). A typical Asch experiment consisted of a number of trials in which each subject in a group expressed his judgment concerning which of three lines was the same length as a standard line. Through seating arrangements and instruction, Asch maneuvered a particular subject into a position where he would hear the reports of several others before giving his own. Unbeknownst to the subject, these other "subjects" were accomplices of the experimenter, instructed to adopt a unanimously incorrect consensus on a number of critical trials. This, of course, placed the subject in a dilemma, for his eyes clearly told him one thing and his companions something different. Asch actually launched his experiments to show the various ways in which people can maintain their independence of judgment in the face of group disagreements. To his surprise he found that there is a considerable yielding to group pressure. Although subjects in isolation rarely made errors on these clear-cut perceptual tasks, when confronted by the conflicting opinion of others, three out of four subjects made at least one error. The average subject made between four and five errors out of a possible twelve. This proportion of yielding has been confirmed in a number of subsequent studies.

When exploring each subject's private experiences in extensive postexperimental interviews, Asch found

"Well, in spite of what all the rest of you say, that's not the way I see it."

ample evidence that some depended on the opinion of others. Many subjects simply discounted the evidence of their own visual sense and concluded that the others, ranging from two to sixteen, in the unanimous majority must be right because they could find no other explanation for the consensus. In their view it seemed more likely that one subject, themselves, was wrong than that two, three, or more equally well-equipped subjects would all be wrong at the same time.

Other subjects revealed that their need for social approval accounted for their behavior. They went along with the majority *in spite of believing that the majority was wrong*. These subjects wanted to avoid appearing odd or being laughed at.

Many subjects made special efforts to reduce the impact of the consensus, to make fewer comparisons of their opinions to those of others, as it were. For example, some subjects developed a "sheep hypothesis" to explain the course of events. The first subject was wrong and the others were merely conforming to his judgment. If the subject could convince himself of this, he was able to reduce the subjective odds that he was wrong. Subsequent research has verified that we accept the opinions of others sometimes because we think that they are right—we depend on them for information; sometimes because we wish to avoid censure or embarrassment—we depend on them for approval. Of course, there is nothing to prevent both dependencies from operating in a given situation, and we suspect that together they are responsible for considerable agreement within a group.

The Asch experiments were deliberately designed to minimize the likelihood of discussion among the group members. As Donald Campbell (1961) has noted, the rational thing for the subject to do in this situation would be to announce what his eyes have told him while conceding that the group is probably correct. This response would give the group the advantage of his input without his questioning their probable wisdom. This adaptive response was apparently very rare in the Asch experiments.

HOW TO CREATE CONSENSUS IN ATLANTIC CITY

The immense success of Resorts International, the first legal gambling casino in Atlantic City, New Jersey, naturally attracted other developers anxious to purchase land near the famed Boardwalk. In one such block of valuable land, the buildings consisted almost entirely of two- and three-story row houses owned largely by Italian-American working people who had purchased them in the forties and fifties for but a few thousand dollars. Richard Bloom, a young real estate man, offered the owners on the block $100,000 each if they would sell him their property. *But* Bloom included an intriguing stipulation: everyone had to sell at that price or no one would get anything! When some owners complained that their houses were bigger or better maintained, Bloom noted that he was only interested in the land under the houses and the condition of the property was immaterial. Initial reactions to the proposal ranged from extreme eagerness to sign to firm reluctance. Within a month, however, all but fifteen owners had signed, and most of them had indicated that they too would sign. People eager to sell had exerted heavy pressure on the reluctant holdouts.

> At one meeting, the son of a home-owner angrily demanded the names of those who had not signed. Bloom declined to provide the names, but the sentiment reflected by the request was an indication that his plan was working. "I'd hate to be last guy," he said to a reporter. "It'd be hard to live here." As

Owners of businesses in Atlantic City must have been under considerable group pressure to sell their properties to developers.

the signers became a majority, "Have you signed yet?" became a common question for people on the block.

Eventually, the signers mounted a bitter petition addressed to the holdouts, accusing them of extreme selfishness. When Bloom's original forty-five-day deadline arrived, only three property owners had failed to sign. The problem, according to Bloom,

> is that the two whose "wishes and needs" are most difficult to satisfy—they simply want more money—live in South Philadelphia, out of range of pressure from the neighbors with whom they could have a common bond.

Quotations and general story line from Calvin Trillin, U. S. Journal: Atlantic City, N.J.: Assemblage, *The New Yorker,* January 8, 1979.

Studies by Festinger and Thibaut (1951) and many others indicate that persuasion is typically directed at the most deviant group member, especially when the topic under discussion is important to the members and when the group is highly "cohesive," that is, when members are attracted to one another and enjoy belonging to the group. Stanley Schachter (1951) has also shown that members of a cohesive group will initially direct most of their communication toward a member with a highly deviant opinion. Then the talk ends, and they reject the person with the deviant opinion. It is as though the group is psychologically redefined without the deviant and, in Festinger's terms, members cease to compare their opinions with his.

In discussions of why great errors are made in planning national policy, Irving Janis (1973) has singled out excessive need for consensus as a major culprit. Great cohesiveness and a desire to preserve unanimity at almost any cost lead to what Janis calls **group think.** He considers it a syndrome of group decision making. Group members are no longer rational and open to information but are directed by a blinders-on spirit of rallying around the flag, the leader, or the previously adopted plan. Speculating why there was a lack of critical debate about Vietnam war policies in the high policy-making circles of the government, Bill Moyers suggests that

> One of the significant problems in the Kennedy and Johnson Administrations was that the men who handled national security affairs became too close, too personally fond of each other . . . great decisions were often made in that warm camaraderie of a small board of directors deciding what the club's dues are going to be for the members next year. . . . So you often dance around the final hard decision which would set you against . . . men who are very close to you, and you tend to reach a consensus (quoted in Janis, 1973, p. 106).

Obedience

At stake in a conformity experiment are subjects' perceptual judgments or opinions concerning a particular issue. But because subjects' concepts of themselves as competent and yet responsive and agreeable human beings are also at stake, the conflict produced can be quite severe, in spite of the fact that subjects know that they are in a psychology experiment. Some subjects in an Asch-type setting have experienced severe anxiety and autonomic disturbances.

The personal anguish of subjects was undoubtedly more extreme and pervasive in the obedience experiment designed by Stanley Milgram (1965). He investigated whether people would conform even when their yielding might have extremely negative consequences for other people. In his experiments participants delivered what they believed to be unendurable and possibly lethal electric shock to other people for apparent failure to learn.

Male participants were solicited by a newspaper advertisement which advised them that the experiment would be "a study of memory and learning." As each volunteer arrived at the laboratory, he encountered a mild-mannered, likable man in his late forties, in reality an accomplice but introduced by the experimenter as another subject. The experimenter, middle-aged, stern, impassive, and dressed in a gray lab coat, gave both men a description of the experiment. One was to be the "teacher" and inflict shock as punishment to the "learner" whenever he failed to remember the correct pairing of words to be taught him by the teacher. A rigged drawing made the naive subject the teacher. The teacher went with the experimenter and learner into an adjacent room where the learner was strapped into an "electric chair," "to prevent excessive movement" during shocks. Electrode paste was applied to his wrist, "to avoid blisters and burns," then the electrode, which led back to a shock generator in the first room. The learner became somewhat apprehensive and confided that he had a history of heart trouble, but the experimenter reassured him.

The shock generator had an impressive keyboard of thirty switches, delivering from 15 to 450 volts. The 195-volt switch was labeled "very strong shock," the 255-volt switch "intense shock," the 375-volt switch "danger: severe shock"; the last two switches were labeled an ominous "XXX." The teacher and learner carried on the learning task via intercom and bulbs lighting up in an answer box at the top of the generator. The naive subject was required to raise the level of shock by 15 volts each time the learner made a mistake, and he made them regularly. Milgram was at the naive subject's side, prodding him on through any demonstration of reluctance as the learner began to express discomfort. In Milgram's words,

> The responses of the victim are standardized on tape and each protest is coordinated to a particular voltage level. . . . Starting with 75 volts, the learner begins to grunt and moan. At 150 volts, he demands to be let out of the experiment. At 180 volts, he cries out that he can no longer stand the pain. At 300 volts, he refuses to provide any more answers to the memory test, insisting that he is no longer a participant in the experiment. . . . In response to this last tactic, the experimenter instructs the naive subject to treat the absence of an answer as equivalent to a wrong answer and to follow the usual shock procedure. If the naive subject protested at any point the experimenter told him, "You have no other choice, you must go on!"

It is difficult to read about these experiments without intensely disliking the subjects, disapproving of the ethics of the experimenter, or both. The most salient incident that led Milgram to conduct these studies was the cold-blooded extermination of millions of victims in the Nazi concentration camps during World War II, a gigantic enterprise carried out not by a few madmen but ultimately through the obedience of many individuals performing the jobs assigned them. Milgram was especially interested in pinning down the aspects of a social situation that make destructive obedience to authority such a routine outcome.

Milgram's results (Figure 13.3) indicate that the unyielding persistence of an authoritative experi-

FIGURE 13.3

Obedience to commands to punish. The graph itself shows the percentage of participants remaining in the experiment as the "punishment" they were required to deliver increased, from mild—a shock of 75 volts—to one of lethal strength. The textual material behind the graph is a verbatim transcript of a portion of one subject's verbal comments, together with Milgram's (1965) observations.

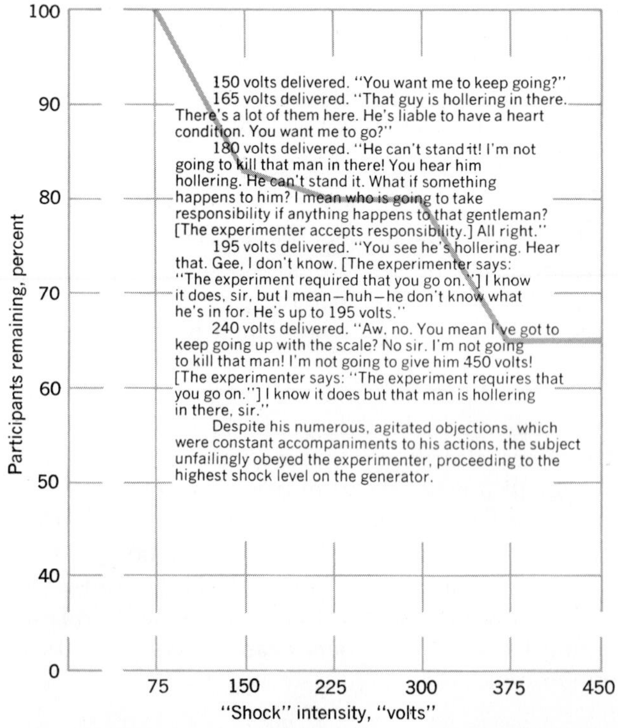
100
90
80
70
60
50
40
0
Participants remaining, percent
75
150
225
300
375
450
"Shock" intensity, "volts"
150 volts delivered. "You want me to keep going?"
165 volts delivered. "That guy is hollering in there. There's a lot of them here. He's liable to have a heart condition. You want me to go?"
180 volts delivered. "He can't stand it! I'm not going to kill that man in there! You hear him hollering. He can't stand it. What if something happens to him? I mean who is going to take responsibility if anything happens to that gentleman? [The experimenter accepts responsibility.] All right."
195 volts delivered. "You see he's hollering. Hear that. Gee, I don't know. [The experimenter says: "The experiment required that you go on."] I know it does, sir, but I mean—huh—he don't know what he's in for. He's up to 195 volts."
240 volts delivered. "Aw, no. You mean I've got to keep going up with the scale? No sir. I'm not going to kill that man! I'm not going to give him 450 volts! [The experimenter says: "The experiment requires that you go on."] I know it does but that man is hollering in there, sir."
Despite his numerous, agitated objections, which were constant accompaniments to his actions, the subject unfailingly obeyed the experimenter, proceeding to the highest shock level on the generator.

menter can induce almost anyone to harm others. Over half of the participants inflicted the most severe shock on the learner. That a person might damage others in a fit of rage, or that a few people with very unfortunate neurotic problems might inflict senseless violence on others may not surprise us. It is more disconcerting and shocking to learn that ordinary citizens, of various ages, educational attainments, and socioeconomic status, show a willingness in a majority of cases to damage an unoffending stranger simply because an experimenter insists that it is "required." This insight into human nature is hardly a pleasant one, but it is better to recognize it than to pretend that ordinary human beings have too much character knowingly to inflict such pain on others.

SUMMARY □

Movement within a group or society toward uniformity of beliefs and behavior is a condition of all social life. The pressures toward uniformity may be found in all cultures and groups, but there is also inevitably some resistance. Even though conformity is often viewed as stultifying, it may or may not be maladaptive for the individual and the group. The Joe McCarthy era, when the slightest deviance in the liberal direction brought down a shower of accusations that the deviant was a "communist," a "fellow traveler," and so on, was an example of conformity carried to a pathological extreme. At a more adaptive level, however, constructive consensus can strengthen group identification and makes possible the achievement of many group goals. The mutual sacrifice and near unanimity of political views during World War II, the coming together of Americans in silent "vigils" after the assassination of Martin Luther King, and the mobilization of talent and commitment to send man to the moon might serve as examples. Conformity is a common way of resolving a conflict between private beliefs and perceptions on the one hand and social pressures on the other. These social pressures can be primarily informational, defining reality, or they may primarily dispense rewards and punishments and have little to do with what is objectively right or wrong. People can also be pressured into an obedience that has extremely negative consequences for others. It is important to study and know the determinants of uniformity and resistance so that we are rational and adaptive in forming a consensus and do not fall into pathological acquiescence to irresponsible authority and mob rule.

ATTITUDES AND BEHAVIOR

In 1935 Gordon Allport wrote that "attitude" was the central concept of social psychology. This is probably no longer true, but for many years it was believed that if we could understand how attitudes were formed and how they could be changed, we would have the key to social progress and the elimination of prejudice. At first social psychologists were concerned with identifying and measuring attitudes. Developments during World War II accelerated a shift to the study of how attitudes are changed. A distinguished group of social scientists addressed the important problem of changing the attitudes of men in the American military services. How could soldiers be made to understand the evils of the Axis powers and feel justified in combating them? How could they be made to realize that the war would be a long one? What are the attitudes of blacks and whites when white and black platoons fight side by side? When they fight together in fully integrated platoons? Work growing out of these war experiences and several years of subsequent research on attitude change culminated in an important book by Carl Hovland, Janis, and Kelley, entitled *Communication and Persuasion* (1953). These authors reported on a variety of experiments studying the credibility of sources of information, one-sided versus two-sided communications, whether it is better for the communicator to draw a conclusion or leave the conclusion to the audience, the immediate versus delayed or "sleeper" effects of persuasion, and how an individual's reference groups may help him resist attempts to persuade him.

These important studies defined new areas for further investigation. Many of the results were quite consistent with common sense: credible, expert, sincere communicators are more effective than their counterparts. Two-sided messages are more effective than one-side communications with better-educated, more skeptical subjects. Group memberships can serve to anchor opinions and to help members resist outside persuasion. These were important "bench mark" findings, but they left ample room for exploring many intriguing subtleties and for making other less obvious findings in the years to follow.

Cognitive Dissonance and Attitude Change

The sixties can reasonably be called the decade of dissonance theory in social psychology. In 1957 Festinger had proposed that when two thoughts or cognitions contradict each other—when one implies the opposite of the other—individuals experience an unpleasant tension, a state of **cognitive dissonance** which leaves them uncomfortable. Dissonance motivates people to try to restore consonance to their clashing thoughts. This might be accomplished by changing one of their beliefs. Let us assume that a young woman has eagerly agreed to go on a blind date, but that her first glance at her companion tells her he is about as unattractive a man as she has ever met. There is clearly potential dissonance between her recognition that she chose, with considerable enthusiasm, to go on the date and the undeniable perception that her date is unattractive. Assuming that there is no way in which she can distort her perceptions enough to convince herself that the young man is physically handsome, she might reduce her discomfort by noting that he has a lively personality, is a laugh-a-minute, and so on.

When Behavior Can Affect Attitudes One of Festinger's crucial insights was that cognitions associated with overt behavior are highly resistant to change. It would be difficult for the young woman to convince herself, for example, that she is not really on a date with this man. Because thoughts about behavior are so resistant, this raises the crucial possibility that our behavior may influence our attitudes—the complement of the traditional assumption that our attitudes predict our behavior. Having made this assumption, dissonance theory goes on to point out that behavior affects attitudes only when people feel fully responsible for their behavior. They must feel that they had freedom of choice, that they were not coerced, and that they could have anticipated the consequences of their actions, or there will be no dissonance. Thus if the young woman had accepted the blind date at the urging of her roommate, who promised that she would return the favor, or if the roommate had insisted persuasively beforehand that the man was very handsome, the young woman would not subsequently have been so prone to emphasize the man's sparkling personality, for there would be little or no dissonance to reduce. In the first instance she would be purchasing a favor in return, one she might need rather desperately at some time in the future. In the second she could hardly have foreseen that her date would be so unattractive, in view of her roommate's insistence on his appeal. In these situations the date's unattractive appearance might be a minor disappointment, but no real dissonance would develop.

A lengthy series of experiments have clearly shown the validity of this reasoning. If subjects are induced for a barely sufficient reward to write an essay that goes against their initial belief, for example, that the marijuana laws should be liberalized when they believe otherwise, they will subsequently show a change in attitude in the direction of that taken in their essay. Such a change does *not* occur if the essay is written for a large reward—an offer they could hardly be expected to refuse—or under conditions allowing them no choice. Actually the important condition is only that the subjects *think* they have a choice, even though this choice is really illusory since the experimenter arranges things so that everyone in fact complies and carries out the dissonance-creating task.

ILLUSION OF CHOICE

Attitude change follows compliance, it would seem, when the complying individual is given the "illusion of choice." In a typical compliance-dissonance experiment subjects who are to experience the crucial dissonance are often assured that they can choose to write an essay consonant with their own attitude rather than the counterattitudinal essay the experimenter prefers that they write. Although all subjects end up writing the counterattitudinal essay, for their attitude to change it is crucial that they believe they could have done otherwise.

The "illusion of choice" may also operate in establishing statewide social policy. After the Supreme Court's desegregation decision of 1954, many Southern states vowed eternal resistance. When schools began to be integrated a few years later, there was often interracial violence and massive public resistance. In 1956 the legislature of the state of North Carolina debated various ways of complying with federal law while avoiding violent confrontations between the races. A controversial law was finally passed that ordered desegregation but offered state tuition aid to any student who wished to attend a private school instead. Although prointegrationists, a minority in the state at the time, were appalled at the potential use of state funds to support prejudice, the massive opposition to desegregation was more or less defused. Over the next several years schools were integrated with surprisingly few incidents of racial confrontation, in spite of the fact that no one took advantage of the tuition support option. In fact, the legal status of the support plan was never clearly established, and funds for its implementation were never appropriated. The people of North Carolina indeed shared an "illusion of choice."

A question that can never be answered is whether more North Carolinians privately became less militant prosegregationists than citizens of other states because of the cognitive dissonance created by their illusion of choice. The theory would hold that there was greater dissonance in North Carolina over this issue because the citizens' cognition that desegregation would harm their children was dissonant with the cognition that they were *freely*—they had the illusion that another course of action was available—sending their children to a desegregated school. One way to reduce this dissonance would be to change their initial belief and to adopt the opinion that desegregated schools would not really harm white children. Changes of this sort *may* have helped to avoid militancy during the desegregation process. It is very doubtful, however, that any legislator voting for the plan was aware that it might change private attitudes.

Insufficient Deterrence Just as dissonance may develop when we are coerced into doing something for reasons that are not clearly sufficient, so will we experience dissonance when we do *not* do something we would otherwise like to do for reasons that are only marginally sufficient. In the classic study by Elliot Aronson and Merrill Carlsmith (1963), three- and four-year-old children were individually brought into a playroom containing a table on which there were five rather attractive toys. After the children had played briefly with each of the toys, the experimenter asked them to rank the toys by preference, from most-liked to least-liked. The toy that turned out to be the second-most-preferred was left on the table, and the remainder were spread around the room on the floor. The experimenter then told the children that he, the experimenter, had to leave for a few mintues but would be back soon.

What else he said at this point varied depending on the situation in which the children were put. In a no-threat situation the experimenter told the children that they could play with any of the toys in the room until the experimenter returned. He took the second-ranked toy with him as he left. In the severe-threat situation the experimenter told the children that they could play with any of the toys *except* the one on the table. Furthermore, they were warned,

> I don't want you to play with the ______. If you play with it, I would be very angry. I would have to take all of my toys and go home and never come back again. You can play with all the others while I am gone, but if you played with the ______, I would think you were just a baby. I will be right back.

In the mild-threat situation the child was also forbidden to play with the second-ranked toy, which was again left on the table, but the admonition was gentler.

> I don't want you to play with the ______. If you played with it, I would be annoyed but you can play with all of the others while I am gone and I will be right back.

The experimenter then observed the subject for ten minutes through a one-way observation mirror. None of the children actually played with the forbidden toy, although some appeared tempted. When the experimenter returned, each child was asked to rank the toys again by preference. If the hypothesis of insufficient deterrence is correct, we would expect the second-ranked toy to be downgraded in the eye of the child who had been mildly admonished not to play with it. This child should be motivated to develop extra reasons for not engaging in forbidden behavior, including the "sour grapes" reason that the toy is not so much fun anyway. The results (Table 13.3) offer strong support for the hypothesis. Children severely threatened or not threatened at all increased their preference for the forbidden toy, whereas children mildly threatened either did not change the toy's preference rank or lowered it.

TABLE 13.3
Change in Preference for Forbidden Toy

	Preference		
Situation	**Increased**	**Unchanged**	**Decreased**
No threat	7	4	0
Severe threat	14	8	0
Mild threat	4	10	8

Adapted from Aronson and Carlsmith, 1963.

The theoretical reasoning behind this finding has been buttressed by many subsequent experiments. Jonathan Freedman (1965) showed that children would not play with a very attractive mechanical robot forty days after a mild prohibition against playing with the toy had been imposed in a totally different setting. Children who had earlier been more severely prohibited from playing with the robot, however, did so later. The children gently admonished had apparently internalized the prohibition.

Mark Lepper (1973) later made an even more striking finding. Children mildly prohibited from playing with an attractive toy, and children severely prohibited from doing so, were asked three weeks later to play a game for prizes. The children soon realized that the game could be won only by cheating. Children who had earlier been mildly admonished were better able to resist the temptation to cheat. Apparently they viewed themselves as honest, moral persons, who had been strengthened by their ability to resist the initial temptation to play with the forbidden toy. The children who had been mildly admonished were personally more responsible for avoiding the attractive toy than children who had been severely admonished. The abstinence had bolstered their self-image.

The Self-Perception Alternative

The experiments done within the framework of dissonance theory, and there were a great many from 1958 to 1973, were often provocative in suggesting that people would change their attitudes, perhaps permanently, after they had been subtly induced to act contrary to their beliefs. The fact that an experimenter could change attitudes to a greater extent by paying a dollar than by paying twenty dollars, as an experiment by Festinger and Carlsmith (1959) had indicated, was a rather startling reversal of notions derived from reinforcement theories of learning.

Even more interesting, however, was Daryl Bem's alternative self-perception explanation of findings supposedly explained by dissonance. He argued that people continue to learn about themselves from their own behavior, just as outside observers do. An observer who notes that a friend always stands by the dill pickles at a party and eats more than his share would probably conlude that the friend likes dill pickles. Bem's twist was in his suggestion that should the observer ask the friend whether he likes dill pickles, the friend might say, "I must like them; I eat them whenever I get the chance."

To apply this argument to the findings from dissonance research, Bem proposed that subjects who for a pittance write an essay contrary to their beliefs must conclude that they do not really feel very strongly against the essay position or they would not have written the essay for so little. Bem argued that subjects do not *change* their attitudes in a dissonance experiment; when asked for their attitudes after the experiment, subjects who were paid very little simply remember them differently than do those who were amply reimbursed for taking a counterattitudinal position. In other words, the position taken in the essay, the subject's most recent act, is more salient than any attitude he or she may have originally held.

After a considerable amount of back and forth in the literature, many social psychologists concluded that the phenomena of attitude change uncovered by dissonance researchers were very interesting, but that there was no way to choose between the dissonance explanation and Bem's explanation in terms of self-perception. The crucial difference between the two theories is that the first depends on a state of tension. According to dissonance theory, people are uncomfortable when they act contrary to their beliefs and this motivates them to change their attitudes. Bem's theory, by contrast, is purely cognitive. People observe their own behavior and attempt to explain it, taking the situation into account. Tension created by inconsistent cognition plays no part in the explanation.

Mark Zanna and Joel Cooper thought that they saw a way to pit the two theories against each other in a crucial test to determine which was correct. In their reasoning they went back to Stanley Schachter's theorizing and research on the labeling of emotion (see page 349). Schachter and Jerome Singer (1962) had shown that subjects who were given an injection causing autonomic arousal and a correct description of what to expect were least likely to interpret it as an emotion when it developed. Those who were given the injection and misinformed about the effects, or not told there would be any, attributed arousal to the situation. They caught the mood of an experimenter's stooge, whether he was playful and full of hilarity or irritated and disgruntled. Zanna and Cooper (1974) thought that these findings could be exploited to distinguish between the dissonance and the self-perception explanations of why people change their beliefs after compromising them for very little purpose.

These experimenters convinced college students that they were to participate in two separate, unrelated experiments. In the first experiment, supposedly dealing with the effects of drugs on memory, subjects were given a powdered-milk placebo. Different groups of participants were told that the pill might make them tense, relax them, or have no side effects. Before the expected memory test, while giving the "drug time to take effect," subjects were to engage in another and entirely separate experiment on opinions. They were asked to write a forceful essay in favor of a ban on inflammatory campus speakers, presumably counterattitudinal for the college student subjects. The experimenter in charge of the opinion experiment then gave some subjects the "illusion of choice," saying that they were completely free not to write the essay. The others heard nothing about such an option, although all subjects did, in fact, write essays.

The subjects who had been given a choice should have felt some dissonance, for they had willingly "decided" to write an essay countering a firmly held private attitude. This dissonance, according to Festinger's theory, should create a state of tension or arousal. But, following the logic of Schachter's emotion-labeling theory, subjects who also thought that they had just ingested a tension-producing pill might quite reasonably attribute any arousal symptoms to the pill itself. If they did this, presumably they would be less motivated to change their attitude on the speaker ban issue than subjects who were given no

TABLE 13.4
Average of Subjects' Later Opinions about Banning Inflammatory Speakers from Campus

	Expected Side Effect of Drug		
Freedom of Decision	**Arousal**	**None**	**Relaxation**
High	3.40	9.10	13.40
Low	3.50	4.50	4.70

Note: The larger this average shift in opinion, the greater the later agreement with the position taken in the essay. The average for the control group—subjects who wrote no essay and took no pill—was 2.30.

Adapted from Zanna and Cooper, 1974.

opportunity to attribute discomfort to a pill. This is exactly what happened (Table 13.4), suggesting that dissonance *is* experienced as an uncomfortable tension and that attitudes are changed in an effort to reduce this tension. Bem would have difficulty incorporating this result into his version of attitude change, although more recent studies (Fazio, Zanna, and Cooper, 1977) have shown that Bem's explanation may be appropriate when the discrepancy between attitudes and behavior is mild, when the behavior is not sufficiently counterattitudinal to create dissonance.

SUMMARY □

The relations between attitude and behavior are complicated, for the one affects the other. That is, not only do attitudes affect behavior—we behave in ways that could have been predicted from our attitudes—but behavior induced by other means can affect subsequent attitudes. It is the great insight of cognitive-dissonance theorists that people who are induced to behave in a manner inconsistent with their beliefs, when they have the option of not doing so, will change their attitudes to bring them more in line with the implications of their behavior. What is more, such changes in attitude appear to have considerable persistence.

Attempts to justify obedience after mild admonishment may be very important in the child's development of morality. Moreover, some people apparently decide what their current opinions are on the basis of their behavior, which may account for periodic changes in attitude in adult life.

There are, of course, many ways to change attitudes that do not involve the subtleties of inducing behavior with "insufficient" justification. Direct persuasion is often very effective. If persuaders are knowledgeable, sincere, and disinterested, they will have high credibility and their arguments will have impact. Various aspects of their arguments are also of critical importance. This subject is very complex, however, and beyond the scope of this chapter.

PEOPLE IN GROUPS

Many human interactions take place in teams, committees, assemblies, and organizations. The importance of group memberships to the average individual can hardly be exaggerated. We are formally educated in groups; we sometimes engage in collaborative work; we play games in groups; we join "societies," clubs, sororities, fraternities; we make plans as a family, which is often viewed as the prototype of a small group; we come together to protest or to bargain for higher wages; and so on. Psychologists have long been fascinated by the complex processes of interaction in groups and have frequently been puzzled by them. One particularly challenging fact is that members of a group sometimes accomplish more than an equal number of isolated individuals acting alone could. The clearest examples are ventures that require highly coordinated, complementary activities such as operating a submarine, launching a new product in the marketplace, and playing a Mozart quartet. In this sense there can be "emergent" or unpredictable phenomena in group activities, which makes us want to identify the processes of effective interaction.

A comprehensive treatment of the psychology of groups would require a lengthy consideration of group structure, communication networks, leadership and power relations, the nature of tasks undertaken by groups, role differentiation or division of labor, and problems of group atmosphere. In the limited space available, perhaps the most constructive approach is to search for generalizations in two areas of group functioning, problem solving and decision making. We shall consider first how groups go about solving cognitive problems that have a correct answer, then how they come to a consensus in formulating judgments, beliefs, and values.

Group Problem Solving

Imagine yourself as a social psychologist working for a large corporation involved in a number of diverse enterprises. You are asked to advise the corporation how various corporate subunits should be organized to complete the tasks assigned to them most efficiently and effectively. What kinds of considerations might go through your mind? Under what circumstances are members of a group going to do a better job at solving a problem than the same number of individuals working in isolation for the same amount of time?

This is actually the oldest experimental problem in social psychology. In 1897 Norman Triplett discovered that children will wind fish reels faster in the presence of others than when alone. This discovery helped to establish a tradition of experimental research on group versus individual performance that has been continuous to the present day. The great volume of completed research has taught us much, but it still would not be easy to counsel you, the corporation advisor, how best to deploy your forces. Nevertheless, both common sense and the literature might tell you to pay attention to four factors.

The Mere Presence of Others Early experiments on subjects working alone versus together generally support the conclusion that the mere presence of others has an energizing effect on performance, causing people to work harder. At the same time, the presence of others often depresses accuracy, either because of the distracting stimulation others provide or simply because people become overconcerned with speed, which affects accuracy. Each of these effects is augmented, apparently, when rivalry is added—that is, when the others who are present are in competition with the performer.

Robert Zajonc (1965, 1966) examined many studies of activities carried out in the presence of others; the research had been done on animals as well as human subjects. He concluded that the presence of others *impairs the learning of new responses but facilitates the performance of those that have already been learned.* It follows that the presence of others is less than helpful when individuals are working on complex or difficult tasks. If the correct responses are readily available to the individual or animal, a greater amount of work will be accomplished in the presence of others, with no loss in quality or accuracy. Zajonc (1965) concluded his review with some tongue-in-cheek advice.

> The student should study all alone, preferably in an isolated cubicle, and arrange to take his examinations in the company of many other students, on the stage, and in the presence of a large audience. The results of his examination would be beyond his wildest expectations, provided, of course, he had learned his material quite thoroughly (p. 274).

Acquiring Correct Information Most problems or tasks confronting a group require the generation and application of information for their solution. Since it is usually the case that the needed information is unevenly distributed throughout the group, and some of it is incorrect, a way must be found to ensure that the correct information is available and prevails over the incorrect. Fortunately, according to ample evidence, the group converges upon the answers held by the most proficient group members. It does so in part because the most proficient members have been found to be right in the past and are therefore taken seriously this time. In addition, many have argued, the most proficient members tend to speak up more quickly and with greater confidence. These two factors probably help explain a successful college quiz team. In a winning team the knowledge of the members is complementary, and there is little dispute over who is likely to know what.

In addition to these social factors, which help push them to the fore, correct information and answers are likely to dominate for two additional reasons. Members can often verify whether answers are correct by checking whether they actually solve the problem. Moreover, correct answers are likely to be more common than incorrect answers. That is, if each of seven group members offer answers, and three of these answers are the same, this answer is more likely to be correct than any of four other different answers. This reasoning is consistent with Marjorie Shaw's classic study (1932). She found that problem-solving groups rejected many more incorrect solutions than correct ones for a problem, even though more correct solutions were actually offered. It seems reasonable to conclude that when the ideas of each group member are made known to each other member, a number of mechanisms operate to promote the frequent adoption of the correct solution. This explains why groups can function much of the time at the level of their most proficient members.

Coordination of Complementary Skills Often, however, even more is expected from groups than functioning at the level of the most proficient member. After all, if this were all groups could do for us, why not simply identify the most competent group member and dismiss the remainder? One reason is that the member who is most proficient on one problem or phase of a problem may not be the most proficient member on the next. On this basis, it is certainly possible to understand how, in fact, a problem-solving group could perform *beyond* the level of its most proficient member. For example, if Mary knows only that $X + Y = 8$, and Helen knows only that $X - Y = 4$, they must join forces to discover the proper values for X and Y. Similarly, if memory is crucial to the task, it is quite likely that all members together can remember more than the single member who recalls the most. Thus members of a jury are generally better able to reconstruct the testimony of a trial than any given jury member can, and they will feel confident of its accuracy. Even though some members cannot spontaneously recall some information, they can readily recognize its accuracy when recalled by someone else.

But are there also circumstances in which the members of a group are able to generate new and creative solutions that were not available to them as individuals beforehand? It seems very likely that there are times when an incorrect suggestion by one group member triggers off an associated response in another member, one which is correct and would otherwise not have come to mind. The possibility of such group-induced creativity underlies the procedure of **brainstorming.** This procedure advocates the suspension of criticism, so that participants will offer all their ideas, no matter how preposterous. It also encourages "free wheeling" or "taking off" from others' ideas, at least during the early phases of discussing a problem. Unfortunately, there are very few well-controlled studies of the effectiveness of brainstorming or, more gener-

Group discussion is effective in solving problems when it increases the number of possible solutions, and when it helps people to weed out poor solutions and to pick good ones.

ally, of the role that groups can play in bringing forth new creative solutions not otherwise available. Brainstorming instructions when given to groups do yield a greater number of creative ideas than instructions emphasizing the quality of suggestions produced, but they also do so when given to individuals working alone (Meadow, Parves, and Reese, 1959). Other investigators have noted that members of brainstorming groups actually produced inferior solutions as compared with those thought up by the same number of individuals working in isolation. Groups tend to pursue a single line of thought for a longer time than individuals do (Taylor, Berry, and Block, 1958; Dunnette, Campbell, and Jaastad, 1963).

Refinement and Objectivity of Thought If brainstorming advocates are impressed by the virtues of **divergent thinking** (page 268), **convergent thinking** also has its place. M.C. Bos (1937) suggested that the very act of formulating an opinion or an idea for communication to the group may help the individual member sharpen and refine the idea. Dean Barnlund (1959) conducted an experiment in which the group had to choose the appropriate conclusion to a series of logical syllogisms. Each syllogism was so constructed that the content of either the premises or the alternative conclusions was attitudinally charged. For example, one correct syllogistic conclusion was "... then some communists are conservative Republicans." Barnlund concluded from his comparisons of how groups and individuals handled these syllogisms that the prospect of group discussion made members more cautious and deliberate in their thinking. They were also less likely than individual problem solvers to act on their prejudices in proposing solutions. Since the members were less distracted by the loaded and irrelevant attitudinal content, group performance was of course better.

Impact of Group Interaction on Decision Making

When we shift from solvable problems to the broader arena of making decisions and forming opinions, wherein no decision is necessarily correct, we enter a different domain of experimental work. From the previous account of research on the social-comparison process, it might be inferred that within a group opinions tend to converge toward the average opinion, as each member tries to increase his or her similarity to each other member. Such convergence would seem reasonable when there is no group leader and when the members do not depend for their opinions on outside **reference groups.** Why should the members reach any consensus other than one somewhere near the initial group average?

The Risky Shift For decades it was assumed that groups making decisions with more or less risky consequences would be more conservative than individuals, or at least that risky individuals would be pulled toward conservatism in response to group discussion. It was therefore very surprising when James Stoner observed, in 1961, that members of his exerimental groups took a *riskier* stance as a result of group discussion.

Stoner asked male students in an industrial management program to make private decisions about the level of risk that they would accept in each of twelve "life dilemmas." For example, each subject was asked to consider what he would do if he had a satisfying, well-paying job with long-range security but was given an opportunity to go into business for himself. There would be some risk of failure but also a chance for great financial gain if successful. The subjects had to decide how sure they must be that the new business venture would be successful before they would resign a secure job and devote their energies to it. The subjects answered a set of questions about twelve such dilemmas working alone. Then these subjects responded to a comparable set of questions after engaging in group discussion. The final decision was made either by members of the group acting together or by each individual acting separately after the group discussion. The question was whether the subject is more willing to make a risky choice—quitting the secure job and going into business for himself—when deciding by himself or after the group discussion. Over a series of hundreds of experiments, far more individuals advocated a riskier solution to the problem afrer group discussion than when deciding on their own. The phenomenon was dubbed "the **risky shift,**" and the tendency was hailed as one of the most robust empirical phenomena in social psychology.

Three hypotheses have been offered to account for the risky shift, and each has received some support. (1) Daring individuals tend to dominate group discussions (for example, Wallach, Kogan, and Burt, 1968). (2) The diffusion of responsibility that takes place in groups makes it possible to share the dangers associated with high risk. (3) Since our culture attaches value to taking risks, advocates of risk have a rhetorical advantage over the advocates of caution (Brown, 1965).

Group Polarization After researchers had accepted the validity of the risky shift, they tried in their research to discriminate among the hypothetical reasons behind the shift. Paradoxically, however, they began to discover that the phenomenon was not so general, universal, and robust after all. Investigators such as Allan Teger and Dean Pruitt (1967) started to pay attention to the fact that the risky shift referred to a score obtained by combining results from many items. Actually, it was noted, for some choice dilemmas group opinion shifted in the cautious or conservative direction. Even more intriguing, a relationship was discovered between the mean initial response to an item and the mean shift on that item. If the mean initial response had been on the risky side, group discussions tended to shift opinion in the direction of even further risk. If the mean initial response had been cautious, however, the groups tended to shift in the direction of even further caution.

Serge Moscovici and his colleagues (for example, Moscovici and Zavalloni, 1969) came to the rescue with the new concept, **group polarization.** According to this concept, the *average* response of group members increases in extremity after discussion. Thus if we imagine an opinion scale ranging from −3 to +3, and a group whose initial, prediscussion ratings average +1.5, discussion might polarize the opinions of the members and the group average might move to +2.3. What support is there for such an effect? Actually, the support is quite remarkable and is not restricted to the domain of choice dilemmas, where the risky shift once ruled the roost.

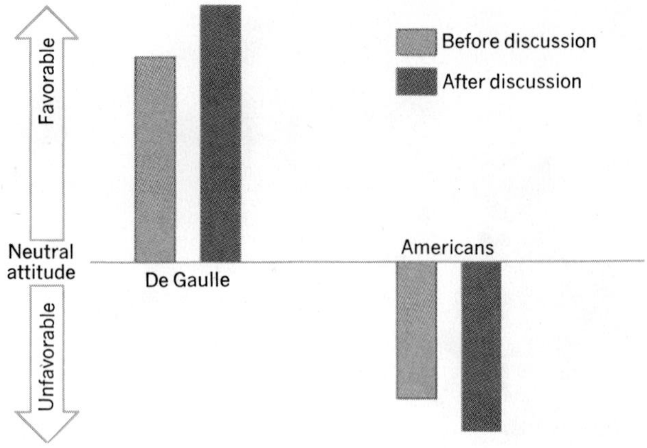

FIGURE 13.4
Effects of discussion on attitudes. Prior to discussion the French students in this study had been favorable toward De Gaulle and unfavorable toward Americans. Discussion made them even more so. When group members are polarized on some issue, discussion may drive them even further apart. (Adapted from Moscovici and Zavalloni, 1969.)

In the realm of attitudes, Moscovici and Marisa Zavalloni (1969) were the first to report the strengthening through discussion of French students' initially positive attitudes toward De Gaulle and negative attitudes toward Americans (Figure 13.4). A variety of other experiments assessing attitudes before and after group discussions indicated the same pattern of results (Myers and Lamm, 1976). Similar experimental findings of polarization have been obtained in studies of ethical dilemmas, decisions of simulated juries about guilt and innocence, and evaluations of persons. Recent experiments on risk taking have shown strong support for Teger and Pruitt's initial hunch; in general, when the betting odds favor risk, groups will take more risks than will individuals. When the odds are against risky bets, groups will take *fewer* risks than individuals.

This is all well and good, but perhaps polarization is still a shaky laboratory phenomenon which holds because of artifacts hidden in the experimental setting. Not so, according to Helmut Lamm and David Myers (1978). They have reported the general finding that, in relation to independents, students who join fraternities become increasingly conservative and prejudiced as they move from sophomore to senior

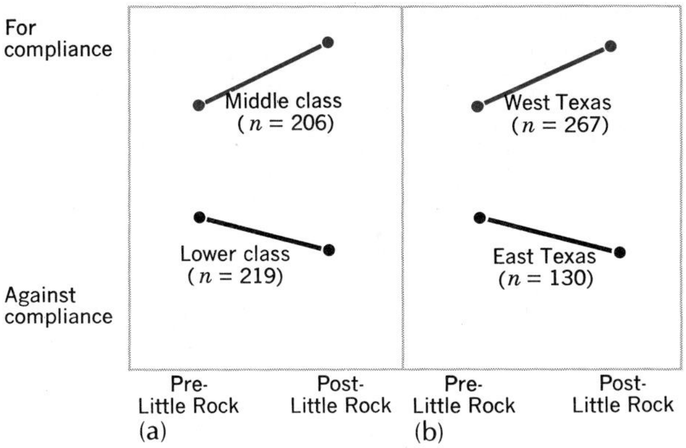

FIGURE 13.5

Effects of dramatic events on polarized attitudes. Before President Eisenhower ordered troops sent to Little Rock to enforce desegregation rulings, Texans were polarized in their attitudes toward compliance (*a*) by socioeconomic class as well as (*b*) geographically. Eisenhower's dramatic order increased the polarization. (Adapted from Riley and Pettigrew, 1976.)

year. The deliberations of natural juries cannot be observed, but at least it is clear (Kalvin and Zeisel, 1966) that 90 percent of the time their eventual decisions are predicted by the initial predeliberation vote, if that vote revealed a majority already in agreement. Robert Riley and Thomas Pettigrew (1976) report data to support the notion that dramatic events tend to polarize groups with different initial biases. Thus a sampling of opinion in Texas shortly before President Eisenhower ordered federal troops to Little Rock, Arkansas, in 1957, indicated that respondents from the lower socioeconomic class were more against compliance with desegregation rulings than respondents from the middle class. After the intervention of troops, opinions shifted to more extreme versions of the earlier inclination. Lower-class respondents were even more against compliance; those of the middle class were more for it. The same tendencies were revealed when samples were reconstituted along regional lines (Figure 13.5). East Texans, originally against compliance, were more against it after the episode at Little Rock. West Texans, originally for compliance, favored it even more.

A number of explanations have been offered for the polarization effect, some of them borrowed from those used to account for the risky shift. The most plausible seem to be the following (adapted from Lamm and Myer, 1978).

The diffusion of responsibility in mobs may encourage behavior that would not be considered were each person to feel individually responsible.

1 *Peculiar Distributions of Initial Positions* If opinions are generally divided into a majority and a minority position, and the positions are on opposite sides of the neutral point, it can be demonstrated that group discussion will shift the minority position toward the majority. There is, however, considerable evidence available to discount this as a major explanation for group polarization. For example, polarization occurs even when there are only two persons in the groups having a discussion.

2 *Responsibility Diffusion* When the members of a group have something to gain personally by acting against the interests of an outside group, responsibility can become diffused through group membership and actions more self-serving. Acting as a group may liberate selfish impulses by neutralizing the conscience or superego. This might well explain the excessive violence of such groups as lynching parties and urban looting mobs.

3 *Strength of Arguments* There is evidence that people's opinions are polarized more during discussions than when they individually list relevant arguments. Although privately written arguments will favor the dominant alternative, arguments presented for discussion favor the dominant alternative to an even greater extent. Thus the consensus in favor of the dominant alternative during a group discussion must seem very strong indeed to group members.

4 *Social Comparison* A simple social comparison theory would predict a convergence of opinion or judgment toward the group mean, but a fair

amount of evidence has accumulated to support the notion that people do not want to be considered average. They want to be just a little different from the others, and in the right direction. People attempt to judge what the group favors and then put themselves out ahead of it. This seems to be one of the strongest factors in polarization. Without such a factor it is difficult to explain Myers and Martin Kaplan's (1976) finding that mere exposure to the true group average will produce polarization. Discussion may enhance the effect, but it is not essential to it.

SUMMARY □

Much of what researchers have learned about the advantages and disadvantages of individuals working in groups rather than separately seems to support a commonsense, logical analysis. The effect on individuals of the mere presence of others seems to be energizing when the work being done is familiar and easy but disruptive when work is unfamiliar and complex. Members of a group can usually summon forth the information required to solve a problem, often when none of the members working alone could do so. The memories, knowledge, and intellects of the group exceed the capacity of any individual member. But studies of brainstorming by group members, sessions in which they offer all their ideas in the hope that perhaps even an incorrect one will bring to mind a brilliant solution, do not indicate this to be a particularly effective procedure. Groups can sometimes encourage refinements in thinking and objectivity, however.

A once widely held assumption that group members would converge toward the average opinion was rudely violated by the consistent finding that they did not do so in situations in which risk was a major consideration. They generally favored taking greater risk after discussing the matter as a group. In attempting to explain this "risky shift" phenomenon, researchers found a more symmetrical tendency toward polarization. Thus there is a shift to the risky position or the conservative one, depending on whether the group members' initial positions favored risk or caution. Moreover, social attitudes also seem to become polarized through group activities, by dramatic events, or even over time. One likely explanation for polarization is that public presentations of a position tend to be more emphatic than arguments thought through in private. People also want to differentiate themselves from the average, in the direction of the majority "leaning."

TO BE SURE YOU UNDERSTAND THIS CHAPTER △

The following concepts are the major ones for this chapter. You should be able to define them and state the points made about each in the text discussion.

Attribution theory
Correspondent-inference theory
Discounting effect
Attribution error
Implicit personality theory
Stereotype
Self-fulfilling prophecy
Applications of social sanctions
Psychological reactance
Social-comparison theory
Cognitive dissonance (theory)
Brainstorming
Divergent thinking
Convergent thinking
Reference group
Risky shift
Group polarization

As you will recognize, the number of concepts is somewhat smaller than in most other chapters in the book; much of the content of the chapter fails to be captured by a listing of concepts. Here are some topics that you should be able to discuss.

When people's behavior seems to reveal a great deal about their personalities
How actors and observers differ in their interpretation of the actor's behavior
How perceived variability within one's own group and other groups relates to prejudice
The effects of prejudicial behavior on the targets of that prejudice
How subjects explain to themselves their conforming to an obviously erroneous judgment of a majority

The procedures, results, and implications of Milgram's studies of obedience
How the theory of cognitive dissonance explains changes in attitudes
Factors that minimize the development of dissonance
The difference between Festinger's cognitive-dissonance theory and Bem's self-perception alternative
Factors affecting the effectiveness of group problem solving

TO GO BEYOND THIS CHAPTER △

In this book This chapter relates the most closely to Chapter 14 on motivation and conflict and to Chapter 15 on social and emotional development.

Elsewhere Recommended textbooks on social psychology are *Principles of Social Psychology,* by Kelly Shaver; *Understanding Social Psychology,* by Stephen Worchel and Joel Cooper; and *Social Psychology in the Seventies,* by Lawrence Wrightsman. Leonard Berkowitz edits the highly respected series, *Advances in Experimental Social Psychology,* now in its eleventh volume. The five volumes of *The Handbook of Social Psychology,* by Gardner Lindzey and Elliot Aronson, are another useful reference.

CH. 14

Motivation, Emotion, and Conflict

One of the most fundamental ideas in psychology is that behavior is the product of two factors: a relatively permanent set of traits, capacities, talents, and abilities, on the one hand; and a second set of conditions which include environmental factors and more temporary states of the individual. Thus each of us has the capacity for producing a knee jerk reflex, for performing at a certain level on an intelligence test, and for displaying whatever expertise we have developed at the piano or on the tennis court. But these are only potential performances. Whether they happen at all, and the vigor of their execution if they do, depends on conditions other than our talents along each of these lines. Doing something depends on the situation, the degree of our alertness, whether we are tired or energetic, and the level of our motivation for engaging in the indicated activity.

As these observations suggest, motives affect a range of activities from our simplest behavior to the most complex. We have seen this importance of motivation from time to time in previous chapters. Here we turn to a more direct discussion of the topic.

Motives as Explanations In his book *The Crime of Punishment,* Karl Menninger tells the story of the beginnings of one man's day as reported by a California newspaper.

> With a defiant roar, he ripped back out of his driveway, across the street, and up onto a neighbor's lawn. Then . . . in forward gear not a block away he side-swiped a car. About a half-hour later police picked up his trail. When another car appeared in front of him he rammed the car in the rear, but instead of stopping, he just kept ramming. The driver in the front car jammed on his brakes but the angry man shoved him 125 feet out into the southbound traffic of the main highway, then backed off and proceeded south on the same highway. A policeman . . . sped after him. When the pursued car and the patrol officer whipped through a red light . . . , another traffic police officer joined in the chase. A car that appeared in front of the pursued driver was rammed, the nearly demolished station wagon bouncing off . . . onto the shoulder of the highway for 500 feet before it ran into a fence and finally stopped.

What is the first question you are prompted to ask as you read this account? Most people ask, "Why did he do it?" When we ask this "why" question, we may be satisfied if the answer is in terms of a motive. The driver is an aggressive, hostile person who must have been angry, perhaps with someone else, and he is taking out his anger on innocent people.

We need to examine further this popular tendency to equate motivation with the *explanation* of behavior. When we ask why a man stole, ran for high office, or assaulted a stranger in the street, the type of answer we are often willing to accept is that these forms of behavior took place *because* the man was covetous, ambitious, or aggressive, failing to recognize that these are not explanations but merely names for the behavior in question. To say that a man hit another man because the first man was aggressive raises the question of how we know that he was aggressive. It turns out that we know he was aggressive because he hit the other man. But this reasoning reduces to "He hit the other man because he hit the other man"—a transparently circular explanation.

Such faulty efforts at explanation were common in instinct theory, promoted by a limited number of psychologists about fifty years ago. Instinct theory maintained that human behavior was driven by **instincts,** which were inborn, unlearned, and universal in the human species. To determine what these instincts were, one consulted one's own experience, literary sources, or the writings of earlier psychologists for suggestions.

Instinct theory was never widely accepted in psychology, partly because of the literary, rather than experimental, source of its ideas. More importantly, it gave too little significance to environmental influences on behavior. In the middle of the 1930s the nature-nurture pendulum was at the extreme environmentalist end of its swing. The concept of instinct was swept away, along with other interpretations of behavior that were strongly biological. But now the pendulum has moved in the other direction, and the concept of instinct has recovered its respectability.

THE STUDY OF ANIMAL BEHAVIOR

After its long rejection the concept of instinct returned to psychology as one of the contributions of an exciting new science, **ethology,** which occupies a position at the boundary between zoology and psychology. Ethology is the scientific study of animal behavior. In this field an **instinct** is a complex, stereotyped, rigidly organized sequence of species-specific behavior. Over the past thirty or forty years the ethologists have provided us with meticulous descriptions of such behavior as courting, nest building, and the defense of territory. Some useful suggestions about the general principles that govern motivated behavior can be gleaned from the courting behavior of a small fish, the three-spined stickleback, and imprinting, a phenomenon which seems related to the affiliative motive.

Courting Behavior of the Stickleback

The stickleback typically mates early in the spring and goes through a complicated sequence of actions

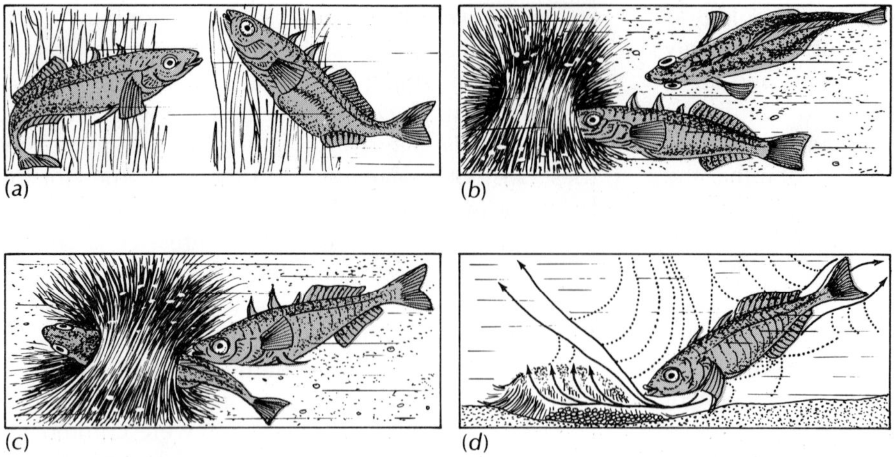

FIGURE 14.1
The courting behavior of the stickleback. (*a*) The male courts the female, (*b*) then he lures her into the nest, where (*c*) he induces her to lay her eggs. After the mating urge has subsided, (*d*) the male stickleback devotes himself to fanning the water over the nest to keep it in motion, as indicated by the arrows. (After Tinbergen, 1952.)

in doing so. The first activity in the sequence is the establishment of a territory, a component of the mating behavior in many species. The male stickleback stakes out such a territory and defends it against all intruders, male and female. Second, it builds a nest out of weeds. When the nest is completed, the color of the stickleback changes. Originally dull gray in hue, the underside becomes a bright red and the back a bluish white. Now a distinct pattern of courtship begins. Whenever a female enters the male's territory, he approaches her with a seductive zigzagging motion and lures her to the nest. She enters the nest, and he induces her to lay her eggs by prodding at the base of her tail (Figure 14.1). The same pattern of courtship may occur with several female fish. At some point, however, the strength of the male's mating urge subsides, his color pales, and from then on he occupies himself with fanning the water over the nest, which increases its oxygen supply. When the young are born, the male stickleback cares for them until they are big enough to join a large school of fish.

Imprinting

There is a tendency in the newborn of many species to follow the first large moving object they see and to behave toward it as though it were its mother. Ordinarily the parent of the young animal provides this stimulus, but a member of some other species or even some inanimate object may accidentally happen to be the first appropriate object the young animal sees. In such an event, this object tends to evoke the behavior in question. In any case, we speak of the general phenomenon as **imprinting** and say that the young animal is imprinted on its parent, on an animal of another species, or on an inanimate object.

Early Observations The more recent discovery of imprinting by European ethologists is actually a case of rediscovery. William James, writing in 1890, described such phenomena as though they were well known and cited Douglas H. Spalding, writing in 1873, as an important investigator. He quoted Spalding as saying that if baby chicks are born in an incubator, they

> . . . will follow any moving object. And, when guided by sight alone, they seem to have no more disposition to follow a hen than to follow a duck or a human being. Unreflecting lookers-on, when they saw chickens a day old running after me, and older ones following me for miles, and answering to my whistle, imagined that I must have some occult power over the creatures; whereas I had simply allowed them to follow me from the first.

Spalding also knew that imprinting occurs only during a **critical period** early in the life of the chick. If such experience was postponed until later, the initial reaction of the animals was not following but fear. As a demonstration of this, Spalding kept three chickens hooded until they were nearly four days old and had this to say about their behavior.

> Each of them, on being unhooded, evidenced the greatest terror to me, dashing off in the opposite direction whenever I sought to approach it. The table on which they were unhooded stood before a window, and each in its turn beat against the window like a wild bird. One of them darted behind some books, and, squeezing itself into a corner, remained cowering for a length of time. We might guess at the meaning of this strange

Konrad Lorenz, a famous European ethologist, and goslings imprinted on him.

> and exceptional wildness; but the odd fact is enough for my present purpose . . . had they been unhooded on the previous day they would have run to me instead of from me. . . .

Nearly a century later, laboratory experiments have fully confirmed both the fact of imprinting and Spalding's interpretation. Eckhard Hess, for example, using ducklings as subjects, showed that it was easy to imprint them on decoys (Figure 14.2). Other investigators, using other species, have shown that even a cardboard cube or cylinder is an adequate imprinting object. Studies of this behavior have shown that (1) the duckling is easily imprinted on the decoy; (2) thereafter, when placed between a male decoy and a female duck, the duckling tends to follow the decoy; (3) in a pond imprinted ducklings congregate around a decoy in preference to a real adult duck; and (4) the duckling will overcome obstacles in order to remain near the object on which it is imprinted, suggesting that the relationship has motivational aspects.

First Following, Then Fear As would have been expected from Spalding's observation that young animals tend first to follow and then to avoid novel objects, there is indeed a critical period during which

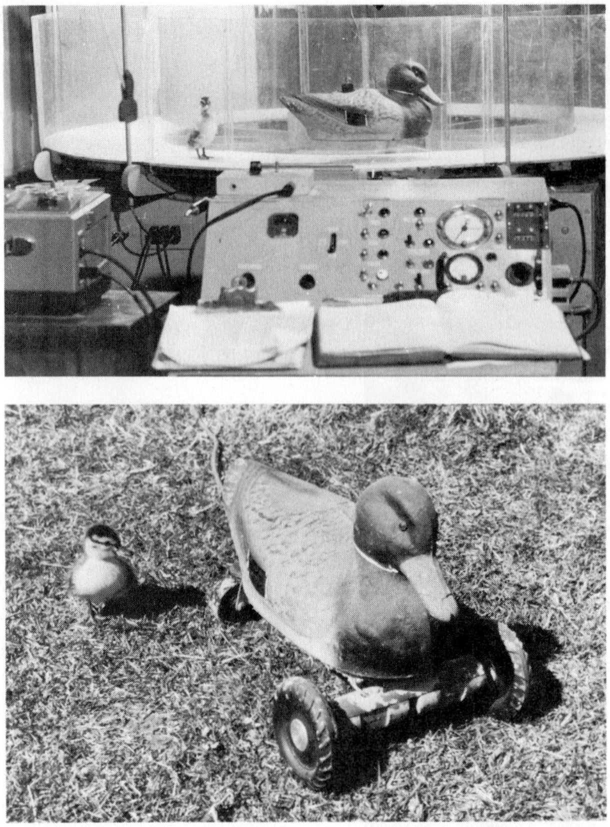

FIGURE 14.2
Imprinting in the duckling. This apparatus (*top*) is used to establish imprinting. A duckling (*bottom*) remains near a male decoy, on which it has been imprinted.

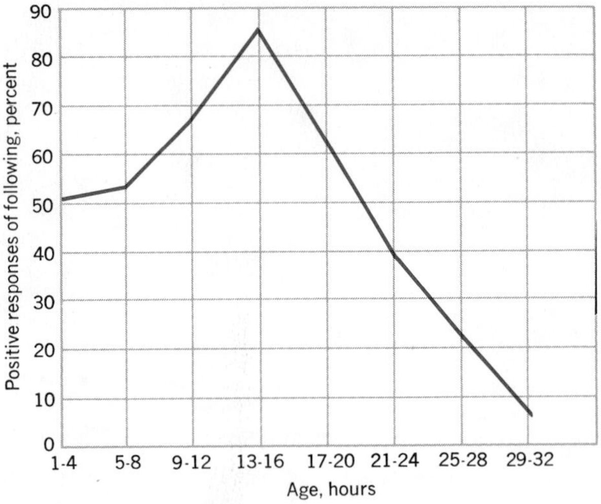

FIGURE 14.3
Age and imprinting in ducklings. Imprinting occurs readily during a very limited age range and then falls off rapidly, beginning about 16 hours after birth. (From Hess, 1958.)

imprinting is the most easily accomplished. Hess has investigated this relationship (Figure 14.3). The ducklings were placed into an apparatus with the decoy at various times after hatching, and a record was kept of whether they followed the decoy. Quite clearly, the tendency to imprint has some strength immediately after birth and increases for a matter of fifteen or sixteen hours, after which there is a decrease. Hess's interpretation, similar to Spalding's, is that the increasing tendency to imprint corresponds to an increasing tendency to follow and reflects increased mobility. The later decreasing tendency reflects the increase in fear of strange objects. In the normal life of the infant animal, this sequence of events is one of great adaptive significance. The infant develops an attachment to a protecting adult and, subsequently, a fear of all strange and potentially threatening objects and a tendency to avoid them. Such instinctive behavior has obvious survival value.

Other studies of imprinting have added to our understanding of the process. This type of early experience has a more permanent and more general effect on the animal's behavior than is at first evident. Much later, when the animal becomes mature, its sexual responses are directed toward the species or the object on which it has been imprinted. Hess, for example, cites one striking case in which a jungle fowl cock was imprinted on a person and kept away from contact with members of its own species for a month. Then it returned to the flock, but, even after five years with members of its own species, it courted human beings exclusively.

We also know some of the factors that facilitate imprinting in ducklings. One important element is the call of the hen of the species as she leads the young from the nest. The young birds appear to be "tuned in" to the distinctive sound of the maternal call. If in the laboratory the maternal call is heard when replicas of different kinds of hens are seen, their visual qualities—size, color, and markings—can be varied markedly without reducing their attractiveness to the duckling. The use of a call different from that species' maternal call does reduce the visual effectiveness of different replicas. Such data affirm that the auditory system of birds develops before the visual system and dominates it early in development (Gottlieb, 1973).

General Principles

With these two examples before us, it will be possible to describe some of the basic concepts and general principles employed by the ethologists in the explanation of instinctive behavior.

Action-specific energy and innate releasing mechanism Two of the most basic concepts in the ethologists' explanation of instinctive behavior are **action-specific energy** and **innate releasing mechanism.** The first concept expresses the idea that the energy for instinctive behavior somehow resides in the nervous system and is available only to the particular instinctive response in question. The second term, innate releasing mechanism or simply *releaser,* refers to the fact that the instinctive reaction is made only to objects in the environment with certain distinctive features. The reaction is "blind" in the sense that it occurs whether or not the object is really appropriate. Thus the male stickleback tends to attack any red object and to court any object with the approximate form of a gravid female. Occasionally the male stickleback takes a male gorged with food to be a female and courts it. As the term *innate* implies, instinctive behavior is released by the appropriate stimulus without earlier training.

Serial organization Ordinarily, the parts of an instinctive act tend to occur in a rigidly fixed sequence; the sequence constitutes what the ethologists called a **fixed-action pattern.** Thus the male stickleback does not build a nest until it has defended its territory for a while; it does not seek to lure females to the nest until the nest is built; and so on. Once the animal has completed a particular stage, the next one tends to ensue whether or not it is appropriate. Thus once a female stickleback is in the nest, she may be stimulated to lay her eggs by any nudging at the base of her tail, and she does so even if the male stickleback who led her to the nest is removed from the tank.

Such observations have led the ethologists to the conclusion that instinctive behavior is initiated through release from some type of inhibitory block. More specifically, it is assumed that each one of the responses in an instinctive chain removes a block to release of the succeeding response.Thus defending territory in the case of the male stickleback removes a block to nest building; nest building removes a block to courting; courting removes a block to tending the nest; and so on.

Hierarchical organization According to a related concept, the hierarchical organization of instinctive behavior, the exact form of instinctive behavior depends on the details of the situation. Thus the hunting behavior of the hawk is somewhat different if the prey is a small mammal than if it is a bird. To explain such variations in instinctive behavior, the ethologists hold that instinctive behavior begins with the arousal of some very general impulse to appropriate action. This general impulse occupies a position at the top of a hierarchy of tendencies. With the general instinctive impulse aroused, the more specific forms of the instinctive behavior, which occupy positions lower in the hierarchy, are released by particular environmental stimuli. The chain of more and more specific released reactions, thus begun, is indefinitely long.

Interaction of instinct and environment This last point implies a very delicate interplay between internal springs to action and environmental events. The studies of imprinting bear out such an interplay. One possible interpretation of imprinting might take a form similar to hierarchical organization. The young animal is born with a very general tendency to follow. What object comes to control this tendency, however, depends on the particulars of the environment.

Frustration and displacement behavior Although instinctive behavior ordinarily proceeds in an orderly way with the sequence of instinctive responses occurring in the right order and to the right stimuli, occasionally there are interesting exceptions. In birds grooming is an instinctive response designed to cleanse the features of dust or water. It happens with great frequency, however, during the course of fighting. Such an out-of-context instinctive act is called **displacement behavior.** Studies of displacement behavior have yielded these interesting facts. (1) It occurs rather frequently under conditions of thwarting and conflict, often during pauses in a fight between two animals. (2) The response itself is characteristically very common, one with a low threshold.

Relevance to Human Motivation

A very interesting question for psychology, of course, is whether these phenomena observed in the behavior of other animals also occur in human behavior. A surprisingly large amount of evidence suggests that parallels do exist. For example, the smiles of infants less than six months old are responses released by a very specific stimulus: well-defined, contrasting spots on a square or round flat background (see page 359). Cardboard constructions containing these essential features are more effective in eliciting smiles than various other stimuli, even a picture of a face.

Babies themselves are to adults a conformation that elicits an affectionate, caretaking reaction. In common with the young of other species (Figure 14.4), they have a head that is large in proportion to the body, large eyes, a protruding forehead, and a soft, rounded body with short, thick extremities. Possibly on an innate basis we find these objects "cute"; we want to pick them up and cuddle them (Eibl-Eibesfeldt, 1970).

Sexuality Because of the wide cultural agreement on standards of male and female attractiveness, there is reason to suppose that sexual responses are naturally released by specific stimuli. In the male broad shoulders in relation to the width of the hips are attractive (Figure 14.5). In the female the shape of the classical Venus is the ideal of beauty. The attractive features of the female are indicators of effective pro-

Children pictured on greeting cards are often drawn to have the features that bring affectionate responses.

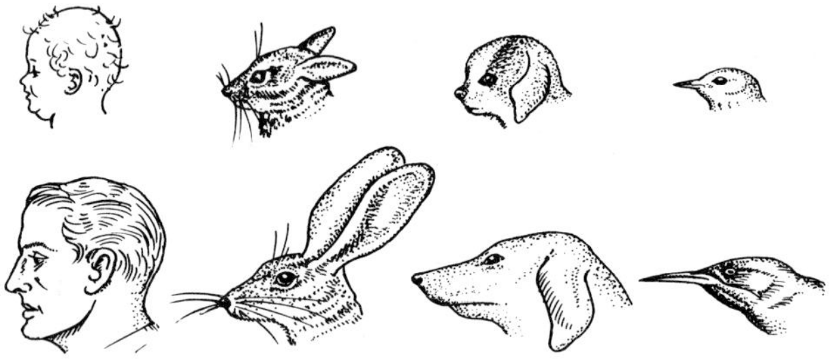

FIGURE 14.4
Biological bases of "cuteness." The differences between the young and adult members of many species are similar.

FIGURE 14.5
Ideals of male and female beauty.

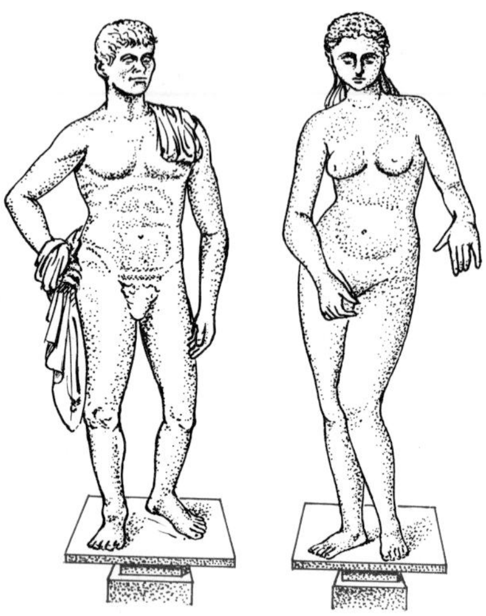

creative and maternal functions. A full bosom promises abundant food for the newborn. Important indicators of health and normal sexual function are a small waistline and red lips and cheeks.

Some sexual releasers are behavioral. Flirting, for example, invokes responses that are common throughout the world.

> The flirting girl at first smiles at the person to whom [the flirt] is directed and lifts her eyebrows with a quick, jerky movement upward so that the eye slit is briefly enlarged. . . . Flirting men show the same movement of the eyebrows. . . . After this initial, obvious turning toward a person, in the flirt there follows a turning away. The head is turned to the side, sometimes bent toward the ground, the gaze is lowered, and the eyelids are dropped. . . . Frequently, but not always, the girl may cover her face with a hand and she may laugh or smile in embarrassment. She continues to look at the partner out of the corners of her eyes and sometimes vacillates between looking at and an embarrassed looking away (Eibl-Eibesfeldt, 1970, pp. 416–420).

Territoriality Like the stickleback, most animals show some form of territoriality. Human beings manifest territoriality in their need for privacy and for a certain amount of control over their immediate surroundings. Experimental study has borne out the deduction of keen observers of social interaction, that people tend to feel uncomfortable if other persons move within the invisible envelope of unoccupied space with which we all like to surround ourselves.

Personal characteristics and the social circumstances affect how large an envelope of space the individual prefers. For example, women choose closer physical proximities than do men (Mehrabian and Diamond, 1971), southern Europeans prefer to stand closer than do northern Europeans (Little, 1968), and people prefer to sit and stand closer to individuals whom they like or know than to strangers. People try to preserve their territory in places such as libraries and cafeterias, even when they are temporarily absent, by laying their personal possessions about on tables and chairs. This manner of commanding space is analogous to the markers animals use to stake their claim to a certain territory.

In general, people prefer to be a certain spatial distance from others. A figure in the neighborhood of five to six feet from nose to nose is a generally comfortable distance between two people conversing. If the other person situates himself either nearer or farther from us, we feel a certain amount of discomfort and react negatively toward the person, even though we are seldom able to attribute the discomfort explicitly to this distance factor. The person who

People riding on a subway maintain as much distance from others as they can manage, but they still sit closer than they would prefer. Birds also space themselves from one another.

comes within this boundary is felt to be intrusive or overbearing or ingratiating, and the one who situates himself or herself farther away is perceived as cold or hostile.

How does a person react to having the preferred "envelope of privacy" encroached upon by another person? To some extent we trade off intrusion in one area by maintaining distance in another (Argyle and Dean, 1965). Thus we can achieve intimacy with another individual by enhanced eye contact, by approaching closer, or by smiling. If the other individual appears intrusive in one of these ways, as when he or she stands too close to us, we can reduce the intimacy by decreasing the amount of eye contact or the amount of smiling we engage in, thus adjusting the composite index of intimacy to the optimal level.

Still another response to the intrusive closeness of another person is, as with other noxious stimuli, flight. Nancy Jo Felipe and Robert Sommer (1966) studied this phenomenon at large tables in a college library. Women students serving as confederates of the experimenters would enter the reading room and sit at various distances from another woman student who was seated alone at one of these tables studying. In the close situation the confederate tried to maintain a shoulder distance of only 12 inches; others sat at distances ranging from 15 inches to 5 feet. Women students who were also studying alone, with the two chairs on either side and the one across from them empty, were watched as controls. In all instances the experimenters measured how long the woman student sat in her chair before leaving the table (Figure 14.6). In the control situation, when no confederate came to occupy a nearby chair, over 90 percent of the women students were, half an hour later, still sitting where they had been when first observed. When the confederate sat within a shoulder distance of 12 inches, however, only 30 percent of the students

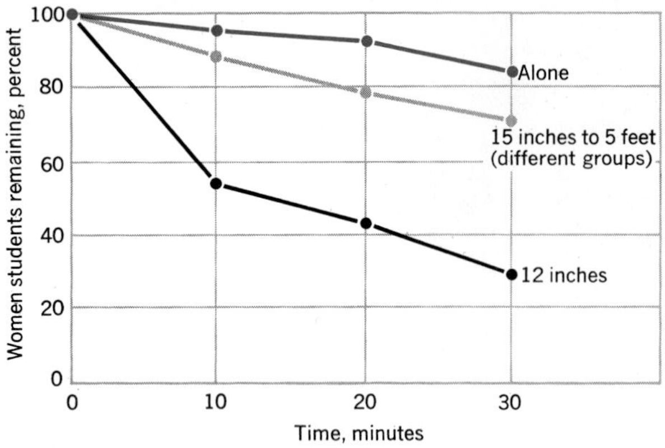

FIGURE 14.6

Territoriality. Women students left the library at various rates when another woman sat down next to them at different distances. When the stranger sat very close (bottom curve), there was a strong tendency to leave. When she sat at greater distances, this tendency was much weaker (middle curve).

were still there half an hour later. In all likelihood the women students who had had neighbors sitting overly close to them left the scene without being quite aware of what had made them uncomfortable.

We might think that since people find crowding so uncomfortable, they would perform less well in highly crowded conditions. Somewhat surprisingly, it has proved difficult to find any impairment of cognitive functioning on simple or complex tasks, even when people are crowded one to every four square feet, as compared to being much more comfortable distances from one another (Freedman, Klevansky, and Ehrlich, 1971).

Aggression In 1932 Albert Einstein, at the request of the League of Nations, wrote a letter to Sigmund Freud soliciting from the founder of psychoanalysis his opinion on why human beings waged wars and whether there were ways to prevent them. Einstein's letter bore his own bias: the only possible answer, he wrote Freud, was that "man has within him a lust for hatred and destruction." In his lengthy reply Freud agreed.

> You express astonishment at the fact that it is so easy to make men enthusiastic about a war and add your suspicion that there is something at work in them—an instinct for hatred and destruction—which goes halfway to meet the efforts of my entire agreement. We believe in the existence of an instinct of that kind and have in fact been occupied during the last few years in studying its manifestations.

Freud's letter was a pessimistic one. He saw no way to rid man of his "aggressive inclinations" other than by encouraging "emotional ties" among people because shared interests produce a "community of feeling" which could inhibit aggression.

Confronted with the same question that Einstein had faced—Why does man go to war?—Nikolaas Tinbergen (1968), professor of animal behavior at Oxford and one of the world's leading ethologists, wrote a provocative piece for a leading scientific magazine, titled "On War and Peace in Animals and Man." Man, he asserted, carries with him his animal heritage of territoriality and aggression in defense of territory.

> In order to understand what makes us go to war, we have to recognize that man behaves very much like a group-territorial species. We too unite in the face of an outside danger to the group; we "forget our differences." We too have threat gestures, for instance, angry facial expressions—and all of us use reassurance and appeasement signs . . . [which] are universally understood; they are cross-cultural; they are species specific (p. 38).

In other species threat gestures alone suffice. Why does man engage in mass murder? Why does his fear not inhibit aggression? Because, Tinbergen says, man has outstripped his own genetic evolution. His discoveries have expanded life, contracted death, and exploded the population on our planet. As a result there is continual intergroup contact, and this provokes recurrent aggression. Threat gestures might still have sufficed except for shifting values and the advances in the technology of war. We have come to believe that fighting is preferable to fleeing, but at the same time we have developed long-range weapons of war in which the push button has supplanted the trigger. Here is Tinbergen's appraisal of modern warfare from an ethologist's point of view.

> . . . the use of long-range weapons prevents the victim from reaching his attacker with his appeasement, reassurance, and distress signals. Very few air crews who are willing, indeed eager, to drop their bomb "on target" would be willing to strangle, stab, or burn children (or for that matter, adults) with their own hands; they would stop short of killing in response to the appeasement and distress signals of their opponents (pp. 40–41).

Not all ethologists agree with Tinbergen's views of an innate aggressive drive in man; some argue that there are innate "bonding drives" which temper and inhibit aggression in human beings. These drives produce social cohesion in groups and are revealed in many different ways: the contact comfort mothers provide for the young, which evokes security rather than fear; the sexual bond, which fosters close relationships; parental care, which is the basic building block for coexistence of human beings; and even joint aggression in the face of common danger, which serves to bind people together. These "natural antidotes" to man's aggressiveness drive form the basis of "our general capacity for social commitment" (Eibl-Eibesfeldt, 1971).

Conclusions

The evidence and argument presented in this section indicate that there probably is a connection between the instinctive activities of lower animals and our own motivated behavior. We should be prepared, however, for differences. The "ascent of man" through evolution has produced an organism with a greater ratio of brain size to body size than in any other organism. Human behavior is therefore more **encephalized,** more dependent on brain function than that of any other animal. Whereas the behavior of lower organisms is dominated by taxis, reflex, and instinct, ours is dominated by learning and reason (Figure 14.7). The simpler forms of behavior are still part of human behavior, but there is a heavy overlay of more highly evolved forms. Human behavior is for this reason much more variable from individual to individual and from culture to culture than the behavior of lower forms of life.

With the understanding that human behavior will be more complex and varied, its ties to instincts nevertheless make us expect human motives to follow certain patterns.

1 The origins of human motivation are likely to be found early in life, much as Freud (page 388) suggested.

2 There may be critical periods when it is easiest to modify motives. Such periods, if they do exist, will be important, for accidents of experience may distort or prevent the development of significant motives. The imprinting of a duckling on an inanimate object is an example of such an untoward happening.

3 Situational factors will be important. Motives cannot be viewed as states that are entirely internal to the human being.

4 The details of motivated behavior will show a hierarchical organization. Studies of human starvation, to be mentioned in the next section, and Abraham Maslow's theory of personality (see page 401) will reveal such an organization of motivated behavior.

5 The relationship between innately given and habitual components of motivation may be essentially that suggested by William James (1890). James argued that instincts exist only to form a basis for the establishment of habits and that, once the habit is formed, the instinct fades away. In the phenomenon of imprinting, the instinctive tendency to follow exists only long enough for offspring to become attached to parents. After that the instinct disappears, allowing the organism much greater behavioral flexibility than would be possible were the instinct to continue to exist.

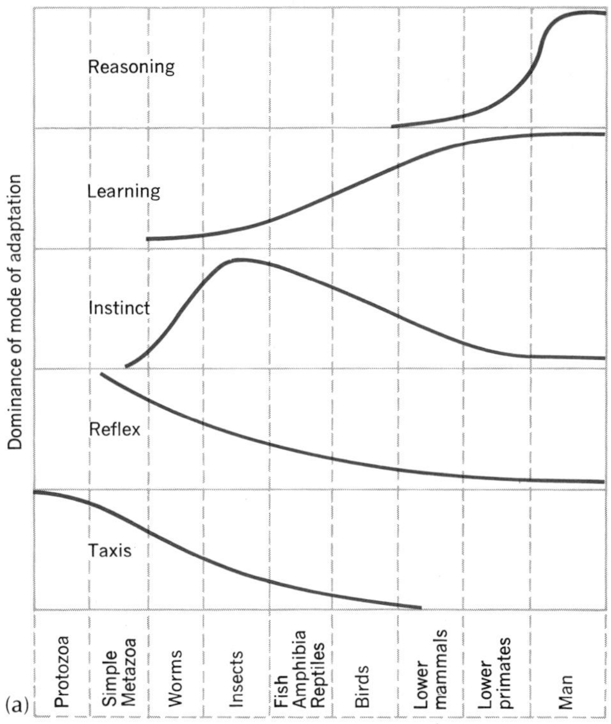

FIGURE 14.7
The importance of different forms of behavior at the various phylogenetic levels. A taxis is a simple movement of a freely moving organism toward or away from the source of stimulation. (Adapted from Dethier and Stellar, 1961.)

SUMMARY □

The concept of instinct figured importantly in early discussions of motivation. In these accounts instinct was defined as an unlearned tendency to seek certain goals. This conception proved unsatisfactory, for it was essentially worthless for explanatory purposes. More recently, the concept of instinct has reappeared in psychology through the important work done by the ethologists, who study the instinctive behavior of animals and find it to consist of a complex sequence of stereotyped acts. These ethological interpretations of instinctive behavior find certain parallels in the motivated behavior of higher mammals and human beings, although we should anticipate more flexibility and a greater effect of experience the higher the animal is on the evolutionary ladder.

THE NATURE OF MOTIVES

Although they differed in many ways, the important instinct theorist William McDougall and the psychoanalytic theorist Sigmund Freud had similar views of motives. Both treated motivation in terms of *energy*, a conception which has persisted in the psychology of motivation down to the present time. This position was clearest in the writings of Freud, who maintained that the energy for all behavior derived from a general reservoir of sexual motivation, the **libido.** This energy, then, was available to any and all of the person's behavior. We shall discuss Freudian theory more concretely later on in this book. At this point we wish merely to call attention to one facet of Freud's position, that libidinal energy was conceived as undifferentiated and undirected. This is the aspect of Freud's theory that had the impact on other psychological theorizing. From the time of Freud, as Donald Hebb put it many years later (1955), motivation has been treated as "an energizer, but not a guide; an engine but not a steering gear." The general idea is that the energy for all behavior is drawn from a single common source.

This general idea is of great importance and, in the history of psychology, provided the rationale for the study of the origins of motivational energy, the varieties of its expression, and the physiological mechanisms through which it operates. Such study has produced an enormous amount of information, which can be organized in the manner shown in Figure 14.8. The most important point conveyed by this representation is the complexity of the concept of motive. A complete discussion of any single motive would treat three kinds of earlier conditions that arouse motives, three aspects of the motivational state itself, three varieties of motivated behavior, and three sets of underlying neurophysiological mechanisms.

Antecedent Conditions

Beginning with antecedent conditions, we can identify the following, recognizing that different motives will depend on these conditions to varying degrees.

Deprivation The chief variable contributing to the intensity of appetitive drives such as hunger and thirst is the length of time the organism has been deprived of the object that is its goal.

Stimulational variables For other motives—avoiding the pain of electric shock being the clearest example—the principal condition determining the strength of the drive is stimulational. A somewhat different set of stimulational variables is related to the availability of the object sought. Sexual arousal, for example, depends for the most part on the accessibility and desirability of appropriate sexual objects. To a lesser extent, but still importantly, the degree of hunger depends on the kinds of food available.

The history of the organism Learning and experience have an influence even on motives that have a reasonably clear physiological basis. Within cultural groups tastes in food vary, as we all know. Between one group and another the differences are even greater. There are people who eat snails, toasted grasshoppers, ants, raw meat, soups made of birds' nests, and each other. There is no evidence that the bodily requirements of these people differ from ours. Obviously particular tastes in food are learned. Much of human motivation derives almost entirely from experience.

Motivated Behavior

The expression of motives is varied. Three categories capture this variety.

Consummatory behavior The most obvious expression of any motives takes the form of **consummatory behavior,** that is, behavior designed to satisfy the motive in question. Thus eating is the consummatory response for hunger, copulatory behavior that for sex, and so on.

Instrumental behavior A second general class of responses associated with any motive are those **instrumental** to its satisfaction. Instrumental behavior consists of the acts that secure what is to be consumed. It is the behavior studied in operant conditioning (page 128). The greater the motivation, the greater the vigor with which we work for whatever satisfies the motive. One interesting incidental point about the instrumental manifestations of motivation is that, sometimes, the instrumental act is the consummatory response for another motive. A child eats, the consummatory response associated with hunger, in order to secure its mother's approval; the prostitute uses the consummatory behavior associated with the sexual motive in order to secure food, clothing, shelter, and sometimes power; a businessman may use aggressive behavior, not to hurt a competitor but to further his ambitions; a student sometimes expresses a scholarly interest in a particular subject, not because he has that interest as his motive but because he hopes to gain the professor's approval.

Substitute behavior Many expressions of human motivation are indirect and substitutive in nature. A study performed at the University of Minnesota dur-

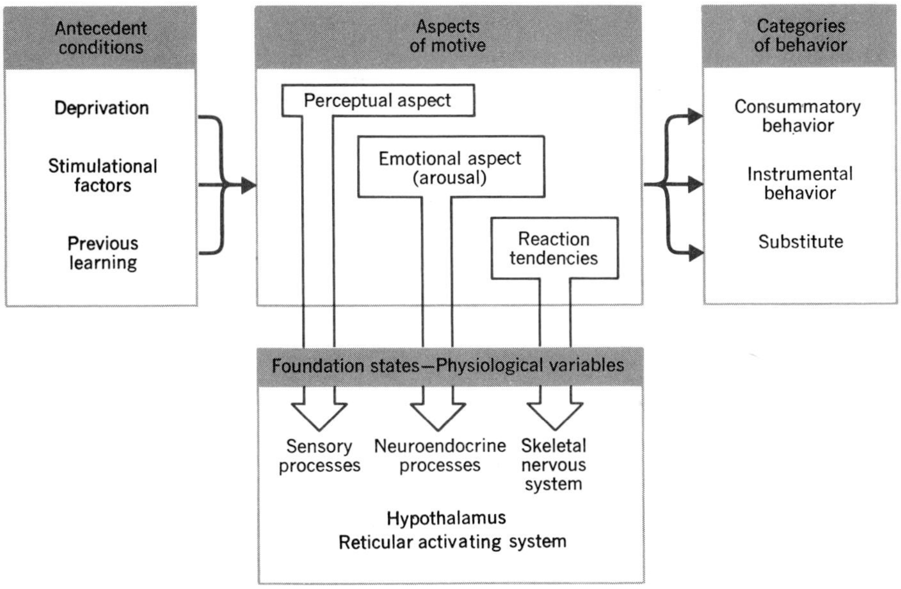

FIGURE 14.8
The nature of motives.

ing World War II serves to make this general point. This investigation was conducted with conscientious objectors who voluntarily submitted to a six-month period of semistarvation. During this time the subjects in the experiment lived on a very restricted diet. Their weight dropped from an average of about 155 pounds to less than 120 pounds, and their daily existence became preoccupied with food. Favorite topics of conversation were food and eating, and cookbooks were fascinating reading material. Motives other than hunger became noticeably weaker. Sexual urges declined; romances collapsed; dancing was too much work. Many of the men were bothered with vivid dreams of breaking the diet. One man expressed his craving for food symbolically by stealing cups from a coffee shop. Thus extreme hunger initiated behavior that was only a substitute for the satisfaction of the hunger drive (Keys et al., 1950).

Physiological Bases and Aspects of Motivation

William McDougall (1926) had this to say in defining the concept of instinct, which, leaving aside the question of innateness, he used about the way we do the concept of motive:

> We may define an instinct as a psychophysical disposition which determines its possessor to perceive and pay attention to objects of a certain class, to experience an emotional excitement of a certain quality upon perceiving such an object, and to act in regard to it in a particular manner . . . (paraphrased slightly).

In this statement McDougall identifies three aspects of a motive or instinct: (1) a perceptual aspect, (2) an emotional aspect, and (3) a behavioral aspect. If we accept this theoretical scheme as providing a framework for the study of the physiology of motivation, we are led to search, not for a single physiological foundation but for a set of them.

With all this complexity before you, it probably requires no special argument on our part to convince you that a complete description of the psychology of motivation is far too large an enterprise to undertake in a single chapter. For this reason we have selected hunger for discussion, and merely mention a few other motives in passing to indicate something of the variety of motivated behavior.

Hunger

The most studied motive is hunger. Hunger depends chiefly on deprivation: it initiates a complex set of chemical and neurological events that cause the organism to seek food with increasing intensity as deprivation progresses.

Behavioral Expressions The effect of deprivation has been extensively studied. With increasing deprivation instrumental and consummatory responses both become stronger (Figure 14.9). The third type of behavioral expression of hunger, substitute behavior, has already been described.

Antecedent Conditions The chief condition with which hunger-related behavior varies is deprivation (see Figure 14.9). Stimulus variables related to the hunger motive are of two kinds, the tastes of food and

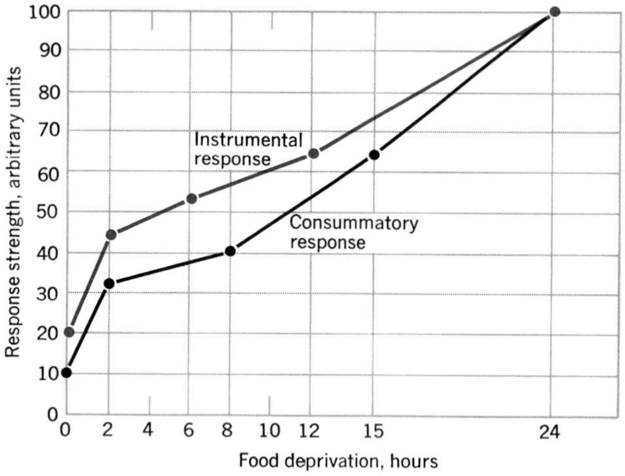

FIGURE 14.9

Response strength and deprivation. In two studies of white rats, the instrumental response was pressing a small panel behind which food was available. The consummatory response was eating, measured by food intake in grams. The arbitrary units are percentages of the response strength after 24 hours of deprivation.

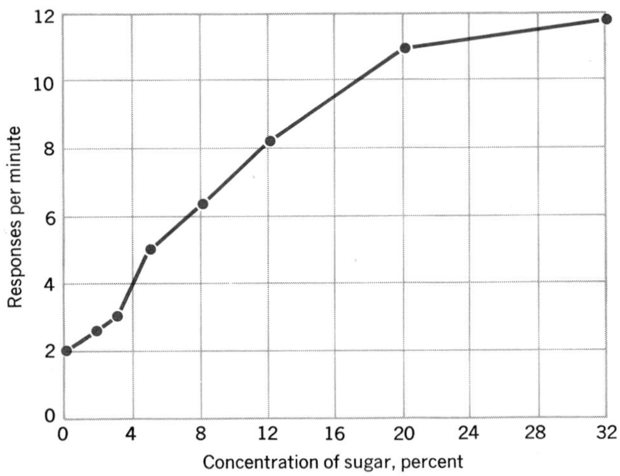

FIGURE 14.10

Sugar concentration and taste incentives. (Data from Guttman, 1949.)

the internal stimuli that inform the animal a state of need exists. Because they play this role, such stimuli are often called **drive stimuli.**

Taste stimuli There is probably no need to dwell on the point that lower animals sense differences in the tastes of foods and have preferences. Rats, for example, have a sweet tooth just as we do. Increasing the percentage of a sugar in the fluid used to reinforce bar pressing increases the rate of bar pressing dramatically (Figure 14.10). As we saw in an earlier chapter (page 139), the term incentive denotes the motivational value of a reinforcer.

Drive stimuli Some drive stimuli come from the environment. Most of us have had the experience of finding ourselves hungry just because we are with others who are eating. Even chickens that have been fed to satiation will resume eating if they are put with other chickens that are eating. As for sexual behavior, it is common knowledge that a male bull who has just mated and whose sexual urge has abated will copulate again if a different receptive female is introduced into his pen. For reasons that are amusing, this is called the **Coolidge effect.** The stimuli for some motives are almost exclusively environmental. These include the stimuli for most acquired human motives, such as aggression, the need to achieve, and the fear of danger or threat.

In the case of hunger, the most important drive stimuli come from the churnings of the stomach, what

THE COOLIDGE EFFECT

University of California, Berkeley
Department of Psychology
Berkeley, California 94720

Dear Greg:

I introduced the term "Coolidge Effect" into the . . . literature as an elaborate hoax just to see if it would get by. In 1955 Lisbeth Jordan and I did an experiment on "sexual exhaustion" in male rats. We found that the average male would ejaculate a certain number of times and then cease copulation for an indeterminate period. One year later at the meetings of the Eastern Psychological Association Alan Fisher reported a replication of our study with a new twist. He got exactly the same results . . . up to the point of our criterion of "exhaustion." However . . . if at this point he provided the male with a new female partner the male might ejaculate another one or two times.

After I moved to Berkeley some of my students and I repeated Fisher's study . . . and obtained essentially the same results. Dick Whalen reported our work at the 1958 meetings of the Western Psychological Association and I primed him to refer to the phenomenon as the "Coolidge Effect" (with no explanation). Dave Krech chaired the session in which Dick spoke and he agreed . . . to emphasize . . . "Coolidge Effect" but to refrain from any comments.

The neologism referred to an old joke about Calvin Coolidge when he was President. You will remember that he was an exceedingly laconic individual and was nicknamed Silent Cal. . . . The President and Mrs. Coolidge were being shown around an experimental government farm. When she came to the chicken yard she noticed that a rooster was mating very frequently. She asked the attendant how often that happened and

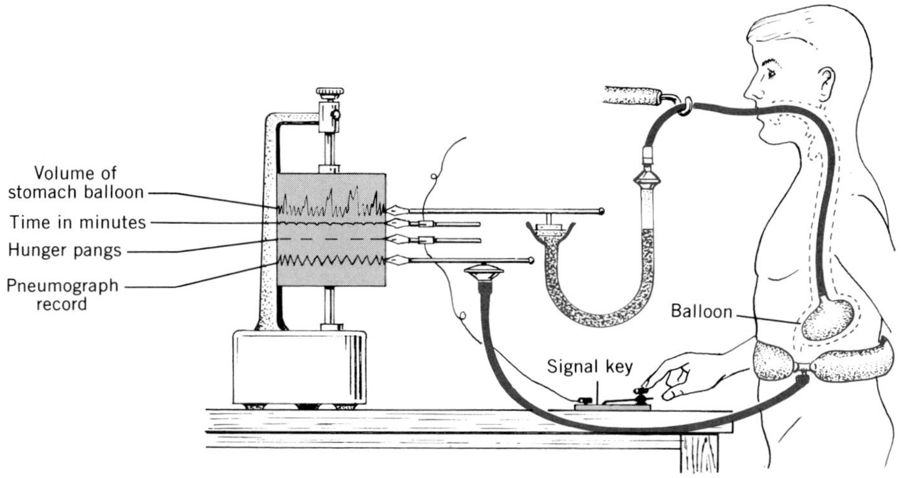

FIGURE 14.11
Recording stomach activity and the experience of hunger pangs. Notice that the record of stomach motility, indicated by fluctuations in the top line, corresponds with that of hunger pangs, indicated by the horizontal straight lines. The subject produced these horizontal lines by pressing a key whenever he felt pangs of hunger. (After Cannon, 1934.)

was told, "Dozens of times each day." Mrs. Coolidge said, "Tell that to the President when he comes by." Upon being told, Coolidge asked, "Same hen every time?" The reply was, "Oh no, Mr. President, a different hen every time." Coolidge: "Tell that to Mrs. Coolidge!"

It has been fun seeing how this silly joke has gotten spread around in the scientific literature without ever being seriously challenged.

Yours as ever,
Frank A. Beach
Professor of Psychology

we experience as hunger pangs. The evidence for this relationship is very straightforward. Many years ago Walter B. Cannon and his colleagues at the University of Chicago had subjects swallow a tube which ended in a balloon. The balloon could be inflated after it was in the stomach, making it possible to record stomach activity (Figure 14.11). The basic discovery made in these experiments was that the stomach contracted at the same moments hunger pangs were reported, indicating that the contractions must be the drive stimuli for hunger.

Obesity: Insensitivity to hunger pangs Although the Chicago group reported a high correspondence between stomach contractions and the experience of hunger, other investigators were less successful and the method fell into disuse. Apparently there are great individual differences in how people react in such situations, and Cannon was probably lucky in his selection of subjects. In particular, we know now that obese people are insensitive to stomach contractions. They respond for the most part to environmental cues that serve as invitations to eating.

Although all people are, to some extent, stimulated to eat by events and circumstances, such temptations are greatly magnified for obese persons. Their eating behavior appears to be heavily under external control. A candy counter, a pastry shop, a hamburger stand is a constant menace to the obese person.

The obese person's victimization by external stimuli has been demonstrated by a number of investigators. In a series of experiments by Stanley Schachter (1971) and his colleagues, obese and normally weighted college students participated in a program of research on the physiological and psychological correlates of hunger. In one study the effects of both high or low fear arousal and food deprivation or satiation were studied. Since fear and satiation inhibit stomach contractions, it was hypothesized that both conditions would reduce the amount of food subsequently consumed by the normally weighted persons but would have no effect on consumption by obese participants.

Under the guise of conducting a taste test, the investigators cautioned the student volunteers not to eat a meal before their scheduled experimental appointment. Upon arrival in the laboratory, some students were offered large roast beef sandwiches but others were not. This "preloading" treatment divided the subjects into fed and unfed groups. In a further subdivision they were assigned to a low-fear or a high-fear arousal situation. Persons tested in the low-fear situation were told that they would receive a minimum bit of electrical stimulation to their skin in order to excite their skin receptors before the taste test. In the high-fear situation concern was aroused by a

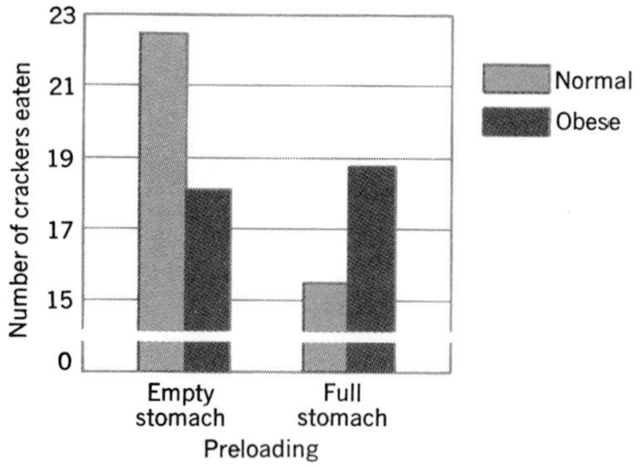

FIGURE 14.12

The eating habits of obese and normal people. Normally weighted students eat more crackers than do the obese when hungry. When both groups have eaten earlier, the obese students eat more crackers than the normal students. (Adapted from Schachter, 1971.)

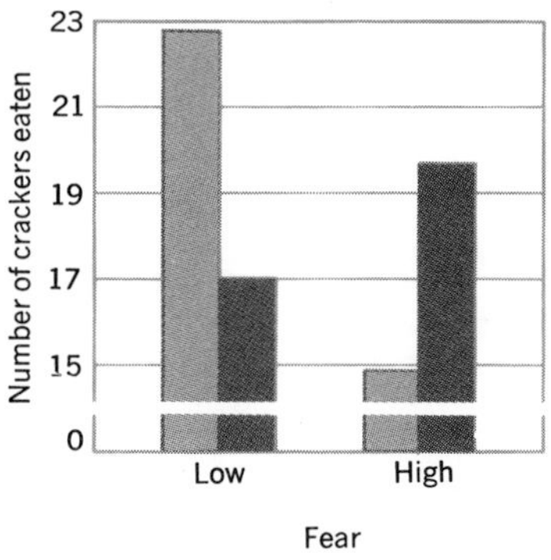

FIGURE 14.13

Fear and eating in obese and normal people. Fear modifies the amounts of food eaten by normal and obese students. When fear is not intense, students of normal weight consume more crackers than do obese students; the relationship is reversed when fear arousal is at a high level. (Adapted from Schachter, 1971.)

large piece of equipment, which presumably housed complicated electrical apparatus required to administer a "painful" shock. Students confronted by this equipment were assured, however, that they would have no "permanent damage" from their shock experience. In this manner the experimenters were able to form both the normal and the obese students into four subgroups: high fear and fed, high fear and unfed, low fear and fed, and low fear and unfed.

After the eight groups had been established, the students were seated before five different bowls of crackers and asked to rate various types of crackers for their taste qualities. Through a one-way vision mirror the experimenters counted the number of crackers consumed, the measure of eating behavior in the experiment. The results of the study (Figures 14.12, 14.13) clearly support the relationship between internal stimulation and hunger in normal persons and the lack of such a relationship in obese people.

Physiological Bases of Hunger In view of the complexity of eating behavior, the physiological bases for it are not surprisingly also complex. Taste sensitivity, stomach contractions, blood sugar level, endocrine condition, and neural mechanisms all play a part, but the exact nature of their roles remains to be worked out.

For example, the stimuli for hunger are usually those coming from the stomach, but these stimuli are not absolutely essential to the experience of hunger. People who have had their stomachs removed report a normal craving for food. Moreover, rats with their stomachs removed learn a maze just as quickly for a food reward as do those with their stomachs in place; and rats whose nerve pathways to and from the stomach have been severed behave about as normal animals do. Clearly physiological factors other than stomach contractions must be involved.

The fact that hunger is somehow dependent on the chemical composition of the blood is inescapable. If blood from a hungry dog is injected into a satiated one, stomach contractions and other symptoms of hunger appear. If blood from a satiated dog is injected into a hungry one, these effects are inhibited. One agent causing such effects might be the sugar in the blood. The amount of sugar in the blood increases soon after eating; with deprivation it decreases. This suggests that blood sugar probably has something to do with hunger. Furthermore, the injection of sugar directly into the bloodstream inhibits stomach contractions; the injection of insulin, which lowers blood sugar, increases them, again suggesting that the blood sugar level and hunger are related.

Other evidence argues against the idea that blood sugar level is the final determiner of hunger. Attempts to establish correlations between blood sugar and various indices of hunger have not been very successful. Some studies have shown a modest degree of relationship. Others, particularly those with human subjects, have been unable to establish any relationship at all. Such evidence has led to the search for other factors in the blood that might control hunger. This search has uncovered important neurological factors.

The most important neural centers for hunger are to be found in the hypothalamus, which is a structure lying at the base of the brain near the pituitary gland (page 40). There can be no doubt that the hypothalamus is important in hunger. Electrical stimulation of the hypothalamus produces stomach contractions. Small lesions in a certain region of the hypothalamus in rats cause eating to increase tremendously. In a period of two months these animals may double their normal body weight. Lesions 1.5 to 2.0 millimeters away cause eating to cease, which suggests that the hypothalamus contains two centers for the control of hunger. The destruction of one, the inhibitory center, causes overeating; when the second, the excitatory center, is destroyed, eating ceases.

There is reason to believe that the frontal cortex has something to do with hunger. Frontal lobotomy, a surgical severing of the connections between the frontal cortex and the rest of the brain, has been considered a way of alleviating certain severe mental illnesses. Some of these lobotomized patients overeat to the same degree as the rats with hypothalamic lesions. Moreover, electrical stimulation of certain portions of the frontal cortex cause stomach contractions; stimulation of other points inhibit them. Neural connections between the frontal cortex and the hypothalamus are assumed and considered responsible.

SUMMARY □

Early conceptions of motivation assigned it the important function of energizing behavior. This idea is overly simple, however, because the determination of motives is complex; motivated behavior takes many forms; motives have a variety of psychological aspects and elaborate physiological bases.

Hunger, for example, is a motive produced for the most part by deprivation, but stimulus conditions contribute to its arousal. Stomach contractions inform the individual of a state of hunger, although these stimuli are not equally effective for everyone. They are particularly ineffective with obese people, who are more sensitive to external stimulation.

On the behavioral side, animal studies have shown how instrumental behavior and eating increase as deprivation proceeds. Extreme deprivation can cause substitute behavior, as demonstrated by studies of human starvation.

At a physiological level hunger is a very complex state depending on gastric motility, blood chemistry, and brain function; hypothalamic activity is of demonstrated importance.

AVERSIVE CONTROL

Hunger is an example of appetitive motives, which cause the organism to seek goals of a certain nature. Thirst and sex are other appetitive motives. Stimuli that punish the organism give it an aversive motive, to avoid such stimuli. Loud noises and aggressive threats are other aversive motives. In terms of the framework we have erected for motivation (see Figure 14.8), the most important antecedent condition for aversive motivation is punishment.

Punishment

The study of punishment lagged behind work on appetitive motivation, for years and for a number of reasons. For one thing, Edward Thorndike had concluded very early in his career—on the basis of totally unimpressive evidence—that punishments were much less effective than positive rewards. William K. Estes (1944) supplied support for this position. He trained rats in a Skinner box and then extinguished their bar pressing either with or without the administration of a slap to the paw. Estes found that the punishment produced only a temporary suppression of responding, and that these rats eventually made just as many responses as unpunished rats did before bar pressing was extinguished. Punishment therefore seemed an ineffective procedure and was little investigated for this reason.

Paradoxically, psychologists were at the same time warning against the use of punishment in child rearing because it was *too* effective. After John B. Watson and Rosalie Rayner's famous experiment in which they conditioned an infant to fear a white rat (page 127),there had been many studies indicating that fear was conditionable. The person who punishes another, in child rearing the parent, can come to be feared, an undesirable side effect of the procedure. Some theorists began to relate neuroses to such patterns of child rearing.

Other investigators demonstrated that painful stimulation causes aggressive behavior (Ulrich, 1967). If two animals of any of several species are put together in an enclosure and subjected to electric shock, they begin to fight. This pain-elicited aggression, together with the fear that pain brings, makes for a very complicated situation. Punishment at the hands of parents appears to have the potential for producing conflicting attitudes of hostility and fear in children. Again, the clinical literature revealed that neurotic individuals have such conflicting reactions toward their parents.

As the literature on punishment grew, its effects were found to depend on so many variables that the outcome of using it seemed very difficult to predict. A brief summary of the most important factors follows.

Strength of punishment For obvious reasons most research on punishment has been done with lower animals. The usual procedure is to train them to make a particular response in some situation, to punish them for making that response—usually with electric shock—and to observe the effect of punishment on behavior. The question is whether the animal ceases to make the punished response.

Aversive control of behavior can be effective, but the many variables of such a situation make the process extremely complex and the outcome doubtful.

Very mild punishment does nothing more than attract attention and produce a slight arousal. Such punishment may even strengthen the punished response rather than suppress it, even though the punishment is somewhat aversive. Karl Muenzinger (1934), for example, found that punishing rats with an electric shock when they made a *correct* turn in a maze facilitated learning. Such punishment seemed only to call attention to significant stimuli in the maze and to emphasize the correct response.

Shocks somewhat stronger than very mild have been found to suppress responses, but later there is complete recovery. After a time the subject begins to make the punished response and does so as dependably as though punishment had not been administered. The punishment used by Estes, slapping the rat's paw, was at this level. Still stronger shocks bring suppression from which there is only a partial recovery. Very strong shocks suppress responses to the extent that there is no recovery.

Delay of punishment As is true of appetitive reinforcers like food, the sooner punishment is delivered after a response is made, the greater the effect on behavior. A mild punishment administered immediately may have as much effect as a harsher punishment that is delayed.

Habituation Animals subjected to a longer series of shocks adapt to them, and the shocks become less effective. Adaptation is particularly likely if the strength of the shock is increased gradually, as it often is in practice, beginning with a very mild punishment and working up to a very harsh one if necessary. In the extreme case punishment can even come to serve as a sign of reward. An experimenter in Pavlov's laboratory succeeded in using electric shock as a CS in a salivary conditioning experiment.

Type of response and its history Although strong, well-established responses are usually more resistant to the effects of punishment than others, one type of strong response is surprisingly susceptible. Consummatory responses, such as male sexual behavior and eating, are easily disrupted by mild punishment. They are probably subject to disruption because they are responses of the parasympathetic division of the autonomic nervous system. Punishment calls up antagonistic responses of the sympathetic division (page 38). The development of *anorexia nervosa* (page 13) in the adolescent daughters of nagging parents is easily understood in terms of autonomic responses.

Responses that are learned through positive reinforcement are easier to disrupt than responses that were based on punishment in the first place. For such responses punishment was one of the conditions of learning. At least temporarily punishment can strengthen responses learned by means of it.

Availability of alternative responses Punishment is the most effective when it works collaboratively with reward. In a famous experiment making this point, John Whiting and Orval Mowrer (1943) first trained animals to take a particular route to a goal. Then they punished the taking of this route but provided a new route which they rewarded. The animals never took the original route again.

Anxiety

Because punishment can create conditioned fears, all of us develop a certain amount of anxiety. We all receive our just punishments in the normal course of growing up. Thus anxiety is a personality trait (see page 384) we all share. There are, however, great differences in the amount of anxiety experienced. Most people have realistic fears of dangerous situations and become anxious about violating social customs. Some people's lives are dominated by anxiety, however. Such individuals are anxious about sexual and aggressive behavior, overeating or undereating, impoliteness, failure in academic subjects or at other important tasks, leaving home, taking a job, being late, being slow, being impulsive, and on, and on, and on.

State and trait anxiety Although every one possesses the *trait* of anxiety to some degree, people may or may not express or experience anxiety, depending on the situation. When anxiety is expressed, the individual is said to be in a *state* of anxiety. This distinction between trait anxiety and state anxiety is an important one (Spielberger, 1966). Trait anxiety is a long-term predisposition to become anxious, with either high or low frequency depending on the strength of the trait. State anxiety is a temporary condition of nervousness and apprehension.

Anxiety in college students The effect of anxiety on academic performances at the college level has been effectively demonstrated by Charles Spielberger (1962). This investigator used a questionnaire to select groups of relatively anxious and nonanxious male undergraduates. By controlling for scholastic ability on the basis of college entrance examination scores, Spielberger was able to evaluate the effects of anxiety on grade-point average, rate of academic failure, and dropout rate from school. He found that at the lowest and highest levels of academic talent, anxiety had little effect on academic performance. Apparently poor students usually fail to do well in college, irrespective of their level of anxiety. Very superior students are sufficiently bright to overcome any adverse effects of anxiety. It may be too that very bright students learn to contain their anxiety through intellectual accomplishment. But within the middle range of intellectual ability (Figure 14.14), anxiety interferes markedly with successful college performance. In addition to poor classroom work, more than 20 percent of a total group of 129 anxious students

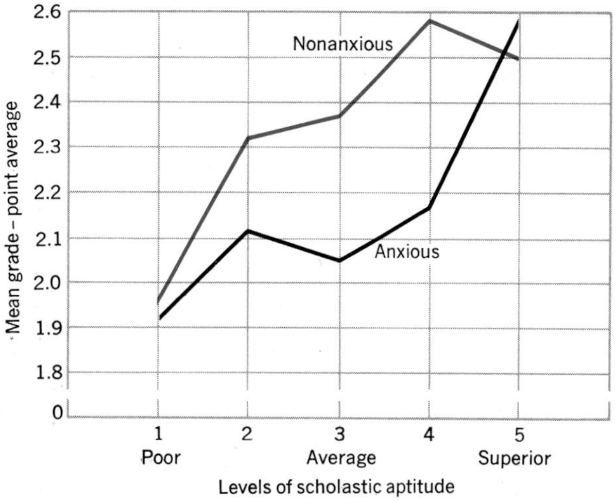

FIGURE 14.14
Relationship of grade-point average, anxiety, and level of scholastic aptitude in college students. Anxiety has its most deleterious effects on students who are intellectually average. (After Spielberger, 1962.)

dropped out for academic failure, whereas only 6 percent of 138 nonanxious students left the university for this reason. Since most college students are in the intermediate ranges of intellectual ability, Spielberger's results suggest that some students who could get through college successfully often fail because of the eroding effects of anxiety.

To determine whether such school failure could be remedied, Spielberger, Henry Weitz, and J. Peter Denny (1962) employed group counseling procedures with anxious college freshmen and then compared their academic performance at the completion of the first year with that of a control group of anxious but uncounseled students. The primary goal of these investigators was one of prevention—to identify the anxious freshmen who could fail out of college and to try to prevent this from happening through counseling. The results of this study were encouraging. Fifty-six student volunteers agreed to participate in a program that required eight to eleven sessions of group therapy. Half of the volunteers were assigned to counseling groups consisting of six to eight students. In the group sessions study habits, vocational goals, social life, problems of personal identity, and the like were examined. For the remainder, the control group, counseling was delayed for a semester. Students in the two groups were carefully matched for entrance examination scores, type of secondary school attended, and other factors that are known to be related to academic performance. The measure used to assess the effects of counseling was improvement in grade-point average from midsemester to the end of the first semester of the freshman year (Figure 14.15). The anxious counseled students showed a sig-

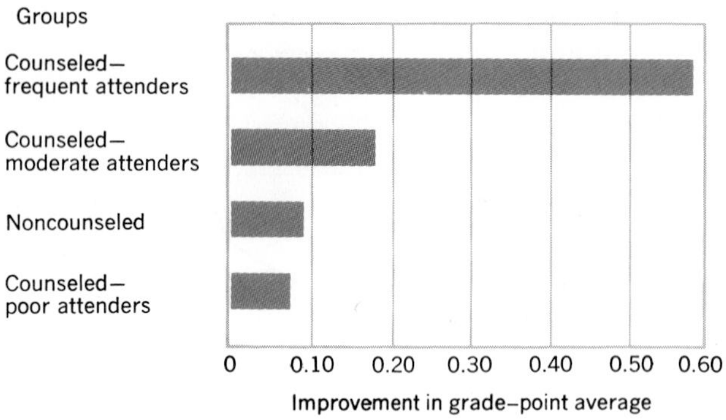

FIGURE 14.15
Improvement in grade-point average for counseled and uncounseled anxious college students. The counseled group was divided into three subgroups—frequent, moderate, and poor attenders—on the basis of how often they went to counseling sessions. The graph reveals that those who came often to counseling showed the greatest improvement in grade-point average. (After Spielberger, Weitz, and Denny, 1962.)

nificantly greater improvement than the uncounseled students. Even more impressive were the differences in improvement that depended on the number of counseling sessions each student in the experimental group had attended. Those who attended two to five sessions did far more poorly than those who came to virtually all sessions of their group. The depressing aspect of the study was that only one third of all the freshmen invited to participate in the program elected to do so.

SUMMARY ☐

Motives may be classified as appetitive or aversive. Hunger is an example of an appetitive motive: punishment and anxiety are examples of aversive motives. Until recently psychology worked on the erroneous assumption that punishment is ineffective in controlling behavior. Research has now shown the error in this way of thinking. Punishment that is intense, immediate, and applied to responses learned through positive reinforcement is very effective, particularly if alternative responses are available to the individual being punished.

The residual effect of punishment is anxiety, a trait for which there are great individual differences. Studies of college students have shown that anxiety may adversely affect academic work. At the same time, however, programs of counseling have improved the grades of highly anxious students.

EMOTION

The individual experiencing an **emotion** is in a stirred-up, agitated mental state, as illustrated by these two classic examples. The first is from the case history of a thirty-six-year-old writer and teacher, William Ellery Leonard. As a small child Leonard had narrowly escaped being run down by a locomotive. This single traumatic experience had effects that lasted for several decades and severely interfered with his later adjustments. Some thirty years after this experience, we find him standing at the shore of a lake and, in his own words,

> I stand looking out over the silent and vacant water, in the blue midday. . . . Then on the tracks from behind Eagle Heights and the woods across the lake comes a freight-train, blowing its whistle. Instantaneously diffuse premonitions become acute panic. The cabin of that locomotive *feels* right over my head, as if about to engulf me. I am obsessed with a *feeling* as of a big circle, hogshead, cistern-hole, or what not, in air just in front of me. The train *feels* as if it were about to rush over me. In reality it chugs on. I race back and forth on the embankment. I say to myself (and aloud): "It is half a mile across the lake—it can't touch you, it can't; it can't run you down—half a mile across the lake."—And I keep looking to *make sure,* so intensely in contradiction to what the eye sees is the testimony of the *feeling* of that cabin over my head, of that strange huge circle hovering at me. . . . Meanwhile the freight chugs on toward Middleton. I rush back and forth on the bluffs. "My God, won't that train go; my God, won't that train go away!" I smash a wooden box to pieces, board by board, against my knee to occupy myself against panic (1927, pp. 304–307).

The second describes the reaction of a monkey, frustrated in her attempts to obtain food in an experiment.

> Sometimes she gazed at the food and at the same time struck the floor with her hand or with a stick. Often she went around touching various objects and at the same time looked up at the food. In case repeated attempts to obtain the food failed, she became more and more affectively disturbed. She went around violently striking the radiator, the floor, or a wooden box, and excitedly uttering a number of sounds. While doing this she again looked towards the food. Finally she got into a state of what might be called a "generalized" affective disturbance, a state in which all reference to the goal was lost. She began throwing things around; she pushed and

> kicked various objects but she no longer threw them in the direction of [the] goal, she did not even look at the goal. It seemed there was a diffuse discharge of energy instead of one specifically directed towards the goal (Klüver, 1933).

Cognitive Bases of Emotion

These examples illustrate another feature of emotional states. Emotional experiences can be qualitatively very different. It is surprising, then, to find that the physiological conditions underlying these experiences are pretty much the same, and that cognitive factors such as the label we apply to the state determine the quality of an emotion.

Physiological Arousal Over half a century ago a Spanish physician, Gregorio Marañón (1924), injected 210 of his patients with adrenaline in an unemotional laboratory situation and asked them to introspect. The effect of adrenaline is to bring on the physiological state of arousal that is characteristic of emotion. In the experiment 71 percent of the patients reported only physical symptoms with no emotional interpretation. The remaining 29 percent responded emotionally. The emotions of this 29 percent were not, however, experienced as "real" emotions. They were reported instead as "cold" emotions or "as if" emotions: "I felt as if I had a great fright, yet I am calm"; or "I felt as if I were awaiting a great happiness." There was, in addition, some evidence that people who had been thinking about an emotional experience, such as sick children or dead parents, before the injection, although dealing with it calmly, became quite emotional about the subject after the injection. These individuals had already had an appropriate context. Apparently providing them with physiological arousal had induced an emotional state. It should therefore be possible to induce a variety of emotional states by manipulating the individual's thoughts and experiences as well as arousal.

Labeling Emotional States In a series of experiments Schachter and Jerome Singer (1962) pursued the lead derived from Marañón's results. Research participants were told that they were in an experiment testing the effect of a new drug, "Suproxin," on vision. When Suproxin, actually epinephrine or adrenaline, was injected, some participants were given an accurate description of the effects of the drug: "What will probably happen is that your hand will start to shake, your heart will start to pound, and your face may get warm and flushed." Other participants received no such information. The physician who gave the injection told them that it was mild and harmless, and that there were no side effects.

After the injection the participants, both those informed of the physiological reactions to expect and those not so informed, were treated in two different ways. Members of one group were individually put in a situation calculated to make them euphoric. They were led into a room which was in a mild state of disarray and introduced to a second "subject," who was actually a confederate of the experimenter. After the experimenter had left the room, explaining that it took time for the Suproxin to take effect, the confederate went through a carefully rehearsed series of antics. He played an imaginary game of "basketball," in which he moved about the room crumpling paper and aiming for the wastebasket. Then he flew paper airplanes. He ended with an exhibition of hula hooping.

In another situation designed to induce anger, each participant was placed with a second "subject," another carefully trained confederate. The participant and the confederate were asked to fill out a questionnaire. The questionnaire was five pages long and began innocently enough, asking for background information. With succeeding pages, however, the questions became increasingly personal and insulting, such as

> With how many men (other than your father) has your mother had extramarital relationships?
> 4 and under ______; 5–9 ______; 10 and over ______.

The two participants worked at this task together. The confederate, however, also made a series of comments expressing increasing irritation. Finally reaching the limits of his patience, he ripped up his questionnaire, threw it on the floor, saying, "I am not wasting any more time, I am getting my books and leaving," and stalked out of the room.

After these experiences, and on the pretext that moods might influence vision, measures of the participants' degree of irritation or happiness were obtained. The general results of the experiment, reflected in these measurements, indicated that (1) the informed individuals, those who had received accurate information about the probable effects of Suproxin, showed little or no tendency to become euphoric in the first situation or angry in the second; (2) uninformed participants, in dramatic contrast, indicated marked happiness following the experience with the euphoric confederate and considerable irritation following the experience with the questionnaire. There is no question that given appropriate physical arousal, emotional experience depends on how the individual perceives the situation. In Schachter's (1967) words,

> Given a state of physiological arousal for which an individual has no immediate explanation, he

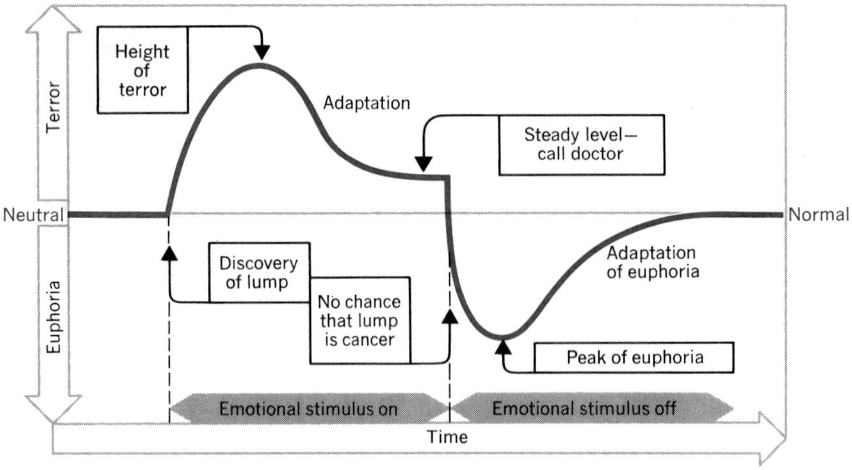

FIGURE 14.16
The dynamics of affect. Noticing a lump in her breast, the woman in the text example is at first terror-stricken. When her fear adapts somewhat, she arranges for an appointment with the doctor and finds that the lump is not malignant. Her reaction is one of euphoria, which also eventually abates. (Ideas from Solomon and Corbit, 1974.)

> will "label" this state and describe his feelings in terms of the cognitions available to him . . . precisely the same state of physiological arousal could be called "joy" or "fury" or any of the great diversity of emotional labels, depending on the cognitive aspects of the situation.

Temporal Dynamics of Affect

Richard Solomon and John Corbit (1974), from whom we have borrowed the title of this section, begin their presentation this way.

> First, we describe the kind of phenomenon which has caught our attention . . . a woman at work discovers a lump in her breast and immediately is terrified. She sits still, intermittenly weeping, or she paces the floor. After a few hours, she slowly regains her composure, stops crying, and begins to work. At this point, she is still tense and disturbed, but no longer terrified and distracted. She manifests the symptoms usually associated with intense anxiety. While in this state she calls her doctor for an appointment. A few hours later she is in his office, still tense, still frightened: She is obviously a very unhappy woman. The doctor makes his examination. He then informs her that there is no possibility of cancer, that there is nothing to worry about, and that her problem is just a clogged sebaceous gland requiring no medical attention.
>
> A few minutes later, the woman leaves the doctor's office, smiling, greeting strangers, and walking with an unusually buoyant stride. Her euphoric mood permeates all her activities as she resumed her normal duties. She exudes joy, which is not in character for her. A few hours later, however, she is working in her normal, perfunctory way. Her emotional expression is back to normal. She once more has the personality immediately recognizable by all of her friends. Gone is the euphoria, and there is no hint of the earlier terrifying experience of that day.

This woman's experience goes through a pattern of changes in time that Solomon and Corbit believe to be typical of emotional reactions (Figure 14.16). An emotional stimulus produces an emotional reaction which first increases to a peak of intensity. Then adaptation occurs, reducing the emotion to a steady level which may be maintained for some time. When the stimulus for emotion is taken away, not only does the emotion disappear but there is a transition to a very different state—from terror to euphoria in the example.

Solomon and Corbit believe that two opposed states or processes, opposed in the sense that they tend to cancel each other, underlie this pattern of emotional experience. They call the first of these hypothetical underlying states state A and the second state B. They believe state B to be a *slave process,* called forth whenever state A is in action (Figure 14.17). In order to understand the details of emotionality, it is necessary to assume that the two states themselves and the relationships between them are different the first time an emotion is experienced than they are after many such experiences.

The first time an emotion is experienced, state B is very weak and is completely overshadowed by state A, until the emotional stimulus is removed. When

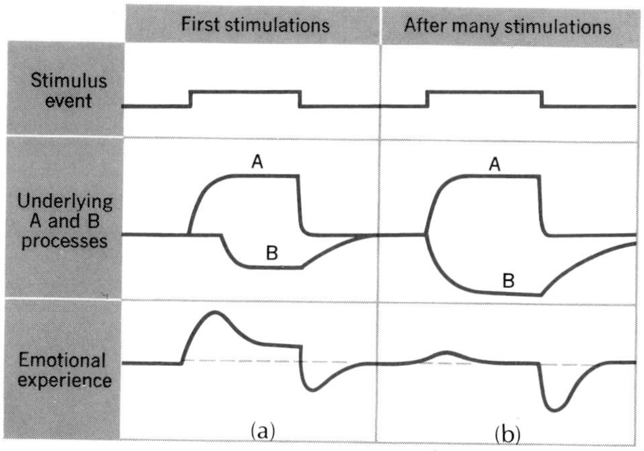

FIGURE 14.17

Opponent process theory of emotional experience. (*a*) An emotional event turns on an emotional response A, to which an opposing reaction B is tied. (*b*) With many stimulations the B process becomes stronger, whereas the A process remains unchanged. Emotional experience is determined by the differences in strength between the A and B processes. The bottom boxes indicate when in time the A and B processes are operating. (Adapted from Solomon and Corbit, 1974.)

this happens, state B is able to express itself (Figure 14.17*a*). Later emotional experiences are different, and Solomon and Corbit explain this by assuming that state B is strengthened with use and weakened with disuse, whereas state A remains unchanged (Figure 14.17*b*). These changing strengths of the two processes imply that after many experiences of the same emotional situation, the B process will dominate (Figure 14.17*b*).

Solomon and Corbit show that the pattern of emotional behavior predicted by their theory applies to many different emotions. They describe the reactions of a dog receiving an intense electric shock in an experiment that went on for many sessions.

> . . . The dog appeared to be terrified during the first few shocks. It screeched and thrashed about, its pupils dilated, its eyes bulged, its hair stood on end, its ears lay back, its tail curled between its legs. Expulsive defecation and urination, along with many other symptoms of intense autonomic nervous system activity, were seen. At this point, the dog was freed from the harness, it moved slowly about the room, appeared to be stealthy, hesitant, and unfriendly. Its "state" had suddenly changed from terror to stealthiness.
>
> . . . When the same dog was brought back for the same treatment day after day, its behavior gradually changed. During shocks, the signs of terror disappeared. Instead, the dog appeared pained, annoyed, or anxious, but not terrified. For example, it whined rather than shrieked, and showed no further urination, defecation, or struggling. Then, when released suddenly at the end of the session, the dog rushed about, jumped up on people, wagged its tail, in what we called at the time "a fit of joy." Finally, several minutes later, the dog was its normal self: friendly, but not racing about.

Solomon and Corbit go on to apply this **opponent process theory** of emotion in many interesting examples. They draw from the work of Seymour Epstein (1967) on the reactions of sport parachutists for one illustration. On their first few jumps novice parachutists react with terror (state A) in the period just before and during the jump; after the jump (state B) they are stunned and stony silent. After many jumps their state A experience is one of tense and eager excitement, much less intense than the fear they felt earlier. Their state B reaction is jubilant exhilaration, very different from their earlier numbness.

Or take the case of a man who has a wife or a lover whom he loses. His early emotional responses to the woman are full of ecstacy, excitement, and happiness. If he loses her at this point, the response to her loss is loneliness. After many years the first reaction (state A) has weakened to one of contentment and comfort. But now the experience of losing her (state B) is agony and grief of long duration.

Solomon and Corbit add to their theory the idea that the opposing emotional states are both conditionable to environmental stimuli, something which we have long known, in a more general way, to be possible. Conditionability complicates the theory, but emotions are complex experiences. Explanations probably need to be complicated. The opponent process theory is the most attractive explanation of emotions available at present.

SUMMARY □

Individuals experiencing an emotion are in a stirred-up state, both mentally and physiologically. Contrary to the evidence of personal experience, it turns out that the condition of physiological arousal is probably the same or similar for all emotions. The emotions we experience are different because of our interpretations of emotional situations. We are particularly able to label emotion by situation when we do not understand why we are physiologically aroused.

Emotions follow a dependable sequence of changes over time. An emotional situation induces an emotional reaction which reaches a peak and then decreases to a steady level. Removal of the emotion-producing stimulus brings an emotional reaction that

"My first and only jump was the most exciting and exhilarating experience I have ever had in my life, but I would never, never, ever jump again." This comment by a sport parachutist who dropped out of training reveals his opposing emotions.

is the opposite of the first reaction. With experience, the initial reaction loses intensity and the later reaction gains in intensity.

CONFLICT

The state of conflict is one with which we are all familiar. We experience conflict when we must forgo one goal in order to attain another. In terms of emotions, conflict is a state in which opposite feelings tug at one another. For instance, sexual and aggressive tendencies run counter to the morals of society. Deciding on the future usually generates conflict—whether to accept a new job, whether to go on to graduate school, whether to have another child, whether to hold ground or retreat before an antagonist, whether to protest the regulations of authority or conform, and so on and so on. Obviously situations generating conflict are so numerous that a way of classifying them by type would help bring order to a chaotic scene. The work of Kurt Lewin, first at Berlin University, then at the University of Iowa, and later at MIT, provided the beginnings of such a classification. Later on Neal Miller at Yale refined the classification.

Types of Conflict

Motives, investigators observed, are always directed toward or away from some object or state of affairs, which makes it possible to refer to them as approach and avoidance tendencies. Conflicts have been classified on this basis. Four major types of conflict, conceived in these terms, can be identified.

Approach-Approach Conflict The first type of conflict is between two attractive alternatives. Suppose you enter a lottery and win the first prize, which is either an all-expenses-paid trip to Europe or an automobile whose value is almost exactly the same as the cost of the trip. Suppose further that for years you have wanted to visit Europe, that the itinerary can be almost entirely of your own devising, and that there are many, many places you would like to see. But suppose, on the other hand, that you have always wanted a car, that this one is almost exactly what you had decided you would like to own, and that there are many ways in which owning a car would simplify your life. Which do you choose? The fact that the choice would be difficult indicates the existence of conflict.

Actually, important approach-approach conflicts are a rarity. More often the conflict is quite a simple one and easily resolved. Shall I wear this outfit or that one? Shall I go to the early movie or the later one? Play poker or go bowling? Read or watch TV? *Scientific American* or *The New Yorker?* Campari or a gin and tonic? Take roses or a bottle of wine? These questions describe approach-approach conflicts of more ordinary proportions. Approach-approach conflicts become serious only when selection of one alternative means the loss of an important second alterna-

Kurt Lewin.

Neal Miller.

tive. Such conflicts are the stuff of which daydreams are made. They seem to exist only in fantasies that begin with expressions like, "Suppose you enter a lottery and win the first prize. . . ."

Avoidance-Avoidance Conflicts Avoidance-avoidance conflicts are common and important. The pain of a toothache makes you suspect you should go to the dentist; you put the visit off, however, because you know it will be unpleasant. It is late and you are tired, but your schedule tells you that you should study for another hour on one of two dull subjects. Which should you study? It is a lovely Saturday morning that deserves to be enjoyed, but the lawn needs mowing and the garden is full of weeds; you really should mow or weed the garden. The term is over and your grades are a disappointment. You have promised to call your mother at home or your father at work to report your marks. Both will be unhappy but in different ways. What do you do?

In all these situations both alternatives are unpleasant; you would rather do neither, but an important consideration—your health, your success in college, the opinion of your neighbors about the appearance of your property, a promise—compels you to take one of the painful courses of action. This is the critical point of an avoidance-avoidance conflict: there is some powerful force in the situation that requires you to do one of two things, both of which you would rather not do.

Approach-Avoidance Conflicts In an approach-avoidance conflict the same object or situation is simultaneously attractive and unattractive; there are tendencies both to approach and to avoid it. Approach-avoidance conflict is often at the base of important problems of adjustment. A young woman is driven toward a sexual affair but is inhibited by moral values. An adolescent would like to have it out with a parent but is prevented from doing so by guilt or the fear of punishment. A student is curious and would like to take a new and difficult subject but is worried about possible failure. In all these situations the conflict is between the pull of positive factors—sexual desire, aggression, curiosity—and the push of negative ones—moral values, fear of punishment, fear of failure.

Multiple Approach-Avoidance Conflicts Most of the important decisions individuals make in life require a choice between two or more alternatives, each of which would, by itself, put them in a simpler approach-avoidance conflict. One such conflict which almost all people face at least once is choosing between two job offers or between keeping a present job and taking a new one. Such decisions can be exceedingly difficult. One job might have certain advantages—desirable location, convenient distance from family, good salary; but it also has disadvantages—little chance of rapid advancement, poor "fringe benefits," long workweek. The alternative position has its own virtues—excellent housing available for employees, initial appointment at a higher level, a prestigious organization; but also its own drawbacks—company's reputation for letting employees go after a few years of service, probability of being required to move often, policies of management undergoing change. On other important matters

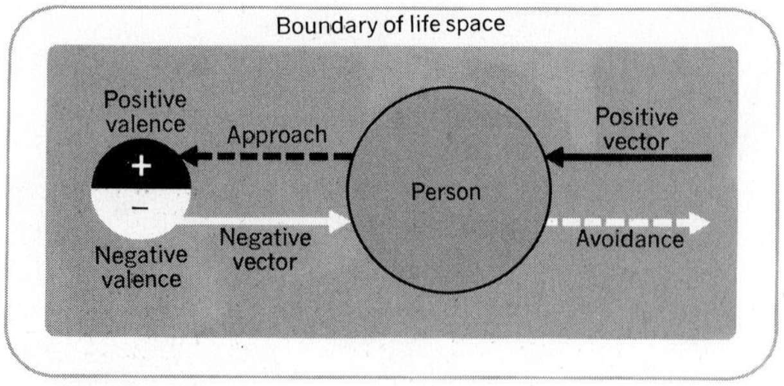

FIGURE 14.18

Approach-avoidance conflict as analyzed by Kurt Lewin. The positive valence in the ambivalent object generates a positive vector which, in turn, creates a tendency to locomote toward or approach the object. The negative valence generates a negative vector and locomotion away from or avoidance of the object. The two sets of positive and negative factors together create the conflict.

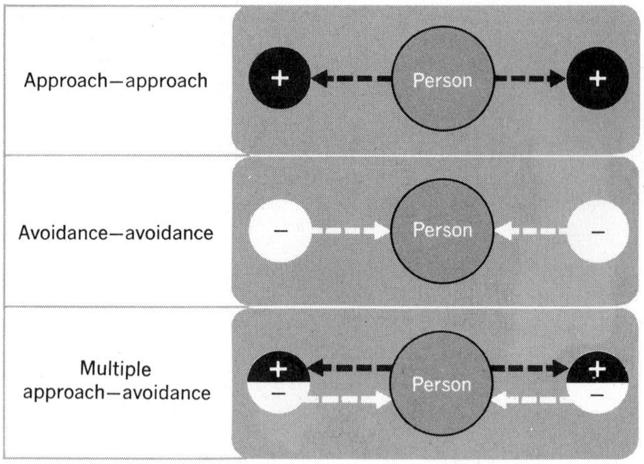

FIGURE 14.19

Simplified diagrams for three forms of conflict. Here arrows represent direction of locomotion, approach and avoidant tendencies, rather than Lewinian vectors.

the opportunities seem about equal. Which job should be selected?

This common example makes two aspects of multiple approach-avoidance conflicts clear: first, the matters being considered are important, and second, the "pros" and "cons" are seldom simple opposites. The second raises the problem of how to weigh the advantages and disadvantages. How much does a desirable location count? Enough to balance some of the long workweeks on the same job or the fact that the other organization has the prestige? Such considerations are seldom resolved easily or without painful second thoughts once a decision has been made.

The Structure of Conflicts

Although they used different vocabularies to describe conflicts, Lewin and Miller developed very similar models for them. In addition, Lewin used a standard type of diagram to represent his model. Figure 14.18 is a Lewin diagram for approach-avoidance conflict, given in some detail. Figure 14.19 consists of simpler diagrams for the other types of conflict. The important concepts in this model of conflict are the following.

- **Valence** (Lewin's term) or *incentive value* (Miller's), indicated by plus and minus signs. These refer to the positive and negative features of objects and activities. In approach-avoidance and multiple approach-avoidance conflicts, positive and negative valences reside in the same objects, making them *ambivalent.*
- **Vector** (Lewin's term) or *drive* (Miller's), indicated by the arrows driving the individual toward or away from the valent object.
- **Locomotion** (Lewin's term) or *response* (Miller's), indicated by the broken arrows labeled approach and avoidance, suggesting the path the person would take if each of the driving forces existed alone in the situation.
- **Life space** or **field** (Lewin's term) or *situation* (Miller's), represented by the boundary of each diagram. In the avoidance-avoidance conflict this boundary is particularly important, for it corresponds to the considerations that require the individual to accept one undesirable alternative or the other. Were it not for these limiting boundaries, neither response would be made and the person would leave the field, that is, avoid the situation entirely.

Conflict Resolution

Conflict puts a person in a painful frame of mind, increasingly painful as the conflicting urges increase in strength. Although there are exceptions to this general rule, approach-approach and avoidance-avoidance conflicts tend to be less painful and therefore easier to resolve than the other two types of conflict. Usually a person quickly chooses one of the desirable or undesirable alternatives and dismisses the other. Approach-avoidance and multiple approach-avoidance conflicts are more complicated and more difficult to handle.

One complicating factor of an object about which we feel ambivalent is that its positive and negative aspects both increase in strength as we approach the object. Simple positive and negative situations will help to make this point clear. When you were small and waiting for Christmas or a birthday, tension and anticipation grew with time until it seemed almost impossible to wait any longer. Escapes from reformatories reportedly increase as the time for normal release approaches. Apparently the desire for freedom increases dramatically as prisoners near the end

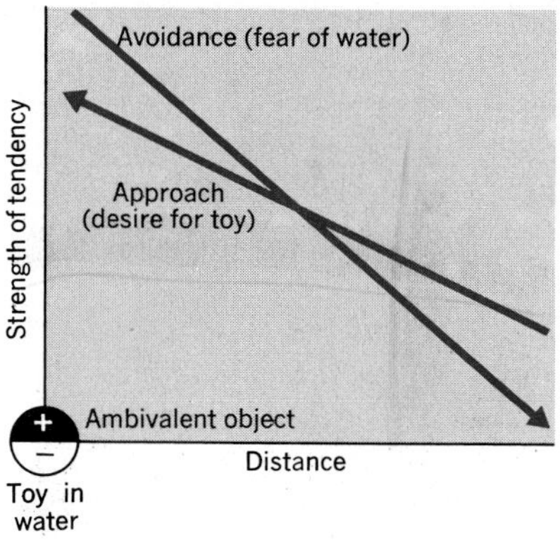

FIGURE 14.20
Approach and avoidance gradients combined form a model for conflict. Tendencies to approach and avoid increase with nearness to the ambivalent object, but the avoidant tendency increases more rapidly and reaches a higher absolute value. In the specific situation cited in the text, ambivalence is made up of the positive value of the the desirable toy and the negative fear aroused by its presence in dangerous waters. (After Miller, 1959.)

of their sentence. If a person is afraid of snakes, wild animals, or insects, even the thought or a picture of the fearful beast may cause a little of the same panic that the animal itself would. The actual presence of the animal heightens fear greatly, however.

To show the operation of such positive and negative tendencies working together, let us deal with Lewin's classical example of approach-avoidance conflict. A little boy at the seashore sees a desirable toy in the water. He wants the toy and goes toward it, but he is also afraid of the water and tends to hold back. As a result the child goes partway to the toy and stops, afraid to go any closer. It is as though the point at which the little boy stops is the spot where the positive tendency to approach and the negative one to avoid are about equal, each canceling the effect of the other.

Neal Miller (1959) has used a graphic method to describe approach-avoidance conflicts (Figure 14.20). As a person nears the ambivalent object, the toy in the water in our example, the approach and avoidance tendencies both become stronger. The function showing the increasing avoidance tendency is steeper than that for the approach tendency, however, and it rises to a higher final level. The result is that the gradients cross. In order to understand the child's behavior, we need only this simple rule. At distances at which approach is stronger than avoidance, the child goes toward the ambivalent object; at distances at which avoidance is stronger than approach, the child retreats. This means that the child will stop his approach partway to the toy—at exactly the point where the gradients intersect.

This theory gains great strength from an additional assumption, that the **approach gradient** and the **avoidance gradient,** as the two functions in Figure 14.20 are called, can be raised or lowered in various ways. Anything that increases the child's fear of the water will raise the gradient and keep him farther away from his goal. Anything that makes the toy seem more attractive or the water less fearful will raise the approach gradient or lower the avoidance gradient, so that the child comes closer. If the approach gradient is raised enough, or if the avoidance gradient is lowered enough, the child will go all the way to the goal and retrieve the toy from the water.

Decisions under Stress

Multiple approach-avoidance conflicts consist of at least two, but usually more than two, simple approach-avoidance conflicts. The psychological processes involved in resolving multiple approach-avoidance conflicts will inevitably be enormously complex. For this reason studies of such conflict resolution have been few.

Yet it is very important to try to understand the behavior of people in multiple approach-avoidance conflicts because it so often goes wrong. A man chooses one job over another, after what he believes is careful deliberation, but finds that he has made a mistake. Now, with the job market difficult, he is stuck with his wrong decision. A gifted woman artist chooses to marry but finds, in a few years, that running a household for husband and children seriously limits the time she can spend painting. Deeply frustrated, she thinks of divorce. President Kennedy, looking back and realizing how badly he had miscalculated in making the conflict-ridden decision approving the Bay of Pigs invasion, asks, "How could I have been so stupid?" (Janis and Mann, 1977a).

A part of the answer to the question President Kennedy asked himself so plainly, and to the questions the people in our other examples must have asked themselves too, is that significant and fateful decisions are made under great stress. Such decisions are of great consequence, which alone makes them stressful. And being in a state of conflict adds to the level of stress.

In recent years Irving Janis of Yale University and Leon Mann of Flinders University of South Australia have begun to make good progress in the analysis of multiple approach-avoidance conflicts (Janis and Mann, 1977a, 1977b). For example, they have identified a mode of resolving conflicts and have described courses to follow in making effective decisions.

Janis and Mann consider, in particular, situations in which some project a person is engaged in seems not to be going well, the future appears ominous, and the individual should at least be considering alternative lines of action. The situation puts the person in conflict. Janis and Mann identify five patterns of coping with such conflict.

1. *Unconflicted adherence.* The decision-maker complacently decides to continue whatever he has been doing, ignoring information about the risk of losses.
2. *Unconflicted change* to a new course of action. The decision-maker uncritically adopts whichever new course of action is most salient or most strongly recommended to him.
3. *Defensive avoidance.* The decision-maker evades the conflict by procrastinating, shifting responsibility to someone else, or constructing wishful rationalizations and remaining selectively inattentive to corrective information.
4. *Hypervigilance.* The decision-maker searches frantically for a way out of the dilemma and impulsively seizes upon a hastily contrived solution that seems to promise immediate relief, overlooking the full range of consequences of his choice because of emotional excitement, repetitive thinking, and cognitive constriction (manifested by reduction in immediate memory span and simplistic ideas). In its most extreme form, hypervigilance is referred to as "panic."
5. *Vigilance.* The decision-maker searches painstakingly for relevant information, assimilates it in an unbiased manner, and appraises alternatives carefully before making a choice.

Only the last of these patterns, vigilance, is an effective mode of conflict resolution. Janis and Mann have developed a number of ways in which they attempt to help people in conflict arrive at decisions in a more vigilant manner. One of their methods is not unlike a procedure described by Benjamin Franklin some 200 years ago. Franklin recommended that people take a sheet of paper and rule it down the middle to make two columns, one for each of the two alternatives. Then, as they think of arguments for and against each, they should write them down in the appropriate column. When they find two positive or negative terms that about balance each other, they cross them off the lists. Or, if they find one item that about balances two on the other side of the ledger, all three are crossed out. The course of action to follow has the balance of positive items in its favor at the end of this process.

Janis and Mann have enlarged upon Franklin's advice. They provide much more detailed guidance for the decision maker by spelling out more of the details. The elements of conflict in any important decision can be classified, they say, into the following four categories. We have illustrated them with items that would apply when a person is choosing between two jobs.

1 *Utilitarian Personal Gains and Losses* This category includes salary, fringe benefits, whether work is interesting, geographical location of company, and other considerations that apply most directly to the decision maker.
2 *Utilitarian Gains and Losses for Significant Others* Such matters as social status of the family, educational opportunities for the children, and effects on relationships with family and friends would be included here.
3 *Self-Approval or Disapproval* Will taking one job or the other enhance or diminish the decision maker's self-image as a moral person, a decisive person, a legal person?
4 *Social Approval or Disapproval* How will family members, close friends, the profession, the media evaluate a decision to take one job or the other?

In the actual process of conflict resolution, Janis and Mann have the decision maker prepare a **balance sheet grid** of the type illustrated in Table 14.1. The individual fills this grid with pluses and minuses to indicate advantages and disadvantages of the alternatives. This procedure assures that the decision maker's course of action will be those Janis and Mann

TABLE 14.1
Balance Sheet Grid for Conflict Resolution

Considerations	Job A	Job B
1. *Utilitarian personal gains and losses* Salary Fringe benefits Chances of advancement Security Location Etc.		
2. *Utilitarian gains and losses for significant others* Status of family Educational Institutions Distance from family Time for family Etc.		
3. *Self-approval or disapproval* Social value of work Creativity of work Self-esteem from selection Requirements for personal compromise Etc.		
4. *Social approval or disapproval* Colleagues Professional organizations Friends Family Etc.		

Adapted from Janis and Mann, 1977a.

find are taken in making all well-thought-out decisions: a thorough consideration of objectives, a thorough canvassing of alternatives, a search for new information if such information turns out to be necessary, a consideration of this information without bias, a periodic reevaluation of consequences as the decision process goes on, and careful planning for implementation of whatever decision is arrived at.

Janis and Mann and various others have used the balance sheet grid in experiments in which people have had to make significant decisions. The result has been better decisions in the sense that, by comparison with members of control groups who did not employ the grid, the subjects have been better satisfied with their decisions later on.

SUMMARY □

Conflict occurs in situations in which incompatible urges are aroused in the individual at one and the same time. The conflicting urges are of two types, to approach and to avoid. Combinations of these approach and avoidant tendencies produce four identifiable types of conflict: approach-approach, avoidance-avoidance, approach-avoidance, and multiple approach-avoidance conflict. The first two types of conflict are usually simple and usually easy to resolve. The second two are more complex and difficult. The complexity stems partly from the fact that the strengths of approach and avoidance urges are both greater the nearer the individual is to an object or state of affairs that arouses them both. In multiple approach-avoidance conflict, the many conflicting elements add further complexity. Attempts to resolve significant and fateful multiple approach-avoidance conflicts are usually made under great stress, often resulting in poor decisions. Recently developed procedures that help clarify the nature of such conflicts and that plan for resolution have been shown to be effective.

TO BE SURE YOU UNDERSTAND THIS CHAPTER △

The following list of important concepts covers most of the substance of Chapter 14. The sections that are not covered are discussions of the nature of motives, punishment, and anxiety.

Instinct (as used in instinct theory)
Ethology
Instinct (as used in ethology)
Imprinting
Critical period
Action-specific energy
Innate releasing mechanism
Fixed-action pattern
Displacement behavior
Encephalization
Libido
Consummatory behavior
Substitute behavior
Drive stimulus
Coolidge effect
Emotion
Opponent process theory
Conflict
Approach-approach conflict
Avoidance-avoidance conflict
Approach-avoidance conflict
Multiple approach-avoidance conflicts
Valence
Vector
Life space
Approach gradient
Avoidance gradient
Unconflicted adherence
Unconflicted change
Defensive avoidance
Hypervigilance
Vigilance
Balance sheet grid

TO GO BEYOND THIS CHAPTER △

In this book Motives developed chiefly through experience are discussed in Chapter 6 under the heading Classical-Operant Interactions. Chapter 16 includes a discussion of Maslow's view of motivation, which in his hands becomes a theory of personality.

Elsewhere Any of several new books on motivation expand on the topics in this chapter. A good reference book for specific topics remains the encyclopedic volume by Charles Cofer and Mortimer Appley, *Motivation: Theory and Research*. Several of the references we have used in this chapter are well within your grasp: Eibl-Eibesfeldt (1970), Janis and Mann (1977a, b), and Solomon and Corbit (1974).

CH. 15

Social and Emotional Development

As children mature, their social and emotional characteristics undergo major changes. The newborn infant is a social being, but indiscriminately so. With development social responses become increasingly specific. The types of experience that generate emotional reactions also change. Social tasks that challenge or distress the young child are very different from those that are difficult for the adolescent or adult. Yet, since some of the most fundamental aspects of personality, such as trust or mistrust of others, appear to be established in the first year or so of life, infants' social and emotional behavior is of special interest to psychologists.

EMOTIONAL BEHAVIOR IN INFANCY

Darwin was one of the first scientists to investigate emotional expressions in infants. In his book *The Expression of the Emotions in Man and Animals* (1872), he suggested that the emotions of the human newborn are innately determined. Some years later John Watson and J. J. B. Morgan (1917) modified Darwin's view and theorized that there are only three innate emotions—fear, rage, and love—and that all other emotional reactions are derived from these primary ones through learning. *Fear,* according to these investigators, could be elicited by an unexpected loud noise or sudden loss of support; *rage* occurred when the infant was immobilized or restrained; and *love* was the response to stroking and gentling.

As popular as Watson and Morgan's theory became, it is now only of historical interest since others have generally been unable to confirm the existence of these emotions by the means suggested. An important reason for this failure is that observers cannot usually agree on what to call a given emotional reaction unless they are told what stimulus or incident brought it on. An infant who is hungry generally cries; observers who do not know the reason for the behavior may call it grief, fear, anger, sleepiness, or other emotions. When the stimulus *is* known, it usually becomes the entire basis for labeling the emotion. An observer who sees an infant restrained is likely to say the baby is angry; if threat is present, the response will be judged as fearful.

A theory that competed with Watson and Morgan's and still enjoys some popularity is that of Katharine Bridges (1932). She maintained that the infant is born with one basic emotion, a generalized excitement. Through a process of maturation, this excitement is differentiated into delight and distress, which in turn lead to more specific emotional expressions. This process of differentiation and the ages at which the various emotions appear are presented in Figure 15.1.

Katharine Banham Bridges.

Smiling

As delightful and intriguing as infants' smiles and laughter may be, psychologists have yet to agree on why children engage in them. These responses are universal in humans and appear to be unlearned. The smile is usually seen sometime in the first month of life, and laughter appears at about four months of age. That these responses have a biological component is suggested by the fact that even children born deaf, dumb, and blind smile and laugh. Experience is also important, however, since the course of smiling in blind infants has been found to be slower than that in sighted children (Freedman, 1964).

The Development of Smiling In the first year of life there appear to be three stages of smiling. Soon after birth there is **spontaneous** or **reflex** smiling, which usually occurs in the absence of appropriate stimuli. The infant will smile in response to stomach disturbance or to high-pitched voices, for example. In the second stage, which begins between two and eight weeks of age, the infant smiles to visual and social stimuli. This is called **nonselective social smiling,** since the infant smiles most readily when a human face appears. At about five or six months of age, **selective social smiling** begins. Now the infant smiles chiefly to familiar faces, and unfamiliar faces sometimes elicit crying.

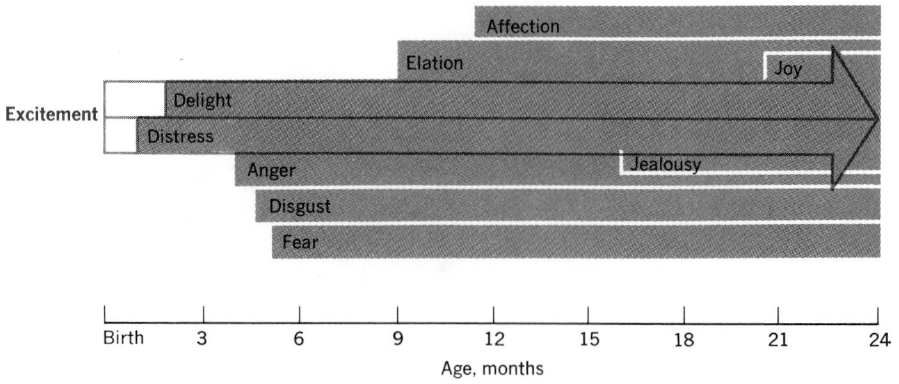

FIGURE 15.1
Approximate ages of differentiation of various emotions. Early in development excitement is first differentiated into general positive (delight) and general negative (distress) affects; these emotions are then differentiated into more specific emotional states. (Adapted from Bridges, 1932.)

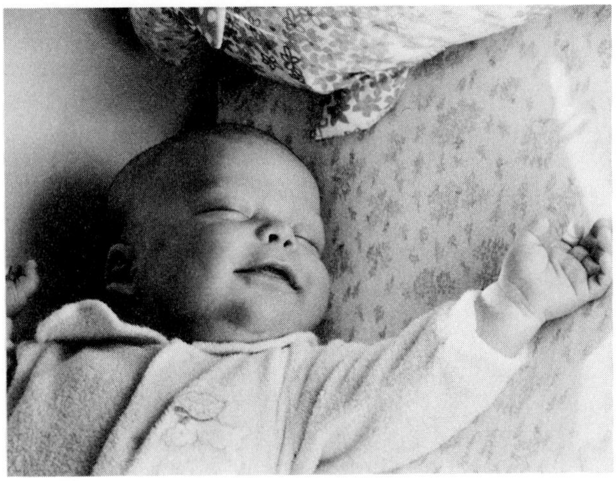

Reflex smiling.

How much a child smiles can be influenced by child-rearing factors. Infants smile more when an adult coos and cuddles and smiles back at them (Brackbill, 1958). Similarly, smiling can be extinguished by the adult's unresponsiveness.

Jacob Gewirtz (1965) examined the smiling of infants raised in different child-rearing settings in Israel. One group lived with their families. Another group resided in an institution where the babies rarely saw their parents. A third were kibbutz infants who were raised in large children's houses with professional caretakers, but whose mothers visited them at feeding times. Gewirtz found that the groups of children varied in how much they smiled to the face of an unfamiliar, unsmiling adult during a two-minute period (Figure 15.2). The children raised in an institution were approximately one month slower than the others in developing a strong smiling response, and then their amount of smiling declined more rapidly. The kibbutz children resembled the family-raised children in the early months, but later the number of their smiles was intermediate between those of the institutionalized and family-raised groups. Gewirtz interpreted these findings in terms of the children's reinforcement histories. Children in family settings are much more likely to be picked up, fondled, and spoken to when they smile than children in an institution or kibbutz. Thus smiling may be enhanced by rewarding children with attention when they smile.

Cognitive Theory of Smiling One theory that attempts to explain why smiling occurs at all holds that a smile reflects an innate emotion of joy experienced by children when they master cognitive tasks (Shultz and Zigler, 1970). This view is derived from Piaget's concepts of assimilation and accommodation (page 292). The infant finds a new visual object puzzling because it cannot be assimilated easily into his or her cognitive framework. The infant must therefore accommodate, or construct an internal representation of it. Once this is done, the child should be able to assimilate the object. This accomplishment provides gratification and leads to smiling.

This theory predicts that a child will take longer to smile to a more complex visual stimulus than to a simpler one. To test this expectation, investigators showed three-month-old infants a clown doll which was either stationary or swinging. The swinging doll was the more complex stimulus, since the contours of an object are more difficult to define when it is moving than when it is stationary. Although the infants smiled in both situations, they smiled more quickly when the clown was stationary. That the smile was preceded by hard cognitive work seemed to be reflected in the very quiet and serious way the infants studied the stimulus before smiling.

A similar phenomenon probably explains the amusement we experience when hearing a joke. Cer-

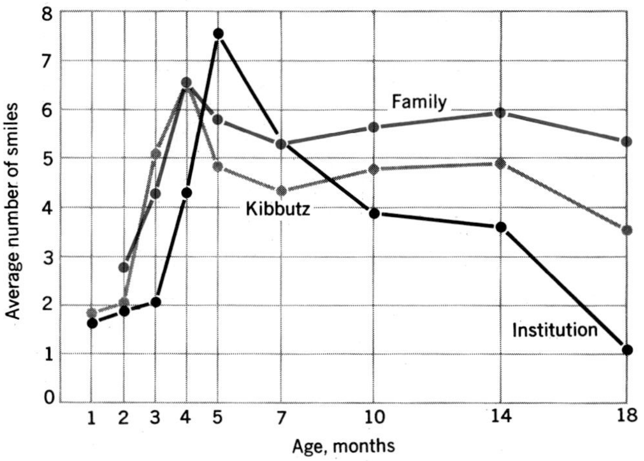

FIGURE 15.2
The amount of smiling at strangers during a two-minute period by infants reared in three different manners. (Adapted from Gewirtz, 1965.)

tainly a portion of our pleasure derives from our success in using our cognitive abilities to "get the point of" the joke. Thus a joke that we have heard and figured out before never seems as funny in the retelling. Analogously, jokes that must be explained to us never strike us as being as funny as those we master on our own.

Evolutionary Theory of Smiling A theory that emphasizes the adaptive and survival value of infant smiling has also been advanced (Freedman, Loring, and Martin, 1967). The baby is born with the ability both to cry and to smile. Crying has obvious survival value, for it usually brings parental behavior that reduces the infant's discomfort. In return, the parent is pleased to have turned off a noxious stimulus, the baby's cry, and to have a sense that all is now well with the infant. The mutuality of emotions of infant and parent in such situations probably represents the beginnings of attachment between child and parent. Any phenomenon that cements this attachment is in the best interest of the infant's survival.

With perhaps the exception of the baby's cry, nothing captures the parent's attention more effectively than the baby's smile. As noted earlier, a parent's face is a particularly strong stimulus for smiling. The infant's smile has survival value because the adult receives pleasure from the smile and increases his or her caretaking and interaction with the infant. Thus the smile, like the cry, assures that the infant's needs will be met and solidifies the attachment between parent and child.

Fear

The Nature of Children's Fears Although Watson's view that fear is an innate response to loud noises or the sudden loss of support is no longer accepted, many psychologists continue to feel that there is an innate component to many fears. In addition to being considered innate, some fears, such as those of darkness and animals, are theorized to mature at different times (Valentine, 1930). For example, Donald Hebb (1949) argued that fear of snakes is a product of psychological maturation rather than of learning. He supported his view with evidence that children about five years old showed little fear of snakes, but adolescents recoiled in horror from a harmless snake. Interestingly, the same pattern is found in chimpanzees—the young do not fear snakes but adults do.

Although there is controversy over exactly what fears are innate, psychologists agree that many fears are learned. For example, pain is a natural stimulus for fear, but things, persons, and events associated with it can also become feared—the pediatrician's needle, the dentist's drill, and the doctors themselves. Fears of objects and events not associated with pain may also be learned, as shown by findings that children adopt the fears that their mothers have (Hagman, 1932).

Cognitive factors are important in determining the nature and intensity of children's fears. The newborn indicates fear of only a very few events, but with development the number of both real and imagined stimuli capable of producing fear increases enormously. At first children tend to be fearful of physical events directly associated with pain. Later the objects of fear remain concrete, such as lions and tigers, but their connection with pain is less direct or absent. Still later children begin to fear abstract events such as failure in school. The changing nature of children's fears between birth and six years of age may be seen in Figure 15.3. That children's fears are related to level of cognitive development is also indicated by the finding that brighter children express more fears than their less intelligent age-mates (Jersild and Holmes, 1935).

Fear of Strangers and Separation Anxiety Two fears that appear toward the end of the first year of life are stranger anxiety and separation anxiety. **Stranger anxiety** refers to the infant's negative response at the approach of a stranger. **Separation anxiety** is the unhappiness, crying, and fretting of the child when a parent or other adult to whom he or she is attached is absent. Both fears have cognitive as well as emotional determinants, since they do not occur until the child has matured enough to discriminate familiar from unfamiliar faces and has achieved object constancy—that is, an awareness that persons continue to exist when not in view.

The developmental course of stranger and separation anxieties can be seen in a study of infants from four to twelve months old (Morgan and Ricciuti, 1969). Each

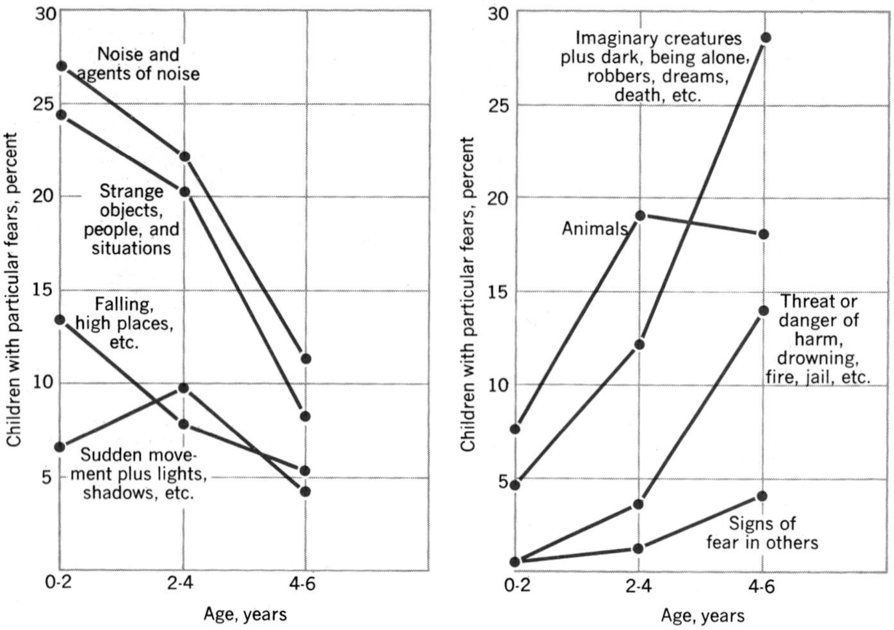

Figure 15.3
Frequency of fears at different ages. (Adapted from Jersild, 1960.)

infant sat either on the mother's lap or four feet away from her when a stranger approached. Before eight months of age the infants cooed, smiled, and were generally positive toward the stranger regardless of how close they were to their mothers (Figure 15.4). Later, however, proximity played a critical role. By twelve months infants who were separated from their mothers showed a much more negative reaction to the stranger than the infants sitting on their mothers' laps.

Many psychologists have treated stranger anxiety as a universal phenomenon which is expected to appear at a certain age and which is even considered a sign of normal development. This widely accepted view has been challenged by Harriet Rheingold and Carol Eckerman (1973). These researchers pointed to methodological flaws in the earlier studies that had supported the universality of stranger anxiety. They also presented evidence that infants between eight and twelve months of age are not always afraid of strangers. In fact, the infants in their study repeatedly looked and smiled at the stranger, played peek-a-boo, and permitted the stranger to hold them whether or not the mother was present.

Rheingold and Eckerman (1970) have also shown that infants are much more ready to leave their mothers in order to carry out exploratory activities than was previously believed. Once children are able to creep, they will leave their mothers, even in a strange environment, in order to explore a distant empty room. The distinction between voluntary and involuntary separation is important, however, for children whose mothers are unavailable to them become very distressed and do not explore. Thus stranger and separation anxieties are complex phenomena which seem to appear only under certain conditions.

SUMMARY □

Emotional development shows a pattern of increasing differentiation from a generalized excitement into progressively more precise emotional reactions. Certain emotions in infants have been studied extensively. Smiling, for example, is an important social response which appears to be universal among human infants. It is easily elicited in young babies by many stimuli but becomes a specific response to particular people as the infant matures. There appears to be a significant cognitive component to smiling, since infants and older children may smile to denote their intrinsic satisfaction in having mastered a challenging task. Smiling, like crying, may also have survival value to the child.

Another emotion with important implications for social development is fear. Some fears may be innate, but many are learned. Children's fears are related to their level of cognitive development: younger children fear concrete objects and events, especially those associated with pain, whereas older children fear more abstract things such as ghosts and failure in school. The most widely studied fears of infants are separation anxiety and fear of strangers. These appear to be related, since infants are more likely to have

Stranger anxiety.

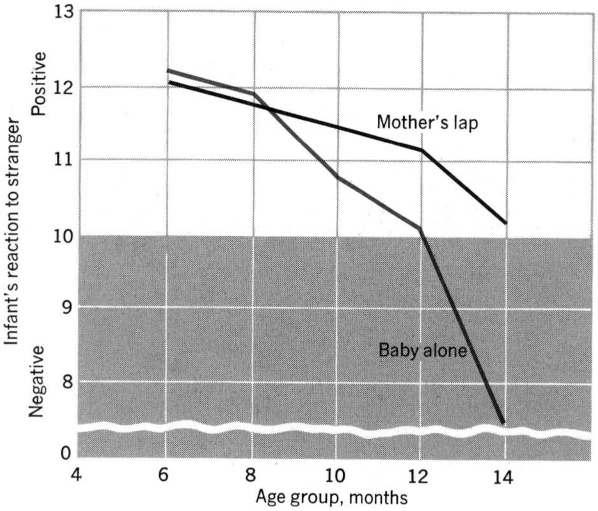

FIGURE 15.4

Reactions to strangers. Infants in various age groups react differently to a stranger, depending on how close they are to their mothers. (From Morgan and Ricciuti, 1969.)

negative reactions to strangers when separated from their mothers.

INDIVIDUALITY IN DEVELOPMENT

So far we have focused on general principles in the development of emotional behavior. In this section we shall examine variations in social and emotional development that stem from the individuals themselves. From the time of birth children differ from one another in many traits. Some of these traits will always distinguish one individual from another. Because of their diverse natures, even children who are exposed to similar environmental conditions and child-rearing practices will not turn out to be the same, for each of them will react differently to the experiences. Moreover, as we shall see, different individuals seem to "invite" different social experiences. Thus, as in Piaget's view of cognitive growth, individuals appear to play an active role in bringing about their own personality development. The parents' attitudes and behavior, the cultural milieu, the educational opportunities are all important in social and emotional development, but so are the individual's own characteristics.

Temperamental Styles

Although the newborns in a hospital nursery may appear very similar, they differ greatly in general activity level, sensitivity to external stimuli, social responsiveness, and sleeping and feeding patterns. Moreover, many of these individual characteristics seem to persist as the infant grows older. There is a remarkable constancy in traits which Alexander Thomas, Stella Chess, Herbert Birch, and their colleagues (Thomas and Chess, 1977; Thomas, Chess, and Birch, 1968) have identified as making up an individual's **temperament** or **temperamental style.** These traits include activity level, regularity of biological functions, approach or withdrawal to new situations, adaptability to changes in routine, level of sensory threshold, intensity of response, mood, attention span and persistence, and distractibility.

In their major research study these investigators observed individuals from infancy through adolescence in an effort to determine the relation between temperament and mental health. They identified three types of temperament in infants, although many babies were not a pure type.

The majority of children were in the first category, called the **easy child.** These children had a pleasant mood and were regular in their hunger, sleep, and excretion patterns. They tended to approach new objects or persons, and the intensity of their responses was generally low or moderate.

The second category consisted of children who were **slow to warm up.** These children were wary of new situations and people and had a slightly negative mood. They were somewhat variable in biological functions, and the intensity of their responses was generally low.

About one in ten babies was in the third category, called the **difficult child.** These children rather quickly became tyrants of the household. They were irregular in feeding and sleeping and slow in accepting new foods or adjusting to new routines or activities. They tended to cry a great deal and quite loudly and seemed to be unhappy, unfriendly, and unpleasant; frustration usually sent them into a tantrum.

These temperamental styles appeared to be independent of sex or intelligence, but they were related to the development of behavioral problems during childhood or adolescence. Of the easy children 18 percent developed behavioral problems judged serious enough to warrant psychiatric attention. In comparison, 40 percent of the slow-to-warm-up children and 70 percent of the difficult children were considered to need help.

Origins of Temperament

What accounts for these differences in temperament among children? Thomas and Chess sought clues in the children's developmental histories and in their parents' traits and child-rearing practices, but none of these factors could predict the type of temperament a child would have. Because differences in temperament are observed so early in life and remain rather fixed, the individual's temperamental style may be a constitutional characteristic—something which he or she is born with and which stems from the very structure of the nervous system or the nature of physiological functioning. Evidence that genetic inheritance may play a role in the development of temperament has been obtained by a Norwegian investigator, A. M. Torgersen (cited in Segal and Yahraes, 1978), who found that identical twins—those who have the same genes—were more likely to have similar temperaments than fraternal twins.

Physiological functioning may reflect other than genetic factors. The results of a study by Arnold Sameroff and Melvin Zax (Sameroff, 1977; Sameroff and Zax, 1973) suggest that temperament may be fashioned by physiological and chemical influences on the brain as it develops before birth. These investigators conducted a longitudinal research project to determine what factors may lead to emotional disorders in children. Women were given a psychiatric interview late in pregnancy, and their children were examined soon after birth and at four, twelve, and thirty months of age on a variety of neurological and psychological tests. Interestingly, children who were labeled difficult at four months of age had mothers who had suffered high levels of anxiety in late pregnancy. Difficult children were also more likely to be black, to be of low socioeconomic status, and to have many siblings. These sociological factors are related to a mother's health and nutrition, which are known to affect the developing fetus. Thus sociological factors may have affected the child's temperament prenatally through these intervening conditions of the mother. Or these factors may have had a postnatal effect in the first three or four months of life.

Implications of Temperamental Differences

Behavioral and temperamental differences observed even in early infancy have at least three significant implications for the child's development. First behavior patterns once thought to be the outcome of poor child-rearing practices may actually be constitutional characteristics of the child. Thomas, Chess, and Birch explain it this way.

> A child who stands at the periphery of the group in nursery school may be anxious and insecure, but he may also be expressing his normal temperamental tendency to warm up slowly. An infant with irregular sleep cycles who cries loudly at night may possibly be responding to a hostile, rejecting mother, but he may also be expressing his temperamental irregularity. A six-year-old who explodes with anger at his teacher's commands may be aggressive and oppositional, but he may also be showing the frustration reactions of a very persistent child when he is asked to terminate an activity in which he is deeply absorbed. A mother's guilt and anxiety may be the result of a deep-seated neurosis, but they may also be the result of her problems and confusion in handling an infant with a temperamental pattern [of] a very difficult child (1968, p. 191).

The second implication is that by knowing and understanding a child's temperament, parents may be better able to guide the development of their children. For example, parents who have slow-to-warm-up children should not pressure them to accept and adapt to new situations very quickly, for this may only strengthen their fears and tendency to withdraw. Yet parents should with sensitivity encourage children to try new things and experiences. Otherwise, a slow-to-warm-up child may turn out like a boy named Bobby (Segal and Yahraes, 1978). Whenever Bobby rejected new food, his parents never again gave it to him; because he shied away from the kids at the playground, they kept him at home. At the age of ten, Bobby had no friends and ate only hamburgers, applesauce, and medium-boiled eggs.

Difficult children are in particular need of special handling. They appear to do best under a kind, consistent, and firm regime. Permissiveness appears to be the wrong strategy, often encouraging the child to become a "holy terror." Thus parents of difficult children must learn to grit their teeth and to ignore the crying sometimes, for continually placating difficult children only teaches them that they can get anything they want by howling. With proper handling, difficult children become better with time and can even develop into positive and charming individuals.

The third implication is that the reactions of parents and others to the child's temperament have important consequences for many areas of development. As already noted, Thomas, Chess, and Birch found that individuals who are difficult as babies are more likely to develop behavior problems later on. The reason for this may not reside in the children's temperaments per se, but rather in the type of interactions they have with their parents. It is well known that the parents' behavior shapes that of the child, but it is also clear that the child's behavior affects that of the parents. Parental response to a difficult child may become as negative as the child's behavior. Thus a vicious circle of bad child behavior–bad parent behavior is formed and can lead to behavior problems later in the child's life.

An example of how this may happen has been suggested by Sameroff. In his longitudinal study Sameroff found that children rated as having difficult temperaments at four months of age were the most likely to score lowest on an intelligence test at thirty months. Although this finding might indicate that temperament and intelligence have a common genetic basis, it is more likely, as Sameroff suggested, that the two are linked behaviorally. He observed children and their mothers at home when the children were twelve months old. He found that the mothers of difficult children tended to stay away from them more and to look at, stimulate, and play with them less than did mothers of other children. In contrast, the children whose mothers spent a great deal of time socializing with them had higher intelligence test scores at thirty months of age. Thus the child with a difficult temperament may "turn off" the mother in the sense that she does not engage the child in many playful and stimulating interactions. This lack of attention may in turn mean decreased intellectual competence in the child later on.

SUMMARY □

Individual differences in infants affect how they are likely to be treated by caretakers and the way in which they will respond to specific child-care practices. One effort to classify infants according to temperament has yielded the three categories of "easy," "slow to warm up," and "difficult" babies. These differences may stem from genetic factors, from physiological and chemical influences on the brain as it develops before birth, and perhaps from some conditions of the mother and environment during the infant's first few months of life. Studies of these three types of temperament suggest that parents would benefit from recognizing their children's temperamental styles and tailoring their child-rearing practices accordingly.

THE NATURE OF SOCIAL ATTACHMENTS

A striking characteristic of infancy is the child's desire to be close to other human beings. Babies enjoy physical contact with and attention from other people and become unhappy when they cannot be near them. This cluster of behaviors defines **attachment.** There is probably no process more basic and more important to later development than the child's attachment to his or her most significant caretaker, typically the mother.

The Formation of Attachments

Psychologists' views of why infants become attached have been changing in recent years. An earlier view based on learning theory held that an infant becomes emotionally attached to the mother because she is a source of relief from discomfort or pain. The mother is originally a neutral stimulus for her child, but after repeated pairings with pleasurable events such as feedings, she takes on rewarding properties and becomes a desired object.

That infant attachment is more complicated than this is suggested by the intriguing studies of rhesus monkeys conducted by Harry F. Harlow and his associates at the Primate Laboratory of the University of Wisconsin. In Harlow's initial experiments infant monkeys were separated from their mothers at six to twelve hours after birth and were raised instead with substitute or "surrogate" mothers made either of heavy wire or of wood covered with soft terry cloth (Figure 15.5). In one experiment both types of surrogates were present in the cage, but only one was equipped with a nipple from which the infant could nurse. Some infants received nourishment from the wire mother, and others were fed from the cloth mother. Even when the wire mother was the source of nourishment, the infant monkey spent a greater amount of time clinging to the cloth surrogate (Figure 15.6). Harlow's studies thus suggested that the contact comfort provided by the mother rather than her association with feeding fostered the infant's attachment, at least in rhesus monkeys.

Later studies indicated that feeding also influences the infant monkey's degree of attachment. When infant monkeys were provided two terry cloth mothers,

Harry F. Harlow.

only one of which was equipped with a nipple, early in life they clearly preferred the milk-giving surrogate (Figure 15.7).

Although the contact comfort provided by the terry cloth mothers seemed to allow normal behavior during infancy, the actions of surrogate-raised monkeys became bizarre later in life. They engaged in stereotyped behavior patterns such as clutching themselves and rocking constantly back and forth; they exhibited excessive and misdirected aggression such as attacking infants or injuring themselves; and they proved to be particularly deficient in their sexual and parenting behavior. Harlow colorfully described the sexual inadequacy of these monkeys.

> Sex behavior was, for all practical purposes, destroyed; sexual posturing was commonly stereotyped and infantile. Frequently when an isolate [surrogage-raised] female was approached by a normal male, she would sit unmoved, squatting upon the floor—a posture in which only her heart was in the right place. Contrariwise, an isolate male might approach an in-estrus female, but he might clasp the head instead of the hind legs, and then engage in pelvic thrusts. Other isolate males grasped the female's body laterally, whereby all sexual efforts left them working at cross purposes with reality (1972, p. 47).

FIGURE 15.5
Two surrogate mothers and the preference of the infant monkey. Although the wire mother provides food, the infant prefers the contact comfort of the cloth mother surrogate.

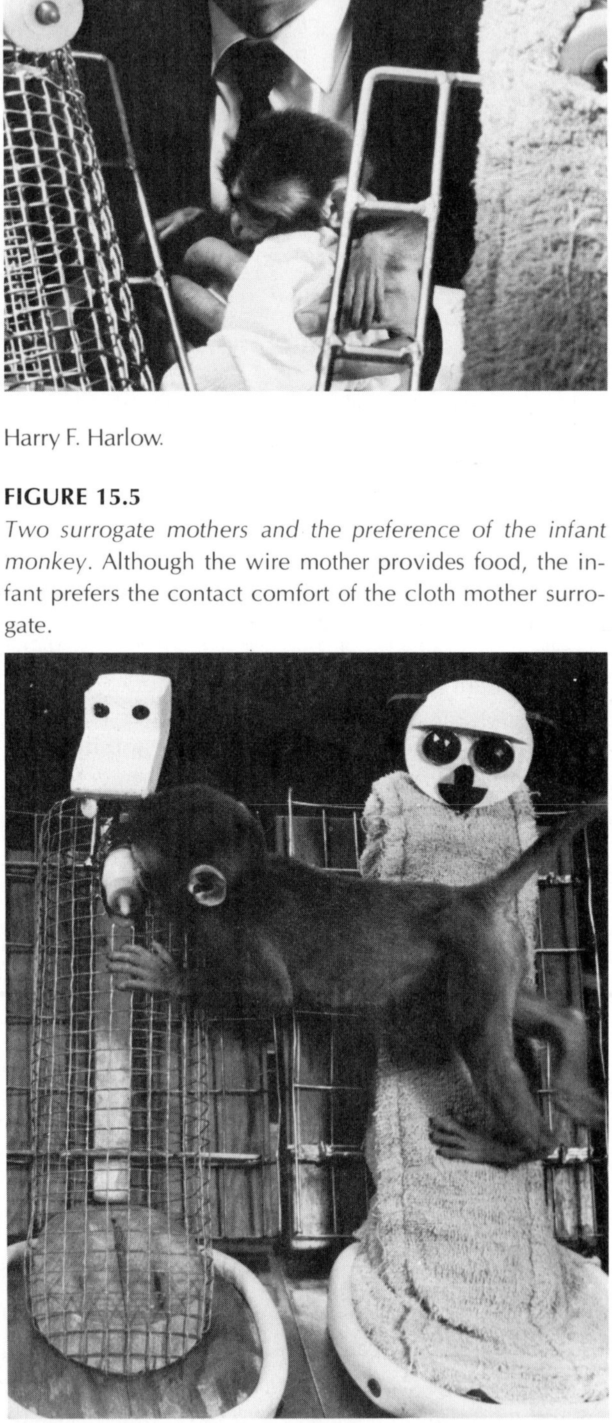

Some of the isolate females were finally impregnated, either through artificial insemination or after repeated and heroic efforts by the most persuasive of the normally raised males in the laboratory. The behavior of these monkeys as mothers—the "motherless mothers" as Harlow called them—proved to be very inadequate. The typical winsome appeal of an infant monkey seeking to be cuddled and the normal maternal response of supporting and protecting the infant may be seen in Figure 15.8. By contrast, Figure 15.9 reveals the motherless mother in full pathological bloom. These mothers tended to be either indifferent or abusive toward their babies. The indifferent mothers did not nurse, comfort, or protect their young, but they did not harm them. The abusive mothers violently bit or otherwise injured their infants, to the point that many of them died.

The rejection and brutality of these mothers raised the question whether their infants would become attached to them. Learning theory predicts that the infant will not become attached, since the mother is associated with pain rather than pleasure. Harlow found, however, that the infants of motherless mothers were unceasing in their efforts to gain maternal contact. Over and over again, the infant would try to reinstate contact with the mother, despite repeated physical rebuffs. Interestingly, these persistent efforts had a rehabilitating effect on some of the motherless mothers. After several months these mothers became

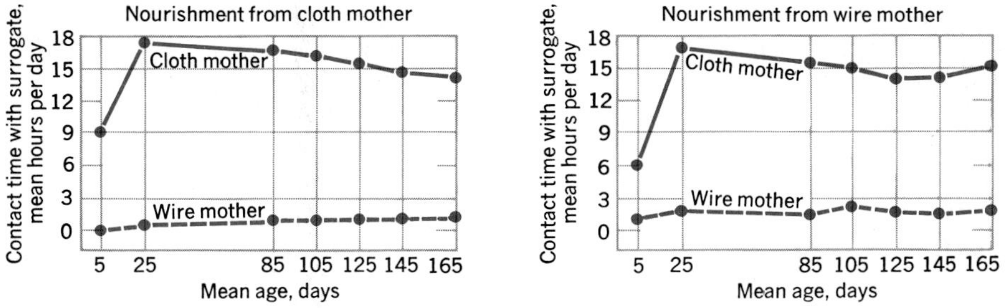

Figure 15.6
Contact time in infant monkeys to their cloth and wire surrogate mothers. (From Harlow and Suomi, 1970.)

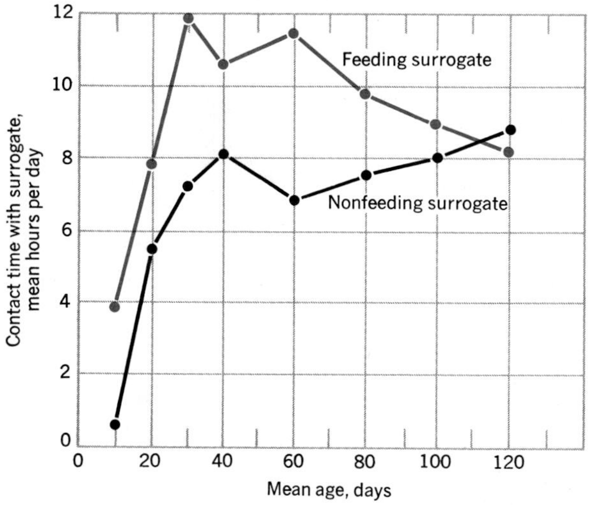

FIGURE 15.7
Preference of infants raised with a feeding cloth mother and a nonfeeding cloth mother. (After Harlow and Suomi, 1970.)

less rejecting and punishing; in fact, some of their infants established more maternal contact than infants of normal mothers. The rehabilitated mothers proved to be adequate caretakers of their later infants. The motherless mothers that never warmed up to their firstborn, however, continued to be inadequate or brutal mothers to their subsequent offspring.

Although Harlow's findings cannot be readily generalized to explain attachment in human infants, some researchers believe that there is a continuity of attachment behavior from lower primates to human beings. John Bowlby (1969), for example, views attachment as an innate response whose function is to protect the young from predators. Consistent with ethological thought (page 335) he believes that the infant seeks contact with the mother when she is present and in frightening situations; these efforts, in turn, elicit protective responses from the mother. Bowlby believes that punishing attachment behavior will not extinguish it but rather will intensify it, for punishment constitutes a threat which will innately incline the infant to attach itself to the mother. Harlow's findings in rhesus monkeys are consistent with Bowlby's theory.

Attachment in Human Infants

H. Rudolph Schaffer and Peggy Emerson (1964a) studied the development of attachment in a group of human infants from the early weeks of life to the age of eighteen months. Attachment was gauged by the infant's reactions to seven common separation situations such as being left alone in a room. They found striking individual differences among the infants. Babies varied in the age at which attachments developed and in the intensity of their attachments. Some focused their attachment on one person, whereas others were attached to several people. The mother's responsiveness to the child's crying and the amount of interaction she initiated with the child were found to be related to the child's attachment, yet the mother's general availability, defined by the amount of time she spent with the child, was not.

The study provided clear evidence against an interpretation in terms of learning theory. In 39 percent of the cases, the principal object of attachment was not the person primarily responsible for the infant's feeding and care; in 22 percent of the cases the person did not participate even to a minor degree in the child's physical care. What seemed to determine the infant's choice for attachment was the amount of stimulation and attention the adult gave the infant, rather than the adult's association with satisfaction of physical needs.

On the basis of their findings, Schaffer and Emerson advanced a view of the development of attachment which, like that of Bowlby, suggests that infants have an innate need to be near other people. This striving for nearness has no single preferred form; it appears in a variety of patterns which may differ from child to child and from one developmental level to the next. Individual variations in the strength of attachment come partly from the inherent characteristics of the individual—children require different optimal levels

FIGURE 15.8
Normal mother's response to infant's need. Physical contact with the mother is constantly sought by the infant monkey. A normal mother responds positively.

FIGURE 15.9
Motherless mother's response to infant's need. The pathological quality of child rearing of the first-born by a "motherless mother" is shown in this rebuff of the infant's need for physical contact. Despite the indifference of a motherless mother to her infant, the infant will continue to make futile but persistent efforts to cling to her.

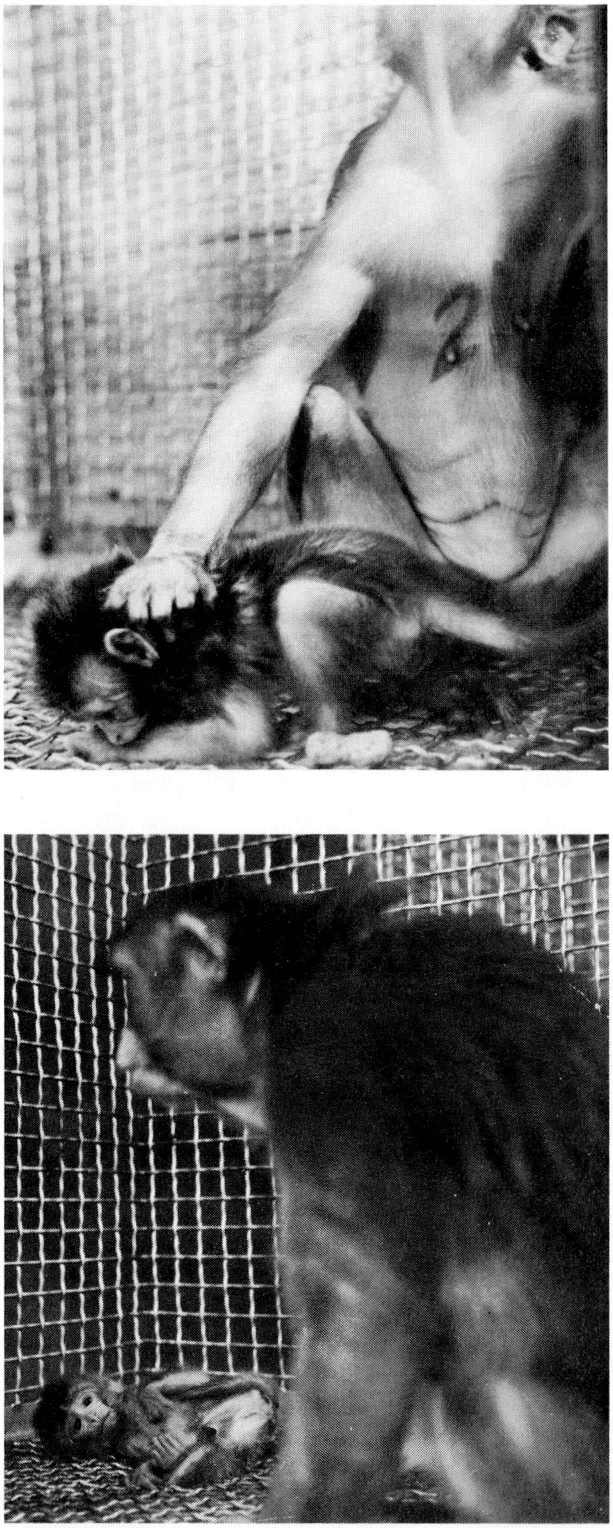

of stimulation—and partly from environmental factors—some people are better "stimulators" than others.

A study by Mary Ainsworth and Silvia Bell (1973) demonstrates how children form different kinds of attachment relationships with their mothers. These researchers found that babies responded in three different ways upon being reunited with their mothers after a brief separation period. The majority of them wanted to be close to their mothers; Ainsworth and Bell interpreted this response to mean that the child had a *secure* attachment to the mother. Another group were termed *ambivalent* in their attachment—they sought contact but at the same time resisted it. A third group, labeled *avoidant,* either did not seek contact with the mother upon her return or, if they did so, then turned and looked away from her. Ainsworth and Bell observed that the mothers of the avoidant children did not like or were indifferent to physical contact with their babies. They also found, interestingly enough, that babies whose mothers did not generally respond promptly to their signals of distress in the first few months of life became fussy, cried a great deal, and were less obedient to their mothers' commands as they grew older. These findings are contrary to the popular belief that mothers who run to answer whenever their children cry will inevitably spoil them.

An intriguing study by Marshall Klaus and his colleagues (1972) suggests that contact with her baby soon after birth may be quite important for the mother's attachment to her child. In their study mothers were allowed an extra sixteen hours of contact with their newborns during their stay in the hospital after giving birth. A control group of women with similar backgrounds were permitted contact only for the brief time periods customary in many hospitals. The results were remarkable. One month later the mothers allowed the extra contact stayed closer to their infants, soothed them more often during a physical examination, fondled them more, and engaged in greater eye-to-eye contact. Similar results were found at one, two, and five years. These investigators suggest an intriguing hypothesis for the high percentage of premature infants who when older are battered by their parents or show the "failure to thrive" syndrome. Because these infants typically require specialized and prolonged medical treatment from the moment of birth, their mothers are prevented from touching them for long periods of time. The early separation may cause a disturbance in the mother's attachment to her infant and consequently lead to these disorders. The results of their study suggest that even the relatively short periods of separation that take place after normal births may be detrimental to the attachment between mother and child.

Importance of Attachment for Later Development

Paradoxically, the process of attachment has important long-term implications for detachment—the child's development into an independent, autonomous human being. Unless the infant forms a secure attachment, he or she cannot develop the trust and confidence necessary to go on to the next stage of development. Attachment behavior usually begins to weaken when infants start to engage in another basic human activity, exploration of their surroundings. In these explorations a child frequently encounters objects and situations which are simultaneously interesting and frightening. Exploration therefore requires a sense on the part of the child that no harm will befall him or her, a confidence which a secure relationship with a caretaker can establish.

The role that attachment plays in encouraging successful exploration was demonstrated at the animal level in Harlow's studies of monkeys raised with surrogate mothers. When confronted with a strange stimulus such as a mechanical toy making unusual sounds, a baby monkey was initially terrorized. If the cloth mother was available, the monkey tended to run and cling to her (Figure 15.10). After a time, as if deriving a feeling of security from this contact, many of the baby monkeys would leave their "mother" to explore the room or fearful object (Figure 15.11). By contrast, the infants raised solely with the wire surrogate showed no signs of overcoming their terror. They ran toward the "mother" but did not cling to her. They either clutched themselves and rocked back and forth or rubbed themselves against the wall, but they never reduced their fear enough to be able to explore the strange toy. The wire mothers were clearly ineffective in producing attachment and providing security for their adopted infants.

The behavior of human infants in the Rheingold and Eckerman study described earlier (page 362) provides strikingly clear parallels with Harlow's results. If placed alone in a room with strange objects, infants appear insecure and frightened; they often remain immobile and do little exploring. If the mother is present, however, they will wander rather far afield to examine strange objects and then return to the mother as a base of security. This process is repeated, with the infant exploring ever greater distances before returning to the mother for reassurance. Thus the mother's presence and the trust that the child has developed make exploration possible. Moreover, Ainsworth's studies have demonstrated that a child's degree of independence and exploration are definitely related to the quality of the mother-child attachment. When put down by their mothers in a strange room, one-year-old children having secure attachments were quite content to wander away and in-

FIGURE 15.10
Infant's reaction to fear. A moving mechanical toy initially arouses fear in the infant monkey.

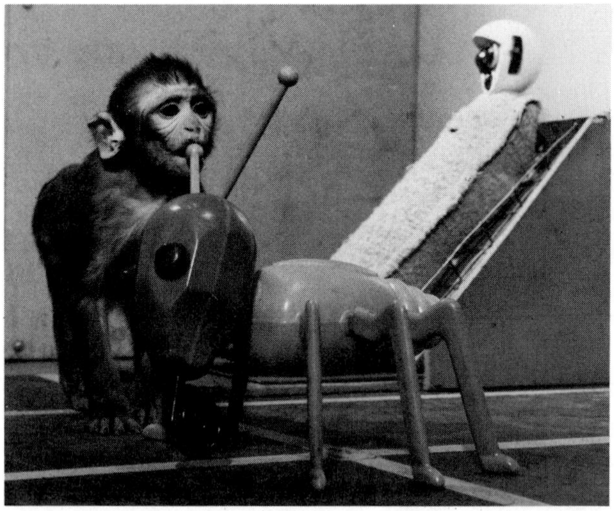

FIGURE 15.11
Effect of "sense of security" on infant's fear. After contact with the cloth mother, the infant is able to explore the fear-arousing toy. This "sense of security" is not apparent in infants reared with the wire mother.

vestigate the surroundings. Children who did not have a secure attachment, however, protested loudly and did not readily go off into independent activity.

Recent studies of rhesus monkeys have elucidated the important chain of events leading from a secure maternal attachment to normal social-emotional development in this species (Suomi, 1979; Suomi and Harlow, 1978). Earlier we described the abnormal adult behavior of rhesus monkeys who had been raised with surrogate mothers. These monkeys were deprived of contact not only with their natural mothers but also with peers and other monkeys—that is, they grew up in complete social isolation. Infant rhesus monkeys normally spend only the first few days of life in intimate physical contact with their mother. Very soon they begin to leave her to explore their surroundings. By the age of three months, the infant spends more time with peers than with its mother or other adults and continues to do so throughout infancy and most of adolescence. The young monkeys spend most of their time together in play. Interestingly, their play contains almost all the elements of deportment making up adult behavior, including aggressive, sexual, and cooperative activites. For example, rhesus monkeys as young as six weeks of age can be seen in sexual postures during play. These behavior patterns tend to be rather clumsy at first, but with time and practice the young monkeys become more proficient at them. These observations suggest that young monkeys learn the social skills they will need as adults in their play with peers.

The importance of peers has been demonstrated experimentally in several ways. Infant monkeys have been raised with their natural mothers but deprived of peer relations. These monkeys do not learn how to play with their age-mates and turn out to be hyperaggressive later in life. In the converse situation, infants are isolated from their mothers but are permitted to interact with peers. Spending as little as thirty minutes a day, five days a week with peers enables such infants to acquire many of the social skills of normally reared monkeys. Perhaps the most significant evidence for the value associating with peers is the ability of play to overcome the detrimental long-term effects of early and complete social isolation. Disturbed monkeys can achieve almost complete recovery by being paired daily with socially competent infants who are three months old at the beginning of treatment. These "monkey therapists" engage the isolates in play which becomes more complex as they grow older. Through these interactions the isolated monkeys gradually learn normal behavior patterns.

What seems to be important for the development of social competence in rhesus monkeys is not merely the availability of peers but the nature of interactions with them. These interactions in turn appear to depend on the quality and stability of the mother-infant relationship. The infants of the motherless monkeys, for example, are so preoccupied with efforts to gain contact with their mothers that they do not establish normal play relationships with their peers and become abnormally aggressive. Similarly, if a normal mother is removed from the social group, her infant will immediately cease all interactions with peers. Once the mother returns, the infant is likely to stay near her or run to her at the slightest external threat; consequently the infant plays less with peers.

All these findings indicate that normal social and emotional development in the rhesus monkey proceeds as a series of events beginning with the formation of a secure attachment to the mother. This attachment provides the infant with the confidence and trust it needs to explore the environment and participate fully and normally in peer relationships. Through its interactions with peers, the young monkey then gradually learns the behavioral skills necessary to function competently as an adult.

Species Differences in Attachment

Although we have discussed some parallels in the attachment behavior of rhesus monkeys and human infants, we must caution against any facile generalizations from the rhesus to the human case. Among the reasons for this, perhaps the most important is that the rhesus pattern cannot even be generalized to all other species of monkey (Lehrman, 1974).

Leonard Rosenblum (1971) has studied attachment in pigtail and bonnet monkeys, two species which are closely related to each other as well as to the rhesus monkey. The young of these species were reared in group pens with their mothers, adult childless females, and an adult male. The pigtail mothers, like the rhesus in similar settings, rarely left their infants, rarely shared them with other group members, and kept themselves apart from others during the three months following the birth of their babies. In contrast, bonnet mothers kept close to other monkeys after giving birth and allowed many members of the group to handle their infants. The pigtail infants spent much less time away from their mothers than did the bonnets of equal age. If separated from their mothers but kept within the social group, the pigtail infants protested vigorously and then became depressed, as do rhesus monkeys. Bonnet infants, on the other hand, did not respond negatively to the separation.

A major reason for this difference lies in the behavior of the other group members. Female pigtails did not pick up and care for a separated infant, but bonnets readily "adopted" an infant and cared for it until the mother returned. Thus the social organization of a **species may be yet another factor determining the nature of an infant's attachment to the mother.**

These findings led Daniel Lehrman (1974) to a broader view of the nature of attachment in monkeys: separation from the mother is extremely distressing, and has severe negative consequences, when the social setting does not provide any compensation. As we will see in the next section, this view also seems to fit human development. Although animal studies cannot give us the complete story on human attachment, they have been extremely valuable in directing our attention to the various factors that could also affect the development of attachment in human beings.

SUMMARY □

The formation of social attachments is an important part of development. Studies show clearly that strong attachments to an individual can be formed, even when the individual does not satisfy the infant's basic physical needs. In rhesus monkeys soft tactile stimulation—what Harlow has called contact comfort—appears to be a major basis for attachment. Contact comfort may also be important in human beings, but sensory stimulation and responsiveness to the infant are critical.

Several theories hold that attachment is an innate response. The fact that rhesus infants persisted in their efforts to be close to their "motherless mothers," even though these females tried to thwart them, is supporting evidence. Human infants whose mothers are not responsive may be ambivalent or avoidant in their relations with them, rather than forming secure attachments. There is some evidence that early postpartum contact between mother and child may promote an optimal attachment bond.

A well-established trust relationship with a caretaker can provide the emotional security a child needs to be able to explore strange surroundings, and to become an autonomous individual. The child's degree of independence depends on the secureness of this attachment, for both human and rhesus monkey infants having insecure relations remain dependent and fearful in novel situations. In rhesus monkeys a secure attachment to the mother enables the infant to interact with peers and thus gradually to learn the behavioral skills necessary to function competently as an adult. Studies of rhesus and other monkeys indicate that the social organization of a species is an important factor in determining the nature of the infant's attachments.

CHILD-REARING PRACTICES AND LATER DEVELOPMENT

During infancy the predominant influences on a child's social and emotional development come from parents and the home environment. As the child grows older and becomes more independent of parental control, many other environmental factors such as peers, school, and socioeconomic status also become important. Because these variables can interact in extremely complex ways, psychologists are still many years away from a satisfying explanation of personality differences. Nevertheless, many fascinating facts and provocative hypotheses have emerged from studies of social and emotional development in children past infancy. We consider the evidence pertaining to parental influences in the present section, that related to the child's culture in the next.

Is Mother Indispensable?

In 1950 John Bowlby was asked by the World Health Organization to study the mental health of homeless children. His report, entitled *Maternal Care and Mental Health,* has had considerable impact on opinions regarding the importance of a mother's care on the later development of her child. In the report Bowlby concluded,

> What is believed to be essential for mental health is that the infant and young child should experience a warm, intimate and continuous relationship with his mother (or permanent mother-substitute) in which both find satisfaction and enjoyment (1952, p. 11).

This view stemmed primarily from studies describing the deleterious consequences of institutionalizing infants and young children. Later research, however, demonstrated that institutionalization does not inevitably have negative effects (Clarke and Clarke, 1960; Yarrow, 1961). Nonetheless, on the basis of the earlier findings, Bowlby (1973) and others have warned that repeated temporary separations—such as those that occur when mothers work—may also have detrimental effects on the child.

The question of whether a mother's continuous care is indispensable for her child's normal development is one of great urgency today, when over half of American mothers with school-age children and about one-third with children under the age of six work outside the home. According to Helen Bee (1974), who has reviewed the research relevant to this question, children of working mothers suffer only if there is instability in the family or in the child care arrangements. For example, boys from unstable families are more likely to be delinquent if their mothers work, but this is not the case for boys from stable families whose mothers hold jobs. Unstable substitute care may also make children more dependent and anxious about being separated from their mothers, whereas stable substitute care does not.

Of course, such different experiences as having a mother who stays home and receiving substitute care while mother works must have some impact on children's development. One of the most extensive studies of the long-term effects of exclusive mothering versus substitute care has been conducted by Terence Moore in England (1975). To relate child care experience to later personality development, Moore used the records of children whose behavior and personality had been assessed at various ages up until fifteen years. Children were divided into two groups. The exclusive mothering group consisted of thirty-one males and twenty-six females who had received full-time care from their mothers up to the age of five. In the diffuse-mothering group were twenty-four males and twenty-four females who had spent at least twenty-five hours per week apart from their mothers for at least one year before the age of five. On the average, the substitute care began at 2.6 years and lasted approximately two years. All the children came from intact homes, and the two groups were matched on several dimensions, including IQ at three years of age. Moore found that boys who had experienced diffused mothering were active, aggressive, independent, and relatively free from fear; they were less likely to study for school examinations and more likely to drop out of school. In contrast, boys who had experienced exclusive mothering showed anxiety for adult approval, little assertive behavior, fear of physical harm, and timidity with peers. They were also more conforming to adult standards than to those of their peer group. Interestingly, Moore found few differences between the girls who had received exclusive mothering and those who had received diffuse.

Moore's study and some others suggest that children, particularly boys, who have mothers providing full-time care tend at a young age to internalize adult standards of behavior, especially in regard to self-control and scholastic achievement. Children in substitute care, on the other hand, tend to be less concerned with adult approval and more interested in approval from peers.

Other research indicates that self-assertiveness and peer orientation may not stem from the mother's absence per se, but rather from the interactions the child experiences during substitute care. In nursery schools where the ratio of the number of adults to number of children is high, the frequency of adult-child interactions is higher and that of peer-peer interactions lower than in nursery schools where the adult-to-child ratio is low (Reuter and Yunik, 1973). Furthermore, children in group care suffer more pain, frustration, and rejection than do children in family day care, which consists of one woman caring for a few children in her own home (Prescott, 1973). The disturbing emotions experienced in group care may lead to more aggressive behavior. With less adult attention and intervention, aggression often achieves the results intended by the child. Thus a group care setting, particulary one with few adults per child, may foster an attitude that the best way to resolve conflicts is to be aggressive.

Substitute care can also have positive effects on a child's social-emotional development. On the basis of cross-cultural studies, anthropologist Margaret Mead (1954) noted that the best personal adjustment is made by children who are cared for by many warm, friendly people. Anthropological evidence also suggests that children who form strong attachments to a single individual, as do children whose contacts are limited to their mothers, grow up able to form only a limited number of intense, exclusive rela-

The role of the father in determining the personality of his child is important but has been too little studied.

tionships in adulthood. Thus children who are temporarily separated from their mothers but who are given love and attention by others may actually become more gracious, sociable, and self-reliant individuals.

Role of the Father

In the study of parental influences on social development, the father remains a relatively neglected subject. Most studies have emphasized early infancy, when many fathers play a relatively minor role. Moreover, it is difficult to secure fathers as research participants. The evidence that has accumulated, however, indicates that the father's personality and behavior are no less important than the mother's to the social-emotional development of the child. This fact was clearly established by a study which compared the attitudes of parents whose children were well adjusted with those whose children had adjustment difficulties (Peterson et al., 1959). The investigators were surprised to discover that both mothers *and fathers* of children with adjustment problems were themselves less well adjusted, less friendly, and less democratic than parents of the well-adjusted children. The maladjusted children who were hyperaggressive tended to have weak and ineffectual fathers, whereas children suffering from shyness and feelings of inferiority tended to have fathers who were dictatorial and unconcerned about their children. How the father treats his child is thus quite important in determining not only whether the child will become maladjusted but what form the maladjustment will take.

The largest body of research involving fathers has examined how their presence in the home or their absence affects children's personality development. Boys from father-absent homes have been found to be less well adjusted and more inept in peer relations than those whose fathers are regularly at home. They also tend to be less masculine, although some may behave at times in an exaggerated masculine manner and at others in a highly feminine fashion (Biller, 1970). Many boys from father-absent homes do not appear to have learned how to be appropriately aggressive. Many think that masculinity consists of constant aggression toward others. This may explain the relationship discovered between father absence and juvenile delinquency. Sheldon and Eleanor Glueck (1950), for example, found that more than 40 percent of the adolescent delinquent boys they studied came from father-absent homes, as compared with less than 25 percent of the boys in a group of nondelinquents.

The usual explanation given for the observed effects of the father's absence is that the boy lacks a masculine model with which to identify. Normally the child develops his **sexual identification**—that is, acquires interests, attitudes, and behavior appropriate to his sex—by imitating or modeling the behavior of the same-sex parent. If the father is not present, the boy has difficulty in forming a strong and appropriate sexual identification.

It now appears that this explanation may not be fully adequate. In many of the father-absent families studied, considerable family discord preceded the divorce which finally led to the father's absence. An analysis by Michael Rutter (1971) suggests that parental conflict and disharmony rather than father absence per se are associated with antisocial behavior in boys. Rutter noted that delinquency is seen twice as often in boys whose fathers are absent through divorce than in boys from unbroken homes. But there is no significant difference in the rate of delinquency of boys whose fathers have died and of boys from intact families.

The effect of father absence has also been studied in girls. E. Mavis Hetherington (1972) found that adolescent girls growing up without fathers had difficulties in heterosexual behavior. Girls whose fathers had died tended to be shy around males and were anxious about sex. Girls whose fathers had divorced or deserted, on the other hand, tended to be promiscuous or inappropriately assertive in their relations with men.

However negative the consequences of a father's absence may be on a child, the father's physical presence alone does not guarantee the child's optimal development. The quality of the father-child relationship is also very important, and it may depend on the father's availability. Mark Reuter and Henry Biller (1973) gave college males a questionnaire to obtain their perceptions of their relationships with their fathers and of the amount of time the fathers had spent at home. They then tried to relate these perceptions with the students' personality adjustment scores. Men who were well adjusted remembered their fathers as either highly nurturant and at least moderately available or only moderately nurturant and very much available. Men who were insecure tended to remember their fathers as either at home a great deal and not paying much attention to them or seldom at home but highly nurturant.

At a time when rising divorce rates and the demands of work are making fathers less available to their children, this body of research has some practical social implications. The father is not merely an economic necessity to his children but a psychological one as well. Certainly we should encourage divorced fathers to spend more time with their children and support organizations such as Big Brother which provide boys with father substitutes. But it is equally important to raise young boys to value their future role as fathers. They should be taught that fatherhood is no less important than motherhood and that their warm and supportive presence can do much to promote the psychological well-being of their children.

Trends in Child-Care Practices

Parents have long sought the advice of experts to aid them with the job of child rearing. The experts in turn have been more than ready to respond. Since time immemorial, they have advised parents on ways of rearing children, inevitably cloaking such advice in the scientific garb of the day. Each shift in expert advice has been accompanied by a certified guarantee that if the prescription is followed, the child will ultimately possess the wholesome habits so avidly sought by the parents. Half a century later, it is difficult to believe that parents in the 1920s and 1930s took seriously the advice of John Watson.

> There is a sensible way of treating children. Treat them as though they were young adults. Dress them, bathe them with care and circumspection. Let your behavior always be objective and kindly firm. Never hug and kiss them, never let them sit in your lap. If you must, kiss them once on the forehead when they say good night. Shake hands with them in the morning. Give them a pat on the head if they have made an extraordinarily good job of a difficult task. Try it out. In a week's time you will find how easy it is to be perfectly objective with your child and at the same time kindly. You will be utterly ashamed of the mawkish, sentimental way you have been handling it (1928, pp. 81–82).

Only twenty years later mothers were being urged to fondle and play with their children and to allow them to initiate feeding, weaning, and toilet training, lest parental rigidity leave inevitable scars on their developing personalities. Ideas on child rearing can change this rapidly and radically because our theories about social development far outrun their empirical supports.

The changing trends in advice on child rearing were documented earlier by Martha Wolfenstein (1953), who analyzed various editions of the bulletin *Infant Care,* issued by the United States Children's Bureau. The bulletin deals primarily with child-rearing practices of traditional concern to American parents, such as weaning, thumb-sucking, bowel and bladder training, and infant masturbation.

In the period 1914 to 1921, parents were warned that if thumb-sucking and masturbation were not promptly curbed, permanent damage to the child was a certainty. Parents were actually advised to pin down infants' nightgown sleeves and to tie their legs to opposite sides of the crib so that they could not suck their thumbs, touch their genitals, or rub their thighs together. In the 1930s focus shifted from these habits to the child's bowel training and weaning. The influence of Watsonian behaviorism was apparent in the emphasis on regularity and "doing everything by the clock." Bowel training and weaning were to be carried out early and with great determination; the baby's resistance was always to be overcome. Child rearing was essentially a struggle between parent and child in which the child was never to be allowed the upper hand or all would be lost. By 1942 Freudian thought had gained popularity. The baby was not viewed as such a dangerous creature, and more permissiveness was recommended. Thumb-sucking and masturbation were not to be interfered with; weaning and toilet training were to be accomplished later and more sympathetically. The 1950s witnessed the child-centered approach championed by Benjamin Spock. Parents were to allow children to shape and pace their own development by responding to their needs, abilities, and readiness for change. Today's child-rearing tactics remain basically child-centered, but the child is expected to accommodate somewhat to the parents' needs and styles.

In view of this ever-changing advice, we might wonder why whole generations of children were not destroyed by the parental practices of certain periods.

The answer appears to be that parental *attitudes* are probably more important than parental *behavior* (Frankiel, 1959; Walters and Stinnett, 1971). For parents who have been led to believe that one misstep in child rearing will result in horrible, lifelong consequences, it should be reassuring to state what experienced grandmothers know intuitively. Even the very young child is a relatively tough human being with a capacity for growth that almost guarantees a normal course of development, provided he or she is protected from physical harm and is given the love and care of devoted parents.

Styles of Parenting

Nonetheless, parents translate their love and concern for their children into very different styles of parenting, especially when guiding and controlling their children's behavior. In 1964 Wesley Becker evaluated the effects of different kinds of parental control practices on children's development. He divided disciplinary techniques into two broad categories, *love-oriented* and *power-assertive*. In the first category were praising and reasoning with the child as well as temporarily withdrawing love and separating the child from the parent. In the second category were all methods involving physical punishment. Children whose parents used love-oriented techniques were more likely to be cooperative with others, to feel responsible for their actions, and to have appropriate feelings of guilt. Children whose parents asserted power tended to be uncooperative and aggressive.

More recently, Diana Baumrind (1975) reported her findings from a longitudinal study that began in 1967 with 150 nursery school children and their families. Baumrind discovered three types of parents, each having a different effect on the child. The **authoritarian parent** "values obedience as a virtue and . . . believes in restricting the child's autonomy." The **permissive parent** seeks "to give the child as much freedom as is consistent with the child's physical survival." The **authoritative parent** "attempts to direct the child's activities in a rational, issue-oriented manner." The authoritative parents are turning out to be the most effective; their children appear to be the most socially responsible, independent, oriented toward success, and vigorous.

Baumrind also finds that corporal punishment—the kind of nonbrutal physical punishment that the parent metes out in response to behavior the child knows is not acceptable—does not inevitably lead to psychological damage. In fact, the authoritative parents who were most effective preferred physical punishment over other negative sanctions. On the basis of her own and other research in this area, Baumrind has specified the following general principles for making punishment an effective tool of discipline. It should be given as soon as possible after the undesirable behavior; it should be consistent and unavoidable; and it should be accompanied by an explanation of why the behavior is unacceptable and what behavior would be more desirable.

CHILD ABUSE

The most bizarre way in which parents treat their children is to abuse them physically. Although once thought to be rare, surveys and child-abuse reporting laws have made it all too apparent that a surprisingly large number of parents, assault, batter, and torture their children. Over 2,000 children are killed each year by their parents or other caretakers, and another half to one and a half million are badly beaten or abused.

In a society that takes for granted the love of parents for their children, the typical reaction to this state of affairs is that a father or mother must be psychotic to brutalize his or her own child. Yet examination of the psychiatric status of child-abusing parents has revealed that only about 10 percent suffer from psychotic mental disorders (Kempe and Helfer, 1972). What characteristics, then, might differentiate the child-abusing parent from the vast majority of parents who would never physically harm their children? In families in which child abuse occurs, instability of the marriage, economic stress, and a sense of isolation from the community in which they live are often evident. Although such difficulties are more common in the lower socioeconomic stratum, it must be emphasized that most families so troubled do not abuse their children. Furthermore, child abuse is also found in middle- and upper-status families (Gelles, in press). These parents were less suspected in the past, perhaps because they are better able to disguise the cause of the injury to their child. But physicians and social service professionals are now on guard for children from affluent families who seem to have an untoward number of "accidents" in the home.

Parents who abuse their children are more likely to have been abused themselves as children. These parents often harbor a deep sense of not having received the care they needed from the very beginning of their lives. As adults, they feel that no one cares for them, that no one is available to help them in periods of stress, and that their spouses offer little nurturance or support. These parents are often hostile in other aspects of their daily lives and may be provoked to violence by ordinary daily stresses. They tend to lack objective knowledge about child rearing and to demand behavior from their child that far exceeds the child's capacities. They also appear to be rigid and cold, rejecting their child, and sometimes they strongly defend their right to abuse their child. Child-abusing parents, of course, differ from one another, and few would have all these characteristics simultaneously.

Brandt Steele (1977) has analyzed some of the consequences of abuse on a child's neurological and psychological development. The children he studied had suffered physical assault, emotional deprivation, nutritional neglect, or sexual abuse. He found that maltreatment can distort the cognitive, social, and emotional development of the child. Blows to the head, for example, can cause bleeding inside a child's skull which may ultimately lead to brain damage. What was particularly surprising and disturbing to Steele is that infants can suffer subtle hemorrhages throughout the brain simply by being shaken. This type of brain damage can cause visual problems, deficits in language and motor skills, and even intellectual impairment ranging from mild to profound retardation. Abused and neglected children also had an extremely low sense of self-esteem, were apathetic and depressed, and lacked joy and spontaneity.

What can be done for child-abusing parents and their children? There is no simple answer; each family must be examined for its strengths and weaknesses. In extreme cases, especially when parents are psychotic or psychopathically aggressive, it may be necessary to remove children from the home permanently to guarantee their safety. In many instances, however, an intensive support program including homemaker services, "crisis nurseries" where parents may leave their children at times of stress, and support groups such as Parents Anonymous may help. The emphasis of all these services is to support parents during crises and to provide them with the nurturance and understanding of which they have long felt deprived.

SUMMARY □

Although many people believe that a mother's continuous care is essential for her child's psychological well-being, there is accumulating evidence that children can thrive despite temporary absences from their mothers, provided they have a stable relationship with warm and attentive adults. If substitute care constitutes a large part of a child's life, we would naturally expect the child to be influenced by the values, attitudes, and behavior of the adults and other children with whom he or she interacts while away from home. Children who during the first few years of life are cared for in family-type settings and those who spend the same years in larger day care groups have been found to have personality differences. And children who receive more individualized attention from adults tend early to internalize adult standards of behavior, whereas those who receive less attention are more self-assertive and peer-oriented.

The attitudes and behavior of mothers have received much more attention than those of fathers. The father's availability, however, and his style of interacting with his child are related to whether the child becomes maladjusted and in what way. A warm relationship with a father figure who is himself an adequate masculine model appears to be particularly significant in helping a boy learn his sex role.

Advice on how to rear children has changed drastically over the years, but it appears that parental attitudes rather than practices ultimately shape the child's development. But parents' disciplinary techniques have been identified as love-oriented and power-assertive, and parents themselves as authoritarian, permissive, and authoritative in guiding their children. Punishment has been found to be an effective method of discipline, but only when it is accompanied by explanations and advice about more appropriate behavior.

CULTURAL INFLUENCES IN SOCIALIZATION

Parents are not totally free agents in the socialization of their children. **Socialization** is inculcating children with the values of the culture to which they belong, and parents are generally expected to assume this responsibility for society as a whole. Sometimes the transmission of cultural values is done by the parent quite consciously; Chinese parents, for example, begin training children in the sayings of their leaders very early in life. More often, however, the effects of culture on child-rearing practices are subtle, having been shaped over a longer period of time. Parents engage in certain child-rearing practices simply because "that is the way that one raises children."

Economic Influences

Child-rearing practices often emanate from the economic needs of a culture and are unconsciously directed at producing children who can make appropriate adaptations to the culture's demands. A study in which more than a hundred societies around the world were classified into categories based on their accumulations of food (Barry, Child, and Bacon, 1959) illustrates well how the basic economy affects child rearing. Societies making large accumulations of food, such as those practicing agriculture and animal husbandry, were found to put strong pressure on their children to be responsible, obedient, and compliant. In contrast, societies with small accumulations of food, such as those relying on hunting or fishing, emphasized achievement, self-reliance, independence, and assertiveness. These findings suggest that the nature of the economy encourages the selection of child-rearing practices that provide training in the motives and behavior necessary for the adult role. If members of a herding society, for example, raised their children to be assertive rather than compliant, they would not later have the patience and cooperative attitude required to tend crops and livestock. On the other hand, societies that engage primarily in hunting and fishing need adult members who are resourceful and develop skill in obtaining food, so they socialize children to be individualistic, assertive, and venturesome. The selection of child-rearing practices is not usually deliberate but takes place gradually through many generations.

Daniel Miller and Guy Swanson (1958) have presented evidence that American parents also seem to foster personality characteristics in their children appropriate to the niche they will fill in the economy. These investigators divided all occupations in the United States into two major categories, **entrepreneurial** and **bureaucratic.** Entrepreneurial occupations are those in which rewards are based solely on the individual's own performance, for example, small-business owners and salespeople whose salary consists of their commissions. Success in these occupations depends on risk taking and competition. It should be noted that entrepreneurial occupations cut across conventional socioeconomic-class lines. Thus an entrepreneur could be a lawyer who has a high income or a small-scale gardener who sells his services door-to-door and earns only a subsistence income.

Bureaucratic positions are in large organizations which employ many kinds of specialists. Incomes are in the form of wages or salary, and rewards are based on specialized abilities rather than on success in risk taking. These economic settings offer employees a degree of security not found in entrepreneurial activities, and working with and getting along with others become most important. Again it should be noted that bureaucratic occupations can cover a wide range of incomes—the employee may be the vice-president of a large bank, a teller, or the custodian.

Miller and Swanson have suggested that parents socialize their children to have traits that will bring success in the economic setting of which the family is a member. Thus entrepreneurial families would adopt child-rearing practices that promote the development of self-control and independence. They might be more severe in toilet training and more inhibiting of the child's sexual activities. The economically more secure atmosphere of the bureaucratic family would favor child-rearing practices that are less severe. In the bureaucratic home stress would be placed on the child's ability to get along well with others and being considerate of others' feelings.

The mode of punishing transgressions would also differ in the two types of families. Individualism would be emphasized in the entrepreneurial home, where the child would be taught to develop internal restraints. Transgressions would be dealt with through appeals to the child's conscience. Bureaucratic families have learned that rewards and punishments flow from sources outside of themselves and therefore would employ more external controls, such as spanking, in dealing with transgressions. Miller and Swanson have found some evidence that child-rearing practices in the two types of families are consistent with these formulations.

Additional evidence is contained in a study of over 300 thirteen-to-sixteen-year-old boys (Berkowitz and Friedman, 1967). On a task requiring cooperation, boys from entrepreneurial homes were found to give help only to the degree that they themselves had received help from their work partner. Boys from bureaucratic families helped their work partner regardless of how much assistance they had received. That is, the entrepreneurial boys employed a philosophy of "Scratch my back, and I'll scratch yours," whereas the bureaucratic boys were organizational in their willingness to help others and in wanting the job to be completed successfully.

Social Class and Poverty

Sophie Tucker, an old-time club entertainer, was once asked how she felt about her life as a child in the ghetto. She answered, "I've been rich and I've been poor. Rich is better." Without benefit of systematic research, Sophie Tucker had summarized the literature.

The socioeconomic status of the family has considerable influence on child-rearing patterns. Poverty represents an extreme case. Poor health, inadequate nutrition, limited education, and occupational instability may foster child-rearing attitudes and practices quite different from those of families with financial security.

Variations in Child-Rearing among Low-Status Families Many myths surround the poor. They are often perceived as lazy and unwilling to work in spite of the fact that the large majority of working-age men classified as poor hold jobs. The poor also tend to be viewed as being all alike. Although many people recognize stratification within the middle class—upper-middle and lower-middle class—they do not recognize diversity in lower-status groups.

Eleanor Pavenstedt (1965), a child psychiatrist, demonstrated the importance of differentiating between extreme poverty and less severe economic deprivation in terms of impact on child development. She conducted intensive clinical studies of the child-rearing practices of two groups representing the economic extremes of a lower-status urban population. In the lowest economic group disorganized family structure was common. Marital separations, divorces, desertions, and neglect and abandonment of the children were quite frequent. The households of many families were chaotic. The youngest child was often found in a crib in a back room, untended and unchanged; his or her crying went unheeded by the mother. There were no set patterns for eating, dressing, bathing, or other daily activities. The mother might leave the home for hours, placing a four- or five-year-old in charge of an infant. Many children owned nothing they could call their own, and a gift made to one child could be appropriated immediately by a sibling. If a child did something wrong, another child might be indiscriminately punished for it.

The results of such disorganization were visible in the children's difficulties in adjusting to school. When they entered nursery school, children from these families concealed their emotions, turning away when frustrated or angry. They often failed to discriminate one adult from another and could not sustain relationships with them. Few learned their teacher's name. The children were not able to carry over things learned on one day to the next. Problem solving was not attempted, questions went unasked, and the children failed to learn from past experience. Pavenstedt adds this description.

> The saddest, and to us the outstanding characteristic of this group with adults and children alike, was the self-devaluation. One little boy, when encouraged by the teacher to have her put his name on his drawing wanted her to write "shitty Billy." Their lack of confidence in their ability to master was painfully reenacted with each new encounter (1965, p. 96).

In striking contrast, Pavenstedt found many families, particularly in the upper-lower class, who showed considerable concern for their children. Many of these families lived in the same skid-row environment as the disorganized multiproblem families, but their homes were stable. Children were shown much affection and were seldom separated from their mothers. These parents emphasized neatness, conformity, and respectability. When the children entered school, parents helped them with their homework and expressed concern about poor achievement. Children from these homes posed few behavior problems in school and learned to read sufficiently well in the first grade to warrant promotion. Pavenstedt's observations indicate that despite the malnutrition, poor health care, and substandard housing which are their common lot, it is not true that the homes of the poor are invariably disorganized.

Comparisons of Child-Rearing across Social Classes From the many studies comparing the child-rearing practices of higher and lower socioeconomic groups, a few reasonably consistent findings have emerged. For example, parents of all social classes have been found to share certain values—wishing their children to be honest, happy, considerate, obedient, and dependable—but the emphasis given these values varies somewhat with socioeconomic class (Kohn, 1959). Middle-class parents are more likely to stress internalized standards or goals such as honesty, self-control, consideration, and curiosity, whereas working-class parents stress qualities that assure respectability, such as obedience, neatness, and cleanliness.

General conceptions of the parent's role have also been found to vary with class (Table 15.1). Working-class mothers tend to feel directly responsible for making their children immediately obey commands, whereas middle-class mothers tend to feel a long-term responsibility for their children's growth, development, affection, and satisfaction. Middle-class parents have more egalitarian relationships with their children and are generally more accessible to the child than parents in the working class. Although the working-class father has been found to be less available to the child than the middle-class father, working-class mothers expect their husbands to be more directive and to play a larger role in imposing constraints.

TABLE 15.1
Behavior and Philosophy of Parents of Two Socioeconomic Classes

Philosophy	Working Class (Lower Class)	Middle Class
Concept of good parent	Elicits specific behavior	Promotes development, affection, satisfaction
Behavioral requirements	Obedience, neatness, cleanliness	Internalized standards
	Qualities assuring respectability	Honesty, self-control
		Boys, curiosity; girls, consideration
Role differentiation	More rigid, more paternalistic	More flexible, more egalitarian
Response to misdeed	Focus on immediate consequences of child's actions	Takes into account child's intentions and feelings
Discipline techniques	More physical punishment	More reasoning, isolation, appeals to guilt
Permissiveness	Less to infant and young child	More to infant and young child
	More to older child	Less to older child
Achievement demands	Less	More
Father as companion to child	Less	More

Adapted from Smart and Smart, 1967; data from Clausen and Williams, 1963.

Some words of caution are in order concerning the relation between child-rearing practices and social class. The child-rearing practices of all social classes have been changing over time, and differences between groups have not remained constant from decade to decade. Possibly for this reason, the literature on the subject contains many inconsistent findings. In toilet training and early independence training, for example, later studies have not shown as many social-class differences as did earlier studies. Secondly, these studies tend to emphasize the homogeneity of child-rearing practices within classes and the heterogeneity across classes. This does an injustice to what actually happens. Often a touted significant difference consists of nothing more than 60 percent of one social class employing a particular practice and 45 percent of another social class doing so. A variety of styles of child rearing are adopted in every social class, and it would be a mistake to conclude that just because parents are of a particular socioeconomic status, they raise their children in a given fashion.

Sex Typing and Implications for Adult Sex Roles

Children in most cultures are subjected to very different child-rearing practices and social expectations on the basis of their sex. In fact, studies indicate that many parents actually perceive major differences between their sons and daughters. For example, when middle-class American parents were asked to describe their seventh-grade children, they spontaneously described their sons as tough-minded activists who were ambitious, energetic, competitive, confident, stable, and capable of being leaders. Daughters were described as expressive and sociable, and the parents approved of qualities such as warmth, charm, popularity, and eagerness to please in them (Hill, 1964). These differences in perception generally mean that treatment accorded sons and daughters is different.

The Nature-Nurture Issue A question of great concern today is the extent to which perceived sex differences come from child-rearing practices and learning and how much they are attributable to biological factors. One way of answering this question is to examine gender roles in various societies in the world. Anthropological evidence indicates that there is considerable variation from culture to culture in the traits and roles of females and males. In her classic studies of three South Pacific societies, Margaret Mead (1935) described some of this variability. In one group, the Arapesh, both males and females had what we would consider typical feminine traits—both sexes were nurturant and unaggressive. Among the Mundugumor people, by contrast, both males and females were hostile and aggressive, traits we describe as masculine. In the Tchambuli there was a reversal of the usual American roles—women were aggressive whereas men were nurturant. The plasticity of gender roles, however, does seem to be limited. In the vast majority of societies males have instrumental roles and females have expressive roles (Munroe and Munroe, 1975). That is, men are the achievers who carry out tasks to ensure that the society runs smoothly, whereas women are concerned with interpersonal relationships and are responsible for binding the family together.

Studying what happens when a child is assigned the wrong sex at birth provides insight into the nature-nurture issue of gender differences. Through some chromosomal or physiological abnormality the external genitals may not develop in accordance with the genetic sex of the child. Thus a genetic female may have masculine-looking genitals and be raised as a boy, and a genetic male with feminine or ambiguous genitals will be raised as a female. John Money and Anke Ehrhardt (1972), who have studied many of these cases, find that sex of rearing appears to be the most important factor in determining sexual identity and gender role. Regardless of their chromosomal sex, children who were raised as girls from infancy onward viewed themselves as females and behaved like females, whereas those raised as boys regarded themselves and acted as males. If the mistake was discovered and the sex reassigned by the age of eighteen to thirty-six months, the children could adjust rather easily. But when sex reassignment was made much later, the child had great difficulty in establishing a secure gender identity.

Sex-role typing begins at birth, when many parents make known their strong expectations of how infant boys should differ from girls. Sex distinctions are made in clothing, toy selections, and even in the identifying colors of pink and blue. As children grow older, pressures for role differentiation escalate. Boys are encouraged to be actively aggressive and to take responsibility, often for their more "fragile" sisters, despite biological evidence contradicting this stereotype of feminine weakness. Girls are taught to be dependent and helpful to others; tomboyishness gains them few rewards. In general, child-rearing practices are directed at preparing the boy for the role of active provider and the girl for that of wife, mother, and homemaker.

The cumulative effect of such differences in experience may be to force artificial limitations on adult personality and behavior in both sexes. Boys who are chided for showing affection or for crying may become men who are unable to feel or express tender emotions. Having learned that housework is a woman's job, men may deprive themselves of more leisure time with their working wives through their

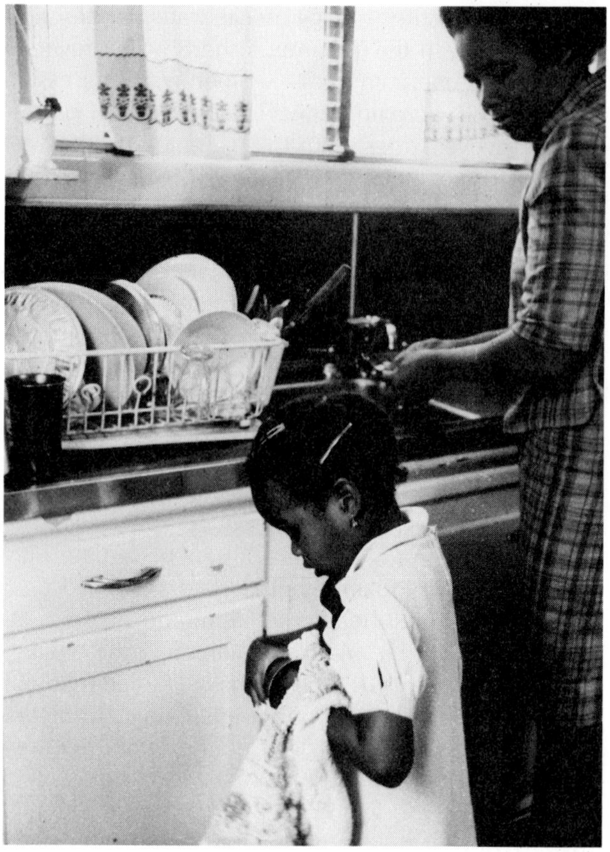

This little girl is acquiring a sex role that will prepare her for certain activities in later life but force her to limit others.

unwillingness to pitch in with the work at home. And believing that mothers are more important to infants, they may detach themselves from their babies' early lives and miss a great deal of joy and pleasure.

The recent women's movement has focused most of our attention on the implications of sex-role expectations for women. Clearly there have been significant limitations on women's educational opportunities and occupational advancement. At one major university women were found to comprise only 5 percent of the faculty members, 15 percent of the graduate students, and 30 percent of the undergraduates (Siegel, 1969). Similar discrepancies are evident in many institutions and professions in the United States. Yet women comprise more than 50 percent of the overall population and have the same distribution of intellect as men. Overt discriminatory practices are unquestionably responsible for such large imbalances in the achievement of men and women. As we have seen earlier, however, motivation can be critically important in how individuals apply their cognitive abilities. Thus, even as formal barriers are removed, some women may retain psychological barriers to exercising freedom in their career choices. They may not be able to overcome years of exposure to cultural sex-role expectations.

CAREER AND LIFE STYLE CHOICES OF WOMEN

The sociologist Alice Rossi (1968) has conducted an extensive study of the life patterns of over 15,000 young women. These women, selected from over 100 colleges, were asked to complete a series of questionnaires over a period of three years following their college graduation. Rossi found that the women could be categorized into three occupational groups: "homemakers," who reported that being a housewife was their total career goal; "traditionals," who indicated a career interest in areas generally considered appropriate for women, such as elementary and secondary school teaching, social work, nursing, and secretarial work; and "pioneers," who indicated serious career interest in fields generally considered to be masculine—the natural sciences, business management, medicine, law, engineering, economics. A very substantial majority of women placed themselves among the "traditionals," whereas three years after graduation only 7 percent of the group saw themselves as "pioneers" (Siegel, 1969).

As Alberta Siegel points out in discussing Rossi's findings, the significance of these different roles can be expected to change as the woman journeys through adulthood. The "traditional" woman makes an occupational choice that is compatible with marriage and a career. She can work, be productive in a meaningful way, and contribute both to society and her family without having questions raised in her own mind and among her friends about her femininity. But her opportunities for major advancement in her chosen field will often be limited.

The "homemaker," if she works at all in the early years of her marriage, does so in a low-level and relatively unproductive job. As she takes on the role of rearing a family, she tends to leave the world of outside work to focus on her job as mother. In time, housekeeping is quite likely to become a bore, and she may find that as her children become more independent her role is relatively unappreciated by society. She may have an identity crisis which deepens as her children leave the nest and her husband begins to reach the peak of his own career. Although she may turn to volunteer community work or acquire a lively interest in some hobby or activity, Siegel observes that, "As her youthful attractiveness fades, this woman often comes to feel serious doubts about her continuing femininity as well as about whether other people really need her, and her self-esteem plummets" (p. 20). The middle years of her adulthood, then, may not be enhancing ones for the homemaker.

As for the "pioneer," her most difficult period comes during the first decade following graduation. Men may resent her ambition and perceive her as intrusive. She may forgo marriage opportunities until her career is established, and then her criteria for a desirable husband are likely to become more stringent. All these factors provide the basis for the conflict "pioneers" often sense between the professional life they have chosen to lead and their femininity. If she marries and has children, she may have to compromise her original level of professional aspiration. If she does not compromise, she may feel guilty about neglecting her children. If her husband is transferred in his job at a time when she is enjoying occupational success, she faces a critical life decision. Is it fair for her to have to relinquish a major position after so many years of education and job preparation? Many a marriage has faltered on this realistic and stressful conflict. As Siegel notes, "Our society offers very few supports for [the pioneer's] life style."

One encouraging sign are studies indicating that a mother's employment has a positive effect on her daughters. If the mother is productive and happy in her work, her daughters tend to view women as more competent and as capable of pursing the joint undertaking of marriage and career. Furthermore, studies of the occupational histories of these women show that they often successfully realize their expectations.

The Female Sex Role and Fear of Success Studies by Matina Horner, a psychologist and President of Radcliffe College, provided evidence that some women have a strong motive to avoid success. Because aggression is not considered a feminine trait and intellectual competitiveness is often viewed as a form of aggression, they develop a **fear of success.** Horner (1968) asked female college students to complete the following story: "After first-term finals, Ann finds herself at the top of her medical school class . . ." Male college students were given a similar line, except that the name "John" and masculine pronouns were substituted in the story cue. Most of the men wrote very positive stories describing John's probable satisfaction with himself and his optimistic plans for the future.

The women's stories, however, contained many negative themes, stressing Ann's unhappiness, her personal conflicts, her probable unattractiveness, and the hostility of other students toward her. Sixty-five percent of the women, in comparison with only 8 percent of the men, wrote stories revealing anxiety about achieving high academic standing. In a follow-up study participants were observed either when they worked alone on a task or when they worked in competition with another participant. Women whose stories had shown fear of success performed well when working on a task alone but poorly if they were in competition with a man.

In a report consistent with Horner's findings, Lois Hoffman (undated paper) has written of the anxiety experienced by bright, competent college women as they become aware of their own capacity for excellence. On many college campuses, Hoffman reports, young women "play dumb" on dates in order to be perceived as more attractive. If they feel themselves to be in intellectual competition with a husband or boyfriend, the anxiety can become intense. Many girls, however, find it demoralizing to maintain this facade in order to be socially accepted.

Hoffman has observed fear of success in girls of the preschool years. She believes that through a long-established pattern the need for affiliation and conformity comes to dominate the motivation of girls, whereas achievement motivates boys. Given a conflict between achievement and affiliation, girls are more likely to give precedence to affiliation, even at the expense of their own self-actualization.

Other studies of women's motivation to achieve have indicated that fear of success is not exclusively a psychological phenomenon but a cultural one as well (Alper, 1974; Monahan, Kuhn, and Shaver, 1974). When a group of nursing students were given the story line that Ann was at the top of her nursing school class, 80 percent of them wrote success stories; when told that Ann was a medical student at the top of her class, only 20 percent did so. Thus women may not fear success in a traditionally feminine role or occupation but only in areas that have been dominated by men. As more women become prime ministers, governors, judges, generals, economists, mathematicians, physicists, and physicians, however, both men and women will come to realize that being feminine does not exclude the possibility of achieving full potential as a human being.

SUMMARY □

Parents' attitudes and child-rearing practices reflect the culture. Cross-cultural studies suggest that child-rearing practices that will enable future adults to meet the economic needs of the society are subtly encouraged. In the United States families whose members are economic entrepreneurs may have different child-rearing attitudes and practices than families taking bureaucratic positions. The entrepreneurs may emphasize individuality, the bureaucratic families cooperation. There may be some social-class differences in child rearing, but goals and practices vary within any class.

In many cultures boys are encouraged to become independent and assertive breadwinners. Girls, on the other hand, are expected to develop social abilities and to become homemakers and mothers. Through cultural sex typing adults of both sexes are constrained in the expression of their individual personalities and abilities.

TO BE SURE YOU UNDERSTAND THIS CHAPTER △

The following concepts are the major ones introduced in this chapter. You should be able to define them and state the points made about each in the text discussion.

Spontaneous or reflex smiling
Nonselective social smiling
Selective social smiling
Cognitive theory of smiling
Evolutionary theory of smiling
Stranger anxiety
Separation anxiety
Temperament (temperamental style)
Easy child
Slow-to-warm-up child
Difficult child
Attachment
Sexual identification
Permissive parent
Authoritarian parent
Authoritative parent
Socialization
Entrepreneurial occupations
Bureaucratic occupations
Sex-role typing
Fear of success

The topics that you might miss in reviewing just this list are these:

Watson's and Bridges's theories of emotional development
Management of children with different temperaments
Harlow's studies of rearing monkeys with surrogate mothers
Child rearing and social development
Cultural influences on development

TO GO BEYOND THIS CHAPTER △

In this book Fear and various forms of anxiety have already been discussed in Chapter 14. Chapters 16 and 18 will delve again into the relation between parental behavior and the child's personality.

Elsewhere Many recent works discuss topics covered in this chapter. Some recommended books are *A Child's Journey,* by Julius Segal and Herbert Yahraes; *The Role of the Father in Child Development,* edited by Michael Lamb; *The Psychology of Sex Differences,* by Eleanor Maccoby and Carol Jacklin; and *Contemporary Issues in Developmental Psychology,* by Norman Endler, L. Boulter, and H. Osser.

CH. 16

Personality: Theory, Assessment, Research

In recognition of the complexity of personality, it has been said that every person is in certain respects like all other people, like some other people, and like no other person. What this means is that, although all human beings share the biological features that are universal to the species, they also hold membership in a particular society and take on the characteristics of certain people in that society. In spite of all these physical, social, and cultural uniformities, however, each person in the world remains wholly unique. You can say about yourself that in the long history of the human race and in the lengthier future that lies ahead, there has never been and will never be anyone quite like *you*. The way you think, feel, perceive, and behave has a pattern which, in its finest details, will never be duplicated. *You* simply cannot be cloned! Your individual personality is created by a combination of unique factors—your biology, constitution, temperament, genetic structure, social development, motivational patterns, specific family and cultural environment, and life experiences. All these contribute both to your individuality as well as to your similarity to others. The idea that you are what you are and that you can never be replicated is mind-boggling, not only for you but also for the personality theorist and researcher whose task is that of integrating these many aspects and dimensions of personality into a coherent framework.

We begin our discussion of the topic of personality with the search for a theoretical framework within which to understand the complexity of human personality. Theorists who have addressed this challenge have adopted one of two alternative orientations or conceptions. The first is a *descriptive* view which emphasizes the *structure* of personality, either in terms of major behavioral dimensions called *personality traits* or in terms of broader categories of *personality types*. The second is a *developmental* orientation in which the task is to describe how personality *develops* and how individuals *adapt* to their diverse environments.

DESCRIPTIVE PERSONALITY THEORIES

Trait Theory

Identifying Traits A **trait** is a stable and enduring attribute of a person that is revealed consistently in a variety of situations. Were a trait theorist to study all possible characteristics that can be used to describe individuals, the number of possibilities would be overwhelming. The most-cited number in the psychology of personality may be 17,953. This is the number of distinguishing adjectives that Gordon Allport and Henry Odbert (1936) were able to extract from the English language when they set out to create a dictionary of trait names that could be used to distinguish one person's behavior from another's. Thirty years later Warren Norman (1963) developed a new pool of some 40,000 trait-descriptive terms. Using experimental and statistical methods, however, Norman was able to reduce this number dramatically. He began his search for simplicity by creating a set of paired polar opposite adjectives from the Allport-Odbert list (Table 16.1). Participants in his study were then asked to rate peers whom they knew well on these word pairs. Statistical analysis revealed that five personality traits seemed to account for the way in which the ratings grouped together. Table 16.1 lists these "basic" traits and some of the adjective pairs that contributed to their definition.

TABLE 16.1
Consistent Trait Dimensions and Polar Adjectives Used When Peers Rate Acquaintances and Strangers

	Polar Adjectives	
Trait Dimension	**A**	**B**
1. Extroversion	Talkative	Silent
	Frank	Secretive
	Sociable	Reclusive
2. Agreeableness	Mild, gentle	Headstrong
	Good-natured	Irritable
	Not jealous	Jealous
3. Conscientiousness	Fussy, tidy	Careless
	Responsible	Undependable
	Scrupulous	Unscrupulous
4. Emotional Stability	Poised	Nervous, tense
	Composed	Excitable
	Calm	Anxious
5. Culture	Polished	Crude
	Imaginative	Simple
	Artistically sensitive	Artistically insensitive

Adapted from Norman, 1963.

Before the five were accepted as *the* basic traits of personality, a follow-up study had to be conducted (Passini and Norman, 1966). The data of the first study had been based on persons rating others they knew. So college students were brought together, one to rate the other after an acquaintance of only fifteen minutes. Each did know that the other was a student. Curiously, these strangers produced the identical quintet of "basic" traits. Do such data mean that these five traits are, indeed, the fundamental components of personality? The answer to this question is "no." When peers rated people they knew, these ratings were consistent with self-appraisals made by the person being rated. This did not hold true in the "stranger" study. Frank Passini and Norman concluded therefore that the similarities in traits obtained in the two studies could not be based on solid infor-

Raymond B. Cattell.

mation about the individuals being rated, but were created by the stereotypic ways in which people label other people. We all use an "implicit personality theory" in our commerce with others (page 310). This is a belief that certain personality attributes or traits go together and are shared in common by people of similar backgrounds. Knowing only that the individuals to be rated were classmates was enough to evoke this set and produce the clusters of ratings.

Source Traits and Surface Traits In another important attempt to classify traits of personality, Raymond Cattell (1965) analyzed the judgments of close acquaintances of a group of people and came up with a list of thirty-five trait clusters. He called these clusters **surface traits** because they were overt expressions of personality. Speaking figuratively, these attributes are close to the surface and are expressions of more basic traits of personality (Table 16.2). Using a statistical method called factor analysis, Cattell isolated sixteen of these more basic factors. He called these **source traits** and developed a self-administered personality questionnaire, the Sixteen Personality Factor Questionnaire (16PF) to measure them.

Over the years, Cattell has given this test to many varied groups of people and reports some interesting findings. For example, in comparing successful and troubled marriages, Cattell has observed that for marriage at least, unlike charges do not attract. Stable marital pairs show greater similarity in personality than unstable marriages which are marked by striking differences between husband and wife. The similarities in stable marriages and the differences in unstable ones seem to produce three important differences in the marital relationship: warmth as opposed to aloofness; trust as opposed to suspiciousness; and self-sufficiency rather than overdependence.

The sixteen factors of Cattell's scale are listed in Figure 16.1, together with a comparison of the test profiles of three different groups of individuals, airline pilots, neurotics, and creative artists and writers. The two artist groups are very similar to each other and both are quite different from the neurotic sample. Creativity and neurosis need not go hand in hand. The fact that personality profiles of creative writers are similar to those of creative artists, suggests that the personality components of creativity are similar wherever the creative spark exists. As for the pilots, they appear to have the traits most plane passengers would find reassuring. They are relaxed, controlled, tough-minded, emotionally stable, self-assured, and practical.

Type Theory

Types are broad inclusive patterns of traits on which some psychologists have attempted to classify people. Perhaps the most famous of all typologies is that of introversion-extroversion first described by Carl Jung (see page 392). According to Jung, the *extrovert* is outgoing, exuberant, lively, and inclined toward direct action. The *introvert* presents the opposite side of the behavioral coin and is more prone to thoughtful reflection. This attractive typology unfortunately shares the two major shortcomings of all simple typologies. First, typologies put people into extreme categories that apply only to a few individuals. As with most dimensions of human variation, the gradation from introversion to extroversion is a continuous one on which people are normally distributed. Most people fall in the middle of the dimension and show both introversion and extroversion to a degree. Second, in their simplicity, typologies ignore one of the most important facts about personality, that it is multidimensional and consists of many attributes.

These shortcomings have been partially overcome in the work of a famous British psychologist, Hans J. Eysenck. Eysenck is a typologist whose focus has been on a small number of personality types, defined by three major dimensions: *introversion-extroversion,*

TABLE 16.2
A Surface Trait and Source Trait with Examples of Their Relevant Dimensions

A. *Surface trait*		
Sociability, sentimentalism	vs.	Independence, hostility, aloofness
Responsive	vs.	Aloof
Affectionate	vs.	Cold
Sentimental	vs.	Unsentimental
Social interests	vs.	Lacking social interests
Home and family interests	vs.	Lacking home and family interests
Dependent	vs.	Independent
Friendly	vs.	Hostile
Frank	vs.	Secretive
Genial	vs.	Cold-hearted
Even-tempered	vs.	Sensitive
B. *Source trait*		
Dominance	vs.	Submission
Self-assertive, confident	vs.	Submissive, unsure
Boastful, conceited	vs.	Modest, retiring
Aggressive, pugnacious	vs.	Complaisant
Extrapunitive	vs.	Impunitive, intropunitive
Vigorous, forceful	vs.	Meek, quiet
Willful, egotistic	vs.	Obedient
Questionnaire items		*Dominance indicators*
Do you tend to keep in the background on social occasions?		No
If you saw the following headlines of equal size in your newspaper, which would you read? (*a*) Threat to constitutional government in foreign country by dictator. (*b*) Physicists make important discovery concerning the electron.		*a*

From Cattell, 1950, 1965.

neuroticism-stability, to which Eysenck later added *psychoticism* as a third factor. During World War II Eysenck used many different types of procedures to classify more than 10,000 individuals, including neurotic soldiers. The symptoms exhibited by this neurotic subgroup helped him to identify the end points of the *introversion-extroversion* dimension. The introverts showed anxiety, depression, apathy, ruminative thinking, and psychologically created physical symptoms. The extroverts exhibited poor occupational histories, imaginary physical complaints, sexual difficulties, and poor performances on intelligence tests. *Neuroticism-stability,* Eysenck's second dimension, is represented at the neuroticism or "unstable" pole by people whose emotions are labile, easily aroused, and strong. These individuals are moody, touchy, anxious, restless. At the other "stable" end of the dimension are individuals with emotional control. They are reliable, even-tempered, calm, and carefree (Eysenck and Rachman, 1965). Figure 16.2 shows Eysenck's diagrammatic illustration of the relationship of various traits to the first two of the three major dimensions.

SUMMARY □

Type and trait theories are ways of describing and systematizing the variability in human personality. Traits are stable and consistent descriptive attributes of individuals. Type theorists have used patterns of such traits to characterize human types. The basic assumption of the trait approach is that individual personalities can be described in terms of a limited number of

FIGURE 16.1
16PF personality profiles. The fact that different groups differ in appropriate ways is evidence of the validity of the test. (After Cattell, 1973.)

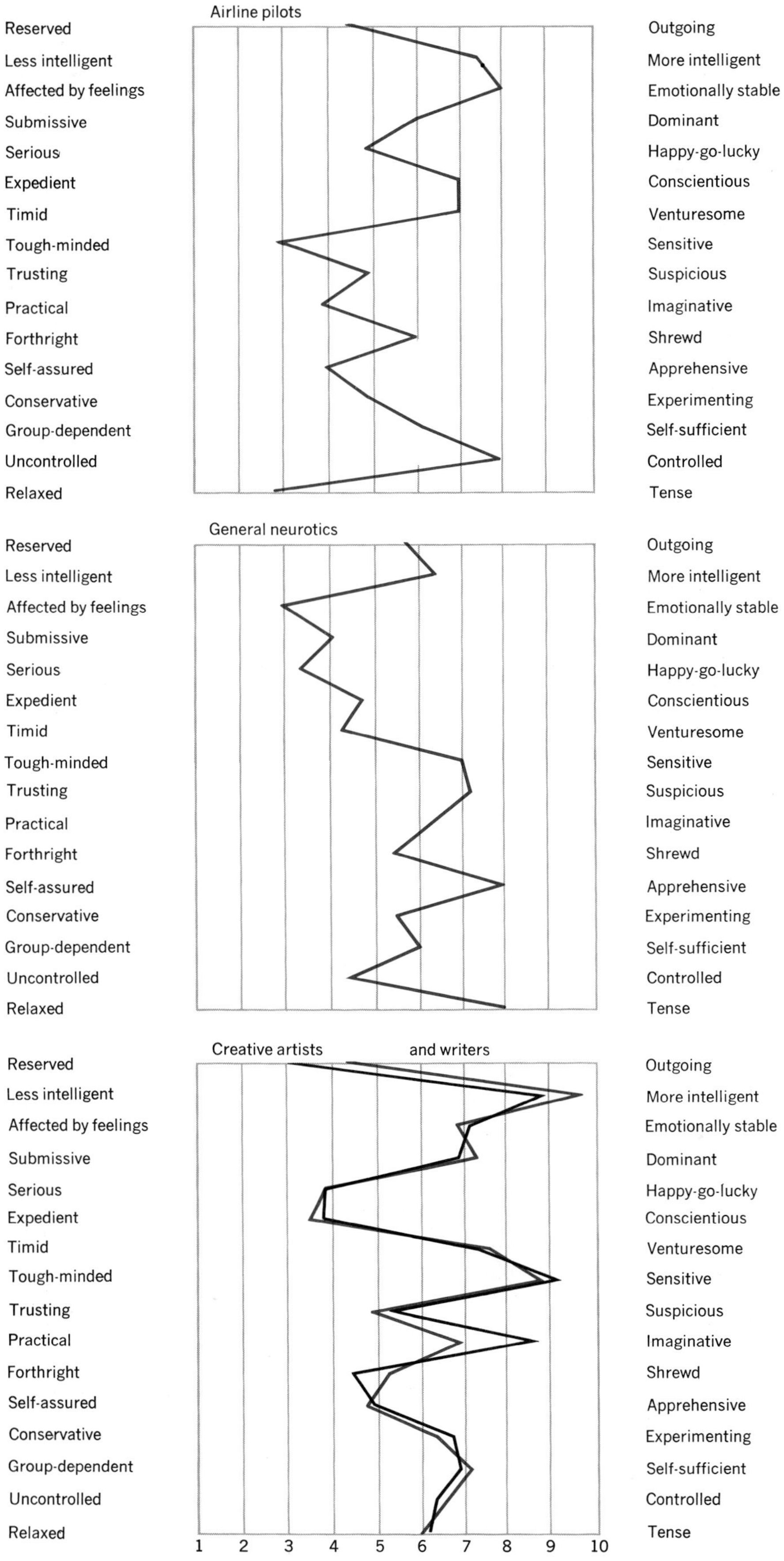
Airline pilots
General neurotics
Creative artists
and writers
Reserved
Less intelligent
Affected by feelings
Submissive
Serious
Expedient
Timid
Tough-minded
Trusting
Practical
Forthright
Self-assured
Conservative
Group-dependent
Uncontrolled
Relaxed
Outgoing
More intelligent
Emotionally stable
Dominant
Happy-go-lucky
Conscientious
Venturesome
Sensitive
Suspicious
Imaginative
Shrewd
Apprehensive
Experimenting
Self-sufficient
Controlled
Tense
1 2 3 4 5 6 7 8 9 10

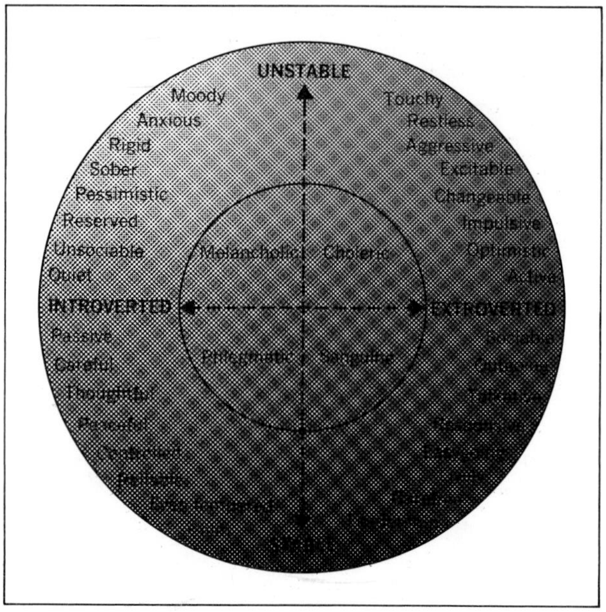

FIGURE 16.2

The results of modern factor-analytic studies of the intercorrelations of traits. To illustrate the long-term nature of such views, Eysenck provided an inner circle showing the classical four temperaments assumed by theorists in ancient Greece. They believed that these temperaments and therefore personality were determined by body fluids. (After Eysenck, 1964.)

dimensions. This view has been criticized as an oversimplification. Typologies, which employ even a smaller number of characteristics, have been criticized for the same reason. Since persons differ in quantitative as well as qualitative ways, efforts to categorize individuals on an "either-or" basis—either introverted *or* extroverted—do an injustice to the variety of behavior. Proponents of type theory, such as Eysenck, have increased the numbers of dimensions employed in their typologies in an effort to make such descriptions applicable to a larger number of people. These accounts remain descriptive, however, and are to be contrasted with developmental approaches to personality.

DEVELOPMENTAL PERSONALITY THEORIES

Freud and Psychoanalysis

The roster of great names in the history of ideas must surely include that of Sigmund Freud if we accept as a criterion of greatness the influence of a person upon society. Freud contributed to psychology and psychiatry, to our language, and to the arts and literature. He put forward theories of personality structure and personality development. He developed a method of psychotherapy. As a result of Freud's work "ego," "unconscious," "repression," and "neurosis" became everyday expressions. In a more general way the lenient social and sexual morals of the twentieth century are attributable in part to Freud's influence.

Freud, born in 1856, spent almost his entire life in Vienna. There over a span of more than fifty years, sitting in his study, surrounded by his books and Egyptian art objects, Freud listened to his patients, observed their distress, and watched their struggles to conquer it. On this basis he formulated, revised, and revised again, his theory of psychoanalysis. When the Nazis moved into Austria, Franklin D. Roosevelt and many others urged Freud to leave Vienna. Reluctantly he finally did so. He traveled to London a dying man, ravaged by the terminal stages of cancer of the mouth and jaw, the result of decades of relentless cigar smoking. When he died in September 1939 within days following the outbreak of World War II, his work had been finally acknowledged, his place in history assured.

The Emergence of Psychoanalysis If one had to point to the first great milestone in the historical development of psychoanalysis, it would have to be Freud's meeting with Josef Breuer, a noted Viennese physician. Breuer was treating a young woman, now celebrated in the psychoanalytic literature as "Fraulein Anna O," who suffered from a variety of hysterical symptoms, including paralysis, an inability to swallow, blurred vision, and visual hallucinations. Breuer, using hypnosis to treat her, would place Anna in a semitrance. During these states Anna would cry out, as though she were going through an anguishing experience. Breuer found that when he asked Anna what was tormenting her, her answers led back to events related to a period during which she nursed her dying father. If Breuer allowed her to "talk out" these experiences, Anna would awaken relaxed and comfortable, her hysterical symptoms obviously relieved. For example, in her waking state one of Anna's complaints was double vision. Under hypnosis she recounted an event in which her dying father asked her for the time. Through her tears the hands of the watch appeared blurred. Her symptom of blurred vision dated from this experience. Several days after recounting this episode, she reported to Breuer that her vision had cleared. In this systematic way Breuer removed Anna's symptoms one after the other.

ANNA O—THE STORY OF BERTHA PAPPENHEIM, FEMINIST

The story of Anna O did not end with her hysterical vision that she was giving birth to Breuer's child. The

Bertha Pappenheim—"Anna O."

new physician who stepped in when Breuer stepped out of the case prescribed morphine to calm Anna. In time Anna became an addict and had to be institutionalized. In a book about this famed patient, Lucy Freeman (1972) traced Anna's subsequent life events in *The Story of Anna O.*

In 1888 Anna, recovered from her addiction, left Vienna to return to Germany. The daughter of a wealthy Jewish family, with a distinguished lineage on both sides, she could have immersed herself in art, music, and handiwork until an eligible man appeared to marry her. She rejected that role and began a distinguished career as one of Europe's first social workers. From volunteer worker in an orphanage for destitute and illegitimate children who were unacceptable to the Jewish community, she rose to the post of director of that institution and set about to create other institutions to train and educate unwed mothers and to provide residences for them, as well as adoption and foster homes for their children.

Orthodox Judaism relegated women to a secondary role, but Bertha Pappenheim (Anna's true name) would not accept such inferior status. She converted her orphanage from a custodial to an educational institution, helped to establish educational seminaries for young women, wrote and translated tracts in favor of women's liberation, fought anti-Semitism in the governments of Europe, founded the Federation of Jewish Women, and became its first President. It was Bertha Pappenheim who broke the power of wealthy Turkish Jews, who were surreptitiously running a white-slave traffic that forced illiterate, impoverished Jewish girls from the ghettos into prostitution and transported them to brothels in South America.

Bertha Pappenheim died in May 1936 and thus escaped witnessing the final desecration of her work by the Nazis, who invaded one of the educational seminaries for young women that she had helped to establish in Poland. Informed that their school would be converted to a brothel, the ninety-three women students in a final act of dignity and courage all took poison and died by their own hands.

Breuer and Freud tried this new method on other cases of hysteria and, in 1895, described their work in a volume, *Studies in Hysteria.* Although the two men agreed on their observations, each wrote his own interpretive section for the book because they were unable to agree on the origins of the disorder. Freud emphasized repressed sexual factors; Breuer tended to blame the "hypnoidal state" of the neurotic. Later these differences were to become very acute and to break up the relationship between the two men. Breuer was evidently disturbed by the sexual implications of their analyses, Freud was not.

Breuer had his concerns accentuated when Anna declared her love for him, an event that forced him to conclude that the method of treatment was dangerous and to abandon it. The specific event that led to Breuer's retreat occurred at the end of eighteen months of treatment during which he had systematically removed symptom after symptom. Breuer had paid his last visit to Anna, before leaving on a vacation trip. He and Anna had said their good-byes. That night Breuer was called from his dinner table, summoned by Anna's mother. A new and extremely disturbing symptom had appeared.

When Breuer came to Anna, she was lying on her bed, writhing about in an agonizing replica of birth pains and muttering, "Now Dr. Breuer's baby is coming! It is coming!" Breuer hypnotized her to get her to sleep and provided the posthypnotic suggestion that when she awakened in the morning she would realize that what she had experienced was entirely in her imagination. But the experience was so frightening to him that he asked a colleague to take over Anna's treatment.

Freud, confronted with similar experiences, brought his intellectual powers to the task of analyzing such fragments of behavior and gradually formulated the concept of **transference**—a view that holds that the analyst acts as a parent substitute, attracting the patient's love for this reason. This was the most basic difference between the men. One was caught in, and under the control of, the morality of his time; the other was freed from such control by a driving desire to know and to understand human behavior. This led to Freud's many contributions, including his theory of personality structure to which we turn next.

The Structure of Personality Freudian theory divides personality into three major components, *id, ego,* and *superego*. The **id** is the original and largest component of mental organization and represents a source of instinctual energy derived from the basic biological needs of sex and aggression. It is the repository of unacceptable thoughts and impulses and is representative of a person's baser nature. The id is governed by the **pleasure principle,** a search for pleasure and immediate gratifications. The **ego** is the rational, conscious component of personality, and unlike the id the ego is governed by the **reality principle.** Its actions are constantly monitored by the demands of reality. The ego serves to keep the id in check by rejecting the primitive and amoral forces that are under the id's direction. In this sense the ego is the instrument of socialization whereby the individual learns to forgo minor immediate gratification for more significant delayed gains. The **superego** is equivalent to conscience and emerges in childhood sometime between ages three and six as a necessary aspect of ego development. It reflects the child's acceptance of the values and morality of society—the ego ideal. In the struggle between id and ego, the superego obviously stands on the side of the ego and assists in containing the pleasure demands of the id.

Anxiety and the Mechanisms of Defense A keynote in Freudian theorizing is that human behavior often has a significance that is not obvious in the overt responses of the individual. Freud's account of the mechanisms people develop to cope with anxiety—called mechanisms of defense—illustrates this point. Since the significance of these functions is not obvious, psychoanalysts speak of them as "unconscious." It should be noted, however, that it is not their behavior of which people are unaware, but rather the motivation for the behavior. It is also important to understand that the mechanisms are adaptive, because they reduce anxiety. Defense mechanisms are neither uncommon nor deviant, but they do represent self-deception. To this extent they prevent an individual from learning more effective and rational ways of coping with frustrations. The most important measures of defense are the following.

Repression is the unconscious banning from memory of traumatic, dangerous, or embarrassing thoughts, events, and desires, thus preventing the arousal of anxiety. Repression differs from *inhibition,* holding back a response for fear of punishment, and also from *suppression,* a conscious exclusion of an unpleasant thought.

Denial, one of the most primitive of the defense mechanisms, is frequently used by children and severely disturbed adults. In denial, the individual rejects an intolerable reality by denying its existence. Persistent denial as an avoidance of reality can, in time, produce more serious signs of disorder.

Repression and denial are designed to block the expression of a wish or thought. A more adaptive form of defensive behavior involves the use of a group of mechanisms in which a wish or thought is expressed but in a modified form designed to disguise its true nature.

Displacement is a mode of defense in which one object is substituted for another as a source of gratification. The point to remember is that an associative link must exist between the original stimulus and the substitute stimulus onto which an emotion or action is displaced. Freud saw dreams as a form of displacement in which the contents of the dream serve as symbols of other actions or persons that evoke severe anxiety and thus require repression.

Introjection, taking onto oneself the beliefs and values of another, and **identification** involve imitation of the attributes and qualities of another person. Identification is the result of introjection. When a child has introjected the attributes of a parent, we say that he or she has identified with the parent. Thus the mechanism of introjection is fundamental to socialization. By assuming the standards, attitudes, and values of the parents, the child's conscience begins to form. Instead of unrestrainedly expressing aggression and hostility, the child learns to inhibit aggressive behavior and, in turn, avoids punishment, gains the love of the parents, and takes on the positive beliefs and values that characterize society. Introjection, however, involves modeling the parents' weaknesses as well as their strengths. The child whose parents are dishonest and have few scruples will also learn to model such antisocial attitudes and behaviors.

Projection is introjection in reverse. It involves a process whereby undesirable traits or impulses in oneself are attributed to others.

Rationalization is the most common and most harmless of the mechanisms probably because it comes closest to representing a conscious way of dealing with unacceptable material. Through rationalization we can fool ourselves by substituting "good" (acceptable) reasons for "bad" (unacceptable) ones in order to make our behavior appear more ethical and more moral than it really is.

There is a final cluster of mechanisms that serve the goal of modifying an objectionable thought or wish by removing its dangerous qualities. In these mechanisms, a new, socially acceptable behavior serves as a defense against the dangerous behavior.

Sublimation is a mechanism whereby the expression of an impulse in its original form is repressed, but the impulse emerges in a socialized manner so that it can be gratified without disapproval. Sublimation has the quality of maturity since it enables a person to meet reality instead of fleeing from it.

Reaction formation is closely related to repression and represents one method for maintaining it. This mechanism consists in developing behavior that is the opposite of some unacceptable personal tendency such as the conversion of hatred of another into expressions of concern and love.

Compensation is a mechanism that is more related to one's status than to the satisfaction of unacceptable impulses and needs. It is a method for handling our deficiencies by "making up" for them in some way. The defect that is being compensated for may be real or imaginary. Sometimes compensation is achieved through the development of a high level of personal skill, sometimes through the achievements of others. Parents who push their children toward specific occupations may be compensating for their own unfulfilled ambitions.

The Psychosexual Theory of Personality Development The individual, according to Freud, has a certain amount of psychic energy or **libido.** The history of **psychosexual development** is the history of the various activities and objects to which the libido attaches itself. In the normal course of development, the individual goes through a number of stages in which the libido is invested first in one kind of activity and then in another. In many cases, however, the libido remains fixated to a degree at one level or another, usually as a result of frustration. In this way libido can remain partially attached to the objects and activities appropriate to an early stage of development. Such **fixations** will then be evident in adulthood in the form of more immature behavior.

Freud associated the sexual instinct in infancy with the manipulation of various body parts for pleasure. Tensions that build up in these areas are reduced by manipulation, and such relief is pleasurable. The major areas for such satisfaction, termed *erogenous zones,* are the mouth, anus, and genitals. Each is associated with a primary drive—hunger, elimination, and sex—and each, in turn, becomes the central focus of the child's activity in a stage sequence of development.

The first period of life, up to the age of seven or eight months, is the **oral stage** in which the baby gains intense pleasures from nursing, sucking, and mouthing. In this stage of development, the libido expresses itself as an oral drive with satisfaction of the drive usually provided by the mother. If this drive is frustrated, as when infants are deprived of adequate mothering, the baby's behavior reveals its distress: breathing is shallow, crying is exaggerated, and there is tension and muscular rigidity. Other babies may become lethargic, their body muscles may grow lax, and tube feeding may even become necessary. A return to adequate mothering will often relieve these acute symptoms.

The second stage of psychosexual development is the **anal stage,** in which the baby derives pleasure from the process of elimination. For the first few months of life, the eliminative processes are automatic; apparently the baby is unaware of them. As the child matures, there is increasing pleasure in excretion. The parent in our society is likely to frustrate this satisfaction by initiating toilet training, often before the child has either the necessary muscular control or the use of language. Parental discomfort with defecation can provide the growing child with a new means of exercising control over the parents. If the child is incontinent, the parents are distressed; if feces are retained and offered at the proper time, the child gains praise and reward. In the Freudian view the experiences of the child during toilet training can exert a profound influence on later adjustment.

The third stage in psychosexual development is the **phallic stage,** occurring between the second and fourth years. In this phase definite signs of sexuality appear in the child, sometimes in the form of overt masturbation, sometimes as a desire for contact with the parent of the opposite sex. At least in our culture, many factors lead to the suppression of this infantile sexuality. Parents may be disturbed by the child's behavior, and they may avoid answering questions that they find embarrassing or even punish this early form of sexual interest.

Partially as a result of parental suppression of early sexuality, the child moves into a **latency stage** in which little direct sexuality is observed. Interests are likely to be centered in sex-typed activities and the child is likely to be negative to members of the opposite sex. The male child often shows strong identification with his father, the girl with her mother. During this period the male child resolves his **oedipal relationship** to his mother. This relationship, generated out of the child's original closeness to the mother, represents a desire for union with her. Freud reasoned that the child rejects this desire out of fear of retaliation from his father, who is a love competitor. This is the **castration complex.** The son then sublimates his affection for his mother and turns to an identification with his father. The onset of puberty, which follows the latency period, sees the reemergence of heterosexual interests as the individual reaches the adult or **genital stage** of psychosexual development.

It is important to understand that when Freud wrote

about "sex" he meant far more than sexual union. Perhaps it would be more appropriate to talk of "love," including love of parents, affectionate behavior, comradeship, and even a love of humankind. But it is equally important to understand that the concept of libido included sexuality in the narrower sense. Libido, for Freud, represented the *life instinct* or *Eros*. Freud also postulated a death instinct, but this construct is far less developed, and less accepted, in psychoanalytic theory.

Evaluation of Freudian Theory Most critics who have read widely in psychoanalysis—whether they agree or disagree with psychoanalytic theory—regard Freud's work as one of the revolutionary milestones in the history of human thought. As observations of the dynamics of human behavior, Freud's insights have never been equaled. Some of the concepts for which we are indebted to him are those of the unconscious, the ego, repression, anxiety, symbolization, regression, and projection. It was not that Freud was the first to use these concepts, and many more, but rather that he showed their potentialities for understanding human personality. In addition, Freud is responsible for a technique of therapy, for the idea that childhood experience can influence adult life, and for the recognition that sexual difficulties are often involved in personality maladjustment and disorders. Whether the connection with Freudian psychology is admitted or not, some sequence of stages is now commonly recognized as characteristic of human development.

Despite these contributions, any appraisal of psychoanalysis must include many criticisms. As a theory psychoanalysis is inexact and literary in emphasis. At a factual level Freudian ideas distort the picture of personality. Freud drew his data from a limited and biased sample of late-nineteenth and early-twentieth-century Viennese upper-middle-class neurotic women who were his patients. There is little in the way of experimental evidence to support his dynamic analysis of behavior. For example, although there is evidence that the so-called oral and anal personalities may have particular identifying traits, little proof links these traits to child-rearing practices or to frustrations during an early period. The theory of infantile sexuality also evokes criticism. Does a boy who expresses a wish to marry his mother or a girl who speaks of being wed to father — we have all heard young children make such statements — do so out of sexual motivation or out of a desire to imitate and model the parents? Contemporary thinking would place the emphasis on the child's strivings to be like the adult parent and to imitate his or her behavior.

Opponents also criticize the rigidity and a narrowness in the stage sequences set out by Freud. They point out that too little attention is paid to the personality changes that come with adulthood. One senses in psychoanalytic theory an entrapment in problems rooted in childhood, without adequate attention to the ever-changing nature of people's adaptations as they grow older. In a similar way the broader social environment is neglected in Freud's theory. Consideration of the social context of behavior was an important addition proposed by analytic thinkers who followed Freud.

Carl Jung.

More Recent Theories

Of Freud's many followers, the names of Carl Jung, Alfred Adler, and Karen Horney represent major contributors to an extension of psychoanalytic thinking. The brief mention we give to them here is not commensurate with either their productivity or their originality.

Carl Jung Jung was Freud's greatest disappointment, for Freud intended him to inherit the mantle of leadership of the psychoanalytic movement after he had passed from the picture. But this was a secondary role that ill-befitted the independent Jung. Jung had been impressed with his reading of Freud's *Interpretation of Dreams* when that important volume first appeared at the turn of the century. He soon became one of Freud's most outspoken supporters, so outspoken that, at one point, Jung's academic career was jeopardized by his public and printed espousal of Freud.

Alfred Adler.

Jung's reply to two German professors who warned him of that danger attests to his scientific ethic and character. "If what Freud says is the truth, I am with him. I don't give a damn for a career if it has to be based on the premises of restricting research and concealing truth" (Brome, 1978, p. 95). In fact, Jung voluntarily relinquished his academic career and retained his independence of action throughout his life—an independence which finally culminated in his break with Freud.

Jung not only challenged Freud's preoccupation with the sexual basis of neurosis but his very concept of the unconscious. Jung argued that sexual thoughts were not alone in being subject to repression. He believed that repression could lead to the forgetting of any frightening experience or threatening event. Jung also believed that these repressions form "complexes" in what Jung termed the **personal unconscious.** As one always interested in myth and mysticism, Jung believed that there also existed an impersonal collective unconscious. The **collective unconscious** contained the images of humanity—the inherited archetypes that reflect the great mythical ideas of the past and involved the repeated experiences of humankind (Hogan, 1976). Part of those experiences are represented in the concept of **persona,** the social mask people use to portray the roles that societal pressures impose on them.

A final point should be made about another major theoretical shift that Jung introduced. He saw human development as growth-oriented, and as such it was aimed not at the resolution of conflict but at goals marked by achievement, maturity, and "self-actualization." The last-named is Jung's term. Abraham Maslow, the humanistic psychologist, elaborated upon it in his own theory of personality growth which has had such a pronounced impact in the sixties and seventies.

Alfred Adler Adler also departed from Freud in his rejection of sexuality as the primary force controlling human behavior. For Adler it was the sense of *inferiority,* not repressed sexuality, that underlay maladjustment. Individuals, therefore, search for ways of compensating for their inferiority and their modes of achievement are established through early conditioning. These patterns, in time, become the individual's life style or most characteristic traits. *Self-esteem,* a contemporary concept, was first elaborated by Adler who saw its sources as both internal, arising out of needs for sex, love, and security, and external, as provided by the family and other social groups. For Adler the level of self-esteem became the basis for how individuals oriented themselves to later situations that shaped their life style.

Adler seems a more contemporary figure than many who took part in the early years of the psychoanalytic movement. His emphasis on the social context of behavior, styles of coping with life stress, the vision of control that individuals can exert over their lives, their motivation toward growth, competence, and superiority—all these convey his view of the coping qualities of people able to meet life's difficulties.

Adler's views on the structure and development of personality proved helpful not only to parents but to some of the major humanistic psychologists such as Carl Rogers, and Abraham Maslow who came later. These views embodying the problems people face in a competitive technological society reflect the practical and applied contributions of Adler that earn him a place among those analytic thinkers who extended significantly the range and content of psychoanalysis.

Karen Horney With the growth of the feminist movement, Sigmund Freud has come to be viewed as the mortal enemy of women. This reaction is understandable because Freud (for example, 1925) cast women in a role inferior to that of men and used the ugly metaphor "penis envy" to summarize what he saw as women's dissatisfaction with their status. In Freud's opinion women envied men both their social roles and their sexual roles.

Since Freud wrote his 1925 paper, things have changed radically. Women have challenged the Freudian assumption of their inferiority. Power in our time has shifted in the family. Outside the family women have taken on many roles, including those of breadwinner, taxpayer, and homemaker. Identification with mother today brings an increment, not a decrement, in power for the young female child in the family. Does this carry with it a new symbolism to replace the only one Freud had available in the era of male power at the opening of the twentieth century? Feminists say "yes," a view that will undoubtedly prevail. But tribute must be paid to the early pioneers who espoused this alternative orientation.

Within the psychoanalytic circle it fell to Karen Horney, one of the first women to be admitted to a medical school in Germany, to challenge Freud's views on female sexuality. Horney came to see that the source of feelings of inferiority in women resided in their powerless position in the society of the 1920s. Outlets for satisfactory expression for women were few, and the few there were were often limited by restrictive male power. For this reason there was a "flight from womanhood," initiated by social restraints that were every bit as important as the psychological constraints they imposed (Rubins, 1978).

Horney saw the distorting effects of masculine influence on feminine development, not only in happenings within the family—favoritism shown a brother, punishment for sexual curiosity; but also in external events—the greater social value placed on maleness, the sense of inferiority and lowered self-esteem which grows out of the unrewarded experience of expressing femininity through achievement, the artificial separation of "sexual" and "romantic" love which forces women to repress one aspect of their emotional responsiveness, the subjugation and debasement of women by the male's need to reaffirm his dominance and need for conquest. Why, Freud had asked, did men often choose hysterical and uneducated women to be their wives or turn to prostitutes to satisfy their sexual drives? Freud's answer: sexuality can only be expressed to one who is inferior to the "pure" mother idealization. Horney's answer: a superior woman would pose too great a threat to masculine pride and therefore debasement becomes the male solution to the problem.

Karen Horney.

Later in her life Horney came to America and wrote papers based on her observations of the social scene as she saw it here. If women suffer, if they develop a lowered sense of self-esteem, if they know greater disappointments and less fulfillment, these are the consequences of a restriction of opportunity, dependence, and other facts of women's economic and social lives, rather than their biology.

> Woman's efforts to achieve independence and enlargement of *her* fields of activity are continually met with a skepticism which insists that such efforts should be made only in the face of economic necessity, and that they run counter to inherent character and natural tendencies. Accordingly, all efforts of this sort are said to be without any vital significance for women, whose every thought should center upon the male or motherhood . . . (1934, p. 605).

For thirteen years (1923 to 1936) Horney wrote in this vein, accentuating a feminine psychology that was positive, although rooted in a social-cultural system which restrained women in the expression of opportunity, interpersonal relations, goals, and aspirations. Her pioneering efforts have served as an impetus to those who have since followed in her courageous path.

Ego Psychology The most important psychoanalytic influence to appear in recent years has been exerted by a group of theorists emphasizing **ego psychology** and the relationship of individuals to the society in which they live. These theorists grew increasingly dissatisfied with the emphasis on conflict and defense that was implicit in Freud's formulation about ego functioning. They also argued that Freudian theory was outdated, that interpretations conceived at the beginning of the twentieth century scarcely seemed the base for constructing an understanding of personality in the closing quarter of the century. These theorists updated psychoanalysis by expanding the conception of ego beyond its identification with the defense mechanisms and by allowing the ego a conflict-free sphere, identified by the operation of such cognitive processes as perception, learning, memory, and attention. This represents a far-reaching change in psychoanalytic theory. Freud had given primacy not to the ego but to the id, which he believed exercised the most important influence throughout an individual's life.

Erik Erikson The psychoanalytic point of view has permeated all his intellectual endeavors, but Erik Erikson is certainly not an orthodox analytic thinker. Although continuing to appreciate the importance Freud ascribed to the instinctual forces and erogenous zones which underlay Freud's psychosexual stages (oral, anal, phallic, latent, and genital), Erikson also emphasized the great importance to personality development of the child's interactions with the social environment. For Erikson any complete understanding of this process of development required a sensitivity to external social forces, as well as to intrapsychic biological factors. Thus, with other neo-Freudians, Erikson has made Freudian thought more social in nature.

Stages of personality development Erikson is best known for his view that personality development proceeds through eight stages, with each stage characterized by a major conflict which must be successfully resolved if healthy development is to take place. These conflicts at successive stages of development are the result of tasks presented by society to the developing individual which interact with the individual's developing biological characteristics. Erikson is also aware that even when a conflict at an early stage is successfully resolved it may recur as a conflict at later stages of development and again need to be conquered. Conversely, a conflict unresolved at an earlier stage can be successfully resolved at any of the later stages of development.

Erik Erikson.

Erikson's anthropological interests led him to do field work among a number of American Indian tribes. His observations of the sense of uprootedness among Indians and the disparities between their cultural history and current life styles set him to thinking about the problems of identity and assimilation and led to his promulgation of the following eight stages of psychosocial development.

Stage 1: Basic trust versus basic mistrust (first year of life). The maternal relationship at this age is critical and children develop trust if their caretaking is characterized by predictability and warmth. These children develop a sense of being loved and of there being rhyme, reason, and predictability in what the parent is doing. If the infant's world is chaotic and unpredictable and the parent's affection cannot be counted upon, the result is a sense of mistrust.

These basic attitudes are not set down in all-or-none fashion in the first year of life. Events in later years can modify the child's basic orientation. Figures other than family members may generate trust in a distrustful child, or the development of trauma in the family later on may rupture a previously developed sense of security and safety.

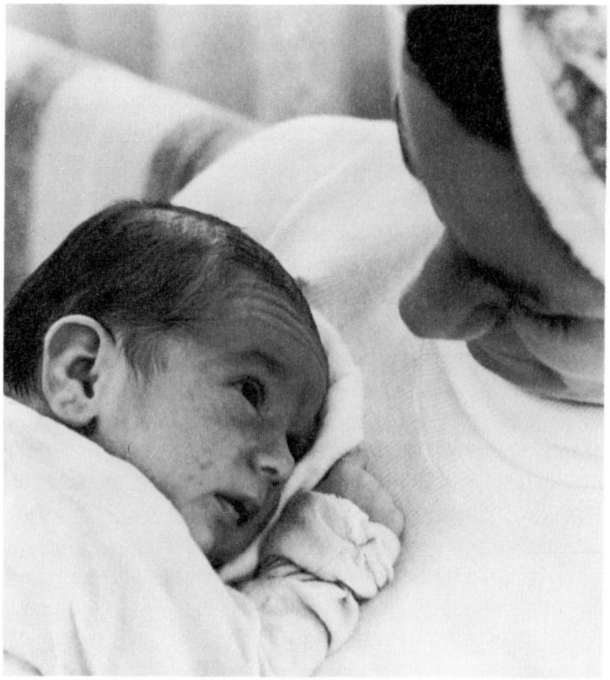

Stage 1: Trust versus mistrust.

Stage 2: Autonomy versus shame and doubt (ages two through three). This stage focuses on the child's growth of autonomy with the development of many skills, such as walking, climbing, exploring, speaking, and countless others. If parents welcome these important steps toward independence, children can continue to explore and master their environments and, in the course of doing so, can begin to exert control over their impulses. If children are not allowed such freedom, if they are overprotected, have things done for them, are criticized for the things they do, shame, doubt, and uncertainty about themselves and their capabilities will dominate their behavior. Such a self-image will be particularly limiting when society demands autonomous behavior years later. The problem is one of a delicate balance between the two extremes of an overly protective home atmosphere and one that provides little or no supervision of the child's activities.

Stage 3: Initiative versus guilt (ages four through five). At this stage the child is ready to engage in a variety of self-initiated motor and intellectual activities. To cope effectively with the environment rather than to be the passive recipient of whatever the environment provides, the child must develop initiative in play, in thought, in activity generally. At this stage the parents must carefully balance their need to protect the child from undercontrolled activities and fantasies while continuing to encourage the initiative the child displays. If the parents downgrade the child's activities or if inquiries are discouraged, future efforts by the child to set and achieve goals will be met with a sense of guilt because the goals will be considered to have little value.

Stage 4: Industry versus inferiority (ages six through eleven). These are the school years during which children widen their array of skills. These skills become the vehicles through which work is accomplished. The child becomes responsible for homework and assignments and develops an awareness that tasks can either be accomplished through industry or they will be failed. If parents reinforce these

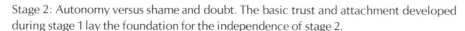

Stage 2: Autonomy versus shame and doubt. The basic trust and attachment developed during stage 1 lay the foundation for the independence of stage 2.

efforts with praise and reward, the child will develop a sense of esteem based upon achievements. If the child's work is derogated, a sense of inadequacy or inferiority may take over. To avoid this, the child needs success and a satisfactory resolution of earlier crises. Such growth results in a sense of trust, autonomy, and initiative. The expansion of the child's world beyond the family implies that other experiences can now begin to modify the child's sense of industry or inferiority.

Stage 5: Identity versus role confusion (ages twelve through eighteen: adolescence). Childhood proper comes to an end at this stage and youth begins. As the number of roles the adolescent is expected to play increases, there is a growing concern with the impression made upon others. Puberty brings on what Erikson has called a "physiological revolution" which adolescents must cope with at the same time that they try to come to grips with the issue of who they are or the nature of their own ego identity. In trying to define themselves, adolescents try out many different identities. But here the danger is one of role confusion in which the individual cannot piece together from the many roles played, a coherent sense of self. It is this striving after a sense of identity that often leads the adolescent to develop a very strong sense of in-group loyalty (the adolescent gang) that is more than matched by an out-group hostility. If, at this stage, the adolescent is permitted some freedom in the exploration of roles with appropriate structuring and advice from adults, a firm sense of ego identity is assured.

Stage 6: Intimacy versus isolation (young adulthood). Only after people have developed a sense of identity and are comfortable with it can they reach out for intimate relationships with other human beings. Forming close relationships, both sexual and nonsexual, offers great potential gratifications but close relationships also pose potential dangers. One can be rejected, or the relationship may fail through disagreement, disappointment, or hostility. If this fear is excessive, one may be tempted not to take a chance on intimate relationships but to opt instead for withdrawal and isolation. Persons who fail to resolve this conflict successfully may engage in a great deal of social activity, but their relations with others are of a superficial sort.

Stage 7: Generativity versus stagnation (middle age). For Erikson *generativity* includes marriage, parenthood, and the sense of working productively and creatively. It also means possessing a degree of selflessness. This generativity is expressed in a concern not only with one's own children but with future generations, and implies a willingness to extend oneself on behalf of all younger people. The generative individual enjoys work and family and is continually ready to express concern for others. The opposite of this person is the individual who cares little about such things and whose life is characterized by stagnation in which pleasure is derived solely from personal gratification.

Stage 6: Intimacy versus isolation.

Stage 8: Integrity versus despair (old age). Toward the end of life, one must take stock of what has been accomplished and of the type of person one has been. This is the stage in which the individual looks back on life either with a sense of integrity and satisfaction or with a sense of despair. There is a period in the lives of all men and women when they realize that major changes in life styles are no longer likely. What they are now and what they do now are what they will always be and do. This is a time of totaling up life's balance sheet and reflecting on what one has achieved. If earlier crises have been met successfully, the ledger reflects integrity; if not, it reflects despair. "Despair," writes Erikson, "expresses the feeling that the time is now short, too short for the attempt to start another life and to try out alternate roads to integrity." To individuals who experience such despair, death is indeed a bitter pill. The parallel between the first and final states of life is seen in Erikson's interesting analogy: "Healthy children will not fear life if their elders have integrity enough not to fear death."

Stage 8: Integrity versus despair. This is Maggie Kuhn, founder of the Gray Panthers, giving a lecture at Harvard.

Evaluation Erikson's theory provides a welcome balance to traditional psychoanalytic theory. His emphasis on adult development does not deny the powerful effects of childhood experience, but it reduces the exclusive preoccupation with the early years that was the outgrowth of Freud's thinking. It assigns a role to experiences outside the family that also contributes to healthy or unhealthy personality formation. It places responsibility on the individual for his or her own maturity and sets forth a climate of hopefulness in its view that at each stage it is possible to modify one's behavior. Erikson's view that there are no fixed and immutable patterns which cannot be changed by time and appropriate experiences is a more positive and less depressive view of personality than orthodox Freudian theory.

Learning Theory

Three decades ago a classic volume was written by two distinguished learning theorists, Neal Miller and John Dollard of Yale University. Their book, *Personality and Psychotherapy,* was one of the most significant efforts to link psychoanalysis and learning theory. Despite the differences between the two orientations, learning theory and psychoanalysis share the assumption that the causes of behavior are to be found in the previous history of an individual. *Personality and Psychotherapy* was by far the most successful of a number of efforts that had been made to translate the concepts of psychoanalysis into the terms of learning theory. Since then the learning point of view has gained increased acceptance in personality theory. In the process the trappings of psychoanalysis have largely been discarded.

We consider now two contemporary orientations that have gained wide acceptance. One is based on the views of B. F. Skinner of Harvard University. The other is social-learning theory, identified with the work of Albert Bandura of Stanford.

The Skinnerian Approach One important contribution of Dollard and Miller (1950) was to treat the learning of neurotic symptoms in the same way that they treated the acquisition of any other behavior. Although this conception was novel in 1950, it now has such general acceptance that it is no longer an issue for debate. If any further support were needed to make this point, it has been provided most forcefully in recent years by psychologists who take the Skinnerian approach to the study of personality development.

The emphasis of the Skinnerian school is on overt behavior—what the organism does in a specified situation. It avoids theory and all inferences of drives, motives, conflicts, traits, and the like. The Skinnerian treatment of personality development emphasizes the gradual shaping of the behavior that takes place as a result of planned or unplanned schedules of reinforcement (page 133).

In contrast to Dollard and Miller, Skinner's rejection of theory in general leads him also to reject psychoanalysis. We take as an example Skinner's criticisms of Freud's views about a significant factor in his own early life.

Freud had suggested that sibling rivalry, which played a significant role in his psychoanalytic theorizing had also been important in his personal relationships with others. He believed important factors related to his early rivalry had been the death of an infant brother when he was one and a half years old and his later experiences with a playmate, older and stronger than he, who was in the ordinarily subordinate power position of being his nephew. Skinner suggests that Freud failed to analyze the origins of his own behavior appropriately.

> An emphasis upon behavior would lead us to inquire into the specific acts plausibly assumed to be engendered by these childhood episodes. In very specific terms how was the behavior of the young Freud shaped by the special reinforcing contingencies arising from the presence of a younger child in the family, by the death of that child, and by later association with an older playmate who nevertheless occupied a subordinate family position? What did the young Freud learn to do to achieve parental attention under these difficult circumstances? How did he avoid aversive consequences? Did he exaggerate any illness? Did he feign illness? Did he make a conspicuous display of behavior which brought com-

> mendation? Was such behavior to be found in the field of physical prowess or intellectual endeavor? Did he learn to engage in behavior which would, in turn, increase the repertoires available to him to achieve commendation? Did he strike or otherwise injure young children? Did he learn to injure them verbally by teasing? Was he punished for this, and if so, did he discover other forms of behavior which had the same damaging effect but which were immune to punishment?
>
> We cannot, of course, adequately answer questions of this sort at so late a date, but they suggest the kind of inquiry which would be prompted by a concern for the explicit shaping of behavior repertoires under childhood circumstances. What has survived through the years is not aggression and guilt, later to be manifested in behavior, but rather patterns of behavior themselves (1972, pp. 244–245).

It is this type of systematic analysis of situations, behavior, and reinforcement contingencies that is necessary, the Skinnerians assert, if we are to understand personality processes. To push the translation of psychoanalytic theory into learning theory any further is a futile task and one that would do little to enhance personality theory or personality research. Personality psychologists, instead, should direct their attention to the utilization of learning principles to achieve their understanding of normal and abnormal personality development. The most significant current efforts along those lines have come from social-learning theory, which does not, however, accept the antitheoretical Skinnerian outlook (Skinner, 1974, 1978).

Social-Learning Theory Social-learning theory receives its name from the emphasis Albert Bandura (for example, 1977) has given it from its very beginning, that the study of individuals must take the social context into account, and that it is by patterns of social interaction that behavior is formed and modified. It is this emphasis that links social-learning theory so intimately to personality development.

Observational learning versus reinforcement A major difference between Skinnerian interpretations and social-learning theory are their assumptions about the conditions that are essential to learning. For Skinner the essential condition is the *direct reinforcement* of behavior. The social-learning theorist concedes the importance of reinforcement but insists that many forms of learning occur simply as a result of *observing* others. In such **observational learning** as espoused by Bandura, direct reinforcement is not essential for learning. One can experience it vicariously by seeing the consequences that result for others who

Albert Bandura.

are behaving in a particular way. This leads to the *imitation* or the **modeling** of the behavior of another, a rapid form of behavior change in which the major factors are observation and cognition. Since the basis for change is cognitive, imitation is not automatic; one *chooses* to imitate a model on the basis of one's perception of the observed consequences of an action or an anticipation of what are likely to be the consequences for behaving in a specific way (Schultz, 1976).

In comparing modeling with direct reinforcement, Bandura argues that direct reinforcement is too inefficient a way to be the primary basis for learning how to behave in a complex world. Do we learn how to find our way to school, or how to drive a car, or the corner on which to wait for a bus by trial and error behavior in which the correct solution is dependent on direct reinforcement? Obviously the answer is "no"; much of our behavior is learned by example. We observe what others do and then proceed to do the same thing. As Duane Schultz (1976) has written,

> Some behaviors can be learned only through the influence of models; language is perhaps the best example of this. How could a child learn to speak if he or she never had the opportunity to

> hear words, phrases, and sentences. If learning to speak could be accomplished by operant conditioning alone, it would mean that the infant would not be reinforced for saying words (or approximations of them) until *after* he or she had said them spontaneously, having never heard them before (p. 303).

Evidence from studies of language acquisition (page 184) attests to the wisdom of this observation.

To broaden our understanding of the power of observational learning, let us look at some of the facts that seem to reflect modeling in our society. There is a relationship between antisocial behavior of children and the antisocial behavior of their parents. Mobs act in concert in ways in which individuals are unlikely to act when alone. Adolescents model peers in ways that often seem aberrant to their families. College students may even model professors, although that type of observational learning seems in short supply these days. There is perhaps a causal relation between watching violence on television—decried by Bandura—and hostility (pages 3 and 506). Given this power of modeling, it is obvious that parents will inevitably transmit their fears, attitudes, and values to their children.

Modeling can even determine what we look at in the environment. In one interesting experiment, college undergraduates were shown a film of nude males and females. Subjects were told that a spot of light that moved about on the film indicated the eye movements of a subject who had previously looked at the film. For one half the subjects the light remained on the background of the picture, for the other half it focused on the nude bodies. Later, when these subjects were shown slides of the nude forms, their own scanning followed the pattern to which they had been exposed. Those who had been told that nude bodies had been looked at did that; the others avoided the nudes and looked at the backgrounds.

Schultz, commenting on the difference between the Skinnerian and the Bandura views, makes a telling point: the control of behavior in Skinner's system resides with whoever controls the reinforcers; in Bandura's system it resides with who controls the models.

Component processes in observational learning What are the requirements for effective modeling to occur? Bandura has described four component processes that govern observational learning.

Attention. One cannot learn by observation unless one attends to the behavior that is to be modeled. Such attentional behavior is related to a wide variety of factors including the observer's characteristics, the activity being observed, the characteristics of the person who is engaging in the activity, and the rewards that accompany the activity.

The explosive impact of television has advanced enormously the availability of models to be emulated. So much so that some psychologists fear that television can attenuate the power of parents as models. Others suggest that the typical middle-class portrayals of life seen on television have led to a rising tide of expectations for viewers which, if left unfulfilled, can lead to a spiraling cycle of frustration and despair in poor people.

Retention. Behavior can be modeled only if it is remembered. The two memory systems discussed in our earlier treatment of dual-coding theory (page 157) are both necessary. The imaginal system allows us to call up an image of modeled behavior. The verbal system serves as a substitute for images. Thus "hot" can warn a child away from a radiator as effectively as can the pain of a burnt finger.

Retention is enhanced by rehearsal (page 166). The more a person mentally rehearses a behavioral pattern, the more proficient will be his or her behavior and the better it will be retained. In one experiment Bandura and his colleagues (1966) had children view a film of a model engaged in a series of novel actions and, according to assigned group, behave in one of three ways while watching: (1) the subject described aloud the sequence of acts as they were performed by the model; (2) the observer merely watched the model carefully as the acts were performed; (3) the subject had to count rapidly while observing the model, thus interfering with learning and retention of the observed acts. Later the subjects were asked to perform the acts, given high and low incentives for correctly imitating them. The quality of performance, from best to worst, followed the order of the assigned ways of watching.

Motor responses. Symbolic representations, images and words, must be converted into action. This requires the organization in sequence, time, and space of the modeled action. These actions must be practiced with corrections made by feedback from one's own performance. Complex behavior patterns may require segmenting the pattern, breaking it into basic components, and practicing these before putting it all back together again in the appropriate sequence.

Motivation. As we have seen previously (page 331), there is an important difference between learning and performance. What is learned becomes overt activity as a result of many influences, one of the most important of which is motivation. In the case of modeling, social-learning theorists believe that rewards are more effective than punishment. It is certain that acts that bring satisfaction are more likely to be modeled than are those that earn disapproval. From our earlier discussion of punishment, however, it is clear that aversive consequences may make children refrain from modeling punishment behavior (page 345). Such effects require further study.

Carl Rogers.

With this background we can now link together the Skinnerian and social-learning points of view in this manner. If we wished to have an individual learn a skill optimally, the first step would be to have the person observe a competent model perform the skill; the next step would be to use reinforcement gradually to bring the skill to a high level of efficiency. How much time to give to modeling and how much to reinforcement will depend on the type of task that is to be acquired.

The Phenomenological-Humanistic Tradition

The phenomenological-humanistic tradition has been called the "third force" in American psychology to identify its recent entry into competition with psychoanalysis and learning theory. The most prominent figures associated with this movement are Carl Rogers and Abraham Maslow.

Rogerian Theory By **phenomenology,** the central focus of Rogerian theory, is meant an emphasis on the conscious experience of individuals and their subjective awareness of themselves and the world in which they exist. We react, asserts Rogers, to the world as we perceive it. These perceptions determine our response to events and to others. If we can keep ourselves open to the world of experience, we have established the basic condition necessary to growth, maturity, and the realization of our potential. Such statements reflect an emphasis that is radically different both from the psychoanalytic view with its stress on unconscious causality and from learning theory with its emphasis on external stimuli and overt measurable responses. This striving for self-enhancement or "actualization" is a process for Rogers which begins at birth and moves forward to fulfillment only if conditions are favorable for doing so.

The concept of "self," or "self-concept," is so important a component in Rogers's theory of personality that his has been termed *self-theory.* How does the self emerge? Its basic roots are to be found in the earliest interactions with parents, for these form the background out of which emerge the perceptions, values, attitudes, and cognitions that mark a person's relationships with others. But the sense of self is not fixed and immutable. Poor parental relationships are modifiable by subsequent experience if the individual can be open rather than defensive, flexible rather than rigid, and strives successfully to gain freedom from external controls (Nye, 1975). How one constructs experiences implies a construction of the self. Thus a constricted sense of one's self can lead to further restrictiveness of experience as the individual shuts out events, experiences, and emotions that are considered to be incompatible with one's self image.

The **humanistic** principle in Rogers's "thinking" is his belief that all human beings are innately good and seek to grow and to expand their horizons. Such growth is dependent on love and acceptance from others—what Rogers calls "unconditional positive regard." Its presence or its absence in the individual's life determines whether that person's self-concept is one of worthiness or unworthiness.

Another basic concept in Rogerian theory is the principle of **congruence-incongruence.** Congruence is a state of internal harmony, incongruence one of disharmony. The achievement of a congruent state implies that one's self-concept is consistent with what one experiences. Successfully achieved consistency makes the "integrated" or whole person. Incongruence reflects basic estrangement. This develops when "unconditional positive regard" is lacking, when love and acceptance are made conditional by others. If conditions are demanded by others before love and acceptance are offered, a phenomenon comparable to repression takes place and a process of denial of the awareness of such experiences, which are unacceptable to the self, further narrows the individual's world.

Maslow: Master of the Self-Actualizing Motive As a humanistic psychologist, Abraham Maslow had long been concerned with psychology's failure to emphasize the positive, health-encouraging aspects of human behavior and to stress the high-order needs of individuals. Maslow, about whom an editor once said that his writing "gave off sparks," commented on this omission:

Abraham Maslow.

> The sad thing is that most students come into psychology with humanistic interests. They want to find out about people; they want to understand love, hate, hope, fear, ecstasy, happiness, the meaning of living. But what is so often done for these high hopes and yearnings? Most graduate, and even undergraduate training, turns away from these subjects, which are called fuzzy, unscientific, tender-minded, mystical.

Toward self-actualization For Maslow a need like love has a position in a hierarchy of motivations which merge into a developmental sequence. Maslow's basic principle is that when the more basic needs are satisfied, other higher needs emerge. From the most basic to the highest level, Maslow proposes the following motivational hierarchy (Figure 16.3).

Physiological needs. In common with many other psychologists, Maslow took the position that all other motives derive from the biological drives. In the expression of human motivation, however, these needs are not very important because they are satisfied most of the time. This means that the motives that are actually expressed in behavior will be those higher in the hierarchy. In the behavior of lower animals and in the starvation study of human subjects (page 341), we can see how the physiological needs dominate behavior when they are allowed to become intense.

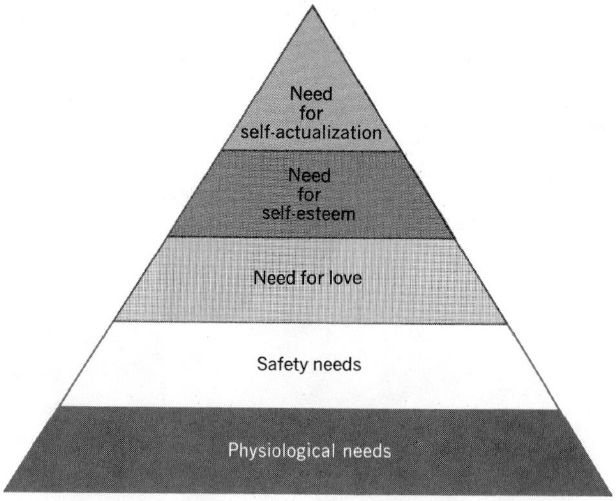

FIGURE 16.3
A hierarchy of motives. Motives at the base of the pyramid must be at least partially satisfied before higher needs can become important. The hierarchy is also an approximate developmental sequence. Most people probably never achieve self-actualization, as defined by Maslow.

Safety needs. These needs, too, tend to be satisfied in our culture. "The peaceful, smooth-running 'good' society ordinarily makes its members feel safe enough from wild animals, extremes of temperature, criminals, assault and murder, tyranny, etc." In childhood the safety needs are of more importance and play a larger role since these relate to the need for security and an environment that has predictability and orderliness. The failure to satisfy these needs results in a fearful, insecure adult unable to cope with the ordinary demands of the environment.

Love needs. If the biological and safety needs are satisfied, the love needs relating to affiliation, acceptance, and "belongingness" will emerge. The secure individual will be able to reach out for friends, affiliate with a group, and ultimately take on the responsibilities in marriage of being both spouse and parent. Frustration of the love needs is, in Maslow's view, one of the prime causes of neurosis in society—a view that is quite consistent with the emphasis given by Freud to the critical importance of sex in its broadest sense.

Self-esteem needs. These needs represent the desire for a positive evaluation of oneself. Such expressions as self-esteem, self-respect, pride, self-confidence, and personal worth identify this set of motives. These needs are associated with achievement behavior, the development of competence skills, the acceptance of approval from others, and the presence of a stable, realistic, positive evalution of oneself.

The need for self-actualization. This, in Maslow's organization, is the highest form of motivation. A person needs an aim in life and a feeling that he is doing things that further this aim. This is the essential quality of self-fulfillment or self-realization, and the act of becoming everything that "one is capable of becoming." As many young people know, the lack of such an aim or the feeling that what one does in college and elsewhere has little value for the achievement of **self-actualization** is one of the most serious problems in our society today. The feeling of alienation is the expression of a mismatch between society's values and the self-actualizing tendencies of the young person.

Later Maslow introduced a significant change in his formulation. Self-actualization, he decided, did not necessarily follow, if all earlier need states had been met. Once self-esteem had been achieved, most people do not extend themselves in a search for greater fulfillment, but the factors that separate the doers from the do-nots is a question that has remained unanswered. Maslow's own major research effort went into the study of self-actualization. He set out to locate people who appeared to him to have realized themselves fully and then through psychological study attempted to define the attributes that they shared. His investigations led him to evaluate personal acquaintances, friends, and even historical figures.

The rare self-actualizer Three thousand college students who came under Maslow's scrutiny yielded only one or two dozen individuals who looked as if they were likely bets to become self-actualizers at some future time. Maslow was led to conclude that, ". . . self-actualization of the sort I had found in my older subjects perhaps was not possible in our society for young, developing people."

Maslow then turned his attention to the healthiest one percent of the college population he could find, selecting people on the negative criterion of the absence of psychopathology and the positive criterion of the self-actualization syndrome, although this syndrome was clearer at the end of the the study than at the beginning. These possible self-actualizers had to have satisfactorily traversed Maslow's hierarchy of needs; they had to feel secure and accepted, be capable of loving and being loved; they had to possess self-esteem and be respected by others; and they had to show evidence that they had begun to develop their own personal philosophy of life. With this restricted group of students, Maslow reported that fifteen types of behavior (Table 16.3) could be observed, yielding a portrait of the self-actualizing type which affirmed his concept of self-fulfillment.

As Maslow studied young people who were moving toward self-fulfillment, he came to a conclusion that has great significance for the study of personality and psychology in general. In Maslow's words,

> . . . healthy people are so different from average ones, not only in degree but in kind as well, that they generate two very different kinds of psychology. It becomes more and more clear that the study of crippled, stunted, immature, and unhealthy specimens can yield only a cripple psychology and a cripple philosophy. The study of self-actualizing people must be the basis for a more universal science of psychology (1970, pp. 179–180).

Maslow and his colleagues have compelled psychologists to look to the strengths in human personality rather than to the weaknesses. They have brought an optimistic view to the study of motivational factors that influence personality functioning and in doing so have emphasized a philosophy that is also beginning to permeate the clinical psychologist's view of the potential that exists even in disordered individuals. This shift to a more positive and enhancing view of people may well become Maslow's and the humanistic psychologists' enduring contribution to psychology.

SUMMARY □

We have looked briefly at three dominant psychological models of personality development. The first was psychoanalysis which brought many changes to psychology's views of the origins of behavior. It emphasized stages in development, the significance of the conflict between pleasure seeking and reality demands, and the significance of sexuality as both the source of these conflicts and the source of human growth. The inflexibility of psychoanalytic doctrine threatened its own viability. This led other psychoanalytic thinkers to introduce new concepts that reduced the power of instinct and stressed the importance of social factors and the role of conflict-free cognition in influencing behavior.

Learning theory of personality is a more recent development. It began in an attempt to translate psychoanalytic concepts into terms that were more acceptable to psychology, an effort that seemed promising because learning theory and psychoanalysis both assume that the causes of personal development are in previous experience. Early learning theory and the Skinnerian approach today lay greatest emphasis on the process of direct reinforcement in personality development. This approach is clearly too narrow, however. On this basis, social learning theory has stressed the importance of observational learning and modeling.

Although the extension of learning theory to a multiplicity of behaviors has been nothing short of phenomenal, there are aspects of human behavior not easily reduced to learning principles: values and beliefs, powerful emotional states such as love and grief, patterns of self-actualization, the sacrificial behavior of people under stress, the quality of humanity in some, its absence in others, and so on. The deficiencies of learning theory define the emphases of the humanistic approaches to personality. Although these theories have provided a renewed emphasis on growth and actualization in human striving, their formulations remain imprecise and their statements of the origins of personality weak and inadequate.

Despite the shortcomings of each of the three major perspectives on personality theory, each point of view has enlarged our understanding of human behavior. Psychoanalysis broadened our awareness of the continuity between infant and adult. Learning theory provided us with insights into how behaviors are acquired, maintained, and extinguished. Humanistic psychology enlarged our horizons by emphasizing human strivings toward self-fulfillment and growth.

A CRUCIAL CONTROVERSY IN PERSONALITY STUDY

For more than a decade personality theorists and researchers have debated whether traits or situations are the determiners of our behavior. This controversy is brought up here because the approaches to personality discussed so far are divided on the issue.

This chapter began with the older trait and psychoanalytic theories and later discussed the more recent phenomenological theory. What the old and the new

TABLE 16.3
The Attributes of Self-Actualizing College Students

1. An efficient perception of reality	The ability to make accurate judgments of self and others which are undistorted by personal needs, fears, anxieties, beliefs.
2. Acceptance of self and others	Freedom from shame, guilt, and anxiety; a lack of defensiveness or pose.
3. Spontaneity; simplicity and naturalness	This implies a flexibility of behavior but not necessarily unconventionality.
4. Problem-centered	A sense of mission and purpose in life which leads one to tasks one feels it is a duty to perform; a concern with philosophical-ethical issues.
5. Quality of detachment; need for privacy	A preference for solitude; dignity under stress; high level of concentration; a responsible self-decision-maker.
6. Autonomy; independence from culture and environment; will; an active agent	The assumption of responsibility for one's own development; a person independent of the opinions of others.
7. Continued freshness of appreciation for nature, art, children, etc.	A sense of recurrent pleasure in one's environment.
8. Mystic experience: the Peak Experience	The capacity to feel ecstacy, wonder, awe; a sense of valued happenings; the intensification of experience.
9. Feeling for mankind	A capacity (or identification) for sympathy and affection toward others.
10. Good interpersonal relations	A capacity for love and identification; the attainment of deep ties with a few individuals or a small circle of friends; a person attractive to others.
11. Democratic character structure	A nonauthoritarian in attitude and behavior; the ability to be friendly with many people of different backgrounds and to learn from others.
12. Discrimination between good and bad means and ends	A sustained and coherent sense of ethics and values with a focus on ends and not on means.
13. Philosophical and unhostile sense of humor	Humor that is not hostile, superior, or authoritarian; the ability to poke fun at oneself and at other humans in general.
14. Creativeness	Originality and inventiveness; a freshness of perception toward the environment.
15. Resistant to enculturation	A reasonable degree of conventionality in how one does things without being either a rebel against authority or lacking the courage to challenge authority when necessary, particularly in the face of injustice.

Adapted from Maslow, 1970.

share is their emphasis on the *person*. Social-learning theory and the Skinnerian point of view shifted the focus to the *environment* and searched for factors in *situations* that might determine whether individuals maintain or change their behavior. These generally different views constitute an obvious basis for controversy.

In 1968 Walter Mischel, in his influential book *Personality and Assessment,* challenged traits as determiners of behavior, maintaining that traits have little power to predict behavior even though they are by their very nature assumed to give it consistency. Trait advocates joined the battle. Jack Block (1971, 1977) of Berkeley, examining evidence from longitudinal research, concluded that behavior had both consistency and continuity over time, but that the degree of consistency and continuity varied with different types of data. The consistency of personality ratings, R-data, and of self-observations, S-data, made by people about their own behavior, temperament, and feelings was "undeniable and impressive." But artificial and contrived test and laboratory studies, T-data, provided erratic and unreliable findings. Block's criticism then was that personality investigations are inadequate.

The intense debate has gradually been resolved in an intelligent compromise. Seymour Epstein (1977) of the University of Massachusetts has observed that a psychology of personality requires the identification of "enduring response dispositions or traits that allow us to predict long-term behavior averaged over many situations without having to specify the nature of particular situations." Individuals need to be studied continually in representative situations in order to determine their traits. The effects of varying circumstances on people must also be studied. Such investigations really call for establishing a number of set situations in which representative samples of individuals might be observed. After situations have been so classified, Epstein proposes studying *interaction* — the behavior of certain types of people in certain types of situations.

In answering the question what determines behavior, we can take a page from the heredity-environment literature. There is no longer a "versus" between the two. Rather they are conceded to interact in providing the bases for our behavior. So too with traits *and* situations. Traits provide the *potentiality* for expression. The strength of a trait will determine the range of situations in which it is likely to be expressed. The distinction between trait and state anxiety (page 347) illustrates the point.

Very powerful traits can be revealed even in neutral situations in which we would not expect them to be evident. The best examples unfortunately are the traits evident in psychopathological conditions (Schalling, 1977). Many of the different forms of deviant behavior described in Chapter 17 are expressed in a great variety of situations and very often over long periods of time.

THE ASSESSMENT OF PERSONALITY

The term **personality assessment** refers to the evaluation of individual personalities, most often with the aid of tests. The development of personality tests has been an active field for many years. There are currently in existence more than 500 different personality tests. These use as varied a collection of stimuli and situations as one can imagine: inkblots, picture stories, figure drawings, play constructions, expressive movement such as writing, walking, and sitting, self-report questionnaires, self-descriptions of interests, inventories of values and attitudes, reactions to humorous cartoons or to cartoons representing frustrating situations, adjective descriptions, aesthetic preferences, and role playing, to cite some of the items in the list.

Constructing Personality Tests

Psychologists who undertake the problem of developing a personality test typically adopt one of three approaches to test construction: the *rational-construct, empirical-criterion,* or *factor-analytic* method (Pervin, 1975). The **rational-construct** method, sometimes called the intuitive method, begins with the psychologist's intuitive consideration of the trait he wishes to measure. For example, a test of introversion-extroversion developed through a rational approach might well begin with the psychologist's considering what an introverted person is like behaviorally. Hesitant? Reflective? Withdrawn? Reserved? Intellectual? Items would then be written designed to reveal these defining characteristics.

The **empirical-criterion** or external approach has as its starting point the identification of groups of people who differ on the dimension the test constructionist wishes to measure. For example, interests are part of the pattern of human personality. Of the interest tests that have been developed, the Strong Vocational Interest Blank (SVIB) is the most popular in use today. The items of this test were created by having people who were engaged in different occupations and were satisfied with their jobs indicate their preferences for different vocational and avocational activities. The patterns of interests of people in various occupations were then identified by determining the items that best differentiated a given occupational group from people in general. No theory was involved in defining what an engineer, a doctor, or an actor liked to do. This was determined empirically by selecting items which best differentiated the groups. When the interests of people who take the Strong test are rated, it is assumed that a person who shares the patterns of interest of a given occupational group will be more likely to enjoy working in that occupation. That is, this individual will have the appropriate personality for the job.

The third approach to personality test construction is based on **factor-analytic** statistical techniques. In this procedure the test developer first selects a wide range of items and administers them to many different types of people. Statistical procedures then make it possible to identify groups of items that cluster together in the sense that answering one item in a given way is correlated with the tendency to answer the others in the cluster in a given way. The items so identified are then formed into a scale which is labeled on the basis of the content of the items and not by any a priori definition entertained by the test's creator. The Cattell 16PF test is an example of a popular personality test based on such factor-analytic techniques.

Types of Personality Tests

The classification of the hundreds of different personality tests now in use is not an easy matter. A classification system that makes sense has been suggested by Donald Campbell (1957). It classifies tests on three polar dimensions, two of which will figure in our discussion. These questions identify the dimensions.

How much freedom does the subject have in responding to the test items? The dimension here is that of *structured versus unstructured (or free) response.* In the **structured test** the person has only a limited set of alternatives set out by the tester; in the **unstructured test** the individual can range far and wide in responding. Examples are

Structured: Do you often feel depressed?
True *False* *Can't say*
Unstructured: What is your mood generally like?

Is the subject aware of the purpose of the test? This dimension is one of *disguised versus undisguised.* The **disguised test** is one in which the purpose of the test is not evident to the subject; the purpose of the **undisguised test** is quite clear. Examples are

Disguised: Please draw me a picture of a person. (The Draw-A-Person Test is not a test of drawing skill but is used to infer a person's view of others or self.)
Undisguised: Most inventories and rating scales as well as diagnostic interviews.

The Minnesota Multiphasic Personality Inventory

The traditional paper-and-pencil tests of the self-rating or inventory type are structured and undisguised. Unfortunately such personality tests are often called "objective" to note their highly structured quality, but this only adds confusion. In taking one of these tests the individual is asked to respond "yes" or "no," or "true" or "false" (or in some cases "can't say") to indicate whether certain statements apply to her or to him. The types of answers allowed show the structure forms of the tests. Examples are

I am easily embarrassed.
I easily become impatient with people.

Such test items hold no mysteries for the test taker, and so they are undisguised.

One of the difficulties of most such questionnaires is that too often the "correct" answer to each question in the sense of suggesting good adjustment readily is apparent, and answers can be "faked" to make a person look good. But a growing sophistication in test construction has done much to remedy this situation, as can be seen by reviewing the structure of the personality test used most extensively throughout the world—the **Minnesota Multiphasic Personality Inventory,** or MMPI. The MMPI consists of 550 statements that respondents must evaluate in terms of their own behavior, reacting to each statement as "true," "false," or "cannot say." The test was created by the empirical-criterion method in which the responses to test items of psychiatrically disturbed and normal people were compared. The range of items chosen for their differentiating power is very wide and includes physical conditions, psychosomatic symptoms, social attitudes, family and marital factors, and psychiatric behavior symptoms. There now exist more than 200 empirically derived scales on which the MMPI can be scored. There are, however, fourteen basic scales that are typically used for personality analysis. Four of these scales are measures of the test-taking attitude of the individual (validity scales); they provide evidence of attempts at deliberate faking. Ten are clinical scales (Table 16.4).

After a person has taken the MMPI, the test is scored for each of the clinical scales, and these scores are plotted in the form shown in Figure 16.4. The ordinate is in terms of standard scales (*T*-scores) that have a mean of 50 and a standard deviation of 10. High scores, especially those of 70 or more—two standard deviations above the mean—are usually taken as particularly significant. It should be mentioned that experts in the use of this test rely very heavily on the patterns of scores and assign special significance to certain combinations of high scores. In general, however, scales to the left of the profile chart—Hs (hypochondriasis), D (depression), and Hy (hysteria)—form the so-called *neurotic triad;* those on the right side—Pa (paranoia), Pt (psychasthenia), Sc (schizophrenia), and Ma (hypomania)—make up a *psychotic tetrad.*

TABLE 16.4
Basic Scales of the Minnesota Multiphasic Personality Inventory

Name of Scale	Psychological Significance	Illustrative Item with Keyed Response
	Validity Scales	
? (Cannot say) scale	Not a scale in the ordinary sense. Failure to answer more than ten items taken as significant.	
L (Lie) scale	Based on fifteen items that reflect minor faults that most people have, such as minor aggressions, temptations, and lack of control. High L means faking in the "good" direction.	Once in a while I put off until tomorrow what I ought to do today. (*False*)
F (Validity) scale	Consists of sixty-four items that are rarely responded to in the scaled direction by normal subjects. High F means an invalid test because of carelessness in answering or deliberate malingering.	It would be better if almost all laws were thrown away. (*True*)
K (Correction) scale	Measures test-taking attitude. High K indicates personal defensiveness; low K, a desire to "look bad" by revealing personal defects, but excessively so.	At periods my mind seems to work more slowly than usual. (*False*)
	Clinical Scales	
(Hs) Hypochondriasis	Largely a scale of physical complaints.	I am bothered by acid stomach several times a week. (*True*)
(D) Depression	Reflects feelings of hopelessness, unworthiness, a lack of self-esteem, and a pessimistic view of life.	I usually feel that life is worthwhile. (*False*)
(Hy) Hysteria	Stresses somatic complaints and a denial of any kind of difficulties.	I can be friendly with people who do things which I consider wrong. (*True*)
(Pd) Psychopathic deviate	The scale measures emotional shallowness in interpersonal relations, a disregard for rules of social conduct, and inability to profit by past experience.	My way of doing things is apt to be misunderstood by others. (*True*)
(Mf) Masculinity–femininity	High scores for men reflect cultural and esthetic interests, passivity, and emotionality; for women, high Mf identifies vigorous, active, and masculine orientation.	If I were an artist, I would like to draw flowers. (*True*)
(Pa) Paranoia	Includes psychotic content, including delusions, and self-reference items. High scores reveal an extreme suspiciousness and excessive sensitivity in interpersonal relations.	I have no enemies who really wish to harm me. (*False*)
Pt) Psychasthenia	A scale designed to indicate phobic or compulsive concerns. High scores suggest vacillation, ruminative behavior, ritualistic concerns, an emphasis on morality, and a lack of esteem.	I usually have to stop and think before I act even in trifling matters. (*True*)
(Sc) Schizophrenia	A scale that reveals bizarre and unusual thinking. Delusions, hallucinations, and evidences of disorientation together with withdrawal are suggested by high scores.	I often feel as if things were not real. (*True*)
(Ma) Hypomania	This scale reflects hyperactivity, an elated mood, flight of ideas, and emotional excitability.	When I get bored, I like to stir up some excitement. (*True*)
(Si) Social introversion	High scores indicate tendencies toward introversion; low scores lean toward extroversion.	At parties I am more likely to sit by myself or with just one other person than to join in with the crowd. (*True*)

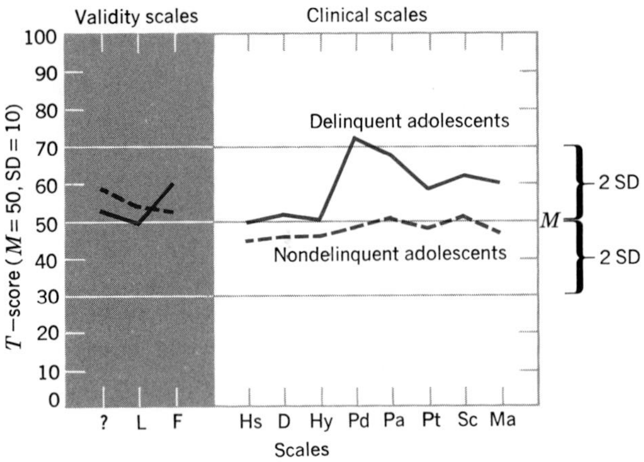

FIGURE 16.4
Plotting a profile of scores from the MMPI. The scores of delinquent adolescents and nondelinquent adolescents are compared. Notice the extreme score on the psychopathic deviate scale. This "Pd spike" is characteristic of delinquents. Scales Mf and Si are omitted. The scale to the right shows the range of scores, 30-70, falling two standard deviations on either side of the mean value of 50. (Adapted from Hathaway and Monachesi, 1953.)

The MMPI has been found useful in a variety of clinical and nonclinical contexts. It has been used for selection purposes, for revealing symptom syndromes, in making diagnostic decisions, in assessing therapeutic potential, and the like. Clearly, the MMPI occupies a favored place in the clinician's techniques for assessment. This favoritisim is worldwide. There are more than fifty translations of the MMPI in approximately twenty-six languages. Some translations require change. In a recently developed Hebrew version for use in Israel (Butcher and Gur, 1974), the American item, *Christ performed miracles such as changing water into wine,* became in the Hebrew version, *God performed miracles such as dividing the Red Sea.*

The California Psychological Inventory

The MMPI has served as the prototype for many other personality inventories but none of these offspring is closer to the parent than the **California Psychological Inventory** (CPI). Although it draws 178 of its 480 items from the MMPI, the CPI has a different purpose and fills a great need. The MMPI as we have seen was created to provide an inventory-based evaluation of psychopathology. One type of objection to the test has been that it describes people almost exclusively in terms of dimensions of psychopathology.

The CPI was constructed to be used with normal populations from age thirteen and up. Retaining the true-false format, the test consists of eighteen scales, three of which are "validity" scales that measure the test-taking attitudes of the respondent (Table 16.5). The fifteen other scales were designed to measure what its creator (Gough, 1960) called "folk concepts, descriptive and classificatory notions concerning behavior and disposition that people everywhere use easily in their daily interaction with one another." As a result the test has little symptom-related content. The language of the items and the interpretive scales are both appropriate for ordinary people.

The CPI was standardized on the responses of 6000 men and 7000 women of different ages, occupational groups, levels of education, and socioeconomic brackets, and from different geographical areas. Scores are reported in the form of a profile. Gough divided the scales into four classes to facilitate interpretation of the test profile, which research has shown permits rich descriptions of personality functioning.

There has been a great deal of research on the CPI, much of which has been brought together in a CPI handbook (Megargee, 1972). The handbook describes the usefulness of the test as a "wide-band" instrument in this summarizing paragraph.

> The studies . . . have found significant associations between the CPI and various measures of achievement in elementary school, high school and college, as well as in military and police training programs, medicine, dentistry, nursing and teaching; moreover, the CPI can identify those who are likely to partake in extra-curricular activities or cheat on exams. The inventory has been found to relate to leadership, managerial ability, employability, and adjustment. It can forecast juvenile delinquency, parole success and can reliably discriminate alcoholics from marijuana and cigarette smokers. It has been found to relate to conformity, creativity . . . physiological responsiveness to stress, . . . political participation, marital adjustment, and to one's choice of family planning methods. The CPI can also be used to predict whether an infant is likely to suffer from colic, and it can chart the short and long term effects on such infants if the marriage should end in divorce (p. 247).

The power of the socialization scale in distinguishing various groups appropriately (Figure 16.5) is one example of how the test functions in actual use.

Projective Techniques

Some of the potentially most powerful techniques for measuring personality come from the evaluation of imaginative productions of various kinds. Collectively, these methods are called the **projective techniques.** These procedures are *unstructured* because they involve tasks such as having the individual make up a story, interpret an ambiguous figure such as an inkblot, create a drawing, or complete an incomplete sentence. The methods are *disguised* because the purpose is not evident to the person taking the test. Psychologists who use these methods assume that the people will project their feelings, desires, and wishes into their reactions on the test. The methods are closely tied to psychoanalytic theories with their emphasis on unconscious factors.

TABLE 16.5
The Psychological Significance and Illustrative Items of the CPI Scales

Name of Scale	Psychological Significance	Illustrative Item with Keyed Response
Class I Scales: Measures of Poise, Ascendancy, Self-Assurance, and Interpersonal Adequacy		
Dominance	Strong dominant, influential person able to exercise initiative and leadership.	I have a natural talent for influencing people. (*True*)
Capacity for Status	Ambition, self-assurance.	I get very nervous if I think someone is watching over me. (*False*)
Sociability	Outgoing sociable participators.	I am a good mixer. (*True*)
Social Presence	Poise, self-confidence, verve, and spontaneity in social situations.	I like to go to parties and other affairs where there is lots of loud fun. (*True*)
Self-Acceptance	Sense of personal worth, self-acceptance, and capacity for independent thinking and action.	I am certainly lacking in self-confidence. (*False*)
Sense of Well-Being (Validity scale)	Health and verve versus inability to meet demands and lack of vitality.	I usually feel that life is worthwhile. (*True*)
Class II Scales: Measures of Responsibility, Socialization, Maturity, and Intrapersonal Structuring of Values		
Responsibility	Conscientious, responsible behavior and belief that reason should govern actions. Importance given to values and controls.	When I work on a committee, I like to take charge of things. (*True*)
Socialization	Degree of social maturity, integrity; Internalized values prevail.	As a youngster in school I used to give the teachers lots of trouble. (*False*)
Self-Control	Adequacy of one's self-control and freedom from impulsivity and self-centeredness.	I would do almost anything on a dare. (*False*)
Tolerance	Permissive, accepting, nonjudgmental social beliefs and attitudes.	I feel sure there is only one true religion. (*False*)
Good Impression (Validity scale)	Infrequent items indicating random responding.	I usually try to do what is expected of me to avoid criticism. (*True*)
Class III Scales: Measures of Intellectual Efficiency and Achievement Potential		
Achievement via Conformance	Strong need for achievement combined with an appreciation of structure and organization.	I always try to do a little better than what is expected of me. (*True*)
Achievement via Independence	Achievement in settings where independence of thought, creativity, self-actualization are rewarded.	For most questions there is one right answer, once a person is able to to get all the facts. (*False*)
Intellectual Efficiency	Personality items highly correlated with measures of intelligence.	I seem to be as capable and smart as most others around me. (*True*)
Class IV Variables: Measures of Intellectual and Interest Modes		
Psychological Mindedness	Psychologically oriented, insightful about how others think and feel.	I have frequently found myself when alone, pondering such abstract problems as free will, evil, etc. (*False*)
Flexibility	Flexible, acceptable, changeable.	I like to have a place for everything and everything in its place. (*False*)
Femininity	Psychological femininity.	I get very tense and anxious when I think other people are disapproving of me. (*True*)

Adapted from Megargee, 1972.

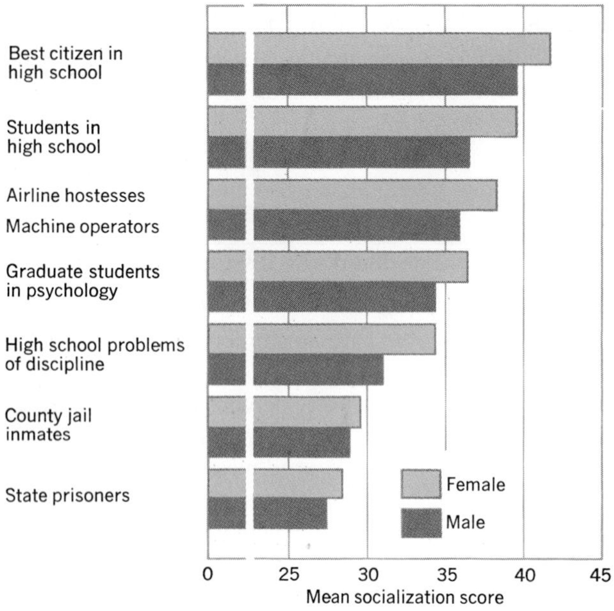

FIGURE 16.5
Validity of the California Psychological Inventory. The score on the socialization scale of the CPI distinguishes in expected directions members of different groups. Notice the separate representations for men and women. (After Gough, 1960.)

FIGURE 16.6
A sample picture from the Thematic Apperception Test.

Thematic Apperception Test The **Thematic Apperception Test** (TAT) consists of a set of twenty pictures (Figure 16.6). The person tested makes up a story about each picture. The instructions indicate that the story should have a past, present, and future; it should describe the events that led up to the scene pictured, what the participants in the story are thinking and feeling, what is currently happening, and how the story will end. The following case study shows how a clinical psychologist used the TAT to achieve a greater understanding of a patient's problem.

> Mrs. T., a twenty-two-year-old white woman was admitted to a hospital because of promiscuity, alcoholism, obesity, and depression. Five months before hospitalization she had taken an overdose of drugs. Then followed an episode in which she was violent and suffered from hallucinations and a sense of unreality regarding herself and her environment. The question of a psychotic disorder was raised.
>
> Six years before hospitalization the patient's parents had separated and her mother subsequently committed suicide. Two years later the patient entered college but subsequently transferred to several other institutions. Two years before her admission she married a student who remained uncertain about his career plans, switched courses of study repeatedly, and was contemplating leaving school at the time of hospitalization. The psychologist was asked to provide a personality assessment after Mrs. T. was admitted to the hospital.

Mrs. T. gave this interpretation of the picture in Figure 16.6 as part of her TAT:

> This is a picture of a woman who all of her life has been a very suspicious, conniving person. She's looking in the mirror. And she sees reflected behind her an image of what she will be as an old woman—still a suspicious, conniving sort of person. And she can't stand the thought that that's what her life will eventually lead her to. And she smashes in the mirror and runs out of the house screaming and goes out of her mind and lives in uh-a- institution for the rest of her life. That's it.

To give you a taste of how a TAT story is interpreted, we reproduce verbatim the clinical psychologist's commentary regarding this story. Remember this is only one story. The full test was given, and all stories were used in a more complete interpretation.

> From a perceptual point of view, looking in a mirror and seeing an image reflected behind oneself is peculiar. One would have to see the image in the mirror. Thus, we see a disruption in the perceptual process. . . . In this case the distortion involves a spatial confusion and may hark back to Mrs. T.'s difficulties in spatial tests of other kinds. Some of the other content in the protocol —suspiciousness and conniving—cannot be fully

Hermann Rorschach, the Swiss psychiatrist who early in this century constructed symmetrical ink blots with which to study personality structure, especially unconscious motivation.

> appreciated in this instance unless we also consider that frank perceptual distortion is evident and, therefore, that projective trends may reach psychotic proportions. Since the older woman is commonly described as a maternal figure, we can assume that the patient is communicating something about her relationship vis-a-vis this maternal figure. There is the attempt to destroy the ties to a dreaded negative maternal figure by violent means, a process which is seen as resulting in the inevitable destruction of the patient as well.
>
> We may speculate further that she may perceive her illness and hospitalization as a direct consequence of her efforts to separate herself entirely from her mother. In that her thinking becomes peculiar on this card, the depth of identification with the mother seems extreme and may reach psychotic proportions.
>
> The feeling of being doomed to become like the maternal figure is of special significance for Mrs. T. since we know that her mother committed suicide. Her need to break the bond with the mother, therefore, becomes even more urgent, in order to free herself from being fated to repeat the mother's suicide.
>
> Over the course of the TAT pictures we are observing increasing signs of disruptions in ego functions, also psychotic trends in Mrs. T.'s thought processes, and the more primitive defenses of projection and denial (Allison, Blatt, and Zimet, 1968, pp. 121–122).

What is revealed about projective test interpretation by this commentary? First, there is the effort to find a pattern in the sequence of interpretations of the TAT cards as indicated in the final paragraph, and to tie the story contents to the results observed on other tests given to the patient. Second, the imaginary production is related to life history data on the assumption that the projective content is, at least in part, a reflection of the patient's interpretation of her own life situations. Third, the clinician's interpretation speaks to two issues, the structural aspect of the patient's disorder—her symptoms, the form of her thought processes, her emotional state—and the content of the patient's thinking.

The themes in the TAT stories play only one part in the clinician's effort to understand the patient; other aspects are equally important. These include the length of the story, its organization, originality, and continuity. Attention is also given to the emotional tone of the stories, the attributes of the hero or central figure as well as the other characters in the story, the kinds of environments portrayed, and the interpersonal situations described.

The Rorschach Test A second widely used personality test of the projective variety is the **Rorschach inkblot test.** The materials used in this test are ten inkblot pictures like the one shown in Figure 16.7, half of which are in color. They are presented to the individual one at a time, in a specific order, with the instruction to describe what the blot looks like or what it might be. Subsequently the clinician makes an inquiry to determine the basis used for the percept.

The average person will give thirty to forty responses to the blots, each of which is scored on three bases: *location, determinant,* and *content.* The location category refers to the part of the inkblot selected by the subject for interpretation. This can be the whole blot, a common (usually large) section, or a small detail that is less frequently reacted to. The scoring for determinant describes the characteristic of the blot responsible for the particular interpretation. Here the possibilities include shape, color, shading, impressions of depth and impressions of movement, singly or in combination. The content of the response is the type of association given by the respondent, such as animal, human, fire, or clouds. Finally, each response is scored plus (+) or minus (−), depending

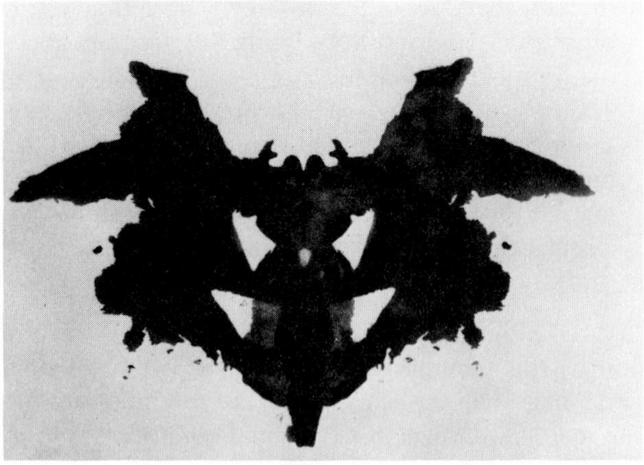

FIGURE 16.7
Card 1 on the Rorschach inkblot test.

on whether the particular association is appropriate to the section of the blot to which it is given.

Both the content of the response and the formal determinant are important in interpreting a Rorschach record. Scoring and interpretation are complex, and we would do a disservice to summarize rules the clinician uses in the analysis. It should be mentioned specifically, however, that the particular significance ascribed to the appearance of a given scoring category in the Rorschach record will depend on other aspects of the record.

A current trend in Rorschach test analysis is to take a page from the MMPI book and to dampen the heavy level of inference that clinicians draw from the test protocol. Recent advocates have suggested that subjective judgments about the test data can be minimized and a variety of carefully defined scales developed that can provide basic quantitative measures of perceptual cognition and personality functioning. If this view gains favor, there may be a resurgence of interest in the projective techniques (Haggard, 1978).

Validity of Personality Tests

It is difficult to establish the **validity** of personality tests, partly because of the problem of deciding on an adequate criterion and partly because of response sets and test-taking attitudes that are likely to affect the responses given to personality test items. Research on personality measures has led to an important distinction between the content of a person's response and the individual's characteristic style of responding and acting. This distinction between what a person says and how it is said has particular relevance for questionnaires and similar objective self-reporting instruments (Bentler, Jackson, and Messick, 1971). The anxious person may be extravagantly cautious, hesitant to guess when uncertain; the uninvolved person may be a cavalier test taker, guessing with complete equanimity whenever an answer is not obvious to him or her. These tendencies toward particular modes of responding have been termed response sets or response biases.

A **response set** may also reflect a person's reaction to the way in which an item is stated rather than to its contents. Response sets, for example, may be tendencies to acquiesce, yea saying, or to dissent, nay saying. The yea-sayer tends to endorse or agree with items; the nay-sayer tends to disagree. The nay-saying tendency itself may be diagnostic, since maladjusted people may often disagree with desirable self-descriptive items (Rundquist, 1966). There are those who argue that the *only* factors responsible for performance on personality tests are these stylistic ones and that the meaning of the items has nothing to do with it.

Criticisms of the content of personality tests that attribute results to stylistic considerations have not gone unchallenged. In a powerful empirical refutation of the response style argument, Jack Block (1965) took twenty-one MMPI scales and randomly eliminated items until each scale had an equivalent number of items keyed "true" and "false," thus rendering an interpretation of his data on the basis of an acquiescence response style untenable. Analysis of these new scales in comparison with the original scales—many of which were biased heavily toward either "true" or "false" answers—indicated that the content and not the response tendencies were the significant properties of the scales. To attribute the responses of patients to a tendency to appear socially undesirable to others rather than to view these as indices of their personal discomfort, anxiety, and distress appears to be inappropriate. It seems much more likely that patients respond in a given manner because the verbal content of the items expresses the nature of their thoughts, or the quality of their emotional responses, or the experiences they have encountered.

Clinical versus Actuarial Prediction

There are two ways of trying to predict from data obtained from tests of personality. One is **clinical prediction.** This involves the formulation of hypotheses based on a clinician's intuition, knowledge, impressions, and judgment about individual cases. The alternative, **actuarial** or statistical **prediction,** involves classifying people on the basis of their test performance and other information such as the person's life history and interview data, and then referring the data to some actuarial table, or "diagnostic cookbook," which gives the "recipe" for interpreting the personality. The basis for this interpretation is a large array of data linking this person's behavior to that of persons who have been classified similarly.

Paul Meehl (1954) one of the first powerful exponents of the actuarial method, finds great strength in actuarial prediction because of its straightforward application of objective rules, mathematical procedures, and tables of data. Robert Holt (1971), who scoffs at such mechanization, calls the clinician's role in this type of analysis that of a "second-rate calculating machine." The predictions made are rather shallow and unsophisticated: college grades, success in specific kinds of training programs, parole violations, and the like. Sophisticated clinical predictions, asserts Holt, require consideration of an individual's needs, conflicts, defenses, and fantasies, and these pose problems far too difficult for an equation or a statistical table to handle. Furthermore, Holt argues, clinical assessment must often be made of unusual people, who are unlikely to be represented anywhere in mathematical equations or tables of data. We now develop the two sides of this argument in more detail.

Actuarial and Clinical Prediction Compared A recent revolution in assessment has been the computerization of personality diagnosis and interpretation. A prime example of this new development is seen in its application to the MMPI. Typically such a system operates on MMPI scale scores together with other data related to variables such as age, sex, and specific case history information. Once the program has been set up, the data for an individual can be fed into the computer and can then be compared mechanically with information that is filed in the computer's memory. The test profile and the psychological analysis of a person's MMPI can be printed out and fed back to the diagnostician. Such programs now provide a test profile, a data sheet indicating the scale scores, and a note about unusual answers to specific items. The main body of such a report is a printout narrative statement that describes the individual's test-taking attitudes and behavioral symptoms. It provides a general diagnostic formulation and a prognostic statement of the person's likely future adaptation.

There are now a number of computer services that offer this service to clinicians, including the Roche Psychiatric Service Institute. A partial computer printout of the results of an MMPI of a forty-one-year-old female client supplied by this organization is presented in Figure 16.8. Remember that all the narrative statements in the printout are derived from data of persons with similar profiles which have been stored in the computer's memory bank.

How good are these computerized accounts? James Butcher (1978), a national expert in MMPI assessments, has recently reviewed a number of the computerized scoring and interpreting services, which have mushroomed over the past decade. Labeling the computerized narratives as "little more than an art (or craft) disguised as a science," Butcher goes on in a negative vein.

> One problem is that computer systems are still pretty rudimentary and most MMPI interpretations made out of context produce either superficial (general) information or highly fallible descriptions. This is the case even when the MMPI is used in settings where gross psychopathology is common. It is even more the case when automated systems are routinely applied in lower base rate psychopathological populations, e.g., for screening in industry, for police, and for graduate school applications.

For Butcher some of the human limitations of the clinician appear not only to be carried over into computer interpretations but to be present to an even greater extent with the mechanical methods. In time these shortcomings may be overcome, but it is important not to mistake computer printouts for science. The experts urge caution in accepting the narrative statements as valid, and see a particular danger in having unqualified persons read and interpret the results.

Is One Method Better? A question, of course, is which of these methods leads to the more accurate prediction. In 1959 Meehl compared thirty-five studies that had appeared in the research literature. He found that the actuarial method was superior in twenty-three studies, and there was no difference in twelve. The clinical method was superior in none. Currently, the count is above seventy, with the actuarial method strongly retaining its manifest superiority.

The studies have covered a wide range. To cite just one example, college football coaches, despite all the paraphernalia of contemporary coaching and their confidence in their judgments, were unable to predict the outcome of the games played by their own teams any better than a mathematical formula based on seven variables: basic team strength, weather, game at home or away, geographical location of game, past schedule, school status, and importance of the game. And this despite the fact that the coaches had the mathematical actuarial predictions available when they made their own ratings (Harris, 1963).

And Suppose It Is? A final caution regarding clinical and actuarial prediction appears to be in order because most of the studies comparing the clinical and actuarial methods have found the actuarial method superior. It would be a grave mistake, however, to decide on this basis that the activities of the clinician are meaningless or the clinical prediction is forever

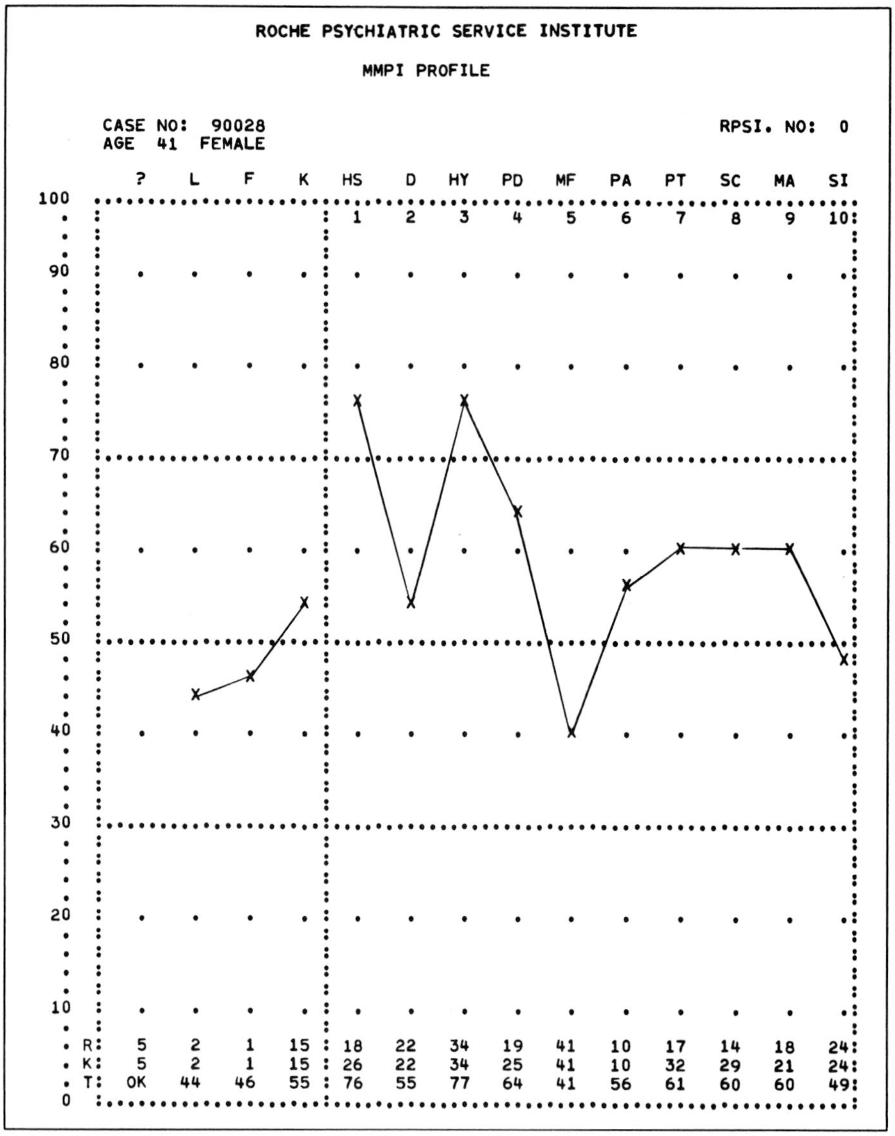

FIGURE 16.8
A computer printout of the MMPI. Profile of a forty-one-year-old woman. (Courtesy of Dr. Raymond Fowler.)

invalid. The problem seems to be to discover the bases of clinical insights and to subject clinical information to the same analysis we employ in evaluating other forms of psychological assessment. Only then will it be possible to pass judgment on the value of clinical prediction.

Psychological Tests and Public Policy

Do tests invade privacy? The growth of the psychological testing movement has been accompanied during the past few years by a rising chorus of criticism aimed at test instruments and their creators. Back in 1965 Congress turned its investigative eye upon the uses and abuses of "psychological tests" following a barrage of criticism that has been labeled as "the most serious attack that has ever been launched by citizen groups or by Government against any part of psychological research or services."

The focus of the attacks was on objective personality tests. Some of the criticisms were justified. Tests of questionable validity and utility had been used to make critical decisions affecting the lives of individuals. In some instances tests had been administered and interpreted by untrained people. Tests appropriate for use with pathologically disturbed individuals had been used inappropriately with children, usually in the absence of the necessary validation studies.

A very specific complaint was that the tests contain objectionable content. For example, the MMPI contains items seen as impertinent, provocative, and unduly disturbing to normal persons by one sample of

COMPUTER ASSESSMENT

A. CRITICAL ITEMS

THESE TEST ITEMS, WHICH WERE ANSWERED IN THE DIRECTION INDICATED, MAY REQUIRE FURTHER INVESTIGATION BY THE CLINICIAN. THE CLINICIAN IS CAUTIONED, HOWEVER, AGAINST OVERINTERPRETATION OF ISOLATED RESPONSES.

334 PECULIAR ODORS COME TO ME AT TIMES. (TRUE)

133 I HAVE NEVER INDULGED IN ANY UNUSUAL SEX PRACTICES. (FALSE)
114 OFTEN I FEEL AS IF THERE WERE A TIGHT BAND ABOUT MY HEAD. (TRUE)

ROCHE PSYCHIATRIC SERVICE INSTITUTE

MMPI REPORT

CASE NO: 90028 RPSI. NO: 0
AGE 41 FEMALE

B. NARRATIVE REPORT

IN RESPONDING TO THE TEST ITEMS IT APPEARS THAT THE PATIENT MADE AN EFFORT TO ANSWER TRUTHFULLY WITHOUT ATTEMPTING TO DENY OR EXAGGERATE.

THIS PATIENT MAY SHOW A WIDE VARIETY OF PHYSICAL SYMPTOMS. SHE HAS RELATIVELY LITTLE MANIFEST ANXIETY AND DEPRESSION AND SHE SHOWS EXTREME DENIAL OF EMOTIONAL PROBLEMS. FREQUENT SYMPTOMS ARE PAIN, ESPECIALLY IN THE HEAD, CHEST OR STOMACH, PROBLEMS IN EATING, LOSS OF APPETITE OR OVER-EATING, AND WEAKNESS, FATIGUE AND INSOMNIA. SHE LACKS INSIGHT INTO HER OWN BEHAVIOR AND IS NOT ABLE TO ESTABLISH STABLE OR MATURE INTERPERSONAL RELATIONS. SHE WOULD BE DIFFICULT TO MOTIVATE FOR PSYCHOTHERAPEUTIC TREATMENT. HER PROGNOSIS, IF TREATMENT IS ACCEPTED, IS FAIR.

SHE HAS DIFFICULTY ACCEPTING AUTHORITY AND RESENTS CONTROL AND SUPERVISION. SHE HAS DIFFICULTY CONTROLLING HER IMPULSES AND MAY ENGAGE IN NONCOMFORMING BEHAVIOR. HER FAMILY RELATIONSHIPS ARE POOR. SHE IS LIKELY TO BE SELF-CENTERED AND MOODY IN HER DEALINGS WITH OTHERS.

SHE IS A RIGID PERSON WHO MAY EXPRESS HER ANXIETY IN FEARS, COMPULSIVE BEHAVIOR AND RUMINATION. SHE MAY BE CHRONICALLY WORRIED AND TENSE, WITH MARKED RESISTANCE TO TREATMENT DESPITE HER DISCOMFORT.

THIS PATIENT TENDS TO EXPRESS EMOTIONAL PROBLEMS AS PHYSICAL SYMPTOMS. SHE MAY BE PRONE TO PSYCHOSOMATIC ILLNESSES.

HER PROBLEMS APPEAR TO FALL WITHIN THE NEUROTIC RANGE. SHE IS USING NEUROTIC DEFENSES IN AN EFFORT TO CONTROL HER ANXIETY.

NOTE: ALTHOUGH NOT A SUBSTITUTE FOR THE CLINICIAN'S PROFESSIONAL JUDGMENT AND SKILL, THE MMPI CAN BE A USEFUL ADJUNCT IN THE DIAGNOSIS AND MANAGEMENT OF EMOTIONAL DISORDERS. THE REPORT IS FOR PROFESSIONAL USE ONLY AND SHOULD NOT BE SHOWN OR RELEASED TO THE PATIENT.

college students (Butcher and Tellegen, 1966). The MMPI was a test being used in job selection. The fact that unprincipled people have sometimes used the tests for personal gain has further darkened the cloud that hangs over programs of personality testing.

The fact that most psychologists have a strong code of professional ethics, and follow the canons of good taste, good sense, and good science, too often seems to fall on deaf ears. Many people fear a world peopled by "brain washers," "brain watchers," and "brain snoopers." Electronic "bugging" and psychological test "bugging" are seen as synonymous. Some right-wing groups view psychological tests as akin to an attempt at "psychological fluoridation" of the American people. Although the congressional hearings failed to uncover "any major story in which many people were doing an injustice to very many other people," doubt and suspicion remain. Critics forget that tests can be used to discover talent that has gone unrecognized or to identify individual potentialities that have never been developed. Tests have reclaimed human resources far more often than they have despoiled them. Michael Amrine (1965), editor of a special issue of the *American Psychologist* devoted to this topic, asked the rather provocative question "Does anyone doubt that security investigators have asked more privacy-invading questions this year than psychologists?" Is it then that a large segment of the public, fearful of the recent revelations of spy scares, the Watergate scandal, electronic listening devices, the growing impersonal nature of our society, the spread of selection procedures to school and industry, and the growth of interpersonal competition in an urbanized technological culture, displace their fears onto psychology and see in the discipline the focus for larger societal concerns that psychology lacks the power to modify?

SUMMARY □

The scientific construction of a personality test usually involves one of three procedures: the rational-construct, empirical-criterion, or factor-analytic methods. In the first procedure the test developer defines the construct to be measured and writes items to fit the definition. The second procedure identifies groups of people who differ in the dimension to be measured and then selects as test items those maximally differentiating the groups. Factor analysis discovers the clustering of items whereby an answer to a given item relates to the answers of others.

Personality tests can be classified in terms of the type of test stimuli, structured versus unstructured, and the revealed or unrevealed purpose of the test, disguised versus undisguised. The MMPI and CPI are structured, undisguised tests. The TAT and the Rorschach tests are unstructured, disguised tests.

The problem of interpreting personality tests is increased by styles of responding that can influence a person's response to the test. Individuals vary in conformity, resistiveness, and acquiescence, which may influence whether they tend to yea-say or to nay-say to test items. Although the psychologist must remain aware of the existence of these influences, their actual importance is still under study. There is some fairly convincing evidence that the content of a test item overrides these various test-taking strategies and attitudes.

The computer has had a great impact on personality study. Programs for the diagnostic analysis of test protocols that have been developed will increasingly ease the task of personality assessment, although, at present computerized interpretations still have serious limitations. Caution is warranted when they are applied to individual cases.

Related to this recent development has been the controversy over clinical versus actuarial prediction. Can an actuarial table beat the sophisticated clinician in predicting behavior? A count of more than seventy studies suggests an affirmative answer to this important question. It should be possible, however, for clinicians to take a page from the actuarial book and develop ways to improve their assessment by making clinical prediction a more objective method.

The development of personality tests with objectionable content, computerized interpretation, and the fading away of personal clinical assessment are all part of a pattern that has led to strong criticism of personality testing. In evaluating this criticism, we should remember that psychologists have misused tests much more rarely than others. Psychologists' behavior in such matters is guided by a strong code of professional ethics developed for the protection of the public.

TO BE SURE YOU UNDERSTAND THIS CHAPTER △

Here are the major concepts presented in this chapter. For this chapter, more than for any other in the book, it is important to know the contributions of individuals: Cattell, Eysenck, Freud, Jung, Adler, Horney, Erikson, Skinner, Bandura, Rogers, and Maslow.

Trait
Surface trait
Source trait
Type
Id
Ego
Superego
Transference
Pleasure principle
Reality principle
Defense mechanism
Repression
Denial
Displacement
Introjection
Identification
Projection
Rationalization
Sublimation
Reaction formation
Compensation
Libido
Psychosexual development
Fixation
Oral stage
Anal stage
Phallic stage
Latency stage
Oedipal relationship
Castration complex
Genital stage
Personal unconscious
Collective unconscious

Persona
Ego psychology
Social-learning theory
Observational learning
Modeling
Phenomenology
Humanism
Congruence-incongruence
Self-actualization
Personality assessment
Rational-construct method
Empirical-criterion method
Factor-analytic method
Structured tests
Unstructured tests
Disguised tests
Undisguised tests
MMPI
CPI
Projective technique
TAT
Rorschach test
Validity
Response set
Clinical prediction
Actuarial prediction

TO GO BEYOND THIS CHAPTER △

In this book The topic of personality is so broad that every chapter in this book has some relation to this one. Among the most pertinent discussions are those of reliability and validity of tests in Chapter 10, of the concept of stages in cognitive development in Chapter 12, and of social and emotional development in Chapter 15. Chapters 17, 18, and 19 are particularly relevant. The first two focus on the development of the abnormal personality, Chapter 17 covering individual responses to stress and anxiety and the role of genetic and environmental factors in psychopathology, Chapter 18 Freud's basic contributions in greater depth, developmental factors in psychopathology, and again gene-environment interaction in forming personality. Chapter 19 has material on psychoanalysis, phenomenological methods, and behavior modification techniques, which translate the views of B. F. Skinner, Albert Bandura, and others into actual clinical practice.

Elsewhere A number of excellent texts provide in-depth coverage of the personality theorists cited in this chapter and others as well. Foremost among the texts are Calvin Hall and Gardner Lindzey's *Theories of Personality* and Salvatore Maddi's *Personality Theories: A Comparative Analysis.* Briefer volumes are provided by Duane Schultz, *Theories of Personality,* and by Larry Hjelle and Daniel Ziegler, *Personality Theories: Basic Assumptions, Research, and Application.* The personological point of view can be found in *Personality Theory: The Personological Tradition,* by Robert Hogan.

If your interest runs to Freudian theory, Philip Holzman has written an excellent paperback, *Psychoanalysis and Psychopathology.* Adler, Jung, and Horney, among others, are discussed by James Brown in *Freud and the Post-Freudians.* The expanding field of ego psychology is described by Gertrude and Rubin Blanck, in *Ego Psychology: Theory and Practice.* Paul Roazen's biography, *Erik H. Erikson: The Power and Limits of a Vision,* will expand your knowledge of this contemporary figure. Carl Rogers and Barry Stevens give Rogers's views in *Person to Person: The Problems of Being Human,* Abraham Maslow his in *The Farther Reaches of Human Nature,* Albert Bandura his in *Social Learning Theory,* and B. F. Skinner his in *About Behaviorism* and *Reflections on Behaviorism and Society.*

Many books provide a broad overview of the field of personality. Some of the best are *Personality: Theory, Assessment, and Research,* by Lawrence Pervin; Pervin's paperback, *Current Controversies and Issues in Personality,* which is excellent on trait versus situation, nature versus nurture, aggression, and gender identity; *Principles of Personality,* by Jerry Wiggins and others; *Personality,* by Robert Liebert and Michael Spiegler; and *The Enterprise of Living,* by Robert White.

Principles of assessment and psychological tests can be reviewed in *Psychological Testing,* by Anne Anastasi; and in *Essentials of Psychological Testing,* by Lee Cronbach. Clinical assessment of personality is covered in *Personality Assessment,* by Richard Lanyon and Leonard Goodstein; in *The Assessment of Persons,* by Norman Sundberg; and in *Assessing Personality,* by Robert Holt.

PART 5

PSYCHOPATHOLOGY AND CLINICAL PSYCHOLOGY

CH. 17

A Casebook of Psychopathology

BREAKDOWN

About three years ago, in my mid-forties, I had a sudden and severe mental breakdown. There was nothing unusual about the breakdown itself, nor about the events in my own life that led up to it. The only exceptional feature was that I am a psychologist and should therefore be able to view the events of my illness from two standpoints—subjectively as the patient and more objectively as the detached professional observer.

Until I broke down I had always regarded myself as reasonably well-balanced: although I had sometimes worried about physical illness, the thought that I might be subjected to the torture and humiliation of a severe mental illness had never entered my head. For many years I had been outgoing, efficient, continually active and reasonably cheerful: I thought of myself as well-meaning, though possibly somewhat insensitive both to my own and others' feelings. It never occurred to me that one day my existence would disintegrate within the space of a few hours. For half a year I lived in mental anguish, a prey to obsessive and agonizing thoughts. I had neither interest in nor ability to cope with the outside world which formerly I had found so fascinating. I hated myself and I hated others, and so unremitting and painful were my thoughts that I was virtually unable to read: I could not even concentrate sufficiently to peruse the daily paper. In five months all I read were a dozen case histories of breakdowns which were sufficiently similar to my own to seize my interest. For someone accustomed to spending most of the day reading and writing, the complete inability to do either was a singularly refined torture.

There were two aspects of the breakdown that were particularly painful, and took me by surprise since I had never experienced anything similar. The onset . . . was marked by levels of physical anxiety that I would not have believed possible. If one is almost involved in a road accident, there is a delay of a second or two and then the pit of the stomach seems to fall out and one's legs go like jelly. It was this feeling multiplied a hundredfold that seized me at all hours of the day or night. My dreams were often pleasant, but as soon as I woke panic set in and it would take a few moments to work out what it was about. The realization brought anguish: an irrevocable and cataclysmic event had occurred from which I could imagine no recovery. Sleep was difficult to come by even with the help of sleeping pills, to which I soon resorted. I would awake in terror twenty or thirty times a night. I would sometimes doze off in the daytime, and dream pleasant dreams for what seemed an eternity only to wake panic-stricken to discover that I had been asleep for no more than a few minutes.

The second unexpected consequence of the breakdown was the most extreme boredom. I could concentrate on nothing except my own pain. At first I would try to go to the theatre, or the cinema, but invariably I had to leave after a few minutes. In my previous existence, there had always been something to look forward to: now there was nothing, except the fitful mercy of sleep. I spent the day longing for the night to come (pp. 1–2).

Professor N. S. Sutherland.

With these words, Professor N. S. Sutherland (1976) of the University of Sussex in Great Britain begins one of the most candid accounts of a mental breakdown available in our literature. It is the story of a very talented psychologist's journey through an *affective disorder,* a depressive episode. The passage we have quoted is an example of what we call **descriptive psychopathology.** It describes the characteristics of mental disorder.

Another approach focuses on the origins of disorder, what we have come to call **developmental psychopathology.** In Dr. Sutherland's case the origins of his disorder remained unresolved.

It is likely that we all have our breaking points, though what destroys one man may barely pierce the skin of another. We all have wishes, conflicts and uncertainties of which we are unconscious, but of what makes one crack under this misfortune, another under that, we know very little. . . . As in all individual cases, one

"I JUST HAVEN'T BEEN EXPERIENCING MY NORMAL FEELINGS OF UNREALITY."

can only speculate about what it was about my background that rendered me liable to a breakdown in middle age (p. 10).

Normal versus Abnormal: The Thin Line That Divides Psychopathology is the scientific study of deviant behavior. Deviant behavior passes under various names, *behavior pathology, behavior disorder, mental disorder, abnormal behavior*—and *psychopathology* too—all carrying the implications of a deviance or departure from normality. But to understand such a departure we must first know something about nondeviant behavior: to understand deviance we must know the norm from which such deviance departs.

In many cases deviant behavior appears to be an extreme version of normality. We have often seen in others neatness that borders on compulsiveness, suspiciousness that seems tinged with irrationality, extreme sensitivity and fear that damages relationships with others or limits freedom and choice. At one time or another almost everyone experiences headaches brought on by nervousness, a vague sense of foreboding, an overwhelming anxiety in the midst of crisis, or uncertainty about his or her own identity and life goals. On the behavioral side the line between normal and abnormal is a thin one, indeed. As we show now, the same is true of environmental conditions and experience.

Several years ago one of us taught a course in Abnormal Psychology in which 185 competent, bright, and healthy undergraduates were enrolled. At the very first class session, the instructor presented the students with this hypothetical situation:

> Imagine that I am capable of dropping a drug into your drink which will, shortly thereafter, induce what appears to be a marked psychosis. You, however, have no awareness of what I have done. Your roommate, several hours later, finding you in a disturbed condition, takes you to the Student Health Service and the Dean's Office is notified of your illness. Your parents are asked to come to the campus and take you home for treatment. Within a day your worried folks take you to a mental health clinic in your community where you are interviewed and asked to fill in the details of your life. Consider this situation tonight. Spend some time reviewing your life and the things that have happened to you in some detail. At the next class session I will ask you whether or not, on the basis of your previous life experiences, you can justify this psychosis.

At the next meeting, when asked for a show of hands by those who believed that their lives justified a psychotic outcome, a sea of hands went up, making a count difficult. The opposite question, "Whose lives can't justify it?" brought two hands into view! Only 2 of 185 students considered a severe breakdown incomprehensible in terms of their past history.

This example illustrates a very important point about attempts to find the causes of psychopathology in reconstructions of a person's past. If you know the outcome of a life history, you will always, in looking backward into that life history, find events and factors that seem to explain the outcome. A successful outcome, normality, presses you toward a stress on the more positive events in that person's life; an unsuccessful one, mental disorder, leads to an emphasis on a person's negative experiences and relationships. For the moment it does not matter whether these experiences actually produce the disorder. The point is that they are available in the lives of most of us, and when needed can be used as possible explanations for our behavior.

TYPES OF PSYCHOPATHOLOGY

DSM-III Listings

In the pages to follow, we will present a brief introduction to descriptive and developmental psychopathology. The presentation makes use of the draft version of the third edition of the *Diagnostic and Statistical Manual of Mental Disorders* (DSM-III) of the American Psychiatric Association. This manual, now being tested, consists of a very extensive classification of the types of psychopathology, the various forms of psychopathology and deviant behavior. A partial summary of these types follows. In later sections we deal in greater detail with several of them.

Organic Mental Disorders Organic mental disorders include brain dysfunctions caused by specific physical and physiological factors. The origins of these disorders are related either to aging or to some form of extensive drug use. Typical of the types of disorders included are *senile dementia* and *withdrawal delirium,* or delirium tremens, from a sudden cutoff in excessive alcohol intake. Opiate, barbiturate, amphetamine, or cocaine intoxication would be included in this group too.

Schizophrenic Disorders Schizophrenic disorders are the classical disorders often characterized by delusions, hallucinations, certain types of thought disorder, and disturbances in language, perception, emotion, social relationships, and the sense of self.

Paranoid Disorders The paranoid disorders involve persistent delusions of persecution and jealousy, in which the associated features of anger can lead to violence. Excessive suspiciousness, a proneness to recurrent use of the courts for litigation may also be indicative when such usage is extreme.

Affective Disorders Affective disorders are serious alterations of mood, typically involving either depression or elation. These can be *episodic* or *chronic.* They can be *unipolar, either* depression or mania of at least two years duration; or *bipolar,* with *both* depressive and manic episodes in the person's history.

Anxiety Disorders Anxiety disorders are marked by the following: acute panic, generalized anxiety, phobias, obsessions and compulsions, each of which indicates a specific anxiety disorder. (This category and the two that follow were previously labeled the *Neuroses,* but the use of this term is discontinued in the DSM-III draft version.)

Somatoform Disorders Somatoform disorders bear physical symptoms but no accompanying organic condition to "explain" the symptoms; psychological conflict is evident. Includes *Somatization Disorder* (previously called "hysteria"), *Conversion Disorder.*

Dissociative Disorders In dissociative disorders there is a sudden temporary alteration of consciousness, resulting in a loss of identity, memory defect (amnesia) for personal information about the self; in *multiple personality* (page 10) several distinct internalized personalities can dominate the individual at one time or another.

Personality Disorders Disorders marked by powerfully habitual, inflexible, and maladaptive behavioral traits are called personality disorders. Examples include chronic suspiciousness and withdrawal—*Paranoid Personality Disorder;* a notable inability to form social relationships accompanied by odd ways of thinking and communicating and perceiving but not marked enough to be diagnosed as schizophrenia—*Schizotypal Personality Disorder;* enormous self-preoccupation, excessive fantasies of success, exhibitionism—*Narcissistic Personality Disorder;* continuous and chronic acting-out—*Antisocial Personality Disorder;* instability in behavior, mood, social relationships, inability to control anger, identity disturbance—*Borderline Personality Disorder.*

"I CAN'T REMEMBER THE LAST TIME I TREATED A CASE OF AMNESIA, AND I CAN'T EVEN REMEMBER IF I EVER DID TREAT ONE."

Psychosexual Disorders Disorders of gender identity (transsexualism), fetishism, zoophilia, pedophilia, exhibitionism, voyeurism, sexual masochism, and sadism are all psychosexual, as are sexual dysfunctions such as impotence, frigidity, vaginismus, premature ejaculation. Homosexuality as a broad term has been a source of great dispute among psychiatrists as to whether or not to consider it a psychosexual disorder. The general term has been excluded from DSM-III, but *ego-dystonic homosexuality* has been included to provide a classification of individuals who seek heterosexuality, but have little or no arousal under such stimulation, but who do have homosexual arousal which for them is both unwanted and distressing.

Reactive Disorders Reactive disorders cover reactions to specific life events. In *Post-traumatic Stress Disorders* symptoms appear after an unusual and powerful stressor such as bereavement, business failure, major disasters, and catastrophes. *Adjustment Disorders* to an identifiable life event are marked by maladaptive reactions such as impairment in social relationships and job functioning.

Disorders of Impulse Control Not Elsewhere Classified Impulse control disorders include *pathological gambling, pyromania* (fire-setting), *kleptomania* (irresistible impulse to steal), *intermittent explosive disorder* (recurrent episodes of explosive aggression, often described by the individual as "spells" or "attacks" which may occur in minutes and as quickly cease, followed by regret and self-blame).

The list as given is incomplete. Even so it is clear that the range of atypical behavior is enormous. This point will become clearer and more impressive as we turn to a more extensive treatment of a variety of psychopathological cases.

Reactive Disorders: Stress and Its Consequences

We begin our casebook of the psychopathologies with personality disturbances that are generated when normal individuals are exposed to severe stress. These are the *reactive disorders,* and they can occur at any point in the life of an individual: infancy, childhood, adolescence, adulthood, and old age. One group of these disorders, the **post-traumatic stress disorders,** require a description of the nature and meaning of stress.

Stress Most students of stress would agree that any definition of the term should contain the following components. First, there is an element of disruption or threat to the individual; second, the sense of threat is created by the person's perception that there is an imbalance between the environmental demand that the stress imposes and the individual's ability to respond adequately to it; third, the failure to meet that demand must be significant for the individual. A mild stress implies a minor imbalance between demand and ability that has insignificant consequences for the individual. Severe stresses—or "extreme situations" as some stress researchers prefer to call them—imply a great imbalance with overwhelming consequences, and it is these two factors that define the nature of "trauma." Catastrophic disasters, witnessing or participating in the carnage of war, the life and death experience of the concentration camps are examples.

Observations of people experiencing such catastrophes indicate that many suffer from a **disaster syndrome** which has a specific sequence of stages. Initially there is a **shock reaction.** In this stage individual variation can be quite marked. Some 10 to 20 percent of people remain calm, another 20 percent show severe panic; but most individuals are confused, stunned, and paralyzed.

The impact of catastrophe was vividly portrayed by Dr. Hachaya, a physician living in Hiroshima when that city was destroyed by an atom bomb on August 6, 1945. Following the bombing, not panic but a "ghostly stillness," a "sense of slow motion" (Lifton, 1967) descended on the city. Hachaya (1955) writes,

> Those who were able walked silently toward the suburbs in the distant hills, their spirits broken, their initiative gone. When asked whence they had come, they pointed to the city and said, "that way"; and when asked where they were going, pointed away from the city and said, "this way." They were so broken and confused that they moved and behaved like automatons.
>
> Their reactions had astonished outsiders who reported with amazement the spectacle of long files of people holding stolidly to a narrow, rough path when close by was a smooth, easy road going in the same direction. The outsiders could not grasp the fact that they were witnessing the exodus of a people who walked in the realm of dreams (p. 54).

The second stage is a **recoil reaction.** The individual becomes aware of the disaster and knows that its consequences must be faced. Depression and hostility are not uncommon, and these lead into a third stage, the **stage of recall,** characterized by tenseness, restlessness, a replaying of the events observed during the disaster, or a repression of such traumatic experiences. Only later does the need for renewal and rehabilitation begin to take form. Typically hospitalization is not required, but high levels of anxiety and distress may continue to debilitate the individual (Kisker, 1977). In the aftermaths of natural disasters, these effects are sometimes quite evident.

On June 9, 1972, disaster struck Rapid City, South Dakota, when a flood of disastrous proportions swept over the city, inundating it and killing many of its inhabitants. Eight months later reporter Harley Sorensen visited the community and wrote a poignant story for the *Minneapolis Tribune* on the mental health problems that flood had left in its wake. There were problems for the individual and for the community.

The individual

> *Anxiety:* A young couple, fleeing the waters of the June 9 flood, struggle to reach high ground. Each carries a child. The water sweeps the children from them. Helpless, they watch as their children are carried away screaming. The father later returns to his job in a water purification system. But he cannot function. The gurgling of the water at his job reminds him of the night his children were lost.
>
> *Fear:* A mother and her two children manage to get to their station wagon. It starts, but flood water takes it away. Caught on debris, it starts to sink. The mother frees the car and it floats away again. It gets caught again. She frees it again. Somehow, the car ends up on a road. The mother drives off with her children. They hear screams and cries for help but they are unable to help. They lose everything. Now, the mother has recurrent nightmares. The children refuse to undress for bed; they fall asleep with their clothes on.

Depression: A mother of five children carries two of her children to safety. She listens with horror while the other three slowly drown. Later she pleads to have her two surviving children taken from her. "I'm a bad mother," she says, "I can't take care of my children. If I keep them, something will happen to them. They'll die. I can't protect them. Please take them."

Panic: It is late July, six weeks after the flood. The Rapid City Girl's Club in North City is meeting. Suddenly, it begins to thunder, lightning and rain. The lights go out. About a dozen of the young girls begin to scream. "The flood is coming," they scream, "the flood is coming." It takes considerable effort to calm the girls down again.

The community

- Marked increases in number of persons committed to Yankton State Hospital over the year previously.
- More husbands and wives "thinking about divorce."
- Overcrowding in hospitals located away from the flood plain; empty beds in hospitals within the area that had been flooded.
- Reports of severe despondency and depression among older people.
- Doctors report a "substantial increase" in subjective physical complaints—headaches, backaches, stomach aches—from people not directly injured in the flood.
- Upsurge in the use of marijuana among young people; increased sales of tranquilizers and sedatives.
- Liquor distributors reported "a tremendous increase" in liquor sales inland around Rapid City.
- Unwanted pregnancies—legitimate and illegitimate—are up, possibly as a result of contraceptives being washed away in the flood.

A final point about stress reactions. It has long been believed that there is a relationship between predisposition to disorder and whether a person will break under a relatively minor as opposed to a very severe stress. Presumably predisposing elements are strongest in those who break under a minor stress, and recovery from such a breakdown will take longer. By contrast, those who break only under the severest of stresses supposedly have much less of a predisposition to mental disorder and are more likely to recover rapidly if and when disorder develops. Irving Janis (1971), a noted researcher in this area who had previously believed that spontaneous recovery usually occurs within a few weeks after an accident or a disaster, now questions this view as overly optimistic.

But the situation is not necessarily a hopeless one. Some studies of survivor behavior in disaster indicate that many do turn to helping and rescuing others. One report of a destructive tornado showed that within half an hour one third of those involved were searching for missing persons and another third were engaged in emergency relief work. Within the next six hours three fourths of the survivors were searching or providing relief and an additional 22 percent were actually engaged in rescue work. Older people are often amazed at the work output of teenagers in a disaster. Furthermore, those who have suffered only minor injuries generally are calm and undemanding and urge rescuers to help the more seriously injured (Tanner, 1976).

Bereavement: The Grieving Spouse Disaster is communal and the company of misery can help to sustain survivors. The death of a spouse, by contrast, is individual and the wife or husband who is left alone to mourn is subject to deep and pervasive stress. Such anxiety is far better known to women than to men, for the greater longevity of women can result in a ratio of widows to widowers in the later years that approximates four to one. In the wake of the death of a spouse comes loneliness and losses of companionship, sex, often a home, comfort, and support, both economic and emotional. There is often loss of friends who, unable to understand or accept the process of grief and mourning, despite the fact that this too is as natural as life itself, gradually drift away from the bereaved person.

Data (Greenblatt, 1978; Parkes, 1972) suggest that the consequences of this stress are very marked. Widows under sixty-five consult physicians at three times the expected rate, spend far more time in bed or in the hospital, use sedatives at seven times the rate of controls, and show an exacerbation of physical symptoms. It has been estimated that widows drink too much alcohol, take too much medication, and have a risk of death—from an illness that often mirrors the dead spouse's—far greater than those of the same age who have not suffered spousal loss.

Recently support programs have been set up to help the surviving spouse combat this stress. In widow-to-widow programs a woman who has lived through the period of grief tries to provide support for the newly widowed.

SUMMARY □

The reactive disorders occur at all stages of life and are produced by extreme environmental stress in persons without any underlying mental disorder. But what is stressful for one person may not be disturbing for another. This simply means that the response to stress is an individual matter. People differ in how they perceive environmental demands, in their degree of confidence in meeting these demands, and in their ability to tolerate the impending threats of failure and frustration. This individual variation in vulnera-

Bereavement.

bility can be seen most clearly within normal limits of stress. But as stress grows more extreme, these individual differences are diminished and the range of adaptation among persons is reduced.

In extreme situations—in the face of natural catastrophes such as floods, earthquakes, tornadoes, and the like; and in those human beings have fashioned for themselves—war, prolonged bombing attacks, concentration camps—the behavior of most people will be deviant. When threat is comparatively mild or moderate, however, some people will be less seriously affected.

Disaster can have a positive effect in bringing survivors together to help less fortunate victims. Here support has a therapeutic quality. By contrast, bereavement through loss of a spouse is a stress in which loss of support can be very profound. More common to women than men, bereavement markedly affects the physical as well as the emotional well-being of the grieving partner.

ANXIETY, SOMATOFORM, AND DISSOCIATIVE DISORDERS

The anxiety, somatoform, and dissociative disorders grouping in the DSM-III draft retitles the neuroses which have occupied an honored place in psychiatry since the turn of the century. As our description of cases in this grouping will show, symptoms are so heterogeneous in this group that it is doubtful that anything useful is accomplished by treating them as though they were a single disorder.

Anxiety Disorders

Panic Disorders The symptoms of a panic disorder are recurrent panic (anxiety) attacks and nervousness, a pervasive sense of anxiety and uncontrollable dread, elevated blood pressure and pulse rate, sweating, and the subjective feelings of breathlessness and dizziness. The attack may be acute, lasting hours or days, or it may become chronic and persist for weeks or months. If the attack lasts six months or longer, the disorder is given the diagnosis of *Generalized Anxiety Disorder*.

A forty-six-year-old businessman who was having serious difficulties in his work and marriage described his anxiety attack.

> I was almost down to work, close to the White House on Pennsylvania Avenue. I got caught in some traffic. Suddenly I began to shake all over. I felt something awful was going to happen. I couldn't go on . . . I wanted to hide my face in may arms. My chest hurt. I was afraid to drive . . . I got a policeman to call up a friend to come down. He drove me home. I thought I was dying . . . I've gotten afraid to drive downtown by myself now and I feel I want to have someone with me (Laughlin, 1967, pp. 91–92).

Obsessive-Compulsive Disorder This disorder takes the form of constantly recurring, often absurd ideas, which are called **obsessions;** or impulses to perform some specific act, called **compulsions.** These actions may be quite simple mechanical movements or very complex rituals such as repetitive hand washing. Efforts to resist performing the compulsion results in heightened anxiety.

A large jewelry firm regularly found one or two of their more perfect diamonds missing at periodic inventories. For a considerable period of time these irregular and seemingly inconsistent losses remained unaccountable. Finally, however, the recurring losses were traced to one of their most devoted and trusted diamond experts. He had not stolen them for himself. His rationale for their appropriation was most interesting and unique. The expert had developed such a tremendous obsessive need for perfection that he simply could not stand an imperfect stone. A diamond *must* be "just-so." As a result, when a customer occasionally brought in a chipped gem for resetting, or an imperfect one, he simply replaced it with a perfect stone from the firm's extensive stock, and threw away the poor or damaged diamond brought in by the customer (Laughlin, 1967, pp. 335–336).

Phobic Disorder This is a fairly common reaction in which a pathological but persistent and irrational fear is attached to an object or situation which is not inherently dangerous. The person may show intense panic even in anticipation of confronting the feared object. The disorder can become increasingly incapacitating as it begins to generalize widely to other objects, ideas, or areas.

A young woman, eighteen, having begun to date seriously, found that simple intimacies such as kissing and embracing aroused intense sexual desires, which were followed by a pervasive sense of guilt and wrongdoing. Reared in a repressive family atmosphere and exposed to strict "moral" training, she had been taught that sex and sinfulness were equivalent and that damnation was the punishment for those who engaged in any form of sexual expression. To contain her guilt she began a slow entry into a pattern of avoidance behavior. First, she stopped seeing the man she was dating. This proved insufficient. Next, she stopped going out with any man because even casual dating made her uncomfortable. Finally, her fears having spread to all social situations, she withdrew entirely from all participation in social functions (Coleman, 1976).

Somatoform Disorders

Somatoform disorders involve disturbances of bodily function. Conversion disorders provide an example. Conversion disorder was formerly termed **hysterical neurosis, conversion type.** It is noted by the presence of physical ailments which have no demonstrable organic basis. Although such physical symptoms—blindness, deafness, mutism, seizures, tics, anesthesias, motor paralysis—would ordinarily be very disturbing, the conversion reactions are usually not accompanied by the expected degree of concern. The incidence of this form of hysteria appears to be declining.

A doctor was called to examine a rancher's adolescent daughter who had lost the use of both legs. The neighbors attributed her paralysis to an epidemic condition which was raging through the ranch animals, but her parents knew this explanation to be untrue. While their daughter was in the house one afternoon, a male relative came in, embraced her, and then attempted rape. The young girl screamed for help, her legs gave way, and she fell to the floor. The man fled. The mother, returning from an errand moments later, found her daughter on the floor. Efforts to help her stand were fruitless, and she was carried to her bedroom. Medical examinations revealed no organic basis for the paralysis which lasted several weeks.

Dissociative Disorders

The dissociative disorders, which are relatively uncommon, involve loss of memory for the past. In *psychogenic amnesia,* for example, there is the sudden inability to recall significant personal information accompanied by severe memory failure. Such behavior is not caused by organic factors or simple forgetting. When the reaction does occur, it is often an object of attention in the media because of its intense dramatic quality.

. . . A twenty-six-year-old druggist lay on a hospital bed and stared blankly at his white-haired mother, who reminded him of his boyhood in an effort to restore his memory. The druggist in answer to his mother's pleas replied:

"I'm sorry but I don't know you. I wish I did know you because I love you better than anything in the world." The entire family gathered around the bed, but the young man did not recognize any of his relatives (Kisker, 1977, p. 211).

The Roots of Anxiety

Most psychologists agree that many of the behaviors just described are learned during the early years of childhood. Their roots appear to lie in the conflict between powerful drives and anxiety aroused by their expression. Typical of such anxiety-inducing conflicts are sexual expression versus sexual inhibition, aggression versus fear of retribution, and a striving for autonomy and independence as opposed to being compliant and dependent. The source of these conflicts is to be found in childhood, when the multiple demands placed upon the child by the parents are particularly heavy: cleanliness training, toilet training, self-feeding, delay over immediate gratifications, achievement pressures, control of sexual and aggressive behavior. Yet such socializing experiences are the typical pattern of our society. Most children are subjected to these demands. Why then do some acquire the burdens of disordered behavior, whereas others remain free of such symptoms?

Two factors appear to be particularly critical, *parental child-rearing attitudes* and *individual vulnerability*. Two forms of early parental attitudes seem to be most important. Either childhood tendencies are excessively indulged, with minimal emphasis on growing up, or they are excessively suppressed, with the expectation that the child can grow up all at once. The slow learnings that result in channeling or renunciation are minimized or ignored.

The second factor, individual vulnerability, has its locus in the child. Children differ in their susceptibility to threat and frustration. Such predispositions are basic factors in anxiety arousal, although it is not entirely clear to what extent this is determined by temperament and to what extent it is determined by the long-term stresses provided by living with inadequate parents. At any rate, it appears that faulty child-rearing practices focused on a vulnerable child and poor parental models form the basis for maladaptive personality formation.

Specific Symptom Patterns

A more specific question remains. How do the specific forms of disordered behavior develop? Why a phobia rather than an obsession? Why amnesia rather than an effort to control anxiety or undo guilt by compulsive hand washing? The answers to such questions can be only speculative, but again we are probably safe in suggesting that a nature-nurture interaction is involved. The typical makeup of the obsessional individual may help to clarify this point.

The symptoms of the obsessional person are intellectual. The obsessional is essentially a thinker, meticulous and rigid, but a thinker nonetheless. One young widow summed up her experiences with a dating service by describing an obsessional "neurotic" she had met.

> He had to count everything, all the time. His small change, the number of cars parked in a street, how many people there were in a room—just everything. Most of the time he couldn't talk, he was that busy counting (Godwin, 1973).

Clearly this is an example of a maladaptive response, but it is important to recognize that it has functional value for the man. The act of counting probably reduces the anxiety that threatens to overwhelm him, perhaps triggered in the dating situation. Thus counting is reinforced and becomes a likely response in social situations that arouse anxiety (page 405).

If counting is to be effective, however, it must be reasonably successful in reducing anxiety. If we could look back into this man's history, we would probably be able to find situations in which counting behavior was first used—and used successfully—to counteract anxiety. Counting is an intellectual activity. To make effective use of a defense of obsessive overintellectualization requires intelligence in a way that many other symptoms do not. Since intelligence is, in part, a genetically determined trait, it can be viewed as an inherited component that can contribute to an obsessive-compulsive disorder.

Nurture's contribution is also essential, however. Obsessive-compulsive people tend to have had meticulous perfectionistic parents of middle-class professional backgrounds. These parents have been described as overambitious for their children, demanding achievements that are appropriate to a later stage of development (Rosen, Fox, and Gregory, 1972). Given this background, we can conjecture about the familial factors that predispose an individual toward an obsessional disorder. The first would be the role played by the parental model. Through modeling the child copies the responses of the parents but typically without the appropriate discriminative ability that is necessary to keep the behavior from becoming a parody of the original model. Imitation is an easy and effortless way for children to acquire a variety of responses, including the disturbed behavior of the parental model.

There is the factor of selective reinforcement to be considered. Middle- and upper-class professional parents tend to reward their children for displays of intellectual achievement, for problem solving by reflection as opposed to action, for verbal skills rather than for motoric ones, and for the inhibition of behavior rather than the expression of impulsive acts. Thus for the child from such a familial background, the aggressive and sexual impulses of childhood are more likely to be displaced into the efforts at orderliness, meticulousness, ritualistic behavior, and overintellectualized rumination. Extended to disorder in the obsessional person, hostility and sexuality may take the form of plaguing and distressing *thoughts—not acts*—of anger or promiscuity.

SUMMARY □

The concept of neurosis in psychiatric classification has now been supplanted by several new categories, including those of anxiety, somatoform disorders, and dissociative disorders. Even under a new term they remain equally debilitating since the behaviors represented by the categories are exaggerated symptoms that presumably serve to modulate and control anxiety arousal. This means that the disordered behavior is presumably learned in situations that arouse distress and is maintained and strengthened by the extent to which it successfully reduces anxiety. Many types of behavior can be reinforced in this manner, including the avoidance of feared objects or situations—phobic disorder; ruminative thoughts or repetitive actions—obsessive-compulsive disorder; physical complaints that lack an organic basis—conversion disorder; amnesias and fugues—psychogenic amnesia or psychogenic fugue disorder; and the like.

These behaviors probably arise as a result of the interaction of environmental and genetic factors. Although psychologists have tended to emphasize the acquisition of behavior by principles of social learning or operant conditioning, a more basic predisposition of the individual could explain why certain forms of behavior tend to become prepotent over others.

PERSONALITY DISORDERS

The personality disorders make up a heterogeneous category characterized by pervasive and maladaptive personality traits. DSM-III describes twelve different types of personality disorders. Three are illustrated here.

Descriptions of Personality Disorders

Paranoid Personality Disorder Paranoid individuals are hypersensitive, rigid, jealous, overaggressive, and envious. They tend to be suspicious of the motives and intentions of others and are prone to emphasize and inflate their own importance.

> A young man was hospitalized after he had viciously beaten his wife two times. He had always been chronically suspicious of her, although there was no evidence of infidelity. This attitude was accentuated when she tried to get close to him and when she requested sexual relations.
>
> He constantly sought reassurance [whether] she "loved him or not," expressing the view that he could accept either if he knew it was the truth. At work he was uncomfortable when his associates attempted to become friendly, accusing them of being overly competitive and taking advantage of his knowledge. He enjoyed his job as an accountant because he preferred working with figures to working with people (Swanson et al., 1970, p. 67).

Introverted Personality Disorder Introverted personalities tend to be seclusive, shy, oversensitive, reserved, and withdrawn. Although given to fantasy, they do not lose their capacity to recognize and to deal with reality. In response to disturbing events, they may detach themselves from the situation. They tend not to show marked emotion, giving the impression of being aloof and distant from others.

> Jeremy Bentham, famed English philosopher, was a sensitive and retiring person from earliest childhood. He disliked play and games, felt inferior to others and hated social activities. He remained solitary in his work and play into adulthood, spending a great part of his time in reading and "gloomy meditation." At college he had no friends, his sense of inferiority being so strong that it led him to remove himself from others. His father often accused him of burying his talents (Menninger, 1947, p. 77).

Antisocial Personality Disorder The antisocial personality has a long-term history of disruptive behavior which brings injury to others. In childhood, lying, fighting, stealing, promiscuity, and running away can be early signs of the disorder. In adulthood the same pattern of behavior is retained. Work efficiency and personal relations are generally poor. The individual is unable to sustain close and meaningful contacts with others. Other psychiatric terms that have been used to describe this pattern include **sociopathy** and **psychopathy** or *psychopathic disorder*.

Several years ago *The New York Times* published a story that can stand as a superb case study of the antisocial personality.

> A thirty-four-year-old man who had tried to extort more than $300,000 from TWA after hijacking one of its jetliners failed to be convicted because of a hung jury. The skyjacker had had a long history of crime. He had robbed seven banks, had forged thousands of dollars in checks, pulled off a $100,000 jewel heist in the Bahamas, had been arrested at least twenty times for major criminal acts, but had spent less than two years in jail.
>
> A singular achievement! How did he manage to do it? By repeatedly assuming the mantle of a *multiple personality*, the skyjacker had recurrently fooled psychiatrists and psychologists who were required to testify at his trials. Basically, he asserted, he was a sane, honest man whose mind was repeatedly taken over by a sinister and criminal alter ago. The crimes were committed by this criminal personality and were not of his own doing.
>
> The skyjacker's past was an interesting one. Both his father, who was a naval officer, and his mother, who came from an old New England family, drank heavily. The father was later dismissed from the Navy for running a brothel in the Caribbean area. The parents were subsequently divorced and the young man, then eleven years old, went to live with his father and stepmother, who threw him out of the house when the father died. The boy, then fifteen, moved into a brothel euphemistically called the "House of Love" and began his long criminal career. But in most cases he avoided criminal prosecution by being sent to a mental hospital from which he equally promptly escaped. At his trial four of six psychiatrists testified that he was mentally ill, the other two indicating that he was sane and "malingering."

The Etiology of the Antisocial Personality

The origins of antisocial personality or sociopathy are not at all clear. The term *sociopath* places emphasis on its possible social roots. What are these social-developmental roots? Clearly implicated are faulty parental models. Case histories of sociopathic individuals often reveal parental behavior that is antisocial—a mother's alcoholism, a father's physical abuse of the child, a familial history of thievery and crime. Often cruel abuse and physical neglect are noted, providing the child with the opportunity to imitate behavior that emphasizes coldness, unconcern, brutality, a lack of involvement, and a rejection of others. Some of this neglect and brutality is apparent in the case history of Derek, which might be considered to describe sociopathy in the making.

> Derek, a seven-year-old boy of average intelligence, was referred for "uncontrollable and aggressive behavior, enuresis and encopresis [lack of bladder and bowel control], speech and sleep disturbances, sexual offenses, jealousy, truanting, stealing, lying, wandering at night, exaggerated masturbation, destructiveness and retardation at school" (Bennett, 1960).
>
> Derek's behavior rightfully earns him the dubious distinction as one of the worst delinquents seen at the tender age of seven in a large-scale British study. Here are some of the behaviors that were recorded by the investigators.
>
> Derek is the oldest of two children; his sister aged four is the object of his cruelty and aggressiveness; he expresses his hatred of her and she, in turn, is terrified of him. The mother reports that he constantly interfered with the sister and at age five achieved sexual intercourse with her which has been repeated several times. Mother has frequently found the children in bed together despite her reproofs. Derek openly masturbates day and night. He remains incontinent even at age seven. He has been unresponsive to toilet training. He is still unable to dress himself. He began to talk with a stutter at age three and it has persisted. Because he was difficult, he was placed in a foster home by a child guidance clinic, but was so troublesome he could not be kept there. At the age of four he ran away from home, he has set fires in hostels on several occasions, has stolen, and although professing a liking for animals, he has stomped two cats to death and has been cruel to other pets. He is a sleepwalker who is beset with night terrors. Sent to school at age four and a half, he refused to learn, truanted, and was the victim of attacks by other children. His teachers report that he seems far away. He performs poorly in all subjects despite his average IQ, although he seems better adjusted at school than in the home. He has peculiar mannerisms, uses only his left hand, interrupts conversations to describe "incomprehensible fantasies and to play weird games." Mother reports that Derek never shows his feelings; he has never wanted affection, kicking her away from him even when very young.
>
> The family picture provides a bleak spectacle. The mother, who is thirty years old, is described as "apathetic and tearful." She married Derek's father at twenty-one and he deserted her when Derek was six years old. Only poverty forced her to return to him when her children were younger. Mother is fatalistic about Derek. Her controls are feeble and inconsistent. Derek has beaten her and remains defiant. At present mother lives with a truck driver, a friendly man whom she would like to marry, but cannot do so without divorcing her husband. The mother wants Derek sent away because she fears that he will be perverted sexually like his father. Derek's father, thirty-one, is a gardener who was dismissed from the army for beating other soldiers. Mother describes him as "sex-mad." He has been brutal, jealous, sexually demanding and likely perverted. While mother was in the hospital having Derek, father impregnated a young girl in the neighborhood. Derek "idolized" his father who treated him severely (he was frequently beaten for masturbation) and preferred the younger sister. The father's family history shows a background of epilepsy, mental retardation, and psychosis.
>
> Treatment of Derek was attempted at a clinic for children but his attendance was irregular because of the chaotic home conditions and the rejection of a treatment plan by the parents. Foster home placement has been achieved with only moderate success. He was brought to juvenile court for stealing and destructive behavior and remanded to the care of education authorities until he is eighteen.

The prognosis is very guarded and the outlook for Derek looks bleak. But can we be confident that Derek is on the path to adult psychopathy? That he is traveling rapidly toward that uncherished goal is suggested by a classic follow-up study of deviant children by Lee Robins (1966). The children of this study—524 of them—had been seen in a psychiatric clinic as youngsters, some thirty years previous to follow-up. Many had been seen because of antisocial behavior, others for different forms of behavior disorders. When traced in their adult life, many showed signs of very poor adaptation, including sociopathic behavior. From her study Robins developed a set of childhood predictors of antisocial behavior in adulthood. We have introduced numbers into the Robins quotation as a count of the criteria against which to apply Derek's history by the age of seven.

Robins's criteria

> If one wishes to choose the most likely candidate for a later diagnosis of sociopathic personality

from among children appearing in a child guidance clinic, the best choice appears to be: [1] the boy referred for theft or aggression who has shown [2] a diversity of antisocial behavior in many episodes, [3] at least one of which could be grounds for a Juvenile Court appearance and whose antisocial behavior involves him with [4] strangers and organizations as well as with [5] teachers and parents. With these characteristics more than half of the boys appearing at the clinic were later diagnosed sociopathic personality. Such boys had a history of [6] truancy, [7] theft, [8] staying out late and [9] refusing to obey parents. They [10] lied gratuitously, and [11] showed little guilt over their behavior. They [12] generally were irresponsible about being where they were supposed to be or [13] taking care of money. They were [14] interested in sexual activities and had experimented with [15] homosexual relationships (p. 157).

Measured against these fifteen criteria Derek's score would be 14, a bleak portent of things to come.

Genetic and environmental factors in the antisocial personality The history of Derek illustrates certain familial factors known to be associated with many antisocial personalities: parental violence, incapacity, inconsistency and indecision with regard to discipline, marital discord, maternal rejection, early separation from home, and a family history of psychopathology. This last factor of a deviant history or defect in relatives raises anew the question of environmental *and* hereditarian influence in psychopathy. Recent research suggests that hereditary factors may be quite important.

A study conducted in Denmark (Schulsinger, 1972) of the biological and adoptive relatives of children who were adopted early in life, and were diagnosed psychopathic when adults, provides some highly relevant data for revealing an interaction between the contributions of genetic and environmental factors. A control group of nondisturbed adoptees was used for comparison purposes. The basic question asked in the study was this. For the two adoptee groups was there a greater proportion of deviance in the biological or the adoptive relatives? If the data indicated a higher incidence in the biological relatives as opposed to the adoptive relatives, it would suggest a genetic linkage, for the children were not raised by their biological parents. Were the reverse true, it would suggest the operation of environmental factors, for the adoptive parents were the primary caretakers of the adoptees. The results showed that the rate of psychopathy among the biological parents was higher than among the adoptive parents for the index group. It was also higher than the rate of psychopathy in both the biological and the adoptive parents of the normal control adoptees (Table 17.1).

TABLE 17.1
Psychopathic-Type Disorders in Biological and Adoptive Relatives of Adoptees with and without a Diagnosis of Psychopathy

	Relatives Showing Deviances, percent	
Status of Adoptees	Biological	Adoptive
Psychopathic	14.4	7.6
Nondisturbed	6.7	5.3

From Schulsinger, 1972.

Another study of convicted male and female felons and their first-degree relatives (Guze, 1976) affirms what is well known: convicted felons come out of severely disordered families and equally disordered social backgrounds in which poverty, parental criminality, alcoholism, and restricted opportunities are inevitably present. Both social *and* familial factors seem to be operating. "It is not yet possible," the author concludes, "to unravel the tangled skein of evidence concerning heredity and environment in sociopathy, but it is difficult to ignore completely the indications of a biological contribution to its etiology" (p. 142).

SUMMARY □

The personality disorders make up a large and heterogeneous collection of psychopathologies that have several attributes in common. First, there are indications of a pervasive trait structure that dominates behavior in many different situations. Second, those traits are maladaptive in many situations that confront the individual. Reactions tend to be rigid, inflexible and stereotyped, and therefore maladaptive. Antisocial personality disorder, sometimes known as sociopathy or psychopathy, is one form of the personality disorders that has received a great deal of attention. Recent findings seem to implicate some hereditary factors, but depriving environments and disorganized families play a very important role as well. Interpersonal functioning in the personality disorders tends to be inadequate, although work and school competence may be sustained.

PSYCHOSES: THE SEVERE MENTAL DISORDERS

Affective Disorders

Affect refers to mood or emotion. Thus in the affective disorders an extreme mood, such as marked depression or elation, dominates the patient's behavior and, if sufficiently excessive, can lead to a loss of contact with the environment. How debilitating such a disorder can be, even in a person of superb intellectual achievement, is seen in the following case.

> A fifty-five-year-old college professor who had been a very productive and meticulous scholar began to ruminate about his past transgressions which were really quite minor in nature, such as taking a towel from a hotel room when a youth. Unable to concentrate and overwhelmed by guilt, he despaired that he would ever work again. He found himself unable to sleep as his anxiety and agitation mounted. He grew more depressed, talked of suicide and cried intermittently.
>
> Increasingly worried about his threats to take his own life, his wife had him admitted to a private psychiatric hospital. To his therapist he repeated his assertion that his career was ended and nothing could be done for him. After a case consultation it was decided to institute a brief course of electric convulsive shock treatments. These were followed by a rapid recovery and return to his home and campus where he was able to resume his research, writing, and teaching activities.

Depression is so commonplace in our country that estimates of the size of the group of people prone to mild or moderate manifestations of these states range up to 20 to 25 percent of the adult population. A figure this large suggests that moods of depression are simply part of the normal human condition that includes "the blues" or being "down-in-the-dumps." At a more severe level there is a growing concern about our suicide statistics (see page 441).

Classification of the Affective Disorders In the current draft of DSM-III, the affective disorders are classified in three broad categories, **episodic, chronic,** and *atypical,* a residual category which will not be discussed here.

The episodic disorder is characterized by periods of disturbance or episodes, which last from a few days to several months. They may be separated by years of normal functioning, or they may recur more frequently. The chronic form is distinguished by sustained and long-lasting disturbance. In either category symptoms may consist of **manic** behavior—a hyperactive pattern of excessive activity, speech, flight of ideas, inflated self-perceptions, grandiosity, and a rapidly changing mood; or **depressive** behavior—a pervasive quality of sadness, tearfulness, discouragement, hopelessness, loss of pleasure, motoric agitation, excessive slowness and retardation, a sense of personal worthlessness, and negative views of the self. In some cases, called **bipolar affective disorders,** both manic and depressive episodes occur. In this group the initial episode is usually a manic one with subsequent manic and depressive episodes tending to be more frequent and of briefer duration than in the episodic forms. The following two cases are representative.

DEPRESSIVE EPISODE, PSYCHOTIC: CASE OF A YOUNG WOMAN'S GUILT OVER THE DEATH OF HER PARENTS

> A twenty-four-year-old woman eloped against her parents' wishes with a young man. As a result they disowned her and refused to communicate with her. The daughter and her husband moved to California. In the year that followed, she had guilt feelings for having failed her parents who had projected a marriage for her to a wealthy young man. When she became pregnant she informed her parents of the impending birth of her child. The parents, in a gesture of rapprochement, sent gifts. The baby died during birth and the arrival of the parents' presents intensified the young mother's grief reaction. The parents made plans to travel to California to visit their daughter and son-in-law; both were tragically killed in an automobile accident while en route. The patient developed a psychotic depression and attempted suicide. She blamed herself for the deaths and remained agitated and expressed the belief that she was the one who deserved to die for having killed her baby and her parents (Coleman, 1976, p. 355).

BIPOLAR AFFECTIVE DISORDER: A CHRONIC CASE OF BOTH MANIC AND DEPRESSIVE BEHAVIOR

> A thirty-eight-year-old woman was admitted to a state hospital for the first time, atlhough since childhood she had had marked mood swings some of which were of a psychotic nature. Her first depression at age seventeen prevented her from working. At thirty-three, pregnant with her first child, a depressed episode recurred. One month after the birth of the baby excitement seized her and she was hospitalized for a brief period. Sent to the seashore to recuperate, she took a hotel room for a night. The next day she signed a lease on an apartment and bought furniture for it, going heavily into debt.
>
> She recovered and for two years functioned reasonably well until she again became overactive, spoke of countless business activities, pawned jewelry and wrote checks indiscriminately although she had no funds with which to cover them. She recovered after several months of hospitalization and resumed her life, but felt mildly depressed. One year later she again had a manic episode and in a single day purchased fifty-seven hats!
>
> She has since been in and out of hospitals with sequences of severely manic and less severe depressive episodes. During one manic episode she became enamored of a physician and sent him the following telegram:

"To: You; Street and No." Everywhere; Place: the remains at peace! We did our best, but God's will be done! I am so very sorry for all of us. To brave it through that far. Yes, Darling—from Hello Handsome. Handsome is as Handsome does, thinks, lives and breathes. It takes clear air, Brother of Mine, in a girl's hour of need. All my love to the Best Inspiration one ever had."

At age fifty-nine this woman is now making an excellent adjustment in home and community. Her ill husband has needed her assistance and she has met these responsibilities admirably. Recurrent episodes of excitement and depression, however, remain a likely outcome (Kolb, 1973, pp. 376–377).

Origins of the Affective Disorders When the affective disorders are more fully understood, it seems likely that a complex interactive explanation will emerge to take into account genetic vulnerability; significant early developmental events, such as loss of a loved object in childhood, for example, parents (Brown et al., 1977); stressful events in adult life that overwhelm the individual's ability to cope, such as childbirth; physiological stressors, such as levels of particular biochemical substances; and specific personality attributes, such as a pessimistic view of life or a low threshold for anxiety arousal under stress.

Twin studies show the importance of genetic factors. If one of a pair of identical twins develops a depression, the likelihood that the other twin will also be depressed has been estimated, in different studies, to range between 50 and 93 percent. The range for fraternal twins is 3 to 38 percent.

Several lines of evidence point to the importance of disrupted attachment and separation from a loved object. A study by Colin Parkes (1964) of more than 3000 psychiatric inpatients of various diagnoses revealed that patients whose psychiatric disorder followed within six months of a family member's death were more likely to develop an affective disorder. Recent research by George Brown and his colleagues (1978) in London indicates that a major loss for women occurring nine months before the onset of psychiatric symptoms tended to precipitate a depressive disorder. Four specific factors were found to heighten vulnerability to depression: (1) loss of mother before the age of eleven, (2) presence at home of three or more children aged less than fourteen, (3) lack of a confiding relationship with a husband, and (4) lack of full- or part-time employment.

With regard to cognitive factors, evidence points to differences between depressive and nondepressive individuals, depressives having negatively distorted views of events. They are pessimistic and have a negative self-concept. The depressives tend to attribute negative outcomes to personal incompetence (Abramson et al., 1978). In performance on a task requiring skill, depressed subjects fail to alter their performance on the basis of prior success, whereas their expectations for other individuals are similar to those of controls (Garber and Hollon, in press). Depressed subjects are also more likely to recall negative events when compared with nondepressives (Lloyd and Lishman, 1975).

Paranoia

We come now to one of the severest of the mental disorders, **paranoia.** The hallmarks of the disorder are delusional themes of *persecution,* a belief that one is being conspired against, spied upon, harassed by others, and thus prevented from achieving long-sought and significant goals; or of *grandiosity,* a belief that one is a religious messiah, the creator of a new world, the inventor of a grand scheme, the instrument for world betterment, has personal immortality, or is a Divine Being; or of both. Associated features are the deep-seated resentments of the individual toward others that can begin in suspiciousness and, in elaboration, be transformed into violence. The absence of schizophrenic symptoms (see page 434) or a manic-depressive syndrome (page 432) helps to delineate the paranoid disorder.

The causes of paranoia and paranoid conditions are not known, but psychological hypotheses that consider early social isolation, marked early frustrations, a sense of being different when a child, and a growing sensitivity to criticism by others to play a predisposing role have been advanced. The early development of great ambition and unattainable goals which bring frustration in adult life, by a person with a low threshold for anger and for suspecting the motives of others, are often added vulnerability factors. Hostile controlling parents who are rejecting and accuse the child of failing to meet their high standards and goals are additional components that have been cited as relevant factors.

In persons prone to paranoid thinking, the dominating personality characteristics include humorlessness, excessive achievement strivings which are not commensurate with one's talents, egotism, tendencies to be sarcastic, embittered, and resentful of others, inflexible thinking, and a mistrustful, impatient, intolerant, and tyrannical attitude toward others (Kolb, 1973). It is difficult to know when these expressions of personality malformation begin to blend into psychosis since an outgoing appearance of normality can cloak the insidious process that is underway. The individual at that point of transformation may nurse secret grievances, develops a growing sense of unease, begins to ruminate at the expense of reason, misinterprets the acts of others, and increasingly perceives an enhanced sense of threat against the self.

Inner fears are then projected against others. Perceiving them as persecutors serves to justify the individual's growing anxiety.

There are sequences or stages in the development of paranoia; the paranoid moves from early manifestations of the disorder through an acute state of inner turmoil to a final stage of what has been called *paranoid crystallization.* This last is the fully blown psychotic state in which the delusional beliefs now rule the individual's behavior. These beliefs may be a conviction that others are seeking to destroy the person, that he (more men than women develop paranoia) is at the mercy of others, and that attack is soon forthcoming from all sides. A period of "paranoid illumination" that follows is marked by the sudden revealing insight that a unified plot, a conspiracy, exists to destroy what the person has achieved (Swanson et al., 1970). With this focusing on the "enemy" and the "plot," the individual's energies are turned to combating the forces arrayed against him (see page 5).

Schizophrenia

Background Every year between 25,000 and 30,000 people enter public or private hospitals with a diagnosis of **schizophrenia.** Although the overall incidence rate for the population approximates one percent, the rate varies among different groups and in different environmental settings. The disorder takes a particularly heavy toll among the poor, nonwhites, and residents of great urban centers; among the nonmarried, separated, widowed, and divorced. Schizophrenia is a malignant disorder with a presence that extends outward to the most distant parts of the world and ranges backward in time to antiquity. Historical records indicate that the disorder was recognized in ancient India as early as 1400 B.C., and in Greece, Rome, and other civilizations of antiquity.

As far back as the seventeenth century, a British anatomist, Thomas Willis, recorded observations of a large number of persons who, initially talented and even brilliant in childhood, deteriorated while still young. Such observations explain why the disorder was first called **dementia praecox.** "Dementia" indicated the deterioration of intellectual abilities; "praecox" referred to the early or precocious appearance of this disorder in the young. The term became firmly established by the great systematizer, Emil Kraepelin (see page 443), when in 1899 in the fifth edition of his major text on psychiatry he brought together a variety of forms of disorder that had been described by others and gave them the status of a single entity, dementia praecox. But the presumed deterioration became an issue that plagued Kraepelin. His follow-up of cases gave evidence that in a considerable number of instances there was a more favorable outcome and a reversibility to the disorder. Furthermore the disorder did not always begin in youth; it also appeared in later life.

In 1911 a famous Swiss psychiatrist, Eugen Bleuler, published a classic volume, *Dementia Praecox or the Group of Schizophrenias,* which represented a significant break with the past. Bleuler introduced the term *schizophrenia* because he did not see the disorder as terminating in dementia, but rather as one characterized by a "splitting off" of various types of mental or cognitive functions. This lack of harmony in portions of the psyche was reflected in the deviant behavior of the schizophrenic. Thus the derivation of the word schizophrenia, which combines two Greek words, *schizein,* to split, and *phren,* mind. Unfortunately, it also gave rise to a common error made by lay persons, namely that a schizophrenic has a "split personality," creating visions of a "Dr. Jekyll—Mr. Hyde" pairing that are entirely false. The split is not one of good versus evil but rather the inappropriateness of a function such as emotion when linked to a thought. An example of this split is seen in a schizophrenic patient who describes a personal tragedy but without the signs of sorrow that one anticipates; in another instance a patient recounts the manner by which he murdered his mother without any emotional expressiveness at all.

Schizophrenic Behavior Bleuler subdivided symptoms of schizophrenia into two groups, the **fundamental** or primary symptoms and a set of **accessory** symptoms. The first he saw as central to the disorder; the second set, which can be very dramatic, are seen in nonschizophrenic patients as well. Of the primary group four stood out for Bleuler. These are the four A's: disturbances of **association**—the cognitive defect; **affect**—the emotional defect; **ambivalence**—the attitudinal defect; and **autism**—the withdrawal and isolation defect.

Association disturbances The schizophrenic is the psychotic who best merits the adjective "strange." There are many indications that thought processes are not normal; speech is rambling, incoherent, and disconnected; weird and unusual associations spill forth; new words, *neologisms,* are constructed to describe peculiar thoughts. The patient may be given to rhyme but without reason. In some instances the rhyme dictates the association, producing a "clang association" readily observable even to the untutored, such as this morning greeting of a patient to a physician who walked through the ward: "Hi guy, my sty is in your eye." The patient may show a tremendous increase in ideas, all of which seem to pour our without self-monitoring; or the opposite may occur in the form of "blocking" and an inability to produce any associations at all. These types of disturbances reveal the lack of a unifying purpose or goal behind the schizophrenic's thinking.

An excellent example of the bizarre nature of schizophrenic thought is provided by a male patient who had the delusion that he was God. Before hospitalization he had been going with a woman for many years but had never had sexual relations with her. Eventually, she turned to another man and became pregnant by him. When she informed the patient of this, the patient maintained that, since he was God, she must be the Virgin Mary and the pregnancy the Immaculate Conception (Rosen, Fox, and Gregory, 1972).

Some patients report their awareness that every thought seems to generate an association, some of which are related only by sound; others are markedly idiosyncratic and based solely on personal experience.

> I couldn't read (newspapers) because everything that I read had a large number of associations with it. I mean, I'd just read a headline, and the headline of this item of news would have . . . very much wider associations in my mind. It seemed to start off everything that I read, and everything that sort of caught my attention seemed to start off, bang-bang-bang, like that, with an enormous number of associations, moving off into things so that it became difficult for me to deal with, that I couldn't read (Laing, 1967, as cited in Freedman, 1974, p. 335).

The comments of former schizophrenic patients as described by Barbara Freedman (1974) provide other forms of disturbed thinking that have been experienced during psychosis: belief in extraordinary cognitive powers—flashes of brilliant insights, great power in generating original creative thoughts, a unifying system to provide greater coherence in thinking; "racing thoughts" which come so swiftly they cannot be sorted out; in others, "slowed thoughts" which creep at a snail's pace; an enveloping awareness in some patients that they can no longer control their thinking and that some external force must be responsible for such an extraordinary event.

On the perceptual side there may be similar distortions in experience: a sense of increased vividness of sensory experiences—lights that are dazzling, the emergence of figure against background with extraordinary clarity; muted awareness of others; the appearance of illusions; changes in depth perception and in the sound of one's own voice. These experiences are reflections of the sensory shifts brought on by an acute schizophrenic episode.

Disturbances of affect Affect refers to emotional responsiveness. Some schizophrenics show "flattened affect," others "inappropriate affect," often both simultaneously. The first of these refers to a shallowness or blunting of emotion, so that situations which normally would be expected to produce an emotional response elicit only apathy from the patient. The second refers to an emotional response that is inconsistent with a situation. Although the patient may speak of some great tragedy, it is without the expected display of sorrow. A female patient, the mother of three children, threw them from a bridge into a river below. Her explanation was that she wished to save them from having to live in a world of evil. In the hospital her manner was bland, her emotional reaction shallow; having saved her children, there was no need for grief. Since her tone was consistent neither with her situation nor her actions, we speak of her affect as inappropriate. The blandness of her response also indicates the blunting of her affect.

Ambivalence The ambivalent patient holds antithetical ideas, wishes, or attitudes toward the same object. For example, the patient may profess love for someone but simultaneously wonder how to kill that person. Or two disparate ideas may occur to the patient simultaneously; a voice may tell him to do this, but another voice admonishes him not to. One patient, asked to describe his mother, began by saying, "My mother is a g____," as if he were about to say "good woman." He stopped and then began again, "My mother is a b____," as if to say "bad woman." For several minutes he alternated the two sentences in the same partial fashion, unable to complete either one (Rosenbaum, 1970).

Autism The schizophrenic is often out of contact with the world; he is apt to be disoriented for time, place, and person, unable to tell what month or day it is or where or who he is. A patient's preoccupation with her own inner world may lead to strange behavior. A young schizophrenic girl who had mislaid her violin case insisted that she must have swallowed it, in spite of reassurances that it would not have been possible for her to do so.

Delusions Bleuler considered delusions or false beliefs to be an accessory symptom, since they occur in mental disorders other than schizophrenia. A German psychiatrist, Kurt Schneider, however, believed delusions to be central to the schizophrenic process and described a set of them. These so-called **first-rank symptoms** (FRS) or *Schneiderian signs* have been widely accepted by British psychiatry (Mellor, 1970). There are eleven such signs, three of which are specific forms of **auditory hallucinations.** The patient (1) hears his thoughts spoken aloud, or (2) hears voices arguing about or referring to him in the third person, or (3) hears voices describing his activities as they take place.

(4) The fourth sign is termed a *delusional percept* and occurs in two stages: a normal perception is given a private meaning by the patient; the perception is then almost immediately elaborated into a delusion. Mellor illustrates this sign with the case of a young man in a boarding house who, while breakfasting with fellow lodgers, had a developing sense of unease that something frightening was about to happen. One of his companions pushed a salt cellar to him and as it moved forward, the young man suddenly developed the conviction that he had to return home to greet the pope, who was going to visit his family to reward them.

The following seven signs reveal the schizophrenic's inability to separate self from environment. (5) *Somatic passivity:* The patient is the reluctant recipient of bodily sensations that are imposed from the outside. For example, a young teacher was convinced that X-rays were entering his neck and passing through his waist and pelvis to prevent his having an erection. (6) *Thought withdrawal:* A female patient had an awareness that her thoughts were being physically extracted from her mind. She complained of a "phrenological vacuum cleaner" that was sucking up all the thoughts she had about her mother. (7) *Thought insertion:* The patient believes that thoughts are put in his mind by some external agency. For example, a female patient, upon looking out onto her garden, had her thoughts interrupted by those of another person who used her mind as a screen onto which to flash these alien thoughts. (8) *Thought broadcast:* The patient believes that his own thoughts are being broadcast to others, usually through some medium such as television or via mental telepathy. For example, a young student believed his mind to be like a ticker tape which could be read by others who merely had to pass the tapes through their own minds to do so.

(9) *"Made" feelings,* (10) *"made" impulses,* and (11) *"made" voluntary acts:* The patient experiences feelings or impulses to act or engages in actions which are seemingly imposed by an external power. Usually a delusion is used to explain the mechanism behind these events. When the patient carries on normal activity, he or she may perceive the self as being a passive automaton commanded by another.

> A twenty-nine-year-old shorthand typist described her actions as follows: "When I reach my hand for the comb it is my hand and arm which move, and my fingers pick up the pen, but I don't control them . . . I sit here watching them move, and they are quite independent, what they do is nothing to do with me . . . I am just a puppet who is manipulated by cosmic strings. When the strings are pulled my body moves and I cannot prevent it" (Mellor, 1970, pp. 17–18).

These are all powerful delusions, but the question remains: How decisively characteristic are they of schizophrenia? Mellor's study conducted in Great Britain indicated that of 166 schizophrenic patients 119 showed one or more first-rank symptoms. Another study (Carpenter and Strauss, 1973), however, using American patients with diagnoses of schizophrenia ($N=103$), affective psychoses ($N=39$), and neuroses and character disorders ($N=23$), found the incidence of first-rank symptoms to be greatest in schizophrenics (51 percent), next most frequent in the affective psychoses (23 percent), and least frequent among the neuroses and character disorders (9 percent). Within the schizophrenic group the presence of such signs was predictive neither of recovery nor of chronicity in schizophrenia. In summary, these signs can be viewed as strong diagnostic indicators of schizophrenia, but they are not exclusively confined to that disorder since they appear with a fair degree of frequency in the affective psychoses as well.

Subtypes of Schizophrenia The subclassification of schizophrenia once occupied a prominent position in discussions of schizophrenia. This is less true today, but the student should have some knowledge of the subtypes of the disorder and some appreciation of the range of behavior reflected. The following classical subtypes are the most dramatic.

Disorganized (hebephrenic) subtype The disorganized subtype of schizophrenia has an early but gradual onset. It is characterized by inappropriate emotional reactions—hebephrenic "silliness"—which consists of giggling, inappropriate laughter, and unexplained weeping; and flat, incongruous, or silly emotional expression. These patients have lively hallucinations and often have delusions of grandeur, but these are usually very bizarre and fragmented. The patient often shows marked regression, soiling, and wetting. Withdrawal tends to accelerate and, when seen years later in the ward, the patient may have suffered profound disintegration of personality. With the advent of phenothiazine medication, however, the depth of such deterioration has been lessened.

Catatonic subtype The catatonic patient has periods in which he or she may be stuporous or highly excitable. There may be posturings in which the patient assumes a position and resists attempts to be moved from it. When in this state, the catatonic reacts only to the most painful of stimuli. This is not to suggest that the patient lacks awareness of what is going on. In some cases catatonic patients have shown a remarkable memory for events that took place when they were in this state. The motor disturbances may take the form of ritualistic motions, repetitive and stereotyped actions. At other times such expressions of the psychosis may be verbal, with simple phrases and words being repeated over and over. Under the impact of the drug therapies, catatonia too has begun to disappear from the psychiatric scene.

Paranoid subtype The most impressive symptom of paranoid schizophrenia is the delusional system. In many instances these delusions are of persecution, the patient believing that some person or group is out to get him. Voices may torment or force the patient to unusual actions. By comparison with other types of schizophrenics, the thought processes of the paranoid are far more adequate. The basis for the patient's thinking may be a little difficult to accept, but, if this is done, the rest of the argument can appear sensible. Their thinking contrasts so sharply with the illogicality and rambling incoherence of other schizophrenic subtypes that some psychiatrists question whether the paranoid subtype should be included among the schizophrenias.

The prepsychotic personality of the paranoid patient is often that of a person who resents and distrusts others and is excessively suspicious and hostile. Such persons have been called "litigious characters." They often feel that they are being wronged; they may seek court action against others on the slightest provocation, or they may demand justice and retribution in situations where others would not perceive injury at all. Onset is later in life than for the other subtypes.

Process schizophrenia versus schizophreniform (reactive) disorder As we have seen, schizophrenia does not necessarily imply deterioration since some patients recover from the disorder. Because of this psychopathologists began a search for the correlates of different outcomes. The results of these studies are so consistent that they have led to a typology aimed at distinguishing process from reactive schizophrenia.

In **process schizophrenia** development of the disorder is a long process. The slow, insidious onset usually begins in the late teens or the early twenties. When the life histories of such patients are reviewed, they show early signs of inadequacy in work, school, and in their sexual and social lives. The process of withdrawal follows, and the person grows apathetic and indifferent and finally must be hospitalized. Before the advent of drug therapy, prognosis for these patients was poor. Their average stay in the hospital was thirteen years. The use of drugs has changed all that, and many of these individuals can now be maintained in the community, often residing with the families or in halfway houses.

By contrast, the patient with **reactive schizophrenia,** called **schizophreniform** in DSM-III, reveals a good premorbid history. It is not unusual to find that the person has been a good student and even a class leader in high school. Such patients are usually married and have been able to raise and support a family. Their breakdown, when it takes place, comes later in life, often when they are in their thirties; occurs suddenly; and often follows evident stress. Most important of all, the response to treatment is good, the patient recovers and returns to family and community, and he or she may never be seen in the hospital or clinic again.

When these two types of patients are studied in the laboratory, the responses of the reactive patients are more similar to those of normal individuals than to those of their process counterparts. Furthermore, genetic studies suggest that hereditary influences are present in process cases, but less so, if at all, in the reactive ones. This has led recently to speculation whether they are forms of the same disorder or quite different disorders, an issue which remains unresolved at the present time. The data seem to tilt in the direction of viewing such reactive cases as different from schizophrenia, but having sufficient similarities to be thought of as a "schizophrenic spectrum disorder" (Kety et al., 1975).

SUMMARY □

The affective disorders, paranoia, and schizophrenia are three of the most serious mental disorders. Severe manifestations of manic or depressive behavior, or a combination of both, signal the affective disorders. Paranoia is revealed by well-formed delusional systems of grandeur, persecution, or both. Formal thought disorder is relatively absent until the contents of the delusional system are tapped or become apparent only in the later stage of the disorder when a paranoid crystallization has taken place.

Schizophrenia is comprised of a group of psychotic disorders evidenced by a general behavioral impairment, disorientation in time and space, and lack of insight. Its causality is complex. Symptoms according to Bleuler are of two types: fundamental symptoms, which are associative disturbances, affective disturbances, ambivalence, and autism—the four A's; and accessory symptoms, of which delusions and hallucinations are most important.

Depending on the symptoms that predominate, it is possible to identify several subtypes of schizophrenia: disorganized or hebephrenic subtype, marked by silliness, hallucinations, and bizarre delusions; catatonic subtype, posturing and ritualistic motions; paranoid subtype, delusional beliefs and systems. A different classification distinguishes two types of schizophrenia on the basis of several factors having to do with their onset, course, and outcome. Process schizophrenia is identified by a gradual onset, poor premorbid history, poor prognosis, and a probable hereditary component; a reactive schizophrenia, or schizophreniform disorder, is identified by a sudden onset, a good premorbid history, a good prognosis, and probably little if any hereditary component. Reactive schizophrenia may be one of a spectrum of related schizophrenic disorders.

TO BE SURE YOU UNDERSTAND THIS CHAPTER △

The major concepts presented in this chapter consist of the disorders and their symptoms.

Organic mental disorder
Schizophrenic disorder
Paranoid disorder
Affective disorder
Anxiety disorder
Neurosis
Somatoform disorder
Conversion disorder
Dissociative disorder
Personality disorder
Psychosexual disorder
Reactive disorder
Disorders of impulse control
Stress
Post-traumatic stress disorders
Disaster syndrome
Shock reaction
Recoil reaction
Stage of recall
Panic disorder
Generalized anxiety disorder
Obsessive-compulsive disorder
Obsession
Compulsion
Phobic disorder
Hysterical neurosis, conversion type
Psychogenic amnesia
Introverted personality disorder
Sociopathy
Psychopathy
Episodic affective disorder
Chronic affective disorder
Bipolar affective disorder
Manic disorder
Depressive disorder
Paranoia
Paranoid crystallization
Schizophrenia
Dementia praecox
Fundamental symptoms
Association disturbance
Disturbance of affect
Ambivalence
Autism
Accessory symptoms
Delusion
Auditory hallucination
First-rank symptoms
Delusional percept
Somatic passivity
Thought withdrawal
Thought insertion
Thought broadcast
Made feelings, impulses, and acts
Disorganized (hebephrenic) schizophrenia
Catatonic schizophrenia
Paranoid schizophrenia
Process schizophrenia
Reactive schizophrenia (schizophreniform)

TO GO BEYOND THIS CHAPTER △

In this book The two chapters that follow enlarge on the theme of disordered behavior. Chapter 18 describes how mental disorders are now being classified, in an effort to improve the reliability of psychiatric diagnosis; it also examines the critical problem of stigma faced by mental patients, even in this "enlightened" era. This chapter will prepare you for Chapter 19, which focuses on various forms of treatment and therapy now being used.

Other material that should help you place Chapter 17 in context is the case history of Jim Jones and its discussion in Chapter 1, illustrating how his mental disturbance precipitated the Jonestown tragedy. Chapter 14 is relevant for its emphasis on motivation, stress, and conflict, Chapter 16 because personality theory and assessment help us understand behavior disorder.

Elsewhere A number of comprehensive textbooks of abnormal psychology can be recommended. Gerald Davison and John Neale's *Abnormal Psychology* is noted both for its broad coverage and for its emphasis on the research literature of psychopathology. James Coleman's *Abnormal Psychology and Modern Life* is one of the most popular compendiums of abnormal behavior. The sixth edition is coauthored by two well-known clinical psychologists, James Butcher and Robert Carson. Barclay Martin has provided another skillfully written text, *Abnormal Psychology*. Peter Nathan and Sandra Harris's

Psychopathology and Society emphasizes the interaction of disordered behavior and the society in which it happens.

Your understanding of stress and its role in psychopathology will be enhanced by these books. Martin Seligman's *Helplessness* gives a theoretical view of possible learned origins of depression and joins animal experimentation to human behavior in speculation about these origins. Hans Selye's *The Stress of Life,* recently revised by this great figure in stress research, is a classic. Ogden Tanner's *Stress,* from Time-Life Books, is superbly informative and lavishly illustrated. In *Everything in Its Path* Kai Erikson perceptively analyzes the destructive effects of a disaster on a community and its citizens. *Madness and the Brain,* by Solomon Snyder, a noted pharmacological-biochemical researcher, is a simple but masterly discussion of schizophrenia and the biochemical factors that may play a central role in the disorder. Irving Gottesman and James Shields, in *Schizophrenia and Genetics,* give an in-depth account of what has come to be regarded as the finest investigation of schizophrenia in twins. In a paperback Joseph Becker covers *Affective Disorders* broadly and in an easily understood manner.

CH. 18

Understanding Psychopathology

When we speak of understanding psychopathology, we have three points in mind—three things we hope you gain from our discussion of these materials. The first is an acquaintance with the forms of deviant behavior. The second is knowledge of how the scientific investigation of psychopathology is carried out. The third is a balanced view of mental disorder as a social problem and fact of life. The previous chapter concentrated on the first of these forms of understanding and paid less attention to the other two, which are the subject matter of this chapter.

THE MENTAL HEALTH PROBLEM

Some Hard Facts

It has been estimated that one in ten persons in the nation—22,000,000 people—are now suffering from some form of mental or emotional disturbance ranging from mild to severe. The President's Commission on Mental Health (1978) indicated that there is new evidence that this figure may be closer to 15 percent of the population. That would boost the number of citizens needing some form of mental health service to 33,000,000. The report of the President's Commission goes on to add that "as many as 25 percent of the population are estimated to suffer from mild to moderate depression, anxiety and other indicators of emotional disorder at any given time." These people too need assistance. They seek it by turning to family, friends, or other persons, for example, ministers, who are outside the mental health system. Were the figure of 25 percent to be reasonably accurate, it would represent 55,000,000 Americans!

Alcoholism is a growing national problem with estimates of prevalence ranging up to 9,000,000 people while 200,000 new cases are added to the rolls annually. The annual cost of problems associated with alcoholism has been placed at approximately $42,000,000,000! In addition to this economic loss alcohol plays a major role in automobile and industrial accidents, crimes of violence, and suicide.

The data on psychoses are frightening. Approximately 2 million Americans, slightly below one percent of our population, are schizophrenic. The Commission report estimates that 4 million Americans will have a schizophrenic-like illness during their lifetime. The estimate for the affective disorders is that more than 10 to 14 million Americans will suffer from depression or mania at some point in their lives. Since these disorders peak in mid-life, generally at the height of a person's productivity, the effect on society is all the more powerful both economically and socially. Half a million children, many as young as two to three years of age, suffer from the most serious forms of mental disorder. It has been estimated that 10 percent of all school age children suffer emotional disorders that are sufficiently severe as to warrant immediate treatment (National Health Education Committee, 1971).

As many as 400,000 people are likely to attempt suicide this year. Among the young, between the ages fifteen and twenty-four, the suicide rate has climbed 67 percent in the past decade. Suicide is the third leading cause of death among college students. Accidents and cancer occupy first and second positions (Shneidman et al., 1970).

It is estimated that up to 16 million Americans suf-

SUICIDE: FACTS, FIGURES, AND FABLES

Before you finish reading this page, someone in the United States will attempt suicide. At least sixty Americans will have taken their own lives by this time tomorrow. More than 25,000 persons in the United States killed themselves last year, and nine times that many attempted to do so. Many of those who attempted will try again, a number with lethal success. And here is the irony: except for a very few, all the people who commit suicide want desperately to live.

- The number of men who kill themselves is three times higher than that of women; but women attempt suicide more frequently.
- The rate for whites is twice that of blacks.
- Suicide is the third leading cause of death among college students. (Accidents and cancer occupy first and second positions.)
- The rate for single persons is twice that of the married.
- Among adults, it is the elderly who most frequently commit suicide.
- The typical American suicide is a white Protestant male in his forties, married with two children, a breadwinner and taxpayer.

Fable	*Fact*
1 People who talk about suicide do not commit suicide.	Of ten persons who kill themselves, eight have voiced their intentions.

2	Suicides happen without warning.	Studies reveal that the suicidal people give many clues and warnings regarding their suicidal intentions.
3	Suicidal people are fully intent on dying.	Most suicidal people are undecided about living or dying, and they "gamble with death," leaving it to others to save them. They almost never commit suicide without letting others know how they feel.
4	Once suicidal, a person is suicidal forever.	Individuals who wish to kill themselves are suicidal only for a limited period of time.
5	Improvement following a suicidal crisis means that the suicidal risk is over.	Most suicides occur within about three months following the beginning of "improvement," when the individual has the energy to put his morbid thoughts and feelings into effect.
6	Suicide strikes more often among the rich—or, conversely, it occurs almost exclusively among the poor.	Suicide is very "democratic" and is represented proportionately among all levels of society.
7	Suicide is inherited "or runs in the family."	Suicide does not run in families. It is an individual pattern.
8	All suicidal individuals are "mentally ill," and suicide always is the act of a psychotic person.	Studies of hundreds of genuine suicide notes indicate that although the suicidal people are extremely unhappy, they are not necessarily "mentally ill."

After Shneidman, Farberow, and Litman, 1970.

fer from exaggerated fears or irrational phobias which limit and interfere with their functioning.

Among the aged, some 1.3 million or 5 percent of those over sixty-five live in institutions such as nursing homes or psychiatric installations. The nursing bill alone for this group of Americans came to $11 billion in 1976.

Exactly what does it mean to say that 22 million Americans are severely mentally disordered? Look at it this way. This group represents the entire present population of the thirteen largest cities of the United States. Can you conceive of all the people who inhabit New York City, Chicago, Los Angeles, Philadelphia, Houston, Detroit, Baltimore, Dallas, Washington, D.C., Boston, St. Louis, Denver, Kansas City—22.3 million people in all suffering from mental or emotional disturbance? Or cast a glance at the map of the United States in Figure 18.1. Were our mental health problem to be concentrated geographically, Figure 18.1 is what a map of the United States would look like. It is not difficult to see why the mental health problem of the nation is public health problem number one and why mental disorder can be considered public enemy number one.

This makes the development of a scientific understanding of psychopathology a matter of prime importance. A scientific account of psychopathology would address itself to the two broad questions mentioned in the introduction to the previous chapter.

What is the best way to describe and categorize disordered behavior? This is the question of **descriptive psychopathology.** What are the causes and origins of psychopathology? This is the question of **developmental psychopathology.** Two giants in the history of psychiatry sought to answer these questions.

One of these giants was Emil Kraepelin, a brilliant descriptive psychiatrist who contributed more to the development of a classification system for mental disorders than any other figure in medical history. Kraepelin believed that "personal investigation and continuous observation of the greatest possible number of different cases" would provide the foundation. Such investigations had to include a study of the language, perceptions, thoughts, and emotions of disturbed people. With such information on hand, first steps could be taken to identify patterns of behavior or syndromes characteristic of different types of patients and to evolve a taxonomy of the mental disorders. But description alone would leave unan-

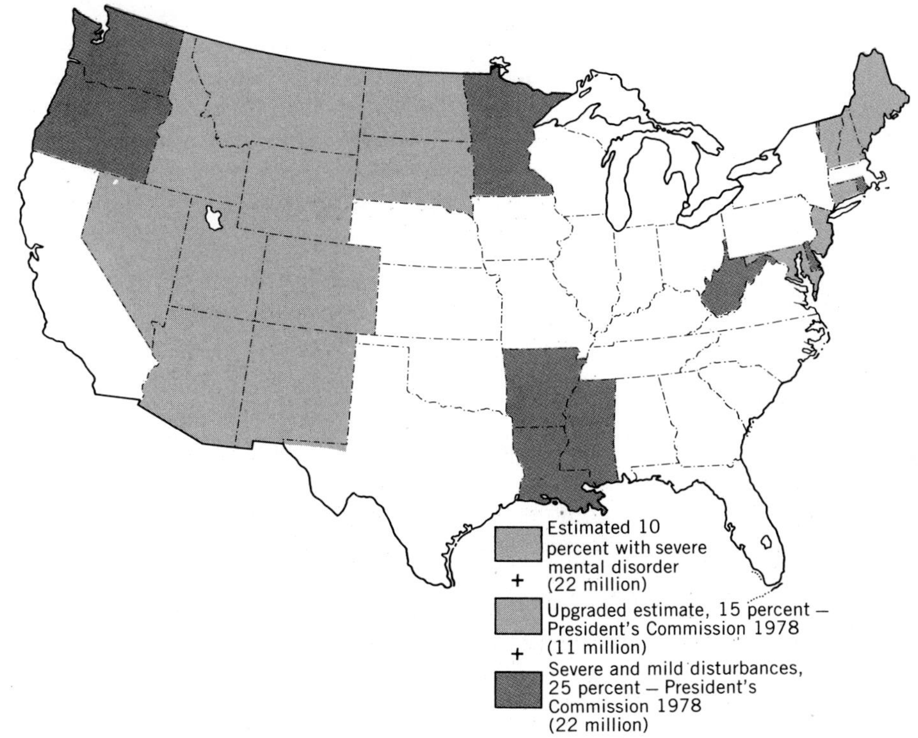

FIGURE 18.1
How a map of the United States might look if the mentally disturbed were concentrated geographically. If 10 percent of the population are mentally disturbed, the entire population of the areas in pink would be included. If the percentage is 15, the gray areas would be added. The purple portions add states to account for a total of 25 percent of our citizenry.

swered the question of how different types of mental disorder develop. A very different figure but one of equal brilliance, Sigmund Freud, struggled to answer this question. It is essential that we contrast these two historical figures and their orientations: Kraepelin, the descriptive psychopathologist; Freud, the developmental psychopathologist.

Kraepelin and Descriptive Psychopathology

In the year 1904 Emil Kraepelin stood at the summit of his profession, occupying the chair in psychiatry at the Medical School in Munich, Germany. His influence was worldwide, his compendium on *Psychiatry* the definitive work of its time. Kraepelin believed that the future of psychiatry rested on observation and careful description, the methods of the natural sciences. His actions had followed his faith. After graduation from medical school, Kraepelin had elected to study with Wilhelm Wundt, the world leader of experimental psychology, in order to learn the procedures of laboratory investigation.

Kraepelin as a master of descriptive psychopathology wrote a case book titled *Lectures on Clinical Psychiatry*. He wrote in the style he would have used were he addressing a medical school class. In the lecture that follows he describes a thirty-year-old woman, suffering from *hysteria* (page 423). We have chosen this disorder because it will allow you to compare Kraepelin's orientation to hysteria with that of Freud, whose views follow. (In DSM-III hysteria would be called a somatoform disorder.)

Here is Kraepelin's presentation of a young woman showing marked symptoms of the disorder.

> Gentlemen, the young lady, aged thirty, carefully dressed in black, who comes into the hall with short, shuffling steps, leaning on the nurse, and sinks into a chair as if exhausted, gives you the impression that she is ill. She is of slender build, her features are pale and rather painfully drawn, and her eyes are cast down. Her small, manicured fingers play nervously with a handkerchief. The patient answers the questions addressed to her in a low tired voice, without looking up, and we find that she is quite clear about time, place, and her surroundings.
>
> After a few minutes, her eyes suddenly become convulsively shut, her head sinks forward, and she seems to have fallen into a deep sleep. Her arms have grown quite limp, and fall down as if palsied when you try to lift them. She has ceased to answer, and if you try to raise her eyelids, her eyes suddenly rotate upwards.

Emil Kraepelin (1856–1926).

Needle pricks only produce a slight shudder. But sprinkling with cold water is followed by a deep sigh; the patient starts up, opens her eyes, looks around her with surprise, and gradually comes to herself. She says that she has just had one of her sleeping attacks, from which she has suffered for seven years. They come on quite irregularly, often many in one day, and last from a few minutes to half an hour.

Concerning the history of her life, the patient tells us that her parents died sixteen years ago, one soon after another. Her father's stepbrother attempted suicide, and her brother is most fantastically eccentric. I must add that two other members of her family give the impression of being very nervous. She did her work easily at school. She was educated in convent school, and passed the examination for teachers. As a young girl she inhaled a great deal of chloroform which she was able to get secretly, for toothache. . .

During her present residence here, so called "great attacks" have appeared in addition to her previous troubles. We will try to produce such an attack by pressure on the very sensitive left ovarian region. After one or two minutes of moderately strong pressure, during which the patient shows sharp pain, her expression alters. She throws herself to and fro with her eyes shut, and screams to us loudly, generally in French, not to touch her. "You must not do anything to me. . ." She cries for help, pushes with her hands, and twists herself as if she were trying to escape from a sexual assault. Whenever she is touched, the excitement increases. Her whole body is strongly bent backwards. Suddenly the picture changes, and the patient begs piteously not to be cursed, and laments and sobs aloud. This condition, too, is very soon put an end to by sprinkling with cold water. The patient shudders, wakes with a deep sigh, and looks fixedly round, only making a tired, senseless impression. She cannot explain what has happened (1904, pp. 252-254).

There are many things to be said about this description. (1) It is meticulously accurate in all details. (2) It illustrates Kraepelin's preference for experimentation and demonstration. Notice how Kraepelin produces an experiment-in-miniature to show how pressure near the genital region generates an attack, a sexualized sensitivity for which the patient will have no memory subsequently. (3) Kraepelin is relatively uncommunicative about the origins of this woman's strange behavior, since such speculations were alien to him. (4) He introduces the patient's family background, but only for the purpose of indicating the hereditary "tainting" he perceives there. Kraepelin believed that the roots of disorder were to be found in biology and in genetics. This hereditarian emphasis led Kraepelin to a fatalism about mental disorders, and virtually guaranteed his loss of influence later in the twentieth century, even as he pressed forward with his formulation and sharpening of the classification system. Looking back, a historian of psychiatry was to write of Kraepelin that "he seems to have been almost unaware that in his careful study he lost the individual" (Zilboorg, 1941).

Freud and Developmental Psychopathology

No one will ever be able to say of Freud that he lost sight of the individual. From the beginning of his career until the closing months of his life, when he began to succumb to cancer of the jaw and cheek, Freud was a practicing clinician who saw patients. His psychoanalytic writings, which were to fill twenty-four volumes, began with five case histories entitled *Studies in Hysteria,* written in collaboration with a Viennese physician, Josef Breuer (page 388).

Although these cases represented the birth of psychoanalysis, to say that their impact was negligible when first published in 1895 is to be charitable. The book was greeted with a stony silence in some medical quarters and with poisonous criticism from others. Why? Certainly not because of the symptoms that were described. Breuer and Freud's description did not differ markedly from Kraepelin's. Rather, it was because Freud set forth a developmental view that stressed the sexual origins of the symptom. Kraepelin could not have been unmindful of the sexual implications of his demonstration that the pressure of his hands on the patient's ovarian region generated a

Sigmund Freud (1856–1939).

response as if "she were trying to escape from a sexual assault." But he ignored their implications. Freud did not turn away from the possibility of sexual trauma as an etiological factor, as the following abridged account from one of the cases in *Studies in Hysteria* clearly reveals.

Here is Freud's account of hysteria in an unmarried eighteen-year-old woman. His approach to the case is as different from Kraepelin's as one can possibly imagine.

> The setting for Freud's observations was not a lecture hall but a mountainside in the Alps, where he had gone to "forget medicine and more particularly the neuroses." But even at 6000 feet Freud could not escape his destiny. As he sat and rested after an arduous hike up the mountain, he was approached by a young woman whom he recognized to be Katharina, the waitress who served him his meals at the inn where he was staying. Katharina, aware that Freud was a physician, solicited his help in alleviating her symptoms, for the medication she was taking provided no relief for her.
>
> Beginning two years previously, she had, on occasion, felt giddy and become breathless without reason. She would then become afraid that she would suffocate and felt a great hammering sensation in her head. Her chest ached as though it were being crushed, and she imagined a figure behind her who threatened to catch her.
>
> After hearing this brief case history, Freud inquired, "When you have an attack, do you think of something?" "Yes. I always see an awful face that looks at me in a dreadful way so that I'm frightened." "Do you recognize the face?" "No." "Do you know what your attacks come from?" "No." Freud then writes: "Was I to make an attempt at an analysis? I could not venture to transplant hypnosis to these altitudes, but perhaps I might succeed with a simple talk. I should have to try a lucky guess. I had found often enough that in girls anxiety was a consequence of the horror by which a virginal mind is overcome when it is faced for the first time with the world of sexuality."

Freud's inner debate is of interest for two reasons. The first is his uncertainty whether to attempt to find the origins of Katharina's physical symptoms; the second is the mention of hypnosis. Breuer had used this method successfully with several similar cases of hysteria. Very early in his career Freud too relied on hypnosis, but he would later discard it as he developed the psychoanalytic techniques of free association and dream interpretation. Having decided to go forward, Freud gives his supposition of a likely early trauma with a rapidity entirely uncharacteristic of later psychoanalysis.

> So I said: "If you don't know, I'll tell you how I think you got your attacks. At that time, two years ago, you must have seen or heard something that very much embarrassed you that you'd much rather not have seen."
>
> Freud's speculation produced an immediate response. Katharina recalled that two years previously she had observed through a window her uncle, the owner of the inn, and a cousin engaged in sexual intercourse.
>
> "I came away from the window at once," she told Freud, "and leaned up against the wall and couldn't get my breath—just what happens to me since. Everything went blank, my eyelids were forced together and there was a hammering and buzzing in my head."
>
> But the face retained its mystery; it remained unclear and unrecognizable to Katharina. And so Freud encouraged her to continue her narrative. Gradually Katharina revealed that this same uncle had on at least two occasions crept into her own bed while she slept and had made sexual advances to her which she had successfully repulsed. She was finally compelled to tell her aunt of her uncle's behavior; the uncle was turned out and a divorce was arranged. Now Katharina could provide the key to unlock the puzzle of the recurring hallucination of the face. Reliving her traumatic experiences, she told Freud the face had now become recognizable. It was her uncle's, who, whenever he saw her, became enraged and made threatening gestures. Some

day she feared he would catch her unawares and injure her.

Freud did not believe that he had effected a cure. His conclusion was appropriately modest; he hoped only that Katharina had "derived some benefit from our conversation" (pp. 125-133).

By contrast with Kraepelin's case history, Freud's is developmental, emphasizing quite different elements. (1) The stress is not on symptoms but on events that seemed to precede the onset of symptoms; (2) the orientation to these events is that they are of etiological significance; (3) their linkage to disorder is twofold: they are initially traumatic, which gives the person who experiences them a reason to repress or forget them; (4) Freud's basic goal is not descriptive but therapeutic—to undo the repression through recall. By the act of recalling the event in a supportive context, Katharina with Freud's help lifted the repression, and the symptom that presumably served as a substitutive response for it was relieved.

Just as Kraepelin searched for regularities in the physical symptoms, Freud looked for psychological regularities in the traumas preceding the hysterical attack and sought a theory that would include these regularities as elements of causation. Reviewing the five cases of hysteria described in the volume on hysteria, plus twelve others, Freud finally concluded that a repulsion against sexuality was always involved. Freud did not come easily to this conclusion. "I regarded the linking of hysteria with the topic of sexuality as an insult—just as the women patients themselves do." But the conclusion seemed inevitable, and Freud courageously set it forth and earned, as he had anticipated, the vilification of society.

It was the similarities in behavior, the symptoms, that led Kraepelin to group the cases and to identify them as hysterical. The puzzle remained, however. Why the lack of a physical basis for the bodily complaints? Freud searched for an alternative basis, a psychological one, which might explain the origins of these unusual physical ailments and found it in the patients' case histories as well as in their behavior. Seventeen of seventeen patients had recalled with great difficulty traumatic events marked with sexual overtones. Freud could only reason that the events and the patients' moral values were incompatible and that the memory of the events had to be driven from consciousness. The forgetting was only partial, however, and thus the conflict between event and values had induced the formation of hysterical symptoms. For Freud, then, the bodily symptom served to symbolize the distressing memory (Holzman, 1970). Thus the foundations for a descriptive and a developmental psychopathology had been put in place at the turn of the century by two great architects of psychiatric thought.

SUMMARY □

In the past and extending up to the present there have been two major approaches to the study of psychopathology. One is to investigate the different forms that mental disorders take. This is the study of the structure of mental disorder and it is a task carried on by descriptive psychopathologists. The second traces the origins of disorder and this task falls to the developmental psychopathologist. We have briefly reviewed the contributions of two of psychiatry's greatest figures—Kraepelin who led the effort to create a descriptive classification system covering all forms of disordered behavior, and Freud whose towering achievements were directed toward tracing the development of disordered behavior.

In Kraepelin's work we saw a greater concern for careful description than for the origins of disorder, a preference for experimental demonstrations, and a leaning toward biological and genetic interpretations of psychopathology. In Freud's work, by contrast, we saw an emphasis on origins, a search for the causes of disorder in experience, and a greater concern for psychological therapy than for classification.

DESCRIPTIVE PSYCHOPATHOLOGY: WHY DIAGNOSE AND CLASSIFY?

Why diagnose has been a basic question raised by some in the mental health movement. What difference does it make, opponents of classification have asked, whether you assign a label of a particular form of mental disorder to a person? Indeed, why label anyone at all? And what justification is there for classifying together individuals simply because they share certain behaviors or experiences in common?

Believers in classification counter by asserting that it is absolutely essential for any field, including psychopathology, that aspires to scientific status to develop some system for describing the phenomena with which that field is concerned. It is difficult to see how there could be any understanding, much less a scientific one, of phenomena that are not described and classified. A science, after all, must be about something! This strongly suggests that achieving a sound descriptive psychopathology is an essential precondition for working out a sound developmental account of different types of mental disorders.

Reliability of Psychiatric Diagnosis

Descriptions are useful only if they are reliable in the same sense that psychological tests must be reliable (page 235). In this case **reliability** means consistency of diagnosis, agreement among two or more clinicians on the diagnostic category to which a patient is

Silent Scream by Richard L. Saholt.

Richard L. Saholt, an artist residing in Minnesota—his works have been exhibited in the Twin Cities area—created this collage at a time when he was under psychiatric care, diagnosed as a chronic schizophrenic. His original efforts at collage were simple constructions using only words. With the support and encouragement of others, including Marshall MacLuhan, whom he visited in Canada, Mr. Saholt began to expand his materials, using photographs and clippings from journals, magazines, and newspapers.

Prominent in the collage are details from the works of the Norwegian artist Edvard Munch (1863–1944), some of whose paintings are reproduced on the next two pages. The central figures from *The Scream, Melancoly,* and *The Day After,* as well as the red-haired *Sin,* arrest the eye with their painterliness and their intensity. Better perhaps than anyone else in the history of art, Munch was able to portray the negative emotions—melancholy, fear, jealousy, despondency—as well as the circumstances of life that he took to be responsible for these reactions.

(continued on last page of insert)

The Scream by Edvard Munch, 1893. Nasjonalgalleriet, Oslo

Weeping Woman by Edvard Munch. Nasjonalgalleriet, Oslo. (Scala—Editorial Photocolor Archives).

Jealousy by Edvard Munch, 1895. Rasmus Meyers Samlinger, Bergen (Scala—Editorial Photocolor Archives).

Evening on Karl Johan Street by Edvard Munch, 1893–1894.
Rasmus Meyers Samlinger, Bergen
(Scala—Editorial Photocolor Archives).

Madonna by Edvard Munch, 1895–1902, Kommunes Kunstsamlinger, Oslo.

(continued)

The final picture in the series, the Halloween collage, is one of Mr. Saholt's later works. Here many of the items used to depict psychosis in the first collage take on a happier meaning. Mr. Saholt believes that collages such as this one, done in a lighter mood, both reflected and contributed to his improvement. He writes, "I began to produce happier scenes in my artwork, and these proved excellent therapy too! I realize that there is no cure for my illness at this stage of the game, but I am coping better today than I ever have before in my whole life. My thoughts and moods are not half as morbid and depressing as they once were."

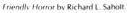

Friendly Horror by Richard L. Saholt.

TABLE 18.1
Percentage of Patients in Each Diagnostic Group Showing Specific Symptoms

Symptom	All Patients (*N*=793)	Schizophrenia (*N*=287)	Manic-Depression (*N*=75)	Neurotic (*N*=152)	Character Disorder (*N*=279)
Depressed	38	28	64	58	31
Suspicious	35	65	25	16	17
Hallucinations	19	35	11	4	12
Suicidal attempt	16	12	24	19	15
Suicidal ideas	15	8	29	23	15
Withdrawn	14	25	4	12	7
Perplexed	14	24	9	9	8
Assaultive	12	5	5	6	18
Threaten assault	10	7	4	11	14
Maniacal outburst	9	12	11	6	7
Bizarre ideas	9	20	11	1	2
Apathetic	8	11	8	8	4
Irresponsible behavior	7	7	3	7	9
Perversions	5	2	0	5	10
Mood swings	5	4	9	5	4
Rape	3	1	0	3	8
Obsessions	3	4	8	3	1
Depersonalization	3	6	4	1	0
Phobias	2	2	4	5	0

Adapted from Zigler and Phillips, 1961.

to be assigned. Unfortunately the evidence has been that the reliability of psychiatric diagnosis is unsatisfactorily low, even when it is done most carefully. In one particularly strong attempt to obtain reliability (Beck et al., 1962) there was agreement on only 54 percent of the diagnoses made. More commonly the reliability of psychiatric diagnosis is even lower than that. There seem to be several reasons for this unsatisfactory state of affairs. Perhaps the most important reason is that symptoms are not unique to given types of psychopathology.

As we saw in the last chapter, specific symptoms can appear in patients with more than one type of disorder. Looking at this point more systematically, Edward Zigler and Leslie Phillips examined the case records of 793 patients and assigned a diagnosis of manic-depressive, schizophrenic, neurotic, or character disorder—a broad term for a subset of the personality disorders, often involving antisocial behaviors—to each case and then tabulated the frequency with which specific symptoms appeared in each case record. A condensed version of their findings appears in Table 18.1.

Looking at the table carefully, you see that there is a considerable overlap of symptoms although certain symptoms do appear most frequently in particular disorders. For example, suspiciousness and perplexity are more marked for schizophrenia than for manic-depression, neurosis, or character disorder. One fifth of the schizophrenics show bizarre ideas, more than any other group, *but* four fifths apparently do not. The character disorder group, with its antisocial emphasis, has the highest percentage of cases showing assaultive behavior, 18 percent, but this percentage is still markedly a minority even within this specific category of cases. From the point of view of diagnostic reliability, this means that no single symptom can uniquely identify a diagnostic category. Obviously this means, in turn, that the clinician must rely on patterns of symptoms, on **syndromes.** This will not be entirely satisfactory either, however. For as the table shows, even the most dependable components of these patterns, such as suspiciousness in paranoid patients, are likely to be missing in about a third of the cases.

Some of the other sources of diagnostic unreliability are the following. (1) Symptoms change spontaneously over time and therapy may also change them. As a result reliability may fade or even vanish completely. (2) On the other hand, severe disorders are diagnosed more reliably than mild ones. Diagnoses made early in the development of a disorder are likely to be less reliable than later on. (3) Diagnoses connoses confined to broad categories are more reliable than highly specific diagnoses. (4) When reliability is based on separate examinations by different clinicians, patients may provide different information to the different examiners. (5) Different clinicians may put different interpretations on, or assign different importance to, the same information. (6) And most important, diagnostic manuals often lack the precision needed to make distinctions among categories. In the study of Aaron Beck and his colleagues (1962), mentioned earlier, this accounted for 62.5 percent of the disagreements.

Improving the Diagnosis of Psychopathology

There are two ways in which to improve the diagnosis of disordered states. The first is to sharpen methods of observing and recording the behavior of disturbed people. Psychologists have had to learn that lesson the hard way, by recognizing that if this was not done inevitably their assessment instruments would lack reliability. Second, there must be greater exactness in defining criteria for the various mental disorders. These two tasks are inextricably linked together. The happy note to be sounded is that psychiatry is now actively engaged in trying to repair these two shortcomings by modifying interview procedures with patients and by the construction of the new diagnostic manual (DSM-III) designed to spell out in great detail specific behavioral definitions for many of the more severe mental disorders.

The Mental Status Examination

The traditional assessment procedure in psychiatry has been the **mental status examination.** In the past this has been a relatively unstructured interview used to arrive at a diagnosis. The psychiatrist inquires, the patient responds in a session that covers a wide range of topics: physical health, personal habits, mood, degree of sociability, thinking disturbances, orientation to time, place, and person, memory and retention, judgment, emotional responsiveness, fears, and anxieties. Note is made of appearance, dress, speech patterns, motor activity, and the like. The word "note" describes the inevitable problem. Since the interview is unstructured, the quality and precision of the interview rests in the hands of the interviewer. Failure to make a proper inquiry, or to probe deeper when given an ambiguous response, and, above all, failure to record fully the contents of the interview can produce glaring omissions in the case record and make for inconsistent diagnostic judgments on the part of those who read the record. This unfortunate situation is now being changed as the greater yield that comes about through a more structured interview becomes apparent to practitioners and investigators.

The Present State Examination

The need to secure a world view of the status of schizophrenia, the most malignant of the mental disorders, has long been recognized by the World Health Organization (WHO). Twenty years ago the WHO sought the advice of an expert committee on the question of how to obtain this comprehensive picture. The committee urged the WHO to initiate studies aimed at refining the techniques of observation, classification, recording, and counting of the mental disorders. In 1973 one outcome of those recommendations was fulfilled with the appearance of a volume on the results of the *International Pilot Study of Schizophrenia* (WHO). This huge effort involved nine nations that varied in language, culture, degree of industrialization, and economic development: Denmark, India, Colombia, Nigeria, the United Kingdom, the U.S.S.R., Taiwan, Czechoslovakia, and the United States.

How was it possible to survey the incidence and prevalence of schizophrenia in what can only be viewed as a United Nations in microcosm? Only by creating a structured diagnostic interview schedule, the **Present State Examination** (PSE), under the direction of a group of psychiatric investigators (Wing et al., 1974), was this goal achieved. We have provided two examples of the type of inquiry specified in the PSE. Figure 18.2 illustrates how the interview begins and how the answers are to be coded. In Figure 18.3 we have illustrated a portion of the interview that focuses on the question of whether a person is in a depressed state. Each question is specifically set down. The interviewer is not expected to depart from the protocol as it appears in Figures 18.2 and 18.3. Initial data on the reliability of the Present State Examination, even under the stringent demands of cross-cultural study, indicate that the interview schedule can be administered satisfactorily in different psychiatric settings and in cultures varying considerably in economic and technological development.

The WHO findings indicate that within a given psychiatric center reliability is high; across centers it is reduced, yet remains high enough to be encouraging. Lowest levels of reliability are for observational items; those based on patient's report are higher. Psychiatric and life history data are more difficult to obtain cross-culturally, since data are gathered in different nations in different ways and the interpretation of terms used to gather such data appear to differ widely. These interview methods are undergoing revision, and with their improvement it is hoped that cross-cultural studies will begin to demonstrate the broad applicability of the classification schema. The presence of a computer program for making PSE diagnoses should also serve to heighten reliability, as will the systematic training of psychiatrists in the criteria for assigning diagnoses and recording the results.

Similar improvements in diagnostic reliability have also been obtained at a local level with the PSE (Duckworth et al., 1967). Using an earlier version of the PSE, two psychiatrists categorized 172 interviews with complete diagnostic agreement in 144 cases for 84 percent concurrence; partial agreement was achieved in another 7 percent. There was disagreement in only 9 percent of the cases. The errors appeared largely in the diagnostic category personality disorders, for which the PSE is not an effective diagnostic instrument.

FIGURE 18.2

The Present State Examination (PSE). This is the initial segment of the PSE used by the World Health Organization for cross-cultural diagnostic psychiatric interviewing. Every question must be checked off and rated. Observe how specific the directions for the interviewer are.

CODE

0	Sign or symptom not present.
1, 2	Sign or symptom present. The degree is indicated on the schedule.
?	Relevant questions have been asked, but examiner is not sure whether symptom is present or not.
NR	No response. Question has been asked but either the subject has failed to respond or the examiner can't rate the response, e.g. the answer was irrelevant.
NA	Question is not applicable and, therefore, will not be asked.
NI	Not inquired.

1. EXPLORATORY PART OF INTERVIEW

		No	Yes	Not known	
	Is patient, at time of interview, under the effects of biological treatment?				
1.01	(a) Drugs. If yes, Specify drug ______ and dosage ______	0	1	4	
1.02	(b) Electric shock treatment If yes, specify how long since last treatment ______	0	1	4	

Interviewer introduces himself, describes purpose of interview and explains any special equipment, e.g. tape or video recorders. Note what was said to patient:

1.03	**Rate whether patient disrupts introduction**	0	1	2	NA

Scoring: 0 Does not disrupt introduction
1 Interrupts, but allows introduction to be continued
2 Disrupts introduction and it cannot be continued
NA No introduction by interviewer

If patient immediately after introduction of psychiatrist spontaneously describes symptoms so that psychiatrist can proceed to rate relevant section, ring NI in items 1.06 - 1.17

EXPLORATORY QUESTIONING

To begin with, I would like you to tell me about the main difficulties (problems, troubles) you have been having in the past month.

If patient does not answer, repeat the question.

Allow patient to talk spontaneously if he is able and to continue from two to five minutes without interruption.

Record verbatim the first few spontaneous sentences and make notes of contents of patient's response.

• • •

A New Diagnostic Manual for Mental Disorders

The basis for diagnosis of mental disorders in the United States is contained in the *Diagnostic and Statistical Manual of Mental Disorders* (DSM) of the American Psychiatric Association. If there is to be an improvement in the precision of psychiatric diagnosis, it will have to come by way of a more adequate description of criteria for such disorders in this manual. Unfortunately, DSM-I, which was published in 1952, and DSM-II, which followed in 1968, failed to accomplish that task. Early in 1978 a pilot form of a new manual, DSM-III, appeared for the purpose of testing its efficiency in field trials all over the country.

Like so many things in contemporary society, DSM-III is inflationary. When DSM-I appeared it contained a listing and descriptions of 60 disorders. By 1968 DSM-II covered 145 disorders. The newest manual approximates 220 disorders (McReynolds, in press) and 11 other conditions such as *child abuse, marital problem, parent-child problem, occupational problem* "not attributable to a mental disorder."

FIGURE 18.3
The Present State Examination focusing on a person's depressive mood. Read items carefully.

7. SECTION ON DEPRESSIVE MOOD

7.01 Have you been very miserable, low-spirited or depressed during the past month? — 0 1 2 ? NR — —

Scoring: 0 No
1 Mild or moderate
2 Severe

7.02 Have you cried at all? How often? — 0 1 2 ? NR

Scoring: Items 7.2 to 7.5
0 Not at all; very seldom
1 A few times
2 Frequently

7.03 Have you felt like crying or wanted to cry, without actually weeping? (How often?) — 0 1 2 ? NR — —

7.04 Do you find yourself brooding over gloomy topics, unpleasant thoughts like disease and death, which happen to other people? — 0 1 2 ? NR — —

7.05 Do you find yourself brooding over the thought of death or illness, which might happen to you? — 0 1 2 ? NR — —

7.06 How do you see the future? — 0 1 2 ? NR — —

Scoring: 0 No particular concern
1 Future seems bleak or dark
2 Can see no future at all, or future seems completely unbearable

7.07 Have you ever felt that life isn't worth living? — 0 1 2 ? NR — —

Scoring: 0 Never
1 Occasionally
2 Frequently

7.08 Did you try to give yourself an injury in the past month (apart from suicidal thoughts)? — 0 1 2 ? NR — —

Scoring: 0 No thoughts about self-mutilation
1 Thought about it
2 Bodily harm to himself

Cut-off. If no evidence that items 7.09 - 7.12 are relevant proceed to Section 8

Cut-off to Section on depressive mood

7.09 Do you stay depressed most of the time or does your mood vary? — 0 1 2 ? NR NA NI

Scoring: 0 No depression
1 Variable depression
2 Unvarying depression

7.10 What does this depression feel like?
Rate presence of depression of a special quality e.g. "like heavy black cloud over my head" — 0 1 2 ? NR NA NI

Scoring: 0 No
1 Sometimes
2 Always

7.11 Did you ever think of ending your life at all? How often? During past month? — 0 1 2 ? NR NA NI

Scoring: 0 No suicidal thoughts
1 Fleeting thoughts only
2 Has deliberately considered methods

7.12 Have you tried to commit suicide in the last month? — 0 1 2 ? NR NA NI

Scoring: 0 No
1 Yes, one or more demonstrative suicidal attempts
2 Yes, one or more serious attempts intended to result in death

Unfortunately, this expanded version includes in the current draft listings of "mental disorders" for children which cover such vague conditions as *"avoidant disorder of childhood,"* initially called *"shyness disorder," "identity disorder"*—summarized in the question, "Who am I?"—and even the category of *"specific arithmetical disorder."* These and similar types of behavior are far removed from the concept of a mental disorder. This overinclusiveness has been sharply attacked by many researchers and clinicians (Garmezy, 1980; Harris, 1979; Schacht and Nathan, 1977; Zubin, 1978).

In spite of these negative features, DSM-III has taken a giant step forward in describing the well-established severe psychiatric disorders. The single paragraph associated with a global description of schizophrenia in the 1968 version of the manual has now been expanded to eleven pages of excellent descriptive content.

In a similar fashion, the affective disorders, which took up two pages of description in DSM-II, now occupy twenty pages in DSM-III. Size itself, of course, is not a criterion of excellence, but a reading of the description of these two historically significant categories of traditional psychiatric disorders suggests that careful, scholarly attention has been paid to the recent findings of researchers in psychopathology.

If it is demanded of a classification system that it spell out not only symptom description but etiology, course, and treatment of disorders, DSM-III falls far short of the mark. But here there is a reality to consider. In some instances *how* the disturbances arose, such as for the organic mental disorders, is known. For most other disorders etiology is not yet known, forcing designers of DSM-III to focus on a description of psychopathological symptoms.

Over the next few years there will be many critical studies forthcoming, and gradually the strengths and the weaknesses of DSM-III will unfold. A distinguished researcher, Joseph Zubin, has pointed to one apparent weakness, namely the assumption that mental disorders are medical disorders. It is apparent that many of the developmental problems exhibited by children are not. Nevertheless, the creators of DSM-III have included reading, arithmetic, and articulation (that is, speech) disabilities of children among the "mental disorders." If this classification is retained in the final version of DSM-III, millions of children could be mislabeled with the pejorative term "mental disorder."

In DSM-II all mental disorders in the United States could be reduced to ten major categories. In DSM-III the categories now number seventeen, with an additional classification for the conditions not attributable to mental disorder. In the previous chapter we have already presented a good many of these categories and case studies that flesh out the description of some of them. You should recognize, however, that DSM-III is not the final word on diagnostic classification. There will be a DSM-IV, a DSM-V, and as many as are needed to solve the problem of the unreliability of psychiatric diagnosis.

SUMMARY □

A sound descriptive psychopathology will be necessary for the development of a scientific understanding of psychopathology. This raises the question of the accuracy of current description, the question of the reliability of psychiatric diagnosis. The evidence is that this reliability is uncomfortably low, for reasons having most importantly to do with precision of the information obtained in the typical, unstructured interviews. Diagnoses are based on this information. New developments are beginning to correct the diagnostic situation.

It has been recognized that to improve the diagnosis of mental disorder requires greater attention to the observation and recording of the behaviors of disturbed people, as well as more exact specification of behavioral criteria to identify specific forms of disorder. The increasing use of structured interviews for determining the mental status of individuals who come to psychiatric attention, together with a new classification manual, DSM-III, are the major current efforts to overcome the unreliability of psychiatric diagnosis. DSM-III does provide improved descriptions of the more severe and traditional psychiatric disorders, such as schizophrenia and the affective disorders; however, a marked weakness is the inclusion as mental disorders many behaviors of children that would more aptly be classified as developmental disabilities or behavioral deficits.

MODELS OF PSYCHOPATHOLOGY

As the term is applied in the field of psychopathology, "model" means the general orientation taken toward the field. The particular model one adopts implies a commitment to certain forms of interpretation and treatment. As we shall see, important consequences depend on the choice of models.

The Medical Model: Pro and Con

The central assumption of the **medical model** is that mental disorder is a *disease,* that people suffering from it are *sick* and thus can legitimately be called *patients,* that the manifestations of their disorder are *symptoms,* which can be evaluated to make a *diag-*

Thomas Szasz, who believes that his own profession of psychiatry has played much too weighty a role in the courtrooms of the nation's various jurisdictions.

nosis, which should in turn bear some relation to *treatment.* These terms are borrowed from the model of physical illness, and the great debate of recent years has centered on the question of whether that model is applicable to deviant behavior. Opponents of the model argue not only that the so-called mental illnesses are not medical diseases but that medical terminology is wrongfully used to cloak "conflict as illness" and to justify coercion of the mentally disturbed under the guise of treatment and under the sanction of law.

Thomas Szasz, a psychiatrist whose antiestablishment views have been expressed in books that bear such provocative titles as *The Myth of Mental Illness, The Myth of Psychotherapy, The Manufacture of Madness, Ceremonial Chemistry, Law, Liberty and Psychiatry,* and *Psychiatric Slavery,* has argued that if a mental disorder is truly a disease, it deserves to be treated like any other illness. He would have mental hygiene laws repealed, court hearings on whether to incarcerate the deviant abolished, and hospitalization of patients against their wills disallowed. "There are no special laws for patients with peptic ulcers or pneumonia," states Szasz (1972). "Why then should there be special laws for patients with depression or schizophrenia?" And with that observation the reasons for the intensity of the debate over the medical model becomes clearer. The issue is not merely a scientific one. It is also a social and political one because it has to do with the civil liberties of patients.

Adding to the controversy over the medical model in recent years has been the argument about who is qualified to treat deviant behavior. Support of a medical model and the concept of illness or disease would seem to suggest that only those with a medical degree should be therapists for the emotionally disturbed. The counter view comes from those who believe that psychotherapy is psychological treatment and must be differentiated from the administration of drugs or the use of shock therapy. Therefore to restrict psychotherapeutic activity to medical doctors is wholly inappropriate. Only in recent years has this view won out; licensing laws in all fifty states affirm the right of psychologists to do therapy. What countless clients of clinical psychologists have subscribed to for years has now been established by law.

An Alternative to the Medical Model

Whereas the medical model treats mental disorder in the same terms as it does physical illness, other approaches take a contrary point of view. We can point to one position which is almost the opposite view. This is the so-called **labeling theory.** Those who espouse this position believe that disordered behavior arises out of the act of assignment of a label of a mental disorder to an individual. Call a person a schizophrenic and that individual will behave the way a schizophrenic is expected to behave. In many respects labeling theory is just as untenable as the medical model in its simplicity, overinclusiveness in explaining all mental disturbance, and failure to recognize certain facts about etiology. Were the act of labeling as powerful as its adherents claim, the consequence of the ever-present name calling, accusation, and innuendo that exist in these litigious times would so raise the incidence of mental disorders that all the nation's wilderness preserves would have to be converted to mental institutions. Fortunately most people are resilient to many of the slings and arrows of outrageous individuals. The contrasting views of supporters and opponents of labeling theory have been examined by Thomas Scheff (1974) and Walter Gove (1975) respectively.

There is an amusing, true story told by one of our colleagues, Paul Meehl, a wise theoretician and a sophisticated clinician in the field of schizophrenia. Meehl had been invited to a department of sociology where he was to present a colloquium on a mathematical model he had generated to enhance our understanding of the genetics of schizophrenia. He was interrupted in his talk by a faculty member who informed him that he thought people behaved in a schizophrenic manner primarily because others had so labeled them. Ignoring some of Meehl's richer language, we quote part of his later comment to us.

> I just stood there and didn't quite know what to say. I was thinking of a patient I had seen on a ward who kept his finger up his ass to "keep his thoughts from running out," while with the other hand he tried to tear out his hair because it really "belonged to his father." And here was this man telling me that he was doing these things because someone had called him a schizophrenic. What could I say to him?

Perhaps what one could say is that labeling theory is questioned for a number of reasons (Gove, 1975). For one thing, family members are more likely to search for justifications of deviant behavior than to label it as mental disorder. Rather than thrusting people into mental hospitals for bizarre behavior, those close to the disordered person tend to deny mental illness until the situation has become completely untenable. Furthermore, institutionalization is now typically so brief that it appears unlikely that hospitalization can account for the profound deviance that more severely disordered patients exhibit. Although we are not prepared to discard the labeling view entirely, we do believe that a reappraisal is definitely in order. That reappraisal would take the form of rejecting it as a factor in the etiology of the severe mental disorders, but perceiving the important role played by labels in maintaining, through stigmatization, the subsequent incapacity of many people who have suffered breakdowns. This is a very important point to which we return at the end of this chapter.

Models for the Times

Models tend to be consistent with the beliefs of the times. In the medieval period when primitive beliefs dominated religion, madness was attributed to demonological possession; astrology brought in its wake the view that the position of the stars affected the "humors," the fluids determining temperament in ancient physiology. When nineteenth-century physiology was influenced by a physics that emphasized concepts such as mass, charges, and the conservation of energy, Freud developed a model of psychopathology based on the science of his time. His early emphasis was on the energy of drives which ebbed and flowed in the human system. Dam up this energy by repression and it will emerge in the symbolic form of a symptom. Bacteriology and the germ theory of disease generated a search for discrete biological conditions responsible for mental disorder, a search which met with utter failure.

In recent times a wide array of models has been proposed. Six broad categories have been identified: three emphasize external factors outside the organism; three others stress factors within the organism (Zubin, 1972). These alternative models are presented in Table 18.2.

SUMMARY □

What is the most appropriate model for attempting to understand mental disorder? The answer to the question is that there is at this point no one correct model. A model is basically an analogy believed by the model's advocates to be a likely structure that may help to explain the phenomenon of mental disorder. Those who espouse a medical model see in mental disorders similarities to the concept of disease. A labeling modelist maintains that derogations of people as being mentally disturbed are self-fulfilling prophecies. Others who see environmental causation at work favor ecological models; the genetically minded opt for hereditary models.

The important point to bear in mind is that the virtues of one model over those of another constitute a competitive enterprise, in which survival depends on the adequacy of the hypotheses that the models generate and the extent to which such hypotheses, when tested, are supported by facts.

DEVELOPMENTAL PSYCHOPATHOLOGY: RECENT TRENDS

The turn to these new models of psychopathology grew out of problems with the traditional methods of study. The genius of Freud lay in part in his insight that mental disorder today is the result of problems the individual has had in the past. For this reason an important part of Freudian psychoanalytic therapy was the effort to uncover these past causes so that, when the patient remembers them, their effects can be handled in the present. But the procedure raises an extremely difficult question. How can anyone (patient or therapist) be sure that the information thus obtained is accurate? As the evidence has accumulated, it has become clearer and clearer that one cannot be sure. The "facts" that a patient dredges up in therapy are, of course, partly facts, but they are also incomplete because of true forgetting, and they are distorted if the patient has created defenses against unacceptable wishes and fantasies.

Perhaps the finest study of the errors in retrospection is one performed with normal children and normal parents. Were the study to be repeated with psychopathological children and disturbed parents, we suspect that the findings would be even more striking. In the study of normal families (Yarrow et al., 1970), researchers had available written detailed in-

TABLE 18.2
Current Models of Psychopathology

Causation Is Internal	
1. Hereditary	Mental disorders are produced by the interaction of genetic and environmental factors. Fundamental to the disorder is a genetic component, but its eventual expression depends on whether an environment is depriving or supportive.
2. Internal environment	The sources of mental disorder are found in the physiology of the body, primarily in its metabolism and biochemical substances.
3. Neurophysiological	Mental disorder is related to deviant brain functioning.
Causation Is External	
4. Ecological	Mental disorders are caused by noxious elements in the environment—poverty, deprivation, discrimination, population density, social disorganization, and social isolation.
5. Developmental	Mental disorders have their origins in unfortunate events that happen during important transitions in the life cycle and prevent the individual from developing attributes necessary for adaptation at a later stage. For example, complications during the mother's pregnancy, birth defects, and severe emotional deprivation in infancy may heighten the risk of later disorder.
6. Learning and conditioning	Deviant behavior is learned, just as normal behavior is. The symptom is the disorder; it is unnecessary to suggest underlying processes to account for the behavior.

After Zubin, 1972.

formation on children who had attended a nursery school where the staff kept meticulous records. The retrospective interviews with the children's mothers were collected three to thirty years after the children had left the school. Comparing mothers' recollections against actual early observational data, the investigators found systematic biases such as these operating. (1) The longer the time interval between retrospective recall and early events, the more positive the past was remembered. (2) The present adjustment of the offspring colored the mothers' recall of the past. Shy offspring were recalled as shy children, outgoing offspring as extroverted in the nursery school. The actual early observations often contradicted the mothers' recall. (3) Mothers' reports conformed to the child-care values that were in vogue at the time of recall of the past. (Never underestimate the power of Spock!)

Longitudinal Study of Children at Risk

Evidence such as this gives the psychopathologist pause. Previous investigations of the origins of deviant behavior that leaned almost exclusively on reconstruction of past events by adult patients and their parents are now seen as a method fraught with error. As a result a major movement is now underway to conduct **longitudinal studies** of children who are believed to be the most likely candidates for psychopathology in adulthood. Such children are described as being **at risk,** and the methods of investigation of these children have come to be identified as the methods of *risk research.*

The question that will occur to you immediately is one that risk researchers quickly came to recognize as their first major research obstacle. Who are the children at risk? A child "at risk" in any community is one who has a higher probability of showing deviant behavior sometime later in life than a randomly chosen child from the same community. As an example of a longitudinal study of children at risk, we can draw upon a British project that followed a sample of forty-one normal London schoolboys from ages eight to eighteen. One fifth of the boys became officially "convicted" delinquents. The study answers the question posed by the title of the volume, *Who Becomes Delinquent?* (West and Farrington, 1973), compared to the nondelinquent members of the sample. Here in a capsule paragraph are some of the risk factors for delinquency. The results parallel American studies.

> Our research has shown that, at least by the age of eight, and probably even before they begin to go to school, some boys are . . . socially and intellectually backward, the product of poor homes with too many children, and reared by parents whose standards of care, supervision and training are woefully inadequate. Perceived by teachers as difficult, resistive children, they fit uncomfortably into the scholastic system. Their parents have little or no contact with the schools and display minimal concern about their children's scholastic progress or leisure pursuits. Aggressive and impulsive in temperament, these boys resist the constraints of school, learn poorly, attend badly and leave early. Unattracted by organized activities or by training schemes, they spend their time on the streets and gravitate to unskilled, dead-end jobs for the sake of the higher wages offered.
>
> . . .Most of those who start off as problem cases in primary schools remain problem cases right through until they leave school and run into difficulties with employers (p. 202).

In addition to providing an example of longitudinal research, this passage shows that no single-factor model is likely to carry us far in our understanding of psychopathology. This study calls our attention to ecological factors, such as poverty, to familial disorganization, and to social learning based on the role model provided by parents. Citation of possible temperamental characteristics like aggressiveness and impulsivity suggests an impact of constitutional factors and probably heredity. In order to show how many different factors bear on the development of mental disorder, we turn now to a more extensive discussion of the origins of schizophrenia.

Origins of Schizophrenia

As the most serious of the psychopathological disorders, schizophrenia has also been the most studied. Various lines of investigation converge on the conclusion that many different factors contribute to the condition. In order to understand schizophrenia we will also have to understand what these variables are and how they interact. Here we shall consider several genetic, psychological, sociocultural, and biochemical determinants of schizophrenia.

Genetic Factors Paul Meehl is a distinguished contributor to the study of the genetics of schizophrenia. In his presidential address to the American Psychological Association during the early sixties, he made the following statement.

Paul E. Meehl.

> Let me begin by putting a question which I find is almost never answered correctly by our clinical students on Ph. D. orals, and the answer which they seem to dislike when it is offered. Suppose that you were required to write down a procedure for selecting an individual from the population who would be diagnosed as schizophrenic by a psychiatric staff; you have to wager $1,000 on being right; you may not include in your selection procedure any behavioral fact, such as a symptom or trait, manifested by the individual. What would you write down? So far as I have been able to ascertain, there is only one thing you could write down that would give you a better than even chance of winning such a bet—namely, "Find an individual X who has a schizophrenic identical twin" (1962, p. 827).

Now that we are in the eighties with twenty additional years of genetics research in schizophrenia behind us, it would be a sad clinical psychology student indeed who would be unable to answer Meehl's question. For in that span of two decades, a series of classic studies of the genetics of schizophrenia have been published that clearly indicate the role heredity plays in the etiology of the disorder. Let us take the case of the family which has a schizophrenic offspring. What is the best estimate we can make that a sibling of that offspring will in turn become schizophrenic? If *neither* parent is schizophrenic, the estimate is 9 to 10 percent. If one *parent* is schizophrenic, it is approximately 17 percent. If *both* parents are schizophrenic, the estimate ranges between 36 and 46 percent. But, you may argue, with two parents so severely disturbed, family life would be so chaotic that an equally strong case for etiology could be made in favor of detrimental environmental influences. This is a good point and more powerful data are needed to deal with it. Some of these data have come from studies of twins.

Twin study In one twin study fifty-seven schizophrenic index cases were drawn from a special twin register of people admitted consecutively over a sixteen-year span to one of the largest and most famous of England's psychiatric hospitals. Of this group twenty-four pairs were identical twins and thirty-three pairs were fraternal sets. Psychiatric diagnosis was checked by a distinguished assemblage of psychiatrists and psychologists. On this basis the investigators have reported an identical-twins concordance rate of 40 percent, compared to 10 percent for the fraternal pairs. The fact that concordance in the identical pairs fell far short of 100 percent is one of the best indicators we have that, although genes may be necessary, they are not apparently sufficient for the later development of schizophrenia. Environmental factors are also important in the etiology of the disorder. Unfortunately on the basis of their available data, the investigators have been unable to fix on any specific environmental factors that may have figured in the life history of the sick member of the discordant pairs of twins and not in that of the well member (Gottesman and Shields, 1972).

Children separated from schizophrenic parents at an early age Another method for studying the relative contributions of genetics and environment to schizophrenia is revealed by this question: Do children born to a schizophrenic parent but separated from their biological parents at an early age tend nevertheless to develop the disorder? This is the question asked in an extraordinary study by Leonard Heston (1966), who learned that a particular foundling home in Oregon had been used as a repository between the years 1915 to 1945 for infants who had been born to schizophrenic mothers confined in a neighboring state hospital. It had been hospital policy at that time to remove the baby from the hospitalized mother within three days and to place it either with members of the father's family or in the foundling home. Later the infants were placed for adoption or settled in foster homes. Heston decided to compare these children with a matched control group made up of children who had also been placed in the same foundling home, but whose mothers had not had an earlier history of institutionalization for a mental disorder. The search for those grown offspring took Heston into fourteen states and Canada. Whenever he located one of the individuals in either group, Heston sought permission to interview the person and to administer both an intelligence and a personality test (MMPI).

The results of the study (Table 18.3) indicate how much more disturbed were the adjustments made in adulthood by the children whose biological mothers had been schizophrenic. Five of the children had already become schizophrenic, many had been arrested for committing thefts and assaults, and for others life had been a marginal existence—they held low-level jobs or had only seasonal employment, lived alone, and remained unmarried.

Adoption studies Hereditary influence when based on studies of the presence of disorder in the relatives of schizophrenics must be tempered by the inability to separate out the possible influence of environmental variables. It was this uncertainty factor that led a group of American and Danish investigators to study the prevalence of schizophrenia in the biological and adoptive relatives of adopted children who later became schizophrenic (Kety et al., 1968, 1978). The reasoning behind the research design is straightforward. Adopted children secure their genetic endowment from the biological parents, their environmental influences from the adoptive parents. The younger the child at the time of adoption, the more striking will be the differentiation. By examining the siblings and half-siblings of thirty-three index cases, adoptees who later became schizophrenic; and a closely matched age group of thirty-four control cases, adoptees who were never admitted to a psychiatric facility, the investigators were able to evaluate the relative weightings of hereditary versus environmental influence (Kety et al., 1975).

This study revealed that 21 percent of the biological relatives of the schizophrenic adoptees fell into a "schizophrenia spectrum" having such disorders as "acute schizophrenia," "uncertain schizophrenia," "inadequate personality," and "schizoid personality." Only 11 percent of the biological relatives of the controls fell into the schizophrenia spectrum. For the *adoptive* relatives the comparable figures were 5 and 8 percent respectively. Examining all these studies of genetic influence, we conclude two things: the case for the role of heredity in schizophrenia has been effectively demonstrated; and the role of environmental influences has also been demonstrated, particularly given the failure to secure 100 percent concordance rates in identical twins. Unfortunately, investigators

TABLE 18.3
Adult Statuses of Children Born to Schizophrenic and Nonschizophrenic Mothers and Removed from Their Care at Birth

	Offspring of	
Adult Outcomes	**Normal Mothers**	**Schizophrenic Mothers**
Number (*N*)*	50	47
Males	33	30
Mean age	36.3	35.8
Schizophrenia	0	5
Mental deficiency (IQ $<$ 70)	0	4
Sociopathic personality	2	9
Neurotic personality disorder	7	13
More than one year in a penal or psychiatric institution	2	11
Felons	2	7
Service in armed forces	17	21
Discharged on psychiatric or behavioral grounds	1	8
Mean IQ	103.7	94
Years in school	12.4	11.6
Total number of children	84	71
Total number of divorces	7	6
Never married; $>$30 years of age	4	9

* Totals greater than *N* are possible because more than one outcome may have applied to the individuals studied.
Adapted from Heston, 1966; Heston and Denney, 1968.

have not been successful in delineating clearly the environmental factors which in interaction with genes can foster or inhibit the behavioral expression of schizophrenia. As for the genetic side, we believe now that genes are implicated in schizophrenia, but the mode of transmission remains unknown.

Psychological Factors Proposed psychological explanations of schizophrenia have taken several forms, most of which have quickly shown themselves to be too narrow and restrictive to account for the complexities of schizophrenic behavior. There is one interpretation, however, which has many strong advocates. It localizes schizophrenic origins in the family.

> We have seen results of research conducted in many parts of the world, and one thing is clear: there has never been a schizophrenic who came from a stable family—at least we can't find any. The hallmark of the thought disorder we identify as a schizophrenic reaction is that it does not lie simply in the patient. There's something wrong in the communication of one or both parents, a disturbing quality in the pattern of the family's interpersonal relations that one can begin to bet on. We can't say this is all there is to it, but patterns are surely apparent.

The author is Theodore Lidz, Professor of Psychiatry at Yale and a prime contributor to the study of the role of the family in schizophrenia. The quotation (Boyers, 1971) captures the essence of the position of many who believe that the essential nature of schizophrenia lies in the transmission of irrationality by parents through deviant rearing patterns and the modeling by the child of the parents' faulty modes of communication and thought.

Lidz is asserting one of three assumptions (Goldstein et al., 1978) underlying the disordered family communication model: (1) that families of schizophrenic patients are discriminably different from other families in terms of their interpersonal role relationships, emotional responsiveness, and communication style; (2) that these attributes must have occurred early and been enduring in the life of the schizophrenic patient in order to have exercised a significant effect on his or her development; (3) that such disordered family relationships are a necessary but not a sufficient condition for the development of schizophrenia.

Who becomes schizophrenic? This last assumption is necessary because not all children in a given family become schizophrenic. But the question then asked is what factors determine which child does succumb. One major contributor, Lyman Wynne, has suggested that within families children are assigned different roles; for example, a child may become the "scapegoat" of the family, or the "weak" one, or the "crazy" one. If these role definitions are affirmed by a psychiatrist, a physician, or a psychologist, the process of role assignment may become so pervasive that it is difficult, if not impossible, for a child to escape from it. This is the act of "labeling" (page 452) in psychopathology about which a great deal has been written (Scheff, 1966).

The question of cause and effect In concluding this discussion, we are left with a problem that relates to the direction of causation. Do the parents of schizophrenic offspring behave differently because they have a sick child or does their behavior cause schizophrenia in their offspring? Pursuing this question, Elliot Mishler and Nancy Waxler (1968) investigated the parent-child interactions of families having both a schizophrenic child and a healthy sibling. On a number of the measures of interaction the parents, when with the disturbed child, differed from the way normal parents interacted with a normal child. When they were with their own well child, however, these parents also behaved the way normal parents do. Disturbed interactions, then, are often limited to exchanges with the disturbed offspring.

Recently, a series of studies have been published in Great Britain that reveal the importance of the emotional atmosphere of the family for the well-being of the schizophrenic patient. These investigators found that there was a greater probability of relapse and return to the hospital for the schizophrenic patient if the family with whom the patient lived behaved in a manner marked by criticism, hostility, and a heavy emotional overinvolvement with the patient. The relapse rate of patients from homes high in these forms of *expressed emotion* was three and a half times the rate of patients from homes low in these forms of behavior. This difference is highly significant statistically, but the explanation of the association remains uncertain. Does the intense emotional atmosphere of the home affect the schizophrenic patient adversely, or do the more disturbed patients make their relatives critical, hostile, and emotionally involved? It is hoped that further study of the family may in time provide the data necessary to answer these critically important cause-effect questions (see page 468).

Sociocultural Factors That schizophrenia and lower social-class status are highly correlated is unequivocal. One hundred years ago Jarvis reported that the "pauper class" in Massachusetts contributed sixty-four times the number of cases to "insanity" as did the "independent" class (Sandifer, 1962). In their classic study of social class and mental illness, Hollingshead and Redlich (1958) located all residents of New Haven, Connecticut, who were in psychiatric treatment during a six-month period from May 31 to December 1, 1950. This group was compared with a control sample drawn from the same community. Subsequently, all patients were sorted into five social classes on the basis of available demographic data. They ranged from unskilled laborers and semiskilled workers (class V) to business and professional leaders who held highly prestigious positions in the community (class I).

The relationship of neurosis and psychosis to social class was attested to by their data. The prevalence—all the existing cases—of psychosis per 100,000 population in class V showed a remarkable increment over the previous four classes. In class V there were nine psychotic patients for each neurotic patient. When the psychotic group was subdivided by disorder, the frequency of schizophrenia soared, being almost nine times the rate in social classes I and II (lesser managerial and professional groups) combined.

What can account for the higher incidence of schizophrenia found in the class V population? Some suggest that the answer lies in the stresses that accompany poverty; others reflect on the powerlessness of the poor. Still other theorists believe that lower class living creates resistance to change, particularly disadvantageous in a rapidly changing technological society; distrust of others; lessened self-esteem; self-deprecation; and heightened anxiety and a belief, which is not unrealistic, that one's efforts bring very little reward (Kohn, 1972). Others have advocated an explanation based on **"social drift"**—schizophrenics drift to the slums as a result of their inadequacy. The problem with both positions is that there is not a universal pattern in all individuals who live in poverty. Individual variation is present in class V just as it is in the other social-class groups. Only by comparative studies of those in class V who resist and those who capitulate to schizophrenia will there be a clearer answer to the question of why a heavy loading of schizophrenia is to be found among the poor.

New evidence may make it necessary to examine the broader sociocultural context for schizophrenia in answering this question. Preliminary analyses of data emerging from the International Pilot Study of Schizophrenia (page 448) suggest that the course of schizophrenia seems more benign in less economically developed countries than is the case in nations noted for their advanced technology. Is the social environment in which people with schizophrenia live in less advanced nations demonstrably less disadvantaging (Wing, 1978)? Would this hold for the poor within such societies as well as for those who are better off economically? For this model, too, new findings generate new questions—an outcome that is common in the search for order in the etiology of this extraordinary disorder (Sartorius et al., 1978).

BIOCHEMICAL MODELS OF SCHIZOPHRENIA AND DEPRESSION

Evidence of a significant genetic factor in schizophrenia and in some forms of depression tell us that somewhere in the brain there must exist a biochemical lesion, since genes are expressed only through biochemical processes. A noted neurophysiologist once expressed this view with a dramatic sentence: "No twisted thought without a twisted molecule." But the search for the "twisted molecule" was endless and seemingly fruitless.

A revolution and new discoveries in neuroscience portend the end of this frustrating search. The synapse, once thought to be simply an electrical junction for the transmission of nerve impulses, is now recognized as a biochemical "switch."

It is these chemical switches that can be affected by hormones, drugs, and metabolic processes and in turn affect behavior. Recent research indicates that the neurotransmitter dopamine may play an important role in schizophrenia. An excess of dopamine may be present in special tracts in the brain. Chlorpromazine, a powerful phenothiazine (see page 473), may block the dopamine receptors, thus containing the transmission of excess dopamine—which accounts for the therapeutic action of this antipsychotic drug.

A similar story is unfolding in the study of depression, in which levels of a group of neurotransmitters, serotonin, norepinephrine, and dopamine, may be abnormally low. These neurotransmitters, which are monoamines, can be destroyed by an enzyme, monoamine oxidase (MAO). Drug treatments are directed to the inhibition of MAO or to increasing the life of the monoamines present in the synapse. The antidepressant drugs that keep norepinephrine from being taken up again by the nerve cell after firing are called tricyclics.

Seymour Kety, Harvard researcher and world-renowned leader in the study of the genetics and biochemistry of mental disorders. In the course of his research on the brain, he has found that a single norepinephrine-bearing neuron in the brainstem sends branches to the cerebral cortex, the cerebellum, the hypothalamus, and the hippocampus (1967).

SUMMARY □

Interpretations of mental disorder were originally based upon the recall of early events by adult patients and family members. Recent studies have indicated that even with normal adult individuals such retrospective reports are full of errors through forgetting defensiveness, and distortion. These errors are accentuated when parents and patients attempt to account for mental disorder in adulthood. As a result of such shortcomings, investigators have begun to do research designed to identify and study the adaptations of children who are presumed to be "at risk" for the later development of psychopathology.

Studies of the concordance rates for identical versus fraternal twins, adoption studies, and pedigree analyses of families with a heavy concentration of schizophrenia strengthen the case for genetic transmission of the disorder. It is equally evident that environmental factors also play a key role, but these have not as yet been unequivocally identified.

Of the psychological models for the etiology of schizophrenia, the most popular focuses on the family. Many parents of schizophrenic patients are manifestly deviant themselves. Thus it is likely that in many cases the family milieu contributes appreciably to the development of schizophrenia.

Still a different model looks to the larger social scene for explanations. The poor bear many burdens, including schizophrenia, which tends to be heavily concentrated in the lowest economic strata. The problem, as with other etiological theories, is how to explain the correlation between poverty and mental disorders. Does it lie in the drift downward of incompetent people, circumstances not uncommon in the life histories of schizophrenic patients? Does poverty add unbearable stresses, disorganization, and a rootlessness which heightens the likelihood of disorder? Or is society, meaning all of us, ever ready to label the poor and the powerless as disordered and thus accentuate disorder in the disadvantaged?

New data emerging from an international study of schizophrenia appear to suggest that some sociocultural factor provided by less developed nations makes the course of schizophrenia more benign than that evident in the more technologically sophisticated nations.

Finally, developments in neuroscience have begun to implicate faulty neurotransmitters in the etiology of schizophrenia and depression.

THE STIGMA OF MENTAL DISORDER

Abstract discussions of classification and models of psychopathology and speculation about the origins of deviant behavior cloak the great human problem associated with mental disorder, the stigma under which many people who have been hospitalized and received psychiatric diagnoses are forced to live out their lives.

Here are some actual television listings drawn from the morning newspaper of a large midwestern city. Identical descriptions of these programs appeared in hundreds of newspapers from coast to coast.

> 8:00 p.m.—A psychotic voyeur is determined to assassinate Detective Hernandez because of jealousy involving Hernandez' girlfriend.
>
> 9:00 p.m.—"Lady Killer." After an exciting courtship, a girl marries a charming, considerate man who, it turns out, wants to kill her.
>
> 10:30 p.m.—"An Echo of Theresa." A couple's second honeymoon in London turns into a nightmare when the man begins to behave in an alarming manner and develops a second personality.

It does not take a great deal of imagination to figure out what any one of the scripts might be—a new marriage torn asunder by a charming husband-turned-psychopath; another husband, gentle and romantic, who suddenly begins to assume the shape of madness, the now-frightened wife growing aware of the horror of her predicament. The mass media portray mental illness largely to excite fear in their audiences. The emphasis is invariably on the most bizarre aspects of mental disorder. In television dramas the mentally ill person stares glassy-eyed, mouth agape, mumbling incoherently, or laughs maniacally and shouts murderous threats. Even an old-fashioned mild neurosis is made lamentable for television viewers through tortured facial expressions and explosions of emotion.

Such images are false and are unsupported by any known facts. Less than 5 percent of mental patients are dangerous to themselves or to others. Instead of being aggressive, disturbed people are typically anxious, passive, and fearful. But a withdrawn and inadequate person will not improve program ratings by keeping millions of people sitting on the edge of their chairs each night in front of their television sets. We take these stereotyped portrayals so much for granted that we fail to realize what an enormous disservice they do the countless millions who have intimately known mental disorder.

The Stigma of Patienthood

Bruce Ennis is a lawyer who participated in a legal project begun in 1968 by the New York Civil Liberties Union to ensure the civil rights of mental patients. The outgrowth of his experience has been a book, *Prisoners of Psychiatry: Mental Patients, Psychiatrists and the Law*. It provides a catalog of case histories detailing the violations of the civil rights of mental patients. One in particular is a poignant account of a young college woman, a distinguished student, who voluntarily spent a year in a mental hospital and then was faced with disastrous curtailment of her career plans after that voluntary commitment.

> Myra, the young woman of this story, graduated *magna cum laude* from the City College of New York. An honors graduate in a combined program in chemistry and psychology, she had been admitted to Phi Beta Kappa in her junior year and had held a National Science Foundation grant to pursue her research studies in chemistry. When she graduated from college in 1969 she applied to thirteen medical schools and although her scores on the Medical College Admission Test had placed her in the 99th percentile on the science and quantitative sections of the test, she was rejected without explanation by each of her thirteen schools.
>
> Some case history background is necessary to trace the probable reason for her rejection. Reared in a strictly orthodox Jewish home, Myra came to find such orthodoxy unacceptable. To her parents, such counter beliefs suggested moral shortcomings and they showed an increasing rejection of her. Their pronouncements indicated that they felt she had been "worthless" from the very day of her birth. Her sense of self-esteem at an abysmally low point, Myra, despite a straight A average at CCNY during her first two undergraduate years, felt she was unable to escape "feelings of loneliness, low self-esteem, and. . . depression." She blamed herself for the stresses of her homelife and yet was unable to leave her parental home, for she feared that she would be unable to survive on her own. Her one escape route as she came to see it was to convince a psychiatrist that she required hospitalization—a task that she felt would be simplified by a suicidal gesture. She hinted at this to the college's psychiatrist but he

did not take her threats seriously. She even took medication designed to make her ill but not to kill, but her family and physician remained unresponsive.

Finally she obtained a nontoxic substance and told a friend she intended to end her life. Mistakenly the friend assumed the substance to be "cyanide" and called Myra's parents. Two hours later the police picked her up in a bus terminal in New York City, where she had busied herself reading a book. The police searched her and found the two capsules of "cyanide" which were confiscated but never subjected to laboratory analysis.

Briefly hospitalized for observation, Myra then had herself voluntarily admitted to Hillside Hospital—an excellent private psychiatric institution in Long Island. A year later she returned to CCNY and completed her junior and senior years with the same outstanding performance that had characterized her first two years of college.

And then came the succession of medical school rejections. Each school had inquired about her hospitalization and clearly each institution was unwilling to take the risk of admitting a former mental patient.

Arguing that a relevant consideration for admission was not solely her past condition, but her present mental status as well, the Civil Liberties Union decided to attack at the most vulnerable point, by challenging the least prestigious (and Myra's last choice) of the schools to which she had applied. It was indicated that Myra would submit to examination and a review of her life history by any three psychiatrists the medical school wished to appoint. Further, the case would be dropped if any one of the three clinicians disputed her eligibility on the basis of her present mental state. The university declined this offer and the Civil Liberties Union was faced with a dilemma. Wide publicity would cripple Myra's chances of acceptance at other medical schools (what better indication of the stigmatizing effect of having been a "mental patient"!). The decision was made to seek a temporary injunction to allow her to audit classes pending a full trial and a test of the case on its merits. Although the judge was visibly moved by Myra's status, the injunction was refused and the case came to trial. Medical experts and clinical psychologists testified in favor of Myra's admission on the basis of an absence of any evidence or symptoms of current maladjustment. Despite the stress of rejections, Myra had stood up under the experience well. Indeed, even while hospitalized she had worked at the hospital doing biochemical research and had taken advanced courses (with A's) at CCNY.

Where had the basis for rejection come from, since the record indicated that one admissions committee member who had interviewed her described her as "impressive"? Apparently a psychiatrist who read her record expressed the view that her probable diagnosis was "latent schizophrenia"—although he did so without interviewing her or conducting a clinical case history or a mental status examination. Indeed the testimony of the psychiatrist has a rather unbelievable ring to it. First he admitted that he was not prepared to diagnose Myra a schizophrenic. What he was prepared to say was "that most hospital admissions carry a diagnosis of schizophrenia. The majority of people who have been in mental hospitals in. . . her age group have a diagnosis of schizophrenia and it was on that, sir, that I made that comment . . . I am not prepared at this point to defend a diagnosis of schizophrenia."

Although the defense of the medical school was insubstantial, the school's arguments that Myra represented "an academic and emotional risk" led the judge to rule against her and the Civil Liberties Union.

But then fate intervened in a more favorable way. A midwestern medical school of considerable prestige offered Myra a substantial fellowship in a combined M.D.–Ph.D. program. Two years after beginning the program, it was reported that Myra has earned "honors in most of her courses and superior grades in all the rest."

Myra has overcome her disadvantaged status. She is one of the lucky ones who has managed to break the web of stigma that surrounds former mental patients. Many others, however, never escape the sense of shame and rejection that accompanies a history of psychiatric hospitalization.

The Mental Patient and the College Student

Who is to blame for this recurring tragedy of prejudice and rebuff? That the mass media can condition a subtle set of attitudes which influences the behavior of the nation toward those who have been hospitalized for mental disorder is unequivocal. If you believe, however, that only persons of lesser understanding and education have disparaging attitudes, the results of a study using college students as participants should provide a realistic antidote to such a simple view (Farina and Ring, 1965). In this study pairs of male undergraduates were brought face to face, presumably to participate in a task that required a cooperative working relationship to ensure good performance. They were to manipulate a box containing a wooden maze, along which were a series of holes. Two knobs on either side of the box could be rotated simultaneously to control the plane and the angle of inclination of the box. The object of the game was to roll a steel ball along the maze without letting it drop into any of the holes. The more holes bypassed, the better the performance. But this could only be achieved by the coordinated play of the two players.

Before they began, each participant was asked to describe himself, his future plans, and anything that he considered to be unusual about himself. Each player was then asked to read in privacy his partner's statements. The investigators, however, substituted for the actual statements information which was designed to suggest that the partner was either "normal" or "sick." The "normal" statement declared that the person was free of "problems," enjoyed college, was "popular," "engaged," had achieved a B average, and planned upon graduation to get married and enter graduate school. The "sick" partner had a sadder story to tell. He had had "adjustment problems" since high school, was a solitary person who lacked "close friends"; on two occasions he had "been placed in a mental institution [for] a kind of nervous breakdown." He, too, was a B student who planned to go on for an advanced degree following graduation.

For purposes of comparison, three groups were formed, a normal-normal pairing (N-N) in which both participants were described by the normal message; a normal-"sick" (N-S) pairing in which one student was described by the normal statement, the other by the "sick" one; and a "sick-sick" (S-S) pairing, with both described as two former "mental patients." After having played the game for fifty trials, each partner returned to his seat to complete a final questionnaire in which he was asked to describe his co-worker. Twenty-seven of thirty students who had believed their colleague "normal" rated him as helpful, whereas only three viewed him as "hindering." By contrast, of the thirty who had presumably had a "sick" partner, only eighteen rated his contribution as a positive one and twelve reported he was a hindrance in doing the task. Twenty-four of the students in this group also indicated that they would have preferred to work alone. In the normal group only thirteen of thirty would have preferred to work alone, the majority favoring the collaboration.

Although the groups had been randomly assigned to one of the three test situations, the S-S pairs performed best, leading the investigators to suggest that if a partner in a joint working relationship has been identified as mentally ill, the colleague works harder, presumably to make up for the "sick" partner's anticipated lacks and lapses. How else to explain the fact that although the S-S duos did better than the other groups, each partner in these duos tended to blame the other for inadequate performance? Conclusion: Negative appraisals of the mentally disordered are made by all segments of society, including well-educated college students.

This, by definition, is what is meant by **stigma.** It is an attribute that demeans the status and the position of any person who is identified with it. To worsen the effect of stigma, this same investigative team (Farina, Holland, and Ring, 1966) later conducted another study and reported that the participants who were reputed to have had a history of mental disorder not only were rated as less adequate, less liked, and less desirable as partners but also had more physical pain inflicted on them under conditions in which the partner administered shock when errors were made during a pseudo-learning task. (Although the participant chose the shock level to be administered, the recipient was the experimenter's confederate and shock was not actually received via the pseudo-apparatus.)

These studies raise a very significant issue. Many persons today question the morality of those who confine people in mental hospitals (see page 460). But one has to look further to a society which derogates mental disorder, to families that reject former patients, to employers who refuse to hire them, to neighbors who fear them. Few in our society are free of the responsibility for the conditions to which the mentally disordered are subjected.

Failure of a Moral Enterprise

Theodore Sarbin and James Mancuso provided the title for this section in an article which they published in 1970. Their moral enterprise that failed was the mental health movement that was unable to change the public's attitudes toward mental illness and deviant behavior. A review of the literature of two decades led them to these conclusions.

1. The public is not sympathetic to persons who are labeled mentally ill.
2. The mental patient is looked upon with disrespect and is relegated to a "childlike, nonperson role."
3. The public tries to place a "sizable" social distance between itself and people labeled "mentally ill."
4. The public has a narrower band than professionals for whom it labels mentally ill. Paranoid patients are so identified as are schizophrenics and alcoholics.
5. The public does not identify unhappiness with mental illness, but rather links unhappiness to concrete problems of living.
6. The public tends to seek help from nonpsychiatric professionals, particularly clergymen, rather than from mental health professionals when they have concrete problems.
7. More financially secure and better-educated persons are more likely to use a mental illness orientation toward unhappiness and deviant behavior. If they seek help, they tend to consult professional mental health personnel.
8. Although the public believes there is a shortage of mental health professionals, it also has

a low opinion of psychiatric treatment and the state of knowledge in the field.

9. The authors have expressed another public attitude in this manner.

> The public . . . has not bought the mental health story as applicable to itself. They feel there are "sick" people, and they should have help, but these are "other" people and not those persons within one's immediate world. They are not sure about how one identifies a mentally ill person. The man in the street will not use this category as freely as do professionals. Nevertheless, the public asserts that mentally ill people should have help available, and in fact, it is a good idea to move them out of the community when they are labeled as mentally ill (p. 170).

It is this last paragraph that sums up some of the many problems that confront those who have had a history of mental disorder. It also points up a massive contemporary problem for former patients. As mental hospitals begin to empty, the placement of patients in the community becomes the central focus for posthospital care. Halfway houses seem to be one solution but the opposition of communities to the placement of mental patients in their midst often has been used to stop their construction. This results in further stigmatization of the mental patient. We return to this critical problem in our discussion of the release of the mental patient to the community in Chapter 19 (see page 468).

SUMMARY □

Stigma, notes the dictionary, is a mark of disgrace, a stain on one's reputation, a characteristic mark or sign of defect—all definitions that are too readily applied to those who are viewed as mentally disordered. Unfortunately, the tendency to stigmatize does not seem to be restricted to any one segment of the population. It is ubiquitous, as evident in the college sophomore enrolled in the introductory course in psychology as it is in the man or the woman you pass on the street. Such attitudes add to the sense of disgrace and the loss of self-esteem which is often present in those who are victims of mental distress. It adds to the heavy burden borne by the mentally disturbed to become aware that friends, employers, and casual acquaintances condemn deviant behavior. The growing recognition of the right to be different does not seem to include most signs of mental aberration. As a result, the vulnerability of the mentally disordered is accentuated by society's attitudes. This view has, unfortunately, carried over to the problem of posthospital treatment of those who have been residents in mental hospitals.

TO BE SURE YOU UNDERSTAND THIS CHAPTER △

The following concepts are the major ones discussed in this chapter. You should be able to define them and state the major points made about each.

Descriptive psychopathology
Developmental psychopathology
Hysteria
Repression
Reliability of diagnosis
Syndrome
Mental status examination
Present state examination
DSM-III
Medical model
Labeling theory
Hereditary model
Internal environment model
Neurophysiological model
Ecological model
Developmental model
Learning and conditioning model
Longitudinal study
At risk
Adoptee study
Social drift
Neurotransmitter
Dopamine receptor
Stigma

As you can see, the list is not long. The content of the chapter is centered for the most part on a set of issues which are described in some detail. They include the following.

Data on the mental health problem
Why psychiatric diagnosis is unreliable
Strengths and weaknesses of DSM-III
How genetic factors related to the origins of schizophrenia are studied
How labeling, although not the entire cause of mental disorder, may contribute
The relationships between socioeconomic class and mental disorder
The biology of mental disorder

TO GO BEYOND THIS CHAPTER △

In this book Chapter 17 was of course a companion piece to this one. You should reread in tandem their sections on schizophrenia. The discussion of structured personality tests in Chapter 16 is paralleled by this chapter's material on the structured mental status examination. Chapter 19, on treatment and therapy, will complete the three-chapter sequence on disordered states. Chapters 12 through 15 stressed adaptive behavior, but they are equally important for understanding maladaptive behavior.

Elsewhere The prevalence of mental disorder in the United States is described more fully in volume 1 of the *President's Commission on Mental Health*. Try your college library for the entire four-volume report.

Many of the comprehensive textbooks of abnormal psychology listed at the end of Chapter 17 discuss diagnosis, classification, and etiology models for psychopathology. You may find an anticlassification bias in some of these texts. A more positive point of view is provided by V. M. Rakoff, H. C. Stancer, and H. B. Kedward, in their *Psychiatric Diagnosis*. A fascinating study, readily understandable to the undergraduate reader, is *Psychiatric Diagnosis in New York and London*, by J. E. Cooper and others. They attempted to learn why American psychiatrists tend to overdiagnose schizophrenia in comparison with British psychiatrists, whereas the reverse is true for depression.

Breuer and Freud's *Studies in Hysteria* is worth reading because it will acquaint you with early Freud and because you owe it to yourself to try something by the master.

The usefulness of the medical model has been challenged by Thomas Szasz in a series of provocative works reflecting his bias against the psychiatric establishment: *The Myth of Mental Illness, Law, Liberty, and Psychiatry, The Manufacture of Madness,* and *Schizophrenia*. A more traditional view is offered by Miriam Siegler and Humphrey Osmond, in their *Models of Madness, Models of Medicine*. A recent volume by Jack Maser and Martin Seligman, *Psychopathology: Experimental Models,* provides an in-depth analysis of various models constructed by researchers, who have then tested their usefulness through laboratory work.

A growing number of developmental psychopathology books have begun to appear; two are *Developmental Psychopathology*, by Thomas Achenbach; and *Psychological Disorders of Children*, by Alan Ross.

For a background of the affective disorders similar to that given for schizophrenia, the paperback *Affective Disorders*, by Joseph Becker, is recommended again. A definitive and contemporary overview of schizophrenia is provided by *The Nature of Schizophrenia: New Approaches to Research and Treatment*, edited by Lyman Wynne, Steven Matthysse, and R. Cromwell, although it is not easy reading.

Two books take opposing sides about labeling theory. Thomas Scheff, in *Labeling Madness*, gives the pro view; Walter Gove, editor of *The Labeling of Deviance*, takes the con view. Erving Goffman's *Stigma* is a classic on the subject, but in *Contemporary Attitudes Toward Mental Illness* Guido Crocetti, Herzl Spiro, and Iradj Siassi question whether the public inevitably stigmatizes the mental patient.

CH. 19

Treatment and Therapy of Disordered States

For 750 years and more the treatment of the mentally disordered has oscillated between neglect and cruelty on the one hand and kindness and concern on the other. In the fifteenth and sixteenth centuries madness was considered in league with witchcraft, evil, and devil possession. An alliance, even extending to "carnal relations," supposedly existed between the afflicted and the devil. Such interpretations were supported by the clergy and by political, academic, and scientific figures of the time. In 1487 two theologians wrote a notorious tract, *Malleus Maleficarum* ("The Witches' Hammer"), which became "the most authoritative and the most horrible document of that age" (Zilboorg, 1941). It gave license to inquisitors who could denounce disturbed behavior as the manifestation of witchery and sorcery. Signs of madness were seen as a threat to the power of the Church in a period when new social forces threatening to the establishment were beginning to emerge. In the foreword to the English edition of the *Malleus,* the objectives of witches were proclaimed to be the abolition of the monarchy, private property, inheritance, marriage, religion and the social order. Any uncommon behavior such as being subject to hallucinations and delusions, was seen as a sign of witchcraft. This conclusion then justified the medieval mode of "treatment": burn the body and save the captive soul.

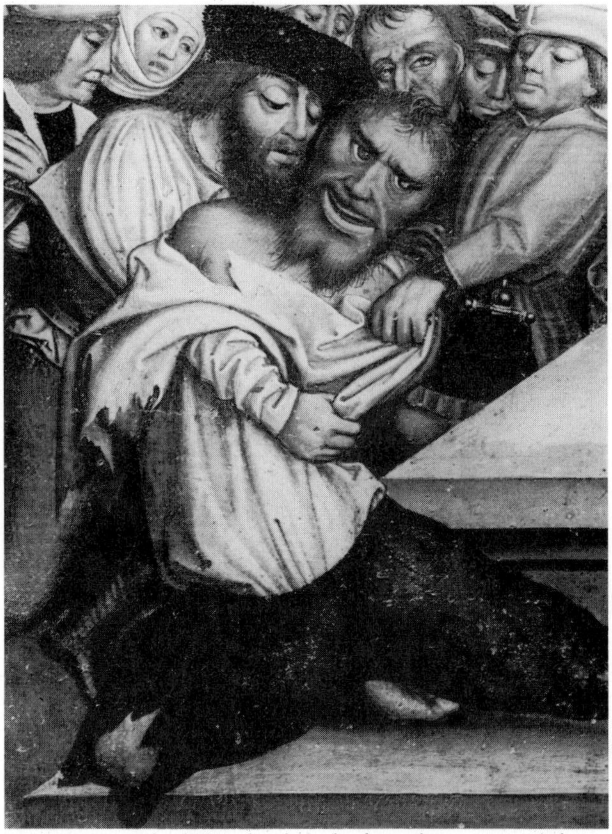

Man possessed of the devil and of madness. Detail from the retable of a Swiss Franciscan church, painted by Hans Fries in 1505 through 1507.

Madhouses, Asylums, and Mental Hospitals The passage of time modified the form of punishment. Instead of burning, patients were beaten, immersed repeatedly in cold water, made to swallow foul-tasting substances—all, of course, to no avail.

By the late eighteenth century a more humane view —madness as sickness—had emerged, and the treatment of the mentally ill turned to sanctuary and care. In the mid-nineteenth century a period of "moral," that is, humane, treatment began. Great emphasis was placed on the need for a warm relationship between physician and patient and for a cheerful and pleasant hospital milieu (Bockhoven, 1963). Wards were made homelike, and patients were treated as though they were members of a family. They were encouraged to rest and to participate in recreational activities in keeping with a view that mental disorder was brought on by being too preoccupied with work. Hospital discharge rates were high, and hospitals competed to see which had the best recovery rate.

With the tidal wave of immigration later in the nineteenth century, racial and ethnic prejudice arose and moral treatment went into decline. The term "foreigners" began to appear in state hospital reports and, on bases that were totally inadequate, psychiatry began to "explain" mental disorder as the result of genetic factors. With this formulation a mood of pessimism about recovery settled over the hospitals. "If madness is genetic, it cannot be cured." Slowly they expanded into monolithic institutions to house the genetically disabled who would be hospitalized for a lifetime. These mental hospitals were located away from population centers and, as they grew overcrowded, treatment became custodial and not therapeutic. Far removed from the outside world, the mentally disturbed suffered the neglect of families and society. For the patient lost in the back wards of hospitals, the phrase "out of sight, out of mind" was tragically apt.

THE MENTAL PATIENT IN SOCIETY

The ever-increasing enrollment in mental hospitals continued until the mid-1950s, when the introduction of the phenothiazines not only stopped the advance but initiated an actual decline in the populations of the state hospitals. In 1955 the resident population of these institutions was 559,000; in 1975 it was 191,000. Length of stay grew shorter and the mental hospitals began to empty, but not always to the advantage of the patients or their families.

Consequences of Early Discharge

By the 1970s the closing down of mental hospitals was in full swing in this country. California was in the

Scene in a state mental hospital, photographed a few decades ago.

vanguard of the movement. As the state hospitals began to discharge even the chronically disordered, a heavy burden was placed on inadequately staffed community mental health centers. With limited facilities they could admit only seriously disturbed persons for very short stays. In the Los Angeles area Eliot Rodnick and Michael Goldstein (1974) of the University of California decided to look at what happened to children when their disturbed mothers were returned home after brief periods of hospitalization, still suffering the effects of an acute schizophrenic disorder. To what extent were the young offspring of these mothers disadvantaged by her condition?

The investigators selected a sample of twenty-seven schizophrenic women, all of whom were mothers, from the roster of a community mental health center. Each patient and a close relative were interviewed to secure data on the quality of the patient's adjustment before breakdown on such indicators of competence as outside activities, participation in community organizations, friendship and leadership patterns with same-sex peers, dating, and a stable sexual attachment. The mothers were then divided into a **good premorbid** group, those having higher competence before disorder, and a **poor premorbid** group, those having lower competence before disorder.

The average period of hospitalization of the patients was ten days, after which they were returned to their homes. Subsequently the investigators held follow-up interviews with the patient and the relative at six months and one year following discharge. A five-point scale was used by clinicians who made blind evaluations of maternal behavior that ranged from warm responsiveness to indifference to the child. The results (Figure 19.1) at two follow-up

Eliot H. Rodnick.

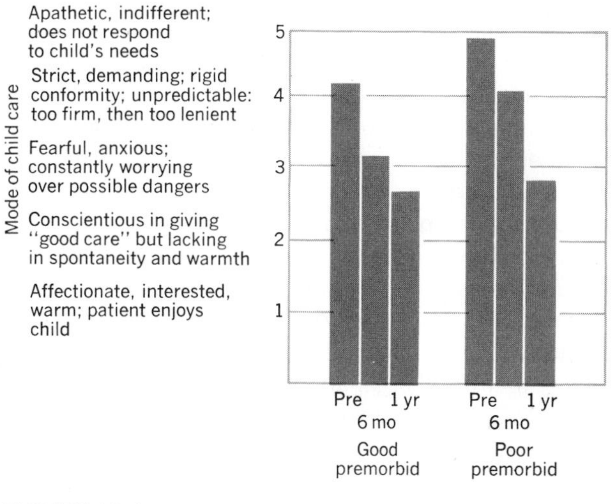

FIGURE 19.1

Ratings of maternal care of good and poor premorbid schizophrenic mothers after early release. The ratings, by interview information, are for three periods before hospitalization (pre) and for six months and one year after release. High scores mean inadequate mothering. (Adapted from Rodnick and Goldstein, 1974.)

points clearly indicate that the poor premorbid group were inferior mothers at six months after discharge when compared with the good premorbid group. At the end of a year there were no significant differences between the groups of patients, all of whom appeared to be "conscientious and giving good care but lacking spontaneity and warmth." The early mothering behavior of the poor premorbid group seems likely to have negative consequences for their children for a number of reasons. The poor premorbid mothers on the average were seven years younger than the more competent mothers. This is to be expected because poor premorbid competence correlates with breakdown at an earlier age. The children of these younger mothers were also younger, of course. They were at an age when mothering is of particular importance. In each family there was at least one child who required intimate physical contact with the mother. Unfortunately, these mothers could not meet their infant's needs because of their "apathy. . . indifference, neglect, or even anxious fearfulness during the baby's first year of life."

Since poor premorbid patients are more likely to have a family history of schizophrenia than good premorbid patients, there is a growing belief among researchers that a genetic factor probably figures in their schizophrenia. Thus the babies whom these poor premorbid schizophrenic mothers tended may have already had a genetic vulnerability, to which was added the stress of inadequate caretaking. Both factors would contribute to the children's risk of developing mental disorder.

The Revolving Door

As mental hospitals began to close and patients went back into the community, only the most chronic cases remained behind. But investigators who checked new admissions data soon began to question the inference that the recovery rate had become remarkable. They detected a "revolving door" pattern of admissions and readmissions. A decade after the downward trend began, a survey (Miller, 1966) of 1045 patients from the San Francisco-Oakland area revealed that 71 percent of them had returned to the hospital at least once during a five-year period following their discharge, and that 24 percent had been rehospitalized an average of 4.4 times.

Other statistics proved equally discouraging. Rehospitalization rates for schizophrenic patients released to the community were 50 to 60 percent in just two years (Mosher, 1971; Talbot, 1974). In another follow-up study 34 percent of patients discharged from mental hospitals had to be readmitted within a year. Elsewhere there has been a 30 percent rise in the readmission rates to state and county hospitals (cited in Liberman, 1979).

Who Comes Back? Who Stays Out?

These findings raise a critical issue. Who returns to the hospital? Recent research provides a number of answers to this important question, at least for schizophrenia. The best indicators for a former patient's remaining in the community seems to be a good work and social adjustment before the disorder, combined with freedom from paranoid thinking during the psychotic state. In general, schizophrenics with more adequate premorbid social and heterosexual adjustment tend to have shorter hospital stays, show more rapid recovery, exhibit greater initiative on discharge, make decisions more readily, and conform to the social rules of society. Such behavior heightens the likelihood that they will be able to remain in the community (Evans et al., 1972, 1973).

One of the most difficult problems for the patients who have been released from a mental hospital is that of obtaining the social support they need to assist them to function more adequately in the outside world. Here the role of the family is critical, and it has been studied and clarified by a team of British investigators (Brown et al., 1972; Leff, 1976; Vaughn and Leff, 1976).

The research began with a survey of male schizophrenic patients who had been discharged from mental hospitals. One surprising finding was an unexpected relationship between adjustment outside the hospital and the patient's type of living arrangements. Severely disturbed behavior was reported for 30 percent of the patients who were living with their families, but it was reported for only 11 percent of the patients who were living alone. Half of the first group, but only 30 percent of the second, were readmitted to the hospital within five years after discharge. Through an intensive and complex interview one factor responsible for this striking difference was finally determined to be the intensity of the emotional atmosphere in the family to which the patient had returned. Hostility, censure, and critical comments about the patients reflecting emotional overinvolvement were the key indicators that a patient might return to the hospital.

These attributes of family atmosphere led to a rating of families on a dimension of **expressed emotionality** (EE). When these ratings were related to relapse rate, it was found that 59 percent of the patients from high-EE homes returned to the hospital compared to 16 percent of those from low-EE homes. Additional interviews indicated that a great deal of emotionality had prevailed in the homes of relapsed patients even before their hospitalization. How, the investigators asked, could the situation be improved?

Patients from high-EE homes seemed to benefit to some extent if they were on tranquilizing drugs; those from low-EE homes had the same low rate of relapse

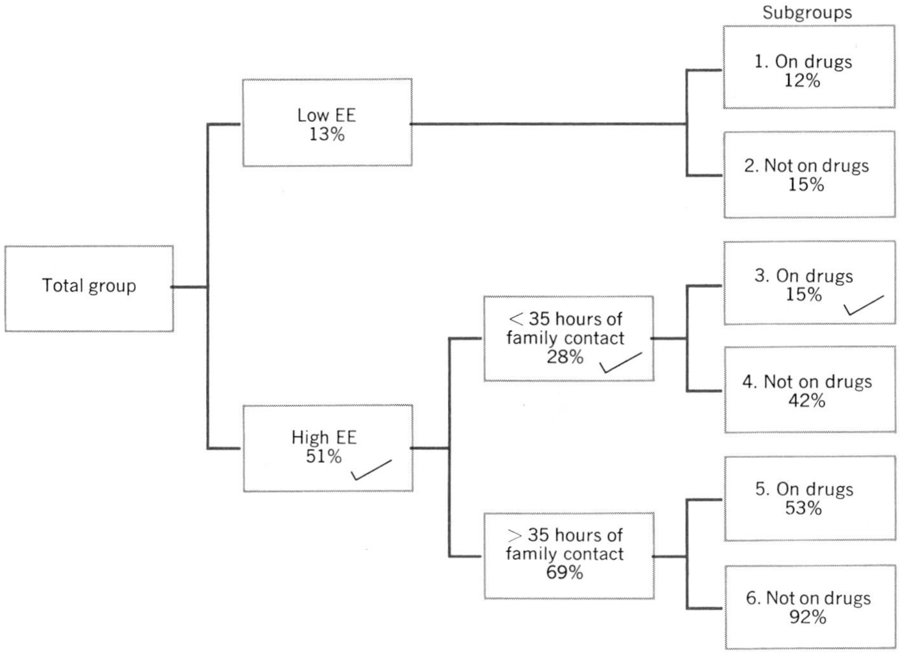

FIGURE 19.2

Nine-month relapse rates for low- and high-EE schizophrenic male patients. The percentages in the boxes are those of patients who had been released and then returned to the hospital. The check marks call attention to the important points. Relapse rates for patients in high-EE homes were high (51 percent), but they were less if these patients had fewer than thirty-five hours of contact with family and were even less if these patients were also using drugs. But hours of family contact and drugs were not important to the relapse rates of patients from low-EE families. (After Vaughn and Leff, 1976.)

whether they were medicated or not. Another important variable was the amount of social contact that patients had with family members. Patients in high-EE homes had a lower relapse rate if they had fewer than thirty-five hours of face-to-face contact with family members during the week and higher rates if they had more than thirty-five hours. The amount of such contact had no significant effect on readmission rates of patients from low-EE families. Figure 19.2 shows the nine-month relapse rates for a group of 128 schizophrenic patients, separated into low- and high-EE families. The category "on drugs" denotes patients receiving tranquilizing medication. A careful scan of this figure provides two important suggestions about measures that might be taken to reduce the relapse rate. Patients should be urged to follow a carefully regulated drug regimen, and efforts should be made to increase the social distance between patient and relatives (Figure 19.3). Day centers or day hospitals provide a supportive environment in which a patient can spend time away from the family. A job or a sheltered workshop are other possible inoculants against another breakdown. Finally, changing the pattern of patient-family interaction and the development of new social skills may serve as a good mental hygiene measure.

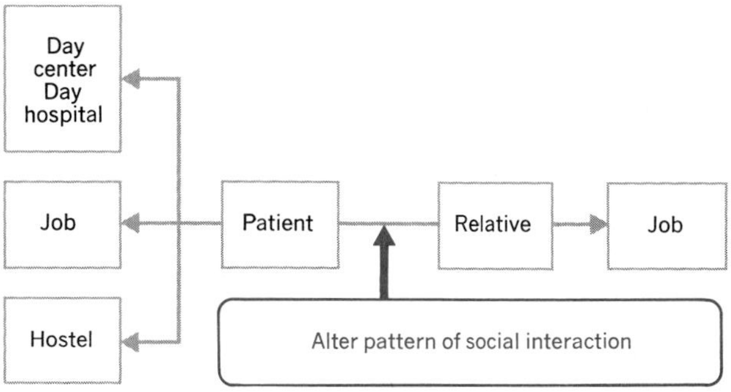

FIGURE 19.3

Increasing social distance from relatives. Released schizophrenic patients usually need to spend time away from the family at day care centers and in outside activities. (After Leff, 1976.)

Social-Skills Training for Patients and Family

Currently a variety of methods are being tested for fostering social skills in patients and members of their families. These include the modeling of the therapist's suggestions for more effective communication and video-taped feedback of actual family interactions to

Acquiring social skills through a family therapy session.

show how emotional situations in the family might be handled with less conflict. Social-skills training of patients may also include teaching ways to express negative feelings, developing better problem-solving techniques, learning how to make requests of others, and practice in listening more effectively and responding more rationally to others.

Contingent reinforcement for positive behavior sometimes helps to achieve these goals. There may be trips into the community under the guidance of a therapist or a well-trained aide, followed by discussions of the patient's performance while away from the hospital. In one project (Liberman, 1979) modeling, rehearsal, coaching, and feedback were used to train families in more adaptive ways of coping. These were taught in a series of ten family therapy sessions held over a five-week span. Before the therapy sessions began, an equal number of meetings were devoted to presentations designed to increase the family's understanding of the nature of schizophrenia. These meetings covered what is known about biological and environmental factors, the value of drugs, and ways to improve the patient's level of social and occupational functioning. These sessions served to expose myths and stereotypes and to prevent misconceptions when specific family problems were aired and discussed later on.

The significance of this didactic component relates to the different ways in which high- and low-EE families interpret family difficulties. When things are going poorly high-EE families blame the *patient* for being thoughtless, provocative, and uncaring. Low-EE families, by contrast, blame the *disorder* and excuse the patient's behavior on the basis of "illness." The latter pattern dampens the criticism directed at the patient; the former pattern aggravates and exaggerates it.

The most extraordinary program of research in the area of training in social skills is the ten-year project of Gordon Paul and his associates at the University of Illinois (Paul and Lentz, 1977). When Paul began his project in 1968, his intention was to compare two forms of psychosocial treatment of typical mental patients in two different wards of a state hospital. One program of therapy was to be milieu therapy, the other a program of therapy based on the principles of social-learning theory. A control group in a similar state hospital was to receive the traditional treatment services available to such patients, including an extensive drug regimen.

Milieu therapy is a type of ward management that emphasizes social interaction among patients, group activities and group pressure directing them toward more normal behavior, relevant communication among patients, and freedom for them to move about. Patients are regarded as responsible people, not as burned-out custodial cases. **Social-learning therapy** emphasizes principles of reinforcement. The physical and social environment of the patient is controlled to ensure that appropriate behavior of the patient receives positive reinforcement and that inappropriate behavior does not.

It is difficult enough to try to maintain a research program for six consecutive months in a state hospital. To do it for a decade is nothing short of incredible! In the course of that decade, the hospital where Paul's study took place emptied in the same way as others did throughout the country. Paul and his col-

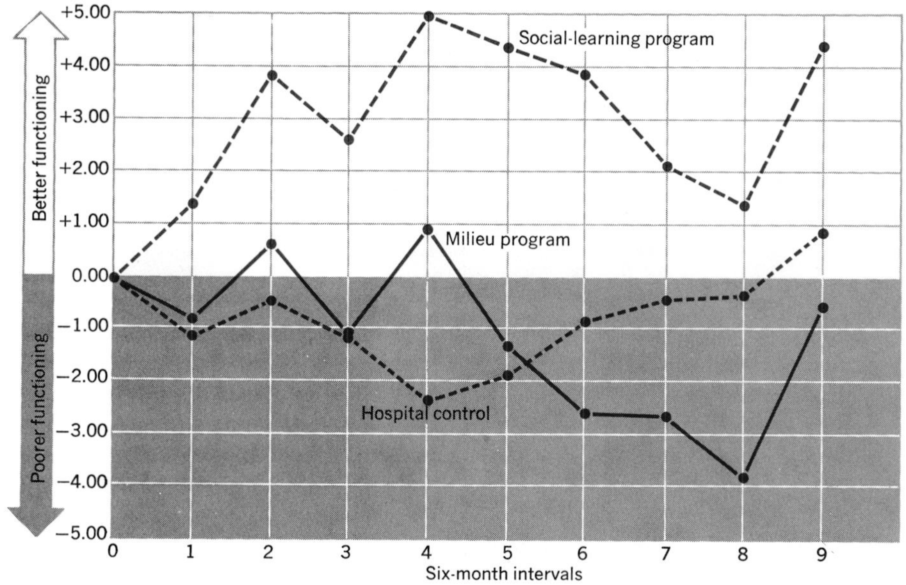

FIGURE 19.4

Improving hospital manners. The general level of hospital functioning of three groups of twenty-eight patients, each undergoing one of three kinds of treatment, was assessed at six-month intervals for signs of improvement. These were the most evident in the patients in the social-learning programs. (Adapted from Paul and Lentz, 1977.)

TABLE 19.1

Status of Three Treatment Groups at Termination of Hospital Programs and at Final Follow-up

Treatment Program	Patients Released by Termination of Hospital Program, percent	Patients Still in Community at Time of Final Follow-up, percent	Condition of Patients in Hospital at Final Follow-up, percent		
			Worse	No Change	Improved
Social Learning	96.4	92.5	2.5	2.5	2.5
Milieu Therapy	67.9	71.0	16.1	9.7	3.2
Hospital Control	46.4	48.4	29.0	9.7	12.9

Adapted from Paul and Lentz, 1977.

leagues saw their most improved patients discharged, until finally they were left with a group of patients for whom the probability of recovery and return to the community was negligible. These patients had been in the hospital for an average of *seventeen* years, about two thirds of their adult lives. Their disorder was the process type of schizophrenia. They had very low levels of social functioning in the hospital. All the patients had a history of unsuccessful treatments of many types, including drug therapy.

Prospects for improvement in such patients are so negligible that the results of the study are very striking. Social-learning therapy proved to be the most effective treatment. Milieu therapy was second best and significantly more effective than traditional hospital procedures. This finding held for improvement in hospital behavior (Figure 19.4), for maximizing release from the institution—all but one social-learning participant achieved release—and for obtaining release in the shortest period of time. The patients improved with relatively little use of antipsychotic drugs and without regard to their individual characteristics or their earlier treatment history. The social-learning ward also cost less per patient than did the other two modes of treatment.

Finally, rehospitalization rates for the social-learning group were less than 3 percent for all patients over a follow-up period that extended from eighteen months after release from the hospital to five years after release, when the study ended (Table 19.1). Paul now believes that a social-learning program such as he conducted would result in community placement of most chronic mental patients within twenty-six to thirty weeks. Given an additional two to three years

Released from the mental hospital, patients often end up alone on deteriorating streets of the inner city.

of continued training in the community, he asserts, these patients would function well enough to live independently and be self-supporting.

Ghettoization of the Mental Patient

Currently we are faced with a situation in the nation's cities that should result in national concern, but does not. This is the *ghettoization* of the mental patient. Here is what Gerald Klerman (1977), Director of the Alcohol, Drug Abuse and Mental Health Administration, has said about the problem.

> New forms of "community chronicity" have been developed in many large urban areas such as New York City, Chicago, Los Angeles, and San Francisco. In the absence of any adequate network of aftercare facilities, community residences and halfway houses, sheltered workshops, or day treatment centers, large numbers of patients are relegated to "lives of quiet desperation" in welfare hotels in segregated neighborhoods. They are subsisting on minimal incomes from social welfare or disability payments, and receiving poorly monitored, often poorly prescribed, psychotropic medication. . . .
>
> . . . Patients often live under conditions of minimum supervision and poor drug management, so that they often may be overdrugged, heavily sedated, stuporous, or dulled. Their limited ability for social interaction often means they wander the streets or sit aimlessly looking at television. . .
>
> In cities, particularly inner city neighborhoods, they are often at the mercy of various predatory groups, such as youth gangs and criminals, and are subject to beatings, robberies, and various forms of abuse (pp. 628-629).

There is evidence to support these assertions. When the state mental hospital in Santa Clara County (California) was closed in 1970, 3000 patients were sent back to the community. The majority grouped together into one square mile in the heart of downtown San Jose where they lived in decrepit board-and-care homes. In 1977 this area had a rate of public mental health treatment services sixty times the average for the county. At the same time, across the country in New York City, 25,000 chronic mental patients were living alone in cubical hotel rooms, in boarding houses, or in run-down seedy motels. Community living for the mental patient has become reinstitutionalization outside the mental hospitals instead of in them (Robitscher, 1976).

SUMMARY ☐

The status of the mentally disordered has always been that of a hapless minority, sometimes persecuted and sometimes cared for by a society that lacks understanding. Recently, with the advent of antipsychotic drugs, the traditional mental hospitals have been emptied. Some former patients have returned to communities that are poorly prepared to house and to provide for them. Others have gone back to families in which conflicts are accentuated or reduced, depending on the presence or absence of a dimension of family life that researchers have called "expressed emotion" (EE). How to dampen these high levels of EE has begun to occupy investigators. Early evidence suggests the importance of a carefully monitored drug regimen and social-skills training of patients and family members.

As for community placement of former mental hospital residents, the ghettoization of these citizens is a growing national problem. They are in effect reinstitutionalized in boarding houses in run-down sections of cities. Here they receive almost no care and are socially isolated. New methods of rehabilitation and social-learning programs are needed to help former patients become more self-sufficient.

SOMATIC TREATMENTS AND PSYCHOTHERAPIES

Two major forms of therapy assist the mental health practitioner in the effort to treat disorder. The first are the **somatic** or **physical** therapies, such as drug and shock therapy. These therapies are based on physiological and biochemical hypotheses of mental disorder. The second group includes the methods of **psychotherapy,** which are based on psychological theories of mental disorder.

Physical or Somatic Therapy

Electroconvulsive Shock Therapy In 1938 Cerletti and Bini introduced the form of **electroconvulsive shock therapy** (ECT) now in use. By means of electrodes fastened to the temples, 70 to 150 volts of electric current pass through the patient's head for 0.1 to 1.0 second (Kalinowsky, 1975). The effect is a convulsion resembling a grand mal epileptic seizure. The use of special muscle relaxants, a general anesthetic, and short-acting intravenous barbiturates has now reduced the likelihood of fractures during treatment, but such injuries sometimes still occur. After the electroconvulsive stimulation, the patient is often confused and usually suffers a *retrograde amnesia* (page 156). The memory loss is not permanent, however, and within a few weeks following treatment the patient's ability to learn and to retain what he has learned appears unaffected. Evidence that ECT might produce permanent brain damage, however, is still equivocal (Salzman, 1978).

Electroshock appears to have its greatest success with severely depressed patients, but not with all types of depression. Current evidence suggests that ECT is not effective with mild long-term depressions, in which the patient complains about many imaginary body ailments, with young people, or with chronic depression associated with the personality disorders. Antidepressant drugs, however, help some of the patients. More systematic studies of treatment are necessary to determine when ECT should be used rather than some other form of therapy.

Psychosurgery The original surgical procedure used in **psychosurgery** was **lobotomy,** a severing of the connections between the thalamus and the frontal lobes. Such procedures have fallen into disrepute for three reasons: (1) the long-term results have been very questionable; (2) the phenothiazines came into use in the mid-1950s and proved to be far more effective as tranquilizers for acutely disturbed patients; and (3) moral objections have been raised against such a radical and irreversible procedure. Today the application of psychosurgery for the control even of violent behavior is a hotly debated topic and has led to court action. As a result there has been a dramatic decline in the use of the procedure, despite improvements in the precision with which psychosurgery is now done.

Drug Therapy The most hopeful advance in the biological treatment of mental patients are a variety of forms of drugs. Among them are the phenothiazines or major tranquilizers, various forms of antidepressant drugs, and *lithium,* which is so effective in controlling mania that its discovery in 1949 has since been called a landmark in psychopharmacology. In this brief description of drug therapy, we concentrate on the most important of the tranquilizing drugs, the **phenothiazine** compounds, of which *chlorpromazine* is the best known. More than ninety-seven drug studies (Baldessarini, 1978) have demonstrated the effectiveness of this drug.

The most successful use of the tranquilizing drugs has been with schizophrenics, often with those who have been long-term chronic patients. Some 15 percent of hitherto inaccessible patients improve to the extent that they can be returned to their communities. Others have become less of a custodial problem despite their failure to recover. Still others can leave the hospital, provided they can receive a maintenance dosage of the drug on an outpatient basis. The phenothiazines, however, are not miracle drugs, and unless some form of environmental support can also be provided for these patients, there is always the possibility of a subsequent relapse and return to the hospital. A special problem with the phenothiazines is that prolonged usage can lead to **tardive** (late) **dyskinesia,** ticlike involuntary movements of the face, mouth, shoulder, and arm, effects which are sometimes irreversible (Baldessarini, 1977).

Determining the efficacy of drugs is complicated by the so-called **placebo effect** (page 17). Research is now beginning to indicate that placebo effects are not general. They lessen some symptoms but not others. For example, the administration of placebos to schizophrenic patients reduced hostility, hallucinations, and persecutory delusions but apathy, flattened and inappropriate effect, and motor retardation were unaffected (Goldberg, Klerman, and Cole, 1965). Unfortunately, the unaffected symptoms are those identified as the fundamental or basic symptoms of schizophrenia (page 434).

Freud's consulting room, splendid with Persian rugs, Egyptian statuary, and other antiquities. These silent figures from the ages must have been evocative companions for those who came here to probe their own pasts.

The Psychological Therapies

Ask the average individual to associate to the word "psychotherapist," and this image is likely to be forthcoming: one person tense and anxious, lying on a couch; another, bearded, sitting slightly behind the couch, busily taking notes or more likely explaining, preferably with a Viennese accent, the childhood roots of a complex and very curious symptom. The image is a caricature. The actual methods of psychotherapy are so varied and so different that no single description can suffice. Psychotherapists, patients, and problems all differ, and so do methods of treatment. In the pages to follow we shall review the major varieties of psychotherapy, describing them in terms that are sympathetic to the approach being described.

Psychoanalysis **Free association** The forerunner of all psychotherapies is Freudian **psychoanalysis.** In the classical psychoanalytic session, the patient reclines on a couch in a softly lighted room and is instructed to talk about everything that comes to mind no matter how trivial, irrelevant, senseless, embarrassing, or vulgar. This is the technique of **free association.** It is one of the keystones of psychoanalytic treatment. The task of free association is more difficult than it may seem. It is something which the patient must learn in the early stages of treatment. During this procedure the analyst is completely passive; the patient is the active contributor to therapy.

The patient at first talks about what appears to be an aimless, directionless stream of topics, but gradually it drifts toward the repressed events that are responsible for the neurosis. When this trend begins, the first of the many problems for the analyst, **resistance,** appears. Psychoanalysis assumes that conflicts and unpleasant events responsible for neuroses are repressed, and that **repression** is a protective device, keeping these events out of the individual's awareness. Repression is not easily abandoned and, as free associations begin to touch upon the repressed material, various things may happen to keep the repressed ideas from being brought to consciousness. A dream may appear with latent content that reveals the resistance, or the patient may say that there are no thoughts, that the mind is a blank, or that the content of thought is too foolish or too meaningless to record. Or a flood of associations may appear, all quite irrelevant but not quite "free," since they are designed to avoid the distressing areas.

Assured that the analyst is interested in everything that comes to mind, the patient may forget appointments—and be charged for the missed session in recognition of the dynamics of such behavior—or begin to feel that the therapy is getting nowhere and should be discontinued. Actually, the opposite is true. The patient is getting too close to repressed material for comfort, and these defenses are designed to prevent the exposure of ego-threatening material.

The transference relationship In psychoanalytic theory it is essential to the therapeutic process that the individual recall and relive the events behind the personality disorder in all their emotional intensity. Thus it is critical that the resistance to such revelation be

The silence of the psychoanalyst acts as a screen on which the young man can project a free flow of thought.

overcome. The most powerful ally of the therapist in this and other phases of analysis is **transference.** This term is used in various therapies and has come to have several meanings, all referring to the therapeutic relationship. In a general sense it refers to the warmth or rapport that exists between patient and therapist. In psychoanalysis it has the more specific meaning of a repetition of past relationships that the patient introduces into the therapeutic relationship, called the **transference neurosis.** By the mechanism of transference the analyst comes to represent an important figure in the person's early life. The emotions originally directed at that figure are now turned toward the analyst. Early in treatment at least, these emotions are most often love responses that were originally directed toward a parent. In **positive transference** the patient unconsciously seeks to recapture the past and to relive it, but with a more satisfactory resolution than had been encountered in childhood.

Since the therapist will not go along with such neurotic behavior, the person is once again doomed to disappointment. As a result the patient's attitude toward the therapist may shift from affection and admiration to one of anger and derogation, called **negative transference.** This marks a critical point in therapy, for here the interpretation of such behavior can reveal to the patient that the repetitive neurotic pattern he or she brings to all relationships originated in unresolved emotional conflicts of childhood. The therapist seeks to analyze these reactions, trying to make clear that the patient's emotions are related to infantile reactions and repressions. The growing awareness and acceptance of these interpretations and a conscious redirecting of attitudes and views toward the self and others are the important elements in the restructuring of personality.

With the interpretation and resolution of the transference neurosis, the analysis begins to move toward its final stages. It is important to understand that neither this interpretation nor others are offered until the analyst is confident that the patient is ready to receive them. Initially the analyst may concentrate on showing connections among certain areas of the patient's verbalizations. Later the interpretations may become more specific, with the analyst indicating how certain dynamic conflicts are being reflected in behavior. At certain points it may be necessary for the therapist to interpret the patient's resistance to facing these contents. The process is a gradual one in which the person "works through" the materials and the interpretations. There is no sudden blossoming of insight and no spontaneous, miraculous "cure," as is so often suggested in a Hollywood movie. The same contents may reappear, resistances may show a type of spontaneous recovery, and interpretations, although previously accepted, may have to be offered again and again. But in a successful analysis the individual moves toward awareness and understanding. Often symptoms are reduced, but sometimes, curiously enough, they remain unmodified during treatment.

The benefit derived from psychoanalysis seems to come about through an emotional catharsis or **abreaction** produced by reliving the traumatic experiences responsible for the patient's maladjustment. This catharsis takes place in a setting in which the therapist is neither disapproving nor distressed by the patient's innermost thoughts. There is a readjustive or reeducative process which gives the patient new responses to replace the neurotic ones.

Client-Centered Therapy In **client-centered** or **nondirective therapy,** as introduced by its founder, Carl Rogers, the stress is on the process of reeducation. The approach is termed nondirective because it leaves responsibility for working a problem through largely up to the client. It is more often used with relatively minor maladjustments. The client-centered procedure consists of a series of interviews in which the therapist's major role is to convey warm support and a sense of unconditional positive regard. (1) The therapist tries to understand what the client—nondirective therapists uniformly prefer the word "client" to "patient"—is trying to communicate and to convey an understanding of the content and feeling that is being expressed. (2) The therapist makes an effort to synthesize what the client has been saying. (3) The therapist accepts what the client says and feels and tries to make the client aware not only of this acceptance but also of the therapist's confidence in the client's ability to deal with his or her problem. In nondirective therapy the counselor accepts, restates, and clarifies the client's statements—and sometimes does little more.

There are also a number of things the therapist does *not* do in nondirective therapy. There is no interpretation of the client's behavior or any effort to promote insight. There is no attempt to offer advice, praise, or blame. The therapist does not probe or explore areas, even those of importance. Unconscious motivation is ignored, and techniques to elicit it such as dream interpretation and free association are not used by the nondirective counselor. The nondirective therapist sees no necessity to have a diagnosis before treatment. In the course of a series of interviews, the clients gradually develop their own insights. They come to accept their problems as something to be faced and handled. At this point it is possible for the individual to begin to work out some positive steps to correct the situation and to make the first tentative gestures in the direction of better adjustment and greater self-sufficiency.

Rogers and his followers have made a major contribution to a scientific analysis of the process of therapy. In their studies, they have observed that characteristic trends take place. For example, analysis of verbatim protocols indicates that the most marked changes occur in the client's self-concept. Negatively toned references to the self give way to more positive evaluations; attitudes of self-esteem and self-regard are generated in later therapy sessions, at least in successful cases. Even more important, clients begin to act on these revised self-perceptions, which Rogers believes is the nub of the therapeutic interchange.

As a therapeutic school the nondirective technique reached its zenith in the mid-1950s. Since that time there has been a marked decline in the use of the method among psychologists. But nondirective therapy has left its impact on psychologists for a number of reasons. For one thing, the Rogerians sparked systematic research into therapeutic processes at a time when the contents of therapy were viewed as sacrosanct. In doing so, they proved that a therapist could be both a responsible and a research-minded clinician. For another, the technique emphasized counseling and therefore came to be used in counseling services in colleges and universities. In this sense Rogers influenced such services to become more therapeutic in their orientation to student problems.

SUMMARY □

Somatic therapies for the mental disorders are drugs, brain surgery, and electroconvulsive shock therapy (ECT). Drugs are the most widely used of these therapies. Powerful beneficial effects of drugs have been demonstrated, particularly of chlorpromazine, but placebo effects complicate research on the effectiveness of drugs. Recently it has been demonstrated that placebo effects alleviate some symptoms but not others.

Psychosurgery is rarely used today. It, along with ECT, has been subjected to strong criticism on moral grounds. Such objections must be evaluated against the demonstrated beneficial effects of ECT when used to relieve certain forms of severe depression.

Psychoanalysis is the respected elder in the family of the psychotherapies. Its fundamental aim is to make unconscious conflicts conscious and thus bring irrational neurotic behavior under rational and constructive control. To this end, the psychoanalyst over an extended period of time uses the transference neurosis to demonstrate the patient's tendency to foist onto people in the present the qualities of important figures of the past who were involved in the development of the neurosis. During treatment the patient may come to view the therapist as one of these past figures, in the hope this time of achieving satisfactions denied in the past. The therapist counters by utilizing such transference to help the patient understand these early conflicts and the disturbance wrought when he or she try to carry them into adulthood. Before this goal can be achieved, however, powerful resistances to such content must be overcome through the analysis of free associations, dreams, fantasies, slips of the tongue, and other symbolic acts that betray the presence of the unconscious.

An outgrowth of humanistic psychology, client-centered, or nondirective, therapy attempts to understand a client's problems, to clarify them, and to help the client work them through. Interpretation and advice are avoided; everything is left up to the resources of the client. A major contribution of nondirective therapy has been a demonstration that the therapeutic process is amenable to research.

BEHAVIOR THERAPIES

> In behavioral research, theoretical advances by some of the world's greatest experimental psychologists have led to new therapeutic techniques. The techniques of behavior therapy and behavior modification have exercised a profound influence in our capacity to treat a wide-ranging set of disordered behaviors: obesity and anorexia; the addictive disorders involving drugs, alcohol, and tobacco; sexual aberrations; obsessive-compulsive neuroses; psychosomatic disturbances; severe phobias and anxiety states; delinquent behavior in the classroom; social incompetence of schizophrenics; severe depression; self-injurious behavior in institutional settings; biopsychological feedback treatments of various somatic disorders; . . . learning disability and hyperactivity due to attentional dyscontrol in children (*Report of the Research Task Panel of the President's Commission on Mental Health,* 1978, p. 1536).

Behavior therapy is the most significant and far-reaching development in psychotherapy in recent decades. Beginning in the 1960s, clinical and experimental psychologists joined by a small band of behaviorially minded psychiatrists set out to modify various forms of behavior disorder by applying the principles of classical and operant conditioning. This revolution in therapy was exclusively psychological in its origins, for its basis lay in a history of laboratory research and theory in the field of learning that extended back to the beginning of the century.

The basic belief of the first wave of behavior therapists was that neurotic behavior stemmed from learning experiences in which responses that were initially acquired as a means of avoiding anxiety subsequently developed into persistent and inflexible habits. Since the aim of both psychotherapy and learning is to produce behavioral change, this commonality suggested that the techniques of classical and instrumental conditioning could be used to help maladjusted people to acquire more adaptive behavior and to extinguish their older, maladaptive habits.

The behavior therapist rejected the psychoanalytic doctrine that the primary task of therapy was to unmask the causes of symptoms as manifestations of unconscious conflicts that required identification and resolution. One leading figure provided a declaration of independence of brevity and force: *"There is no neurosis that underlies a symptom, but merely the symptom itself. Get rid of the symptom and you have eliminated the neurosis!"*

We can sense in this declaration the view that there was no need to search for the roots of disorder in childhood trauma, no necessity for dream interpretation or free association to escape the bonds of repression, no two to five years of tenure on a psychoanalytic couch. The task to be accomplished was to effect change, through learning principles, in disturbing habits that others called symptoms.

In the 1970s behavior therapists have ceased to rely exclusively on the methods of classical and operant conditioning to effect change. They have begun to incorporate procedures designed to help clients understand how certain thoughts and beliefs that they harbor about themselves and others and their problems add to their distress. The goal of these *cognitive behavior therapists* is to help individuals to make more realistic appraisals and evaluations of their experiences, their expectations, and the consequences that stem from their beliefs.

Behavior Therapy Based on Classical Conditioning

Systematic Desensitization In 1958 Joseph Wolpe, a psychiatrist, reported experiments in which he had induced experimental neurosis in cats by shocking them for food-approach behavior in an experimental cage. He then tried to overcome the neurosis by therapy. His technique involved *counterconditioning,* in which the principal element was to get the cats to feed in the presence of stimuli which only minimally evoked distress and then gradually to expose the animal to stimuli which formerly had aroused greater and greater intensities of anxiety.

This was Wolpe's principle of **reciprocal inhibition,** and it consisted of the following components. (1) In the presence of anxiety-evoking stimuli provide a means whereby (2) a response antagonistic to anxiety can be made, so that (3) the anxiety response is suppressed resulting in (4) a weakening of the bond between these stimuli and the anxiety responses which they have produced in the past.

Because the procedure involved a systematic method of *desensitizing* the organism to situations that aroused anxiety, the therapeutic method was called **systematic desensitization.** The therapy was performed according to a certain set technique. First, the therapist had to know the specific stimulus events that triggered the person's anxiety. With an anxious

Joseph Wolpe.

person, one had to know exactly what situations the client feared and how intense these fears were. There could be no guessing about this; the person who came for treatment had to spell out the stimuli that created fear. This, then, became the first step in the treatment process: requiring the client to list in rank order a hierarchy of stimuli to which he or she responded with ever-increasing degrees of anxiety.

The second step was to train the person to make a response incompatible with anxiety whenever these stimuli were present. Wolpe decided that the response would be deep relaxation, and he set about to train patients in how to achieve it. Subsequently sexual responses and assertive responses have also been used successfully as incompatible responses. The third step was to join the feared stimuli in the hierarchy with the incompatible response of relaxation. This last step is the heart of the procedure of desensitization. The patient in the treatment room must first relax deeply and then imagine the situations that are feared. Wolpe has the patient begin with an image of the least threatening situation. Being already relaxed, the patient responds to the image with relaxation rather than tension. In this way he or she gradually extinguishes the anxiety with which the imagined event had been associated. The important factor is for the client to begin with the most weakly feared event or object and in subsequent therapy sessions to move up the hierarchy gradually, visualizing and extinguishing in turn the stronger and more feared stimuli.

Table 19.2 lists one college student's **anxiety hierarchy** over being tested. The hierarchy has two components; one is the type of test feared and the other is the closeness in time to having to take a test. The fear ratings given by the student on two separate occasions appear in the left-hand columns. Two things are notable, the reliability of subjective judgments and the preciseness of item descriptions. The latter requires the therapist to be a sophisticated interviewer with good clinical skills. Expressed in another way, systematic desensitization is not a simple-minded technique that can be performed by just any believer in behavior therapy. Carelessness in creating a hierarchy can result not only in a treatment failure but in heightened anxiety for the client.

If the client begins to feel anxiety as a scene is visualized, then imagery is to cease, the person is asked to relax, and a pleasant scene is then substituted. If fear does not occur, visualization is continued for 10 to 15 seconds followed by 15 to 30 seconds of relaxation. The scene may be repeated for two or three trials and then the next item in the hierarchy is presented. If fear is aroused, a less disturbing stimulus is repeated, then the distressing item until its anxiety-arousing properties have been extinguished.

Although Wolpe interpreted the mechanism at work in systematic desensitization to be counterconditioning, it is not at all clear that approach to a feared stimulus becomes possible because the response competition of relaxation gradually supplants anxiety. The effect, it has been argued, may be produced primarily by the exposure of a person to a feared stimulus. It is the successful victory over one's fear that may be the major factor facilitating extinction of the anxiety and avoidance behavior.

The Effectiveness of Desensitization One of the best comparative studies of the effectiveness of desensitization procedures was performed as a doctoral study by Gordon Paul, who was soon to conduct the decade-long mental hospital study of social-learning–milieu therapy described earlier. Paul (1966) chose five carefully matched groups of college students who shared a strong fear of public speaking. These "clients" were assigned to one of five treatment programs: (1) *insight-oriented psychotherapy,* traditional interviewing aimed at the development of insight into the basis of the problem; (2) *systematic desensitization,* in which the hierarchy for anxiety aroused by public performance was graded; (3) *attention-placebo,* a "pseudotherapy" consisting of attention from a therapist plus prescription of a placebo

TABLE 19.2
A Mixed Desensitization Hierarchy for Test Anxiety in a College Student

First Fear Ratings	Second Fear Ratings	Anxiety Hierarchy Items
0	0	Beginning a new course
15	10	Hearing an instructor announce a small quiz two weeks hence
20	25	Having a professor urge you personally to do well on an exam
35	40	Trying to decide how to study for an exam
40	45	Reviewing the material you know should be studied, listing study to do
60	50	Hearing an instructor remind the class of a quiz one week hence
60	65	Hearing an instructor announce a major exam in three weeks and its importance
75	75	Hearing an instructor announce a major exam in one week
80	70	Standing alone in the hall before an exam
80	80	Getting an exam back in class
80	80	Anticipating getting back a graded exam later that day
80	85	Talking to several students about an exam right before taking it
90	85	Studying with fellow students several days before an exam
90	90	Hearing some "pearls" from another student which you doubt you'll remember, while studying in a group
90	90	Cramming while alone in the library right before an exam
90	95	Thinking about not keeping up in other subjects while preparing for an exam
95	95	Talking with several students about an exam immediately after taking it
100	100	Thinking about being generally inadequately prepared
100	100	Thinking about not being adequately prepared for a particular exam
100	100	Studying the night before a big exam

Ratings: 0 = "totally relaxed"; 100 = "as tense as you ever are."
From Kanfer and Phillips, 1970.

described as a "fast-acting tranquilizer." This third treatment also included participation in a task described as stressful and anxiety-inducing, one which would reduce anxiety once the client had learned to cope with it. Actually the task also involved fakery, since experience had shown that it not only failed to arouse anxiety but actually made some people drowsy. Two no-treatment control groups were also used. To control for therapist differences all therapists administered all forms of therapy.

Each person who received therapy delivered a pretreatment test speech and then entered into a series of five hours of individual therapy extending over a period of six weeks. At the end of that time, a post-treatment test speech was also required of them. One pattern of results—observable manifestations of anxiety during test speeches—is presented in Figure 19.5. All measures tended to favor the desensitization group; "attention-placebo" and "insight" students also benefited from their therapy, whereas the no-treatment controls did not benefit at all (Table 19.3).

Implosion Therapy Instead of beginning with the least anxiety-arousing scene in a hierarchy of graded stimuli, this desensitization procedure begins with the most fear-arousing, hair-raising stimulus imaginable in an effort to provide intensive and dramatic extinction. In this technique there is no counterconditioning or relaxation and no hierarchy of stimuli. The model is Pavlovian, and the emphasis is on extinction by

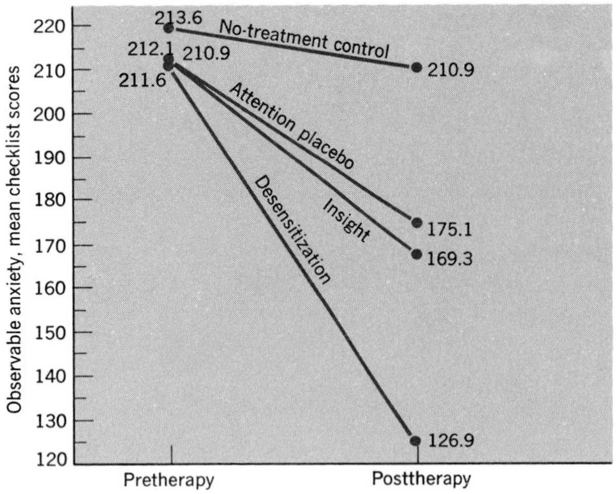

FIGURE 19.5
The effectiveness of three psychotherapies in reducing stage fright. The mean scores for observable signs of anxiety are based on checklist measures obtained when speeches were made before and at the end of psychotherapy. (Data from Paul, 1966; graph adapted from Strupp, 1971.)

presenting the feared CS in the absence of the US. In the view of its founders, Thomas Stampfl and Donald Levis (1967), the most rapid extinction takes place if the stimulus used most closely resembles the stimulus to which anxiety was originally conditioned. The emphasis, therefore, is on "forced reality testing" and therein lies the danger of the technique, for if the anxiety that is generated is so excessive that the client cannot cope with it, the anxiety itself may be exacerbated (Yates, 1970).

If the desensitization involves rapid exposure to a real rather than an imagined stimulus, the method is called **flooding;** the term **implosion** is used for flooding conducted with imaginary stimuli.

In contrast to the desensitization hierarchy for a test-anxious student provided in Table 19.2, Isaac Marks (1978), a well-known British behavioral psychiatrist, describes in his book *Living With Fear* an actual implosion procedure used with a young male student who had failed a previous exam because of an attack of panic. The therapist with the student's collaboration decided to have the client experience his examination anxiety fully without providing an escape from it.

> The student was made to sit up in bed and try to feel his fear. He was asked to imagine all the consequences that would follow his failure—derision from his colleagues, disappointment from his family, and financial loss. At first as he followed the instructions, his sobbings increased. But soon his tremblings ceased. As the effort needed to maintain a vivid imagination increased, the emotion he could summon began to ebb. Within half an hour he was calm. He was instructed to repeatedly experience his fears. Every time he felt a little wave of spontaneous alarm he was not to push it aside but was to enhance and try to experience it more vividly. The patient was intelligent and assiduously practiced his exercises methodically until he became almost unable to feel frightened. He passed his examinations without difficulty (p. 212).

Marks (1972) compared desensitization with flooding in treating chronic phobic hospital patients. Both treatments produced improvement but flooding was more successful. Despite the high level of anxiety arousal it generated, it proved to be a "surprisingly acceptable treatment" to the patients. Anxiety levels that were high in the first session dissipated quickly over subsequent sessions. It is Marks's view, based on years of experience, that rapid prolonged exposure to the feared real-life public situation is the treatment of choice with phobic individuals. It is simply quicker and more effective than using fantasied exposure through the medium of imagery.

Paradoxical Intention The **paradoxical intention** procedure is a variation of flooding. The client is asked to stop fighting his fears and instead to express them openly and even to exaggerate them (Marks,

TABLE 19.3
Proportion of Cases in Various Improvement Categories Following Treatment for Stage Fright

Treatment	*N*	Unimproved	Slightly Improved	Improved	Much Improved
Desensitization	15	0%	0%	14%	86%
Insight	15	7	47	27	0
Attention-Placebo	15	20	33	47	0
No-Treatment Control	29	55	28	17	0

From Paul, 1966.

TABLE 19.4
Four Forms of Behavior Therapy Based on Operant Conditioning Principles

Increasing Desirable Behavior	Decreasing Undesirable Behavior
Positive Reinforcement	*Extinction*
Desirable behavior is followed by the *occurrence* of a positive rewarding event.	Undesirable behavior is followed by the *omission* of a positive rewarding event.
Avoidance Training	*Punishment*
Desirable behavior is followed by *escape* from or *omission* of a painful, noxious event.	Undesirable behavior is followed by the *occurrence* of a painful, noxious event.

1972). For example, a patient who lived in fear of having a heart attack was told by the therapist, "Go ahead. Right now. Try to make your heart go so fast that you will die of a heart attack right on this spot." The patient laughingly said, "Doc I'm trying but I can't do it." With repeated instructions to try to die three times a day, the patient began to supplant fear with laughter. Marks writes,

> In the moment he started laughing at his symptoms and when he became willing to produce them (paradoxically) intentionally, he changed his attitude toward his symptoms . . . [and] interrupted the vicious cycle and strangled the feedback mechanism (p. 179).

The Power of Operant Conditioning

The operant methods help the therapist achieve therapeutic goals. The first is *to strengthen desirable behavior;* to do this the therapist must await its occurrence and then either provide a rewarding event or remove a painful or aversive stimulus. The second is *to decrease an undesirable activity;* to do so the therapist must either fail to provide a desired stimulus or event, by omitting it, or see to it that the negative behavior is followed by an aversive stimulus. These four alternatives for therapist-initiated action are summarized in Table 19.4.

Positive Reinforcement There are four steps in using **positive reinforcement** (Leitenberg, 1972): (1) the behavior to be rewarded must be carefully defined so that reinforcement can follow the appropriate response; (2) there must be clear specification of the reinforcers which are valued by the subject; (3) the situation should be arranged to heighten the likelihood that the desirable behavior will be emitted; (4) the behavior when generated should be maintained by an appropriate reinforcement schedule.

Positive reinforcement has been used to shape the responses of deviant children and adults. For example, psychotic patients whose level of delusional speech has been high have engaged to a greater extent in nondelusional talk when rewarded with tokens for rational speech. The tokens are then exchangeable for television watching time, candy, and so on.

The power of reward training is to be found on a broader and far-reaching scale in the development of token economies. A **token economy** is a broadly based institutionalized program of behavior modification in which all personnel make use of generalized reinforcers, the "tokens," which the client earns for desirable behavior. The tokens may then be exchanged for specific gifts, activities, privileges, goods, or services. Such token economies have now been successfully set up in schools, mental hospitals, clinics, reformatories, homes for the mentally retarded, and other institutional settings. In the token economy teachers, aids, guards, nurses—all persons who are in active contact with the client—are legitimately viewed as "behavioral technicians."

An effort to change the delinquent careers of adolescents by creating just such a token economy in a reformatory has been described in a volume appropriately titled *A New Learning Environment* (Cohen and Filipczak, 1971). In his preface to the book, B. F. Skinner declares the results a potential landmark in penal reform, and they may well be so. The setting was the National Training School (NTS) in Washington, D.C., a "reform school" in which teenage delinquents convicted of crimes ranging from auto and house theft to rape and murder were housed. Most of the youths were school dropouts with no interest in schooling or any sort of an academic training program. The investigators, wedded to behavior modification, set out to change all that by establishing an incentive system in which monetary rewards were given for academic achievement. They succeeded not only in increasing the school achievement of these unlikely candidates but did so at a rate two to four times the average of most public school students in the country.

For one full year the juvenile offenders were allowed to participate in a project that provided a twenty-four-hour-a-day learning environment. Reinforcements in the form of money were paid out to the youths for demonstratable academic competence; in turn, the money could be used to buy gifts, pay for better rooming arrangements (a private room cost $8 per week) or clothing (from the Sears catalog), or admit them to a recreational lounge. If a youth did not want to participate in the project, he could live the life of a typical inmate with the drabness that ordinarily entailed.

If a student was unwilling or unable to pay for his room and board, he went "on relief." He moved to an open area in which there were two double bunks; he had to wear the NTS khaki clothing issue, eat standard NTS meals on a metal tray—with enough points students could dine in more attractive surroundings—and go to bed when lights went out. He could not visit in private rooms or meet with his family in the lounge on visiting days. Nor could he buy showcase items in the store or from the mail order catalogs which were used for more elaborate purchases. Not a single youth voluntarily spent more than four weeks in such a status while the project was in effect.

The inmates who participated were given a special label; they were called Student Educational Researchers. The comprehensive educational program consisted of sixteen courses ranging from the American Revolution to electricity and electronics to remedial training in reading and mathematics. Short-term seminars and courses were added to the curriculum later. Programmed instruction manuals were used in the courses, and a grade of 90 percent or better was required to earn additional points.

There were no long waiting periods to earn such reinforcement, for the course materials were broken down into units with points awarded for the successful completion of each course component. Commendation for successful completion was announced to the entire group, maximizing the rewards that had been achieved. In addition, correctional officers were allowed to give points for exemplary behavior. Gradually this bonus-awarding system was extended to other staff members. But in such a setting material incentives became only a small part of the total reward system. Mutual respect and peer approval also came to play an important role in sustaining the behavior of the youths.

The changes that were observed support the significance of reward training. Social judgment and adjustment improved; the students handled themselves with dignity; vulgarity and violence disappeared; student government began to parallel the structure of a democratic society; the youths even began to dress to please the female staff and their families and guests when they came to visit.

Academically, the students showed marked progress. Achievement test scores rose more than two grade levels over an eight-month period. After eleven months of the program, the average IQ increase was 12.5 points (Figure 19.6). Perhaps of even greater importance, the students stayed out of trouble for some time following discharge. Recidivism during the first year was two thirds less than the average. But by the third year it was near the norm, suggesting the need to carry the structure and the commitment of the project into the world beyond the reformatory's walls.

Extinction The method of **extinction** removes an undesirable response by removing the positively reinforcing stimulus that maintains it. Teodoro Ayllon (1963) reports the case of a forty-seven-year-old chronic female schizophrenic patient who was the bane of the ward's nursing personnel because of three undesirable activities: she stole food, hoarded towels in her room, and insisted on wearing an excessive amount of clothing. To control her food-stealing behavior, the nurses and attendants had in the past coaxed, wheedled, cajoled, and finally forcibly induced the patient to return the food. Ayllon secured the staff's cooperation to discontinue these attentions and had the nursing staff carefully record all such food-stealing episodes over a period of one month. The patient was then assigned to sit alone at a table in the dining hall; whenever she approached another table or attempted to take food from the counter, she was removed from the cafeteria and deprived of her meal. Thus a positive reinforcement, food, was made contingent on the patient's ability to refrain from stealing it. Results of this regimen were dramatic (Figure 19.7). Within two weeks food stealing had ceased; and at the end of fourteen months the patient's weight had satisfactorily declined from 250 to 180 pounds. Over a one-year period following "training," on only three occasions was there subsequent food stealing, and it was rapidly extinguished again by the alert staff.

Aversion Therapy The **aversive therapies** are used when certain self-destructive or acting-out behavior must be brought under rapid control. In instances such as these extinction or the reinforcement of competitive responses may be too time-consuming. But as will become apparent, aversive training techniques raise a critical issue, namely whether it is ethical to use shock or other forms of aversive stimulation in an effort to eliminate an undesirable behavior.

In general, there are three principal methods used in aversion therapy: *classical conditioning,* in which a noxious stimulus is paired with a stimulus that elicits the maladaptive behavior; *punishment,* in which the behavior is followed by the noxious stimulus; and *avoidance training,* in which punishment is avoided if the individual does not engage in the maladaptive behavior.

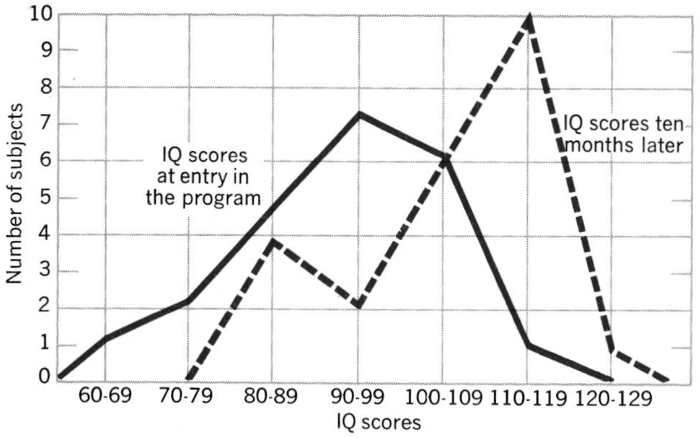

FIGURE 19.6
Effect of a token economy on test IQs of teenage delinquents. The frequency distribution of IQ test scores for twenty-four students had moved upward after ten months of therapy. (From Cohen and Filipczak, 1971.)

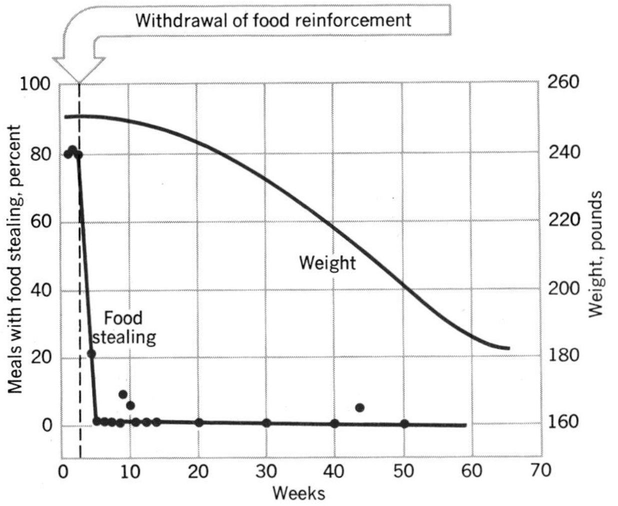

FIGURE 19.7
Successful extinction of food stealing. Food stealing (*lower curve*) disappeared almost as soon as food was withdrawn by sending the woman from the cafeteria whenever she attempted to steal. The dots not on the curve indicate that food stealing recurred on only three occasions. The upper curve indicates the decline in the patient's weight. (Adapted from Aylion, 1963.)

The varieties of aversive stimuli include shock, nauseants, and verbal descriptions of aversive scenes; payment of fines, such as making a "charitable" contribution to a detested organization—the Ku Klux Klan or the American Nazi Party—for weight gain in a weight reduction program; or "time out" from positive reinforcement, for example, removing children to an isolated room for misbehavior (Agras, 1972).

Avoidance training Alcoholism can be treated by **avoidance training**. An alcoholic drink is placed in front of an alcoholic patient with electric shock programmed to follow its presentation ten seconds later. If the patient pushes the drink away, refusing it, the shock is not administered. Presumably by this method of prolonged avoidance conditioning the individual will develop a habit of avoiding alcohol.

An alternative method is to pair cessation of an aversive stimulus with a neutral stimulus in an effort to make that stimulus pleasurable. To increase responsiveness to heterosexual stimuli in individuals with low heterosexual drives, therapists deliver ongoing shocks except when they show their clients scenes of heterosexual activity.

Punishment Administering **punishment** in order to eliminate undesirable behavior is a form of aversion therapy that has been used primarily in alcohol and drug addiction and in cases of markedly deviant sexual behavior.

A typical example of such a treatment and the ethical issue it presents is provided by C. B. Blakemore and his colleagues (1963), who reported a successful attempt to treat a male transvestite.

> The patient was a healthy, intellectually superior thirty-three-year-old with normal primary and secondary sexual characteristics but with a history of transvestitism which extended back to childhood. From the age of twelve he had taken pleasure in dressing as a woman, masturbating while he did so. He obtained further sexual satisfaction by viewing himself in the mirror while dressed in feminine attire. Subsequently, as his sexual preoccupation grew, he began to appear in public dressed as a woman, complete with wig and cosmetics—an act which brought momentary relief from sexual tension. He married—transvestites frequently do—but sexual relations with his wife could only be consummated if he were first permitted to dress in her clothing. His wife's revulsion hastened his search for treatment, which initially took the form of six years of more traditional therapy. When this proved unsuccessful, he appeared at a hospital clinic which had an active behavior therapy program.
>
> There his treatment consisted of standing, facing a full-length mirror, on an electrified grid that permitted electric shocks to be delivered to the soles of his feet through the grid floor. The patient was instructed to begin dressing in his favorite woman's clothing while standing on the grid. Slits had been cut in the feet of his nylon stockings and a metal plate inserted into the soles of his shoes. As he dressed, he received a shock and a buzzer sounded to signal that he should begin to divest himself of his clothing. These stimuli remained on until he had removed his feminine attire. Over 400 such trials were repeated during a six-day span, a procedure the patient found "unpleasant, arduous and stressful." A follow-up six months after treatment indicated that the patient no longer indulged in any

transvestite behavior, nor did he desire to experience this previously satisfying form of sexual outlet.

The extension of punishment procedures to other forms of sexuality—child molestation, sadism and masochism, homosexuality—has aroused strong opposition. Recently, a newspaper carried a story describing aversion therapy with a child molester. In this treatment an electric shock to the forearm followed presentation of slides of a nude boy or male-male sexual activity. This aroused the ire of gay rights activists on a nearby campus. The issue took this form. Gays drew stern parallels between the treatment procedure and Nazi barbarity; the mild electric shock was likened to Hitler's gas chambers and the therapy to concentration camp research. The gay community, confusing the mild electric shock administered to the forearm as an aversive stimulus with the electroconvulsive shock therapy that is administered in mental hospitals, charged that political and social repression were inherent in the procedure. Most of all, the activists were angered by the "peculiar eagerness" of psychiatrists and psychologists to change the sexual orientations of gays.

In a reply to these accusations, the therapist pointed out that a behavior therapist in agreeing to alter a client's sexual interest would do so only if five conditions were met.

1 That the client strongly desires the change and enters the program voluntarily.
2 That the desired behavior change was not ethically objectionable to the therapist.
3 That the psychologist believed that permanent change was feasible, that the therapeutic change could not only be established but maintained.
4 That the short- and long-term results of the therapy would make the client a happier person.
5 That other persons would not be adversely affected by such changes in the client.

Despite these constraints, the ethics of using aversion therapy continue to be debated, for punishment can produce negative effects: it can create disruptive emotional states; generate antipathy toward therapist and treatment; bring on counteraggression; decrease self-esteem; reinforce escape rather than coping behavior. But sometimes people face even more threatening alternatives—prison, disgrace, loss of employment and loved ones, a lifetime of regret and self-condemnation. Such conflicts often lead people to seek help. Should the behavior therapist withhold procedures which could conceivably produce behavior changes that would ensure a sense of greater personal security in clients? That issue is still hotly debated because it seems to involve value judgments by society's majority about different methods of sexual expression.

But if we move away from sexual behavior and ask the question whether we should use punishment techniques to try to save the life of an infant, debate diminishes. This was the question faced by Peter Lang and Barbara Melamed (1969), who were called in for consultation about the treatment of a nine-month-old male infant whose life was seriously endangered by persistent vomiting and chronic ruminative rechewing of the vomitus. The case was unusual because of the extreme youth of the patient and because the conditioning procedure was attempted only after all other physical and psychological treatments had been ruled out or proved unsuccessful.

The infant had been hospitalized three times for persistent vomiting, which began in the fifth month of life, and failure to gain weight. The mother related the onset to a broken ankle she had suffered which forced the family to live with her parents for several weeks. There followed a period of conflict between mother and grandmother over the care of the baby; the parents were also having marital difficulties at this time.

During the infant's hospitalizations all medical tests had proved negative; exploratory surgery had been performed; dietary changes had produced no changes nor had the use of antinauseants. Intensive nursing care to provide security and warmth for the infant was eliminated when it seemed to heighten the baby's anxiety and restlessness. The psychologists were called in as a last resort when the infant's weight had declined to twelve pounds and feeding had to be continued through a nasogastric pump.

After two days of observation, treatment began. It took the form of administering a brief repeated sequence of shocks—one second in duration, one second apart—to the infant's calf whenever he started vomiting after feeding. A tone signal was sounded before shock, as soon as vomiting began, and stopped when vomiting ceased. The pairing of vomiting, signal, and shock was managed by a nurse who observed the infant and signaled when he was beginning to vomit. After two sessions shock was needed only rarely; the infant would cry when he heard the noxious tone, but vomiting would cease. Shock was then administered not just after feeding but whenever the baby vomited during the rest of the day, while he was lying down, playing, or being held. Weight started to increase steadily as soon as treatment began (Figure 19.8). After the last conditioning trial had ended, the mother was reintroduced into the picture and gradually took over the responsibility of feeding and caring for her young son. The infant was discharged from the hospital five days later. On follow-up the infant was eating well and gaining weight, sought attention from others, and was declared to be fully recovered by the family physician. A year later the baby was continuing to thrive, and there was no evidence that another symptom had been substituted for the vomiting.

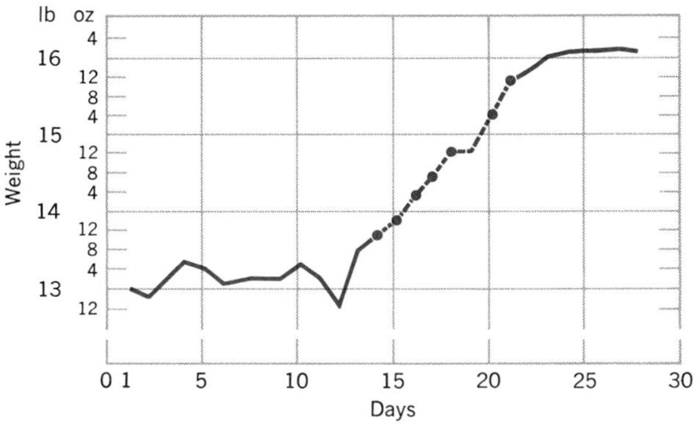

FIGURE 19.8
Changes in body weight of an infant hospitalized and treated for chronic vomiting. Conditioning began on day 13. Dots indicate days on which shock was administered. Notice the weight gain from days 13 to 18. On day 19 the infant started to vomit again. Additional conditioning on days 20 and 21 reinstituted weight gain. (From Lang and Melamed, 1969.)

Rational-Emotive Therapy A Cognitive Approach

Albert Ellis (1962, 1971, 1977), the creator of **rational-emotive therapy** (RET), is one of the pioneering figures in **cognitive behavior therapy.** For Ellis cognition and emotion are closely linked. To control one's thoughts is to provide control over one's emotions. Neurotics are so because they think irrationally, engage in "self-sabotaging" behavior, and either cannot or will not behave more appropriately. RET is a cognitive therapy, as can be seen by looking at what Ellis (1977) has called the ABC's of the method.

First, A represents an *activating* experience or event —you are fired from a job; C represents the emotional and behavioral *consequences* that follow—you can go home, become depressed, and sit around the house, your self-esteem nearing the zero point. Does A cause C? No, says Ellis, because interpolated between A and C is B, your *belief* about A. It is B that causes C—if you loved the job, you are depressed; if you disliked it, you are noncommittal or even relieved. So beliefs are the essential element that gives rise to the irrational views that people have about themselves and the situations they encounter.

Here is a taste of Ellis (1962) as he confronts a patient who has failed to carry out a work assignment which he was given as part of his therapy. The harsh language is designed for its shock value in jolting the patient out of his lethargy.

> If a patient says to me, "You know, I just don't feel like doing the homework assignment you gave me, and I didn't like you for giving it to me, so I just forgot about it," I rarely nondirectively reflect back to him: "So you didn't like the as-

Before aversion therapy the infant was debilitated, his body fat gone and his skin hanging in loose folds. The tape on his face holds the tubing for nasogastric feeding. Thirteen days later, after behavior modification and immediately before discharge, body weight had already increased 26 percent. The child's face had filled out, and his arms and trunk were rounded and substantial.

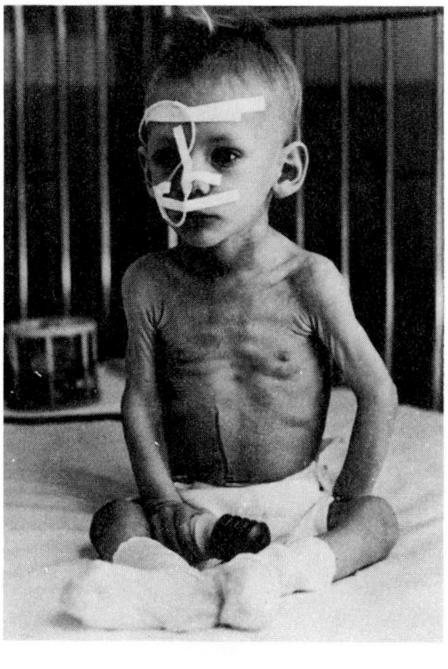

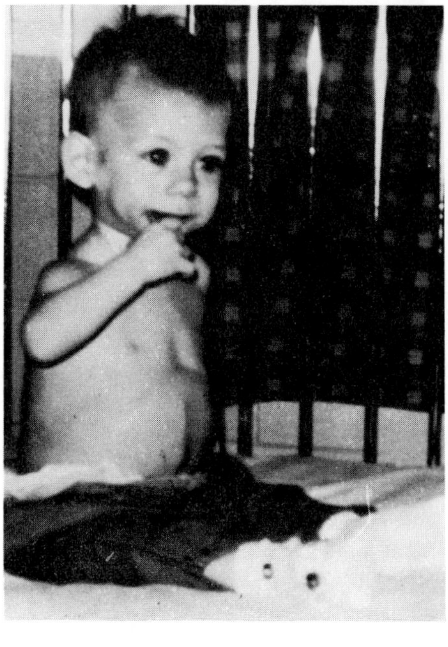

TABLE 19.5

The Rational-Emotive Therapist's View of Some Irrational Beliefs That Create "Neurosis"

Irrational Beliefs	Rational Transformations
1. Individuals must be loved or approved by virtually everyone for the things they do. People should consider what others think of them and depend on others.	1. There is nothing horrible or catastrophic in not being loved by everyone. True self-respect comes not from the approval of others but from liking yourself and following your interest. "What do I want to do in life?" is more important than choosing an action on the basis of what others wish you to do.
2. To be worthwhile people must be thoroughly competent, adequate, and achieving in all respects.	2. This confuses extrinsic and intrinsic values. The principal goal in life consists of discovering what are your own most enjoyable and rewarding interests in life.
3. Human unhappiness has its roots in external events, and people cannot control their sorrows.	3. Unhappiness comes from within and is created by the individual; you therefore must forthrightly face the fact that since you create, you too can eradicate your own unhappiness.

Adapted from Ellis, 1962.

Albert Ellis believes that people are often governed by unreasonable, hidden expectations, such as "I must make everyone like me." He helps patients to search out, admit to, and question these silent sentences.

signment and hated me for giving it to you?" And I often fail to say, in an approved psychoanalytic manner: "What is there about the assignment and about me that you didn't like?"

Rather, I am likely to say: "So you didn't feel like doing the assignment. Tough! Well you're goddam well going to have to do it if you want to overcome the nonsense you keep telling yourself. And you didn't like me for giving you the assignment. Well, I don't give a shit whether you like me or not. We're here not to have a lovey-dovey relationship—and thereby to gratify you for the moment so that you don't have to work to get better—but to convince you that unless you get off your ass and do that assignment I gave you and many equivalent assignments, you're probably going to keep stewing in your own neurotic juices forever. Now when are you going to cut out the crap and do something to help yourself? (p. 198).

In order to change a destructive pattern, Ellis will cajole, attack, lecture, upbraid, direct, suggest, support, criticize, evaluate, and argue during his therapeutic exchanges with patients. He has no hesitancy in contradicting the patient, in denying the validity of his self-defeating behavior, or in combating his illogicalities and demanding that he follow an alternate form of action—all with the professed aim of educating the patient in the direction of developing a new, more positive, better reasoned, and less self-destructive set of beliefs. Several of the irrational ideas that create neurotic disturbances and the rational transformations that Ellis seeks to induce via therapy are listed in Table 19.5.

Ellis's mode for coping directly with the patient's illogicalities in therapy is revealed in the following passage.

> Convincing oneself, if one is a therapist, that the usual concepts of self-worth are illogical and illegitimate and convincing one's patients of this fact are, unfortunately, two different things. I must say that I have had the devil of a time, in recent years, showing many of my clients that they are not as worthless as they think they are. . . I. . . put the onus on them of proving that they are valueless. . .
>
> I, therefore, often say to my patients: "Look, you insist that you are worthless, valueless, and no damn good. Now give me some evidence to prove your hypothesis." Of course they can't. They almost immediately come up with some statement such as: "Well, I am worthless because I'm no good at anything.". . .but as I soon show them, these are tautological sentences which say nothing but: "I am worthless because I consider myself to be worthless". . .
>
> I then go through a whole battery of reasons with these clients which indicate why it is untenable for them to consider themselves worthless. [By the same token, I usually attempt to show them that they (that is, their totality or essence) cannot be legitimately rated at all, but only their many traits, deeds, and performances can be accurately given some kind of rating or worth] (1962, p. 154).

This description captures Ellis's view of how he uses the therapeutic exchange to extinguish an old belief system while reinforcing another. He has called this method **insightful countersuggestion** to describe how he teaches the client to understand the forces that have shaped his or her behavior, thereby providing some degree of control over actions. Such procedures are consistent with the methods used by a new breed of cognitive behavior therapists.

SUMMARY □

The current psychotherapeutic scene has been invigorated by one of the genuine revolutions of our time—behavior therapy. The roots of these new forms of therapy are to be found in the principles of classical and operant conditioning. Their impact is evident in the diversity of conditions to which behavior therapists have turned their attention with results that are impressive. Some of the methods based on classical conditioning include systematic desensitization, flooding and implosion, and paradoxical intention. Others based on operant conditioning principles include positive reinforcement, extinction, avoidance training, and punishment. The second two have raised questions about the ethics of using aversive procedures in therapy. More recent additions to the group of behavior therapies place great emphasis on the client's cognitions, expectations, and problem-solving strategies and are identified as cognitive behavior therapies.

The breadth of the psychotherapies is striking. The nondirective therapy of Rogers and Ellis's rational-emotive therapy provide a contrast that is little less than startling. Where Rogers "accepts," Ellis will "challenge"; where Rogers "reflects and clarifies," Ellis will "cajole, abuse, deny and repel" the patient's illogicalities. Yet both produce change. What Rogers and Ellis share is their attitude of involvement in what is happening to their clients, concern about their distress, and a hopeful optimism regarding their future. Both believe in the potential for growth in their patients; and, if one clarifies while another commands, both provide the reinforcements that sustain those who come for assistance in their first tentative steps toward maturity and self-realization.

THERAPY IN GROUPS

Group Therapy

Individual psychotherapy, the one-to-one confrontation of a client and therapist, is the dominant force in therapeutic practice. In recent years, however, this traditional method of treatment has been challenged by a group of brash newcomers—the group therapies. **Group therapy** came to the fore during World War II when the shortage of therapists available to soldiers who had broken in combat made it necessary to introduce more efficient treatments. That shortage is still in evidence today and, together with the growing expense of individual treatment, has fostered the development of short-term group therapy.

Whatever the forces that impel the growth of group therapy, there is an important justification for the movement. People are social beings. They can exist only marginally when alone. When they experience distress, it is often a product of their relationships with others. If people are to learn new methods of relating to others, what better way is there for them to do so than by using a group as a place to practice and develop the necessary skills? Furthermore, retraining in a group should promote the generalization of adaptive behavior to the social world beyond the treatment setting. Irvin Yalom (1975), one of the nation's leaders in group therapy, sees a more intimate function for group therapy. He observes that "without exception, patients enter group therapy with the history of a highly unsatisfactory experience in their first and most important group—their primary family" (p. 14). An aim of group therapy must be to remove the effects of such experience. To foster the identification with the family, a male-female cotherapist team leads many groups. Group members often assign them the symbolic roles of parents. Members of the group interact with these group leaders and members as they once interacted with parents and siblings. For this reason group therapy invites an enormous number of possibilities for emulating past relationships. Yalom continues,

> There are an infinite variety of patterns: They may be helplessly dependent upon the leaders, whom they imbue with unrealistic knowledge and power; they may defy the leaders at every step because they regard them as individuals who block their autonomous growth or strip them of their individuality; they may attempt to split the cotherapists and to incite disagreements or rivalry between the two; they may compete bitterly with other members in their efforts to accumulate units of attention and caring from the therapists; they may search for allies among the others in an effort to topple the therapists; they may forego their own interests in a seemingly selfless effort to appease or provide for other members (pp. 14-15).

Groups detect such manipulations and group correctives are applied. Behaviors are challenged, new relationships develop, the group encourages different and more adaptive behaviors; a new pattern of social learning is achieved and new social skills are acquired, sometimes through imitation and modeling, sometimes by rapid and personal feedback. Yalom observes that the senior members of a therapy group acquire marked social skills in which they help others, withhold judgments, assist in conflict resolution, and become capable of being empathic and compassionate. Skills such as these go beyond the therapy room and transfer to the social world beyond.

Encounter Groups

Group therapy and **encounter groups** are *not* the same. First, they differ in group composition. Group therapy members often share a common type of maladjustment and a search for common solutions to their problems. Although this may be true of some members of the encounter group, it is certainly not true of most. The orientation of the members of the two groups also differs. Self-disclosure is slow and difficult in group therapy. Encounter groups aim for rapid exposure of themselves and their coparticipants. Moreover, there is greater fragility in a group formed for long-term therapy than in the casual assemblage of strangers in a short-term encounter session. Finally, the group therapist does not move toward emotional intimacy with participating members, whereas the encounter leaders are likely to reinforce members' explorations of the therapists' thoughts and feelings.

Encounter groups have flown under many flags, among them *human relations groups, T-groups, marathon groups, sensory awareness groups,* and *sensitivity groups* (Yalom, 1975). Five years ago the sensitivity training movement could be found on every campus, with itinerant group leaders passing through town holding group sessions in much the way a traveling preacher may have once held an on-the-road revival meeting. Today the peak of the movement seems to have passed. Encounter groups are fewer in part because reports of psychological casualties have dampened the enthusiasm of potential participants (Liberman et al., 1973).

What was the orientation of these encounter groups when they were at the height of their popularity? Typically, stress was placed on intensive encounter as a means of increasing the self-actualization of normal individuals who elected to participate. This emphasis on normality had another facet. Although those who came to such groups were reasonably well-functioning individuals, it was believed that they had erected a facade, an image, that was designed to ward off self-evaluation, while maintaining the regard of their peers. The result was said to be a loss of creative potential, a sense of unfulfillment, a distance between self and others that made social exchanges shallow and not entirely honest.

The encounter group was to undo all this and bring about a new confrontation with the true self. The group would become the champion of honesty and the individual members would come to see that the facade was unnecessary and constricting. To remove the facade and to be willing to describe and elaborate on personal "weaknesses" would bring the group's reward for self-disclosure. Such acceptance would bring in its wake still other disclosures, and thus encounter group participants would abandon their dishonest ways of relating to self and to others. Perhaps there is reason in this stance, but the movement was not to have a chance to find out. A new and dangerous mentality began to evolve in the encounter groups.

> If something is good, more is better. If self-disclosure is good in groups, then total immediate, indiscriminate disclosure in the nude must be better; if involvement is good, then prolonged, continuous, marathon involvement must be better. If expression of feeling is good, then hitting, touching, feeling, kissing, and fornicating must be better. If a group experience is good, then it is good for everyone in all stages of the life cycle, in all life situations. The excesses are often offensive to public taste and may be dangerous to some participants (Yalom, 1975, p. 482).

The failure to protect participants from such excesses led to a rising tide of criticism. Some industrial organizations discontinued the practice of sending their staffs to training groups. Sensitivity training was denounced in the halls of Congress as "brainwashing." Many psychologists began to view the movement with marked misgivings. Some attacked the intrusiveness of the group and the indignity generated by the group's insistence on exposure by its participants. Others pointed to the meaninglessness, the superficiality, and the stereotype of the games and techniques that characterize many encounter sessions. It was on this note that the encounter movement began to lose its momentum and its multitudes.

SUMMARY □

Group therapy meets a need not served by individual psychotherapy. It provides a format for portraying the role of the family, in the interchanges within the group. Sometimes these interactions reflect earlier patterns of members' family interactions. Members of successful therapy groups may detect manipulative behavior and encourage the adoption of new social skills.

One type of group that rose to prominence in the 1960s and now appears to have passed its peak of popularity is the encounter group. Reports of psychological casualties within such groups and other excesses may have dampened the enthusiasm of some advocates.

THE EFFECTIVENESS OF PSYCHOTHERAPY

Research in psychotherapy often begins with a very basic question. Does psychotherapy work? Some psychologists, considering the results of many studies, have taken a pessimistic view, suggesting that, except possibly for behavior therapy, there is little evidence that psychotherapy is effective at all.

One of the strongest critics, Hans Eysenck (1961), reviewed nineteen studies that covered more than 7000 cases seen in psychoanalysis and other types of treatments. Patients were divided into four groups: cured, much improved; improved; slightly improved; unimproved, discontinued treatment, died, and so on. On the basis of his survey, Eysenck reported that only 44 percent of those treated by psychoanalysis showed improvement, whereas 64 percent of those treated by other psychotherapeutic methods and 72 percent of those who received primarily custodial care improved. Eysenck takes a dismal view of the field and concludes that recovery and psychotherapy seem to be inversely related: the more psychotherapy, the lower the recovery rate.

Eysenck's analysis did not go unchallenged. A reappraisal of his analysis by Allen Bergin and Michael Lambert (1978) suggests that Eysenck's original judgments of improvement were far too harsh, and that there are too many differences among the studies cited to permit ready comparison. Types of cases, measures of improvement, and extent of follow-up all varied considerably. In contrast with Eysenck, Bergin finds the results "encouraging" and concludes that the best results of psychotherapy occur with longer and more intense treatment. Psychotherapy, he asserts, has "modestly positive effects" with a larger proportion of studies, cited by Eysenck, reporting favorable outcomes than chance alone would suggest.

Therapists and Clients as Variables

One criticism of many outcome studies has been the use of inexperienced therapists. The importance of this criticism can be seen in an interesting bit of data. Bergin (1971) analyzed fifty-two studies of the effects of therapy and concluded that twenty-two showed positive effects of treatment, fifteen were ambiguous, and fifteen were negative. Significantly, however, in twenty of the twenty-two studies showing positive outcomes the therapy had been conducted by experienced therapists. The success rate was far lower for inexperienced therapists.

Similar problems exist with patients. Some of them, such as schizophrenics, sociopaths, and the brain-damaged, are poor therapeutic risks. Much better are the YAVIS type (Schofield, 1964)—Y(outhful), A(ttractive), V(erbal), I(intelligent), and S(uccessful)—who are highly competent people. Any study of outcome which includes many such individuals is bound to demonstrate the effectiveness of treatment. They routinely profit from therapy.

Here, then, are two sets of factors—variations in the talents of therapists and variations in the likelihood that clients will benefit from therapy. Effectiveness of therapy will depend on the right combination of these two individuals. If that combination is not present, therapy will be unsuccessful. Studies of the outcomes of therapy in which, for the most part, inexperienced therapists have treated poor risks will indicate that therapy has very little effect.

What is the probability of a good therapist–good client match? On the basis of a relatively conservative estimate of the actual fractions involved, Paul Meehl (1965) suggests,

> Now let us suppose that 1/4 represents an upper bound on the proportion of patients currently receiving conventional therapy who are appropriate, and let 1/4 represent an upper bound on the proportion of therapists who are much good at their job. Assuming the essentially random model

The patient ear and understanding of a friend can help a troubled person talk through an emotional problem.

of patient-therapist pairing, the joint probability of a suitable patient getting to a suitable therapist is around .06 (.25 × .25), a very small tail to wag the statistical dog in outcome studies.

Such observations lead one to conclude that to ask whether psychotherapy is effective or ineffective is to ask the wrong question. Future studies of the effectiveness of therapy will undoubtedly ask a more complex question, namely

> *What* treatment, by *whom* is most effective for *this* individual with *that* specific problem, and under *which* set of circumstances (Paul, 1967).

You and Psychotherapy

Three lengthy chapters on behavior pathology and its treatment may cause some concern in students regarding their own mental health. In the case of mental disorder such concerns can easily be brought on by similarities between normal and disordered behavior. This is not to deny that minor and severe maladjustments exist on the college campus, but in the individual case the probabilities always favor health and effectiveness, and the ability to adapt to college life does serve as one criterion of good mental health.

Suppose you are concerned with your psychological state. Does this reflect a morbid attitude on your part? Not necessarily. It may be one of the realistic self-appraisals you make as you move toward maturity. And it may be that you will conclude, after such an appraisal, that you can profit from psychological help. This is not a sign of weakness and it may well be a sign of strength to seek such counsel. If you feel a sense of pervasive unhappiness, a lack of accomplishment, marked self-dissatisfaction, a counseling center on your campus—or a casework agency or a clinic in your community—may help you to achieve greater comfort, self-understanding, and self-acceptance.

For others, help may be found in friendship. Freedom to talk about your feelings and concerns—not indiscriminately but with a trusted friend, relative, or adviser in whom you have confidence—may help you to clarify your situation and see solutions that you might otherwise have missed or misevaluated. This, of course, is the way most people in our society gain help. Psychotherapy at present exists only for the few. The availability of a mature person who will honor your confidences is one alternative that can be helpful.

The advice to rely on friends is one of several suggestions that mental health experts have provided as ways of managing personal problems. These may be self-evident but they may also be helpful.

- Do not hesitate to share your concerns with a trusted and respected person. You can choose a professional, a teacher, a faculty adviser, a friend. It is not a sign of weakness to choose *judiciously* someone with whom to discuss what is troubling you, what your options are, how you might solve the problem you face.
- Be aware that there may not be a present solution to your problem. If it is beyond your control at the moment, live with the problems until you can resolve it.

- Stay away from drugs, alcohol, and those other addictive substances designed to make you forget. You will not forget and you will feel worse in the morning.
- Take care of your physical self. Physical debility and mental disablement go hand in hand.
- Try getting outside yourself. Do things with others or, better yet, try doing some things *for* others. It will serve to boost your self-esteem at a time when such a boost is needed.
- Try to order your priorities. If a number of troubles have hit you simultaneously, tackle the ones that need handling first—after you have thought through what your hierarchy should be.
- Try getting exercise as an outlet for relieving some of the anxiety you feel. A few studies suggest that jogging is psychotherapeutic.
- If you are going to read self-help books, stay away from those whose covers promise to solve all your problems. Self-help books are flooding the market and most of them are worthless. But there are some that have been written by wise people. Browse in the library; compare the credentials of the authors. Avoid the ones that make promises, promises, promises. If there is anything you do not need when you are under stress, it is soft-mindedness and fakery.

Questions Frequently Asked about Psychotherapy

Q: *What sort of qualities should I look for in a therapist?*
A: There is no universal set of desirable attributes. What is important is the relationship you develop with the therapist. It helps to know, however, that certain characteristics go with successful therapy: a solid level of experience, evident skills, a quality of empathy, similarities in values, attitudes, and interests with your own.

Q: *Who is most likely to benefit from psychotherapy?*
A: The person who is highly motivated to change, who has had a previous history of achievement, who is competent in terms of work, social, and sexual history, and who has the good fortune to secure an able, experienced, empathic therapist.

Q: *Can people be injured by therapy?*
A: There are reports of what have been called "deterioration effects" or "negative effects" (Strupp et al., 1977). Some clients worsen with therapy. Those who do are more fragile and disturbed to begin with and are made more vulnerable by the ministrations of inept, careless, or primitive clinicians. There are some forms of therapy that foster "leave-taking" by clients. These include flooding, implosive therapy, and aversive conditioning. There have been unfortunate reports of the development of depression in some phobics treated by desensitization. More traditional approaches in the hands of a competent, experienced therapist generally show positive effects (Bergin and Lambert, 1978).

Q: *Is one type of therapy superior to another?*
A: There is virtually no evidence of the superiority of any one traditional school of psychotherapy over another traditional school. Behavior therapy has the best track record.

Q: *Are there any things I should watch out for?*
A: Yes, never pay much attention to therapists who advertise in the media. The shoddier the newspaper or magazine in which the advertisement appears, the more cautious you should be. Never join an encounter group impulsively. Beware of a group that is given to excessive bullying of its members, seeks to exploit specific individuals, uses jargon, or overinterprets the behavior of its participants.

SUMMARY □

Evaluations of the effectiveness of psychotherapy have sometimes been very negative, seeming to show that these procedures have an impact that is either nil or negative. Reevaluations of the bases of these conclusions reveal that they have not taken into account an essential condition for successful therapy, securing an appropriate combination of client and therapist.

The chapter ends with a brief discussion of the options that are open to a student in need of psychological help. The most important point we make is that the need for such help is nothing to be ashamed of. Almost everyone has problems now and then.

TO MAKE SURE YOU UNDERSTAND THIS CHAPTER △

Here is a list of the most important concepts in this chapter. You should be able to define these terms and state the points made about each in the text discussion.

Good premorbid schizophrenic
Poor premorbid schizophrenic
Expressed emotionality (EE)
Milieu therapy
Social-learning therapy
Somatic or physical therapy
Psychotherapy
Electroconvulsive shock therapy (ECT)
Psychosurgery
Lobotomy
Phenothiazines
Tardive dyskinesia
Placebo effect
Psychoanalysis
Free association
Resistance
Repression
Transference
Transference neurosis
Positive transference
Negative transference
Abreaction
Client-centered (nondirective) therapy
Behavior therapy
Reciprocal inhibition
Systematic desensitization
Anxiety hierarchy
Implosion therapy
Flooding
Paradoxical intention
Positive reinforcement
Token economy
Extinction
Aversion therapy
Avoidance training
Punishment
Encounter group
YAVIS type
Insightful countersuggestion
Rational-emotive therapy (RET)
Cognitive behavior therapy
Group therapy

TO GO BEYOND THIS CHAPTER △

In this book A rereading of Chapter 6 should be helpful in understanding the basic processes of behavior therapy. The section on punishment in Chapter 14 will help you understand aversive therapy. The theories underlying a number of other therapies—reward training, social-learning therapy, the token economy, psychoanalysis, and Rogerian therapy—are given in Chapter 16. Chapters 17 and 18 on psychopathology obviously link strongly to treatment and therapy.

Elsewhere The crisis in state mental hospital systems is described by Paul Ahmed and Stanley Plog in *State Mental Hospitals: What Happens When They Close. The Mental Health Industry,* by Peter Magaro and others, treats the same and related problems.

For an overview of thirteen different psychotherapies, see Raymond Corsini's *Current Psychotherapies.* Innovative therapies, some significant, others not, are covered in a paperback by Robert Harper, *The New Psychotherapies.* As for specific forms of therapy described in this chapter, we recommend these books: Karl Menninger and Philip Holzman, *Theory of Psychoanalytic Technique;* Albert Ellis, *Humanistic Psychotherapy;* Carl Rogers, *On Becoming a Person;* David Rimm and John Masters, *Behavior Therapy;* Irvin Yalom, *The Theory and Practice of Group Psychotherapy;* and M. A. Lieberman and others, *Encounter Groups: First Facts.*

If you seek assistance for yourself or others, these books may be helpful: Isaac Marks, *Living with Fear;* Joel Kovel, *A Complete Guide to Therapy;* and Clara Park and Leon Shapiro, *You Are Not Alone.*

Statistical Appendix

H. G. Wells once described the importance of statistics this way: "Statistical thinking will one day be as necessary for efficient citizenship as the ability to read and write." For all of us Wells's "one day" appears to be near at hand; for psychology it arrived a long time ago. Most of psychology is an inexact science at best. In such a discipline, which must muster and make sense of ill-assorted materials, the methods of statistics are the most important tools available, because they provide the means of dealing with imprecision and uncertainty.

In psychology statistical methods serve two basic purposes. (1) They offer efficient ways of describing sets of data. (2) They make it possible to evaluate the confidence that can be placed on data and to draw general conclusions from limited information. **Descriptive** and **inferential** statistics, named for these uses, are the subjects of this appendix. We hope that the presentation will demonstrate three things. (1) Statistics has some very useful things to say and clarifies important issues. (2) Statistics is more a way of reasoning than a branch of mathematics. (3) There is nothing very difficult about the subject. The presentation of whatever we need to know, in an elementary introduction to the topic, requires only grade school arithmetic.

DESCRIPTIVE STATISTICS

Benjamin Disraeli's and Fiorello LaGuardia's views of statistics were different from that of Wells. LaGuardia claimed that "Statistics are like psychiatrists—they will testify for either side." Disraeli was more unkind; he insisted that "There are three kinds of lies: lies, damned lies, and statistics." LaGuardia and Disraeli were talking about problems raised by descriptive statistics. In its most common meaning, to lie is to misrepresent the facts in some situation, or to describe them incorrectly, with intent to deceive. Descriptive statistics are especially subject to misrepresentation, but the distortion of truth may come either through innocent misunderstanding or through deliberate trickery. The materials in this section will include examples of both these mishaps in usage.

Incidence and Frequency

In everyday life the statistics we encounter most often are rates of the occurrences of things. Crime rates, rates of automobile accidents, and rates of unemployment are all vital pieces of information. Psychology provides comparable statistics. Fifteen percent of the American public are overweight. Ten percent of the population have some form of mental disturbance. Two percent of the children in school stutter. Every thirty minutes someone in America commits suicide. The rate of mental illness throughout the world has been relatively stable for fifty years. One out of every twenty adults is an alcoholic.

All statistical statements of this type share a particular problem. The rate referred to will go up or down, depending on how other terms that contribute to the determination of the rate are defined. Take the last case as an example. The frequency of alcohol abuse increases with age. To make the rate of alcoholism higher or lower, we need only raise or lower the age that defines adulthood. The definition of alcoholism adds to the problem. If having been drunk once is considered alcoholism, the rate will be very high indeed—even if we ignore the subsidiary problem of how being drunk is defined. If only people whose problems with alcohol have required medical or psychological help are considered alcoholics, the rate of alcoholism is considerably lower. Obviously it will often be important to give close attention to the meaning of the terms employed when making statements about the rate at which phenomena occur.

Trends in Data

Measures of the type we have been discussing often change with time or with other conditions. Frequently such materials are presented graphically. You have already discovered that psychology uses this mode of presentation frequently. With the aid of an example, we shall use this section to make some points about the use and misuse of graphs.

The example, which will be important to readers of this book, concerns apparent trends in the intellectual caliber of students coming to college. Measured by such instruments as the Scholastic Aptitude Test (SAT), which most students take before admission to college, it is declining. Figure A.1 depicts this widely discussed trend. The horizontal axis, the **abscissa** of the graph, represents the years 1969 through 1977. The vertical axis, the **ordinate,** is the average SAT score. This graphic presentation makes its sad point eloquently.

Lies! Damn Lies! The first question to ask about the decline in SAT scores shown in Figure A.1 is whether it is big enough to worry about. The answer to this question is "Yes," for reasons that you will understand better after you have read the rest of this appendix. The decline is about a third of a standard deviation of these scores, and that is a large decline.

In the meantime it is worth noting that the decline can be made to *seem* large or small by some simple graphic trickery. Figure A.2 will show you how to perform such statistical magic, or how to expose it for what it is, depending on your purposes. The top half of the figure makes the decline all but disappear by

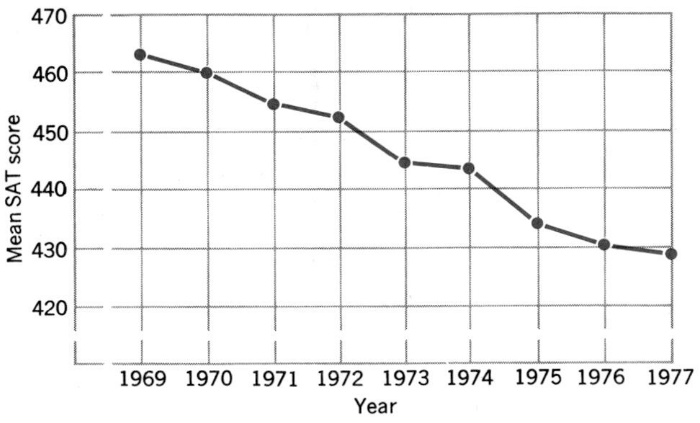

FIGURE A.1
Nine-year trend in SAT scores.

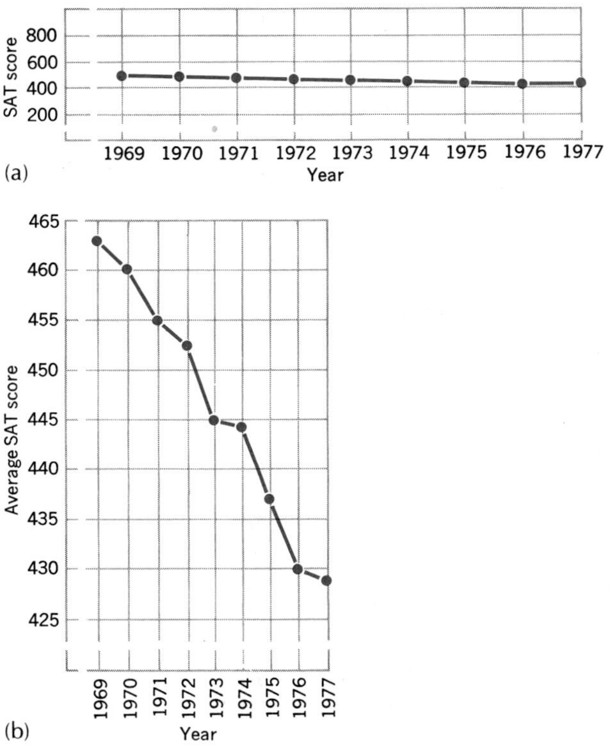

FIGURE A.2
Figures don't lie but liars sometimes figure. The significant decline in SAT scores over the years (*a*) can be made to disappear, or (*b*) it can be exaggerated by manipulation of axes.

compressing the ordinate. The bottom half of the figure is what Darell Huff (1954) calls a "gee-whiz graph" in his book *How To Lie with Statistics*. Expanding the ordinate exaggerates the decline unrealistically.

Searching for Explanations The second question to ask about the decline in SAT scores is the most important question, "Why?" Several answers have appeared in the newspapers, including one from which we wish to dissociate ourselves immediately. According to this explanation, SAT scores are diminishing because of liberalized sexual mores and too much sex in the younger generation. There is absolutely no evidence to support such an interpretation. Other explanations have pointed the finger of blame at our national addiction to television, the deteriorating quality of secondary education, and the selection of the students whose scores have been studied. The last possible interpretation goes something like this. Most of the students who took the SAT test earlier, when it was first developed, were applying to the Ivy League colleges and other highly selective institutions. The more recent scores are those of an increasingly more heterogeneous group of applicants to a group of much less selective institutions. On the average, these students are less able and, as the proportion of them increases, the average SAT score declines.

Which explanation is correct? Unfortunately for those who seek simple answers, probably all of them —except for the one blaming too much sex. This is the typical state of affairs in psychology. Any important psychological fact has many causes. A crude way to make the point is to warn you that, if you will show us a person who advocates any pat and simple answer to important questions about behavior, we will show you a fraud.

Frequency Distributions

A graphical representation of data that is basic to a number of statistical concepts is the frequency distribution. We shall begin with an example. The scores below were obtained by a hundred college students on a twenty-one-item test.

19	16	18	19	12	18	15	15	15	14
16	13	15	15	13	15	14	19	20	18
14	15	17	16	18	19	18	16	10	19
15	11	20	14	13	12	19	13	18	15
13	16	13	16	21	16	16	16	14	13
18	12	19	18	15	11	13	17	15	15
17	19	17	13	14	17	20	18	19	18
21	17	14	16	16	16	17	17	16	17
16	18	17	16	19	16	11	14	17	16
19	14	16	17	12	17	15	15	17	18

Because of the large number of scores in this array, it is difficult to get an accurate grasp of them. A cursory glance tells us that the scores vary somewhat and that the typical student probably made a score of 15, 16, or 17. For many purposes, however, these statements are not precise enough. One way of bringing greater clarity to such collections of numbers is to put them into a **frequency distribution,** which presents the data graphically. In Figure A.3*a*, one version of a frequency distribution, the range of test scores has been marked off on the horizontal axis from low to high. Then single x's for each of the hundred scores have been put above the proper numbers. The graph thus

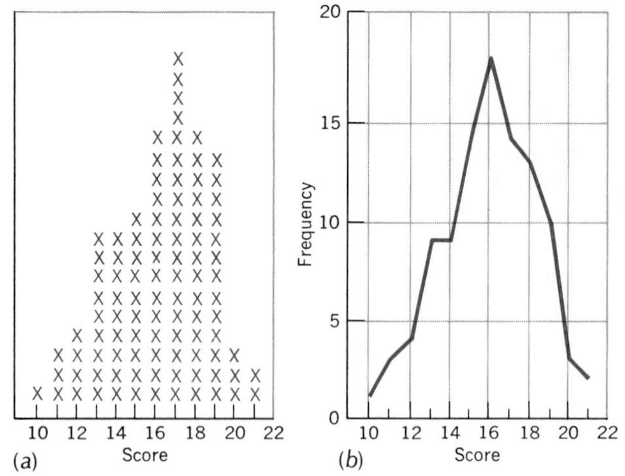

FIGURE A.3

Two forms of frequency distribution. (*a*) An x indicates the performance of each individual. Such figures are never actually used because they are tedious to construct. (*b*) A frequency polygon employs points and lines to present the same data. Notice that a scale has been added on the ordinate.

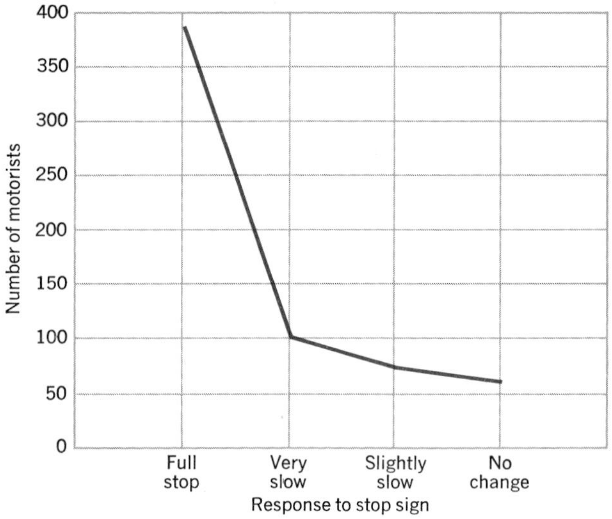

FIGURE A.4

A J-curve. This frequency distribution shows the number of motorists behaving in different ways at a stop sign. The experimenters sat in a parked car at an intersection and observed the motorists' reactions. Most of them came to a full stop.

shows us in a detailed way how the students distribute themselves by their scores. A more common frequency distribution is presented in Figure A.3*b*. This figure is a **frequency polygon.** The horizontal axis is the same as in Figure A.3*a*, but here a vertical axis has been added. And, instead of counting x's, we simply refer to this vertical axis to read the number of individuals who made a particular score.

Measures of Central Tendency

The shape of the graphs in Figure A.3 indicates that these scores tend to pile up in the middle of the distribution. This is typical of most psychological and biological data. Several different measures can be used as an index of this clustering or central tendency, but three of them are very common. Two of these measures can be determined by inspecting the set of data in Figure A.3. The third you already know about. The first and easiest number to determine is the **mode.** In Figure A.3 you will find that the most frequent score is 17. The mode of this distribution is 17. The mode is the most frequent score in a given distribution.

The second single number representative of the distribution and its clustering is the **median,** or the middle score. The scores of the distribution must be ordered by rank to determine the median. The middle score in Figure A.3 would fall between the fiftieth and fifty-first, since there are a hundred of them. If you count the x's in Figure A.3*a* from either end of the distribution, you will find that the median falls at the score of 16.

The third representative number, the **mean,** is the familiar arithmetical average. It is obtained by adding up all the scores and dividing by the number of scores. The mean of the test scores is 15.97, a value very close to those previously obtained for the mode and median.

Symmetry and Skewness

To be useful, any measure of central tendency should indicate the typical. Depending on the situation, and the shape of the frequency distribution, different measures of central tendency are differentially useful. The distributions of scores in Figure A.3 were symmetrical; that is, there were just about as many below the mean as there were above it. In such distributions the mode, mean, and median will have nearly the same value; they all describe the central tendency of the distribution quite well. For distributions that are not completely symmetrical but not remarkably asymmetrical either, the mean is the most useful measure of central tendency because it is familiar to everyone and it also allows other statistical manipulations.

In other situations one of the other measures of central tendency may be more appropriate. Let us start with an extreme case, the behavior of the American motorist at stop signs. The motorist will come to a full stop, decelerate to a very slow speed, slow down only slightly, or keep going at the same speed. These four categories of behavior, ranging from "full stop" to "no change in speed," can be arranged along the abscissa, the number of motorists falling into each category along the ordinate (Figure A.4). The resulting curve is sometimes called a **J-curve.** Although some

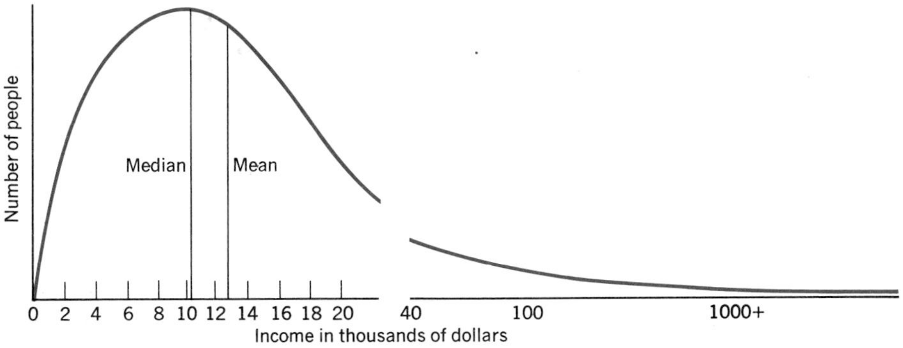

FIGURE A.5
Taxable income in the United States. Points on the abscissa are placed arbitrarily after $20,000. Median and mean have been indicated to show their relationship in a positively skewed distribution.

motorists behave in other ways, the great majority of them conform to the law and stop completely at traffic signals. The mode of the distribution describes the typical behavior most exactly.

An asymmetrical distribution like the J-curve in Figure A.4 is said to be **skewed.** Distribution of yearly taxable income in these United States is always skewed in another way, because individual incomes can range from nothing to enormous. Although in the late 1970s some families had yearly incomes between $5000 and 10,000 and even more earned between $10,000 and $20,000, some incomes are considerably higher (Figure A.5). The highest single yearly income in the United States may be something like $6,000,000, skewing the distribution far, far to the right. The mean income in the United States during this period was approximately $12,500, whereas the median income was only $10,500. In the computation of the mean, the extreme values of the distribution, those of its very long tail, have pulled the mean toward them. But the median is obtained by counting, which means that extreme values are no more important than any other. Earnings of many times $6,000,000 would have no greater effect on the median than any other income above the median. Because it is unaffected by the extremely high incomes of the few, as is the mean, the median is a much more accurate measure of typical income.

A distribution like that in Figure A.5, which has a tail to the right toward the high numbers, is said to be **positively skewed.** Distributions in which the tail is to the left, toward the low numbers, are said to be **negatively skewed.** The median is again the better measure of central tendency. Scores on course examinations often have a negatively skewed distribution (Figure A.6). A number of students make a nearly perfect score on the test, which creates a ceiling effect, a bunching at the top scores. The usual test does not give the very best students a chance to show how good they are. They are not separated out but instead

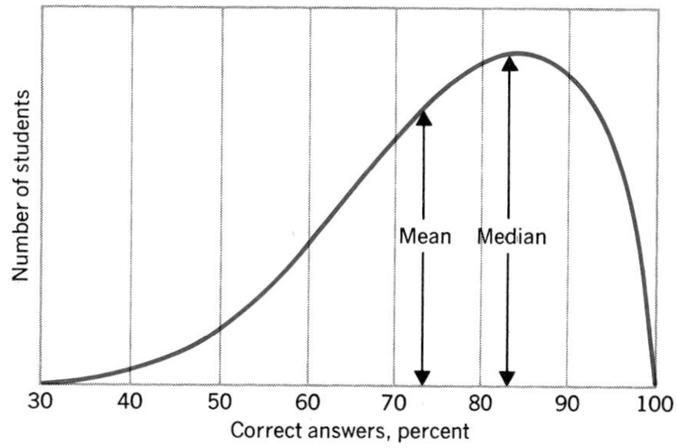

FIGURE A.6
Distribution of grades on a typical course examination. This distribution is negatively skewed. Notice, as in Figure A.5, how skewness affects the relationship between median and mean.

are part of the substantial group whose scores pile up toward the high end of the distribution. The only straightforward solution to this problem is to make tests much longer than they usually are, but the limitations of time generally rule out this possibility.

Variability

The frequency distributions already presented have provided you with a glimpse at one of the most obvious facts of human nature. People vary enormously on almost every dimension you can think of. This simple observation is so basic that it identifies one way of expressing the whole purpose of psychology. Our aim is to account for the variance in human and animal behavior.

Variance and Standard Deviation Two closely related measures of variability are important in statistical thinking. The reason for the existence of two measures is that each has a useful feature that the other does not. The two measures are *variance* and

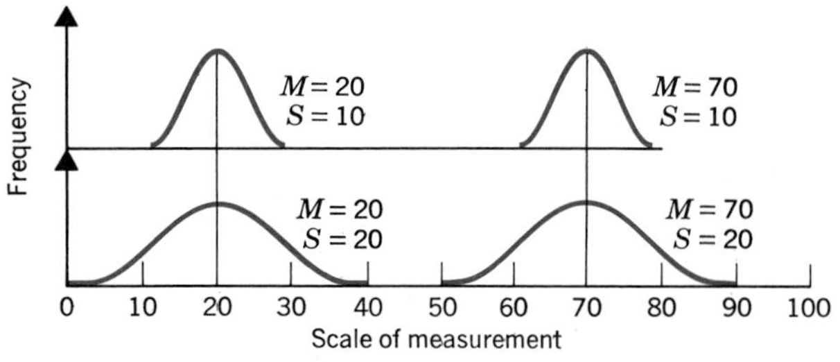

FIGURE A.7

Features of frequency distributions. A frequency distribution is a plot of the number of individuals (ordinate) receiving each score on some scale of measurement (abscissa). Cases cluster around the mean but also scatter around it. The two distributions to the left have the same mean but differ in variability. The same is true of the two distributions to the right. The two upper and two lower distributions each have the same variability but differ in their means.

standard deviation. We shall describe these measures now and explain their useful features in later sections. Both measures serve the same descriptive purpose. They indicate the degree to which measurements cluster about the mean. The mean centers the distribution and the curve that expresses it. The variance and standard deviation indicate how measures spread out from the mean. The less the measures in a distribution cluster, the wider is the dispersion, and the larger are the variance and standard deviation (Figure A.7).

Both variance and standard deviation are numbers obtained by simple calculations. To find the **variance** of a set of scores, first obtain the mean—by adding the scores and then dividing the sum by the number of scores. Then determine the deviation of each of the scores from the mean—by subtracting the mean from each of these numbers. For scores below the mean, these deviations will be negative; for those above the mean, the deviations will be positive. Having obtained the deviation of each score from the mean, next square them all. Then add the squared deviations, whose signs will all have become positive in the process of squaring them. Finally obtain the mean squared deviation by dividing by the number of them. The statistic obtained is the variance of the distribution. The **standard deviation** is just one short step beyond variance. It is the square root of the variance.

The numbers in which variances and standard deviations are stated are in the same point system as the measurements on which they were based. The principal thing you need to know about variance and standard deviation is that these measures express something factual about a distribution. They do not come from on high but must be calculated. Such calculations have yielded the following values for some distributions with which you are familiar.

1. As measured by most IQ tests, the average IQ is 100 points. Scores range from near zero to over 200, with a mean of 100. The variance of the distribution of IQ scores is about 225 points and the standard deviation is about 15 points.
2. The range of SAT scores is some 600 points, from a little less than 200 to a little more than 800. On the original sample of students who took this test, the mean was 500. Reflecting the large range of scores, their variance was 10,000 and the standard deviation ($\sqrt{10{,}000}$) was 100.
3. For data in Figure A.3, with a mean of 15.97 and range from 10 to 21, the variance is 5.66, the standard deviation 2.38.

Symbols Although it is possible, as we have been doing, to present statistical ideas in words, it is much more efficient to put them in symbolic form. This step is essential to the presentation of calculations.

The mean The formula for the mean, *M,* is

$$M = \frac{\Sigma X}{N}$$

where Σ stands for the process of addition, *X* refers to each and every individual score, and *N* is the number of scores for which the mean is computed.

As you can see, this formula describes simply and quickly the methods used to calculate the mean: add up (Σ) all the scores (*X*) and divide by the number of scores (*N*).

Variance and standard deviation The formula for variance, S^2, sometimes symbolized *V*, is

$$S^2 = V = \frac{\Sigma d^2}{N}$$

where Σ stands for the process of addition and *d* refers to the difference between each and every individual score (*X*) and the mean (*M*). Thus $d = X - M$ and $d^2 = (X - M)^2$. The process of squaring makes all terms in the equation positive. As before, *N* is the number of measurements for which variance is computed.

The formula for the standard deviation is

$$S = \sqrt{\frac{\Sigma d^2}{N}}$$

where all terms have the meanings previously presented.

Computations Since the formulae for the standard deviation and variance include terms that depend on knowing the mean, the calculation of either of these will illustrate the calculation of the mean as well. The following sets of numbers will provide two simple examples: (*a*) 1, 2, 3, 4, 5, 6, 7; and (*b*) 46, 47, 48, 49, 50, 51, 52. Please note that the two sets are very dif-

TABLE A.1
Computation of Variance and Standard Deviation

X	d	d^2
46	46 − 49 = −3	9
47	−2	4
48	−1	1
49	0	0
50	+1	1
51	+2	4
52	+3	9
343	0	28

$$M = \frac{\Sigma X}{N} = \frac{343}{7} = 49$$

$$S^2 = \frac{\Sigma d^2}{N} = \frac{28}{7} = 4, \text{ the variance } (V)$$

$$S = \sqrt{\frac{\Sigma d^2}{N}} = \sqrt{4} = 2, \text{ the standard deviation}$$

X	d	d^2
1	1 − 4 = −3	9
2	−2	4
3	−1	1
4	0	0
5	+1	1
6	+2	4
7	+3	9
28	0	28

$$M = \frac{\Sigma X}{N} = \frac{28}{7} = 4.0$$

$$S^2 = \frac{\Sigma d^2}{N} = \frac{28}{7} = 4, \text{ the variance}$$

$$S = \sqrt{\frac{\Sigma d^2}{N}} = \sqrt{4} = 2, \text{ the standard deviation}$$

ferent in the sizes of the individual numbers. You should expect the means to be different. The ranges of the two sets of scores are the same, however, and you should not be surprised to find that S and S^2 are the same for the two sets. The calculations appear in Table A.1.

Having dealt with two sets of numbers for which the means differ and variability is the same, we present for comparison examples for which the reverse is true, for which the means are the same and variability differs. The two sets of numbers in the left-hand column of Table A.2 have these properties.

SUMMARY ☐

The data of psychology commonly take the form of descriptive statistics that tell us what we need to know about behavioral phenomena—their frequency, the relation of one phenomenon to another,

TABLE A.2
Computation of Variance and Standard Deviation

X	d	d^2
4	4 − 16 = −12	144
8	−8	64
12	−4	16
16	0	0
20	+4	16
24	−8	64
28	+12	144
112	0	448

$$M = \frac{\Sigma X}{N} = \frac{112}{7} = 16$$

$$S^2 = \frac{\Sigma d^2}{N} = \frac{448}{7} = 64, \text{ the variance } (V)$$

$$S = \sqrt{\frac{\Sigma d^2}{N}} = \sqrt{\frac{448}{7}} = \sqrt{64} = 8, \text{ the standard deviation}$$

X	d	d^2
10	10 − 16 = −6	36
12	−4	16
14	−2	4
16	0	0
18	+2	4
20	+4	16
22	+6	36
112	0	112

$$M = \frac{\Sigma X}{N} = \frac{112}{7} = 16$$

$$S^2 = \frac{\Sigma d^2}{N} = \frac{112}{7} = 16, \text{ the variance}$$

$$S = \sqrt{\frac{\Sigma d^2}{N}} = \sqrt{\frac{112}{7}} = \sqrt{16} = 4, \text{ the standard deviation}$$

their distribution, their "average" values, and their variability. Most of the time descriptive statistics are useful and informative. Through innocent misunderstanding or otherwise, however, they can sometimes distort and mislead. Rate measurements may vary, depending on definitions of the terms that enter into the computation of the rate. The meaning of a given rate is unclear unless these definitions are given. Graphic representations of rates can be misleading if the vertical axis is made too long or too short.

A frequency distribution arranges the set of numerical data from lowest to highest and shows the number of measures at each value. Most distributions of data tend to pile up at the middle. There are three measures of this central tendency: the mean, the well-known arithmetic average; the mode, the most common value in the distribution; and the median, the middle score. Depending on the shape of the distribution curve, one or the other measure of central tendency will be the most appropriate. For symmetrical distributions the mean, mode, and median will all have the same value. In such situations the mean is the most useful measure. For skewed distributions that have a long tail, with data piled up at one end, the mean will be pulled too high by the extreme values in the tail and will not represent typical performance. Then the median or sometimes the mode becomes the better measure of central tendency.

Variance and the standard deviation are the most important indices of the degree to which measurements cluster about or spread out from their mean.

MORE DESCRIPTIVE STATISTICS

Variance and standard deviation have different special properties that make them useful in different ways. The variance for any set of scores can be broken down into additive components in order to estimate the degree to which several different variables contribute to the variation in a trait or aspect of behavior. We deal with this idea in the next section (see page 505). The usefulness of the standard deviation derives from its precise relationship to the normal curve.

The Normal Curve

The normal distribution is actually a complex mathematical function, but almost everyone has seen the graphic version of it. The familiar bell shape and mirror-image symmetry of the **normal curve** describe the frequency distribution of many biological and psychological traits. Among the real-life happenings described by the normal curve are most body measurements, such as chest sizes, and reaction times in stopping a car. The normal curve in Figure A.8 is a

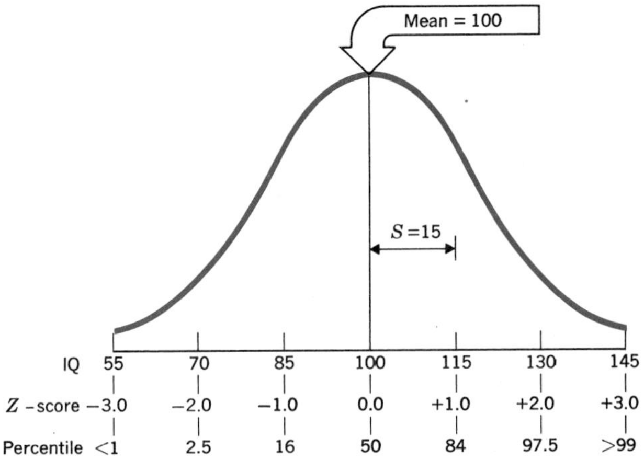

FIGURE A.8
IQs, Z-scores, and percentiles. This idealized distribution of IQs indicates their relation to Z-scores and percentiles.

somewhat idealized distribution of the IQs for the white population of the United States. The mean of the distribution of IQs is 100, the standard deviation of the distribution about 15. Once we have these facts and are aware that IQs are normally distributed, we know a great deal about the distribution of intelligence. It should be understood that knowledge about this distribution applies generally to any normal distribution.

Z-Scores In Figure A.8 the abscissa is marked off into units corresponding to 15 IQ points. In other words, it is marked off in units of the standard deviation (*S*). We can now understand the second row of numbers beneath the abscissa, the one labeled ***Z*-score.** The numbers on this scale represent deviations of scores from the mean in *S*-units. Since the mean does not deviate from itself, it has a *Z*-score of zero. An IQ of 85 is 15 IQ points, or one standard deviation, below the mean and therefore has a *Z*-value of −1.0. For an exactly analogous reason, an IQ of 115 corresponds to a *Z*-score of +1.0; an IQ of 70 is the equivalent of a *Z*-score of −2.0; and so on. A *Z*-score is computed by dividing the deviation of a raw score by the standard deviation. That is, from any raw score (*X*) subtract the mean (*M*) and divide by the standard deviation (*S*). The mathematical formula is very simple, $Z = (X - M)/S$. To illustrate the conversion of raw IQ scores to standard deviation units, let us take an IQ that does not appear in Figure A.8, for example, an IQ of 110: $110 - 100 = 10 \div 15 = +.667$. Our computation tells us that an IQ of 110 falls two-thirds of a standard deviation above the mean, making the *Z*-score +.667. A more exact understanding of *Z*-scores requires an appreciation of the areas under the normal curve as they are marked off by various *Z*-score ranges. We shall present the important points in two slightly different ways.

Percentile Ranks The **percentile rank** of a score is the percentage of other scores in a distribution that the particular score equals or exceeds. Thus if a score is at the fiftieth percentile (the median), it equals or exceeds 50 percent of the scores; if it is at the thirty-seventh percentile, it equals or exceeds 37 percent of the scores. Now look at the very bottom scale in Figure A.8, which ranges from <1 (percent) to >99 (percent), and compare it with the middle scale, which is in terms of Z-scores. As you can see, percentiles and Z-scores are very definitely related. Each Z-score has a particular percentile rank; for example, a Z-score of −1.0, which corresponds to a raw IQ of 85, has a percentile rank of 16. Another way to put it is to say that 16 percent of the area in a normal curve falls below a Z-score of −1.0.

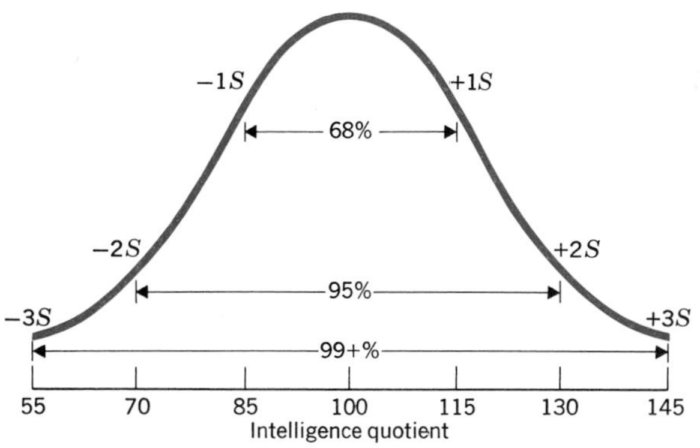

FIGURE A.9
Areas under the normal curve. This idealized distribution of IQs indicates what percentage of them fall within various S-ranges. If you understand this figure, you can derive Figure A.8 from it. A small fraction of one percent of the population have IQs over 145 and below 55.

Standard Deviations and Areas The relationship of areas within the normal curve to Z-scores can be expressed in another way, one which is in terms of the standard deviation on which the Z-score is based. Figure A.9 shows the percentages of total area falling within a normal distribution curve as they are marked off by different S-distances on either side of the mean. The range from −1S to +1S covers 68 percent of the area under the curve, and of the distribution of scores. The range from −2S to +2S covers about 95 percent of the area and the scores, and the range from −3S to +3S covers over 99 percent of them. For any curve to be a normal curve, the areas bounded by the various standard deviation markings must be exactly these particular percentages of the total area beneath the curve. We know a normal curve only by these percentages; inspection alone will not tell us that a bell-shaped curve describes a normal distribution. For later purposes it will also be important to note that the percentages of area and of scores *not* included in each of the three standard deviation ranges shown in Figure A.9 are 32, 5, and 1.

Correlation

Until now we have been examining the statistics that describe one set of measurements. The methods of **correlation** tell us whether and how closely different psychological processes are related by allowing us to compare two sets of measurements. A typical correlational question, whether there is a relation between speed of learning and retention, will serve as an example. To answer this question, we would need first to teach a number of people something and to measure the amount of training they required to learn it. Then, after some standard length of time, these same people would be tested to find out how much they had remembered. The question, then, would be whether people who learn fast tend to forget quickly, as we sometimes hear, or whether those who learn easily also retain things well.

In an imaginary, but realistic, study of this question, let us suppose that there were ten individuals in the experiment and that they were required to learn a passage of poetry. Let us further assume that the measure of learning was the number of readings required to learn the passage. Finally, let us assume that after one month the participants tried to recall the poem. The measure taken was the number of mistakes they made when reciting it. If these participants were typical, the results of this experiment might approximate those shown in Table A.3. The middle column of the table gives the number of readings each individual required to learn the poem. The right-hand column indicates the number of mistakes that these same individuals made on the recall test. In general, the people who learned quickly tended to make few mistakes on the recall test, discounting the popular idea that so-called quick learners soon forget what they have learned.

Scatter Diagrams One way to present the meaning of correlation is by graph. The points on the graph in Figure A.10, which is called a **scatter plot** or **scatter diagram,** represent the performances of the ten participants. The number near each point is that of the specific individual; you can identify each person's record in Table A.3 and figure out how the plot was made.

The arrows leading to the point for participant number 9 will help you to understand. If you refer back to Table A.3, you will see that he required twenty-eight readings to master the passage—hence the arrow from 28 on the abscissa. On the recall test he made seventeen mistakes, so another arrow is drawn from 17 on the ordinate. The point for this per-

TABLE A.3

Hypothetical Learning and Recall Data

Participant	Number of Readings Required To Learn	Number of Mistakes Made on a Recall Trial One Month Later
1	12	3
2	14	7
3	15	6
4	17	12
5	18	8
6	21	12
7	23	14
8	25	13
9	28	17
10	31	22

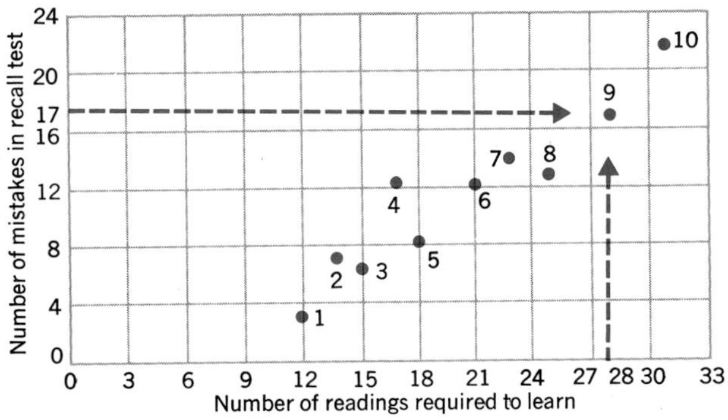

FIGURE A.10

Plotting a scatter diagram. This figure shows the relationship between learning and recall for each of ten subjects. Each point represents the scores for one subject and is plotted at the spot where lines drawn from the subject's scores on the ordinate and on the abscissa would intersect. The method is illustrated for subject number 9, who took 28 readings to learn the material and made 17 mistakes in attempting to recall it.

son appears at the spot where the paths of these arrows would cross. Each of the other points was plotted in the same way.

When high scores on one measure are associated with high scores on a second in this way, the scores are said to be **positively correlated.** Sometimes high scores on one measure are associated with low scores on another. Such pairs of scores are said to be **negatively correlated.** Figure A.11 presents an example of a negative correlation, that between the time required to press a button when one of two lights is brighter and the difference in brightness of the two lights, ranging from a small difference to a large one. The smaller the difference in brightness, the greater the amount of time required to decide that there was a difference and to press the button.

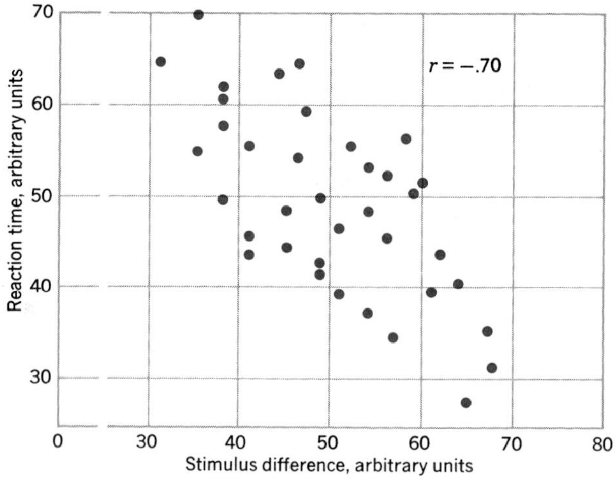

FIGURE A.11

A negative correlation. The *x*-measures on the abscissa are differences in the brightness of two lights. The *y*-measures on the ordinate are the times required by subjects to press a button to indicate that they detected a difference in brightness. The greater the stimulus difference, the less time required to detect it. (Data from Blommers and Lindquist, 1960.)

Correlation Coefficients The relationships presented verbally and graphically so far in this section are more commonly expressed numerically. Called **correlation coefficients,** these numbers range in value from +1.00, indicating a perfect positive correlation, through zero or no correlation, to −1.00, indicating a perfect negative correlation (Figure A.12).

The correlation coefficient can be computed with the help of *Z*-scores, which allow us to put measures as different as reaction times and differences in the brightness of two lights on the same scale and compare them. Whatever the scales of measurement in which scores are expressed, they can be converted to *Z*-scores and meaningfully compared with each other, for *Z*-scores state positions within distributions. The *Z*-score is sometimes called a standard score for just this reason.

In the computation of a correlation coefficient, we call the two sets of measures to be correlated *x* and *y*. The calculations proceed in these steps. First compute each person's two *Z*-scores for raw scores on *x* and *y*. The mean and standard deviation will of course have to be computed first. The *Z*-scores above the mean will have positive values and those below will have negative values. Then multiply each person's two *Z*-scores together. The processes of multiplying positive by positive and negative by negative *Z*-scores will both yield positive products, but multiplying negative by positive and positive by negative *Z*-scores will yield negative products. Finally, add together the *Z*-score products for all individuals and

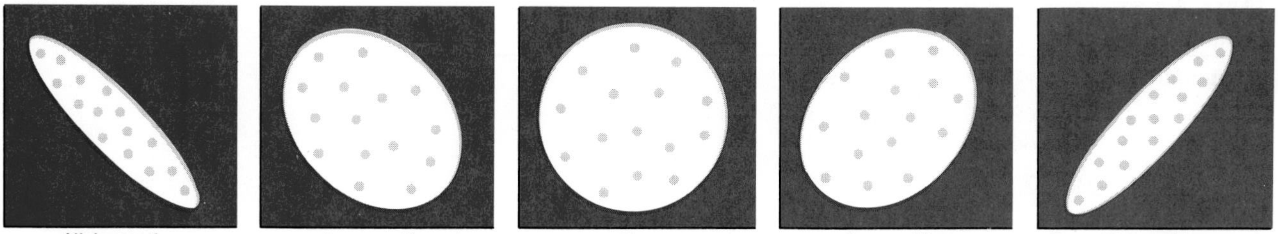

FIGURE A.12
Ellipses showing five different patterns of correlation. The ovals sloping downward represent negative correlations. Those sloping upward to the right represent positive correlations. The "fatter" the ellipse, the nearer the correlation is to zero.

divide by the number of individuals. In other words, average these Z-score products. Their average is the correlation coefficient, denoted by *r*. The formula for the computation just described is

$$r = \frac{\Sigma(Zx \cdot Zy)}{N}$$

If you think through these calculations, keeping in mind the meanings of positive and negative correlations, you will see that correlations will be positive when high scores on x go with high scores on y and low scores on x go with low scores on y, for positive will be multiplied by positive and negative by negative. Correlations will be negative when high scores on either measure are associated with low scores on the other, for positive will be multiplied by negative. The final two steps, adding Z-score products that are positive or negative, or that are for the most part one or the other, and dividing them by their number, will obviously not change their signs.

Another measure of correlation, a rank-order coefficient called rho (*R*), may add to your understanding. The formula for rho is

$$R = 1 - \frac{6\Sigma D^2}{N(N^2 - 1)}$$

In this formula, instead of converting to Z-scores, the x and y measures are converted to rankings. The subjects are ranked 1, 2, 3, . . . , *N* on x and 1, 2, 3, . . . , *N* on *y*, from high to low, or vice versa. Then the individual's rank on x is subtracted from his or her rank on *y* or vice versa. The term *D* in the formula refers to the difference in each individual's rank on the x and y measures. With *D* defined, the meaning of the formula for *R* should be clear.

An Example A professor gave his first examination to a small undergraduate class, graded it, and, addressing the class later, described the problem that the grades had created in this way. "Either I gave a rotten examination that was way too hard, or else you students didn't study. Since it is important for my examinations to be reasonable from your point of view, and it is just as important for you to understand my expectations, I will give another examination on the same materials a week from today. For my part, I will try to adjust the level of the exam. For yours, you should do a bit more studying if your conscience tells you that you did less for this exam than you should have."

One week later the second test was given. Table A.4 lists the scores of the thirteen students who took the two examinations, each sixty items long. As you can see, performance on the second exam was uniformly better than on the first, but there is also a positive correlation between the scores. The rest of the materials in the table make this point by computing *r* and *R*. For the computation of *r*, it is necessary, first, to compute the means and standard deviations for the two tests. Without going through the mechanics, the values obtained were these: for test 1, $M = 34.00$ and $S = 10.59$; for test 2, $M = 48.38$ and $S = 6.43$. Next it is necessary to compute Z-scores for each student's x and y scores. The scores for student 1 are taken as an example. Recalling that $Z = (x - M)/S$, we have

$$Z_x = \frac{24 - 34}{10.59} = \frac{-10}{10.59} = -.94$$

$$Z_y = \frac{49 - 48.38}{6.43} = \frac{+.62}{6.43} = +.10$$

With these values computed, the next steps are to multiply Z_y by Z_x for each student and to average these products, as required by the formula for *r*. The result is $r = +.77$ (Table A.4).

The calculation of *R* begins by converting the scores to ranks. Then differences between ranks are obtained. These differences are squared and added, and the sum is entered into the formula for *R*. The result of the computation is +.72, which approximates the value of *r*.

Uses and Misuses of Correlation The existence of a correlation between two variables tells us that the two measures are associated, that values on one measure are related to those on the other according to some definite pattern. What else does a correlation tell us?

TABLE A.4
Computation of *r* and *R*

Computation of *r*

Student	First Exam Score (x)	Second Exam Score (y)	Z_x	Z_y	$Z_x \cdot Z_y$
1	24	49	−.94	+.10	−.09
2	45	55	+1.04	+1.03	+1.07
3	26	38	−.76	−1.61	+1.22
4	30	47	−.38	−.21	+.08
5	33	49	−.09	+.10	−.01
6	20	37	−1.32	−1.77	+2.34
7	18	39	−1.51	−1.46	+2.20
8	54	58	+1.89	+1.50	+2.84
9	39	51	+.47	+.41	+.19
10	26	54	−.76	+.87	−.66
11	44	48	+.94	−.06	−.06
12	42	54	+.76	+.87	+.66
13	41	50	+.66	+.25	+.17
				total	+9.95

$$r = \frac{\Sigma(Z_x \cdot Z_y)}{N} = \frac{9.95}{13} = +.77$$

Computation of *R*

Student	First Exam Score (x)	Second Exam Score (y)	Rank on x	Rank on y	D	D^2
1	24	49	3	6.5	3.5	12.25
2	45	55	12	12	0	0.00
3	26	38	4.5	2	2.5	6.25
4	30	47	6	4	2	4.00
5	33	49	7	6.5	0.5	0.25
6	20	37	2	1	1	1.00
7	18	39	1	3	2	4.00
8	54	58	13	13	0	0.00
9	39	51	8	9	1	1.00
10	26	54	4.5	10.5	6	36.00
11	44	48	11	5	6	36.00
12	42	54	10	10.5	0.5	0.25
13	41	50	9	8	1	1.00
					total	102.00

$$R = 1 - \frac{6\Sigma D^2}{N(N^2-1)} = 1 - \frac{6(102)}{13(169-1)} = 1 - \frac{612}{2184} = 1 - .28 = +.72$$

We shall see that it can predict one value from the other with an accuracy that depends on the size of the correlation coefficient.

Correlation and prediction Before you were admitted to college, it is quite likely that you took a college aptitude test. Scores on such tests are meant to predict the grades you are likely to make in college. Accurate prediction depends on the size of the correlation. When a correlation is perfect, +1.00 or −1.00, it is possible to make a perfectly accurate prediction. As the size of the correlation decreases, the accuracy of prediction also decreases. A correlation of zero has no predictive value at all. For example, the height of a college student cannot be used to predict grade point average. The correlation between height and college grades is zero. What about the correlations in between zero and +1.00 or −1.00? In making predictions, we need to understand that the lower the correlation, the less accurate the prediction. In order to be more exact, however, we need first to explain what is meant by the accuracy of prediction.

Accounting for variance Take the case of SAT scores and college grades with which this discussion began. Consider first the distribution of grades for the entire freshman class in some college. Their distribution might be that in Figure A.13 labeled "All SAT

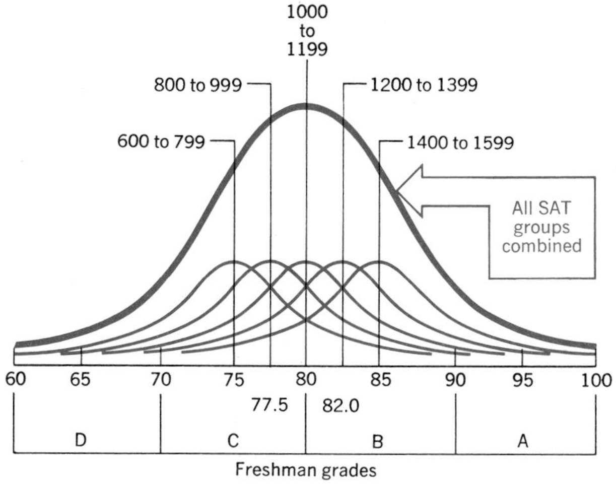

FIGURE A.13

Accounting for variance. Students with differing SAT scores receive different freshman grades on the average. The SAT scores account for these average differences. Each subgroup shows considerable variance around its individual mean, however. This variance is unaccounted for. The small distributions added together would reproduce the total distribution. The variance in the means of the groups plus the variance within individual groups equals total variance.

groups combined." This large distribution of course includes the scores for students with very different SATs. Suppose now that we look at the distribution of grades for five groups of students who have the similar SAT scores, identified in Figure A.13 by the labels 800 to 999, 1000 to 1199, and so on. There would of course be fewer of them in each group and their distributions would be smaller. Notice that the means of grades for these groups differ; they are 75, 77.5, and so on. But the range of grades within each small group is very wide. One way to describe what we see in Figure A.13 is to say that SAT scores predict grades to a degree, reflected by the different means of the five subgroups, but the prediction of grades for individual students is seldom accurate, reflected by the wide range of grades within individual SAT subgroups.

Another way to describe the situation is in terms of the useful property of variance, to which we have finally come. Variance can be separated into additive components that are assignable to different causal factors. Figure A.13 shows that the total distribution of grades has been broken down into two components. The first component is the variation in mean grades for the five subgroups. The second component is the variation in grades within each subgroup. It would be reasonable to say that the first of these components is *accounted for* by SAT scores; the second component is *unaccounted for*. If the small distributions were all added back together, they would recreate the large distribution. This should begin to give you a feel for what it means to say that variance can be broken down into additive components. Accounted-for variance plus unaccounted-for variance, in this case, equals total variance.

What does all this have to do with correlation? The connection is surprisingly direct. If the correlation between x and y is r, the proportion of variance in y accounted for by x is r^2. In our example x is SAT scores, y is freshman grades. The proportion of variance of grades accounted for by SAT scores is whatever fraction the variance in the means of the grades of the five subgroups (variance accounted for, as we have already seen) is of total variance. These calculations, performed on actual data, yield values that range from about .09 to about .16. Since the proportion of variance accounted for is r^2, r will be the square root of the proportion of variance accounted for. This means that the correlation between SAT scores and freshman grades is in the neighborhood of $\sqrt{.09} = .30$ to $\sqrt{.16} = .40$. Clearly the correlation between SAT scores and grades accounts for only a small proportion of the variability of grades. This explains why college administrators do not put much faith in any except extremely high and low SAT scores—or at least why they should not.

Correlation and causation Knowing that there is a correlation between two variables, particularly when it is a positive one, makes it very tempting to conclude that one variable causes the other. For example, we mentioned in Chapter 1 that there is a strong positive correlation between the price of an American jug wine and its cost, which tempts us to say that a particular wine costs what it does because of its quality. Whatever the plausibility of this particular conclusion, the mere fact of a correlation does not necessarily imply causation.

This point may be illustrated by a number of correlations for which it is obvious that no causal relationship exists. There is, for example, a positive correlation between the softness of asphalt paving and the mortality rate of infants. There is a positive correlation between the number of ice cream cones consumed in New York City day by day and the death rate in Bombay. Heat is responsible for both these correlations. There is a positive correlation between the lengths of boys' trousers and their mental ages, chronological age being responsible for both. There is a positive correlation between the sizes of boys' feet and the quality of their handwriting for the same reason. A final illustration may tickle the fancy most of all. There is reported to be a positive correlation, year by year, between the number of storks' nests and the number of births in northwestern Europe.

These somewhat amusing examples have the advantage of making the point very concretely. The existence of a correlation between two variables implies nothing about causality. Some relationships, such as

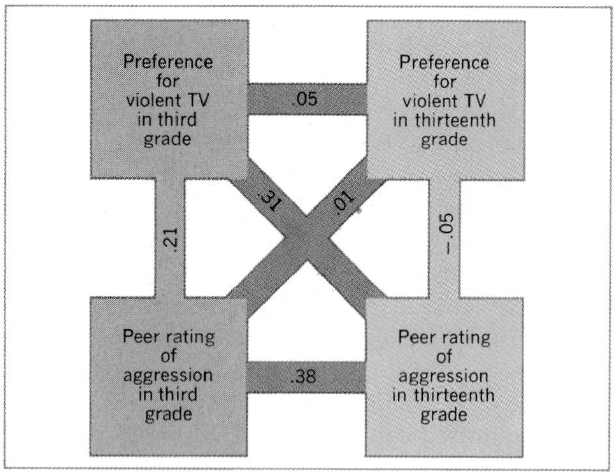

FIGURE A.14
Cross-lagged correlation coefficients. The correlation of .31 has been used as an argument for the causal dependence or later aggression on earlier preference for violent television shows. (Data from Eron et al., 1972.)

that between the quality of jug wines and their cost, probably are causal. For others, such as the relation between the length of a boy's trousers and his IQ or the size of his feet and the quality of his handwriting, a third factor, in this case chronological age, is responsible. Or a causal relationship, should there be one, may not be in the supposed direction. Take the correlation between the number of storks' nests and the birthrate in northwestern Europe. As population and hence the number of buildings increase, the number of places for storks to build their nests would also increase.

New developments in statistics have begun to give us a clearer picture of when *patterns* of correlation support statements of causality. The procedure used is the method of **cross-lagged** correlation coefficients. An important application was in a study of the relationship between viewing violence on television and aggression on the part of the viewer. In this study Leonard Eron and his colleagues (1972) obtained two measures on a group of third-grade children, a measure of the strength of their preference for violent television programs and a measure of their aggressiveness as rated by their peers. Ten years later comparable measures were obtained for the same individuals.

These data allow the calculation of six correlation coefficients (Figure A.14). The two coefficients on the two horizontal lines of the figure indicate the stability of television preferences and aggression over the ten-year period. The preference for violent television was not stable at all ($r = +.05$), but aggressiveness was moderately so ($r = +.38$). The two correlations on the vertical lines ($r = +.21$ and $r = -.05$) show the relationship between preferences for violent television and aggression at the two different times.

The cross-lagged correlations on the two diagonals are *crossed* because they are of different measures and *lagged* because they are separated in time. Early ratings of aggression did not predict later preferences for violent television at all ($r = +.01$). Early preference for violent television, however, did show a modest correlation ($r = +.31$) with later aggression. On this basis and a number of other analyses, it was concluded that watching violent television is one of the causes of aggressiveness later on.

SUMMARY □

The normal curve is a symmetrical, bell-shaped frequency distribution. It describes the distribution of most biological and psychological traits. The most important aspect of the normal curve is the relation of proportions of area beneath it to Z-scores.

A Z-score is a number that tells us, in units of standard deviation, where a raw score of the distribution falls with respect to the mean. That is, it tells us that a score is so and so many standard deviations above or below the mean. For any normal curve there is a precise and known correspondence between proportions of the distribution and Z-scores: 68 percent of the distribution falls between Z-scores −1.0 and +1.0; 95 percent of it between Z-scores −2.0 and +2.0; 99.7 percent of it between Z-scores −3.0 and +3.0.

A correlation coefficient is a number between −1.0 and +1.0 that indicates the direction and degree of relation of two distributions of measurements obtained on the same individuals. The most direct interpretation of the meaning of a correlation coefficient is that it allows the prediction of one measure from another. A less direct interpretation is that the existence of a correlation, r, between x and y means that a proportion of the variance equal to r^2 in one variable is accounted for by variation in the other.

Simple correlations have nothing to say about causality, neither that a causal relationship exists nor that one does not exist. Certain patterns of correlation obtained from longitudinal data have been put forward as supporting causal statements.

INFERENTIAL STATISTICS

It will be understandable if, by now, you have forgotten a major point with which this chapter began, that statistics is a tool for dealing with imprecision and uncertainty. Having seen a parade of means, standard deviations, and correlations presented with two-decimal precision, you may have come to the conclusion that statistics must be pretty accurate measures after all. It is time now to explain why this is an erroneous conclusion and how the other part of the statistical enterprise, inferential statistics, is able to manage imprecision.

Samples and Populations

The procedures of inferential statistics provide a means whereby information obtained on a sample is used to draw conclusions about a larger population. That is why the procedures are called **inferential statistics:** data on samples are used to draw inferences about populations. The terms population and sample mean about what you would expect them to. A **population** is the entire universe of individuals, objects, or events potentially available for study; a **sample** is a smaller set of individuals, objects, or events drawn from the population.

The general rule for drawing inferences about populations from sample data is straightforward. The statistic obtained on a sample provides an estimate of the same measure for a population. If the mean IQ of a sample of college students is 110, an estimate of the mean IQ of the entire population of college students would also be 110. If the correlation between the IQs of parents in a sample and of their children is +.60, we would infer that the same correlation applies to the IQs of parents and of children in the population. If 52 percent of a sample of voters say that they will vote Democratic in the next election, Dr. Gallup uses this percentage as his best estimate of the outcome of the election, even if it is an estimate in which he has little confidence.

The Accuracy of Estimates As this *last* example suggests, the estimates based on samples must carry two cautious provisos. *First,* it is important to understand that, since samples *are* samples, the measure obtained on a given one will almost certainly differ from that obtained on another. In other words, measures obtained on samples are subject to error. If the values obtained on two samples differ, at least one of them and probably both must differ from the value for the population. It is the recognition of such errors that may lead Dr. Gallup to decide that the outcome of an election is "too close to call," in spite of the 52 percent majority who say they plan to vote one way or the other. *Second,* these estimates assume that the sample upon which they are based is representative of the population for which conclusions are being drawn. If the sample is not representative, the estimate may be very much in error.

No doubt the most famous error of this sort is that committed by the 1936 Literary Digest Poll. In that year the magazine *Literary Digest* mailed out ten million ballots on the presidential election and received over two million of them in return. On the basis of these straw votes, *Literary Digest* predicted the election of Alfred M. Landon to the presidency of the United States. But November 2, 1936 came and went and President Franklin D. Roosevelt received 60 percent of the popular vote in a landslide victory.

In the Literary Digest Poll ballots had been mailed to subscribers of the magazine, to individuals selected from telephone directories, and to persons on lists of automobile registrations. This meant that the sample contained far too many well-to-do people. The year 1936 was a depression year, a year in which many people could not afford an automobile or a telephone, much less the *Literary Digest.* In all years there is some tendency for individuals with high incomes to vote Republican. It was this basic failure to obtain a **representative sample** that led to the downfall of the Literary Digest Poll and the magazine itself.

Randomization We have just seen that one of the great dangers in making inferences about a population from samples is that the sample selected may not be representative of the population. Furthermore, we have seen that large numbers of cases do not protect against this danger. The ideal procedure, in research, would be to select members of samples at random. A **random sample** is one in which each individual in the population and every combination of individuals have an equal chance of being selected. Selecting a truly random sample is rarely possible, because this would require the identification of every individual in a population and devising a scheme to give every person an equal chance of being selected. Because of the obvious difficulties in such procedures, investigators usually take liberties with randomness by selecting haphazardly from a phone book, advertising for volunteers in the newspaper, contacting people living at different addresses, or approaching people as they pass by some location. The representativeness of samples suffers as a result. Any lack of representativeness limits the confidence we can place in the outcomes of research, for reasons which will become clear as the discussion proceeds.

The Significance of a Difference

In recent years a feud has been raging between the bottlers of Coca Cola and Pepsi Cola over the question of which drink tastes better. Although it is hard to imagine anyone other than the two corporations taking sides on this issue, suppose that someone actually does become interested enough to do an experiment, to try to answer the question with data.

There are eighteen participants in all, nine who will rate the taste of Pepsi, the other nine the taste of Coke. The experimental design is a double-blind one (page 17). The drinks are poured into identical glasses, so that the participants do not know which they receive. Someone else does the pouring so that the experimenter is also in the dark. The instructions direct the subjects in the experiment to rate the unidentified drink on a scale from zero to 100, with 100 the value that they would give to their most favorite taste in any food or drink. When the results are in, it turns out that the mean rating for Coca Cola is 53.5, that for Pepsi Cola 48.5. Apparently Coke tastes better than Pepsi—or does it?

Any experimental result of this type is subject to two interpretations. (1) The result obtained is a true one. It represents a difference that exists in the population. (2) The difference obtained is a misleading result. No difference exists in the population, and one was found only because the samples selected just happened to be unrepresentative.

The second of these two interpretations is called the **null hypothesis,** the hypothesis of no difference. The commonest procedure for determining whether an experimental difference is significant, that is, whether it has been caused by something other than mere chance, is to test the null hypothesis, almost always with the hope that the hypothesis can be rejected. If the null hypothesis can be rejected, whatever two situations were used in the experiment must have had, by implication, two distinguishable outcomes. Since we cannot say that there is *no* difference, the one found must truly exist and must be attributable to the difference between the two situations explored in the course of the experiment.

A test of the null hypothesis really asks this question. If the null hypothesis is true, what is the probability that a difference as large as the one obtained in the experiment would occur by a chance error in sampling? Statistical procedures provide an estimate of the probability. Through appropriate analyses it is possible to say that this probability is one in two (.50 or 50 percent), in ten (.10 or 10 percent), in twenty (.05 or 5 percent), in a hundred (.01 or 1 percent), or one in some other number. These probabilities define the **level of confidence** with which the null hypothesis can be rejected. To reject the null hypothesis at the .03 (or 3 percent) level of confidence is to say that if no difference actually exists in the population as a whole, the one obtained would occur by accident only three times in a hundred. It is more reasonable to conclude that the null hypothesis is false and that the experimental result is true. In practice, experimenters tend to reject the null hypothesis if they can do so at the .05 level of confidence or less.

The *t*-Test

In order to introduce the *t*-test, one of the most common statistical tests employed to evaluate the significance of a difference, let us stipulate the results of the Coke–Pepsi-tasting experiment in a little more detail. The numbers in Table A.5 are contrived to simplify as many calculations as possible.

TABLE A.5
Data for Determining Significance of Difference

Statistic	Coke Tasters	Pepsi Tasters
Mean rating	53.5	48.5
Σd^2	648	1152
N	9	9

The first and third rows in the table require no comment. The reason for including Σd^2 is related to a point that will be made after we compute the standard deviations for the two sample groups, using the formula $S = \sqrt{\Sigma d^2/N}$. For the Coke tasters

$$S_{\text{Coke}} = \sqrt{\frac{648}{9}} = \sqrt{72} = 8.49$$

And for the Pepsi tasters

$$S_{\text{Pepsi}} = \sqrt{\frac{1152}{9}} = \sqrt{128} = 11.31$$

As inferential statistics, that is, as estimates of the standard deviations for whole populations, there is a problem with these numbers. Standard deviations for sample groups slightly underestimate the standard deviations for populations, for reasons that are beyond the purposes of this presentation. A new statistic, $\hat{S}$ (sometimes called "S-hat"), must be calculated to correct for this small error and to obtain a better estimate of the population standard deviation. The formula for $\hat{S}$ is almost the same as that for S:

$$\hat{S} = \sqrt{\frac{\Sigma d^2}{N-1}}$$

For the Coke tasters this value is

$$\hat{S}_{\text{Coke}} = \sqrt{\frac{648}{8}} = \sqrt{81} = 9$$

And for the Pepsi tasters

$$\hat{S}_{\text{Pepsi}} = \sqrt{\frac{1152}{8}} = \sqrt{144} = 12$$

These numbers are slightly larger than the values for S and are better estimates of the population standard deviations, usually symbolized by sigma, σ, the lowercase Greek letter equivalent to s.

Accuracy of the Estimate of the Mean The mean calculated after the testing of a sample group is a fair estimate of the population mean, provided the people in the sample were randomly chosen. It is, however, only an estimate. If a very large number of sample groups were drawn and tested, the means of these many group testings would form a normal distribution. And the *mean* of this distribution of sample

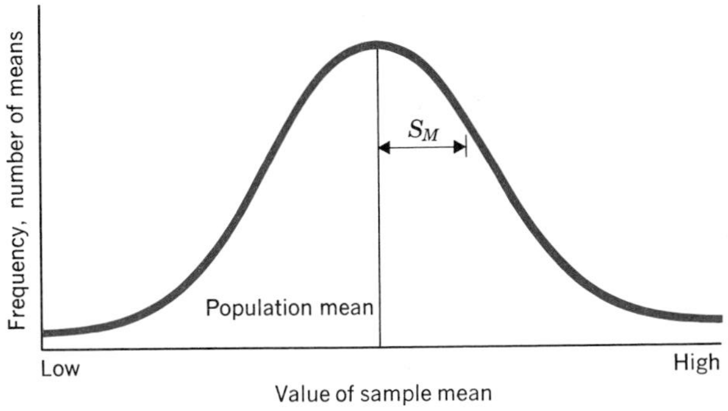

FIGURE A.15
Sampling distribution of the mean. If a large number of samples were drawn, their means determined, and these means plotted in the form of a frequency distribution, the distribution would be normal. The standard deviation of this distribution of means is the standard error of the mean.

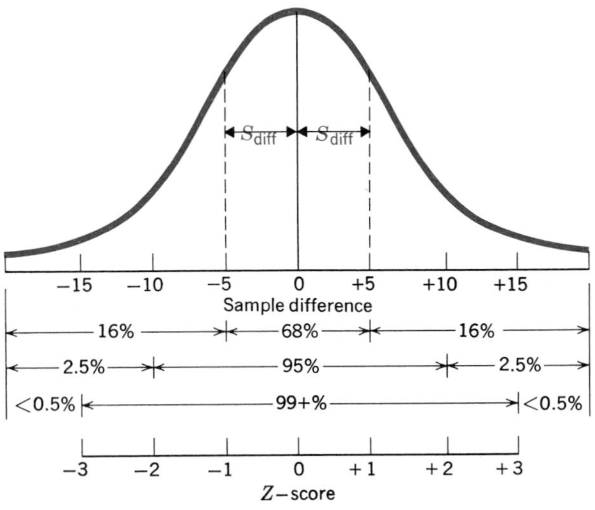

FIGURE A.16
Sampling distribution of differences. The distribution of differences between a large number of pairs of sample means would be normal. The distribution in this figure is for the test experiment, in which the standard error of the difference was 5.0 by calculation. If the null hypothesis is true, differences of 5.0 or larger would be obtained by chance in 32 of 100 pairs of samples. Such an outcome is therefore too likely to allow rejection of the null hypothesis.

group means would be a very good estimate of the population mean. From this normal distribution of sample means, the **sampling distribution of the mean** as it is called, a standard deviation could be figured. It is referred to as the **standard error of the mean** and is symbolized by S_M. Figure A.15 gives these statements pictorial meaning.

In actual practice, of course, it is almost never possible to test sample after sample to obtain the sampling distribution of a mean and calculate its standard error. Fortunately this value can be estimated. The standard error of the mean, which would really be the standard deviation of a large number of sample means from *their* mean, is estimated by dividing the population standard deviation by the square root of the number of individuals in the sample:

$$S_M = \frac{\sigma}{\sqrt{N}}$$

Since the value of σ is rarely known, the working formula substitutes $\hat{S}$, our best estimate of σ, and thus becomes

$$S_M = \frac{\hat{S}}{\sqrt{N}}$$

For the Coke drinkers in our tasting experiment,

$$S_{M,\ \text{Coke}} = \frac{9}{\sqrt{9}} = \frac{9}{3} = 3$$

For the Pepsi tasters

$$S_{M,\ \text{Pepsi}} = \frac{12}{\sqrt{9}} = \frac{12}{3} = 4$$

These numbers are needed in the next step of our test of the null hypothesis.

Accuracy of the Estimate of Difference To repeat a point, the difference between the average ratings of Coke and Pepsi was 5 points (53.5 − 48.5) in favor of Coke. This is only an estimate of a population difference, however. Since the means of samples will vary with the testing of one sample group and another, so too will the difference between these means. If a very large number of pairs of sample groups were drawn and tested, and if the differences between means were calculated for each and every sample pair, then put into a frequency distribution, the result would be a normal **sampling distribution of differences.** Its mean would be a very good estimate of the population difference. The standard deviation figured from this distribution would be the **standard error of the difference,** symbolized by S_{diff}. Again, it is possible to estimate this value without having data on large numbers of pairs of samples.

The standard error of the difference would really be the standard deviation of a large number of sample pair differences from *their* mean. It is calculated by squaring the standard error of the mean (S_M) for each of the two samples actually drawn and tested and compared, then adding these two squared terms, and finally taking the square root of their sum:

$$S_{diff} = \sqrt{S_{M1}^2 + S_{M2}^2}$$

With statistics for the tasters in the Coke-Pepsi experiment inserted, this becomes

$$S_{diff} = \sqrt{3^2 + 4^2} = \sqrt{9 + 16} = \sqrt{25} = 5$$

The meaning of this number is presented pictorially in Figure A.16.

Testing the Null Hypothesis With S_{diff} available, we are finally in a position to use normal curve statistics to ask the following question. If the true difference between means that would be obtained by testing large numbers of pairs of sample groups were zero, what is the probability of obtaining by chance a difference as large as that revealed by our experiment? More concretely for our example, if people in the general population would give the same tastiness ratings to Coke and Pepsi, what is the probability of obtaining a difference in rating as large as the 5.0 points we obtained?

The answer to this question involves the ***t*-test,** a statistic which under certain circumstances is exactly the same as a Z-score. The formula for t is

$$t = \frac{\text{mean difference}}{S_{diff}}$$

For our example

$$t = \frac{53.5 - 48.5}{5} = \frac{5}{5} = 1.0$$

As Figure A.16 may help you see more clearly, this value of t tells you that a difference rating of 5.0 points or more, in *favor of one drink or the other,* would occur by chance in 32 of 100 comparisons, almost a third of the time. In terms developed earlier, we can reject the null hypothesis at only the 32 percent (or .32) level of confidence. In practice no one rejects the null hypothesis when the probability of a difference being found through unfortunate chance sampling is this high. More commonly the .01 (1 percent) or .05 (5 percent) levels are required.

SUMMARY ☐

The term "inferential statistics" refers to a set of procedures for drawing conclusions about populations from measures obtained on samples. In most cases—the standard deviation is the most important exception—statistics obtained on a sample can be taken as estimates of the corresponding values for the population. An important point to understand, however, is that these estimates are merely estimates. The statistics obtained on different samples would vary from sample to sample. A second important point to understand is that these samples must be representative if statistics collected from them are to be fair estimates. The most straightforward procedure for assuring representativeness is through the selection of random samples.

Our discussion has concentrated on applying inferential statistics in the evaluation of experimental data. A difference obtained in an experiment may be either a true one brought about by the different conditions of the experiment or an accident of unfortunate sampling. The second possibility, that there is actually no difference—the "null hypothesis"—is evaluated in the most common statistical tests. These procedures allow us to calculate the probability of finding a difference of the order obtained in the experiment should the null hypothesis be true. If that probability is low, the null hypothesis is rejected at a level of confidence corresponding to the probability. Rejecting the null hypothesis then lends support to the alternative, that the different situations explored by the experiment have different outcomes.

TO BE SURE YOU UNDERSTAND THIS APPENDIX △

Here are the most important concepts in the materials just presented. You should be able to define and apply them.

Descriptive statistics
Inferential statistics
Abscissa
Ordinate
Frequency distribution
Frequency polygon
Mode
Median
Mean
J-curve
Skewed distribution
Positive skew
Negative skew
Variance
Standard deviation
Normal curve
Z-score
Percentile rank
Correlation
Scatter plot
Positive correlation
Negative correlation
Correlation coefficients
Cross-lagged correlation
Population
Sample
Representative sample
Random sample
Null hypothesis
Level of confidence
Sampling distribution of the mean
Standard error of the mean
Sampling distribution of differences
Standard error of the difference
t-test

The list just given omits symbols and formulae, which have been collected for presentation.

$$M = \frac{\Sigma X}{N}$$

$$S^2 = \frac{\Sigma d^2}{N}$$

$$S = \sqrt{\frac{\Sigma d^2}{N}}$$

$$\hat{S} = \sqrt{\frac{\Sigma d^2}{N-1}}$$

$$S_M = \frac{\hat{S}}{\sqrt{N}}$$

$$S_{\text{diff}} = \sqrt{S^2_{M1} + S^2_{M2}}$$

$$t = \frac{\text{mean difference}}{S_{\text{diff}}}$$

In addition to these terms and equations, you should be able to handle these materials.

Constructing and interpreting graphs, including frequency distributions and scatter diagrams.
Relationships between mean and median under conditions of symmetry and skew.
These relationships between Z-scores and areas under a normal curve: $-Z = 1.0$ to $+Z = 1.0$, 68 percent; $-Z = 2.0$ to $+Z = 2.0$, 95 percent; $-Z = 3.0$ to $+Z = 3.0$, 99 percent.
Relationships between correlation and (1) variance accounted for, (2) prediction, and (3) causation.
The argument used in rejecting the null hypothesis and interpreting experimental data: since there is no difference, the obtained difference must be real.

TO GO BEYOND THIS APPENDIX △

In this book Statistical considerations come up in almost every chapter, most importantly in Chapters 1, 9, 10, and 17. It seems likely, however, that you will review materials in this appendix in connection with those chapters, rather than the other way round.

Elsewhere Any of a number of introductory statistics books will provide further discussion of most of the topics in this chapter. The most useful recommendation we can make, if you want to go further into the study of statistics, is to select a book that applies statistics to your major field of interest. A general book that will be well within your grasp is *How To Use (and Misuse) Statistics,* by Gregory A. Kimble.

DICTIONARY OF PSYCHOLOGICAL TERMS

This Dictionary goes beyond the usual glossary of terms that appear in introductory textbooks. We have included, in addition, psychological terms the student is likely to come across in lectures and outside readings. To do so we have culled a range of sources to produce a list of definitions that is based on our collective judgments of the significance and the frequency of usage of a term or concept. We have omitted psychological terms that are used essentially in their usual dictionary meaning.

For further definitions we recommend the following three standard technical dictionaries:

English, H. B., and English, A. C. (1958) *A comprehensive dictionary of psychological and psychoanalytic terms*. New York: Longmans, Green and Co.

Eysenck, H. J., Arnold, W., and Meili, R. (Eds.) (1972) *Encyclopedia of psychology*. 3 vols. New York: Herder and Herder.

Hinsie, L. E., and Campbell, R. J. (1970) *Psychiatric dictionary*. (4th ed.) New York: Oxford University Press.

A

ABAB design. An *experimental design* of the *small-N type*. ABAB refers to a sequence of treatments in which A stands for a baseline condition, without the experimental treatment, and B stands for a condition in which the experimental treatment has been introduced.

Ability. Present level of performance on some task. Contrast with *aptitude*.

Abreaction. In psychoanalysis, removal of emotional tension stemming from *repression* by reliving the situation originally causing conflict.

Abscissa. The horizontal or x-axis in a graph. Usually represents the values of the independent variable. Contrast with *ordinate*.

Absolute threshold. Minimal level of stimulation that the organism can detect. Sometimes referred to as detection threshold.

Absolute refractory phase. Period immediately after firing, during which a *neuron* is completely unresponsive to stimulation.

Absorption. A cognitive trait characterized by a capacity for total attending.

Abstract reasoning. The ability to comprehend relationships among things; to respond to concepts and symbols as opposed to concrete elements.

Acceptance acquiescence. A response set notable for a ready acceptance of all characteristics as self-descriptive. An acceptance–acquiescent individual would say "true" to all test terms that describe personality attributes, while rejecting as "false" items that deny them.

Accessibility of memory. An individual may have information *available* in memory but at the same time be unable to obtain access to the memory without some special hint. See *cued recall*. Contrast with *availability of memory*.

Accessory symptoms. The secondary symptom effects of schizophrenia suggested by Bleuler.

Accommodation. (1) In vision, the flattening and bulging of the lens of the eye that serve to produce a sharp image of objects on the retina. A primary cue to depth and distance. (2) As used by Piaget, the process by which the organism adapts to the demands of the environment by modifying its internal structures.

Acetylcholine. Chemical that facilitates the transmission of nerve impulses from one neuron to another; a chemical neurotransmitter.

Achievement motive. A need to achieve for its own sake rather than for the benefits derived from such achievement.

Acquiescence set. A response style characterized by a tendency to yea-say when responding to test items, whether or not the answer is a validly descriptive one.

Acquired drive. A learned motive. Contrast with *primary drive*.

Acquisition. *Learning:* the establishment of a learned response.

Action potential. The electrical changes accompanying a nerve impulse, muscle contraction, or gland secretion.

Action-specific energy. An ethological term. Refers to the proposition that the energy for instinctive behavior is specifically available to certain reactions in the presence of certain stimuli called "releasers."

Active avoidance. A form of *operant conditioning* in which a specified response avoids some noxious stimulus. Contrast with *passive avoidance*.

Active vocabulary. The words a person actually uses in speech. Contrast with *passive vocabulary*.

Actuarial prediction. Statistical prediction through known probabilities that certain patterns of test behavior are associated with particular behavioral signs. Contrast with *clinical prediction*.

Adaptation. The adjustment of the senses to environmental conditions. In dark adaptation the eye adjusts to low levels of illumination. Often adaptation involves a shift in the absolute threshold.

Adaptation, evolutionary. Determinants of the survival characteristics of a species that facilitate its existence in an ever-changing environment.

Adaptation level. A concept that refers to the fact that the judgment of the value of a stimulus depends on the context in which it occurs. Closely related to frame of reference.

Adaptive behavior deficit. Decreased ability to meet the standards of personal independence and social responsibility expected of an individual's age and cultural group.

Additive mixture. In vision, the mixture of lights, each contributing its wavelengths to the color seen. Contrast with *subtractive mixture*.

Adoptee study. A method for the study of genetic factors in which environmental factors are separated out by selecting individuals who have early in life been adopted and thus escaped the environmental influences of their biological parents.

Adrenal glands. A pair of endocrine glands at the top of the kidneys. The source of adrenaline.

Adrenaline. A hormone secreted by the adrenal glands under conditions of strong emotion. Its action is like that of the sympathetic nervous system.

Aerial perspective. A cue to depth from the blurring by the atmosphere of the images of distant objects.

Affect. In psychiatric terminology, emotion.

Affect, disturbances of. Disturbances of mood and emotional responsiveness such as flattened or inappropriate affect. The emotional state is not consonant with cognitions involved.

Affect, flattened. Lack of emotional responsiveness, particularly when emotion is appropriate. Typically used to describe the schizophrenic patient's behavior.

Affect, inappropriate. A distortion in the emotional component of a pattern of behavior, making it incongruent in relation to its cognitive quality.

Affectional systems. Harlow's term for the complex patterns of biological and psychological response that reflect attachment to various classes of stimulus objects (e.g., mothers, peers).

Affective disorder, bipolar. Severe disorders of mood in which the same individual has both manic and depressive episodes. Such episodes tend to be more frequent and of briefer duration that in the episodic form of the affective disorder.

Affective disorder, chronic. Sustained and long-lasting mood disturbances of elation or depression.

Affective disorder, episodic. Extreme mood state, such as marked elation or depression, which may last for relatively brief periods of time and may not recur again for months and even years.

Affective disorders. Mental disorders marked by great emotionality, such as depression or elation so extreme that the individual loses contact with the environment.

Affective reaction. Technically, a psychotic reaction characterized by extreme swings of mood. See *manic-depressive disorder*. More generally, any emotional reaction.

Afferent neuron. A neuron that conducts impulses toward the central nervous system. Contrast with *efferent neuron*.

Affiliative motivation. The need to be associated with other persons.

Afterimage. In vision, after looking at a stimulus for several seconds and then removing it, the perceiver has an image that is like the original stimulus in shape but is of a complementary color.

Age norms. The representative performance of children of a given age with regard to some specific characteristic, e.g., IQ, height.

Age scale. A type of intelligence test in which items are arranged in order of difficulty, and credit for passing is assigned in age units. Contrast with *point scale*.

Aggression anxiety. Anxiety instigated by one's own aggressive tendencies.

Agnosia. Inability to recognize objects. Usually results from brain damage. See *aphasia* and *apraxia*.

Allele. A variation of form a gene may take at a given locus on a chromosome.

All-or-none law. The property of a neuron, muscle cell, or gland cell, after any stimulus, either to respond to its fullest extent or not to respond at all.

Alpha rhythm. A rhythm of the electroencephalogram, or EEG, typically obtained from the occipital region of the cortex; has an average frequency of about 10 cycles per second.

Altered states of consciousness. A mental state that is characterized by markedly different subjective experiences and psychological functioning than is typical of an individual during the normal waking state.

Alternate-forms method. A method of establishing the *reliability* of a test by correlating the scores obtained on two versions of the test.

Amacrine cells. Interconnecting cells in the retina.

Ambivalence. In conflict theory and elsewhere, a reaction toward an object that is simultaneously one of approach and avoidance.

Ambivert. In type theory, a person who is both introverted and extroverted.

Amnesia. Loss of memory. May occur as a result of physical injury or psychologically as the result of repression.

Amniocentesis. The procedure of withdrawing amniotic fluid from the uterus in order to detect biochemical and chromosomal abnormalities in the fetus.

Amphetamine. A central nervous system stimulant which induces euphoria and has proved effective in the treatment of narcolepsy. The drug may, however, pose dangers when taken indiscriminately to achieve a "high."

Ampulla. A swelling at the base of each semicircular canal. It contains hair cells embedded in a gelatinous mass. When the head turns, rotates, or comes to rest, the hair cells are displaced by the lagging endolymph and register the motion.

Anagrams. Letters which must be rearranged to construct a word.

Anal stage. In Freudian theory, a stage of psychosexual development in which the infant's most intense pleasures are derived from activities associated with elimination. Also see *oral stage, phallic stage,* and *latency stage.*

Anal triad. The syndrome of parsimony (stinginess), pedantry (meticulousness), and petulance (ill humor) assumed in psychoanalytic theory to result from fixation at the anal stage of development.

Analytic concept. Sorting of objects on the basis of similarity or of a component that is a part of the total stimulus.

Analytic-relational style. Cognitive styles employed by children; the analytic style uses as a basis for categorization similarities in some manifest quality of the class members (e.g., "Both have fur"); the relational employs as a basis for similarity some thematic relation between class members (e.g., "A match is used to light a cigarette").

Anorexia nervosa. Self-inflicted starvation.

Antagonistic muscles. Pairs of muscles so arranged that contraction in one member of the pair produces stretching in the other member.

Anthropomorphism. Interpreting animal behavior in terms of human psychological processes.

Anticipation method. In serial rote learning, the method in which the subject must respond to each item in a list with the one that follows. Contrast with *free recall.*

Antidromic impulse. An impulse from axon to dendrite in a single neuron. The opposite of the normal direction of conduction.

Antigravitational rigidity. Rigidity resulting from a contraction of antigravitational muscles that follows a transsection of the nervous system in between the hindbrain and the midbrain. The limbs and neck are in a state of stiffened extension.

Antisocial personality. The behavior disorder of the guilt- and anxiety-free individual whose impulsive and often destructive behavior repeatedly brings this offender into conflict with society. Also called sociopathic personality.

Anxiety. A fearful response attached by conditioning to previously neutral stimuli. Can be defined by intensity as in normal or pathological anxiety; by focus of response as in somatic or psychological anxiety; or by locus of arousal as in objective or neurotic anxiety.

Anxiety, state. A more transitory experience of fear arousal and apprehensiveness.

Anxiety, trait. A stable, long-term predisposition to the rapid arousal and maintenance of a state of apprehensiveness.

Anxiety disorder. Disorders marked by acute panic and generalized anxiety that appears to have no specific cause. In *DSM-III* this category also includes *phobias, obsessions,* and *compulsions* in which anxiety is a key component.

Anxiety disorder, generalized. Panic disorders that last six months or longer (*DSM-III*). See *panic disorder.*

Anxiety hierarchy. The description of a sequence of events which are ordered for their ability to evoke anxiety in an individual and which are to be neutralized by the method of systematic desensitization.

Anxiety proneness. A predisposition to the ready arousal of anxiety under numerous stimulating conditions; a threshold phenomenon.

Aphasia, expressive. A speech disturbance in which the patient knows what he wishes to say but cannot utter the word because of an inability to coordinate the muscles. Usually a result of damage or disease to the cerebral cortex.

Aphasia, receptive. A speech disturbance resulting from an inability to understand the meaning of spoken speech symbols or sometimes of written or tactile speech symbols because of damage or disease of the secondary auditory, visual, or somesthetic sensory centers in the cerebral cortex, or of Wernicke's area.

Apparent motion. Perception of motion under conditions in which no physical movement occurs. See *phi phenomenon.*

Application of social sanctions. The enforcement of social norms through expressions of approval and disapproval.

Approach-approach conflict. Conflict produced by the necessity of choosing between two desirable objects.

Approach-avoidance conflict. Conflict produced when a single object or activity is simultaneously attractive and unattractive.

Approach gradient. In conflict theory, the concept (often depicted graphically) that the tendency to approach a positive goal increases with nearness to the goal. Contrast with *avoidance gradient.*

Apraxia. Inability to execute skilled movement, usually as a result of brain damage. See *aphasia* and *agnosia.*

Aptitude. The capacity to profit from training in some particular skill. Contrast with *ability.*

Aqueous humor. A fluid transparent to light filling the space between the lens and the cornea of the eye.

Artifact. The outcome of a study in which the arbitrary treatment of the data leads to spurious conclusions rather than to a true explanation of the phenomenon.

Assimilation. The process, as used by Piaget, whereby the organism's interaction with the environment results in a modification of its internal structures. A child gives meaning to an act by assimilating it to something the child already knows.

Association (area or neuron). An area or neuron in the nervous system that allows communication from relatively sensory structures to relatively motor structures.

Association disturbance. A symptom most frequently observed in schizophrenia (one of Bleuler's fundamental symptoms) in which the individual is unable to retain a train of thought. Cognitions appear to be confused, illogical, and bizarre.

Associative meaning. Meaning in terms of what is associated with an item.

Astigmatism. An imperfectly formed *cornea* that leads to blurred vision.

Asymptote. A limit that a mathematical (or graphic) function approaches but never reaches.

Attachment. The closeness of the tie of infant usually to mother. Initially, the infant's response to strangers is an indiscriminate one; as he learns to discriminate more adequately the stimulus figures in his environment, the close tie to mother is accentuated, and fear of separation becomes manifest. Some investigators (Bowlby) believe that the attachment response is innate and is elicited by specific stimuli.

Attention. The name applied to the tendency of the organism to focus its activity in a certain direction.

Attention defects. Disturbances in the ability to maintain a set or a goal-directed idea.

Attitude. A tendency to respond positively or negatively to other individuals, to institutions, or to courses of activity.

Attitude scale. A device for measuring attitudes toward any of a variety of objects.

Attribution error. Tending to discount the importance of situational factors and to overestimate personal characteristics in judging the causes of another person's behavior.

Attribution theory. The conception that our evaluation of a person's behavior depends on the motives we attribute to it.

Audiogenic seizure. Usually in lower animals (e.g., mice) an epileptiform attack brought on by auditory stimulation. Depends in important ways on hereditary factors.

Audiogram. A graphic representation of a person's pattern of sensitivity to sounds of different frequencies. In cases of deafness shows where the individual's loss of hearing occurs.

Audiometry. Procedure for determining degree of hearing loss.

Auditory threshold. The intensity of an auditory stimulus which is just barely able to be heard.

Authoritarian parent. A parent who places great value on a child's obedience.

Authoritarian personality. A type of personality identified by rigid adherence to middle-class values, extreme awareness of authority relationships, denial of personal sexuality, a tendency to exploit others but also to feel exploited, categorical thinking, and a tendency toward *projection.*

Authoritative parent. A parent who seeks to guide a child's behavior in a logical and issue-oriented manner.

Autism. Absorption in fantasy to the exclusion of interest in reality. A primary symptom of schizophrenia.

Autokinetic effect. A small light in a completely dark room appears to move (*-kinetic*) by itself (*auto-*).

Autonomic nervous system. The part of the nervous system that includes the visceral motor system, nerves to the small glands in the skin, nerves to the small muscles at the base of hairs, nerves to tear ducts and salivary glands, nerves to eye muscles, etc. Consists of sympathetic and parasympathetic divisions and is involved in control of body's internal environment.

Autoshaping. A procedure, most commonly used with pigeons, in which a window in a Skinner-type apparatus is illuminated, and food is made available a few seconds later. Under this procedure the pigeon comes to peck the window without special training.

Availability of memory. A memory is available if it can be called up either on command or with the aid of a special cue or hint. A memory may be available without being *accessible.* See *cued recall.*

Aversion therapy. A form of behavior therapy based upon punishment.

Aversive control. The use of negative reinforcement to induce escape or avoidance conditioning.

Aversive stimulus. A negative, unpleasant, or punishing stimulus.

Avoidance. Tendencies to withdraw.

Avoidance-avoidance conflict. Conflict produced by the necessity of choosing between two undesirable alternatives.

Avoidance gradient. In conflict theory, the concept that the tendency to move away from an undesirable object or state of affairs decreases with distance from this object. Contrast with *approach gradient.*

Avoidance learning. Instrumental learning in which an individual learns to prevent the occurrence of a noxious stimulus by responding appropriately to a warning signal.

Axon. A thin extension of a neuron's protoplasm, which acts as the communicative part of a neuron. Usually sheathed in insulating myelin.

B

Backward association. In verbal learning, an association between the response term and the stimulus term so that, given the former, the subject can produce the latter.

Backward conditioning. An arrangement or paradigm in classical conditioning in which the US precedes the CS. Little or no conditioning actually occurs.

Balance sheet grid. A systematic visual technique for categorizing positive and negative consequences of alternative choices when in a conflict situation.

Bar graph. A form of frequency distribution in which bars are used to indicate numbers of cases.

Barbiturates. Drugs that act as central nervous system depressants (e.g., phenobarbital).

Basal ganglia. Large nuclei in the old forebrain that subserve motor functions.

Basal mental age (basal level). In the Binet-type test, the highest age level at which all tests are passed.

Base-rate problem. A problem sometimes encountered in experimental study whereby the frequency with which some type of behavior occurs in the absence of the experimental treatment is difficult to estimate.

Basilar membrane. A membrane in the cochlea of the inner ear that supports the organ of Corti. Its movement stimulates the hair cells of this structure.

Beat. In audition, the tendency for two tones of similar pitch to be heard as a single tone that waxes and wanes in intensity. The frequency of these beats is equal to the difference in frequency between the two tones. Contrast with *summation tone*.

Behavior modification. See *behavior therapy*.

Behavior therapy. A variety of psychotherapeutic techniques based on learning and conditioning principles. It includes classical and instrumental conditioning procedures, the use of reinforcements to shape behavior.

Belongingness, principle of. The tendency of a grouping of items to be perceived as a whole if the items appear, in some way, to belong together.

Between-subject experiment. An experiment in which different groups of participants receive different experimental treatments. Contrast with *within-subject experiment*.

Bilateral transfer. The effect of practice with one hand on learning (usually) the same skill with the other.

Bimodal distribution. A frequency distribution with two modes, i.e., two points at which there is a piling up of frequencies.

Biofeedback. Voluntary bodily regulation through the feedback of information from internal organs. Biofeedback techniques are based on the principle that an organism can voluntarily modify responses when it receives information feedback designed to adjust or correct such responses until a desired goal is reached.

Biological constraints (on learning). The inborn characteristics of the organism limit what it learns readily. See *principle of preparedness*.

Bipolar cell. In the retina, a cell connecting the rods and cones with ganglion cells.

Blind spot. A region of the retina where a person is effectively blind. Fibers leave the retina at this point to become the optic nerve.

Blocking. A sudden cessation in a train of thought or verbal expression. The person may be unable to explain the reasons behind sudden cognitive stoppages.

Blocking of alpha rhythm. Disappearance of the alpha rhythm upon the presentation of visual (or other) stimuli.

Boilermaker's deafness. Deafness produced by long-term exposure to high-intensity auditory stimulation. Also called *stimulation deafness*.

Bonding drives. A term used by ethnologists to designate drives that facilitate attachment behavior and social cohesion in group members.

Bony labyrinth. A name for the *vestibule* and *semicircular canals* which contain the receptors for vestibular sensitivity.

Bound morpheme. A *morpheme* that has meaning only in combination with another, the pluralizing "s," for example. Contrast with *free morpheme*.

Brain. All the central nervous system except the spinal cord.

Brainstem. The forward extension of the spinal cord to which the cerebrum and cerebellum are attached.

Brainstorming. An undisciplined free-wheeling situation in which groups attempt to solve a problem.

Brainwashing. Techniques of influence used to modify the thinking of those who stand in a subjugated status to some control agent (e.g., prisoners of war, concentration camp victims). The goal of such persuasion is to induce an individual to do things or accept values that he ordinarily would not.

Brain waves. See *electroencephalogram*.

Branched program. In programmed learning, a program that allows participants who master certain information at a given point to proceed further in the programmed series while others, who have not mastered the materials, return to previously learned material to review it.

Brightness. A dimension of visual experience that depends for the most part on the energy of the stimulus. An experience of intensity, identifiable as the dimension from black to white. Contrast with *hue* and *saturation*.

Brightness constancy. The fact that objects retain their relative brightness under various levels of illumination.

Broca's area. An area in the frontal cortex hypothesized by Broca to be responsible for speech. Contrast with *Wernicke's area*.

Bureaucratic. Type of occupation in which income is in the form of wages or salary, and specialized abilities rather than success in risk taking are needed. See *entrepreneurial*.

C

California Psychological Inventory (CPI). A popular, carefully designed, well-standardized test to measure personality functioning of normal individuals.

Canalization. Return to the original growth curve following stressful experiences; a manifestation of the physical integrity of the body.

Case history method. The investigation of psychological problems through the examination of the biographies of human subjects.

Castration complex. In Freudian theory, a fear on the part of a boy that his father will castrate him because of his sexual attraction toward his mother.

Catalepsy. The molding and retention of a part of the body in a given position.

Cataract. A clouding of the *cornea* that impairs vision to the point of effective blindness. In severe cases only differences in brightness in different areas of the visual field are perceived.

Categorical perception (of ***phonemes.***) The abrupt shift in perception of phonemes as a sound is gradually altered from that of one to that of another. The sound is perceived first as one phoneme and then as the other. The gradual transformation is not perceived.

Category scale. A psychological scale formed by requiring individuals to sort stimuli into categories that represent equal intervals on the psychological scale.

Catharsis. In psychoanalysis, elimination of a complex by bringing it to consciousness and allowing it expression. More generally, any relief from emotional disturbance that follows expression of the emotion. See *abreaction*.

Cathexis. Psychic energy invested in an idea, object, or person.

Ceiling level. The age level in Binet-type intelligence tests at which an individual fails all the tests of a given age.

Cell body (of a neuron). The part of the **neuron** that contains the nucleus and nutritional mechanisms.

Centering. Riveting of a person's attention on a particular perceptual attribute of a problem or stimulus array. *Decentering* refers to the ignoring of irrelevant aspects of a problem or array of stimuli.

Central nervous system. The portion of the nervous system that is encased in bone. Includes the brain and the spinal cord.

Central tendency (measure of or type). Clustering of set of values to the middle; different statistics are identified as the mean (arithmetic average), median (middle-value), and mode (most frequent value).

Cephalocaudal sequence. A sequence of maturation in which the pattern of development is from the head downward.

Cerebellum. That division of the central nervous system just below and behind the cerebrum and above the hindbrain. The cerebellum is involved in the maintenance of muscle tonus and in the coordination of movements.

Cerebral arteriosclerosis. Hardening of the arteries of the brain, which produces marked neurological and behavioral changes in the individual.

Cerebral dominance. The concept that one hemisphere of the cerebral cortex controls the person's behavior and thus dominates the other hemisphere.

Cerebral peduncles. Bulges in the bottom of the midbrain consisting of axons of cells whose bodies are in the cerebral cortex.

Cerebrotonia. In Sheldon's theorizing, a personality type characterized by thought rather than action, restraint in social relations, introversion, and need of privacy. Associated in theory with *ectomorphy*.

Cerebrum. The main division of the brain in vertebrates, consisting of a left and right hemisphere.

Channel capacity. The number of items an observer can report exactly after a brief exposure.

Character disorder. A defect of personality structure characterized by immaturity, antisocial reactions, and lack of social responsibility.

Chloretone. A drug that inhibits movement without disturbing growth.

Chlorpromazine. One of the tranquilizing drugs.

Cholinergic. The physiological functions and bodily processes that are stimulated by acetylcholine; also refers to a group of nerve fibers which act upon effectors (muscles, glands) by the release of acetylcholine.

Chromatic. Possessing *hue*.

Chromosomes. Small particles that are located in the nucleus of the cell and play a central role in heredity. The genes—the genetic determiners—are to be found in the chromosomes. The human cell contains twenty-three pairs of chromosomes. One of each pair has been derived from the sperm cell (father), the other from the egg cell (mother).

Chromosomes X and Y. These determine sex characteristics. An XX pair produces a female offspring; an XY combination, a male.

Chronological age. Age in years and months. Used in computing IQ.

Chunking. Grouping items as an aid to memory.

Clang association. In a word association test, a reaction based on the sound of the stimulus word rather than its meaning. For example, *table–Mabel* rather than *table–chair*.

Classical conditioning. A learning procedure in which an organism is presented with a neutral stimulus (CS) and a biologically significant stimulus (US) in fixed order, without respect to the organism's behavior. Contrast with *instrumental conditioning*.

Client-centered therapy. Nondirective therapy devised by Carl Rogers in which the emphasis is on increasing awareness of the client through clarification of the problem, therapist acceptance of disturbing recountals, and the client's ensuing self-growth.

Clinical prediction. Prediction of behavior in terms of hypotheses developed from all available evidence about the dynamics of a particular personality. Contrast with *actuarial prediction*.

Cloning. Asexual form of reproduction in which all progeny are genetically identical.

Clustering in free recall. If an individual tries to recall a list of items, typically words, they are remembered in groups or clusters. Frequently the basis for clustering is categories—animals, professions, musical instruments, etc.

Cocaine. A drug that serves as a central nervous system stimulant.

Cochlea. A bony, fluid-filled canal, coiled like a snail, containing within it a smaller membranous fluid-filled spiral passage, wherein lie the receptors for hearing.

Cocktail party phenomenon. The ability to sort out two or more messages coming to the individual simultaneously and to attend to only one of them

Coding. See *encoding*.

Cognition. Thinking; more broadly, a term for any process whereby an organism acquires knowledge.

Cognitive behavior therapy. The linkage of cognitive and emotional components in therapy. The purpose of such efforts is to help an individual to evaluate many of the irrational beliefs and values that exacerbate distress.

Cognitive dissonance, theory of. The general proposition that bits of knowledge that fail to fit or harmonize produce a strong negative motive.

Cognitive stages. Qualitatively different levels of cognitive development. In cognitive stage theories, intellectual development is assumed to proceed by a sequence of stages, each one representing a different way of processing information about the world.

Cognitive style. A style of perceiving the environment and responding to stimuli within it that has the habitual and consistent quality of a personality trait.

Cold emotion. An emotional experience produced by the injection of adrenalin. The individual reports feeling as though he should have a certain emotional experience.

Cold spot. Area on the skin particularly sensitive to cold stimuli below 32° C.

Collective unconscious. Jungian term for the portion of the unconscious common to all humankind. See *unconscious* and *personal unconscious.*

Color circle. A schematic arrangement of colors in which the spectrum is bent back against itself to form a circle.

Commissure. Tracts connecting corresponding areas in the hemispheres or bilateral divisions of the brain or spinal cord.

Communication disorder/deviancy. The attribute of speech assumed to be characteristic of the parents of schizophrenic patients in which imprecision, illogicality, irrelevance, and conflicting messages are communicated by parents to offspring.

Communicative action of nervous system. The activity of the nervous system that allows stimuli impinging on organs in one part of the body to evoke responses from organs in another part of the body.

Community psychology. Clinical psychology freed from its traditional concerns with individual assessment and treatment and focusing on the individual's adaptation within the community structure of which he is a part.

Compensation. The act or result of seeking a substitute for something unacceptable or unattainable. Occasionally takes the form of an unusually high level of development of an originally unattainable trait or skill.

Competence motivation (effectance motivation). A concept suggested by Robert White whereby the individual strives to acquire skills that facilitate effective functioning in the environment.

Complementary colors. Colors that, when mixed, produce an achromatic.

Complex cell. A single cell in the visual cortex of the cat that responds to stimuli registering in a number of retinal locations and responds vigorously to moving stimuli. See *simple cell* and *hypercomplex cell.*

Complex indicator. In the word association test, an indication of an emotional difficulty (complex) associated with the stimulus word. May take the form of a very unusual response, a protracted latency, or other indication of upset.

Complication experiment. In studies of reaction time the bases for reacting may be made more and more complex. Adding such complexity increases reaction time, and this provides a measure of the time required to do the additional processing. See *subtraction procedure.*

Compromise formation. A mechanism of defense in which an act or thought expresses two, often incompatible, impulses.

Compulsion. An irresistible impulse to perform some act (e.g., handwashing). Together with obsessions, a symptom of obsessive-compulsive reaction.

Concept. A representation of the common properties of objects, events, or ideas that are otherwise distinguishable.

Concept formation. The grouping of individual objects, events, or ideas, all of which share a common attribute or property.

Conceptual intelligence. In Piaget's developmental theory of intelligence, the period of intellectual development extending from two years to maturity.

Concordance. A term in behavior genetics to describe the relationship between family members or twins with respect to a given characteristic or trait. If both show or fail to show the trait in question, the pair is described as concordant; if only one shows the trait, the pair is discordant for that trait. Usually expressed in terms of the percentage of a sample showing concordance.

Concrete operations. A stage in Piaget's developmental theory of intelligence extending from ages seven to eleven years, characterized by conservation, ability to reverse thought, coherent play, flexible thinking, and evaluativeness.

Concurrent validity. *Validity* established by comparing scores on a test with those obtained on another test of established validity.

Condensation. A process of compressing the emotion associated with several different ideas into some new content or idea.

Conditioned emotional response (CER). A form of conditioned fear produced in rats by pairing a neutral stimulus with electric shock. Its effect is demonstrated by a reduction in the rate of bar pressing for food. See *suppression ratio.*

Conditioned reinforcer. A reward which is satisfying as a result of its pairing with reinforcement.

Conditioned response (CR). A response resembling the UR that is evoked by the CS as a result of repeated pairings of CS and US.

Conditioned stimulus (CS). A neutral stimulus that, for experimental purposes, is presented to an organism together with a nonneutral stimulus (US) for the purpose of studying the development of conditioned responses.

Conduction deafness. Deafness produced by imperfections in the mechanisms that conduct sound stimulation from the outer ear to the inner ear. Contrast with *sensory-neural deafness.*

Cones. Retinal elements that respond in terms of color.

Configural pattern. The distribution of subtest scores of a standardized test instrument such as the WAIS or MMPI. The purpose of pattern analysis is to find better predictors of a criterion measure by composites of scores rather than individual scores.

Conflict. The situation in which there is simultaneous instigation toward two or more incompatible responses. See specific types (e.g., *approach-approach conflict*).

Congruence-incongruence. A Rogerian principle that emphasizes the internal harmony or disharmony between the concept of the self and the nature of one's experience.

Conjunctive concept. A concept for which all examples have in common two or more attributes.

Connotative meaning. Meaning in terms of emotional tone.

Conservation. The ability of a child to maintain such concepts as number, substance, and quantity, despite perceptual cues that seem to deny them.

Consolidation. A theoretical process that occurs for several minutes after learning, in which memories become more firmly established. During the period of consolidation a blow to the head may obliterate the unconsolidated memory.

Construct validity. *Validity* established when scores on a test conform to what is generally understood about the trait being tested.

Consummatory behavior. Behavior that fulfills (consummates) some motive. Involves consumption (e.g., of food) only part of the time.

Content validity. *Validity* established when a test has adequate and appropriate coverage of a given area.

Context theory of meaning. The theory that the meaning of a specific item such as a word depends on the situation (context) in which it occurs.

Contiguity. The occurrence of two events together in time, for example, CS and US or response and reinforcement. Contrast with *contingency*.

Contingency. A term used in connection with *operant conditioning* procedures. Refers to the dependence of reward on the occurrence or nonoccurrence of a specified response.

Contingent reward. A reward is said to be contingent on behavior if it follows a specific behavior.

Continuity. The consistency of behavior across stages of development.

Continuous reinforcement. A schedule of reinforcement in which a subject is rewarded for every correct response. Contrast with *partial reinforcement*.

Control group. A reference group in an experiment. Typically subjected to the measurements performed on the experimental group, but not given the experimental treatment.

Controlled variable. A variable whose value is held constant for all groups in an experiment.

Convergence. A cue to depth and distance provided by kinesthetic stimuli, produced when the eyes turn to obtain clear images on both retinae.

Convergent thinking. Thinking that has the goal of selecting the best or most appropriate or most conventional solution to a problem.

Conversion disorder. A *somatoform disorder* (*DSM-III*) marked by a variety of bodily symptoms such as paralysis and loss of sensation, sensory disturbances, and insensitivity to pain.

Conversion hysteria. A term formerly used for *conversion disorder*.

Coolidge effect. An increase in sexual activity *of a male animal* following satiation when the male is presented with a new female partner.

Coordination of secondary schemas. A stage in Piaget's developmental theory of intelligence extending from eight to twelve months of age, reflecting the beginning of purposive, goal-directed, problem-solving behavior.

Cornea. The outermost transparent coating at the front of the eye.

Corpus callosum. A mass of white matter that links the two cerebral hemispheres.

Correct rejection. In signal detection procedures, indicating that no signal is present on trials when the signal is, in fact, absent.

Correlation. Co-relation. The way in which pairs of measures obtained on the same individuals are related. See *correlation coefficient*.

Correlation coefficient. A number that indicates the degree of correspondence of two measures obtained on the same unit, usually an individual.

Correlational method. A method of psychological investigation in which the goal is to discover the interrelationships among response measures.

Correlational study. *See correlational method.*

Correspondent-inference theory. A theory according to which we assume that a person's behavior tells us something more important about him when there are few reasons for engaging in the behavior than when there are many strong reasons. See *attribution theory*.

Cortex, rind or bark. A layering of cells near the surface of any organ. Thus cerebral cortex is the surface layer of cells in the cerebrum.

Co-twin control. A method of experimentation used in research on the nature-nurture problem in which a pair of twins is involved, one twin being assigned to the experimental condition, the other being assigned to the control condition.

Counterconditioning. The replacement of one conditioned response by the establishment of an incompatible response to the same conditioned stimulus.

Countertransference. A form of transference recognized in psychoanalytic practice in which the analyst develops strong emotional attachments for his patient.

CR. Conditioned response.

Cranial nerves. The twelve pairs of peripheral nerves containing fibers running to and from the brainstem.

Craniosacral system. In anatomical terms, the *parasympathetic nervous system*.

Creativity. The ability to produce new ideas and products.

Cretinism. A form of mental retardation caused by an inborn failure of the individual to metabolize thyroxin.

Criterion. A comparison base for judgment; often a score, behavior, or goal against which the predictive quality of a test is judged.

Criterion situation. Performance in a situation external to a test or any other measure against which test performance is evaluated, thus providing an indication of the validity of the test.

Critical period. A stage in development in which the organism is optimally ready to acquire certain forms of learned responses.

Crossing-over. The exchange of corresponding segments of a pair of chromosomes during meiosis.

Cross-lagged correlation coefficients. Correlations evident between two different measures obtained at different times on the same individuals. Under some circumstances these correlations reveal a causal relationship.

Cross-sectional studies. Research studies that compare the performance of groups of people of various ages to determine how a particular characteristic changes with age. Contrast with *longitudinal method.*

Crystalline lens. The lens of the eye.

Crystallized intelligence. Term used by Raymond Cattell to denote cognitive capacities that depend on learning. Contrast with *fluid intelligence.*

CS. Conditioned stimulus.

Cubical model of intelligence. J. P. Guilford's view of intelligence as consisting of three dimensions—the contents, the operations, and the products of thought. The model postulates 120 separate intellectual abilities.

Cued recall. An experimental procedure in which the individual receives some cue as an aid to recall. *Paired-associate learning* would be an example, but the term is used more frequently in connection with *free recall,* in which a category name may be provided as a cue.

Cultural-familial retardation. Mild retardation that is nonorganic and likely results from gene (familial)–environment (cultural) interaction.

Culture-fair test. A test that is free of cultural bias; in intelligence testing, one that is free of contents that would favor middle- and upper-class individuals.

Cumulative response curve. A record of performance in instrumental conditioning in which every response of the participant moves a pen a step of a certain size on a constantly moving paper.

Curare. A drug that immobilizes the skeletal musculature by blocking the junction between nerve and muscles.

Cutoff score. A score below which applicants for some job or training are rejected. The cutoff score is selected to maximize the number of successes and to minimize the number of failures.

Cyclothymic personality. A form of personality disorder in which moods of elation and depression alternate.

D

Dark adaptation. Adaptation of the eye to low levels of illumination.

Db. The abbreviation for decibel.

Deactivating enzyme. A chemical that breaks up a *neurotransmitter substance* following *synaptic transmission.*

Death instinct. Basic instinct or drive of an aggressive, destructive nature (Thanatos); a psychoanalytic concept.

Decenter. The ability to focus attention simultaneously on several perceptual attributes of a stimulus.

Decibel. A measure of the intensity of an auditory stimulus. The intensity of any stimulus in decibels (db) is ten times the common logarithm of the ratio of the sound in question to a standard reference intensity which is typically in the region of the absolute threshold.

Decontextualization. The ability of a person to perceive objects irrespective of the context in which they occur or are embedded.

Dedifferentiation. Regression in thought in which a mature individual engages in undifferentiated thought processes characteristic of an earlier age.

Deep structure. Noam Chomsky's term for basic, underlying meaning of a sentence, however it is stated in its *surface structure,* in active or passive voice, in question form, etc.

Defense mechanism. Some type of behavior designed to protect a person from uncomfortable anxiety.

Defensive avoidance. Avoidance of decision making when in conflict by rationalization, shifting responsibility, or being unresponsive to new information.

Degeneration. Deterioration of a neuron following damage. Degeneration is a "method" for studying connections in the nervous system. Damage created in one area leads, by degeneration, to damage in the cell bodies of neurons connected to the damaged area.

Delta waves. EEG brain waves that are characteristically slow and of high amptitude. Seen to occur in stage 3 (deep) sleep.

Delusion, grandiosity. A false belief in one's power and greatness; a false sense of omnipotence.

Delusion, persecutory. A false belief that others seek to destroy or take advantage of the perceiver, or in some manner render him incompetent.

Delusional percept. A *first-rank symptom* in which a normal perception is given private meaning and rapidly elaborated into a delusional belief.

Delusions, somatic. Perception by schizophrenic patients that their bodies are disturbed or distorted in some extremely aberrant manner (e.g., a snake in one's intestine).

Demand characteristic. A participant's perception of what is demanded of him by an experimental procedure. Frequently, the participant's perception may be very different from the experimenter's intention.

Dementia. A term of multiple meanings; originally used as equivalent to madness and later to delirium. The term today is used to stress severe intellectual deficit, often irreversible and frequently suggestive of deterioration of mental processes.

Dementia praecox. A term used earlier in psychiatry's history to describe schizophrenia. It emphasizes the attributes of early onset and unavoidable deterioration.

Demographic data. Vital and social statistics related to such factors as birth, death, marriage, residence patterns, disease and disorder distributions, etc.

Demoralization hypothesis. Jerome Frank's view of the universal element in all persons who seek therapy, namely their awareness that they can no longer cope with a life situation.

Dendrite. Relatively thick extension of a neuron's protoplasm on which the terminal buttons of other neurons synapse.

Denial mechanisms. Mechanisms of defense in which an unpleasant external reality is rejected and replaced by a more pleasurable and wish-fulfilling fantasy pattern.

Denotative meaning. The thing, event, or relationship that a word stands for.

Dependent variable. In psychology, any aspect of behavior that the psychologist attempts to predict or control. More generally, the events that any science attempts to predict or control.

Depersonalization. A form of neurotic behavior in which a sense of unreality and of estrangement from one's body and surroundings predominates.

Depressive disorder. An emotional state consisting of marked sadness, fearfulness and apprehension, extreme sense of guilt, self-condemnation, withdrawal from others, and loss of sleep, sexual interest, and appetite. The person may be highly agitated or extremely withdrawn and lethargic.

Descriptive psychopathology. The study of the structural aspects of various forms of behavior disorder.

Descriptive statistics. Measures (e.g., *mean, standard deviation, correlation coefficient*) that describe the characteristics of some set of data. Contrast with *inferential statistics.*

Detection threshold. See *absolute threshold.*

Deterioration (dementia). A chronic and progressive disorganization of personality.

Determinism. In its most general sense, the philosophical point of view which denies the existence of free will and asserts that all phenomena can be explained in terms of their antecedents. Determinism asserts that if one knew all antecedent conditions one could predict behavior.

Deuteranopia. A form of partial color blindness in which the person is unable to distinguish red and green, apparently as a result of a weakness in the perception of green. Contrast with *protanopia.*

Development quotient (DQ). Similar to intelligence quotient, but typically based on infant developmental tests.

$$DQ = \frac{\text{Tests passed (in months)}}{\text{Chronological age}} \times 100$$

Developmental psychopathology. The study of the origins and longitudinal development of various forms of behavior disorders.

Deviation IQ. A measure of an individual's relative position within his age group as revealed by intelligence test performance. The score is based on a measure of variability—the standard deviation—and is expressed as a Z-score that ranges from −3.0 to +3.0. Equivalent in interpretation to the original IQ measure defined by Mental age ÷ Chronological age.

Diathesis-stress theories. The theories of psychiatric disorder that emphasize the interaction of fundamental biological predispositions with life stresses, which potentiate them into disorder. Important etiological theories of mental disorder.

Dichotic listening. A technique for studying attention and information processing in which simultaneous but differing messages are presented to each ear via earphones.

Dichromatic color vision. Describing the vision of many color-blind persons, for whom the various hues in the visual world depend on the mixing of two colors. For normal trichromatic color vision, three hues are necessary.

Difference threshold. The smallest difference between two stimuli that can be detected dependably. Compare with *absolute threshold.*

Differentiation, cognitive. Applied to cognitive development, differentiation refers to the shift with age from gross, all-or-none types of thinking to complex, highly discriminative thought.

Difficult child. A child whose temperament is disrupted by an unpleasant mood, difficulty in accepting and adjusting to new situations, and irregularity in biological functions.

Diffuse projection. A neurological expression for the fact that stimulation brings a general state of arousal in the cerebral cortex. This effect is produced by the ascending reticular formation and is to be contrasted with stimulation in more limited primary projection areas of the cortex.

Disassociative disorder. Disorders marked by sudden temporary alterations of consciousness that result in loss of identity and memory defect (amnesia) for personal information about oneself and one's previous life history.

Disaster syndrome. A specific sequence of reactions often characteristic of people in natural or man-made disasters. Includes initial *shock reaction,* which is followed by *recoil reaction* and a stage of *recall* of the traumatic experience.

Discounting effect. In our interpretations of the whys of another person's behavior, we may play down a given cause if other causes are plausible.

Discriminative stimulus (S^D). A stimulus that evokes an operant response and signals that a reinforcer is available (the ring indicating that one should answer a telephone).

Disguising mechanisms. Mechanisms of defense such as displacement, in which an anxiety-arousing wish or thought is expressed in modified form to disguise its true nature.

Disjunctive concept. A concept which includes examples in which one or another of several characteristics is present.

Displaced aggression. Hostility directed at a person or object not directly responsible for the frustration that produced it. See *frustration–aggression hypothesis.*

Displacement. The expression of any behavioral tendency in response to some stimulus other than the one that usually instigates the behavior in question. See *displaced aggression* and *displacement behavior.*

Displacement (dream distortion). A process whereby the contents of the dream camouflage unacceptable thought.

Displacement behavior (ethology).

The elicitation of common instinctive behavior in inappropriate circumstances, usually thwarting ones.

Distal stimulus. The energy in the physical world that excites a sense organ. Contrast with *proximal stimulus*.

Distributed practice. In learning, practice which includes substantial rest pauses between trials. Contrast with *massed practice*.

Divergent thinking. Thinking characterized by a search for a variety of ideas or multiple solutions to a problem.

Dizygotic twins. Twins that develop from two fertilized ova. "Fraternal" twins.

DNA (deoxyribonucleic acid). Molecules found in the cell nucleus that are the fundamental determiners of the heredity of the organism. This "chemical master," which provides the master plan for the organism's genetic code, is composed of a sugar (deoxyribose), a phosphate group, and four nitrogenous bases (adenine, guanine, cytosine, and thymine).

Dominant gene. A gene that expresses itself in trait or appearance, even when paired with a recessive gene.

Dopamine receptor. Dopamine is a *neurotransmitter substance* in the CNS believed to play a prominent role in schizophrenia, when produced in excess. The dopamine receptor is a site on the postsynaptic neuron that is activated by dopamine and passes on the impulse transmitted by it.

Doppler effect. When a sound passes us, its pitch rises as it approaches and lowers as it moves away.

Double blind. An investigational procedure best exemplified by studies of the effects of drugs on psychopathological states in which neither the investigator nor the patient knows whether he is in the drugged or undrugged group. Applied more generally to all studies of therapy.

Down syndrome. A form of mental retardation induced by a genetic anomaly, usually trisomy in the twenty-first chromosome.

Drive. A motive.

Drive-reduction theory. A theory holding that reinforcement consists of the reduction of a motive. Food, for example, is a reinforcer because it reduces hunger.

Drive stimulus. A stimulus associated with a drive, for example, the hunger pangs associated with hunger.

Drug therapy. Intervention efforts aimed at alleviating disturbing symptoms of a disorder through the use of pharmaceutical agents.

Drug withdrawal. Symptoms attendant on removal of a drug with addictive powers.

DSM-III. The revised Diagnostic and Statistical Manual of the American Psychiatric Association now undergoing field trials.

Dual-coding theory. Theory that materials in memory are represented in two systems, a system of images and a verbal system.

Duplicity theory of vision. The theory, which has essentially the status of fact, that vision consists of two separate senses. See *rods* and *cones*.

E

Eardrum. The membrane at the entrance to the middle ear that is set into vibration by sound waves striking it.

Easy child. A child whose temperament it is to have a pleasant mood, to approach new stimuli, and to be regular in biological functions.

Echoic memory. A very brief memory for auditory stimuli corresponding to *iconic* memory in vision. In both cases the memory persists for a second or so.

Ectomorphy. One of the body types identified by Sheldon. The long, thin, angular type of person has this one. Contrast with *endomorphy* and *mesomorphy*.

EEG. Electroencephalograph or electroencephalogram.

Effectance motivation. See *competence motivation*.

Effective stimulus. A stimulus that affects an appropriate receptor in detectable strength. Contrast with *distal stimulus*. See *proximal stimulus*.

Effector. An organ capable of producing a response; a muscle or gland.

Efferent neuron. A neuron that conducts impulses away from the central nervous system toward an effector. Contrast with *afferent neuron*.

Ego. In psychoanalytic theory, the portion of the personality that behaves realistically, postponing pleasures of the id and directing the energies of the id into socially acceptable channels.

Ego psychology. Revisions in psychoanalytic theory emphasizing the functions of the ego as opposed to those of the id. Ego theory stresses reality functioning rather than the disguised but overt representation of repressed thoughts and wishes.

Ego strength. The ability of the individual to perform effectively those functions necessary for coping in the environment.

Egocentricity. Behavior characteristic of children in which there is little differentiation of self from others in the external world. In Piaget's theory, egocentrism refers to the appraisal of objects and events in terms of one's self-interest, personal needs, and values.

Eidetic imagery. The ability to evoke a clear, vivid, and identical image of an object or event after it has been experienced. People capable of such imagery are called *eidetikers*. Eidetic imagery is often, but inaccurately, referred to as photographic memory.

Elaborative rehearsal. Rehearsal in which the individual relates an item to be remembered to other items with which it can be associated. A useful procedure for putting the item in long-term memory. Contrast with *maintenance rehearsal*.

Electroencephalogram. A record, typically ink-written, of the spontaneous electrical activity of the brain, obtained by attaching electrodes to the scalp and greatly amplifying the voltage changes. Commonly referred to as a record of "brain waves."

Electroshock (electroconvulsive) therapy. A therapeutic procedure often used with manic-depressive reactions, in which convulsions are produced by passing an electric current through the head.

Elicited behavior. In conditioning, behavior that is part of the organism's existent behavioral repertoire and is made in response to a readily recognized physical stimulus.

Embryo. In the human species, the organism from the second to the eighth week following conception.

Emitted behavior. Behavior without a known stimulus. What is popularly called voluntary behavior.

Emotion. A "stirred up" state of the organism. Physiologically, the functions of the autonomic nervous system and endocrine system are important.

Empirical-criterion method. A method for developing personality inventories or tests that ignores theory initially and relies exclusively on empirical methods to select test items (e.g., the MMPI).

Enactive representation. First stage in Jerome Bruner's theory of cognitive growth, during the first half year, when infants know the world only by their actions, thus representing objects and past events through motor responses.

Encephalization. The concept that, in the higher levels of phylogenetic development, the cerebral cortex becomes increasingly important in the control of behavior.

Encoding. Putting materials into a form that the memory system can handle. More generally, the process of translating messages into signals (codes) which can be transmitted through a communication channel.

Encoding specificity. The tendency for memories to be stored or encoded in terms of a specific context and to be accessible only in that context.

Encounter group. Small therapeutic group that emphasizes personal growth through emotional expressiveness, candor, and interpersonal honesty within the group. Also termed *sensitivity training* and *T-group*.

Endocrine system. A glandular system that excretes its products directly into the bloodstream.

Endogenous psychosis. A psychotic state which arises primarily from hereditary–constitutional factors, the antecedants of which, therefore, are to be found within the individual.

Endolymph. A fluid within the membranous labyrinth of the vestibular system. Within the sacs of the *vestibule*, it contains small crystals of calciurn carbonate which lag against and stimulate hair cells, giving us a sense of motion whenever the head tilts or changes in acceleration.

Endomorphy. One of the body types identified by Sheldon. The round, corpulent person has this one. See *ectomorphy* and *mesomorphy*.

Engram. A hypothesized memory trace formed and stored during learning that will decay and be lost unless transferred to a long-term memory storage system.

Entrepreneurial. Type of occupation in which rewards are based on the person's performance, such as business ownership or selling, the salary for which consists of commissions. See *Bureaucratic*.

Environmental variance. The range of expression of a particular trait in a population that is attributed to different environmental conditions and experiences.

Enzyme. Organic compound that produces chemical changes and other compounds through catalytic action.

Epilepsy. Name for a variety of disorders brought on by widespread discharge of neurons in the brain. See *grand mal epilepsy*, *petit mal epilepsy*, and *psychomotor epilepsy*.

Epinephrine. A hormone secreted by the adrenal medulla implicated in emotional arousal. *Adrenaline* is sometimes used as a synonym.

Episodic memory. Memory for temporally dated personal events. Contrast with *semantic memory*.

Equilibrium. As used by Piaget, describes the organism's need to achieve a balance with its environment. The effect is a reciprocal one in which both organism and environment modify each other in the course of the individual's adaptation.

Erogenous zone. Areas of the body capable of producing sexual excitement or libidinal gratification when stimulated.

Ethology. A branch of zoology concerned with the behavior of animals, and in this sense allied to psychology.

Etiology. Cause or origin.

Eugenics. The study and application of principles to improve the genetic qualities of a population.

Evoked potential. An electric discharge in a neural center produced by stimulation elsewhere.

Excitation. A general term used to refer to positive influences favoring the occurrence of a response. Contrast with *inhibition*.

Excitatory stimulation. Stimulation that tends to fire a neuron. Contrast with *inhibitory stimulation*.

Existential psychology. A psychology that emphasizes human experience as the basic reality rather than psychical events and overt behavior.

Experimental design. The plan of an experiment. The simplest design involves two groups of subjects, an *experimental group* and a *control group*. It proceeds in three stages devoted to equating groups, introducing the experimental treatment and evaluating the effect of this treatment.

Experimental group. In an experiment, the group to which some special manipulation is applied. Contrast with *control group*.

Experimental neurosis. Emotional disturbance produced (usually) in a lower animal by establishing the conditions of conflict. In Pavlov's demonstration, the need to make a very fine discrimination brought about the conflict.

Experimenter bias. Distortions of experimental results produced by the investigator's tendency to see wished-for effects in the data. A source of experimental error.

Explosive personality. A personality disorder in which there are outbursts of rage and aggression and a loss of control.

Expressed emotionality (EE). A construct used to characterize the families of schizophrenic patients whose behavior to the patient is marked by intense criticism, hostility, and anger. Such families appear to increase the likelihood that a released schizophrenic family member will return to the hospital.

Extinction. The (1) procedure and (2) result of eliciting a conditioned response without reinforcement.

Extirpation. The removal of brain tissue for experimental purposes.

Extrapunitive aggression. Aggression directed outward, toward other persons.

Extrasensory perception (ESP). Awareness of thoughts and objects without direct participation of the senses.

Extrovert. In type theory, the personality that is oriented outward, requiring continual stimulation from the environment. Contrast with *introvert.*

Eyedness. The tendency for one eye to dominate the other in vision. The two eyes receive different views of an object. When these are very different, we "see" the view obtained by the dominant eye. Otherwise things would be seen double.

F

F_1. First filial generation. The first generation of descent from a given mating.

Face validity. The appearance of validity produced by the fact that a test requires a performance very similar to the job for which it is designed to make predictions.

Factor analysis. A statistical technique, employing the methods of correlation, designed to detect the components (factors) that contribute to a complex trait.

False alarm. In signal detection experiments, the report of a signal on trials when none is there. Contrast with *hit.*

False recognition. Reported recognition of an item or even never seen previously by the reporting person.

Family pedigree study. Intensive multi-generational study of families of affected individuals identified by specific attributes, or predisposition to disease or disorder.

Fantasy. Daydreaming, imagining another private and pleasant world.

Fear of success. Motive to avoid success found in some women because intellectual competitiveness is seen as unfeminine.

Fechner's law. $S = K \log I + A$. The perceived intensity of a stimulus (S) varies with the logarithm of physical intensity (I). A is an intercept constant.

Fetus. The unborn human organism from the eighth week following conception to birth.

Field independence–dependence. A cognitive style and its personality correlates, as described by Witkin and his associates. Its central components are individual differences in perceiving and orienting oneself to the environment. Field-independent types require fewer cues from the visual field for orientation to it; field-dependent types depend on the visual field for their orientation.

Figure–ground relationship. In the visual world, figures tend to stand out sharply and definitely against an extended background.

Final common path. In reflex physiology, the motor pathway upon which many neural pathways converge.

First-rank symptoms (FRS). Hallucinatory experiences and delusional beliefs believed by Kurt Schneider, psychiatrist, to be the prototypic indicators of schizophrenia, hence called Schneiderian signs, of which there are eleven.

Fis phenomenon. The refusal of a child who mispronounces a word (e.g., "fis" for "fish") to accept that pronunication when it is used by someone else.

Fixation. (1) Stereotyped response developed as a consequence of conflict. (2) In psychoanalytic theory, an attachment of the libido to some particular stage of psychosexual development.

Fixed-action pattern. In ethology, a stereotyped instinctive act.

Fixed-interval schedule. In instrumental conditioning, a schedule of partial reinforcement in which the subject is rewarded for the first response after a certain fixed amount of time.

Fixed-ratio schedule. In instrumental conditioning, a schedule of partial reinforcement in which reward occurs after a certain fixed number of responses.

Flooding. A form of implosion therapy in which individuals confront real rather than imagined stimuli in order to densensitize themselves to feared objects or situations. See *implosion therapy.*

Fluid intelligence. Term used by Raymond Cattell to denote cognitive ability that is not influenced by prior learning.

Forebrain. The uppermost portion of the brain which shows its most advanced development in the higher vertebrates; comprises the cerebrum, thalamus, hypothalamus, and related structures.

Formal operations. A stage in Piaget's developmental theory of intelligence extending from eleven years to maturity and characterized by the full development of reasoning and judgment.

Fovea. Region in the retina that is closely packed with cones; the region stimulated by the image of an object at which one looks directly.

Frame of reference. The background of experience against which one's judgments are made. See *adaptation level.*

Free association. In psychoanalysis, the technique of having the patient report all thoughts as they occur.

Free floating anxiety. Anxiety that is not attached to specific objects.

Free morpheme. A *morpheme* which has meaning when it stands alone, a word for example. Contrast with *bound morpheme.*

Free recall. A method of studying memory in which the participant, after the presentation of materials, is allowed to reproduce them in any order. Contrast with the procedures used in *paired-associate learning* and *serial learning.*

Free responding. In instrumental conditioning, an experimental arrangement in which the participant is allowed to respond spontaneously rather than just on trials.

Frequency distribution. A graphic representation of the number of measures (often individuals) of each value or class of values.

Frequency polygon. A frequency distribution in which the *x*-axis is the measure or score and the *y*-axis is the number of measures (frequency). Values are connected by straight lines. Contrast with *bar graph*.

Frontal lobes. Approximately the upper or forward half of the cerebral hemispheres.

Frustration. Any object or state of affairs that prevents a person from obtaining a desired goal object.

Frustration–aggression hypothesis. The theory that aggression is always the consequence of frustration. (The reverse relationship does not hold: frustration has a variety of consequences, including frustration.)

Frustration tolerance. The amount of frustration that a person can undergo without a disintegration of behavior.

Fugue state. A dissociative reaction in which a person relinquishes his identity and activities and establishes a new identity with amnesia for the former life.

Functional autonomy. The hypothesis that sometimes habits become drives, that is, ends in themselves, free of their original motivational basis.

Functional disorder. A form of psychopathological reaction without a known physiological basis.

Fundamental symptoms. Bleuler's basic symptoms of schizophrenia: association and affect disturbances, ambivalence, and autism.

Fundamental tone. The lowest tone in a complex tone. Contrast with *overtone*.

G

Galvanic skin response (GSR). A change in the resistance of the skin to the passage of electric current. Occurs in emotional states.

Gamete. A cell of either sex (egg or sperm) that combines with a cell of the opposite sex to form a new organism.

Ganglion cell. In the retina, nerve cells whose fibers form the optic nerve.

Ganzfeld. A field of vision without objects and with homogeneous illumination.

Gate-control theory of pain. A theory of pain perception that attributes pain to the joint function of two sets of neurons. Activity in large-diameter fibers closes a gate determining whether stimulation to be experienced as painful will be transmitted; activitity in small-l-diameter fibers opens it.

Gene. The basic unit for the transmission of hereditary attributes located on chromosomes. Typically, chromosomes exist in pairs, one having been contributed by the father, the other by the mother.

Gene pool. The total collection of genes in a particular population.

General adaptation syndrome. A sequence of physiological reactions produced by protracted periods of stress. Consists, in order, of the alarm reaction, the stage of resistance, and the stage of exhaustion.

General factor. A factor that statistical analysis suggests is involved in all tests for a particular trait. Spearman's *g factor* in intelligence is an example.

Generalization. The automatic transfer of a response conditioned to a particular stimulus to all similar stimuli.

Generalization decrement. The loss of response strength that occurs when a response is elicited by a stimulus other than the original conditioned stimulus. Contrast with *generalization*.

Generalization gradient. The degree of response evoked in an organism to stimuli that vary in similarity to a stimulus to which the organism has been previously trained to respond.

Generalization of extinction. *Extinction* of a response to one stimulus lowers response strength to a similar stimuli.

Generation-recognition theory. A theory of *retrieval* suggested by studies of the *tip-of-the-tongue phenomenon*. According to this theory retrieval consists of the examination of a set of possible answers generated from those available in a certain semantic category. The answer produced is the answer recognized as having the physical features of the desired answer.

Generative grammar. The rules of grammar by which a sentence can be constructed.

Genetic engineering. Processes and techniques for changing the structure of individual genes or sections of DNA or for changing the genetic makeup of individuals or populations.

Genetic variance. The range of expression of a particular trait in a population that is due to different *genotypes*.

Genital stage. In psychoanalytic theory, a stage of psychosexual development characterized by heterosexual interests. See *anal stage* and *oral stage*.

Genius. Person of unparalleled achievements; formerly, a person with an IQ exceeding anywhere from 150 to 180, but this criterion fails to capture the essence of a concept best limited to supreme accomplishment.

Genotype. In genetics, the characteristics of an organism that are hereditarily determined and hence capable of being transmitted biologically.

Germ cells. Reproductive cells (i.e., a sperm or an egg) that unite to form a new individual of a species.

Germinal period. The first two weeks of prenatal development in the human species.

Gestalt psychology. A school of psychology that emphasized the wholeness of behavior, especially perception. Responsible for the expression, "The whole is greater than the sum of its parts." The whole according to this school dominates and gives meaning to the parts.

Giftedness. Having very high intelligence.

Glial cells or Glia. Literally "glue"; nonactive cells in the nervous system that perform supportive, nutritive, and phagocytic (i.e., ingests microorganisms) functions throughout the brain and spinal cord.

Glove anaesthesia. A form of hysteria in which an insensitivity to touch on the hand is so localized as to make evident that the sensory nerves are not involved.

Gradient of texture. A cue to depth and distance resulting from the fact that detail disappears in the distance.

Grand mal epilepsy. A form of *epilepsy* characterized by loss of consciousness and violent convulsions.

Gray matter. Areas of the *central nervous system* that contain unmyelinated nerve cell bodies and dendrites and are integrative in function. Contrast with *white matter.*

Group polarization. Discussion leads to an average increase in the extremity of the position taken on a controversial issue. Groups with opinions that differed before discussion draw further apart.

Group therapy. Therapeutic intervention in which group interaction is the central focus for understanding the behavior of individuals.

Group think. A symptom of group decision making in which the behavior of the group rallies around the leader, an earlier plan or slogan, rather than solving a problem.

Growth curve. A graphic representation of growth in which the abscissa of the graph is represented by age units and the ordinate by progressive or incremental units.

Guinea pig effect. The behavior of people who know they are being observed or experimented on differs from what it would be under more natural conditions.

H

Habit-family hierarchy. An expression referring to the fact that any stimulus tends to elicit a group of responses (habit family) that vary in strength (hierarchy).

Habituation. The process of allowing an organism to become accustomed to a particular situation. Often used to control the fearful reactions of experimental participants to experimental situations. More technically, the fact that repeated elicitation leads to the weakening of a response.

Hair cell. A hearing receptor in the organ of Corti; so called because the cell contains hairlike projections.

Halfway house. A physical setting within a community devised as a living, self-governing unit for persons who are or have been mentally disordered.

Hallucination. A sensory experience without known physical basis. Distinguish from *illusion.*

Hallucinogen. A drug that produces hallucinatory experiences.

Halo effect. In making judgments of people, the tendency to rate an individual high or low on all traits because of the knowledge that he is high or low on one or a few.

Hemiplegia. "Half paralysis" of one side of the body from brain damage.

Heritability ratio. An estimate of the relative contribution of heredity to the total variance of a given trait in a specific population.

Hertz (Hz). Unit of frequency of a periodic process equal to one cycle per second.

Heterozygous. With respect to a trait, a gene pair containing a dominant and a recessive gene. Either may be transmitted to the offspring.

Hierarchical organization. Patterns of instinctive behavior under stimulation that begin with initial general arousal followed by more specific behavioral tendencies that vary in their probability of response.

Hierarchical structures. An aspect of the stage of concrete operations in which the child is able to classify stimuli on the basis of specific attributes or dimensions.

Hierarchy of needs. Maslow's concept of the sequential emergence of motives: physiological, safety and security, love, self-esteem, and self-actualization.

Higher-order conditioning. Classical conditioning in which the US is the CS from a previous experiment.

Hindbrain. The lowest portion of the brain stem just above and continuous with the spinal cord and just below and continuous with the midbrain. Consists of medulla oblongata, pons, and cerebellum.

Hit. In signal detection experiments, the report of a signal on trials where one is present.

Homeostasis. The tendency of the body to maintain certain physiological constancies.

Homograph. Two or more words that are spelled the same and pronounced the same but mean different things; e.g., (1) The Brooklyn *Bridge* and the game of *bridge,* (2) *cardinal* numbers, the bird *cardinal,* the church official called a *Cardinal,* and the St. Louis ballplayer called a *Cardinal.*

Homozygous. With respect to a trait, a gene pair made up either of two dominant or two recessive genes.

Homunculus. A miniature human being who was believed in earlier times to reside in the sperm cells and to grow with nourishment and time to babyhood.

Horizontal cells. Interconnecting cells in the retina.

Hormone. A substance excreted by any of the endocrine glands.

Hue. Chromatic color determined by the wave length of the light stimulus. Distinguish from *brightness* and *saturation.*

Humanistic psychology. A view of human functioning that emphasizes the uniqueness of individuals, their strivings and potential for growth. Often identified as a third force in psychology, in contrast to psychoanalysis and behaviorism.

Hurler syndrome. A disorder of metabolism transmitted as a recessive trait associated with a characteristic facial appearance and mental retardation.

Hydrocephaly. Literally "water head," a condition produced by an accumulation of cerebrospinal fluid in the cranial cavity. When this happens early in life, it leads to enlargement of the head. The condition is associated with mental retardation.

Hypercomplex cell. Cells in the visual cortex of the cat that fire to complex stimuli such as corners.

Hyperkinesis. Marked overactivity and distractability in younger children, the causes of which are unknown.

Hyperphagia. Literally "overeating," produced by injury to certain regions of the hypothalamus.

Hypervigilance. Frantic search for a decision governed more by emotion than a careful consideration of alternatives. In its most extreme form hypervigilance is converted into a "panic" state.

Hypochondriasis. A form of neurosis characterized by preoccupation with the state of one's body accompanied by multiple physical complaints.

Hypothalamus. A region in the forebrain that controls many emotional and motivational processes.

Hypothesis. (1) An implication of a theory subjected to an experimental test. (2) In lower animals, a systematic mode of behavior that appears prior to the solution of a problem.

Hysterical neurosis (conversion type). Physical ailments that lack a demonstrable organic base. These ailments which might be expected to elicit alarm in a person are often responded to with unconcern. This is *la belle indifference* of the hysteric to the debilitating symptom.

Hz. See *hertz*.

I

Iconic memory. A very brief memory for visual stimuli corresponding to *echoic memory* in audition. In both cases the memory persists for a second or so.

Id. In psychoanalytic theory, the portion of the personality that is concerned with the immediate gratification of basic bodily urges.

Ideas of reference. A morbid belief that the activities of others have a direct reference to oneself.

Identification. The process by which the child assimilates the values of the parents and sees himself in some sense as "the same" as the parents. See *introjection*. Also, a mechanism of defense that involves imitating the acts of another.

Identification with the aggressor. A mechanism of defense used by children to control the arousal of anxiety by imitating in fantasy or action the behavior of an aggressive and significant adult figure.

Identity constancy. Cognitive awareness that an object remains qualitatively the same despite alterations in form, size, and general appearance.

Ideographic law. Lawfulness within the behavior of a single individual. Contrast with *nomothetic law*.

Ikonic representation. The second stage of Jerome Bruner's theory of congnitive development, in which information is processed in the form of imagery.

Illusion. A distorted perception. Distinguish from *hallucination*.

Imagery. The process of imagination and the formation of mental images.

Imitation/modeling. The copying of an action by another, usually, but not necessarily, implying a measure of identification.

Immediate memory. Memory lasting only a second or so. Contrast with *short-term memory*.

Implicit personality theory. The collection of expectations that each of us has about people in general and groups of people. The expectations are not well formulated or spelled out and are, therefore, implicit. See *stereotype*.

Implosion therapy. A form of behavior therapy in which the individual imagines himself at once in the most frightening circumstances in order to extinguish anxiety and fear.

Impression formation. In social psychology, the process of forming opinions of people. Sometimes referred to as interpersonal perceptions or person perception.

Imprinting. The development in the young of many species of a filial attachment to the first large moving object they see.

Incentive. Any goal object or external condition that impels an organism to action or goal activity.

Incidence. In epidemiology a statistic that refers to the frequency of new cases of a given disorder that occur within a given period of time. This term contrasts with *prevalence* which refers to all existent cases of a given disorder at some particular time.

Incus. Commonly termed the *anvil;* the middle bone of the middle ear that transmits sound stimulation from the eardrum to the cochlea.

Independent variable. (1) Any variable that serves as a basis for making a prediction. (2) In an experiment, a factor that can be manipulated for the purpose of determining the effect of such manipulation. Contrast with *dependent variable*.

Induced color. A colored surface produces its complementary color in a small achromatic patch placed on it.

Inferential statistics. Statistics that are used to generalize findings from a representative sample to a broader population.

Inferior colliculus. The hindmost pair of bulges in the tectum of the midbrain; part of the auditory system.

Information-processing model. A model built on the flow of information through some hypothetical communication system.

Inhibition. In general, any temporary interference with a response. Used more specifically in many contexts: (1) in motor learning, to the suppressive effect of massed practice; (2) in reflex physiology, to the diminished strength of the reflex under various circumstances; (3) in personality (especially psychoanalytic) theory, an interference with the expression of some tendency or with the recall of some event; (4) in Pavlovian theory, forgetting the CR during extinction; in discrimination learning, acquiring the ability not to respond to the nonreinforced stimulus; termed "internal inhibition."

Inhibitory stimulation. Stimulation that tends to inhibit the firing of a neuron. Contrast with *excitatory stimulation*.

Innate releasing mechanism. In ethology, the mechanism that releases instinctive behavior in the presence of appropriate stimuli. See *action-specific energy*.

Inner ear. The internal portion of the ear that includes the cochlea, semicircular canals, and vestibular sacs.

Inoculation (against persuasion). A technique for developing resistance to persuasion by exposing persons to brief counteragruments against their own beliefs. They are stimulated to find refutations.

Insight. The fact of, or the process assumed to be responsible for, the sudden solution of a problem.

Insight-oriented therapy. Therapy aimed at helping an individual to discover the nature of his symptoms and their origins.

Insightful countersuggestion. A method used by Albert Ellis in rational – emotive therapy in which old and inappropriate value systems are extinguished and newer, less self-punitive ones are reinforced under the directing guidance of the therapist.

Instigation. That which sets the occasion for behavior; a combination of appropriate stimuli and motivation.

Instinct. An unlearned biologically based form of behavior. (1) For psychologists such as McDougall, a rough equivalent of biological or primary drive. (2) In ethology, a rigidly stereotyped complex bit of behavior that is specific to a species.

Instinct theory. Theory that emphasizes the unlearned, biologically rooted basis for behavior. Such theories typically emphasize the organism's selective response to specific environmental objects. In psychoanalysis, instinct theory refers to the impetus to action to eliminate or modify stimuli that arouse impulses. Ethological views of instinct stress the rigid, stereotyped behavior patterns characteristic of many species and the energy that is associated with these instinctive acts.

Instinctive drift. What the organism learns in a situation gradually takes on the characteristics of the responses that are normally used as reactions to the reinforcer.

Instrumental behavior. Behavior that leads (is "instrumental") to the attainment of a goal.

Instrumental conditioning (or learning). The modification of behavior under circumstances where reward or the avoidance of punishment is contingent upon the occurrence of a specified response. Contrast with *classical conditioning.*

Integrative action of nervous system. The activity of the nervous system that allows the weighing of simultaneous or persistent stimuli originating in organs throughout the body.

Intelligence A and B. Terms used by psychologist Donald Hebb to denote the innate potential for the development of intellectual capacities (A) as opposed to the actual level of intellectual functioning (B).

Intelligence Quotient (IQ)

$$\frac{\text{Mental age}}{\text{Chronological age}} \times 100$$

See *deviation* IQ.

Interference theory. A theory that proposes that forgetting of old information is caused by interferences generated by the input of new information.

Intermittent (partial) reinforcement. Reinforcement given irregularly rather than on every conditioning trial. Also *intermittent schedule.*

Internalization. Adopting the ideals, values, and goals of another person (usually admired) as one's own.

Internuncial neuron. Neurons that connect sensory and motor neurons within the central nervous system.

Interoceptive conditioning. Classical conditioning in which some important component in inside the body.

Interposition. The obstruction of the outline of one object by that of another, which is seen as closer; a principal cue in judging distance.

Interstimulus interval. In classical conditioning, the interval separating CS and US.

Introjection. The acceptance of the values of another (typically a parent) into the self. See *identification.*

Intropunitive aggression. Aggression directed against oneself. Contrast with *extrapunitive aggression.*

Introspection. The process of examining and reporting the content of one's own consciousness.

Introversion–extroversion typology. The theory that persons may be divided into two types of personalities: introverts and extroverts.

Introvert. A person who shows a strong tendency to find satisfaction in an inner life of thought and fantasy. Contrast with *extrovert.*

Involutional psychosis. An affective disorder of women who are going through menopause and of men somewhat older whose sexual adequacy is diminishing. Their symptoms are depressive and sometimes regressive and paranoid.

IQ. See *Intelligence quotient.*

Iris. The set of autonomically innervated muscles that controls the amount of light entering the eye.

J

***J*-curve.** A frequency distribution in which the modal value is the most extreme measure, typically zero.

James–Lange theory. The theory of emotion according to which emotional experience follows a reaction to a stimulus: We see the bear, run, and then experience fright. As opposed to: We see the bear, are frightened, and then run.

Just noticeable difference (j.n.d.). The smallest difference between two stimuli that can be detected reliably.

K

Karyotype. A systematic array of the chromosomes of a single cell in drawing or photographic form.

Kibbutz. Communal, typically agricultural setting in Israel in which children live in quarters separate from those of the parents. They are watched over by professional caretakers and see their parents in the evening.

Kinesthesis. Sensory impressions arising in the muscles and joints that provide information about the positions and movements of parts of the body.

Klinefelter syndrome. A disorder of males in which an extra x chromosome keeps the testicles small at puberty, disrupts hormonal balance, and is likely to cause sterility.

Kwashiorkor. A nutritional disorder resulting from severe protein deficiency.

L

La belle indifference. In hysteria, an expression of the fact that the patient appears to enjoy his illness and to be indifferent to his symptoms.

Labeling theory. The view that mental disorder has its etiology in the act of naming or identifying a person as disordered by attaching a disease label (e.g., schizophrenia) to the individual.

Lactation. The secreting or forming of milk.

Latency. The time between the presentation of a stimulus and the occurrence of the response.

Latency stage. In psychoanalytic theory, a period of psychosexual development in which the person shows little or no interest in heterosexual matters.

Latent dream content. The inaccessible repressed information of the dream which is camouflaged by the manifest content of the dream itself.

Lateral connection. Connections across the *retina,* involved in the sharp definition of objects.

Law of effect. (1) In its empirical form (empirical law of effect), a statement of the fact that animals learn responses that are rewarded. (2) In its theoretical form (theoretical law of effect), the proposition that reward is necessary for learning to occur.

Law of independent assortment. A Mendelian law that a pair of genes governing a single trait segregate independently of other gene pairs in the formation of germ cells. The trait is inherited separately.

Law of segregation. A Mendelian law that the paired paternal and maternal alleles governing a trait separate in the formation of germ cells.

Learned helplessness. Following experience with unavoidable punishment, the organism is unable to avoid punishment when avoidance becomes possible.

Learning. A fairly permanent change in behavior which occurs as a result of experience.

Learning curve. Function relating performance in a learning situation to practice. What is actually plotted is performance, learning presumably being the underlying state.

Learning set. Learning to learn, that is, learning to master certain types of problems as a result of previous experience with problems of the same type.

Lens. A transparent structure of the eye that focuses light rays directly on the retina by changes in convexity.

Lesion. Destruction of tissue as a result of injury or disease.

Level of aspiration. Goal set by an individual with expectancy of achievement. Attaining the goal is perceived as success, the inability to do so as failure.

Level of confidence. In testing the *null hypothesis,* the confidence with which the hypothesis can be rejected. Low probabilities mean a high level of confidence that a statistic was not obtained by chance.

Level of processing. An item to be remembered exists in a physical form (visual shape or sound) and as an item that may be processed at several different "depths" by rhyming, or making meaningful associations. This observation defines a set of levels from superficial to deep. The deeper the processing, the better the item is remembered.

Leveling/sharpening. A cognitive style characterized by undifferentiated (levelers) or differentiated (sharpeners) perception of objects that have been retained in memory.

Libido. In Freudian theory, general sexuality that provides the energy for all behavior.

Lie detector. An apparatus that measures blood pressure, pulse, respiration, and skin resistance changes during the course of questioning an individual. The hypothesis is that lying is accompanied by changes in these emotional indices.

Life instinct. Psychoanalytic concept used to describe the basic instinct or drive under the control of the pleasure principle (Eros).

Life space. A term used by Lewin to denote the total environment of an organism that helps to determine its behavior.

Limbic system. A set of structures in and around the core of the old forebrain that supposedly integratres motivational-emotional patterns such as arousal, sleep feeding.

Limen. See *threshold.*

Linear perspective. A secondary cue to depth or distance provided by the fact that parallel lines appear to converge in the distance.

Linear program. In programmed learning, materials in which all learners proceed from beginning to end without review or practice on related materials at difficult points. Contrast with *branched program.*

Linguistic competence. Mastery of the rules of language. The ability to create and understand an indefinitely large number of expressions.

Linguistic determinism. Part of the *Whorfian hypothesis.* The general conception that the thoughts that are possible are determined by language.

Linguistic object. Language treated as a physical event without respect to semantic properties. Studies of rote memorization treat language that way.

Linguistic relativity. Part of the *Whorfian hypothesis.* The conception that the content of thought depends upon how the language categorizes objects and events in the world.

Lithium carbonate. A naturally occurring chemical compound which has proved effective in the treatment of manic states.

Lobotomy. A psychosurgical procedure, now used sparingly, in which the white nerve fibers connecting the frontal lobes with the thalamus are cut.

Local-stimulus theory of drive. The hypothesis that motives are intense stimuli.

Lock-and-key specificity. A way of describing the fact that a *neurotransmitter* can affect only one type of receptor site and the *receptor site* can be affected by only one type of neurotransmitter.

Locomotion. In conflict theory, the representation of movement from one point to another; therefore, the change in the relationship of an organism to its environment.

Long-term memory (*LTM*). The permanent aspect of the memory system, as opposed to short-term memory.

Longitudinal method. The method whereby changes in a person are studied over time. By contrast the cross-sectional method infers changes over time by studying different persons of different ages at a given point in time.

Loudness. A dimension of auditory perception related to the intensity of the stimulus.

LSD (lysergic acid diethylamide). A hallucinogenic drug that can induce vivid perceptual experiences, hallucinations, and disorganized thinking.

M

MA. See *mental age.*

Mach bands. Light and dark edges of a visual pattern, the lightness and darkness of which is intensified as a result of what is called *lateral inhibition* (stimulated cells inhibit adjacent cells).

Macrocephaly. An abnormally large head; a condition which causes mental retardation.

Made feelings, impulses, acts. *First-rank symptoms* in which the person believes that one's feelings, impulses, or actions are not voluntary but are being imposed by an external power or force.

Magazine training. The use of a periodically presented reinforcer irrespective of the organism's actions to establish it as a conditioned reinforcer.

Mainstreaming. The principle of integrating handicapped with nonhandicapped persons in schools and the community whenever possible.

Maintenance rehearsal. Repeating an item over and over, thus keeping it in short-term memory until needed. *Not* a useful procedure for the establishment of the item in long-term memory. Contrast with *elaborative rehearsal.*

Malleus. One of three bones of the middle ear. See *incus* and *stapes.*

Manic-depressive disorder (affective disorder, bipolar). A psychosis characterized by extreme swings of mood, from elation to depression and back again. More often, the psychosis takes a predominantly manic or a predominantly depressive form.

Manic disorder. Intense emotional state in which elation, flight of ideas, distractibility, purposeless frenetic activity, and grandiosity and expansiveness characterize the individual's behavior.

Manifest dream content. The overt content of a dream, without reference to its symbolic or wish-fulfillment quality.

Maple Syrup Urine disease. A disorder in the ability to metabolize certain amino acids causing mental retardation.

Marasmus. Profound physiological decline in infants, usually associated with severe restriction of caloric intake or deprivation of activities (rocking, soothing) typically associated with good mothering behavior.

Marked expressions. In pairs of words (e.g., short–tall), one of them may imply an end of the continuum when used in the question, "How ____ is he?" Such words are said to be marked. Contrast *unmarked expressions.*

Masking. In hearing, the obliteration of one tone by another.

Mass-action-differentiation sequence. In psychological development, a progression from activity that involves the entire body to a more precise control over parts of the body.

Massed practice. A practice situation in which the trials are crowded closely together. Contrast with *spaced practice.*

Maternal deprivation. Lack of adequate mothering of the infant, often with severe psychological and physiological consequences for the child.

Maturation. Changes in behavior that occur as a result of physiological (probably chiefly neural) growth.

Maturational readiness. A stage of development where the organism is optimally prepared to acquire some particular kind of habit. See *critical period.*

Mean. The average: the sum of the measures divided by the number of measures.

Median. A measure of central tendency. The middle score, or fiftieth percentile.

Mediated generalization. Stimulus generalization that occurs because the new stimulus evokes a (mediating) response that, in turn, evokes the conditioned response. See *semantic generalization.*

Mediation. Internal processes that are presumed to occur between an observed stimulus and an observed response. See *verbal mediation.*

Medical model. A model of mental disorders which assumes that such disorders are *diseases* similar to the traditional physical diseases treated by medical practitioners.

Meditation. Reflectiveness in thought as characterized by marked motor stillness and prolonged contemplation; typically associated with mystic and religious Eastern practices.

Medulla. The hindmost part of the brain stem. The lower part of the hindbrain containing major ascending and descending tracts between the spinal cord and higher centers.

Meiosis. A particular form of cell division involving the gametes. When egg and sperm cells are formed, the chromosomes do not double, so that each germ cell receives only half the number of chromosomes characteristic of all other cells of the organism. Thus, when a sperm and egg cell are formed during fertilization, the newly fertilized ovum then has the full complement of chromosomes, half contributed by the mother (via the egg cell) and the other half by the father (via the sperm cell).

Membranous labyrinth. A structure within the bony labyrinth. See *bony labyrinth.*

Mental age. For a tested person, the mean age of individuals who obtain the same score on the test as he does. More generally, the score on an individual test of intelligence, expressed in terms of years and months.

Mental combinations. A stage in Piaget's developmental theory of intelligence extending from eighteen to twenty-four months of age and characterized by the emergence of conceptual—symbolic thought.

Mental retardation. A condition of significantly subaverage intellectual functioning and of deficits in adaptive behavior which are first manifested during childhood.

Mental status examination. A structured or unstructured psychiatric interview designed to reveal the behavior and physical appearance of an individual. Aspects examined are personal habits, health and appearance, mood state, quality and trend of thought, speech and expressiveness, motor and mental activity, judgment, etc.

Mentally retarded, educable. Retarded persons whose intellectual level indicates that they are capable of acquiring self-help skills, of becoming socially adaptive, and of handling unskilled or semiskilled jobs.

Mentally retarded, trainable. Retarded persons who are expected to learn self-care skills and to maintain a social adjustment within a relatively restricted social environment.

Mescaline. A psychotomimetic drug derived originally from a variety of cactus.

Mesomorphy. In Sheldon's typology, the vigorous, powerful-muscled type of person. See *ectomorphy* and *endomorphy*.

Methadone. A dependence-inducing narcotic with morphine-like effects. Chiefly used in rehabilitating heroin addicts since the drug blocks the craving for heroin and its euphoric effects.

Methamphetamine ("Speed"). A synthetic drug that acts as a stimulant.

Method of fractionation. A psychophysical method in which a subject selects the stimulus that, to him appears to be a certain fraction (typically one-half) of a second stimulus.

Method of limits. A psychophysical method in which stimuli are presented in increasing and decreasing orders of intensity, trial by trial. Some trials begin below absolute threshold; others begin above.

Method of loci. A memory device to recall people or objects by imagining them in specific locales known to the individual.

Microcephaly. An abnormally small head and brain area caused by disease, trauma, or a pair of defective recessive genes; a condition which brings mental retardation.

Midbrain. The middle section of the brain stem continuous with and just above the hindbrain and just below the forebrain.

Midbrain syndrome. A set of symptoms resulting from a transsection of the brain stem between the midbrain and the forebrain levels in which an animal can right itself and make walking or running movements but is devoid of voluntary movements.

Middle ear. The air-filled space between the eardrum and the inner ear. Contains the three auditory bones (*hammer, anvil,* and *stirrup*).

Milieu therapy. A form of therapy in which the climate and management of the wards of a mental hospital stress group activities, freedom of the patients to move about, and more adequate communication among patients and staff. Responsibility for the ward is housed to some extent in the patients.

Milwaukee Project. A cognitive, social and parental intervention program designed to prevent cultural-familial retardation in children at risk.

Miss. In signal detection procedures failure to detect a signal when one is presented.

Mitosis. A process of cell division involving duplication of the chromosomes that then line up in pairs within the cell nucleus. The pairs, split, with one member of each duplicated pair going to the daughter cell that has been formed following division of the original parent cell.

MMPI. The Minnesota Multiphasic Personality Inventory. The most widely used objective test of personality.

Mnemonic devices. Artificial techniques for helping an individual to remember items to be learned; these methods bear no formal relationship to the material being learned.

Mode. A measure of central tendency: the most frequent score.

Model psychosis. An externally drug-induced psychosis which appears to be markedly similar in its symptom forms to a more traditional form of psychotic disorder.

Modeling. In social-learning theory, the process by which much of personality is formed, through the child's observation and *imitation* of others.

Modifying mechanisms. Mechanisms of defense such as sublimation in which an anxiety-arousing thought or wish is modified by removing its objectionable or dangerous qualities.

Mongolism. See *Down syndrome.*

Monotonic relationship. Any relationship in which steady increases or decreases of the dependent variable are associated with increases of the independent variable.

Monozygotic (identical) twins. Twins that develop from a single egg, hence genetically identical.

Moon illusion. A visual illusion in which the moon appears larger the closer it is to the horizon.

Moral treatment. A method of treatment of the nineteenth century whereby patients were released from restraints and treated with compassion and dignity.

Morpheme. A unit of meaning in language. Basic words are well as prefixes and suffixes which change the meaning of the basic word are examples.

Motion parallax. Apparent motion. seen when the eye is fixed on a particular stimulus and the body is in motion. For example, in riding in an automobile, the individual has the illusion that objects nearer than the point of fixation are moving in a direction opposite to the direction in which the person is traveling. Distant objects appear to move in the same direction.

Motivation (drive). An intervening variable that energizes behavior.

Motivation, primary. The energizing of behavior on the basis of biological drives such as thirst, hunger, etc.

Motivation, secondary. The energizing of behavior on the basis of acquired or learned drives such as achievement, affiliation, etc.

Motor neuron. A neuron that transmits neural impulses from the central nervous system to muscles and glands. Also *efferent neuron.*

Motor theory of consciousness. The theory that mental experience depends on stimulation from muscular activity.

Müller–Lyer illusion. A visual illusion in which two lines of equal length are perceived to be unequal if one has ends marked with arrowheads (perceived as smaller) as opposed to the other in which the arrowheads are reversed and appear as "feathers" (perceived as larger).

Multiple approach-avoidance. Complex approach-avoidance conflicts in which a choice of one positive alternative has the negative quality of requiring a person to relinquish another desirable alternative. In this form of conflict alternative choices have both positive and negative qualities.

Multiple personality. A form of dissociation in which a person may assume alternate personalities, with the acts and memories associated with each not within the awareness of the others.

Muscle action potential. An electrical discharge associated with the activity of muscles.

Mutation. An unusual and abrupt change in gene structure that subsequently generates a new organismic form. A change in DNA.

Myelin sheath. A fatty covering that encases the axons of larger motor and sensory neurons.

Myopia. Nearsightedness as a result of the focusing of images on the lens in front of the retina rather than on it. Near objects in this condition can be approximately properly focused by accommodation.

N

Narcissim. In psychoanalysis, erotic feelings associated with one's own body or self. More generally, a feeling of egotistical pride.

Narrative story. A mnemoric device. The individual trying to remember a large number of items links them together in sequence in a story.

Natural language mediator. A verbal link used to relate items for purposes of remembering them. For example, a participant in a *paired-associate learning* experiment might recall the pair of *nonsense syllables,* COL—JUN by constructing the phrase, "A COLD day in JUNE." The translation uses the phrase structure and the extra words and letters as natural language mediators.

Natural selection. The Darwinian proposition that the inheritance of structures is determined by its utility for the species in the struggle for survival. It is those individuals of the species who can best meet environmental demands who survive and reproduce.

Naturalistic experiment. A type of naturalistic observation in which the investigation pays systematic attention to the behavior occurring in unmanipulated normal circumstances.

Naturalistic observation. The observation of behavior under natural conditions of life.

Nature-nurture interaction. The interplay between heredity or what is inborn and environment on the development of individual traits and behavior.

Nature–nurture problem. The pervasive question of whether behavior is the result of heredity (nature) or environment (nurture).

Negative afterimage. An image that is complementary in color to that of the original stimulus, seen after looking long at the original stimulus and then at an achromatic surface.

Negative correlation. A relationship between two measures of behavior in which high values of x are associated with low values of y, and vice versa. Contrast with *positive correlation*.

Negative reinforcer. A punisher. An event that an organism will learn to escape or avoid.

Negative relationship. A relationship in which increases in the independent variable are associated with decreases in the dependent variable. Contrast with *positive relationship*.

Negative skew. Describes a *skewed distribution* with the long tail toward the left, toward low numbers. Contrast with *positive skew*.

Negative transfer. Transfer in which practice in one task interferes with the learning of another task. Contrast with *positive transfer*.

Neocortex. Literally new cortex. That part of the cerebral cortex that is unique to mammals.

Neologisms. New words sometimes made up by schizophrenic patients.

Neonate. A newborn infant.

Nerve. A bundle of axons in the peripheral system, generally with a protective and supportive sheath.

Nerve impulse. A chemical reaction in the walls of a nerve cell that allows the cell body and dendrites to communicate with the terminal buttons by way of the axon.

Nerve tract. A collection of axons in the central system.

Neurasthenia. Neurotic complaints of weakness, fatigue, and exhaustion.

Neuromuscular junction. The point of contact of a motor neuron with a muscle.

Neuron. Nerve cell; the active elements of the nervous system.

Neurosis. A large group of nonpsychotic disorders (formerly part of the psychiatric Diagnostic and Statistical Manual II) in which anxiety is paramount.

Neurosis: anxiety reaction (DSM-II). A neurotic disorder characterized by pervasive anxiety, both in the psychological sense of dread and accompanying physiological symptoms of marked autonomic activation. High levels of anxiety may border on a panic state.

Neurosis: depressive reaction (DSM-II). A form of neurosis in which anxiety and apprehensiveness are prominent and depression is pervasive. Accompanied by loss of interest in the environment, sleeplessness and tension, and a sense of loneliness and helplessness.

Neurosis: dissociative reaction (DSM-II). A neurotic reaction in which there is a loss of memory for some traumatic nonphysical event or situation of the past.

Neurosis: obsessive-compulsive (DSM-II). A neurosis characterized by troublesome persistent thoughts (obsessions) and/or irresistible urges to perform certain apparently meaningless acts (compulsions).

Neurosis: phobic reaction (DSM-II). A neurosis marked by pathological persistent and irrational fear attached to a nondangerous object or situation.

Neurotic paradox. The use of responses that, although they momentarily reduce anxiety, have the long-range effect of inducing greater anxiety.

Neurotic triad. *MMPI* designation of three scales that measure hypochondriasis (H), depression (D), and hysteria (Hy).

Neuroticism–stability. A factor, after extroversion, in the personality model espoused by Eysenck. At one pole is a "genotypical proneness" to neurosis; at the other, stability or normality.

Neurotransmitter substance. A chemical released from an axon into a synapse that subsequently changes the membrane of the cell beyond, thus carrying the neural impulses.

Nitrous oxide. A chemical substance, sometimes euphemistically called "laughing gas," capable of altering consciousness.

Nominal realism. An aspect of the stage of preoperational thought in which the child assumes that the name of an object is a concrete and essential attribute of the object.

Nomothetic law. A law that applies generally to groups of persons. Contrast with *ideographic law.*

Nondirective therapy. See *client-centered therapy.*

Nonmonotonic relationship. A relationship in which increases in the independent variable are associated first with increases (or decreases) in the dependent variable and then with decreases (or increases). Contrast with *monotonic relationship.*

Nonreversal shift. An experimental procedure on concept formation in which a participant first learns two discriminations and having learned them, shifts to the learning of two more featuring previously irrelevant dimensions. Contrast with *reversal shift.*

Nonsense syllable. Relatively meaningless three-letter sequences often used in studies of rote learning.

Norepinephrine. A catecholamine that acts as a neurotransmitter and has some of the properties of epinephrine; (also called noradrenalin).

Normal curve. The bell-shaped function characteristic of frequency distributions of many psychological measures.

Norm of reaction. The range of phenotypes which are possible for a given genotype under different environmental circumstances.

Normalization. The principle of providing mentally retarded and other handicapped persons with environmental conditions that are as close as possible as those of the rest of society.

North Carolina Abecedarian Project. A medical, social and cognitive intervention program currently in progress whose goal is to prevent mental retardation in children at risk.

Nucleus. In cytology, the area within a cell that contains the genetic material. In neuroanatomy, a relatively compact collection of the cell bodies of neurons.

Null hypothesis. The hypothesis that there is no significant difference between experimental and control groups after they have been treated differently during the course of the experiment.

Numerical peg system. A mnemonic procedure in which the memorizer uses some numerical system like "One is a bun, etc." and hangs other items to be remembered on the numerical pegs thus provided.

O

Object concept. The cognitive awareness that an object exists and has permanence even when it is not in view.

Object constancy. The perception of objects as relatively unchanged despite variations in such factors as placement, illumination, distance from the perceiver, etc. Comparable concepts specific to aspects of a stimulus include *color constancy, size constancy,* and *shape constancy.*

Objective tests of personality. Tests that take the form of questionnaires or rating scales. Contrast with *projective tests of personality.*

Observational learning. Acquisition of information and behavior by observing the actions of another individual.

Obsessions. Recurring, intrusive and uncontrollable thoughts.

Obsessive-compulsive disorder. An *anxiety disorder (DSM-III)* in which the mind is flooded with constantly recurring and often absurd ideas—*obsessions;* or the individual has impulses to perform a specific act repetitively—*compulsions.*

Occipital lobe. A major division (the hindmost part) of either cerebral hemisphere; involved in the processing of visual information.

Oedipal relationship. In Freudian theory, the emotional (sexual) attachment of a boy for his mother.

Old forebrain. The more primitive parts of the forebrain. Consists of olfactory apparatus, basal ganglia, limbic system, etc.

Olfactory bulbs. Protrusions of the old forebrain that receive the olfactory nerve and project to the pyriform cortex.

Olfactory rod. Receptor for smell.

Omission training. In instrumental conditioning, a procedure in which reward fails to follow a designated response. Extinction.

Ontogenesis. Development in the individual from conception to death.

Operant conditioning. A form of training in which responses are strengthened through positive or negative reinforcement. Also *instrumental conditioning.*

Operation. In Piaget's theory of cognitive development, actions which an individual performs mentally, such as reversibility, transformation, negation.

Operationism. A position in the philosophy of science that maintains that scientific concepts acquire their meaning in terms of publicly observable operations.

Opponent-process theory. (1) The theory of color vision originally proposed by Hering which accounts for color vision in terms of a three-component system. The three components are black-white, blue-yellow and red-green (2) A theory of motivation that emphasizes that specific emotional experiences are followed by their physiological opposites. These opposing responses are assumed to be conditionable to environmental stimuli.

Optic nerve. A pair of cranial nerves connecting the retina with the visual centers.

Oral stage. A stage in psychosexual development in which the infant acquires its most important pleasures from activities that involve the mouth —chewing, sucking, biting etc. Contrast with *anal stage, latency stage,* and *genital stage.*

Ordinal scale. A scale in which items are assigned numbers to indicate rank order along some dimension.

Ordinate. The vertical or *y*-axis on a graph.

Organ of Corti. A structure located on the basilar membrane of the spiraling cochlea of the inner ear; contains the hair cells for hearing.

Organ vulnerability. A predisposing weakness in a given organ system of the body that lowers its resistance to disease.

Organic mental disorder. Mental disorder marked by impairment of intellectual and/or emotional functioning resulting from brain pathology. The dysfunction can be caused by aging, excessive drug usage, or specific physical or physiological factors.

Organic retardation. Mental retardation due to a physiological disorder; examples are Down syndrome, phenylketonuria, microcephaly.

Organization in recall. Particularly in free recall the participant may use a variety of devices to bring order to the process, for example, by *clustering.* As a result the order in which items appear in free recall is not random but is consistent with this organization.

Orienting reaction. A response that permits the organism to attend to novel stimuli by altering its position with respect to the location of that stimulus.

Orthogenetic principle. Werner's principle that development proceeds from a relatively global undifferentiated response toward one of increasing differentiation and hierarchical organization of elements that constitute the response.

Ossicles. The three small bones in the middle ear that transmit movements of the eardrum to the fluids of the inner ear.

Otosclerosis. A condition in which a spongy growth immobilizes the *stapes* at the point where it transmits sound to the *oval window,* resulting in deafness.

Outer directedness. An orientation to the world in which an individual's action tendencies are determined from without (i.e., by environmental events) rather than from within the self.

Oval window. Membranous "window" at the entrance to the cochlea.

Overintellectualization. A symptom of the obsessional—compulsive neurosis in which an elaborate pattern of thought is used to deny unacceptable impulses and affects.

Overlearning. Practice beyond the point of mastery in learning a set of materials.

Overregularization. The tendency of the child to use regular verb and plural inflections during the course of acquiring language for irregular words: "I comed" rather than "I came," "foots" rather than "feet."

Overtone. In a complex tone, any of the tones of higher pitch. The frequencies of the overtones are multiples of those of the fundamental tone.

P

Paired-associate learning. Learning pairs of terms after the manner of a foreign language vocabulary. The learner's task is to give the second member of the pair (response term) when presented with the first (stimulus term)

Panic disorder. Sudden and inexplicable fear or anxiety with attendant physiological symptoms that overwhelm the individual and limit behavior to an extreme focus on the anxiety. In such states individuals find it difficult to engage in constructive activity.

Paradoxical cold. Cold felt when a warm object stimulates cold receptors.

Paradoxical intention. A variation of flooding in which the client is urged not merely to express fears but to exaggerate markedly confrontation with the feared situation. See *flooding, implosion.*

Paradoxical sleep. Stage 1 dreaming. Such sleep is called "paradoxical" because the EEG record suggests the person is only lightly asleep but the presence of REMs denotes the difficulty of arousal.

Paradoxical warmth. Warmth felt when the stimulus is typically cool (29°–31°C).

Paranoia. A form of severe psychosis characterized by systematic delusions of a persecutory or grandiose nature. These delusions are typically isolated from the rest of the personality and intellect.

Paranoid crystallization. The final stage in the development of a paranoid psychosis in which the delusional belief now becomes very evident as truth to the individual and begins to rule behavior. Paranoid illumination which follows is marked by the sudden revealing insight into the plot that threatens the person.

Paranoid disorder. A psychotic disorder involving persistent delusions of persecution, jealousy, grandiosity, excessive suspiciousness of others. Overt behavior may appear normal but the delusional thinking that characterizes the individual can become evident upon questioning or by specific environmental events that trigger the belief system.

Paranoid ideas. Thoughts of grandeur or persecution that typify the thinking of paranoid patients.

Paranoid personality disorder. A form of personality disorder typified by hypersensitivity, rigidity, jealousy, overaggressiveness, and overbearing attitude, and enviousness.

Parasympathetic ganglion (plural: ganglia). Cluster of nerve cell bodies in the head and alongside the sacral cord serving parasympathetic functions of the autonomic system.

Parasympathetic nervous system. A division of the autonomic system concerned with protecting and conserving the body resources, preserving normal functions, and maintaining a calm emotional state. Contrast with *sympathetic nervous system.*

Paresis. The tertiary form of syphilis in which organic damage to the brain by invading microorganisms produces profound mental and neurological symptoms.

Parietal lobe. A major division of either cerebral hemisphere lying between the frontal and occipital lobes and above the temporal lobe.

Partial reinforcement. Reinforcement that occurs at a rate less often than for every correct response or on every trial.

Partial reinforcement effect. The fact that resistance to extinction is greater following partial reinforcement than following continuous reinforcement.

Passive-aggressive personality disorder. A form of personality disorder in which the person expresses hostility in passive ways, such as dependence and resistance.

Passive avoidance. A form of *operant conditioning* in which making a specified response leads to punishment. The participant learns not to make that response and in this passive way avoids punishment. Contrast with *active avoidance.*

Passive vocabulary. All the words a person understands. Contrast with *active vocabulary.*

Patterns of light and shade. A cue to depth and distance provided by the fact that the world is lighted from above by the sun. Dependable patterns of illumination provide the cues.

Pavlovian conditioning. See *classical conditioning.*

Payoff matrix. (1) In social psychology, a diagrammatic representation of the gains and losses that occur under various combinations of acts on the part of persons in a situation of competition. (2) In signal detection experimentation, the gains for reporting correctly that a signal is present when there is one and absent when there is none as well as the losses for reporting that a signal is present when there is none or absent when one is present.

Peak experience. A powerful emotional experience bordering on ecstasy that serves to transform the individual's perception of self and environment.

Pellagra. Nicotinic acid deficiency which induces physical and psychological changes in the individual. Mania, convulsions, memory loss, dementia, and stupor may become an end point unless treated with high doses of nicotinic acid and other B vitamins.

Percentile rank. The percentage of scores in a total distribution that a given score equals or exceeds.

Perception. The interpretation of sensory information.

Perceptual constancy. The tendency for a perceiver to perceive the correct sizes, shapes, and colors of objects in spite of great variations in the pattern of proximal stimulation.

Perceptual defense. A hypothetical, but not fully validated, tendency for a person to fail to perceive obscene or otherwise threatening stimuli.

Perceptual learning. (1) Most often, the hypothesis that learning is a matter of developing new perceptions or of seeing new relationships. (2) Also, the fact that perception is influenced by learning.

Performance IQ. An IQ score that is based primarily on nonverbal tests of intelligence. Such tests place a premium on factors involving motor skills, spatial abilities, speed, etc.

Performance test. In intelligence testing, a nonverbal test, a test that requires no language. Contrast with *verbal test.*

Perilymph. The fluid between the bony and membranous labyrinths of the ear.

Peripheral nervous system. That portion of the nervous system that connects receptors with the central nervous system or the central nervous system to glands and muscles.

Permissive parent. A parent who gives a child as much freedom as is consistent with his or her physical safety.

Perseveration deficit. An effect of damage to *perfrontal association cortex.* Once started on an activity the patient perseverates—shows an inability to stop and shift to something else.

Person perception. Inferences made about the disposition, motives, and intentions of a person. See *impression formation.*

Persona. Jung's concept of the socially conforming mask of the person.

Personal unconscious. Jungian term for that portion of the unconscious that is based on specific experiences of the individual. See *unconscious* and *collective unconscious.*

Personality. The unique organization of fairly permanent characteristics that set the individual apart from other individuals and, at the same time, determine how others respond to him.

Personality assessment. The systematic study and appraisal of an individual's attributes to assess the degree of integration and the dominant configuration of characteristic abilities, interests, values and behavior dispositions.

Personality disorders. A heterogenous category of pervasive and maladaptive personality traits. The addiction disorders and various sexual deviation are included in this group. Persons with personality disorders often have minimal subjective anxiety.

Personality inventory. Tests of personality which consist of objective items that require true or false answers from the respondent.

Petit mal epilepsy. Form of *epilepsy* characterized by brief losses of consciousness.

Phallic stage. In psychoanalytic theory, a stage in psychosexual development in which the child develops an interest in its sexual organs.

Phenomenology. An emphasis on subjective awareness and experience. May also refer to naive reports of experience of untrained individuals. See *humanistic psychology.*

Phenothiazines. A group of antipsychotic drugs that reduce anxiety and distress; particularly effective with schizophrenic patients.

Phenotype. In genetics, the characteristics that actually appear in a living organism. Differentiated from genotypes, which are hereditary in their determination but not overtly manifested.

Phenylketonuria (PKU). A disorder in the ability to metabolize the amino acid phenylalanine, which is inherited as a recessive trait and causes mental retardation. The mental retardation can be largely prevented by a special diet.

Phi phenomenon. Apparent motion of what is regarded as a single light, seen when two lights a short distance apart are flashed alternately in rapid succession.

Phobia. An unreasonable (neurotic) fear.

Phobic disorder. A disorder marked by pathological, persistent and irrational fear that is attached to an object or situation that is not inherently dangerous.

Phoneme. The smallest unit of sound that signals a difference in meaning in a particular language.

Phonetics. The branch of linguistics that is concerned with the analysis of the sounds employed in speech.

Phonetic symbolism. Meanings conveyed by the sound of an utterance.

Phonology. The study of language in terms of sounds.

Photopic vision. Vision as it occurs under illumination sufficient to permit a full discrimination of colors; dependent upon the cones.

Phylogenesis. Evolution of a genetically related group of organisms. The higher the phylogenetic level of organism, the more complex the behavior. Contrast with *ontogenesis.*

Physical primary color. In vision, a color that, when mixed with other primaries, contributes to the production of all visible hues. Contrast with *psychological primary.*

Physiological nystagmus. A continuous small tremor of the eyes.

Physiological zero. The temperature that is experienced as neither warm nor cold.

Pitch. The psychological attribute that depends mainly upon the frequency of the physical stimulus. See *loudness.*

Pituitary gland. A gland of the endocrine system located at the base of the brain. It is the "master gland" or "key gland" because its hormones control the secretions of many other glands of the system.

Place (resonance, piano, harp) theory. Helmholtz's theory that a particular place and resonating fibers on the basilar membrane are stimulated by a particular frequency of sound waves.

Placebo. Originally, a medicine without medicinal value given merely to satisfy a patient. More recently, a treatment (usually a pill, but could be any form of treatment) that is identical in all respects with a treatment under experimental test, except that it lacks the active ingredient. See *placebo effect.*

Placebo effect. In studies of psychotherapy, an error introduced by the fact that patients often improve as a result of the attention they receive as participants in the study even though they are in the control (placebo) group.

Placenta. The vascular structure within the uterus in mammals to which the fetus is attached by the umbilical cord, and through which the fetus receives nourishment and oxygen via the mother's bloodstream.

Pleasure principle. In Freudian theory, the principle that the individual impulsively seeks to satisfy id urges, either directly or in fantasy. Contrast *reality principle.*

Point scale. In intelligence testing, a test in which credit is given directly in terms of number of items passed. Contrast with *age scale.*

Polygenic inheritance. Inheritance that is determined by a linked set of genes all affecting the same characteristic.

Pons. The upper part of the hindbrain.

Population. A concept in statistics that refers to all of the individuals in some real or imagined universe.

Population genetics. The distribution of genetic determiners throughout a given population.

Positive correlation. A correlation in which high measures on one trait are associated with high measures on the second trait, and low values on one are associated with low values on another. Contrast with *negative correlation.*

Positive reinforcer. A reward; an event that increases the probability that the response it follows will be made again in similar circumstances.

Positive relationship. A relationship in which increases in the independent variable produce increases in the dependent variable. Contrast with *negative relationship.*

Positive skew. Describes a *skewed distribution* with the long tail toward the right, toward high numbers. Contrast with *negative skew.*

Positive transfer. Transfer in which learning of one skill aids in the learning of a second. Contrast with *negative transfer.*

Posthypnotic suggestion. A suggestion given to a hypnotized person by the hypnotist that he perform a prescribed act later when in the waking state.

Postsynaptic neuron. In synaptic transmission the receiving neuron. Contrast with *presynaptic neuron.*

Post-traumatic stress disorder. Personality dysfunction created in the aftermath of severe trauma or intense personal stress.

Potential stimulus. Energy from the environment that would be detected if it struck an appropriate receptor. See *distal stimulus.* Contrast with *proximal stimulus* and *effective stimulus.*

Pragmatics. The rules that govern the use of language by real people in real situations.

Precocious puberty. Extremely early sexual maturity due to brain lesion that disturbs normal regulation.

Predictive validity. Validity established by the capability of a test to predict performance on some later task.

Prefrontal association cortex. Large area of frontal cerebral cortex that is neither sensory nor motor in function and is often assumed to serve an associative purpose.

Premise of equipotentiality. The false assumption that associations are formed with equal ease between any and all stimuli or between any and all stimuli and responses. Contrast with *principle of preparedness.*

Preoperational stage. In Piaget's theory of cognitive development, the stage in which children become capable of symbolic activities such as mental imagery and language and come to understand identity constancy and functions.

Present State Examination. A carefully designed, structured mental status examination that has improved the reliability of psychiatric diagnosis. Used in the International Pilot Study of Schizophrenia, WHO, Geneva, Switzerland.

Presynaptic neuron. In synaptic transmission, the transmitting neurons. Contrast with *postsynaptic neuron.*

Prevention, primary. A public health term to denote procedures designed to *prevent* the development of disorder in vulnerable populations.

Prevention, secondary. A public health term emphasizing early diagnosis of disorder in an effort to shorten its duration and impact.

Prevention, tertiary. A public health term to denote intervention efforts aimed at limiting disabilities induced by irreversible disorders through rehabilitation.

Preventive mechanisms. Defense mechanisms such as repression, which serve to keep anxiety out of awareness.

Primacy effect. In memory, a tendency to remember first-learned things best. Contrast with *recency effect.*

Primary circular reactions. A developmental substage in Piaget's theory of intelligence, extending from one to four months, in which the infant repeats again and again the movements in his repertoire.

Primary colors (color primaries). Any of a set of three colors from different thirds of the spectrum that can be mixed to make all hues. Particular wavelengths for red, green, and blue are usually chosen.

Primary cues to distance. Cues derived from the functioning of the visual system. See *accommodation, convergence, retinal disparity* and *motion parallax.*

Primary drive. An unlearned biological motivation. Contrast with *acquired drive.*

Primary memory. The retention of the image of an object that persists for a very brief period following its presentation. Contrast with *secondary memory.*

Primary mental abilities. Thurstone's subdivision of Spearman's general factor into the primary abilities of spatial perceptions, perceptual speed, verbal comprehension, numerical ability, memory, word fluency, and reasoning.

Primary motor cortex. Areas of the cerebral cortex most closely connected to the muscles, in terms of number of intervening synapses. Contrast with *secondary motor cortex, primary sensory cortex* and *secondary sensory cortex.*

Primary process. In Freudian theory, means of the id to secure immediate and direct satisfaction of an instinctual wish, making no sharp distinction between imagination and reality. Contrast with *secondary process.*

Primary projection area. An area in the brain to which the neural effects of stimulation are conducted (projected) directly. Contrast with *diffuse projection.*

Primary reinforcement. Reinforcement that depends little or not at all upon previous learning. Contrast with *secondary reinforcement.*

Primary reinforcer. Any stimulus or event that is innately reinforcing because of its biological significance to the organism, such as food, water, sex, and termination of pain.

Primary sensory cortex. Areas of the cerebral cortex most directly connected to the receptors, in terms of number of intervening synapses. Contrast with *secondary sensory cortex, primary motor cortex* and *secondary motor cortex.*

Primary sex characteristic. Those physiological and structural sexual characteristics that make reproduction possible.

Primary taste qualities. Salty, sweet, sour, and bitter.

Principle of preparedness. The biological makeup of the organism predisposes it to form associations between certain events or between certain responses and their consequences. Contrast with *premise of equipotentiality.*

Prisoner's dilemma. A game involving two people that permits the study of cooperation and competition.

Proactive inhibition. A term to summarize the fact that learning prior to current learning interferes with the later recall of the materials currently being learned.

Proband. In genetic studies, the person who bears the trait or diagnosis in which the investigation is interested.

Production deficiency. In studies of verbal mediation, the failure to use labels of objects to facilitate performance. This deficiency is typical of kindergarten-age children.

Programmed learning. The presentation of materials to be learned in carefully planned sequences, often with the aid of a teaching machine.

Project Head Start. A national preschool educational, social and health intervention program for economically disadvantaged children.

Projection. Seeing one's own (usually undesirable) traits in others.

Projective tests of personality. Tests allowing relatively free responding to situations, requiring interpretation on the assumption that the nature of the interpretation reveals the important aspects of personality.

Proximal stimulus. The effect of a potential stimulus or distal stimulus upon the receptors.

Proximodistal sequence. A sequence of development that proceeds from near the trunk outward to the extremities.

Psychasthenia. A disordering inability to resolve doubts and uncertainties and to resist phobias, obsessions, and compulsions though the individual is aware of their irrational nature.

Psychedelic drug. The hallucinogens perceived as providing a "mind-expanding" experience.

Psychoanalysis. The theory and practice of thereapeutic methods developed by Freud and his followers to account for and to deal with the neuroses.

Psychodynamics. The study of motives and drives as explanations of behavior, usually in a psychoanalytic context.

Psycholinguistics. The study of the psychological aspects of language and its acquisition.

Psychological primary colors. Red, green, blue, and yellow, hues that seem pure and antinged by neighbors in the spectrum. Contrast with *physical primary color.*

Psychological reactance. People tend to assert their freedom when others threaten to control them.

Psychometrics. The techniques and theories of mental measurement. Psychometric intelligence refers to intelligence as measured by mental tests.

Psychomotor epilepsy. Form of *epilepsy* in which the individual loses contact with the surroundings but appears conscious and engages in confused, repetitive acts.

Psychoneurosis (DSM-II). Behavior pathology in which anxiety always plays a part. Relatively less severe than a psychosis. Symptoms in addition to anxiety define such specific types of neurosis as hysteria and psychoasthenia.

Psychopathic personality. See *sociopathic personality.*

Psychopathy. Behavior that is marked by antisocial activity without evident guilt. Psychopathic personalities are constantly in conflict with the law, lack an ability for loyalty or allegiance to others, are markedly selfish, and motivated by personal gain. See *antisocial personality.*

Psychopharmacology. That area of psychology centered on the effects of drugs on behavior.

Psychophysical correlation. A general term used to refer to the dependence of some psychological attribute of sensory experience upon a dimension of physical stimulation, for example, the dependence of brightness upon the intensity of visual stimulation.

Psychophysics. The procedures used in the study of the relationships between physical stimulation and psychological judgment. Also the science resulting from such study.

Psychosexual disorder. A *DSM-III* category of disorders formerly viewed as sexual perversions or sexual dysfunctions. Includes disorders of gender identity, fetishism, exhibitionism, voyeurism, sexual masochism or sadism, impotence, frigidity, premature ejaculation and the like.

Psychosexual stages. The psychoanalytic viewpoint that development occurs in stages: oral, anal, phallic, latent, and genital. Each stage has a focal bodily point for stimulation (e.g., in the oral stage the mouth plays a central role) and specific external objects for sexual attachment.

Psychosis. A general term to indicate severe mental disorders which adversely affect mental functioning and social competence. Most psychoses are identified in terms of (a) severity, (b) extended withdrawal from social relationships, (c) marked deviance in affect expression, (d) severely disordered thought, and (e) pervasive regressive behavior.

Psychosocial retardation. *Mental retardation* for which no organic cause has been identified, usually of mild degree and prevailing in lower socioeconomic classes.

Psychosomatic disorders. Physical disorders that are precipitated or aggravated by emotional stress and other psychological factors. Contrast with *hysterical neurosis.*

Psychosomatic medicine. The branch of medicine concerned with the study of psychophysiological disorders.

Psychosurgery. Brain surgery sometimes used in the treatment of mental disorder.

Psychotherapy. The treatment of mental and emotional disorders by psychological methods such as direction, suggestion, reconstruction, persuasion, and counseling.

Psychotic depressive reaction (DSM II). A psychosis characterized by "blueness" and feelings of worthlessness.

Psychotic tetrad. *MMPI* designation of four scales that presume to measure paranoia (Pa), psychasthenia (Pt), schizophrenia (Sc), and hypomania (Ma).

Psychotomimetic drug. Drugs that induce psychotic-like features. The most important is LSD-25.

PTC. Phenyl-thio-carbamide, a substance to which some individuals are "taste blind."

Puberty. The time of transition from sexual immaturity to maturity.

Puberty praecox. Early onset of puberty as a result of a glandular disturbance.

Punishment. The application of a painful or discomforting stimulus in order to decrease the probability that the undesirable behavior it follows will persist. See *negative reinforcer; avoidance learning.*

Pupil. The opening surrounded by the iris through which light enters the eye.

Purkinje phenomenon. The shift in the relative brightness of colors that occurs with the shift from rod to cone vision.

Pyriform cortex. Cerebral cortex in the old forebrain that gains sensory input from the olfactory bulbs.

R

r. See *correlation coefficient.*

Race. A breeding population distinguished by the greater frequency of a collection of inherited bodily traits than is found in other populations of the same species.

Racist. A person having a constellation of beliefs indicative of racial prejudice including: (a) the assumption that race is the primary determiner of negative psychological traits; (b) that the members of a particular race do not vary from one another; and (c) that some races are biologically superior to others and thus dominant.

Random sample. A sample chosen so that every individual and every combination of individuals in the population stand an equal chance of being selected.

Range. The measure of variability indicated by the highest and lowest scores in a distribution.

Rapid eye movements. See *REM.*

Rating scale. A device which permits a rater to record the estimated magnitude of expression of a trait or quality. A graphic rating scale defines, qualitatively, different points along the dimension.

Ratio scale. In psychophysics, a scale in which the unit of measurement is a fraction of a certain standard perceptual difference, so that one can speak of "twice as loud," "one-half as sweet," etc.

Rational-construct method. A method for developing personality inventories or tests in which the test developer initially defines the construct represented by his test and then creates items reflecting behaviors that are subsumed under that definition (e.g., Allport-Vernon-Lindzey Study of Values).

Rational–emotive therapy. A form of therapy associated with Ellis, in which the therapeutic goal is the modification of the patient's inappropriate cognitions regarding his self-concept and his relations with others.

Rationalization. Providing oneself with "good" reasons for one's undesirable behavior or position in life.

Reaction formation. Engaging in behavior that is the opposite of some unacceptable unconscious wishes in order to protect against them.

Reaction time. The interval between the onset of a stimulus and the beginning of the individual's response.

Reactive depression. A state of sadness and self-deprecation induced directly by an external event; usually transient.

Reactive disorder. Disorders marked by acute distress that are reactions to specific, traumatizing life events. These events can include personal loss, bereavement, separation, natural disasters, and catastrophies.

Reactive effects of measurement. The unwanted side effects of psychological investigations, for example, the "guinea pig" effect produced in many participants in experiments.

Reality contact. An appropriate sense of awareness of the environment as evidenced by appropriate social, emotional, and cognitive responsiveness to objects and stimulus figures within it.

Reality principle. In Freudian theory, the principle that the ego becomes aware of and adapts to the realities of life situations, thereby inhibiting or delaying the expression of the id's impulses or drives.

Reality testing. In Freudian theory, the exploratory probing by which the young person learns about the environment.

Rebound effect. The increase in the amount of time spent dreaming following REM or Stage 4 sleep deprivation.

Recall, stage of *(disaster syndrome).* The third stage of the disaster syndrome in which the traumatic event is recalled and reviewed with tenseness, and restlessness. Or the event is repressed. High levels of anxiety and distress may continue even after the need for renewal and rehabilitation begins to dominate the individual's thinking.

Recall test. A test in which the individual, provided with a cue or sometimes nothing more than a request to do so, must produce an answer.

Recency effect. In memory, the tendency to remember best the last learned things in a list. Contrast with *primacy effect.*

Receptor. A cell or group of cells that receives stimulation.

Receptor site. Locations on a postsynaptic neuron which receive neurotransmitter substance in synaptic transmission.

Recessive gene. A gene that will not express itself in a trait or appearance unless paired with another recessive gene. If paired with a dominant gene, the action of the recessive will be masked.

Recidivism. A chronic tendency to repeat anti-social behavior.

Reciprocal inhibition. In Wolpe's theory, weakening anxiety to certain stimuli by providing a means of responding that inhibits anxiety. See *systematic desenitization.*

Reciprocal innervation. The innervation of antagonistic muscles to provide for relaxation of one as the other contracts.

Recoding. The reorganization of perceptual or other materials that makes it possible to deal with a collection of units as a single item.

Recognition memory. Memory for materials or events reflected in the ability to recognize them as items encountered previously. Also, an experimental procedure in which participants first see a collection of materials and then attempt to pick these old materials out of a list that contains some new items.

Recoil reaction. A second stage of the disaster syndrome in which there is a growing awareness of the traumatic event, with an attendant sense of depression, helplessness, and anger.

Reference group. In social psychology, a group that provides an individual with attitudinal and behavioral standards.

Reflex. A relatively simple, rapid, and automatic unlearned response to a stimulus.

Reflex arc. A pathway followed by a neural impulse that extends from a receptor to an effector to produce a reflex.

Reflex schemas. The earliest period of intellectual development, in Piaget's theory, extending from birth to one month, during which the infant's reflexes, such as sucking and grasping, are practiced.

Refractory period. The three- or four-millisecond interval immediately following a nerve impulse in which the neuron is first absolutely and then relatively incapable of generating another impulse.

Regression. A return to a simpler or earlier form of behavior as a consequence of frustration.

Regression fallacy. Because of regression to the mean, which operates in the case of correlated measures, the score (*Y*) associated with an extreme score (*X*) is always less than *X*. Occasionally, as in the case of two measures of intelligence of gifted persons separated in time, this reduction in the second score is taken as a true loss in intelligence when it is not.

Regression to the mean. A statistical concept referring to the fact that the measure predicted from another measure on the basis of a correlation is less extreme than the measure from which the prediction is made.

Reinforcement. In operant conditioning the satisfying state of affairs that follows the response, increasing the frequency of the response. In classical conditioning, the pairing of a CS with a US.

Reinforcing stimulus. A stimulus that brings about a satisfying state of affairs.

Relative refractory period. A brief period following stimulation of a nerve or muscle during which it is unresponsive to all but a very strong stimulus.

Relative size. A cue to depth in which an object producing a smaller retinal image is seen as farther away than an object that is known to be of the same size but produces a larger retinal image.

Releaser. An ethological term to designate a stimulus that initiates ("releases") an instinctive behavioral cycle.

Reliability. The extent to which a measuring instrument yields consistent results each time the same individual is tested. Contrast with *validity*.

REM (rapid eye movement). Eye movements that occur during sleep and usually denote dreaming. The movements of the eyeball generate electrical activity which can be recorded by attaching electrodes near the eye.

REM rebound. The increment in the amount of dreaming on a successive night after the individual has been deprived of REM sleep.

Reminiscence. An improvement in a practiced act after a period of no practice. Differs from spontaneous recovery only in that the act has not earlier undergone extinction.

Repetition compulsion. A Freudian concept referring to the neurotic compulsion to relive traumatic experiences.

Replication. The repetition of an experiment under the identical conditions followed in the original study.

Representative sample. A sample whose characteristics match those of the population.

Repression. The exclusion from memory of traumatic experiences, without the individual's awareness.

Repression–sensitization. A dimension of personality characterized by a selective tendency to deny or to be vigilant toward potentially anxiety-arousing stimuli.

Reproduction method. A method of studying retention in which the learner must reproduce materials previously learned.

Resistance. In psychoanalytic therapy, the common tendency of a patient to use many kinds of behavior to avoid unpleasant topics.

Respondent conditioning. Learning in which the reaction to an eliciting stimulus is an involuntary response; the behavior is respondent because it is identified by the specific eliciting stimulus, not by its effect on the environment. See *classical conditioning;* contrast to *operant conditioning.*

Response bias. A predisposition to respond in a particular way and, for example, (a) respond with "false" to items on a personality test, or (b) turn left at a choice point in a maze.

Response set. A tendency (set) on the part of an individual to respond to test questions in characteristic ways without regard to content of the question.

Resting potential. The electrical charge between the inside and outside of a nerve cell, muscle, or gland cell. Usually about −70 millivolts.

Retention. The ability to recall material previously learned.

Retention curve. A curve depicting the retention over time of previously learned material. The abscissa indicates elapsed time, the ordinate the amount remembered. The typical curve form is one of an initially rapid decline followed by a slower decline.

Reticular activating system. A general facilitative system originating in the reticular formation of the brain stem that, when stimulated, activates the entire nervous system. Regulates alertness, attention, wakefulness, and perceptual associations.

Reticular formation. The innermost portion of the brain stem that appears reticulated or netted under the microscope.

Retina. The light-sensitive layer in the eye that contains the receptors (rods and cones) for vision.

Retinal disparity. The fact that the two eyes receive slightly different images of the same object. Provides a very sensitive primary cue to depth.

Retrieval. The process of calling an item up from memory.

Retroactive inhibition. The interference with retention by learning interpolated between original learning and attempted recall.

Retrograde amnesia. Forgetting of events immediately preceding some injury or other traumatic experience.

Retrospective report. Reports based on memory of an event.

Reversal shift. An experimental procedure in which a participant first learns two discriminations and, having learned them, shifts to the learning of two more discriminations requiring a positive response to stimuli to which the response was negative earlier. Contrast with *nonreversal shift.*

Reversibility. As a principle enunciated by Piaget, the ability to move back and forth in a sequence of thought without distorting the individual elements of the sequence. (In logical mathematical operations, $2 + 4 = 6$, and $6 - 4 = 2$.) In problem solving, the ability to interrupt a sequence of thought at any point and to return to the beginning of the sequence without changing the nature of the problem. Related to *conservation* and *concrete operations.*

Reward training. A form of instrumental conditioning employing a positive reinforcer.

Rhodopsin. A light-sensitive substance found in the rods.

Risk population. In psychopathology, used to denote a group that has a higher probability of developing a mental disorder in comparison to a randomly selected sample.

Risk research. The study of groups of individuals with a higher probability of developing mental disorder than people in general. See *risk population*.

Risky shift. The tendency for people in groups to take bigger risks when engaged in collective decision making than would the members as individuals.

RNA (ribonucleic acid). Complex molecules that are believed to be the "enforcers" of the genetic code by directing the formation of enzymes out of amino acids found in the cell.

ROC (receiver–operating characteristic) curve. In signal detection research, a function in which the probability of a "hit" is plotted against the probability of a "false alarm."

Rod–cone break. In the curve of dark adaptation, the sudden increase in sensitivity (drop in the curve) that occurs after a few minutes, Reflects the transition from primarily cone vision to primarily rod vision.

Rods. Visual receptors of the retina extremely sensitive to low intensities of light and thus employed in twilight and night vision; but insensitive to hue. Contrast with *cones*.

Role. The behavior expected of an individual by reason of his membership in a particular group.

Role playing. A method for studying the attributes of a specific role by concretely acting out the details of that role in a hypothetical but staged situation which allows for a systematic observation.

Rorschach test. One of the projective tests of personality. The inkblot test.

Rote learning. Verbal learning involving fixed, mechanical sequences. Typically, there is little attention to meaning.

Round window. Located just below the oval window, the membranous "window" separating the tympanic canal of the cochlea from the middle ear.

S

***s* factors.** Specific intellectual abilities in Spearman's two-factor theory of intelligence.

Sample. A group from some population selected from special study.

Sampling distribution of the mean. A distribution of *means* that theoretically would be obtained if a very large number of samples of the same size were selected, their means determined and these means cast into a frequency distribution.

Saturation. The "richness" of a color; the dimension from gray to full color.

Savings method (relearning method). An experimental procedure for studying retention in which the learner relearns materials previously learned, and the measure is the decrease in errors and in time or number of trials needed for relearning as compared with original learning.

Scapegoating. The displacement of hostility by directing it against the innocent, sometimes as anger toward a particular person, but more often as prejudice toward all members of a minority group. See *displacement.*

Scatter diagram. A graphic representation of a correlation.

Scatter plot. See *scatter diagram.*

Schedule of reinforcement. The pattern of reinforcement employed in a condition of partial reinforcement. See *fixed interval schedule, fixed ratio schedule, variable interval schedule,* and *variable ratio schedule.*

Scheme. In Piaget's theory of cognitive development, an organized pattern of physical action.

Schizoid personality. A form of personality disorder in which the personality displayed is one of seclusiveness, oversensitivity, isolation, and detachment. Schizotypal personality disorder (DSM III).

Schizophrenia. See *schizophrenic disorder.*

Schizophrenia, catatonic subtype. A form of schizophrenia characterized by unusual postures and stereotyped, repetitive movements and speech.

Schizophrenia, childhood (DSM II). A form of psychosis in childhood often occurring between one and eleven years of age in which the chief disturbance is autistic thinking and an inability to establish affective contact with other people.

Schizophrenia (hebephrenic) disorganized subtype. A type of schizophrenia characterized by bizarre ideas and silliness.

Schizophrenia, paranoid subtype. Schizophrenia in which the major symptom is a set of delusions.

Schizophrenia, process. Characterized by early onset in a poorly integrated individual. Typically, the prognosis is unfavorable.

Schizophrenia, pseudoneurotic. A form of schizophrenia in which the defenses appear to be neurotic, and a pervasive anxiety is the dominating quality.

Schizophrenia, reactive. Characterized by late onset of the disorder in a fairly well-adapted individual. Typically, the prognosis is favorable.

Schizophrenia, schizo-affective (DSM II). A form of schizophrenia in which thought and affect disorder are both markedly present. In DSM-III designated schizoaffective disorder.

Schizophrenia, simple (DSM-II). Schizophrenia in which the chief symptoms are apathy and withdrawal.

Schizophrenic disorder. A group of disorders marked by major dysfunctions of thinking, emotion, and behavior. Disturbances in thinking take the form of illogicality, numerous faulty associative interferences, and delusional beliefs. Perception is also disturbed, with hallucinations—auditory, visual, and tactile—common. Affect is flattened or extremely labile, and often inappropriate. Motor behavior can be faulty and bizarre. Social relationships are minimal; withdrawal from others is the more characteristic pattern.

Schizophrenic, good premorbid. A term used to denote a schizophrenic patient whose life course before the disorder was socially, sexually, and economically adequate. In this group breakdown usually follows an evident stress. Recovery prospects are good. Such conditions are also called *reactive* or *schizophreniform.*

Schizophrenic, poor premorbid. A term used to denote a schizophrenic patient whose life course before the disorder was socially, sexually, and economically inadequate. In these patients the disorder often takes a chronic course.

Schizophreniform disorder. Formerly the reactive type of schizophrenia marked by acute onset, strong affective components, and a history of considerable premorbid competence in the social, sexual, and economic spheres. Typically these patients have a favorable prognosis and recover rapidly. The disorder is now segregated from schizophrenia because it is so atypical.

Schizophrenogenic mother. A powerful, domineering, and possessive mother who might, according to the view advanced by some clinicians, intensify stress in the mother-child relationship and play a role in the schizophrenic breakdown of her offspring.

Scotopic vision. Vision that occurs under conditions of faint illumination.

Secondary cues to distance. Cues that derive from features of the environment. See *linear perspective, aerial perspective, interposition, gradient of texture* and *patterns of light and shade.*

Secondary circular reactions. A period of heightened intellectual activity extending from four to eight months of age in Piaget's developmental theory of intelligence. Characterized by the infant's preoccupation with the effects its activity produces on the environment.

Secondary drive. A learned or acquired drive.

Secondary memory. Long-term memory. Contrast with *primary memory.*

Secondary motor cortex. Areas of the cerebral cortex indirectly connected to the muscles, in terms of number of intervening synapses. Contrast with *primary motor cortex, primary sensory cortex* and *secondary sensory cortex.*

Secondary process. In Freudian theory, behavior that is reality-oriented and under the control of the ego. Contrast with *primary process.*

Secondary reinforcement. Learned reinforcement; any rewarding event or state that derives its effectiveness from earlier conditioning. Contrast with *primary reinforcement.*

Secondary reinforcer. A stimulus that becomes a reinforcer as a result of previous association with a reinforcing stimulus.

Secondary sensory cortex. Areas of the cerebral cortex indirectly connected to the receptors in terms of number of intervening synapses. Contrast with *primary sensory cortex, primary motor cortex* and *secondary motor cortex.*

Secondary sex characteristics. Physical attributes distinguishing mature males from females other than reproductive organs, such as deepness of voice and body build.

Secular trend. Changes in patterns of development for populations over an extended period of time.

Selective breeding. The method of investigation of genetic factors in which subjects with specified characteristics are mated for the purpose of studying the transmission of these characteristics to the offspring.

Selective reinforcement. In operant conditioning, the use of reinforcing stimuli to strengthen an operant response.

Self-actualization. The highest-order need in Maslow's hierarchy, characterized by the desire for self-fulfillment and realization of one's potential.

Self-concept. The individual's awareness of his or her identity as a person, starting with the infant's discovery of bodily parts and becoming eventually an encompassing organized perception of the person's thoughts, feelings, attitudes, views, and goals.

Self-fulfilling prophecy. The prophecy that an event will happen increases the probability that the event actually will happen. See *labeling theory.*

Self-reflexive character of language. The power that true language has to be about itself. Signing may exist (for example, in lower animals) without this quality, but such accomplishments, in the view of the textbook, are not true language.

Self-stimulation. Electrical stimulation of the brain produced by a subject's activities. Depending upon the location of the stimulation animals may work to receive it or cease responding. In the former case the site is referred to as a "pleasure center."

Self-theory. A personality theory (Rogerian) that emphasizes an individual's self-concept and the role of the self in shaping the individual's destiny.

Semantic differential. A rating scale by which a concept is located in one of seven positions between polar adjectives, good-bad, strong-weak and active-passive, for example. These ratings yield measures of *connotative meaning.* The three dimensions above (strong-weak, etc.) are the most important.

Semantic generalization. A form of mediated generalization that occurs because of a similarity in meaning between the original CS and the new test stimulus.

Semantic memory. Knowledge of the world, including the knowledge of language and how it is used. Contrast with *episodic memory.*

Semantics. The study of the meaning of words. See *denotative meaning, associative meaning,* and *connotative meaning.*

Semicircular canals. Three curved and tubular fluid-filled canals of the inner ear, perpendicular to one another and registering three planes; they sense the turning of the head and its coming to rest.

Sensation level. The intensity of sensory experience.

Sensorimotor intelligence. In Piaget's developmental theory of intelligence, the period extending from birth to two years, during which the child comes to realize that objects exist independently of his or her perceptions.

Sensory deprivation. An experimental procedure in which the participant experiences markedly reduced or monotonous stimulation for a relatively long period of time.

Sensory–neural deafness. Deafness caused by damage to the structures of the inner ear or auditory nerve. Contrast with *conduction deafness.*

Sensory neuron. Neurons which are in contact with receptors and carry messages to the central nervous system.

Separation anxiety. Crying, fretting,

and discomfort reflective of unhappiness that occurs when a child is separated from an adult (typically a parent) to whom he or she is attached.

Serial anticipation method. A method of rote learning employing a serial list. The subject must respond to each item the one that comes next.

Serial learning. The learning of a list of stimuli in a specific order.

Serial position curve. A graph showing the ease of learning each item in a serial list.

Set. A preparedness to respond in a particular way.

Sex-linked trait. A trait that is determined by a gene transmitted on the sex chromosome.

Sex-role typing. The reinforcement and emphasizing of stereotypic behaviors and attitudes presumed to be characteristic of males and females.

Sexual identification. Discriminating among interests, attitudes, and behaviors that are appropriate for males and females and adopting those that are perceived as appropriate for one's own sex.

Shadowing. A procedure in which a subject repeats a message as it is heard. This assures that the individual attends to the shadowed message although interest is in the extent to which an unshadowed message delivered at the same time is processed.

Shape constancy. A form of perceptual constancy. Objects viewed from different angles produce different retinal images. In spite of this they are seen as having a constant shape.

Shaping. Through operant conditioning reinforcement is provided for responses which initially only approximate the desired response. On subsequent conditioning trials, even closer approximations to the desired behavior are reinforced until the specific operant has been elicited and rewarded.

Shock reaction. Initial phase of the disaster syndrome in which the individual in disaster is confused and unable to act under the impact of the stunning event; the individual seemingly remains unaware of the magnitude of the disaster.

Shock therapy. A form of therapy for mental illness employing convulsions produced by electric shock or a drug.

Short-term memory (STM). Memory that lasts for about fifteen to thirty seconds. Contrast with *immediate memory*.

Sidman avoidance schedule. Punishment, usually electric shock, is scheduled to occur at regular intervals but a response in this interval postpones punishment.

Signal detectability theory. A theory of the sensory and judgmental processes involved in psychophysical determinations.

Significant difference. In statistics, a difference that is unlikely to have occurred by chance.

Significate. Piaget's term for an external object or some aspect of reality.

Signifier. Piaget's term for the internal or symbolic representation of an external object.

Simple cell. Cells in the visual cortex of the cat that respond to simple stimuli like lines or edges registered in certain locations on the retina.

Size constancy. The tendency for objects to be seen as their correct size from different distances.

Size discrimination problem (two choice). A procedure used in learning experiments employing two stimulus objects varying in size which are shifted from trial to trial in terms of placement, but with selection of a given size consistently rewarded.

Skewed curve. An asymmetrical frequency distribution in which the range of scores on one side of the mode is greater than on the other.

Skin map. A diagram showing the spots on the skin that are sensitive to cold, warmth, touch, etc.

Skinner box. A device for the study of operant conditioning: (a) a barpressing apparatus used with rats or (b) a window pecking apparatus used with pigeons.

Slave process. Opposing physiological process following elicitation of an emotional state. See *opponent process theory* (2).

Sleep stages. The four stages of sleep that have been described by sleep researchers.

Sleeper effect. A change in public opinion that occurs after a survey has been conducted. Typically, the data of the survey is made to seem inaccurate.

Slow-to-warm-up child. A child whose temperament is characterized by wariness of new situations, a variable pattern of biological functions, and slightly negative mood.

Small-N design. An experimental design devised for use with a small number (N) of participants. Whereas traditional experimental designs subject some individuals to the experimental treatment and withhold it from others, all subjects receive the experimental treatment in small-N designs. See *between-subject experiment* and *within-subject experiment.* Small-N experiments are within-subject experiments.

Smiling, nonselective social. Smiling in the human infant which occurs between two and eight weeks and is generated in response to a variety of visual, social stimuli, particularly the human face.

Smiling, selective social. The third phase of smiling in the human infant. It occurs at about five or six months of age in response to familiar faces.

Smiling, spontaneous or reflex. The first stage of smiling in the earliest weeks of life in the human infant in which smiles are elicited without appropriate stimuli, perhaps even to stomach disturbances.

Social breakdown syndrome. The deterioration in social and interpersonal skills that accompanies chronic mental disorders and is accentuated by long-term institutional placement.

Social class. A grouping of people on a dimension of social status. Often conceived as ranging from upper–upper downward to lower–lower.

Social-comparison theory. A social psychological theory asserting that an individual verifies socially derived knowledge by comparing his or her opinions with those of others.

Social competence. A general term intended to reflect the social, vocational, and sexual adaptation patterns of individuals. Everyday effectiveness in dealing with the environment.

Social desirability. A response style that results in subjects responding to items in personality tests on the basis of the degree of social approval these elicit.

Social drift hypothesis. A sociological hypothesis of the relationship of lower-class social status to the incidence of schizophrenia. Social drift suggests that positive correlation is not causative, but correlational. Inadequate people, such as schizophrenics, migrate into the slums because of their inability to cope in a complex society.

Social environment. A general concept in social psychology referring to the many important social factors in the environment.

Social exchange theory. The concept that we react to a person in terms of the rewards and costs of the encounter.

Social isolation hypothesis. A sociological hypothesis that assumes the high correlations between lower-class status and schizophrenia to be causally related. Presumably, the isolation of slum living serves as a social stress that heightens the probability of breakdown.

Social-learning therapy. The utilization of learning principles and a controlled physical and social environment to enhance the social adaptation of persons.

Social-learning theory. The view that much of personality is formed through observation and imitation of others. This theory, identified with Bandura, emphasizes *modeling* and *observational learning.*

Social mobility. The movement of an individual from one social class to another.

Social-skills training. A form of therapy designed to train schizophrenic patients and other less competent individuals in more adequate ways of responding to other people and to environmental demands.

Socialization. The child's acquisition by experience of the values of his culture.

Sociopathic personality. Character disorder in which the individual's behavior is not governed at all by the usual social conventions. See *antisocial personality.*

Somatic nervous system. All the peripheral nerve structures not in the autonomic system; the sensory fibers serving the sensory receptors and the motor fibers serving skeletal muscles.

Somatic motor fibers. Axons that carry commands from the central nervous system to the muscles attached to bones.

Somatic passivity. A first-rank symptom of schizophrenia in which the patient suffers the delusion that bodily sensations are being controlled and imposed by outside forces.

Somatic-sensory fibers. Axons that carry information from the receptors to the central nervous system; afferent neurons.

Somatic therapy. The treatment of mental and emotional disorders by physical methods acting on bodily processes, e.g., shock, psychosurgery, and drugs.

Somatoform disorder. A new category in DSM III marked by physical symptoms for which there is no evident accompanying organic disorder, strengthening the assumption that psychological conflict underlies the behavior. Includes *somatization disorder* (formerly hysteria) and *conversion disorder.*

Somatotonia. The personality associated in Sheldon's system with mesomorphy. Characteristics are (a) a tendency toward action rather than thought, and (b) extroverted behavior.

Somatotype. Body type as in typologies based upon physique.

Sound spectrograph. An electronic device that indicates changes in intensity–frequency patterns of sounds as a function of time.

Spaced (distributed) practice. Practice with relatively long pauses between trials. Contrast with *massed practice.*

Span of apprehension. The number of items that can be perceived in a single glance.

Span of immediate memory. The number of items that can be remembered following a single brief presentation. The span tends to be about seven with a range from five to nine.

Spatial summation. Two or more subthreshold stimuli applied to different parts on a neuron add together and produce a neurve impulse when none of the stimuli alone is strong enough.

Species-specific. Patterns of response that are characteristic of a given species under the same or markedly similar conditions.

Specific energies of nerves. Johannes Mueller's law that afferent nerves, being connected to specific receptors, can respond only to certain types of stimulation and can yield only certain types of experience.

Specific factor. In the factor analysis of intelligence, a skill that is applied when taking a particular kind of test. Contrast with *general factor.*

Spectrum. The range of physical stimuli to which a receptor responds. Most often used in connection with visual stimuli.

Spinal cord. The nervous tissue within the vertebral column.

Spinal nerves. Thirty-one pairs of peripheral nerves extending from spaces between the vertebrae of the spinal column to various parts of the body.

Spinal reflex. A complete reflex circuit that passes through the spinal cord but not directly through a higher center. If the control of brain centers is removed, the spinal reflex will still be evident.

Split brain. A brain in which the two hemispheres are no longer joined together as a result of the cutting of the corpus callosum.

Split-half method. A method of establishing reliability of a test by comparing a person's performance on two halves of it, such as on all odd- and all even-numbered items.

Spontaneous recovery. Reappearance of an extinguished conditioned response after a lapse of time. See *reminiscence.*

Spotlight dream. A dream within a series of dreams that illuminates the basic content of the dream sequence.

Stabilized image. An image on the retina presented in a way to eliminate the small movements usually produced by physiological nystagmus.

Standard deviation. The most commonly used measure of dispersion or variability.

Standard error of the estimate. The standard deviation of the distribution of scores theoretically associated by correlation with a single score. Thus, in predicting a score from this latter score, it is possible to describe a hypothetical distribution of predicted scores.

Standard error of the mean. The standard deviation of a frequency distribution of means that would be obtained in theory from a series of samples all selected (or treated) in the same way.

Standard error of the difference. The standard deviation of a sampling distribution of differences.

Standardization. In test construction, the process of trying the test out on a group representative of the people for whom the test is meant, in order to establish appropriateness of items and later standard methods of scoring and interpretation.

Standard score. A score expressed in terms of standard deviations from the mean.

Standardization sample. A sample of persons used to pretest the adequacy of a test or tests and to establish norms for test performance.

Stanford–Binet tests. One of the most frequently used tests for children. Originally created by Binet and revised for use in the United States at Stanford University, the test is based upon age norms and is constructed in terms of age levels.

Stapes. One of the three bones of the middle ear (*malleus, incus* and *stapes*) that transmit sound vibrations from the eardrum to the inner ear.

Statistical inference. Drawing more general conclusions about populations from data obtained with a sampling of individuals.

Statistical significance. The extent to which data obtained from studies permit rejection of the null hypothesis of no differences between groups; the likelihood, expressed in probability terms, that if the null hypothesis was correct, the experimental results would obtain.

Stereochemical theory. The lock-and-key theory of olfaction. According to this theory, the molecules of particular odorous substances are shaped so as to fit certain depressions in the olfactory receptors.

Stereotype. Expectations and opinions about large groups of people. A stereotype is overly concrete, specific and resistant to disconfirming evidence. See *implicit personality theory.*

Stereotypy. Persistent thinking in stereotypes; or a condition in which the individual makes repetitive movements, as in catatonic schizophrenia.

Stimulation deafness. Deafness produced by long-term exposure to high-intensity auditory stimulation. Also called *boilermaker's deafness.*

Stimulus. In general, any antecedent condition or "cause" of behavior. More specifically, environmental energy. See *distal stimulus, proximal stimulus, effective stimulus,* and *potential stimulus.*

Stimulus generalization. See *generalization.*

Storage. Putting materials into memory. Some accounts refer to short-term and long-term storage depending upon the stage of memory involved.

Strabismus. Inability of one eye to focus on a spot with the other, usually because of imbalance in the eye muscles.

Stranger anxiety. A fear of strangers which appears at about eight months of age in the human infant.

Stress. A generic term for any situation that threatens the adaptation of an organism; and the physiological and psychological responses of an individual to a threat to his or her integrity.

Stroboscope. A device that turns a light on and off in very rapid and controllable flashes.

Strong Vocational Interest Blank. One of the most widely used interest inventories employed in vocational, educational, and industrial counseling.

Structuralism. A school of psychology which saw the task of psychology as that of attempting to understand the structure of the mind. The major method of structuralism was introspection. Mind was reduced by this school to a set of sensory elements.

Structured test. A test that provides the individual with only a limited set of response alternatives.

Subjective organization. The organization of materials to be remembered that a person creates for himself as opposed to an organization imposed by the nature of materials. See *organization in recall.*

Sublimation. Conversion of one's unacceptable impulses into socially acceptable outlets.

Substitute behavior. Any behavior that provides indirect or symbolic satisfaction of a need.

Subtraction procedure. In the *complication experiment reaction time* is longer if the observer must react in a special way depending upon the characteristics of the stimulus than if he must merely react as quickly as possible when the stimulus occurs. The difference between these two reaction times (obtained by subtraction) provides an estimate of the time required for the added information processing.

Subtractive mixture. Mixture of pigments, each of which absorbs some of the wavelengths reflected by the other pigments. Contrast with *additive mixture.*

Successive approximations. A method of training in which successively more nearly exact performances of the correct response are required.

Summation. The addition of the intensities of nerve impulses so that, for example, the combined effect is strong enough to fire a neuron.

Summation tone. A third tone sometimes heard when two tones are sounded together. Its pitch is that which corresponds to the total of the two component frequencies.

Superego. In Freudian theory, the portion of personality containing the parental and social standards internalized by the ego; the individual's conscience and ego ideal or aspiration.

Superior colliculus. The foremost pair of bulges in the tectum of the midbrain; part of the visual system.

Suppression. The forcible and intentional exclusion of unpleasant thoughts from consciousness. Differs from repression, in which the process is beyond awareness.

Suppression ratio. A quantitative measure of the degree to which a conditioned emotional response (CER) interferes with bar pressing. Letting *B* stand for the number of responses in the presence of the CS for the CER and *A* for the number of responses in the immediately preceding period of the same length, the formula for the suppression ratio is $B/(A + B)$.

Surface structure. In Noam Chomsky's theory, the structure of language as spoken or written. Surface structure is a transformation of materials in *deep structure,* the intended meaning, by a set of rules which put it into a sentence in active voice or passive voice, into question or implied question form, or into some other sentence structure.

Surrogate mother. Substitute mother figure; also pseudomother, as in Harlow's use of cloth and wire mother-substitute forms.

Symbiosis. The close tie, often of pathological dimensions, existing between two individuals—typically, but not exclusively, mother and child.

Symbolic representation. Third stage in Jerome Bruner's theory of cognitive growth, beginning at age three, when children use language, and symbols in general, to process their experiences.

Symbolization. Disguised representation in consciousness of repressed thoughts, acts, or ideas (psychoanalytic); in a broader sense, the process of using symbols.

Sympathetic ganglia. Chains of clustered nerve cell bodies alongside the thoracic and lumbar spinal cord that subserve the sympathetic functions of the autonomic system.

Sympathetic nervous system. A division of the autonomic system concerned with emotional excitement. Prepares the organism for emergency and, in general, acts in opposition to the parasympathetic system.

Superstition. In operant conditioning, a false conception of causation brought on in pigeons by reinforcement at fixed intervals of whatever the birds were doing.

Synapse. The junction between neurons.

Synaptic cleft. The space between postsynaptic and presynaptic neurons.

Synaptic transmission. The transmission of nerve impulses from one neuron to an adjacent neuron.

Syndrome. A pattern of symptoms characteristic of a disease or a disorder.

Synesthesia. Registration of a stimulus by both its own and another sensory system (e.g., a passage of music that produces in an individual a combined auditory and visual sensation). Synesthesias are more common in early perceptual stages of development.

Syntax. The rules by which words may be combined into phrases and sentences. Grammar is the most familiar example.

Systematic desensitization. A form of behavior therapy devised by Wolpe and based upon the principle of counterconditioning. A hierarchy of progressively fearsome situations are imagined by a person in deep relaxation, which acts to inhibit anxiety.

T

***t*-test.** A statistical test to determine whether a difference is significant.

Taste bud. Flask-shaped mass, usually lying in the wall of a tongue papilla, made up of supporting cells and of taste cells which project short hairlike processes into the pore of the structure.

TAT (Thematic Apperception Test). A projective technique, devised by Murray, consisting of vague pictures for which an individual is required to create stories.

Taxis. Reflex movement by a simple organism that is a positive or negative response to stimulation such as light, temperature or a chemical agent.

Tay-Sachs Disease. A disorder of metabolism transmitted as a recessive trait and causing mental retardation. It is confined mainly to children of northeastern European Jewish ancestry.

Tectum. The roof of the midbrain consisting of superior and inferior colliculi.

Temperament. An aspect of personality typically associated with mood, adaptability, etc., in ways considered to have marked stability; increasingly, a constitutional factor is cited as underlying the behavioral manifestations.

Temporal lobe. That part of the cerebral hemisphere lying in front of the occipital lobe.

Temporal summation. A form of summation in which two subthreshold stimuli occurring in rapid succession succeed in firing a neuron.

Terminal button. The responsive parts of a neuron at the end of its axon. The terminal buttons store transmitter substance and discharge it upon arrival of a nerve impulse.

Territorial instinct. A form of innate behavior, characteristic of many infra-human species, in which the organism or a group demarcates a physical area as exclusively its own personal habitat and will defend aggressively against invasion by members of its own species.

Tertiary circular reaction. A stage in Piaget's developmental theory of intelligence extending from twelve to eighteen months of age and involving the infant's "active experimentation" with his surroundings.

Test–retest method. A method of establishing reliability that involves giving the test twice to the same sample of persons.

Therapeutic community. A form of therapy encompassing all ongoing activities and personnel of the hospital so that the patient's environment may contribute to the cure of mental illness.

Thoracicolumbar system. In anatomical terms, the *sympathetic nervous system*.

Thought disorder. A symptom of schizophrenia characterized by intellectual incoherence, tendencies to neologisms, association defects, peculiar speech forms, and an inability to abstract.

Thought broadcast. *A first-rank symptom* in which the person believes that his thoughts are being broadcast to others through some medium such as television.

Thought insertion. *A first-rank symptom* in which the person believes that thoughts are being put into his mind by some external force or agent.

Threshold. That point, statistically determined, at which a stimulus is just barely adequate to elicit a specific response (absolute threshold) or at which it differs sufficiently from another stimulus to elicit a different response (differential threshold).

Timbre. The quality of sounds that enables us to tell one kind of sound from another. Depends upon the set of overtones associated with the fundamental tones.

Tip-of-the-tongue phenomenon. The failure to recall a word or name that is quite well known to the speaker.

Token economy. A technique used in institutional or familial settings in which rewards (tokens) are given for positive prosocial behaviors and which can later be exchanged for material goods and privileges.

Toxic reation. Poisonous reaction to drug ingestion.

Trait. An enduring attribute of a person that is manifested in a variety of situations.

Trait, source. The basic, underlying determiners of surface traits.

Trait, surface. An overt behavior pattern that is consistently revealed in comparable situations.

Trait theory. A theory that emphasizes the existence of traits as enduring and persistent aspects of the personality. These are viewed as dimensional and measurable by a person's scores on a variety of scales that are presumed to reflect behaviors characteristic of such traits.

Tranquilizers. Drugs designed to reduce anxiety and manifestations of psychotic behavior.

Thought withdrawal. *A first-rank symptom* in which the person believes that *thoughts* are being physically extracted from his mind by powerful external forces.

Transactional model of development. A theoretical model which holds that the development of personal traits and behavior occurs through reciprocal actions between the individual and the environment over time.

Transfer of training. The effect (beneficial or interfering) of learning one thing upon the learning of another.

Transference. The close emotional attachment of the patient in psychoanalysis to the analyst.

Transference neurosis. A phenomenon encountered in psychoanalytic therapy in which the affect originally directed at another person (often a parent) is directed at the analyst.

Transformational rules. In Noam Chomsky's theory, the rules by which the intended meaning in *deep structure* is processed into a sentence of particular *surface structure* by choosing one of several possible syntactical arrangements.

Transient situational disturbances (DSM II). Emotional disturbances that are temporary or transient in nature and are triggered by sudden catastrophe or prolonged stress. In DSM-III, termed post-traumatic stress disorder.

Transposition. Having learned to discriminate two stimuli, the organism responds to a new pair of stimuli as if the original learning had consisted of the learning of a relationship.

Transvestite. A person who derives erotic satisfaction by cross-dressing, i.e., dressing as a member of the opposite sex.

Traumatic neurosis. Neurotic disorder induced by a specific event, usually of markedly stressful proportions. Also termed transient situational neurosis.

Treatment milieu. The total physical, occupational, and psychological qualities of an environment in which therapy occurs; usually applied to clinic and hospital settings.

Trichromat. An individual showing a retinal response to three colors.

Trichromatic color vision. Normal color vision, in which all visible hues can be reproduced by appropriate mixtures of three primary colors.

Trichromatic theory. The Young-Helmholtz theory of color vision which assumes that color vision can be accounted for by three elementary processes.

Trick vocabulary. The use of language, as in the case of children (and probably birds), without respect to meaning.

Trisomy 21. A condition of having three rather than two of the number 21 chromosome and the major cause of *Down syndrome*.

Truncated distribution. A distribution that covers less than the complete range of scores.

Turner's syndrome. A disorder of females in which the absence of an X chromosome keeps the breasts incompletely developed and brings sterility.

Two-factor theory. A theory of learning that makes the assumption that classical and instrumental learning are different with respect to the principle of reinforcement.

Type theory. In personality theory, any position that views persons as members of categories rather than as having many dimensions.

U

Unconditioned response. A response that occurs to the US without special training. US → UR.

Unconditioned stimulus. A stimulus that produces a consistent response (UR) at the ontset of training US → UR.

Unconflicted adherence. A method for coping with conflict marked by a continuation of ongoing activity without regard to risk or loss.

Unconflicted change. Uncritical acceptance of a new course of action when in conflict.
Unconscious. A general term to signify classes of activities that are not open to conscious awareness.
Unmarked expressions. In pairs of words (e.g., short-tall), one of them merely asks for information when used in the question, "How ____ is he?" Such words are unmarked. Contrast *marked expression.*
Unobtrusive measures. Measures of which the participants in research are unaware—for example, obtaining a measure of alcohol consumption in a neighborhood by counting empty containers in garbage cans. These measures are designed to minimize the *reactive effects of measurement.*
UR. See *unconditioned response.*
US. See *unconditioned stimulus.*
Unstructured test. A test in which the range of response is determined by the individual with minimum restriction imposed by the test stimuli.

V

$V_{environmental}$. The variance, or range of expression, of a population trait due to different environments.
$V_{genetic}$. The variance, or range of expression, of a population trait due to different genotypes.
$V_{phenotypic}$. The total variance, or range of expression, for a given population trait.
Vacuum activity. Instinctive activity that occurs in the absence of characteristic releasing stimuli.
Valence, positive or negative. The attractive (positive) or unattractive (negative) properties of an object that imply movement toward or movement away from the object by an organism.
Validity. The extent to which the measurements obtained in a test correlate with behavior in some other situation.
Variable interval schedule. A schedule of partial reinforcement in which the participant is rewarded for the first response following amounts of time that vary from reward to reward.
Variable ratio schedule. A schedule of partial reinforcement in which the participant is rewarded for the first response following numbers of previous responses that vary from reward to reward.
Variance. A measure of variability; the square of the standard deviation.
Vector. A force of a given intensity that impels behavior in a specific direction.
Verbal I.Q. Intelligence test score derived from test measures that require language usage, reasoning, vocabulary, informational content, comprehension, etc.
Verbal mediation. The use of language to intervene between perception of outside events and acting upon them.
Verbal test. A test that requires the use of language. Contrast with *performance test.*
Vertical–horizontal illusion. A tendency for vertical lines to seem longer than horizontal lines of the same length.
Vestibular sensitivity. The "sense of balance" and detection of motion in relation to gravity conveyed by the two sacs of the *vestibule* and the *semicircular canals.*
Vestibule. Two fluid-filled sacs in the *membranous labyrinth* containing otoliths or crystals which lay against hair cells when the head is tilted or the body is in straight-line motion.
Vicarious functioning. The assuming of function by another area of the brain after the portion usually responsible has been destroyed.
Vigilance. (1) Careful search for and review of relevant information about alternatives in a conflict situation. An adaptive response. (2) In signal detecting situations, level of attention devoted to search.
Visceral motor fibers. Axons that carry commands from the central nervous system to the internal organs of the body. See *autonomic nervous system.*
Viscerotonia. In Sheldon's classification, the personality type associated with endomorphy: gluttonous, comfort-loving, and extroverted.
Visual acuity. The ratio between the distance at which the tested eye can make a discrimination and that at which a normal eye makes it.
Visual cliff. A device used to study infants.
Visual purple. Rhodopsin.
Vitreous humor. The transparent jelly-like substance filling the eyeball between the retina and the lens.

W

WAIS (Wechsler Adult Intelligence Scale). The most widely used individual intelligence test for adults which provides for verbal, performance, and composite I.Q. scores. An analogous Wechsler Intelligence Scale for Children (WISC) is also extensively used for evaluating children's intellect.
Warm spot. A point-like spot on the skin that is particularly sensitive to warm stimuli.
Weber's law. $\Delta I/I = K$, where I is a reference stimulus magnitude and ΔI is the amount of change necessary to produce a just noticeable difference.
Wechsler scales. Intelligence tests created by the psychologist David Wechsler. These include the Wechsler Adult Intelligence Scale (WAIS) and the Wechsler Intelligence Scale for Children (WISC). Subtests measuring verbal and performance abilities are a distinguishing feature of these scales.
Wernicke's area. An area in the temporal lobe of the left hemisphere brain associated with the control of speech.
White matter. Areas of the central nervous system containing the myelinated axons of neurons. It is communicative in function. Contrast with *gray matter.*
White noise. Noise composed of sound waves of all frequencies.
Whorfian hypothesis. The hypothesis of Benjamin Lee Whorf according to which thought is determined in part by language. See *linguistic determinism* and *linguistic relativity.*
Withdrawal. A defensive response to stress in which the person is profoundly listless and indifferent and

avoids contact with others.

Within-subject experiment. An experiment in which a single participant, on different occasions, receives the several experimental treatments of the study. Contrast with *between-subject experiment.*

Word-association test. A test sometimes used for personality diagnosis in which a person gives the first word that comes to mind in response to a series of stimulus words spoken by the examiner.

X

***x*-axis (abscissa).** The horizontal axis on a graph; usually represents the independent variable.

XYY males. Males having an extra Y chromosome in their genetic makeup. It remains unclear whether these men have criminal tendencies.

Y

YAVIS type. A term used by Schofield for the person who has a good chance of benefiting from therapy—young, attractive, verbal, intelligent and successful.

***y*-axis (ordinate).** The vertical axis on a graph; usually represents the dependent variable.

Yoked control. An experimental method in which the control participant receives the same treatment as the experimental participant on the same schedule. Usually, the two procedures are run at the same time, and the experimental participant's reactions control the events presented to the control participant.

Young–Helmholtz theory. A theory of color vision that assumes three types of receptors in the retina maximally responsive to red, green, and blue, respectively.

Z

***Z*-score.** A number that expresses the distance of a particular score (X) above or below the mean (M) in units of standard deviation: $Z = (X - M)/S$.

Zeigarnik effect. The tendency to remember incomplete tasks better than completed tasks.

Zygote. A cell formed from the union of male and female gametes. In higher animals, the union of sperm and egg cells to form a fertilized egg that will grow to a new individual.

PHOTO CREDITS

Chapter 1

2	Bettmann Archive.
3	Jason Lauré/Woodfin Camp.
4	American Airlines.
6	(top) V. Rouse/Sygma.
	(middle) Frank Johnston/Woodfin Camp.
	(bottom) Michelle Vignes/ICON.
10	Culver Pictures, Inc.
12	Michael Hardy/Woodfin Camp.
17	Jim Anderson/Woodfin Camp.
20	Courtesy of Dr. Stuart W. Cook.

Chapter 2

40	Courtesy Dr. James Olds.
45	From "The Split Brain in Man" by Michael S. Gazzaniga. Copyright © August 1967 by *Scientific American, Inc.* All rights reserved.

Chapter 3

49	New York Public Library Picture Collection.
55	Bettmann Archive.
59	Photo by John Foraste, Brown University Bulletin.

Chapter 4

75	Sidney Harris.
77	(left) B. Escher Foundation/Haags Gemeente Museum; The Hague, Amsterdam.
	(right) Teri Leigh.
80	Michael Stratford.
81	(top) Reproduced with permission of the Trustees of the Pierpont Morgan Library.
	(bottom) Pierre Berger/Photo Researchers.
82	William Reaves/EPA-Documerica.
83	American Meteorite Lab.
86	Kathy Bendo.
87	(top) Kathy Bendo.
	(bottom) Teri Leigh.
89	George Gerster/Rapho-Photo Researchers.
90	Photo by Philip Clark, from R. L. Gregory, *The Intelligent Eye,* George Weidenfeld and Nicolson, Ltd. London.
91	The William Hood Dunwoody Fund, The Minneapolis Institute of Arts.
94	Courtesy Dr. Alan Hein, MIT.
95	Photo by William Vandivert. From *Scientific American,* April, 1960.

Chapter 5

99	Culver Pictures, Inc.
103	Rene Burri/Magnum.
105	Michal Heron/Woodfin Camp.
109	Culver Pictures, Inc.
112	Ken Heyman.
115	New York Historical Society, New York City.

Chapter 6

125	Culver Pictures, Inc.
128	Public Relations, Teachers College, Columbia University.
129	(top) Harvey S. Zucker.
	(bottom) Kathy Bendo.
130	Courtesy B. F. Skinner, Harvard University.
131	Joel Gordon.
135	Elliot Erwitt/Magnum.
139	Yerkes Primate Research Center of Emory University.

Chapter 7

151	Gilles Peress/Magnum.
152	Van Bucher/Photo Researchers.
155	(left) Courtesy of Dr. Craik, University of Toronto.
	(right) Courtesy of Dr. Tulving, University of Toronto.
158	Courtesy of Dr. Paivio, University of Western Ontario.
159	Walter Kintsch, University of Colorado.
161	Center for Advanced Study in the Behavioral Sciences.
162	Bettmann Archive.

Chapter 8

173	New York Public Library Picture Collection.
174	Courtesy Dr. A. M. Liberman of Haskins Laboratory and University of Connecticut.
175	
177	New York Public Library Picture Collection.
179	From K. von Frish, "Decoding the Language of the Bee," Science 185 (August 23, 1974) 663-68. Copyright 1974 by The American Association For The Advancement of Science.
181	(top) Courtesy of Dr. Beatrice Gardner.
	(bottom) Yerkes Primate Research Center of Emory University.
183	Yerkes Primate Research Center of Emory University.
184	Rodney Smith.
186	Suzanne Szasz.
192	C. Bonington-Daily Telegraph Magazine/Woodfin Camp.

Chapter 9

201	American Museum of Natural History.
203	Lynn McLaren/Rapho-Photo Researchers.
207	Arthur D. Bloom MD-University of Michigan Medical School.
214	Harvey Stein.
215	From Kallmann and Jarvick, 1959, Fig. 9.
222	NASA.

Chapter 10

227	Brown Brothers.
231	(top) Courtesy of David Wechsler.
	(bottom) Courtesy The Psychological Corporation.
232	Drawing by C.E.M.; © 1974 The New Yorker Magazine, Inc.
233	Suzanne Szasz.
242	Yale University Archives, Yale University Library.

Chapter 11

253	David Roberts/Photo Researchers.
256	Michael Weisbrot.
261	(top) Bruce Roberts/Rapho-Photo Researchers.
263	Courtesy One-to-One.
265	(top left) Ernst Haas/Magnum.
	(top right) Dan Budnick/Woodfin Camp.
	(bottom left) Culver Pictures, Inc.
	(bottom right) New York Public Library Picture Collection.
272	Joel Gordon.

Chapter 12

288	Courtesy of Ann and Will Branch and Elizabeth Katz.
289	Courtesy Harvard University News Office.
291	Yves de Braine/Black Star.
292	By Etienne Delessert from "How the Mouse Was Hit On The Head By A Stone And So Discovered The World", Doubleday.
295	From DeVries, 1969, pp. 8, 9.
298	Burt Glinn/Magnum.

Chapter 13

314	(top) Eve Arnold/Magnum.
	(bottom) Ellis Herwig/Stock, Boston.
316	Photo by William Vandivert. From *Scientific American,* November, 1955.
317	Gilles Peress/Magnum.
325	Joel Gordon.
327	Alon Reininger/Woodfin Camp.

Chapter 14

333	Nina Leen/Life Magazine © Time Inc.
334	Courtesy of Professor E. H. Hess, University of Chicago.
336	Courtesy of Hallmark Cards.

337 (top) Donald Dietz/Stock, Boston.
(bottom) Jen and Des Bartlett/Photo Researchers.
346 Bruce Roberts/Photo Researchers.
352 Jose A. Fernandez/Woodfin Camp.
353 (left) Wide World Photos.
(right) Stella Kupferberg.

Chapter 15

359 Courtesy of Katherine Banham.
360 Suzanne Szasz.
363 Joel Gordon.
366 (top) Nina Leen/Life Magazine © Time, Inc.
(bottom) Dr. H. F. Harlow, Regional Primate Research Center.
368 Dr. H. F. Harlow, Regional Primate Research Center.
370
373 Suzanne Arms/Jeroboam.
380 Yan Lukas/Photo Researchers.

Chapter 16

385 Courtesy of Raymond B. Cattell.
392 Henri Cartier – Bresson/Magnum.
393 Erich Solomon/Magnum.

Chapter 17

394 Courtesy Karen Horney Clinic, Inc., New York City.
395 Courtesy of Eric Erikson.
396 (top) Ellen Shub/The Picture Cube.
(bottom) Emilio A. Mercado/Jeroboam.
397 Fredrick D. Bodin/Stock, Boston.
398 Jean Boughton/Stock, Boston.
399 Courtesy of Albert Bandura.
401 Photo by Antony di Gesu. Courtesy Carl Rogers.
402 Courtesy Brandeis University.
410 Reprinted by permission of the publishers from Henry A. Murray, *Thematic Apperception Test,* Cambridge, Massachusetts; Harvard University Press. © 1943 by the President and Fellows of Harvard College, 1971 by Henry A. Murray.
411 Dr. Henri Ellenberger, University of Montreal.
412 Used with permission of Hans Hubert, Publisher, Berne, Switzerland.
421 Courtesy of Stewart Sutherland.
422 Sidney Harris.
423 Sidney Harris.
427 Costa Manos/Magnum.

Chapter 18

444 National Library of Medicine.
452 Gabor Szilasi.
455 Courtesy of Paul E. Meehl.
459 Christopher S. Johnson.

Chapter 19

466 Photo by Bulloz.
467 (left) Jerry Cooke/Photo Researchers.
(right) Courtesy of Eliot H. Rodnick.
470 Linda Ferrer Rogers/Woodfin Camp.
472 Michael Weisbrot.
474 Plate 53 from BERGGASSE 19: Sigmund Freud's Home and Offices, Vienna 1938, The Photographs of Edmund Engleman, Basic Books, Inc., Publishers, New York.
475 Stella Kupferberg.
478 Temple University, Department of Psychiatry.
485 Courtesy of Dr. Peter Lang.
486 Courtesy of Albert Ellis.
490 Owen Franken/Stock, Boston.

Author and Reference Index

Note: Number appearing in *italics* are for text reference only. Numbers appearing in roman refer to Journal entries.

Abel, G. G. See Agras et al. (1974).
Abelson, W. D. See Zigler et al. (1973).
Abramov, I. See DeValois et al. (1966).
Abramson, L. Y., Garber, J., Edwards, N. B., and Seligman, M. E. P. (1978) Expectancy changes in depression and schizophrenia. *Journal of Abnormal Psychology,* 87, 102–109. *433*
Achenbach, T. M. (1974) *Developmental psychopathology.* New York: Wiley. *464*
Achenbach, T., and Zigler, E. (1968) Cue-learning and problem-learning strategies in normal and retarded children. *Child Development,* 39, 827–848. *259*
Adler, A. Psychoanalysis *393*
Agnew, H. W., Jr. See Webb and Agnew (1968).
Agras, W. S. (1972) *Behavior modification: Principles and clinical applications.* Boston: Little, Brown. *483*
Agras, W. S., Barlow, D. H., Chapin, H. N., Abel, G. G., and Leitenberg, H. (1974). Behavior modification of anorexia nervosa. *Archives of General Psychiatry,* 30, 279–286. *13*
Ahmed, P. I., and Plog, S. C. (1976) *State mental hospitals. What happens when they close.* New York: Plenum Press. *492*
Ainsworth, M. D. S., and Bell, S. M. (1973) Mother-infant interaction and the development of competence. In K. Connolly and J. Bruner (Eds.), *The growth of competence.* New York: Academic Press. *369*
Albrecht, D. G. See DeValois et al. (1979).
Allen, L. See Honzik et al. (1948).
Allen, N. E., Hart, B., Buell, J. S., Harris, F. R., and Wolf, M. M. (1964) Effects of social reinforcement on isolate behavior of a nursery school child. *Child Development,* 35, 511–518. *11*
Allison, J., Blatt, S. J., and Zimet, C. N. (1968) *The interpretation of psychological tests.* New York: Harper and Row. *411*
Allport, G. W. (1935) Attitudes. In C. Murchison (Ed.), *A handbook of social psychology.* Worcester, Mass.: Clark University Press. *319*
Allport, G. W. (1954) *The nature of prejudice.* Reading, Mass.: Addison-Wesley. *310*
Allport, G. W., and Odbert, A. S. (1936) Trait names, a psycholexical study. *Psychological Monographs,* 47, 1–171. *384*
Alper, T. G. (1974) Achievement motivation in college women: A now-you-see-it-now-you-don't phenomenon. *American Psychologist,* 29, 194–203. *381*
Amabile, T. M. See Ross et al. (1977).
American Psychological Association. (1973) Ethical principles in the conduct of research with human participants. Washington, D.C.: The Association. *20*
Amrine, M. (Ed.) (1965) *American Psychologist,* 20 (11). *415*
Anastasi, A. (1976) *Psychological testing.* (4th ed.) New York: Macmillan. *417*
Anderson, D. and Rosenthal, R. (1968) Some effects of interpersonal expectancy and social interaction on institutionalized retarded children. *Proceedings of the 76th Annual Convention of the American Psychological Association,* 479–480 *313*
Appley, M. H. See Cofer and Appley (1964).
Argyle, M., and Dean J. (1965) Eye-contact, distance and affiliation. *Sociometry,* 28, 289–304 *337*
Arieti, S. (1976) *Creativity: The magic synthesis* New York: Basic Books, 1976. *271*
Armor, D. J., Polich, J. M., and Stambul, H. B. (1976) *Alcoholism and treatment.* Santa Monica, Calif.: Rand Corporation. *113*

Aronson, E. and Carlsmith, J. M. (1963) Effect of the severity of threat on the devaluation of forbidden behavior. *Journal of Abnormal and Social Psychology,* 66, 584–588. *321*
Asch, S. E. (1956) Studies in independence and conformity: A minority of one against a unanimous majority. *Psychological Monographs,* 70 (19). (Whole 416.) *315*
Aserinsky, E., and Kleitman, N. (1953) Regularly appearing periods of eye mobility and concomitant phenomena during sleep. *Science,* 118, 273–274. *104*
Ashby, W. R., and Walker, C. C. (1968) Genius. In P. London and D. Rosenhan (Eds.), *Foundations of abnormal psychology.* New York: Holt, Rinehart and Winston. *264, 266*
Asratyan, E. A. (1953) I. P. Pavlov: His life and work. Moscow: Foreign Languages Publishing House. *127*
Atkinson, G. See Tellegen and Atkinson (1974).
Ayllon, T. (1963) Intensive treatment of psychotic behavior by stimulus satiation and food reinforcement. *Behavior Research and Therapy,* 1, 53–61. *482, 483*

Bacon, M. K. See Barry et al. (1959).
Bagby, E. (1928) *The psychology of personality.* New York: Holt, Rinehart and Winston. *128*
Baggett, P. (1975) Memory for explicit and implicit information in picture stories. *Journal of Verbal Learning and Verbal Behavior,* 14, 538–548. *159*
Bahrick, H. P., Bahrick, P. Q., and Willinger, R. P. (1975) Fifty years of memory for names and faces: A cross-sectional approach. *Journal of Experimental Psychology: General,* 104, 54–75. *162*
Bahrick, P. Q. See Bahvick et al. (1975).
Baird, D. See Birch et al. (1970).
Baker, C. T. See Sontag et al. (1958).
Baker, J. P., and Crist, J. L. (1971) Teacher expectancies: A review of the literature. In J. D. Elashoff and R. E. Snow, *Pygmalion reconsidered.* Worthington, Ohio: Charles A. Jones. *275*
Bakkestrom, E. See Witkin et al. (1976).
Baldessorini, R. J. (1977) *Chemotherapy in psychiatry.* Cambridge, Mass.: Harvard University Press. *473*
Baldessarini, R. J. (1978) Chemotherapy. In A. M. Nicholi Jr. (Ed.), *The Harvard guide to modern psychiatry.* Cambridge, Mass: The Belknap Press of Harvard University Press, 387–432. *473*
Balfour, G. See Donaldson and Balfour (1968).
Bandura, A. (1977) *Social learning theory.* Englewood Cliffs, N.J.: Prentice–Hall. *398, 417*
Bandura, A., Grusec, J. E., and Menlove, F. L. (1966) Observational learning as a function of symbolization and incentive set. *Child Development,* 37, 499–506. *400*
Bandura, A., Ross, D., and Ross, S. A. (1963) Imitation of film-mediated aggressive models. *Journal of Abnormal and Social Psychology,* 66, 3–11 *3*
Barker, R., Dembo, T., and Lewin, K. (1941) Frustration and regression: An experiment with young children. University of Iowa Studies in Child Welfare 386. *14*
Barlow, D. H. See Agras et al. (1974).
Barnlund, D. C. (1959) A comparative study of individual, majority, and group judgment. *Journal of Abnormal and Social Psychology,* 58, 55–60. *325*
Barron, F. (1958) The psychology of imagination. *Scientific American,* 199, 150–66. *269*
Barry, H., Child, I. L., and Bacon, M. K. (1959) Relation of child training to subsistence economy. *American Anthropologist,* 61, 51–63. *376*
Bartlett, F. (1958) *Thinking.* New York: Basic Books. *190*
Bauer, J. A., Jr. See Held and Bayer (1967).
Baumrind, D. (1975) The contribution of the family to the development of competence in children. *Schizophrenia Bulletin,* Fall, 1 (14), 12–37. *375*
Bayley, N. (1955). On the growth of intelligence. *American Psychologist,* 10, 805–818. *244*
Bayley, N., and Schaefer, E. S. (1964) Correlations of maternal and child behaviors with the development of mental abilities: Data from the Berkeley Growth Study. *Monographs of the Society for Research in Child Development,* 29 (6). (Whole 97.) *242*
Beach, F. A. The Collidge effect. *342–343*
Beck, A. T., Ward, C. H., Mendelson, M., Mock, J. E., and Erbaugh, J. K. (1962) Reliability of psychiatric diagnosis: II. A study of consistency of clinical judgments and ratings. *American Journal of Psychiatry,* 119, 351–357. *447–448*
Becker, J. (1977). *Affective disorders.* Morristown, N.J.: General Learning Press. *439, 464*
Becker, W. (1964) Consequences of different kinds of parental discipline. In M. L. Hoffman and L. Hoffman (Eds.), *Review of child development research,* Vol. 1. New York: Russell Sage Foundation. *375*
Becker, W. C. See Peterson et al. (1959).
Bee, H. L. (1974) The effect of maternal employment of the development of the child. In H. L. Bee (Ed.), *Social issues in developmental psychology.* New York: Harper and Row. *372*
Bee, H. L. See Maccoby and Bee (1965).

Beez, W. V. (1968) Influence of biased psychological reports on teacher behavior and pupil performance. *Proceeding of the 76th Annual Convention of the American Psychological Association,* 605–606. *313*

Bekesy, G. von (1967) *Sensory inhibition.* Princeton, N.J.: Princeton University Press. *86*

Bell, S. M. See Ainsworth and Bell (1973).

Bellugi, U. See Brown et al. (1969).

Bem, D. J. (1972) Self-perception theory. In L. Berkowitz (Ed.), *Advances in experimental social psychology,* Vol. 6. New York: Academic Press. *321–322*

Bendfeldt, F. See Ludwig et al. (1972).

Bennett, E. C. See Krech et al. (1954).

Bennett, I. (1960 *Delinquent and neurotic children.* New York: Basic Books. *430*

Bentler, P. M., Jackson, D. N., and Messick, S. (1971) Identification of content and style: A two-dimensional interpretation of acquiescence. *Psychological Bulletin,* 76, 186–204. *412*

Bercovici, S. See Edgerton and Bercovici (1976).

Bergin, A. E. (1971) The evaluation of therapeutic outcomes. In A. E. Bergin and S. L. Garfield (Eds.), *Handbook of psychotherapy and behavior change.* New York: Wiley. *489*

Bergin, A. E., and Lambert, M. J. (1978) The evaluation of therapeutic outcomes. In S. L. Garfield and A. E. Bergin (Eds.), *Handbook of psychotherapy and behavior change.* (2nd ed.) New York: Wiley. *489, 491*

Berkeley, M. A. (1978) Vision: Geniculocortical system. In R. B. Masterton (Ed.), *Handbook of behavioral neurobiology.* New York: Plenum Press *41*

Berko, J. (1958) The child's learning of English morphology. *Word,* 14: 150–77. *188*

Berko, J., and Brown, R. (1960) Psycholinguistic research methods. In P. H. Mussen (Ed.), *Handbook of research methods in child development.* New York: Academic Press. *188*

Berkowitz, L. (1964) The effects of observing violence. *Scientific American,* 210, 2–8. *3*

Berkowitz, L. (1970) The contagion of violence: An S–S mediational analysis of some effects of observed aggression. In W. J. Arnold and M. M. Page (Eds.), *Nebraska Symposium on Motivation,* Vol. 18. Lincoln: University of Nebraska Press, 95–136. *3*

Berkowitz, L., and Friedman, P. (1967). Some social class differences in helping behavior. *Journal of Personality and Social Psychology,* 5, 217–225. *377*

Berkun, M. M., Bialek, H. M., Kern, R. P., and Yagi, K. (1962) Experimental studies of psychological stress in man. *Psychological Monographs,* 76, 534. (Whole 15.) *14*

Berman, P., Waisman, H., and Graham, F. (1966) Intelligence in treated phenylketonuric children: A developmental study. *Child Development,* 37, 731–747. *255*

Berry, P. C. See Taylor et al. (1958).

Berschied, E. See Snyder et al. (1977).

Bialek, H. M. See Berkun et al. (1962).

Biller, H. B. (1970) Father absence and the personality development of the male child. *Developmental Psychology,* 2, 181–201. *373*

Biller, H. B. See Reuter and Biller (1973).

Binet, A. (1903) *The experimental study of intelligence.* *227–228*

Birch, H. G., Richardson, S. A., Baird, D., Horobin, G., and Illsley, R. (1970) *Mental subnormality in the community: A clinical and epidemiological study.* Baltimore: Williams and Wilkins. *256*

Birch, H.G. See Thomas et al.(1968).

Birely, J. L. T. See Wing et al. (1967), Brown et al. (1972).

Blaine, J. D. See Janowsky et al. (1976).

Blakemore, C. J., Thorpe, J. G., Karker, J. C., Conway, C. G., and Lavin, N. I. (1963) The application of faradic aversion conditioning in a case of transvestitism. *Behavior Research and Therapy.* 1, 29–34. *483*

Blanck, G., and Blanck, R. (1974) *Ego psychology: Theory and practice.* New York: Columbia University Press. *417*

Blanck, R. See Blanck and Blanck (1974).

Blane, H. T., and Hewitt, L. E. (1976) *Alcohol and youth: An analysis of the literature, 1960–1975.* Report for NIAAA Contract, ADM 281–75–0026 *113*

Blatt, B. (1970) *Exodus from pandemonium.* Boston: Allyn and Bacon. *262*

Blatt, B. (1973) *Souls in extremis.* Boston: Allyn and Bacon. *262*

Blatt, B., and Kaplan, F. (1966) *Christmas in purgatory.* Boston: Allyn and Bacon. *262*

Blatt, S. J. See Allison et al. (1968).

Bleuler, E. (1911) *Dementia praecox or the group of schizophrenias* New York: International Universities Press, 1950. (English translation.) *434*

Block, A. J., Boysen, P. G., Wynne, J. W., and Hunt, L. A. (1979) Oxygen desaturation in normal subjects. *The New England Journal of Medicine,* 300 (10), 513–517. *108*

Block, C. H. See Taylor et al. (1958).

Block, J. (1965) *The challenge of response sets.* New York: Appleton-Century-Crofts. *412*

Block, J. (1971) *Lives through time.* Berkeley, Calif.: Bancroft Books. *405*

Block, J. (1977) Advancing the psychology of personality: Paradigmatic shift or improving the quality of research? In D. Magnusson and N. S. Endler

(Eds.), *Personality at the crossroads: Current issues in interactional psychology.* Hillsdale, N.J.: Lawrence Erlbaum Associates, 37–63. *405*

Block, N. J., and Dworking, G. (Eds.) (1976) *The IQ controversy.* New York: Pantheon. *225*

Blommers, P., and Lindquist, E. F. (1960) *Elementary statistical methods in psychology and education.* Cambridge, Mass.: Riverside Press. *502*

Bloom, B. S. (1964) *Stability and change in human characteristics.* New York: Wiley. *272*

Bloom, L. M. (1970) *Language development: Form and structure in emerging grammars.* Cambridge, Mass.: MIT Press. *187*

Blum, J. E. See Jarvik et al. (1973).

Bockhoven, J. S. (1963) *Moral treatment in American psychiatry.* New York: Springer. *466*

Bodmer, W. F. See Cavalli-Sforza and Bodmer (1971).

Bogen, J. E. See Gazzaniga et al. (1965).

Bohnert, P. J. See Swanson et al. (1970).

Borden, R. See Freeman et al. (1975).

Boring, E. G. (1950) *History of experimental psychology.* New York: Appleton-Century-Crofts. *150*

Bos, M. (1937) Experimental study of productive collaboration. *Acta Psychologia,* 3, 315–425. *325*

Boulter, L. R. See Endler et al. (1976).

Bousfield, W. A. (1953) The occurrence of clustering in the free recall of randomly arranged associates. *Journal of General Psychology,* 49, 229–240. *161*

Bower, G. H. (1970) Analysis of a mnemonic device. *American Scientist,* 58, 496–510. *165*

Bower, G. H., and Clark, M. C. (1969) Narrative stories as mediators for serial learning. *Psychonomic Science,* 14, 181–182. *168*

Bowers, K. S. See Meichenbaum et al. (1969).

Bowlby, J. (1952) Maternal care and mental health. Geneva: World Health Organization. *372*

Bowlby, J. (1969) *Attachment and loss,* Vol. 1, *Attachment.* New York: Basic Books. *367*

Bowlby, J. (1973) *Attachment and loss,* Vol. 2, *Separation: Anxiety and anger.* New York: Basic Books. *372*

Boyers, R. (1971) R. D. Laing and antipsychiatry. *Salamagundi* (16). Saratoga Springs, N.Y. *457*

Boysen, J. See Savage-Rumbaugh et al. (1978).

Boysen, P. G. See Block et al. (1979).

Bozzetti, L. P. See Janowsky et al. (1976).

Brackbill, Y. (1958) Extinction of the smiling response in infants as a function of reinforcement schedule. *Child Development,* 29, 115–124. *360*

Brady, T. See Magenis et al. (1977).

Brainerd, C. J. (1978) *Piaget's theory of intelligence.* Englewood Cliffs, N.J.: Prentice-Hall. *303*

Brandsma, J. M. See Ludwig et al. (1972).

Bransford, J. D., and Johnson, M. K. (1972) Contextual prerequisites for understanding: Some investigations of comprehension and recall. *Journal of Verbal Learning and Verbal Behavior,* 11, 717–720. *167*

Brauch, A., Brauch, W., and Katz, E. *288*

Brecher, E. M., and Editors of Consumer Reports. (1972) *Licit and illicit drugs.* Boston: Little, Brown. *115*

Brehm, J. W. (1966) *A theory of psychological reactance.* New York: Academic Press. *313*

Breland, K., and Breland, M. (1961) The misbehavior of organisms. *American Psychologist,* 16, 681–684. *145*

Breland, M. See Breland and Breland (1961).

Brener, J., and Kleinman, R. A. (1970) Learned control of decreases in systolic blood pressure. *Nature,* 226, 1063–1064. *130*

Breuer, J., and Freud, S. (1895) *Studies in hysteria.* New York: Basic Books, 1957. (Translated from the German and edited by James Strachey in collaboration with Anna Freud, assisted by Alex Trachery and Alan Tyson.) *110, 444, 464*

Bridges, K. M. B. (1932) Emotional development in early infancy. *Child Development,* 3, 324–341. *359*

Brome, V. (1978) *Jung.* New York: Atheneum. *393*

Bronfenbrenner, U. (1974) *A report on longtiduinal evaluations of preschool programs,* Vol. 2, *Is early intervention effective?* Washington, D.C.: Department of Health, Education and Welfare, Publication (OHD) 74–25. *273*

Bronfenbrenner, U. (1975) Is early intervention effective? In H. Guttentag and E. Struening (Eds.), *Handbook of evaluation research.* Beverly Hills, Calif.: Sage Publication. *274*

Brooks, L. R. (1968) Spatial and verbal components of the act of recall. *Canadian Journal of Psychology,* 22, 349–368. *158*

Brown, B. See Deutsch and Brown (1974).

Brown, B. L., Strong, W. J., and Rencher, A. C. (1974) Fifty-four voices from two: The effects of simultaneous manipulations of rate, mean fundamental frequency and variance of fundamental frequency on ratings of personality from speech. *Journal of the Acoustical Society of America,* 55, 313–318. *175*

Brown, G. W., Birley, J. L., and Wing, J. K. (1972) Influence of family life on the course of schizophrenic disorders: A

replication. *British Journal of Psychiatry,* 121, 241–258. *468*
Brown, G. W., Harris, T., and Copeland, J. R. (1977). Depression and loss. *British Journal of Psychiatry,* 130, 1–18. *433*
Brown, H. O. See Smith et al. (1947).
Brown, J. A. C. (1961) *Freud and the Post-Freudians.* Baltimore: Pelican Books. *417*
Brown, R. (1973) *A first language: The early stages.* Cambridge, Mass.: Harvard University Press. *187*
Brown, R. See Berko and Brown (1960).
Brown, R., Cazden, C. B., and Bellugi, U. (1967) The child's grammar from I to III. *Symposia on child psychology,* Vol. 2. Minneapolis: University of Minnesota Press, 28–73. *184*
Brown, R. W. (1959) *Words and things.* New York: Free Press. *177*
Brown, R. W. (1965) *Social psychology.* New York: Free Press. *326*
Brown, R. W., and McNeill, D. (1966) The "tip of the tongue" phenomenon. *Journal of Verbal Learning and Verbal Behavior,* 5, 325–337. *157*
Brozek, J. See Keys et al. (1950).
Bruiniks, R. H., Rynders, J. E., and Gross, J. C. (1974) Social acceptance of mildly retarded pupils in resource rooms and regular classes. *American Journal of Mental Deficiency,* 78, 377–383. *261*
Bruner, J. S. *279, 289*
Bruner, J. S. See Connally and Bruner (1974).
Bruner, J. S., and Kenney, H. J. (1966) On multiple ordering. In J. S. Bruner, R. R. Olver, and P. M. Greenfield (Eds.), *Studies in cognitive growth.* New York: Wiley. *290*
Budoff, M. See Gottlieb and Budoff (1973).
Buell, J. S. See Allen et al. (1964).
Burns, R. S. See Lerner and Burns (1978).
Burt, C. (1955) The evidence for the concept of intelligence. *British Journal of Educational Psychology,* 25, 158–177. *264*
Burt, R. B. See Wallach et al. (1968).
Burton, V. R. See Yarrow et al. (1970).
Butcher, H. J. (1970) *Human intelligence: Its nature and assessment.* London: Methuen. *249*
Butcher, J. N. (1978) Minnesota Multiphasic Personality Inventory. Reviews of computerized scoring and interpreting services. In O. K. Buros, (Ed.), *The eighth mental measurements year book.* Highland Park, N.J.: Gryphon Press, 938–962. *413*
Butcher, J. N., and Gur, R. (1974) A Hebrew translation of the MMPI: Assessment of translation adequacy and preliminary validation. *Journal of Cross-Cultural Psychology,* 5, 220–227. *408*
Butcher, J. N., and Tellegen, A. (1966) Objections to MMPI items. *Journal of Consulting Psychology,* 30, 527–534. *415*
Campbell, D. T. (1957) A typology of tests, projective and otherwise. *Journal of Consulting Psychology,* 21, 207–210. *406*
Campbell, D. T. (1961) Conformity in psychology's theories of acquired behavioral dispositions. In I. A. Berg and B. M. Bass (Eds.), *Conformity and deviation.* New York: Harper, and Row. *316*
Campbell, D. T. See Webb et al. (1966).
Campbell, J. See Dunnett et al. (1963).
Campbell, J. D. See Yarrow et al. (1970).
Cannizzo, S. R. See Keeney et al. (1967).
Cannon, W. B. (1934) Hunger and thirst. In C. Murchison (Ed.), *Handbook of general experimental psychology.* Worcester, Mass.: Clark University Press. *343*
Carey, G. L. (1958) Sex differences in problem-solving performance as a function of attitude differences. *Journal of Abnormal and Social Psychology,* 56, 256–260. *245*
Carlsmith, J. M. See Aronson and Carlsmith (1963), Festinger and Carlsmith (1959).
Carpenter, M. B. (1976) *Human neuroanatomy.* Baltimore: Williams and Wilkins. *41*
Carpenter, W. T., Jr. Strauss, J. S., and Muleh, S. (1973) Are there pathognomonic symptoms in schizophrenia? *Archives of General Psychiatry,* 28, 847–852. *436*
Carroll, L., Language. *173*
Cattell, James McK. (1887) The time it takes to think. *The Nineteenth Century,* 31, 827–833. *150*
Cattell, R. B. (1949, 1953) *Culture fair measures of intelligence.* *238*
Cattell, R. B. (1950) *Personality: A systematic theoretical and factual study.* New York: McGraw-Hill. *386*
Cattell, R. B. (1963) Theory of fluid and crystallized intelligence: A critical experiment. *Journal of Educational Psychology,* 54, 1–22. *239*
Cattell, R. B. (1965) *The scientific analysis of personality.* Chicago: Aldine. *385, 386*
Cattell, R. B. (1973) Personality pinned down. *Psychology Today,* 7, 40–46. *386*
Cattell, R. B. See Horn and Cattell (1967).
Cavalli-Sforza, L., and Bodmer, W. F. (1971) *The genetics of human populations.* San Francisco: W. H. Freeman. *205*
Cazden, C. B. See Brown et al. (1969).
Chamberlain, J. See Magenis et al. (1977).
Chandler, M. J. See Sameroff and Chandler (1975).
Chapin, H. N. See Agras et al. (1974).

Charlesworth, W. R. (1976) Human intelligence as adaptation. In L. B. Resnick (Ed.), *The nature of intelligence*. Hillsdale, N.J.: Lawrence Erlbaum Associates. *240*

Cherry, E. C. (1953) Some experiments on the recognition of speech, with one and with two ears. *Journal of the Acoustical Society of America*, 25, 975–979. *151*

Chess, S. See Thomas et al. (1968).

Chess, S. See Thomas and Chess (1977).

Child, I. L. See Barry et al. (1959).

Chomsky, N. (1957) *Syntactic structures*. The Hague: Mouton Publishers. *173*

Christiansen, K. O. See Witkin et al. (1976).

Clark, A. M. See Clark and Clark (1960).

Clark, D. H. See Lesser et al. (1965).

Clark, E. V. (1973) What's in a word? On the childs acquisition of semantics in his first language. In T. E. Moore (Ed.), *Cognitive development and the acquisition of language*. New York: Academic Press. *189*

Clark, E. V. See Clark and Clark (1977).

Clark, H. H., and Clark, E. V. (1977) *Psychology and language*. New York: Harcourt Brace Jovanovich. *185, 197*

Clarke, A. D. B., and Clarke, A. M. (1960) Some recent advances in the study of early deprivation. *Journal of Child Psychology and Psychiatry*, 1, 26–36. *372*

Claussen, J. A., and Williams, J. R. (1963) Sociological correlates of child behavior. *Yearbook of the National Society for the Study of Education*, 62, 62–107. *378*

Clayton, R. R. See O'Donnell et al. (1976).

Cleland, C. C. (1978) *Mental retardation: A developmental approach*. Englewood Cliffs, N.J.: Prentice-Hall. *251, 262*

Clements, R. J. (1963) *Michelangelo: A self-portrait*. Englewood Cliffs, N.J.: Prentice-Hall. *267*

Clove, G. L. See Wiggins et al. (1976).

Cofer, C. N. (1961) Experimental studies of verbal processes in concept formation and problem solving. *Annals of the New York Academy of Sciences*, 91, 94–107. *193*

Cofer, C. N., and Appley, M. H. (1964) *Motivation: Theory and research*. New York: Wiley. *357*

Cohen, H. L., and Filipczak, J. (1971) *A new learning environment*. San Francisco: Jossey-Bass. *481*

Cohen, S. See Ray (1978).

Cole, J. O. See Goldberg et al. (1965).

Cole, V. Effectiveness of methadone. *115*

Coleman, J. C. (1972) *Abnormal psychology and modern life*. (4th ed.) Glenview, Ill.: Scott, Foresman. *432*

Coleman, J. C. (1976) *Abnormal psychology and modern life*. (5th ed.) Glenview, Ill.: Scott, Foresman. *427, 438*

Collings, V. B. See McBarney and Collings (1977).

Connolly, K. J., and Bruner, J. S. (Eds.) (1974) *The growth and competence*. New York: Academic Press. *303*

Conrad, R. (1964) Acoustic confusions in immediate memory. *British Journal of Psychology*, 55, 75–84. *153–154*

Conway, C. G. See Blakemore et al. (1963).

Cook, W. Code of ethics for research with human subjects. See American Psychological Association (1973). *20*

Cooper, J. See Fazio et al. (1977), Ward et al. (1974), Wing et al. (1974), Zanna and Cooper (1974).

Cooper, J. E. See Wing et al. (1967), (1974).

Cooper, J. E., Kendell, R. E., Gurland, B. J., Sharpe, L., Copeland, J. R. M., and Simon, R. (1972) *Psychiatric diagnosis in New York and London*. London: Oxford University Press. *464*

Cooper, M. See Lemkan et al. (1941).

Cooper, R. M., and Zubek, J. P. (1958) Effects of enriched and restricted early environment on the learning ability of bright and dull rats. *Canadian Journal of Psychology*, 12, 159–164. *210*

Copeland, J. R. See Brown et al. (1977).

Copeland, J. R. M. See Cooper et al. (1972).

Corbit, J. See Eimas and Corbit (1973), Solomon and Corbit (1974).

Coren, S., Porac, C., and Ward, L. M. (1978) *Sensation and perception*. New York: Academic Press. *73*

Cornsweet, J. C. See Riggs et al. (1953).

Cornsweet, T. N. (1970). *Visual perception*. New York: Academic Press. *58*

Cornsweet, T. N. See Riggs et al. (1953).

Corsini, R. J. (Ed.) (1979) *Current psychotherapies*. (2nd ed.) Itasca, Ill.: F. E. Peacock Publishers. *492*

Cowles, J. T. (1937) Food tokens as incentives for learning by chimpanzees. *Comparative Psychology Monographs*, 14 (71). *139*

Cox, C. M. (1926) The early mental traits of three hundred geniuses. In L. M. Terman (Ed.), *Genetic studies of genius*, Vol. 2. Stanford, Calif.: Stanford University Press. *267*

Craik, F. I. M., and Tulving, E. (1975) Depth of processing and the retention of words in episodic memory. *Journal of Experimental Psychology: General*, 104, 268–294. *154, 156*

Crick, F. Genetic code. *206*

Crist, J. L. See Baker and Crist (1971).

Crocetti, G. M., Spiro, H. R., and

Siassi, I. (1974) *Contemporary attitudes toward mental illness.* Pittsburgh, Pa.: University of Pittsburgh Press. *464*
Crome, L., and Stern, J. (1972) *Pathology of mental retardation.* (2nd ed.). London: Churchill Livingstone. *253*
Cromwell, R. L. See Wynne et al. (1978).
Cronbach, L. J. (1970) *Essentials of psychological testing.* (3rd ed.) New York: Harper and Row. *417*
Crovitz, H. E. (1970) *Galton's walk.* New York: Harper and Row, 1970. *194*
Cunitz, A. R. See Glanzer and Lunitz (1960).

Dallenbach, K. M. See Jenkins and Dallenbach (1924).
Danks, J. H. See Gloucksberg and Danks (1975).
Darwin, C. (1872) *The expression of the emotions in man and animals.* *359*
Dasen, P. R. (1975) Concrete operational development in three cultures. *Journal of Cross-Cultural Psychology,* 6, 156–172. *300*
Dasen, P. R. (1977) Introduction. In P. R. Dasen (Ed.), *Piagetian psychology: Cross-cultural contributions.* New York: Gardner Press. *299*
Davids, A., and DeVault, S. (1962) Maternal anxiety during pregnancy and childbirth abnormality. *Psychosomatic Medicine,* 24, 464–470. *19*
Davies, S. P., and Ecob, K. G. (1959) *The mentally retarded in society.* New York: Columbia University Press. *260*
Davis, A. See Eells et al. (1951).
Davis, K. E. See Jones et al. (1961), Jones and Davis (1965).
Davison, G. C., and Neale, J. M. (1978). *Abnormal psychology.* (2nd ed.) New York: Wiley. *438*
Dean, J. See Argyle and Dean (1965).
Dembo, T. See Barker et al. (1941).
Dement, W. C. (1960) The effect of dream deprivation. *Science,* 131, 1705–1707. *106*
Dement, W. C. (1974) *Some must watch while some must sleep.* San Francisco: W. H. Freeman. *108, 121*
Demone, H. W., Jr., and Wechsler, H. (1976) Changing drinking patterns of adolescents since the 1960's. In M. Greenblatt and M. A. Schuckit (Eds.), *Alcoholism problems in women and children.* New York: Grune and Stratton. *113*
Dennis, W. (1973) *Children of the crèche.* New York: Appleton-Century-Crofts. *246*
Denny, J. P. See Spielberger et al. (1962).
Dethier, V. G., and Stellar, E. (1961) *Animal behavior.* Englewood Cliffs, N.J.: Prentice-Hall. *339*
Deutsch, M., and Brown, B. (1964) Social influences in Negro-white intelligence differences. *Journal of Social Issures,* 20, 20–35 *219*
DeValois, R. L., Abramov, I., and Jacobs, G. H. (1966) Analysis of response patterns of LGN cells. *Journal of the Optical Society of America,* 56, 966–977. *56, 57*
DeValois, R. L., Albrecht, D. G., and Thorell, L. G. (1979) Cortical cells: Bar and edge detectors, or spatial frequency filters? In S. Cool (Ed.), *Frontiers of visual science.* New York: Springer-Verlag. *75*
DeVault, S. See Davids and DeVault (1962).
DeVries, R. (1969) Constancy of generic identity in the years three to six. *Monographs of the Society for Research in Child Development,* 34, (3), Serial 127. *294, 295*
Diamond, E. (1962) *The science of dreams.* Garden City, N.Y.: Doubleday. *103*
Diamond, S. G. See Mehrabian and Diamond (1971).
Dobzhansky, T. (1955) *Evolution, genetics, and man.* New York: Wiley. *202, 225*
Dobzhansky, T. (1964) *Hereditary and the nature of man.* New York: Harcourt Brace Jovanovich. (Paperback: Signet Science Library.) *205*
Dobzhansky, T. (1968) Genetics and the social sciences. In D. Glass (Ed.), *Genetics.* New York: Rockefeller University Press and Russel Sage Foundation. *212*
Dobzhansky, T. See Sinnott et al. (1958).
Dodge, S. H. See Walk and Dodge (1962).
Dollard, J., and Miller, N. E. (1950) *Personality and psychotherapy: An analysis in terms of learning, thinking and culture.* New York: McGraw-Hill. *140, 194, 398*
Domino, E. F. (1978) Neurobiology of phencyclidine—an update. In R. C. Petersen and R. C. Stillman (Eds.), *Phencyclidine (PCP) abuse: An appraisal.* National Institute of Drug Abuse Research Monograph 21, Rockville, Md., 18–43. *116*
Donaldson, H. H. (1900) *The growth of the brain.* New York: Charles Schribner's Sons. *27*
Donaldson, M., and Balfour, G. (1968) Less is more: A study of language comprehension in children. *British Journal of Psychology,* 59, 461–472. *188*
DSM-III Draft (1978) *Diagnostic and statistical manual of mental disorders.* Washington D.C.: The Task Force on Nomenclature and Statistics of the American Psychiatric Association (January 15, 1978). *422, 449*
Dugdale, R. (1877). *The Jukes: A study in crime, pauperism, disease, and heredity.* New York: G. P. Putnams Sons, 1910. *257*
Dumaret, A. See Schiff et al. (1978).
Duncan, C. P. (1942) The restroactive effect of electroshock on learning. *Journal of Comparative and Physiological Psychology,* 42, 32–44. *156*
Dunn, L. C. See Sinnott et al. (1958).
Dunnette, M. D., Campbell, J., and

Jaastad, K. (1963) The effect of group participation on brainstorming effectiveness for two industrial samples. *Journal of Applied Psychology,* 47, 30–37. *325*
Duytme, M. See Schiff et al. (1978).
Dworking, G. See Block and Dworking (1976).

Ebbinghaus, H. (1913) *Memory: A contribution to experimental psychology.* (Translated by H. A. Ruger and C. E. Bussenius.) New York: Columbia University Press. *162*
Eckerman, C. O. See Rheingold and Eckerman (1970), (1973).
Ecob, K. G. See Davis and Ecob (1959).
Edgerton, R. B. (1967) *The cloak of competence.* Berkeley, Calif.: University of California Press. *277*
Edgerton, R. B., and Bercovici, S. (1976) The cloak of competence: Years later. *American Journal of Mental Deficiency,* 80, 485–497. *277*
Edwards, A. (1971) *Individual mental testing: I. History and theory.* Scranton, Pa.: Intext Publishers. *249*
Edwards, N. B. See Abramson et al. (1978).
Eells, K., Davis, A., Havighurst, R. J., Herrick, V. E., and Tyler, R. (1951) *Intelligence and cultural differences.* Chicago: University of Chicago Press. *247*
Ehrhardt, A. A. See Money and Ehrhardt (1972).
Ehrlich, P. R. See Freedman et al. (1971).
Eibl-Eibersfeldt, I. (1970) *Ethology: The biology of behavior.* New York: Holt, Rinehart and Winston, 1970. *335–336*
Eibl-Eibesfeldt, I. (1971) *Love and hate.* New York: Holt, Rinehart and Winston. *339*
Eichorn, D. H. See Stedman and Eichorn (1964).
Eimas, P. D., and Corbit, J. (1973) Selective adaptation of linguistic feature detectors. *Cognitive Psychology,* 4, 99–109. *176*
Eimas, P. D., Siqueland, E. R., Jusczyk, P., and Vigorito, J. (1971) Speech perception in infants. *Science,* 171, 303–306. *176*
Eisdorfer, C. See Jarvik et al. (1973)
Elashoff, J. D., and Snow, R. E. (1971) *Pygmalion reconsidered.* Worthington, Ohio: Charles A. Jones. *275*
Elias, C. See Moulton et al. (1978).
Elkind, D. (1973) Giant in the nursery—Jean Piaget. In *Annual editions, readings in human development '73–74.* Guilford, Conn.: Dushkin Publishing Group. *294*
Ellis, A. (1962) *Reason and emotion in psychotherapy.* New York: Lyle Stuart. *485, 487*
Ellis, A. (1971) *Growth through reason.* Palo Alto, Calif.: Science and Behavior Books. *485*
Ellis, A. (1973) *Humanistic psychotherapy* New York: McGraw-Hill. *492*
Ellis, A. (1977) The basic clinical theory of rational-emotive therapy. In A. Ellis and R. Grieger (Eds.), *Handbook of rational-emotive therapy.* New York: Springer, 3–34. *485*
Emerson, P. E. See Schaffer and Emerson (1964a).
Endler, N. S., Boulter, L. R., and Osser H. (Eds.) (1976) *Contemporary issues in developmental psychology.* (2nd ed.) New York: Holt, Rinehart and Winston. *382*
Ennis, B. J. (1972) *Prisoners of psychiatry.* New York: Harcourt Brace Jovanovich. *460*
Epstein, S. M. (1967) Toward a unified theory of anxiety. In B. A. Maher (Ed.), *Progress in experimental personality research.* New York: Academic Press. *351*
Epstein, S. (1977) Traits are alive and well. In D. Magnusson and N. S. Endler (Eds.), *Personality at the crossroads: Current issues in interactional psychology.* Hillsdale, N.J.: Lawrence Erlbaum Associates, 83–98. *405*
Erbaugh, J. K. See Beck et al. (1962).
Erickson, B., Lind, E. A., Johnson, B. C., and O'Barr, W. M. (1977) Speech style and impression formation in a court setting: The effects of "powerful" and "powerless" speech. *Journal of Experimental Social Psychology,* 14, 266–279. *9*
Erikson, E. Ego psychology. *395–397*
Erikson, K. T. (1976) *Everything in its path.* New York: Simon and Schuster. *439*
Erlenmeyer-Kimling, L., and Jarvik, L. F. (1963) Genetics and intelligence: A review. *Science,* 142, 1477–1478. *213*
Eron, L. D., Huessman, L. R., Lefkowitz, M. M., and Walker, L. O. (1972) Does television violence cause aggression? *American Psychologist,* 27, 253–263. *506*
Eron, L. See Lefkowitz et al. (1972).
Estes, W. K. (1944) An experimental study of punishment. *Psychological Monographs,* 57. (Whole 263.) *345*
Evans, J. R., Rodnick, E. H., Goldstein, M. J., and Judd, L. L. (1972) Premorbid adjustment, phenothiazine treatment, and remission in acute schizophrenia. *Archives of General Psychiatry* 27, 486–490. *468*
Evans, J. R., Goldstein, M. J., and Rodnick, E. H. (1973) Premorbid adjustment, paranoid diagnosis and remission. *Archives of General Psychiatry* 28, 666–672. *468*
Evans, R. I. (Ed.) (1973) *Jean Piaget: The man and his ideas.* New York: E. P. Dutton. *303*
Eysenck, H. J. (1961) *The effects of psychotherapy.* In H. J. Eysenck (Ed.), *Handbook of abnormal psychology.* New York: Basic Books. *489*
Eysenck, H. J. (1964) Principles and

methods of personality description, classification and diagnosis. *British Journal of Psychology,* 55, 284–294. *388*
Eysenck, H. J., and Rachman, S. (1965) *The causes and cures of neurosis.* San Diego, Calif.: Robert R. Knapp. *386*

Fantz, R. L. (1961) The origin of form perception. *Scientific American,* 204, 66–72. *95*
Farberow, N. L. See Shneidman et al. (1970).
Farina, A., Holland, C. H., and Ring, K. (1966) Role of stigma and set in interpersonal interaction. *Journal of Abnormal Psychology,* 71, 421–428. *462*
Farina, A., and Ring, K. (1965) The influence of perceived mental illness on interpersonal relations. *Journal of Abnormal Psychology,* 70, 47–51. *461*
Fawl, C. L. (1963) Disturbances experienced by children in their natural habitats. In R. G. Barker (Ed.), *The stream of behavior.* New York: Appeleton-Century-Crofts. *14*
Fazio, R. H., Zanna, M. P., and Cooper, J. (1977) Dissonance and self-perception: An integrative view of each theory's proper domain of application *Journal of Experimental Social Psychology,* 13, 464–479. *322*
Fechner, G. T. Measurement of sensation *71*
Feingold, J. See Schiff et al. (1978).
Felipe, N. J., and Sommer, R. (1966) Invasions of personal space. *Social Problems,* 14, 206–214. *337*
Festinger, L. (1954) A theory of social comparison processes. *Human Relations,* 7, 117–140. *315*
Festinger, L. (1957) *A theory of cognitive dissonance.* Evanston, Ill.: Row and Peterson. *319*
Festinger, L., and Carlsmith, J. M. (1959) Cognitive consequences of forced compliance. *Journal of Abnormal and Social Psychology,* 58, 203–210. *321*
Festinger, L., and Thibaut, J. (1951) Interpersonal communication in small groups. *Journal of Abnormal and Social Psychology,* 46, 92–99. *317*
Fifer, G. See Lesser et al. (1965).
Filipczak, J. See Cohen and Filipczak (1971).
Finkelstein, N. W. See Ramey and Finkelstein (1978).
Fisher, C. (1965) Psychoanalytic implications of recent research of sleep and dreaming. *Journal of the American Psychoanalytic Association,* 13, 197–303. *107*
Flavell, J. H. (1963) *The developmental psychology of Jean Piaget.* Princeton, N.J.: Van Nostrand. *299*
Flavell, J. H. (1970) Developmental studies of mediated memory. In L. P. Lipsitt and H. W. Reese (Eds.), *Advances in child development and behavior,* Vol. 5. New York: Academic Press *287*
Flavell, J. H. (1977) *Cognitive development.* Englewood Cliffs, N.J.: Prentice-Hall. *296, 303*
Flavell, J. H. See Keeney et al. (1967).
Fowler, R. Computerized test evaluation. *414*
Fox, R. E. See Rosen et al. (1972).
Frankiel, R. V. (1959) *A review of research on parent influences on child personality.* New York: Family Service Association of America. *375*
Freedman, D. G. (1958) Constitutional and environmental interactions in rearing four breeds of dogs. *Science,* 127, 585–586. *210*
Freedman, D. G. (1964) Smiling in blind infants and the issue of innate vs. acquired. *Journal of Child Psychology and Psychiatry,* 5, 171–184. *359*
Freedman, D. G., Loring, C. B., and Martin, R. M. (1967) Emotional behavior and personality development. In Y. Brackbill (Ed.), *Infancy and early childhood.* New York: Free Press. *361*
Freedman, J. L. (1965) Long term behavioral effects of cognitive dissonance. *Journal of Experimental Social Psychology,* 1, 145–155. *321*
Freedman, J. L., Klevansky, S., and Ehrlich, P. R. (1971) The effect of crowding on human task performance. *Journal of Applied Social Psychology,* 1, 7–25. *338*
Freeman, L. (1972) *The story of Anna O.* New York: Walker. *389*
Freeman, S., Walker, M. R., Borden, R., and Latané, B. (1975) Diffusion of responsibility and restaurant tipping: Cheaper by the bunch. *Personality and Social Psychology Bulletin,* 1, 584–587. *15*
Freud, S. (1885) *Cocaine Papers* New York: New American Library, 1974. (Edited by R. Byck.) *114*
Freud, S. (1900) The interpretation of dreams. *The standard edition of the complete psychological works of Sigmund Freud,* Vols. 4, 5. London: The Hogarth Press and the Institute of Psychoanalysis, 1953. *105*
Freud, S. Psychoanalysis, psychoanalytic therapy, view of motivation *388–392*
Friedman, P. See Berkowitz and Friedman (1967).
Frisch, K. von (1950) *Bees: Their vision, chemical senses and language.* Ithaca, N.Y.: Cornell University Press. *179*
Frisch, K. von (1965) Tanzprache und orientierung der beinin. New York: Springer. *208*
Frisch, K. von (1974) Decoding the language of the bee. *Science,* 185, 663–668. *179*
Frost, N. (1971) Clustering by visual shapes in the free recall of pictorial stimuli. *Journal of Experimental Psychology,* 88, 409–413. *169*
Fuller, J. L. (1967) Experiential deprivation and later behavior. *Science,* 158, 1645–1652. *210*
Fuller, J. L., and Thompson, W. R.

(1978) *Foundations of behavior genetics*. Saint Louis, Mo.: C. V. Mosby. *225*

Garber, H., and Herber, F. R. (1977) The Milwaukee project: Indications of the effectiveness of early intervention in preventing mental retardation. In P. Mittler (Ed.), *Research to practice in mental retardation*, Vol. 1, *Care and intervention*. Baltimore: University Park Press. *274*

Garber, J. See Abramson et al. (1978).

Garber, J., and Hollon, S. D. (1978) Universal versus personal helplessness in depression: Belief in uncontrollability or incompetence? *Journal of Abnormal Psychology*. *433*

Gardner, B. T. See Gardner and Gardner (1975).

Gardner, E. J. (1975) *Principles of genetics*. (5th ed.) New York: Wiley. *222,225*

Gardner, H. (1978) *Developmental psychology*. Boston: Little, Brown. *301*

Gardner, R. A., and Gardner, B. T. (1975) Communication with a young chimpanzee: Washoe's vocabulary. In R. Chauvin (Ed.), Edition du Centre National de la Recherche Scientifique, Paris. *181, 182*

Garmezy, N. (1978) DSM-III: Never mind the psychologists. Is it good for the children? *American Psychologist*. *451*

Gazzaniga, M. S. (1967) The split brain in man. *Scientific American*, 217, 24–29. *45*

Gazzaniga, M. S. (1970) *The bisected brain*. New York: Appleton–Century–Crofts. *46*

Gazzaniga, M. S., Bogen, J. E., and Sperry, R. W. (1965) Observations on visual perception after disconnection of the cerebral hemispheres in man. *Brain*, 88 (part 2), 231–236. *46*

Gazzaniga, M. S., Steen, D., and Volpe, B. T. (1979) *Functional neuroscience*. New York: Harper and Row. *47*

Gelles, R. J. (In press) A profile of violence towards children in the United States. In G. Gerbner, C. J. Ross, and E. Zigler (Eds.), *Reconsidering child abuse: An analysis and agenda for action*. New York: Oxford University Press. *375*

Gelman, R. (1969) Conservation acquisition: A problem of learning to attend to relevant attributes. *Journal of Experimental Child Psychology*, 7, 167–187. *300, 301*

Gergen, K. J. See Jones et al. (1961).

Gerwirtz, J. L. (1965) The course of infant smiling in four child-rearing environments in Israel. In B. M. Foss (Ed.), *Determinants of infant behavior*, Vol. 3. New York: Wiley. *360, 361*

Gibson, E. J., and Walk, R. D. (1960) The visual cliff. *Scientific American*, 202, 2–9. *95*

Gibson, J. J. (1950) *The perception of the visual world*. Boston: Houghton Mifflin. *82*

Gill, T. V. See Rumbaugh et al. (1974).

Ginsburg, B. E. (1971) Developmental behavioral genetics. In N. B. Talbot, J. Kagen, and L. Eisenberg (Eds.), *Behavioral science in pediatric medicine*. Philadelphia: Saunders. *218*

Glanzer, M., and Cunitz, A. R. (1960) Two storage mechanisms in free recall, *Journal of Verbal Learning and Verbal Behavior*, 5, 351–360. *153*

Glaserfeld, E. von See Rumbaugh et al. (1974).

Glucksberg, S., and Danks, J. H. (1975) *Experimental psycholinguistics*. Hillsdale, N.J.: Lawrence Erlbaum Associates. *176*

Glueck, E. See Glueck and Glueck (1950).

Glueck, S., and Glueck, E. (1950) *Unraveling juvenile delinquency*. New York: Commonwealth Fund. *373*

Goddard, H. H. (1912) *The Kallikak family: A study in the heredity of febble-mindedness*. New York: Macmillan. *257*

Goddard, H. H. (1946) What is intelligence? *Journal of Social Psychology*, 24, 51–69. *240*

Godwin, J. (1973) *The mating trade*. Garden City, N.Y.: Doubleday. *428*

Goertzel, M. G. See Goertzel and Goertzel (1962).

Goertzel, V., and Goertzel, M. G. (1962) *Cradles of eminence*. Boston: Little, Brown. *264, 268*

Goffman, E. (1963) *Stigma*. Englewood Cliffs, N.J.: Prentice-Hall. *464*

Goldberg, S. C., Klerman, G. L., and Cole, J. O. (1965) Changes in schizophrenic psychopathology and ward behavior as a function of phenothiazine treatment. *British Journal of Psychiatry*, 111, 120–133. *473*

Goldsby, R. A. (1971) *Race and races*. New York: Macmillan. *218*

Goldstein, M. J., Rodnick, E. H., Jones, J. E., McPherson, S. R., West, K. L. (1978) Familial precursors of schizophrenia spectrum disorders. In L. C. Wynne, R. L. Cromwell, and S. Matthysse (Eds.), *The nature of schizophrenia. New approaches to research and treatment*. New York: Wiley, 487–498. *457*

Goldstein, M. J. See Evans et al. (1972), (1973), Rodnick and Goldstein (1974).

Goodenough, D. R. See Witkin et al. (1976).

Goodenough, F. L., and Maurer, K. M. (1942) *The mental growth of children from two to fourteen years: A study of the predictive value of the Minnesota Preschool Scales*. Minneapolis: University of Minnesota Press. *244*

Goodman, L. S. See Smith et al. (1947).

Goodstein, L. D. See Lanyon and Goodstein (1971).

Goodwin, D. W. (1976). *Is Alcoholism hereditary?* New

York: Oxford University Press. *121*
Goodwin, D. W. (1979) Genetic determinants of alcoholism. In J. H. Mendelson and N. K. Mello (Eds.), *The diagnosis and treatment of alcoholism*. New York: McGraw-Hill, 59–82. *114*
Gordon, W. See Price-Williams et al. (1969).
Gottesman, I. (1963) Genetic aspects of intelligent behavior. In N. R. Ellis (Ed.), *Handbook of mental deficiency*. New York: McGraw-Hill. *204*
Gottesman, I. I., and Shields, J. (1972) *Schizophrenia and genetics*. New York: Academic Press. *439, 456*
Gottlieb, G. (1973) Neglected developmental variables in the study of species identification in birds. *Psychological Bulletin*, 29, 362–372 *334*
Gottlieb, J., and Budoff, M. (1973) Social acceptability of retarded children in nongraded schools differing in architecture. *American Journal of Mental Deficiency*, 78, 15–19. *261*
Gough, H. G. (1960) *Manual for the California Psychological Inventory*. (Rev. ed.) Palo Alto, Calif.: Consulting Psychologists Press. *408, 410*
Gove, W. R. (Ed.) (1975) *The labelling of deviance*. New York: Sage Publications and Halstead Press. *453, 464*
Graf, R., and Torrey, J. W. (1966) Perception of phrase structure in written language. *American Psychological Association Convention Proceedings*. Washington, D.C., American Psychological Association. *176*
Graham, F. See Berman et al. (1966).
Graham, P. See Wing et al. (1967).
Gray, C. R., and Gummerman, K. (1975) The enigmatic eidetic image: A critical examination of methods, data, and theories. *Psychological Bulletin*, 82, 383–407. *286*
Greenblatt, M. (1978) The grieving spouse *American Journal of Psychiatry*, 135, 43–47 *425*
Greenfield, P. M. (1976) Cross-cultural research and Piagetian theory: Paradox and progress. In K. Riegel and J. Meacham (Eds.), *The developing individual in a changing world*. The Hague: Mouton Publishers. *299*
Gregory, I. See Rosen et al. (1972).
Gregory, R. L. (1970) *Eye and brain: The psychology of seeing*. New York: McGraw-Hill. *73, 90*
Gregory, R. L. (1973) *The intelligent eye*. New York: McGraw-Hill. *73*
Gregory, R. L., and Wallace, J. G. (1963) Recovery from early blindness: A case study. *Experimental Psychological Social Monograph* (2). *92*
Gripp, R. See Magaro et al. (1978).
Grize, J. B. See Piaget et al. (1968).
Gross, J. C. See Bruininks et al. (1974).
Grossman, H. J. (Ed.) (1973) *Manual on terminology and classification in mental retardation*. Washington, D.C.: American Association on Mental Deficiency. *252*
Groves, P., and Schlesinger, K. (1979) *To biological psychology*. Dubuque, Iowa: W. C. Brown. *47*
Gruen, G. E., Ottinger, D. R., and Ollendick, T. H. (1974) Probability learning in retarded children with differing histories of success and failure in school. *American Journal of Mental Deficiency*, 79, 417–423 *261*
Grusec, J. E. See Bandura et al. (1966).
Guilford, J. P. (1959) Three faces of intellect. *American Psychologist*, 14, 469–479. *240*
Guilford, J. P. (1967) *The nature of intelligence*. New York: McGraw-Hill. *239*
Guilford, J. P., and Hoepfner, R. (1971) *The analysis of intelligence*. New York: McGraw-Hill. *239*
Gummerman K. See Gray and Gummerman (1975).
Gur, R. See Butcher and Gur (1978).
Gurdon, J. B. (1968) Transplanted nuclei and cell differentiation. *Scientific American*, 219 (6), 24–35. *223*
Gurland, B. J. See Cooper et al. (1972).
Guthrie, E. R. (1952) *The psychology of learning*. (Rev. ed.) New York: Harper. *126*
Guttman, N. (1949) Equal reinforcement values for sucrose and glucose compared with equal sweetness values. *Journal of Comparative and Physiological Psychology*, 47, 358–361. *342*
Guze, S. B. (1976) *Criminality and psychiatric disorders*. New York: Oxford University Press. *431*

Hachaya, M. (1955) *Hiroshima diary*. Chapel Hill: University of North Carolina Press. *424*
Hager, J. L. See Seligman and Hager (1972).
Haggard, E. A. (1978) On quantitative Rorschach scales. *Educational and Psychological Measurement* 38, 703–724. *412*
Hagman, E. R. (1932) A study of fears of children of preschool age. *Journal of Experimental Education*, 1: 110–130. *361*
Haldane, J. B. S. (1946) The interaction of nature and nurture. *Annals of Eugenics*, 13, 197–205. *211*
Hall, C. S. (1951) The genetics of behavior. In S. S. Stevens (Ed.), *Handbook of experimental psychology*. New York: Wiley. *208, 209*
Hall, C. S., and Lindzey, G. (1978) *Theories of Personality*. (3rd ed.) New York: Wiley. *417*
Hall, C. S., and Van de Castle, R. L. (1966) *The content and analysis of dreams*. New York: Appleton-Century-Crofts. *105*
Harlow, H. F. (1972) Love created—love destoyed—love

regained. *Modeles animaux du comportement humain*. Edition du Centre National de la Recherche Scientifique, Paris, 198, 13–60. *366*
Harlow, H. F. See Suomi and Harlow (1978).
Harlow, H. F., and Suomi, S. J. (1970) Nature of love—simplified. *American Psychologist*, 25, 161–168. *367*
Harper, R. A. (1975) *The new psychotherapies*. Englewood Cliffs, N.J.: Prentice-Hall. *492*
Harrell, M. S. See Harrell and Harrell (1945).
Harrell, T. W., and Harrell, M. S. (1945) Army general classification test scores for civilian occupations. *Educational and Psychological Measurement*, 5, 229–239. *246*
Harris, F. R. See Allen et al. (1964).
Harris, J. G., Jr. (1963) Judgmental versus mathematical prediction: An investigation by analogy of the clinical versus statistical controversy. *Behavioral Science*, 8, 324–335. *413*
Harris, S. (1978) DSM-III: Its implications for children. *Child Behavior Therapy*, 1, 37–46. *451*
Harris, S. H. See Nathan and Harris (1980).
Harris, T. See Brown et al. (1977).
Hart, B. See Allen et al. (1964).
Harter, S. See Zigler and Harter (1969).
Hathaway, S. R., and Monachesi, E. D. (1953) *Analyzing and predicting juvenile delinquency with the MMPI*. Minneapolis: University of Minnesota Press. *408*
Havighurst, R. J. See Eells et al. (1951).
Hayes, K. (1951) *The ape in our house*. New York: Harper and Row. *180*
Hebb, D. O. (1949) *The organization of behavior: A neuropsychological theory*. New York: Wiley. *361*
Hebb, D. O. (1955) Drives and the CNS (conceptual nervous system). *Psychological Review*, 62, 243–254. *340*
Hebb, D. O. (1972) *Textbook of psychology*. (3rd ed.) Philadelphia: Saunders. *239*
Heber, F. R. See Garber and Heber (1977).
Hecht, F. See Motulsky and Hecht (1964).
Heidbreder, E. (1947) The attainment of concepts: III. The problem. *Journal of Psychology*, 24, 93–138. *190, 192*
Heider, F. (1958) *The psychology of interpersonal relations*. New York: Wiley. *307*
Hein, A. See Held and Hein (1963).
Held, R., and Bauer, J. A., Jr. (1967) Visually guided reaching in infant monkeys after restricted rearing. *Science*, 155, 718–720. *94*
Held, R., and Hein, A. (1963) Movement-produced stimulation in the development of visually guided behavior. *Journal of Comparative and Physiological Psychology*, 56, 872–876. *93*
Helfer, R. E. See Kempe and Helfer (1972).
Hellmer, L. A. See Peterson et al. (1959).
Helmholtz, H. von Trichromatic color theory. *55*
Helson, H. (1948) Adaptation-level as a basis for a quantitative theory of frames of reference. *Psychological Review*, 55, 297–313. *78, 79*
Henschel, A. See Keys et al. (1950).
Hering, E. Opponent process color theory. *55*
Herrick, V. E. See Eells et al. (1951).
Hess, E. H. (1958) "Imprinting" in animals. *Scientific American*, 198, 81–90. *333, 334*
Hess, E. H. (1970) *Ethology and developmental psychology*. In P. H. Mussen (Ed.), *Carmichael's manual of child psychology*. (3rd ed.) New York: Wiley, 1–38. *334*
Heston, L. L. (1966) Psychiatric disorders in foster home reared children of schizophrenic mothers. *British Journal of Psychiatry*, 112, 819–825. *456, 457*
Heston, L., and Denny, D. (1968) *Interactions between early life experience and biological factors in schizophrenia*. In D. Rosenthal and S. Kety (Eds.), *The transmission of schizophrenia*. Oxford: Pergamon Press. *457*
Hetherington, E. M. (1972) The effects of father absence on personality development in adolescent daughters. *Developmental Psychology*, 7, 313–326. *373*
Hilgard, E. R. (1965) *Hypnotic susceptibility*. New York: Harcourt Brace Jovanovich. *110*
Hilgard, E. R. (1968). *The experience of hypnosis*. New York: Harcourt Brace Jovanovich. *121*
Hilgard E. R. See Weitzenhoffer and Hilgard (1962).
Hilgard, E. R. (1977). *Divided consciousness*. New York: Wiley Interscience. *121*
Hilgard, J. R. (1970) *Personality and Hypnosis*. Chicago: University of Chicago Press. *110, 121*
Hill, J. P. (1964) Parental determinants of sex-typed behavior. Unpublished doctoral dissertation, Harvard University. *379*
Hirsch, J. (1970) Behavior-genetic analysis and its biosocial consequences. *Seminars in Psychiatry*, 2, 89–105. *221*
Hirschhorn, K. See Witkin et al. (1976).
Hjelle, L. A. and Ziegler, D. J. (1976) *Personality: Theories, basic assumptions, research and applications*. New York: McGraw-Hill. *417*
Hoepfner, R. See Guilford and Hoepfner (1971).
Hoffman, L. W. (undated) Early childhood experiences and women's achievement motives. Unpublished paper. *381*
Hofstaetter, P. R. (1954) The

changing composition of "intelligence": A study in technique. *Journal of Genetic Psychology*, 85, 159–164. *242, 243*
Hogan, R. (1976). *Personality theory: The personological tradition*. Englewood Cliffs, N.J.: Prentice-Hall. *392, 417*
Holland, C. H. See Farina et al. (1966).
Hollingshead, A. B., and Redlich, F. (1958) *Social class and mental illness*. New York: Wiley. *458*
Hollon, S. D. See Barber and Hollon (1978).
Holmes, F. B. See Jersild and Holmes (1935).
Holt, R. R. (1971) *Assessing personality*. New York: Harcourt Brace Jovanovich. *413, 417*
Holzman, P. S. (1970) *Psychoanalysis and psychopathology*. New York: McGraw-Hill. *417, 446*
Honzik, M. P. (1957) Developmental studies of parent-child resemblance in intelligence. *Child Development*, 28, 215–228. *216*
Honzik, M. P., Macfarlane, J. W., and Allen, L. (1948) The stability of mental test performance between two and eighteen years. *Journal of Experimental Education*, 18, 309–324. *244*
Hook, E. B. (1973) Behavioral implications of the human XYY genotype. *Science*, 179, 139–150. *207*
Horn, J. L., and Cattell, R. B. (1967) Age differences in fluid and crystallized intelligence. *Acta Psychologica*, 26, 107–129. *239*
Horner, M. (1968) Sex differences in achievement motivation and performance in competitive and noncompetitive situations. Unpublished doctoral dissertation, University of Michigan. *381*
Horney, K. (1934) The overevaluation of love: Study of a common present-day feminine type. *Psychoanalytic Quarterly*, 3, 605–638. *394*
Horney, K.
Psychoanalysis *394–395*
Horobin, G. See Birch et al. (1970).
Hovland, C. I., Janis, I. L., and Kelley, H. H. (1953) *Communication and persuasion*. New Haven: Yale University Press. *319*
Hubel, D. H., and Wiesel, T. N. (1959) Perceptive fields of single neurons in the rat's striate cortex. *Journal of Physiology*, 148, 574–591. *75*
Huesmann, L. R. See Lefkowitz et al. (1972), Eron et al. (1972).
Huff, D. (1954) *How to lie with statistics*. New York: W. W. Norton. *495*
Hunt, E., and Love, T. (1972) How good can memory be? In A. W. Melton and E. Martin (Eds.), *Coding processes in human memory*. New York: Wiley. *148, 164*
Hunt, L. A. See Block et al. (1979).
Hurvich, L. M., and Jameson, D. (1957) An opponent-process theory of color vision. *Psychological Review*, 64, 384–404. *55*
Huston-Stein, A. (1978) Televised aggression and prosocial behavior. In H. L. Pick, Jr., H. W. Leibowitz, J. E. Singer, A. Steinschneider, and H. W. Stevenson (Eds.) *Psychology: From research to practice*. New York: Plenum Press. *3*
Illsley, R. See Birch et al. (1970).
Isaacs, A. D. See Wing et al. (1967).
Iscoe, I. See Stevenson et al. (1955).
Itard, J. M. G. (1807). *The wild boy of Aveyron*. (Translated by G. Humphrey and M. Humphrey.) New York: Appleton-Century-Crofts, 1932. *259*

Jaastad, K. See Dunnette et al. (1963).
Jablensky, A. See Sartorius et al. (1978).
Jacklin, C. N. See Maccoby and Jacklin (1974).
Jackson D. N. See Bentler et al. (1971).
Jacob, G. H. See DeValois et al. (1966).
Jacobsen, B. See Kety et al. (1975), (1978).
Jacobson, L. See Rosenthal and Jacobsen (1968).
James, W. Imprinting. *332*
Jameson, D. See Hurvich and Jameson (1957).
Jameson, D. H. See Ludwig et al. (1972).
Janis, I. L. (1971) *Stress and frustration*. New York: Harcourt Brace Jovanovich. *425*
Janis, I. L. (1973) *Victims of group think*. Boston: Houghton Mifflin. *317*
Janis, I. L. See Hovland et al. (1953).
Janis, I. L., and Mann, L. (1977a) Coping with decisional conflict. In I. L. Janis (Ed.), *Current trends in psychology*. Los Altos, Calif.: William Kaufman *355, 356*
Janis, I. L., and Mann, L. (1977b) *Decision making*. New York: Free Press. *355, 356*
Janowsky, D. S., Meacham, M. P., Blaine, J. D., Schorr, M., and Bozzetti, L. P. (1976) Marijuana effects on simulated flying ability. *American Journal of Psychiatry*, 133, 384–388 *117*
Jarvik, L. F. See Erlenmeyer-Kimling and Jarvik (1963).
Jarvik, L. F., Klodin, V., and Matsuyama, S. S. (1973) Human aggression and the extra Y chromosome. *American Psychologist*, 28, 764–782. *207*
Jarvik, L. F., Eisdorfer, C., and Blum, J. E. (Eds.) (1973) *Intellectual functioning in adults*. New York: Springer. *249*
Jenkins, J. G., and Dallenbach, K. M. (1924) Oblivescence during sleep and walking. *American Journal of Psychology*, 35, 605–612. *163*
Jenkins, J. J., and Paterson, D. G. (1961) *Studies in individual differences: The search of intelligence*. New York:

Appleton-Century-Crofts. *249*
Jensen, A. R. (1969) How much can we boost IQ and scholastic achievement? *Harvard Educational Review*, 39, 1–123. Reprinted in *Environment, heredity and intelligence*. Cambridge, Mass.: Harvard Educational Review Reprint Series 2. *219*
Jerauld, R. See Klaus et al. (1972).
Jersild, A. T. (1960) *Child psychology*, (5th ed.) Englewood Cliffs, N.J.: Prentice-Hall. *362*
Jersild, A. T., and Holmes, F. B. (1935) *Studies of children's fears*. Child Development Monograph 20. New York: Bureau of Publications, Teachers College, Columbia University. *361*
Johnson, B. C. See Erickson et al. (1977).
Johnson, M. K. See Bransford and Johnson (1972).
Johnson, R. C. See Zelhart and Johnson (1959).
Jones, E. E., and Davis, K. E. (1965) A theory of correspondent inferences: From acts to dispositions. In L. Berkowitz (Ed.), *Advances in experimental social psychology*, Vol. 2. New York: Academic Press. *308*
Jones, E. E., Davis, K. E., and Gergen, K. J. (1961) Role playing variations and their informational value for person perception. *Journal of Abnormal and Social Psychology*, 63, 302–310. *308, 309*
Jones, E. E., and Nesbett, R. (1971) *The actor and the observer: Divergent impressions of the causes of behavior*. New York: General Learning Press. *309*
Jones, E. E. See Synder and Jones (1974).
Jones, J. *5–7*
Jones, J. E. See Goldstein et al. (1978).
Judd, L. L. See Evans et al. (1972).
Jung, C. Psychoanalysis. *392–393*

Kagan, J. (1971) The beneficiaries of change. Paper presented at Symposium on Crises on Our Conscience, October 1971. Washington, D.C.: Joseph P. Kennedy, Jr. Foundation. *237*
Kagan, J. (1972) Cross-cultural perspectives on early development. Paper presented to the Annual Meeting of the American Association for the Advancement of Science, Washington, D.C., December, 1979. *246*
Kalinowsky, L. B. (1975) Electric and other convulsive treatments. In D. X. Freedman and J. E. Dyrud (Eds.), *American handbook of psychiatry*, Vol. 5. (2nd ed.) S. Arieti, Editor-in-Chief. New York: Basic Books *435*
Kalvin, H. G., Jr., and Zeisel, H. (1966) *The american jury*. Boston: Little, Brown. *327*
Kamiya, J. (1969) Operant control of the EEG and some of its reported effects on consciousness. In C. Tart (Ed.), *Altered states of consciousness*. New York: Wiley *131*
Kanfer, F. H. and Phillips, J. S. (1970) *Learning foundations of behavior therapy*. New York: Wiley. *479*
Kaplan, F. See Blatt and Kaplan (1966).
Kaplan, M. F. See Myers and Kaplan (1976).
Karker, J. C. See Blakemore et al. (1963).
Karlsson, J. L. (1974) Inheritance of schizophrenia. *Acta Psychiatrica Scandinavica*, Supplement 247. *266*
Karnes, M., and Teska, J. (1975) The effects of early intervention programs. In J. Gallagher (Ed.), *The application of child development research with exceptional children*. Reston, Va.: Council for Exceptional Children. *274*
Katz, I. (1968) Factors influencing Negro performance in the desegregated school. In M. Deutsch, I. Katz, and A. R. Jensen (Eds.), *Social class, race, and psychological development*. New York: Holt, Rinehart and Winston. *220*
Katz, P., and Zigler, E. (1967) Self-image disparity: A developmental approach. *Journal of Personality and Social Psychology*, 5, 186–195. *268*
Kedward, H. B. See Rakoff et al. (1977).
Keenan, J. M., and Kintsch, W. (1974) The identification of explicitly and implicitly presented information. In W. Kintsch, *The representation of meaning in memory*, Hillside, N.J.: Lawrence Erlbaum, Associates. *159, 160*
Keeney, T. J., Cannizzo, S. R., and Flavell, J. H. (1967) Spontaneous and induced verbal rehearsal in a recall task. *Child Development*, 38, 953–966. *287*
Keiser, S. (1969) Superior intelligence: Its contribution of neurogenesis. *Journal of the American Psychoanalytic Association*, 17, 452–473. *268*
Kelley, H. H. (1971) *Attribution in social interaction*. New York: General Learning. *308*
Kelley, H. H. See Hovland et al. (1953).
Kelley, H. H., and Stahelski, A. H. (1970) The inference of intention from moves in the prisoner's delemma game. *Journal of Experimental Social Psychology, 6, 401–419*. *311*
Kellogg, L. A. See Kellogg and Kellogg (1933).
Kellogg, W. N., and Kellogg, L. A.(1933) *The ape and the child*. New York: McGraw-Hill. *180*
Kempe, C. H., and Helfer, R. E. (Eds.) (1972) *Helping the battered child and his family*. Philadelphia: Lippincott. *375*
Kendall, R. E. See Cooper et al. (1972).
Kendler, H. H., and Kendler, T. S. (1962) Vertical and horizontal processes in problem solving. *Psychological Review*, 69, 1–16. *287*
Kendler, H. H., and Kendler, T. S.

(1970) Developmental process in descrimination learning. *Human Development*, 13, 65–89. *287*
Kendler, T. S. See Kendler and Kendler (1962), (1970).
Kennel, J. H. See Klaus et al. (1972).
Kenney, H. J. See Bruner and Kenny (1966).
Keppel, G., and Underwood, B. J. (1962) Proactive inhibition in short-term retention of single items. *Journal of Verbal Learning and Verbal Behavior*, 1, 153–161. *164*
Kern, R. P. See Berkun et al. (1962).
Kessen, W. (1962) "Stage" and "structure" in the study of children. In W. Kessen and C. Kuhlman (Eds.), Thought in the young child. *Monographs of the Society for Research in Child Development*, 27 (2). (Whole 83.) *300*
Kety, S. S. (1967) Psychoendocrine systems and emotions: Biological aspects. In D. C. Glass (Ed.), *Neurophysiology and emotion*. New York: Rockefeller University Press. *459*
Kety, S. S., Rosenthal, D., Schulsinger, F., and Wender, P. H. (1968) The types and prevalence of mental illness in the biological and adoptive families of adoped schizophrenics. *Journal of Psychiatric Research*, Supplement 1, 254–362. *456*
Kety, S. S., Rosenthal, D., Wender, P. H., Schulsinger, F., and Jacbsen, B. (1975) Mental illness in the biological and adoptive families of adopted individuals who have become schizophrenic: A preliminary report based upon psychiatric interviews. In R. Fieve, D. Rosenthal, and H. Brill (Eds.), *Genetic research in psychiatry*. Baltimore: Johns Hopkins University Press, 147–165. *437, 456*
Kety, S. S., Rosenthal, D., Wender, P. H., Schulsinger, F., and Jacbsen, B. (1975) The biologic and adoptive families of adopted individuals who became schizophrenic: Prevalence of mental illness and other characteristics. In L. C. Wynne, R. L. Cromwell, and S. Matthysse (Eds.), *The nature of schizophrenia: New approaches to research and treatment*. New York: Wiley, 25–37 *456*
Keys, A. B., Brozek, J., Henschel, A., Mickelson, O., and Taylor, H. L. (1950) *The biology of human starvation*. Minneapolis: University of Minnesota Press. *341*
Kimble, G. A. (1978) *How to use (and misuse) statistics*. Englewood Cliffs, N.J.: Prentice-Hall. *512*
King, F. A. (Ed.) (1978) *Handbook of behavioral neurobiology*. New York: Plenum Press. *47*
Kintsch, W. (1977) *Memory and cognition* (2nd ed.) New York: Wiley. *171*
Kintsch, W. See Keenan and Kintsch (1974).
Kirschner Associates. (1970) A national survey of the impacts of Head Start centers on community institutions. Report prepared for the Office of Child Development, May 1970. *273*
Kisker, G. W. (1977) *The disorganized personality*. (3rd ed.) New York: McGraw-Hill. *424, 427*
Klatzky, R. L. (1975) *Human memory: Structures and processes*. San Francisco: W. H. Freeman. *171*
Klaus, M. H., Jerauld, R., Kreger, N. C., McAlpine, W., Steffa, M., and Kennel, J. H. (1972) Maternal attachment: Importance of the first post-partum days. *New England Journal of Medicine*, 286, 460–463. *369*
Kleinman, R. A. See Brener and Kleinman (1970).
Klerman, G. L. (1977) Better but not well: Social and ethical issues in the deinstitutionalization of the mentally ill. *Schizophrenia Bulletin*, 3, 617–631. *472*
Klerman, G. L. See Goldberg et al. (1965).
Klevansky, S. See Feedman et al. (1971).
Klodin, V. See Jarvik et al. (1973).
Klonoff, H. (1974) Marijuana and driving in real-life situations. *Science*, 186, 317–324. *117*
Klüver, H. (1933) *Behavior mechanisms in monkeys*. Chicago: University of Chicago Press. *349*
Knodel, J. (1977) Breast-feeding and population growth. *Science*, 198, 1111–1115. *18*
Kogan, N. See Wallach et al. (1968).
Kohlberg, L. (1969) Stage and sequence: The cognitive-developmental approach to socialization. In D. A. Goslin (Ed.), *Handbook of socialization theory and research*. Chicago: Rand McNally. *282*
Kohlberg, L. (1971) Early education: A cognitive-developmental view. In P. S. Sears (Ed.), *Intellectual development*. New York: Wiley. *281*
Köhler, W. (1925) *The mentality of apes*. New York: Harcourt, Brace and World. *177*
Kohn, M. L. (1959) Social class and parental values. *American Journal of Sociology*, 64, 337–351. *378*
Kohn, M. L. (1972) Class, family and schizophrenia: A reformulation. *Social Forces*, 50, 295–313. *458*
Kolb, L. C. (1968) *Modern clinical psychiatry*, (8th ed.) Philadelphia: Saunders. *433*
Kovel, J. (1976). *A complete guide to therapy*. New York: Pantheon. *492*
Kraepelin, E. Descriptive psychopathology. *443–444*
Kraepelin, E. (1904) *Lectures on clinical psychiatry*. London: Bailliere, Tindall and Cox. *443*
Kraft, C. L. (1978) A psychophysical contribution to air safety: Simulator studies of visual

illusions in night visual approaches. In H. L. Pick, H. W. Leibowitz, J. E. Singer, A. Steinschneider, and H. W. Stevenson (Eds.), *Psychology: From research to practice*. New York: Plenum Press. *4*

Krasner, L. (1976) The operant approach in behavior modification. In J. T. Spence, R. C. Carson, and J. W. Thibaut (Eds.), *Behavioral approaches to therapy*. Morristown, N.J.: General Learning Press. *139*

Krech, D., Rosenzweig, M. R., Bennett, E. C., and Krueckel, B. (1954) Enzyme concentrations in the brain and adjustive behavior-patterns. *Science*, 20, 994–996. *209*

Kreger, N. C. See Klaus et al. (1972).

Krueckel, B. See Krech et al. (1954).

Krueger, W. C. F. (1929) The effect of overlearning on retention. *Journal of Experimental Psychology*, 12, 71–78. *166*

Kugel, R. B. (1967) Familial mental retardation—fact or fancy? In J. Hellmuth (Ed.), *Disadvantaged child*, Vol. 1. New York: Brunner/Mazel. *256*

Kugel, R. B., and Parsons, M. H. (1967) *Children of deprivation: Changing the course of familial retardation*. Washington D.C.: Department of Health, Education and Welfare, Children's Bureau. *256*

Kuhn, D. See Monahan et al. (1974).

Laing, R. D. (1967). *The politics of experience*. New York: Ballantine Books *435*

Lamb, M. (Ed.) (1976) *The role of the father in child development*. New York: Wiley. *382*

Lambert, M. S. See Bergin and Lambert (1978).

Lamm, H. See Myers and Lamm (1976).

Lamm, H., and Myers, D. G. (1978) Group-induced polarization of attitudes and behavior. In L. Berkowitz (Ed.), *Advances in experimental social psychology*, Vol. 11. New York: Academic Press. *326, 327*

Lane, H. (1976) *The wild boy of Aveyron*. Cambridge, Mass.: Harvard University Press. *259*

Lang, P. J., and Melamed, B. E. (1969) Avoidance conditioning therapy of an infant with chronic ruminative vomiting: Case report. *Journal of Abnormal Psychology*, 74, 1–8. *484, 485*

Lanyon, R. I., and Goodstein, L. D. (1971) *Personality assessment*. New York: Wiley. *417*

Latané, B. See Freeman et al. (1975).

Laughlin, H. P. (1967) *The neuroses*. Washington, D.C.: Butterworths. *426–427*

Laurendeau, M., and Pinard, A. (1962) *Causal thinking in the child*. New York: International Universities Press. *282*

Laurendeau-Bendavid, M. (1977) Culture, schooling, and cognitive development: A comparative study of children in French Canada and Rwanda. In P. R. Dasen (Ed.), *Piagetian psychology: Cross-cultural contributions*. New York: Gardner Press. *300*

Lavin, N. I. See Blakemore et al. (1963).

Lawrence, K. A. See Ross and Lawrence (1968).

Lee, E. S. (1951) Negro intelligence and selective migration. *American Sociological Review*, 16, 227–233. *220*

Leff, J. P. (1976) Schizophrenia and sensitivity to family environment. *Schizophrenia Bulletin*, 24, 566–574. *468, 469*

Leff, J. P. See Vaughn and Leff (1976).

Lefkowitz, M., Eron, L., Walder, L., and Huesmann, L. R. (1972). Television violence and child aggression: A follow-up study. In G. A. Comstock and E. A. Rubinstein (Eds.), *Television and social behavior*, Vol. 3, *Television and adolescent aggressiveness*. Washington, D.C.: U.S. Government Printing Office, 35–135. *3*

Lefkowitz, M. M. See Eron et al. (1972).

Lehrman, D. (1974) Can psychiatrists use ethology? In N. F. White (Ed.), *Ethology and psychiatry*. Toronto: University of Toronto Press. *371*

Leibowitz, H. W. See Pick et al. (1978).

Leitenberg, H. (1972) Positive reinforcement and extinction procedures. In W. S. Agra (Ed.) *Behavior modification: Principles and clinical applications*. Boston: Little, Brown, 27–57. *481*

Leitenberg, H. See Agras et al. (1974).

Lemkau, P., Tietze, C., and Cooper, M. (1941) Mental-hygiene problems in an urban district. *Mental Hygiene*, 25, 624. *253*

Lentz, R. N. See Paul and Lentz (1977).

Leonard, W. E. (1927) *The locomotive god*. New York: Appleton-Century-Crofts. *348*

Lepper, M. (1973) Dissonance, self-perception and honesty in children. *Journal of Personality and Social Psychology*, 25, 65–74. *321*

Lerner, S. E. and Burns, R. S. (1978) Phencyclidine used among youth: History, epidemiology and acute and chronic intoxication. In R. C. Petersen and R. C. Stillman (Eds.), *Phencyclidine (PCP) abuse: An appraisal*. National Institute of Drug Abuse Research Mongraph 21, Rockville, Md., 66–118. *116*

Lesser, G. S., Fifer, G., and Clark, D. H. (1965) Mental abilities of children from different social-class and cultural groups. *Monographs of the Society for Research in Child Development*, 30, Serial 102. *241*

Levis, D. J. See Stamfl and Levis (1967).

Lewin, K. Classification of conflict. *352*
Lewin, K. (1936) *A dynamic theory of personality.* New York: McGraw-Hill. *281*
Lewin, K. See Barker et al. (1941).
Lewis, M. (Ed.) (1976) *Origins of intelligence: Infancy and early childhood.* New York: Plenum Press. *249*
Liberman, A. M. Sound spectrogram. *174, 175*
Liberman, R. P. (1979) *Social skills and rehibilitation for schizophrenics.* NIMH Program Project Grant. Mental Health Clinical Research Center for the Study of Schizophrenia, Camarillo State Hospital and University of California at Los Angeles. *468, 470*
Lidz, T., The family in schizophrenia. *457*
Lieberman, M. A., Yalom, I. D., and Miles, M. B. (1973) *Encounter groups: First facts.* New York: Basic Books. *492*
Liebert, R. M., and Spiegler, M. D. (1978) *Personality.* (3rd ed.) Homewood, Ill.: Dorsey Press. *417*
Lifton, R. J. (1967) *Death in life.* New York: Random House. *424*
Lind, E. A. See Erickon et al. (1977).
Lindquist, E. F. See Blommers and Lindquist (1960).
Lindsay, Ph. H. and Norman, D. A. (1977) *Human information processing.* (2nd ed.) New York: Academic Press. *171*
Lindzey, G. Hall, and Lindzey (1978). See Loehlin et al. (1975), Spuhler and Lindzey (1967).
Lippsitt, L. P. (1978) Assessment of sensory and behavioral functions in infancy. In H. L. Pick, Jr., H. W. Leibowitz, J. E. Singer, A. Steinschneider, and H. W. Stevenson (Eds.), *Psychology: From research to practice.* New York: Plenum Press. *2*
Lishman, W. A. See Lloyd and Lishman (1975).
Litman, R. L. See Shneidman et al. (1970).
Little, L. (1968) Cultural variations in social schemata. *Journal of Personality and Social Psychology,* 10, 1–7. *336*
Lloyd, G. G., and Lishman, W. A. (1975) Effect of depression on the speed of recall of pleasant and unpleasant experiences. *Psychological Medicine,* 5, 173–180. *433*
Locke, J. (1690) *An essay concerning human understanding.* London. *49, 91*
Loehlin, J. C., Lindzey, G., and Spuhler, J. N., (1975) *Race differences in intelligence.* San Francisco: W. H. Freeman. *219*
Loftus, E. F., and Palmer, J. C. (1974) Reconstruction of automobile destruction: An example of the interaction between language and memory. *Journal of Verbal Learning and Verbal Behavior,* 13, 585–589. *161*
Loftus, E. F. See Loftus and Loftus (1976).
Loftus, G. R., and Loftus, E. F. (1976) *Human memory: The processing of information.* Hillsdale, N.J.: Lawrence Erlbaum Associates, 1976. *171*
Lorenz, K. Imprinting.
Loring, C. B. See Freedman et al. (1967).
Love, T. See Hunt and Love (1972).
Lovrien, E. See Magenis et al. (1977).
Luce, G. G., and Segal, J. (1966) *Sleep.* New York: Coward-McCann. *104, 106*
Luchins, A. S. (1942) Mechanization in problem solving. *Psychological Monographs,* 54. (Whole 248.) *195*
Ludwig, A. M. Multiple personality. *102*
Ludwig, A. M., Brandsma, J. M., Wilbur, C. B., Bendfeldt, F., and Jameson, D. H. (1972) The objective study of a multiple personality. *Archives of General Psychiatry,* 26, 298–310. *101*
Lundsteen, C. See Witkin et al. (1976).
Lunneborg, P. W. (1978) *Why study psychology?* Monterey, Calif.: Brook/Cole. *22–23*
Luria, A. *279*
Luria, A. R. (1957) The role of language in the formation of temporary connections. In B. Simon (Ed.), *Psychology in the Soviet Union.* Stanford, Calif.: Stanford University Press. *289*
Luria, A. R. (1961) *The role of speech in the regulation of normal and abnormal behavior.* New York: Liveright. *289*

McAlpine, W. See Klaus et al. (1972).
McBarney, D. H., and Collings, V. B. (1977) *Introduction to sensation/perception.* Englewood Cliffs, N.J.: Prentice-Hall. *73*
McCandless, B. R. (1964) Relation of environmental factors to intellectual functioning. In R. Heber and H. Stevens (Eds.), *Mental retardation: A review of research.* Chicago: University of Chicago Press. *212*
McClearn, G. E. (1962) The inheritance of behavior. In L. Postman (Ed.), *Psychology in the making.* New York: Knopf. *225*
Maccoby, E. E., and Bee, H. L. (1965) Some speculations concerning the lag between perceiving and performing. *Child Development,* 36, 367–377 *188*
Maccoby, E. E., and Jacklin, C. N. (1974) *The psychology of sex differences.* Stanford, Calif.: Stanford University Press. *382*
McConnell, C. A. See Stevenson et al. (1955).
MacDonald, N. (1960) Living with schizophrenia. *Canadian Medical Association Journal,* 82, 218–221. *100*
McDougall, W. (1926) *An introduction to social psychology.* Boston: Bruce Humphries. *340, 341*

McDowell, D. J. See Magaro et al. (1978).

MacFarlane, J. W. See Honzik et al. (1948).

McGuire, W. J. (1964) Inducing resistance to persuasion. In L. Berkowitz (Ed.), *Advances in experimental social psychology*, Vol. 1. New York: Academic Press, 191–229. *313, 315*

McKay, D. G. (1973) Aspects of the theory and comprehension memory and attention. *Quarterly Journal of Experimental Psychology*, 25, 22–40. *152*

McLaughlin, M. M. See Ross and McLaughlin (1949).

McNeill, D. (1966) Developmental psycholinguistics. In F. Smith and G. A. Miller (Eds.), *The genesis of laungage*. Cambridge, Mass.: M.I.T. Press. *185*

McNeill, D. See Brown and McNeill (1966).

McNemar, Q. (1942) *The revision of the Stanford-Binet scale*. Boston: Houghton Mifflin. *247*

MacNichol, E. F. (1964) Three pigment color vision. *Scientific American*, 211, 48–56. *56*

McPherson, S. R. See Goldstein et al. (1978).

McReynolds, W. T. (1977) Diagnostic and statistical manual of mental disorders (3rd ed.) and the future of clinical psychology. *Catalog of Selected Documents in Psychology*, 8, 69. *450*

Maddi, S. R. (1976) *Personality theories: A comparative analysis*. (3rd ed.) Homewood, Ill.: Dorsey Press. *417*

Magaro, P. A., Gripp, R., and McDowell, D. J. (1978). *The mental health industry*. New York: Wiley. *492*

Magenis, R. E., Overton, K. M., Chamberlain, J., Brady, T., and Lovrien, E. (1977) Parental origin of the extra chromosome in Down's syndrome. *Human Genetics*, 37, 7–16. *254*

Magoun, H. W. (1952) An ascending reticular activating system in the brain stem. *Harvey Lectures*, 47, 53–71. *37*

Maher, B. A. (1963) Intelligence and brain damage. In N. R. Ellis (Ed.), *Handbook of mental deficiency*. New York: McGraw-Hill. *252*

Maier, S. F., and Seligman, M. E. P. (1976) Learned helplessness: Theory and evidence. *Journal of Experimental Psychology: General*, 105, 3–46. *142*

The Malleus Maleficarium of Heinrich Kramer and James Sprenger (1487) New York: Dover Publications, 1971 *466*

Mancuso, J. C. See Sarbin and Mancuso (1970).

Mann, L. See Janis and Mann (1977a), (1977b).

Marañón, G. (1924) Contributions a l'etude de l'action émotive l'adrenaline. In *Revue francaise d'endocrinologie*, 2, 301. *349*

Marden, P. G., and Kolodner, K. (1977) *Alcohol use and abuse among adolescents*. NCAI Report NCA 1026533, NIAAA. *113*

Marks, I. M. (1972) Flooding (implosion) and allied treatments. In W. S. Agras (Ed.), *Behavior modifications: Principles and clinical applications*. Boston: Little, Brown. *480*

Marks, I. M. (1978) *Living with fear*. New York: McGraw-Hill. *480, 492*

Marks, J. (1925) *Genius and disaster: Studies in drugs and genius*. New York: Adelphi Co. *266*

Marks, L. E. (1975) On colored-hearing synesthesia: Cross modal translations of sensory dimensions. *Psychological Bulletin*, 82, 303–327. *285*

Martin, B. (1977) *Abnormal Psychology* New York: Holt, Rinehart and Winston. *438*

Martin, E. Preface. (1978) In M. C. Reynolds (Ed.), *Futures of education for exceptional children: Emerging structures*. Minneapolis: National Support Systems Project. *261*

Martin, R. M. See Freedman et al. (1967).

Maser, J. D., and Seligman, M. E. P. (eds.) (1977) *Psychopathology: Experimental models*. San Francisco: W. H. Freeman. *464*

Maslow, A. H. Self actualization. *401–403*

Maslow, A. H. (1970) *Motivation and personality*. (2nd ed.) New York: Harper and Row. *403*

Maslow, A. H. (1971) *The farther reaches of human nature*. New York: Viking Press. *417*

Masters, J. C. See Rimm and Masters (1979).

Masterton, R. B. See Thompson and Masterton (1978).

Masterton, R. B., and Glendenning, K. (1978) Phylogeny of the sensory systems. In R. B. Masterton (Ed.), *Handbook of behavioral neurobiology*. New York: Plenum Press.

Matsuyama, S. S. See Jarvik et al. (1973).

Matthysse, S. See Wynne et al. (1978).

Maurer, K. M. See Goodenough and Maurer (1942).

Meacham, M. P. See Janowsky et al. (1976).

Mead, M. (1935) *Sex and temperament in three primitive societies*. New York: Morrow. *379*

Mead, M. (1954) Some theoretical considerations on the problem of mother-child separation. *American Journal of Orthopsychiatry*, 24, 47–483. *372*

Meadow, A., Parves, S. J., and Reese, H. (1959) Influence of brainstorming instructions and problem sequence on a creative problem solving task. *Journal of Applied Psychology*, 43, 413–416. *325*

Mednick, S. A. See Witkin et al. (1976).

Meehl, P. E. On labeling theory. *452–453*

Meehl, P. E. (1954) *Clinical versus statistical prediction*. Minneapolis: University of Minnesota Press. *413*

Meehl, P. E. (1959) A comparison of clinicians with five statistical methods of identifying psychotic MMPI profiles. *Journal of Counseling Psychologists*, 6, 102–109. *413*

Meehl, P. E. (1962) Schizotaxia, schizotypy, schizophrenia. *American Psychologist*, 17, 827–838. *455*

Meehl, P. E. (1965) Comment on Eysenck's "The effects of psychotherapy." *International Journal of Psychiatry*, 1, 156–157. *489*

Megargee, E. I. (1972) *The California psychological inventory handbook*. San Francisco: Jossey-Bass. *408, 409*

Mehrabian, A., and Diamond, S. G. (1971) Seating arrangement and conversation. *Sociometry*, 34, 281–289. *336*

Meichenbaum, D. N., Bowers, K. S., and Ross, R. R. (1969) A behavioral analysis of teacher expectancy effects. *Journal of Personality and Social Psychology*, 13, 306–316. *313*

Melamed, B. E. See Lang and Melamed (1969).

Mellor, C. S. (1970) First rank symptoms of schizophrenia. *British Journal of Psychiatry*, 117, 15–23. *435–436*

Melzack, R., and Wall, P. D. (1965) Pain mechanisms: A new theory. *Science*, 150, 971–979. *65*

Mendel, G. Laws of genetics. *201–202*

Mendelson, J. H., and Mello, N. K. (Eds.) (1979) *The diagnosis and treatment of alcoholism*. New York: McGraw-Hill. *113*

Mendelson, M. See Beck et al. (1962).

Menlove, F. L. See Bandura et al. (1966).

Menninger, K. (1947) *The human mind*. (3rd ed.) New York: Knopf. *429*

Menninger, K. (1968) *The crime of punishment*. New York: Viking Press. *331*

Menninger, K., and Holzman, P. S. (1973) *Theory of psychoanalytic technique*. (2nd ed.) New York: Basic Books. *492*

Menyuk, P. (1971) *The acquisition and development of language*. Englewood Cliffs, N.J.: Prentice-Hall. *185*

Mercer, J. R. (1975) Sociocultural factors in educational labeling. In M. J. Begab and S. A. Richardson (Eds.), *The mentally retarded and society: A social science perspective*. Baltimore: University Park Press. *237*

Merrill, M. A. See Terman and Merrill (1960), (1973).

Merton, R. K. (1948) The self-fulfilling prophecy. *Antioch Review*, 8, 193–210. *311*

Mesmer, F. A. Animal magnetism. *109*

Messick, S. See Bentler et al. (1971).

Mettler, F. A. (1956). *Culture and the structural evolution of the neural system*. James Arthus Lecture, American Museum of Natural History. *27*

Mickelson, O. See Keys et al. (1950).

Miles, C. C. (1954) Gifted children. In L. Carmichael (Ed.), *Manual of child psychology*. (2nd ed.) New York: Wiley. *268*

Miles, M. B. See Lieberman et al. (1973).

Milgram, S. (1965) Some conditions of obedience and disobedience to authority. *Human Relations*, 18, 57–75. *318, 319*

Miller, D. (1966) Worlds that fail. *Trans-action* (2), 36–41. *468*

Miller, D. R., and Swanson, G. E. (1958) *The changing American parent: A study in the Detroit area*. New York: Wiley. *377*

Miller, G. A. (1956) The magical number seven plus or minus two: Some limits on our capacity for processing information. *Psychological Review*, 65, 81–97. *149*

Miller, G. A. (1965) Some preliminaries to psycholinguistics. *American Psychologist*, 20, 15–20. *184*

Miller, G. A. (1969) Psychology as a means of promoting human welfare. *American Psychologist*, 24, 1063–1075. *184*

Miller, N. E. Classification of conflict. *352*

Miller, N. E. (1959) Liberalization of basic S-R concepts: Extensions to conflict behavior, motivation, and social learning. In S. Koch (Ed.), *Psychology: A study of a science*, Vol. 2. New York: McGraw-Hill, 196–292. *355*

Miller, N. E. See Dollard and Miller (1950).

Milner, B. (1962) Laterality effects in audition. In V. B. Mountcastle (Ed.), *Inter-hemisphere relations and cerebral dominance*. Baltimore: Johns Hopkins University Press. *43*

Milner, B. See Olds and Milner (1954).

Milunsky, A. *Know your genes*. Boston: Houghton Mifflin, 1977. *225*

Mischel, W. (1968) *Personality and assessment*. New York: Wiley. *405*

Mishler, E. G., and Waxler, N. E. (1968) *Interaction in families: An experimental study of family*. New York: Wiley. *458*

Mittler, P. (Ed.) (1977) *Research to practice in mental retardation*, Vol. I, *Care and intervention*; Vol. II, *Education and training*; Vol. III, *Biomedical aspects*. Baltimore: University Park Press. *277*

Mock, J. E. See Beck et al. (1962).

Monachesi, E. D. See Hathaway and Monachesi (1953).

Monahan, L., Kuhn, D., and Shaver, P. (1974) Intrapsychic versus cultural explanations of the "fear of success" motive. *Journal of Personality and Social Psychology*, 29, 60–64 *381*

Money, J., and Ehrhardt, A. A. (1972) *Man and woman, boy and girl*. Baltimore: John Hopkins University Press. *379*

Moore, L. T. (1924) *Isaac Newton*.

New York: Charles Scribner's Sons. *268*
Moore, T. W. (1975) Exclusive early mothering and its alternatives: The outcome to adolescence. *Scandinavian Journal of Psychology*, 16, 255–272. *372*
Morgan, G., and Ricciti, H. N. (1969) Infants' responses to strangers during the first year. In B. M. Foss (Ed.), *Determinants of infant behavior*, Vol. 4. New York: Wiley. *361, 363*
Morgan, J. J. B. See Watson and Morgan (1917).
Morton, J. T. (1942) The distortion of syllogistic reasoning produced by personal convictions. Unpublished doctoral dissertation, Northwestern University. *195*
Moscovici, S., and Zavalloni, M. (1969) The group as a polarizer of attitudes. *Journal of Personality and Social Psychology*, 12, 125–135. *326*
Mosher, L. R. (1971) Madness in the community. *Attitude*, 1, 2–21. *468*
Moskowitz, B. A. (1978) The acquisition of language. *Scientific American*, 239, 92–108. *185, 193*
Motulsky, A., and Hecht, F. (1964) Genetic prognosis and counseling. *American Journal of Obstetrics and Gynecology*, 90, 1227–1241. *254*
Moulton, J., Robinson, G. M., and Elias, C. (1978) Psychology in action: Sex bias in language use: "Neutral" pronouns that aren't. *American Psychologist*, 33, 1032–1036. *194*
Mowrer, O. H. See Whiting and Mowrer (1943).
Muenzinger, K. F. (1934) Motivation in learning: I. Electric shock for correct responses in the visual discrimination habit. *Journal of Comparative Psychology*, 17, 267–277. *346*
Munoz, R. See Feighner et al. (1972).
Munroe, R. H. See Munroe and Munroe (1975).
Munroe, R. L., and Munroe, R. H. (1975) *Cross cultural human development*. Monterey, Calif.: Brooks/Cole. *379*
Murray, H. A. (1943) *Thematic apperception test manual*. Cambridge, Mass.: Harvard University Press. *410*
Myers, D. G. See Lamm and Myers (1978).
Myers, D. G., and Kaplan, M. F. (1978) Group-induced polarization in simulated juries. *Personality and Social Psychology Bulletin*, 2, 63–66. *328*
Myers, D. G. and Lamm, H. (1976) The group polarization phenomenon. *Psychological Bulletin*, 83, 602–607. *326*

Naeslund, J. *211*
Naranjo, C., and Ornstein, R. (1977) *On the psychology of meditation*. Baltimore: Penguin Press. (New York: Viking, 1971.) *101*
Nathan, P. E. See Schacht and Nathan (1977).
Nathan, P. E. and Harris, S. H. (1980) *Psychopathology and Society*. (2nd ed.) New York: McGraw-Hill. *438*
Neale, J. M. See Davison and Neale (1978).
Nelson, V. L. See Sontag et all. (1958).
Newman, H. H., Freeman, F. N., and Holzinger, K. J. (1937) *Twins: A study of heredity and environment*. Chicago: University of Chicago Press. *215*
New York State Department of Mental Hygiene. (1955) *Technical Report*. *253*
Nirje, B. (1969) The normalization principle and its human management implication. In R. B. Kugel and W. Wolfensberger (Eds.), *Changing patterns in residential care*. Washington, D.C.: President's Commission on Mental Retardation. *260*
Nisbett, R. See Jones and Nisbett (1971).
Noble, C. E. (1952) The role of simulus meaning *(m)* in serial verbal learning. *Journal of Experimental Psychology*, 43, 437–446. *178*
Norman, D. A. See Lindsay and Norman (1977).
Norman, W. T. (1963). Toward an adequate taxonomy of personality attributes: Replicated factor structure in peer nomination personality ratings. *Journal of Abnormal and Social Psychology*, 66, 574–583 *384*
Norman, W. T. See Passini and Norman (1966).
Nye, R. D. (1975) *Three views of man. Perspectives from Sigmund Freud, B. F. Skinner and Carl Rogers* Monterey, Calif.: Brooks/Cole. *401*
Nyswander, M. Effectiveness of methadone. *115*

O'Barr, W. M. See Erickson et al. (1977).
Odbert, A. S. See Allport and Odbert (1936).
O'Donnell, J. A., Voss, H. L., Clayton, R. R., Slatin, G. T., and Room, R. G. W. (1976) Young men and drugs—A nation-wide surgey. National Institute of Drug Abuse Research Monograph 5, Rockville, Md. *112*
Office of Economic Opportunity. (1968). *Head Start: A community action program*. Washington, D.C.: U.S. Government Printing Office. *273*
Olds, J., and Milner, P. (1954) Positive reinforcement produced by electrical stimulation of septal area and other regions of the rat brain. *Journal of Comparative and Physiological Psychology*, 47, 419–427. *40*
Ollendick, T. H. See Gruen et al. (1974).
Opper, S. (1977) Concept development in Thai urban and rural children. In P. R. Dasen (Ed.), *Piagetian psychology:*

Cross-cultural contributions. New York: Gardner Press. *300*

Orne, M. T. (1962) On the social psychology of the psychological experiment: With particular reference to demand characteristics and their implications. *American Psychologist,* 175, 776–83. *16*

Ornstein, R. E. (1974). *The nature of consciousness.* New York: Viking Press. *121*

Ornstein, R. E. (1977) *The psychology of consciousness.* New York: Harcourt Brace Jovanovich. *121*

Ornstein, R. See Naranjo and Ornstein (1977).

Osgood, C. E., and Suci, G. J. (1955) Factor analysis of meaning. *Journal of Experimental Psychology,* 50, 325–338. *178*

Osmond, H. See Siegler and Osmond (1974).

Osser, H. See Endler et al. (1976).

Ottinger, D. R. See Gruen et al. (1974).

Overton, K. M. See Magenis et al. (1977).

Owen, D. R. (1972) The 47, XYY male: A review. *Psychological Bulletin,* 78, 209–233. *207*

Owen, D. R. See Witkin et al. (1976).

Page, E. B. (1972) Miracle in Milwaukee: Raising the IQ. *Educational Researcher,* 1: 8–10, 15–16. *274*

Paivio, A. (1971) *Imagery and verbal processes.* New York: Holt, Rinehart and Winston. *157*

Palmer, F. H., and Andersen, L. W. (1979) The effectiveness of early childhood intervention: Findings from longitudinal studies. In E. Zigler and J. Valentine (Eds.), *Project Head Start: A legacy of the war on poverty.* New York: Free Press. *274*

Palmer, J. C. See Loftus and Palmer (1974).

Park, C. C., and Shapiro, L. (1976) *You are not alone.* Boston: Little, Brown. (Paperback: Consumers Union.) *492*

Parkes, C. M. (1965) Recent bereavement as a cause of mental illness. *British Journal of Psychiatry* 110, 198–204. *433*

Parkes, C. M. (1972) *Bereavement: Studies of grief in adult life.* New York: International Universities Press. *425*

Parsons, M. H. See Kugel and Parsons (1967).

Parves, S. V. See Meadow et al. (1959).

Passini, F. T., and Norman, W. T. (1966) A universal conception of personality structure? *Journal of Personality and Social Psychology,* 4, 44–49. *384*

Paterson, D. G. See Jenkins and Paterson (1961).

Pattie, F. A. (1967) A brief history of hypnosis. In J. E. Gordon (Ed.), *Handbook of clinical and experimental hypnosis.* New York: Macmillan, 10–43. *109*

Paul, G. L. (1966) *Insight and desensitization in psychotherapy: An experiment in anxiety reduction.* Stanford, Calif.: Stanford University Press. *478, 479, 480*

Paul, G. L. (1967). strategy of outcome research in psychotherapy. *Journal of Consulting Psychology* 21, 109–118. *490*

Paul, G. L., and Lentz, R. J. (1977) *Psychosocial treatment of chronic mental patients. Milieu versus social-learning programs.* Cambridge, Mass: Harvard University Press. *470, 471*

Pavenstedt, E. (1965) A comparison of the child-rearing environment of upper-lower and very low-lower class families. *American Journal of Orthopsychiatry,* 35, 89–98. *377–378*

Pavlov, I. P. Historical background. *125–126*

Pavlov, I. P. (1927) *Conditioned reflexes: An investigation of physiological activity of the cerebral cortex.* London: Oxford University Press. *146*

Peele, T. L. (1977) *Neuroanatomical basis for clinical neurology.* New York: McGraw-Hill. *43*

Pellegrino, J. Organization and memory. *167*

Penfield, W., and Rasmussen, T. (1950) *The cerebral cortex of man.* New York: Macmillan. *42*

Penrose, L. S. (1963) *The biology of mental defect.* London: Sidgwick and Jackson. *258*

Pervin, L. A. (1975). *Personality: Theory, assessment and research.* (2nd ed.) New York: Wiley. *405, 417*

Pervin, L. A. (1978) *Current controversies and issues in personality.* New York: Wiley. *417*

Peskin, H. (1964) Ego autonomy at optimal and minimal levels of intellectual functioning. Unpublished manuscript, San Francisco State College. *245*

Petersen, R. C. (Ed.) (1977) Marihuana research findings. National Institute of Drug Abuse Research Monograph, 14, Rockville, Md. *117*

Petersen, R. C. & Stillman, R. C. (1978) Phencyclidine: An Overview. In R. C. Petersen and R. C. Stillman (Eds.), *Phencyclidine (PCP) abuse: An appraisal.* National Institute of Drug Abuse Research Monograph 21, Rockville, Md. *116*

Peterson, D. R., Becker, W. C., Hellmer, L. A., Shoemaker, D. J., and Quay, H. C. (1959) Parental attitudes and child adjustment. *Child Development,* 30, 119–130. *373*

Peterson, L. R., and Peterson, M. J. (1959) Short-term retention of individual verbal items. *Journal of Experimental Psychology,* 58, 193–198. *153, 154*

Peterson, M. J. See Peterson and Peterson (1959).

Pettigrew, T. F. See Riley and Pettigrew (1976).

Philip, J. See Witkin et al, (1976).

Phillips, L. See Zigler and Phillips (1961).
Piaget, J. *279, 291*
Piaget, J. (1932) *The moral judgment of the child.* New York: Collier Books, 1962. (Translated by M. Gabain.) *296*
Piaget, J. (1952) Autobiography. In E. G. Boring (Ed.), *A history of psychology in autobiography,* Vol. 4. Worcester, Mass.: Clark University Press. *292*
Piaget J. (1971) Forword to Delessert, E. How the mouse was hit on the head and so discovered the world. New York: Doubleday.
Piaget, J. (1973) States of cognitive development. In R. I. Evans (Ed.), *Jean Piaget: The man and his ideas.* New York: E. P. Dutton. *293*
Piaget, J. (1977) Preface. In P. R. Dasen (Ed.), *Piagetian psychology: Cross-cultural contributions.* New York: Gardner Press. *299*
Piaget, J., Grize, J. B., Szeminska, A., and Vinh Bang. (1968) *Epistémologie et psychologie de la fonction.* Paris: Presses Universitaires de France. Etudes d'Epistémologie Génétique Series, Vol. 23. *295*
Pick, H. L. Jr., Leibowitz, H. W., Singer, J. E., Steinschneider, A., and Stevenson, H. W. (Eds.) (1978) *Psychology: From research to practice.* New York: Plenum Press. *2*
Pinard, A. See Laurendeau and Pinard (1962).
Pisani, P. See Rumbaugh et al. (1974).
Plog, S. C. See Ahmed and Plog (1976).
Porac, C. See Coren et al. (1978).
Posner, M. I. (1969) Abstraction and the process of recognition. In G. H. Bower and J. T. Spence (Eds.), *The psychology of learning and motivtion, 3,* 43–100. *150*
Premack, D. (1972) Teaching language to an ape. *Scientific American, 227,* 92–99. *180*
Premack, D. (1976) *Intelligence in ape and man.* Hillsdale, N.J.: Lawrence Erlbaum Associates. *181*
Prescott, E. (1973) *A comparison of three types of day care and nursery school–home care.* Paper presented at a meeting of Society for Research in Child Development, Philadelphia, March 1973. *372*
The President's Commission on Mental Health. (1978) *Report of the Commission,* Vols. 1–4. Washington D.C.: U.S. Government Printing Office. *441, 464, 477*
Price-Williams, D. R., Gordon, W., and Ramirez, M. (1969) Skill and conservation. *Developmental Psychology,* 1, 769. *30*
Pruitt, D. G. See Teger and Pruitt (1967).
Purkinje, J. E. Purkinje shift. *58*

Quay, H. C. See Peterson et al. (1959).

Rachman, S. See Eysenck and Rachman (1965).
Rakoff, V. M., Stancer, H. C., and Kedward, H. B. (Eds.) (1977). *Psychiatric diagnosis.* New York: Brunner/Mazel. *464*
Ramey, C. T., and Finkelstein, N. W. (1978) *Psychosocial mental retardation: A biological and social coalescence.* Background paper for the Conference on Prevention of Retarded Development in Psychosocially Disadvantaged Children, Madison, Wis., July 23–26, 1978. *274*
Ramey, C. T., and Smith, B. J. (1977) Assessing the intellectual consequences of early intervention with high-risk infants. *American Journal of Mental Deficiency,* 81, 318–324. *274–275*
Ramirez, M. See Price-Williams et al. (1969).
Ratliff, F. See Riggs et al. (1953).
Ray, O. S. (1978) *Drugs, society and human behavior.* (2nd ed.) St. Louis, Mo.: C. V. Mosby. *114, 116, 121*
Rayner, R. See Watson and Rayner (1920).
Redlich, F. See Hollingshead and Redlich (1958).
Reed, E. W., and Reed, S. (1965) *Mental retardation: A family study.* Philadelphia: Saunders. *257*
Reed, S. See Reed and Reed (1965).
Reese, H. See Meadow et al. (1959).
Rencher, A. C. See Brown et al. (1974).
Renner, K. E. See Wiggins et al. (1976).
Rescorla, R. A. (1967) Pavlovian conditioning and its proper control procedures. *Psychological Review, 74,* 71–80. *141–142*
Resnick, L. B. (Ed.) (1976) *The nature of intelligence.* New York: Wiley. *249*
Reuter, J., and Yunik, G. (1973) Social interactions in nursery schools. *Developmental Psychology,* 9, 319–325. *372*
Reuter, M. W., and Biller, H. B. (1973) Perceived paternal nurturance: Availability and personality adjustment among college mates. *Journal of Consulting and Clinical Psychology,* 40, 339–342. *374*
Rheingold, H. L., and Eckerman, C. O. (1970) The infant separates himself from his mother. *Science,* 168, 78–83. *362*
Rheingold, H. L., and Eckerman, C. O. (1973) Fear of the stranger: A critical examination. In H. W. Reese (Ed.), *Advances in child development and behavior,* Vol. 8. New York: Academic Press. *362*
Riccuiti, H. N. See Morgan and Riccuiti (1969).
Richardson, S. A. See Birch et al. (1970).
Riecken, H. See Thibaut and Riecken (1955).
Riggs, L. A., Ratliff, F., Cornsweet, J. C., and Cornsweet, T. N.

(1953). The disappearance of steadily fixated visual test objects. *Journal of the Opthamology Society of America,* 43, 495–501—Riggs portrait in chapter 3.
Riley, R. T., and Pettigrew, T. F. (1976) Dramatic events and attitude change. *Journal of Personality and Social Psychology,* 34, 1004–1015. *327*
Rimm, D. C., and Masters, J. C. (1979) *Behavior therapy.* (2nd ed.) New York: Academic Press. *492*
Ring, K. See Farina and Ring (1965), Farina et al. (1966).
Roazen, P. (1976) *Erik H. Erikson: The power and limits of a vision.* New York: Free Press. *417*
Robins, L. N. (1966) *Deviant children grown up.* Baltimore: Williams and Wilkins. *430–431*
Robinson, G. M. See Moulton et al. (1978).
Robinson, P. W., and Foster, D. F. (1979) *Experimental psychology: A small-N approach.* New York: Harper and Row. *11*
Rodnik, E. H. and Goldstein, M. J. (1974) Premorbid adjustment and the recovery of mothering function in acute schizophrenic women. *Journal of Abnormal Psychology,* 83, 623–628. *467*
Rodnick, E. H. See Evans et al. (1972), (1973), Goldstein et al. (1978).
Rogers, C. R. Nondirective therapy. *476*
Rogers, C. R. (1961) *On becoming a person.* Boston: Houghton Mifflin. *492*
Rogers, C. R., and Stevens, B. (1967) *Person to person: The problem of being human.* New York: Pocket Books. *417*
Room, R. G. W. See O'Donnell et al. (1976).
Ropp, R. S. (1957) *Drugs and the mind.* New York: St. Martin's Press. *116*
Rosch, E. (1973) On the internal structure of perceptual and semantic categories. In T. E. Moore (Ed.), *Cognitive development and the acquisition of language.* New York: Academic Press. *191*
Rosch, E. (1977) Human categorization. In N. Warren (Ed.), *Advances in cross-cultural psychology,* Vol. 1. London: Academic Press. *191*
Rose, R. J. See Wiggins et al. (1976).
Rosen, E., Fox, R. E., and Gregory, I. (1972) *Abnormal psychology.* (2nd ed.) Philadelphia: Saunders. *428, 435*
Rosenbaum, C. P. (1970) *The meaning of madness.* New York: Science House. *435*
Rosenblum, L. A. (1971) The ontogeny of mother-infant relations in macaques. In H. Moltz (Ed.), *The ontogeny of vertebrate behavior.* New York: Academic Press. *371*
Rosenthal, D. See Anderson and Rosenthal (1968), Kety et al. (1968), (1975), (1978).
Rosenthal, R., and Jacobson, L. (1968) *Pygmalion in the classroom.* New York: Holt, Rinehart and Winston. *275*
Rosenzweig, M. R. See Krech et al. (1954).
Ross, A. O. (1980) *Psychological disorders of children.* (2nd ed.) New York: McGraw-Hill. *464*
Ross, J., and Lawrence, K. A. (1968) Some observations on memory artifice. *Psychonomic Science,* 13, 107–108. *168*
Ross, J. B., and McLaughlin, M. M. (Eds.) (1949). *A portable medieval reader.* New York: Viking. *183*
Ross, L. (1977) The intuitive psychologist and his shortcomings: Distortions in the attribution process. In L. Berkowitz (Ed.), *Advances in experimental social psychology,* Vol. 10. New York: Academic Press. *309*
Ross, L., Amabile, T. M., and Steinmetz, J. L. (1977) Social roles, social control, and biases in social-perception processes. *Journal of Personality and Social Psychology,* 35, 485–494. *309*
Ross, R. R. See Meichenbaum et al. (1969).
Rossi, A. S. (1968) Head and heart: Career and family in the lives and plans of women college graduates. Unpublished paper. *380*
Rothkopf, E. Z. (1971) Incidental memory for location of information in text. *Journal of Verbal Learning and Verbal Behavior,* 10, 608–613. *286*
Rubin, D. B. See Witkin et al. (1976).
Rubins, J. L. (1978) *Karen Horney: Gentle rebel of psychoanalysis.* New York: Dial Press. *394*
Rumbaugh, D. M. See Savage-Rumbaugh et al. (1978).
Rumbaugh, D. M., Glaserfeld, E. von, Warner, H., Pisani, P., and Gill, T. V. (1974) Lana (chipanzee) learning a language: A progress report. *Brain and Language,* 1, 205–212. *181*
Rundquist, E. A. (1966) Item and response characteristics in attitude and personality measurement. *Psychological Bulletin,* 66, 166–177. *412*
Rutter, M. (1971) Parent-child separation: Psychological effects on the children. *Journal of Child Psychology and Psychiatry,* 12, 233–260. *373*
Rynders, J. E. See Bruininks et al. (1974).

Salzman, C. (1978) Electroconvulsive therapy. In A. M. Nicholi, Jr. (Ed.), *The Harvard guide to modern psychiatry.* Cambridge, Mass.: The Belknap Press of Harvard University Press, 471–479. *473*
Sameroff, A. J. (1977) Concepts of humanity in primary prevention. In G. Albee and J. Rolf (Eds.), *Primary prevention of psychopathology,* Vol. 1. Burlington, Vt.: Waters. *364*
Sameroff, A. J., and Chandler, M. J. (1975) Reproductive risk and the

continum of caretaking casualty. In F. D. Horowitz (Ed.), *Review of child development research,* Vol. 4. Chicago: University of Chicago Press. *211*

Sameroff, A. J., and Zax, M. (1973) Neonatal characteristics of offspring of schizophrenic and neurotically-depressed mothers. *Journal of Nervous and Mental Diseases,* 157, 191–199. *364*

Sandifer, M. G. (1962) Social psychiatry a hundred years ago. *American Journal of Psychiatry,* 118, 749–750. *458*

Sarbin, T. R., and Mancuso, J. C. (1970) Failure of a moral enterprise: Attitudes of the public toward mental illness. *Journal of Consulting and Clinical Psychology,* 35, 159–173. *462*

Sartorius, N., Jablensky, A., Stromgren, E., and Shapiro, R. (1978) Validity of diagnostic concepts across cultures: A preliminary report from the International Pilot Study of Schizophrenia. In L. C. Wynne, R. L. Cromwell, and S. Matthysse, (Eds.), *The nature of schizophrenia. New approaches to research and treatment.* New York: Wiley, 657–669. *458*

Sartorius, N. See Wing et al. (1974).

Sattler, J. M. (1970) Racial "experimenter effects" in experimentation, testing, interviewing, and psychotherapy. *Psychological Bulletin,* 73: 137–160. *220*

Savage-Rumbaugh, E. S., Rumbaugh, D. M., and Boysen, S. (1978) Symbolic communication between two chimpanzees. *Science,* 201, 641–644. *182*

Scarr, S., and Weinberg, R. A. (1978) Attitudes, interests, and IQ. *Human Nature,* 1, 29–36. *218*

Schacht, T., and Nathan, P. E. (1977) But is it good for the psychologists? Appraisal and status of DSM-III. *American Psychologist,* 32, 1010–1025. *451*

Schachter, S. (1951) Deviation, rejection, and communication. *Journal of Abnormal and Social Psychology,* 46, 190–207. *317*

Schachter, S. (1967) Cognitive studies on bodily functioning: Studies of obesity and eating. In D. C. Glass (Ed.), *Nerophysiology and emotion.* New York: Rockefeller University Press. *349*

Schachter, S. (1971) *Emotion, obesity, and crime.* New York: Academic Press. *343, 344*

Schachter, S., and Singer, J. E. (1962) cognitive, social and physiological determinants of emotional states. *Psychological Review,* 69, 379–399. *322, 349*

Schaefer, E. S. See Bayley and Schaefer (1964).

Schaffer, H. R., and Emerson, P. E. (1964a) The development of social attachments in infancy. *Monographs of the Society for Research in Child Development,* 29(3). (Whole 94.) *367*

Schaie, K. W., and Strother, C. R. (1968) A cross-sequential study of age changes in cognitive behavior. *Psychological Bulletin,* 70: 671–680. *243*

Schalling, D. (1977) The trait-situation interaction and the physiological correlates of behavior. In D. Magnusson and N. S. Endler (Eds.), *Personality at the crossroads: Current issues in interactional psychology.* Hillsdale, N.J.: Lawrence Erlbaum Associates, 129–146. *405*

Scheff, T. J. (1966) *Being mentally ill: A sociological theory.* Chicago: Aldine. *458*

Scheff, T. J. (1974) The labelling theory of mental Illness. *American Sociological Review,* 39, 444–452. *464*

Schiff, M., Duytme, M., Dumarent, A., Stewart, J., Tomkiewicz, S., and Feingold, J. (1978) Intellectual status of working-class children adopted early into upper-middle-class families. *Science,* 200, 1503–1504. *247*

Schiffman, H. R. (1976) *Sensation and perception: An integrated approach.* New York: Wiley. *73, 83, 84*

Schlesinger, K. See Groves and Schlesinger (1979).

Schlosberg, H. See Woodworth and Schlosberg (1954).

Schmidt, G. W., and Ulrich, R. E. (1969) Effects of group contingent events upon classroom noise. *Journal of Applied Behavior Analysis,* 2, 171–179. *12*

Schneider, K. (1959) *Clinical psychopathology.* New York: Grune and Stratton. *435*

Schneidman, E. S., Farberow, H. L. and Litman, R. L. (1970) *Psychology of suicide.* New York: Science House. *442*

Schofield, W. (1964) *The purchase of friendship.* Englewood Cliffs, N.J.: Prentice-Hall. *489*

Schorr, M. See Janowsky et al. (1976).

Schulsinger, F. (1972) Psychopathy: Heredity and environment. In M. Roff, L. Robins, and M. Pollack (Eds.), *Life history research in psychopathology,* Vol. 2. Minneapolis: University of Minnesota Press, 102–119. *431*

Schulsinger, F. See Kety et al. (1968), (1975), (1978), Witkin et al. (1976).

Schultz, D. (1976) *Theories of personality.* Monterey, Calif.: Brooks/Cole. *399, 417*

Schwartz, B. (1978) *Psychology of learning and behavior.* New York: W. W. Norton. *146*

Schwartz, R. D. See Webb et al. (1966).

Scientific American. (1972) *Altered states of awareness.* San Francisco: W. H. Freeman. *121*

Searle, L. V. (1949) The organization of hereditary maze brightness and maze dullness. *Genetic Psychology*

Monographs, 39, 279–325. *209, 210*
Sears, P. (1976) Does a high I.Q. mean happiness? Dr. Pauline Sears says yes. *People,* Jan. 12, 1976, 5, 55–57. *268*
Sechrest, L. See Webb et al. (1966).
Segal, J. See Luce and Segal (1966).
Segal, J., and Yahraes, H. (1978) *A child's journey.* New York: McGraw-Hill. *364, 382*
Seitz, V. See Yando et al. (1979), Zigler et al. (1973).
Seligman, C., and Darley, J. M. (1977) Feedback as a means of decreasing residential energy consumption. *Journal of Applied Psychology,* 62, 363–368. *8*
Seligman, M. E. P., and Hager, J. L. (1972) *Biological boundaries of learning.* New York: Appleton-Century-Crofts. *143–144*
Seligman, M. E. P. (1975) *Helplessness.* San Francisco: W. H. Freeman. *439*
Seligman, M. E. P. See Abramson et al. (1978), Naier and Seligman (1976), Maser and Seligman (1977).
Selye, H. (976) *The stress of life.* (Rev. ed.) New York: McGraw-Hill. *439*
Shapiro, L. See Park and Shapiro (1976).
Shapiro, R. See Sartorius et al. (1978).
Sharpe, L. See Cooper et al. (1972).
Shaver, P. See Monahan et al. (1974).
Shaw, M. E. (1932) A comparison of individuals and small groups in the rational solution of complex problems. *American Journal of Psychology,* 44, 491–504. *324*
Shields, J. See Gottesman and Shields (1972).
Shneidman, E. S., Farberow, N. L., and Litman, R. L. (1970) *Psychology of suicide.* New York: Science House. *441–442*
Shoemaker, D. J. See Peterson et al. (1959).
Shultz, T., and Zigler, E. (1970) Emotional concomitants of visual mastery in infants: The effects of stimulus movement on smiling and vocalizing. *Journal of Experimental Child Psychology,* 10, 390–402. *360*
Siassi, I. See Crocetti et al. (1974).
Sidman, M. (1953) Avoidance conditioning with brief shock and no exteroceptive warning signal. *Science,* 118, 157–185. *142*
Siegel, A. E. (1969) Education of women at Stanford University. *The Study of Education at Stanford,* 7, 1–32. *380*
Siegel, R. K. (1978) Phencyclidine, criminal behavior, and the defense of diminished capacity. In R. C. Petersen and R. C. Stillman (Eds.) *Phencyclidine (PCP) abuse: An appraisal.* National Institute of Drug Abuse Research Monograph 21. Rockville, Md. *116*
Siegler, M., and Osmond, H. (1974) *Models of madness, models of medicine.* New York: Macmillan. *464*
Simmelhag, V. L. See Staddon and Simmelhag (1971).
Simon, R. See Cooper et al. (1972).
Singer, J. E. See Pick et al. (1978), Schachter and Singer (1962).
Sinnott, E. W., Dunn, L. C., and Dobzhansky, T. (1958) *Principles of genetics.* (5th ed.) New York: McGraw-Hill. *203*
Skeels, H. M. (1966) Adult status of children with contrasting early life experiences: A follow-up study. *Monographs of the Society for Research in Child Development,* 31 (3). (Whole 105.) *245, 256*
Skeels, H. M. See Skodak and Skeels (1949).
Skinner, B. F. Approach to personality. *398–399*
Skinner B. F. Skinner boxes. *128–130*
Skinner, B. F. (1938) *The behavior of organisms: An experimental analysis.* New York: Appleton-Century-Crofts. *129*
Skinner, B. F. (1948) Superstition in the pigeon. *Journal of Experimental Psychology,* 38, 168–172. *144*
Skinner, B. F. (1972) *Cumulative record.* (3rd ed.) New York: Appleton-Century-Crofts. *398–399*
Skinner, B. F. (1974) *About behaviorism.* New York: Knopf. *417*
Skinner, B. F. (1978) *Reflections of behaviorism and society.* Englewood Cliffs, N.J.: Prentice-Hall. *417*
Skodak, M., and Skeels, H. M. (1949) A final follow-up study of one hundred adopted children. *Journal of Genetic Psychology,* 75: 85–125. *216*
Slatin, G. T. See O'Donnell et al. (1976).
Smart, M. S., and Smart, R. (1967) *Children: Development and relationships.* New York: Macmillan. *378*
Smart, R. See Smart and Smart (1967).
Smith, B. J. See Ramey and Smith (1977).
Smith, C. U. M. (1970) *The Brain.* New York: G. P. Outnam's Sons. *47*
Smith, J. A. See Swanson et al. (1970).
Smith, S. M., Brown, H. O., Thomas, J. E. P., and Goodman, L. S. (1947) The lack of cerebral effects of *d*-tuboceurarine. *Anesthesiology,* 8, 1–14. *196*
Smoke, K. L. (1932) An objective study of concept formation. *Psychological Monographs,* 42. (Whole 191.) *190*
Snow, R. E. See Elashoff and Snow (1971).
Snyder, F. (1970) The phenomenology of dreaming. In L. Madow and L. H. Snow (Eds.), *The psychodynamic implications of the physiological studies on dreams* Springfield, Ill.: Charles C. Thomas. *105*
Snyder, M., and Jones, E. E. (1974) Attitude attribution where behavior is constrained. *Journal of Experimental Social Psychology,* 10, 585–600. *309*

Snyder, M., and Swann, W. B. (1978) Behavioral confirmation in social interaction: From social perception to social reality. *Journal of Experimental Social Psychology,* 14, 148–162. *312*

Snyder, M., Tanko, E. D., and Berscheid, E. (1977) Social perception and interpersonal behavior: On the self-fulfilling nature of social stereotypes. *Journal of Personality and Social Psychology,* 35, 656–666. *311*

Snyder, S. H. (1974) *Madness and the brain.* New York: McGraw-Hill. *439*

Solomon, R. L., and Corbit, J. D. (1974) An opponent-process theory of motivation: I. Temporal dynamics of affect. *Psychological Review,* 81, 119–145. *350, 351*

Sommer, R. See Felipe and Sommer (1966).

Sontag, L. W., Baker, C. T., and Nelson, V. L. (1958) Mental growth and personality development: A longitudinal study. *Monographs of the Society for Research in Child Development,* 23 (2). (whole 68.) *245*

Spearman, C. (1904) General intelligence" objectively determined and measured. *American Journal of Psychology,* 15, 201–93. *239*

Sperling, G. (1960) The information available in brief visual presentations. *Psychological Monographs,* 74. (Whole 498.) *149*

Sperry, R. W. See Gazzaniga et al. (1965).

Spiegler, M. D. See Liebert and Spiegler (1978).

Spielberger, C. D. (1962) The effects of manifest anxiety of the academic achievement of college students. *Mental Hygiene,* 46, 420–426. *347*

Spielberger, C. D. (Ed.) (1966) *Anxiety and behavior.* New York: Academic Press. *347*

Spielberger, C. D., Weitz, H., and Denny, J. P. (1962) Group counseling and academic performance of anxious college freshmen. *Journal of Counseling Psychology,* 9(3), 195–204. *347, 348*

Spiro, H. R. See Crocetti et al. (1974).

Spuhler, J. N. See Loehlin et al. (1975).

Spuhler, J. N., and Lindzey, G. (1967) Racial differences in behavior. In J. Hirsch (Ed.), *Behavior-genetic analysis.* New York: McGraw-Hill. *220*

Staddon, J. E. R., and Simmelhag, V. L. (1971) The "superstition" experiment: A re-examination of its implications for the principles of adaptive behavior. *Psychological Review,* 78, 3–43. *144*

Stamfl, T. G., and Levis, D. J. (1967) Essentials of implosive therapy: A learning-theory-based psychodynamic behavior therapy. *Journal of Abnormal Psychology,* 72, 496–503. *479*

Stancer, H. C. See Rakoff et al. (1977).

Stedman, D. J., and Eichorn, D. H. (1964) A comparison of the growth and development of institutionalized and home-reared mongoloids during infancy and early childhood. *American Journal of Mental Deficiency,* 69, 391–401. *253*

Steele, B. F. (1977) *Psychological Dimensions of Child Abuse.* Paper presented to the American Association for the Advancement of Science, Denver, Colo., February 1977. *376*

Steffa, M. See Klaus et al. (1972).

Steinmetz, J. L. See Ross et al. (1977).

Steinschneider, A. See Pick et al. (1978).

Stellar, E. See Dethier and Stellar (1961).

Sterling-Smith, R. S. (1976) *A special study of drivers most responsible in fatal accidents.* Summary for Management Report, Contract DOT HS 310-3-595. *117*

Stern, J. See Crome and Stern (1972).

Stevens, B. See Rogers and Stevens (1967).

Stevenson, H. W. See Pick et al. (1978).

Stevenson, H. W., Iscoe, I., and McConnell, C. A. (1955) A developmental study of transposition. *Journal of Experimental Psychology,* 49, 278–280. *283*

Stewart, J. See Schiff et al. (1978).

Stillman, R. C. See Petersen and Stillman (1978).

Stinnett, N. See Walters and Stinnett (1971).

Stocking, M. See Witkin et al. (1976).

Stoner, J. A. F. (1961) A comparison of individual and group decisions involving risk. Unpublished M.A. thesis, Sloan School of Management, M.I.T. *325*

Stratton, G. M. (1897) Vision without inversion of the retinal image. *Psychological Review,* 4, 341–360, 463–481. *93*

Stromgren, E. See Sartorius et al. (1978).

Strong, W. J. See Brown et al. (1974).

Stroop, J. R. (1935) Studies of interference in serial verbal reactions. *Journal of Experimental Psychology,* 18, 643–662. *91*

Strother, C. R. See Schaie and Strother (1968).

Strupp, H. H. (1971) *Psychotherapy and the modification of abnormal behavior.* New York: McGraw-Hill. *480*

Strupp, H. H., Hadley, S. W., and Gomes-Schwartz, B. (1977) *Psychotherapy for better or worse. The problem of negative effects.* New York: Jason Aronson. *491*

Sundberg, N. (1977) *Assessment of persons.* Englewood Cliffs, N.J.: Prentice-Hall. *417*

Suomi, S. J. (1979) Peers, play, and primary prevention in primates. In M. W. Kent and J. E. Rolf

(Eds.), *The primary prevention of psychopathology,* Vol. 3, *Social competence in children.* Hanover, N.H.: University Press of New England. *370*

Suomi, S. J., and Harlow, H. F. (1978) Early experience and social development in rhesus monkeys. In M. E. Lamb (Ed.), *Social and personality development.* New York: Holt, Rinehart and Winston. *370*

Sutherland, N. S. (1976) *Breakdown.* New York: Stein and Day. *421*

Swann, W. B. See Snyder and Swann (1978).

Swanson, D. W., Bohnert, P. J., and Smith, J. A. (1970) *The paranoid.* Boston: Little, Brown. *429, 434*

Swanson, G. E. See Miller and Swanson (1958).

Szasz, T. S. (1961) *The myth of mental illness.* New York: Harper and Row, Hoeber Medical Division. *452, 464*

Szasz, T. S. (1963) *Law, liberty and psychiatry.* New York: Macmillan. *452, 464*

Szasz, T. S. (1970) *The manufacture of madness.* New York: Harper and Row. *452, 464*

Szasz, T. S. (1972) Preface. In B. J. Ennis, *Prisoners of psychiatry.* New York: Harcourt Brace Jovanovich. *452*

Szasz, T. S. (1976). *Schizophrenia: The sacred symbol of society.* New York: Basic Books. *464*

Szeminska, A. See Piaget et al. (1968).

Talbot, J. A. (1974) Stop the revolving door: A study of recidivism to a state hospital. *Psychiatric Quarterly,* 48, 159–167. *468*

Tanko, E. D. See Snyder et al. (1977).

Tanner, O. (1976) *Stress.* New York: Time-Life Books. *425, 439*

Tart, C. T. (Ed.) (1969) *Altered states of consciousness.* New York: Wiley. *117*

Taylor, D. W., Berry, P. C., and Block, C. H. (1958) Does group participation when using brainstorming facilitate or inhibit creative thinking? *Administrative Scence Quarterly,* 3, 23–47. *325*

Taylor, H. L. See Keys et al. (1950).

Teger, A. I., and Pruitt, D. G. (1967) Components of group risk taking. *Journal of Experimental Social Psychology,* 3, 189–205. *326*

Tellegen, A., and Atkinson, G. (1974) Openness to absorbing and self-altering experiences ("Absorption"), a trait related to hypnotic susceptibility. *Journal of Abnormal Psychology, 83, 268–277.* *111*

Terman, L. M. (1917) The intelligence quotient of Francis Galton in childhood. *American Journal of Psychology,* 28, 208–215. *264*

Terman, L. M. (1925) *Genetic studies of genius,* Vol. 1, *Mental and physical traits of a thousand gifted children.* Stanford, Calif.: Stanford University Press. *267*

Terman, L. M., and Merrill, M. A. (1960) *Stanford-Binet intelligence scale: Manual for the third edition,* Form L-17. Boston: Houghton Mifflin. *230*

Terman, L. M., and Merrill, M. A. (1973) *Stanford-Binet intelligence scale: Manual for the third revision.* Boston: Houghton Mifflin. *234*

Terman, L. M., and Oden, M. (1947) *The gifted child grows up.* Stanford, Calif.: Stanford University Press. *267*

Terman, L. M., and Oden, M. (1959) *The gifted group at mid-life.* Stanford, Calif.: Stanford University Press. *267*

Teska, J. See Karnes and Teska (1975).

Thibaut, J. See Festinger and Thibaut (1951).

Thibaut, J., and Riecken, H. (1955) Some determinants and consequences of the perception of social causality. *Journal of Personality,* 24, 113–133. *308*

Thomas, A., and Chess, S. (1977) *Temperament and development.* New York: Brunner/Mazel. *363*

Thomas, A., Chess, S., and Birch, H. G. (1968) *Temperament and behavior disorders in children.* New York: New York University Press. *363, 364*

Thompson, D. M. See Tulving and Thompson (1973).

Thompson, G., and Masterton, R. B. (1978) Brainstem auditory pathways involved in reflexive head orientation to sound. *Journal of Neurophysiology,* 41, 1183–1202. *41*

Thompson, W. R. See Fuller and Thompson (1978).

Thorell, L. G. See Valois et al. (1979).

Thorndike, E. L. (1911) *Animal intelligence.* New York: Macmillan. *7, 128*

Thorpe, J. G. See Blakemore et al. (1963).

Thurstone, L. L. (1938) Primary mental abilities. *Psychometric Monographs,* Vol. 1. *239*

Thurstone, L. L. (1941) *The primary mental abilities tests.* Chicago: Science Research Associates. *216*

Tietze, C. See Lemkau et al. (1941).

Tinbergen, N. (1952) The curious behavior of the stickelback. *Scientific American,* 182, 22–26. *332*

Tinbergen, N. (1968) On war and peace in animals and man. *Science* (June 28), 24–49. *338*

Tomas, J. E. P. See Smith et al. (1947).

Tomkiewicz, S. See Schiff et al. (1978).

Torrey, J. W. See Graf and Torrey (1966).

Triplett, N. (1897) The dynamogenic factors in pacemaking and competition. *American Journal of Psychology,* 9, 507–533. *323*

Tryon, R. C. (1942) Individual differences. In F. A. Moss (ed.), *Comparative psychology.* (Rev.

ed.) Englewood Cliffs, N.J.: Prentice-Hall. *209*

Tulving, E. (1972) Episodic and semantic memory. In E. Tulving and W. Donaldson (Eds.), *Organization of Memory*. New York: Academic Press. *160*

Tulving, E. See Craik and Tulving (1975).

Tulving, E., and Thompson, D. M. (1973) Encoding specificity and retrieval processes in episodic memory. *Psychological Review*, 352–373. *160*

Turnure, J., and Zigler, E. (1964) Outer-directedness in the problem solving of normal and retarded children. *Journal of Abnormal and Social Psychology*, 69, 427–36. *258*

Tyler, L. (1965) *The psychology of human differences*. (3rd ed.) New York: Appleton-Century-Crofts. *215*

Tyler, R. See Eells et al. (1951).

Ulrich, R. E. (1967) Pain-aggression. In G. A. Kimble (Ed.), *Foundations of conditioning and learning*. New York: Appleton-Century-Crofts. *345*

Ulrich, R. E. See Schmidt and Ulrich (1969).

Underwood, B. J. (1957) Interference and forgetting. *Psychological Review*, 64, 49–60. *164*

Underwood, B. J. See Keppel and Underwood (1962).

U. S. Office of Education. (1971) *Education of the gifted and talented*, Vol. 1. Report to the Congress of the United States by the U.S. Commissioner of Education. Washington, D.C.: U.S. Government Printing Office. *268*

Valentine, C. W. (1930) The innate bases of fear. *Journal of Genetic Psychology*, 37, 394–420. *361*

Valentine, J. See Zigler and Valentine (1979).

Van de Castle, R. L. See Hall and Van de Castle (1966).

Vandenberg, S. G. (Ed.) (1965) *Methods and goals in human behavior genetics*. New York: Academic Press. *211*

Vandenberg, S. G. (1917a) The genetics of intelligence. In L. C. Deighton (Ed.), *Encyclopedia of education*. New York: Macmillan. *214, 217*

Vandenberg, S. G. (1917b) What do we know today about the inheritance of intelligence and how do we know it? In R. Cancro (Ed.), *Intelligence: Genetic and environmental influences*. New York: Grune and Stratton. *215*

Vaughn, C. E., and Leff, J. P. (1976) The influence of family and social factors on the course of psychiatric illness. *British Journal of Psychiatry*, 129, 125–137. *468, 469*

Vernon, P. E. (Ed.) (1970) *Creativity*. Baltimore, Md.: Penguin Books. *277*

Vierck, C. J., Jr. (1978) Somatosensory system. In R. B. Masterton (Ed.), *Handbook of behavioral neurobiology*. New York: Plenum Press. *41*

Vinh Bang See Piaget et al. (1968).

Voss, H. L. See O'Donnell et al. (1976).

Waber, D. P. (1977) Sex differences in mental abilities, hemispheric lateralization, and rate of physical growth at adolescence. *Developmental Psychology*, 13, 29–38. *245*

Waisman, H. See Berman et al. (1966).

Walder, L. See Lefkowitz et al. (1972).

Walk, R. D. See Gibson and Walk (1960).

Walk, R. D., and Dodge, S. H. (1962) Visual depth perception in a 10 month old monocular human infant. *Science*, 137, 529–530. *95*

Walker, C. C. See Ashby and Walker (1968).

Walker, L. O. See Eron et al. (1972).

Walker, M. R. See Freeman et al. (1975).

Wall, P. D. See Melzack and Wall (1965).

Wallace, J. G. See Gregory and Wallace (1963).

Wallach, M. A., and Kogan, N. (1965a) A new look at the creativity-intelligence dimension. *Journal of Personality*, 33, 348–369. *271*

Wallach, M. A., and Kogan, N. (1965b) *Modes of thinking in young children*. New York: Holt, Rinehart and Winston. *271*

Wallach, M. A., Kogan, N., and Burt, R. B. (1968) Are risk takers more persuasive than conservatives in group discussion? *Journal of Experimental Social Psychology*, 4, 76–88. *326*

Wallach, M. A., and Wallach, L. (1976) *Teaching all children to read*. Chicago: University of Chicago Press. *10*

Walter, J., and Stinnett, N. (1971) Parent-child relationships: A decade review or research. *Journal of Marriage and the Family*, 33, 70–111. *375*

Ward, C. H. See Beck et al. (1962).

Ward, C. O., Zanna, M. P., and Cooper, J. (1974) The nonverbal mediation of self-fulfilling prophecies in inter-racial interaction. *Jornal of Experimental Social Psychology*, 10, 109–120. *311*

Ward, L. M. See Coren et al. (1978).

Warner, H. See Rumbaugh et al. (1974).

Watson, J. B. Genetic code. *206*

Watson, J. B. Language. *195*

Watson, J. B. (1913) Psychology as the behaviorist views it. *Psychological Review*, 20, 158–177. *99*

Watson, J. B. (1928) *Psychological care of infant and child*. New York: Norton. *374*

Watson, J. B., and Morgan, J. J. B. (1917) Emotional reactions and psychological experimentation.

American Journal of Psychology, 28, 163–179. *359*
Watson, J. B., and Rayner, R. (1920) Conditioned emotional reactions. *Journal of Experimental Psychology,* 3, 1–14. *127*
Waxler, N. E. See Mishler and Waxler (1968).
Weaver, T. R. (1946) The incidence of maladjustment among mental defictives in military environment. *American Journal of Mental Deficiency,* 51, 238–246. *258*
Webb, E. J., Campbell, D. T., Schwartz, R. D., and Sechrest, L. (1966) *Unobtrusive measures: Non-reactive research in the social sciences.* Chicago: Rand McNally. *18*
Webb, W. B. (1969) Partial and differential sleep stage deprivation. In A. Kales (Ed.), *Sleep: Physiology and pathology.* Philadelphia: Lippincott, 221–231. *107*
Webb, W. B. (1975) *Sleep, the gentle tyrant.* Englewood Cliffs, N.J.: Prentice-Hall. *106, 121*
Webb, W. B., and Agnew, H. W., Jr. (1968) In L. E. Abt and B. F. Reiss (Eds.), *Progress in clinical psychology.* New York: Grune and Stratton. *104, 107*
Weber, E. H. Weber's law. *70–71*
Weinberg, R. A. See Scarr and Weinberg (1978).
Weitz, H. See Spielberger et al. (1962).
Weitzenhoffer, A. M., and Hilgard, E. R. (1962) *Stanford hypnotic susceptibility scale.* Stanford, Calif.: Stanford University Press; distributed by Consulting Psychologists Press. *110, 111*
Wender, P. H. See Kety et al. (1968), (1975), (1978).
Werner, H. *283*
Werner, H. (1957a) *Comparative psychology of mental development.* (Rev. ed.) New York: International Universities Press. *285*
Werner, H. (1957b) The concept of development from a comparative and organismic point of view. In D. B. Harris (Ed.), *The concept of development: An issue in the study of human behavior.* Minneapolis: University of Minnesota Press. *283*
West, D. J., and Farrington, D. P. (1975) *Who becomes delinquent?* London: Heinemann. *454*
West, K. L. See Goldstein et al. (1978).
Westinghouse Learning Corporation. (1969) *The impact of Head Start: An evaluation of the effects of Head Start experience on children's cognitive and affective development.* Ohio University, Report to the Office of Educational Opportunity, Clearinghouse for Federal, Scientific, and Technical Information, Washington, D.C. *273*
White, R. W. (1976) *The enterprise of living.* (2nd ed.) New York: Holt, Rinehart and Winston. *417*
Whiting, J. W. M., and Mowrer, O. H. (1943) Habit progression and regression—a laboratory study of some factors relevant to human socialization. *Journal of Comparative Psychology,* 36, 229–253. *346*
Whorf, B. L. (1940) Science and linguistics. *Technology Review,* 49, 229–248. *191–193*
Whorf, B. L. (1956) *Language, thought, and reality.* New York: Wiley. *192*
Wiesel, T. N. See Hubel and Wiesel (1959).
Wiggins, J. S., Renner, K. E., Clore, G. L., and Rose, R. J. (1976) *Principles of personality.* Reading, Mass.: Addison-Wesley. *417*
Wilbur, C. B. See Ludwig et al. (1972).
Williams, J. R. See Clausen and Williams (1963).
Willinger, R. P. See Bahrick et al. (1975).
Wing, J. K. (1978) Social influences on the course of schizophrenia. In L. C. Wynne, R. L. Cromwell, and S. Matthysse (Eds.), *The nature of schizophrenia. New approaches to research and treatment.* New York: Wiley, 599–616. *458*
Wing, J. K. See Brown et al. (1972).
Wing, J. K., Cooper, J. E., and Sartorius, N. (1974) *The measurement and classification of psychiatric symptoms.* London: Cambridge University Press. *448*
Wing, J. K., Bireley, J. L. T., Cooper, J. E., Graham, P., and Isaacs, A. D. (1967) Reliability of a procedure for measuring and classifying "Present Psychiatric State." *British Journal of Psychiatry,* 113, 499–515 *448*
Witkin, H. A., Mednick, S. A., Schulsinger, F., Bakkestrom, E., Christiansen, K. O., Goodenough, D. R., Hirschhorn, K., Lundsteen, C., Owen, D. R., Philip, J., Rubin, D. B., and Stocking, M. (1976) Criminality in XYY and XXY men. *Science,* 193, 547–555. *207*
Witty, P. A. (1940) A genetic study of fifty gifted children. *Yearbook of the National Society for the Study of Education,* 39, 401–408. *268*
Wohlwill, J. F. (1970) The place of structured experience in early cognitive development. *Interchange,* 1, 13–27. *301*
Wolf, M. M. See Allen et al. (1964).
Wolfe, J. B. (1936) Effectiveness of token-rewards for chimpanzees. *Comparative Psychology Monographs,* 12 (60).
Wolfenstein, M. (1953) Trends in infant care. *American Journal of Orthospychiatry,* 23, 120–130. *374*
Wolpe, J. (1958) *Psychotherapy by reciprocal inhibition.* Stanford, Calif.: Stanford University Press. *477*
Woodworth, R. S., and Sclosberg, H. (1954) *Experimental*

psychology. New York: Holt, Rinehart and Winston. *156*
World Health Organization. (1973) *The international pilot study of schizophrenia,* Vol. 1. *448*
Wundt, W. *2*
Wynne, J. W. See Block et al. (1979).
Wynne, L. C., Cromwell, R. L., and Matthysse, S. (Eds.) (1978) *The nature of schizophrenia. New approaches to research and treatment.* New York: Wiley. *464*

Yagi, K. See Berkun et al. (1962).
Yahraes, H. See Segal and Yahraes (1978).
Yalom, I. D. (1970) *The theory and practice of group psychotherapy.* New York: Basic Books. *488*
Yalom, I. D. (1975) *The theory and practice of group psychotherapy.* (2nd ed.) New York: Basic Books. *487, 488, 492*
Yalom, I. D. See Bieberman et al. (1973).
Yando, R., Seitz, V., and Zigler, E. (1979) *Intellectual and personality characteristics of children: Social class and ethnic group differences.* Hillsdale, N.J.: Lawrence Erlbaum Associates. *247*
Yarrow, L. J. (1961) Maternal deprivation: Toward an empirical and conceptual reevaluation. *Psychological Bulletin,* 58, 459–490. *372*
Yarrow, M. R., Campbell, J. D., and Burton, V. R. (1970) Recollections of childhood: A study of the retrospective method. *Monographs of the Society for Research in Child Development,* 35 (5), Serial 138. *453*
Yates, A. J. (1970) *Behavior therapy*. New York: Wiley. *480*
Young, T. Trichromatic color theory. *55*
Yunik, G. See Reuter and Yunik (1973).

Zajonc, R. B. (1965) Social facilitation. *Science,* 149, 269–274. *324*
Zajonc, R. B. (1966) *Social psychology: An experimental approach*. Belmont, Calif.: Wadsworth. *324*
Zanna, M. P. See Fazio et al. (1977), Ward et al. (1974).
Zanna, M. P., and Cooper, J. (1974) Dissonance and the pill: An attributional approach to studying the arousal properties of dissonance. *Journal of Personality and Social Psychology,* 29, 703–709. *322, 323*
Zavalloni, M. See Moscovici and Zavalloni (1969).
Zax, M. See Sameroff and Zax (1973).
Zeisel, H. See Kalvin and Zeisel (1966).
Zelhart, P., and Johnson, R. C. (1959) An investigation of eidetic imagery. Paper presented at the meeting of the Western Psychological Association, San Jose, Calif. *286*
Zigler, E., Abelson, W. D., and Seitz, V. (1973) Motivational factors in the performance of economically disadvantaged children on the Peabody Picture Vocabulary Test. *Child Development,* 44, 294–303. *220, 237*
Zigler, E., and Harter, S. (1969) Socialization of the mentally retarded. In D. A. Goslin (Ed.), *Handbook of socialization theory and research*. Chicago: Rand McNally. *253*
Zigler, E., and Phillips, L. (1961) Psychiatric diagnosis and symptomatology. *Journal of Abnormal and Social Psychology,* 63, 69–75. *447*
Zigler, E., and Valentine, J. (Eds.) (1979) *Project Head Start: A legacy of the war on poverty*. New York: Free Press. *277*
Zigler, E. See Achenbach and Zigler (1968), Katz and Zigler (1967), Schultz and Zigler (1970), Turnure and Zigler (1964), Yando et al. (1979).
Zilboorg, G. A. (1941) *A history of medical psychology*. New York: Norton. *444, 466*
Zimet, C. N. See Allison et al. (1968).
Zubek, J. P. See Cooper and Zubek (1958).
Zubin, J. (1972) Scientific models for psychopathology in the 1970's. *Seminars in Psychiatry,* 4, 283–296. *453, 454*
Zubin, J. (1978) But is it good for science? *The Clinical Psychologist,* 31, (2), 1–7. *451*

Index of Subjects